THE O… OF

THE HISTORY OF NATIONALISM

The Oxford Handbook of the History of Nationalism comprises thirty six essays by an international team of leading scholars, providing a global coverage of the history of nationalism in its different aspects—ideas, sentiments, and politics. Every chapter takes the form of an interpretative essay which, by a combination of thematic focus, comparison, and regional perspective, enables the reader to understand nationalism as a distinct and global historical subject.

The book covers the emergence of nationalist ideas, sentiments, and cultural movements before the formation of a world of nation-states, as well as nationalist politics before and after the era of the nation-state, with chapters covering Europe, the Middle East, Northeast Asia, South Asia, Southeast Asia, sub-Saharan Africa, and the Americas. Essays on everyday national sentiment and race ideas in fascism are accompanied by chapters on nationalist movements opposed to existing nation-states, nationalism and international relations, and the role of external intervention into nationalist disputes within states. In addition, the book looks at the major challenges to nationalism: international socialism, religion, pan-nationalism, and globalization, before a final section considering how historians have approached the subject of nationalism.

Taken separately, the chapters in this Handbook will deepen understanding of nationalism in particular times and places; taken together they will enable the reader to see nationalism as a distinct subject in modern world history.

John Breuilly is Emeritus Professor of Nationalism and Ethnicity at the London School of Economics. His main interests are in the history and theory of nationalism and in modern European, especially German history. Recent book publications include *Austria, Prussia and the Making of Modern Germany, 1806–1871* (2011), *Nationalism, Power and Modernity in Nineteenth-Century Germany* (2007), and articles and chapters on charismatic leadership and nationalism and on nationalism and global history. He is currently working on a book on the global history of nationalism, also to be published by Oxford University Press.

'Taken at once, the book juxtaposes advances from numerous regional and thematic subfields to open up theoretical vistas for specialists. At the same time, its chapters decorate this theoretical tableau with rich detail. As such the book will engage both students and lay readers.'

Eric Kaufmann, *LSE Review of Books*

'an impressive volume of easy-to-read, clear and concise essays . . . an extremely thorough and illuminating book.'

Gilles Andréani, *Survival*

'All students of nationalism will want to possess this volume. Not only are the individual contributions excellent, with useful up-to-date bibliographies, but there is a bonus in the form of helpful chronologies and maps showing the worldwide spread of nationalism.'

Krishan Kumar, *International Affairs*

THE OXFORD HANDBOOK OF

THE HISTORY OF NATIONALISM

Edited by

JOHN BREUILLY

OXFORD
UNIVERSITY PRESS

OXFORD
UNIVERSITY PRESS

Great Clarendon Street, Oxford, OX2 6DP,
United Kingdom

Oxford University Press is a department of the University of Oxford.
It furthers the University's objective of excellence in research, scholarship,
and education by publishing worldwide. Oxford is a registered trade mark of
Oxford University Press in the UK and in certain other countries

First published 2013
First published in paperback 2016

Published in the United States of America by Oxford University Press
198 Madison Avenue, New York, NY 10016, United States of America

British Library Cataloguing in Publication Data
Data available

Library of Congress Cataloging in Publication Data
Data available

ISBN 978–0–19–920919–4 (Hbk.)
ISBN 978–0–19–876820–3 (Pbk.)

Acknowledgements

The editor would like to acknowledge the help and advice of Christopher Wheeler at OUP in developing the idea for this book into a practical proposal. Matthew Cotton at OUP provided essential support during the process of getting from that proposal to the book. Richard Mason has been a model copy-editor: efficient, thorough, and sensible. I thank all the contributors to the volume for their cooperation as well as the quality of their chapters. Joya Chatterji lent me the Congress Party poster which is used on the front cover. I am especially indebted to John Hutchinson with whom I work on the nationalism programme at LSE, not only for his chapter but for general support and advice. Finally I would like to mention Fred Halliday—an outstanding scholar and public intellectual—who died shortly after completing his chapter for this book.

Contents

PART III: NATIONALISM IN A WORLD OF NATION STATES: POLITICS AND POWER

PART IV: NATIONALISM IN A WORLD OF NATION STATES: IDEAS, SENTIMENTS, AND INTERNATIONAL RELATIONS

PART V: CHALLENGES TO THE WORLD OF NATION STATES

PART VI: NATIONALIST HISTORIOGRAPHY

List of Contributors

Cemil Aydin is Associate Professor of History at the University of North Carolina at Chapel Hill. He studied at Boğaziçi University, İstanbul University, and the University of Tokyo before receiving his PhD degree at Harvard University in 2002. His recent publications include *Politics of Anti-Westernism in Asia: Visions of World Order in Pan-Islamic and Pan-Asian Thought* (New York: Columbia University Press, 2007); and a co-edited volume on critiques of the 'West' in Iran, Turkey, and Japan in *Comparative Studies of South Asia, Africa and the Middle East*, 26:3 (Fall 2006). He is currently working on a book project on the intellectual history of the idea of the 'Muslim World' (forthcoming, Harvard University Press).

Erica Benner is Fellow in Ethics and the History of Philosophy at Yale University. Her publications include *Really Existing Nationalisms* (Oxford: Oxford University Press, 1995); *Machiavelli's Ethics* (Princeton, NJ: Princeton University Press, 2009); and *Thucydides' Moral and Political Philosophy* (Princeton, NJ: Princeton University Press, forthcoming).

Bruce J. Berman is Professor Emeritus of Political Studies and History at Queen's University, Kingston, Ontario, and was Director and Principal Investigator of the Ethnicity and Democratic Governance programme from 2006 to 2012. His publications include *Control and Crisis in Colonial Kenya* (London and Athens: James Currey and Ohio University Press, 1990); *Unhappy Valley: Conflict in Kenya and Africa*, with John Lonsdale (London and Athens: James Currey and Ohio University Press, 1992); and *Ethnicity and Democracy in Africa*, edited with Dickson Eyoh and Will Kymlicka (London and Athens: James Currey and Ohio University Press, 2004). He was President of the Canadian Association of African Studies (1990–1) and the African Studies Association (2004–5).

John Breuilly is Professor of Nationalism and Ethnicity at the London School of Economics and Political Science. His publications include *Nationalism and the State*, 2nd edn. (Chicago and Manchester: University of Chicago Press and Manchester University Press, 1993), *Austria, Prussia and the Making of Modern Germany, 1806–1871* (London: Pearson, 2011); and 'On the Principle of Nationality', in *The Cambridge History of 19th-Century Political Thought* (Cambridge: Cambridge University Press, 2011), edited by Gareth Stedman Jones and Gregory Claeys. He is currently writing a global history of nationalism for Oxford University Press.

Peter Burke studied at St John's College and St Antony's College, Oxford; taught at the new University of Sussex (1962–78); and occupied a chair in Cultural History, University of Cambridge, until his retirement in 2004. He remains a fellow of Emmanuel College. His books, translated into more than thirty languages, include *Culture and Society in Renaissance Italy* (London: Batsford, 1972); *Popular Culture in Early Modern Europe* (New York: Harper & Row, 1978); *The Fabrication of Louis XIV* (New Haven, CT: Yale University Press, 1992); *Languages and Communities in Early Modern Europe* (Cambridge: Cambridge University Press, 2004); and *A Social History of Knowledge*, 2 vols. (Cambridge: Polity Press, 2000 and 2012).

Richard Caplan is Professor of International Relations and Director of the Centre for International Studies (CIS) at Oxford University, where he is also a fellow of Linacre College. He is the author of *International Governance of War-Torn Territories: Rule and Reconstruction* (Oxford: Oxford University Press, 2005) and *Europe and the Recognition of New States in Yugoslavia* (Cambridge: Cambridge University Press, 2005); the editor of *Exit Strategies and State Building* (Oxford: Oxford University Press, 2012); and the co-editor of *Europe's New Nationalism: States and Minorities in Conflict* (Oxford: Oxford University Press, 1996).

Joya Chatterji is Reader in Modern South Asian History at the University of Cambridge and a fellow of Trinity College. She is the editor of the journal *Modern Asian Studies*. Her publications include *Bengal Divided: Hindu Communalism and Partition, 1932–1947* (Cambridge: Cambridge University Press, 1994; South Asia edition, 1995); *The Spoils of Partition: Bengal and India 1947–1967* (Cambridge: Cambridge University Press, 2007); and (with Claire Alexander and Annu Jalais) *The Bengali Muslim Diaspora: Migration, Displacement and Settlement in Bangladesh, India and Britain* (London: Routledge Press, forthcoming).

John Darwin is a fellow of Nuffield College, Oxford, where he teaches imperial and global history. His recent publications include *After Tamerlane: The Global History of Empire since 1405* (London: Allen Lane, 2007), which won the Wolfson Prize in History; and *The Empire Project: The Rise and Fall of the British World-System 1830–1970* (Cambridge: Cambridge University Press, 2009), which won the Trevor Reese Prize for the best book published in Imperial and Commonwealth History 2007–10.

Yves Déloye is Professor of Politics at the University of Paris I Panthéon-Sorbonne, member of the Institut Universitaire de France (2000–5), and General Secretary of the Association Française de Science Politique. He specializes in the historical sociology of politics, the study of political socialization, and the theoretical perspectives on the historical emergence of European citizenship. His publications include *Sociologie historique du politique*, 3rd edn. (Paris: La Découverte, 2007); *Les Voix de Dieu. Pour une autre histoire du suffrage électoral: le clergé français et le vote XIXe–XXe siècle* (Paris: Fayard, 2006); *Encyclopaedia of European Elections*, edited with M. Bruter (New

York: Palgrave, 2007); and *L'acte de vote*, in collaboration with O. Ihl (Paris: Sciences Po, Les Presses, 2008).

Don H. Doyle is the McCausland Professor of History at the University of South Carolina and Director of ARENA, the Association for Research on Ethnicity and Nationalism in the Americas. Together with Marco Pamplona he edited a collection of essays, *Nationalism in the New World* (Athens, GA: University of Georgia Press, 2006. His publications include *Nations Divided: America, Italy, and the Southern Question* (Athens, GA: University of Georgia Press, 2002). He is presently editing a collection of essays on *Secession as an International Phenomenon* and writing a book on the creation of US nationalism between the Revolution and the Civil War.

Roger Eatwell is Professor of Comparative European Politics and Dean of Humanities and Social Sciences at the University of Bath. He has published widely on interwar and post-war fascism and the extreme right, including *Fascism: A History* (London: Chatto and Windus, 1995) and, as co-editor, *Charisma and Fascism in Interwar Europe* (London: Routledge, 2007).

Andreas Eckert is Professor of African History at Humboldt University Berlin and Director of the International Research Institute's Work and Human Life Course in Global History. He is editor of the *Journal of African History*. His publications include *Kolonialismus* (Frankfurt: Fischer Taschenbuch Verlag, 2006); *Herrschen und Verwalten. Afrikanische Bürokraten, staatliche Ordnung und Politik in Tanzania, 1920–1970* (Munich: Oldenbourg, 2007); and *Vom Imperialismus zum Empire*, edited with Shalini Randeria (Berlin: Suhrkamp, 2009).

Susan-Mary Grant is Professor of American History at Newcastle University, UK. Her book publications include *North Over South: Northern Nationalism and American Identity in the Antebellum Era* (Lawrence, KS: 2000); *The War for a Nation: The American Civil War* (New York: Routledge, 2006); and *Themes of the American Civil War: The War between the States* (New York: Routledge, 2010).

Montserrat Guibernau, MPhil, PhD, University of Cambridge, is currently Professor of Politics at Queen Mary, University of London, and Visiting Fellow at the Centre for Global Governance, LSE. Her recent books include *Per un catalanisme cosmopolita* (Barcelona: Angle Editorial, 2009); *The Identity of Nations* (Cambridge: Polity Press, 2007); *Catalan Nationalism* (London: Routledge, 2004); *Nations without States* (Cambridge: Polity Press, 1999); and *The Ethnicity Reader*, 2nd edn., with John Rex (Cambridge: Polity Press, 2010).

Fred Halliday† at the time of his death in April 2010 was ICREA Research Professor at the Barcelona Institute for International Studies. His book publications include *Nation and Religion in the Middle East* (London: Saqi, 2000) and *100 Myths About the Middle East* (London: Saqi, 2005).

David Henley is Professor of Contemporary Indonesia Studies at the University of Leiden. His publications include *Nationalism and Regionalism in a Colonial Context: Minahasa in the Dutch East Indies* (Leiden: KITLV Press, 1996); *Jealousy and Justice: The Indigenous Roots of Colonial Rule in Northern Sulawesi* (Amsterdam: VU Uitgeverij, 2002); and, as co-editor and contributor, *The Revival of Tradition in Indonesian Politics: The Deployment of Adat from Colonialism to Indigenism* (New York: Routledge, 2007).

Miroslav Hroch is Professor of History at Charles University, Prague. His publications in English include *Social Preconditions of National Revival in Europe* (Cambridge: Cambridge University Press, 1985, and Columbia, NY, 2000); *In the National Interest: Demands and Goals of European National Movements* (Prague: Charles University, 2000); and *Comparative Studies in Modern European History* (Aldershot: Ashgate Variorum, 2007).

John Hutchinson is Reader in Nationalism in the Government Department at the London School of Economics. He has written widely on nationalism, including *The Dynamics of Cultural Nationalism: The Gaelic Revival and the Creation of the Irish Nation-State* (London: Allen and Unwin, 1987); *Modern Nationalism* (London: Fontana, 1994); and *Nations as Zones of Conflict* (London: Sage, 2005). He is currently completing a monograph on Nationalism and War.

Christophe Jaffrelot is Senior Research Fellow at CERI-Sciencs Po/CNRS and Professor of South Asian Politics and Society at the King's Indian Institute. His books include *The Hindu Nationalist Movement and Indian Politics* (New York: Columbia University Press, 1996); and, as editor, both *Pakistan: Nationalism Without a Nation?* (Delhi: Manohar; London and New York: Zed Books, 2002) and *Hindu Nationalism: A Reader* (New Delhi: Permanent Black, and Princeton, NJ: Princeton University Press, 2007).

Paul Lawrence is a senior lecturer in history at The Open University. His research interests include theories of nationalism, the relationship between historiography and nationalism, and the history of crime and policing in Europe. His main publications to date include *Nationalism: History and Theory* (London: Longman, 2005); *Crime and Justice 1750–1950* (Cullompton, UK: Willan Press, 2005), written with Barry Godfrey; and *History and Crime* (London: Sage, 2008), written with Barry Godfrey and Chris Williams. He has published articles in *French History*, *Contemporary European History*, *Immigrants and Minorities*, *Déviance et société*, and *Crime, histoire et sociétés*.

John M. Lonsdale is Emeritus Professor of Modern African History at the University of Cambridge and Fellow of Trinity College, Cambridge. His publications include *Unhappy Valley: Conflict in Kenya and Africa* (London: Ohio University Press, 1992), with Bruce Berman; *Mau Mau and Nationhood: Arms, Authority and Narrative* (Oxford: James Currey, 2003), co-edited with Atieno Odhiambo; and *Writing for Kenya: The Life and Work of Henry Muoria* (Leiden: Brill, 2009), co-edited with Wangari Muoria Sal, Bodil Folke Frederiksen, and Derek Peterson. He is currently working, with Bruce Berman, on the intellectual histories of Jomo Kenyatta and Louis Leakey, with a focus on their imagination of Kikuyu ethnicity.

James Mayall, Emeritus Sir Patrick Sheehy Professor of International Relations, University of Cambridge. His publications include *Nationalism and International Society* (Cambridge: Cambridge University Press, 1990); *World Politics: Progress and its Limits* (Cambridge: Polity Press, 2000); with Krishnan Srinivasan, *Towards the New Horizon: World Order in the 21st Century* (New Delhi: Standard Publishers, 2009).

Nicola Miller is Professor of Latin American History at University College London. Her publications include *Soviet Relations with Latin America, 1959–1987* (Cambridge: Cambridge University Press, 1989); *In the Shadow of the State: Intellectuals and the Quest for Identity in Twentieth-Century Spanish America* (London: Verso, 1999); *Reinventing Modernity: Latin American Intellectuals Imagine the Future, 1900–1930* (New York: Palgrave Macmillan, 2008).

Rana Mitter is Professor of the History and Politics of Modern China at Oxford University. He is the author of *The Manchurian Myth: Nationalism, Resistance and Collaboration in Modern China* (Berkeley, CA: University of California Press, 2000); *A Bitter Revolution: China's Struggle with the Modern World* (Oxford: Oxford University Press, 2004), for which he was named *Times Higher Education Supplement* Young Academic Author of the Year; and *Modern China: A Very Short Introduction* (Oxford: Oxford University Press, 2008). His articles have appeared in scholarly journals including *The China Quarterly*, *The Historical Journal*, and *Modern Asian Studies*. In 2007–12 he ran a major project funded by the Leverhulme Trust on the experience, legacy, and memory of World War II in China. He is a regular broadcaster on BBC radio, and has written for publications including the *Financial Times*, *Times Literary Supplement*, and *History Today*.

Aaron William Moore is a lecturer in East Asian history at the Department of History, University of Manchester. His first book, *The Peril of Self-Discipline* (Cambridge, MA: Harvard University Press, 2012) examines over two hundred diaries by Chinese, Japanese, and American soldiers during WWII. He is currently writing a second monograph analysing the personal documents of children and adolescents during the 1930s and 1940s in China, Japan, England, and the USSR. Other publications include 'The Chimera of Privacy: Reading Self-Discipline in the Diaries of Japanese Servicemen from the Second World War (1937–1945)'; 'Talk about Heroes: Expressions of Self-Mobilization and Despair in Chinese War Diaries (1911–1938)'; and 'The Problem of Changing Language Communities: Veterans and Memory Writing in China, Taiwan, and Japan'.

Jürgen Osterhammel is Professor of Modern and Contemporary History at the University of Konstanz (Germany). His publications include *Colonialism: A Theoretical Overview* (Princeton, NJ: Princeton University Press, 2005); with Niels P.

Petersson: *Globalization: A Short History* (Princeton, NJ: Princeton University Press 2005); *Die Verwandlung der Welt: Eine Geschichte des 19. Jahrhunderts* (Munich: C. H. Beck, 2009, American edition forthcoming).

Aviel Roshwald is Professor of History at Georgetown University, Washington, DC, where he directs the Master of Arts in Global, International, and Comparative History program (MAGIC). His most recent book is *The Endurance of Nationalism: Ancient Roots and Modern Dilemmas* (Cambridge: Cambridge University Press, 2006). His previous publications include *Estranged Bedfellows: Britain and France in the Middle East during the Second World War* (New York: Oxford University Press, 1990) and *Ethnic Nationalism and the Fall of Empires: Central Europe, Russia and the Middle East, 1914–1923* (London: Routledge, 2001). He is also the co-editor, with Richard Stites, of *European Culture in the Great War: The Arts, Entertainment, and Propaganda, 1914–1918* (Cambridge: Cambridge University Press, 1999).

Michael Rowe is Lecturer in Modern European History at King's College London. His publications include *From Reich to State: The Rhineland in the Revolutionary Age, 1780–1830* (Cambridge: Cambridge University Press, 2003) and, as editor, *Collaboration and Resistance in Napoleonic Europe* (London: Palgrave, 2003).

Sabine Rutar is a research fellow at the Südost-Institut, Regensburg. She is the managing editor of *Südosteuropa: A Journal of Politics and Society*. Her publications include (ed.) *Beyond the Balkans: Towards an Inclusive History of Southeastern Europe* (Münster: Lit Verlag, 2012 [Studies on South East Europe, 10]); 'Labor and Communism in Yugoslavia and Italy. Trieste and the Northeastern Adriatic During the Cold War (1945–1975): A Contribution to the Renewal of Workers' History', in *Acta Historiae*, 18 (2010), 1–2, 247–74; *Kultur—Nation—Milieu. Sozialdemokratie in Triest vor dem Ersten Weltkrieg* (Essen: Klartext Verlag, 2004).

John Schwarzmantel is Senior Lecturer in Politics, and Director of the Centre for Democratisation Studies, at the University of Leeds. His main research interests are in the field of political ideologies and theories of democracy. His major publications include *Socialism and the Idea of the Nation* (New York: Harvester Wheatsheaf, 1991); *The State in Contemporary Society* (New York: Harvester Wheatsheaf, 1994); *The Age of Ideology: Political Ideologies from the American Revolution to Modern Times* (Basingstoke: Palgrave Macmillan, 1998); *Citizenship and Identity* (London: Routledge, 2003); and most recently *Ideology and Politics* (London: Sage, 2008). He has also contributed a chapter on 'Karl Renner and the Problem of Multiculturalism' to the collected volume *National Cultural Autonomy and its Contemporary Critics* (London: Routledge, 2005).

John T. Sidel is the Sir Patrick Gillam Professor of International and Comparative Politics at the London School of Economics and Political Science. He is the author of *Capital, Coercion, and Crime: Bossism in the Philippines* (Stanford, CA: Stanford

University Press, 1999); with Eva-Lotta Hedman, *Philippine Politics and Society in the Twentieth Century: Colonial Legacies, Postcolonial Trajectories* (London: Routledge, 2000); *Riots, Pogroms, Jihad: Religious Violence in Indonesia* (Ithaca, NY: Cornell University Press, 2006); and *The Islamist Threat in Southeast Asia: A Reassessment* (Washington, DC: East-West Center Washington, 2007).

Eric Van Young is Professor of History in the University of California, San Diego. His books include *Hacienda and Market in Eighteenth-Century Mexico: The Rural Economy of the Guadalajara Region, 1675–1810* (Berkeley, CA: University of California Press, 1981; rev. edn., 2006); *La crisis del orden colonial. Estructura agrarian y rebeliones populares en la Nueva España, 1750–1821* (Mexico City: Alianza Editorial, 1992); and *The Other Rebellion: Popular Violence, Ideology, and the Struggle for Mexican Independence, 1810–1821* (Stanford, CA: Stanford University Press, 2001).

Peter van der Veer is Director of the Max Planck Institute for the Study of Religious and Ethnic Diversity in Göttingen and University Professor at Utrecht University. He was awarded the Hendrik Muller Award for outstanding contributions to Social Science Research and has been elected a fellow of the Royal Netherlands Academy of Arts and Sciences. His books include *Imperial Encounters: Religion and Modernity in India and Britain* (Princeton, NJ: Princeton University Press, 2001); *Nation and Religion* (Princeton, NJ: Princeton University Press, 1999); and *Religious Nationalism: Hindus and Muslims in India* (Berkeley, CA: University of California Press, 1994). He is currently doing comparative research on religion and society in India and China.

Theodore R. Weeks is Professor of History at Southern Illinois University at Carbondale, where he teaches European, world, and Russian history. Among his major publications are *Nation and State in Late Imperial Russia* (DeKalb, IL: Northern Illinois University Press, 1996); *From Assimilation to Antisemitism: The 'Jewish Question' in Poland, 1850–1914* (DeKalb, IL: Northern Illinois University Press, 2006); and *Across the Revolutionary Divide: Russia and the USSR 1861–1945* (Chichester: Wiley-Blackwell, 2011). He is currently working on a history of Vilnius as a multicultural city, 1795–2000.

Oliver Zimmer teaches Modern European History at University College, Oxford. A former Humboldt fellow, he is the author of *A Contested Nation: History, Memory and Nationalism in Switzerland 1861–1891* (Cambridge: Cambridge University Press, 2003); *Nationalism in Europe 1890–1940* (London: Palgrave, 2003); and co-editor (with Len Scales) of *Power and the Nation in European History* (Cambridge: Cambridge University Press, 2005). He is currently working on a book entitled *The Nation in the Town: Nationalism and the Reshaping of German communities, 1860–1900.*

Chronologies

These are very selective. They are intended to help readers follow political events involving nationalist movements in non-national states and state-led and oppositional national movements in nation states. I have organized the chronologies in terms of the regions and cases covered by the chapters in Parts 3 and 4. The chronologies go back no further than the eighteenth century and do not go beyond 2000.

Europe until 1918 (Excluding Habsburg and Ottoman Europe)

DATE	EVENT
1707	Union of England and Scotland
1756–63	Seven Years War involves global conflict between Britain and France and is associated with patriotic discourse and movements in both countries
1772	First partition of Poland
1787	Fiscal measures proposed by French Crown lead to demands for an Estates General to be called
1789	Estates General called; Third Estate declares itself National Assembly; Declaration of Rights of Man and Citizen
1792	France: First Republic declared; war between France and other states, which extends with short breaks until 1815
1793	Second partition of Poland; execution of Louis XVI
1794	Rising in rump state of Poland suppressed
1795	Third and final partition of Poland
1796	Napoleon begins reorganization of Italian lands, first as republics and later as monarchies
1799	Napoleon becomes French First Consul
1804	Napoleon declared Emperor
1806–7	French defeat of Prussia; end of Holy Roman Empire; formation of Confederation of the Rhine; formation of Grand Duchy of Warsaw
1814–15	Defeat of Napoleon; Congress of Vienna confirms partition of Poland; organizes German lands under a Confederation, organizes Italian lands under Austrian domination; restores monarchy in France
1821	Austrian military intervention in Italian states
1830–1	July Revolution in France; insurrection in Congress Poland suppressed by Russia; disturbances in various German and Italian states; uprising against Dutch rule leads to establishment of Belgium

1832	Mazzini founds Young Italy
1834	Formation of German Customs Union under Prussian leadership
1846	Failed nationalist uprisings in Galicia and Posen
1848–9	Revolutions, with many national demands, followed by counter-revolution in France, the Habsburg Empire, the German, Italian, and Polish lands
1857	Formation of Italian National Society
1859–60	France and Piedmont defeat Austria in war, sparking off a chain of events leading to unification of Italy (except the Papal States and Venetia) under Piedmontese rule; formation of German National Association
1862	Bismarck appointed Minister President of Prussia
1863–4	Insurrection in Congress Poland suppressed by Russia, leading to direct incorporation of the territory under Russian rule; beginning of 'Russification' policy by Tsarist state
1864	Austria and Prussia defeat Denmark and take over Schleswig and Holstein
1866–7	Prussia and Italy defeat Austria and other German states; Prussian annexes Schleswig-Holstein and Hannover; creates North German Confederation; Italy acquires Venetia
1870–1	Franco-Prussian War leads to formation of the German Second Empire; Third Republic formed in France; Italian troops enter Rome and take over Papal States
1881	Three Emperor's League hardens control over the Polish lands
1890	Resignation of Bismarck as German Chancellor; Three Emperor's League not renewed
1894	Franco-Russian alliance
1898	Germany embarks on a battleship fleet building programme as part of an imperialist strategy
1904	Unrest in Finland in response to tightening of Russian control; war between Russia and Japan
1905	Revolution in Russia stimulates nationalist movements
1907	Elections to Russian Duma encourage nationalist organizations
1914	Start of World War I
1916	Austria and Germany create an autonomous Poland; ethnic uprising against Russian rule in Turkestan
1917	Russian revolutions in February and October; Lenin supports 'national liberation' and Woodrow Wilson 'national self-determination'
1918	Germany ends war against Bolshevik Russia with draconian treaty of Brest-Litovsk; launches offensive on Western Front, which fails, and sues for peace in September; national and other uprisings throughout Europe
1918–19	Peace Conference in Versailles leads to formation of new nation states in central Europe

Habsburg Empire

DATE	EVENT
1780	Joseph II becomes Emperor, introduces enlightened reforms
1789	The first Czech patriotic newspaper founded
1791–2	Magyar and Bohemian nobility demand repeal of reforms
1792	Slovak Learned Society founded; wars against France begin
1804	Francis II, Holy Roman Emperor, declares himself Francis I, Emperor of Austria
1806	Abolition of the Holy Roman Empire
1808–9	'Patriotic' war against Napoleon

DATE	EVENT
1809	Illyrian provinces created by Napoleon; philologist J. Kopitar proposes the name 'Slovene'
1818	Czech Patriotic Museum founded
1825	Hungarian Diet begins national reforms
1830	First Slovene literary almanack
1841	Magyar liberals led by Kossuth enter Hungarian Diet
1843	Slovak patriots approve new version of Slovak written language
1847	Liberals achieve majority in the lower chamber of Hungarian Diet
1848	Magyar national revolution; publication of Czech political programme; Slovenes officially approved as a nationality in Austria
1848–9	Austrian Constitution proclaimed but never implemented; Magyar revolution suppressed
1851–9	Neo-absolutist government in Austria
1861	Start of constitutionalist era
1866	Concept of Unified Slovenia approved; Austria defeated in war with Prussia
1867	Austro-Hungarian compromise creates dualist monarchy
1867–8	Mass protests in Bohemia against dualism
1868	Magyar-Croatian agreement; start of Magyarization
1871	First unsuccessful attempt at German-Czech compromise
1874	University in Zagreb opened
1907	Universal direct suffrage for Austrian and Bohemian lands
1918	Dissolution of Habsburg Empire; formation of Czechoslovakia and Yugoslavia; Transylvania incorporated into Romania

Ottoman Empire and Middle East to 1923

DATE	EVENT
1791	Sultan Selim III starts rationalizing reforms in the empire
1789	First steps toward state organization in Montenegro
1792	Declaration in favour of 'Romanian nation' published in Transylvania
1804–13	Serbian peasant uprising leads to autonomy (George Karadjordje)
1815	New Serbian upheaval (Milos Obrenovic)
1821	Start of Greek revolt
1822	Greek independence and first Constitution
1826	Serbian Matica founded in southern Hungary
1827	British, French, and Russian intervention in favour of Greeks
1829	Greek independence approved by Great Powers
1830–1	Autonomous Serbian Principality approved
1835	Establishment of first school with Bulgarian as language of education
1839	Formal declaration of equality between Muslims and Christians
1848	Russia invades Danubian principalities
1852	Independence of Montenegro under Russian protection
1859	Unification of Wallachia and Moldavia into one independent state
1861	Danubian principality becomes Kingdom of Romania
1862	Bulgarian government in exile formed
1875–8	Eastern Crisis (from Bosnian revolt through suppression of Bulgarian uprising to Ottoman-Serbian and Ottoman-Russian War)

1876	23 December: Promulgation of Ottoman Constitution
1878	14 February: Suspension of Ottoman Constitution; Prizren League, first Albanian national association
1878	Treaty of Berlin: Great Powers approved independence of Serbia, Montenegro, Romania, and Bulgaria; Bosnia and Herzegovina occupied by Austria
1882	British occupation of Egypt following rising under Arabi Pasha
1893	Underground Army for Macedonia's liberation established
1897	First Zionist Congress (Basel, Switzerland)
1903	Ilinden revolt in Macedonia; linguistic definition of Macedonian nation
1911	Italian invasion and occupation of Ottoman-ruled Tripolitania (Libya) and the Dodecanese islands
1912–13	First and Second Balkan Wars; independent Albania recognized by Major Powers; takeover of Ottoman territory by Greece and Serbia
1914	November: Ottoman entry into war on side of Central Powers
1917	2 November: Balfour Declaration
1918	Formation of Yugoslavia
1919	Transylvania becomes part of Romania; uprising in Egypt
1920	Treaty of Sèvres (ending state of war between Allies and Ottoman Empire); San Remo Conference (formal Anglo-French partition of Middle East); Iraqi Revolt
1920–2	Turkish-Greek War
1922	Britain recognizes kingdom of Egypt
1923	Treaty of Lausanne (granting Turkey much more favourable terms than the now defunct Treaty of Sèvres); 29 October 1923: Proclamation of Turkish Republic, with Mustafa Kemal (later Atatürk) as president

Europe after 1918

1919	Formation of Weimar Republic
1922	Formation of USSR initially with six 'national republics': Russia, Ukraine, Belorussia, Armenia, Azerbaijan, Georgia; Mussolini becomes prime minister of Italy
1923	Failure of putsch in Munich led by Hitler
1927	Romanian Fascist organization the Iron Guard established
1932	USSR: Nationality to be entered on passports
1933	Hitler appointed German chancellor; Nazi takeover
1936–9	Spanish Civil War ends with Franco's military dictatorship
1938	USSR: National republics now reached fifteen; plus thirteen autonomous Soviet Socialist Republics and seventeen national regions and autonomous provinces; Austria merged with Germany; Munich agreement on Czechoslovakia
1939	Start of Second World War
1941	German attack on USSR; renewed Russification policy by Stalin and deportation of whole peoples
1945	USSR confirms and extends its direct or indirect control over Eastern Europe
1948	Tito-Stalin split; break between Albania and Yugoslavia
1949	Establishment of NATO; constitutions for the Federal Republic of Germany and the German Democratic Republic
1953	Death of Stalin
1955	Establishment of Warsaw Pact

1956	Khruschev's speech at 20th Congress of Soviet Communist Party; Hungarian Revolution
1957	Treaty of Rome establishes European Economic Community, forerunner of the European Union
1961	Non-aligned movement formed in Belgrade; Albania breaks off relations with USSR
1963	Third Yugoslav Constitution grants right of secession to republics
1965	Ceausescu takes over in Romania
1968	Prague Spring
1972	Albania breaks with China; now totally isolated
1980	Death of Tito
1984	Forced Bulgarization of Turkish people
1985	Death of Enver Hoxha, ruler of Albania; Mikhail Gorbachev party leader in USSR
1987	Gorbachev publishes *Perestroika*; warns of threat of nationalism in USSR; Slobodan Milosevic comes to power as head of Serbian League of Communism
1988	Start of large anti-communist demonstrations in USSR and other communist states in Eastern Europe
1989	Collapse of communist regimes throughout Eastern Europe
1991	End of Soviet Union; Croatia and Slovenia declare independence; war between 'Yugoslavia' (effectively Serbia) and Croatia
1992	European Union recognizes Croatia and Slovenia; Bosnia-Herzegovina declares independence and at war with Serbia
1996	Dayton Agreement ends war between Bosnia and Serbia
1998–9	War between Serbia and Kosovo; ended following NATO bombing
1999	Death of Croatian President Franjo Tudman
2000	End of Milosevic's rule in remainder of Yugoslavia (Serbia and Montenegro)

Middle East and North Africa after 1923

1924	Turkey abolishes Caliphate
1925–7	Syria's Great Revolt
1928	Muslim Brotherhood founded in Egypt
1929	Western Wall riots in Palestine
1930	Anglo-Iraqi treaty (implemented 1932); name of Constantinople changed to Istanbul
1932	Turkey admitted to League of Nations
1936	Anglo-Egyptian treaty; Arab High Committee formed to combat Jewish claims; Franco-Syrian treaty (never ratified by French); Bakr Sidqi's coup in Iraq
1937	Assassination of Bakr Sidqi; British Royal Commission on Palestine recommends establishment of Jewish and Arab states
1936–9	Arab Revolt in Palestine
1939	British White Paper on Palestine; the British plan for an independent Palestine by 1947 denounced by both Arabs and Jews
1941	Rashid Ali's Revolt in Iraq; demand for British military withdrawal from Iraq; British and Free French seize Syria and Lebanon from Vichy France
1942	Egypt cleared of Germans
1944–5	Formation of Arab League
1947	British proposal to divide Palestine rejected by Arabs and Jews and matter referred to United Nations
1948	Formation of state of Israel, which defeats Arab attacks

1949	Israel admitted into United Nations
1952	Anti-British riots in Egypt; King Farouk abdicates in favour of his son, Fuad
1954	Gamal Abdel Nasser takes power in Egypt
1956	Suez crisis: Anglo-French forces land in Egypt; soon removed following Egyptian resistance and pressure from USA; Sudan, Morocco, and Tunisia declare independence
1958	Syria and Egypt form the United Arab Republic (UAE) with Nasser as president; monarchy overthrown in Iraq
1961	Syria leaves UAE
1967	Six-Day War
1969	Yasser Arafat elected chairman of Executive Committee of the Palestine Liberation Organization
1970	Death of Nasser
1973	Renewed Israel-Arab War
1975	Onset of civil war in Lebanon
1978	Camp David accord signals withdrawal of Egypt from united Arab front against Israel
1979	Iranian Revolution; Saddam Hussein becomes president of Iraq
1982	Israel invades Lebanon; start of war between Iraq and Iran
Late 1980s	Palestinian revolt in occupied West Bank and Gaza; formation of Hamas
1990	Iraqi invasion of Kuwait defeated by military forces led by USA; end of Iraq-Iran war

Sub-Saharan Africa after 1800

DATE	EVENT
1814	Cape of Good Hope becomes British colony
1836	Beginning of 'Great Trek'
1838	Battle of Blood River: Boers defeat Zulus
1869	Opening of Suez Canal
1873	Ashanti War
1879	British-Zulu War
1883	Germany begins settlements in south-west Africa, France taking over upper Niger
1884	Berlin Conference of fourteen states to agree on territorial claims in Africa
1885	King Leopold takes over Congo; Germany annexes Tanganyika and Zanzibar; British protectorates over North Bechuanaland and Niger river region
1886	Anglo-German agreements on areas of control in west and east Africa; German-Portugese agreement in south-west Africa
1887	Britain annexes Zululand; British East Africa Company chartered
1890	Cecil Rhodes premier of Cape Colony; Lugard occupies Uganda for British East Africa Company
1895	Creation of Rhodesia and East African Protectorate
1896	Kenya incorporated into East African Protectorate
1899	Second Boer War
1901	Ashanti kingdom annexed to Gold Coast colony
1902	End of Second Boer War
1910	Union of South Africa established
1918	Britain takes over Germany's East African colonies
1920	Colony of Kenya created
1945	First parties formed in Uganda
1946	New Constitution in Gold Coast; first British African colony with African majority in legislature

DATE	EVENT
1947	Nigeria acquires modified self-government
1948	National Party wins general election in South Africa
1952	Formation of Uganda National Congress; state of emergency declared in Kenya following murders by what British identify as the 'Mau-Mau'
1953	Federal constitution of Rhodesia and Nyasaland
1954	Nkrumah forms government in Gold Coast following electoral victory of Convention People's Party
1957	Ghana becomes independent
1960	Independence for Belgian Congo: France agrees to independence for Dahomey, Niger, Upper Volta, Chad, Ivory Coast, Central Africa, and French Congo; Nigerian independence
1961	Independence for Sierra Leone
1962	Independence for Uganda and Tanganyika
1963	Kenyan and Zanzibari independence
1964	Zambia (formerly Northern Rhodesia) and Malawi (formerly Nyasaland) become independent; creation of Tanzania
1965	White regime in Southern Rhodesia unilaterally declares independence
1967	Civil war in Nigeria, which lasts until Biafran defeat in 1970
1975	Angola, Mozambique, and other Portugese African colonies independent
1979	Southern Rhodesia becomes independent as Zimbabwe under majority rule
1990	Release of Nelson Mandela
1994	Introduction of majority rule in South Africa; Mandela becomes president

India from the Late 18th Century

DATE	EVENT
1793	East India Company introduces the Permanent Settlement
1802	Start of a series of victories by the Company leads to its control of large parts of India
1857	Revolution in India ('Indian Mutiny')
1858	Powers of Company transferred to British Crown
1877	Queen Victoria declared Empress of India
1886	First meeting of Indian National Congress
1906	All India Moslem League formed
1909	Indian Councils Act gives greater powers to legislative councils and ensures appointment of an Indian to Viceroy's executive council
1919	Constitutional reforms increase Indian participation in government and widen franchises to local legislative councils; troops fire on demonstrators in Jallianwala Bagh; martial law declared in Punjab; Mahatma Gandhi starts first non-cooperation campaign
1921	First Indian Parliament meets
1922	Gandhi sentenced to six years' imprisonment for civil disobedience
1925	Establishment of Hindu nationalist organization Rashtriya Swayamsevak Sangh (National Volunteer Corps)
1929	Round Table Conference between Viceroy and Indian leaders on dominion status
1930	Gandhi opens civil disobedience campaign; Simon Report on India published
1931	Delhi pact: civil disobedience campaign suspended, Congress promises to recognize Round Table Conference, political prisoners released

1932	Indian Congress declared illegal; Gandhi arrested; third India conference in London
1934	Gandhi suspends civil disobedience campaign
1935	Government of India Act reforms government; separates Burma and Aden from India; grants provinces greater self-government; creates central legislature in Delhi to come into operation on 1 April 1937
1937	Congress wins elections to provincial governments but abstains from forming a government, demanding full independence
1940	Congress rejects Viceroy's invitation to serve on War Advisory Board
1942	Gandhi arrested
1945	Congress demands Britain 'Quit India'; Congress and Muslim League win most seats for Central Legislative Assembly
1946	Constituent Assembly, boycotted by Muslim League, discusses independence
1947	Independence declared; country partitioned into India and Pakistan, with many deaths and refugees in Punjab and Bengal
1948	Gandhi assassinated
1950	Indian Constitution recognizes fifteen official languages
1951	Jana Sangh, Hindu nationalist political party, formed
1956	Reorganization of Indian provinces along linguistic lines agreed
1959	Ayub Khan bans political parties in Pakistan
1970	Victory for East Pakistan Awami League in general election
1971	East Pakistan becomes independent state of Bangladesh
1977	Jana Singh merges with Janat party to win general election
1980	Bharatiya Janata (BJP) Hindu nationalist party formed
1984	Assassination of Indira Gandhi by one of her Sikh bodyguards
1992	Destruction of Ayodhya mosque; violent Hindu-Muslim conflict

Southeast Asia from the Mid-18th Century

1740	First of series of wars and annexations by Dutch East India Company
1819	Sir Stamford Raffles of British East India Company establishes trading post on Singapore island
1863	French take formal control over Cambodia
1867	France annexes Cochinchina; the Straits Settlement (Singapore, Malacca, Penang) becomes a British Crown colony
1884	French take formal control of Vietnam
1885	British takes formal control of Burma
1898	USA takes control of the Philippines
1904	Phan Boi Chau founds Viet Nam Duy Tan Hoi (Vietnam Reformation Society)
1908	Formation of nationalist organization Budi Utomo in Java
1920	Formation of Indonesian Communist Party
1927	Formation of Vietnamese Nationalist Party; Sukarno founds Indonesian Nationalist Party
1930	Vietnamese Communist Party changes name to Indochinese Communist Party
1940–4	Japanese conquest of Southeast Asia
1945	Japanese forces surrender, nationalist leaders proclaim independence in Indonesia and Vietnam
1946	Philippine independence proclaimed; French troops arrive in Vietnam, Dutch troops in Indonesia

1949	Dutch acknowledge Indonesian independence
1954	Geneva Accords: Independence for Cambodia and Laos, French withdrawal from Vietnam; Democratic Republic of Vietnam confined to north, with US-backed regime created in the South, reunification postponed
1957	Federation of Malaya granted independence
1959	Singapore granted independence
1962	Military coup establishes Army rule in Burma
1963	Singapore, Sabah, and Sarawak join Federation of Malaysia
1965	Singapore expelled from Malaysia; Army coup topples Sukarno, sparks anti-communist pogroms in Indonesia
1969	Ethnic riots in Malaysia lead to authoritarian controls, New Economic Policy; Indonesia absorbs West Papua
1972	President Marcos proclaims martial law in the Philippines
1973	Student-led protests end military rule in Thailand
1975	Reunification of Vietnam, incorporation of South into DRV; Communist victories in Cambodia and Laos; Indonesian invasion of East Timor, initiating twenty-four years of occupation
1976	Army coup restores military rule in Thailand
1978–9	Vietnamese invasion of Cambodia, onset of ten-year occupation
1986	'People Power' revolt ends authoritarian rule in the Philippines, oligarchical democracy restored
1988	Election of civilian prime minister in Thailand
1989	Vietnamese withdrawal from Cambodia
1991	Military coup in Thailand
1992	Civilian rule restored in Thailand
1993	UN-supervised elections in Cambodia, incumbent Hun Sen remain in office
1997–8	Asian economic crisis
1998	Indonesian President Suharto forced to resign
1999	UN-supervised referendum for independence in East Timor, Indonesian military occupation ends

Northeast Asia from 1840

DATE	EVENT
1839–42	First Opium War
1850–5	Tai'ping Rebellion
1854	USA makes first trade treaty with Japan
1857	Royal Navy destroys Chinese fleet; British and French forces take Canton
1858	End of Anglo-Chinese War; further ports opened up to Britain and France; opium trade legalized; Anglo-Japanese commercial treaty providing for unsupervised trade and setting up of a British residency
1860	Anglo-French forces defeat Chinese at Pa Li Chau
1864	British, French, and Dutch fleets attack Japan in reprisal for closing ports and expelling foreigners; Japan made to pay indemnity
1868	Shogunate abolished; Meiji dynasty restored

1871	Abolition of domains and replacement by prefectures
1877	Satsuma rebellion crushed
1887	China cedes Macao to Portugal
1889–9	Japanese Constitution followed by first general election
1893	China-Japan War
1895	Japan gains port facilities and ceded areas at end of war
1897	German and Russian occupations in China
1898	Formation of 'The Boxers', an anti-Western organization; emperor starts extensive reforms but removed by dowager empress who revokes reforms
1900	Boxer uprising; many foreigners killed and the occupying powers suppress uprising
1901	China made to pay indemnity to occupying powers
1904–5	Russo-Japanese War ends with substantial cessions by Russia
1905	Sun Yat Sen founds union of secret societies to expel Manchus from China; Korea made a Japanese protectorate
1908	Dowager empress dies
1910–45	Korea under Japanese rule
1911	Establishment of Chinese Republic with Sun Yat-sen as president and Chiang Kai- shek his military adviser
1919	4 May: Student demonstration in Beijing against treatment of China at Versailles Peace Conference
1922	Nine-power treaty in Washington preserves principle of 'open door' in trade with China; civil war
1924	First Kuomintang Congress includes Communists
1925	30 May: Worker demonstration in Shanghai against foreign firms
1927	Conflict between Chiang Kai-shek and communists who are massacred in Shanghai
1928	Clashes between China and Japan; China annuls 'unequal treaties'; Chiang Kai-shek elected president of China
1933	Japan occupies China north of Great Wall and withdraws from League of Nations
1934–5	Long March led by Mao Zedong
1936	Chiang Kai-shek enters Canton and declares war on Japan
1937	Japan seizes Beijing, Tienkin, Shanghai, Nanking, and Hangchow; Kuomintang and Communists declare common front against Japan
1938	Japan installs puppet government of Chinese Republic of Nanking
1941	Japanese attack on Pearl Harbour; China allied with USA
1942	Major Japanese advances, including in Singapore and Burma, Indo-China, and the Dutch East Indies
1943	Churchill, Roosevelt, and Chiang Kai-shek meet in Cairo
1945	USA drops two atom bombs on Japan, which surrenders a week later; fighting breaks out between communists and nationalists in north China
1946–52	US occupation of Japan
1948	Chiang Kai-shek re-elected president by Nanking Assembly and granted extensive powers; communists announce formation of North China People's Republic
1949	Chiang Kai-shek forced to withdraw to Formosa (renamed Taiwan); Communist People's Republic proclaimed under leadership of Mao Zedong
1958–61	'Great Leap Forward' in China
1966–76	Cultural Revolution; death of Mao Zedong in September 1976
1978	Deng Xiaoping launches economic reforms
1979	Formal diplomatic relations between China and USA
1989	June: Suppression of protest in Tiananmen Square
1997	Hong Kong incorporated into China

Colonial and Post-Colonial America

1754–63	French and Indian War, North America
1759	Charles III (*r.*1759–88) accedes to Spanish throne; era of Bourbon Reforms
1762	British capture and briefly hold Havana
1764	British Sugar Act imposed on Thirteen Colonies
1765	British Stamp Act imposed on Thirteen Colonies, Stamp Act Congress formed
1767	British Townshend Duties on selected imports prompt colonial boycott; Jesuits expelled from Spanish America
1773	Boston Tea Party, colonials protest by dumping tea in harbour
1774	British Coercive Acts shut down Boston harbour, ban public meetings, and end local government; first Continental Congress meets
1775	April 19: Battles of Lexington and Concord begin armed conflict
1776	January: Tom Paine's *Common Sense* published; July 4: Declaration of Independence of the United States of America signed
1777	Articles of Confederation establish national government for USA
1778	British defeated at Battle of Saratoga; French form alliance with USA; Spanish colonial trading system partially opened as measure of Bourbon Reforms
1780–1	Tupac Amaru revolt in Peru; Comunero revolt in Colombia
1781	British surrender after Battle of Yorktown
1783	Treaty of Paris formally ends British-USA conflict
1788	Charles IV (*r.*1788–1808) accedes to Spanish throne
1789	Constitution of USA establishes stronger federal government and adds Bill of Rights; French Revolution sparks revolts in French, Portuguese, and Spanish American colonies; anti-Portuguese Tiradentes Conspiracy in Brazil
1791–1804	Slave revolt in Saint Domingue wins independence for new Republic of Haiti
1794	Colombian patriot Antonio Nariño publishes French revolutionary 'Declaration of the Rights of Man'
1803	Louisiana Purchase
1806	British invade and briefly hold Buenos Aires
1807	King João VI and court flee Portugal to Brazil to escape Napoleonic invasion
1808	Napoleon places his brother Joseph on the Spanish throne; Peninsular War begins; US termination of external slave trade
1810	Creoles establish ruling juntas in Venezuela, Chile, and Argentina; Miguel Hidalgo's 'Grito de Dolores' in Mexico; Hidalgo executed in 1811
1812	Constitution of Cádiz promulgated; US at war with Britain (until 1815)
1814	Ferdinand VII returns to Spanish throne
1815	Simón Bolívar retreats to Jamaica; execution of José María Morelos in Mexico
1821	Mexico becomes independent; King João VI returns to Portugal from Brazil
1822	José de San Martín and Simón Bolívar confer in Guayaquil, Ecuador; San Martín goes into self-imposed exile in France; King Pedro I declares independence of Brazil
1824	Bolívar defeats Spanish forces at Junín, and José Antonio Sucre does the same at Ayacucho, consummating independence of Spanish South America
1829–52	Argentina: Confederation of Río de la Plata run by arbitrary power as dictator Rosas establishes dominance of Buenos Aires
1830	Disintegration of Gran Colombia (est. 1819) into Colombia, Venezuela, and Ecuador; US Indian Removal Act
1830–42	Mexico: Civil war between conservatives and liberals; in 1836 secession of Texas, which becomes a US state in 1845

1838–40	Disintegration of United Provinces of Central America (est. 1823–4) into Costa Rica, El Salvador, Guatemala, Honduras, and Nicaragua, the independent states of today
1846–8	Mexican-American War: US acquires over one-third of Mexico's territory, including California
1860	Republicans (Abraham Lincoln) win presidential election; South Carolina secedes
1861	Start of US Civil War
1862	Mexico: Napoléon III supports conservatives and installs the Hapsburg Maximilian as emperor
1863	1 January: US Emancipation Proclamation
1865	Robert E. Lee surrender to Ulysses Grant at Appomattox; 14–15 April: Abraham Lincoln assassinated
1865–70	War of the Triple Alliance: Argentina, Brazil, and Uruguay defeat Paraguay
1867–76	Mexico: Maximilian defeated by Liberals with help of United States
1868–78	Cuba: First war of independence
1879–83	Chile: War of the Pacific—Chile seizes nitrate deposits from Peru and Bolivia, which is left landlocked; Argentina and Chile: War of the Desert; 'Pacification' of the Mapuche (extermination of indigenous peoples)
1886	Cuba: Slavery abolished
1888	Brazil: Slavery abolished
1889	Brazil: Army overthrows emperor and a republic is founded; First Inter-American Conference held in Washington at US instigation
1895	Cuba: Second War of Independence launched
1898	Spanish-American War: US intervenes in Cuban independence struggle and expels Spain from Cuba, Puerto Rico, and the Philippines; US military occupation of Cuba
1902	Cuba: Inaugurates Republic, but Platt Amendment to Constitution gives US right to intervene, which it does militarily in 1906–9, 1912, and 1917
1903	US intervenes to secure Panama's independence from Colombia; Canal; Treaty signed immediately (Canal opens 1914); Dominican Republic: US assumes control of customs' house
1905	Honduras: US marines intervene, and again in 1907 and 1911
1910–20	Mexico: Revolution; US sends troops twice (1914 and 1916–17)
1915–34	Haiti: US military occupation
1916–24	Dominican Republic: US military occupation
1927–33	Nicaragua: Augusto Sandino leads guerrilla struggle against US military occupation (since 1912, with short interruptions); Sandino killed 1933; US withdraws in 1934 but leaves behind pro-US dictator Somoza
1930	Argentina: Fascist coup gives way to restored oligarchic rule from 1932; Brazil: Oligarchic government overthrown in Liberal Revolution led by Getúlio Vargas, who dominated Brazilian politics until death in 1954
1938	Mexico: Nationalization of oil industry pioneers wave of economic nationalism across the region
1938–52	Chile: Popular Front governments (Communist Party in alliance)
1941–2	Latin American countries support US in declaring war on the Axis powers (Chile in 1943; Argentina in 1945)
1947	Inter-American Treaty of Reciprocal Assistance (Rio Treaty) signed by US and Latin American countries—a mutual assistance pact
1948	Organization of American States (OAS) founded as section of the United Nations
1952	Bolivia: Revolution carried out by MNR (National Revolutionary Movement)
1954	Guatemala: Reformist government led by Jacobo Arbenz overthrown in uprising orchestrated by CIA, after land reform that affected United Fruit Company (UFCO)

1959	Cuba: Revolution led by Fidel Castro and Che Guevara; attempts to imitate it in many other Latin American countries
1960	Cuba: US economic embargo declared; later supported by OAS states (except Mexico)
1961	Cuba: Bay of Pigs invasion by exiles organized by CIA fails; President Kennedy launches Alliance for Progress ($20 billion development aid over ten years, plus counter-insurgency training for Latin American militaries)
1962	Cuba: Alliance with Soviet Union sealed although no formal treaty signed until 1989; Missile Crisis
1965	Dominican Republic: US secures OAS support for military invasion to ensure 'No more Cubas'
1970–3	Chile: Popular Unity government led by Salvador Allende; overthrown by coup, which leads to military rule by Augusto Pinochet until 1990
1976	Argentina: Coup initiates seven years of military rule and 'Dirty War'; Venezuela: Nationalization of oil industry (negotiated)
1979	Nicaragua: Sandinista Revolution; Brazil: Formation of Workers' Party (PT) led by 'Lula' da Silva

Maps

A central theme of this Handbook is that the history of nationalism needs to be treated as distinct from national history. However, a second central theme is that nationalism is fundamentally altered with the formation of nation states, which are then projected as national achievements by nationalist 'winners' as well as national setbacks by nationalist 'losers'. This sequence of maps traces over time from the early eighteenth century to the present the growth in the territorial extent of 'state societies', then the combination of European nation-state formation and overseas empire, and then the decline of imperial states combined with further nation-state formation. The graph at the end provides an overview of the territorial dimensions of these changes.

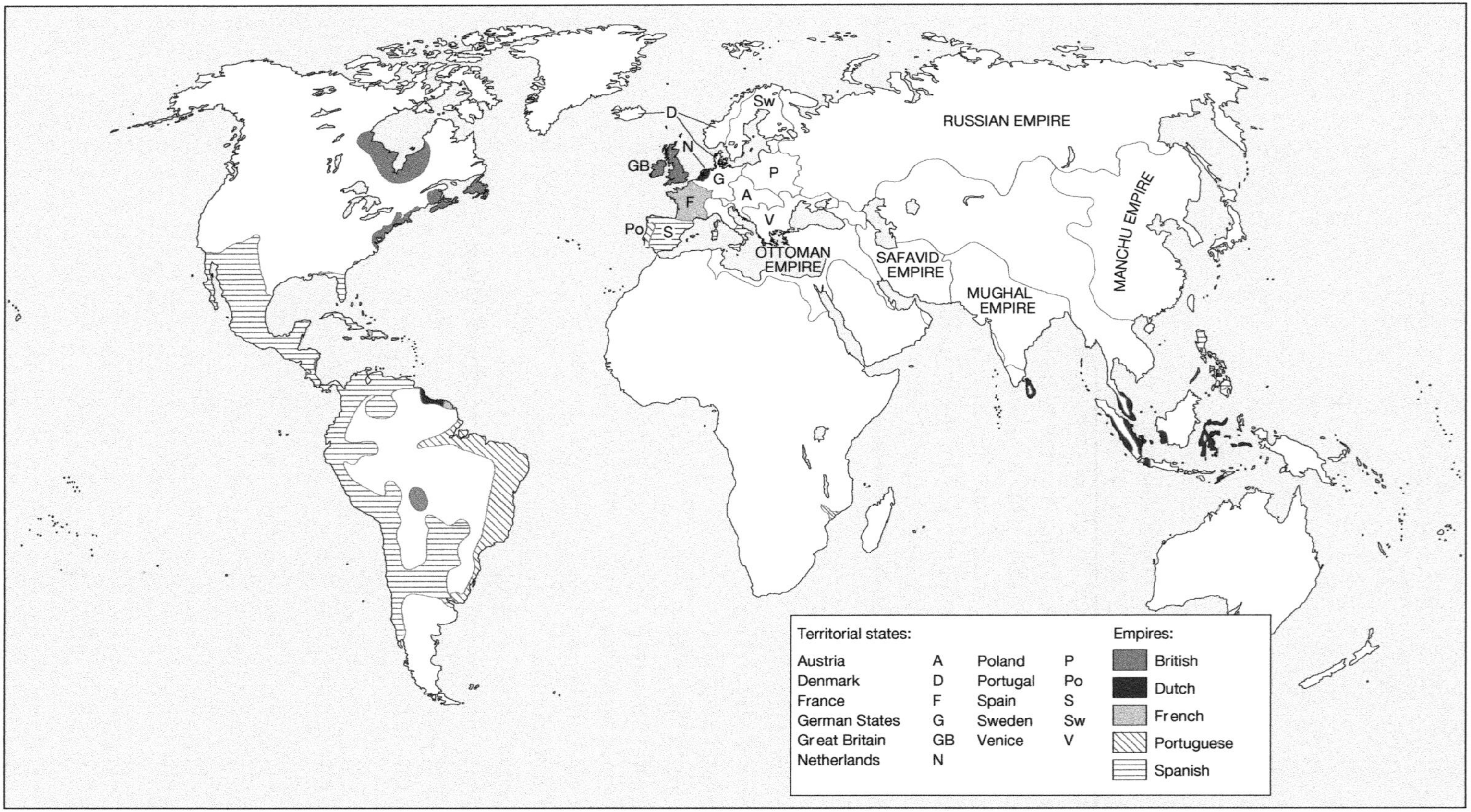

Map. 1. World Map, 1715

This map shows the European states as well as non-European empires in the world in 1715, along with the non-European territories under the control of European states.

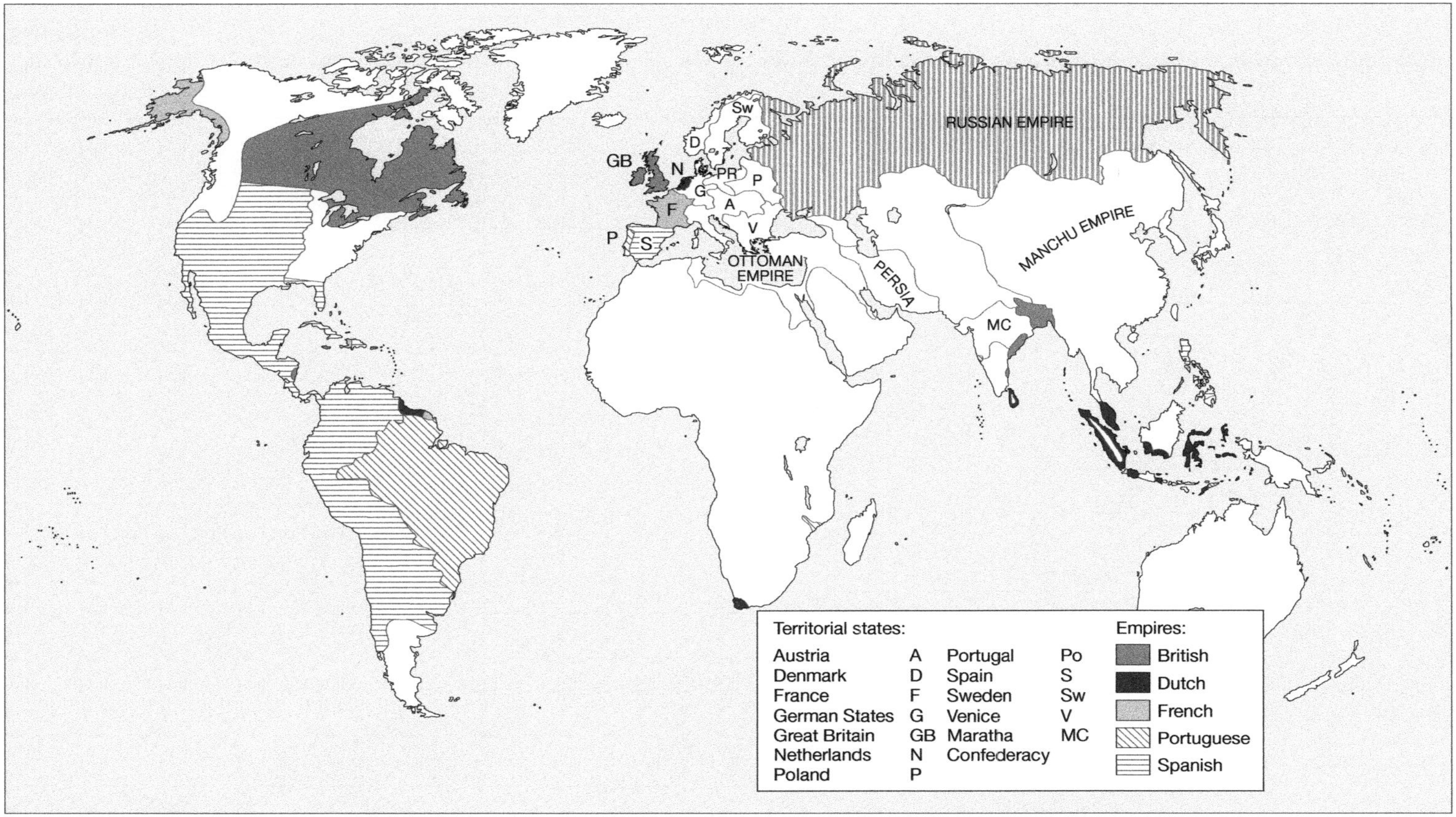

Map. 2. World Map, 1783

This map shows the European states as well as non-European empires in the world in 1783, along with the non-European territories under the control of European states.

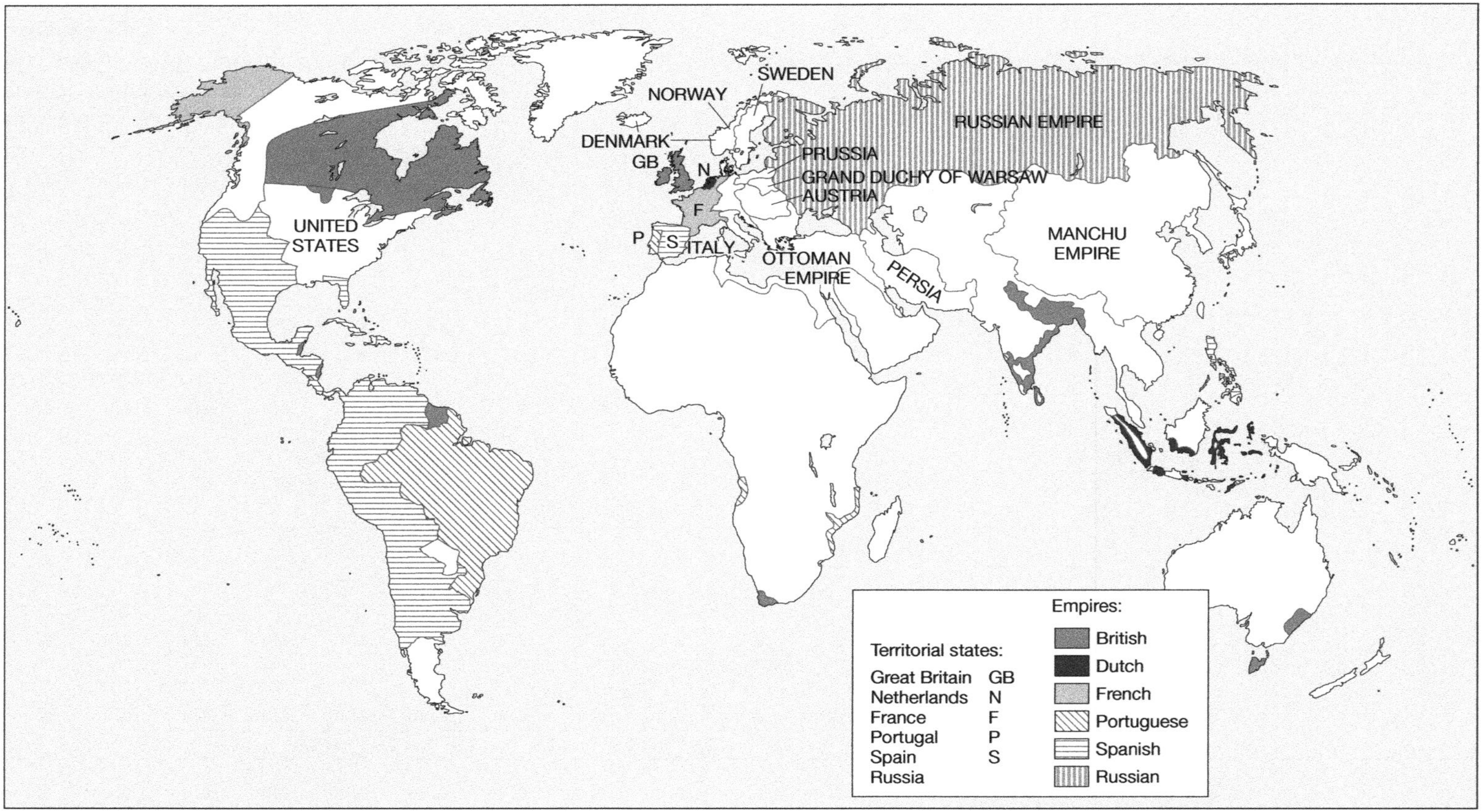

Map. 3. World Map, 1812

This map shows the European states as well as non-European empires in the world in 1812, along with the non-European territories under the control of European states.

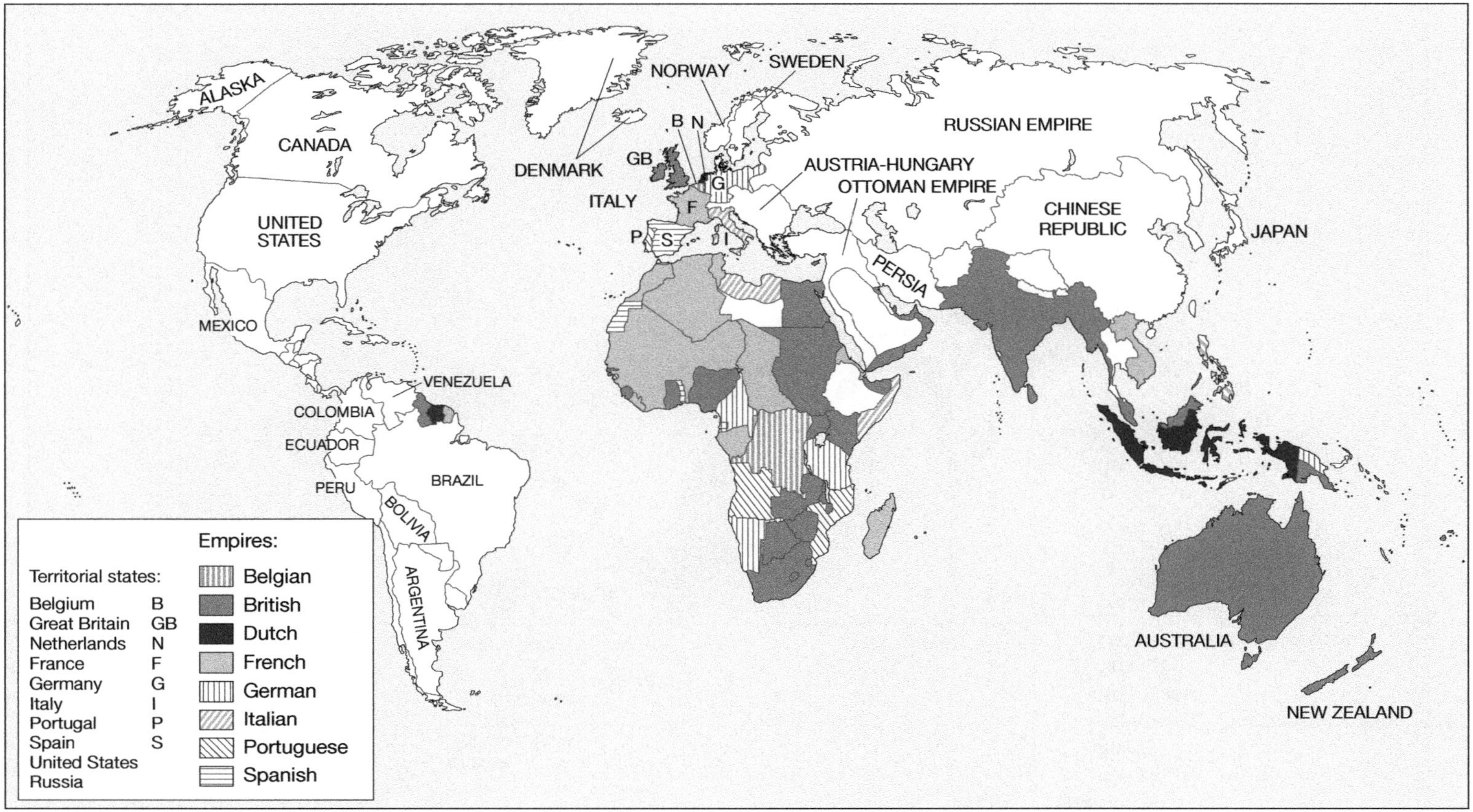

Map. 4. World Map, 1914

This map shows the European states as well as non-European empires in the world in 1914, along with the non-European territories under the control of European states.

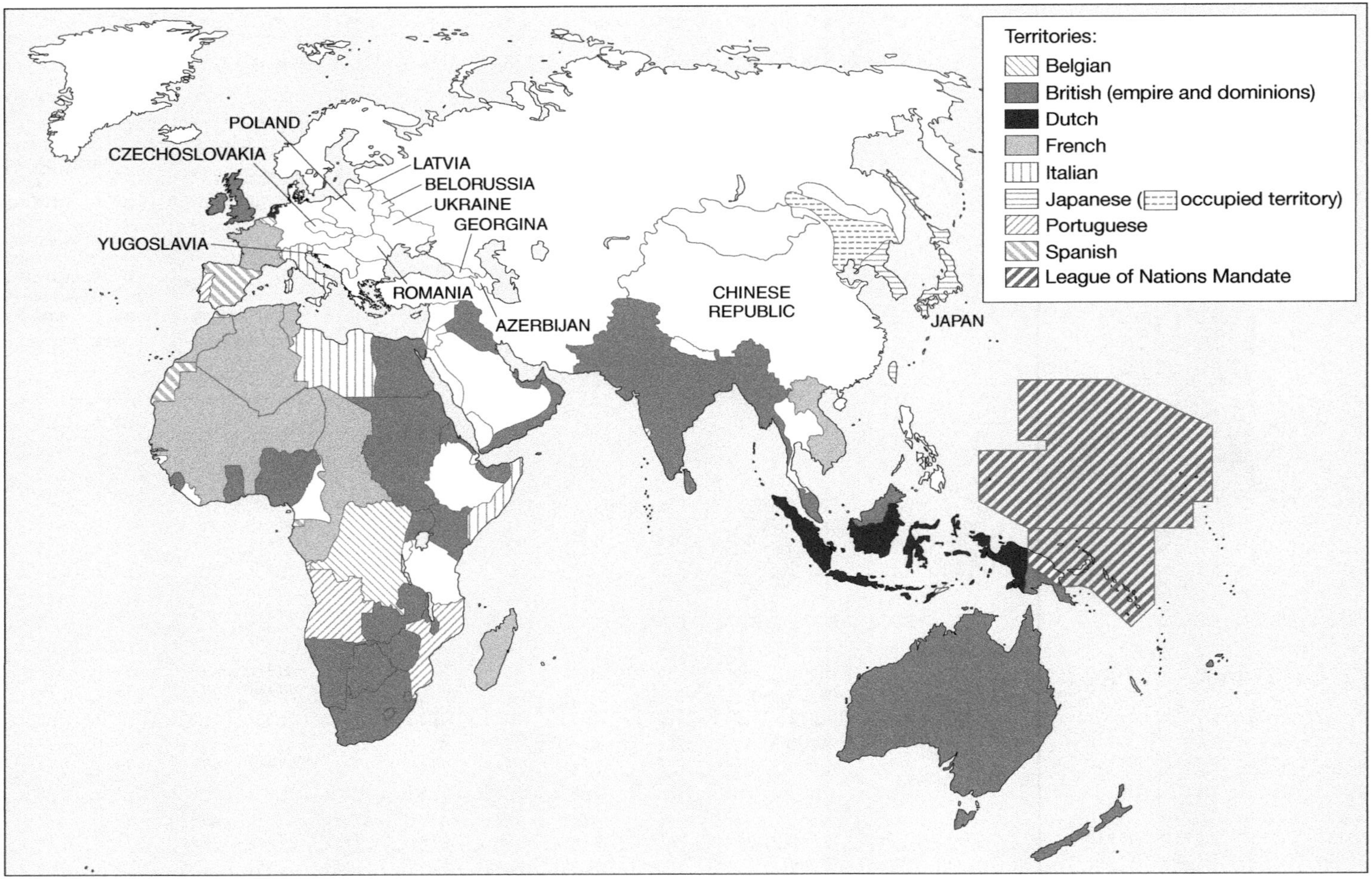

Map. 5. World Map, 1920

This map shows the European states as well as non-European empires in the world in 1920, along with the non-European territories under the control of European states.

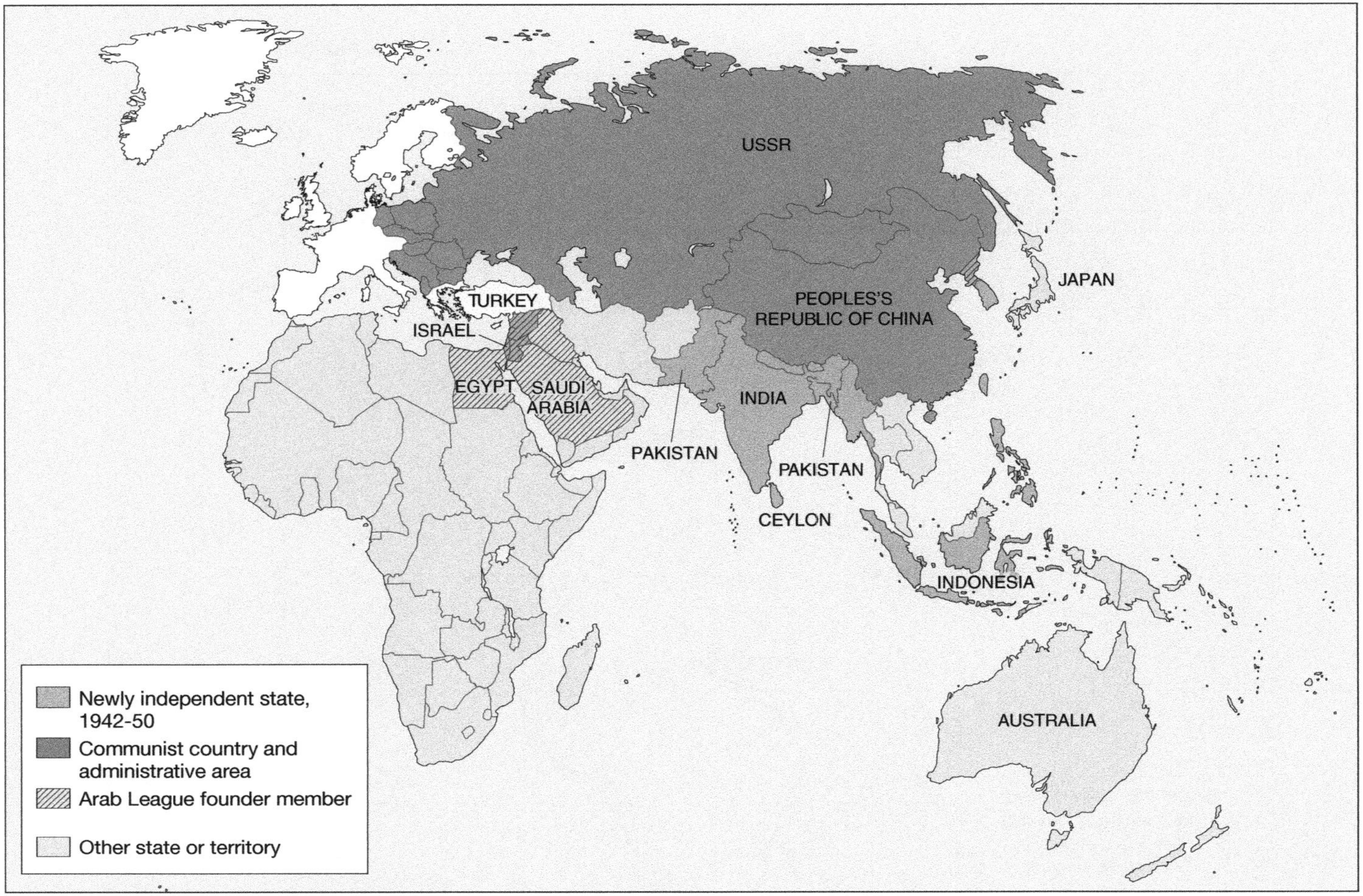

Map. 6. World Map, 1950

This map shows the European states as well as non-European empires in the world in 1950, along with the non-European territories under the control of European states, and non-European territories which had acquired independence.

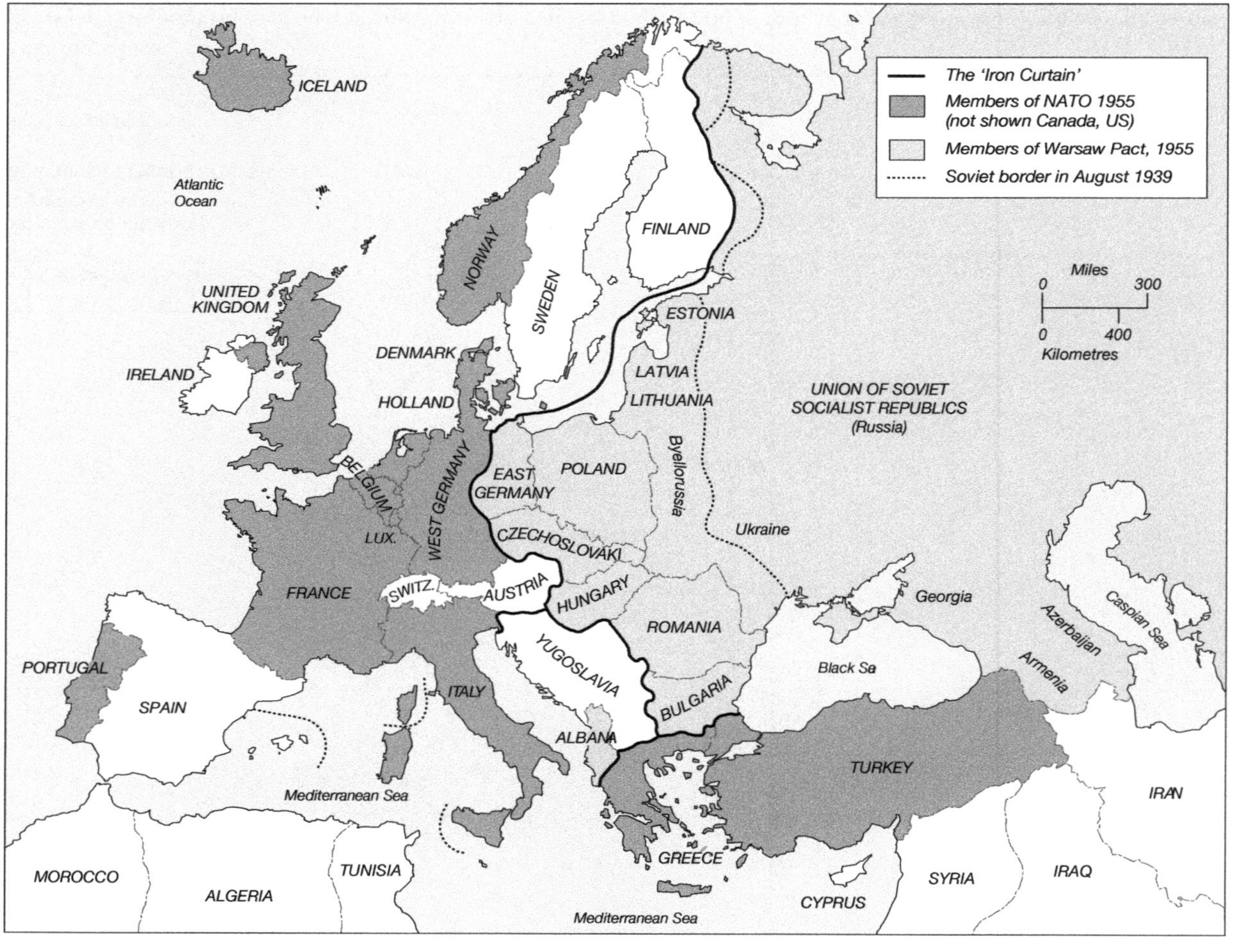

Map. 7. Cold War Europe

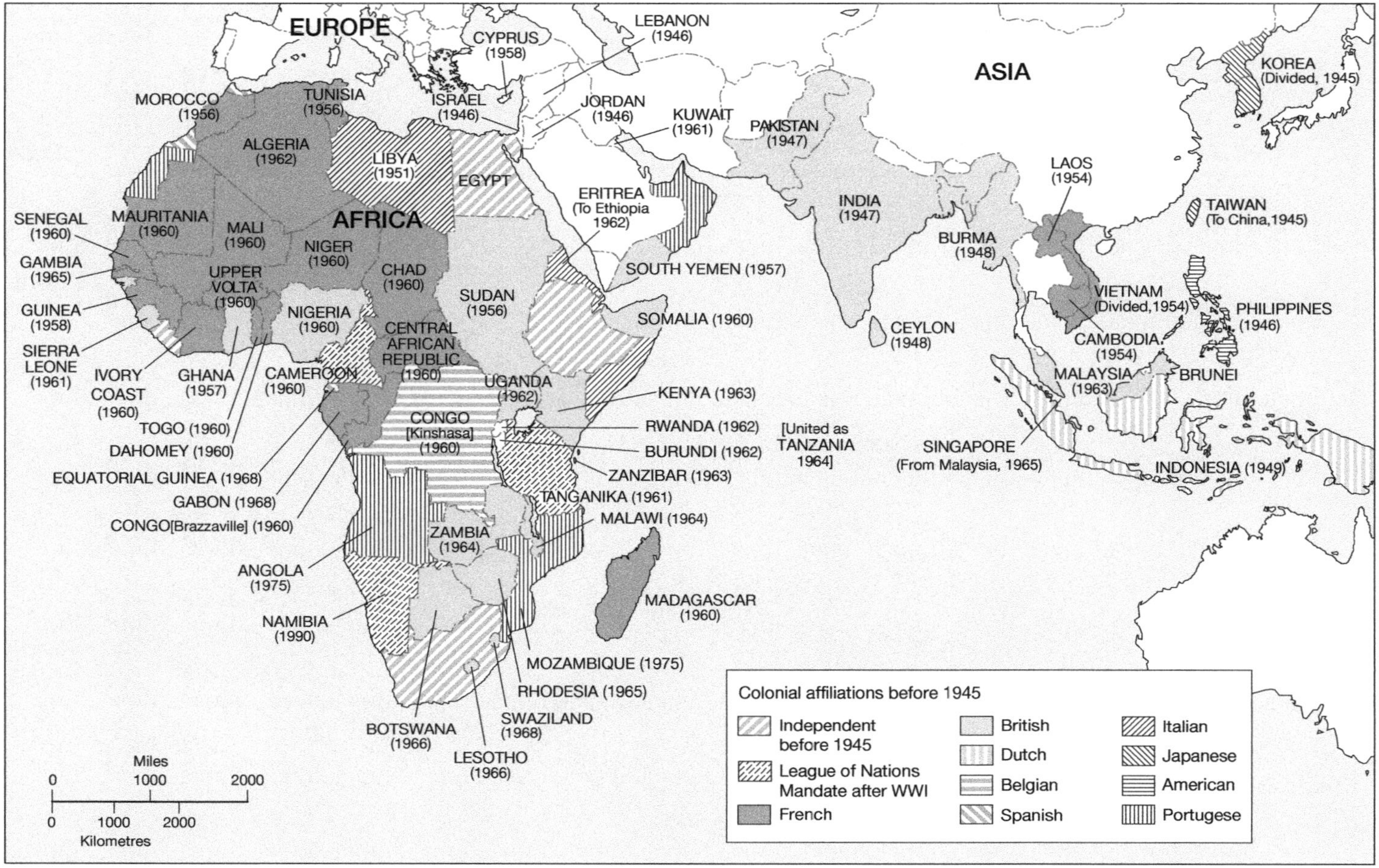

Map. 8. Decolonization

MAP. 9. Soviet Union Break-up

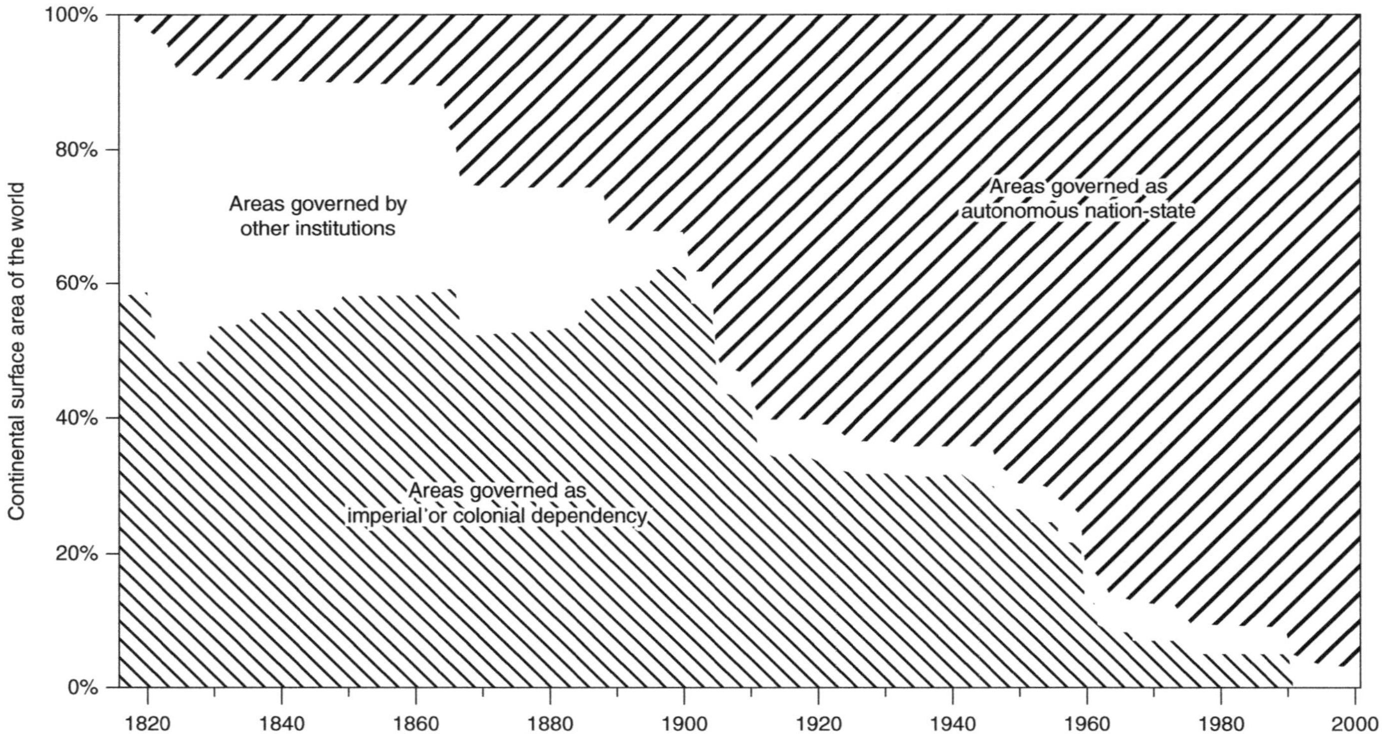

Map. 10. Graph showing the growth of modern empires followed by the growth of modern nation states

CHAPTER 1

INTRODUCTION: CONCEPTS, APPROACHES, THEORIES

JOHN BREUILLY

The Challenge

Some years ago Oxford University Press suggested to me the idea of editing a handbook on nationalism. I declined the proposal on the grounds that there were already a number of good handbooks on the subject and that in any case, as an historian, I was not competent to deal with the many non-historical aspects of nationalism. However, on looking more closely at those handbooks, I realized that they contained little history, and most of that was contemporary.[1] So I suggested a handbook on the history of nationalism.

I begin with this point because it poses a challenge. Of all modern political ideologies, nationalism appears to be the most through and through historical. Political ideologies oriented to religious beliefs have transhistorical referents. Liberalism, democratic radicalism, and socialism are based on universal values of individual freedom, democracy, and social justice. Conservative ideology does present itself in historical form but typically by shifting from an implicit endorsement of customary social relationships to an explicit defence of tradition against challenges from non-conservative ideologies. Nationalism shares with liberalism, radicalism, and socialism a claim to universal validity—the world is divided into a series of nations—and like them begins as a challenge to the status quo. Paradoxically, however, the claim to validity takes the form of an insistence on the unique character of each nation, even if nationalists wax most lyrical about their own nation. We can succinctly define the political ideology of nationalism as one which claims that there exists a unique nation, that this nation has a special value and therefore right to existence and recognition, and that to secure this right the nation must possess autonomy, often understood as a sovereign nation state.[2] The most basic tenet of nationalism—the unique nation—is grounded historically. In principle one could identify a nation non-historically (genetic make-up, language, foundational moment) but that identity is soon embedded within the unique history which produced that phenotype, language group, or revolutionary act.[3]

This historical grounding of nationalism was reinforced by its close ties with the emergence of professional academic historical writing.[4] To this day, the most basic divisions between modern historians are national. When someone says she is a German historian, that refers to the nationality of the history, not of the historian.

Yet, while there are good general studies of liberalism, radicalism, socialism, and conservatism, they are lacking for nationalism. This is a sweeping claim, but I think it can be sustained. What purport to be general studies of nationalism can be placed in one of three categories. (I omit historical surveys of the literature on nationalism.) First, general theories of or approaches to nationalism selectively cite historical evidence in their support.[5] Second, historical surveys usually take the form of a collection of national histories, treating nationalism as one aspect of these histories. A distinguished example is by Hugh Seton-Watson.[6] Third, there are histories of ideas that make few detailed connections to the role nationalism plays in political movements and organizations (including nation states) and in providing people with a sense of identity.[7] Some comparative historical studies try to combine elements of these approaches but they are selective in their range of cases.[8] By contrast, general studies of the other ideologies combine attention to ideas, politics, and sentiments, often by focusing on the history of political parties associated with those ideologies.[9]

The short explanation for this absence is that the history of nationalism—except when treated as a history of ideas—is conflated with national history. By contrast, because liberalism, radicalism, and conservatism can be treated as political positions within the national framework, they can be considered as distinct from that framework. The great strength of history as a discipline is its attention to the particular. The concept of the nation serves to delimit a field of modern history but, having done that work, national historians labour away in their respective fields without paying much attention to what is going on elsewhere.[10] Thus nationalism is neither a specific object of study within or beyond the national frame. The object of study becomes national history rather than the history of nationalism. It is perfectly possible for historians to write national histories that treat nationalism negatively, yet such studies deepen rather than challenge the sense that each national history is unique, along with its ill-defined nationalism.[11]

To write any general history of nationalism one must break this conflation of national and nationalism. Unfortunately, making this break usually takes one away from history. Other disciplines such as sociology, psychology, political science, anthropology, literary and art history start to take centre stage. Much of this work is non-historical either because it uses ahistorical concepts such as those of identity and interest or because of a contemporary or even near-future perspective. Social scientists frequently generate their own data in such forms as surveys, participant-observation, and experiments. The main exception is historical sociology, which has produced valuable work on nationalism.[12] Nevertheless, historical sociology with its explicit use of theory, comparative perspective, and principal dependence on secondary literature, differs even from those historians who explicitly use social-science concepts, by virtue of their engagement with original sources from which they construct accounts of sequences of events. That usually takes us back to national history. To understand how we might escape from these positions, we need to consider more closely how historians came to the study of nationalism.[13]

Nationalism as such first attracted the attention of historians because of its political significance in the aftermath of the First World War. The war aims of the states involved were formulated in nationalist or anti-nationalist terms.[14] The Habsburg fear of Slav nationalism accounts for its drastic response to the assassination of Archduke Franz Ferdinand on 28 June 1914, triggering the sequence of events that rapidly transformed a local conflict into general war. The post-war settlement that emerged from the Versailles Treaty included the establishment of new 'nation states' in central Europe, justified by US President Woodrow Wilson's doctrine of national self-determination. The publicity given to this doctrine raised nationalist expectations across the world, also stimulated by the near-simultaneous declarations by Vladimir Ilich Lenin and the Bolsheviks in favour of national liberation. Disappointment with the (inevitably) partial and biased implementation of the principle of national self-determination served to intensify such nationalism.[15]

The challenges confronting nation states in central Europe—winners and losers—generated increasingly extreme nationalist claims. Apart from disputes about national boundaries, there developed national minorities within the various states, minorities that then looked to their 'homeland' state for support.[16] To this can be added the economic problems in the post-war period, especially the great depression from the late 1920s that brought fascist movements to prominence and, in two deadly instances, power.

All this made it apparent that nationalism had acquired a character and significance which took it beyond this or that national history. Among the first historians to rise to the challenge of writing a history of this nationalism was Carlton Hayes. From the perspective of the USA, Hayes saw nationalism combining with other ideas such as Jacobinism, Anglo-American liberalism, imperialism, and fascism (his term was 'integral nationalism'), shifting from one combination to the next from the late eighteenth to early twentieth century. Hans Kohn, writing during the Second World War, saw the liberal democratic nationalism of Britain, France, and the USA pitted against the imperialist-racist nationalism of the Third Reich, Fascist Italy, and Imperial Japan. (Kohn found no place for nationalism in the last major participant: the USSR.)[17]

Treating nationalism as ideology enabled Hayes and Kohn to write a general, transnational history, but this had its limitations. How does one explain origins, changes, and varieties as outlined by Hayes and Kohn? Hayes did it by turning nationalism into a function of other ideologies, so that the task was to explain the shifts from Jacobinism to liberalism to imperialism and so on. Kohn reverted to conflating nation and nationalism, linking his two types of nationalism to two types of nation: the western and the eastern.[18] Intellectual conservatives like Elie Kedourie treated nationalism as an ideology that spreads like a disease, first infecting alienated intellectuals and then large groups disoriented by war, economic upheaval, or rapid social change. Nationalism is either reduced to a function of something else (other ideologies, the nation) or is depicted as an incredibly powerful idea that can shape the world in its image.

There is another option. This is to devise a general approach that does not commence with national history or ideology. An attempt in this direction was made by Marxist politicians in the late Habsburg Empire who engaged with rather than dismissing the manifest existence of nationalist conflicts within the empire's labour and socialist movement. Otto Bauer and Karl Renner argued that the growth of popular political participation had promoted and would continue to strengthen national identity, which was grounded in language. This bound members of different classes into a 'community of fate' while simultaneously dividing members of the working class. This went against orthodox Marxism, which envisaged working-class consciousness growing at the expense of national consciousness. Bauer and Renner argued that the challenge for socialists was to insulate national cultural differences from economic and political class conflict. They sought the answer in a programme of 'national cultural autonomy' based on personal identity.[19]

The Austro-Marxists failed. Marxism after 1918 followed the Bolshevik path, which accepted national difference as a matter of objective cultural identity that was to be recognized and valued but always subordinated to the higher priorities of socialism. However, Bauer's idea that national consciousness was rooted in communication was taken up by non-Marxist social science. Karl Deutsch, not coincidentally an émigré to the USA from the former Habsburg Empire, moved away from the organic, romantic language of Bauer ('communities of fate') to explore the relationship between nationalism and 'social communication'.[20] In the early 1980s the two most important contributions to a modernist social-science understanding of nationalism, by Ernest Gellner and Benedict Anderson, elaborated on this relationship between communication and nationalism. Gellner highlighted the impact of industrialism on communication, or what he called 'culture', while Anderson emphasized 'print capitalism' and its capacity to generate imaginings of national community. Subsequent debates about nationalism are responses to these arguments, seeking variously to deepen and expand them, to challenge them by disputing the modernity of nationalism, and to move beyond them to postmodern arguments about nationalism as discourse.[21]

However, little of this debate engages closely with historical research. The preoccupations of most social scientists are with contemporary issues and they see little need to ground these in a deep historical perspective. If nationalism is understood, for example, as an ideology used instrumentally by elites, one needs to concentrate upon those elites and their interests. Political-science studies of contemporary ethnic conflict generally construct mass datasets that are used to test for relationships. Apart from neglecting history, this approach is often suspicious of narrative history, regarding it as an arbitrary selection of anecdotes that cannot be subjected to scientific tests concerned with causal explanation.

If, by contrast, nationalism is related to enduring ethnic identity based on the construction and reproduction of myths and memories, this leads towards contemporary ethnography or long-run accounts of myths and memories. However, these accounts are usually oriented to what one might call folklore studies and detached from the political focus of most national history. There is additionally the danger that material used in such studies was actually generated by earlier nationalist efforts at a recovery of national culture in such forms as collections of national epics and folk song. When an author advances a general argument about nationalism on the basis of such material, it is usually handled in highly selective ways. Specialist historians, if they take note of such writing, often dismiss it as simplistic and inaccurate. When historians do contribute to debates on nationalism, it is usually to insist on the special relevance of their field of study without placing it within the larger framework of such debates.[22]

We constantly find ourselves between a rock and a hard place. Studies of nationalism as a distinct subject are non-historical or produce historical work that is speculative by professional historiographical standards. Professional historians working within national fields, including the study of nationalism, do not use the concepts and methods of the social scientists in their work. National historiography grows richer and generates its own debates but these are rarely generalized beyond the national frame or used for explicit comparison.[23]

Comparative history apparently offers a way out of this dilemma but it has its limitations, some of which I have already mentioned. Historians falter when moving from their special field to look at more cases over time and/or space. As the cases and their variations multiply, they outrun the capacity for systematic comparison. Then one reverts to narrative history in which 'nationalism' means either the politics leading to nation-state formation or aggressive interactions between nation states. This tends to produce two kinds of historical work, one focused on oppositional movements and one on states, but both embedded within the national frame. However hard one tries, the starting point is the 'nation'. To write a history of Japanese or German, Serbian or Romanian, Iraqi or Egyptian, Nigerian or Indonesian nationalism, one starts with the territory that comprises the state which later acquires that national name.

It quickly becomes apparent that some names have a long history whereas others do not. This leads to a distinction between 'old' and 'new' nations.[24] Already questionable assumptions have been made. Just because a word naming a nation has a long history, does that mean it has some stable referent with an equally long history? The problem is clear when one tries to write a long-run national history of Nigeria or Indonesia, but is it any less problematic to write such a history of France or Japan? What do such national names have to do with nationalism? How do we write about nationalism without treating it as one aspect of a larger 'national history'? How do we deal with nationalisms without nation states or any kind of autonomy? How do we detach the history of nationalism from that of the nation state?

The Plan

There are no perfect answers to these questions but there are partial ones. They start with three decisions arrived at in the planning of this volume:

1. The subject of the Handbook is the history of nationalism, not nationalism as an aspect of the history of nations or nation states.
2. The history of nationalism is primarily a history of politics, of a political ideology, and of the movements and organizations (including states) that subscribe to nationalist ideology.
3. Such nationalism is specific to the modern era.

All three propositions are debatable. The first decision was taken so as to avoid 'methodological nationalism', that is, placing nationalism within a national framework rather than leaving open to question the nation/nationalism relationship. The second is a matter of emphasis. Nationalism can be treated as doctrine (as in the history of ideas), as sentiment or identity (as in studies of 'everyday' or 'banal' nationalism), and as cultural movement. Chapters in the book consider these topics. However, detailed historical studies of nationalism are concerned with politics, for reasons already outlined. As for the third proposition, although there are many persuasive advocates of pre-modern nationalism, they address themselves mainly to ideas and sentiments as well as discourses in which national terms figure, rather than to politics. Peter Burke's chapter (Chapter 2) touches upon these issues, but otherwise I found it difficult to envisage a contribution to this Handbook that would go beyond summarizing relevant studies.[25]

Emphasizing nationalism as modern politics makes pivotal the moment of nation-state formation, as this changes the relationship of nationalism to the major power-container of modern times: the territorial state. The two distinctions—ideas/sentiments and politics, before and after the nation state—provide the basis for the book's organization in Parts I to V, with a final chapter examining historical writing and nationalism.

The next question concerned the character and content of individual chapters. So far as the first was concerned, as this is a handbook, not an encyclopaedia, there was no attempt at comprehensive coverage—even if this were possible. The probable result would be many short and disconnected descriptions that can easily be obtained elsewhere. Instead I asked each author to write an interpretative essay, even if at the cost of excluding relevant cases and narrative detail. Such essays illuminate those cases that are considered and provide ideas for readers seeking to understand comparable cases.

CONTENTS

Part I: The Emergence of Nationalism: Ideas and Sentiments

This section considers nationalism as ideas, sentiments, and cultural movements before the era of nation states. Peter Burke (Chapter 2) looks at ideas about the nation in late medieval and early modern Europe, paying particular attention to the impact of religion and the increasing use of vernacular languages in print. Chapters 3 and 4 by by Erica Benner and Andreas Eckert belong to the sub-discipline of the history of ideas. Benner analyses concepts of nation and nationalism in the work of major European thinkers such as Jean-Jacques Rousseau and Johann Gottlieb Fichte, arguing that these are ideas to take seriously in their own right. Eckert's chapter analyses the national idea as developed by various African and Asian intellectuals, arguing that rather than contrasting 'western' with 'non-western' thought one should approach this as a transnational history of ideas. John Hutchinson (Chapter 5) looks at nationalism as a cultural movement, emphasizing both its integrity (it is not a disguised form of politics) and also its relationship to political nationalism.

Parts II and III: Politics and Power: The Emergence of Nationalism and Nationalism in a World of Nation States

The challenge of avoiding methodological nationalism was greatest for these two sections. The obvious and easy decision is for chapters on French and German, US and Brazilian, Chinese and Indian, Nigerian and Kenyan nationalism, and so on. Apart from the danger of going into encyclopaedic mode, and even then failing to be comprehensive, this would establish a presumption in favour of successful cases, defined as those that ended up with their 'own' nation state. Not every nationalism manages to achieve autonomy, let alone a nation state, but that does not make those cases less real as examples of nationalism. Selecting only nationalisms that resulted in a nation state and writing their history as one of origins, rise, and success can make it appear that they were bound to succeed, which is precisely what their nationalist apologists claim. It can also make nationalism appear strong where autonomy has been achieved and weak where it has not. There is also the danger of neglecting entirely 'vanished' nationalisms.

Historians cannot and should not entirely give up the advantage of hindsight, but any effort to outline alternative futures is severely constrained by the decision to call the subject 'French' or 'Nigerian'. It is admittedly no more possible to prove that events might have taken a different course as that they were inevitable. Historians cannot replay the past as a series of experiments, testing for causal relationships. However, they can establish that even the most committed nationalists did not see their success as preordained. There were powerful obstacles in the path of every nationalist project as well as conflicts of values and visions within every nationalist movement. Contemporaries anticipated and worked towards different futures than the one that came into being, and were often surprised by the actual outcome. The challenge for the historian of nationalism is to retain that sense of contingency while drawing on a rich national historiography and making the actual sequence of events appear as something more than chance.

The strategy adopted has been to select regions both before and after they became organized along nation-state lines. The notion of a 'region' is itself problematic. It might be based on long-established polities (China, Japan); new imperial domains (British India, Dutch East Indies); projections by the powerful (Southeast Asia as a US-designated strategic region;[26] the 'East', whether Near, Middle, or Far, as a view from the 'West'); or a geographical zone (the Americas, sub-Saharan Africa). Names and concepts of regions have been proposed, contested, and changed over time, such as the post-Soviet notion of 'Central Europe' or the rejection of the term 'Balkans' as a demeaning term for south-east Europe. Nevertheless, such regional designations, however arrived at, enable one to gain distance from the political geography of nation states while drawing upon the historiography of national and area studies.

To regional focus was added the selection of types of nationalism. Miroslav Hroch and Theodore Weeks (Chapters 9 and 10) look at separatist nationalist movements in the multinational states of the Habsburgs and Ottomans, the Romanovs and the Soviets. Hroch draws comparisons between such nationalisms in two different empires at the same time; Weeks within one region but across time as one imperial state was succeeded by another. My own Chapter 8 analyses another type of nineteenth-century nationalism—unification nationalism—comparing German, Italian and Polish nationalism.

Michael Rowe (Chapter 7) deals with a European region but defined by the key events of the period, that of the French Revolution and Napoleon Bonaparte. The common challenges posed by France as bringer of war and empire to those living in territories that subseqently became such nation states as Spain, Germany, Italy, and Poland enable Rowe to transcend the national frame. Oliver Zimmer (Chapter 21) writes about Europe during another period that witnessed the rise of distinctive forms of nationalism, those generated in the aftermath of the First World War and culminating with the end of the Second World War. Likewise, Sabine Rutar (Chapter 26) deals with another set of European nationalisms that took shape in the transition in south-east Europe from communist nation states to post-communist nation states, accompanied in the case of former Yugoslavia by violent nationalist conflict and the formation of new nation states. More generally, John Darwin (Chapter 17) looks at nationalism in the major European nation states, as this relates to global imperialist conflict between those states.

In the Middle East, there is a complex interlinking of pre-modern empire (principally that of the Ottomans) and modern empire, above all British and French. Both within and beyond that region (in north Africa) pan-nationalism—principally Arab but also African and Islamic—has drawn the attention of historians as well as the nationalisms associated with nation states such as Egypt, Iraq, and Syria. This enables a series of overlapping chapters. Aviel Roshwald (Chapter 11) looks at the emergence of nationalism in the Middle East under Ottoman as well as Western imperial rule, including Zionism and Arab nationalism. Readers can compare the nationalisms of the Ottoman Middle East with those of Ottoman Europe considered by Miroslav Hroch in Chapter 9. Another comparison can be made between Roshwald's regionally focused treatment of Arab nationalism and Cemil Aydin's chapter on pan-nationalism (Chapter 34), where Arab nationalism in turn is related to Pan-Asianism, Pan-Africanism, and Pan-Islam. Fred Halliday (Chapter 22) writes about the different forms nationalism took in the post-colonial Middle East, stressing its close links to earlier and continuing anti-imperialism and the fundamental importance of the Arab-Israeli conflict.

In Northeast Asia the principal cases are Japan and China (with some consideration for Korea), well-established imperial-monarchical states before the era of nationalism. By comparing these cases Rana Mitter and Aaron Moore (Chapters 14 and 23) escaped the constraints of the national frame. Their essays also make it clear that the history of nationalism within this region is one of constant entanglement, from Chinese and Korean nationalism being shaped by Japan as both model and enemy, to post-1945 Japanese nationalism responding to the rise of a powerful China.

David Henley (Chapter 13) compares two imperial zones within Southeast Asia: French Indochina and the Dutch East Indies. He poses the question of why these zones moved out of the colonial era on different trajectories: one towards a plurality of nation states (Vietnam, Cambodia, Laos), the other to one nation state (Indonesia), something that was not widely anticipated at the time. John Sidel (Chapter 24), dealing with the post-colonial period in the region, selected three pairs of cases for comparative analysis in order to understand why nationalism took different forms.

In the case of India there was both an extensive pre-modern state (Mughal India) and a modern imperial state (the British Raj). Given its size, complexity, and rich historiography, it was not practical to place India within a larger region. Joya Chatterji (Chapter 12) introduces a comparative perspective by considering the alternative forms of nationalism that took shape under the Raj: Hindu and Muslim, secular and religious, and the reasons for their varied achievements, often unanticipated, by 1947. For the subcontinent in the post-colonial period Christophe Jaffrelot (Chapter 25) continued such comparisons, now in relation to the three distinct cases of nationalism in India, Pakistan, and Bangladesh.

European imperial rule in sub-Saharan Africa took yet a different form. There was a relative absence of pre-modern empire compared to those of the Mughals or Ottomans. (However, there were kingdoms such as those of the Ashanti, Ganda, and Zulus.) European states made formal imperial claims (unlike in China and Japan) but in fragmented ways (unlike in Indochina, the East Indies, and India), with the formation of Belgian, British, Dutch, French, German, Portuguese, and Spanish colonies. The region is instead defined in terms of geography and climate: sub-Saharan Africa. John Lonsdale and Bruce Berman wrote separate chapters for the colonial and post-colonial periods (Chapters 16 and 18) but also co-authored a common introduction (Chapter 15) and took careful account of each other's chapters. They identified particular kinds of nationalism, linked to pre-colonial legacies, the forms of colonial rule, and the continued global pressures exerted in the post-colonial era. They also placed this history within a wider context, making comparisons with earlier 'Western' nationalism, challenging the influential view of African nationalism as special, a variant on methodological nationalism.

Finally, we move beyond the interconnected land masses of Africa, Asia, and Europe to their long, entangled histories with the Americas. Though there is a shorter historical connection with Europe, European imperial rule came to this region earlier than in Africa and Asia. In an age before steamships and railways, telegraphs and industrialization, it had a different character. For the colonial period two historians, Don Doyle and Eric Van Young, brought together their expertise in North and South American history respectively to co-author a chapter that transcends the usual frames of colonial American historiography (Chapter 6) and thereby illuminates the study of nationalism in the whole region. With the end of formal colonial rule in most of the Americas by the early nineteenth century, the focus shifts to the different forms that nationalism took in the USA and the multiple states of South America. Susan-Mary Grant (Chapter 20) emphasizes the relative unimportance of the central state in the USA or even a clear delimited territory until the Civil War and later, raising the important questions of whether 'US' nationalism was also of little importance in that earlier period, whether other nationalisms mattered more, and how subsequently nationalism developed. Nicola Miller (Chapter 19) also stresses the weakness of independent states in Latin America for much of the nineteenth century (also accompanied by boundary shifts and inward penetration) and considers the intertwined histories of nationalism and state-building.

Part IV: Nationalism in a World of Nation States: Ideas, Sentiments, and International Relations

We return to nationalism as a series of ideas and sentiments but now in a world of nation states. Chapters in this Part also look at how nationalism is handled in the international order and the character of nationalist movements opposed to the existing nation state. James Mayall (Chapter 27) considers nationalism and international relations, especially the relationship between principles of state sovereignty and national self-determination, the first formulated before the era of nation states and at odds with nationalist claims made against existing nation states. This raises issues about external intervention into the affairs of a sovereign state, especially in relation to internal nationalist conflicts. Richard Caplan (Chapter 28) looks at changes in the principle and practice of external intervention, especially since the end of the Cold War that had frozen the political geography of nation states in many parts of the world. Montserrat Guibernau (Chapter 30) looks at one internal dimension of this—nationalist challenges within nation-states—in relation to the cases of Scotland and Catalonia.

The idea that humankind is divided into races has a long pedigree, but more as a cultural than a biological concept. Initially it was distanced from nationalist ideas that highlighted differences *within* broad race groups, especially white Europeans. That changed in the twentieth century, and Roger Eatwell (Chapter 29) analyses how race came to play a role in the ideas of fascist and other extreme forms of nationalism. Finally, nationalism as sentiment becomes a mass phenomenon following the creation of nation states that become increasingly implicated in the lives of their citizens. The ways in which national identity figure in everyday life is the subject of the final chapter in this section by Yves Déloye (Chapter 31).

Part V: Challenges to the World of Nation States

Nationalism is not the only powerful political ideology or movement at work in the modern world. Nationalism, nation states, and an international order based on the principle of nation-state sovereignty have always been challenged. From the nineteenth into the twentieth century one such challenge came from socialist internationalism, which made class instead of nation the keystone of its social theory and projected a vision of a classless society rather than a series of nation states. John Schwarzmantel (Chapter 32) shows how misleading it is to see the relationship between nationalism and socialism as one of simple opposition but rather considers the interactions and combinations involved. Nationalism has also been regarded as a political religion, displacing in a secular age the loyalties and values attached to traditional religion. Others have argued that religion and nationalism complement, even reinforce, each other. Peter van der Veer (Chapter 33) takes the argument beyond such notions of competition or complementarity, showing how modernity shaped concepts of both religion and nationalism in similar ways.

Pan-nationalism has often been treated as a failure, given that no African, Asian, Arab, Slav, or Islamic state has been founded. Cemil Aydin (Chapter 34) argues that pan-nationalism was of major significance as a response to the global imperialism of the late nineteenth and early twentieth century. It was also a powerful influence upon 'successful' nationalist movements. Finally, nationalism is often depicted as belonging to a stage in modern world history associated with the creation of an order of nation states, a stage that is being brought to an end by the more recent processes of globalization. Jürgen Osterhammel (Chapter 35) shows how misleading is this view, first because the two concepts are incommensurable (nationalism is a distinct orientation to the world, globalization is a range of processes) and second because nationalism can only be understood as an aspect of globalization.

Part VI: Nationalist Historiography

In the last section we return to the starting point of this introduction, the relationship between nationalism and historians. Paul Lawrence (Chapter 36) considers not just the national focus of modern professional historical writing but also the ways in which nationalism has been treated by historians and how it relates to a distinctively modern way of regarding the past.

Concluding Points

As already mentioned, this Handbook does not attempt a comprehensive, encylopaedic coverage of its subject. Instead it is organized in relation to aspects of nationalism (ideas, sentiments, politics), the division between nationalism before and after the nation state, and considers nationalist politics in relation to distinct regions and types of nationalism. Authors have written interpretative essays rather than narrative accounts, using comparison to show how nationalism works historically.

This organization led to many empirical omissions that were unavoidable, which was not in itself a major problem. Other kinds of omission are more serious. Certain regions have been neglected. With the exception of some parts of Russia and the USSR in the essay by Theodore Weeks, central Asia is not considered. A chapter comparing nationalism in Afghanistan and in Persia/Iran would have fitted well into the Handbook, but I could not find a suitable author. Lands of white settlement that did not engage in nationalist opposition to the homeland state (Canada, Australia, New Zealand, South Africa) also merited consideration.

There are also types of nationalism that a regional focus cannot capture. The original plan of the Handbook included a chapter on 'settler nationalism', cases where populations of European origin, regarding themselves as still connected to the 'homeland', developed a distinctive form of nationalism in relation to that homeland and to indigenous peoples. Examples would be Algerian *pieds noir*, Ulster Protestants, British settlers in east-central Africa. However, such a chapter did not materialize. There has also been a growing interest in the closely related subject of 'diaspora nationalism', though here the focus is on involvement with the 'homeland' (e.g. Ireland and Irish-Americans, Israel and Jews living in other countries). Aspects of both kinds of nationalism are touched upon in the chapters on the Americas (settler nationalism) and the Middle East (Zionism).

There is little in this Handbook on what one might call state-led nationalism. There are a couple of reasons for this. First, it is impossible to detach the history of such nationalism from that of the individual nation state. Apart from the fact that this is well covered in national historiographies, it is difficult to see how state-led nationalism could go beyond the individual nation state and the particular interactions it has with its citizens. One could in principle try to identify broader themes such as education and nationalism, economy and nationalism, immigration and nationalism, irredentism and nationalism, but it would be the nation state that was at the centre of attention, not nationalism. Only when one can explore a distinct form of nationalism shared by a number of states, such as John Darwin's treatment of imperialism (Chapter 17) or Oliver Zimmer's of fascism (Chapter 21), could I see a case for a chapter.

I am less concerned about thematic omissions. There are more potential themes than could ever be covered. Many are considered, albeit usually with little historical perspective, in various handbooks on nationalism.[27]

I did not ask the authors to take a particular approach towards their subject. Historians are not easily shepherded, precisely because they are sensitive to the complexities and nuances of the subjects about which they write. Different authors have different views of nationalism. Some consider 'nations' as realities distinct from nationalism that in turn condition that nationalism; others see nationalism as preceding, even constructing nations; yet others are sceptical as to whether 'nation' has meaning beyond its uses by nationalists. Some historians emphasize the destructive and irrational features of nationalism; others its contribution to promoting cultural diversity and autonomy; whereas for yet others it is always Janus-faced. Some historians regard nationalism as an analytic concept rather than a force in the world with moral qualities, be they good or bad or both. In part such disagreements relate to the types of nationalism about which different historians write, in part to the concepts and methods they bring to bear, in part to their moral perspective.

What mattered was not such differences of approach or perspective but that the authors be good historians with expertise in the subject about which they were writing. In addition they needed that rare capacity to distil their knowledge and understanding into a short, well-organized, clearly written essay which advanced an interpretation that took one beyond simple narrative.

As for what readers might learn from this book, that is for readers to decide and not for the editor to suggest. Instead I will finish by briefly stating some of the things I have learnt, starting with some background arguments.

I have suggested we can distinguish between nationalism as ideas, politics, and sentiments. Conceptually we might consider this the basic sequence in the historical development of nationalism: the formulation of the idea, its translation into politics and, especially following the creation of nation states, its diffusion to large numbers of people as sentiment. This resembles Miroslav Hroch's distinction between three phases of nationalism: intellectual and cultural, elite politics, and mass movement.[28]

One can trace pre-modern versions of the idea (not just the terminology) of nation, although this is rarely if ever presented as comprehending the whole of a society but only privileged elements, or translated into an explicit political programme, let alone a movement. The idea of the nation as inclusive and participatory is a democratic one. In pre-modern societies democratic arrangements were small-scale, as in the ancient Greek *polis*, and one can detect anticipations of later nationalist ideas, underpinned by broader distinctions between the Greeks and barbarians.

However, only with the formation of territorial states with large populations and pressures to extend participation beyond privileged elites is there a systematic shift of the national idea to be inclusive and participatory and political. These conditions were met in abundance on the Atlantic seaboard of Europe in the early modern period as a plurality of such states competed both in and beyond Europe, as commercial capitalism reshaped the relationship between old power and new wealth, as dissident religious movements challenged the hierarchical and privileged position of established Churches. It is no coincidence that the most persuasive accounts of pre-modern nationalism are about this region.

Furthermore, groups exhibiting nationalist sentiments can be located in these contexts—those demanding parliamentary reform in Britain, enlightenment radicals in France, and the British and Spanish settlers in the Americas. Both competition between these states (above all, at a global level, Anglo-French conflict) and internal conflict increasingly used the language of nationalism.

However, this is only a *conceptual* sequence. This is because the history of nationalism is transnational. A nationalist idea used to good effect in one place can be taken up somewhere else but, given a different set of conditions, will work in a very different way. Not only ideas can travel in this way but also styles of political organization and action and even sentiments and senses of identity. C. A. Bayly, for example, has argued that nationalist ideas, politics, and sentiments translated into India by British imperial rule interacted with existing forms of 'patriotism' to give a distinctive character to nationalism.[29] One can identify typical shifts from one period to another in modern global history, but at best this is only a rough template for tracing the transnational history of nationalism.[30] One can see something of this shifting, complex history in the chapters of this book. The power of nationalism resides precisely in this flexible capacity to combine ideas, politics, and sentiments in a variety of modern contexts, enabling people to identify friends and enemies and to orientate themselves quickly to the mass politics of the emergent territorial state as well as the conflicts between such states.

Yet despite all these variations, nationalism is an historical subject distinct from national history. If the Handbook persuades readers of that basic point alone, it will have been worth producing. So understood, nationalism matters. It is not just a reflex of non-national material and ideal interests such as class or race or state. However, one must not go to the other extreme and treat nationalism as some deeply felt idea, sentiment, or political commitment that operates independently of, even against, such interests. Detailed consideration of how nationalism works historically in particular regions and periods is the best way of bringing out the complex interrelations between the different aspects of nationalism and the other interests and conditions with which it combines.

Once one treats nationalism as an historical subject distinct from the nation or nation state, it can also be seen as global. This does not just mean that, by contributing to the formation of a world of nation states, nationalism demonstrated its global reach, but that nationalist intellectuals, politicians, and citizens were constantly responding to other nationalists on a global scale. This theme crops up again and again and so I will just select examples at random. Roger Eatwell (Chapter 29) writes of the impact that Japanese nationalism had upon race ideas in Italian fascism. Cemil Aydin (Chapter 34) demonstrates how Pan-Asianism influenced Pan-Islamism. Michael Rowe (Chapter 7) shows how forms of nationalism developed in revolutionary and Napoleonic France were diffused to other regions of Europe. John Sidel (Chapter 24) argues that the ways in which different states in Southeast Asia either were or were not integrated into a US-dominated global economy, political system, and culture shaped the nationalism of those states. Nationalism also changes globally over time. Nationalism in mid-nineteenth-century Europe, shaped by the dominant examples of Britain and France, takes a different form from that of the period in the decades up to 1914 when global imperialism and ideas of the state harnessing modern science and industry play a bigger part. In the epoch of world wars nationalism in Europe was associated with ethnic and race ideas and a propensity for violence. As the European imperial order was dismantled under the aegis of the two new superpowers after 1945, nationalism took on yet other shapes.

Although one can argue that nationalism is a distinct global historical subject that needs to be considered outside the frame of national history, it is so various in time and space and combines ideas, sentiments, and politics in so many different ways, that it is difficult to see how there could ever be a satisfactory account, let alone theory, of 'nationalism as such'. Just as it was impossible for a contemporary in 1850 to predict the forms nationalism would assume by 1900, and in turn for someone then to predict its forms in 1950, so I doubt those who make predictions today, such as about the inevitable decline of nationalism in the face of globalization. Nationalism is a distinct, complex, and significant subject, and the best—perhaps the only—way of understanding it is historically.

Notes

1. A good example is G. Delanty and K. Kumar (eds.) (2006) *The Sage Handbook of Nations and Nationalism*, London. This is divided into three sections: theories and approaches; themes; contemporary historical studies under the general heading of 'Nations and Nationalism in a Global Age'.
2. There is a good section on definitions on the web page 'The Nationalism Project' <http://www.nationalismproject.org/> as well as at the start of J. Hutchinson and A. D. Smith (eds.) (1994) *Nationalism*, Oxford.
3. One debate within nationalism concerns the possibility of 'civic' nations defined as a voluntary commitment to a set of political values and institutions, in contrast to 'ethnic' nations. It is generally agreed that no nationalist ideology has ever proposed such a nation. From a large literature on the subject, see R. Brubaker (2004) 'The Manichean Myth: Rethinking the Distinction between "Civic" and "Ethnic" Nationalism', in R. Brubaker (ed.) *Ethnicity without Groups*, Cambridge, MA.

4. See Chapter 36 by Paul Lawrence. The links are traced out in detail in I. Porciani and L. Raphael (eds.) (2010) *Atlas of European Historiography: The Making of a Profession, 1800–2005*, Basingstoke.
5. Such as B. Anderson (1991) *Imagined Communities: Reflections on the Origins and Spread of Nationalism*, London; E. Gellner (2006) *Nations and Nationalism*, Oxford.
6. H. Seton-Watson (1977) *Nations and States: An Inquiry into the Origins of Nations and the Politics of Nationalism*, London.
7. The pioneering work is E. Kedourie (1961) *Nationalism*, London. I have analysed this in some detail in J. Breuilly (2000) 'Nationalism and the History of Ideas', *Proceedings of the British Academy*, 105, 187–223.
8. J. Breuilly (1993) *Nationalism and the State*, Manchester; E. Hobsbawm (1992) *Nations and Nationalism since 1780: Programme, Myth, Reality*, Cambridge; M. Hroch (1985) *Social Preconditions of National Revival in Europe: A Comparative Analysis of the Social Composition of Patriotic Groups among the Smaller European Nations*, Cambridge. Hroch's study is unique in that it is based on original research and makes detailed comparisons within a rigorous theoretical framework. However, this was only possible because Hroch concentrated on a particular set of cases—'small-nation nationalism' in nineteenth-century Europe—and adopted a Marxist approach. See Chapter 9 by Miroslav Hroch.
9. Admittedly not always satisfactorily, as when historians of liberalism treated as a history of liberal parties write rather differently from historians of liberalism defined as a set of political ideas or as an aspect of a political culture.
10. As for interactions between national histories, that is assigned to the sub-discipline of 'international history' which usually ignores the internal affairs of the individual states. 'Nation' thereby acquires a double meaning—national society and nation state—but just how these two meanings relate to each other is rarely explored.
11. I develop this point in relation to just such a type of German historical writing. J. Breuilly (2011b) 'Theories of Nationalism and the Critical Approach to German History', in S. O. Müller and C. Torp (eds.) *Imperial Germany Revisited: Continuing Debates and New Perspectives*, Oxford.
12. Such as by Rogers Brubaker, Michael Mann, and Charles Tilly.
13. This next section overlaps with Chapter 36 by Paul Lawrence.
14. British and US aims were initially framed in the universal language of liberal democracy, typically dismissed by German writers as Anglo-Saxon humbug, but the rhetoric of everyday propaganda took the self-referential form of nationalism.
15. For the global impact of Wilson's 'Fourteen Points' and subsequent declarations, see E. Manela (2007) *The Wilsonian Moment: Self-Determination and the International Origins of Anti-Colonial Nationalism*, Oxford. One could do with another study entitled 'The Leninist Moment'.
16. R. Brubaker (1996) *Nationalism Reframed: Nationhood and the National Question in the New Europe*, Cambridge.
17. C. Hayes (1931) *The Historical Evolution of Nationalism*, New York; H. Kohn [1944] (2005) *The Idea of Nationalism: A Study in its Origins and Background*, New York.
18. This relates to the debates about civic and ethnic nationalism, for which see note 3 above.
19. O. Bauer (2000) *A Question of Nationalities and Social Democracy*, Minneapolis; E. Nimni (ed.) (2005) *National Cultural Autonomy and its Contemporary Critics*, London. See also Chapter 32 by John Schwarzmantel.

20. K. Deutsch (1966) *Nationalism and Social Communication*, New York.
21. The literature is huge. For a good introduction, see U. Ozkirimli (2016) *Theories of Nationalism*, London.
22. Thus some historians of Anglo-Saxon England claim that this was the first nation or nation state without much concern for what these concepts mean, and then are often cited by generalist writers on nationalism as providing 'proof' for the early existence of nations or nation states. See J. Breuilly (2005) 'Changes in the Political Uses of the Nation: Continuity or Discontinuity?', in O. Zimmer and L. Scales (eds.) *Power and Nation in European History*, Cambridge.
23. A good example is in the field of Risorgimento historiography where the recent work of Alberto Banti has stimulated vigorous and fascinating debates about the nature and role of nationalism in the process of Italian unification, but largely confined to Italian historiography. See my Chapter 8 on unification nationalism for references.
24. As made by Seton-Watson (1977). One can add a third category of nations that so far have not achieved autonomy, whether as a sovereign nation state or in some lesser form such as federalism.
25. One such study is by a contributor to this volume, Aviel Roshwald. See A. Roshwald (2006) *The Endurance of Nationalism: Ancient Roots and Modern Dilemmas*, Cambridge. A debate on his book, in *Nations and Nationalism*, 14/4 (October 2008), 637–63, features contributions from Roshwald, myself, and another author in this book, Susan-Mary Grant. A recent study making a case for pre-modern nationalism is C. Hirschi (2012) *The Origins of Nationalism: An Alternative History from Ancient Rome to Early Modern Germany*, Cambridge.
26. See the introduction to B. Anderson (1998) *The Spectre of Comparisons: Nationalism, Southeast Asia and the World*, London.
27. The *Sage Handbook* (see note 1 above) devotes 20 of its 45 chapters to 'Themes' and many of the other chapters take the form of 'nationalism and X'.
28. Apart from his chapter in this book (Chapter 9), see his short presentation of the argument in M. Hroch (1996) 'From National Movement to the Fully-Formed Nation: The Nation-Building Process in Europe', in G. Balakrishnan, G. (ed.) *Mapping the Nation*, London.
29. See the essays by Chatterji, Eckert, and Osterhammel, as well as C. A. Bayly (2004) *The Birth of the Modern World 1780–1914*, Oxford.
30. I have tried sketching out such an argument in J. Breuilly (2011a) 'Nationalism as Global History', in D. Halikiopoulou and S. Vasilopoulou (eds.) *Nationalism and Globalisation: Conflicting or Complementary?*, Basingstoke.

Suggested Further Reading

Anderson, B. (1991) *Imagined Communities: Reflections on the Origins and Spread of Nationalism*, London.

Anderson, B. (1998) *The Spectre of Comparisons: Nationalism, Southeast Asia and the World*, London.

Bauer, O. (2000) *A Question of Nationalities and Social Democracy*, Minneapolis.

Bayly, C. A. (2004) *The Birth of the Modern World 1780–1914*, Oxford.

Breuilly, J. (1993) *Nationalism and the State*, Manchester.
Breuilly, J. (2000) 'Nationalism and the History of Ideas', *Proceedings of the British Academy*, 105, 187–223.
Breuilly, J. (2005) 'Changes in the Political Uses of the Nation: Continuity or Discontinuity?', in Zimmer, O. and Scales, L. (eds.) *Power and Nation in European History*, Cambridge.
Breuilly, J. (2011a) 'Nationalism as Global History', in D. Halikiopoulou and S. Vasilopoulou (eds.) *Nationalism and Globalisation: Conflicting or Complementary?*, Basingstoke.
Breuilly, J. (2011b) 'Theories of Nationalism and the Critical Approach to German History', in Müller, S. O. and Torp, C. (eds.) *Imperial Germany Revisited: Continuing Debates and New Perspectives*, Oxford.
Brubaker, R. (1996) *Nationalism Reframed: Nationhood and the National Question in the New Europe*, Cambridge.
Brubaker, R. (2004) 'The Manichean Myth: Rethinking the Distinction between "Civic" and "Ethnic" Nationalism', in Brubaker, R. (ed.) *Ethnicity without Groups*, Cambridge, MA.
Delanty, G. and Kumar, K. (eds.) (2006) *The Sage Handbook of Nations and Nationalism*, London.
Deutsch, K. (1966) *Nationalism and Social Communication*, New York.
Gellner, E. (2006) *Nations and Nationalism*, Oxford.
Hayes, C. (1931) *The Historical Evolution of Nationalism*, New York.
Hirschi, C. (2012) *The Origins of Nationalism: An Alternative History from Ancient Rome to Early Modern Germany*, Cambridge.
Hobsbawm, E. (1992) *Nations and Nationalism since 1780: Programme, Myth, Reality*, Cambridge.
Hroch, M. (1985) *Social Preconditions of National Revival in Europe: A Comparative Analysis of the Social Composition of Patriotic Groups among the Smaller European Nations*, Cambridge.
Hroch, M. (1996) 'From National Movement to the Fully-Formed Nation: The Nation-Building Process in Europe', in Balakrishnan, G. (ed.) *Mapping the Nation*, London.
Hutchinson, J. and Smith, A. D. (eds.) (1994) *Nationalism*, Oxford.
Kedourie, E. (1961) *Nationalism*, London.
Kohn, H. (2005) *The Idea of Nationalism: A Study in its Origins and Background*, New York.
Manela, E. (2007) *The Wilsonian Moment: Self-Determination and the International Origins of Anti-Colonial Nationalism*, Oxford.
Nimni, E. (ed.) (2005) *National Cultural Autonomy and its Contemporary Critics*, London.
Ozkirimli, U. (2016) *Theories of Nationalism*, London.
Porciani, I. and Raphael, L. (eds.) (2010) *Atlas of European Historiography: The Making of a Profession, 1800–2005*, Basingstoke.
Roshwald, A. (2006) *The Endurance of Nationalism: Ancient Roots and Modern Dilemmas*, Cambridge.
Seton-Watson, H. (1977) *Nations and States: An Inquiry into the Origins of Nations and the Politics of Nationalism*, London.

PART I

THE EMERGENCE OF NATIONALISM: IDEAS AND SENTIMENTS

CHAPTER 2

NATIONALISMS AND VERNACULARS, 1500–1800

PETER BURKE

'Rien de plus international que la formation des identités nationales'
Anne-Marie Thiesse

THIS chapter is situated at the meeting point between political theorists and political historians who are interested in nationalism, and linguists and cultural historians who are interested in vernaculars. In this field, one of the best-known theses is that of the 'Great Divide', around the year 1800, a major watershed in various respects according to a number of scholars, from Michel Foucault to Reinhart Koselleck, marked by the rise of a new sense of time, for instance, a new sense of society, and a new sense of the nation.[1]

THE GREAT DIVIDE

According to this thesis, put forward in different forms by Benedict Anderson, Ernest Gellner, Eric Hobsbawm, and others, it has been argued that national consciousness was essentially a nineteenth-century phenomenon—indeed, that it was unthinkable before the French and Industrial Revolutions.[2]

In the traditional 'agro-literate polity', so Gellner argued, in a characteristically elegant and lucid essay, the elites belonged to a larger community than the nation—Europe, or at least western Europe—while the peasants belonged to a smaller community than the nation, their native region, or even village.[3] The languages of these two groups both reflected and encouraged their particular collective consciousness. Elites often spoke a foreign language in addition to their own, French in Russia or The Netherlands, for instance, or German in Scandinavia, while the peasants spoke their local dialect. Before 1789, it was rare for a government to concern itself with the language that ordinary people living in the state actually spoke. There are a few exceptions to this rule in the form of recently conquered territories. In 1678, for instance, King Karl XI of Sweden ordered the inhabitants of former Danish provinces such as Skåne to use Swedish. However, the reason for this order appears to have been pragmatic, not ideological.[4]

Even the term 'nation' in its precise modern sense was lacking, since the word might be used to describe a wide variety of groups. Dante wrote of the 'Florentine nation', Machiavelli of the 'ghibelline nation' (or faction, as we would call it), Edmund Spenser of the 'nation of birds', and Ben Jonson of the 'nation of lawyers'. Even when the word 'nation' was used about Germans, for instance, or Poles, it might refer to the nobility alone (an early modern Polish myth described the nobles and the peasants as two different races, descended from Japhet and Cham respectively). It is instructive to contrast Martin Luther's *Address to the German Nobility of the German Nation* (1520) with Johann Gottlieb Fichte's *Address to the German Nation* (1807–8), which evoked Luther but was more inclusive.

It is only after 1800 that we find what has been called 'the normative isomorphism of language, nation and state'. In other words, the linguistic community coincides or is supposed to coincide with the political community.[5] In theory at least, despite the continuing existence of multilingual empires, each nation was supposed to be organized into one state, and its inhabitants to speak one language, what J. G. Herder called the *Nationalsprache.* During the French Revolution, the abbé Henri Grégoire was already advocating uniformity of language throughout France for political reasons. What he wanted was 'to fuse every citizen into a national mass', with the aim of 'simplifying the mechanism and facilitating the working of the political machine' (*fondre tous les citoyens dans une masse nationale, simplifier le mécanisme et faciliter le jeu de la machine politique*).[6]

According to the scholars cited above, the twin ideals of national consciousness and uniformity of language depended for their realization on new developments in communications, from the railways to the daily newspaper, together with other social, political, and cultural changes. 'Contrary to what Marxism has led people to expect,' Gellner put it, 'industrial society strengthens the boundaries between nations rather than those between classes'. Urbanization was uprooting many people from their native regions. The centralized state, often a national state, was making itself felt at the village level. The spread of literacy encouraged what Anderson calls 'the convergence of capitalism and print technology on the fatal diversity of human language', permitting and indeed encouraging the process of standardization, what Thiesse describes as 'the fabrication of national languages'. Universal education was to a considerable extent an education in national consciousness, since the school curriculum often emphasized the national language, literature, history, and geography, and

Breton children, for instance, were punished for speaking their native language, even in the playground.[7]

This contrast between two periods in European history has the advantage of clarity and it systematizes important insights. The railways, the daily newspaper, urbanization, political centralization, and universal education all contributed to the transformation of 'imagined communities'—to quote Anderson's happy and successful phrase—from religious to secular and from regional to national.

Critical Reactions

All the same, the thesis of the 'Great Divide' has come under scholarly fire.[8] It is vulnerable to criticism on two main counts.

In the first place, there were many continuities across the divide. For example, 'print-capitalism', as Anderson himself admits, did not begin in 1800 but around 1450, while even newspapers go back to the seventeenth century.[9] More generally, what we tend to call the European 'old regime' persisted in important respects until as late as 1914.[10] The great multilingual empires—Habsburg, Romanov, Ottoman—continued to exist until the First World War. The internationally oriented nobility and the locally oriented peasantry of the Gellner model could still be found in many parts of nineteenth-century Europe. Turning peasants into Frenchmen proved to be a problem, and turning peasants into Frenchwomen was probably even more difficult, since they were not required for military service, a means like the school of unifying the nation.[11] As for Italy, it has been calculated that when it became a nation in 1860, only 2.5 per cent of the population knew and used the standard language. Only in the age of radio and television did the majority of the population learn to speak Italian.[12]

In the second place, it would be mistaken to view Europe before 1800 as an undifferentiated static old regime. In fact, as this chapter will show, the early modern regime (1500–1800 or better, perhaps, 1450–1750) varied a good deal so far as religion, vernaculars, or national consciousness were concerned. The regime was also continually changing.

So far as variety is concerned, a number of distinctions need to be made. One important distinction is that between older nations such as England and France, for instance, and newer nations such as Britain or the United Provinces of the Dutch Republic, which has a better claim than the United States of America to be the 'first new nation', since it was founded nearly two hundred years earlier.[13] A second distinction separates small nations such as the Swedes or the Venetians from larger ones such as France or Spain. (The Venetians were surely as much a nation as anyone in early modern Europe, since the city state was independent, and its inhabitants spoke a distinctive language, now classified as a dialect, while expressions of Venetian patriotism were common.) A third is the distinction between nationalism, in the sense of an organized social and political movement, and a more diffuse national sentiment, national consciousness, or national identity—which may be stronger or weaker in different places and times and among different social groups. The fact that in French, for instance, the term *patriotisme* came into use around the middle of the eighteenth century, while the term *nationalisme* emerged in the 1790s, suggests that important cultural changes were taking place at that time.[14] It should be added that although the term 'nation' was used more rarely and more vaguely before the late eighteenth century than it has been since that time, proud references to the English, French, Spaniards, Germans, and so on are not difficult to find in the sixteenth and seventeenth centuries, as will be seen later in this chapter, even if the question as to who is Dutch, Swedish, Polish, et cetera, was rarely if ever raised in this pre-passport age.

Yet another useful distinction is that between what might be called 'positive' and 'negative' national consciousness. Negative national consciousness, or not to put too fine a point on it, xenophobia, was all too common in early modern Europe, whether the targets were neighbours or invaders. Anti-Italian, anti-Spanish, and anti-French feelings were particularly widespread, a tribute to cultural as well as political hegemony. In Italy, for instance, the contemptuous terms *hispanizare* and *spagnolare* were used to refer to the imitation of Spanish customs and fashions, while Oliver Cromwell once described English Catholics as 'Spaniolised'.

On the other hand, positive national consciousness, defined as a sense of solidarity between people from different regions, was relatively rare in the old regime.[15] It was generally confined to moments of resistance to invasion or conquest, so that it may be useful to describe it as 'defensive' or 'conjunctural' national consciousness as opposed to a consciousness that was permanent or 'structural'. The moments of resistance might be relatively brief, as in the case of Italy after its invasion by the French in 1494, the context for Machiavelli's famous appeal to his ideal prince to drive the 'barbarians' from the Peninsula; or England at the time of the Spanish Armada in 1588, for instance, a context in which we should read Shakespeare's famous verses spoken by John of Gaunt in *Richard II*—'This other Eden, demi-paradise... This blessed plot, this earth, this realm, this England'.

Other moments of resistance were relatively long, like the Dutch resistance to Spain between 1568 and 1648, the Irish resistance to England or the Polish resistance to her various invaders (Prussian, Austrian, Russian, or Turkish) from the seventeenth century onwards. These moments or movements of resistance were led by elites, but there is evidence, particularly strong in the Dutch case, for the involvement of ordinary people as well, especially in the towns. The famous *Geuzenlieder*, or 'Beggar Songs', which spread in the form of printed broadsides as well as orally, often express anti-Spanish sentiments and sometimes describe the Spaniards as *marranos*, in other words Jews disguised as Christians.

Taking a long-term view, what is especially clear is the importance for the construction and maintenance of an imagined community (whether local, national, or international) of sharing two major items of culture: a religion and a language.

Religion and National Consciousness in Early Modern Europe

A discussion of the early modern period needs to take the late Middle Ages as a baseline. Without creating another 'Great Divide', around the year 1500, we should note the importance at this time of the imagined community of Latin Christendom, supported by the dominance of the Catholic Church in western Europe, using a single sacred language, Latin, and defined against Muslims, Jews, pagans, and also against the Eastern Christians whose sacred language was Church Slavonic or Greek.

However, Latin Christianity sometimes had a local or even a national colouring. Some nations, like cities, had their patron saints: England had St George, Spain St James (San Diego), while France had a whole array of saints from St Denis and St Michel to the royal saints St Clovis and St Louis. France was known at this time as the 'most Christian kingdom', while Spain was the 'Catholic monarchy'.[16] At the other end of Europe, in Eastern Christendom, Russia was becoming 'Holy Russia' and Moscow the 'Third Rome' (replacing the 'Second Rome', Constantinople, after that city was captured by the Turks in 1453).[17]

Reformers of the Church appealed to the laity, hence to the vernacular and on occasion to popular xenophobia as well. In the fifteenth century, for instance, the Czech reformer Jan Hus exploited anti-German feeling and advocated a vernacular liturgy. At the Reformation, Luther and his followers and rivals went still further in this direction. Luther exploited anti-Italian feeling in his *Address to the Christian Nobility of the German Nation* (1520). Following Luther's success in parts of Germany, national Churches were organized in England, Denmark, Sweden, and elsewhere, complete with foundation myths such as the story that the Anglican Church had been founded independently of Rome by Joseph of Arimathea, the man described in the New Testament as preparing Christ's body for burial.

Calvinism, on the other hand, was an international movement. All the same, like the Lutherans, the Calvinists adopted vernacular liturgies as well as placing more emphasis than Catholics had done on the study of the Bible by the laity and so on the vernacular. Protestant emphasis on the Bible encouraged the spread of literacy, most spectacularly in Sweden in the seventeenth and eighteenth centuries, where the clergy carried out regular inspections in order to test the proficiency of everyone (young or old, male or female) at reading passages from Scripture. It is therefore no surprise to discover that by 1800 the most literate parts of Europe were generally Protestant ones. As the author of a recent survey puts it, 'The case for connecting Protestantism and literacy seems compelling', although other factors were also at work—townspeople tended to be more literate than peasants and men more literate than women, for instance, the north of Europe more literate than the south and the west more literate than the east.[18]

Translations of the Bible into German, Italian, Catalan, and Czech had all appeared in print before 1500 (indeed, the German Bible of 1466 had gone through fourteen editions by 1518).[19] However, at the final sessions of the Council of Trent in 1563, the Catholic Church officially rejected vernacular translation as an encouragement to private judgement and so to heresy. On the other side, Luther's translation of the Bible into German (1522–34) was followed by a wave of Protestant translations. By 1600, translations of the New Testament had been published in German, English, Danish, Swedish, Dutch, Italian, French, Spanish, Polish, Czech, Hungarian, Welsh, Icelandic, Basque, Romansch, and a South Slav language akin to what is now called 'Croat' or 'Slovene' (the Spanish translation was made by an exiled Protestant, Francisco de Enzinas, and published at Antwerp, designed to be smuggled into Spain). By the end of the seventeenth century, translations of all or part of the Bible had been published in more than fifty languages.[20]

Luther made his translation in a form of German that was intended to be intelligible from his native Saxony to the Rhineland (although western Germans experienced some difficulties with his vocabulary, so that glossaries were added to some editions). Luther's example was followed by later translators of the Bible into Swedish (1541), Dutch (1637), and Finnish (1642). These later translations, like the English Authorized Version, were created by teams of scholars, and efforts were made to have different regions represented on the team, precisely in order to produce a text that would be as widely intelligible as possible. In the case of Sweden, for instance, the chief translators came from Stockholm and Uppsala but others from Vadstena in Östergötland, in the south-east of the country.[21]

One effect of the rise of Bible reading by the laity, thanks to these translations, was the appropriation and spread of the idea of the 'chosen people' or 'elect nation', an idea that was incorporated into a number of national narratives. In the Middle Ages, some of the French clergy had already described France as a Holy Land and the French as a Chosen People, like the Jews in the age of the Old Testament—who might therefore be described as the first nation.[22] Around the year 1500, when the prophet Girolamo Savonarola briefly dominated Florence, some of the Florentines saw themselves as an Elect Nation.[23]

From the middle of the sixteenth century, however, the idea that a given nation was a Chosen People became increasingly common, thanks to Protestant emphasis on the Bible. For example, the Polish Protestant Stanisław Orzechowski described his fellow countrymen as a people chosen by God. The writer John Lyly called England 'a new Israel' and the English God's 'chosen and peculiar people'. In the seventeenth century, John Milton would also describe 'this Nation' as 'chosen before any other' and claim that God usually revealed himself first to 'his English-men'. For their part, Scottish Calvinists saw Scotland as a new Israel, especially in the age of the Covenanters. The National Covenant of 1638 to keep the Anglican form of worship out of Scotland consciously followed the Old Testament model of a pact with God.[24]

The Dutch, who became aware of themselves as a new nation when the seven provinces of the Northern Netherlands (unlike their former compatriots in the Southern Netherlands) declared their independence from the empire of Philip II, also viewed themselves in biblical terms as a New Zion. For example, in his *Nederlandsche*

Gedenck-Clanck (*Anthem of Commemoration*) of 1626, Adriaan Valerius told the story of Dutch enslavement and liberation, reminding God that he had 'dealt kindly with us, even as you have led the Children of Israel from their Babylonian captivity; the waters receded before us and you brought us dry-footed, even as the people of yore, with Moses and with Joshua, were brought to their Promised Land'.[25] Given the number of Protestants from the South who took refuge in the new republic, the Book of Exodus seemed to have been written with the Dutch in mind.

Positive identifications with the Chosen People were accompanied by negative definitions of 'the other'. An early seventeenth-century painting in the monastery of Sucevița in Moldavia represents the passage of the Red Sea by the Israelites, with Pharaoh's troops in hot pursuit. These troops wear Polish costume, thus identifying the Romanians in the age of Michael the Brave with the Israelites and their Polish enemies with the Egyptians. In the 'Beggar Songs' current in the course of the Dutch Revolt, Philip of Spain was described as a new Pharaoh—or sometimes a new Herod, giving the Dutch the role of the massacred Innocents. The English Protestant majority defined themselves against what they called 'Popery' and more specifically against Catholic Spain, France, and Ireland.

For their part, Spaniards defined themselves against foreign heretics. This may seem surprising in the case of a country that lacked a strong Protestant movement and was free from the threat of invasion, but the 'Catholic Monarchy' of Spain had been defined against the numerous Muslims and Jews who had lived in the Iberian Peninsula in the Middle Ages. After 1492, these groups were given the alternative of conversion or expulsion. Many were officially converted, but other Spaniards tended to believe that the conversions were at best superficial and at worst a mask.

It would be rash to assume that the majority of early modern Protestants had actually read through the Bible, though some parts of Scripture, notably the Psalms and the New Testament, were better known than the rest, while sermons gave their audiences considerable familiarity with the text at second hand. Better known in both the Protestant and the Catholic worlds were the catechisms that children were often required to learn by heart, notably the ones written by Luther and the Italian Jesuit Roberto Bellarmino, each of them translated into numerous vernaculars. (Bellarmino was translated into twenty European vernaculars, as well as some non-European ones, intended for the mission field.) Catechisms were the first books to be printed in a number of languages, among them Estonian (1535), Romanian (1544), Lithuanian (1547), Slovene (1551), and Latvian (1585). Adapting Anderson's argument, we might suggest that print religion in general and printed catechisms in particular encouraged the crystallization of imagined communities based on a common language.

After the Reformation, when the variety of forms of Christianity allowed individuals or their masters to make a choice between them, the choice often followed lines that now appear to be national but might be better described as linguistic. In Transylvania, for instance, where three ethnic groups had long coexisted, German speakers followed Luther, Hungarian speakers turned Calvinist, and Romanian speakers remained in the Orthodox fold. Religion thus amplified the cultural differences that already existed between the three groups. Transylvania was a special case, since it came under Ottoman hegemony after the battle of Mohács in 1526, but it is also an eloquent case, revealing what might have happened elsewhere if there had been more freedom of choice in the age of 'confessionalization', in which rulers determined the official religion of their subjects.

Conversely, certain forms of language became badges of religious allegiance, especially in the Protestant world. The penetration of everyday writing and even speech by biblical phrases, whether in German, Dutch, English, French, or Czech, revealed that the writer or speaker was one of the 'godly'.[26]

Returning for a moment to the resistance of the Dutch to Spain, the Irish to England, and the Poles to their different enemies, it is worth noting that the Protestant leaders of the Dutch Revolt came to regard Catholics as traitors, while the Catholic Irish expressed similar sentiments about Protestants, and the Poles about Orthodox Christians and Jews. To some extent, therefore, these movements support the recent argument that early modern nationalism was the product of the exclusion of internal enemies, generally people with a different religion, thus drawing sharper group boundaries than before. However, the religious 'glue' was often insufficient to hold together people from different regions or different social classes, once the immediate threat was removed.[27]

In the age of the religious wars, especially the 'Eighty Years War' (1568–1648), religion divided nations rather than uniting them. However, the situation changed from the later seventeenth century onwards. In France, for example, the main religious minority, the Calvinists or Huguenots, were given the alternatives of conversion or expulsion in 1685. After this time, religion became more of a unifying factor. In the eighteenth century, for instance, as we have seen, Protestant 'Britons' defined themselves against Catholics or 'Papists'.[28]

In the case of eighteenth-century France, it has been argued that nationalism derived both 'out of, and in opposition to, Christian systems of belief'. Speaking more generally, it has been suggested that the languages of national identities in Europe 'have drawn much of their power from the languages of the Judaeo-Christian tradition'.[29] It should be added that the secular religion of nationalism did not so much replace traditional religion—rather it coexisted and interacted with it. Nineteenth-century European nationalism, like Marxism, may be viewed as a secular religion, but the contribution of Christianity to this rival is undeniable. Polish nationalism had a Catholic colouring, Russian nationalism had an Orthodox one, while English xenophobia was fuelled by a Protestant hatred of 'Popery'. Nationalism was supported by a system of symbols parallel to and in competition with religious symbols: national anthems in the place of hymns, and statues of the leaders of the nation or 'martyrs' in the cause of national freedom in the place of images of the saints. The idea of national destiny derived from—although gradually lost—its traditional associations with the biblical Chosen People.

Language and National Consciousness in Early Modern Europe

In the case of language, 1450 makes a better baseline than 1500, distinguishing an old regime of manuscript communication from the new age of print.

Around 1450, there was little sense of what we now call 'language loyalty'. In public and private writing as well as in speech, a good many people were both willing and able to switch from one language to another: from Latin to the vernacular, from a regional dialect such as Venetian to an inter-regional language such as Italian, or in border areas from French to Spanish, German to Polish, and so on. Thus the humanist Claude Chansonette (otherwise known as Claudius Cantiuncula), who came from Metz, translated Erasmus into French and Thomas More into German, in both cases from a Latin original. Some major poets wrote in more than one vernacular. In the sixteenth century, Gil Vicente wrote in Spanish as well as Portuguese, just as John Gower, in the fourteenth century, had written in both English and French.

Another important point concerns variety, especially regional varieties, within what we retrospectively perceive as different vernaculars. Italian might be spoken or written in a Lombard as well as a Tuscan manner, for instance, as well as in a more or less Latinized form. Dialects of what we think of as the 'same' language were not always mutually intelligible, and they symbolized regional allegiances.

In some parts of Europe, notably Italy, medieval writers, Dante among them, had already discussed the possibility of a standard written language. All the same, the coming of the printing press, and especially of what Anderson calls 'print-capitalism', was a powerful force towards standardization. By the year 1499, printed books had appeared not only in Latin, Greek, and Church Slavonic but also in thirteen vernaculars (in chronological order: German, Czech, Italian, English, Catalan, French, Flemish, Croat, Spanish, Portuguese, Danish, Swedish, and Breton). In the sixteenth century, eighteen more vernaculars would be added to the list.

Printers were naturally interested in selling books in the vernacular in more than one region and so they—like the translators of the Bible, if for different reasons—encouraged a written language in a kind of 'lowest common denominator' of dialects. Some printers were extremely interested in language, among them the German Sebastian Franck, the Hungarian Gáspár Heltai, the Englishman William Caxton, and the Frenchman Geoffroy Tory, whose aim was 'mettre et ordonner par règle notre langage françois' ('to regulate our French language'). In short, 'Having fortified the 'language walls' between one nation and another, the printers proceeded to break down the minor differences of speech . . . within any given language group'.[30] A standard language, first for writing and later for speaking, helped unify the area in which it was used.

Dialect, a badge of regional consciousness, was downgraded, coming to be regarded as a barbarous or impure form of the language. It also came to be associated with the common people at a time when elites were withdrawing from participation in other forms of what we know as popular culture.[31]

Princes were thinking along similar lines to the printers and the Protestants, since they too needed their messages to be understood by people who spoke different and at times mutually unintelligible dialects. In the late Middle Ages, some German rulers, including the Holy Roman Emperor, and their officials were already communicating with their subjects in the vernacular as well as in Latin. Where the vernacular was used, the imperial, Saxon, and other chanceries eliminated regional terms to produce something like a standard language in which rulers communicated with their subjects, mainly in order to tell them what to do. The Saxon chancery, as Luther admitted, was his inspiration when he translated the Bible into an inter-regional form.

Standardization also brought prestige, allowing other languages to compete with Latin, Italian, and later French. Some degree of standardization was a necessary condition for the competition between languages that becomes increasingly visible in print from the sixteenth century onwards, with different writers singing the praises of their own vernaculars. João de Barros and Pero Magalhães de Gândavo praised Portuguese (1540, 1574); Alessandro Cittolini and Sperone Speroni, Italian (1540, 1542); Etienne Dolet, Joachim Du Bellay, Jean Tahureau, and Henri Estienne, French (1540, 1549, 1555, 1579); Martin Viziana, Castillian and Valencian (1574); Simon Stevin and Hendrik Spiegel, Dutch (1582, 1584); Jan Rybyński, Polish (1589); Richard Carew, English (1615); and Martin Opitz, German (1617). As in the case of the topos of the Chosen People, so in that of the eulogy of the vernacular, 'nothing is more international than the formation of national identities'.[32]

These various languages were praised in similar and contradictory terms as the richest, or the closest to ancient Greek or Hebrew, or the oldest (the language of Adam in some cases), or the most noble, elegant, pure or lucid form of speech or writing. On the other hand, rival languages were condemned as poor in vocabulary, barbarous in expression, as broken, patched, a mere 'mingle-mangle' or 'hotchpotch', or as sounding like the cries of animals rather than human speech. Spanish was denounced as the language of the devil in some German texts, while a Swedish bishop complained that the Danes 'do not trouble to speak like other people', but 'force their words out as if they wish to cough, and seem almost on purpose to twist their words in their throats before they come out'.

Some writers complained that their own vernacular was being invaded by words from abroad (French by Italian, German by French, and so on), and so needed to be purified. If 'linguistic nationalism' is an anachronistic description, we may at least speak of linguistic pride and also of a kind of linguistic xenophobia, a nativist reaction against foreign words associated with the idea that indigenous resources were sufficient and foreign words unnecessary or even a form of pollution.

In the fifteenth century, the Czech reformer Jan Hus already felt the need to resist German influences and so he coined the term *radnice*, for instance, to replace the obviously Germanic word for 'town hall', *ratusa* (from *Rathaus*). Again, the Netherlander Jan van de Werve, for instance, condemned the corruption of Dutch by French words in his *Tresoor der Duitsche Tale* (1553). A sixteenth-century German physician, Laurentius Fries, advocated the vernacularization of medical terms, while the schoolmaster and pastor Valentin Ickelsam opposed the introduction of foreign words such as *Policey* (discipline), *Podagra* (gout), *Recept* (recipe), and *Syndicus* (burgomaster).[33]

Linked to the increasing pride in certain vernaculars was the pride in literary achievements revealed by the first national bibliographies and biographies, especially biographies of writers, among them John Bale's *Scriptores britanniae* (1548); François de la Croix du Maine's *Bibliothèque françoise* (1584); Marquard Freher's *Germanicarum rerum scriptores* (1600–11); and Andreas Schott's *Hispaniae Bibliotheca* (1608). Whether or not a written vernacular literature is necessary to the development of a nation, there can be little doubt that it stimulates national pride and helps form a national identity.[34]

Myths of the Nation and National Character

Religion and language were not the only domains in which an increasingly sharp national consciousness may be seen in the early modern period. The rise of national histories both expressed and in turn encouraged such a consciousness. Among the best known of these histories were Paolo Emili's *De Rebus Gestis Francorum* (1516–20) and Polydore Vergil's *Anglica Historia* (1534), both written by expatriate Italian humanists, and the Jesuit Juan de Mariana's *De Rebus Hispaniae* (1592). Mariana's history of Spain was soon translated into Spanish, while other national histories made a greater impact by being written in the vernacular, among them Francesco Guicciardini's great *Storia d'Italia*, 1561–4, transcending the political fragmentation of the Peninsula, and P. C. Hooft's *Nederlandsche histoorien* (1642–54). Some histories of this kind had already been written in the Middle Ages, but many more contributions to the genre were made after 1500.

Although the term 'ethnicity' did not exist in early modern times, myths of the descent of particular peoples were common. The idea that both the French and the English were descended from the Trojans goes back to the Middle Ages (readers may wonder why there was such an interest in the losers of the Homeric wars, and the answer seems to be that the ancient Romans believed in their descent from Trojans). The Dutch, however, claimed descent from the ancient Batavians, who had resisted Rome (for this reason, the city now known as Jakarta was christened 'Batavia'). The Swedes claimed descent from the Goths and in the seventeenth century in particular there was an officially encouraged cult of the Goths in Sweden. The Scots claimed to be descended from Scota, the Pharaoh's daughter, the Hungarians from the Huns, and the Poles from the Sarmatians, a people who migrated from Iran and settled in eastern Europe. Indeed, in Poland, the seventeenth century was the time of a fashion now known as 'Sarmatism', a movement to distinguish Poles (or at least the nobility) from their western neighbours by adopting the clothing and weapons of their traditional enemies the Turks, notably the kaftan and the scimitar, treating these objects as if they were ancestral accoutrements.[35]

Even sports might be associated with particular peoples. In 1366 the Statute of Kilkenny had already prohibited hurling and recommended archery, in an attempt to weaken Irish and strengthen English identity.[36] In this context, the idea that the cleanliness of Dutch houses, so often mentioned by foreign travellers, was an expression of the identity of a new nation, appears less far-fetched than it may have done at first sight.[37] In the early modern period, the idea of national character was crystallizing, with manners and customs as its signs.

In 1617, for instance, a minor Spanish writer, Carlos García, published a book about the opposition or 'antipathy' between the French and the Spaniards, extending to the way they dressed, walked, and spoke.[38] The book was translated into French a few years later and into Italian and German before the end of the century. In the eighteenth century the phrases 'national genius' and 'national character' came into regular use. The philosopher Christian Thomasius, for instance, criticizing the German fashion for imitating the French, remarked that every nation 'has its special character' (*hat ihren absonderlichen Character*).[39] Montesquieu wrote of the 'genius' of a nation, while David Hume published an essay 'Of National Characters', arguing against Montesquieu's and other geographical explanations for differences in the manners and customs of different peoples and offering political explanations instead. Hume denied the existence of immutable national characters, but supported the idea of differences in what we would call national 'cultures'.[40]

One of the most vivid illustrations of the idea of national character comes from a remarkable series of visual documents produced in early eighteenth-century Styria. The best known of these images, the *Table of Peoples* (*Völkertafel*), may be seen in the Museum für Volkskunde in Vienna. At the top of the large painting may be seen men from ten nations—Spanish, French, Italian, German, English, Swedish, Polish, Hungarian, Russian, and, intriguingly, 'Turkish or Greek', each wearing his distinctive costume. Below, the differences in the ten national characters are classified under seventeen categories (customs, clothes, illnesses, worship, and so on). It has been argued that classifications of this kind not only express a sense of differences between nations but also amplify them, since all the slots have to be filled.[41]

The case of Thomasius illuminates the context in which the idea of national character arose: the reaction against Spanish and French cultural hegemony in the seventeenth century. The Dutch playwright Gerbrand Bredero's *Spanish Brabanter* is a critique of Netherlanders who adopt Spanish ways. A romance, *The Hired Carriage* (*La carrozza da nolo*, 1647) by the Italian Agostino Lampugani referred to 'the madness' of some of his compatriots, who forget 'to be Italians' and follow fashions of Spain or France. The Italian natural philosopher Lorenzo Magalotti described what he called the mania of European nations to imitate the French 'even in their defects'. Thomasius himself denounced his countrymen's taste for French food, French clothes, the French language, French manners, and 'French sins'. In the eighteenth century, Frederick the Great—writing in French—would complain that 'French taste ruled our kitchens, our furniture, our clothes', at once accepting and resenting French dominance in the arts of civilization. Like language, material culture was a domain in which both foreign influence and 'nativist' or national reactions against foreign influence are clearly to be seen.

These examples from material culture are a reminder of the importance of the visual in imagining communities. In similar fashion, the importance of printing cannot be reduced to the printed word. As Anderson noted, imagined national communities were reinforced by the spread of maps—and, one might add—by that of prints representing and often caricaturing the 'Other', whether the neighbours or the inhabitants of exotic lands, against whom viewers might define their identity or identities.

The word 'identity' is best used in the plural, possibly at all times and definitely in the early modern period, given the collective identities that competed with the nation at this time, not only those of gender and class but also city or region. The term 'patriotism' only came into use in the eighteenth century, but civic or regional loyalty was extremely strong in the sixteenth and seventeenth centuries, and not only among the lower classes. When the poet Pierre de Ronsard published his *Amours* in 1552, he described himself on the title page as 'gentilhomme Vendomois', in other words by his region. For the development of inter-regional solidarity, especially in large states such as France, it was necessary to wait for the age of conscription, railways, and cheap daily newspapers. In that limited sense the supporters of the 'Great Divide' theory are surely right. On the other hand, as I have been suggesting throughout this essay, we should not be thinking in crude binary terms of the presence or absence of national consciousness or national pride in modern or indeed in medieval Europe, but rather of their changing salience. National consciousness has become more widespread in recent centuries, as well as penetrating deeper into everyday life (including language). At the same time, national loyalties have come to take priority over loyalties to region, class, or religion.

Notes

1. M. Foucault (1966) *The Order of Things: An Archaeology of the Human Sciences*. English trans. (1974), London; R. Koselleck (1979) *Futures Past: On the Semantics of Historical Time*. English trans. (1985), Cambridge, MA.
2. B. Anderson (1983) *Imagined Communities*. Revised edn. (1991), London; E. Gellner (1983) *Nations and Nationalism*. 2nd edn. (2006), London; E. Hobsbawm (1990) *Nations and Nationalism since 1780*. 2nd edn. (1992), Cambridge; J. Breuilly (1982) *Nationalism and the State*. Revised edn. (1993), Manchester.
3. For comments and criticisms, see J. A. Hall (ed.) (1998) *The State of the Nation: Ernest Gellner and the Theory of Nationalism*, Cambridge.
4. P. Burke (2004) *Languages and Communities in Early Modern Europe*, epilogue, Cambridge.
5. T. Kamusella (2008) *The Politics of Language and Nationalisms in Central Europe during the 19th and 20th Centuries*, Aldershot.

6. M. de Certeau, J. Revel, and D. Julia (1975) *Une politique de la langue*. Paris; cf. D. A. Bell (2001) *The Cult of the Nation*, 169–97, Cambridge, MA.
7. Gellner, *Nations*, 12; Anderson, *Communities*; A.-M. Thiesse (1999) *La création des identités nationales, Europe 18e–20e siècle*, 67–82, Paris; E. Weber (1979) *Peasants into Frenchmen: The Modernisation of Rural France, 1870–1914*, London, 303–38.
8. J. A. Armstrong (1982) *Nations before Nationalism*, Chapel Hill, NC; A. D. Smith (1986) *The Ethnic Origins of Nations*, Oxford; A. Hastings (1997) *The Construction of Nationhood: Ethnicity, Religion and Nationalism*, Cambridge.
9. Anderson, *Communities*, 37–46.
10. A. Mayer (1981) *The Persistence of the Old Regime: Europe to the Great War*, London.
11. Weber, *Peasants*.
12. T. de Mauro (1963) *Storia linguistica dell'Italia unita*. Revised edn. (1991), Rome, 14, 43, 78.
13. Compare S. M. Lipset (1979) *The First New Nation: The United States in Historical and Comparative Perspective*, New York, with S. Schama (1987) *The Embarrassment of Riches*, 51–125, London. Cf. L. Colley (1992) *Britons: Forging the Nation, 1707–1837*, New Haven.
14. Smith, *Ethnic Origins*; Bell, *Cult*, 3. On national movements and their mobilization, M. Hroch (1985) *Social Conditions of National Revival in Europe: A Comparative Analysis of the Social Composition of Patriotic Groups among the Smaller European Nations*, Cambridge. First published in German in Prague in 1968.
15. This is, I think, the decisive argument against L. Greenfeld's (1992) discussion of a precocious sixteenth-century English 'nationalism' in her *Nationalism: Five Roads to Modernity*, Cambridge, MA. Cf. the critique of this argument by K. Kumar (2003) *The Making of English National Identity*, Cambridge, 95–120.
16. C. Beaune (1985) *The Birth of an Ideology: Myths and Symbols of Nation in Late-Medieval France*. English trans., revised edn. (1991), Berkeley, CA, 264, 284ff.
17. M. Cherniavsky (1961) *Tsar and People: Studies in Russian Myths*, 101–27, New Haven and London.
18. R. A. Houston (2002) *Literacy in Early Modern Europe*. 2nd edn., London, 158, and more generally, 141–72.
19. Hastings, *Construction*, 108.
20. S. L. Greenslade (1963) (ed.) *The Cambridge History of the Bible*, vol. 3, *The West from the Reformation to the Present Day*, Cambridge.
21. Burke, *Languages*, ch. 4.
22. A. Roshwald (2006) *The Endurance of Nationalism: Ancient Roots and Modern Dilemmas*, 15. Cambridge. Cf. A. D. Smith (2003) *Chosen Peoples*, Oxford.
23. Beaune, *Birth*, 293ff; L. Polizzotto (1994) *The Elect Nation: The Savonarolan Movement in Florence, 1494–1545*, Oxford, 367.
24. W. Haller (1963) *Foxe's Book of Martyrs and the Elect Nation*, London. On the role of Protestantism in the formation of British identity, see Colley, *Britons*, 11–54.
25. Schama, *Embarrassment of Riches*, 98, 104; cf. G. Groenhuis (1981) 'Calvinism and National Consciousness: The Dutch Republic as the New Israel', in A. C. Duke and C. A. Tamse (eds.) *Church and State since the Reformation*, The Hague, 118–33.
26. M. van Beek (1969) *Enquiry into Puritan Vocabulary*, Groningen.
27. A. W. Marx (2003) *Faith in Nation: Exclusionary Origins of Nationalism*, New York. See also the critique by P. Sahlins (2004) in *American Historical Review*, 109.
28. Colley, *Britons*, 11–54.

29. Bell, *Cult*, 7; M. A. Perkins (1999) *Nation and Word, 1770–1850: Religious and Metaphysical Language in European National Consciousness*, xiv, Aldershot.
30. S. H. Steinberg (1955) *Five Hundred Years of Printing*, 88, Harmondsworth.
31. This point is argued in P. Burke (1978) *Popular Culture in Early Modern Europe*, ch. 9. 3rd edn. (2008), Aldershot.
32. 'Rien de plus international que la formation des identités nationales': Thiesse, *Création*, 11. On the praise of individual languages, J. A. Fishman (1977) *In Praise of the Beloved Language: A Comparative View of Positive Ethnolinguistic Consciousness*, Berlin; and Burke, *Languages*, ch. 3.
33. Burke, *Languages*, ch. 6.
34. Hastings, *Construction*.
35. S. Cynarski (1968) 'The Shape of Sarmatian Ideology in Poland', *Acta Poloniae Historia*, 19, 5–17.
36. Hastings, *Construction*, 46. Cf. P. Palmer (2001) *Language and Conquest in Early Modern Ireland*, Cambridge.
37. Schama, *Embarrassment of Riches*, 375–97.
38. C. García (1617) *La oposición y conjunción de los dos grandes luminares de la tierra o la antipatía de Franceses y Españoles*, ed. Michel Bareau (1979), Edmonton, AL.
39. C. Thomasius (1687) *Nachahmung der Französen*. Reprint (1894), Stuttgart.
40. On France, Bell, *Cult*, 140–68.
41. F. K. Stanzel (ed.) (1997) *Europäischer Völkerspiegel: Imagologisch-ethnographische Studien zu den Völkertafeln des frühen 18. Jhts*, Heidelberg; J. Leerssen (2006) *National Thought in Europe: A Cultural History*, Amsterdam, 64.

Suggested Further Reading

Anderson, B. [1983] (1991) *Imagined Communities*, 3rd edn, London.
Armstrong, J. A. (1982) *Nations before Nationalism*, Chapel Hill, NC.
Baggioni, D. (1997) *Langues et nations en Europe*, Paris.
Bell, D. A. (2001) *The Cult of the Nation*, Cambridge, MA.
Burke, P. (2004) *Languages and Communities in Early Modern Europe*, Cambridge.
Fishman, J. A. (1997) *In Praise of the Beloved Language: A Comparative View of Positive Ethnolinguistic Consciousness*, Berlin.
Gellner, E. (2006) *Nations and Nationalism*, Oxford.
Hastings, A. (1997) *The Construction of Nationhood: Ethnicity, Religion and Nation*, Cambridge.
Hobsbawm, E. (1990) *Nations and Nationalism since 1780: Programme, Myth, Reality*, Cambridge.
Leerssen, J. (2006) *National Thought in Europe: A Cultural History*, Amsterdam.
Ranum, O. (ed.) (1975) *National Consciousness, History and Political Culture in Early Modern Europe*, Baltimore.
Thiesse, A.-M. (1999) *La création des identités nationales, Europe 18e–20e siècle*, Paris.

CHAPTER 3

NATIONALISM: INTELLECTUAL ORIGINS

ERICA BENNER

In modern social science, the word 'nationalism' is generally used to describe any movement that seeks to make state boundaries correspond with those of self-proclaimed 'nations', or any doctrine that gives national interests priority over other considerations. Such uses aspire to value-neutrality. They do not assume that nationalism must have stronger affinities with some political ideologies than others, but recognize its capacity to link up with a wide range of values: internal freedom and internal control, liberation from foreign dominion and imperial self-assertion. Historically, however, national ideas have always carried highly controversial and conflicting political implications. Most of the concepts that are now regarded as basic elements of nationalist doctrine—nation-building, national identity or consciousness, national self-government—were first elaborated in the late eighteenth century by thinkers with strong republican sympathies. The term 'nationalism' itself was scarcely used before the second half of the nineteenth century. The 1866 edition of *Larousse* defined it as a 'blind and exclusive' preference for one's own nation, or a degenerate form of reasonable *patriotisme*. Today this pejorative meaning remains standard throughout continental Europe: especially when applied to larger states, but also to movements of historically subordinate nations. A more positive sense emerged in anti-imperial circles around 1900 in the English-speaking countries, where until the First World War 'nationalist' meant a supporter of independence for Ireland and other subject peoples.

This essay traces some of the main intellectual developments behind these divergent understandings of nationalism. There are two distinct ways to study nationalism's intellectual origins. One focuses on broad intellectual movements, political networks, and rhetoric, and examines the contexts in which they emerged and operated. The other focuses on the ideas of a few highly reflective writers who discussed national issues in a general way, and who developed key concepts and arguments used in nationalist politics. The second approach is adopted here. I take philosophical or philosophically informed texts as my main source, rather than a wider cross section of programmatic or historical works written to support particular nationalist causes.

It has been said that nationalism lacks any outstanding defenders among classical philosophers and political thinkers.[1] This claim presupposes a narrow view of what constitutes a defence of nationalism. If one assumes that such a defence must be wholehearted, or treat national values as more fundamental than individual freedom or international justice, it is true that few early discussions of nationality looked like this. Some of nationalism's first philosophical defenders were also its most perceptive critics. They saw the formation of national polities as a necessary, yet by no means unproblematic, solution to urgent problems of internal legitimacy and external defence. On the one hand, they proposed various national means to make units of government more representative or popular, or to protect populations from unwanted intrusion by foreign powers. At the same time, they understood that nation-building raised difficult questions about the claims of minorities, the distribution of national territories, and the rights of states to decide whether considerations of national interest might take precedence over international standards. This ambivalence notwithstanding, the most profound thinkers of the late eighteenth and nineteenth centuries did offer powerfully reasoned arguments in defence of national values and politics. Rousseau, Herder, Kant, Fichte, Hegel, and Mill all saw national forms of legitimacy, independence, and resistance as among the most important corollaries of their ethical commitments. These philosophers did a great deal to articulate a distinctive and influential language of nationalism, together with what became its characteristic values and political prescriptions.

A close reading of early philosophical works can help to correct two misleading types of generalization found in historical and theoretical studies of nationalism. One assumes that particular nations or regions have their own highly distinctive forms of national doctrine, stressing their coherence and stability over time.[2] While such generalizations may be illuminating, they may also encourage exaggerated distinctions between ideal-typical Western and Eastern or English, French, German conceptions of nationality. Further, they often underestimate the extent to which the same ideas, social movements, and international pressures influenced national thinking across countries and regions. It is easier to avoid national stereotypes by focusing on the arguments of independent-minded thinkers who, though politically interested, sought to examine the moral and political implications of nationhood from a general standpoint rather than simply to advance a particular nationalist cause.

The second kind of generalization posits idealized contrasts among different types of national doctrine—'civic' and 'ethnic', liberal and authoritarian, anti-expansionist and imperial—while playing down their interconnections. If we presume that civic nationhood is clearly distinct from ethnic, or that liberal individualism must preclude imperialist or racist forms of nationalism, we may overlook the combinations and alliances formed among these doctrines during the past three centuries. Historically ill-informed typologies create the impression that some forms of nationalism were more absolute in their value commitments or resistant to compromise than they often were;

or that other forms, conversely, carried built-in immunity to extremism, intolerance, or injustice. A more nuanced account emerges from reading the texts discussed here, especially if readers do not impose today's standard typologies on more complex ideas developed in the past. Early philosophical writings furnish an invaluable source for understanding the pressures that gave rise to nationalism in its different forms, and the complex moral issues that it continues to raise.

From Peoples to Nations: Jean-Jacques Rousseau

The modern political idea of the nation has ancient and early modern sources. The Latin word *natio* meant place of origin. It had lacked strong political connotations in ancient times, but was sometimes used in the Middle Ages as a near-synonym for *gens*, signifying the high-ranking or true 'people' in Roman and medieval usage. Early modern republicans ascribed this sense of *natio-gens* to the whole free male population of a city or state. The concept of 'nation' was thus linked to the normative idea of sovereignty by identifying the people who were entitled to hold ultimate authority within a polity. At the same time, the word 'nation' retained the older sense of birthplace or paternal home, evoking the idea of an ancestral territory. This sense of 'nation' drew on a rich repertoire of ancient arguments defending the value of self-government (*autonomia*, *liberta*) for any city or people, in its traditional homeland (*patria*). Through its identification with patriotic values—which Greeks, Romans, Jews, and other ancient peoples held sacred—the term 'nation' acquired religious and emotional connotations. In relation to members of the same nation, the bond between sovereign people and homeland was sometimes expressed in quasi-religious terms as a bond between spiritual and organic aspects of the same 'body'. In relation to non-members, the same bond served as a barrier—ideally rooted in both popular will and material power—against attempts by foreigners to control independent nations. Although English republicans first used the language of nationhood to refer to politically constituted 'peoples', it was readily extended to currently stateless ones. English and Italian political theorists frequently invoked Old Testament references to the Hebrew nation whose members lacked a territorial state, yet were bound together by their own written laws, religion, and historical memories. The fusion of Greek and Roman-era rhetoric of anti-imperial resistance with biblical examples lent force to the idea that stateless nations might have divine authority to constitute their own polities, casting off unwanted foreign control.

These internally legitimating and externally defensive values can be found in most national doctrines, however they differ from one another in other respects. If the early modern language of nationhood expressed a core idea, it was that legitimate authority should be conferred by a popular mandate, not by a monarch or narrowly based elite;

and determined by the sovereign body within a nation, not imposed from without. Until the second half of the eighteenth century, however, the concept of nationhood remained marginal even in republican theory. The Genevan philosopher Jean-Jacques Rousseau (1712–78) was the first writer to give it a larger role in a theory of political legitimacy. He grounded this role in what would become a highly influential argument about the moral importance of national sovereignty.

In the *Social Contract* (1762) Rousseau offered an exceptionally pure, voluntarist form of the civic national ideal. Its main elements were further developed by Immanuel Kant (1724–1804).[3] Rousseau identified the nation as a 'people' constituted by individuals who, deliberating without distinction of birth, religion, or wealth, voluntarily establish their own governing authority. The primary bond among members of such a national community—indeed the only necessary one—is their agreement to obey the political authority they have created for themselves. Historical, cultural, or religious affinities may supplement uncoerced agreement as sources of legitimacy, but never substitute for it. In so far as authority is established under procedures that all see as fair, it is reasonable to consider individuals as obligated to follow its dictates for the sake of the common freedom. This version of civic nationhood rests on individualistic premises. It deliberately omits any reference to particular religious, regional, or social identities of contracting individuals; its guiding principle is equal respect for their powers of choice, limited only by respect for the same powers in others.[4] It is also egalitarian. Rousseau implied that any people who choose to constitute themselves as a nation have moral claims to independence that must be taken equally seriously, irrespective of their size, military strength, cultural characteristics, or whether they currently have a government of their own. Obviously, the legitimate claims of other peoples limit the territorial claims any nation may reasonably make. But facts of geography or current power may not override any people's right to seek some form of independence.

This thoroughgoing egalitarianism set Rousseau's argument apart from most other forms of civic nationhood advanced during the late eighteenth and nineteenth centuries.[5] By comparison with earlier contract theories, moreover, his arguments gave more consistent support to the independence claims of peoples living under or vulnerable to foreign domination. For example, nearly a century earlier John Locke (1632–1704) had argued that contracting individuals have natural rights to form new sovereign polities. But Locke proposed a non-contractual, inegalitarian criterion for distributing contested territory: if two or more peoples lay claim to the same land, it should go to those who use land in a more 'rational and industrious' manner. This criterion elevated a particular definition of progressive civilization above individuals' equal rights to authorize or reject their governments. It gave the advantage to peoples who could claim to be introducing superior civilization, trumping historical claims of prior occupation. Rousseau rejected all teleologies that assigned unequal rights to independence or territory on the basis of claims to superiority in religion, civilization, or economic progress. This principled stance was rooted in political realism, not utopian naivety. Rousseau realized that notwithstanding their claims to objectivity, all theories that posit particular ends to justify overriding some people's rights are controversial. Moreover, they tend to be defined in ways that give an advantage to the theorist's own cause. The same is true of various empirical criteria that might be proposed as a basis for deciding which peoples may form independent nations. So long as unequal rights are justified in terms that some perceive as arbitrary and unjust, subordinate peoples will be restive, and dominant peoples insecure in their dominance.[6]

At the same time, Rousseau recognized that international pressures made it difficult to implement contractarian principles in any single nation. For weaker peoples confronted by expansionist Great Powers, it was tempting to embrace defensive, collectivist, and exclusionary forms of nation-building instead of individualist ones. Rousseau outlined what these might involve in his constitutional projects *Corsica* (1765) and *Poland* (1772). Both were written at the behest of reformers in those countries, who hoped that more modern forms of government and administration might help to avert foreign invasion.[7] Noting that the impetus for such reforms came from insecurities created by competition among the preeminent states, Rousseau supported Corsican and Polish efforts to cultivate national particularities as insurance against foreign conquest. His advice to Corsicans stressed economic policies aimed at achieving independence from wealthier neighbours. His initial advice to the Poles was to play culture politics against power politics: they should use education and public rituals to implant a strong sense of national identity in their population. Rousseau acknowledged that the call to build up cultural barriers involved regrettable moral trade-offs. The intrinsic goodness or badness of a national practice might seem less important than how effectively it preserves the distinction between Poles and their conquerors. Even if practices are 'in some respects bad', they 'will still have the advantage of making the Poles fond of their country and give them a natural revulsion to mingling with foreigners'.[8]

Here Rousseau came close to presenting a justification for ethnic nationalism, which defines national identities in exclusive terms by grounding them in characteristics or sentiments that are said to be natural. He did not, however, *defend* it unequivocally. For Rousseau the choice of contractual or ethnocentric forms of nationhood was just that: a choice, and not one strongly predetermined by history or cultural traditions. National affinities and differences may be constructed in order to foster belief in their naturalness, and there may be good defensive reasons to do this. Rousseau understood that political choices are always constrained by conditions not of their agents' own choosing; and that in his own times, ethnocentric nation-building might well seem like sound defensive strategy for weaker polities and peoples. Beleaguered Poles—whose country would soon be occupied and divided up between three powerful neighbours[9]—could reasonably see xenophobic revulsion as a rational means of self-preservation. External threats made it difficult for Poles to undertake internal reforms in line with Rousseau's preferred republican principles. Instead of extending Poland's narrow franchise and reinforcing local and religious freedoms, many reformers were tempted to remodel the constitution on the pattern of centralized absolute monarchy, and to impose more uniformity on the country's diverse populations. Rousseau acknowledged the appeal of these options for Polish reformers, yet did not conclude that Poles and other vulnerable peoples should abandon contractarian principles and embrace ethnocentric practices. Instead he went on to suggest political and administrative reforms that would improve national defences while paving the way for eventual, far-reaching republican legislation.

Rousseau's writings remain a valuable source for historians seeking to examine the origins of nationalism, and for political scientists and philosophers interested in elucidating the motives that fuel it. He offered equally penetrating accounts of the reasoning behind civic voluntarist and defensive ethnic forms of nationalism, and implied that the two are not fundamentally opposed. Both, he suggested, stem from the same basic human desires: to be treated as equally free and competent agents who ought willingly to confer legitimacy on their own political orders, and who have reason to feel insulted if others deny them this right. But if ethnic nationalism is an understandable reaction to external pressures, for Rousseau it was never a morally satisfactory response or one likely to improve local or international stability. The only durable solutions are based on contractual principles, applied to relations between polities as well as within them. So long as the fundamental causes of defensive nationalism—rampant Great Power competition and imperialism—were not addressed, national claims would continue to proliferate and become more uncompromising.

Nationalism and Language: Johann Gottfried Herder

Like his mentor Kant, the German philosopher Johann Gottfried Herder (1744–1803) was strongly influenced by Rousseau's writings. But whereas Kant built on Rousseau's contractual principles, Herder elaborated a new, non-contractual conception of nationhood. His analysis of contemporary international pressures that provoked defensive nation-building resembled Rousseau's. Expansionist rivalries among the larger Powers, he argued, threatened the very survival of weaker peoples both in and beyond Europe. Herder also shared Rousseau's egalitarian commitments. He denied that a handful of western European countries constituted models of superior civilization, or had better claims to independence than other peoples, currently stateless or not.

Despite these affinities, Herder's defensive conception of nationhood was fundamentally different from Rousseau's. Nations for Herder were constituted by common bonds of language, which drew legitimating force not from acts of consent but from nature and historical evolution. And whereas Rousseau countered the self-serving hierarchical ideologies of the Great Powers by insisting on universal and unchanging principles of right, Herder opposed the same ideologies with a rival teleological theory of history: one that supported the independence of weaker peoples against incursions by the strong. Criticizing German and other elites who mimicked French or English languages and cultures, he argued that the diversity of language communities was part of a Providential plan for the moral advancement of humanity. For Herder, language was mankind's most distinctive and ennobling faculty, the foundation of sociability and sound morals, and the means for expanding human rational and spiritual capacities. Each language community, moreover, develops these capacities in its own unique way, thus discovering diverse and equally valuable routes to general truths. Since all languages embody legitimate interpretations of the common human experience, none may be ranked as superior to others—least of all because its speakers inhabit what are at present the most powerful states. In so far as he made judgements about their comparative value, Herder provocatively inverted the dominant standards of his era. Echoing Martin Luther, he suggested that vernacular languages—spoken in purest form by the lower social orders—were closer to nature and God's truth than the 'dead' Latin of priests, or the stilted French favoured in many German courts.

Although Herder said less about national politics than about national culture, his arguments implied a novel theory of legitimacy. No previous philosopher had suggested that identities based on language should be regarded as the primary source of legitimate political authority or locus of political resistance. His conception of the ideal relationship between language communities and political units is ambiguous, and thus inspired very different types of national programme. With suitable qualifications, Herder may fairly be seen as the father of both pacific multiculturalism and exclusive ethnic nationalism. He never stated a preference for sharply bounded, monoglot states, or implied that these are a condition for human advancement. His mature writings call for the toleration of cultural differences, not the formation of mono-ethnic states. Yet Herder was keenly aware that in an age of increasing literacy and social consciousness among European middle classes, language and culture could become powerful weapons in political conflicts, wielded by dominators and resisters alike. No previous writer had so fully considered how shared identity based on language might serve as a political resource, especially a defensive resource for weaker peoples seeking to resist conquest, cultural assimilation, or persecution.[10] Empires that tried to 'weld together' diverse provinces and language groups would, Herder warned, inevitably provoke resistance; for 'he who would suppress my language would also rob me of my reason and my way of life, and my people of honour and rights'.[11]

Herder's opposition to assimilation and conquest was unequivocal. It is less clear whether his criticisms imply that vulnerable language communities should respond by trying to build culturally unified states for themselves, or to establish military defences similar to those of existing stronger powers. The idea that cultural self-preservation depends on state power is intimated in Herder's programmatic 'Idea for the First Patriotic Institute for the Common Spirit of Germany' (1787).[12] Language is described here not just as the expression of a people's spirit and unique virtues. It is also a means of projecting power over others without having to lift a gun. In contemporary Europe, the French language exerted a 'secret preponderance' over other languages and cultures. No one forced Germans, Poles, or Russians to mimic French cultural norms; the glamour of power was enough to make people emulate them of their own accord. In the longer term, however, this uncoerced cultural dominance paved the way for French elites to impose 'universal monarchy' on Europe as a whole. Herder called on German princes and men of letters to resist this threat by forming a Patriotic Institute, charged with devising a common cultural and language policy for all the separate German states. Its aim should be to ensure that compatriots felt no shame or fear of 'being Germans on our own well-protected piece of territory'. Since 'the peoples of Europe (not excluding other parts of the world) are now in a contest of, not physical, but mental and artistic forces with each other,' Herder declared, each 'must advance with those others; in our time one can no longer be a barbarian; as a barbarian one gets cheated, trodden upon, despised, abused.' No contemporary people could opt out of this global competition 'even if it wanted to'.[13] In short, by the end of the eighteenth century national self-preservation had come to depend on cultural prestige as well as military and economic strength, and national political institutions had become necessary to defend distinct cultural identities.

Herder said almost nothing about the military dimensions of national statehood. He avoided explicit endorsements of military action in defence of nationality, and never directly enjoined weaker peoples to build up armies. Yet he sometimes hinted at the need to develop military defences as a condition for cultural survival. For example, he wrote that the historically 'submissive and obedient' conduct of non-Russian Slavs had long facilitated their oppression by the neighbouring empires. The time had now come, he told them, to 'awaken from your long and heavy slumber' and 'be freed from your enslaving chains'. Shedding their aversion to 'permanent military establishments', the Slavs should seek to realize their historical destiny: to 'use as their own' the vast territories now dominated by Habsburg Germans and Ottoman Turks.[14] These remarks hardly amount to a call to arms against the latter, let alone to Pan-Slavic expansionism. Nevertheless, they indicate one of the many ambiguities in Herder's practical legacy. Amid the conflicting national claims that emerged in the next century, many nationalist intellectuals and activists would interpret such comments as world-historical justification for asserting their claims by force, rather than by pursuing multinational coexistence.

Another ambiguity concerns the appropriate motives for pursuing defensive cultural nationalism. In his *Treatise on the Origins of Language* (1772), Herder distinguished between primitive and modern motives for sharpening divisions of language among groups that may have been closely related. Among primitive peoples, identity-defining wars arose from emotions connected with 'family feeling'; their aim was not to assuage 'hunger and thirst' but to despoil enemies as a 'sacrifice to the shades of their fathers'. Feelings of 'jealousy, feeling of honour, pride in their race and their superiority' drove people to separate their branch of a group from others and to form new, distinct language-cultures as a means of confirming the divorce. Herder identified three 'slogans' that served as the basis for differentiating communities, leading them to represent their differences as absolute. The first degrades the status of enemies: *Whoever is not with and of us is beneath us! The foreigner is worse than us, is a barbarian.* The second naturalizes enmities, making 'national hatred . . . eternal in perpetual, bitter wars': *Whoever is not with me is against me.* The third slogan asserts the 'complete division and separation' of rival groups. As Herder put it:

> who wanted to have anything in common with . . . the contemptible barbarian? No familial customs, no remembrance of a single origin, and least of all language [should be held in common]. . . . Language could not possibly, therefore, remain of one kind. And so the same familial feeling that had formed a single language, when it became national hatred, often created . . . complete difference in language.

According to Herder, these primitive motives are rooted 'more in noble weakness than base vice'. In the long run, he expected wise nature to tame divisive impulses: over time different peoples would stop treating each other like 'national animals' (*Nationaltiere*) and recognize diverse but complementary ways of being human.[15] It is not always clear, however, whether Herder thought that nature had moved the politics of his own times beyond primitive attitudes. His early and late writings condemn 'the barbaric system of war and conquest' treated by contemporary statesmen as 'the sole, immovable basis of all the states of Europe'.[16] If the conquering Great Powers still exhibited primitive impulses in their treatment of weaker peoples, how should the latter defend themselves, if not by similar means? Defensive nationalists might well take from Herder the idea that national egoism or even 'hatred'—however deplorable—should be judged a 'noble weakness' inflicted by the times, rather than denounced as 'limited nationalism' (*eingeschränkten Nationalismus*).[17]

Despite Herder's commitment to future goals of national toleration, then, the immediate political implications of his ideas were complex. In contrast to Rousseau and Kant, he said little about the legal or moral restraints that should guide nationalist efforts to forge new national states. Rousseau saw international law and institutions as the only realistic foundation for national freedom. Herder doubted whether formal laws could ever have obligatory force in relations between nations, and so did not advise peoples or states to put themselves under common restraints. His lack of interest in wider political and legal frameworks for adjusting different national claims was underwritten by the teleological structure of Herder's theory of history. He assumed that history is directed by a wise, purposive nature that would ultimately 'compensate' for injustices committed in the present. This assumption elicited Kant's objection that Herder's theory of history was too speculative and optimistic to support his vision of human coexistence. Providential nature may never help men evolve better moral dispositions; their only realistic hope, Kant argued, was to impose stronger and fairer restraints on themselves.[18]

Moreover, Herder's language-based criterion for nationhood raised a host of practical issues that he himself did not address. The idea of a national language is inherently controversial, and could be interpreted and applied in self-serving ways. For example, in 1808 Fichte suggested that German nationality encompassed a broad language family including speakers of Dutch as well as the Germanic Scandinavian languages. Such expansive uses of the language criterion illustrate its potentially explosive political implications. Herder himself did not specify which peoples should constitute the

German nation, or distinguish clearly between German-speaking, Germanic, or Teutonic *Völker*. But even if he had, this would have stirred up more arguments than it resolved. As Rousseau and Kant recognized, there is a fundamental difficulty in applying any theory that locates the source of political legitimacy in pre-defined group identities, rather than in the wishes of its members. Someone has to decide what count as the pertinent forms of identity, and what particular cases meet their criteria; and this is never a matter of objective judgement, but involves controversial political interests.

German Reactions to the Revolutionary Wars

The revolutions in America and France claimed to found new national forms of legitimacy on universal, republican principles.[19] Some of the most interesting intellectual reactions to these movements, especially to the French revolution, came from Germany. By 1800, the confederation of German states known as the Holy Roman Empire had begun to disintegrate under pressure from the revolutionary wars. In 1806 Napoleon invaded Prussia. These events led two young German philosophers, Johann Gottlieb Fichte (1762–1814) and Georg Wilhelm Friedrich Hegel (1770–1831), to suggest alternatives to the crusading republican concept of nationhood that prevailed in revolutionary France.

Fichte's early and late philosophical writings maintain strongly cosmopolitan positions. Like many German intellectuals, he supported the French Revolution in its first years. In the 1790s he defended a unitary concept of the nation based on republican principles, and argued that republican revolutionaries were entitled to use forcible intervention to advance the cause of freedom in other countries. But when Napoleon invaded Prussia, Fichte recanted these views. His *Addresses to the German Nation* (1808) were delivered in French-occupied Berlin as public lectures permitted by French authorities. Here Fichte urged Germans to reject occupation and mobilize around a common national identity, casting out 'foreign artifices'.

While his arguments have sometimes been seen as foreshadowing extremist ethnic nationalism in Germany, this view needs careful qualification.[20] The *Addresses* combined a Machiavelli-inspired doctrine of resistance to conquest with Rousseau-like arguments about how to construct a political and cultural sense of nationhood. Fichte pointed out that few Germans at the time had political allegiances transcending their separate states. A sense of nationality must 'be instilled in them' by deliberate policies. The most important of these should establish a system of education designed to inculcate a shared cultural identity. Fichte did add a non-voluntarist element that had not appeared in any of his earlier writings, and vanished again after the *Addresses*: he described language as the key feature distinguishing one nation from another and, like Herder, considered language-based identities as a fundamental source of political legitimacy. Indeed, Fichte may have been the first author to argue explicitly that language communities have a right to self-government. 'Whenever a separate language is found,' he declared, 'there a separate nation exists, which has the right to take independent charge of its affairs and to govern itself.'[21] He went well beyond Herder in postulating a moral hierarchy among nations, based on the extent to which their languages had been corrupted by foreign borrowings. Emulating Luther's crusade against foreign corruption, Fichte insisted that national self-liberation should be conjoined with a mission to seek the 'salvation' of 'the whole human race'. But while the Protestant idea of 'elect' nations granted some the right to lead others, Fichte's conception of national leadership was largely innocent of power-political ambitions. The Germans' humanitarian mission should not, he insisted, be pursued by military or political means involving the domination of other peoples, but by spreading the system of rational education outlined in the *Addresses*.

If there are morally dubious elements in Fichte's national thinking, they are rooted less in ethnocentrism than in the priority he gave to ends of national unification over restraints on the means that may be used to pursue it. Fichte rejected the unitary French model of nation-statehood. He praised the separation of state and cultural nation in German-speaking lands, which he saw as a more natural condition for Germans and a better guard for individual liberties. Ultimately, however, external pressures meant that German independence would be compromised without political unification. The envisaged German nation state should protect civil liberties, giving 'freedom as wide a field as possible, even at the risk of securing a smaller degree of uniform peace and quietness'. But in the face of foreign threats, 'the devouring flame of a higher patriotism' must have 'an undisputed right to summon and to order everyone concerned'.[22]

Hegel too withdrew his initial support for the French Revolution after witnessing its violence and expansionist zeal. In texts later published as *The German Constitution* (1798–1802), Hegel deplored the political disunity that had allowed some German states to 'come under the rule of the conquerors, and hence also of foreign laws and customs', while 'many others will lose what is their highest good, namely their existence as independent states'. In response, he urged the formation of a unified German state with a national 'centre . . . in which all powers are concentrated', and reorganizing 'the whole military strength of Germany into a single army'. Political unity and common defences were the main prerequisites for nation-building; the question whether Germans should opt for a monarchy or a republic was a secondary issue. Hegel admitted that unification might only be achieved by force, not mainly because of disagreements among leaders, but because the idea of unification was 'utterly alien' to most German people.[23] In keeping with this anti-populist stance, he did not regard a common popular culture as essential for the envisaged *Nationalstaat*.

Hegel's later works outline a conception of national unity based on combining traditional institutions with modernizing reforms. According to his philosophy of history, the principal agents of human rational development are distinct peoples

(*Völker*). Echoing Herder, he proposed a distinctive account of political legitimacy based on the idea that *Sittlichkeit*—or 'ethical life'—can develop only in the life of particular peoples, and only through particularity can it contribute to the universal progress of reason. Modern, sovereign states with sharply bounded territories were the best means of protecting and nurturing particular *Sitten*. Writing in the 1820s, Hegel argued that such national states represented the highest development of human reason and ethical development. The most important distinguishing features of these nations were generated through common political life, and sustained by the defensive needs of the state. They had no necessary roots in language or religion.

Hegel's mature political theory had universalistic foundations: unlike Herder, he proposed standards of rational order that any modern state should strive to meet. Yet in one key respect, Hegel's version of Enlightenment universalism was considerably more particularistic than that of Rousseau, Kant, Herder, or Fichte. These philosophers called for an end to what they saw as a historically transient or corrupt and unnatural state of war among nations. Both Rousseau and Kant exhorted all societies to put themselves voluntarily under universal legal restraints, and Fichte too envisaged a future condition of international right among formally equal states. By contrast, Hegel argued that the state of war was the natural and hence the permanent condition of international relations. One condition for national independence was a clear 'awareness of one's existence as a unit in sharp distinction from others'; and war could play a useful role in strengthening this sense of identity. This view had particularistic and illiberal implications. It inflated the rights of nation states in their external relations, while undermining restraints on their actions. This, in turn, created a tension between Hegel's principles of internal political order—which respected the rights of individuals, corporations, regions, and minorities—and the more collectivist virtues he saw as necessary in relations among modern states. Maintaining the 'independence and sovereignty of the state' was the individual's highest duty, 'at the risk and the sacrifice of property and life, as well as of opinion and everything else naturally comprised in the compass of life'.[24] These views were rooted not in authoritarian attitudes, but in concerns about external defence that persisted even after the Revolutionary wars.

Hegel's conception of nationality was inegalitarian as well as ethically particularistic. His theory of history picked out specific peoples in each epoch who contributed more than the rest to the rational development of the species. In other respects, the theory resembled Herder's attempts to identify Providential purposes that have directed human history in all times and places, and that are destined to bring the disparate national parts of humanity to accept common standards of reason—making it unnecessary to subordinate themselves to formal international laws. Herder, however, had insisted on the equal value of different national contributions to human progress. He placed special emphasis on the rich cultural life of *Völker* such as the Baltic peoples and non-Russian Slavs who, lacking states of their own, were judged history's losers by criteria of *Realpolitik*. Hegel adapted Herder's teleological account of world history to the hierarchical thinking that would dominate discussions of nationality in the nineteenth century. He argued that only peoples with a history of political independence were entitled to form national states. Hegel's metaphysical account of history's ultimate ends reflected the power-political anxieties of his times. 'In the existence of a nation,' he wrote, 'the substantial aim' set by history 'is to be a state and preserve itself as such.' According to this criterion, the most advanced nations were those that currently possessed their own state. Any people who sought to form a new state must have had one in the past, and meet various geographical and political criteria of viability. 'A nation with no state formation (a *mere* nation),' Hegel argued, 'has, strictly speaking, no history—like the nations which existed before the rise of states and others which still exist in a condition of savagery.'[25] Peoples thus denied rights to self-government were bound to regard such criteria as arbitrary reflections of particular interests. Nevertheless, similar claims that nations could be ranked as more and less 'historical', and thus deserving of independence, were proposed by republicans such as Giuseppe Mazzini, liberals such as John Stuart Mill, and socialists such as Karl Marx and Friedrich Engels. In different ways all these thinkers built on the republican anti-imperial legacies of Rousseau and Herder. But they diluted or abandoned their predecessors' national egalitarianism, which rejected any criteria grounding rights to self-government on facts created by past conquests, accidents of geography, or size.

Self-Government and Empire

The revolutions of 1848–9 swept national issues to the forefront of political debates in Europe. The uprisings were sparked by liberal and left-wing movements for constitutional and social reform. But in the Habsburg Empire with its large Hungarian, Slav, and Romanian populations, the revolutions soon turned into revolts by stateless 'nationalities', as they were called, against foreign and imperial rule. This threat to the survival of one of Europe's venerable Great Powers gave fresh urgency to discussions about which peoples were entitled to national independence. Though couched in the language of general principles, the discussions were highly politicized. In 1848 the French Foreign Minister Alphonse de Lamartine announced that a universal '*principe de nationalité*' authorized France to give military aid to any movement of subject nationalities in Europe. As a young Karl Marx (1818–83) was quick to observe, any such 'principle' defined and declared unilaterally was sure to be invoked in opportunistic ways. Each competing Great Power—a rank at that time comprising the French, British, and Russians, with the multinational Austrian and Ottoman empires threatened with disintegration—would use it selectively to support national movements that weakened their rivals.[26]

Marx's British contemporary John Stuart Mill (1806–73) offered a far less cynical analysis of the newly articulated *principe de nationalité*. Though some of his views are widely criticized today, Mill's attempt to evaluate national claims according to general principles, rather than particular political interests, was unusually sensitive for his times. During and after the 1848 Revolutions, Mill sought to defend aspirations for self-government, especially against authoritarian empires, without encouraging ethnocentric nationalism. In 1861 he outlined a complex set of standards that combined moral principles with pragmatic considerations. One key principle was that 'the question of government ought to be decided by the governed'. A corollary was that where 'the sentiment of nationality exists in any force, there is a prima facie case for uniting all the members' under a single government 'to themselves apart'.

Had Mill made this principle of consent to government the non-negotiable bedrock of his criteria, his position would have resembled Rousseau's. But he went on to argue that the general principle of consent should be weighed against other, equally compelling considerations, both moral and pragmatic. The moral considerations were expressed in Mill's notion of 'utility', which he claimed embodied the highest 'interests of humanity'. The most important such interests are advanced by the expansion of individual liberty and forms of government that promote that liberty. Mill proposed that specific national claims should be judged against this standard. This suggested pragmatic criteria for deciding which national claims should be given priority. One condition for national independence was geographical, and called for the integration of diverse populations into one national state. Since countries such as Hungary had populations 'so mixed up as to be incapable of local separation', they must try 'to make a virtue of necessity, and reconcile themselves to living together under equal rights and laws'. Another criterion linked considerations of geopolitical viability—which favoured the formation of larger, culturally integrated political units—with the 'moral and social consideration' that human progress required the gradual absorption of less advanced peoples into the more advanced. The principle of nationality should not hold out vain hopes of survival to peoples who formed 'an inferior and more backward portion of the human race' such as Bretons, Welshmen, and Basques, who could only benefit from assimilation to larger, more powerful nations.[27]

While in Europe Mill's concept of utility advised the absorption of smaller nationalities, matters were less straightforward in the non-European colonies. A civil servant who worked for many years on colonial issues, Mill understood that assimilation was impossible where the ostensibly more civilized nation was much less populous than the less, as with the English in India. In such cases it was clearer to Mill than to many of his contemporaries that colonial rule was ultimately untenable. However backward at present, native majority populations were bound to demand self-government sooner or later. If they achieved it through means that also improved local standards of civilization, this would serve the overall utility of the human species. Distinguishing between countries whose population was already 'in a sufficiently advanced state to be fitted for representative government' and 'others which have not attained that state', Mill urged the European Powers and 'colonies of European race' to 'use their superiority' to try to prepare the latter—mainly non-European peoples—'for a higher stage of improvement', including eventual self-government. Thus Mill's criteria were more generous to non-European aspirations for independence than to those of the less progressive European 'nationalities'. But his utilitarian standard was still paternalistic. For peoples deemed unready for self-government, he wrote, 'it is often better for them to be under the despotism of foreigners than of natives, when those foreigners are more advanced in civilization' than themselves.

Despite Mill's commitments to general principles of freedom and consent of the governed, then, his final touchstone for evaluating national claims was the teleological standard of utility. In deciding how to address national claims, consent could be trumped by contestable judgements about the 'highest good for the human race', or about what cultural or geopolitical facts identified a people as capable of self-government. These standards sharply limited the application of his principles of self-government. But as with any teleological standards that give particular ends precedence over other moral claims, Mill's were inherently controversial, and therefore tended to provoke more arguments than they settled. Mill expressed little concern about the resentments and conflicts that might arise from such inegalitarian national principles. In contrast to Marx, he did not anticipate the proliferation of frustrated national claims, or expect them to produce ever more violent conflicts. Nor did he seem to realize that the nationality principle itself could become a plaything of both liberal and despotic powers, as all parties and their intellectual spokesmen sought to define and apply it in ways that helped their own cause. Instead Mill assumed—despite evidence to the contrary—that rising national demands would somehow be adjudicated by a fair-minded club of civilized nation states, led by a wholly impartial Britain.[28]

The presumption that a few Western Powers were entitled to determine whether and when to grant other peoples self-government provoked resistance, intellectual as well as political, in less highly ranked nations. One of the most balanced critiques of such paternalistic doctrines came from a non-European admirer of Mill, the best-selling Japanese liberal philosopher Yukichi Fukuzawa (1835–1901). In his *Outline of a Theory of Civilization* (1874) Fukuzawa accepted Mill's distinction between progressive and backward peoples, placed the Japanese in the latter category, and outlined far-reaching reforms aimed at ending his country's backwardness. But he rejected the notion that backward nations must be educated by the more civilized before they could demand independence on terms of equality. Even the least advanced peoples must undertake reforms of their own accord, and pursue progress in education and representative government without the tutelage of supposedly advanced nations. Imposed by foreigners, any measures taken toward advancement would be seen as illegitimate, and foster xenophobic backlashes. Mill and other Western liberals dangerously underestimated 'how hateful, how infuriating, and how painful' was the 'imbalance of power' for the backward, especially when their Western mentors paid 'lip service . . . to equality of rights between nations'.[29]

While pursuing reforms on largely western models, some modernizing nationalists drew on an earlier British argument that stressed the continuity of older national bonds. In a treatise widely read throughout Europe and beyond, the Anglo-Irish philosopher and Whig MP Edmund Burke wrote in 1790:

> We wished to derive all we possess as an inheritance from our forefathers. . . . In this choice of inheritance we have given to our frame of polity the image of a relation in

> blood; binding up the constitution of our country with our dearest domestic ties; adopting our fundamental laws into the bosom of our family affections . . .[30]

Burke described this conception—at once historical and ethnic in its emphasis on natural ties of blood—as a choice made by generations of Britons aimed at strengthening subjects' loyalty toward the state. This came to be seen as a pragmatic, evolutionary 'English model' of nationhood that others might try to emulate. It exerted a tremendous influence over nation-builders in many countries, especially those with monarchies, whose political elites wanted to implement modernizing reforms in a controlled way 'from above'. The most successful nation states, these reformers believed, were those that could represent their 'body' of subjects through images of familial ties, thereby fostering affectionate respect for traditional authorities. Moderate anti-republican German authors such as Hegel adopted elements of Burke's organic-historic conception. When in the 1870s and 1880s Japanese imperial authorities sought foreign advice on drafting a new constitution, German advisers suggested the English parliamentary system as a constitutional ideal, and key Japanese authors of the Meiji Constitution cited Burke's treatise as an important source for their concept of nationality.

Imperialism, Radical Nationalism, and Race

It makes little sense to examine the rise of radical *fin de siècle* nationalism in any country or region without considering the wider context of competition for empire. Radical nationalism can take many forms, but all involve perceptions of threats to a nation's survival or standing. Typically, it seeks to intensify efforts to promote strong forms of identity through national education, media, and administrative centralization. But unlike garden-variety defensive nationalism, which aims above all to erect barriers against foreign interactions, radical nationalism lashes out against actual or potential foes by adopting policies of international activism. These include intensified commercial, territorial, and military expansion, often combined with a dismissive attitude to moral and legal restraints. Radical nationalism in the late nineteenth century was not primarily the product of ethnic or revolutionary politics in particular countries; it was an international phenomenon whose spokesmen included moderate liberal and republican thinkers. In the 1840s Alexis de Tocqueville (1805–59) argued that only an aggressive colonial policy could preserve France's global influence and national standing vis-à-vis rival powers. Requisite measures included the transfer of a large 'European population that will protect and guarantee the territory we have conquered', the systematic desolation of local tribes, and the 'interdiction of commerce'. Significantly, de Tocqueville dispensed with any justifications invoking the higher good of humanity;

in the struggle to defend France's standing among rival European empires, the overriding good was particular and national.[31]

In the century's last decades, radical nationalism gained momentum from the idea that national hierarchies were determined by the quality of biological 'races' in which nations partook. Racial doctrines gained a wide following in academic, political, and military circles throughout Europe, and the language of racial inequality began to seep into nationalist doctrines across the political spectrum. Race doctrine had two main elements. One was a radicalized version of earlier empirical criteria for discriminating among national claims: an assertion of natural inequality among human groups identifiable by observable characteristics. By tying inequalities to deterministic biology, racial doctrines helped to naturalize claims of superiority and inferiority between national groups, making them more absolute. The other element was a regressive, paranoid teleology: inferior race groups were thought to possess a brutish power that endangered the survival of higher races and their civilizations. The targets of these fears included rebellious colonized populations, but also other major European 'races' that were deemed more or less progressive as forces for empire: the Germanic, the Gallic, the Slavic, the Jewish. Precise definitions of these races and the ranks assigned to them constantly altered in different countries, according to the social conflicts and alliances of the day. Playing on social and international anxieties about loss of status in relation to newly assertive populations, racial thinking came to serve as one of the main ideological strategies of international positioning and repositioning, and as a justification for aggressive imperialism. Far from being simply a new variant of defensive ethnocentrism or authoritarianism, doctrines of racial inequality dovetailed just as well with radicalized civic and liberal nationalism, which had already become less egalitarian over the course of the nineteenth century.

Deploring these developments in the late 1880s, Friedrich Nietzsche (1844–1900) opined that national values had become mere herd-thinking, 'bovine nationalism'. The quest for strong group identities had degenerated into a demand for cultural, then racial unity, producing an irrational fear of minorities—especially those like the Jews whose time-tested identity appeared threatening to nations 'whose type is still weak and undetermined'.[32] By the early 1930s the term 'nationalism' was associated almost exclusively with movements that placed the ends of particular nations above wider considerations of order or justice.[33] Nietzsche expected the politics of radical nationalism in Europe to be succeeded by a European union, in which national rights would be limited by confederal and supernational duties. The earliest defenders of nationalism, notably Rousseau, had called for similar limits on national claims. With nationalism as with many political ideas, sometimes the oldest versions see furthest ahead.

Notes

1. R. Beiner (ed.) (1999) 'Introduction', *Theorizing Nationalism*, Albany, NY, 2.
2. L. Greenfeld (1992) *Nationalism: Five Roads to Modernity*, Cambridge, MA.

3. See E. Benner (2011) 'The Nation State', in A. Wood (ed.) *The Cambridge History of Nineteenth-Century Philosophy*, Cambridge, ch. 23.
4. Rousseau's concept of the General Will has often been interpreted in a collectivist manner, starting with French revolutionaries who claimed Rousseauian inspiration for forms of republican nationalism that were intolerant of individual and minority rights. Nothing, however, could be further from the tenor of Rousseau's own basic principles. These required respect for equal individual freedom, and hence protection for conscientious disagreements expressed within the limits of law.
5. Excepting those of Kant and Paine.
6. John Locke's arguments reflected and reinforced contemporary British justifications for colonial expansion in the Americas. Rousseau sharply criticized Locke's and other inegalitarian doctrines that purported to be based on natural law.
7. In the eighteenth century, the ancient Greek idea that philosophers could give valuable advice on how to found or reconstitute polities was not considered utopian. Rousseau's arguments did influence nation-building policies in Poland as well as in republican France, albeit not always in ways that adhered to his deepest principles. Polish reformers asked several well-known Francophone philosophers to submit advice on a new constitution, and there is no evidence that Rousseau's proposals were well received at the time. This is unsurprising, since he urged Poland's aristocratic lawmakers to adopt far-reaching reforms that would make the constitution more popular and representative. His ideas were, however, cited as an influence on the Polish constitution of May 1791.
8. J.-J. Rousseau (1997) 'Considerations on the Government of Poland', in V. Gourevitch (ed.) *The Social Contract and Other Later Political Writings*, Cambridge, 177–60.
9. Poland underwent three partitions between Austria, Prussia, and Russia, first in 1772—the year Rousseau completed his Project—and the last in 1795. Poland was thereby deprived of independence until 1918. This alleged injustice committed by Great Powers against a large, long-established polity became the first major *cause célebre* for the idea of national freedom.
10. See Chapter 2 by Peter Burke for earlier ideas about language and nation.
11. J. G. Herder (1877–1913) 'Briefe zu Beförderung der Humanität' ('Letters for the Advancement of Humanity'), in B. Suphan (ed.) (1877–1913) *Sämtliche Werke*, vol. 7, Berlin, 65–8.
12. J. G. Herder, 'Idee zum ersten patriotischen Institut für den Allgemeingeist Deutschlands', in Suphan (ed.) *Sämtliche Werke*, vol. 16, 600–12.
13. Herder (2002) 'Letters for the Advancement of Humanity', in M. N. Forster (ed.) *Herder: Philosophical Writings*, Cambridge, 377.
14. J. G. Herder (1997) 'The Slavs', in H. Adler and E. A. Menze (eds.) *Herder on World History: An Anthology*, New York, 300–1.
15. J. G. Herder (2002) 'Treatise on the Origin of Language', in Forster (ed.), 150–4.
16. Herder (2002) 'Letters Concerning the Progress of Humanity', in Forster (ed.), 365.
17. J. G. Herder (2002) 'This too a Philosophy of History', in Forster (ed.), 297. This is one of the first recorded uses of the word 'nationalism' in any language.
18. I. Kant (1991) 'Reviews of Herder's Ideas on the Philosophy of the History of Mankind', in H. Reiss (ed.) *Political Writings*, Cambridge, 201–20.
19. For the role of nationalism in these revolutions, see Chapter 6 by Don Doyle and Eric Van Young and Chapter 7 by Michael Rowe.

20. This view is more reasonably based on one of Fichte's earlier, pre-nationalist texts where, echoing French Jacobin doctrines, he defended a strongly unitary form of republican nationalism and attacked various types of 'state within the state'—including that allegedly formed by the Jews.
21. J. G. Fichte, *Addresses to the German Nation* trans. and ed. G. A. Kelly (1968), New York, 184. There is now a more recent English version available in the *Cambridge Texts in the History of Political Thought* series edited by Gregory Moore (2008).
22. Fichte, *Addresses to the German Nation*, 118–20, 126, 184.
23. G. W. F. Hegel (1999) 'The German Constitution', in L. Dickey and H. B. Nisbet (eds.) *Hegel: Political Writings*, Cambridge, 6–101.
24. G. W. F. Hegel, *Philosophy of Right*, ed. T. M. Knox (1967), Oxford, 208–23, 297.
25. Hegel, *Philosophy of Right*, 217–19; G. W. F. Hegel, *Philosophy of Mind*, ed. W. Wallace (1971) Oxford, 279.
26. For more detail on Marx, Marxist and socialist views of nationalism, see Chapter 32 by John Schwarzmantel.
27. J. S. Mill (1991) 'Considerations on Representative Government', in J. Gray (ed.) *On Liberty and Other Essays*, Oxford, 430–3, 217.
28. Mill, 'Considerations on Representative Government', 449–67.
29. Y. Fukuzawa (1970) *An Outline of a Theory of Civilization*, ed. David A. Dilworth and G. Cameron Hurst, Tokyo, 171–98.
30. E. Burke, *Reflections on the Revolution in France*, ed. F. G. Selby (1890), London, 34–7.
31. A. de Tocqueville, *Writings on Empire and Slavery*, ed. J. Pitts (2001), Baltimore, 145, 70–1. In 1841 de Tocqueville wrote to Mill that a nation like France 'must not be suffered to believe that its place in the world is diminished . . . and to console herself . . . with peaceful prosperity at whatever cost, and with the well-being of each individual'. Mill's stern reply criticized the French obsession with national status. Even 'the most stupid and ignorant person' in England, he insisted—inadvertently exposing his own national blind spot—was unconcerned with such insubstantial things as national glory. H. O. Pappé (1998) 'Mill and Tocqueville', in G. W. Smith (ed.) *J. S. Mill's Social and Political Theory*, London, 123–5.
32. F. Nietzsche, *Beyond Good and Evil*, trans. and intro. R. J. Hollingdale (1991), Harmondsworth, 102–3, 162–9. Nietzsche suggested that in order to calm the hysteria 'it would perhaps be a good idea to eject the anti-Semitic ranters from the country'.
33. See Chapter 21 by Oliver Zimmer and Chapter 29 by Roger Eatwell.

Suggested Further Reading

Arendt, H. (1951) *The Origins of Totalitarianism*, New York.

Barnard, F. M. (1988) *Self-Direction and Political Legitimacy: Rousseau and Herder*, Oxford.

Benner, E. (1995) *Really Existing Nationalisms*, Oxford.

Berlin, I. (1955) 'Nationalism: Past Neglect, Present Power', in Hardy, H. (ed.) *Against the Current: Essays in the History of Ideas*, Oxford.

Dahbour, O. and Ishay, M. R. (eds.) (1995) *The Nationalism Reader*, New York.

Engelbrecht, H. C. (1933) *Johann Gottlieb Fichte: A Study of his Political Writings with Special Reference to his Nationalism*, New York.

Hont, I. (1994) 'The Permanent Crisis of a Divided Mankind: "Contemporary Crisis of the Nation State" in Historical Perspective', *Political Studies*, 42, 166–231.
Kamenka, E. (ed.) (1976) *Nationalism: The Nature and Evolution of an Idea*, London.
Kedourie, E. (1960) *Nationalism*, London.
Varouxakis, G. (2002) *Mill on Nationality*, New York.

CHAPTER 4

ANTI-WESTERN DOCTRINES OF NATIONALISM

ANDREAS ECKERT

Introduction

Critiques of 'the West' voiced by non-Western intellectuals and public leaders have attracted considerable interest in recent years.[1] This is taking place in a context in which we face on the one hand the acceleration of economic globalization and rates of migration, and on the other hand the growing trend towards national and other forms of cultural essentialism. A strong resurgence of nationalism can be observed, for instance, in East Asia and Latin America. In the West, Islamic fundamentalism is usually regarded as the most important (and most threatening) case of anti-Westernism. Radical Islamism is a highly modern ideology that defines itself against internationalism and secularism—including the institution of the secular nation state—in the Islamic world. The disquiet in the West about the supposed erosion of the nation state[2] and about the rise of radical ethno-nationalisms has to do with the fact that the conflicts and tensions linked to it are not only a problem of 'underdeveloped states', but take place in the heart of Europe. As Anthony Hopkins put it: '... the unpredicted appearance of a virulent strain of assertive ethnicity has engulfed not just very different and very distant peoples but also societies whose proximity to our own is sufficiently close to suggest, not just that the barbarians are inside the walls, but that we are the barbarians'.[3] Partha Chatterjee even suggests that:

> nationalism is now viewed as a dark, elemental, unpredictable force of primordial nature threatening the orderly calm of civilized life. What had once been successfully relegated to the outer peripheries of the earth is now seen picking its way back

> towards Europe, through the long-forgotten provinces of the Habsburg, the Czarist, and the Ottoman empires. Like drugs, terrorism, and illegal immigration, it is one more product of the Third World that the West dislikes but is powerless to prohibit.[4]

This chapter discusses the history (and historiography) of anti-Western doctrines of nationalism. It begins by focusing on the development of ideas about the 'West' within non-Western societies during the nineteenth century and outlines the growth of more critical and alternative discourses with the globalization of nationalism. Such debates were usually limited to small elites. The 'West' was not the only point of reference. For example, around 1900 Japan began to serve as a metaphor for Asian modernity for the Ottomans, Egyptians, and Indians. The ambiguities of non-Western nationalism will be considered in relation to Gandhi and Senghor, who both combined indigenous and Western ideas of nationalism in specific, complex ways. Some reflections on 'Western' readings of nationalism in the era of decolonization in the 1950s and 1960s, characterized by rather optimistic notions of nation-building, are followed by a final section on alternative ways of understanding the nationalism of this period, for instance, as in Bengal and in Tanzania, in terms of indigenous discourse and patterns of collective action.

Nationalism, Globalization, and Critiques of 'the West'

The assumption that nationalism is a Western product and the question of what has been made of it in the non-Western world are familiar topics in academic as well as political discourses. For a long time, 'nationalism was generally considered as one of Europe's most magnificent gifts to the rest of the world'. Most historians of colonialism and area specialists agreed that nationalism was a European import: 'the debates in the 1960s and 1970s in the historiographies of Africa or India or Indonesia were about what had become of the idea and who was responsible for it'.[5] The rejection of 'Westernization' in the name of authentic cultural traditions was a common theme in much of this literature. Anti-Western ideas in the non-Western world have a long history, much of which is linked to nationalism. What was meant by 'the West', and what was criticized about it, varied considerably over time and space. In this context, the suggestive term 'Westernization' cannot really catch the complexity of mutual influence, hybridization, and cross-cultural entanglement that characterized the world in the era of imperialism and colonialism. Still, the idea that the non-Western world had to incorporate aspects central to European culture and its political order was shared by most elites outside Europe and the United States. While during the mid-nineteenth century, these elites could try to uphold the myth of cultural and political autonomy, things had changed around 1900. Western dominance and the imperialist grip on the world had conjoined local, regional, national, and international politics all over the world. Ideas and concepts about the domestic order had become increasingly linked to ideas of the global order.[6]

Many concepts and institutions began to spread globally, 'nation' and 'nationalism' among them. The nationalization of the world in the nineteenth century did considerably affect the colonized and semi-colonized parts of the globe. One could argue that nationalism and colonialism were at once products and agents of a Eurocentric globalization. However, at first glance the emergence of the nation state in its territorial presuppositions seems to contradict the imperatives of globalization.[7] The various nationalist movements that mushroomed around 1900 in many non-European areas posed a serious challenge to the international order based on large overseas empires and international law. Outside the West, nationalism soon emerged as the leading ideology and privileged form of political discourse, and eroded more encompassing definitions of belonging in places as diverse as Egypt and India. In some regions, for instance Europe and Latin America, nationalism had a longer history dating back to before 1800. In other parts of the world, for example Japan and China, early formations of nationalism emerged during the first part of the nineteenth century. Nationalism was the product of a complex set of social conditions and political discourses within a society and its regional contexts. Besides these long-standing, more or less 'internal' traditions of nationalism, the fast-growing entanglement of the world since the late nineteenth century worked as an additional, 'external' factor that decisively influenced the trajectories of nationalism worldwide. The emergence of a world order of nation states went hand in hand with the spread of nationalism, and even in those societies in which the nation state looked back to a longer history, the discourse of nationalism was frequently shaped by the new waves of globalization.[8]

More recently, some historians have suggested 'that the nation-state itself was a product of the prior emergence of inter-state relationships, which more or less forced nationhood on a previously diverse set of political systems, ranging from the tribal to the imperial'.[9] The global spread of the nation state beginning in the mid-nineteenth century in turn shaped further the processes of globalization. On the one hand, juridical principles regulating both relationships between states and between states and their subjects were diffused globally. On the other hand, there were strong efforts to erase local differences and varieties within the nation in the name of national cultural homogeneity. Increases in global mobility especially shaped discourses of nationalism.[10] As the example of Chinese migration shows,[11] in the face of a growing number of migrants, around 1900 many countries strengthened their immigration controls and devised ways of enforcing control over the mobility of people, including passports, fingerprints, and other biometrical devices. The Chinese Exclusion Act in the United States in 1882 is such a case. Chinese mobility also contributed to the ethnicization of notions of national belonging. In essence, mass migration influenced and defined a sense of nation both for the host country and the country of origin. The existence of Chinese communities in places such as the United States prompted questions concerning the cohesion and composition of the nation and fed into discourses of nationalism. One could argue that 'the particular form that nationalism and the representation of the nation-state took around the year 1900, were not mere invented traditions, but rather at least partly the effects of interactions and entanglements on a global scale'.

The spread of nationalism and the nation state was characterized by a striking ambiguity. On the one hand, it was part and parcel of the Westernization of the world; on the other hand it undermined a system of large Western overseas empires. Nationalism was often closely linked to anti-colonialism: local groups and individuals seeking power in a colonial state, aiming at the 'political kingdom' (Kwame Nkrumah). Anti-colonial nationalism was an important driving force of the decolonization process that shaped the mid-twentieth century.[12] An exception is Latin America, where some twenty states (except one: Cuba) have enjoyed formally independent existences since they emerged from the dissolving Spanish and Portuguese empires in the 1810s and 1820s. As such, they are even older than most European states. However, Frederick Cooper stresses the fact that it would be wrong to present nationalism as subsuming all other struggles in the period preceding national independence. Such a perspective, Cooper writes, does 'miss a lot of history, notably the tension—at times a creative one—between the national question and other sorts of social questions'.[13]

Elites, Westernization, and Anti-Western Nationalisms

From the mid-nineteenth century the debates of cultural and political elites in China, Japan, India, Africa, and the Ottoman Empire often (though not exclusively) referred to 'Europe' and the 'West'. From the perspective of non-European observers, 'Europe' appeared more homogenous and consistent than as experienced from within. However, this image considerably contributed both to Europe's external effects and its identity.[14] The 'non-Western' preoccupation with the 'West' took various forms. In India the Brahmin prohibition against crossing the 'black waters' (*kala pani*) remained valid until the nineteenth century, and Gandhi was accused of breaking the taboo when he went to study in England. By contrast, in Japan coming to terms with the West had started in the pre-modern period in the form of 'Dutch studies' (*rangaku*). In specific schools, for a long time seen as subversive, texts in Western military, medical, and agrarian sciences were studied.[15]

'European studies' in the non-Western world and non-Western perspectives on Europe must be located within an asymmetrical world order characterized by colonial structures and a capitalist world economy. Here it is important to note that non-Western ideas about Europe cannot be reduced to purely negative criticism. Japanese and Ottoman elites strongly criticized the modern city, capitalism, and the 'Western spirit.' However, these critical views did not represent the whole spectrum of non-Western ideas about Europe. Moreover, the anti-Western views cannot be exclusively traced back to the ideas of European romanticism. Neither should the agency of non-Western elites be reduced to the translation and cultural colouration of ideas that were 'born in Europe, before [they were] transferred to other parts of the world'.[16]

Non-European actors had various ways of selectively appropriating European 'achievements'. References to the 'West' were mainly restricted to educated groups and intellectual and political elites. Such elites pursued different goals, whether it be 'self-strengthening' (*yangwu* was the slogan in Qing China) in the face of colonial threat, or the effort to assert their own interests within their societies. The intensified preoccupation with the West was closely linked to the growth of exchanges transcending borders and the parallel formation of a global consciousness. Technological innovations, especially the 'information revolution' since the 1850s, were crucial here.[17] New public spheres emerged, especially in parts of Asia, Latin America, and the Ottoman Empire, which flourished in existing discussion fora.[18] The emergence of the press contributed to the spread of ideas and formed an important basis for coming to terms with the 'West'.[19]

Tapan Raychaudhuri has proposed a typology of the attitudes of intellectual elites in order to analyse the Indian 'xenology of Europe', which can roughly be applied elsewhere.[20] Raychaudhuri first identifies 'traditional elites', both Brahmin and Muslim, whose view of the world initially was hardly influenced by their encounter with the West. During the nineteenth century, this group declined relative to elites who were more influenced by the West. Most Indians who expressed their views in public, in principle came to agree with British politicians and Orientalists who regarded India as a backward society. Consequently many of them advocated firm reform politics: One interesting example was the group 'Young Bengal' led by the schoolteacher Henry Derozio, which called with great enthusiasm for the acceptance of Western customs, clothes, and eating habits, and made fun of the 'irrational character' of local customs. However, the modernizing impulse was usually linked to reservations about colonialism. Moreover, admiration for the West was seldom unqualified. Rammohan Roy (*c.*1770–1833), a pioneer of Indian modernity, argued for Indian wisdom and against increasingly hostile Evangelicals while also campaigning against Indian customs such as *sati* (suttee) and polygamy. He endorsed universalism and rationality and criticized irrational and non-universal aspects of Western culture.[21] Raychaudhuri stressed 'the well-known fact that the Indian national consciousness developed initially alongside a great enthusiasm for British rule in India. The colonial projection that the British conquest was the best thing that ever happened to India was widely accepted until the 1890s.'[22]

Members of the small group of mission-educated West Africans such as James Africanus Horton (1835–83) also called for British intervention. Horton, the son of a freed slave, had studied medicine in London and Edinburgh and returned to Sierra Leone as a military doctor and administrator. He considered himself a citizen and African, regarded Christianity as a civilizing force and European colonization as a means to found modern democracies and constitutional monarchies. For him, technology and schools were the most important instruments of progress. He saw

European colonization as a means to an end, a first step towards achieving independence as soon as possible. Horton repeatedly argued for the establishment of a University for West Africa that would demonstrate the intellectual equality of Africans to Europeans and help modernize Africa at technological, economic, and social levels. It was completely natural for Horton to take over ideas and institutions coming from Europe. At the same time he criticized those Europeans who promised 'civilization' but refused to provide Africans 'civilizing' institutions such as universities.[23]

Horton can be seen as a forerunner of Pan-Africanism. Edward Blyden (1832–1912) was an early key contributor to the ideologies of Pan-Africanism (and West African nationalism), articulating a notion of 'African personality' and the uniqueness of the 'African race'. Blyden constantly travelled back and forth across the Atlantic. From Sierra Leone, he travelled to England and encouraged both the Church Missionary Society and the British government to expand their activities into Sierra Leone's hinterland. He believed that the expansion of 'Christian civilization' throughout the region could create the basis for the emergence of a large and influential West African state. In *Christianity, Islam and the Negro Race*, published in 1887, Blyden expressed the conviction that underlies later explicit formulations of Pan-Africanism: 'Among the conclusions to which study and research are conducting philosophers, none is clearer than this—that each of the races of mankind has a specific character and specific work.' Blyden argued explicitly that what he called Africa's current 'state of barbarism' did not reflect any innate deficiency in the 'Negro': 'There is not a single mental or moral deficiency now existing among Africans . . . to which we cannot find a parallel in the past history of Europe'.[24] Blyden's ideas became particularly influential amongst Western-educated West Africans. The Nigerian intelligentsia, for instance, adopted these ideas to defend itself.[25] The vague, unformed sense of being 'Black Englishmen' was displaced by a sense of being black, part of the rising community of diasporan Africans. The members of the educated community could become a genuine elite not by serving as agents of the Western penetration into the African darkness but by combining Western knowledge with their putative racial characteristics, acting in concert with black elites of similar mind. For West Africans this identity could assume many forms—they could see themselves as Yoruba, West Africans, Africans, or 'Negroes'—but in what has been called the 'cosmopolitan black ethos' of the period, all these identities were subsumed under their 'common historical and racial identity with the Negroes of Black America'.[26] Whatever Yoruba or West African qualities they held, were claimed as virtues of the race affirmed against claims of European hegemony and superiority. Similarly, accomplishments by any black—West African or not—were taken as evidence of ability that pertained to all. The intelligentsia adopted this racial community as their own in diverse contexts, in the pursuit of what Blyden termed 'race organisation and race consolidation'.[27] Accepting the premise of innate racial distinctions but proclaiming that African differences were not inferiorities, Blyden as well as members of the West African coastal elites sought to establish African standards of civilization by which European contributions might be judged valuable or not. The vision was that Africa would create a unique civilization on its own terms, learning from the West but not betraying its racial existence. The 'inspiration of the race is in the race', Blyden argued. Each race had its own particular genius and future, and 'that only [sic] way must be found before there can be peace and harmony and progress'.[28]

In the course of the nineteenth century, there was a growing protest directed not against Western values and norms but rather specific Western practices such as British colonial rule in India. This critique was often based upon the assumptions of the European Enlightenment. It referred to the lack of political freedom and democracy, to Christian intolerance, aggressive nationalism, colonial rule, and, especially, the growing influence of racial discourses that put into question the emancipation promises of the Enlightenment. Ottoman and Japanese elites 'perceived the late nineteenth century European discourses on the yellow race, the Muslim world and Orientals, in connection with the predominant notions of Darwinism and other scientific paradigms, as a judgment that they could never perfectly fulfill all the required standards of civilization due to defects in the racial makeup, religious beliefs or cultural character'.[29] Many Western-educated elites in Japan and the Ottoman Empire became increasingly disillusioned and expressed a strong sense of being rejected by the European centres to which they looked for inspiration. However, Ottoman and Japanese writers often accepted at least partly Western ideas of 'race hierarchy', especially for the 'races' deemed below them. While European authors perceived emerging Islamic solidarity as xenophobic anti-Westernism, Muslim writers usually denied the existence of any reactionary alliance against the West or noted that it was the only way to overcome the unjust Eurocentric world order. More or less in parallel with this, East Asian intellectuals were increasingly emphasizing the conflict between 'the white and the yellow races'. A notion of a shared Asian-Eastern identity emerged. It was, however, not the legacy of common culture, history, or religion, but the geopolitics of Western imperialism that was shaping the imaginations of non-Western intellectuals to conceptualize an anti-Western alliance. In other words: anti-Western critiques emerged from an ongoing engagement of Asian thinkers with a global circulation of ideas and exemplified the global character of debates over modernity, culture, and nationalism. Asian critiques of the materialism of the modern West echoed ideas that were widespread at the time in the West itself, as were essentialist notions of a refined Asian 'spirituality' adopted by Asian thinkers in something like a 'reverse orientalism'.[30] In the field of international politics, Asian and Muslim critics of the West did not reject the universal standards of the Enlightenment; rather, they employed those standards to condemn the European powers of hypocrisy in violating, with their racist, exclusionary, and imperialist practices, the very ideals they claimed to uphold in their 'civilizing mission'.

Critique of the West on the basis of traditional values also gained importance. Preference for local customs and ways of living led to a rejection of Western consumerism, industrialization, and factory work, the mechanization of modern life, the apotheosis of the nation state and, above all, individualism that was interpreted as egoism. A specific dichotomy worked here: readiness to appropriate the practical abilities of Europeans went hand in hand with the conviction that Eastern civilizations, as represented for instance by Rabindranath Tagore, were 'spiritually' superior to the West.[31] In Japan, many authors evoked the complementary relationship between Western techniques and Japanese 'spirit' (*wakon yôsai*).[32] Especially since the last quarter of the nineteenth century, the rapid appropriation of science, empiricism, and technology was accompanied by references to 'traditional' values; these traditions, however, were often 'invented' or at least 'reconfigured'.[33]

Around 1900 these debates only engaged a small part of the population. Beyond urban centres, there was barely any idea about 'the West'; furthermore, debates in India or Japan were much more intense than in Africa. Moreover, 'the West' was not the only point of reference for the elites. In China, reformist circles regarded Japan as a model for aspirations to modernization. Japan began also to serve as a metaphor for Asian modernity for the Ottomans, Egyptians, and Indians. The Japanese victory over Russia in 1905 was a turning point in the history of anti-Western critiques. The contradictions of the legitimacy structures of the international order became more obvious. Anti-colonial nationalists and intellectuals in Asia, as well as in other parts of the world, used the Japanese victory to counter earlier discourses of white-race supremacy and the backwardness of the non-Western world. Nationalist movements all over Asia embraced the anti-Western internationalism of Pan-Asian and Pan-Islamic thought as a potential form of empowerment in their demands for autonomy and equality in the international order.

The Ambiguities of Non-Western Nationalism: Gandhi and Senghor

Nationalism in the non-Western world cannot be reduced either to anti-Western doctrines based on traditional values or the simple appropriation of Western models. There are numerous nuances of this position. Prasenjit Duara stresses the fact that nationalists in the colonies and semi-colonized regions like China usually posited an alleged ancient unity of the nation which granted them and the nation state the right to make a number of transformations. He does not deny indigenous foundations of nationalism, but argues that nationalists outside the West adapted the evolutionary assumptions of their colonial masters. Nationalist historians located their interpretations of the local pasts within an evolutionary paradigm framed around the argument that all developments inevitably led to modern capitalism and nationalism.[34] Christopher Bayly takes a different perspective. He identifies patriotism as the central concept of India's regional and pan-Indian nationalist movements that emerged at the end of the nineteenth century. According to Bayly's definition, patriotism entails attachment, ideologies, and theories of government that engaged the rulers and populations of the regional homeland before and during the early phase of colonial rule. He suggests that traditions of remembered patriotism during this period formed the basis of the ideas and institutions of later Indian nationalism.[35] The positions of Duara and Bayly represent interesting, but not incompatible, contrasts. While the first tends to the 'invention of tradition' approach, the latter focuses less on discourse than collective action responses to colonialism, seeing later nationalism as based on earlier patriotism.

Two individual cases can serve to further illustrate the ambiguities of non-Western nationalism. Mohandas Karamchand Gandhi (1869–1948) is one of the most written-about personalities in modern history; his advocacy of non-violent action and his pioneering techniques of non-violent resistance and mass civil disobedience resonate in many parts of the world. Gandhi's reputation as the 'father' or 'maker' of independence was generally accepted during the later stages of the Indian nationalist movement, and in India and elsewhere since independence. He was credited with providing India's nationalist movement with a mass base, which essentially consisted of peasants. More recent historiography, however, argues that not all of Gandhi's ideas and activities promoted national unity or advanced the cause of national independence. 'In a nationalist movement spread over many decades and involving a variety of different personalities and approaches, including constitutionalism, terrorism and mass protest, Gandhi and his political techniques can hardly be credited with having had more than a partial share in wresting India's independence from the British.'[36] Thus the related debate focuses on two different questions: how far did Gandhi inhibit the nationalist cause, and how far did other factors advance it?

What is relevant here is the extent to which Gandhi's nationalist views and practices can be labeled anti-Western and how much he referred to local political traditions. At first glance, much of his nationalism seemed to be shaped by a substantial critique of the West or at least Britain. In his book *Hind Swaraj* (the Freedom of India), published in 1909, Gandhi offered a negative assessment not only of British rule in India but more generally of modern industrial civilization and the Western concept of civil society.[37] 'India's salvation,' he wrote, 'consists in unlearning what she has learnt during the past fifty years or so. The railways, telegraphs, hospitals, lawyers, doctors and such like have all to go, and the so called upper class have to learn to live consciously and religiously and deliberately the simple life of a peasant.' Western representative institutions did not make much sense to him. He even compared Parliament with 'a sterile woman and a prostitute', because according to him this institution could never enact a law according to its own judgement and shifted its allegiance from one set of ministers to another, depending on which set happened to be more successful. Instead Gandhi's model for India was the Ram Rajya (the Kingdom of Rama) of the Hindu epic *Ramayana*. Ram Rajya was a patriarchy in which the ruler, the embodiment of moral virtue, always gave voice to the collective will. David Arnold aptly summarizes 'Hind Swaraj' as 'an odd (even eccentric) combination of Victorian anti-industrialism and Indian tradition (the latter in turn filtered through Western writers like Maine), which repeatedly castigates the dark side of modern civilization but sees none of its cultural or material benefits. Nor does it recognize the oppression and inequality, the violence and intolerance, the poverty, ignorance and disease, also to be found in pre-modern societies.'[38]

Gandhi's thinking has been described, among other things, as a 'reinvented discourse created out of modernity and influenced by the thinking of the colonial world'. There are many aspects in Gandhi's writings that refer to well-known Western classics of moral rearmament and social idealism. He created something like a counter-eugenicist language which inverted that of the pre-war nationalist leadership: we Indians are better fitted for the war of all nations against all, because our character and substance is not polluted with violence, lust, and love of pleasure. However, when he talked of communities as moralized networks of giving and receiving or the charisma of land, Gandhi also drew from a continuing indigenous tradition of political and moral philosophy that provided a hermeneutic link for the more abstract sense of nation.[39]

Léopold Sédar Senghor (1906–2001), who later became the first president of independent Senegal, was the main protagonist of the doctrine of Négritude. Négritude was a cultural project that emerged through intense discussions and intimate friendships among a diasporic peer group based in Paris whose members shared similar colonial backgrounds and metropolitan challenges, as well as an interest in Africa.[40] Senghor was a product of colonial assimilation. Before leaving home to join the transnational group of colonial students and activists living in continental France in the 1930s, he was trained in an overseas French school in Senegal to become a member of the native elite at home. Négritude in the 1930s was not a self-consciously organized movement. It consisted primarily of 'interminable discussions' among students who shared ideas, explored Paris, and began to write poetry. Senghor engaged contemporary currents of colonial thought, French culture, and black politics in order to fashion relationships to the colonial system in which he had been trained, to the French nation in which he now lived, and to the African societies to which he felt deeply connected. Over the course of his public life, Senghor would develop a complex conception of racial consciousness and cultural nationalism, but he would always argue that Négritude was a rejection of assimilation, the identification with blackness, and a celebration of African civilization that was conceptualized as a distinctive culture.

A good example of Senghor's ambivalent position is his attitude toward language. Senghor, who in his later life was the first African to be elected member of the prestigious Académie Française, often praised the French language for being, among other things, a highly poetic language. 'French prose,' he wrote, 'has taught us to rely on facts and ideas to clarify the universe in order to express the inner world through a coherent re-structuring of the universe.'[41] Yet he insisted that 'every African should be able to read and write in his own language' and that this 'is a sine qua non of the harmonious development of Black African society'.[42] While Senghor argued for cultural syncreticism, he also attempted to construct Négritude as something that separates the African spirit from the Western one: 'L'émotion est négre comme la raison est hellène.' Senghor's ideas about Africa were deeply shaped by European writings on Africa—namely the works of Leo Frobenius and Maurice Delafosse as well as the thoughts of the French colonial administrator Robert Delavignette. During the 1950s, as Senegalese representative in the French National Assembly, Senghor was one of the most effective African nationalists who harshly criticized French colonial politics and helped to get new labour laws for Africa through Parliament. The central vision behind the reflections and activities of Senghor was to unify and integrate peoples of African descent all over the world and to challenge Western superiority. He combined a critique of Western politics and culture with a modernization project that—although conceptualized as an alternative modernity—included many elements of Western ideas and concepts.

It would be wrong, however, to conceptualize the indigenous traditions evoked by Gandhi and Senghor simply as non-Western variants on a common Western trope of anti-modernism, or to limit the analysis to the 'deconstruction' of these men's explicit insistence that their ideas are indigenously rooted. Senghor, for instance, could be described as a cultural broker and a good example for Frederick Cooper's observation that 'in between is as much a place to be home as any other'.[43] His specific position enabled Senghor to play with different cultural registers and repertoires. From that resulted a specific understanding of authority, power, culture and, for that matter, nationalism, which was neither traditional nor modern, neither Western nor anti-Western, but rather a specific *bricolage*.

Accounts of Nationalism in the Non-Western World after World War II: The Example of Africa

As Christopher Bayly rightly emphasized, it was 'in all former European colonies [that] intellectual elites have sought in history a body of myths of origin to legitimate their independence. This has been the most powerful influence on the development of post-colonial historiography.'[44] Since the rise of non-European historiography after World War II, nationalism ranks high among the central concerns of historians of and in Africa, Asia, Latin America, and the Middle East. The interest in nationalism and related historiographical debates has undergone various conjunctures and differed from region to region. The idea of nationalism as an exclusively Western export and the opposite concept of an authentically African, Chinese, or Indian nationalism largely untouched by Western influence represent the extreme poles of a discussion that has been shaped by many paradigms. Most of the earlier accounts of nationalism in the non-Western world followed an approach that stressed the central role of Western-educated elites for which nationalism represented an important tool to mobilize resistance to colonial rule. In other words: the degree of Westernization determined the power of the nationalist project. In the context of African history James S. Coleman's *Nigeria: Background to Nationalism* (Berkeley 1958) provides a good example of this trend. To Coleman, 'modern' nationalism of the 1940s and 1950s, which he distinguished sharply from earlier revolts against colonialism (labelled 'traditional nationalism'), implied sentiments, activities, and organizations that explicitly aimed at taking over the government and at achieving independence in a nation state. According to Coleman, the main characteristics of nationalism were: a) the explicit goal of self-government; b) the concept of a national unity; c) the dominance of a Western-educated elite in political decision-making; d) the formation of permanent political associations and parties to pursue national ideas and aims; and e) the dominance of 'modern' (= Western) political values.

This approach was directed against widespread judgements that the principle of national self-determination was not applicable to the cultural realities of non-Western areas. Arnold Toynbee argued in 1953, building partly on one of his older arguments:

> During the last century and a half we have seen our Late Modern Western political institution of 'national states' burst the bounds of its birthplace in Western Europe and blaze a trail of persecution, eviction, and massacre as it had spread abroad into Eastern Europe, South-West Asia, and India—all of them regions where 'national states' were not part and parcel of an indigenous social system but were an exotic institution which was deliberately imported from the West, not because it had been found by experimentation to be suitable to the local conditions of these non-Western worlds, but simply because the West's political power had given the West's political institutions an irrational yet irresistible prestige in non-Western eyes.[45]

Against this view, African nationalists and nationalist historians could soon develop a general narrative of nationalist triumph.[46] One important form of this narrative focused on the issue of social mobilization and highlighted the ways in which the Western-educated elites were able to use the institutions and symbols of the colonial state for their own purpose, to mobilize the masses, and to instil a sense of national identity in the people of each African colony. The other crucial version of the nationalist narrative was the revolutionary one, represented most powerfully by Frantz Fanon, who denounced the anti-colonial nationalism of the Western-educated intellectuals or 'bourgeois nationalists' as 'false'. Fanon hoped for the revolutionary dynamic of peasants and the lumpenproletariat to overthrow the colonial regime with violence.[47]

Most members of the African elites espoused European ideas of progress and development. One important project of these elites was the creation of 'another' Africa, using science and technology. Oriented towards Western concepts of democracy, political organization, national self-determination, and economic growth, they set as their goals the ending of colonial rule and the creation of nation states. Aside from the dominant criticism of colonial politics, the political program of the nationalist elites fell back upon the heritage of African culture. Partly as a reaction to the European denial that there was any African history worth knowing, the Westernized elite has developed a high esteem of African culture and its past. In the view of the nationalist elite, the positive and usable elements of this culture and history were necessary to build up the new African nations.[48] However, the nationalist perspective implied crucial aspects of the colonial discourse, for instance the sharp divide between pre-colonial and colonial cultures or the representation of peasants as backward people. The past was identified with prominent leaders, usually the founders and heads of African states. The bottom line was struggle over the control of modern institutions such as churches, professions, and ultimately government posts, and finally the tracing of a genealogy of nationalism. Within the nationalist-modernization ethos, it was state-formation that received the greatest attention. The terms in which political events of the past were presented tended to be those that most closely resembled the political systems of the present. 'In short, an indigenous past, with its own social forms and mythological values often very different from those in Europe was now being remythologized to fit an alien model and one which was not even working very well in contemporary Africa.'[49] The unitary nation state became the favoured child of both modernizers and socialists. Frantz Fanon even called for the 'liquidation' of all tribalisms and regionalisms, because otherwise the unity of the people would remain a chimera. For African nationalists of the 1950s and 1960s, 'Europe' and the 'West' were important points of reference. However, both in Africa and in India, there were alternative ways of understanding nationalism, for example in terms of indigenous discourses and patterns of collective action.

Nationalism beyond Westernized Elites

In the case of South Asia, various scholars have argued that there was nothing like a local 'proto-nationalism', but that the Indian national leadership was totally appropriated by the discourse of power of the Western nation state.[50] Partha Chatterjee stresses that nationalism is a 'derivative discourse' in the colonial world, a discourse that originates in Europe.[51] He points to a basic contradiction, at the discursive level, within the nationalist discourse. On the one hand, he argues, this discourse was universal, because it posited the basic equality of all peoples in the world. On the other hand, at the level of its ethical and epistemological framework of knowledge, nationalist discourse was restricted to the patterns of Western thought, with its colonial constructions of Reason and Other, West and East. The contradiction between 'universal' and 'Eurocentric' became, according to Chatterjee, an important source of tension and dynamism in how nationalist discourses and movements were constructed in history. It led to important limits on what was even considered possible within nationalist politics. Chatterjee's main project seemed to be the demystification of famous nationalists such as Gandhi and Nehru. He tells the story of a kind of 'autonomous' or 'pure popular culture' that was betrayed by unscrupulous or tortured nationalist allies keen on building a new hegemony. Chatterjee later argued that 'religion' and the 'domestic sphere' served as pristine redoubts from which Indians could fight back against the colonial state and Westernization. Reacting largely to Benedict Anderson and a perception of the literature on nationalism as Eurocentric, Chatterjee attempts to demonstrate that nationalism in Bengal and India was not constructed according to a European model or even in direct reaction to a European model. He claims that cultural national identity in these places pre-dated any nationalist political action directed against the imperialist powers. Instead, cultural identity was divided into spiritual and material realms. According to Chatterjee, the material identity was largely determined in relationship with colonial powers and it has been mistaken by many as the dominant strain of national identity. Much more crucial, in his view, was the spiritual area that was comprised of cultural content and was completely separate from any discourse with the colonizers. This spiritual identity provided the building blocks for later nationalist movements. Thus for Chatterjee there seem to be two kinds of nationalism: derivative and authentic. But how to explain why the domestic sphere and religion were less affected by colonialism and Western thoughts and practices than other aspects of Indian life and society?

Some historians have focused on forms of radical nationalist ideology in India, which seemed more suited to the country's social complexity than the derivative discourse of Western nationalism. A number of nationalists, for instance, propagated an idea of nation that stressed the nurturing aspect of nation rather than its rational ordering aspect. In Bengal around 1900, nationalism—neither 'dominated' nor 'derivative'—was apparently legitimized in terms of female virtue and power: 'Nationalist thought, even at the moment of departure, may well have found idioms of articulation that overlapped with European forms and yet at the same time opposed both the problematic and the thematic of colonial knowledge.'[52] Swadeshi songs, which were performed by singers in small towns and the countryside during the political upsurge after the partition of Bengal in 1905, referred to the affective relations created by the surviving routines of exchange and interdependence in rural Bengal. The songs underlined the force of the idea that people should buy the produce of local looms and other artisan products. Thus one element of nationalist ideology and action at the turn of the twentieth century—the support of the local textile production against imports from Manchester—was firmly rooted in Bengali society. As Christopher Bayly suggests, it drew not on invented traditions but on old ones, and thus stood for the ability to adapt genuine traditions to modern circumstances.[53]

In Africa, much anti-colonial opposition was inspired, organized, and directed by peasants. There were broad-based radical movements, national in scope, anti-colonial in focus, in which peasants played an essential, if not a determinant, role. Such movements, of course, contained ambiguities and contradictions, and were often themselves terrains of struggle.[54] In Tanzania, in the period of transition to independence, 'peasant intellectuals' who had articulated rural discourses on healing the land, anti-slavery, and democracy, became active and dynamic partners in the formation of a nationalist coalition. Some of the rural discourses, such as healing the land, were old but constantly reorganized at moments of political transition. Other discourses, for instance on anti-slavery and democracy, were products of the colonial period. Taken together, reorganized and modified by peasant intellectuals, these discourses became regional emancipatory ones and formed a dynamic core element of the Tanzanian nationalist movement. However, peasant leaders did not possess the bureaucratic skills to position themselves strategically during the final scramble for state power. Thus it was the small educated elite working for the colonial administration, not the peasants, who came to power when independence was achieved in 1961.[55]

Julius Nyerere, the first president of Tanzania and a former teacher, represented this tiny group of African bureaucrats taking over state power from their colonial predecessors. In the 1960s and 1970s, Nyerere acquired an international reputation for propagating an African socialism opposing Western values:

> It is opposed to capitalism, which seeks to build a happy society on the basis of the exploitation of man by man; and it is equally opposed to doctrinaire socialism which seeks to build its happy society on a philosophy of inevitable conflict between man and man. We, in Africa, have no more need of being 'converted' to socialism than we have of being 'taught' democracy. Both are rooted in our own past.... Modern African socialism can draw from its traditional heritage the recognition of 'society' as extension of the basic family unit. But it can no longer confine the idea of the social family within the limits of the tribe, nor, indeed, of the nation.... Our recognition of the family to which we all belong must be extended yet further—beyond the tribe, the community, the nation, or even the continent—to embrace the whole of mankind.[56]

However, as so often with non-Western nationalist concepts, Nyerere's African socialism, too, was only at first glance an anti-Western doctrine, but also contained many elements of concepts deriving from the West.

Conclusion

This chapter has highlighted some aspects of the complex history of anti-Western doctrines of nationalism since the nineteenth century. It argued that anti-Western ideas in regions outside Europe and the United States have a long history that is often linked to issues of nationalism. However, what was meant by the 'West', and criticized about it, varied a lot. Moreover, for a long time debates about the 'West' only concerned small groups of non-Western intellectual elites. Gandhi and Senghor represent two examples for the main argument of this chapter, that nationalism in the non-Western world cannot be reduced either to anti-Western doctrines based on 'traditional' values or the simple appropriation of Western models. Both men combined in their ideas about nationalism a critique of the West based on references to the value of indigenous traditions with many Western concepts. Thus their specific understanding of nationalism was neither traditional nor modern, neither Western nor anti-Western, but a kind of bricolage and an ongoing effort to negotiate what is 'traditional' and what is 'modern', what is 'indigenous' and what is 'foreign', and what is 'right' and what is 'wrong'. However, an account on non-Western doctrines of nationalism should extend beyond elites. Peasants in Asia and Africa have also shaped the ways in which nationalism was conceptualized and organized. The current wave of an apparently anti-Western nationalism voiced by intellectuals and political leaders in many non-European regions exhibits once more the ambiguities of non-Western nationalism.

Notes

1. A widely discussed but largely unsuccessful attempt to understand the rise of anti-Westernism is I. Buruma and A. Margalit (2004) *Occidentalism: A Short History of Anti-Westernism*, New York. On this book, see also below.
2. A number of authors find arguments about the radical decline of the nation state exaggerated: see A. Ong (1999) *Flexible Citizenship: The Cultural Logics of Transnationality*, Durham and London; F. Cooper (2001) 'What Is the Concept of Globalization Good For? An African Historian's Perspective', in *African Affairs*, 100, no. 399, 189–213.
3. A. G. Hopkins (1999) 'Back to the Future: From National History to Imperial History', in *Past and Present*, no. 164, 201–2.
4. P. Chatterjee (1993) *The Nation and its Fragments: Colonial and Postcolonial Histories*, Princeton, NJ, 4.
5. Both quotes, Chatterjee, *The Nation and its Fragments*, 4.
6. See S. Conrad and D. Sachsenmeier (eds.) (2007) 'Introduction', *Competing Visions of World Order: Global Moments and Movements, 1880s–1930s*, New York, 6.
7. See A. Dirlik (2006) 'Globalization Now and Then: Some Thoughts on Contemporary Readings of Late 19th/Early 20th Century Responses to Modernity', *Journal of Modern European History*, 4, no. 2, 141.
8. Two recent global histories of the long nineteenth century see nationalism as one of its most important features, especially during the later part of this era. See C. A. Bayly (2004) *The Birth of the Modern World 1780–1914: Global Connections and Comparisons*, Oxford, esp. ch. 6; J. Osterhammel (2009) *Die Verwandlung der Welt: Eine Geschichte des 19. Jahrhunderts*, Munich, esp. ch. 8.
9. Dirlik, 'Globalization Now and Then', 141. One impressive example of this historiography is S. Conrad (2010) *Globalization and the Nation in Imperial Germany*, Cambridge.
10. A. McKeown (2004) 'Global Migration, 1846–1940', *Journal of World History*, 15, no. 2, 155–90.
11. The following paragraph relies on S. Conrad and K. Mühlhahn, 'Global Mobility and Nationalism: Chinese Migration and the Reterritorialization of Belonging, 1880–1910', in Conrad and Sachsenmeier, *Competing Visions*, 181–211 (quote: 204).
12. D. Rothermund (2006) *The Routledge Companion to Decolonization*, London and New York.
13. F. Cooper (1996) *Decolonization and African Society: The Labor Question in French and British Africa*, Cambridge, 7.
14. S. Conrad (2006) '"Europa' aus der Sicht nicht-westlicher Eliten, 1900–1930', in *Journal of Modern European History*, 4, no. 2, 159.
15. See G. K. Goodman (2000) *Japan and the Dutch, 1600–1853*, Richmond, VA.
16. These are the arguments of Buruma and Margalit, *Occidentalism* (quote: 6).

17. See D. Headrick (1998) *The Tentacles of Progress: Technology Transfer in the Age of Imperialism, 1840–1914*, New York, and (1991) *The Invisible Weapon: Telecommunications and International Politics, 1851–1914*, Oxford.
18. See, for South Asia, the groundbreaking study by C. Bayly (1996) *Empire and Information: Intelligence Gathering and Social Communication in India, 1780–1870*, Cambridge.
19. For the case of China, see B. Mittler (2004) *A Newspaper for China? Power, Identity, and Change in Shanghai's New Media, 1871–1912*, Cambridge, MA; R. G. Wagner (ed.) (2007) *Joining the Global Public: World, Image, and City in Early Chinese Newspapers, 1870–1910*, Albany, NY.
20. T. Raychaudhuri (1999) *Perception, Emotions, Sensibilities: Essays on India's Colonial and Post-colonial Experiences*, New Delhi. See also Conrad, 'Europa', 163–5.
21. See P. Robb (2002) *A History of India*, Basingstoke, 223.
22. Raychaudhuri, *Perception*, 19.
23. See C. Fyfe (1972) *Africanus Horton 1835–1883: West African Scientist and Patriot*, New York. Horton's most important publications were 'Political Economy of British West Africa' (London, 1865) and 'West Africa Countries and Peoples' (London, 1868).
24. E. W. Blyden (1887, repr. 1967) *Christianity, Islam and the Negro Race*, Edinburgh, 140.
25. The following paragraph is based on P. S. Zachernuk (2000) *Colonial Subjects: An African Intelligentsia and Atlantic Ideas*, Charlottesville, VA. For the general context, see R. Rathbone, 'West Africa: Modernity and Modernization', in J.-G. Deutsch et al. (eds.) (2002) *African Modernities: Entangled Meanings in Current Debates*, Oxford, 18–30.
26. M. J. Echeruo (1978) *Victorian Lagos: Aspects of Nineteenth-Century Lagos Life*, London, 109.
27. Blyden, *Christianity*, 140. Zachernuk, *Colonial Subjects*, 67ff, and (2001) 'Critical Agents: Colonial Nigerian Intellectuals and their British Counterparts', in C. Youé and T. Stapleton (eds.) *Agency and Action in Colonial Africa*, New York, 156–71.
28. First quote from E. W. Blyden (1890) *The African Problem and the Method of its Solution*, second quote from Blyden (1908) *African Life and Customs*, both quoted by Zachernuk, *Colonial Subjects*, 70ff.
29. C. Aydin (2006) 'Beyond Civilization: Pan-Islamism, Pan-Asianism and the Revolt against the West', *Journal of Modern European History* 4, no. 2, 207. For the following paragraphs, see Aydin, 'Beyond Civilization'; (2007) *The Politics of Anti-Westernism in Asia: Visions of World Order in Pan-Islamic and Pan-Asian Thought*, New York, chs. 2 and 3; as well as Chapter 34 in this volume.
30. Aydin, 'Politics of Anti-Westernism', 89, 203.
31. See U. das Gupta (2004) *Rabindranath Tagore: A Biography*, Oxford.
32. See Conrad, 'Europa', 164.
33. Since E. Hobsbawm and T. Ranger (eds.) (1983) *The Invention of Tradition*, Cambridge, it became—at least in the context of African history—nearly common sense that most traditions in Africa were 'invented' or 'imagined'.
34. P. Duara (ed.) (2004) *Decolonization: Perspectives from Now and Then*, London; and (1997) *Rescuing History from the Nation: Questioning Narratives of Modern China*, Chicago.
35. C. A. Bayly (1998) *Origins of Nationality in South Asia: Patriotism and Ethical Government in the Making of Modern India*, New Delhi.
36. D. Arnold (2001) *Gandhi*, Harlow, 8.

37. For this and the following paragraphs (incl. the quotes from Gandhi), see S. Bose and A. Jalal (1998) *Modern South Asia: History, Culture, Political Economy*, London and New York, ch. 13; Arnold, *Gandhi*, 64ff.
38. Arnold, *Gandhi*, 70.
39. Bayly, *Origins of Nationality*, 120ff (quote: 121).
40. There is a vast literature on Négritude. One of the more recent publication is G. Wilder (2005) *The French Imperial Nation-State: Négritude and Colonial Humanism between the Two World Wars*, Chicago and London. For the following paragraph, see esp. 151–7. An excellent biography of Senghor is J. G. Vaillant (1990) *Black, French, and African: A Life of Léopold Sédar Senghor*, Cambridge, MA.
41. Léopold Sédar Senghor (1979) 'French—Language of Culture', in J. A. Langley (ed.) *Ideologies of Liberation in Black Africa 1856–1970: Documents on Modern African Political Thought from Colonial Times to the Present*, London, 381–2.
42. Léopold Sédar Senghor, 'The Problems of African Language', in Langley (ed.) *Ideologies of Liberation*, 374–6.
43. F. Cooper (1994) 'Conflict and Connection" Rethinking African Colonial History', *American Historical Review*, 99, 1539.
44. C. Bayly, 'Modern Indian Historiography', in M. Bentley (ed.) (1997) *Companion to Historiography*, London and New York, 677.
45. A. Toynbee (1953) *The World and the West*, New York and Oxford, 70–1.
46. For the following paragraph, see Cooper, *Decolonization*, 6–7.
47. F. Fanon [1961] (1966) *The Wretched of the Earth*, New York.
48. See for instance A. A. Mazrui and M. Tidy (1984) *Nationalism and New States in Africa*, Nairobi.
49. R. A. Austen (1993) "'Africanist' Historiography and its Critics: Can There Be an Autonomous African History?', in T. Falola (ed.) *African Historiography: Essays in Honour of Jacob Ade Ajayi*, Harlow, 207.
50. See P. Chatterjee (1986) *Nationalist Thought and the Colonial World: A Derivative Discourse?*, London; A. Nandy (1984) *The Illegitimacy of Nationalism*, Delhi.
51. For the following, see F. E. Mallon (1993) 'Dialogues Among the Fragments: Retrospect and Prospect', in F. Cooper et al. (eds.) *Confronting Historical Paradigms: Peasants, Labor, and the Capitalist World System in Africa and Latin America*, Madison, WI, 390ff.
52. See S. Bose (1997) 'Nation as Mother: Representations and Contestations of "India" in Bengali Literature and Culture', in S. Bose and A. Jahal (eds.) *Nationalism, Democracy, and Development: State and Politics in India*, Delhi, 50–76 (quote: 60); Bayly, *Origins of Nationality*, 117f.
53. Bayly, *Origins of Nationality*, 118.
54. See A. Isaacman (1990) 'Peasants and Rural Social Protest in Africa', *African Studies Review*, 33, 1–120.
55. S. Feierman (1990) *Peasant Intellectuals: Anthropology and History in Tanzania*, Madison, WI; Feierman's main argument is aptly summarized by Mallon, 'Dialogues', 391. My account follows her summary.
56. J. Nyerere (ed.) (1966) 'Ujamaa: The Basis of African Nationalism', *Freedom and Unity/ Uhuru na Umoja: A Selection from Writings and Speeches 1952–65*, Dar es Salaam.

Suggested Further Reading

Aydin, C. (2007) *The Politics of Anti-Westernism in Asia: Visions of World Order in Pan-Islamic and Pan-Asian Thought*, New York.

Bayly, C. A. (1998) *Origins of Nationality in South Asia: Patriotism and Ethical Government in the Making of Modern India*, New Delhi.

Chatterjee, P. (1993) *The Nation and its Fragments: Colonial and Postcolonial Histories*, Princeton, NJ.

Conrad, S. and Sachsenmeier, D. (eds.) (2007) *Competing Visions of World Order: Global Moments and Movements, 1880s–1930s*, New York.

Dirlik, A. (2007) *Global Modernity: Modernity in the Age of Global Capitalism*, Boulder, CO.

Duara, P. (1997) *Rescuing History from the Nation: Questioning Narratives of Modern China*, Chicago, IL.

Feierman, S. (1990) *Peasant Intellectuals: Anthropology and History in Tanzania*, Madison, WI.

Guichard, S. (2010) *The Construction of History and Nationalism in India: Textbooks, Controversies and Politics*, London and New York.

Pecora, V. P. (ed.) (2001) *Nations and Identities*, Oxford.

Zachernuk, P. S. (2000) *Colonial Subjects: An African Intelligentsia and Atlantic Ideas*, Charlottesville, VA.

CHAPTER 5

CULTURAL NATIONALISM

JOHN HUTCHINSON

Introduction

Much scholarship focuses on what I call 'political nationalism', namely those projects aimed at the establishment of an independent nation state. In this chapter I argue that we also need to give attention to cultural nationalist movements whose primary aim is the formation of national *communities*. Originating amongst historicist intellectuals,[1] these movements typically precede or accompany political nationalism and take the form of ethno-historical 'revivals' that promote a national language, literature and the arts, educational activities and economic self-help. Cultural nationalism has often been dismissed as a surrogate politics, as socially reactionary and as a transient phenomenon that fades after independence. This, however, misrepresents the goals and significance of such movements. They do have political effects, but their aim is not so much political as the formation of a moral community. They use the idiom of regeneration, but to promote social and political innovation. Although they give way to state-oriented movements, they recur periodically even after independence has been achieved, seeking to redefine the identity of political communities.

The Idea-World and Practices of Cultural Nationalism

How do we define 'cultural nationalism'? It is often hard in practice to separate cultural and political nationalisms. Cultural nationalists often engage in political, even insurrectionary activities, and nationalists whose goal is for political independence may justify their claims by arguments that their nation has an ancient and distinctive culture that is threatened by foreign rule. Many cultural nationalists view the possession of independent statehood as essential for the defence of the identity of the nation, for example, by establishing an educational system that will school citizens in their language and history. Nonetheless, I argue that cultural and political nationalisms derive from different sources, with the former concerned with the meaning and the identity of the nation as a distinctive moral community.

I have previously distinguished between a cultural nationalism imbued with an '*organic*' romantic conception of the nation as a historical community and a political nationalism, arising from an enlightenment '*voluntarist*' vision of the nation as a political autonomous community of will built on the rational decision making of equal citizens and expressed through the mechanism of the territorial state.[2] But this is too simple. Both nationalisms encouraged the rise of a civil society, of an educated citizenry engaged in a diversified 'public' sphere in which all could participate no matter what their social, economic, religious status. All nationalists appeal to the nation as historically determined and as moulded by human will.[3] Cultural nationalist intellectuals in some contexts view themselves as giving authentic voice to a collective historical consciousness, but in others as *magi* constructing a new nation. The demarcation between cultural and political nationalism is whether the primary concern is with the establishment of a strong community or a strong territorial state, as the basis of the nation. Many cultural nationalist revivals emerge out of or are in close alliance with movements of religious reform, attempting to reconcile traditional belief systems with ideas of progress. This is not to say, as we shall see, that identity-building activities are necessarily separate from political ones.

Should we differentiate 'cultural nationalism' from projects of ethnic revival that long pre-date the modern period? We can find many ethnocultural revivals throughout history.[4] In Renaissance and early modern Europe, humanist scholars, under the influence of the Roman historian Tacitus, claimed 'national' descent of their populations from the vigorous barbarian peoples (the Gauls, Goths, the Belgae, and Germanic tribes) who had fought the Romans, ideas that informed nascent republican currents. Such descent myths combined with religious conceptions of being a Chosen People during the wars of religion of the seventeenth century: in the Dutch revolt against Habsburg Spain, Netherlanders invoked as ancestors the ancient Batavians, and by the seventeenth century anthropological taxonomies of 'national characteristics' were widespread in much of Europe.[5]

Nonetheless, by the late eighteenth century such identity-construction was given a quite novel *political* dynamism by the coming together of neo-classical and pre-romantic European intellectual currents. Out of this emerged a polycentric *Weltanschauung* that presented a pantheistic conception of the universe, in which all natural entities were animated by a force that individualized them and endowed them with a drive for realization. The nation was one such life-force, a primordial, cultural, and territorial people through which individuals developed their authenticity as moral and rational beings. One of its influential advocates was the German philosopher Johann Gottfried von Herder, who portrayed humanity as essentially diverse, and world progress as a result of the mutual interactions of nations, each of which had its own unique contribution to make.[6]

This vision had revolutionary implications and the ideological movements it inspired diverged from their precursors by seeking through the idiom of 'revival' and 'regeneration' an unprecedented demotic transformation of social and political life. In the decades after 1780 cultural societies sprang up across Europe: the Russian Academy (1783), the Royal Irish Academy (1785), the Royal Bohemian Society of Sciences (1794), the Welsh *Eisteddfod* (1789), the Magyar National Museum (1807), the Finnish Literary Society (1831). From such beginnings historical scholars, philologists, and artists during the nineteenth century established a network of learned academies, literary and language societies, theatres and publishing houses, and choral and athletic clubs to 'revive' their respective nations. Similar phenomena began to appear outside Europe, in India by the mid-1870s, China by the 1890s, the Arab Middle East in the 1920s. One scholar has described the stages of these revivals as first identifying the nation, elaborating it in space and time, forming permanent representative organizations (cultural and political), and mustering the people.[7]

In the following sections I will elaborate on revivalist ideas and practices, transnational and national. They prescribed a duty to recover and sustain all 'national' cultures, for the loss of one was a loss to humanity. History became the teacher of humanity and a resource for social innovation. These intellectuals intensified and extended identification with territorial homelands that were perceived as a reservoir of sacred energies. They vernacularized cultures in order to creating a common set of values that would unite a socially differentiating collectivity. They politicized the national community, arguing it was imbued with an innate activism. The goals and practices of such revivalism included the 'salvage' of cultural remains, the employment of such remains to construct a regenerative vision and programme, and formation of national communities by uniting all members in historically authentic sentiments and practices.

Regenerating a National Humanity

Early revivalism was as much transnational as national and spread worldwide from its original centres in the metropolitan cities of Europe such as London, Paris, Berlin, Amsterdam, and Copenhagen. A vision of a human family tree based on ethno-cultural principles spurred an international network of thinkers and scholars to rediscover and record the most distant origins of peoples of the world and their interrelationships, as a way of making sense of the present, thereby stimulating the rise of archaeology, philology, folklore, and comparative religion. One important outcome was the 'discovery' in the 1780s by British Orientalist scholars in Calcutta, led by Sir William Jones and Henry Colebrooke, of a Hindu Aryan Sanskrit civilization in North India developing from the second millennium BC, which they proclaimed as the 'original' civilization of humanity.[8] Jones's conjecture that Sanskrit was the mother language of Europe was given 'scientific' status in Franz Bopp's Indo-European language classification in 1816. These ideas, when reaching a receptive constituency, had far-reaching consequences.

Firstly, they undermined hierarchies of authority within Europe and between Europe and the rest of the world. Within Europe prestige had been based previously on the relationships of rulers and peoples to biblical figures or Greco-Roman antiquity. Jones's discovery was interpreted by the Schlegel brothers as declaring the Asian origins of the European peoples who had migrated in successive waves, the Greeks, Romans, Celts, Germans, and Slavs.[9] German romantics, in claiming their direct descent from 'pagan' Aryans, sought to wrest the cultural leadership of contemporary Europe from France, which under Napoleon legitimized itself as the new Roman imperium. The 'rediscovery' of non-European civilizations undermined imperialist claims that portrayed subject peoples as backward barbarians and legitimized anti-colonialist nationalists who asserted rights to freedom as heirs of the founding civilizations of humanity. Egyptian nationalists were inspired by a pride in their ancient Pharaonic heritage after the discovery of Tutankhamen's tomb in 1922 by British and French archaeologists.

A second effect was the transfer of modern academic resources from the advanced cultures of Europe to the peripheries, 'training' intellectuals in the 'hinterland' to reconstruct their own histories and cultures. Developing an ethnic model of the nation against the 'civic' or political model of France, German intellectuals made their country the heartland of romantic nationalism, and its thinkers and universities provided inspirations for the intellectuals of the stateless peoples of Europe, from Finland to Slovak territories, and beyond. Most early Russian nationalists were educated in German territories. French and German scholars concerned with discovering their Celtic past were active in resurrecting the scientific study of Gaelic culture in Ireland as the last bastion of the Celts.

Sentiments of ethnic or cultural affiliation led romantic intellectuals to participate in the cultural and political struggles of 'reviving' nationalities. A sense of indebtedness to their Greek heritage inspired cooperation among European intellectuals, who rallied public opinion in support of the Greek struggle for independence against the Ottoman Empire, depicting this as the struggle of European liberty against Oriental despotism. After establishing Young Italy in 1831, the nationalist patriot Giuseppe Mazzini developed international organizations that promoted the regeneration and freedom of all the major nationalities of Europe.

Finally, the depiction of world civilization as the product of national cultures, each of which played a special role, justified a mutual borrowing of cultures. Nationalists might claim that although currently backward, their nation had once been a teacher of the nations, so that borrowing from the advanced was no more than reclaiming their patrimony. Such a perspective encouraged nationalist groups within independent non-European states such as Japan, the Ottoman Empire, and China to look worldwide for models by which to reconstruct their societies to stave off the European imperial challenges.

History and National Mission

Ethnocultural revivalism offered a new vision of history whereby power was transferred from God (or his representatives) to originating peoples and their myths. History replaced religion as the guide to collective identity and destiny. Historical scholars, Jules Michelet for France, Frantisek Palacky for Czechs, Mikhail Hrushevsky for Ukrainians, Nicolae Iorga for Romanians, became avatars of the nation. It became an imperative to discover the nation's history in all its manifestations, resulting in locating earlier, multiple pasts with alternative repertoire and role models, and, above all, in identifying a golden age that inspired emulation.

Because documented history was largely the story of elites, romanticism stimulated an explosion of genetic sciences, including philology, archaeology, folklore, and topography to excavate the life of the people. Historians through publications, academies, and museums sought to recover all aspects of the national heritage, to present it as a distinctive ancient civilization, and to defend its achievements against foreign detractors. History was expanded, deepened, and systematized as historians sought to identify an underlining meaning in the past, in spite of apparent discontinuities, that would offer direction to the present and establish a repertoire of options and role models.

There was a concern with origins, with a golden age and a period of decline from which nationalists could gain clues about national regeneration. In search of collective authenticity, romantics focused on the earliest emergence of peoples when their primordial character is most clearly displayed. The Norwegian poet Henrik Wergeland in 1834 declared in a famous speech 'In Praise of the Ancestors' that the Snorri's Norse sagas translated in the late eighteenth century were 'the Norwegian patent of nobility among the nations'.[10] The golden age was one where the creative genius of the nation flowered, harmonizing all dimensions of human experience (religious, scientific, artistic, military, and economic), when the nation was in active contact with the other great centres, and making a permanent contribution to human civilization. Late nineteenth-century Indian nationalists evoked a democratic Aryan civilization that had allegedly instructed two of the great world centres of learning (Greece and Persia) and that had denied there were inherent barriers between the sexes, castes, or between religious and secular learning.[11]

Historical 'memory' was used to stimulate revival through invidious comparisons with the decadent present. The golden age provided an inspiration for a rising generation who, returning to its energies, would throw off the paralysis of tradition, recreate it as a politically autonomous and self-reliant society, and make it a model to the world. Periods of decline from this high point even through disaster had their lessons. Serbs commemorated their defeat on the plains of Kosovo in 1389 and subsequent servitude at the hands of the Ottoman Turks, just as Greeks portrayed the fall of Constantinople in 1453 as a catastrophe brought about by a combination of external betrayal and inner weakness.

Historians were map-makers of collective identity, but (for cultural nationalists) the past had also to become a living experience. Commemorative festivals and pageants, often organized around historical monuments, were central to most nationalist movements and were used to evoke a call to action. By rooting themselves in an ancient and self-renewing collectivity that had survived countless disasters, a new educated middle class found confidence they could master a world undergoing revolutionary change and were inspired to heroic sacrifice. They acquired stature in the modern world by membership of a nation whose heroic age had contributed to the civilization of humanity. They found their own special mission as a generation who would restore the links in the chain to this great past, thus renewing the historical destiny of their nation.

Creating Homelands

Although ethnic groups throughout history have viewed themselves as linked 'ancestrally' to the land, romanticism intensified, extended, diffused, and embedded this sense of belonging, imbuing the defence and the regaining of the national territory as a sacred duty. It attracted a sense of devotion in the deracinated young in the cities and towns who viewed the countryside as a spiritual resource rather than as a livelihood.

In pantheist fashion revivalists viewed the territorial homeland as a repository of a moral vision and primordial energies, and each nation's homelands had unique characteristics that gave the community its individuality. Scandinavians and Canadians celebrated the darkness and austerity of their Arctic wastes as imbuing their peoples with an inner mysticism; and the Swiss the ruggedness of the Alps, the protectors of their republican freedoms.[12]

Intellectuals from the cities undertook cultural journeys as part of the 'recovery' of their collective self to record the distinctive qualities of their habitat and its peoples. This extended spatially the sense of homeland, filled out a sense of the life and activities of the communities who worked the land, and historically deepened the sense of attachment by exploring the layers of the past that were embedded in the land. In nineteenth-century Denmark archaeological discoveries of the lur and golden horn (musical instruments), the sun wagon, and the 'barrow' burial mounds became important symbols of a primordial folk culture.[13]

This resulted in the unexpected 'discovery' of remote areas, sometimes marked by natural beauty, sometimes of great cultural significance, which because of their 'wildness' and 'hidden' quality became mysterious and sacred reservoirs of the national spirit. The poet William Wordsworth and painter J. M. W. Turner constructed the Lake District as a site of unique moral vision, just as the painter, musician, and antiquary George Petrie and the poet W. B. Yeats promoted the west of Ireland, and the composers Bedrich Smetana and Antonin Dvorak the Bohemian woods.

Topographical artists publicizing scenic beauties of their nation contributed to a burgeoning nationalist tourist industry amongst an emerging middle class.

Such regions became fortresses of the nation to which groups, especially alienated urban educated middle classes, could turn to escape assimilation to foreign values and experience moral regeneration, thereby embedding themselves in the land. They provided pilgrimage sites through which young nationalists from different regions found a common national identity, celebrating seasonal festivals, founding educational colleges, and sometimes even forming settlements as in the Zionist kibbutz in Palestine. The defence of these regions from foreign cultural or political threat galvanized powerful nationalist movements. The cult of the land had an integrating effect, binding a new mobile middle class of the cities to larger territorial unit, by rooting them in a defence of a highly individualized homeland.

Vernacularizing Culture

Although popular cultures pre-dated the era of nationalism, the romantics pioneered a general vernacularization of high culture, seeking to construct a collective ethos by which new educated elites sought to integrate a society differentiated through the division of labour.

Herder's plea to the European peoples to preserve their national vernaculars as the lifeline of their heritage had a major impact, particularly on the Slavs. In eastern Europe there was an explosion of philological research and the publication of dictionaries and grammars, as nationalists sought to identify the authentic language of the people, purified of foreign borrowings, and to make it the public medium of modern science and culture. The transformation of 'dialects' into a common literary standard was employed to unify dispersed populations into communities and differentiate them from neighbouring 'others'. Such linguistic nationalism had different roots. Liberal clergy, seeking to communicate a vision of their religion as compatible with the spirit of improvement, produced written forms of the dialects of the people. The major triggers, however, were the attempts of (often imperial) centralizing states to impose on ethnic minorities an alien official language in the religious, educational, and administrative institutions of their territories, for purposes of administrative efficiency or cultural homogenization.[14]

For cultural nationalists, nevertheless, language 'revival' itself was but a means. The goal was resurrection of the *Volksgeist* that expressed the unique creative energies of the nation, the memory of which sophisticated society had lost. This was to be found in the wild imaginative life of rural folk living close to nature. There were many sources of the national charisma: fairy tales; songs, melodies, and proverbs, but James Macpherson's 'discovery' of the Ossianic Lays (1762) triggered a competitive enthusiasm throughout Europe to rediscover early epic literature, whose myths and legends were portrayed as the earliest and purest expression of the anonymous genius of the people.[15] The Irish responded by rediscovering their ancient Celtic Red Branch and Finn Cycles; Norwegians the Edda (translated 1766–8); and Germans rekindled in 1813 their interest in the thirteenth-century *Nibelungenlied.*

Artists perceived themselves as having a special mission to restore the ancient unity of being lost to the modern world by the division of labour, returning individuals to their national archetype and thereby recreate a unified way of life. The poets Jan Kollar for Slovaks, Adam Mickiewicz for Poles, W. B. Yeats for the Irish, Haim Bialik for Zionists, and the composer Richard Wagner for Germans, all had iconic status within their national movements.

Once again nationalist writers were concerned not just to recover and classify cultural remains but to fashion new genres and institutions that expressed the national ethos in ways appropriate to their changing society, one that was increasingly literate but also increasingly diverse. They created several genres including the lyric poem and ballad, often modelled on traditional oral literature, but notable was the 'epic' historical novel, in the hands of writers like Walter Scott and Leo Tolstoi, which set heroic individuals against the backdrop of key historical moments (foreign invasion or civil war) in exploring the struggle of national progress against tradition.

Another influential genre was the drama, because of its capacity to activate a collective experience. Here William Shakespeare was a model—criticized in the eighteenth century for his 'barbaric' breaches of the classical rules, but now likened by intellectuals in revolt against French classicism to Homer and Ossian in his artlessness, protean energy, sense of mystery, and social range.[16] German thinkers were impressed by the Elizabethan drama's nation-building effects, especially the history plays: the poet and playwright Friedrich Schiller argued that a German national theatre would provide a means of promoting a national myth to the people, and his play, *Wilhelm Tell* (1804), based on Swiss legends, became a coded plea for German freedom. Wagner established his Bayreuth Theatre in the belief that his legendary operatic cycle based on the *Nibelungenlied* would dissolve everyday reality and reveal to Germans their heroic collective essence. Yeats, influenced by Wagner, claimed that a theatre, by bringing individuals into a collectivity and immersing them in the national legends, could perform for a literate age the equivalent of the ancient epics, whose communal recitations had bound older oral societies. He founded the Abbey Theatre to present the heroes and gods of the Irish epic cycles, above all the warrior-seer Cuchulain.[17]

Such artists hoped to create a single collective national personality. Their project, however, was more than about language or the arts. They were often encyclopaedic intellectuals, recorders of folk culture, dabblers in mystical cults, founders of cultural institutions (theatres, opera houses, schools of art), and active supporters of the reformation of everyday life. They established societies to promote native dress, national sporting associations, gymnastic and arts and crafts societies. All aspects of the human personality were to be explored and brought into balance with each other.

They hoped to form a new educated elite to express a distinctive vision based on popular traditions that that would guide a society undergoing rapid differentiation under the impact of technological change. Indeed, vernacular revolution pervaded all aspects of social life: 'authentic' designs informed new city centres, parliaments, railway stations, housing estates, and, in the private sphere, the domestic furniture of burgeoning bourgeois life that incorporated 'national' designs.

The Politics of Community

Revivalist intellectuals had a politics, but one distinct from political nationalists for whom state independence and/or citizenship within a national state were central to their ambitions. For cultural nationalists, political institutions were only a means to preserve the national community and should arise from it. They viewed the centralizing state as a bureaucratic threat to life forces of the nation, conceived as a 'spontaneous' order. Their politics, we shall see, was incoherent and oscillated between a populist communitarianism and a revolutionary elitism.

In the first place, theirs was a moral enterprise to regenerate the nation from within and from below, by appealing to the memory and practices of a golden age and encouraging an upsurge of populist energies. The indicators of national decline were moral rather than political—for example, levels of alcoholism, illegitimacy, criminality, emigration—and the earliest alliance of the intellectuals was with religious reformists, whose impetus was to recover a collective spirituality by rooting it in the material advancement of their communities. The Grundtvig 'meeting movement' of Lutheran peasant intellectuals in Denmark, the Bernacacina movement of Slovak lower clergy in the early nineteenth century, the Arya Samaj in late nineteenth-century India, and Protestant theosophical societies in late nineteenth-century Ireland were important allies and incubators of a cultural nationalism in their respective countries.[18]

Their core constituency, however, comprised young middle-class men (educated professionals such as civil servants, teachers, lawyers, journalists) and sometimes women, who became the political cadres of nationalist organizations. As the names of these organizations suggest (Young Italy, Young Poland, Young Ireland, Young Egypt), nationalism was an ideology of the educated young.[19] Alienated from their traditional values by their secular education, imbued with new expectations of social and political mobility, they sought to reconnect with their society by leading it from backwardness. Finding themselves only too often blocked from power by established holders of power and status, nationalism offered them an alternative moral vision of integration achieved by a novel form of training, conveyed by the term *Bildung*, a drawing out of the essence of the individual through an immersion in the life energies of the nation, as captured in its history, arts, customs, and whole way of life. It offered them an alternative vocation as nation-builders. The effect was to create a new moral community, based on disaffected male youth, organized around a cult of national sacrifice, inspired by heroic myths of the past.

Revivalists envisaged a grass-roots strategy of educational permeation of each sector of national life. They spoke of a return to the people and valorized those whom they regarded as the custodians of the nation's continuity, usually the peasantry. In practice the future of the nation lay in nationalizing the leaders of society and its dominant institutions, social, economic, and cultural. This was the real legacy of revivalist movements.

Although cultural nationalism has often been portrayed as illiberal, its political characteristics varied greatly during the nineteenth century.[20] The Grundtvigian movement of Lutheran pastors and folk high-school teachers in Denmark found a positive reception from the prosperous farmers. It became a major training centre for Danish political elites and thereby helped to form the distinctive populist and libertarian character of that nation state.[21] In many agrarian societies, however, the educated stratum was tiny, and to obtain social leverage they had to appeal to the gentry and clergy. Where these strata responded, as in Poland and Croatia, the nationalism took on a conservative hue. In much of eastern Europe, however, the gentry were ethnically or linguistically distinct from the working population, and nationalists were forced to turn to a peasantry that had low political consciousness. Here revivalism took on the form of a populist self-help movement. In the Galician Ukraine and Latvia nationalists (in the late nineteenth and early twentieth century) attempted to construct a modern vernacular literary and scientific culture out of a largely illiterate oral culture, promoting a vigorous lay movement among the peasantry, establishing libraries, agricultural and credit cooperatives, and newspapers.[22] In the twentieth century the communitarianism of cultural nationalism also conjoined with socialist ideologies, as exemplified in the work of Mexican intellectuals such as the painter Diego Rivera and in James Connolly's Irish communist movement.

A communitarian politics, however, that emphasizes moral transformation was likely to have only a limited effectiveness, particularly against states that controlled the apparatus of coercion and access to public employment and education. Its real significance was to form an elite of young people from different sectors of the nation into a counter-cultural society that was capable of resisting the norms of the dominant society. It did so by creating a new symbolism and set of ceremonies and an overlapping range of cultural and social agencies (literary societies, musical choirs, sporting associations, et cetera), in which status was gained by preparedness to serve the nation. The size of this counter-culture varied according to the resources it could mobilize and the social and institutional alliances it could form. Although romantic nationalists were in general peaceful and reformist, conflict was seen as a necessary part of the nationalism, for the young must overthrow the established order in order regenerate the nation. This conflict was generally envisaged as cultural (at least initially), but the heroic past revealed to young romantic nationalists by historians and artists provided powerful role models that could inspire a revolutionary activism. Moreover, nationalism emerged as a potent ideology in the period of the French Revolution, a time of war and social upheaval. The cult of the fallen soldier, celebrated in songs and commemoration ceremonies, was central to romantic nationalism.[23] Where nationalists were confronted by a repressive (and also foreign) regime, the ideal of heroic sacrifice could organize young men into revolutionary brotherhoods, and from this into rebellion. Such uprisings (even when they were minor skirmishes) were dramatized by poets and artists as part of a lineage of national martyrdom.

This elitism was enhanced where revivalists were outsiders to the societies they wished to transform. Many were of mixed ethnic descent and conscious of this: Patrick Pearse was one of many Irish nationalists born to mixed English and Irish parentage, Thomas Masaryk the Czech historian was of Slovak birth, and Adam Mickiewicz was of Polish and Jewish descent. Nationalists sometimes saw themselves as not so much reviving an old as forging a new nation, like the Anglo-Irish who hoped to weld the Gaelic and English populations, or the Mexican and Peruvian intellectuals who hoped to yoke indigenous with European invaders into a *mestizo* nation.[24]

Well-educated religious minorities were over represented in the early stages of many revivalist movements: Protestants in Slovak and Irish nationalisms, Copts in Egyptian and Maronite Christians in Lebanese nationalisms. A sense of marginality created a drive to find a secular ethnic past preceding and relativizing the religious traditions of the majority that would give this minority a role in the political community. Such feelings were possibly increased by the gradual march of democracy that would undermine the status of the minority. Egyptian Copts who perceived themselves to be the truest descendants of ancient Egypt were active in asserting the claims of the Pharaonic era against the prestige of the later Arab-Islam period.[25] In similar fashion, Syrian Christians championed the Aramaeans as the original descendants of their nation; Maronite Christians claimed the Phoenicians as ancestors of Lebanon to establish a national identity not identified with the Arab Muslim majority.[26]

Others came from diaspora or overseas populations. Some combined a sense of nostalgia for a homeland with a sense of shame at its backwardness compared with the free institutions and vigour of their host society. A Greek neo-classical nationalism formed in the late eighteenth century amongst scholars and merchants in the Balkans, many of whom were educated or travelled widely in Europe. Conscious of the backwardness of their homeland compared with Europe, they funded cultural societies, libraries, and literary publications in order to regenerate their 'fallen' kinsmen.[27] Pan-Africanism originated among the descendants of black slaves in the USA seeking roots and dignity, and developed a second base among African intellectuals in France.[28] Other diasporas were radicalized by the spread of democratic principles that made their status increasingly precarious. A cultural Zionism was born in Jewish diasporas of western and eastern Europe, triggered by the rising tide of anti-Semitism from the mid-nineteenth century that in western Europe eroded liberal hopes of assimilation offered by the Enlightenment and that in Russia and eastern Europe resulted in waves of pogroms.[29]

All this indicated the transformational energies of people from 'outside' traditional society. But they have often been interpreted, notably in the classic works of Hans Kohn and Ernest Gellner, as essentially reactionary figures, in flight from modernity. Moreover, Kohn believed that they had significance primarily in the early phases of nationalism, as definers of identity, but left the stage to political or state-oriented nationalists once that task was done.[30] To what extent are such intellectuals conservative, even regressive, in their return to the past? Do they have more than a transient role in the formation of territorial nation states?

Moral Innovators

What allowed national revivalism to challenge traditions were the continuous and unpredictable external and internal shocks to the existing social order unleashed by secular modernization. A crisis developed that was perceived to be both internal and external, when a society was threatened by technologically and culturally more dynamic competitors and there was intense social polarization between traditionalists and modernists over how to respond. Traditional autocratic regimes, first in central and eastern Europe, then, as European states expanded, in the rest of the world, regarded with horror the liberal democratic legacy of the French Revolution, but recognized the mobilizing capacities (especially military) of the national model. Tsarist Russia was defeated in the Crimea (1853–6); Japan was forced to open its ports by the US Admiral Matthew Perry in 1854; and China, the greatest of the non-European states, was humiliated in the Opium Wars (1839–60) and facing the prospect of partition by European powers by the early twentieth century.

In response, these regimes felt compelled to introduce limited reforms (expanding education, emancipating serfs, opening access to public offices, and sponsoring technological innovation) to ensure their survival. As they reformed, conflicts erupted between traditionalists and modernizers. I argue that the significance of cultural nationalists is that they present populations with new maps of identity and political prescriptions that claim to combine the virtues of historical tradition and modern progress at times of crisis when established practices and identities were shaken.

The traditionalists initially sought to block out 'the West' and the ideas of progress that threatened to destroy indigenous values. Modernizers in nineteenth- century Russia, China, and India adopted a radical anti-traditionalism, many taking up the ideas of political nationalism, arguing that the only salvation of their society was to copy the models of the advanced West, if needs be abandoning the great traditions of Orthodoxy or Confucianism or Hinduism that doomed their peoples to backwardness and poverty. But these internal conflicts, as well as threatening social breakdown, could result in demoralization by creating a sense of inferiority before foreigners.

National revivalism offered a third way, by preaching a modernization from within. We find national revivalists regularly establishing formal institutions at times of conflict. Their ideas may be adopted by dissident social groups, alienated from the dominant social order or co-opted by regimes fearing for their legitimacy. I have mentioned their affinity with liberal religious reform movements that wished to revise dogmas, laicize teachings, and develop vernacular languages and 'scientific' agriculture in order to make (religious) tradition a living force. Both nationalists and reformists sought a solution to the internal conflict by evoking a national golden age and studying the experience of other countries.

For this reason I have described such nationalists as *moral innovators*, providing new directions at times of social crisis. The golden age of such nationalists was a time when the nation was a dynamic high culture harmonizing all dimensions of human experience (religious, scientific, artistic, military), in active contact with the great centres and making a permanent contribution to human civilization. This evolutionary historical vision claimed to present an innovative solution that would reconcile the interests of traditionalists and modernizers, thereby redirecting energies away from destructive conflict into a cooperative reconstruction of the national community. The golden age was used to transform the accepted meanings of 'tradition' and 'modernity' so that in their 'authentic' national forms they were one and the same, and thereby persuade their adherents to ally in the national project. The aim was to reform ossified tradition and to articulate the options by which modernization should be pursued.

We observe this occurring after the demoralizing controversy that divided secular liberals and orthodox Hindu during the late 1880s and early 1890s over the British colonial administration's proposal (supported by the former) to outlaw the custom of child marriage. A revivalist Hindu nationalism crystallized, hostile to both sides, in Swami Vivekananda's neo-Vedantic movement, which sought to undermine the authority of Hindu tradition by evoking as the authentic India its Aryan heritage. Not only child marriage was alien: Vivekananda rejected the religious taboos on contacts with foreigners and the caste hierarchies as later inventions of the Brahmin priesthood, which were deviations from this dynamic democratic civilization. At the same time he rejected reforms initiated by British liberalism: India had to be reformed on native lines. In effect such movements are internalizing as essential components of ethno-religious tradition the ideals and institutions of civil society and liberal democracy.[31]

To traditionalists national revivalists argued that it was a misunderstanding to conceive of tradition as a passive repetition of custom. Traditionalists must recognize that tradition has continually to be renewed, sometimes by adapting the ideas of others, and its authentic expression is to be found in the golden age when the national community was a dynamic modernizing civilization confidently exchanging ideas and technologies with other cultures. To modernizers who uncritically admired foreign models, revivalists argued that the greatest embodiment of a successful modernity was to be found in the golden age of their nation, which had instructed the then backward 'West'. Whatever the West now had was borrowed from their nation, and hence they should look to their own traditions for inspiration.

In China the late nineteenth-century reform movement broke with an ethnocentric perspective of China as a unique Confucian civilization, to view it as one among other nations of the world, from whose history one could learn. They directed their message to a growing literate public, influenced by Social Darwinist ideas and aware of the foreign threat to China. In search of solutions, revivalists engaged in historical studies of polities ancient and modern, and analysed in journals contemporary movements of colonized peoples against western empires (including the Boers and Indians against the British), the struggles of the Young Turks to modernize the Ottoman Empire, and the successes of the Meiji Reformers in Japan, especially after Japan's defeat of the Tsarist Empire in 1905. The Chinese reformers offered competing diagnoses, some stressing the importance of a strong state, others the creation of a powerful ethnic consciousness, but by 1911 educated opinion had come to believe that the answer to the Chinese crisis was the transformation of a foreign-led (Manchu) dynastic empire into a national state, led by a patriotic elite. Increasingly they saw China as the leader of an Asian civilization against the West.[32]

Revivalists oscillated across a modernist-traditionalist continuum in articulating 'solutions'. By attracting support from modernizers and traditionalists, they imported competing ideas into their movements over the balance to be struck between conserving distinctive traditions and the promotion of socioeconomic progress. They might inconsistently adopt opposing positions, or shift from one to the other, either for instrumental or affective reasons. In the early years of the twentieth century, the Gaelic revival had something of a modernizing thrust, directed against the otherworldly passivity encouraged by the Catholic Church and attempting to create a vigorous lay Irish Catholic middle-class culture. But, faced with the continued sway of English culture over urban Ireland and the eruption of class conflict across Britain and Ireland, by 1913 its lower middle-class intelligentsia, many of rural origins, allied increasingly with fervent neo-traditionalist movements that sought to mobilize the urban poor and the peasantry to shore up a crumbling community from foreign temptations.[33] In this regard, cultural nationalists have never been outright modernists or traditionalists, but rather ideological innovators. They articulate the shifting options for societies seeking to determine their path to modernization, in a manner that balances their concern to preserve a distinctive identity with a drive for progress.

Communitarian and State-Oriented Movements

All this suggests a small-scale and elitist discussion forum, often limited to a few members of the intelligentsia, whose communitarian strategies can go only so far. They may flare into a revolutionary activism (as we have noted) but are as likely to fizzle out or be co-opted by states or state-seeking political nationalists. Certainly the assumption is that revivalists are a pre-political force, influential in the early stages of nationalism but who give way to more concrete state-oriented movements. Miroslav Hroch's classic studies of the activism of non-state nationalisms suggest this. He argues that nationalist movements have three main demands: for a separate national culture; for political autonomy; and for a complete class structure or national society.[34] Typically there are three phases: (a) gestation, where intellectuals excavate cultural remains and reconstruct them for their own sake, with no national claims in mind; (b) patriotic agitation, where cultural claims such as language recognition are tied to political demands by nationalist organizations, led by a middle-class intelligentsia and attempts are made to awaken the masses; and (c) mass mobilization, where nationalism mobilizes urban and rural masses, often with separatist political demands.[35]

Hroch is aware that historical sequences will vary from case to case, but in this schema the intellectuals, after having the role as identity formers, retire as significant actors from the scene to be replaced by more political agents. This, however, is too static, for defining the nation may be a recurring process because of changing relations of a given population with its neighbours.

Indeed, in my work on national revivals in eighteenth- and nineteenth-century Ireland, I found that that there was a long-running concern with national identity and cultural regeneration that surfaced *episodically* in three national revivals, each of which emerged at a time of growing political nationalism in the form of state-seeking movements and shared their hostility to the intervention of a centralizing state in national life. *Each* revival had three phases: *gestation* led by *historicist* intellectuals; *crystallization* in the form of cultural institutions propounding a new historico-cultural conception of the nation; and *socio-political articulation* when more *modernizing* intellectuals translated into concrete sociopolitical programmes (some of) the communitarian themes of the revival, appealing to a disaffected rising educated generation that felt excluded from power. In this third phase, revivalism could develop a broader-based movement, offering an alternative grass-roots politics to that of established statist organizations. Each Irish revival ended in revolt, and the third time (the Easter rebellion of 1916) with long-term success.[36]

Hroch is right to say that there is generally a developing social momentum. But the relationship between identity formulation and political power is more dynamic than his model indicates, and the intellectuals may remain significant throughout the period of nationalist agitation. Although where there was a degree of political freedom, state-oriented movements are likely to be more effective in marshalling large-scale coalition, we find what can be called a contrapuntal relationship between the identity politics of cultural nationalism and the drive for state power, with one movement often alternating with the other where that fails, and in turn becoming the platform for political mobilization. The revivals in Ireland *crystallized* at times of crisis for larger political nationalist movements, notably when the latter were plunged into internal conflict between traditionalist and modernist supporters. Moreover, the sociopolitical phase of revivalism formed when a new nationalist intelligentsia perceived themselves blocked not only by the state but also by established political nationalist organizations.[37] (To add to the complexities, there are often tensions *within* revivalist movements, between the historicist intellectuals of the early stages, the historians, poets, and language enthusiasts engaged in the 'rediscovery' of the nation in its diverse complexity, and the modernizing leaders of the sociopolitical phase whose interest in culture is in the provision of useful stereotypes for the purposes of collective mobilization.)[38]

Nonetheless, one might ask whether revivalist movements are significant only in the pre-independence phase of nationalism, since the major task for nationalists after political independence is to build a viable state to protect the nation, that is, effective administrative, economic, judicial, educational, and military institutions. In the course of this, 'statism' may come to replace nationalism as post-independence regimes are perceived to be increasingly detached from the interests of their citizens, and to have lost the original moral vision (its charisma) of the nation. In fact, tensions between overmighty centralizing states (which are often perceived to take on an 'imperial' character) and their citizens are endemic to the modern world, generating revivalist movements in established polities that extol the virtues of a nation of localities. There are many examples. A significant English cultural nationalism formed in the mid- to late eighteenth century, extolling Anglo-Saxon liberties against aristocratic oligarchy, and again in the late nineteenth century, rejecting the corruptions of British Empire. In the 1960s amidst the increasing disillusionment with the Soviet state, the All-Russian Society for the Protection of Historical and Cultural Monuments formed, attracting over 20 million members. This expressed a concern about environmental degeneration and the demographic decline of the Russians compared with the Muslim 'Asians'. It promoted the preservation of Russia's architectural and cultural heritage and a return to the historic Russia of neo-Slavophile and Orthodox rural traditions, organizing pilgrimages to sacred centres such as ancient towns, monasteries, and churches.[39]

The resurgence of revivalist projects seeking to renationalize the state is the more likely where there are long-running cultural differences about what constitutes the authentic national vision, and where there is therefore an alternative conception ready to challenge the established ideal. In Russia competition between Slavophiles and Westerners, the first as defenders of Russia's distinctive Orthodox traditions and the second looking to western European models, originated in the early nineteenth century and continues into the present. In France the struggle between Republicans and clerico-legitimists in France since the French Revolution recurs in various forms, most visibly in the campaigns of Jean-Marie Le Pen's National Front against the Fifth Republic. Such differences may go back to traumatic historical episodes such as Peter the Great's assault on Orthodoxy, or the legacy of revolutionary civil war. They may also reflect powerful regional divisions, as in Norway, split between the more rural populist west and the metropolitan east, dominated by Oslo, with rival versions of the Norwegian language.

Whatever their origins, these divisions that often erupt into 'cultural wars' can offer radically different views of the structure of politics, the status of social groups, relations between regions, the countryside, and the city, economic and social policies, and foreign policy. They persist since they reflect the diverse heritages of populations whose geopolitical setting continues to expose them to unpredictable impacts from several directions. Modern Russia has been shaped by interactions with western and central Europe, Byzantium, and the Asian steppes. These rival national visions have alternated in power both at the level of the state and of 'educated society'. As communism in the USSR collapsed, so one saw the re-emergence of rival projects, with a western orientation becoming dominant under Boris Yeltsin that included a radical reconstruction of the Russian economy. But after its failure there occurred a resurgence of neo-Slavophile ideas, under Vladimir Putin, expressing a support for authority, Russian distinctiveness, and a deep suspicion of the West.

Conclusion

I have suggested that a focus on the identity of the nation as moral community goes alongside the drive for political autonomy. Cultural activism inevitably flows into the field of politics and may result in attempts to seize state power, but this is not the primary goal of cultural nationalists. Rather, their concern is to define and revise the content of the nation that the state nominally serves and to rebalance state and community (often by advocating regional decentralization). Typically, cultural nationalism like political nationalism crystallizes in institutional form as a reaction against state centralization. There is, nonetheless, often a pattern of alternation between cultural and political nationalisms, for while communitarianism by itself will fail against a hostile state, a mobilization of all collective energies to achieving or building a state can lead to a sense of deracination, and in turn a further wave of revivalism.

Cultural nationalists use the idiom of regeneration to describe their enterprise. This idiom implies an emphasis on history to validate that enterprise, but in doing this cultural nationalists smuggle values and practices into 'tradition' that are often innovative and exotic. They thereby enable the co-option of traditionalist and religious forces to the nationalist cause. As I have argued, however, there is never any finality to this enterprise because of the unpredictability of the modernization process itself.

National tradition has to be regularly redefined because of the new demands of the present. The turn to a nation's history offers material for this task when it results in the 'discovery' of 'forgotten' multiple and competing pasts, cultural artefacts and heritages, and sacred sites. Although this may generate conflict over what is truly authentic to the nation, as in the prolonged cultural wars in France and Russia, it also offers options for societies when the existing ideas and legitimations are discredited. Nation-formation is frequently a long drawn-out process of trial and error or fierce contestation. In cases such as the Slovaks, where there was little sense of an earlier ethnic identity, nationalists seem to have more scope for invention, but their problem is that they have insufficient material with which to appeal to the apathetic masses. They themselves are unsure who they are, and Slovak nationalists have oscillated between advocating a Slovak, Pan Slav, Czecho-Slovak, and now again Slovak identity. We might suggest that where ethnic traditions are absent, the problems of nationalists are still more difficult: they have greater room for manoeuvre, but without the raw materials on which to build they are dependent on long drawn-out processes of intergroup conflict in order to achieve a sense of collective identity.

Notes

1. By historicism I mean an understanding of the world by how it came to be. History takes on the character of being a surrogate religion.
2. J. Hutchinson (1987) *The Dynamics of Cultural Nationalism*, London, ch. 1.
3. O. Zimmer (2003) 'Boundary Mechanisms and Symbolic Resources: Towards a Process-Oriented Approach to National Identity', *Nations and Nationalism*, 9, no. 2, 73–93.
4. J. Armstrong (1993) *Nations Before Nationalism*, Chapel Hill, NC.
5. J. Leerssen (2006) *National Thought in Europe*, Amsterdam, 25–70. See also, for this early modern period, Chapter 2 by Peter Burke in this volume.
6. The leading study of Herder is F. M. Barnard (2003) *Herder on Nationality, Humanity and History*, Montreal and Kingston.
7. W. J. Argyle (1976) 'Size and Scale as Factors in the Development of Nationalist Movements', in A. D. Smith (ed.) *Nationalist Movements*, London, 31–53.
8. R. Schwab (1984) *The Oriental Renaissance: Europe's Rediscovery of India and the East 1680–1880*, New York, 51.
9. L. Poliakov (1974) *The Aryan Myth*, New York, 198.
10. Ø. Sørensen (1994) 'The Development of a Norwegian National Identity during the Nineteenth Century', in Ø. Sørensen (ed.) *Nordic Paths to National Identity in the Nineteenth Century*, Oslo, 26–9.
11. C. Heimsath (1964) *Indian Nationalism and Hindu Social Reform*, Princeton, NJ, ch. 6.
12. E. Kaufmann and O. Zimmer (1998) 'In Search of the Authentic Nation: Landscape and National Identity in Canada and Switzerland', *Nations and Nationalism*, 4, no. 4, 483–510.
13. M. L. Sørenson (1996) 'The Fall of a Nation, the Birth of a Subject: The National Use of Archaeology in Nineteenth-Century Denmark', in M. Diaz-Andreu and T. Champion (eds.) *Nationalism and Archaeology in Europe*, London, 24–47.
14. J. Breuilly (1993) *Nationalism and the State*, Manchester, ch. 5.
15. Leerssen, *National Thought in Europe*, 122–6.
16. Jonathan Bate (1997) *The Genius of Shakespeare*, London, ch. 6.
17. Hutchinson, *The Dynamics of Cultural Nationalism*, 134.
18. See U. Ostergard (1994) 'Nation-Building Danish Style', in Ø. Sørensen (ed.) *Nordic Paths to National Identity in the Nineteenth Century*, Oslo; P. Brock (1976) *The Slovak National Revival*, Toronto; Heimsath *Indian Nationalism and Hindu Social Reform*; Hutchinson, *The Dynamics of Cultural Nationalism*, ch. 5.
19. E. Kedourie (1960) *Nationalism*, London, 99–102.
20. H. Kohn (1946) *The Idea of Nationalism*, New York, 3–4, 329–41, 429–30.
21. Ostergard, 'Nation-Building Danish Style', 46–7.
22. A. Plakans (1974) 'Peasants, Intellectuals, and Nationalism in the Russian Baltic Provinces 1820–90', *Journal of Modern History*, 46, 464–9; I. L. Rudnytski (1977) 'The Ukrainian National Movement on the Eve of the First World War', *East European Quarterly*, XI, no. 2, 141–54.
23. G. Mosse (1976) 'Mass Politics and the Political Liturgy of Nationalism', in E. Kamenka (ed.) *Nationalism: The Nature and Evolution of an Idea*, London, 38–54; G. Mosse (1990) *Fallen Soldiers: Reshaping the Memory of the World Wars*, Oxford.

24. N. Miller (1999) *In the Shadow of the State: Intellectuals and the Quest for National Identity in Twentieth-Century Spanish America*, London, ch. 4. So the Anglo-Irish poet G. W. Russell wrote in 'On Behalf of Some Irishmen not Followers of Tradition': 'We would no Irish sign efface,/But yet our lips would gladlier hail/The firstborn of the Coming Race/Than the last splendour of the Gael.'
25. D. Reid (1997) 'Nationalising the Pharaonic Past: Egyptology, Imperialism and Egyptian Nationalism 1922–52', in J. Jankowkski and I. Gershoni (eds.) *Rethinking Nationalism in the Arab Middle East*, New York, 140.
26. B. Lewis (1998) *Multiple Identities of the Middle East*, New York, 74.
27. G. Jordanis (2001) *The Necessary Nation*, Princeton, NJ, 122–33.
28. See Cemil Aydin's Chapter 34 on pan-nationalism.
29. Z. Sternhell (1999) *The Founding Myths of Israel*, Princeton, NJ, 12–13.
30. Kohn, *The Idea of Nationalism*, 3–4, 329–41, 429–30; E. Gellner (1983) *Nations and Nationalism*, Oxford, 55–61.
31. Heimsath, *Indian Nationalism and Hindu Social Reform*, ch. 6.
32. R. E. Karl (2002) *Staging the World: Chinese Nationalism at the Turn of the Twentieth Century*, London, chs. 2, 4–6.
33. T. Garvin (1987) *Nationalist Revolutionaries in Ireland 1858–1928*, Oxford, chs. 5 and 6.
34. See Miroslav Hroch's Chapter 9.
35. M. Hroch (1985) *Social Preconditions of National Revival in Europe*, Cambridge, ch. 6; M. Hroch (1996) 'From National Movement to the Fully-Formed Nation: The Nation-Building Process in Europe', in G. Balakrishnan (ed.) *Mapping the Nation*, London, 78–81.
36. Hutchinson, *The Dynamics of Cultural Nationalism*, 47–50.
37. Hutchinson, *The Dynamics of Cultural Nationalism*, ch. 8.
38. A classic example is the confrontation between W. B. Yeats and Arthur Griffith over the satirical comedies of John Synge, deemed by Griffith to be an assault on the virtue of Catholic Ireland. This is discussed in F. S. L. Lyons (1979) *Culture and Anarchy in Ireland*, Oxford, 66–71.
39. D. Popielovsky (1989) 'The "Russian Orientation" and the Orthodox Church', in P. Ramet (ed.) *Religion and Nationalism in the Soviet Union and Eastern Europe*, Durham, NC.

Suggested Further Reading

Barnard, F. M. (2003) *Herder on Nationality, Humanity and History*, Montreal and Kingston.
Befu, H. (1993) *Cultural Nationalism in East Asia*, Berkeley, CA.
Chatterjee, P. (1993) *The Nation and its Fragments*, Princeton, NJ.
Hroch, M. (1985) *Social Preconditions of National Revival in Europe*, Cambridge.
Hutchinson, J. (1987) *The Dynamics of Cultural Nationalism*, London.
Hutchinson, J. (2005) *Nations as Zones of Conflict*, London.
Jordanis, G. (2001) *The Necessary Nation*, Princeton, NJ.
Kohn, H. (1946) *The Idea of Nationalism*, New York.
Kohn, H. (1976) *Prelude to Nation-States: The French and German Experience,1789–1815*, Princeton, NJ.
Kopf, D. (1969) *British Orientalism and the Bengali Cultural Renaissance*, Berkeley, CA.
Leerssen, J. (2006) *National Thought in Europe*, Amsterdam.

Leerssen, J. (2006) 'Nationalism and the Cultivation of Culture', *Nations and Nationalism*, 12, no. 4, 559–78.
Smith A. D. (1986) *The Ethnic Origins of Nations*, Oxford, ch. 8.
Smith A. D. (1995) 'Gastronomy or Geology? The Role of Nationalism in the Reconstruction of Nations', *Nations and Nationalism*, 1, no. 1, 3–23.
Yoshino, K. (1992) *Cultural Nationalism in Contemporary Japan*, London.

PART II

THE EMERGENCE OF NATIONALISM: POLITICS AND POWER

CHAPTER 6

INDEPENDENCE AND NATIONALISM IN THE AMERICAS

DON H. DOYLE AND ERIC VAN YOUNG

Introduction

INSOFAR as nationalism connotes a desire for sovereignty as a state and separate existence as a people, it would seem that any movement for independence, wherever it might occur, presupposes nationalist consciousness and purpose. When such a movement involves protracted military conflict and significant sacrifice from the populace struggling for sovereignty, as exhibited in most American independence movements, it would seem all the more to imply a strong undercurrent of popular nationalist sentiment. Yet in all the independence movements of the Americas, the first such colonial revolts of the modern era, the role of nationalism as a motivating force is far more complicated than this logical proposition would suggest.

The independence movements that erupted in the Americas between 1776 and 1825 did not result from a rising national consciousness within the colonies, whether among the populace or elites. Nor is it clear that the wars for independence and subsequent struggles to establish viable national constitutions and governments gave birth to coherent, durable national identities, at least not immediately. Everywhere the new nation states of the Americas were confronted with multi-ethnic populations, in many cases vast territories, and fractious politics, all of which challenged ongoing efforts to build enduring states and nourish cohesive national identities. Although there were notable social conflicts within the colonies before the outbreak of the imperial crises and independence movements, and signs of burgeoning 'national' identifications among elite groups, especially, the independence struggles of the Americas emerged not from popular nationalist movements but from multiple crises in European imperial systems of power over their colonies. Nor does the idea of parallel and intersecting 'imperial crises' (especially among Britain, France, and Spain) by itself provide anything like a comprehensive explanation for the political outcomes of these struggles, since historical contingencies—the accidents of a battle here, events in the metropolis, a different ethnic mix of the colonial population there—shaped the nature of intra-imperial conflict, inter-imperial rivalries, and the nature of the polities that emerged from the movements for independence.

The independence process in the Americas reveals both substantial similarities and great differences between the Anglo-American and Ibero-American colonies. One problem in framing comparisons, however, is the number of administrative units into which the New World realms of the Iberian powers (including Portuguese Brazil) were divided, giving rise to the twenty or so nations of Latin America. The sheer size and diversity of the Iberian New World realms make direct comparison between Anglo- and Ibero-America difficult. Spanish and Portuguese America embraced not only the densely populated indigenous areas (once state-level societies) of the Andes and Mesoamerica, but also the vastnesses of northern Mexico, the Argentine pampas, Patagonia, and the Amazonian interior of Brazil, and a population of about 17 million people by the early nineteenth century—about three times that of the British North American colonies, including African slaves and indigenous peoples. Finally, the conditions under which Ibero-American independence took shape were different from those surrounding the separation of the Anglo-American colonies from Great Britain, not least among them the demonstration effect on colonial political thinkers and revolutionary leaders of the American and French Revolutions. By the time the Spanish Americans thought about liberation, beginning in 1808 or so, the presence in the western hemisphere of a young but firmly established republican state provided a model, albeit a long controversial one, of how the new polities might reconfigure themselves from colonial possessions. This 'cross-case contamination' makes it impossible to look at the two areas as distinct instances of colonial liberation processes, therefore, rather than as points along a continuous narrative of American nation-making.

However, there were a number of similarities in the imperial situations of Britain, Spain, and Portugal. There was, first of all, the problem of geography common to all far-flung imperial systems. The Atlantic Ocean was a formidable barrier to communication and control, the friction of distance raising the costs and reducing the efficiency of metropolitan governance. Furthermore, where the Spanish and British empires bumped up against each other in the Atlantic shipping lanes and the Caribbean, inter-imperial conflict in time of war could loosen control especially by the weaker power, Spain, over its overseas realms, as with the British occupation of Havana during the Seven Years War and the shipping interdictions of the Napoleonic period. The influence of Enlightenment ideas on notions of human freedom, forms of governance, and emergent nationalism, although they can easily be exaggerated for the Iberian colonies, nonetheless acted powerfully in both imperial spheres to legitimate the idea of independence. Finally, the natural inclination of European-descended people in settler colonies to diverge in interests and outlook from the metropolis as their societies matured was common to both Anglo- and Ibero-America.

British North America

For the thirteen colonies of British North America the road to independence involved a long, slow, halting march over the course of two decades. Beginning in 1763, when British imperial policy began a decided shift, it was not until 1775 that armed conflict began. Hostilities dragged on to 1781, and the Treaty of Paris that finally settled the conflict and granted recognition of the United States by Britain was not signed until 1783. It would be another six years before the US Constitution, ratified in 1789, established what proved to be a strong and durable federal system of government over the states.

Nationalist mythology in the United States typically identifies the foundation of the future nation in the New England Puritans' flight from England beginning in 1620 to escape religious persecution. Thanksgiving Day, a popular national holiday in the US, commemorates this foundation myth in a national holiday of feasting. The New England Puritan leader, Jonathan Winthrop, in 1630 famously connected the Puritan mission in America to the biblical image of a 'City Upon a Hill' that would set an example before the world. Later, this would become frequently cited by modern historians as prophetic evidence of a self-conscious role for an American people. But Thanksgiving was a modern invention of the mid-nineteenth century, and there is little to suggest Winthrop's idea of America as a refuge and model was an important part of American identity until the idea began to appear in revolutionary propaganda. The Puritans saw themselves on the margins of the English and Christian worlds, but by no means separate from either.

Nor was there any indication during more than a century and a half of development of any popular sentiment among the colonists anticipating eventual independence from Britain. On the contrary, settlers in British North America welcomed the protection that membership in the British Empire afforded against incursions from the Spanish, French, and indigenous peoples that endangered them. The British imperial system encouraged local self-government, permitted remarkable ethnic and religious diversity among colonial settlers, and fostered a flourishing trade with the colonies. The Navigation Acts introduced in the mid-seventeenth century were intended to restrict British American trade to British (including British North American) ships and to or through British ports, but they also protected American exports from foreign rivals. In any case, enforcement of the Navigation Acts was lax and penalties were rarely imposed; the result was a lively commerce in smuggling between American colonists and the French, Dutch, Portuguese, and Spanish over the next century. Before 1763 the British ruled their North American colonies with a light hand, and there were at most a few episodic, local protests coming from the North American colonists against British rule and rulers. It was a policy the famous Whig politician and political theorist Edmund Burke, in his 1775 defence of the American colonists in Parliament, characterized as 'wise and salutary neglect'.[1]

As with all the American independence movements, we argue below, instead of a story of inevitable conflict and long-anticipated independence, the British North American rebellion came about rather unexpectedly and could probably have been averted altogether by more skilful leadership on the British side and more persuasive efforts among the Loyalists on the American side. What began essentially as a tax protest in 1765 evolved into a major constitutional crisis during the ensuing decade. British American colonists remained hopeful of resolution even after military conflict had begun in April 1775. By 4 July 1776 when independence was formally declared, a large majority of colonists had come over to the side of full-blown independence, but only because they saw it as a last resort when other solutions seemed no longer possible. By then, the rudiments of a North American nationalist sentiment had begun to take recognizable form. This was a product rather than a cause of a prolonged conflict during which colonists pressed their rights as members of the British nation, not their separateness as a people.

Far more unpredictable was the evolution of British North American protest from legalistic and constitutional quarrels over the right of Parliament to tax or govern the colonies into the invocation of radical Enlightenment ideas of universal human equality, natural rights, and the right to revolution. Employed first to justify American rights *within* the empire, natural rights and equality soon became the basis for independence *outside* the empire. The success of the American Revolution in eventually winning for the colonies independence as a nation against the most powerful empire in Europe was itself a remarkable achievement that caught the attention of intellectuals and revolutionaries elsewhere, notably in Europe and Latin America. More than the example of military success, it was the ideas of natural rights, human equality, government by consent, and the right to revolution, first applied to a revolutionary movement in the thirteen colonies, which proved such a powerful fuel for the coming age of revolutionary nationalism in the Atlantic world. One of the main reasons for the widespread contagion of these revolutionary ideas was that they were detached from any particular nationalist identity or ideology and instead based on notions of universal human aspirations. Scores of new nations and would-be nations would announce their existence with their own declarations of independence, many of them lifted verbatim from the American template of 1776, which, in turn, came from the common currency of European Enlightenment thinkers.

Among the most important of the contingencies affecting the move toward independence in the British and Spanish colonies were imperial efforts to introduce economic and administrative reforms into the overseas empires of Spain and Britain. The Spanish Bourbon Reforms, beginning in an inchoate fashion early in the century, and reaching a crescendo during the reign of Charles III (1759–88) and the years immediately following, and the British reforms, led by Lord Grenville and others in Parliament after 1763, were parallel efforts to enhance imperial control and profit from the American colonies.

The British reforms took place at the close of a protracted trans-Atlantic military conflict between Britain and France, which left France vanquished as an imperial power in North America. Known as the Seven Years War (1756–63) in Europe, the conflict began two years earlier in the American theatre of war, where it became known as the French and Indian War. The conflict brought British and colonial American soldiers and officers together in common cause against the French, and Britain's triumph was a great source of pride among American colonists. The removal of the French as a major power in North America also opened the trans-Appalachian interior of North America, into which the fast-growing colonial population could spread. Few would have predicted this victory as the beginning of the end of the British Empire in America.

Britain's victory over France came at tremendous expense, however, and a new corps of economy-minded politicians sought to shift some of the costs of imperial administration and defence to the prosperous American colonies. They would bring a decided break with the long tradition of salutary neglect and self-government in the thirteen colonies. The Navigation Acts, in place with few modifications over the previous century and more, provided the main guidelines for economic regulation of the British American colonies. They put into operation the basic mercantilist motivation of overseas colonization: colonies existed to enhance the empire, to extend its domain and enrich its resources. In theory, colonial trade was to remain largely contained within the British Empire using British ships and British ports; trade to or from other countries was subject to duties and restrictions. In practice, however, British trade regulations were loosely observed and American merchants conducted a large trade in smuggled goods, particularly with the French sugar islands to which Americans exported food in exchange for molasses for rum manufacturing. Even during the French and Indian War, many American merchants were profiting handsomely from trade with the French enemy. Britain's policy had been to encourage colonial prosperity and thereby enrich the empire at large, even if this required turning a blind eye to a degree of illegal trade.

The Sugar Act of 1764 was the first major shift away from the British tradition of salutary neglect. It sought to tighten up the entire imperial system of trade regulation, particularly the illegal trade with the French sugar islands. The Act in fact lowered the duties imposed on sugar products, but at the same time put in place a vastly more rigorous system of customs collections, prosecution, and fines. In brief, it took the enforcement of colonial trade out of the hands of colonial jurists and handed it over to the British Navy and its Vice-Admiralty courts. Americans protested mightily against the new regulations, the corruption of local customs officials, and the unfairness of the vice-admiralty courts, but they could not logically protest the constitutionality of British trade regulations since they had been in place for more than a century without constitutional challenge and formed the foundation of British imperial policy.

The Anglo-American crisis was fueled largely by a second new imperial policy, which aimed at increasing revenues through the direct taxation of American colonists. The introduction of new taxes, imposed by the British Parliament, provoked violent protest and thorough debate about Parliament's very right to impose taxes and legislation of any kind on the American colonists. In particular, the Stamp Act of 1765 introduced an unprecedented tax on consumption. The British had long practised the imposition of duties and regulations on trade, but the stamp tax was a revenue-raising device that required British government stamps on a wide variety of consumer items. This policy set off a cycle of violent American protests, including the cry 'No taxation without representation', partial British retreat followed by the introduction of new revenue measures, then escalating colonial opposition.

The Stamp Act provoked the first signs of inter-colonial protest in which historians might retrospectively see the initial glimmer of a proto-nationalist movement. Protest leaders quickly called for a Stamp Act Congress with delegates from most of the colonies to organize a collective protest against the tax. Protest groups calling themselves the Sons of Liberty emerged in very similar form and enacted more or less the same kind of theatrical protests in every major city from Boston in Massachusetts down to Savannah in Georgia.

Yet, no sooner did this inter-colonial protest succeed, resulting in the repeal of the Stamp Act by Parliament within a year of its passage (March 1766), than the whole institutional structure of inter-colonial protest quickly melted away. The Sons of Liberty along with the Stamp Act Congress disbanded, and Americans returned to being loyal, obedient British citizens. A sense of common cause had generated the first real inter-colonial cooperative movement in whose language of opposition and conspiracy one might locate the beginnings of American nationalism. But such protest, violent and radical in its implications, remained very much a utilitarian weapon that was brandished not to push the cause of nationhood *outside* the British Empire so much as to advance the American cause *within* it.

According to Albert Hirschman's classic account, people dissatisfied with their relationship to a political state, a firm, or any other human organization calculate the relative costs of 'exit, voice, and loyalty'.[2] Voice, not exit, was the main strategy to which British North American colonists adhered, precisely because the bonds of loyalty and identity with the British Empire made separation an unthinkable alternative. In 1765 even the most radical colonists were intent on restoring traditional liberties within the empire; none dared speak of an American future outside the protection of Britain. The option of independence would come into play only after several more cycles of American protest gave rise to British vacillation and intransigence. First in Boston, later in other parts of the thirteen colonies, colonists saw their choices narrowing to loyalty or exit (independence).

The next cycle of policy and protest came when the British officials, mindful of the arguments against internal taxes but intent on raising revenue from their American colonies, decided to impose new duties on trade. In 1767 Charles Townshend, British Chancellor of the Exchequer, introduced new import duties on glass, lead, paper, paints, and tea. Americans objected that these were not conventional duties whose purpose was to regulate trade, the underlying principle of the Navigation Acts, but were instead taxes in disguise imposed without American consent. Protest over these measures escalated the conflict and inflamed the American rhetoric against the corrupt motives of British officials and their conspiratorial designs to 'enslave' Americans and crush their traditional liberties.

The Townshend duties inadvertently gave the colonists another weapon of protest, and one that had the effect of enlisting in the American cause a broader public outside the merchant elite. This was a consumer boycott that began against the specific items in the Townshend Act, and then became a general embargo against all British imports. Tea was the primary consumer item listed in the Townshend Acts, and it became a mark of American patriotism not to drink British imported tea. Protest meetings, speeches, broadsides, and newspaper articles called upon American colonists to shun British imported goods, boycott merchants who imported them, and buy American-made products. Habits of everyday life affecting diet and clothing had become linked to American patriotism. Drinking tea or wearing fancy dress became a socially scorned sign of submission to British tyranny; wearing American-made clothing and drinking coffee or local herbal teas, in turn, became a proud emblem of patriotic defiance. These non-importation and non-consumption campaigns took on a proto-nationalist tenor as Americans extolled the patriotic virtue of American homespun clothing and denounced British imported finery as effeminate, aristocratic, and, above all, unpatriotic.

The boycott also broadened the popular base of patriotism by enlisting women both in their roles as consumers and as producers. Women organized sewing groups to make clothing, and in cities and towns throughout the colonies they formed local chapters of the Daughters of Liberty, a counterpart to the street demonstrators known as the Sons of Liberty. Boycott leaders lavished praise on women who, by banning tea and forsaking other imported fineries, would convince the British 'that American patriotism extends even to the Fair Sex, and discourage any future Attempts to enslave us'.[3]

The revolution in British North America may present the best example of Benedict Anderson's theory about the abstract idea of a national community first being imagined through print, and in this case imagined as shared opposition against imperial rulers.[4] Not only in print, but also in speeches, street demonstrations, banners, and broadsides, a language of common grievance and patriotic resistance had become formulated and integrated into daily life. A stream of pamphlets and newspaper articles articulated the arguments against each British policy and how it violated American traditions of self-government and taxation by local consent. Literacy rates were unusually high in the British North American colonies, at least among the free white population; estimates range from 70 to 100 per cent of adult white males. A sense of shared grievances against a common adversary, essential ingredients for any nationalist movement, took form in these pre-revolutionary publications well ahead of the military conflict.

Even without the printed word, the British North American protest movement had created a set of images and symbols in banners, flags, engravings, and effigies that provided colonists with vivid symbols of their cause. One of the most famous was

Benjamin Franklin's cartoon depicting a snake cut in pieces labelled New England, New York, South Carolina, et cetera, and the motto: 'Join or Die'. Ironically, Franklin first drew this cartoon in a call for unified American support of the British at the outset of the struggle against the French in 1754. Ten years later, beginning with the Stamp Act protests, various versions of Franklin's 'Join or Die' snake became a common image on flags, posters, and in newspapers—now in calls for unity *against* the British. A similar image on many militia flags showed an American rattlesnake, typically coiled and ready to strike, with the mottos: 'Liberty or Death' and 'Don't Tread on Me'.

Since 1765 a deeply suspicious, even paranoid understanding of the conflict was taking hold in the minds of colonists who saw in British policy a deep design to 'enslave' the colonists. References to British plots to 'enslave' became commonplace in American rhetoric before the Revolution, and no less among southern slaveholders as among New England radicals. British officials interpreted this as unreasonable American hyperbole. There is little in the British debates before 1776 to indicate awareness that they were dealing with anything more than a few quarrelsome colonists who had long been accustomed to running their own affairs and naturally resented the changing order of things. Nor did either side indicate, even after the Declaration of Independence, that the conflict, though very deep and serious, involved irreconcilable alienation or fundamental differences between *peoples*. The British commonly referred to 'Americans' during parliamentary debates and newspaper commentary, but not with any implication that they constituted a distinctive or coherent people. It was simply a geographic qualifier that distinguished British subjects on the other side of the Atlantic.

For their part, most British American colonists sustained strong identification both with Britain and with their colony, but nothing in their experience caused them to see themselves as members of the inter-colonial entity that would be declared in 1776. That changed, especially among elites, during a decade of pre-revolutionary protest when their growing awareness of shared grievances and new inter-colonial cooperation and organization helped foster a proto-national American identity. The persistence of British policy worked to forge a sense of common cause among Americans who might otherwise have continued as disunited and quarrelsome as ever. Still, on both sides of the dispute, there was little awareness that this antagonism was heading toward the independence of the thirteen colonies, until 1776.

British officials were keenly aware of provincial differences and disunity within the colonies, and they underestimated the capacity of their own punitive measures to unify the colonists and incite their rebelliousness. Boston was long the starting point for the most vociferous and troublesome protests, and the British deliberately sought to isolate it and its surrounding region with harsh measures intended to cow the other colonies, if not bring Boston to terms. This had just the opposite effect, for many colonists came to see in Boston a preview of what was in store for all of them if they did not show solidarity with New England. The American motto 'Join or Die' took on more plausible meaning as the British clamped down hard on New England.

During the decade of tumult since 1765, Boston had produced an effective corps of mob leaders and their followers, together with a number of persuasive propagandists who stood ready to interpret every British policy as yet more proof of the tyrannical conspiracy against liberty in the colonies. British persistence, American resistance, and the growing American tendency to interpret obnoxious policies and stubborn leadership as definitive proof of a deep conspiracy, all helped to escalate the tensions on both sides. After the British rescinded all of the Townshend duties, except those on tea, Bostonians dumped a shipload of imported tea into their harbour in 1773. The British retaliated with the Coercive Acts, which included provisions to shut down the port, ban all local government assemblies in Massachusetts, protect British officials accused of crimes from trial in Massachusetts, and require all colonies to quarter British troops at their expense.

Armed conflict began in April 1775 when British forces stationed in Boston advanced toward Concord, a few miles in the interior, to destroy an arsenal they learned was being assembled there. Local citizens had formed armed militia units, styled 'Minutemen', and they assembled on 19 April to meet the advancing British troops. A brief skirmish on the town commons of Lexington that morning resulted in the slaying of several Minutemen by British troops. Later that morning, at Concord's North Bridge, the British encountered resistance and decided to retreat to Boston. American militia swarmed over the retreating British troops during a long, bloody day of sniper fire and skirmishes. A few weeks later, the British met with another military disaster trying to dislodge American militia from an arsenal outside Boston. The Battle of Bunker Hill on 17 June 1775 was the first full-pitched military engagement between American and British forces, and the American victory surprised both sides. British forces withdrew from Boston early in 1776 and redeployed to New York with a revised strategy that involved isolating New England, occupying the middle and southern colonies, and appealing to Loyalist support. It was still uncertain that this was the beginning of a sustained war and it was by no means clear that the stakes involved independence for the thirteen colonies.

The turn toward independence was influenced by the power of agitators who interpreted events and pointed to British aggression as clear proof that no peaceful solution was at hand. None were more influential in the recalculation of loyalty than Thomas Paine and his immensely popular pamphlet, *Common Sense*, published in January 1776. Paine had arrived from England a little more than a year earlier, with a checkered career behind him that included dismissal from his post as an excise officer. In London, Paine had met Benjamin Franklin who recognized his penchant for writing and reform and suggested he leave for Philadelphia.

To Paine goes the credit for being the first to set forth publicly a vision of a new American nation and for turning much of his American audience from loyal British subjects into rebel nationalists. It may have been his newness and his obliviousness to differences and conflicts among the thirteen colonies that permitted Paine to imagine America as a nation in the making. He portrayed America as a society set apart from the corrupt ways of the Old World, a refuge for immigrants fleeing European tyranny, an 'asylum for mankind' in his deft phrase. Paine articulated the future nation and its historic mission in ways not even the most visionary colonial patriot dared imagine.

Part of what made Paine's booklet so popular was that he told Americans what they wanted to hear. Full of vitriol and outrage, *Common Sense* made the American case against the British in melodramatic terms that vilified British tyranny and sanctified its American victims. But Paine went well beyond the current limits of discourse by calling for independence, denouncing the king for his role in American oppression, and ridiculing the entire idea of inherited monarchy.

Common Sense was the first widely influential appeal to American national independence. It went through twenty-five editions in its first year of publication alone, and was widely copied in newspapers, read in taverns, and shared among friends. It is arguably one of the best-selling publications of all times, more than 150,000 copies being sold in a population of over 2.5 million.[5] Paine argued forcefully that the British-American conflict was much more than a dispute over taxes and trade regulations, and more than a matter of bad policy and poor leadership. He heralded the beginning of a new American republic that would define itself in opposition to Old World corruption and oppression. Paine set out to demolish all the cautionary arguments against independence and insisted that only by becoming a nation could America end the underlying cause of the conflict with Britain. Much of his argument for independence was based on the pragmatic calculation that by proclaiming American sovereignty, it would transform the Anglo-American conflict from an internal civil war into an international conflict, one in which America could find alliances with other countries.

Paine assaulted traditional ties of loyalty to king and country that until this point had prevented so many Americans from even considering independence. He challenged the British Crown's *right to rule*, not just the fairness of its policies or even the constitutionality of British imperial rule. Up to this point most American protests had assailed Parliament's bad policy and misguided leaders for abusing the king's loyal subjects in America. Paine now launched a direct attack on the king as the main source of British misrule of the American colonies. Though he avoided personal attacks on King George III (who goes unmentioned by name in *Common Sense*), he ridiculed the entire principle of hereditary rule on which all monarchs' authority rested. Most dynasties could be traced back to the 'principal ruffian of some restless gang . . . chief among plunderers'. 'One of the strongest natural proofs of the folly of hereditary right in Kings, is that nature disapproves it,' Paine observed, 'otherwise she would not so frequently turn it into ridicule, by giving mankind an ASS FOR A LION'.

Paine assaulted the traditional acceptance of social hierarchy as something natural and perpetual, and he applied the same irreverence for the existing order of things to national affairs. Britain would not always be superior to America either in population or in power, he proposed: 'there is something very absurd, in supposing a continent to be perpetually governed by an island'.

Paine also cast America's future as an inspiring model that people everywhere would strive to emulate. It would be a republic, free of monarchy and aristocracy, and one that others would see both as a refuge from Old World tyranny they could flee to and as a beacon of hope for restoring liberty to their own lands. 'Every spot of the old world is overrun with oppression,' he wrote. 'Freedom hath been hunted round the globe. Asia, and Africa, have long expelled her.—Europe regards her like a stranger, and England hath given her warning to depart. O! receive the fugitive, and prepare in time an asylum for mankind.' 'We have it in our power to begin the world over again.'

It was Paine who urged a formal manifesto of independence be issued, and by July 1776 the Declaration of Independence carried out this idea. Much of the Declaration echoed Paine's rhetoric: it employed the Enlightenment notion of natural rights and the right to revolution whenever such rights are abused. Though it placed primary responsibility on the king for Britain's 'long train of abuses' against the colonies, nothing in the Declaration decried monarchy per se nor anticipated an American commitment to any particular form of government. Nor did the Declaration suggest that the conflict between America and Britain was rooted in fundamental antagonisms between peoples, or even in insurmountable problems of distance. The US Declaration of Independence does not seem to fit the usual mold of a nationalist document proclaiming nationhood as essential to peoplehood, yet it would become the template for hundreds of similar independence movements that followed.

If nationalism was more the child than parent of the independence movement in British North America, that young and unsteady child was now burdened with responsibilities that seemed to many far beyond its capacity. Achieving independence and building a durable national state proved to be a long and uncertain ordeal. The armed struggle dragged on until 1781, and the final peace treaty followed in 1783. The British sought to drive wedges into every crack in the fragile North American society, not least by offering amnesty and protection to Loyalists, and freedom to slaves who would take up arms against their masters. Loyalists made up about one in five of the white population, about 500,000 according to the best estimates of recent historians. A much smaller group, about 80,000, fled to Canada during or after the Revolution.[6] The social origins of Loyalist opposition varied from one local context to another, but the impulse to oppose independence drew from a combination of material interests in the perpetuation of British rule and the sheer horror of revolutionary social upheaval. Though at each extreme the identity of Patriots and Loyalists was strong, there were large numbers in between who were cautious and no doubt calculating about their commitment to either side and remained vacillating in their loyalties throughout the conflict. When the British army invaded New Jersey, for example, hundreds of Americans accepted their offer of amnesty and declared their loyalty to the Crown. When American forces under George Washington regained control, many found themselves in the perilous gap between patriotic adherence to the new nation and loyalty to the former. The British overestimated the strength of Loyalist support outside New England, for they were counting on Loyalists to oppose the Revolution and join forces with them. In Virginia royal governor Lord Dunmore offered freedom to all slaves of Patriot masters if they would join what came to be known as Dunmore's Ethiopian Regiment. Hundreds of slaves acted on this offer, and it terrified many southern slave owners who now saw the Revolution opening up the genuine possibility of massive slave unrest. Though Dunmore's plan was foiled by the ravages of disease, the weapon of slavery laid waiting for future application.

In the first major American victory of the war, British troops were forced to surrender at Saratoga, New York, in October 1777. Early in 1778 the French, who had been calculating the verdict of the battlefield, now joined in alliance with the United States. Soon the British launched a new southern military strategy that involved capturing Charleston, invading South Carolina, and sweeping northward to Virginia. The British expected strong support from slave-owning Loyalists and runaway slaves, thousands of whom fled to British lines during the invasion. But Loyalist support proved indecisive, and Patriot forces utilized guerrilla tactics to thwart British gains in the South. The British retreated to Yorktown, Virginia, where in October 1781 American and French forces surrounded them and forced a surrender. The military struggle was essentially finished at Yorktown, though peace negotiations dragged on until late in 1783 with final approval by the United States in early 1784.

Meanwhile, the political apparatus of the newly minted nation remained weak. Soon after the Declaration, what it referred to as the 'united States of America' formulated the Articles of Confederation (1777) as the constitution for the central government, which was now empowered to finance the war and represent the collective interests of the thirteen states in domestic and international affairs. A deep distrust of strong central government and disputes over how the states should apportion taxes and voting crippled the national government. Washington's army was woefully under-supplied, starving, and ill-equipped; it came dangerously close to outright mutiny more than once. However, a combination of timely victories, effective propaganda, French support, and the incalculable advantage of fighting against an invading army on native soil, combined to favour the eventual success of the United States. After 1781 many diehard Loyalists felt compelled to flee for Canada, which diminished at least one important counterforce to national unity.

But victory and independence did as much to undermine as consolidate nationalist feeling in the United States. Some considered the central government more like a military alliance than a coherent and enduring nation, and many were prepared to abandon it and let the states go their separate ways after 1783. Many pointed to fundamental economic and social differences among the thirteen states that would prevent coherence under one government. Some predicted that they would break up over conflicts dealing with western lands or over economic differences between the plantation South and the mercantile interests of the North.[7]

The union of states held together until 1860 in large part because of the fear that fragmentation would come at higher risk than continued union. Moreover, the original thirteen states rapidly multiplied as the US expanded its domain into the Mississippi Valley and to the Pacific Ocean within a few decades. One unifying element was the ongoing presence of rival foreign powers surrounding the young nation. The British had no intention of giving up their claims to North America and continued to attempt to limit, if not roll back, US expansion, most notably during the War of 1812. The French under Napoleon briefly threatened to reestablish a French American empire in Louisiana and the Caribbean before deciding to sell their remaining North American territory to the US in 1803. During the American Civil War (1861–5) both Britain and

France schemed to reestablish their power in North America, most notably with France's establishment of a puppet regime in Mexico. The ongoing threat from hostile European powers served as a counterforce to internal divisions among the states during the first half of the nineteenth century.

Another important source of nationalist feeling was the deliberate effort by cultural nationalists, educators, clergy, and politicians to inculcate in the American mind a sense of national identity and purpose. Long after independence, the US remained culturally dependent on Britain. Especially after the War of 1812 nationalists, such as the philosopher and essayist Ralph Waldo Emerson, called upon Americans to establish their cultural independence through artistic and intellectual expression. In this endeavour, the history of the struggle for independence, the battles, military heroes, and the Founding Fathers of the nation became the most important wellspring of national identity. When the Union ultimately did break apart in the 1860s, it was telling that President Abraham Lincoln summoned Americans to the cause of Union, and slave emancipation, as the completion of the American Revolution.

Nearly two generations were to separate the beginning of the independence struggles in British North America from those in Ibero-America. What accounts for this lag? While the demonstration effect of the British anti-colonial movement was certainly important in the Spanish and Portuguese overseas realms, the French Revolution (1789–94) was even more so, and it took time for the ripples of Europe's Napoleonic wars to swamp the Iberian monarchies and work their way across the Atlantic. Furthermore, the ethnic and social divisions *within* the Spanish and Portuguese colonies militated against the formation of even fragile and fleeting anti-colonial popular alliances until a sudden shock to the imperial system—Napoleon's invasion of the Iberian Peninsula—posed a profound question of where colonial loyalties lay, and how far they could be stretched without snapping. Finally, the peculiarly confederative nature of the Spanish Empire, in particular, meant that when imperial political structures were shaken at their foundations, autonomy within the universal Spanish monarchy was the first posture to be adopted by American Spaniards, only later to give way to Creole ambitions for definitive independence when metropolitan intransigence put the question to the test of force.

Spanish America and Brazil

The political life of the new states of Spanish and Portuguese America during the nineteenth century strongly suggests that the shared horizontality of vision commonly believed to be an essential element in national identification among citizens was very slow to develop in most of Latin America, and was certainly little in evidence in the movements for independence at the start of the century. Strong centrifugal tendencies materialized in the form of federalist-centralist struggles, as in Mexico and Argentina, even while these conflicts might be accompanied by patriotic discourses, and by the carping of intellectuals intent on evangelizing for the linkage between modernization and nationalism. Loyalties to the clan, natal village, or town, or even region, seem to have been stronger than those to the new national units, although when this changed is hard to determine. There is much to be said for the arrival of the railroads all over Latin America after about mid-century in deepening market relationships and therefore national integration, opening the possibilities of travel and exposure to a 'national space' for individuals, extending the policing and propagandistic capacities of the state, and in general reducing the friction of distance. Warfare against neighbouring states, and the accompanying mass mobilizations of militia and regular armies, played their roles in consolidating a nationalist sensibility among common people, even those living in isolated areas. The Mexican-American War (1846–8), the War of the Triple Alliance (1864–70) pitting Paraguay against the coalition of Argentina, Brazil, and Uruguay, and the War of the Pacific (1879–83), between Chile and a Peru-Bolivia alliance, for example, did as much to foment Mexicanness, Paraguayanness, or Peruvianness as any policy that the respective states might consciously have adopted. The full arsenal of nation-making instruments—the telegraph, the spread of print media and literacy, schooling and textbooks, uniform national celebrations and historical monuments, nationalist historiography, and so forth—were turned to the cause of nation-building immediately after independence was achieved, although they were limited by technological and fiscal constraints and came into their own only in the late nineteenth or early twentieth centuries. Still, as late as the early twentieth century it is likely that most Andean peasants living in the highlands knew or cared little about the fate of the nation in which they occupied a status of diminished citizenship. And when the good works done by President Lázaro Cárdenas (r. 1934–40), known widely as *Tata* (Father) Lázaro, were remembered almost raptly by Mexican rural people in the 1930s, and even long after his death, it is likely that their veneration for him echoed at least distantly the messianic sentiment focused by humble people on the absent Spanish King Ferdinand VII ('*El Deseado*', 'The Longed-for One') during the insurgency of 1810–21, as direct protector of the poor and Indians, rather than an appreciation of Cárdenas's role as a public servant of the Mexican nation. As in British North America, especially among common people a national sensibility was more the product of independence than its cause.[8]

Absent a widespread and deeply rooted sense of national identification, therefore, before the onset of the independence process, how is that process to be explained? If there was at least some sense of an 'imagined' national community either before or following independence, was it localized according to social and geographic divisions? How are political factors to be related to economic and social changes in the Iberian colonies and the protracted episodes of large-scale violence that separated them from the mother countries? What was the mix in the various American regions between exogenous and endogenous factors leading to sustained political violence, organized rebellion, and ultimately to independence?

The question of exogenous versus endogenous causal factors is easiest to answer, albeit schematically, insofar as the externalities are concerned. Hovering over all the processes of independence in Ibero-America was the long shadow of the French Revolution, not only in ideological and political terms, but also in the history of the hemisphere itself. Although the Caribbean region does not otherwise play a major role in this account of national independence movements in the Americas, the slave uprising and revolution on the French sugar island of St Domingue, which began in 1791 and concluded with the independence of Haiti in 1804, had a far-reaching influence in all the American independence movements that followed. A direct outgrowth of the French Revolution, the Haitian revolution (along with earlier large-scale indigenous uprisings in the Andean region) frightened Spanish Creole autonomy—and independence-minded elites (and also those of Brazil, where the slave population was proportionally even larger) with the spectre of mass social violence by people of colour. This prompted them to withhold their support after 1808 from a number of popular movements in the colonies—as in New Spain, for example—that might otherwise have garnered their alliance against the colonial regime. The Anglo-American colonies, of course, had already had their revolution and established a new republican state and constitution before 1791. But the events in St Domingue, particularly the large-scale massacre of white people and the destruction of the island's plantation economy, strongly influenced discussions of governmental forms in the fledgling United States. Events in Haiti alarmed the attitudes of the southern elite groups who so dominated the public life of the new nation. The political dimensions of citizenship—who was to be a citizen and who was not—and thinking about racial difference in the new nation also reflected the Caribbean upheaval. The Haitian episode, in fact, points to one of the chief questions of the independence and post-independence eras bearing on the development of national sensibilities in the new polities: how was the intersection of race, citizenship, and class to be dealt with, and beyond that how inclusive was the idea of the 'nation' to be?[9]

Long before the advent of the French Revolution, however, since the opening of the New World, the rivalries among European powers had been habitually played out in colonial theatres (one thinks, for example, of the papal arbitration embodied in the Treaty of Tordesillas in 1494 to establish Portuguese and Spanish spheres of domination, at the very dawn of the Columbian enterprise; or of the later privateering of Sir Francis Drake while England and Spain headed toward war nearly a century later). But these rivalries became more overt, more heated, and extended even to a continental scale (for example, the Seven Years War, 1756–63) in the eighteenth century, both growing out of events in Europe itself, and exacerbated by them. The virtual bankruptcy of the French monarchy arising from its intervention in the American Revolution, which in turn laid the groundwork for the French Revolution, the rise of Napoleon, Bonaparte's strategic 1808 invasion of the Iberian Peninsula and usurpation of the Spanish Crown, and the flight of the entire Portuguese court to Brazil, led to the crisis of Spanish monarchical institutions and legitimacy in particular, and the eventual breakaway over about two decades of most of the New World possessions of Spain and Portugal. Furthermore, the shock waves directly set off in the Spanish metropolis by the violence of the French Revolution itself resonated loudly in the colonies, provoking reactions by colonials against government measures intended to suppress revolutionary contagion of all kinds. These measures included zealous efforts to exclude from the colonies subversive writings (a long-standing practice in a system that leaked like a sieve, anyway), the building up of military forces in key colonial areas, the investment of public funds in improving Spanish naval and military capabilities on a worldwide scale, and an increase in public security vigilance aimed at neutralizing real and imagined conspiracies against royal rule.

Finally, the convocation in French-occupied Spain of a parliament (*Cortes*) under the protection of British naval power in the southwestern city of Cádiz (1810), with the inclusion of at least some American deputies, laid bare the issues of imperial adjustment within the universal Spanish monarchy in the absence of the king, Ferdinand VII. These included the forms and proportionality of American representation, what degree of autonomy the overseas kingdoms would enjoy, whether there was to be a written constitution to constrain the powers of the monarchy when it should be restored, et cetera. This body was to develop a charter (the constitution of Cádiz, 1812) for monarchical Spain and its overseas realms that included some liberal elements, and was briefly applied to several of the colonies (most notably New Spain, largely ignored in Peru) before it was abrogated by Ferdinand VII on his restoration to power in 1814. Not only did the enactment of this constitution change the political ground rules in the Spanish New World colonies, at least briefly, but its suppression after only a few months (it would be reinstated briefly between 1820 and 1823 when a military rebellion in Spain itself forced Ferdinand VII to swear allegiance to it once more) also created widespread ill feeling among the politically aware in the overseas possessions, and the charter served as a model for post-independence republican experiments among the former colonies.

Much of the 1812 constitution, it is true, grew from an indigenous political tradition in Spain itself going back at least to the sixteenth century, including ideas of residual popular sovereignty, compactual agreements between monarch and people, and the right to resist tyranny. But although in traditional interpretations of Latin American independence the role of Enlightenment ideas from the rest of Europe has been somewhat exaggerated, they did filter into Spain, Portugal, and their New World dominions. This thinking stimulated movements for curricular reform in Ibero-American universities and the application (or at least the discussion) of selected elements of the new political economy (beginning with Adam Smith's work) to trans-Atlantic commerce and colonial economic development. There came to exist in general an atmosphere of intellectual ferment in which the eyes of the educated elites of Spanish America and Brazil turned increasingly toward a greater Atlantic world. The great Venezuelan independence leader Simón Bolívar (1783–1830), for example, travelled widely in Europe beginning in 1799, was much impressed by what he saw there, and later ardently espoused republican ideas of an essentially classical type. A few years earlier a republican, pro-independence plot in the Brazilian colony (the 'Tiradentes' conspiracy of 1789) invoked the works of Jean-Jacques Rousseau, which circulated widely in the New World colonies despite strict prohibitions; the French revolutionary

Declaration of the Rights of Man was to be printed by Colombian independence leader Antonio Nariño (1765–1823) in 1794; and the parish of Dolores, in central Mexico, presided over by Father Miguel Hidalgo y Costilla (1753–1811), the father of Mexican independence, was known as 'Little France' because of the curate's public pronouncements and reading propensities. There really was no figure in the Ibero-American Atlantic world, however, equivalent in passion and reach of influence to Thomas Paine in the Anglo-American colonies. With few exceptions the great figures of Spanish American independence did not survive to develop through writing, public debate, and policy measures their ideas about republicanism, political economy, and national identity in the manner of Hamilton, Jefferson, Adams, Madison, and others. It is nonetheless undeniable that the effects of demonstration and intellectual ferment in the North Atlantic world during the Age of Revolution affected Spanish and Portuguese America.

Closer to the core workings of the Spanish Empire, although still to be counted among the exogenous factors, was the problem of realizing more revenues from the colonies, especially as Spain was recurrently embroiled in her French alliance and therefore opposed to the British (Brazil had been a British client state since the Methuen Treaty of 1703), after the accession of the Bourbons to the Spanish throne in the early eighteenth century. The British captured Havana in 1762, near the close of the Seven Years War, and held it for nearly a year, opening the port and notably stimulating commerce in ways still being eschewed by Spanish policy. About the same time there was a good deal of internal critique within Spain focused upon the creaky political, economic, and administrative system of the empire, pushing the Spanish monarchy to embark on a program of defensive modernization. One of the central features of this project was the piecemeal promulgation of the so-called Bourbon Reforms in the New World colonies, a largely inchoate set of economic and political reform measures intended to stimulate the silver-mining industry in Mexico and Peru, expand trade, increase fiscal receipts, fend off European rivals, and so forth. These initiatives included broader, deeper, and more efficient taxation (for example, the rationalization of the tribute system embracing Indians and people of mixed race), the establishment of lucrative Crown monopolies (on tobacco products, for example), and the institution of the French-inspired intendancy system in government along with the creation of new units of territorial administration. Furthermore, the Spanish monarchy placed at least small standing-army units in the colonies, initiated regalist policies directed not only against the Church hierarchy but also intended to purge popular forms of religious ritual of their more florid and undecorous Baroque elements, and eventually decreed a tentative and incremental opening of the trading system beginning in 1778.

Reforms instituted in Portugal's Brazilian colony during the ministry of the Marquis of Pombal (r. 1750–77) paralleled in some ways those in the Spanish American realms. Taxes were rationalized and tightened, the trading system made more advantageous for merchants in the metropolis (to the cost of Brazilians), manufactures in the colony severely discouraged, the Jesuit order expelled (1759–60), and the border with Spain's territories settled and made less porous, among other measures. The policies bear some resemblance to those imposed by the British Crown on the North American colonists during roughly the same time, arising from the same set of circumstances of European rivalries—policies famously resisted as 'tyrannous' by many colonial groups under the banner of 'No taxation without representation!'

While events in the larger system of European colonies and power relations, both long and short term, must therefore be accorded great weight in the advent of independence movements in the Ibero-American colonies, endogenous factors also prepared the ground for what happened after 1808 or so, although it is risky to interpret the response to them as having forged a proto-national sensibility in the overseas realms. Here local or regional traditions of uprising or smaller-scale popular protest played a role, if not as direct precursors to the independence movements, then certainly as establishing a modality of 'bargaining by riot' to reestablish disequilibrated political and fiscal balances within an absolute monarchy. In other words, the repertoire of political behaviour that would be drawn upon during the wars of independence, particularly by indigenous people in the Andean and Mesoamerican regions, was already well established by centuries of practice. Areas within Spanish America where indigenous populations remained densest after their recovery from the early colonial hecatomb of disease-induced mortality, during which up to 90 per cent of the contact populations perished, developed a tradition of uprisings, some of them strongly marked with millenarian-messianic beliefs and associated 'world-turned-upside-down' scenarios projecting the end of Spanish rule and the return of native monarchs and deities.

Although these episodes began immediately in the wake of the conquest (for example, the Taki Onqoy or 'dancing sickness' native movement in the Peruvian highlands in the mid-sixteenth century, and similar contemporaneous outbursts in Mexico), they reached something of a crescendo in the late colonial period. Mexico saw the Tzeltal Rebellion in the Chiapas area (1712–13) and the Jacinto Canek uprising in Yucatán (1761), mobilizations involving thousands of primarily indigenous peasants, not to mention the nearly 150 well-documented incidents of collective violence ranging from local riots to mini-rebellions that dusted the central and southern parts of the colony, many of them in the last decades of the eighteenth century. In the Andes the Juan Santos Atahualpa movement (1742) initiated what has been called 'the age of pan-Andean rebellion', wracking the interior parts of the Peruvian highlands with violence in the 1740s. The early 1780s, however, saw an even larger uprising of indigenous people led by José Gabriel Condorcanqui, who called himself Tupac Amaru, claimed lineage from the last of the Inca sovereigns, and initiated an anti-Spanish insurrection that eventually embraced hundreds of thousands of Peruvian and Bolivian highlanders. Although the uprising found some allies among non-Indians, its fearful anti-Spanish violence was underwritten by a complex ideological amalgam of Christian and native religious beliefs. Among these were Indian irredentism, racial antagonism, resistance to economic exploitation by whites, and paradoxically a reverence for the distant Spanish monarch who, it was widely believed, would surely take steps to correct injustices suffered by his native subjects if only he knew what his corrupt colonial officials were doing. The Tupac Amaru uprising was still invoked both by loyalist authorities and the rebellious Creole elite thirty years later in the Andean area and in New Spain as an example of the destructive force of popular rebellion by non-whites, much as the St Domingue slave uprising of a decade later played the role of a bogeyman during the movements for independence.

Nor were economic and social stressors absent from the generalized scenario of inter-ethnic antagonism, even if they were unevenly distributed over the vast Ibero-American realms. During the late eighteenth century indigenous people, in particular, were under pressure from domestic, commercial agricultural economies in the colonies expanding to meet the requirements of growing cities and some export activities, tensions most often translated into conflicts over land between peasant villages and the market-oriented estates known as haciendas or plantations. In some areas of New Spain, for example, these conflicts were endemic and violent, could last for many decades, and pitted village against village, peasant against estate owner, landlord against landlord. Rising prices for goods of wide popular consumption (maize and other cereals, for example), growing population in the countryside, and increasing commercialization combined to create potentially Malthusian pressures in which nominal wages were stable and real wages dropped—in the Mexican case as much as 25 per cent in the last quarter or so of the eighteenth century. Lacking sufficient land to produce marketable surpluses, therefore, many rural people withdrew from the market as sellers of agricultural products, in which position they had enjoyed a relative advantage in the seventeenth century, only to re-enter it in the eighteenth as sellers of wage labour whose value was increasingly discounted by market forces. Furthermore, institutionalized forms of colonial exploitation of indigenous people and other groups of commoners (the so-called *castas*), such as the notorious *reparto de mercancías*, drained resources from the countryside, pressing ever more heavily upon subsistence economies already close to the line. Particularly fierce in the Andean highlands but widely known elsewhere, as well, the *reparto* worked through the forcible sale by local royal officials with commercial backers of manufactured goods and livestock at inflated prices, unloading on rural people items they could ill afford and would probably not have purchased had they not been coerced to do so. Although the independence movements in most areas of Ibero-America were not to feature strong elements of agrarian redress or redistributive programs (with some exceptions noted below), these stressors certainly created something like a political hyper-sensitivity that helped to energize ethnic and political conflict.

None of these political, economic, or ideological forces individually, nor all of them in combination, however, were sufficient to forge that sense of an inclusive, horizontal identification we have come to think essential to national sensibility, and whose seeds Benedict Anderson famously located in *the origins* of the Spanish American independence movements rather than among their consequences.[10] Among the secondary elite groups who generally led the movements—the white lawyers, professional men, town councilmen, landowners, priests, militia officers, and others—one sees at most what has been called 'Creole patriotism'. This loose ideological position consisted of an attachment to the colonial homeland compounded of sentimentality, invented and embellished collective memories, some elements of class solidarity and the need to maintain domination over humbler people, and economic interests that diverged increasingly from the metropolis. One major source of Creole patriotism in the political sphere was the weakness of the Iberian crowns in the seventeenth century (they were joined between 1580 and 1640). This reduced state capacity arose from political and military overcommitments in Europe, state fiscal mismanagement, flagging dynastic energies, and in the case of Spanish America the decline of treasure remissions from the silver mines of New Spain and Peru. Always implicit in the long distances and difficult communications between Europe and the New World realms, the degree of colonial autonomy from the metropoli had increased as administrative control over the colonies flagged, public offices were auctioned to ambitious Creoles to fill emptying royal coffers, and the colonists' sense grew that they could handle their own affairs without supporting the imperial overhead costs they felt weighed upon them excessively. The expulsion in 1654 of the Dutch interlopers who had occupied some of the richest areas of the northeastern Brazilian sugar littoral for a generation, for example, was achieved almost exclusively by the Portuguese planters and their domestic forces, leaving in its wake a new-found sense of competence and autonomy. A second major source of Creole patriotism was the burgeoning sense of difference between New World and Old World Spaniards, American and European nature, and of culture more generally. This was nourished in large measure by reaction to European claims of superiority over the New World, and by the nostalgic and patriotic natural and political histories of the Spanish American realms, published in their exile by the generation of Jesuit intellectuals expelled in the 1760s from both Portuguese and Spanish America, in keeping with the regalist policies of enlightened monarchy.

Finally, after the mid-eighteenth century, reforms were initiated by the Marquis of Pombal in Portuguese Brazil, as we have seen, to increase the economic benefits flowing to the metropolis. A succession of Bourbon ministers in the Spanish dominions, among them the famous José de Gálvez, reasserted political controls by wresting the slackening reins of trans-Atlantic government from American Spaniards, and extracting more wealth from the colonies, a need that became ever more critical as the costs of warfare escalated during the Napoleonic era. These policies affected different social groups differently, so that linking them directly to the impulse for independence is difficult. Among Spanish American Creoles, for example, the incremental replacement of native-born ecclesiastical, political, and administrative officials by peninsular Spaniards was collectively regarded in many quarters as constituting a second conquest, a painful disenfranchisement that in part gave rise to calls for colonial autonomy in the initial phases of the post-1808 political environment. Among all groups the increased rates of fiscal extraction—the closing of loopholes in the indigenous tribute system, for instance—signified the violation of a colonial pact, a sort of colonial moral economy felt to keep exploitation of the overseas realms within reasonable limits in exchange for loyalty to the universal Spanish monarchy. The Pombaline reforms in Brazil produced similar though more muted effects. Issues of taxation as such were less prominently discussed in the Iberian than in the British North American colonies because the mechanisms of protest—provincial legislative bodies, chiefly—were non-existent beyond the municipal level. In the Spanish and Portuguese colonies many of these policies were bitterly resented by elite groups who had come to think of themselves as Americans, but not yet as Mexicans, Colombians, Peruvians, Argentines, or Brazilians.

Although racist categories were in practice somewhat porous in the New World, the chief cultural barrier to the horizontal imagining characteristic of a national sensibility was the ethnic difference between white Creoles and the people of colour who made up the vast majority of the populace—indigenous groups, the growing sector of mixed-race population, and freed and enslaved Africans and their descendants. These were the people whose labour formed the basis of the colonial economy, and whose emergence into political life through forms of mediated citizenship, the vote, and an increasing awareness of their own human value was one of the major problems of nation-making to be solved during the decades following independence. Among popular groups, and especially the Indians who at the end of the colonial era still made up the majority of the total population in Mesoamerica and the Andean region, and lower but still important percentages elsewhere, feelings of racial fear, mistrust, and otherness reciprocal to those of American-born whites posed a nearly insuperable obstacle to the formation of a nationalist fellow-feeling. Rates of monolingual speech among indigenous peoples were very elevated in many regions, and rates of literacy correspondingly low. The literacy skills of adult males reached perhaps 10 per cent overall in New Spain, probably less in the Andes, and were higher in the Rio de la Plata, as opposed to an estimated 70 to 90 per cent among adult men in British North America. Educational opportunities long remained very limited (village-supported rural schools barely functioned in many places, and were unknown in many others) and printing not widespread, with the exception of major cities. Under such conditions the reach of print media in fostering an imagined horizontal community, the most important element in Benedict Anderson's well-known formulation, remained severely limited. Physical mobility was limited, so that most Indian peasants lived within circumscribed political and knowledge horizons emphasizing localism, loyalty to the natal ethnic village, and an intense piety focused on local religious cults (village patron saints, for example) and celebratory life. Certainly there was considerable regional variation in this situation, and some general factors operating to attenuate it. Information from the urban world or from abroad, including insurgent propaganda, was not limited to what one could read oneself, but might travel along chains of oral transmission from city to countryside and back again. Furthermore, widespread market relations reduced the chronic isolation of village life, and the claims of wage labour, kinship, and other forces drew many people out of their villages over some distances. Still, the double helix of religious sensibility and political community that constituted rural villages was strongly reinforced by ethnic difference and an ancient racist discourse of Indian inferiority. This posture stressed localism and distrust of outsiders, and naturally restricted the channels of information and mobilization through which many rural people might be drawn into the insurgent cause at all, let alone around the banner of an emergent national sensibility. The way this worked out on the ground in Mexico between 1810 and 1821, for example, was that while indigenous people did engage in political violence that sometimes merged with the Creole-directed insurgency, their participation tended to be transitory, their collective behaviour modelled strongly by a pre-insurgency political repertoire (the classic village riot, for instance), and their spatial sphere of action—that is, the reach of their participation—anchored markedly in their villages of birth. Other groups in the colonial population (subject to great regional variation), such as the mixed-blood *mestizos* and people of African origin, were less strongly rooted in village life, their collective identities more malleable. They ranged further, fought longer, and were concomitantly more attached to programmatic pronouncements that eventually foreshadowed ideological, ethnic, and political alliances broader than simple Creole patriotism.

The political crisis triggered in the Anglo-American colonies by late and relatively fortuitous taxation policies finally left the British metropolis untouched, the monarchy intact and poised for the imperialist adventures of the nineteenth century. Parallel events in the Iberian colonies, however, stripped away most of the Spanish and Portuguese empires, forcing the peninsular monarchies to their knees, if not quite yet onto the imperial scrapheap. Napoleon's invasion of the Iberian Peninsula in 1807 and his usurpation of the Spanish throne in the name of his brother Joseph Bonaparte set off a political chain reaction stretching far beyond the guerrilla resistance by Spaniards that ravaged Spain itself for the next several years.[11] When the French armies crossed Spain to Portugal and were already in sight of Lisbon, King João VII fled with the entire Portuguese court to Rio de Janeiro under the protection of a British fleet, remaining there for the next fourteen years and effectively inverting the centuries-long centre-periphery relationship. In the case of Brazilians the familiarity on home ground with the monarchy, and the positive changes the regime wrought in the colonial capital (the encouragement of industries previously prohibited under mercantilist policies, the establishment of schools of higher learning, the freeing-up of the trade system) meant that when dynastic politics forced the king's return to Portugal in 1821, his son Dom Pedro I was able to declare the independence of Brazil in 1822, virtually without bloodshed, as an empire with a dynast of the legitimate ruling house—himself—already in place. Had Ferdinand VII been able to elude Napoleon's grasp and flee to New Spain, Peru, or even Cuba, things in the Spanish colonies might have turned out quite differently. But as it was he remained for many years under house arrest and the French emperor's thumb until restored by domestic loyalists and British expeditionary forces in the Peninsular War (1808–14) under the command of Arthur Wellesley, who would later become the Duke of Wellington.

The counterpoint to the calm of the Brazilian colony was found in the mounting chaos that engulfed the Spanish overseas realms with King Ferdinand's forced abdication and Joseph Bonaparte's usurpation of the Spanish throne. In Spain itself a succession of juntas established by local notables claimed to rule temporarily in the usurped king's name, residual sovereignty eventually coming to be widely recognized among anti-French elements as residing in the Cortes of Cádiz. In Spanish America the situation was a good deal more complicated, which is understandable given the diversity of the colonies. There, too, governing juntas were organized in the major political capitals (Montevideo, 1808; La Paz and Quito, 1809; Caracas, Buenos Aires, and Santiago de Chile, 1810; and so forth), while Peru remained a royalist stronghold for nearly fifteen years. In Mexico City strongly conservative elements among the Spanish merchant and landowner groups staged a pre-emptive coup in the fall of 1808 against a viceroy deemed too sympathetic to rumblings of colonial autonomy among liberal Creole politicians and lawyers whose ostensible loyalties still lay with the absent King Ferdinand. At this early stage the public discourse, and behind it the genuine sentiment, of the Creole political class generally asserted (with a few exceptions) the loyalty of the Spanish realms to the monarchy. What these patriots protested were oppressive colonial policies, the regime of carpet-bagging peninsular officials who had gradually replaced New World-born Spaniards in high governmental and ecclesiastical office during the eighteenth century, and the violation of their rights as Spanish subjects (something akin to the rights of 'free-born Englishmen') equal to those born in Spain itself. The political agenda was quite clearly focused more on an enhanced autonomy within the structure of the universal Catholic monarchy than upon the national independence of the successor states that could be imagined taking shape from the fragments of the empire. This is why the convening of the Cádiz parliament with American deputies, the ensuing elections in the colonies, and the debates over a Spanish constitution provided a political opening eagerly seized upon by perhaps the majority of New World Spaniards.

The ten to fifteen years following the Napoleonic usurpation of the Spanish throne in 1808 saw the Spanish American realms scourged with violence on a vast scale. The deaths in battle of American loyalists, peninsular troops, insurgents, and innocents caught in the crossfire of what often appeared a civil conflict, although significant, figured less in overall mortality than the absence of medical care and the depredations of epidemic disease, all of which affected untold numbers of the 17 million inhabitants of the colonial realms, disproportionately among young men, of course. Equally widespread was destruction of productive capacity in agriculture, mining (the silver mines in Mexico, for example, would not recover their levels of pre-insurgency production for several decades after independence), manufactures (what there were of them, mostly on a small scale), the wreckage of infrastructure, and a rapidly escalating public debt (mostly on the part of debts owed by insurgent governments to the British) that would plague the new states for decades to come. Tough Spanish regular army commanders carried out a *guerre à outrance* against the civil population as well as insurgent armies and guerrilla forces, regularly seized property from people suspected of insurgent sympathies, and extracted forced loans from merchant groups under the putative authority first of the Cádiz government, then of the restored King Ferdinand VII. Along with continually disrupted trans-Atlantic shipping, all this had the effect of eventually alienating many American Spaniards and of undermining the moral, if not the legal, legitimacy of the restored monarchy. These were not auspicious signs under which to establish new states.

On 9 December 1824 insurgent forces under the command of José Antonio de Sucre, a lieutenant of Simón Bolívar, defeated a Spanish loyalist army near Ayacucho, in the Peruvian highlands, thus achieving the independence of Peru and ensuring that of Spanish South America. Much of the region had already effected its freedom from colonial control as early as 1819, forming the new republic of Gran Colombia (the later Colombia, Venezuela, Ecuador, and Panama), and what would later come to comprise Chile, Bolivia, Paraguay, and Argentina. Mexico (as New Spain came to be called) emerged from its independence struggle in 1821 into a short-lived monarchy under the Creole military politician Agustín de Iturbide (Emperor Agustín I—and last), while Central America, falling bloodlessly into independence, came for a time as a unit to form part of Mexico. Although not all the great figures of the Spanish American wars between 1806 and 1824 were necessarily cast in a heroic mold (the various movements had their share of opportunists, criminals, ex-smugglers, and even a few psychopaths), they did eventually consummate the national independence of their regions and furnish the primary material for the mythology upon which nationalism later flourished. One of the peculiarities of Mexican independence was that its two greatest avatars were Catholic priests—Father Miguel Hidalgo y Costilla, a Creole, and his sometime disciple Father José María Morelos y Pavón, a former mule-driver and talented military commander of mixed racial background. In Spanish South America the great figures included Bolívar, whose faith in republican institutions drained away along with his health until his death in 1830; José de San Martín (1778–1850), Bolívar's sometime collaborator and competitor, the liberator of Argentina and Chile; and Bernardo O'Higgins (1778–1842; son of an Irish-born father in Spanish service who had come to be Viceroy of Peru), for a time supreme dictator of Chile. There were even an enterprising foreigner or two, chief among them Thomas Cochrane, 10th Earl of Dundonald (1775–1860), a brilliant Scottish naval commander (and reputedly the model for the fictional Captains Hornblower and Jack Aubrey) who served successively in the navies of Chile and Brazil, and later of Greece during its own independence struggles.

A cultish veneration came to be accorded these men in the family romances of the new nation states. Most of them were white landowners, military politicians (whose counterparts among loyalist Creoles were by no means absent—Iturbide, until his eleventh-hour volte-face in favour of independence for Mexico, being a prime example), lawyers, priests, and even a few intellectuals. But the histories of these mythified figures have come to obscure the role of ordinary people in the wars of liberation and civil conflicts from which the nations of Latin America emerged. Here the story becomes almost incomprehensibly complex. The cracks and schisms in the various insurgencies along ethnic, class, and regional lines make it quite clear that different groups of people had different goals in mind when they picked up their weapons ostensibly to liberate the fatherland(s) from colonial oppression. The imagined community of the nation was essentially a hypertrophied Creole patriotism with little room in it for the people of colour who comprised the majority of the population. The new states confronted enormous obstacles involving economic reconstruction, negotiating the terms of re-entry into the world of sovereign nations as newly independent polities, and the management of huge national debts in the face of reduced or non-existent state fiscal capacity. But the Creole elites that emerged as the directorate of the new states also faced problems of maintaining some sort of social hierarchy and control, of establishing political stability in the face of weak nascent institutions, and of sowing viable, legitimate, but ultimately limited notions of citizenship within the new polities. The problem, in short, was that of stuffing humble people of indigenous and African extraction back into the boxes from which they had burst into the political vacuum during wartime.

Numerous examples existed of movements heavily tinged with class and ethnicity that coalesced with anti-colonial movements but really embodied other social ambitions. These foreshadowed the political conflicts of the post-independence period but had little to do with nation-making themselves, or actually ran counter to it. The case of Mexican Indian villages, for which there is ample evidence that localism and defence of community trumped longings for an imagined national community when they participated in the insurgency, has already been mentioned. Such movements might even be localist, populist, and loyalist at the same time. The famous *llanero* army of the Spanish-born one-time smuggler José Tomás Boves, for instance, composed of mixed-race and working-class men from the interior grasslands (*llanos*) of Venezuela, wreaked havoc on various towns in support of the royalist cause until his death in 1814. Boves's movement was driven primarily by plebeian ambitions for local freedom and property redistribution from wealthy landowners to the poor, in what has been called a 'Venezuelan Vendée'. The llanero chieftain recruited Afro-Venezuelans by promising freedom to slaves who fought to defend the royalist cause, a technique adopted on the opposite side of the struggle, as well (and used by the British in the Anglo-American colonies). Half a continent away, not coincidentally in the great grasslands (*pampas*) of the Río de la Plata, José Artigas came to lead a largely cowboy guerrilla army in the Banda Oriental (what would later become Uruguay) against the Spanish colonial regime. Artigas aimed less at nation-making than a federalist model emphasizing local freedoms, social radicalism, and redistribution of wealth, programmatic elements that would prove anathema to monied and socially well-placed Creole rebels. Nor were these turbulent side-eddies of populist, localist insurgency and counter-insurgency limited to white and mixed-blood leaders. In the old Inca capital of Cuzco, in the Andean highlands, an Indian leader of Inca descent, Mateo Pumacahua, led an anti-Spanish rebellion for several years (until his defeat, trial, and execution in 1815) that at one time captured the important Andean cities of La Paz and Arequipa. Originally encouraged by Creole patriots, the uprising quickly got out of hand, targeting the property of whites in general and claiming to vindicate the political rights of Indians as such, especially their liberation from tribute obligations as prescribed by the 1812 Constitution but later ignored in practice. Similar to indigenous participation in the independence struggles in Mexico, this movement was less about realizing any vision of a nation than about asserting ethnic identity and class interest in a setting of civil conflict.

Concluding Remarks

By the time the United States was emerging as a major power in global terms, at the end of the nineteenth century, most of the Latin American states (with the exception of Brazil, whose slavocratic regime and stable monarchical institutions insulated it from endemic civil conflict) were only beginning to consolidate themselves after three generations of widespread internal political struggles, economic instability, and social tensions. The nature of the independence process itself in the two regions of the Americas accounts for some of this difference, but so do the accidents of geography, resource endowment, cultural traditions, human capital, and relations with the colonial metropoli that kicked off the movements in the first place. Nonetheless, there were important features in common between the two great upheavals. That colonial societies in general tended eventually to diverge in their interests from the metropolitan centres as they matured is a descriptive truism worth keeping in mind. Beyond this, in both the British North American and Ibero-American cases the crises of empire radiating outward from the Euro-Atlantic core provided much of the impulse toward autonomy and eventually independence in the colonial world. Attempts in Britain, Spain, and Portugal to extract more resources from the colonies through fiscal means played a major role in mobilizing groups across the colonial societies and in crystallizing evolving notions that colonial pacts were being violated. The ideals of classical republicanism provided an ideological template for state formation in both cases, while the solvent forces of Enlightenment thinking more generally led colonials to question the structures of authority in many areas of life.

Differences between the British and Iberian regions were also striking. Certainly the historical moment was very different for the Anglo-American colonies, which had no ready model for their revolution, while that same revolution profoundly influenced the Iberian colonies by demonstrating the range of the possibilities in state formation. The thirty-five years intervening between the two independence movements saw the eruption of the French Revolution, an epochal event even more destabilizing to the European and colonial *ancien régime*. The 'rights of free-born Englishmen' were more readily deployed against the exercise of arbitrary monarchical and ministerial power than any notions of Creole rights or residual popular sovereignty in the Iberian overseas realms. This at least partially explains why the impulse for a radical break with Spain took some time to develop beyond initial ideas of autonomy within a reconfigured Spanish monarchy. The vast differences in the social structures of Anglo- and Ibero-American societies, the latter with a far smaller proportion of European to indigenous and African peoples, also tempered enthusiasm for revolutionary rhetoric and state-building, especially in light of the Haitian example. Of major challenges faced by the new nations of both Anglo- and Ibero-America the incorporation of non-European populations into the nation was one, remaining so long after independence was achieved. Another was the legitimization of the new states themselves. Here constitution-making was conspicuously less successful in Spanish America (Brazil, of course, remained a monarchy until very near the close of the nineteenth century) than in the former British colonies. The traditional corporatist forms of social organization characteristic of colonial life (the privileged status of Army and Church, the strength of religious sodalities and guilds, the strong ethnically marked identities of rural communities in many areas) remained largely intact for decades, preserving a mediating stratum of power and loyalty between people and nation states and concomitantly weakening civil society. National cults of patriotism, public celebratory life, and some spread of education worked to attenuate the cellular nature of society in the new polities, and warfare with neighbouring states played its part, as well, in ramping up nationalist sentiments. But the sort of riotous and intense engagement with politics at all levels, and therefore the importance of the nation state as a venue for the performance of political life that Alexis de Tocqueville noted in the young United States, took much longer to develop in Latin America outside the larger urban areas.

The new nations that emerged from the American independence movements offer prime examples of what is by now the familiar adage that nations produce nationalism, not the other way around. More precisely, it was the military, political, and social struggle to achieve independence and the prolonged effort to build the apparatus of state government that required former colonists to forge a new sense of nationhood at least sufficient to wage successful war and constitute new states. Historians of all the new American nations typically emphasize the slow development of national identity, the limited reach of the central government, the persistence of provincial politics and identity, and the marginalization of those outside the European core population. Though all of these symptoms of national weakness bear out in varying degrees in the new American nations, particularly the Spanish American republics, no less remarkable was the capacity of these young nations to endure. All the nations that came into being between 1776 and 1825 continue to exist today, despite a massive civil war in the United States and chronic political instability in many of the Latin American nations.

The creation of these new American states also must be considered a seminal moment in the history of nationalism, one rarely acknowledged by historians who see modern nationalism coming out of the French Revolution. Though many scholars of nationalism have debated Benedict Anderson's ideas about the central importance of 'print culture' to imagining the national community, far less attention has been given to his suggestion that the new American nations served as '*creole* pioneers' for the modern age of nationalism: 'Not only were they historically the first such states to emerge on the world stage, and therefore inevitably provided the first real models of what such states should "look like," but their numbers and contemporary births offer fruitful ground for comparative enquiry.' In the new nations of the Americas, he continued, 'a "model" of "the" independent national state was available for pirating'. Whether

American independence movements inspired or followed European nationalist movements is less important than our understanding that all were part of a broad trans-Atlantic exchange of ideas, people, and state models that marked the first epoch in the history of modern nationalism.

Notes

1. E. Burke (1834) 'Speech for Conciliation with the Colonies', given in the House of Commons 22 March 1775, *The Works of the Right Hon. Edmund Burke*, London, I: 186.
2. A. O. Hirschman (1970) *Exit, Voice, and Loyalty: Responses to Decline in Firms, Organizations, and States*, Cambridge, MA.
3. W. Tennent, III (1774) 'To the Ladies of South Carolina', *South Carolina Gazette*, 2 August, quoted in Mary Beth Norton (1980) *Liberty's Daughters: The Revolutionary Experience of American Women, 1750–1800*, New York, 159.
4. B. Anderson (1991, 1983) *Imagined Communities: Reflections on the Origin and Spread of Nationalism*, London. (A third edition was published in 2006.)
5. E. Foner (2005) *Tom Paine and Revolutionary America*, New York, 79.
6. R. Middlekauf (2005, 1985) *The Glorious Cause: The American Revolution, 1763–1789*, New York, 63–4.
7. J. Greene (2006) 'State and National Identities in the Era of the American Revolution', in D. H. Doyle and M. A. Pamplona (eds.) *Nationalism in the New World*, Athens, GA.
8. For a discussion of Latin American nationalism in the nineteenth and twentieth centuries, see Chapter 19 in this volume by Nicola Miller, 'Latin America: State-Building and Nationalism'.
9. For the fears of Creoles, both loyalists and revolutionaries, of mass uprisings by people of colour in light of the events during the Haitian revolution at the end of the century, see R. Graham (1994) *Independence in Latin America: A Comparative Approach*, 2nd edn., New York, 59 (Brazil), 149 (Cuba), 46 (Venezuela), and 34–5 (Spanish America in general); J. E. Rodríguez O. (1998) *The Independence of Spanish America*, Cambridge, 116, 122, 163; and more generally, D. P. Geggus (ed.) (2001) *The Impact of the Haitian Revolution in the Atlantic World*, Columbia, SC. For a recent treatment of the Haitian revolution itself, see L. Dubois, (2004) *Avengers of the New World: The Story of the Haitian Revolution*, Cambridge, MA.
10. On B. Anderson's ideas concerning the 'imagined community' specifically in relation to the Latin American independence movements, in addition to the essay by C. Lomnitz cited in Nicola Miller's Chapter 19 in this volume, see E. Van Young (2006) 'A Nationalist Movement without Nationalism: The Limits of Imagined Community in Mexico, 1810–1821', in D. Cahill and B. Tovías (eds.) *New World, First Nations: Native Peoples of Mesoamerica and the Andes under Colonial Rule*, Brighton, 218–51.
11. See Chapter 7 by Michael Rowe in this volume dealing with nationalism in Napoleonic Europe.

Suggested Further Reading

The United States

Albanese, C. L. (1976) *Sons of the Fathers: The Civil Religion of the American Revolution*, Philadelphia.
Armitage, D. (2007) *The Declaration of Independence: A Global History*, Cambridge, MA.
Breen, T. H. (1997) 'Ideology and Nationalism on the Eve of the American Revolution: Revisions Once More in Need of Revising', *Journal of American History*, 84, no. 1, 13–39.
Doyle, D. H. and Pamplona, M. A. (2006) *Nationalism in the New World*, Athens, GA.
Greene, J. P. (1993) *The Intellectual Construction of America: Exceptionalism and Identity from 1492 to 1800*, Chapel Hill, NC.
Greenfeld, L. (1992) *Nationalism: Five Roads to Modernity*, Cambridge, MA.
Kammen, M. G. (1978) *A Season of Youth: The American Revolution and the Historical Imagination*, New York.
Lipset, S. M. (1963) *The First New Nation: The United States in Historical and Comparative Perspective*, New York.
Middlekauf, R. (1982, 2005) *The Glorious Cause: The American Revolution, 1763–1789*, rev. edn., New York.
Morgan, E. (1977) *The Birth of the Republic, 1763–89*, Chicago, IL.
Murrin, J. M. (1987) 'A Roof without Walls: The Dilemma of American National Identity', in *Beyond Confederation: Origins of the Constitution and American National Identity*, ed. R. Beeman, S. Botein, and E. C. Carter, II, Chapel Hill, NC.
Norton, M. B. (1980) *Liberty's Daughters: The Revolutionary Experience of American Women, 1750–1800*, Boston.
Royster, C. (1979) *A Revolutionary People at War: The Continental Army and American Character, 1775–1783*, Chapel Hill, NC.
Waldstreicher, D. (1997) *In the Midst of Perpetual Fetes: The Making of American Nationalism, 1776–1820*, Chapel Hill, NC.
Wood, G. S. (220) *The American Revolution: A History*, New York.
Zelinsky, W. (1988) *Nation into State: The Shifting Symbolic Foundations of American Nationalism*, Chapel Hill, NC.

Latin America

Adelman, J. (2006) *Sovereignty and Revolution in the Iberian Atlantic*, Princeton, NJ.
Archer, C. I. (ed.) (2003) *The Birth of Modern Mexico, 1780–1824*, Wilmington, DE.
Bushnell, D. and Langley, L. D. (eds.) (2008) *Simón Bolívar: Essays on the Life and Legacy of the Liberator*, Lanham, MD.
Doyle, D. H. and Pamplona, M. A. (eds.) (2006) *Nationalism in the New World*, Athens, GA.
Earle, R. (2000) *Spain and the Independence of Colombia, 1810–1825*, Exeter.
Graham, R. (1994) *Independence in Latin America: A Comparative Approach*, 2nd edn., New York.
Henderson, T. J. (2009) *The Mexican Wars for Independence*, New York.
Lynch, J. (ed.) (1994) *Latin American Revolutions: Old and New World Origins*, Norman, OK.
McFarlane, A. and Posada-Carbó, E. (eds.) (1999) *Independence and Revolution in Spanish America: Perspectives and Problems*, London.

Pimenta, J. P. G. (2007) *Brasil y las independencias de Hispanoamérica*, trans. V. and P. García Guerrero, Castellón de la Plana, Spain.
Rodríguez O., J. E. (1998) *The Independence of Spanish America*, Cambridge.
—— (ed.) (2005) *Revolución, independencia y las nuevas naciones de América*, Madrid.
Uribe-Urán, V. M. (ed.) (2001) *State and Society in Spanish America during the Age of Revolution*, Wilmington, DE.
Van Young, E. (2001) *The Other Rebellion: Popular Violence, Ideology, and the Mexican Struggle for Independence, 1810–1821*, Stanford, CA.
Vázquez, J. Z. (ed.) (1976) *Dos revoluciones: México y los Estados Unidos*, Mexico City.

CHAPTER 7

THE FRENCH REVOLUTION, NAPOLEON, AND NATIONALISM IN EUROPE

MICHAEL ROWE

Introduction

This chapter focuses on nationalism in the period 1789–1815. It starts with a consideration of the impact made by the rise of the public sphere, and of a newly critical and politicized public opinion in the period immediately before the outbreak of the French Revolution in 1789. The Revolution, and its invocation of the 'nation' as sovereign, is the subject of the following section which also looks at how this new concept shaped French foreign policy. This policy contributed to the outbreak in 1792 of over twenty years of warfare that eventually engulfed all Europe. The remaining sections look at the impact of this conflict on the development of nationalism, starting with an analysis of the changing relationship between the French army and the French nation, followed by a survey of the increasingly supra-national ethos of Napoleon's empire, and then moving on to a consideration of the national component in the resistance to Napoleonic hegemony.[1] The concluding section highlights some overarching themes, and in particular, how states in this period confronted new hurdles in justifying themselves in the eyes of their subjects.

The historical significance of nationalism lies in its ability to mobilize people not merely in defence of hearth and home, or even for prince or religion, but for a wider, imagined community whose members have a disinterested and constant sense of obligation to one another. Nationalism is associated with the large territorial state: an entity sufficiently big that its interests are not obviously coincidental with its subjects with whom it strives to establish a direct, unmediated relationship. For the sociologist and political economist Max Weber, the defining feature of the modern state is its effective monopoly of violence. States not in possession of this monopoly are now labelled 'failed'. Nonetheless, successful states endure because of a sense of mutual obligation between themselves and their inhabitants, and because they are regarded as legitimate. The undoubted success of the modern state as an entity capable of mobilization rests less on its ability to employ force, necessary though this element is, than on its capacity to associate itself with the national community so that the two are indistinguishable.

Nations are communities bound by mutual obligations. Collective memories are immensely important in sustaining such communities, and historians of Europe's nation states identify the Revolutionary/Napoleonic period (1789–1815) as incredibly rich in forging such memories. This is obviously so with France, whose national symbols—the tricolour flag, *Marseillaise*, Bastille Day—all come from this period. Elsewhere in Europe regimes subsequently drew on the memories of this era to bolster their own legitimacy—typically by associating ruling dynasties with 'national awakenings' in response to Napoleon—something especially apparent in Russia and Prussia/Germany in the years immediately before World War I. In the past, mainstream historians, locked within national traditions and dependent upon official archives, lent the credibility of scientific scholarship to the enterprise.[2] In the twentieth century, in contrast, the World Wars displaced the French Revolution and Napoleon as defining moments in national stories, though even today references to the Revolutionary/Napoleonic era persist in monumental form in most European capitals, from Nelson's Column in London's Trafalgar Square to Moscow's recently reconstructed Cathedral of Christ the Saviour a few blocks from the Kremlin. Historians today spend their time deconstructing national myths rather than creating them, and recent scholarship distinguishes between the relative insignificance of nationalism in the period 1789–1815 as compared to the 'myths' that developed later.[3]

Rise of Public Opinion

Nationalism demands public engagement with politics beyond a particular locality. This has been the focus of a vast amount of recent research by scholars of the eighteenth century, much of it inspired by Jürgen Habermas's seminal *The Structural Transformation of the Public Sphere*.[4] The eighteenth century emerges from this research as the era that gave birth to a form of critical public opinion that increasingly saw itself as the legitimate final arbiter on matters ranging from artistic taste to affairs of state. Originally, scholars linked this process to the rise of the bourgeoisie and with progressive politics, but this is increasingly contested: nobles, clergymen, craftsmen, as well as professionals and capitalists, participated in the public sphere, a forum in which religious bigots and the peddlers of smut—the latter motivated by commercial considerations—were equally at home as the polite and tolerant.[5] Indeed, recent studies concerned with the degree of popular involvement in the public sphere point to its social breadth, something that lends force to the argument of historians who challenge the notion that political authority and ideas, including nationalism, were simply things imposed on people from above by states and/or intellectuals.[6]

The public sphere was neutral at one level. However, it was also fundamentally subversive of the existing order, and encouraged ideas whose triumph was a precondition of modern nationalism. The belief in a basic equality when it came to participation in the public sphere challenged the existing sociopolitical order based upon people divided into distinct corporations; the notion that rational discussion produced a *single* public opinion was in harmony with the absolute claims of national sovereignty and endowed it with immense political force; and the claim that the 'tribunal' of public opinion was the final arbiter challenged existing governing institutions.

Eighteenth-century France remains the classic example of the Ancien Régime failing to adapt to this new political culture.[7] The challenge posed here was especially strong: France's relative prosperity meant that the 'hardware' of the public sphere—the media—was well developed, only lagging behind Britain and the Netherlands. France's well-established statehood meant that public opinion was 'French', in the sense that it quite naturally took the territory of France as its point of reference despite the obvious cultural differences between different provinces. This was not the case in composite monarchies, of which the Habsburg Empire was the most striking example, where patriotism was centred on particular territorial sub-components.[8] From today's perspective composite monarchies might appear unwieldy. However, the challenge their regimes faced from the public sphere was fragmented, and this allowed their rulers to suppress 'patriotic' uprisings piecemeal. This is one reason why the Habsburgs survived their crisis of 1789–90 but the French Bourbons did not.

A history of unified statehood coupled with a vibrant, critical public sphere were not the only reasons for the crisis in France: had they been, the British monarchy would also have succumbed to revolution. Other things went wrong for the French monarchy, including defeat in war. Ultimately, there was little that could be done about this, given that the French position was unnaturally inflated at the beginning of the eighteenth century. Its relative decline was more about others—notably, Britain, Prussia, and Russia—expanding than France contracting. What made this dimension so damaging was its nature—the fact that the Austrian alliance of 1756 that formed the cornerstone of French policy was deeply unpopular, including in elite circles, and that it was embodied in the royal family. The litany of foreign-policy failure, starting with the Seven Years War (1756–63) and culminating with the failure of France to assist its allies in the Netherlands during the Prussian invasion of that country in 1787, had an especially damaging impact on the morale of the patriotically inclined officer corps, that small but crucial group whose refusal to defend the monarchy in 1789 proved decisive.[9] Foreign-policy failure in combination with the Habsburg dynastic alliance made it all the easier for the *Parlementaire* opposition to royal absolutism to portray itself as 'national' and hence, by implication, paramount, and the monarchy as somehow alien. The fiscal/institutional failings of the French monarchy—not least, its physical isolation in Versailles and the personal shortcomings of Louis XVI, especially his lack of charisma—completed the list of problems.[10] In Britain, in contrast, a generally good foreign-policy record, a constitutional system that placed greater distance between expendable ministries and the monarchy itself, and George III's successful self-projection as a national symbol resulted in survival, despite a public sphere and political culture even more rumbustious than that of France.[11] Whilst in France Louis XVI became detached from the nation, in Britain George III discovered that magical formula of combining occasional spectacular ceremonial with an avoidance of ostentation.[12]

Triumph of the Nation

Keith Baker argues convincingly that in terms of the political ideas that underpinned the French Revolution, everything was already in place by the time of Louis XVI's accession in 1774. It was the coincidence of these ideas with a series of events that created the explosion of 1789. One of the brains behind the Revolution, Abbé Sieyes, provided a suitable pithy statement illustrating the French revolutionary concept of national sovereignty: 'The nation exists before everything, it is the object of everything. Its will is always legal, it is the law itself.'[13] For Sieyes the Third Estate, which numerically was dominated by farmers, craftsmen, and merchants, was the nation and hence everything because it alone was productive. It was on this basis that the Third Estate transformed itself into the National Assembly in 1789. Such a fundamentalist outlook left no room for 'loyal' political opposition, which became by definition *lèse nation*. Nor did it leave room for the First (clerical) and Second (noble) Estates, or the world of historically accrued privilege that underpinned the old order of autonomous corporations and provinces. Up to this point these had served as the most effective barrier against the state-building activities of absolute monarchs. Now, these corporations were swept aside by the new institution embodying national sovereignty, the National Assembly. The key measures were the so-called August (1789) laws, which abolished 'feudalism' (notably, manorial courts and fiscal privilege), the law of 4 March 1790 replacing provinces with *départements*, and the *Loi le Chapelier* (17 June 1791) abolishing corporations (including trade guilds). These were the kind of measures of which absolutist monarchs would previously have approved. Now, however, they were theoretically underpinned by the powerful concept of nationhood that left no room for institutions that discriminated between citizens, or stood between them and the state. The world of privilege was not simply abolished in 1789–91 on grounds of administrative convenience or because it got in the way of resource mobilization, though this last dimension was the most immediate consequence as France (in 1792) embarked upon a generation of war that would transform Europe.

France's declaration of war on 20 April 1792, first against Austria, contradicted earlier pacifist statements by the revolutionaries, who apparently agreed with Jean-Jacques Rousseau's assertion that wars of conquest were for kings, not free peoples. Initially, policy followed this principle, with Paris rejecting Spanish requests for assistance against Britain during the Nootka Sound crisis.[14] Yet foreign policy was an area where one of the numerous contradictions that characterized the French Revolution manifested itself: the idea, on the one hand, that there are certain universal principles applicable to humanity as a whole, something that tended towards cosmopolitanism; on the other hand, the growing realization that France was special because it was where these principles had first triumphed. The new French constitution (1791), with its pledge that the 'French nation renounces to undertake any war with a view to make conquests, and will never employ its forces against the liberty of any people', suggested the triumph of cosmopolitanism.[15] The failure from the start of that constitution to end the Revolution, the connection between the ongoing domestic political crisis in 1791–2 and a deteriorating foreign-policy situation that left France more vulnerable, combined with pre-existing Austrophobia, paranoia, émigré plotting, obdurate Alsatian princes, and the persuasiveness of Brissotin rhetoric, swung the pendulum towards chauvinism and propelled France into war.[16]

Not that the internationalist idealism of the revolutionaries was smothered immediately by war. French defeat of the Austro-Prussian invasion at Valmy in northeastern France and Jemappes in Belgium in the autumn 1792, followed immediately by a rapid offensive into Belgium and the Rhineland, brought closer the revolutionary dream of liberating Europe's peoples from princely tyranny and thus creating a new order in which relations between nations would naturally be fraternal rather than confrontational. This euphoric moment was marked by a series of French declarations to Europe's peoples, including the National Convention's decree of 19 November 1792 promising fraternity and assistance to all people wishing liberty.

This optimism did not long endure. French expansion provoked Spain and Britain into joining the First Coalition, and Austrian and Prussian armies succeeded in blunting the French advance into Germany. Worse, as it fundamentally challenged the revolutionaries' perspective, was the realization that ordinary Europeans in territories occupied by France—not just priests and nobles—rejected the 'fraternity' offered them. This combination of factors in early 1793 hastened the pace at which the newly instituted French Republic shed its internationalist aspirations and instead adopted a policy of revolution in one country. The implications of this were felt first by the foreign idealists gathered in Paris, the most prominent of whom—the Prussian Anarcharsis Cloots—was guillotined on 24 March 1794. In the occupied territories, revolutionary fraternity made way for unembellished exploitation. The French treated even native 'patriots' in places like the Rhineland and Low Countries with the contempt appropriate to peoples who had failed to make any contribution to their own 'liberation'.[17] In Spain, which the French invaded in 1794, the sense that the native population was incapable of receiving the fruits of liberty was even more pronounced, as reflected in the comments of one soldier engaged on that front: 'The peasant's cottage should no more be respected than the palace of a *seignor* because the popular class is as much an enemy of the French as those who wear monks' hoods or velvet mantles.'[18]

Army and Nation

By 1793–4, French republican discourse was distinguished by revolutionary chauvinism: the French nation was distinct and superior because it alone had liberated itself from tyranny. It was surrounded by (and indeed, riddled with) enemies, according to this same discourse. The Republic's unprecedented mobilization in face of the threat is easily portrayed as the energy of the French nation being 'released'. To do so *is not* to project current values onto the past, as people at the time spoke in these terms. Certainly, the French Republic's energy and success in reversing the course of war was impressive. Its commitment to waging total war—a conflict in which the nation in its entirety was directly committed—is best expressed in the National Convention's decree of 23 August 1793:

> From this moment until that in which our enemies shall have been driven from the territory of the Republic, all Frenchmen are permanently requisitioned for service in the armies.
>
> The young men shall fight; the married men shall forge weapons and transport supplies; the women will make tents and clothes and will serve in the hospitals; the children will turn old linen into lint; the old men will have themselves carried into the public squares to rouse the courage of fighting men, to preach the unity of the Republic and hatred of Kings.[19]

The growth of the French army reflects the effort: at about the time of the decree, it stood at 351,000 men. By August 1794 this had leapt to at least 750,000, an unprecedented force by French standards.[20]

'National awakening' is nonetheless a misleading term to describe what occurred in 1793–4, as it implies that the mobilization was primarily a voluntary effort. This was not the case. Rather, the mobilization was the result of state initiative, enabled by the destruction of the obstructive privileged corporate order in 1789–91. This is not to claim that all young Frenchmen remained unmoved by the mass propaganda unleashed by the authorities warning of the terrors awaiting France should the Coalition invade. For some, no doubt, this was persuasive, but for most not enough. Indeed, the shortfall in volunteers forced the French government to rely on compulsion to fill the ranks from the very start of the war: already in May 1792 the Legislative Assembly ordered the employment of a ballot system in those departments failing to meet their quota of 'volunteers' for the national levy of 74,000, and the same method was employed for the levy of 300,000 in spring 1793, by which time it was quite clear that the voluntary system was totally inadequate. We must accept that national sentiment was insufficiently strong in France to provide enough manpower to defend the Republic. This is hardly startling: all the major armies committed in the World Wars of the twentieth century were similarly dominated by conscripts rather than volunteers, but that does not mean nationalism was absent from the factors that encouraged them to fight.[21]

The French revolutionaries envisaged that the instrument for fighting—the army—should be very different from the old royal army. Even before the outbreak of war in 1792, they acted upon their vision of the army as an extension of the nation. The 1790 reform of military justice enshrined the soldier's right to be tried by a properly constituted court martial that included a jury and abolished harsh sentences. The 'French' character of the army was also asserted. On the eve of the Revolution, Louis XVI's army counted 102 line regiments, 23 of which were foreign. In June 1791 the National Assembly stripped these regiments of their foreign identity, though foreigners continued to serve throughout the revolutionary wars. Citizen-soldiers also enjoyed every right to engage in politics. Even before coming to power, local Jacobin clubs started propagandizing in units stationed in their areas. Once in power, the Jacobins availed themselves of the resources of government to flood the army with patriotic publications celebrating the virtues of fighting for the nation.[22]

To what extent did these efforts create a new-style army motivated by nationalism? The rapidity with which the French army shrank from the 1794 peak due to desertion—it was down to 484,000 in August 1795, and in 1796 fell to under 400,000, where it remained for some years—indicates the limits of nationalism as a motivator.[23] Nonetheless, there are also sufficient soldiers' letters from this period indicating not only familiarity with revolutionary rhetoric, but also an acceptance of its precepts. Acknowledging that some soldiers were genuinely committed to the principles of the Revolution, including the duty of the patriotic citizen to fight for the nation, does not mean that one need deny the importance of other less abstract factors: loyalty to unit, and to comrades.[24] There is no reason why the two might not coexist in perfect harmony, making it impossible, methodologically, to abstract the one from the other. A final consideration is that by 1794–5 roughly 95 per cent of serving soldiers had enrolled since the outbreak of the French Revolution.[25] One might deduce from this fact that the importance of patriotic sentiment would be greater than had the army been composed mainly of old veterans long since alienated from civilian life.

However, paradoxically as the revolutionary wars progressed there are good reasons for believing that the army became less rather than more national. The longer soldiers served the more attached to their units they became. Also, as the revolutionary wars progressed French military success propelled the army ever further from the borders of the Republic. National survival as a motivating factor receded as a consequence. By the mid-1790s the average French soldier was more likely to worry about his own physical survival given the breakdown of military logistics.[26] This too had ideological consequences, as the republican ideal of national unity binding all citizens was only sustainable if it could be demonstrated that the whole nation was ready to sacrifice itself for the men at the front. This could not be done, especially when government was no longer in the hands of virtuous Jacobins but the sleazy politicians who came to dominate the Directory (1795–9). Indeed, even under the Jacobin Republic there were signs that the army's own self-image was beginning to change, with the soldier emerging as a distinctly virtuous type endowed, unlike the civilian, with honour. The organizational genius behind the 1793–4 mobilization, Lazare Carnot, was in part responsible for this development: a consequence of his drive to restore discipline and morale was to set the army apart, detach it from factional politics, and imply that it and not the nation as a whole was the repository of republican virtue. The French army now gradually 'praetorianized', with soldiers owing allegiance to their comrades, units, and above all generals so long as these provided for them.[27] Successful generals well understood this and masterminded the wholesale plunder of occupied territories to supply their armies. The young Napoleon Bonaparte, taking command in 1796 of the Army of Italy, was the ultimate example, and shamelessly played up his role as sole provider and keeper of his troops.[28]

In November 1799 the French army's estrangement from the nation resulted in what was arguably history's first military coup, that propelling Napoleon Bonaparte into power. Napoleon's Consulate (1799–1804) and Empire (1804–14) reconciled military and civilian France only at the apex, in the person of Napoleon himself. Evidence of the army's further 'de-nationalization' followed, including even the recreation of foreign regiments (Swiss, Irish, German) within the regular French army.[29] This was, so far as Napoleon was concerned, not detrimental to military efficiency, the only criteria he was concerned about. Charismatic leadership, unit loyalty, comradeship based upon an unwritten (but ruthlessly enforced) moral code and, above all, a cult of honour sustained Napoleon's army. This was a force that in its composition reflected the increasing cultural and linguistic diversity of the empire. By 1809, when France again found itself at war against Austria, regiments supplied by the German satellite states made up about a third of the total Napoleonic host. The French element shrank further still by the time of the Russian campaign, when the proportions were reversed: about one third of Napoleon's invasion force was French, and two thirds were made up of Germans, Poles, Italians, Dutch, Croats, Swiss, Spaniards, and Portuguese.[30]

Napoleon's Empire

Napoleon's victories in 1799–1800 saved France from invasion and preserved the 'natural frontiers' acquired up to 1797. His victories of 1805 and 1806, against Austria and Prussia, pushed the boundaries of effective French power into Germany and Italy. The empire was less French, though labelling it European, Carolingian, or Roman is not helpful either.[31] At its greatest extent, at the beginning of 1812, it extended to 130 departments, only about 90 of which covered the territory traditionally occupied by France. The rest were new acquisitions, stretching in a crescent from what is now northern Germany, through the Low Countries and Rhineland, to the northwestern and central parts of Italy, with an additional but detached stretch of territory along the Adriatic Coast. In addition, Catalonia in northeastern Spain was on the point of incorporation into France.[32] The vast majority of 'new Frenchmen' living in these departments did not speak French as their native language, nor enjoy the sense that they naturally belonged to France. In other ways, they were more or less integrated into the French Empire, though there were variations from region to region. At least a proportion of the large number of 'new Frenchmen' who served in Napoleon's army were, judging by the few remaining memoirs, inculcated by the spirit of glory that infused this force, but as already argued, this was not really nationalism: the cult was focused on Napoleon, not France.[33] 'New Frenchmen' appear to have fought as well as their 'old French' comrades, motivated as they were by loyalty to their units and leader. That said, when units and leadership collapsed, as happened on the terrible retreat from Moscow in 1812, stragglers tended to congregate in linguistically defined groups: survival demanded the ability to communicate, and this was quite naturally easiest with people from one's own locality.

The loss of men, and more importantly horses, in the Russian campaign of 1812 was something from which Napoleon never recovered. Indeed, the extent to which he managed to mobilize forces in 1813 to stem the coalition of Russians, Prussians, Austrians, and Swedes advancing through central Europe is noteworthy. It is this stage of the Napoleonic wars, culminating in the Battle of Leipzig (or 'Battle of the Nations') in October 1813, that German nationalists subsequently portrayed in terms of a national awakening. There is some evidence to support the claim that 'new Frenchmen'—not only German speakers—were not as loyal as the inhabitants of 'old France'. 'New Frenchmen' deserted, with whole regiments of Belgians and Dutch affected. Napoleon took the threat sufficiently seriously to disarm and intern remaining 'foreign regiments', and also avoided mobilizing the National Guard in the new departments. On the other hand, most of the 'new departments' remained relatively calm as Napoleonic power collapsed.[34]

Quiescence rather than nationalism best describes responses in the 'new departments'. This is not surprising, for at least two reasons. The first is that most of the 'new departments' had previously belonged to an arc—stretching from the North Sea to northern Italy—distinguished by its territorial fragmentation. This was a zone dominated by city states, Church states, small principalities, and the peripheral holdings of larger composite monarchies. In short, it was a part of Europe that had escaped relatively unscathed from the kind of early modern state-building that distinguished other parts of the continent, including France, Scandinavia, Prussia, and Britain. The loyalties of the inhabitants of this arc of polities were very much locally focused, and the kind of sacrifices demanded by larger states and indeed nationalists correspondingly alien.

The second reason for the passivity of the 'new departments' relates to the nature of Napoleonic-style government, both within the French Empire and to an extent within the penumbra of satellite states located to the east of the Rhine and in the remainder of Italy. The French revolutionaries—the Jacobins, at least—had envisaged a Republic composed of politically active citizens acting selflessly for the French nation of which they were a part. The Napoleonic agenda, in contrast, involved the depoliticization of France. It was a change best reflected in official terminology, with 'citizens' becoming '*administrés*' ('the administered') in government documents. It was also reflected in education policy, which under Napoleon was designed to turn the elite into technocrats for the state rather than to expose the population at large to a curriculum that might produce politically aware citizens.[35]

The Napoleonic constitution of Year VIII (13 December 1799) avoided general statements of principle regarding national sovereignty and the rights of citizenship. Napoleon himself avoided such subjects, which for him belonged to the realm of 'metaphysics'. He was especially aware of the dangers posed by any representative or legislative body describing itself as sovereign, or acting as representative of the nation. This is the reason why he adopted a tricameral legislative structure, with legislative power divided between the Tribunate, Legislative Body, and Senate.[36] So far as Napoleon was concerned none of these bodies, either individually or collectively, was 'sovereign'. Instead, the exercise of sovereignty resided in all the official institutions of France collectively. The ambiguities were further revealed in the formula adopted for the imperial title Napoleon created for himself in 1804: 'Emperor, through the Grace of God and the Constitution', something that implied Napoleon owed his position only partially to the French nation, even though the latter ratified his elevation through plebiscite. One might compare Napoleon's views on sovereignty with contemporary opinion on nuclear power generation: its potential to generate power is too immense to easily set aside, but the associated dangers require elaborate containment structures lest the energy be released in a way that is unintended.

Thus, the issues of nationality, sovereignty, and citizenship were effectively bound within a powerful set of institutions that represented Napoleon's greatest legacy to France and Europe. The issues were also masked in the image that the regime projected of itself. This was traditional rather than revolutionary in that it stressed monarchical and imperial as opposed to national and republican elements. This process started even before Napoleon made himself emperor: as early as 1802, Napoleon—as First Consul—exercised the right of pardon, surrounded himself with a functioning court and guard, and sat in the place previously occupied by Louis XVI whilst attending Mass.[37] As this final point indicates, religion helped fill the vacuum left by the marginalization of republican political concepts of nationhood, something displayed in especially spectacular form in Napoleon's coronation in 1804. The justification for investing the head of state in what was essentially a religious ceremony was spelt out in the planning sessions held by the Council of State. The view expressed by one of the councillors, Jean-Étienne-Marie Portalis, reflected the majority opinion:

> You do not wish to divorce Heaven and Earth. Everything that tends to make sacred he who governs is of great benefit. The problem of our time is that one speculates too much about power. When the people believe it conferred by God, then they regard it as sacred.[38]

Napoleon might have been agnostic when it came to the precise historical provenance of the emblems adopted for his monarchy—those eventually adopted fused Roman, Byzantine, and Carolingian elements—but he was firm on the need for a religious component, not least because nothing else would do for the large minority of 'new Frenchmen'. The essentially supra-national character of Napoleon's *imperium* increased further after 1804, both because of territorial expansion and because of Napoleon's dynastic policy that culminated with his marriage to Marie Louise of Austria in 1810. By then, it was hardly surprising that members of the old French elite were grumbling at the prominence of new Frenchmen in an imperial court that was growing more European and less French by the day.[39]

Napoleon's imperial monarchy stood contrary to the republican concept of the nation in another respect. Republican nationalism stressed the equality of citizens, national unity, and the direct relationship between citizens and their government. The most obvious manifestation of this republican vision had been the abolition of 'supra-national' institutions that infringed upon national sovereignty (notably, the Roman Catholic Church), and 'sub-national' institutions (provinces, universities, trade/craft guilds) that mediated relations between the central government and the individual. Napoleon had no interest in re-establishing a system of corporate privilege, not least because it would have undermined his capacity to mobilize resources for waging war. On the other hand, Napoleon believed that a strong set of institutions loyal to but nonetheless apart from the state were essential for social stability. In his own words, effective government is founded upon masses of granite and not grains of sand.

In practical terms, Napoleon's reversal of republican social atomization led to the creation/re-establishment of institutions that to an extent divided French citizens from one another: religious organizations, Masonic lodges, the *Légion d'Honneur*, imperial nobility, chambers of commerce, guards of honour, and so on. Napoleon believed that individuals within society each had their place—albeit determined in part by merit, and not just birth—and in addition that markers needed to be re-established following the meltdown of the 1790s so that everyone knew where they stood. Hence, for example, the meticulous attention to matters one might label official etiquette; precedence at official functions and ceremonies, heraldry, and so forth. Historians keen to emphasize the republican nature of Napoleon's regime highlight some fundamental differences between its new social hierarchy and that of the old regime: the fact that the new institutions did not override the basic legal equality of all citizens and that they were dependent upon the state. Nonetheless, republican opponents of Napoleon's social re-hierarchization made the fundamental point that this policy undermined the notion that citizens were basically equal, that their loyalty must overwhelmingly be directed towards the nation and not diverted towards other institutions. The Napoleonic model of society composed of a set of blocs held in a state of healthy competition with one another for the favour of the emperor—rather like the regiments of the army—was hardly an appealing alternative vision of a nation of homogeneous and unanimous citizens held by committed republicans.[40]

French republicans might well grumble at the supra-national, imperial, and dynastic direction that events were heading under Napoleon. Conversely, an important social strata of new-Frenchmen and indeed non-Frenchmen (the inhabitants of the satellite states bound to the French Empire proper) were thus more easily attracted to the Napoleonic civilizing mission, and enthusiastically collaborated with it. Thousands of Germans, Italians, Belgians, Poles, and Dutch did so, finding more or less prominent positions within the military or civilian administrations of an empire that was more open than the average modern nation state to the recruitment of the talented, irrespective of national background.[41] Imbued with the culture of the Enlightenment, they shared in the vision, held also by 'old-Frenchmen' of similar social background, of spreading progress to the ignorant and unenlightened, irrespective of whether this be within the frontiers of 'old France' or in more exotic outposts of empire like Illyria or Calabria. The self-perception of this breed of frankly arrogant imperial bureaucrat was profoundly unimpressed by the kind of German (and other) nationalism sprouted by a small but disproportionately influential minority during the crisis years of 1813–14. It is indicative of how things had developed since 1789 that these officials, serving France, labelled their enemies in the European Coalition 'revolutionary' for sponsoring nationalist rhetoric.

Resistance to Napoleon

The Coalition that brought Napoleon down in 1813–14 consisted of all the other major European powers: Austria, Britain, Prussia, and Russia. Britain, despite mobilizing to an unprecedented degree against the Revolutionary/Napoleonic challenge, followed a distinctive path. Its representative institutions, though grounded in the same corporate order as existed elsewhere in Europe, had nonetheless evolved to the extent that they had effectively broken with that order. In this period they included a critical mass of the population, and hence could cope with the vast mobilization of resources necessitated by the 'Second Hundred Years War' against France. These institutions were taken for granted. That is not to say that the public consensus was against reform, or indeed that a minority did not favour radical change. However, for the majority debate was contained within the existing institutional framework that furthermore proved eminently suited, albeit with some tweaking, to the demands set by war. Nationalism in this period was by no means uncontested, as recent studies have shown: a variety of social and regional groups with differing political agendas availed themselves of patriotic rhetoric and perhaps even believed genuinely that their particular interests coincided with those of the wider 'national' community. At the same time, the monarchy's relative aloofness and increasing representational function meant that it could, by and large, serve as a unifying rather than divisive force. Changes in policy could be affected through replacement of Cabinets; they did not require threats of military coups or assassination.[42]

Britain's relatively secure geographical position, wealth, and institutional strength meant it weathered the Revolutionary/Napoleonic storm without the necessity of far-reaching reform. The least geopolitically secure power—Prussia—in contrast, was compelled to embark upon fundamental reform. Prominent figures within this kingdom believed the only way of defeating Napoleon was to mobilize the energy of the people in a way not dissimilar to France in the 1790s. This radical position was forced upon them by the nature of Prussia's collapse in the face of the Napoleonic onslaught in 1806. This had resembled more a complete moral collapse of an existing system, and not just another defeat on the battlefield to a numerically superior foe.

The most important assumption that united the Prussian reformers, of whom the statesmen Heinrich Friedrich Karl vom Stein and Karl August von Hardenberg were the most prominent, was the belief that the Prussian state could only be regenerated through involving more actively society's most talented in the work of government. This was the message behind Stein's famous memorandum of June 1807 (the so-called *Nassauer Denkschrift*), which stressed the importance of re-establishing 'harmony between the spirit of the nation ["Geist der Nation"], its opinions and needs, and those of the state administration'. In December 1807, Stein wrote to Hardenberg that it '. . . is essential that the nation become accustomed to managing its own affairs, so that it will emerge from this state of infancy in which an anxious and officious government attempts to keep the people'.[43] Similarly, Hardenberg called for bringing the 'nation' into a closer relationship with government.

How might this be achieved? Here the reformers differed, though few considered emulating 1790s French-style democracy. Hardenberg, who was less hostile to the professional state bureaucracy than was Stein, dismissed (in his *Rigaer Denkschrift*) 'pure democracy' as something appropriate for the very distant future (if ever), and instead proposed the 'amalgamation' of national representatives with particular administrative bodies. Stein was less enamoured of the virtues of the bureaucracy, but this resulted not so much in a stronger commitment to democracy than advocating the revitalization of the old corporate order, albeit one now based firmly on utilitarian principles. These ideas found expression in government policy following Stein's appointment as prime minister and in particular in his civic ordinance granting a greater degree of self-government for towns and an edict emancipating the peasantry. Hardenberg's reform plans, in contrast, attacked more fundamentally the social order based on privileged estates, though even he stopped short of the abolition of the nobility. What both Stein and Hardenberg undoubtedly furthered was the centralization of the Prussian state, at the expense of provincial and local autonomy. This was particularly apparent on the fiscal front, where Hardenberg's reforms—especially the consolidation of war debts into a single state-wide account—was, in his own words, motivated 'because we want not to perpetuate *provincialism,* but rather establish *nationalism*'.[44]

The Prussian reformers' biggest misjudgement was to assume that creating some form of constitutional representation would result in disinterested mobilization for an uncontested 'national [Prussian] interest', and that Prussia's elite would automatically break out of their old 'egotistical' corporate way of thinking. Such, of course, was not to occur, and this jeopardized the whole reform project. One might well understand the reformers' frustration as particular social groups, and the nobility in particular, 'misused' the new representative organs and adopted the new patriotic discourse to bolster their traditional interests, arguing that these rather than the reforms conformed with the national interest. This last argument was reinforced by reference to both Stein and Hardenberg's non-Prussian backgrounds.[45]

Any group, whether that of reforming bureaucrats or conservative nobles, equating itself with the national interest was dangerous from the perspective of the Prussian king, Frederick William III. It potentially implied a distinction between the national interest and the king. The parallels with what had happened in France in 1789, when sovereignty was transferred from the Crown to a representative body (the National Assembly), were obviously not lost on the Prussian king.[46] The danger was magnified when such sentiment spread from civil servants, conservative landowners, and romantic writers to senior officers of the army, the ultimate guarantor of the existing order. Plans by the military reformers to transform the Prussian army into a repository of virtuous patriotism might be appealing from the perspective of reversing the defeat of 1806 and re-establishing Prussia as a great power. It was unappealing to those, the king foremost amongst them, fearful that the military might slip the royal leash.

Fears of a military coup were not exaggerated. Frederick William's determination to keep Prussia out of war in 1809 was deeply unpopular amongst the officer corps chaffing at the bit to get back at Napoleon. The apparent success of the Spanish insurgency, together with the appeal to German national solidarity issuing from Vienna upon the outbreak of war, only intensified the sentiment. The government's cautious neutrality in 1809 provoked widespread frustration and restlessness within the officer corps, and the king's own cousin—Prince August—dared warn that the 'nation' would act without him. In the end, nothing came of the mutterings or wild plans for a national rising apart from a few relatively small-scale freelance raids against the French and their allies conducted by Prussian units acting on their own authority. However, it is significant that senior Prussian officers were now supporting their argument for confronting Napoleon with references to public opinion, and thus trying to bounce their monarch into adopting a policy with which he was in disagreement. During one of his more morose moments, Frederick William even considered abdication in favour of someone else 'whom the nation believes worthier'.[47]

Things went a stage further in 1812–13. The Franco-Prussian offensive alliance (24 February 1812) forced upon Frederick William by Napoleon in advance of the Russian invasion provoked an unprecedented spate of high-profile resignations from government and army. At grass-roots level, massive requisitioning by Napoleon's host caused popular francophobia that manifested itself in spontaneous attacks against French soldiers as they staggered back from Russia after the failure of the invasion. However, what really stands out as extraordinary is the Convention of Tauroggen (30 December 1812). This was concluded between the effective commander of the Prussian corps attached to Napoleon's *Grande Armée*, General Yorck, and the Russians he was supposed to be fighting against. Yorck, along with his entire staff and the corps, switched sides without authorization from his king. In so doing Yorck—a conservative—appealed to the higher authority of the Prussian nation.[48] Stein, now in Russian service, urged Yorck on and convened the East Prussian estates—or 'representatives of the nation' as they were referred to at the time—to organize resistance against

Napoleon. This amounted to insurrection against the Prussian king, whose order that Yorck be dismissed from the service and arrested was known but ignored by the estates which proceeded to raise the whole nation—all men capable of bearing arms, irrespective of class or creed—against the French. Even worse for the king, the spirit of insurrection started to spread westwards, to other Prussian provinces, thereby lending force to the argument of even the most conservative of advisors that the 'general will of the nation' was for war against France, and that if Frederick William refused to lead he would be removed.[49] It is in this context that Frederick William finally opted, in March 1813, for the Russian alliance and made his famous appeal 'To My People'.

The bare details of the Prussian mobilization against Napoleon that followed indicate the magnitude of the effort, which was comparable to Jacobin France in 1793–4. About 6 per cent of the entire Prussian population eventually found itself in active service. Though not the largest of the Coalition contingents, the Prussians in 1813 did distinguish themselves in their determination to destroy the enemy. The extent to which this effort represented a broader popular nationalism—Prussian and/or German—encompassing the masses is a question historians have sought to answer. What is clear is that the degree of mobilization varied regionally and socially. Those with a high level of formal education—university students, teachers, and so forth—were over-represented, providing about 12 per cent of the 27,000 volunteers in the Prussian forces, though representing only 2 per cent of the population. Some served in Lützow's *Freikorps*, whose black uniforms, red facings, and golden buttons inspired the banner of the German national movement, and subsequently the German national flag. Artisans were also over-represented, accounting for 41 per cent of volunteers though only 7 per cent of the population. Peasants, in contrast, were under-represented. However, what is noteworthy is that no group was absent from the mobilization effort, with even those previously on the margins engaged. For example, Jews also volunteered for the forces, and were active in the general fund-raising effort; and women were appealed to specifically by the Prussian government, and responded by joining patriotic associations with names such as the *Vaterländische Frauenverein*.[50]

Clearly, what happened in Prussia in 1813 was not simply a top-down phenomenon: the poet Heinrich Heine's crack that people were patriotic because they were told to be so does not explain grass-roots spontaneity clearly evident in the effort; and it also ignores that the starting point—Tauroggen—was an unprecedented act of disobedience, not obedience. This consideration in itself does not turn the volunteers of 1813 into Prussian—and still less, German—nationalists. As noted earlier, the historical significance of nationalism lies in its ability to mobilize people in furtherance of interests that are not obviously tangible. It is not so much a question of nationalism requiring people to give up local interests and allegiances, and of sacrificing hearth and home in defence of a wider community. Rather, nationalism's strength in part lies in its linking of the local with the national; its encouragement of the belief that tangible (local) interests and values are best preserved within the framework of the larger 'imagined community'. An element of reciprocity must exist for this to be credible: even if hearth and home are not directly threatened, members of the community feel a sense of obligation towards those under threat. The evidence for Prussia in 1813 is mixed. Data pointing to a correlation between the degree of voluntary mobilization and the damage inflicted by French requisitioning suggests that there were limits to the sense of mutual obligation between the inhabitants of Prussia: reactions to Napoleon were primarily determined by the degree of personal suffering inflicted by the French occupation, and this varied between provinces and social groups. This consideration applies less to the students and teachers, a fraction amongst the volunteers, but a group that does appear to have been motivated by the more 'elevated' consideration than the mere personal; the over-representation of craftsmen, in contrast, is explicable by the damage caused by Napoleon's Continental System and requisitioning by the French army.[51]

The 'Borussian' (Prussian) school that dominated German historiography by the end of the nineteenth century argued that Prussian power and German cultural nationalism merged during the 'Wars of Liberation' of 1813. This is difficult to sustain: the Prussian reformers for the most part paid little attention to defining the cultural parameters of the national community and geographically thought in terms of the Prussian state.[52] Their caution in this matter is hardly surprising given Prussia's 'acquisition' of approximately three million Polish-speaking subjects in the eighteenth-century partitions.[53] Even strident nationalists like the philosopher Johann Gottlieb Fichte associated Germany's cultural flowering with its political fragmentation (something that distinguished it from 'French' bureaucratic centralization); most German speakers lived not in Prussia but in one of the other states, and amongst these Prussia's image was often as bad if not worse than that enjoyed by the French (something not assisted by Prussia's abandonment of the anti-French coalition in 1795). The experience of Napoleonic rule rather added to this element of divisiveness that obstructed the development of a German imagined community beyond the mere cultural. This was recognized by commentators at the time, who pointed to the largely negative impact of Napoleonic domination in Prussia and the Hanseatic cities—areas hit especially hard by the Continental System—but recognized the beneficial aspects (notably, the Napoleonic Code) in the west and south, areas where the patriotic call to arms (notably, Ernst Moritz Arndt's *Landwehrkatechismus*) in 1813–14 fell on deaf ears. The Borussian myth required that such differences be forgotten or trivialized.

Nationalism's Revolutionary Potential

The Revolutionary/Napoleonic crisis was a Europe-wide phenomenon. Its legacy for the subsequent development of nationalism was important. At the institutional level, the era saw the further strengthening of the large, uniform territorial state, an entity that through its very remoteness came to depend upon nationalism as an essential legitimating prop. The French revolutionaries started this process in 1789, by eliminating intermediate corporate bodies and provincial privileges, and by asserting the sovereignty of the French state over 'foreign' princes in Alsace and Avignon. They did all this for ideological reasons. There followed in the generation after 1789 the Europe-wide elimination of alternatives to large territorial states, a process in part driven by ideology but also by the dynamic of war. Thus did city states, ecclesiastical states, the Holy Roman Empire, and small principalities fall by the wayside; composite monarchies like Britain, Austria, and Prussia survived by becoming less composite. The Europe that emerged from all this in 1815 was thus far less heterogeneous than that of 1789.

These changes had an impact at grass-roots level. To many Europeans government became more remote; for most, it became more demanding. Governments taxed more, and some introduced military conscription. Borders became 'harder' and frontier controls less easy to evade. States paid greater attention to nationality law, a consequence in part of the French Republic's reaction to royalist emigration, but also of the necessity to police cross-border movement to prevent draft evasion. In short, borders between states meant more in 1815 than they had done previously. And, for a sizeable number of people, including Belgians, Genoese, Venetians, Poles, and a fair proportion of Germans, who found themselves annexed by states in this period, these borders enjoyed no historical legitimacy. All this gave rise to centre-periphery tensions as governments after 1815 attempted to integrate new populations. Especially in Germany and Italy, many of the states that emerged in 1815 suffered from legitimacy deficits, and this facilitated the spread of nationalism in those two areas later in the nineteenth century.[54]

The Revolutionary/Napoleonic period also had an impact at the level of ideas and rhetoric. The public sphere expanded even further, with contemporaries from various parts of Europe reporting the craving for news by even those nearer the bottom of the social pyramid. The rhetoric of nationalism in this period was without precedent in terms of its scope. Much of it was sponsored by government—in revolutionary France after 1789, in Britain (especially during the invasion scare of 1803–4), Spain (after 1808), Austria (in 1809), Russia (1812), and Prussia (1813). Historians have shown in some detail how reality was often at variance with this officially inspired rhetoric. At the time, the practical impact of the rhetoric was limited, as was its duration. However, it did have a tendency to take on a life of its own, with language not so much reflecting as shaping reality. Thus, nationalist rhetoric initially sponsored by government to aid mobilization was taken over to further very different agendas: the protection of particular local, confessional, social, or provincial interests, against attempts by government to centralize, conscript, and tax; or to challenge government on its handling of war and foreign policy, or even to demand greater participation in government affairs. Furthermore, the political conflicts in the decades after the Napoleonic Wars drew on the conflicting interpretations of what had happened in them. Memories of the wars were instrumentalized to further political agendas throughout Europe for the rest of the nineteenth century.

Europe's rulers recognized the subversive potential of nationalist ideas and rhetoric. Napoleon did so earlier than most, and spent much of his time squeezing the nationalist genie back into its bottle. He avoided dwelling on the dangerous issue of sovereignty, discouraged active citizenship, and avoided calling on the French nation, as the Jacobins had been compelled to do, by drawing on the resources of a vast empire. His props were soldiers inspired by glory, imperial bureaucrats motivated by a civilizing mission that was more urban, elitist, and European than French, and passive *administrés* who paid their tax. In the 1790s, Jacobin France briefly confronted the rest of Europe with the rhetoric and reality of the mobilized nation in arms; by 1813, Napoleonic France, in ironic contrast, condemned foreign nationalists attempting the same as revolutionary disturbers of the imperial peace.

Napoleon's main continental opponents—Francis of Austria,[55] Frederick William III of Prussia, and Alexander I of Russia—followed the French pattern of briefly encouraging and then containing national enthusiasm. Austria had briefly flirted with nationalism in 1809 hoping to emulate the Spanish example in Germany. Nothing much came of this other than a minor rebellion against the Bavarians in Tyrol and yet another crushing defeat. Thereafter, under Klemens von Metternich, Austria became Europe's leading opponent of nationalism, which it rightly regarded as incompatible with the monarchical principle. Prussia faced a greater challenge than Austria: it was more thoroughly defeated in 1806–7 than Austria in 1805 and 1809. Unlike in Austria, there were signs that a Prussian nationalism was emerging in which the higher ideal of the state was abstracted from the king who became, as it were, an expendable element. No doubt only a minority were imbued with this sense of Prussian *Staatspatriotismus*, but they were sufficiently well placed to mount what was in effect a military coup. Like Metternich in Austria and Napoleon in France, Prussia's king sought to bury the national enthusiasm released in 1813 at the earliest possible moment, a pattern also followed closely in Alexander's Russia. After Napoleon's defeat, all three eastern monarchies thus defaulted back to the best way of combining efficient government with stability: bureaucratic absolutism of the type that romantic nationalists in those countries had previously condemned as 'French'. After 1815 the Revolutionary/Napoleonic wars became an officially taboo subject, and would remain so until the passage of a generation inserted sufficient distance for the selective celebration of those aspects that best reinforced the existing order.

Notes

1. The focus of the section on resistance is primarily Prussia, with a brief look at Britain. Constraints of space prevent analysis of reactions to French imperialism in other parts of Europe. For these, the reader is referred to the extensive and growing secondary literature. For a European focus, T. C. W. Blanning (1985) 'The Role of Religion in European Counter-Revolution, 1789–1815', in D. Beales and G. Best (eds.) *History, Society and the Churches: Essays in Honour of Owen Chadwick*, Cambridge, 195–214; also, C. Esdaile (ed.) (2005) *Popular Resistance in the French Wars: Patriots, Partisans and Land Pirates*, Basingstoke. This second publication is especially strong on Spain, and on the motives of the guerrillas there fighting French forces. For German-speaking Europe, see H.

Schulze (1991) *The Course of German Nationalism: From Frederick the Great to Bismarck 1763–1867*, Cambridge; for the Russian Empire, see A. M. Martin (1997) *Romantics, Reformers, Reactionaries: Russian Conservative Thought and Politics in the Reign of Alexander*, DeKalb, IL. Specialized studies are curiously lacking for the Habsburg Monarchy in this period. For this polity, the reader is referred to C. A. Macartney (1971) *The Habsburg Empire, 1790–1918*, London. Napoleonic-era Italy, in contrast, has attracted more scholarly attention recently: M. Broers (2005) *The Napoleonic Empire in Italy, 1796–1814: Cultural Imperialism in a European Context?*, Basingstoke; and J. A. Davis (2006) *Naples and Napoleon: Southern Italy and the European Revolutions (1780–1860)*, Oxford and New York.

2. On historical writing and nationalism, see Chapter 36 by Paul Lawrence.
3. For Napoleonic memories in Germany, see the special issue of *Central European History* 39, no.4 (2006), which includes articles by K. Aaslestad, K. Hagemann, U. Planert, and M. Rowe. K. Hagemann is project director of 'Nations, Borders and Identities: The Revolutionary and Napoleonic Wars in European Experiences and Memories', which brings together scholars working in the field. For Britain, see H. Hoock (ed.) (2007) *History, Commemoration, and National Preoccupation: Trafalgar 1805–2005*, Oxford.
4. J. Habermas (1989) *The Structural Transformation of the Public Sphere: An Inquiry into a Category of Bourgeois Society*, Cambridge.
5. R. Darnton (1971) 'The High Enlightenment and the Low-Life of Literature in Pre-Revolutionary France', *Past and Present*, 51, 81–115.
6. J. Van Horn Melton (2001) *The Rise of the Public in Enlightenment Europe*, Cambridge.
7. T. C. W. Blanning (2002) *The Culture of Power and the Power of Culture: Old Regime Europe 1660–1789*, Oxford, ch. 8.
8. É. H. Balázs (1997) *Hungary and the Habsburgs 1765–1800: An Experiment in Enlightened Absolutism*, Budapest.
9. J. Egret, *La pré-révolution française, 1787–1788*, Paris, 71–3.
10. K. M. Baker (1978) 'French Political Thought at the Accession of Louis XVI', *The Journal of Modern History*, 50, no. 2, 279–303; M. Ozouf (1988) 'Public Opinion at the End of the Old Regime', *The Journal of Modern History*, 60 supplement, 1–21; R. R. Palmer (1940) 'The National Idea in France before the Revolution', *Journal of the History of Ideas*, 1, 89–111; M. Price (1995) 'The Dutch Affair and the Fall of the *Ancien Regime*, 1784–1787', *The Historical Journal*, 38, 875–905.
11. J. Brewer (1973) 'The Misfortunes of Lord Bute: A Case-Study in Eighteenth-Century Political Argument and Public Opinion', *The Historical Journal*, 16, 3–43; J. C. D. Clark (2002) 'Protestantism, Nationalism and National Identity', *The Historical Journal*, 43, 249–76.
12. L. Colley (1984) 'The Apotheosis of George III: Loyalty, Royalty and the British Nation 1760–1820', *Past and Present*, 102, 94–129.
13. M. Forsyth (1987) *Reason and Revolution: The Political Thought of the Abbé Sieyes*, Leicester, 76.
14. P. W. Schroeder (1994) *The Transformation of European Politics 1763–1848*, Oxford, 170.
15. My translation of the original, taken from C. Debbasch and J.-M. Pontier (eds.) (1989) *Les Constitutions de la France*, 2nd edn., Paris, 37.
16. T. C. W. Blanning (1986) *The Origins of the French Revolutionary Wars*, London, chs. 3–4; Schroeder, *Transformation*, 93–9. 'Brissotin' refers to the followers of Jacques Pierre Brissot (1754–93), who advocated war.

17. T. C. W. Blanning (1983) *The French Revolution in Germany: Occupation and Resistance in the Rhineland 1792–1802*, Oxford; S. Schama (1977) *Patriots and Liberators: Revolution in the Netherlands, 1780–1813*, London, ch. 4.
18. J.-P. Bertaud (1988) *The Army of the French Revolution*, Princeton, NJ, 250.
19. T. C. W. Blanning (1996) *The French Revolutionary Wars 1787–1802*, London and New York, 100–1.
20. Bertaud, *Army*, 82, 272.
21. A. Forrest (2002) *Napoleon's Men: The Soldiers of the Revolution and*, London and New York, ch. 4.
22. Bertaud, *Army*, 32, 126, 134, 192–3.
23. Ibid., 272.
24. J. A. Lynn (1984) *The Bayonets of the Republic: Motivation and Tactics in the Army of Revolutionary France, 1791–94*, Urbana, IL.
25. Bertaud, *Army*, 169.
26. P. Griffith (1998) *The Art of War of Revolutionary France, 1789–1802*, London, 73–4. Also P. Wetzler (1985) *War and Subsistence: The Sambre and Meuse Army in 1794*, New York.
27. Bertaud, *Army*, 158, 219, 271, 316.
28. A. Herriot (1957) *The French in Italy 1796–1799*, London, 86–7.
29. J. G. Gallaher (1991) 'The Prussian Regiment of the Napoleonic Army', *The Journal of Military History*, 55, 331–44.
30. J H. Gill (1992) *With Eagles to Glory: Napoleon and his German Allies in the 1809 Campaign*, London, 23; C. Esdaile (2007) *Napoleon's Wars: An International History 1803–1815*, London, 452.
31. 'Lotharingian' might be closer to the mark: M. Broers (2001) 'Napoleon, Charlemagne, and Lotharingia: Acculturation and the Boundaries of Napoleonic Europe', *The Historical Journal*, 44, 135–54. See also P. G. Dwyer, 'Introduction', and G. Ellis, 'The Nature of Napoleonic Imperialism', in P. G. Dwyer (ed.) (2001) *Napoleon and Europe*, London, 1–21 and 97–117, respectively.
32. Napoleon decreed Catalonia's incorporation into France as four newly instituted departments on 26 January 1812. However, in legal terms annexation never took effect.
33. M. Rowe (2003) *From Reich to State: The Rhineland in the Revolutionary Age, 1780–1830*, Cambridge, 191.
34. Rowe, *Reich* 8.
35. I. Woloch (1994) *The New Regime: Transformations of the French Civic Order, 1789–1820s*, London and New York, chs. 6–7.
36. I. Collins, (1979) *Napoleon and his Parliaments, 1800–1815*, London.
37. J. Tulard (2004) *Le sacré de l'empereur Napoléon. Histoire et légende*, Paris, 6.
38. For the original (French) quotation, see Tulard, *Le sacré de l'empereur Napoléon*, 15.
39. P. Mansel (1988) *The Court of France, 1789–1830*, Cambridge, 57–69.
40. The literature on Napoleonic France is vast. Amongst the most accessible items that have not already been cited are the following: R. B. Holtman (1967) *The Napoleonic Revolution*, Philadelphia, PA; M. Lyons (1994) *Napoleon Bonaparte and the Legacy of the French Revolution*, Basingstoke; G. Ellis (1997) *Napoleon*, Harlow; J. Tulard (1984) *Napoleon: the Myth of the Saviour*, London. For the wider Napoleonic empire, M. Broers (1996) *Europe under Napoleon 1799–1815*, London and New York; S. Woolf (1991) *Napoleon's Integration of Europe*, London.
41. Napoleon was less tolerant of Frenchmen serving foreign princes. Rowe, *Reich*, 188–9.

42. It is not even clear whether the wider community was essentially English or British. For the argument that this period of war contributed more to a sense of Englishness, see J. C. D. Clark (2000) 'Protestantism, Nationalism and National Identity, 1660–1832', *The Historical Journal*, 43, no. 1, 249–76. For the view that it was a British identity that was forged, see L. Colley (1992) *Britons: Forging the Nation 1707–1837*, New Haven and New York. For the regional and social dimension in particular, M. Philp (ed.) (2006) *Resisting Napoleon: The British Response to the Threat of Invasion, 1797–1815*, Aldershot. Also, C. Emsley (1979) *British Society and the French Wars, 1793–1815*, London; and J. E. Cookson (1989) 'The English Volunteer Movement of the French Wars, 1793–1815: Some Contexts', *The Historical Journal*, 32, no. 4, 867–91. For the Irish dimension, and the 1798 rebellion in particular, see T. Bartlett, D. Dickson, D. Keogh, and K. Whelan (eds.) (2003) *1798: A Bicentenary Perspective*, Dublin.
43. Stein to Hardenberg, 7 December 1807. Quoted from M. Levinger (2000) *Enlightened Nationalism: The Transformation of Prussian Political Culture, 1806–1848*, Oxford, 46.
44. Levinger, *Enlightened Nationalism*, 57–8, 62.
45. R. M. Berdahl (1988) *The Politics of the Prussian Nobility: The Development of a Conservative Ideology, 1770–1848*, Princeton, NJ.
46. Levinger, *Enlightened Nationalism*, 83–5, 89, 91, 99–101, 113–14.
47. C. Clark (2006) *Iron Kingdom: The Rise and Downfall of Prussia, 1600–1947*, London, 346–50.
48. For more on Yorck, see P. Paret (1966) *Yorck and the Era of Prussian Reform, 1807–1815*, Princeton, NJ.
49. Clark, *Iron Kingdom*, 358–62.
50. Clark, *Iron Kingdom*, 374–6.
51. It must be noted that the vast majority of Prussian soldiers were conscripts, not volunteers. At the peak of the mobilization effort, in August 1813, volunteer 'Jäger' battalions numbered approximately 10,000 men, a tiny proportion of the 300,000-strong army. D. Gates (1997) *The Napoleonic Wars*, London, 229.
52. Levinger, *Enlightened Nationalism*, 63–5.
53. Most of these were lost in the 1807 Tilsit settlement imposed by Napoleon. However, a return of these Polish territories constituted one of Prussia's war aims in 1813.
54. For more on citizenship and the control of movement across borders, see A. Fahrmeir (2007) *Citizenship: The Rise and Fall of a Modern Concept*, New Haven, CT, and London.
55. He held two imperial titles: as Francis II he was Holy Roman Emperor, a title abolished along with the empire in 1806; and as Francis I of the new Austrian Empire he founded.

Suggested Further Reading

Alexander, R. S. (2001) *Napoleon*, London.

Bell, D. A. (2001) *The Cult of the Nation in France: Inventing Nationalism, 1680–1800*, Cambridge MA.

Blanning, T. C. W. (1983) *French Revolution in Germany: Occupation and Resistance in the Rhineland 1792–1802*, Oxford.

Blanning, T. C. W. (2002) *The Culture of Power and the Power of Culture: Old Regime Europe 1660–1789*, Oxford.

Broers, M. (1996) *Europe under Napoleon 1799–1815*, London and New York.
Colley, L. (1992) *Britons: Forging the Nation 1707–1837*, New Haven and London.
Esdaile, C. (ed.) (2005) *Popular Resistance in the French Wars: Patriots, Partisans and Land Pirates*, Basingstoke.
Fletcher, I. (ed.) (1998) *The Peninsular War: Aspects of the Struggle for the Iberian Peninsula*, Staplehurst.
Forrest, A. (2002) *Napoleon's Men: The Soldiers of the Revolution and Empire*, London and New York.
Laven, D. and Riall, L. (eds.) (2000) *Napoleon's Legacy: Problems of Government in Restoration Europe*, Oxford.
Levinger, M. (2000) *Enlightened Nationalism: The Transformation of Prussian Political Culture, 1806–1848*, Oxford.
Lovett, G. H. (1965) *Napoleon and the Birth of Modern Spain*, New York.
Martin, A. M. (1997) *Romantics, Reformers, Reactionaries: Russian Conservative Thought and Politics in the Reign of Alexander I*, DeKalb, IL.
Muir, R. (1998) *Tactics and the Experience of Battle in the Age of Napoleon*, New Haven, CT, and London.
Philp, M. (ed.) (2006) *Resisting Napoleon: The British Response to the Threat of Invasion, 1797–1815*, Aldershot.
Schama, S. (1989) *Citizens: A Chronicle of the French Revolution*, New York.
Schulze, H. (1991) *The Course of German Nationalism: From Frederick the Great to Bismarck 1763–1867*, Cambridge.
Woolf, S. (1991) *Napoleon's Integration of Europe*, London.

CHAPTER 8

NATIONALISM AND NATIONAL UNIFICATION IN NINETEENTH-CENTURY EUROPE

JOHN BREUILLY

INTRODUCTION

FROM today's perspective a map of Europe in 1810 is notable for one great absence: nation states. Europe was dominated by multi-ethnic dynastic states, whether old (Romanov, Habsburg, Hohenzollern, Ottoman) or new (Napoleonic). Transforming this political geography into nation states can take three forms.[1] First, state-led or nation-building nationalism 'nationalizes' the population and government without changing the boundaries of a state.[2] Or second, state-opposing nationalism aims to form a separate nation state from an existing state.[3] In nineteenth-century Europe significant nationalist movements took the third form: aiming to unify a fragmented nation into a single state.

This chapter considers the role that German, Italian, and Polish nationalism played in nation-state formation. I use the term 'unification nationalism', but arguably 'pan-nationalism' is better. Pan-nationalism implies failed unification nationalism (for example, Pan-Africanism, Pan-Arabism) while unification nationalism implies successful pan-nationalism.[4] However, until the moment of success (unification) there is no difference between the two. 'Unification' is a retrospective judgement that informs historical understanding. Appreciating that this is hindsight helps us reflect on the particular challenges which confronted pan-nationalisms in nineteenth-century Europe.

The Background

The eighteenth century ended with the destruction of a great European state that carried a national name. In 1795 the third and final Polish partition gave rise to protests about national servitude. Lord Acton judged the partition an injustice, which also marked the starting point of modern nationalism.[5] The beneficiaries of that extinction were three multi-ethnic dynasties: Hohenzollern, Habsburg, Romanov. The French Revolution generated militant nationalism in France but its medium-term consequence was yet another multi-ethnic dynasty: Napoleon's empire.[6] The Habsburg and Hohenzollern dynasties collaborated with Napoleon in destroying small states in central Europe and, having defeated Napoleon, confirmed much of his territorial reorganization, even sometimes retaining 'national' terminology.[7] The German lands were given a political roof in the shape of the German Confederation, dominated by Habsburg and Hohenzollern, though legal sovereignty was vested in thirty-odd princely states (plus four city states). The Italian lands had been politically simplified but Habsburg domination over the peninsula was secured variously by direct rule (Lombardy-Venetia), dynastic ties (Tuscany, Parma, Modena), formal agreements on rights of military intervention, and Austria's proximity. Finally, despite boundary alterations (Prussia ceded Polish lands to Russia, receiving German territories as compensation), the partition of Poland was confirmed. The historic kingdom of Poland roughly divided into four parts: territory annexed by Russia ('Russian Poland'); 'Congress Poland' (named after the Congress of Vienna, 1814–15, and bound in personal union with Russia); the Grand Duchy of Posen in Prussia; the Habsburg province of Galicia.

These arrangements suited the three dynasties. Despite public sympathy for these nationalist causes in Britain, the settlement satisfied concern for stability and balance in Europe, leaving Britain free to pursue commercial and naval supremacy beyond Europe. French liberals and radicals nursed dreams of supporting oppressed national movements but were implacably opposed by the restored Bourbon monarchy. Such movements were easily suppressed. The obstacles in the way of a Europe of nation states appeared insuperable.

Pan-Nationalism: Doctrines and Sentiments

I define nationalism as a politics that seeks autonomy for the nation. This politics claims there is a distinct nation (usually comprehending all or most social groups in a certain territory) whose interests and values are embodied in the nationalist programme. One can distinguish between nationalism as intellectual claim (doctrine), shared sense of identity (sentiment), and strategy and organization (politics). The three are closely linked but such distinctions enable comparison that moves beyond a series of narrative national histories.

The construction of nationalist doctrine was a transnational process. The 'discovery' of national epics such as the German *Nibelungenlied* proceeded from a European network of scholars.[8] The perception that such epics were relevant to contemporaries centred on the rejection of the Voltairean judgement that post-Roman Europe until the seventeenth century was a dark period best left obscure. It was informed by the romantic sense that these texts were less individual compositions than expressions of national culture. This transnational character should be understood not as individual 'national awakenings' but as a pan-European intellectual movement. However, the very conceit of discovering, restoring, and cultivating unique national cultures meant intellectuals applied their energies mainly to their 'own' nation in ways that accentuated variety.

Polish nationalist discourse thus displayed specific features. A state called Poland existed until 1795.[9] Polish nobles defended this state as that of the Polish nation. However, it had long ceased to be effective. With an elective monarchy, a parliament dominated by great magnates, populated by a numerous gentry and incapable of making decisions, it was controlled from outside. Hitherto those external powers calculated it was better to keep Poland nominally in existence rather than to annex its territories.[10] A state-focused patriotism sought reforms to restore genuine autonomy. These rarely extended beyond political measures, such as voting procedures of the parliament (*Sejm*) or reshuffling power between magnates and gentry. Such patriotism was doomed to failure, given the corruption of the existing regime. Marked by its absence was any serious attempt to include the mass of the subjects in the national movement, especially through land reform. Some patriots turned to insurrection, which the partitioning powers crushed. Subsequent nationalist discourse commenced its story with this 'martyrdom'. Hopes of resurrection flared briefly when Napoleon formed the Grand Duchy of Warsaw, reflecting European nationalist ideas about Poland. Poles formed an important element in the Grand Army that invaded Russia in 1812. Consequently they shared in Napoleon's defeat.

Many Polish nationalists could only express themselves freely in exile.[11] Following Russian repression of insurrection in Congress Poland in 1831, Paris and London became major centres. Nationalist activity polarized between restorationists and radicals. Restorationists, led by Prince Czartoryski, were anti-Russian, aimed to retain the privileged hierarchy of pre-partition Poland and saw in diplomacy the main instrument of change. Radicals, regarding nationalism as inclusive and egalitarian, preached reform (especially peasant emancipation) to appeal beyond the privileged, and saw popular insurrection as the way forward. All nationalists infused their programmes with a romantic sensibility most eloquently expressed by the exiled poet Adam Mickiewicz. Poland as martyr conjured up a Catholic imagery of blood sacrifice and redemption. Historians constructed narratives of glory, decline, and suffering, pointing to renewed glory in the future. Although little concrete was undertaken to help the

Polish cause, public opinion in Britain and France treated these doctrines with credulous sympathy.[12]

Polish exiles were not alone, as suppression of unrest in the late 1820s and early 1830s extended to German and Italian lands.[13] Exiles supported and influenced each other, seeing their movements as similar and complementary. In the 1820s the Greek uprising sparked nationalist enthusiasm, in particular functioning for some Germans as a disguised form of their own nationalism. French and British radicals vociferously championed the Polish cause, especially against reactionary Russia. The most systematic advocacy of a Europe of nations asserted against dynasties came from Mazzini's 'Young Europe'. Giuseppe Mazzini embodied and cultivated the romantic image of political exile as hero-martyr; a political asset in the battle for public support in Britain and France and for securing leadership of notoriously factious exile networks.[14]

As with Poland, Italian nationalist doctrine first found detailed expression under Napoleon, even if such nationalists were torn by ambivalent feelings towards Napoleon as revolutionary and despot. A call for national resistance to dynastic Europe came in March 1815 from Joachim Murat, Napoleon's brother-in-law and King of Naples, in the 'Rimini proclamation': 'Italians! The hour has come to engage in your highest destiny.' Murat was executed in May but his conversion to 'Italian nationalism' impressed writers like Alessandro Manzoni. 'Muratism' raised its head again as late as 1859–60.

Nationalist ideas were elaborated not just as political doctrine but as poetry, novels, paintings, sculptures, and music. Alberto Banti has identified a 'Risorgimento canon' with a vision of Italy that motivated many to risk life and liberty.[15] Along with its emotional affinities with Polish romantic nationalism, there is a similar distinction between moderates and radicals. The former, usually from privileged backgrounds, counselled diplomacy and incremental liberal reform such as tariff reductions, constitutionalism, and voluntary land reform. The latter, with professional men prominent, operated in secret societies and/or exile, penned appeals to the 'people', and conspired to spark insurrection.

The distinction works less well for German nationalism. It was not possible to portray Germany as groaning under a foreign yoke because Austria and Prussia were ruled by German princes and there was a rudimentary political system in the German Confederation. The national movement focused instead on how to 'nationalize' the Confederation. German nationalists looked to nationwide institutions such as universities and elite secondary schools with common curricula and students drawn from different states; newspaper, periodical, and book publishers; inter-state agreements on tariffs, cross-border movement, and currencies. At the extremes there were radicals seeking rapid transformation through revolution and moderates aiming for gradual reform such as customs unions and alliances between like-minded elites in different German states. However, in between were many shades of opinion, for example those who saw Prussia as an agent of unity against Austria and the smaller German states.

Polish nationalism is most easily framed as opposition to foreign rule, whereas German nationalism is most difficult to see in this way. Italian nationalists occupied an intermediate position, with much of the peninsula ruled by native princes but

'German' Habsburg power seen as dominant. Some nationalists did look to Piedmont or the Papacy as agents of national reform but these hopes were less substantial than those vested in Prussia. Unsurprisingly, radical insurrectionism was strongest in Polish and weakest in German nationalist discourse.

These pan-nationalist doctrines assumed that they expressed not merely an authentic but a dominant culture. Their exponents drew upon well-established literary languages predominating in the government administration and established Churches.[16] Influential was a distinction between 'nation' as bearer of culture and rulership, entitled to a state, and 'nationality' as referring to vernacular cultures of largely non-literate masses who did not merit political independence.[17] Mazzini's Europe of nations had no place for Ruthenes, Slovaks, or Romanians. Polish nationalists dismissed, even if they acknowledged, national claims in the names of Ruthenes, Ukrainians, and Lithuanians. Germans nationalists rejected political claims by Czech and other Slav nationalists.[18]

This type of nationalism confronts two challenges when trying to mobilize popular support. The first is social inclusion. Nationalists did not come from humble backgrounds. Censorship and limited literacy constrained mass appeal, especially in the countryside. If nationalists failed to propose social and economic reform, it is difficult to see why their arguments would have had any popular resonance. Claims made for the popularity of such nationalism are weak. Banti cites support for Pope Pius IX between his election in 1846 and the revolution of 1848 as evidence of nationalist mass appeal. However, Banti's own argument that nationalism clothed itself in well-entrenched sentiments of family and Catholicism suggests that it was these that achieved popular resonance. Once Pius IX turned against nationalism, mass support for it swiftly faded away.[19]

The second challenge—ethno-national inclusion—was less important for Italian nationalists.[20] However, restoring the Polish state envisaged rule over a multi-ethnic world. Yet if Polish nationalism could only be effective through popular appeal, the danger was that such mobilization would promote non-Polish nationalist sentiments. A similar response to German nationalism could develop in multi-ethnic zones such as Prussian Posen with its Polish-speaking majority and Habsburg Bohemia with its Czech-speaking majority.

Pan-Nationalist Politics

Before 1848

Pan-nationalist politics were poorly developed before 1848, except for in Poland where they varied regionally. Cultural nationalism was easiest to cultivate in Congress Poland in the 1820s. In the 1830 insurrection nationalists gained control of the kingdom's army, drawing leadership from political elites. The emotional pull of restorationist nationalism inhibited moderate opposition. Nevertheless, nationalists were divided over whether and how to use violence and on framing a popular reform programme. They had limited success mobilizing in Russian Poland, where Lithuanian and Ruthene peasants proved unreceptive. Russia crushed the uprising in 1831, removed much of the kingdom's autonomy, and ended constitutional rule.

In Posen, Prussia had long worked with Polish magnates but enhanced military security on the border with Congress Poland in 1830. In Galicia the government cooperated with Polish landowners. Nationalist organization was concentrated amongst the numerous smaller gentry (*szlachta*) as well as students in towns like Cracow but was largely isolated from magnates and peasants. When *szlachta* nationalists sought to spark insurrection in 1846, peasants turned against them, often in league with the Habsburg authorities, killing an estimated one to two thousand gentry. This *jacquerie* was concentrated in western Galicia where the peasants spoke Polish. *Szlachta* nationalism could not transcend class, let alone ethnic difference. The uprising was linked to a conspiracy in Posen that was betrayed and repressed, although the nationalist cause received good publicity from mass trials in 1847.

Following Russian repression many nationalists went into exile. The middle third of the century was the heyday of émigré politics, divided between moderates and radicals, in different locations, highly factionalized yet sharing a transnational language of romantic nationalism. Émigrés did not coordinate well with those at home; and nationalists in the different regions cooperated poorly with one another. There was no significant external support beyond expressions of sympathy that were far outweighed by implacable opposition from the three dynasties.

Italian nationalist politics was less developed. There was no recent statehood from which to draw ideas, elites, and institutional practices. One had to look back centuries for 'Italian' resistance to foreigners, and that principally from city states. Writers like Carlo Cattaneo and Jean de Sismondi made the urban commune the focus of historical interpretation and contemporary strategy but were at odds with those who looked to an existing state (Papacy, Piedmont) or a popular movement led by nationalist heroes (Mazzini, Garibaldi). Meanwhile the Habsburg Empire demonstrated its power by repressing disturbances. Beyond a few half-baked conspiracies hatched by Mazzini little was achieved beyond additions to the roll call of martyrs.

German elite national sentiment was better developed though less overtly political. Exile politics was dominated by radicals cut off from the domestic mainstream. By the mid-1840s there were nationwide liberal and democratic associations. There were differences between those who looked to leadership from Prussia or Austria, those hoping to develop a popular politics building upon the constitutional regimes of the medium states, and those focused on economic or political reforms with unifying consequences. Governments prosecuted overt nationalist politics. However, elements within those same governments agreed on the need for reform and that current arrangements could not be sustained indefinitely. Nevertheless, these divisions and the opposition of Prussia and Austria kept nationalist politics weak.

Mid-Century Revolution

The revolutions of 1848 were not initially about the national question but a combination of political reform demands and widespread discontent with short-term economic hardship due to harvest failures and long-run problems of economic development.[21] These remained major concerns throughout the revolutions. It was growing differences over such matters as instituting parliamentary government and democratic franchises, implementing peasant emancipation and tackling mass unemployment, which aided successful counter-revolution. What made the 'national question' important for many was its bearing on such concerns. Where Polish or Magyar nobles controlled Slav or Romanian peasants, the national question was a social question.

The rapid spread of revolution allowed new political movements to flourish, including nationalist ones. Polish nationalism was the most developed but also the most divided and opposed. In Russian and Congress Poland absence of revolution inhibited nationalist action. In Galicia the recent repression of 1846 had similar effects. The best prospects lay in Posen, especially after a liberal ministry in Berlin declared in favour of a restored Poland, freed those imprisoned after the 1846 conspiracy, and granted autonomy to Posen.[22] This policy was opposed not only by the temporarily paralyzed monarchy but increasingly by Germans in Posen. The government in Berlin retreated from its initial Polonophilia, covering its tracks with a partition between Germans and Poles, though one vastly favouring Germans. The German National Assembly supported this policy in a debate that included strong expressions of anti-Polish sentiment.

What we might today call ethnic conflict arose in other places. Czech nationalists in Bohemia and Moravia, part of the German Confederation, called for a boycott of elections to the German National Assembly. The Croatian leader Joseph Graf Jellačić opposed Magyar demands for an autonomous Hungary that would subject Croatians to rule from Budapest. Romanian nationalists took the same line in Transylvania. Conflict was along class as well as ethnic lines. Such conflict also expressed itself as mutual hostility between national groups in different states, for example between Germans and Danes over Schleswig-Holstein, or German support for continued Habsburg power over Italians, Hungarian, and Slavs. However, the main obstacles to nationalist success in the German and Italian lands lay less in inter-ethnic or inter-state conflict as in the difficulties of obtaining unity of purpose and identity within one's 'own' nation.

German nationalism was initially the best organized, as demonstrated in the calling and running of democratic elections to a national Parliament that met for a year in Frankfurt am Main from May 1848. The deputies, overwhelmingly from bourgeois, especially professional and academic, backgrounds, could quickly cooperate despite having had few previous connections, by dint of a common conception of German nationality and commitment to establishing a national state.[23] However, they were distanced from the popular politics emerging in the individual states. Moderates were anti-democratic and favoured negotiation with existing states to achieve national goals. They were divided between those who looked to Prussia or Austria for leadership (Prussians tended to be pro-Prussia, Austrians pro-Austria, other Germans sceptical), a division overlapping with that between Protestant and Catholic. As old regimes regained confidence, appealed to reservoirs of support—taking credit for popular measures such as peasant emancipation—exploited divisions between their opponents, and turned ultimately to their armies, so Frankfurt parliamentarians found themselves at odds with each other and unable to summon popular or military force to oppose counter-revolution.

However, one cannot write off the German national movement as failure. The work of the National Assembly laid bare obstacles to unification. Proposals such as freedom of movement throughout the national territory or the abolition of guild and communal controls over local occupational and residence rights evoked opposition, often from people who proclaimed national ideals. Plotting the detailed division of powers between national government and member states, or between Church and State, revealed further disagreements. Beyond certain elites and groups such as mobile skilled workers, it turned out that 'Germans' agreed on very little. Drafting a constitution was a considerable political as well as intellectual achievement that moved debate beyond vague ideas of unity based on shared identity.[24] It also raised one final problem: who would hold power in this nation state?

Once it was clear that unification was only possible in cooperation with existing power holders, the central issue was the relationship between Prussia and Austria. In March 1848, Frederick William IV of Prussia, under pressure from insurgents in Berlin, declared that his country would 'go forth' into Germany. His liberal ministers were sincere in their national values. However, as Posen showed, liberals soon backed away from such values. The focus shifted to German, even Prussian concerns, although they were seen differently from radical, liberal, and conservative perspectives. As the old order reasserted itself, conservative anti-national views became more important. As the Habsburg dynasty regained authority in the summer and autumn of 1848 in its Austrian heartland, then Bohemia and Moravia, then north Italy, its leaders made clear their opposition to any German nation state that excluded Habsburg Germany and equally to any dismemberment of the empire into 'national' segments.[25]

The National Assembly shifted position with the changing political climate. First, it proposed a 'greater' Germany including Habsburg Germany. Then it devised the idea of an inner and outer Germany, one including and one excluding Habsburg Germany. Finally it gambled on a Prussia-dominated, 'lesser' Germany, offering the emperorship of the new state to Frederick William IV. However, a majority for this offer was only attained by making concessions to radicals so that the constitution stipulated a sovereign Parliament elected on universal manhood suffrage. The Prussian king rejected this poisoned chalice, at which point most deputies went home. Radicals stepped into the breach and there were 'second revolutions' in the spring of 1849 invoking the Imperial Constitution, but these were opposed by moderate nationalists and crushed by Prussian troops.

Politically the weakest movement was that of Italy. There was no Italian political system like the German Confederation or recent state tradition as with Poland. The revolutions mainly proceeded in their own way in each Italian territory, even divided within the same state. Throughout the period of revolution, revolutionaries in Milan and Venice acted independently of each other, even cut off from rural hinterlands. The Kingdom of the Two Sicilies reflected its title as Sicilians rose up separately from mainland rebels. Pius IX turned against the national movement after increasing unrest forced him to flee Rome in November 1848. The subsequent radical revolution in Rome did bring Mazzini and Giuseppe Garibaldi to the fore, turning the newly declared republic into a nationalist vanguard. Piedmont apparently rallied to the national cause, going to war against Austria in April 1848, briefly incorporating Lombardy-Venetia and evoking nationalist enthusiasm. However, the rigidly conservative king of Piedmont-Sardinia, Charles Albert (1798–1849), was bent on dynastic expansion and therefore regarded with great suspicion by nationalists who only supported him for pragmatic reasons. Those reasons evaporated with Piedmont's military defeat at the battle of Custozza in July 1848. It renewed war in March 1849 but was even more quickly defeated.

The predominance of local concerns, rivalries between cities like Turin and Milan, Venice and Rome, Palermo and Naples; the failure to develop a social programme with popular appeal, indeed the hostility of moderates to any such programme: all this meant the nationalist goal in Italy had no chance of success without external intervention. Britain made sympathetic noises but nothing more. France was the great hope, but its revolution faltered with the election of Louis Napoleon in December 1848 and then his coup in December 1851. The new ruler put Catholic populism ahead of a Europe of nations. French soldiers were amongst those (also Neapolitan, Spanish, Austrian, and Papal) who suppressed the Roman republic and hunted Garibaldi across the peninsula. It was not enough to have an idea of '*italianata*', embodied in a canon of inspiring works of art; without coordination between regions and nationalists of different hues, popular support, and external intervention, nationalist politics remained weak and incoherent.

The most formidable national movement of 1848–9 was in Hungary. It did not have the problem endemic to pan-nationalism of being divided between different states. It shared with Polish nationalism a landowning leadership and, as in Congress Poland until 1831, access to administrative and military resources. It confronted the Habsburg Empire which was in a state of general collapse. As events drifted towards conflict, many Hungarian nationalists reluctantly decided upon rebellion. They framed a popular reform programme. Only outright repression, with Russian troops crossing the border to aid the Habsburgs in April 1849, ended this revolution, accompanied by the ominous emergence of counter-nationalist movements amongst Romanians and Slavs. The Hungarian case points up specific weaknesses in the three pan-nationalist movements.[26]

By contrast, Slav pan-nationalism never got much beyond words. In the Czech case, there was a cultural movement and limited politics. However, Czech nationalists were reluctant to work with less developed movements. Polish nationalists kept their distance from pan-Slavism, which might challenge Polish assumptions of dominance in multi-ethnic regions. Slav efforts to construct written language led to disagreements, for example, over which dialect(s) to choose. Slav movements had different views of political strategy. Russia sponsored its own brand of pan-Slavism that was at odds with Austro-Slavism, which regarded Russian Tsarism as a threat. Austro-Slavism took different forms in Galicia, Hungary, Bohemia, and Moravia, and was distanced from south Slav ideas associated with gaining autonomy from the Ottoman Empire.

From Pan-Nationalist Failure to Successful Unification

Failure in 1848–9 changed nationalism and the national question. Counter-revolution in Prussia and Austria crushed Polish nationalist politics for two decades. Radicals went into exile to plot again but, given the weaknesses revealed in diplomatic and insurrectionary strategies, the emphasis was on building popular support. Peasant emancipation provided the key condition for 'organic work'.[27] This meant turning from 'high' to 'low' politics, becoming absorbed in local conditions that varied from region to region, and taking on 'vernacular' forms that extolled popular culture. It involved peasants, village schoolteachers, and the clergy of non-privileged churches (Greek Catholic in Galicia, Catholic in Posen). That differentiated Polish-speaking peasants from others, especially in eastern Galicia, promoted by Habsburg support for peasant emancipation, improved elementary schooling and rising literacy rates, commercialization, provincial autonomy, and electoral politics.[28]

This was less important in Russian and Congress Poland where the absence of revolution (and hence counter-revolution) and peasant emancipation enabled some continuity for traditions of romantic, gentry nationalism, culminating in the insurrection of 1863. With its repression, the imposition of direct Russian rule and some measure of peasant emancipation, conditions should have been laid for a similar shift towards 'organic work'.[29] However, peasant emancipation was less thoroughgoing than in Galicia and Posen, and direct Russian rule, combined with aggressive Russification, provided less space for popular national identity. Ukrainian nationalism was stronger in eastern Galicia than Russian Poland, though the latter subsequently became a core region of modern Ukraine.

All these developments had negative consequences for pan-nationalism. Polish movements in Posen and Galicia were more exercised by ethno-national challenges—in Posen from better-placed German groups and a German state, in Galicia from national movements amongst hitherto subordinate groups. Polish nationalism in

Congress Poland[30] and Russian Poland had lost its gentry leadership but this had not yet been replaced by peasant-based nationalism. A potential base developed with urban-industrial growth but this would be fragmented and much pulled toward socialism. The international situation worsened prospects for unification, especially after the German chancellor Bismarck engineered a dynastic alliance between Austria, Germany, and Russia in 1888.

Prospects did not appear much better in 1850 for German, Italian, and Hungarian nationalists. Yet twenty years later there were German and Italian nation states, and Hungary possessed internal autonomy and influence on Vienna over foreign and military policy. Nationalist doctrines, sentiment, and politics were not obviously stronger than in the Polish lands, indeed arguably weaker. Nationalist politics in Germany and Italy did change and in certain respects grew stronger, but what was crucial was how they combined with wider forces tending to nation-state formation.

Nationalist movements became more realistic. There remained exiles who dreamed of popular uprisings but they were marginalized. Imprisonment, repression, and emigration dissipated radical nationalism, some finding new outlets in socialism or on the Union side in the American Civil War (1861–5). Active nationalists who remained were either moderate or disciplined their radicalism to work in wider coalitions. Whereas in the Polish lands pan-nationalism disappeared in the local effort of 'organic work', in Germany and Italy new political possibilities opened.

Counter-revolution could not endure. Early industrialization in the 1850s, led by investment in railway construction, meant that regions with resources such as coal and iron ore, and prepared to give entrepreneurs freedom, developed rapidly. Tariff reductions, customs unions, freedom to form limited-liability companies made small Italian and German states look absurd and strengthened the influence of bourgeois groups favouring national liberal reforms. Piedmont and Prussia appeared as promising agents of this change. Elite organizations such as the *Società Nazionale* (established 1857) and the *National Verein* (established 1859 and borrowing the name of its Italian counterpart) used a sober language of realism and progress and sought to work with, not against, governments.[31] Not only moderates ran these influential pressure groups but also former radicals who saw them as the only way forward.

The major opponent of German and Italian as well as Hungarian nationalism was the Habsburg regime. This did not, contrary to retrospective nationalist accounts, stagnate in the 1850s and early 1860s. Vienna was massively rebuilt; the Habsburg economy grew more rapidly than earlier. In relative terms it was less dynamic than the German states in the *Zollverein* (the German Customs Union founded in 1834) but more than most Italian states. However, the Habsburg Empire as a major power was overstretched in ways that did not apply to Prussia and Piedmont. The Crimean War (1853–6) imposed a financial toll even though Austria was officially neutral. That neutrality, effectively anti-Russian, ensured the loss of the conservative alliance with Russia but did not bring closer ties with the Western Powers. Louis-Napoleon reverted to the French tradition of supporting national movements and in 1859 France went to war in northern Italy against Austria, with Piedmont very much a junior ally.

Rapid victory enabled Prime Minister Cavour to expand Piedmontese control into other parts of northern Italy. Unexpectedly, this led to the fall of governments in central and southern Italy, culminating by the end of 1860 in the Piedmontese-led unification of the peninsula, except for Venetia and the Papal States.

Defeat in 1859 led to constitutionalism and financial retrenchment in Austria. This weakened her militarily in relation to Prussia, which by contrast had embarked on an ambitious military modernization programme in the early 1860s. Liberal nationalists looked to Prussia to take the lead, although remaining anxious to avoid war or the exclusion of Habsburg Germany from a nation state. That these unwished-for events came about in 1866 makes it clear how much the national movement followed rather than led unification. The Austro-Prussian war of that year completed Habsburg exclusion from the Italian and German lands, thereby strengthening Hungary within the reduced empire. Moderate nationalists, not the radicals prominent in 1848, led in negotiating autonomy. Finally, the war of 1870–1 between France and Prussia-Germany in alliance with Italy ended with the formation of the German Second Empire and the completion of Italian unification except for a small Papal enclave in Rome.

To understand how this rapid transformation came about in the Italian and German lands and what role nationalism played, we need to analyse this sequence of events. The most obvious similarity was the leading role of Piedmont and Prussia. Both states had reactionary reputations before and during 1848. Both signalled leadership of the national movement during the revolution, even if motives were dynastic rather than national. Both went to war—Piedmont with Austria, Prussia with Denmark—and both had been defeated or forced to withdraw. After 1848 both retained (Piedmont's 'Statuto') or granted a constitution. Both initiated free-trade agreements and other liberal economic reforms. Both thereby became poles of attraction for the liberal, 'realistic' tendency in the national movement. Both could only envisage expansion within their 'national' lands. Prussia was limited by France, Russia, and Austria to the west, east, and south respectively. She had success in 1864 in the north, in the war fought alongside Austria against Denmark, but that only secured Schleswig-Holstein. The greatest gains to be made were in the German lands. Likewise Piedmont was constrained by French power to the west and looked to northern Italy as its potential zone for expansion. For both states the principal obstacle was the Habsburg Empire, protector of the smaller German and Italian states. Unification for Piedmont and Prussia was only achieved after war against Austria; Piedmont in 1859 and 1866, and Prussia in 1866. The great fear for national liberals was that that they might end up just replacing one dynastic power by another.

There were also important differences. Prussia was far more powerful than Piedmont. Prussia required only non-intervention by the other major powers when she fought wars against Austria and France. Bismarck was able, by a combination of skill and luck, to localize the two wars and to settle them decisively before the possibility of external interference.[32] The problem for Piedmont was the opposite. She could not challenge Habsburg hegemony in Italy without a powerful ally. Cavour entertained ideas of British help but that never extended beyond diplomatic support. France was the only candidate, and 1859 was effectively a Franco-Austrian war. Piedmont was shut out of subsequent peace negotiations and initially looked likely to gain just Lombardy in exchange for ceding Nice and Savoy to France. The extension of Piedmontese rule throughout Italy was entirely unexpected and will be considered below. In the wars of 1866 and 1870–1, Italy was junior partner to Prussia.

It is difficult to integrate state interest, international diplomacy, and dynastic warfare with nationalism, if we see the latter as a popular movement of the 'nation'. Historians tend to one pole or the other. 'National' historians see Bismarck and Cavour as unwitting instruments, stressing the role of nationalism whether as progressive national liberalism, the power of national discourse in international relations, or mobilizing popular movements. 'Sceptics' see nationalism as either a rationalization of non-national interests or as failure, contending that the new nation states were not really national. This either/or approach is problematic. I will briefly consider the arguments for a powerful popular and/or radical nationalist role in unification before returning to this debate between the 'national' and 'sceptical' interpretations.[33]

Although national liberalism dominated Italian and German nation-state formation, there was a role for radical nationalism. Leading radicals, having learnt the lessons of the failure of 1848, allied themselves with national liberalism. Daniele Manin, leader of the Venetian uprising of 1848–9, was a key figure in the Italian National Society, as was Francisco Crispi who was instrumental in Garibaldi's invasion of Sicily in May 1860. Garibaldi had in 1859 put himself at the service of Victor Emannuel. There were similar radical figures in the *National Verein* and the Progressive Party, although they are less well known to posterity.[34] Such men organized the Italian plebiscites and undertook the detailed construction of national institutions in the North German Confederation (1867–71) and Second Empire.

Furthermore elite national liberal organization connected to many other associations, often ostensibly non-political like workers' educational associations, consumer and producer cooperatives, choral societies, shooting clubs, and occupational organizations. These were more densely developed in the German lands. They became important during and after unification rather than before, partly because the 1860s were more propitious as regimes grew milder and standards of living improved, in part because of popular enthusiasm produced by nation-state formation.

Here though was a major difference between the cases. In Italy unification came swiftly and unpredictably; until then nationalist organizations were small and fragmented, unable to see a clear way forward. In Germany by the mid-1860s unification under Prussian leadership was being intensely anticipated and provided a focus for most of the national movement.[35] So radical and popular nationalism was important. However, these movements were dominated by national liberals and had a more organized and popular base in the German lands.[36]

This makes it difficult at first glance to explain the one great exception to this rule of effective, if antagonistic cooperation between the leading state and the national liberal movement. This is the part played by Garibaldi and radical nationalism in Italian unification. Following Austrian defeat, by the end of 1859 the most likely scenario was

Piedmontese expansion into north Italy—definitely Lombardy, possibly Venetia—and perhaps parts of central Italy, notably Tuscany, Parma, and Modena, in return for ceding Nice and Savoy to France. The Papal States had too much internal and external Catholic support and the Kingdom of the Two Sicilies was too remote to constitute objects of Piedmontese ambition. Anyway, France would oppose the creation of too powerful a Piedmont. Even if Cavour in his less stable moments (of which he had plenty) thought he could act unilaterally, that was impossible. Also, perceptive national liberals were averse to Piedmont swallowing what they saw as the clericalist centre and the primitive south of the peninsula, thereby endangering secular liberal progress.[37]

However, renewed upheaval in Sicily provided radical nationalists with a chance to play more than a supporting role to Piedmont. The dramatic story of the expedition of Garibaldi and his one thousand Redshirts to Sicily in May 1860, his rapid takeover of the island and then the mainland of the kingdom, is well known, as is how it triggered a Piedmontese move southwards, culminating in the invasion of the Papal States to prevent Garibaldi bringing radical nationalism up the peninsula. Garibaldi stuck to his policy of serving Victor Emmanuel and the outcome was the incorporation of the south (legitimized by another manipulated plebiscite) into the Kingdom of Italy under the House of Savoy. Garibaldi's role points to the strength of radical nationalism, giving the lie to those who argue that Italians were not yet 'made' and that unification was a top-down elite affair.[38]

Garibaldi was a radical nationalist and played a crucial role in national unification. However, that does not mean that radical nationalism played so central a role.[39] Sicily and the mainland south had the least developed popular or elite nationalist sentiment. Sicilian resistance to rule from Naples might opportunistically utilize nationalism but it was an autonomist movement. The rising in April 1860 aimed to remove the corrupt, vicious, but also incompetent Bourbon regime. This crisis provided Garibaldi with his opportunity. Cavour sought to prevent Garibaldi raising a well-equipped military force and sailing for Sicily. Almost all his volunteers came from northern Italy where radical nationalism was strongest.

Garibaldi's success was due to his military talent and the incompetence of Bourbon forces. He was welcomed and gathered increasing support as he registered one victory after another. The two components to that welcome stood in tension with each other. Many peasants hoped that Garibaldi, this messianic figure arriving like a bolt out of the blue, would free them from their servitude. The combination of Bourbon collapse and Garibaldi's arrival sparked off land seizures. Landowners therefore were anxious that Garibaldi restore law and order. In a confused and fast-moving situation Garibaldi and those he placed in day-to-day control of government shifted positions, but generally the main thrust was in the direction of law and order. 'Brigandage', difficult to distinguish from peasant activism, was savagely repressed. There was no fundamental land reform. Garibaldi may have been sympathetic to peasant demands but his priority was nationalism. He needed swiftly to secure the island of Sicily and move to the mainland. Working with established agents of local order was the best way to do that.

The story is similar once Garibaldi crossed to the mainland, finally taking Naples in September 1860.

This is not a story of nationalism as popular and even radical but of a contingent relationship between an extraordinary radical nationalist leader with his small following and the political space opened up by the simultaneous collapse of Habsburg power in the north and Bourbon power in the south. That this was a contingent rather than what one might call an organic relationship became manifest in subsequent events. Garibaldi surrendered leadership and handed over to Piedmont in November 1860. This was not simply an individual decision but an act of political realism. Garibaldi did not control the expertise and institutions to administer the south or the political connections and machinery to form a national government. That could only come from a combination of Piedmontese state officials, the national liberal politicians in the National Society, and local propertied elites. There would be no Garibaldian political movement. Individuals like Crispi would make successful political careers but within structures built under Piedmontese auspices. The weakness of Piedmont in the unification process—dependent on contingent interventions by Louis Napoleon in the north and Garibaldi in the south—explains the formally highly centralized nation state that was established, one superimposed upon rather than displacing regionalized political arrangements and loyalties. By contrast, the powerful Prussian state, having annexed other parts of north Germany in 1866–7, felt able to tolerate a federalist constitution in 1871 that combined with a steady growth in the power of Berlin over the following decades.

This brings me back to debates between 'national' and 'sceptical' historians and the need to restate the terms of this debate. Nationalist movements are concrete ensembles of interests and values. To point to the importance of material interests and non-nationalist values does not diminish the importance of nationalism, unless one starts with a fantastic notion of a political ideology and movement powered purely by a disinterested commitment to the nation, the Mazzinian vision. Rather the issue is whether nationalism as doctrine, sentiment, or politics plays an integral role in legitimating, coordinating, and mobilizing forces that seek national autonomy, or whether it is contingently appropriated by those whose language and concerns are not framed in national terms at all.

Nationalist discourse was coming to be dominated by a rhetoric of realism and progress, rather than idealism and abrupt change. This was not just because such language was 'convenient' for certain interests but also because the rapid growth of free-market industrial capitalism and the associated rise of bourgeois groups made this a 'natural' way of envisaging change. The related growth of literacy, a freer and more mobile labour force, better communications and urbanization, generated significant popular support for such movements. This was most marked in the German lands, especially in north and central Germany, and in northern Italy, as well as in some Habsburg regions such as Vienna and Bohemia. It was weaker in central and southern Italy, in the eastern half of the Habsburg Empire, and in Congress and Russian Poland. Unsurprisingly, one can map the strength of national liberalism onto these regional differences. In economically backward regions nationalism was either still associated with a gentry class (Congress and Russian Poland, Galicia) with little popular resonance or was developing a peasant base that drew attention to ethno-national differences. Neither form of nationalism could integrate interests with the discourse of liberal pan-nationalism.

Nationalist discourse equally should not be seen as a 'reflection' of the social forces most supportive of it. These forces cannot invent such ideas and movements but at best only select from and promote what exists. Amongst Habsburg Germans, for example, although there was a discourse of liberal nationalism, given the overwhelming interest in remaining dominant in an imperial state, these would never select pan-nationalism. The importance of this 'natural' fit between discourse and interests can be seen in the connections to Piedmont and Prussia. Against the wishes of bourgeois interests and the liberal discourse, unification did not come about in a peaceful liberal manner but by means of large-scale violence. Properly understood these were not wars of unification but of conquest. The story had to be re-presented to legitimize the extension of state power when Piedmont 'amalgamated' with other Italian states or Prussia annexed Hannover. The liberal discourse of national unification did this. It satisfied external supporters such as France and Britain whose governments and public opinion were most comfortable when they could perceive these new states as liberal and progressive. It chimed with a politics that, even if dependent on warfare at crucial movements, needed to harness 'national opinion' to control parliaments which were part of that legitimation and also necessary instruments for raising loans and taxes and implementing liberal reforms. Bismarck, an authoritarian conservative who saw elections and parliaments in manipulative terms, nevertheless had concluded that without such institutions it was not possible to rally the 'social forces' needed for modern states to remain strong. Likewise, Cavour and those who blatantly manipulated the plebiscites throughout Italy that backed fusion with Piedmont, needed the legitimation these provided.[40]

Pan-Nationalism after 1871

By 1871 Italian and German nation states had been formed and national movements had played a key role. However, especially after the negotiation of the Three Emperor's League in 1881, there was no prospect of a Polish nation state. Polish national effort had shifted from high politics to 'organic reform', taking explicit national form mainly in relation to ethno-national conflicts either with well-established opponents such as Germans in Posen or new ones like Lithuanians in Russian Poland and Ukrainians in Galicia. In Galicia Polish nationalists constantly feared the government playing the 'Ruthene' card to undermine them. In Prussia Polish national politics expanded beyond Posen, exploiting Reichstag elections but this pulled it further away from pan-nationalism. In Russian Poland gentry nationalism declined but little arose to take its place. One could anticipate that Polish nationalism would become inward looking and take either a conservative and fearful or an increasingly populist and ethnic form. This is largely what happened in Galicia.

However, another factor played a key role in Germany and Russia: state-led nationalism. When Prussian Poles confronted a German emperor instead of a Prussian king (even though the same person) and militant German nationalism, they saw themselves as a threatened national minority. This sentiment was increased by Bismarck's policies. His deep hostility to Polish nationalism had contributed to his early decision as Prussian prime minister ostentatiously to support Russian suppression of the 1863 rising. He subsequently backed limited measures of Germanization over issues such as language use in schools and administration. In the 1870s he initiated, with strong support from the National Liberal Party, a campaign against the Catholic Church in Germany—the 'struggle for culture' (*Kulturkampf*). As Prussian Poles were overwhelmingly Catholic, measures such as arrests of priests from archbishops down, intervention in church schools, and supervision of theological education and clerical appointments, created massive hostility. Although the *Kulturkampf* was abandoned in the early 1880s, there followed an even more dangerous attack through government sponsorship of German colonization, including forced purchase of Polish estates. The objective appeared to be not only the destruction of the Polish gentry as a class but also to block the formation of a free Polish peasantry. The campaign failed but only because of a fierce Polish response. After a brief relaxation following Bismarck's resignation in 1890, the campaign was renewed.[41] By 1914 Polish national minority politics were well established.

It is not surprising when a new nation state pursues nationalist policies. More interesting is that imperial states followed suit.[42] In the western half of the Habsbug Empire there was a positive recognition of language as the basis of nationality that was given political expression. In the eastern half of the empire forced Magyarization, and in the Ottoman Empire Turkification, worked in a negative way. So too did Russification policies, affecting groups who did not speak Russian and saw themselves as non-Russian. The most important of these were Poles. Russification and Germanization sustained a strong sense of Polish nationality and of injustice. There continued to be links across the three zones between small groups of nationalist activists who hoped to build on such sentiments.

After 1890 diplomatic prospects opened up with the Franco-Russian alliance. Following the emergence of mass politics in Austria from the 1890s and in Russia following the 1905 Revolution, there were further possibilities for popular nationalism. Industrial growth—especially in Russian Poland—provided another source of support for a Polish national movement. Although mainly focused on the Russian zone, there remained minorities of activists operating across all three states seeking to keep alive pan-nationalism.

In this effort a major division emerged associated with the figures of Roman Stanislaw Dmowski (1864–1939) and Józef Klemens Pilsudski (1867–1935). Dmowski politicized the tradition of 'organic work', stressing the need to cooperate with Russia against

Austria and Prussia, seeking to exploit diplomatic opportunities, and campaigning against non-Polish ethno-nationalism, not just Lithuanian and Ukrainian but also the large and increasingly politicized Jewish minority. Pilsudski drew upon the tradition of direct action, including violence, but fused it with socialist ideas. He was anti-Russian, favouring cooperation with Austria and Germany. However, neither tendency got much support from their target governments before 1914 and only limited assistance after war broke out.

The restricted importance of such nationalsm was demonstrated by the smooth mobilization of Poles in all three states.[43] The unchallenged power of the states until the Russian collapse in 1917, along with rapid territorial changes as armies swept one way and then the other, made impossible any significant politics not promoted by government. There were such initiatives, as with the formation by Germany and Austria of an autonomous Poland in 1916, and Austrian permission for Pilsudski to recruit and drill a Polish legion. Each state sought to exploit anti-state nationalism in the territories of its opponents, but this was limited by concern about possible repercussions in its own land and the need to think about eventual negotiations with the enemy. What mattered was that governmental policies kept alive Polish national, if not nationalist, sentiment in all three states, that Dmowski and Pilsudski sustained organized pan-nationalism, and that their efforts kept alive the 'Polish question' in international diplomacy. Dmowski quickly recognized that initiative was shifting to the Western Powers and he moved to Paris to influence this. Pilsudski speculated in 1914 on prospects for Polish pan-nationalism if first Russia and then the Central Powers were defeated. That was precisely the situation from September 1918. With the US entry into the war (April 1917) and Woodrow Wilson's declaration in favour of national self-determination—with explicit mention of Poland in his 'Fourteen Points'—Polish nationalists needed to exploit this unique and unexpected opportunity. The first outcome was the formation of the Polish Republic in November 1918. However, despite strong and widespread Polish national sentiment and leadership able quickly to build a strong army, this nation-state formation was principally due to the near simultaneous collapse of Russian, Austrian, and German power and the decision of the Western Powers to reconstruct central Europe as a series of nation states. The Polish state came into conflict with Lithuanian and Ukrainian nationalists. The new Weimar Republic and Soviet Union refused to recognize Polish boundaries. In part Poland was able to assert itself against these powers, especially in war with the USSR, but the drawing of its boundaries elsewhere were largely decisions taken in Paris.[44] Hard-headed nationalists like Dmowski were under no illusions about the dangers Poland would confront as the USSR and Germany recovered and Poles could not depend on Western support forever. That is what happened. The Polish nation state lasted just twenty years and had to wait another fifty years before a new form of independence was possible.

Conclusion

Pan-nationalism or unification nationalism, like all forms of nationalism, exhibits doctrines, sentiments, and politics focused on the nation and the need for national autonomy. As with all studies of nationalism there is the danger of exaggerating its importance in the attainment of such autonomy, especially nation-state formation. Equally, there can be overreactions against 'national' interpretations and a move towards 'sceptical' ones that downplay the role of nationalism. I have suggested ways of avoiding this either/or approach.

Unification nationalism confronts specific challenges. Nationalism seeking change within one existing state, or to separate from one occupying power, has a clear state and territorial focus. However, when unification nationalism is spread across more than one state, its ideal boundaries are often unclear. Such challenges were greatest for Polish nationalism, when confronting three occupying powers that were major powers and themselves represented either non-national dynastic or non-Polish national ideas. That pan-nationalism could be sustained at all was remarkable and the principal explanation for that was the recent existence of Poland as a state. As that moment receded into the past, the elites directly linked to that legacy died out, the privileged social basis for restorationist nationalism declined and the common experience of exiles was marginalized, Polish nationalism took on different and inward-looking forms in the various regions. Social change created a potential popular base amongst peasants and workers, especially where the occupying state itself pursued policies of national discrimination, but again this was not focused on unification. Elite pan-nationalism did persist, but only following a crisis in which all three dynasties collapsed was it able to use international and popular support to form a nation state.

German and Italian nationalism confronted only one foreign and occupying power: the Habsburg Empire. Once Prussia and Piedmont came to support a national policy, this provided a focus for both political opposition and coordination. Integration between leading state and national movements was most developed by the doctrines and politics of national liberalism. However, the integration was always imperfect and tense. In the German case a major problem was the dependency upon Prussian political and military power. In the Italian case it was dependency upon state collapse in the north and south of the country brought about by the contingent interventions of France and Garibaldi's invasion of Sicily.

All three nationalist movements saw themselves as expressions of a dominant culture. They did not have to construct a national culture from scratch and took for granted that the dominant elites throughout the national territory belonged to the nation (even if they opposed nationalism). In this respect they differed both from most small-nation national movements and from other forms of pan-nationalism such as Pan-Africanism and Pan-Slavism.

The major social challenge was to extend nationalist sentiments and politics from the elite to the popular level. This very process could generate counter-nationalist movements. Probably a more serious but less well studied problem was encountering indifference rather than hostility in societies with highly regionalized popular cultures and great inequality.[45] Counter-nationalism was a major problem for Polish nationalists; indifference was a major problem for German and especially Italian nationalists.

All three movements needed international support. As they aimed to create large states and employed national liberal discourse, they were generally looked upon with favour by public opinion in Britain and France. Whether this would lead to active support from governments depended also on perceived state interest. When interest and sentiment converged, as with France in Italy in 1859 or the Western Allies in 1918, this could prove crucial.

The nation states that were formed were seen as flawed by many nationalists. German historiography using the concept of the 'special path' (*Sonderweg*) argues for a unique set of defects linked to unification that would have fateful consequences. Italian historiography influenced by Antonio Gramsci's concept of the 'passive revolution' argues that Italy was never truly national.[46] The very short periods of a sovereign Polish nation state in modern times (1918–39, 1989 to the present) perhaps accounts for less sustained critiques. Such critiques often take for granted the path to the nation state but imagine it could have taken a better form. In that sense they themselves express yet another version of nationalism.

Notes

1. These are logical types based on whether the nation state is smaller, identical with, or larger than the territory of the non-national state(s) from which it is formed. Nation-state formations usually combine the types. However, given the role of existing states as agents or opponents of nation-state formation, nationalist movements tend to be dominated by features associated with one of these types.
2. As argued in the classic study by E. Weber (1976) *Peasants into Frenchmen: The Modernisation of Rural France*, London.
3. See the chapters by Hroch (9), Doyle and Van Young (6), Chatterji (12), Moore (23), Lonsdale (15), Henley (13), and Roshwald (11).
4. See Chapter 34 by Cemil Aydin. The success/failure judgement relates to the formation of a nation state, but one can define and evaluate nationalism by other criteria such as promoting national identity or culture.
5. See Erica Benner's Chapter 3 on Rousseau's model constitution for Poland; Lord Acton (1862) 'Nationality', *Home and Foreign Review*, July; reprinted in (1909) *The History of Freedom and Other Essays*, London, 270–300.
6. See Chapter 7 by Michael Rowe.
7. Napoleon imposed his rule on non-French territory using names such as the Kingdom of Italy, Grand Duchy of Warsaw, Illyrian provinces, and Confederation of the Rhine.

After 1815 two such names were perpetuated in the Kingdom of Poland and the German Confederation.

8. There is a fine line to be drawn between discovery and invention (forgery) as fragmentary manuscript sources in archaic languages were translated into texts accessible to contemporary readers. See J. Leerssen (2006) 'Nationalism and the Cultivation of Culture', *Nations and Nationalism*, 12, 559–78; and J. Breuilly (2011b) 'On the Principle of Nationality', in G. S. Jones and G. Claeys (eds.) *The Cambridge History of Nineteenth-Century Political Thought*, Cambridge; as well as the chapters by Benner (3) and Hroch (9).
9. N. Davies (2001) *Heart of Europe: The Past in Poland's Present*, Oxford, uses the term *Rzeczpospolita*, or United Republic of Poland-Lithuania, 1569–1795 [451]. Poland and Lithuania were first united by dynastic marriage in 1386. A brilliant study of the changing meanings of 'Poland' and 'Lithuania' between then and the twentieth century is T. Snyder (2003) *The Reconstruction of Nations: Poland, Ukraine, Lithuania, Belarus, 1569–1999*, New Haven.
10. For the complex reasons for the successive partitions, see J. Lukowski (1999) *The Partitions of Poland: 1772, 1793, 1795*, London.
11. There was limited freedom until 1830 in Congress Poland and in Galicia for a good deal of the nineteenth century, especially after 1867.
12. For background, see P. Wandycz (1974) *The Lands of Partitioned Poland, 1795–1918*, Seattle and London; for a survey of nationalist ideas and movements, see N. Davies (2005) *God's Playground: A History of Poland. Volume 2: 1795 to the Present*, Oxford, 3–60. For nationalist historians, including Joachim Lelewel (1786–1861), who played a leading political role, see M. Baar (2008) *Historians and the Nation in the Nineteenth Century: The Case of East-Central Europe*, Oxford; and on Polish national historiography, see P. Brock, J. D. Stanley, and P. J. Wróbel (eds.) (2006) *Nation and History: Polish Historians from the Enlightenment to the Second World War*, Toronto.
13. There is no general study of political exile communities in Paris and London but instead the subject is divided by city and nationality. For Germans in London, see R. Ashton (1986) *Little Germany: Exile and Asylum in Victorian England*, Oxford; for Italian exiles see M. Isabella (2009) *Risorgimento in Exile: Italian Emigrés and the Liberal International in the Post-Napoleonic Era*, Oxford. Studies of individuals, such as that by D. M. Smith (1994) *Mazzini*, New Haven, on Mazzini (London), or W. J. H. Zawadzki (1992) *A Man of Honour: Adam Czartoryski as a Statesman of Russia and Poland, 1795–1831*, Oxford, on Czartoryski (Paris), provide detail on exile communities.
14. L. Riall (2007) *Garibaldi: Invention of a Hero*, New Haven and London, argues that in this sense Garibaldi was Mazzini's 'invention'. The Hungarian exile Kossuth had a similar popular, heroic image.
15. Banti's major works are not available in English translation, but for an introduction to and critique of his interpretation, see L. Riall et al. (2009) 'Alberto Banti's Interpretation of Risorgimento: A Debate', *Nations and Nationalism*, 15, 396–454. This 'cultural turn' has recently become especially strong in Italian national historiography, as can be seen in two recent collections of essays: S. Patriarcha and L. Riall (eds.) (2011) *The Risorgimento Revisited: Nationalism and Culture in Nineteenth-Century Italy*, Basingstoke, and A. R. Ascoli and K. V. Hennenberg (eds.) (2001) *Making and Remaking Italy: The Cultivation of National Identity around the Risorgimento*, Oxford.
16. The language point is debatable for the Italian case, as there was a strong predilection for French and a greater diversity of dialects, even amongst elites.

17. Some writers framed the distinction in terms of 'historical' and 'historyless' peoples. See Breuilly, 'On the Principle of Nationality'.
18. In this regard we can also include Hungarian nationalist discourse, even if that was not pan-nationalist. For the perspective of the 'nationalities' or 'small nations', see Chapter 9 by Hroch.
19. For scepticism about popular nationalism, see I. Porciani, 'On the Uses and Abuses of Nationalism from Below: A Few Notes on Italy', in M. V. Ginderachter and M. Beyen (eds.) (2012) *Nationhood from Below: Europe in the Long Nineteenth Century*, Basingstoke, 73–95; and D. Laven's contribution in Riall et al., 'Alberto Banti's Interpretation of Risorgimento Nationalism'.
20. Sicilians and Sardinians did not share an 'ethnic culture' with mainland Italians but never managed to frame a separate sense of identity in ethno-national terms. Something similar to the problems encountered by Polish and German nationalism can be found in the north, for example in the Austrian Tyrol.
21. For a good overview, see J. Sperber (1994) *The European Revolutions, 1848–1851*, Cambridge; for more detail, see various essays in D. Dowe et al. (eds.) (2001) *Europe in 1848: Revolution and Reform*, Oxford. Chapters by Soldani, Langewiesche, Koralka, and Hahn deal with revolution in the Italian, German, Habsburg, and Polish lands, respectively.
22. There was a long-standing and widespread belief that Russia would oppose any liberal, let alone democratic, transformation in central Europe, and that supporting the Polish cause as well as waging war against Russia was essential for success.
23. For this shared sense of nationality, see B. Vick (2002) *Defining Germany: The 1848 Frankfurt Parliamentarians and National Identity*, Cambridge, MA, and London. On the practical problems of cooperation between strangers who have never sat in a parliament before, see F. Eyck (1968) *The Frankfurt Parliament 1848–49*, London.
24. M. Hewitson (2010) *Nationalism in Germany, 1848–1866*, Basingstoke, goes further and argues that the National Assembly set the model for the actual unification of 1870–1.
25. The epileptic Ferdinand abdicated in December 1848 in favour of his energetic young nephew Franz Josef who brought in tough ministers, especially Minister-President Schwarzenberg.
26. See I. Deak (1979) *The Lawful Revolution: Louis Kossuth and the Hungarians, 1848–49*, New York.
27. This was the term used for nationalist engagement with peasant concerns. See A. Bromke (1967) *Poland's Politics: Idealism versus Realism*, Cambridge, MA, esp. ch. 1.
28. For a detailed examination of these processes, see J.-P. Himka (1988) *Galician Villagers and the Ukrainian National Movement in the Nineteenth Century*, Basingstoke; and (1999) *Religion and Nationality in Western Ukraine: The Greek Catholic Church and the Ruthenian National Movement in Galicia, 1867–1900*, Montreal-Kingston.
29. Wandycz calls this absorption in local politics 'Triple Loyalism'.
30. This state had now been officially abolished and the territory renamed 'Vistulaland'.
31. On these associations and their role in the nationalist movements and nation-state formation, see R. Grew (1963) *A Sterner Plan for Italian Unity: The Italian National Society in the Risorgimento*, Princeton, NJ; and Hewitson, *Nationalism in Germany, 1848–1866*, ch. 5, 'Prussia, the Nation and the Constitution'.
32. The war of 1870–1 was more protracted than that of 1866, but it was already clear by the end of 1870 that France had been defeated.

33. For 'national' views of the Risorgimento, see chapters in Patriarcha and Riall (eds.), *The Risorgimento Revisited*, especially chapters by Ginsborg and Banti who have pioneered this approach in recent historiography. For a popular English version, see C. Duggan (2007) *The Force of Destiny: A History of Italy since 1796*, London. (The title of his study indicates the approach.) For the 'sceptical' view, see D. Laven's chapter 'Italy', in T. Baycroft and M. Hewitson (eds.) (2006) *What is a Nation? Europe 1789–1914*, Oxford, and the pioneering studies of Mack Smith from which I select just two: D. M. Smith (1954) *Cavour and Garibaldi, 1860: A Study in Political Conflict*, Cambridge, and (1994) *Mazzini*, New Haven. I discuss the German historiography in J. Breuilly (1996) *The Formation of the First German Nation-State, 1800–1871*, London, and, more recently, (2011a) *Austria, Prussia and the Making of Germany, 1806–1871*, London, esp. 6–9. A standard national view is H. Schulze (1991) *The Course of German Nationalism: From Frederick the Great to Bismarck, 1763–1867*, Cambridge; an explicitly sceptical view, M. Hughes (1988) *Nationalism and Society: Germany 1800–1945*, London. For the 'national' view in Polish historiography, see Davies, *Heart of Europe*. In English I do not know of a general 'sceptical' account, but R. F. Leslie (1963) *Reform and Insurrection in Russian Poland, 1856–1865*, London, and (1956) *Polish Politics and the Revolution of November 1830*, London, debunks nationalist interpretations of the two major insurrections.
34. This is indicative of the greater dominance of Prussia and national liberals in the German unification movement. The office manager of the *National Verein*, Feodor Streit, is a good example of such a radical. See Hewitson, *Nationalism in Germany, 1848–1866*, especially 223–53.
35. The shift in the balance of power in favour of Prussia came late and was not fully appreciated until after unification. Indeed that was a key element in Prussian success, for it meant opponents did not organize as effectively as they might have done. See J. Breuilly and R. Speirs (eds.) (2004) *Germany's Two Unifications: Anticipations, Experiences, Responses*, London, especially the introduction and conclusion which argues that the same contrast can be made between the anticipation of 1871 and the lack of anticipation of German reunification in 1991.
36. For Germany the studies by T. Hamerow (1969) *The Social Foundations of German Unification, 1858–1871. I: Ideas and Institutions*, Princeton, NJ, and (1972) *The Social Foundations of German Unification, 1858–1871. II: Struggles and Accomplishments*, Princeton, NJ, and J. Sheehan (1995) *German Liberalism in the Nineteenth Century*, Chicago, IL, and London, remain valuable. Among more recent studies, see D. Langewiesche (2000) *Liberalism in Germany*, London. There is not much on Italy in English, but, see I. Porciani in Ginderachter and Beyen (eds.), *Nationhood from Below*, esp. 83–5, dealing with urban case studies of popular associations.
37. D. Laven in a forthcoming book argues that the record of Cavour's government in Sardinia and the attitudes of the Milanese political elite towards the language, culture, and people of Sardinia should have given pause to anyone in the Italian south wishing to be ruled by the House of Savoy.
38. The famous phrase 'Italy is made, now we must make Italians' is usually but probably wrongly attributed to Massimo d'Azeglio. See D. Laven in Baycroft and Hewitson (eds.), *What is a Nation?*, 256.
39. I initially developed some of these arguments in J. Breuilly (1993) *Nationalism and the State*, Manchester, 112–15.

40. Just how manipulated they were can be gauged from the fact that the plebiscites held in Nice and Savoy equally massively supported being annexed to France, this being Louis Napoleon's territorial reward.
41. See W. Hagen (1980) *Germans, Poles, and Jews: The Nationality Conflict in the Prussian East, 1772–1914*, Chicago, IL.
42. See J. Leonhard and U. V. Hirschhausen (eds.) (2009) *Empires und Nationalstaaten im 19. Jahrhundert*, Göttingen.
43. Davies, *Heart of Europe*, takes the 'national' perspective which makes even more jarring his short comment (231) that Polish students from all three states at the Jagellionian University in Cracow all returned 'home' to join their respective armies when war commenced in 1914.
44. For a clear and short account of the Paris Peace Conference and the formation of the Polish Republic, see M. Macmillan (2003) *Peacemakers: The Paris Peace Conference of 1919 and its Attempt to End War*, London, ch. 17.
45. The idea of national indifference has been pursued interestingly for Czech and German nationalism in Bohemia. Historians of the late Habsburg Empire have also drawn attention to 'centripetal' tendencies such as dynastic loyalism. For a good survey, see L. Cole (2012) 'Differentiation or Indifference? Changing Perspectives on National Identification in the Austrian Half of the Habsburg Monarchy', in Ginderachter and Beyen (eds.), *Nationhood from Below*.
46. This perspective is interestingly reviewed in M. Cabo and F. Molina (2009) 'The Long and Winding Road of Nationalization: Eugen Weber's *Peasants into Frenchmen* in Modern European History (1976–2006)', *European History Quarterly*, 39, 264–86.

Suggested Further Reading

For a general overview of nineteenth-century Europe set within a global framework one still cannot better the trilogy by E. Hobsbawm: *The Age of Revolution* (1962), *The Age of Capital* (1975), and *The Age of Empire* (1987). A good collection of essays on nationalism in nineteenth-century Europe is *What is a Nation? Europe 1789–1914*, ed. T. Baycroft and M. Hewitson (2006); unfortunately there is no chapter on Polish nationalism.

For a good survey of Polish history, see P. Wandycz (1974) *The Lands of Partitioned Poland, 1795–1918*. An account more focused on nationalism and organized by chapters that go backwards in time is N. Davies (3rd ed., 2001) *Heart of Europe: The Past in Poland's Present*, esp. ch. 4. Davies (2005) has treated the same subject at greater length in *God's Playground: A History of Poland. Volume 2: 1795 to the Present*.

A good introduction to Italian history for this period is H. Hearder (1983) *Italy in the Age of the Risorgimento, 1790–1870*. A broader social framework is provided by S. Woolf (1979) *A History of Italy 1700–1860: The Social Constraints of Political Change* (1979). More thematic and historiographical is L. Riall (2009) *Risorgimento: The History of Italy from Napoleon to Nation State*.

For a general introduction to nineteenth-century German history, see *19th Century Germany: Politics, Culture and Society 1780–1918*, ed. J. Breuilly (2001). *The Oxford Handbook of Modern German History*, ed. H. W. Smith (2011), contains much of interest and relevance, especially 'The Formation of German Nationalism, 1740–1850' by C. Jansen, and 'Nation State, Conflict Resolution, and Culture War, 1850–1878' by S. Weichlein.

Other Reading Suggestions

Ascoli, A. R. and Hennenberg, K. V. (eds.) (2001) *Making and Remaking Italy: The Cultivation of National Identity around the Risorgimento*, Oxford.

Ashton, R. (1986) *Little Germany: Exile and Asylum in Victorian England*, Oxford. Baar, M. (2008) *Historians and the Nation in the Nineteenth Century: The Case of East-Central Europe*, Oxford.

Breuilly, J. (1993) *Nationalism and the State*, Manchester.

Breuilly, J. (1996) *The Formation of the First German Nation-State, 1800–1871*, London.

Breuilly, J. (2011a) *Austria, Prussia and the Making of Germany, 1806–1871*, London.

Breuilly, J. (2011b) 'On the Principle of Nationality', in Jones, G. S and Claeys, G. (eds.) *The Cambridge History of Nineteenth-Century Political Thought*, Cambridge.

Breuilly, J. and Speirs, R. (eds.) (2004) *Germany's Two Unifications: Anticipations, Experiences, Responses*, London.

Brock, P., Stanley, J. D., and Wróbel, P. J. (eds.) (2006) *Nation and History: Polish Historians from the Enlightenment to the Second World War*, Toronto.

Bromke, A. (1967) *Poland's Politics: Idealism versus Realism*, Cambridge, MA.

Cabo, M. and Molina, F. (2009) 'The Long and Winding Road of Nationalization: Eugen Weber's *Peasants into Frenchmen* in Modern European History (1976–2006)', *European History Quarterly*, 39, 264–86.

Deak, I. (1979) *The Lawful Revolution: Louis Kossuth and the Hungarians, 1848–49*, New York.

Dowe, D. et al. (eds.) (2001) *Europe in 1848: Revolution and Reform*, Oxford.

Duggan, C. (2007) *The Force of Destiny: A History of Italy since 1796*, London.

Eyck, F. (1968) *The Frankfurt Parliament 1848–49*, London.

Ginderachter, M. V. and Beyen, M. (eds.) (2012) *Nationhood from Below: Europe in the Long Nineteenth Century*, Basingstoke.

Grew, R. (1963) *A Sterner Plan for Italian Unity: The Italian National Society in the Risorgimento*, Princeton, NJ.

Hagen, W. (1980) *Germans, Poles, and Jews: The Nationality Conflict in the Prussian East, 1772–1914*, Chicago, IL.

Hamerow, T. (1969) *The Social Foundations of German Unification, 1858–1871. I: Ideas and Institutions*, Princeton, NJ.

Hamerow, T. (1972) *The Social Foundations of German Unification, 1858–1871. II: Struggles and Accomplishments*, Princeton, NJ.

Hewitson, M. (2010) *Nationalism in Germany, 1848–1866*, Basingstoke.

Himka, J.-P. (1988) *Galician Villagers and the Ukrainian National Movement in the Nineteenth Century*, Basingstoke.

Himka, J.-P. (1999) *Religion and Nationality in Western Ukraine: The Greek Catholic Church and the Ruthenian National Movement in Galicia, 1867–1900*, Montreal-Kingston.

Hughes, M. (1988) *Nationalism and Society: Germany 1800–1945*, London.

Isabella, M. (2009) *Risorgimento in Exile: Italian Emigrés and the Liberal International in the Post-Napoleonic Era*, Oxford.

Langewiesche, D. (2000) *Liberalism in Germany*, London.

Leerssen, J. (2006) 'Nationalism and the Cultivation of Culture', *Nations and Nationalism*, 12, 559–78.

Leonhard, J. and Hirschhausen, U. V. (eds.) (2009) *Empires und Nationalstaaten im 19. Jahrhundert*, Göttingen.

Leslie, R. F. (1956) *Polish Politics and the Revolution of November 1830*, London.

Leslie, R. F. (1963) *Reform and Insurrection in Russian Poland, 1856–1865*, London.

Lukowski, J. (1999) *The Partitions of Poland: 1772, 1793, 1795*, London.

Macmillan, M. (2003) *Peacemakers: The Paris Peace Conference of 1919 and its Attempt to End War*, London.

Patriarcha, S. and Riall, L. (eds.) (2011) *The Risorgimento Revisited: Nationalism and Culture in Nineteenth-Century Italy*, Basingstoke.

Riall, L. (2007) *Garibaldi: Invention of a Hero*, New Haven and London.

Riall, L. et al. (2009) 'Alberto Banti's Interpretation of Risorgimento Nationalism: A Debate', *Nations and Nationalism*, 15, 396–454.

Schulze, H. (1991) *The Course of German Nationalism: From Frederick the Great to Bismarck, 1763–1867*, Cambridge.

Sheehan, J. (1995) *German Liberalism in the Nineteenth Century*, Chicago, IL, and London.

Smith, D. M. (1954) *Cavour and Garibaldi, 1860: A Study in Political Conflict*, Cambridge.

Smith, D. M. (1994) *Mazzini*, New Haven, CT.

Sperber, J. (1994) *The European Revolutions, 1848–1851*, Cambridge.

Vick, B. (2002) *Defining Germany: The 1848 Frankfurt Parliamentarians and National Identity*, Cambridge, MA, and London.

Wandycz, P. (1974) *The Lands of Partitioned Poland, 1795–1918*, Seattle and London.

Weber, E. (1976) *Peasants into Frenchmen: The Modernisation of Rural France*, London.

Zawadzki, W. J. H. (1992) *A Man of Honour: Adam Czartoryski as a Statesman of Russia and Poland, 1795–1831*, Oxford.

CHAPTER 9

NATIONAL MOVEMENTS IN THE HABSBURG AND OTTOMAN EMPIRES

MIROSLAV HROCH

BACKGROUND: THE TWO EMPIRES

IN central and south-east Europe the path from pre-modern empire to modern nation state took two basic forms. The first involved struggles for the unification of politically divided national communities that already possessed well-established cultural traditions and a national language as well as a full social structure. This was the case with German, Italian, and Polish 'unification nationalism'.[1]

The second involved national movements acting on behalf of subordinate ethnic groups and seeking to achieve all the attributes of a fully fledged nation. It is this form of nationalism that will be analysed in this chapter. These movements had three main aims: the development of a national culture based on the local language; the achievement of some degree of political rights and self-administration (not necessarily an independent state); the formation of a full social structure of equal citizens from its own ethnic group. The precise way in which these aims were pursued varied from case to case.

Such national movements operated in both the Habsburg lands (after 1804 the Austrian Empire) and the Ottoman Empire. In the Austrian Empire the German language dominated administration and public life, but ethnic Germans constituted only a small minority within the population. The remainder of the population was made up of various ethnic groups (Magyars, Czechs, Slovaks, Slovenes, Croatians) as well as ethnic minorities whose core territory was located outside the empire (Serbians, Romanians, Italians, Poles, Ruthenes).[2] The table below provides estimates of the size of various ethnic groups within the Habsburg Empire.

Nationality	1850–1	%	1910	%
Germans	6.3 mill.	28.6	9.9 mill.	26.7
Magyars	5.0 mill.	22.7	10.1 mill.	27.3
Poles	2.0 mill.	9.1	4.9 mill.	13.2
Czechs	4.1 mill.	18.6	6.4 mill.	17.3
Croatians	1.6 mill.	7.3	2.4 mill.	6.5
Slovenes	1.1 mill.	5.0	1.2 mill.	3.5
Slovaks	1.8 mill.	6.8	2.0 mill.	5.4

The dominant group in the European part of the Ottoman Empire were the Turkish-speaking Muslims. Much of the population consisted of Christian ethnic groups, like Greeks, Serbians, Romanians, Montenegrins, Bulgarians, Albanians, as well as Slavic-speaking Muslims (Bosniaks).

Political, social, and cultural conditions in these two empires differed in many respects and these were important in shaping specific national movements. One major difference concerned how the two empires were established. The Habsburg dynasty had expanded since the late Middle Ages by combining dynastic claims, diplomatic treaties, and the threat or actual use of military force. Their rule in almost all their lands was based on contracts and conventions with local elites who pledged loyalty to the dynasty and empire. Insofar as national movements could identify themselves with specific historical lands (and hence with 'national histories' linked to those lands), they could formulate demands in terms of their violated constitutions, lost historical rights and traditions. Consequently, their claims could be presented in terms of a different interpretation of historical rights from that of the dynasty, sometimes backed up by mass demonstrations. Extensive violence was limited to the revolutions of 1848, although these were less concerned with national aims than with the removal of political oppression by the old regime.

By contrast, the Ottoman Empire was formed by conquest and force, and the new rulers continued to display their military supremacy over the following centuries. In most cases, they destroyed pre-existing state institutions and the local nobility within the conquered territory. National claims therefore could not base themselves on old rights or agreements and their success depended rather on the whims of local or central Ottoman authorities.

A second important difference concerns the role of religion. The Ottoman conquerors accentuated their superiority by emphasizing the supremacy of Islam. However, they did not aim at general conversion to Islam; indeed, they maintained religious barriers dividing Muslims from non-Muslims. This division provided the Christian population with the opportunity to create separate institutions. National movements (except Albanians and Bosniaks) defined themselves and their enemies in terms of confessional difference. As a consequence, the clergy always played an important role in national movements.

By contrast, Habsburg support for the Counter-Reformation achieved a good deal of confessional homogenization throughout the empire. This meant that in most cases national movements could not use religious difference as the basis for national mobilization. However, the Catholic Church was usually organized in relation to the historical lands that gave a national dimension to the clergy. Confessional differences—or the memory of such differences—could play a part in national struggles, but this was a secondary element.

Third, in economic terms, the key difference was that capitalism and industrialization started much earlier in central Europe than in the Balkans. Consequently, both forms of production and social structures in the Ottoman Empire were pre-modern with strong traces of patriarchalism and privileged social relations. Differences in economic and commercial growth related to differences in the intensity of social communication.

Fourth, since the Enlightenment had already penetrated into central Europe by the mid-eighteenth century, there was a strong tradition of scientific research on the history, language, habits, and characteristics of ethnic groups in the Habsburg Empire. This in turn promoted the cultivation of national identity within these groups. By contrast, in the Ottoman Empire, higher secular education was very weak. Most scholarly research on ethnic groups was conducted abroad, partly by members of the Christian ethnic groups, partly by foreign—French, British, German—scholars.

Consequently, the early national movements in central Europe had clearly defined ideas of the nation. They knew (or believed they knew) who were Czechs, Magyars, Slovenes, et cetera, and what were the forms taken by their language, culture, and history. In the Balkans, the understanding of ethnic groups and their pasts was more often based on myths, interpreted by misunderstandings and modified by power policy. These provided conditions for nationalists making overlapping claims and often engaging in aggressive conflicts of interests in the Balkans.

Fifth, basic differences in education in the two empires have their roots in the medieval period. While the central European secular educational system developed into a sophisticated hierarchy of village elementary schools, higher urban schools, and universities, the Ottoman Empire only possessed religious schools. Relics of higher education survived from Byzantine times but they were also concerned with religious matters and their language of education was exclusively Greek. A small number of wealthy Christians had been studying abroad since the end of the eighteenth century, but the general rate of literacy—both Christian and Muslim—was much lower than in central Europe.

Sixth, the different position of the two empires in the system of international relations, and how they were regarded by 'public opinion' within the other major states, influenced how national movements and secessionist nationalism were utilized in foreign policy. While national movements inside Austria were—at least at first—largely ignored by the other powers, national movements in the Ottoman Empire quickly provided welcome pretexts for diplomatic and military interventions.

All these differences between the two empires shaped the various claims and methods of national movements and their outcomes. Furthermore, if and when national movements aimed to achieve power, they put less emphasis on cultural and social demands and instead stressed political demands, even extending to secessionism.

The Magyars

In 1526 the medieval Kingdom of Hungary, which included also the autonomous Kingdom of Croatia and the Great Duchy of Transylvania, became, through a dynastic marriage, part of the Habsburg domains. At this time, eastern and central Europe were endangered by Ottoman expansion. Core territories of the Kingdom of Hungary were, until the end of the seventeenth century, occupied by the Ottomans. Transylvania fell under Ottoman 'protection'. By exploiting this situation, the Hungarian nobility successfully resisted Habsburg centralism as well as the Counter-Reformation until the eighteenth century. Hungary remained an autonomous part of the Habsburg Empire.

Hungary was a multi-ethnic territory, where Magyar speakers made up the largest group but nowhere near the majority of the population, which included Croats, Serbs, Slovaks, Germans, Romanians, Jews, and Ruthenes (see the table on p. 176). Such ethnic diversity did not necessarily create problems, since Latin was, until the end of the eighteenth century, the exclusive language of public life, administration, and education. The majority of the numerous nobility, however, was Magyar speaking and it retained a strong political consciousness of being the privileged 'Natio Hungarica'. The Hungarian Diet, accessible exclusively to nobles, protected the Kingdom's autonomy. With some aristocratic support, enlightened scholars from the mid-eighteenth century began to study the history of the Kingdom, the ethnography of its inhabitants, as well as to celebrate and modernize the written form of the Magyar.

The Hungarian nobility openly opposed the enlightened rationalist reforms introduced by Joseph II in the 1780s. They rejected the abolition of serfdom and protested against the replacement of Latin by German in administration and schools. A growing number of lower nobility proposed replacing both Latin and German by their Magyar mother tongue. Even though the Diet did not succeed in most points, the conflict strengthened the coherence of the nobility and stimulated its search for a new identity. Step by step, the opposition of Estates used national rhetoric and gave up the exclusive aristocratic concept of the 'Natio'. As a result, the early national movement was dominated by the nobility and its programme combined old historical political demands for Hungarian state rights with new demands in favour of Magyar language and culture. This interconnection was demonstrated during the 'reform diet' of 1827, when the introduction of the Magyar language into all spheres of life was advocated and a new concept of the nation formulated. The most influential spokesman of this concept was one of the richest magnates, Stephen Szechényi, who regarded the Magyar nation as a community of citizens irrespective of birth or property. In order to make a reality of this nation, Szechényi recommended reforms of the relationship between landlords and peasants, including the abolition of seigneurial privileges. He believed that defence of political autonomy required such reforms and that these concessions would not undermine the economic position of nobles. Most Magyar patriots were of noble origin, even though many of them owned no land and supported themselves as members of the free professions and government officials.

In the two decades following the Diet of 1827, Magyar national agitation made important progress, above all among the nobility and the urban population. The Magyar language was introduced into the schools. Magyar poetry and literature achieved important goals and there were publications in Magyar in the humanities and sciences, supported by the well-funded Hungarian Academy of Sciences. During the 1840s a new generation of Magyar intellectuals developed a liberal programme aiming at the emancipation of the Hungarian political nation, which was understood to include both Magyars and non-Magyar-speaking inhabitants of the Kingdom. However, this idea was rejected by the other nationalities in Hungary with the possible exception of Jews.

This disagreement between Magyars and non-Magyars played an important role during the revolution of 1848, when Magyar political leadership took advantage of the breakdown of the Metternich regime and as early as April announced important reforms such as the abolition of labour services and the integration of Transylvania into the rest of the Kingdom. These 'April Laws' were the first step towards a constitutional state that would enjoy a great deal of autonomy in the form of personal unions under Habsburg rule. The Magyar political leadership envisaged a centralized nation state with Magyar as the official language. This provoked strong opposition among those non-Magyar groups in which national movements had already started to form, such as the Croatians, Romanians, Serbs, and Slovaks. Once the government in Vienna had survived the political crisis of spring 1848, it could exploit these national movements—above all, those of Croatians—to support military action against Magyar revolution. Further Magyar military successes over the following year led the Austrian emperor to request military help from the Russian tsar. The defeated Magyar revolutionaries were persecuted in the ensuing counter-revolution.

Nevertheless, Magyar national mobilization was strong enough to survive Austrian oppression during the 1850s. As soon as Austria introduced constitutional reforms from about 1860, Magyar liberals again took up their struggle for an autonomous Hungarian state, only this time aiming to attain their goal by negotiation, not revolution. Under the leadership of Ferenc Deak, they were able to exploit Austrian weakness following its defeat by Prussia in the war of 1866 to achieve the so-called Compromise (*Ausgleich*) of 1867. The state was transformed into a dual monarchy—Austria-Hungary. In effect, Magyars had achieved statehood. The major drawback was that they regarded all inhabitants of historical Hungary (except Croatians), whatever their language, as members of one political Hungarian nation. In pursuit of this goal, the Hungarian government soon embarked on a policy of Magyarization that provoked further serious internal conflicts. However, the bulk of the Magyar political elite after the Compromise gradually came to feel a genuine loyalty towards the Monarchy, which they strongly supported until the end of the First World War.

The Czechs

The formation of a Czech national movement was a process concentrated on the territory of the formerly independent medieval Kingdom of Bohemia. As a result of dynastic policy, in the fourteenth century Bohemia had fallen under Habsburg rule, along with Moravia, Silesia, and Lusatia, which together were known as the 'Lands of the Crown of Bohemia'. Czech culture flourished in the sixteenth century, including a rich literature. Tension between the Protestant majority represented in the Estates and the Catholic Habsburg rulers resulted in rebellion that was defeated in 1620. It was followed by severe repression. Leading politicians and intellectuals were sentenced to death or forced into exile; the dominant Czech language in cultural and public life and administration was steadily replaced by German; the country was forcibly converted to Catholicism; its autonomy was undermined and later virtually abolished.

From the last third of the eighteenth century, enlightenment scholars began researching the history of Bohemia, the Czech language (still spoken by two thirds of inhabitants—peasants, artisans, the lower urban classes), and Czech literature from before 1620. This research received support from aristocrats as well as part of the Catholic hierarchy, motivated by a shared opposition to the far-reaching social, administrative, and religious reforms introduced by Joseph II. By contrast, most members of the Bohemian and Moravian Estates, being German speakers or bilingual, were not greatly upset by the Germanization of the administration and school system.

Important changes resulting from these reforms, together with what they heard about the French Revolution (although this was condemned by the authorities), motivated some young intellectuals of artisan and peasant origins to search for a new identity in the nation, understood as the community of all Czech-speaking inhabitants, irrespective of birth or position. In their view, confirmed by personal experience, Czech-speaking members of the lower classes were disadvantaged by their lack of knowledge of German. From the first two decades of the nineteenth century, Czech activists began agitating in the name of the nation-to-be, trying to persuade their co-nationals to accept Czech national identity based on common language and shared destiny, while also urging the Austrian authorities to permit Czech to be used as a language of higher education and public life. Even though this demand remained unfulfilled until 1848, Czech activists were allowed to publish in their language non-political texts except those deemed to be incompatible with Catholicism and state absolutism.

The first success for such agitation came in 1818 with the founding of the 'Patriotic Museum' and its journal in 1827, the first scientific journal written in Czech. During the

1830s, other journals appeared and it was possible to print scientific works with financial support based on collections organized by the 'Czech Matice'.[3]

In the 1840s a new Czech-speaking elite developed and national agitation succeeded in gaining an audience within the urban lower middle classes. The aims of the Czech social programme included peasant emancipation and improvements in the training of craftsmen. An extension of the programme to political goals was first formulated in March 1848. This programme was addressed to the government in Vienna and accepted by both German- and Czech-speaking liberals. It demanded above all civil and constitutional rights and, as an integral element of these, equal rights for the use of the Czech language. Since Bohemia and Moravia belonged to the German Confederation, Czechs were invited to participate in elections to the German National Assembly, but there was a successful boycott. This started a split between Czechs and an increasing portion of the German-speaking population of Bohemia and Moravia who identified themselves with the German nation. The counter-proposal of a federal Austrian constitution (part of what was known as the Austroslav programme), which was supported by Czech representatives, failed in the face of absolutist centralization implemented during the counter-revolution.

The constitutional regime after 1860 created the opportunity for national mobilization. Czechs won in municipal elections in Prague and many Czech-speaking towns but were unable to achieve a majority in the Bohemian Diet because the electoral system favoured the nobility and industrialists who generally rejected Czech identity. In response, the Czech political programme was extended to include demands for autonomy based on the historical rights of Bohemia and Moravia, and for democratization (universal suffrage) that could secure political power based on the support of the Czech majority.

The Czech national movement achieved mass support, demonstrated above all in the wave of meetings called to protest against the *Ausgleich* of 1867. Czech politicians demanded the same political status as had been granted to the Magyars. In the world of everyday politics the Czech national movement made progress in various cultural, social, and linguistic matters. Prague University, which had been exclusively German speaking, was divided into a Czech and a German university. New Czech high schools were founded. There was industrialization in Czech-speaking areas. The use of the Czech language in state administration was enlarged, although it did not achieve full parity with German.

Assertion of Czech identity in Moravia, an autonomous part of the historical lands of the Crown of Bohemia, only gained mass support some two or three decades later than in Bohemia. By the end of the nineteenth century, Czech speakers constituted a fully formed social structure, with its own middle classes and educated elites.

Until 1914 the ultimate political goal of the Czech national movement was autonomy within the Monarchy. No significant national political group sought secession and an independent nation state. However, during the First World War, an increasing number of Czech politicians came to view dynastic ties to the empire as obsolete and supported the secessionist program of Czech émigrés, led by T. G. Masaryk. Following the defeat of Austria and the end of the war in 1918, these politicians persuaded the Entente powers to permit the birth of a new state—Czechoslovakia.[4]

The Slovaks

The Slavic-speaking inhabitants of northern Hungary were descendants of a local population dating from the time before the Magyar invasion of 900. This population had no political autonomy and the only broader cultural contacts made in the late medieval and early modern periods were those with Czechs in Moravia and Bohemia. While German speakers in Hungary accepted the Lutheran Reformation from Germany, Slovak speakers were inspired by the Czech Reformation. The Protestant minority of Slovaks used Czech into the nineteenth century—which all Slovaks could understand—as their language of liturgy and education. Consequently, a complicated combination of identities emerged in the eighteenth century: educated Slovak speakers regarded themselves politically as Hungarians, but at the same time as ethnic Slovaks (or Slavs) and—in the case of Protestants—as participants in Czech cultural life.

As long as Latin was the official language in Hungary, ethnic identity did not play an important role. The situation changed in the 1780s when a group of Slovak Catholic clergymen, stimulated by Magyar opposition to Germanization, chose the West Slovak dialect as the basis for constructing a written form of Slovak. Printed texts in this language were published up to the mid-nineteenth century. At the same time, Slovak Protestants, above all pastors, used Czech in their printed texts. Young Slovak intellectuals in the 1830s regarded this split as dangerous for the future of their ethnic community. Over the next decade, they constructed—under the leadership of a Protestant, Ludovit Štúr—a new linguistic norm based on dialects from central Slovakia and established a national movement to agitate for the use of this distinctive language, regarded as a guarantee of national identity. However, most Czech intellectuals, who considered Slovaks to be part of the Czech nation, refused to accept this Slovak 'separation'.

During the revolution of 1848 Slovak patriots tried to mobilize popular support for the struggle against Magyarization, but with little success. Initial successes for the national movement were only registered from the beginning of the 1860s, when constitutional reforms allowed the foundation of Matice Slovenská, which acted as a centre for Slovak national agitation and provided support for the publication of books in the Slovak language. National demands were limited to language issues and a measure of autonomy for Slovak culture, and the national movement began to receive more support, as demonstrated in petitions and meetings. The Slovak language was introduced into elementary schools and even into three high schools (*Gymnasien*).

However, these small successes were annihilated after 1867, when the politics of Magyarization started. The Slovak language disappeared from public life and most schools, and national agitation was forbidden. Slovak culture was allowed only in the forms of non-political poetry and fiction. The only way to receive a non-Magyar higher education was in the seminaries for Catholic priests. The small group of secular Slovak intellectuals were mainly educated in Prague, where they collaborated closely with Czechs, often expressing overlapping Slovak and Czechoslovak (usually called 'Czechoslavic') identities. Thus, the concept of one Czechoslovak nation can be traced back to the first half of the nineteenth century. This concept of one nation with an accepted Slovak variant of the Czechoslovak language would provide the official legitimation of the new state of Czechoslovakia. Between the two World Wars, this concept was implemented in the schools with the support of a majority of Slovak voters. It was opposed by the Slovak Peoples Party, led by Catholic priests, who mobilized a strong minority of Slovak voters in support of a concept of the Slovak nation. Following the destruction of independent Czechoslovakia by Nazi Germany in 1939, this party declared an 'independent' Slovak nation state, allied to Germany. The new Republic in 1945 was organized as a state of two nations—Czechs and Slovaks—opening the way for the promotion of a genuine Slovak national culture.

The Slovenes

In the late medieval period, the Habsburg lands in Styria, Carinthia, and Carniola were inhabited by Slavic as well as German speakers. The Slavic speakers were concentrated in the countryside, a minority in Styria and Carinthia, and a majority in Carniola.

Even though they had no common name, one of the Slovene dialects was used during the Reformation as the basis for a translation of the Bible and other religious texts. This dialect could be understood by all Slavic groups in the eastern Alps, including those who lived in the territories of the Veneto and Trieste.

At the end of the eighteenth century, enlightenment scholars, historians, and philologists concluded that all these dialects were components of one single language, and consequently, that all speakers of these dialects had been a nation already in the medieval period. They invented a name for these speakers —Slovenes—and published a Slovene dictionary and grammar. During the short existence of the 'Illyrian Provinces', created by Napoleon after his military triumph over Austria in 1809, almost all speakers of Slovene dialects lived under one unified administration.[5] This promoted the formation of a Slovene ethnic identity.

However, the path to modern national identity was complicated after 1830 by the new and attractive concept of 'Illyrism' formulated by the Croatian Ludovit Gaj. He regarded all southern Slavic dialects as similar and proposed there be one common language, arguing that Slovenes, Croatians, Bosniaks, and Serbs were all members of one 'Illyrian nation'. After some disputes, Slovene intellectuals rejected Illyrism (only Gaj's orthography was accepted) and formulated instead the cultural concept of a 'unified' Slovene nation. In the name of this nation, they sought unsuccessfully during the revolution of 1848 to bring all Slovenes into one administrative unit under

Habsburg rule. However, this early national agitation was complicated by a split between the majority of conservative patriots (represented above all by Catholic clergy in the countryside) and liberals. A unified national program that commanded support from both streams was only devised in 1865.

In the new constitutional context of the 1860s, national agitation achieved its first successes. Slovene parties gained a majority in the Diet in Carniola in 1867. By the end of the 1860s, thousands of citizens—partly due to the influence of the Czech example—participated in protest meetings against the *Ausgleich* of 1867. In the 1870s the national movement had to confront an accelerating policy of Germanization, especially in Carinthia and Styria. Its leadership temporarily gave up the aim of a unified Slovenia but successfully achieved more limited goals in the fields of cultural and school policy. As a result of economic prosperity, a stronger Slovene urban middle class developed in the last decades of the nineteenth century, above all in Carniola and its capital Ljubljana, which became centres of a mass national movement.

Slovenes were, however, not strong enough to pursue an independent political programme during the First World War, and the post-war arrangements were decided by negotiations between the Entente powers and Serbia. Slovene-speaking regions of Carniola and southern Styria were included as an acknowledged nation in the newly created Kingdom of Serbs, Croatians, and Slovenes. The Slovenes in Gorica, Istria, and Trieste remained under Italian rule and those in Carinthia under Austrian rule, where they subsequently became a target for a strong and successful Germanization.

Even though the oppressive Serbian policy did not allow Slovenes to play any important role in political life, their national culture and economy grew significantly in the interwar period. Slovenia became the highest developed part of Yugoslavia, as the state was renamed in 1930. This prosperity was then interrupted during the Second World War.

The Croatians

Eighteenth-century Croatia was a small remnant of the medieval kingdom (Croatia proper, Slavonia, Dalmatia) that was unified in 1102 in the form of a personal union with Hungary. One of its three parts, Dalmatia, was lost to Venice at the beginning of the fifteenth century, and in the seventeenth century almost half of the remaining territory of Slovenia and of Croatia proper was turned into a 'military border' region designed to provide a defence against Ottoman attacks. The military border regions were governed directly from Vienna by the army and were settled by immigrants fleeing Ottoman territories. The Orthodox among these settlers were identified as Serbs. The resistance of the Croatian Estates to this division of their territory was defeated by the end of the seventeenth century and punished by the confiscation of the most important landholdings. With only a weak sense of political or ethnic identity the Croatian Diet in 1790 voluntarily accepted the 'protection' of the Hungarian Estates and supported them in their struggle against the reforms introduced by Joseph II. This included opposition to the official use of the German language. In the Croatian Diet, Latin continued to be used as the official language until 1830. Then the Diet approved the Hungarian decision to introduce the Magyar language into Croatian schools.

The linguistic situation in Croatian territories was complicated by the fact that its population used dialects that belonged to two different groups. 'Kai' dialect was spoken around the capital Zagreb and had possessed a written form since the time of Renaissance humanism. Other Croatians used a vernacular belonging to the 'Što' dialects, which were spoken also by inhabitants of Bosnia and Serbia. Since in the eyes of Romantic patriots a single language formed the basis of a nation, a group of Croatian intellectuals led by Ludovit Gaj decided to codify a common literary language based on 'Što' dialects, regarding this language as that of one potentially united 'Illyric nation', which would include not only Croatians but also Slovenes and Serbs. However, this project failed. Later the project became counter-productive when Serbian politicians used it in support of their vision of a 'Great-Serbian' nation, which would include all 'Što' speakers, including Bosnians and some Croatians. In the 1850s moderate intellectuals from both sides formally came to a compromise, accepting the idea of one Serbo-Croat language to be used by these two nations, albeit with two different alphabets, Latin for Croatians and Cyrillic for Serbs.

Despite these differences, the Croatian national movement took its first significant steps in the 1840s. The first journals were published, Illyrian (later Croatian) *Matice* were founded to support literary and scientific life. A Croatian 'national party' was informally constructed with these campaigns and became a leading political force in the 1848 revolution. Its programme included civil rights and national aims, above all, unification with Dalmatia and abolition of the military border regions in order to form an autonomous state with Croatian as the language of administration and education. Even though Croatian troops supported Vienna in its war against the Magyar revolution, Croatian national demands remained unfulfilled. After the failure of the revolution, Magyarization in Croatia was replaced by Germanization. Croatia continued to be an economically underdeveloped region.

With the introduction of constitutionalism in the 1860s, the Croatian national movement resumed its activity, although the national idea had only a weak reception at mass level. Croatian politics was divided into three streams: the pro-Hungarian 'Magyarons', represented above all by the nobility; the National Party, which maintained the idea of South-Slavic cooperation; the movement (later party) of 'historical right', which demanded the unification of all the territories of the medieval Croatian kingdom. After the *Ausgleich* of 1867, Croatians achieved under the leadership of the National Party recognition as a 'political nation' and some degree of autonomy, including the military border that was regained in 1881. While the National Party included an idealistic Yugoslav wing, the Party of Rights focused on 'national interests', including both a radical anti-Serbian policy and the struggle for peasant interests against Magyarized landlords. This political orientation became stronger in the last two decades of the nineteenth century. Some radicals from its ranks developed the Greater-Croatia idea, claiming the inclusion of Bosnia into their national territory.

After the defeat and breakup of the empire, Croatia was included within the Kingdom of Serbs, Croatians, and Slovenes, even though many, probably most, Croatian politicians opposed this. In the weak and turbulent democratic period of the 1920s, Croatian nationalists struggled against Greater-Serbian policies, and even though they were not very successful, they did succeed in a mass mobilization of Croatians. King Alexander sought to settle the crisis by abolishing democracy and introducing an authoritarian regime in 1921.[6] As a reaction against this policy, the demand for Croatian independence became stronger, especially among right-wing politicians, and received support from Germany.

After the occupation of Yugoslavia in April 1941, Adolf Hitler created a Croatian state ruled by a puppet government composed of admirers of the Nazi regime. Cruel persecution of all non-Croatians, above all Serbs, provoked a strong reaction on the Serbian side, above all among partisans under the leadership of Josip Broz-Tito.[7] After their victory in 1945, Croatia, with its historical borders, became an autonomous republic within the new federal state of Yugoslavia.

The Serbians

By the eighteenth century all that remained of the medieval Kingdom of Serbia, which had been destroyed by Ottoman invasion, was the autonomous Orthodox Patriarchate. This provided a source of cultural identity for a rural population organized as patriarchal families and clan lineages. Serbians had openly resisted Ottoman rule several times from the sixteenth century. Most important was the uprising linked to the conquest of southern Hungary by Habsburg armies at the end of the seventeenth century.

Meanwhile the Ottoman authorities persecuted Serbians, but there were limits to how far this could go. During the time of reforms introduced during the 1790s by Sultan Selim III, Serbians, especially in the district of Belgrade, exploited tensions between the sultan and janissaries (a special military force) to prepare an insurrection. This broke out in 1804 and continued until 1812, thanks largely to Russian support. This was followed by further unrest until—around the same time as Greek independence was declared—in 1830 Serbians achieved autonomous status as a principality. This was only the first step towards a modern Serbian nation, since three important obstacles remained. First, only about 20 per cent of Serbians lived in the territory of the principality. Second, its traditional patriarchal society lacked a nobility and middle class and was subject to the power of the Orthodox Church. Third, the new state elite lacked modern political education and only slowly and unwillingly accepted elements of civil rights and constitutionalism.

The most striking feature of the Serbian national movement was the territorial division between its political and cultural wings. The Serbian cultural revival began not in the principality but in southern Hungary (later named the Vojvodina), led by Serbians with higher levels of modern economic development and education than their counterparts in the principality. The interest in national emancipation motivated a group of Serbian merchants and educated men to establish in 1826 *Matica Srpska*, an institution that provided financial support for cultural activities. Serbian books were mainly published in Vienna and Pest. During the 1848 revolution, the Serbians in southern Hungary formed a powerful opposition to both Habsburg centralism and Magyarization.

Only gradually did educated elites take shape in Serbia, mostly coming from outside the principality. Serious constitutionalism began with the constitution of 1869, which was introduced shortly after the country achieved full independence. The internal political life of this state (which became a kingdom in 1882) was frequently punctuated by coups and violence. Nevertheless, it was during the 1840s and 1850s that the modern concept of the Serbian nation was born. Rejecting Illyrism as a tactical manoeuvre by the Habsburgs, the first generation of educated Serbians defined their nation by two criteria that were not fully compatible: Orthodox religion and the Serb language. The problem of sharing a written language with the majority of Croatians was partially solved by stipulating that the constructed 'Serbo-Croat' language be written by Catholic Croatians in the Latin alphabet and by Orthodox Serbians in the Cyrillic alphabet.

It was with this confusing combination of religious and linguistic criteria that the Greater-Serbian concept was formulated as the ideological basis for the Serbian state policy of bringing all Serbians into one nation state. Muslims in Bosnia were regarded as Islamized Serbians because they spoke što dialect. In the most extreme version of the Greater-Serbian idea Croatians who spoke što dialects were also regarded as Catholic Serbs. Thus all Bosnia was considered to belong to Serbia, and the Austrian occupation of this region in 1878 was rejected as an act of aggression against the Serbian nation. The struggle for a Serbian nation state had taken on the character of a 'unification nationalism' in the name of the Greater-Serbian idea. The success enjoyed by this idea after the First World War was, especially due to conflict with Croatian nationalism, the reason for much of the instability in the newly created multinational state of Yugoslavia.

The Montenegrins

The small mountainous territory called Montenegro was the one region in the Balkans that was never fully brought under the Ottoman yoke. Living in a traditional patriarchal society, its inhabitants had developed over several centuries a strong sense of identity based on clan lineages. The country was ruled by princes together with the heads of the various clans. In the first half of the nineteenth century, Montenegro became de facto an independent state with support from Russia. During the 1850s Montenegrins successfully resisted Ottoman attacks and in 1860 obtained an agreement guaranteeing their borders. This was the first step towards international recognition agreed at the Congress of Berlin in 1878. At the same time, Montenegro enlarged its territory and achieved access to the Adriatic.

During the 1870s the absolutist princes of Montenegro initiated important reforms. The administration was improved and a few dozen elementary schools were founded as well as two high schools. The first newspapers were also published.

In the settlement following the First World War Montenegro was incorporated into the Kingdom of Serbs, Croatians, and Slovenes, and its were inhabitants treated as a specific part of the Serbian nation. Nevertheless, Montenegrins preserved some important elements of their national identity, based on common memory and geographical exclusivity and, after 1945, achieved the status of an autonomous republic.

The Greeks

The Greek national movement was the only one in the Balkans that could build on cultural and linguistic continuity since the medieval period. Ottoman conquest had destroyed the Byzantine Empire but the Ottomans tolerated the Greek Orthodox Church (which used Greek as its language) and Greek literature. A group of Greek merchants and aristocrats survived, above all in Constantinople, and became the core of a rich and powerful class of 'Phanariots', who played an important role in running Ottoman foreign policy as well as naval, trade, and financial affairs in the seventeenth and eighteenth centuries. The Phanariot class cooperated closely with the Greek Orthodox hierarchy to maintain a Byzantine-Greek identity. In the eighteenth century their cultural ambitions extended to cultivating the Greek language as the lingua franca for all Christians in the Balkans.

From the eighteenth century an expanding Greek diaspora lived in Russia and central and western Europe, maintaining contacts with each other and with Greek centres in the Ottoman Empire. This enabled the diffusion of enlightenment ideas into the Balkans. A younger generation of Greeks took up the ideas of humanity and constitutionalism, and even the principles of the French Revolution with its civic concept of the nation defined by common language and the equality of all citizens. As a consequence there developed two competing views of the Greek future based on different concepts of Greek national identity. The Phanariots considered themselves as representatives and future rulers of the nation. Enlightenment intellectuals envisaged the creation of a nation state bringing together all ethnic Greeks. They grounded this idea in a view of the Greek past inspired by western humanist philologists and other scholars, an idealized image of ancient Greece as the motherland of democracy.

Both national movements gave priority to political goals but differed in their social programmes and their view of political power. Significant also was the difference in the linguistic programme. Whereas the Phanariots favoured the modernized written Greek (*kathareusa*), which non-educated people could not understand, the democrats formulated a linguistic norm based on the spoken language (*dimotiki*).

Anti-Ottoman feeling grew in all classes of society during the Napoleonic Wars. Greeks were resentful of Ottoman repression, inspired by the Serbian uprising and encouraged by the support Russia gave to the Serbians. Leading Phanariots and local Greek oppositional groups discussed the possibility of an armed rising against Ottoman rule. The Phanariot aristocracy under the leadership of Alexander Ypsilanti, who was a principal figure in the Russian diaspora, prepared a military campaign directed at the Danubian principalities. The other centre was organized by urban middle-class groups in the Greek peninsula, in contact with small rebellious peasant groups, above all in the Peloponnese.

While the Ypsilanti campaign failed and was defeated by the summer of 1821, the insurgency in the Peloponnese enjoyed great success, taking control of all the peninsula and penetrating into central Greece. Many volunteers from other parts of Greece came to fight against the Ottomans. In December 1821 an assembly of national representatives met and agreed a liberal constitution, inspired by the French constitution of 1795.

The Ottoman regime had been taken by surprise. After a period of confusion, Ottoman forces launched a successful offensive against the uprising. The decisive act was military intervention in favour of the Greek insurgents: a joint French and British fleet defeated the Ottoman navy in 1827 near the Peloponnesian coast. Russia declared war on the Ottoman Empire in spring 1828. Thus the new Greek nation state was created under the joint protection of three of the four European powers (Austria alone remained aloof) in the years 1828–30.

This nation state, however, did not correspond to the expectations of Greek liberal nationalists as it included only a small part of ethnic Greek territory and was turned into an autocratic monarchy under the rule of King Otto, a member of a cadet branch of the Wittelsbach (Bavarian) dynasty. The struggle for constitutional government and the liberation of all Greeks from Ottoman rule continued throughout the nineteenth century until 1914. Leading Greek politicians aimed at a unification of all Greek-inhabited territories, including parts of the western coast of Asia Minor. The most radical form of this nationalism also claimed the historical capital of the Byzantine Empire, Constantinople.

The Romanians

The term Romanian[8] did not exist in the early modern period. The formation of a Romanian national movement proceeded in different ways in the territory of three political units. In the principalities of Wallachia and Moldavia almost all the population, including the aristocracy, were Romanian speakers, whereas in Transylvania, Romanian-speaking peasants were a subordinate ethnic group under the rule of

Magyar-speaking nobles. Romanians also had their separate religion divided into the two confessions of Greek Orthodoxy and Greek Catholicism (also known as the Uniates, this breakaway Church maintained an Orthodox ritual but acknowledged the leadership of Rome).

The first studies of the Romanian language and history were undertaken in Transylvania in the last decades of the eighteenth century by what is known as the 'Transylvanian school', who were mainly Uniates. These scholars identified the Romanian language as 'Latinist' and sought to purify it by removing non-Latin (in other words, Slavic and Greek) elements. The first steps towards linguistic emancipation were also taken in the principalities, even though the *boyar* (nobility) Academy in Bucharest continued to use Greek. While the cultural definition and project of the Romanian nation was constructed in Transylvania, the political programme of unification developed in the principalities.

Wallachia and Moldavia were semi-independent principalities, ruled by Greek Phanariots under the protection of the Ottoman Empire. The struggle for emancipation was led by the nobility (*boyars*), who regarded themselves as a 'nation' in the sense of a privileged elite, similar to the view taken by Magyar nobles. Opposition by boyars in 1821 supported the idea of a general upheaval of all Balkan Christians, led by the Greek Prince Ypsilanti. Their goal was not a civic nation but an independent state-nation ruled by the Estates, meaning the nobility.

Consequently, the national movement in the principalities focused on political aims and managed to increase their autonomy in 1831–2. Inspired by French revolutionary ideas, radical patriots in Wallachia advocated social reforms in 1848, but the revolutionary movement was unable to withstand Russian occupation. What survived was the programme of unifying the two principalities, which was supported by the more conservative Moldavian liberals. This unification was inspired by the historical tradition of 'Latinism', and its form was envisaged as a liberal state ruled by a younger generation of boyars.

With the end of Ottoman domination, the political elite of both states divided into pro-Russian and pro-Western factions. The most important cultural and to some extent also political support came from France, which was regarded by pro-Western intellectuals as their most important ally. This was more the case in Wallachia; in Moldavia the Russian influence was stronger. The crisis during the Crimean War (1853–6), when the principalities were occupied by Austria, strengthened the unification programme in both principalities. The first step was taken under Alexandru Ion Cuza in 1859, when conservatives accepted the liberal idea of a national state, although without any important social reforms that would damage their interests. The newly established nation state took the form of a monarchy—Romania—under the rule of kings drawn from a branch of the Hohenzollern dynasty. Only after unification, and especially from the 1880s, did there begin a process of national mobilization from above, accompanied by political emancipation and liberalization.

By contrast national mobilization in Transylvania began as a movement for linguistic goals, since the Orthodox and Uniates found a common identity as ethnic 'Vlachs'.

A petition of 1792 to the Magyar-dominated Transylvanian Diet demanded the use of the Romanian language in the Diet as well as representation of Romanian interests. An effective national agitation did not start before the 1830s. The first signs of its success came during the revolution of 1848, when Romanian political leaders opposed the Magyar concept that treated them as members of a unified Hungarian political nation. However, the movement only achieved mass mobilization in the constitutional era from the 1860s. The political programme of the national movement adopted the idea of unification with the existing Romanian nation state. This goal was finally realized following the defeat and collapse of the Habsburg Empire in 1918.

The Bulgarians

After the Ottoman conquest in the late fourteenth century, nothing survived of the medieval Bulgarian state. The Orthodox Church used the Greek language, and merchants, though ethnic Bulgarians, used Greek as their language of communication and education. Some scholar-clergymen 'discovered' around 1800 the glorious past of the Bulgarian state and reflected upon the ethnic specificity of the population. Some Russian and Austrian scholars also contributed to studies of the Bulgarian language, history, and ethnography.

The first expressions of Bulgarian identity were linked to Church organization and activity. From about 1830, some clergymen, Bulgarian by origin, requested permission from the Ottoman administration to use the Church Slavonic language in services and to have their own Church organization. Small concessions were made, such as introducing the Bulgarian language into elementary schools. In 1840 there existed twenty elementary schools and one high school using Bulgarian as the language of education.

In order to use Bulgarian in schools and to print and publish Bulgarian texts, it was necessary to codify the language. However, it took some decades before writing in various dialects could be replaced by one standard norm. Almost all books published in the 1830s and 1840s were translations of religious texts into Bulgarian. The first journals appeared in 1840s. Tellingly, books were published outside Bulgaria, in Constantinople, Pest, and Vienna.

The successful struggle for Church autonomy developed in the 1850s into a movement for Bulgarian national revival. Young intellectuals, most of them educated in Russia or Austria and living outside the Ottoman Empire, argued that the national movement should be secular, based less on a confessional and more on an ethnic concept of the Bulgarian nation. During the 1860s a secular Bulgarian literature appeared in the forms of poetry, novels, and educational books. In 1869 the Bulgarian Literary Society was founded.

Moderate patriots wished to come to some arrangement with the Ottoman Empire, but radicals set up a 'Bulgarian government' sitting in Belgrade (later in Bucharest) and tried—inspired by Garibaldi's success in Italy—to unleash popular uprisings against

Ottoman rule. When these attempts totally failed, the protagonists came to the view that they must make the national idea attractive not only to peasants but also to craftsmen and wealthy merchants in the towns, and also must wait for a favorable situation. Erroneously, they thought such a moment had come in 1875 and they initiated an insurrection. This was defeated but the Ottoman repression that followed provoked, in 1877, a new upheaval, this time supported by a large part of the population. However, the decisive force in the conflict was the Russian tsar who dispatched a strong army to the Balkans and forced the Ottoman Empire to capitulate.

The decision made by the major powers at the Congress of Berlin in 1878 did not satisfy the original goals of the Bulgarian movement. Yet this partial success prepared the way for a unification of almost all ethnic Bulgarian territory. The new state was established in 1879 as a constitutional monarchy with guaranteed civil rights. However, it had much to do to build up its educational system and state administration, helped above all by Austria.

The Macedonians

The ancient name 'Macedonia' disappeared during the period of Ottoman rule and was only restored in the nineteenth century, originally as a geographical term designating a vast territory between the towns of Salonika and Skopje. The urban population of this territory was Greek Slavic and Turkish speaking, along with many Albanians in the west. The question of national identity became relevant only in the 1870, when the Bulgarian national movement claimed all Slavic territories in the western part of the Balkans. However, Macedonian territory remained under Ottoman rule and the Slavic inhabitants were mobilized both by local intelligentsia and by agents coming from Bulgaria for the liberation of Macedonia. This movement expressed a dual sense of identity, demanding unification with Bulgaria while also advocating a regional Macedonian identity. By 1900 some intellectuals had formulated the concept of a Macedonian nation, based on linguistic differences from Bulgarian as well as specific historical developments and geographical location. This concept was rejected by Bulgarian nationalists who considered Macedonians to be part of their nation, and also by Greek nationalists who regarded all Macedonia as ancient Greek territory that had to be united with the rest of Greece. In 1918 Macedonia was occupied by Serbia, which justified this by claiming that Macedonians were really Serbs speaking a different dialect.

The situation changed with the formation of an anti-German resistance during the Second World War. Macedonian partisans played an active role in this, which in turn influenced the decision to create an autonomous republic of Macedonia within the new post-war state of Yugoslavia. As a result of this, language, culture, and science were cultivated as expressions of Macedonian national identity, which was accepted by most Slavic speakers in this territory.

The Albanians

The Albanian national movement began very late, even though Albanians (calling themselves *shquiptare*) had been recognized as a distinct ethnic group since the early medieval period, living under the rule of various governments. Their resistance to Ottoman expansion was only temporarily successful in the fifteenth century. In the following centuries, a majority of Albanians became Muslims.

In the nineteenth century only a very few educated Albanians showed any interest in notions of an Albanian identity or culture. The first signs of a national movement came with war in the Balkans in 1878 when some of these people founded the Prizren League, which proclaimed political and cultural goals. The movement had only limited success with its attempts at promoting Albanian culture, above all in the written language and education. The League was banned and persecuted by the Ottoman government in 1881 and again in 1897. Nevertheless, the national movement survived, in part due to support from Albanians abroad and the Albanian colony in Constantinople. Its liberal leaders hoped to gain an advantage by supporting the Young Turks movement, but in this they were disappointed. In 1908 they came to an agreement on using the Latin alphabet (instead of Arabic or Greek) for written Albanian. They were, however, unable to unify the two variants of literary language, which corresponded to the two main dialects.

During the first year of the Balkan Wars (1912–13), Albanians exploited the weakness of the Ottoman Empire and declared an independent state in November 1912. This was recognized by the major powers in the following year. After the turmoil of World War I, during which Albanians had lived under various occupying armies, independence was restored in 1920. This new state included only about half of the Albanian speakers of the Balkans, the other half becoming minorities in Yugoslavia and Greece. It is difficult to consider Albania as a nation state at this time, as it was governed by a semi-feudal aristocracy of landowning *beys* who successfully suppressed attempts by liberals to introduce constitutional government and civil rights. Instead, with Yugoslav and later Italian support, a dictatorship under King Zog was established in 1928. Only after 1945 was Albanian national identity able to spread both in Communist Albania and in Kosovo, despite differences of dialect and religion.

The Muslims/Bosniaks

The emergence of a 'Muslim nation' in Bosnia is linked to one of the most recent national movements to form in Europe. Its historical background is usually taken to be the Slavic Kingdom of Bosnia, which emerged in the medieval period on the margins of the Western Church but also with some degree of Orthodox infiltration from the east.

Its geographic location and low level of state power allowed the heretic *Bogomils*, who had been expelled from the Byzantine Empire, to settle down and even to win over a sizeable portion of the local population to their faith. They created a specific 'Bosnian Church' and resisted persecutions and even crusades organized from Hungary. The Ottoman conquest of Bosnia in the late fourteenth century altered the religious situation. Eventually a strong Slavic-speaking Muslim community formed, whose members were privileged and played an important role in the economic and military life of the empire. During the seventeenth and eighteenth centuries the Christians in Bosnia were differentiated according to confession.

The renewed Christian resistance of the nineteenth century was inspired by the successes enjoyed by national movements in Serbia and Montenegro. They culminated in the uprising of 1875, which in turn helped bring about what is often referred to as the Near Eastern crisis. The rising was defeated, but Bosnia and Herzegovina were occupied by Austria-Hungary in 1878 and governed directly from Vienna until the outbreak of war in 1914.

While Bosnian Serbs opposed the Habsburg occupation and demanded unification with Serbia, many Croatians became effective collaborators of Vienna, playing a part in modernizing the school system, roads, and the administration. In an effort to divide the opposition, Austria supported the concept of Bosnian identity and the idea that the Muslim 'Bosniaks' were a specific ethnic group. After 1918, when Bosnia was incorporated into Yugoslavia, the Muslims were defined only as a religious community. During the German occupation in the 1940s, many Muslims were active in the partisan resistance and were subject to brutal treatment by the occupiers. After 1945, Bosnia became a republic within the federal state of Yugoslavia, inhabited by Muslims, Croatians, and Serbians. Muslims were granted official recognition as a national group only as late as 1968.

Conclusion

All these national movements that originated in the Habsburg and Ottoman Empires share one important feature. Sooner or later, the efforts of a small group of 'nationalists' to cultivate a distinct sense of national identity reached the stage of mobilizing mass support. Even though only some of these movements initially aimed at independent statehood, the trend in this direction steadily increased so that, by the end of the twentieth century, all of them had attained their nation state. On the path towards autonomy or statehood, the leadership of national movements had to confront the problem of overlapping political and ethnic borders. In some cases the political border divided a homogeneous ethnic territory (Slovenes, Serbs). In other instances historic borders included members of different ethnic groups (Serbs and Croatians, Germans and Czechs). In almost all cases, there existed a tension, even a contradiction, between earlier ethnic borders and current political ones, whether real or imagined in collective memory. It was difficult, if not impossible, to find solutions where borders would satisfy all national claims. Consequently, the path towards nationally defined autonomous territories was always accompanied by the formation of ethnic minorities. Once nation states were established, issues of minority status and minority rights created serious problems both within states and frequently in international relations.

Can we identify general reasons or preconditions for this successful path from national agitation to mass movement and later on, to autonomy or independence? We cannot explain this solely in terms of the enthusiasm of a small number of activists or the sheer appeal of national ideas to the broader population. If we inquire into the circumstances that were favourable for national mobilization, we discover that national agitation started soon after or in the midst of deep internal conflicts in both empires. These were above all related to the modernizing reform projects of Joseph II and Selim III in the late eighteenth century. Before this there was a 'Phase A' of the national movements, which was an elite and scholarly project to define and elaborate a concept of national identity, above all based on ethnicity.[9] This phase was stronger in the Habsburg monarchy, and weaker in the Ottoman Empire. The degree to which this idea of a new national identity spread depended on the level of social communication and on the ability of the broader population, conditioned by the degree of formal education, to understand and internalize new ideas about a community based on equality and solidarity. Last but not least, the acceptance of national appeals was stronger where the idea of national solidarity could be linked to a community of interests, above all economic and social, but also political. Only when we have identified these various conditions can we make sense of differences in timing and intensity of the different national movements.

The chronology and structure of the process of national emancipation differed a good deal. Some national movements started at the end of the eighteenth century (Magyars, Czechs, Greeks, Serbians); some of them in the first half of the nineteenth century (Slovaks, Slovenes); some later (Albanians, Bosnian Muslims). This corresponds to the asynchronous development of coherence within those ethnic groups which became objects of national agitation. To use the terms of Anthony Smith, some of them had already become 'ethnic communities' by 1800 (Magyars, Czechs, Greeks), whereas others were still at the level of 'ethnic categories' (Slovaks, Slovenes, Bulgarians).[10] However, the fact that some movements (Greek, Serbian, but also Romanian, Bulgarian, Magyar) achieved statehood early, and others much later, cannot be explained either in terms of the different times they began or by differences in level of education or degrees of economic backwardness.

These different paths to statehood correspond to the differences in the structure of national programmes. Some national movements began with linguistic and cultural goals, and even later when they developed a political program that did not include independence. Other movements emphasized political objectives very early in their development and soon came to demand an independent state. The first type of national programme was found principally within national movements in the Habsburg Empire (with the major exception of the Magyars). The second type characterized the movements within the Ottoman Empire. In other words, secessionist nationalism was decisive in national movements under Ottoman rule, whereas under Habsburg rule secessionism dominated only in the Magyar case.

How can we explain this difference? First, we must recall the differences in the political systems and political culture of the two empires, which were considered in the introduction. Second, we must analyse the social structure of national movements. Where the ethnic group as 'nation-to-be' included all social classes corresponding to the given level of economic development (as was the case with the Greeks, Magyars, and Serbians), national movements demanded statehood almost from their start. By contrast, where a subordinate ethnic group lacked a full social structure, especially a ruling class (bourgeoisie, nobility), national movements formulated political goals only later, and these usually took the form of demands for autonomy, not full independence.

Seen within a European context, the national movements in the Ottoman Empire appear as one specific type of secessionist nationalism, often using force and with an important role played by religious claims. By contrast, national movements in the Habsburg Empire were so diverse that it is impossible to see them as representing one specific type. Here we find the various kinds of national programmes and 'nationalisms' that also developed elsewhere in Europe. The unification nationalisms of the Poles and Germans have their parallels in Italy.[11] The secessionist nationalism of the Magyars has its counterparts not only in the Ottoman Empire but also in Norway, Ireland, and Belgium, as well as in Polish areas under Russian rule.

As for 'cultural nationalism', one can distinguish two forms. First, there were the movements that used national history to construct a political argument, such as those of the Czechs and Croatians. They are similar to movements in Catalonia, Wales, and Flanders. Then there were movements that did not employ historical arguments, such as the Slovaks and Slovenes. In this respect, these resemble national movements in Finland, Estonia, and Latvia.

Finally, the fact that these national movements also went on to achieve their own nation states was not the result of their long-term aims but instead a consequence of the sudden collapse of the Austro-Hungarian and German Empires, and the final breakdown of the Ottoman Empire, at the end of the First World War, and of the post-war decisions made by the triumphant powers of Britain, France, and the USA.

Notes

1. See above, Chapter 8, on nationalism and unification in Europe.
2. The term 'Ruthene' applies to eastern Slavic-speaking people in Eastern Galicia. During the nineteenth century the national identity of Ruthenes came to be closely associated with the more distinctive and larger group of Ukrainians inhabiting territory in the Russian Empire.
3. The name 'Matice' means in Serbian 'mother' and was borrowed from Matica Srbska, which, founded in 1826, was the central cultural institution of the Serbian national

movement in Hungary. Similar cultural institutions were founded with this name in other Slavic national movements.

4. This was part of a general programme of 'national self-determination', expressed for example in the 'Fourteen Points' drawn up before the end of the war by US President Woodrow Wilson, and envisaged as the basis for the post-war order in place of the defeated empires.
5. 'Les Provinces Illyriennes' included not only the territory of Slovene speakers but also Croatia, Istria, and Dalmatia. This was a formally independent state unit, although decisive executive power was held by French officials. Some elements of this administrative system survived the fall of Napoleon.
6. It was with his assumption of power that the new name of Yugoslavia was adopted for the state.
7. This partisan movement was not the only resistance to fascism and was not confined to Serbians. Indeed, Tito himself was Croatian.
8. There have been two spellings of this word in English: Romanian and Rumanian. The established spelling is now Romanian, and that of the name of the country and state Romania.
9. For the idea of phases A, B, and C in the development of national movements, see M. Hroch (ed.) (2007) 'Real and Constructed: The Nature of the Nation', *Comparative Studies in Modern European History*, London, part VII, 95.
10. See A. D. Smith (1991) *National Identity*, Harmondsworth.
11. The Polish and German national movements have a Habsburg component although they are mainly located in other states. They and the Italian movement are considered in the previous chapter.

Suggested Further Reading

Habsburg Empire

Agnew, H. (1976) *The Czechs and the Lands of the Bohemian Crown*, Stanford, CA.

Brock, P. (1976) *The Slovak National Awakening*, Toronto.

Despalatovič, E. M. (1975) *Ludevit Gaj and the Illyrian Movement*, New York.

Gross, M. (1979–80) 'Croatian National-Integrational Ideologies from the End of Illyrism to the Creation of Jugoslavia', in *Austrian History Yearbook*, 3–33.

Kann, R. (1950) *The Multinational Empire: Nationalism and National Reform in the Habsburg Monarchy, 1848–1918*, 2 vols., New York.

Kořalka, J. (1991) 'The Czechs 1840–1918', in A. Kappeler (ed.) *The Formation of National Elites*, New York, 41–76.

Niederhauser, E. (1981) *The Rise of Nationality in Eastern Europe*, Budapest.

Szabad, G. (1977) *Hungarian Political Trends between the Revolution and the Compromise 1848–1867*, Budapest.

Ottoman Empire

Adanir, F. (1992) 'The Macedonians in the Ottoman Empire, 1878–1912', in A. Kappeler (ed.) *The Formation of National Elites*, New York, 161–92.

Banac, I. (1984) *The National Question in Jugoslavia*, Ithaca, NY.

Clogg, R. (1992) *A Concise History of Greece*, Cambridge.
Crampton, R. J. (1997) *A Concise History of Bulgaria*, Cambridge.
Hitchins, K. (1985) *The Idea of Nation: The Romanians of Transylvania 1691–1849*, Bucharest.
Jelavich, C. and B. (1977) *The Establishment of the Balkan National States, 1804–1820*, Seattle.
Lampe, J. R. (1982) *Balkan Economic History, 1550–1990*, Bloomington, IN.
Todorova, M. (1997) *Imagining the Balkans*, Oxford.
Petrovich, M. B. (1976) *A History of Modern Serbia, 1804–1918*, New York.

CHAPTER 10

SEPARATIST NATIONALISM IN THE ROMANOV AND SOVIET EMPIRES

THEODORE R. WEEKS

INTRODUCTION

THE Russian Empire was famously described by V. I. Lenin as a 'prison of nations', and very similar language was used in the 1990s referring to the Soviet Union in its final days. The continuities at first appear striking but, after a closer look, even more overwhelming are the differences between relations between national minority and state in the Romanov and Soviet Empires. In this short essay, I would like to set down the main challenges that nationalism posed for these two multinational states (the USSR, of course, never identified itself as an 'empire'), the responses chosen by Russian/Soviet political leaders to deal with nationalism, and finally the role that nationalism played in undermining the Russian Empire and the USSR.

Before looking into the historical peculiarities of the Russian case, some definitions are in order. In Russian it is possible to distinguish between 'Russian' as an ethnic and cultural designation (*russkii*) and as a geographical and political one (*rossiiskii*). Unfortunately, usage of the two terms was never very precise or consistent, aside from official designations such as the *Rossiiskaia Imperiia* and the present *Rossiiskaia Federatsiia*. During Soviet times, *sovetskii* was often used where in the pre-revolutionary context one might have expected *rossiiskii*. Despite all imprecision in actual usage, the Russian language reflects the reality of a multinational state where neither the leaders (the mainly German-by-blood tsars or Georgian Stalin) nor the population could be consistently expected to be ethnically Russian. Both the Russian Empire and the USSR recognized that separatist nationalism posed a serious threat to their continued political stability, indeed to their very existence.

In the Russian Empire, religion was a much more important element of identity than 'nationality', a term that most subjects would not have understood. In a preliterate society (and literacy remained below 50 per cent throughout the imperial period, though rates differed markedly among different national groups) the language one spoke was less important for group identity than the religion one practised. Thus it was logical for peasants in the western part of the Russian Empire to speak of the 'Polish faith' (Catholicism), 'German faith' (Protestantism), and 'Russian faith' (Orthodoxy). And the Jews constituted their own special national-religious group, speaking their own languages (Yiddish and Hebrew), and living according to the rhythms of their own religious precepts. To be sure, religion could go along with nationality, and few could conceive of a non-Catholic Pole or a non-Orthodox Russian except as a special 'exception'. Clergy, especially at the parish level, played an important role in spreading national identity (in particular the Lithuanian, Ukrainian, and Polish examples come to mind), but organized Churches (in particular the Catholic) often looked askance at national agitators, who were seen as aggressive, anti-clerical, and irreligious.

Both national consciousness and political organization remained at a very low level of development in the Russian Empire until 1905 at least. No political parties of any kind—even monarchical ones—were permitted until that year, most identities remained religious and local (rather than national), and while cultural activities were not specifically forbidden per se, censorship was strict, even of Russian-language materials, and anything that smacked of separatism was frowned upon and driven underground. The 1905 Revolution brought significant changes: the existence of a Parliament, the Duma, a reduced level of censorship, and a more tolerant policy toward civil groupings of all kinds. Increasing literacy and political mobilization meant that national identity and national organizations were gaining strength in different parts of the empire on the eve of World War I.

Nationalities and Nationalism in the Period of Russification (Post-1863)

The last half-century of the Russian Empire's existence, dating from the failed Polish Insurrection of 1863–4, is often characterized as a period of 'russification'. Such a characterization is fine as long as we recognize what this term does—and does not—signify. The Russian government certainly did not regard 'diversity' as a strength: they (and other contemporary Europeans) would not have even understood such a concept. For all their suspicion of the ideology of the French Revolution, Russian administrators did accept the idea of political centralization and, ideally, a state in which one national-cultural group dominated. In the Romanov Empire that nation and culture would be, of course, Russian. The use of a single language of administration throughout the empire was seen as inevitable and desirable for an efficient bureaucracy. This did not, however, mean that Russia actively attempted to 'de-nationalize' non-Russians. The Russian government had neither the ability nor the will to embark upon such a massive program of social engineering, all the more so when most Russians could not read or write.

Still, from the non-Russian perspective, policies of the later nineteenth century did seem to threaten other cultures. The Russian government would no doubt have been delighted if, say, Poles and Kazakhs abruptly abandoned their native tongues and taught their children Russian. Over time, it was hoped, many peoples, particularly those without their own written language, would abandon their 'pagan' tongues and draw closer to Russian culture. But even the most zealous russifier knew that the most problematic nationalities in the empire—Poles and Jews—would never become Russians. Even as a small but growing number of Jews adopted Russian as their native tongue by the early twentieth century, this phenomenon was regarded with deep suspicion by the Russian authorities.[1] Such suspicions were increased when significant numbers of these young Russian-speaking Jews (by origin, most had abandoned the religion) figured among the radical movements of the day, like one Lev Davidovich Bronshtein, better known to history as Trotsky.[2]

Russification certainly did restrict the further development of non-Russian culture, in particular in the western parts of the empire. Poles were not allowed to use their language freely in the so-called 'Western provinces' (more or less present-day Lithuania, Belarus, Ukraine) where they made up a significant portion of the landowning class. The University of Warsaw was shut down and it became impossible to obtain higher education in Polish. Education in Polish was restricted by the government, though these restrictions were widely flouted by 'secret' (illegal) schools.[3] Lithuanians lost the right to publish their language in Latin letters (a measure aimed to reduce Polish influence), which retarded cultural development of that nation. The Russian government never considered Belarusians and Ukrainians to make up separate nations: rather, they were seen as branches of the Russian people speaking dialects of the Russian language. This policy was more strictly enforced after 1863, with the Minister of Internal Affairs Petr Valuev famously stating that 'there is not, nor could there be... a Ukrainian language'.[4] In the 1880s a campaign was launched to reduce the power and privileges of the Baltic Germans despite the fact that this group of landowners played a very positive and overwhelmingly loyal role in the tsarist bureaucracy and officer corps. This aspect of russification points to the complications inherent in the policy: reducing German rights, among other things forcing the German university of Dorpat to adopt Russian as the language of instruction, produced the unexpected consequence of emboldening the Latvian and Estonian national movements.[5]

In the Grand Duchy of Finland, attached to the Russian Empire through the tsar who was simultaneously the Grand Duke of that territory, the Swedish-speaking upper class wisely decided to share power with the Finnish masses. Despite the efforts of St Petersburg to reduce Finnish prerogatives, until 1910 Finland enjoyed far more cultural and even political autonomy than other non-Russian regions.

From the point of view of non-Russian nationalists, russification appeared to threaten the very existence of their nation. Indeed, even today one can find this interpretation—russification as a form of total cultural assimilation—in Polish and Lithuanian historiography. But there is little evidence to back up this extreme claim. Russification had two primary goals: to bind non-Russians to the imperial (Russian) centre, in part by obliging them to learn Russian if they wished to rise in the world and to prevent further uprisings. After all, for all the restrictions on the Polish elites (in land purchasing, education, government employment), St Petersburg specifically—at least *de jure*—exempted Polish peasants from such restrictions and indeed provided them with much more generous terms of emancipation (from serfdom) than the Russian peasantry received. The main change in the treatment of Poles after 1863 was the abandonment of previous attempts to co-opt Polish elites; henceforth educated Poles would have to leave their native region if they wished to rise in government service. But of course it was precisely these frustrated, underemployed middle-class Poles who would support separatist Polish nationalism with great fervour from the last decades of the nineteenth century.

To sum up, after the failed Polish Insurrection of 1863 the Russian government adopted policies aimed to stymie separatist tendencies among non-Russians. While Polish autonomy (in the Kingdom of Poland) had already been eliminated after the Insurrection of 1830–1, now even Polish culture, especially outside of homogenously Polish areas, came under attack. The main target of this policy of 'russification' was the Poles, but in different ways Lithuanians, Ukrainians, and—somewhat later—Germans and Finns also felt its impact. The aim was to strengthen the hold of the Russian centre, primarily in the political and administrative fields, but also culturally in the sense of spreading knowledge of the Russian language as the lingua franca of the empire. These policies had little impact on the southern and eastern borderlands of the empire, where separatist national movements were seen as a far less urgent threat than the Poles in the west.

Toward a 'Nationality Problem' (1890–1914)

From the final decade of the nineteenth century, separatist nationalism was increasingly recognized as a growing threat for the stability of the Russian Empire. But this threat was in most cases more potential than immediate. In the newly conquered regions of Central Asia, local and religious identities predominated; the lack of standardized languages and a modern educational system further stymied the growth of national movements. In the Caucasus, also largely conquered in the course of the nineteenth century, a great variety of national groups and religions presented a problem more by complicating administration than as separatist nationalists. The Armenians formed the main exception to this rule: by the early twentieth century they had created a significant national movement, often linked with revolutionary goals. Still, in the context of a very mixed ethnic region, the growing level of Armenian national consciousness did not directly threaten tsarist rule, in particular when counterbalanced by generally loyal Georgian elites and large groups of Muslims (then called 'Tatars', today's Azeris) whose hostility toward the Christian Armenians was notorious.

The separatist threats that the Russian Empire faced in the decades before World War I were to some extent the unwanted outcome of centralizing, or more precisely, 'russifying' policies. For example, the effort to limit Finnish autonomy and force Finns to serve in the Russian Army led to widespread discontent and the assassination of the Russian governor general N. I. Bobrikov in 1904. The tsar's traditionally very loyal Baltic German subjects felt slighted by the policies since the 1880s to limit their cultural and economic hegemony over Latvians and Estonians. The unification of Germany in 1871 and the worsening relations with that burgeoning power from the 1890s further cast German subjects in a negative light, but such suspicions were rarely based on any actual threat.

One of the largest potential threats, if mobilized nationally, was the Ukrainians, who made up nearly 18 per cent of the Russian Empire's population in 1897. Before 1900, however, only the first stages of national identity had begun to develop among this mainly peasant people. To employ the schema developed by Czech historian Miroslav Hroch, Ukrainians remained somewhere between Stage A and B of nationalist development: it had not become a mass movement, but had progressed beyond narrow intellectual circles. The Russian government, however, steadfastly refused to see in Ukrainians (whom they termed 'Little Russians') anything but a branch of the Russian people, speaking a Russian dialect. The laws forbidding printing or schooling in Ukrainian further restricted the development of national consciousness. At the same time, across the border in Austrian Galicia (where the term 'Ruthenian' was often used instead of Ukrainian) the more liberal conditions prevailing there helped the development of a standardized Ukrainian language and encouraged the creation of a Ukrainian 'high culture', including the use of Ukrainian in certain faculties at L'viv (Lwów) University. Still, even after 1905 when publications in Ukrainian were allowed in the Russian Empire, the high rate of illiteracy among Ukrainian speakers and the persistence of local and religious rather than national identity were continuing weaknesses. Among Belarusians the level of national consciousness was lower still.

The one national group that could plausibly present a separatist threat to the Russian Empire was the Poles. From the late nineteenth century two Polish political parties took shape—abroad and underground—that specifically threatened the status quo. One was the Polish Socialist Party (PPS), the other the so-called National Democrats ('Endeks'). Both envisioned an independent Poland, though the Endeks were willing (by the early twentieth century, in any case) to work within the framework of the Russian Empire. The PPS's vision of a future Poland included many nationalities living together in a socialist republic where ethnicity and language would be less crucial than loyalty to the Polish state. The Endeks, on the other hand, followed a strictly ethnic-Polish line tinged with social Darwinism. In particular they insisted that the majority of Poland's Jews (over 10 per cent of the population of Russian Poland in 1900) must emigrate to allow the 'healthy' development of a Polish middle class. While neither of these parties could (nor, in the case of the endeks wanted to) directly challenge Russian rule before 1914, their programmes and organizations represented a potential threat.

The Jews presented a special case. Restricted by government policy in their place of residence, access to education, and employment opportunities, Jews (in particular of the younger generation) were highly visible as members of radical parties. Most Jews, of course, continued to live traditional religious lives and wanted most of all to be left alone by the government, not to confront it. But as nationalists—Zionist or otherwise—the Jews did not directly threaten the status quo. While the Zionist leader Theodor Herzl (1860–1904) received a warm welcome from Russian Jews in 1903, it is doubtful that the cheering masses at railroad stations saw in him a national leader. The fundamentally secular nature of Zionism could not be accepted by most Russian Jews, and most young socialists of Jewish descent rejected with special vehemence the idea that Jews constituted a nation.

The Revolution of 1905 brought about a fundamental reorientation in Russian politics that was not yet played out by 1914. While the new Parliament, the Duma, was a pitifully weak institution, its very existence—and elections to it—encouraged the development of modern political give and take. In areas of mixed nationality, elections to the Duma, despite the restricted franchise, tended to split along ethnic-national lines. In particular, Polish-Jewish relations were severely strained by the Duma elections of 1907 and essentially ruptured by the subsequent electoral campaign in 1912. The electoral law of 3 June 1907 specifically stated that the tsar regarded himself first and foremost as protector of Russian interests; non-Russian representation in the Duma was consequently severely curtailed. Tsar Nicholas II was also personally close to the anti-Semitic and nationalist Union of Russian People (known popularly as the 'Black Hundreds'), despite his condemnations of anti-Jewish violence. One may speculate that, given another decade or two of peace, the Russian Empire may well have developed a truly Russian-nationalist policy of cultural and administrative russification, but the outbreak of World War I in the summer of 1914 presented the tsar and his government with problems far more immediately pressing than the eternal 'national question'.

World War I and Early Soviet Policies (to 1923)

With the descent of Europe into all-out war in early August 1914, issues of national separatism were initially swept from the attention of governments and the public. Quickly, however, governments incorporated 'nationality policy' into their war plans. On 14 August the Russian commander-in-chief, Grand Duke Nikolai Nikolaevich, issued a manifesto in which he stated the intention of the Russian government to resurrect the Polish state. But the extremely vague wording of the manifesto did not explain just what form the future Poland would take except that it would be closely linked with Russia. The manifesto was an all too transparent attempt to win over Polish public opinion with fairly empty promises and as such failed to create much pro-Russian feeling among Poles. Brutal actions of Russian soldiers and what were seen as anti-Polish policies in Galicia further exacerbated Polish-Russian relations.

While Poles were being wooed—however ineffectually—by St Petersburg, Jews and German subjects of the tsar bore the brunt of increased government suspicion and surveillance. As the German army advanced eastward (taking Warsaw in early August 1915 and Wilno-Vilnius two months later), the Russian military forced the evacuation of hundreds of thousands on suspicion of espionage and collaboration with the enemy. These evacuations hit Jews particularly hard and further exacerbated already abysmal relations between Poles and Jews in view of the military authorities' obvious unequal treatment of the two groups. As for Germans, while the government's official position was one of unity among all the tsar's subjects, the violent attacks on businesses and the sacking of the German embassy in the first days of the war made speaking German or having a German name a risky business. In late May 1915 a riot directed against a German-owned factory in Moscow escalated into a mass attack on any stores or businesses bearing foreign names. The total damage from this three-day riot, it has been argued, probably exceeded that of any other pogrom in Russian history. While the main targets of these attacks were *foreign*-owned businesses, even loyal German subjects of the tsar could hardly count on careful discrimination between them and *Reichsdeutsche* by hostile mobs. The Russian government also undertook mass evacuations of German settlers in the western and southern regions (adjacent the eastward-moving front), stepped up the liquidation and confiscation of German assets, and worked to strengthen the link between the Orthodox faith, Russian culture, and political loyalty. The increasingly 'national-Russian' policy of the tsarist government increased significantly during the war years and, it can be argued, so did feelings of Russian national identity.[6]

There is certainly nothing unusual about an upsurge in patriotic sentiment in wartime. At the same time, already in autumn 1914 the Russian Army experienced setbacks from which it never really recovered. The government attempted to rally public opinion among Russians through encouraging patriotic exhibitions, posters, concerts, and other such performances.[7] Still, it was hard going to present the Romanov dynasty as entirely 'Russian' and of course the tsarina was herself German by birth, though she had been raised at the court of her grandmother, Queen Victoria. The contemporary effort by King George V to enhance the patriotic profile of the newly christened 'House of Windsor' by savvy public relations was quite unthinkable for the hidebound Tsar Nicholas II. His own conservative temperament and his wife's shy, seemingly haughty, personality precluded any serious effort by the Romanov rulers to translate Russian patriotic feeling into support for the tsarist regime.

The single most devastating ethnic uprising against Russian rule during the war occurred in Turkestan (Central Asia) in 1916. By the war's second year, the Russian government was faced with enormous material and manpower shortages. Hitherto Muslim subjects of the tsar had not been subject to the military draft, though Kazakhs and Kyrgyz did volunteer (usually to serve in the cavalry) and Turkmens had their own division in the Russian Army. While drafting Central Asian Muslims into the army was not seriously considered (both out of practical concerns and from a desire not to provoke Muslims who might refuse to serve in a war against the Ottoman sultan), the Russian authorities came up with a plan to oblige male Central Asian Muslims to serve in labour battalions.

Despite the serious misgivings of local officials, including the governor general of Turkestan, obligatory labour service for Muslim men between the ages of nineteen and thirty-one was decreed in late June 1916. As soon as the government's plans became known, riots ensued. While the riots were not based on 'national' feeling, they did draw on Muslim and tribal identities and as such can be seen as a kind of 'proto-national' protest. In the next several months anti-government and anti-Russian (against recent settlers) attacks, followed by bloody reprisals on the part of the authorities, claimed tens of thousands of lives. Hundreds of thousands of Kazakh and Kyrgyz fled across the border to China with their flocks, many perishing in the process. The outcome of the government's ill-planned attempt to harness Muslim labour for the war effort was uniformly negative: enormous bloodshed, plummeting harvests of grain and animal products, greatly increased Muslim hostility toward all things Russian. The Muslim attacks on Russian settlers were motivated not so much by nationalist demands—though the fault lines were defined by ethnicity and religion—but more simply by the resentment of local people at new settlers and the government's imperial policy favouring Russians over local Muslim peoples.[8]

The war and the Russian Empire's military failures emboldened national movements throughout the empire to demand not just cultural rights but autonomy or even independence. As the empire weakened in 1916, national separatist movements got stronger. With the collapse of Romanov rule in March 1917 (new style) and the advent of a liberal Russian government (the so-called 'provisional government'), national leaders from Helsinki in Finland to Erevan in Armenia called for autonomy or independence. The provisional government leaders, as good liberals and good Russian patriots, were trapped between their liberal ideals and a strong desire to keep the Russian Empire intact, though quite possibly with some measure of autonomy for non-Russians. The worsening political and military situation did not give the provisional government time to formulate an explicit 'nationality policy', and with the Bolshevik Revolution of November 1917, Russia entered an entirely new political era.

As Marxists, the Bolshevik leaders considered nationalism to be at best a secondary phenomenon or at worst a mask used by conservatives to preserve the exploitative status quo. All national groups were to enjoy respect, equal rights, and even cultural autonomy under Bolshevik rule. Yet the writings of both Lenin (in his dealings with the Jewish Socialist Party, the Bund) and Joseph Stalin ('Marxism and the National Question', 1913) showed definite limits to Bolshevik toleration of national demands. In his polemics against the Bund, which claimed the right to represent Jewish workers,

Lenin staunchly supported a centralized party, seeing the Bund's demands for special rights to propagandize Jewish workers as un-Marxist and impractical. Stalin's famous pamphlet (his one significant pre-revolutionary theoretical work) followed in Lenin's path by furiously denouncing the Bund and Caucasian socialists who opposed a centralized 'all-Russian' Social Democrat Party. While both Lenin and Stalin claimed that they did not aim to restrict non-Russian rights, their insistence on the primacy of central party rule pointed to the limits of political—and even cultural—rights for non-Russians.

Upon coming to power in November 1917, the Bolsheviks had to deal with separatist movements on all sides. In nearly all cases, the independence movements—in Finland, Ukraine, the Caucasus, and elsewhere—legitimized their separation from the former Russian Empire on the basis of President Woodrow Wilson's call for 'national self-determination'. While refraining from rejecting national self-determination in every case, Bolshevik policy in their first months of rule specifically spoke out against this slogan being used to support anti-Soviet 'bourgeois' regimes. Thus independence struggles could be deemed progressive if they furthered the interests of the working people of a given nation and, conveniently for the new Communist leaders of Russia, this meant *ipso facto* that the leaders of such struggles would be favourably disposed toward the new Soviet state. However, it needs to be emphasized that the Bolsheviks were reacting to a real and threatening situation: the governments of the newly independent states, from Finland to Poland, were all (to varying degrees) hostile to Communist rule in Moscow. The Communist Party (the Bolsheviks changed the party name in March 1918) was not inherently hostile to the development of non-Russian cultures: its main objective was to maintain its position as the single and unitary source of power in the country.

As long as central power was concentrated in their hands, the Communists did not object, at least in principle, to different degrees of local autonomy, often based on cultural and economic differences between regions. Already before the Bolshevik Revolution, in June 1917, the Petrograd Soviet had set up the organization that would become under Bolshevik rule 'Narkomnats': the People's Commissariat of Nationalities. Narkomnats's main task was to mediate between national groups, encourage cultural development, and help decide how best to coordinate national-cultural and economic interests on the local level. The commissariat contained sections entrusted with the affairs of specific regions and national groups, for example, the Caucasus, Jews, Muslims, Belarusians. In the first years of Communist rule dozens of autonomous regions for ethnic groups as diverse as Volga Germans and Bashkirs were set up; this process culminated with the formation of the Union of Soviet Socialist Republics in the new Soviet constitution ratified in early 1924.

Differences on nationality policy in the Caucasus led to a major clash between Lenin and Stalin. By the early 1920s Lenin was increasingly concerned that overly brutal measures used by local Communists among the Georgians in the Caucasus had taken on a 'Great Russian chauvinist' tinge, even though these repressions were led by Grigorii ('Sergo') Ordzhonikidze, supported by his fellow Georgian, Stalin. This was an argument more over tactics than strategy: Lenin and Stalin agreed that Communist rule had to be extended to the region, but Lenin felt that violent methods would alienate local sentiment and thus be counterproductive in the long term. Lenin's worries about the spread of 'Great Russian chauvinism' reflected the strength of Russians among Communists and the industrial working class in areas of mixed nationality such as the Caucasus (in particular the oil boomtown, Baku) and Central Asia. Supporting local Communists often meant inadvertently supporting local Russians and taking a position against traditional, often religious non-Russian society. This situation was worsened for Lenin by the fact that enforcing central rule over the national periphery often could not help but resemble previous efforts at russification under the tsars.

It would not, however, be correct to conclude that nothing had changed. The Bolshevik mindset was vastly more activist and energetic—'modern'—than that of the tsar's administrators. While pre-revolutionary authorities primarily embraced the status quo and worked to keep order, the Bolsheviks wanted to create a new world. They were, in Stalin's celebrated words, 'the engineers of the human soul', and this 'human engineering' would also have a major impact on the non-Russians after Lenin's death in 1924.

The Era of Soviet Activism in Nationality, 1924–45

Traditionally students of Soviet nationality policy have tended to distinguish between the 1920s and early 1930s, when developing modern socialist ethno-cultural nations was stressed, and the period from approximately the mid-1930s to Stalin's death (1953), when national repressions were the order of the day, combined with (especially from the period of World War II) increasing anti-Semitism and Russian chauvinism. This distinction is certainly valid, but another way to approach the issue is to consider the two decades beginning with Lenin's death as an era of state activism in the field of nationality. At first this activism was characterized by a desire to mold or even create new, modern, socialist nations and to incorporate members of these nations into the Soviet Communist system (party, hierarchy, professions, et cetera). Terry Martin aptly described the USSR in this period as an 'Affirmative Action Empire'; Yuri Slezkine argued that Soviet efforts to define and develop separate nationalities in Central Asia created a kind of 'communal apartment' of distinct nationalities.[9] From the mid-1930s onward, possibly reacting to fears that efforts at mobilizing national identity had succeeded all too well, less benevolent policies including mass arrests of 'national intelligentsia' and even mass resettlement of national groups. What both the earlier ('benevolent') and later ('repressive') periods had in common was an activist stance, a desire to intervene with cultural, economic, and political measures, first in favour of more cultural-national diversity and then to strengthen the Russian-Soviet (the two cannot always be distinguished) centre vis-à-vis the 'national' (in other words non-Russian) periphery.

During the 1920s, Soviet nationality policies aimed to delineate and develop 'proper' cultural nations, among other things by codifying languages, establishing alphabetical systems, and translating major works (including, but not limited to, classics of Marxism-Leninism) into these tongues. For example, in Central Asia linguists carefully delineated 'correct' forms of Kazakh, Kyrgyz, Turkmen, and Tadzhik (only the latter being readily distinguishable as the sole non-Turkic language prominent in the region), and devising writing systems for each language using (initially) Latin letters and (in the later, more russifying period) Cyrillic orthography. These linguistic efforts at differentiation between Central Asian nationalities were reinforced by the drawing of administrative boundaries and creation of separate Soviet Socialist Republics.[10] All of these efforts aimed to replace previous religious (Muslim) and local identities with national and Soviet ones.

Along with these cultural and administrative measures, the policy that perhaps best characterizes the 'benevolent' activist period was *korenizatsiia*, sometimes translated as 'indigenization'. The primary aim of indigenization was to bring non-Russians, in particular those from traditionally peasant and nomadic nationalities like, say, Ukrainians and Kazakhs, into the mainstream of Soviet life, including efforts to recruit them into both the local and the All-Union Communist Party. Tellingly, there was never a 'Russian' Communist Party, though there were Ukrainian, Uzbek, Armenian (et cetera) branches of the All-Union Party (CPSU). It is this policy that Terry Martin refers to in his striking phrase 'affirmative action empire'. In the 1920s and into the 1930s schools were set up using national languages and non-Russians received preferential treatment (including specific national quotas) for admission to the party, higher education, and professional positions. Russians living in national republics (in other words Ukrainian, Belarusian, et cetera, Soviet Socialist Republics) often felt—and resented—pressure to learn the local language and have their children educated in it. Indigenization also pushed for non-Russian women to get educated, work outside the home, and join the party, a shocking development for traditional peasant and Muslim societies. Indigenization was successful in creating a cadre of Ukrainian, Uzbek, Armenian (et cetera) Communists, but also aroused the anger of Russians who saw themselves as the victims of 'reverse discrimination'. This resentment, coupled with misgivings in Moscow that national identity—even among Communists—could develop into national separatism, helped bring an end to *korenizatsiia* in the 1930s.

The policy of indigenization implicitly took for granted that the new national cultures being nurtured by the Soviet state would strengthen not just national-particularist identities but also an all-Soviet identity. When members of national minorities came to challenge central policies or simply to champion local interests, Moscow was annoyed and disturbed. A sign of the shift in policy is provided by the fate of the Ukrainian Old Bolshevik and national Communist, Mykola Skrypnyk. In the 1920s Skrypnyk had supported a policy of strict Ukrainization in education, the workplace, and the party. As a long-standing member of the Bolshevik Party (having joined in 1899), Skrypnyk could hardly be suspected of disloyalty. In 1932–3, however, in the wake of mass collectivization, peasant resistance, and a disastrous harvest (in part at least engineered by Bolshevik policy) causing mass famine in the Ukrainian SSR, Skrypnyk came under attack. The Ukrainian Bolshevik was accused of theoretical errors that strengthened Ukrainian nationalists wishing to separate from the USSR. In the face of furious personal attacks and the demand to recant his policies publically, Skrypnyk instead chose to commit suicide at his desk in July 1933. Stalin made certain that no other would-be 'national Bolshevik' (as Skrypnyk termed himself) would miss the point of Skrypnyk's fall from grace by remarking at the XVIIth Congress of the CPSU in January–February 1934 that 'Many people think that the Biblical Fall of Skrypnyk was an isolated instance, an exception to the rule. This is not true.'[11]

During the Great Purges of the mid to later 1930s, non-Russian Communists were especially hard hit. From mid-1933 onward, Central Committees in union republics from Belarus to Central Asia denounced nationalism as the 'greatest danger'. These attempts at damage control did not prevent mass arrests and purges. Local Communists attempted to save themselves, sometimes successfully, by furiously persecuting 'national chauvinism' and cooperating with Russian Communists at all levels. An uneasy compromise was reached by which local languages continued to be used, but local Russians rarely felt any pressure to learn them. Union Communist parties continued to try to gain members among under-represented nationalities (very often the 'titular nationality', in other words Uzbeks in the Uzbek SSR, Belarusian in the Belarus SSR, et cetera), but without pressing for quotas.

One may interpret the motivations for this shift in policy in different ways. Certainly the increased tension of the international situation played a role; the Soviet leadership was shaken by Adolf Hitler's rise to power in Germany in 1933 and Japanese incursions into China from 1937. But perhaps indigenization was simply a victim of its own success: when it became clear that encouraging the development of national identities could lead to potentially 'separatist' demands, the Soviet state moved emphatically to strengthen the centre at the expense of non-Russians.

The shift in the mid-1930s away from a benevolent attitude toward developing national-cultural difference was accompanied by an increasing suspicion of non-Russian national groups as at least potentially disloyal to the Soviet state. The introduction of the internal passport with an entry for nationality (in other words, Russian, Jewish, Uzbek, Korean, Armenian, et cetera) in 1932 aided the Soviet state in targeting members of suspicious minorities. From 1934 Poles, Koreans, Latvians, Germans, Finns, and other national minorities living in proximity to the borders of the USSR were singled out for arrest and deportation. With the shift in autumn 1939–summer 1940 of the Soviet border to the west, incorporating former eastern regions of Poland and swallowing up the previously independent Baltic states (Estonia, Latvia, Lithuania), hundreds of thousands were arrested, deported, and even murdered, as most infamously at Katyń, partly as members of potentially dangerous nationalities, partly to decapitate any potential resistance to Soviet power. In many cases (particularly with the Poles) national and social-political suspicions went hand in hand.

Arrest and deportation of national groups were carried out in even more sweeping form after the German invasion of the USSR in June 1941. Entire nationalities, including Chechens, Ingush, Crimean Tatars, and Volga Germans were summarily rounded up and forcibly deported to Central Asia, with very significant loss of life. These deportations were, so to speak, preemptive strikes against all members of these nationalities, not a reaction to any actual disloyal deeds or words. These deportations, combined with the mass murder of Jews by the Nazis and a post-war 'transfer of populations' (in particular the expulsion—voluntarily or otherwise—of the bulk of Poles remaining in 1944 along the western frontiers of the USSR), increased the level of national homogeneity there. On the other hand, expelled Poles were not infrequently replaced by Russian immigrants, both temporary and permanent. If any doubt remained about the privileged position of the Russian language and of ethnic Russians in particular within the USSR at war's end, it was dispelled by Stalin's famous speech a fortnight afterwards to military commanders in the Kremlin. Stalin's toast praised the Russian people, among other things, as 'the most outstanding of all the nations that constitute the Soviet Union' and 'the guiding force among all the peoples of our country'.[12] Stalin's words were a clear indication that while non-Russian nationalities would not be obliged to give up their separate culture and identity, all would be expected to look up to and emulate the Russians.

Nationality and Nationalism in Post-War USSR (1945–85)

By placing the Russian nation foremost among Soviet peoples, Stalin implicitly set up a hierarchy of national culture and identity. Non-Russians were expected (and, at least in school, obliged) to learn the Russian language; few Russians learned other languages, even when they lived in other union republics. Ironically, the national group that in the first three decades of Soviet rule most enthusiastically learned Russian and assimilated to Russian culture, the Jews, were hit by anti-Semitic policies in the final years of Stalin's rule. But perhaps the irony is more apparent than real. With the establishment of the State of Israel in 1948 (an event welcomed—at least on the official level—by the USSR), Soviet Jews unwittingly found themselves in the same position as Soviet Poles, Finns, and Germans in the 1930s: as a possible 'Fifth Column' within Soviet society, their loyalties divided between Moscow and Tel Aviv. Of course, any such suspicions were based on paranoia and anti-Semitism, not on any actual 'separatist threat' from Soviet Jews. Whatever the reason, however, Jewish cultural institutions were shut down, prominent Jews arrested or killed in suspicious accidents, and Zionism was accused of producing agents for American intelligence services; most grotesque of all, in early 1953 an article in *Pravda* accused a group of doctors with Jewish surnames of being participants in a vast conspiracy to poison Kremlin leaders. The so-called Doctors' Plot appeared to signal a new party purge aimed primarily at Jewish Communists, but Stalin's death in early March prevented any such development.

In the period 1939–44 the USSR had extended its borders to the west, incorporating lands taken from Finland, Poland, Czechoslovakia, and Romania into the Soviet state. The mass murders and population transfers of the war period and its immediately aftermath (to approximately 1948) had considerably 'simplified' and 'homogenized' the ethnic makeup of this region. At the same time, armed bands of partisan fighters continued to operate in the Baltic provinces and western Ukraine until the late 1940s, violently resisting the establishment of Soviet rule. These guerrilla forces had no chance against the Red Army and the Soviet security forces, and were arrested, killed, or forced into exile. At the same time the NKVD carried out mass arrests and deportations of Estonians, Latvians, Lithuanians, and Ukrainians who had been politically active (and anti-Communist) in the interwar period or who were suspected of nationalist sentiment or an anti-Soviet political stance. After the collapse of the USSR in 1989 it has become fashionable in the Baltic countries to speak of an attempted 'genocide' of these nations under Soviet rule. The term is not, however, appropriate: for all the suffering these mass arrests caused, they had a political logic to them and did not aim to destroy the Lithuanian, Latvian, or Estonian nations. The Communist Party apparatus in these Soviet republics, after all, was led by individuals of the republic's 'titular nationality', such as Antanas Sniečkus in the Lithuanian SSR.

After the population transfers of the immediate post-war years, with the partial exception of the Doctors' Plot, the USSR abandoned radical, activist measures to influence national cultures, opting instead for more gradual bureaucratic measures to neutralize national separatist threats and create a Soviet identity. National languages and cultures were tolerated and even actively supported, but expressions of national separatism—for example, display of the interwar Lithuanian or Estonian flags—was strictly forbidden. In the post-Stalin era, practical motives (not to say cynicism) tended to play a far more important role in official policy and everyday life than did ideology. So it was too in matters of national identity and cultures. Generally children could be educated in their native tongue (at least in regions where this language was commonly spoken), but the higher one went up the educational ladder, the more important Russian became. PhD dissertations, for example, were usually written in Russian throughout the USSR.

Ideologists of the post-Stalin period spoke of the 'Friendship of Nations' ('Druzhba Narodov') that prevailed in the USSR. This 'friendship' had something of an imperialist tinge in its unexamined presupposition that the Russian language and political influence from Moscow were both obvious and beneficial to non-Russians throughout the USSR. Speaking slightingly of any national group was considered bad form, though one could detect a degree of condescension in Soviet fulminations (in Russian) about the enormous advantages that Soviet rule had brought, for example, to Central Asian peoples or Ukrainian peasants. On a practical level, youngsters throughout the USSR were required to learn Russian in school. While every union republic had its own radio and, from the 1960s, television stations using native languages, many programmes (including the most important All-Union news programme, 'Vremia' ['Time']) were carried throughout the USSR—of course in Russian. It thus became of practical importance for Soviet citizens of all nationalities, in particular if they wanted to succeed professionally, to perfect their Russian.

In the two Slavic republics (Belarusian and Ukrainian SSR), the proximity of their languages and culture to that of Russia posed special problems. When faced with the expense and complication of, say, setting up parallel schools or courses in two languages, administrators were often tempted to opt 'for practical reasons' for a single school using Russian. This course was particularly often followed in regions with a significant number of ethnic Russians. When, for example, Ukrainian parents protested against such 'practical measures' and insisted on their rights as Soviet citizens to have their children educated in Ukrainian, such protests could bring negative consequences (reprimands at the party and workplace level, expulsion from the party, loss of one's job, and in extreme cases even arrest). Most parents preferred not to protest openly in order not to jeopardize their own position and their children's education.

The post-war decades also witnessed a significant out-migration of Russians to other union republics. While some non-Russian scholars, both then and (far more) now, see in this phenomenon a planned programme of russification, probably practical issues were more important. The USSR was dedicated to industrializing the entire country (after all, Lenin had famously remarked, 'Communism is Soviet power plus the electrification of the whole country'). In regions like Central Asia, the Caucasus, the Ukrainian countryside, or—to a somewhat lesser extent—the Baltic republics, engineers, skilled industrial workers, and university-educated administrators were more plentiful in the Russian centre than on the periphery. Thus many educated Russians migrated to Central Asia and industrial cities like Baku on the Caspian Sea to take up jobs in industry, administration, health care, and the like there. The party also sent significant numbers of Communist cadres to the union republics both for surveillance and training purposes. It became an unwritten law that the First Secretary of, say, the Turkmen Communist Party (the head of the party hierarchy) would be a member of the titular nationality (in this case, a Turkmen), but he (this was an almost exclusively all-male club) would be 'assisted' by a Russian (possibly a russified Belarusian or Ukrainian) second in command. In this way Moscow and the All-Union Party could keep tabs on the situation in non-Russian regions. The fundamental centralism (which waxed and waned at times, but remained important throughout) of the Soviet economy and political system also enhanced the place of Russian throughout the country.

Because of the major role played by Russian in Soviet science and scholarship, military and party affairs, culture and everyday life, assimilation to Russian was far from rare. This process was most marked among individuals of nationalities living among Russians (the Volga Tatars, for example), offspring of mixed marriages (particularly when residing in regions of Russian culture), and the Slavic nationalities (Belarusians and Ukrainians). Jews present a special case: even before the Holocaust, most Jewish parents were not educating their children in Yiddish. After the war, a youthful native speaker of Yiddish became an extreme rarity in the USSR; the great majority of Soviet Jews spoke Russian as a native tongue. Central Asians who gained a university degree frequently spoke Russian on the job, for example knowing technical terms only in that language. On the other hand, the Baltic and Transcaucasian (Georgian, Azeri, Armenian) nationalities vigorously preserved their national culture, often pressuring Russians living in their republics to learn the local language. But even in these regions, a high level of pride and interest in local culture did not, in most cases, translate into active involvement in illegal patriotic activities.

From the 1960s the relative political relaxation (relative, that is, to the harsh Stalinist regime) allowed the development of the dissident movement. These rare and courageous individuals organized and spoke out against the failings of the Soviet system, from civil rights to environmental degradation to the repression of national cultures. Lithuanian dissidents, for instance, began in 1972 to publish the underground *Chronicle of the Catholic Church in Lithuania* whose content was at least as much patriotic as religious. The victory of Israel in the Six-Day War (June 1967) energized the national identity of many Jews. Some organized to support so-called 'refuseniks' (those whose application to emigrate had been denied), put together illegal Hebrew classes, and in one case plotted to hijack a Soviet airliner to Israel, then used their trial to publicize the prejudice and restrictions faced by Soviet Jews. In the Ukrainian SSR, insisting on using Ukrainian could easily lead to accusations of 'anti-Soviet behaviour'.

While national identity and diverse ethnic cultures and language use did not significantly fade in the USSR, before 1985 there were no serious threats to political stability from dissident groupings organized along national lines. To be sure, demographic trends, in particular the high birth rate among Muslim Central Asians, were disturbing to the mainly Russian (and Ukrainian) leadership of the Communist Party. The idea that increased numbers of non-Russians, mainly in Central Asia, would 'explode' the USSR was advanced by the French Sovietologist Hélène Carrère de'Encausse in 1978, but despite her book's alarmist title, in fact the text did not predict any *rapid* destabilization.[13] Nearly a decade later, American political scientist Alexander Motyl published a book entitled *Will the Non-Russians Rebel?*, a question he answered with a resounding, 'No'. Basing his thesis almost exclusively on Ukrainian data, Motyl argued that the USSR would remain stable mainly due to the efficiency of the KGB at repressing national dissent.[14] It is easy in hindsight to mock Motyl's inability to see the threat of national separatism when literally months after his book's publication citizens in the Baltic, Caucasus, and elsewhere rallied along ethnic lines against the USSR, but in one sense he was quite correct. It was only the easing of the USSR's repressive apparatus (and the will to use it) that allowed the emergence of the national-separatist movements of the late 1980s.

Gorbachev and the Nations

To start with an obvious fact, since it is so often ignored: the nationality problem did not destroy the USSR. In fact, national-separatist movements, while destabilizing, in no way threatened the continued existence of the USSR even in the first years of the 1990s. Mikhail Gorbachev, who came to power in 1985, had spent his entire career as a party functionary in his native Stavropol region (southern Russia) and in Moscow. He had no direct experience with nationality issues nor had he ever lived for a significant period in an ethnically mixed region. This lack of experience showed when in December 1986 Gorbachev clumsily appointed a Russian as First Secretary of the Kazakh Communist Party, violating the unwritten law that the First Secretary of every union republic would be drawn from the republic's titular nationality. The appointment set off three days of violence in Almaty, leaving hundreds dead. In 1987–8, long-suppressed tensions between Muslim Azeris and Christian Armenians, in particular over the Armenian-dominated territory within the Azerbaijan SSR, Nagorno-Karabakh, led to strikes, protests, and disturbances. During the historic year 1989 the Baltic republics took the lead in passing language laws requiring all residents to master the titular nationality's language within a certain number of years. By year's end most republics from the Moldova to Central Asia had passed such laws, which were clearly aimed primarily at Russian speakers who rarely bothered to learn, say, Moldovan, Estonian, or Kyrgyz. In May 1989 the Lithuanian and Estonian SSRs took the further step of declaring themselves sovereign, followed by Latvia in July. By the end of 1990 all fifteen republics of the USSR (including the Russian republic) had declared themselves sovereign, that is, affirmed that laws passed by the republic parliaments had priority over All-Union laws from Moscow.

The collapse of the USSR's 'external empire' in late 1989 further encouraged national separatism. Lithuania declared itself independent on 11 March 1990; Gorbachev insisted that such a declaration was illegal and cut off fuel supplies to the republic for several months until the Lithuanian Parliament agreed to suspend—but not to cancel—the affirmation of independence. With increasingly violent riots in Armenia and Azerbaijan (resembling in some localities a state of war), unrest in Central Asia, and the Baltic republics' open defiance of Moscow, Gorbachev was faced with a stark choice in dealing with separatist nationalism. He could either embrace the hard line and attempt to quell the rebellions with violence or he could reconcile himself to the loss of at least the Baltic and probably Caucasian republics and attempt to salvage Soviet control over the Slavic republics and Central Asia. In 1991, in a manner of speaking, he took both courses at once and thereby made the break-up of the USSR (or massive bloodshed) very likely if not inevitable.

The year 1991 began with troops from the Ministries of the Interior and Defence being sent to seven republics (the Baltic three, Georgia, Armenia, Moldova, and western Ukraine), ostensibly to seek out deserters. Many young men of draft age had refused to show up for service in the Red Army on the grounds that their loyalty was to their sovereign republic, not to the USSR as a whole. Many suspected that these troops would also be used to re-establish Moscow's control. In mid-January, Soviet troops occupied media sources (television tower, newspaper printing plants) and closed down the airport in the Lithuanian capital, Vilnius, while Moscow-loyal Communists announced the formation of a 'committee of national salvation'. But when this attempted seizure of power was met with mass protests and the killing of several civilians, Gorbachev apparently lost his nerve or, following his own account, was informed of the use of force and called off the troops. In any case, the ineffective use of violence galvanized nationalist movements throughout the USSR to organize and demand not just autonomy or a vague 'sovereignty' but actual independence.

But how was this independence to come about? Military and police power was concentrated overwhelmingly in the hands of Moscow, not the republics. Gorbachev attempted to finesse this issue by holding a union-wide referendum in March 1991. All Soviet citizens were to answer the single question: 'Do you consider necessary the preservation of the Union of Soviet Socialist Republics as a renewed federation of equal sovereign republics, in which the rights and freedoms of an individual of any nationality will be fully guaranteed?' The long and complex sentence allowed voters either to concentrate either on the first half (preserve the USSR) or the second ('rights and freedoms . . . of any nationality . . . guaranteed'). The six most problematic (from Moscow's standpoint) republics (the Baltic three, Armenia, Georgia, Moldova) boycotted the referendum, in Ukraine and Russia more than 70 per cent of voters agreed, and in the Central Asian republics the 'yes' vote was over 90 per cent. But probably more important than the vote on the referendum was the fact that Gorbachev's primary rival, Boris Yeltsin, was elected as Russian president—a newly created post—at the same time.

Having no stake in the continued existence of the USSR, Yeltsin quickly opened dialogue with politicians in the other republics on an equal basis. But it is anyone's guess how long the USSR would have bungled along had several of Gorbachev's ministers not decided in August 1991 to seize power and attempt to return to a more centralized, authoritarian USSR. Their failure brought with it the humiliation of Gorbachev, the rise of Yeltsin, and in December 1991, the end of the USSR. The 'Commonwealth of Independent States' (including twelve former Soviet republics, but not the Baltics) set up in its place was a weak organization to help coordinate practical issues in dividing up Soviet assets and liabilities.

The collapse of the USSR brought forth fifteen independent states—but was it a triumph of nationalism? Depending on what one wishes to emphasize, the answer is 'yes', 'maybe', and 'no'. Yes, in the Baltic provinces the memory of recent independence, well-organized citizens' protests, and (relatively) quick switch of local Communists to the patriotic front certainly may be termed a victory of the national principle. Probably the same may be said in Armenia and Georgia, where national feeling remained strong throughout the Soviet period. In Ukraine and Russia, organizations emphasizing cultural-linguistic and religious traditions certainly played some part in undermining support for the Soviet state. In the Muslim republics and Belarus, however, it is difficult to discern much popular support or organized groups that advocated national independence—indeed, more than a decade after the demise of the USSR most of these republics continue to be ruled by former Communists. Furthermore, even in the Baltic provinces it was the *republic* that gained independence and no attempt was made anywhere to redraw republic boundaries along ethnic-national lines. For example, if linguistic criteria were followed, the city of Narva would certainly be included in Russia and not form part of Estonia. To be sure, the decision to keep republican boundaries was undoubtedly a wise one, and also facilitated the recognition of the newly independent republics by foreign powers, but it was not a 'national' one. The USSR was not destroyed by nationalism or separatist nationalists: it collapsed primarily from internal weaknesses. Certainly nationalism was one factor that weakened the cohesiveness of the USSR under Gorbachev, but the declining economy and failure to reform the political system quickly enough were much more crucial factors in the Soviet collapse. But in a broader way, the Soviet nationality policies followed since the early 1920s, which created would-be national units, encouraged (Soviet) national symbols, and allowed the creation of Soviet national elites, may well have paved the way for the ultimate collapse of the USSR.

Epilogue and Conclusions

Since 1992, one may note a growth in nationalist sentiment throughout the former USSR. Frictions in the Baltics (especially Estonia and Latvia) with Russian-speaking residents is one example of this phenomenon, though in recent years new identities as Russian-speaking Estonians or Latvians seem to be improving. Certainly the admission of the Baltic republics to the European Union in 2004 has encouraged peaceful solutions to nationality disagreements, but positive developments could be discerned even before that date. Millions of non-Russians continue to reside within the borders of the Russian Federation, from Tatars who enjoy significant autonomy to Chechens who have suffered brutal and catastrophic military attacks from Moscow. Former Communists in a number of Muslim republics have reinvented themselves as religious patriots, most remarkably in the figure of Saparmurat Niyazov who dubbed himself 'Türkmenbaşy', or 'leader of the Turkmen'. In the Russian Federation, President Vladimir Putin—like many other former Communists—has embraced both Russian nationalism and the Russian Orthodox faith. Among Russians, Putin's neo-patriotic stance has been popular; many Russians bewail the collapse of the USSR as a Russian national tragedy and see Putin as the man who can prop up Russia's reputation in the international community.

From the 1860s to the early twenty-first century nationality and the fear of national separatism has played a constant—if not primary—role in Russian politics. The tsars wished to neutralize perceived threats from Poles, Jews, Finns, and others, while the

Soviet authorities actually mobilized state resources to arrest and deport hundreds of thousands of non-Russians, in particular during the 1940s. During the Soviet era national-culture difference was ostensibly welcomed, but separatist nationalism was dealt with severely. The Soviet period saw both significant developments (in literacy, publishing, educational systems) among many national cultures and a spreading of Russian as a second and even first language among Soviet citizens of non-Russian ethnicity. Fears of general de-nationalization under Soviet rule were just as wrong as Polish worries that their culture would be wiped out by russification in the late nineteenth century. It remains to be seen whether the forces of globalization will prove more of a threat to these national cultures than the Russian or Soviet state ever was.

Notes

1. B. Nathans (2002) *Beyond the Pale: The Jewish Encounter with Late Imperial Russia*, Berkeley.
2. On Jewish participation in the Russian radical movement, see E. Haberer (1995) *Jews and Revolution in Nineteenth-Century Russia*, New York.
3. T. R. Weeks (1996) *Nation and State in Late Imperial Russia: Nationalism and Russification on the Western Frontier, 1863–1914*, DeKalb, IL.
4. A. Miller (2003) *The Ukrainian Question: The Russian Empire and Nationalism in the Nineteenth Century*, Budapest.
5. Edward C. Thaden (ed.) (1981) *Russification in the Baltic Provinces and Finland, 1855–1914*, Princeton.
6. P. Gatrell (2003) *A Whole Empire Walking: Refugees in Russia during World War I*, Bloomington, IN; E. Lohr (2003) *Nationalizing the Russian Empire: The Campaign against Enemy Aliens during World War I*, Cambridge.
7. H. Jahn (1995) *Patriotic Culture in Russia during World War I*, Ithaca, NY.
8. D. Brower (2003) *Turkestan and the Fate of the Russian Empire*, London.
9. Y. Slezkine (1994) 'The USSR as a Communal Appartment, or How a Socialist State Promoted Ethnic Particularism', *Slavic Review*, 53 (Summer), 414–52; T. Martin (2001) *The Affirmative Action Empire: Nations and Nationalism in the Soviet Union, 1923–1939*, Ithaca, NY.
10. F. Hirsch (2005) *Empire of Nations: Ethnographic Knowledge and the Making of the Soviet Union*, Ithaca, NY.
11. Quoted in Martin, *The Affirmative Action Empire*, 350.
12. Cited at <http://www.great-victory1945.ru/victory.htm>, consulted 10 November 2007.
13. H. Carrère de'Encausse (1978) *L'empire éclaté. La révolte des nations en U.R.S.S.*, Paris.
14. A. J. Motyl (1987) *Will the Non-Russians Rebel? State, Ethnicity, and Stability in the USSR*, Ithaca, NY.

Suggested Further Reading

Beissinger, M. (2002) *Nationalist Mobilization and the Collapse of the Soviet State*, Cambridge.
Blank, S. (1994) *The Sorcerer as Apprentice: Stalin as Commissar of Nationalities, 1917–1924*, Westport, CT.
Brower, Da. (2003) *Turkestan and the Fate of the Russian Empire*, London.
Chinn, J. and Kaiser, R. (1996) *Russians as the New Minority: Ethnicity and Nationalism in the Soviet Successor States*, Boulder, CO.
Kappeler, A. (2001) *The Russian Empire: A Multiethnic History*, Harlow, Essex.
Lohr, E. (2003) *Nationalizing the Russian Empire*, Cambridge.
Martin, T. (2001) *The Affirmative Action Empire: Nations and Nationalism in the Soviet Union, 1923–1939*, Ithaca, NY.
Pipes, R. (1964) *The Formation of the Soviet Union, Communism and Nationalism, 1917–1923*, Cambridge.
Smith, J. (1999) *The Bolsheviks and the National Question, 1917–23*, New York.
Suny, R. and Martin, T. (eds.) (2001) *A State of Nations: Empire and Nation-Making in the Age of Lenin and Stalin*, Oxford.
Weeks, T. R. (1996) *Nation and State in Late Imperial Russia: Nationalism and Russification on the Western Frontier, 1863–1914*, DeKalb, IL.

CHAPTER 11

NATIONALISM IN THE MIDDLE EAST, 1876–1945*

AVIEL ROSHWALD

Seeds of Change in the Ottoman Empire

On 23 December 1876, amidst a Serbian-supported rebellion in Ottoman-ruled Bosnia-Herzegovina and a revolt in Bulgaria,[1] Sultan Abdülhamit II acquiesced in the promulgation of a liberal constitution for the Ottoman Empire. This appeared at the time as a dramatic, watershed moment, the liberating culmination of nearly four decades of government-initiated economic, administrative, military, and educational reform efforts. The new dispensation proved short-lived, however. Within just over a year, Russian military intervention against the Ottomans in what Europeans dubbed the 'Eastern Crisis' had given the sultan an opportunity (on 14 February 1878) to declare an emergency, prorogue the newly elected Parliament, and suspend the constitution.[2]

In agreeing to the constitution's promulgation, the newly enthroned sultan had sought to kill two birds with one stone: The move preempted European plans to resolve the Eastern Crisis by imposing new reforms on the Ottoman Empire. It also met the demands of the group of radical reformers—loosely referred to as the Young Ottomans—who had helped place Abdülhamit II in power in the first place.

The Young Ottomans were members of the educated, Western-influenced elite that earlier sultans' reform programmes had brought into being. The main impetus for the modernization effort had been the ever growing encroachment of the European Great Powers on the once formidable Ottoman Empire and the steady erosion of Ottoman

* My thanks go to Avi Beker for his helpful comments on this piece. All shortcomings remain my own responsibility of course.

power in the largely Christian-populated Balkans. Even the viceroy of an overwhelmingly Sunni Muslim province such as Egypt, Muhammad Ali (an Albanian officer in the Ottoman military who was installed as governor in 1805 and went on to found a hereditary dynasty of rulers titled *khedives*), had dared to challenge Ottoman authority. It was first Russian, then British, military intervention that saved the rest of Ottoman territory from outright conquest by this nominal subject of the sultan in 1833 and 1840, respectively.[3] In the Crimean War (1853–6), it was Anglo-French intervention that stood in the way of Ottoman subjection to the Russian Empire.

In other words, not only had various of the European Great Powers been pushing the Ottomans against the ropes, but the once feared empire suffered the further indignity of having to rely on the fickle support of Great Power allies and the vagaries of balance-of-power politics to avoid falling to the mat. The sense of humiliation was highlighted by the set of treaties referred to collectively as the Capitulations, which granted the citizens and subjects of European powers quasi-diplomatic immunities during stays in the Ottoman Empire, with no reciprocity for Ottoman subjects. Finally, every major European power seemed to have its own favourite group of non-Muslim Ottoman subjects (mostly Christians of various denominations), over which it sought to extend some form of special protection.

Constitution or no constitution, the Ottoman Empire continued to fray at the edges in the years that followed. The 1878 Congress of Berlin ended the war with Russia at the price of Ottoman territorial losses in the Balkans and Transcaucasus. In 1882, Britain occupied Egypt. Even though Egypt had been effectively free of Ottoman control for decades, and remained theoretically subject to Ottoman sovereignty until 1914, its functional subjection to British rule was a blow to Ottoman prestige. Moreover, under its new masters, Cairo became a safe haven for many of the harshest critics of Sultan Abdülhamit II's arbitrary rule, alongside some of the most innovative articulators of an Islamic modernist school of thought, and the earliest exponents of Arabism and outright Arab nationalism.

Islamic modernists sought to reconcile their interest in various aspects of modernization with their commitment to Islam by claiming that the original, ancestral Islam had been a religion that complemented and reinforced reason, rather than clashing with it. According to them, the latter-day *ummah* (the universal community of believers) suffered from the accretion of centuries of politically dictated and hence distorted interpretations of the Prophet's teachings and of the traditions of the original Islamic society. These interpretations, the modernists argued, served the narrow self-interest of authoritarian rulers rather than the well-being of the *ummah*. The Islamic modernists' line of reasoning represented an attempt to reconcile a sense of timeless Islamic identity and community with an embrace of potentially far-reaching educational, economic, legal, and political reforms.[4]

At the turn of the twentieth century, the intellectual movement dubbed by latter-day scholars as Arabism emerged as one of several offshoots of Islamic modernism. A leading figure here was Rashid Rida (1865–1935), a Syrian-born student of Egypt's most prominent Islamic modernist thinker, Muhammad Abduh (1849–1905). Rida pointed out that it was among the Arabs that the seeds of Islam had first been planted and flourished. Arabic was, after all, the language of the Qur'an. It was the Arab caliphates' subjection to foreign conquerors, culminating in the triumph of the Ottoman Turks, that had weakened the foundations of Islamic civilization. Any renewal and revitalization of Islam was therefore dependent on a revival of Arab culture and identity.

Rida's writings appealed to what might be termed Arab national pride, but did so in a manner that linked it to a broader concern with Islamic civilization. Yet this approach obviously held the possibility of turning towards outright Arab nationalism, especially if the Ottoman Empire continued to prove incapable of effectively defending the realm of Islam against the depredations of the infidels. The possibility of replacing the Ottoman Empire (whose nineteenth- and twentieth-century sultans highlighted their claim to be caliphs—leaders of the universal Sunni Muslim community) with an Arab-led caliphate certainly held appeal for some of the early Arabists.

Mention should also be made of a small group of Western-educated[5] Christian Arab intellectuals from latter-day Lebanon and Syria who articulated a secular vision of Arab nationalism in the last decades of the Ottoman Empire's existence. Publicists and writers such as Najib Azouri—a Uniate Christian from Syria whose writings from exile in Paris and Cairo date from 1904 to his death in 1916—looked forward to a day when the Arab nation would break free of Ottoman control and transcend its internal Christian-Muslim divide.[6] A shared language (at least a shared literary language—spoken dialects of Arabic are widely divergent) and common history would replace religious affiliation as the critical marker of sociopolitical identity and belonging among Arabs. The establishment of a secular Arab nation state (to include all the Arabic-speaking regions east of Egypt in Azouri's vision) would do away with the aura of second-class status that still surrounded Christian minorities in the waning days of the Ottoman Empire and that, in the view of these early nationalists, hampered the progress of Arab civilization as a whole. But although some of these figures undoubtedly helped lay the ideological groundwork for later secular nationalist movements in the Arab world, their influence remained very limited among their contemporaries. The central role in the genesis of Arab nationalism once ascribed to early Christian Arab activists by historian George Antonius[7] has been questioned in the historiography of recent decades. It was the religiously inflected Arabism of figures such as Rashid Rida, this scholarship suggests, that struck a more responsive chord among disaffected members of the Sunni Muslim elites in the Fertile Crescent.[8]

Islamic modernists, Arabists, and Christian Arab nationalists were not the only critics impatient with the inefficacy of the Ottoman government and the inconsistency and double-faced character of its modernization efforts. In the first decade of the twentieth century, the Committee of Union and Progress (CUP), informally known as the Young Turks, represented a much more serious and direct challenge to the authority of the sultanate. This movement, operating underground and from exile, was originally constituted in 1889 as a multi-ethnic coalition of activists who shared a common demand for the restoration of the 1876 constitution. Yet even before it came to power, the CUP split over the question of how a truly reformed Ottoman Empire should be organized—on a centripetal, Turko-centric basis or with territorial and cultural autonomy for diverse ethnic and religious groups?

In principle, all the various factions within the CUP embraced the slogan of 'Ottomanism', which called for the cultivation of a common, quasi-national identity among the entire population of the empire. But the slogan merely begged the question: was this to be a culturally and linguistically assimilationist identity that utterly erased all internal divisions or a loosely civic one that allowed for the simultaneous cultivation of diverse ethno-religious traditions and communal autonomies? For a majority of the Turkish speakers of Muslim background in the CUP, it was self-evident that Turkish identity should form the core ingredient in any Ottomanist recipe. It was this faction that refounded a fragmented CUP on its own terms in 1902 and proceeded to penetrate the Ottoman army's officer corps. This was a critical factor in the success of the Young Turks' 1908 revolution, which was followed by the restoration of the 1876 constitution and, in 1909, the suppression of a reactionary counter-coup and the deposition of Sultan Abdülhamit II in favour of a more pliant member of the ruling family. In the wake of a questionably conducted parliamentary election in 1912, further turmoil ensued, culminating in a 1913 putsch organized by a group of military officers belonging to the CUP. This placed the soon-to-be notorious, authoritarian triumvirate of Enver Pasha, Talat Pasha, and Jemal Pasha firmly in the political saddle, where they were to stay to the end of the First World War.

The reinstatement of the constitution in 1908 raised enormous expectations in all corners of the empire, but the turmoil that ensued came at further cost to Ottoman territorial holdings and raised serious questions about what the long-term basis was to be for the empire's internal cohesion. Foreign powers responded to the revolution by grabbing yet more Ottoman territories in the Balkans and North Africa. A continued perception of Ottoman vulnerability contributed to the onset of the bloody Balkan Wars of 1912–13, which left the Ottomans' European holdings reduced to those of present-day Turkey.

From a very dispassionate, ethno-strategic perspective, the Balkan losses could be seen as a potential gain for the Ottoman Empire. They came as the culmination of a long-drawn-out process that left the empire shorn of territories whose populations were largely Christian (with some notable exceptions, such as parts of Bosnia-Herzegovina and newly independent Albania). To be sure, there were still millions of Armenians and Greeks in Anatolia and Constantinople, as well as various Christian minorities in the Arab Middle East, and small pockets of Jewish population throughout (including the still tiny, but growing, Zionist settlement in Palestine, of which more below). But Muslim demographic preponderance within the empire was now greater than ever, and, especially in the eyes of some Arab politicians and publicists, this religious streamlining held forth the possibility of making the dream of Ottomanism a reality. That is, their common Islamic heritage could bind Arabs and Turks (and Kurds, to the extent that anyone was paying attention to them) in a common civic identity, allowing an effective refounding of the empire on the basis of some form of popular sovereignty and shared religio-cultural heritage. By the same token, Arab advocates of

Ottomanism insisted that a decentralized, federal system of government was the most appropriate means of creating a new, progressive political order. Such a system would allow the Arabs to enjoy a considerable degree of home rule in their native provinces while gaining equal access with Turks to positions of power at the centre.

In practice, however, the humiliation of losing additional territory in the Balkans and North Africa, aggravated by the domestic political instability of the years following the 1908 Revolution, only served to reinforce the inclination of the CUP's leading circles to centralize power and to cultivate the identity of what they saw as the empire's Turkish core nationality. In public, the Young Turks still spoke the inclusive language of Ottomanism, while periodically resorting to Islamist and jihadist propaganda when it served their purposes (notably during World War I). But in their private deliberations and in various aspects of their public policy, they behaved ever more obviously like Turkish nationalists.[9]

By the time the Young Turk military triumvirate seized power in 1913, a gulf of suspicion had begun to open up between the CUP's central leadership and members of Arab elites concerned about the growing centralization and Turkification of administrative and political power in the empire. Arab dissent took open political form in the safety of British-controlled Cairo, where advocates of federalization founded the Ottoman Administrative Decentralization Party at the end of 1912. This organization maintained links with activists in Syria and Mesopotamia (Iraq) who formed secret Arab nationalist societies, al-Fatat[10] in Syria and al-'Ahd (The Covenant) in Mesopotamia. It should be noted that at this stage these remained tiny conspiratorial organizations consisting of a few score members.

The First World War and its Aftermath

In November 1914, as the CUP triumvirate brought the Ottoman Empire into the war against the Allies, the gloves came off on the domestic front as well. Within a year, the Young Turk regime had launched a carefully planned anti-Armenian ethnic-cleansing campaign that rapidly assumed genocidal qualities and proportions. Somewhere in the range of 600,000 to over a million Armenian men, women, and children were murdered or allowed to die amidst their forced transportation from eastern Anatolia to the Syrian desert.[11] The Armenian genocide was the most extreme manifestation of an overarching effort by the CUP leadership to re-engineer the ethno-demographic structure of Anatolia along cohesive Turkish-nationalist lines. This process reached its culmination after the war with the forced transfer of some 380,000 Muslims and 1.1 million Greek Orthodox between Greece and Turkey, in the wake of Turkish nationalist leader Mustafa Kemal's defeat of Greek and other Allied forces that had attempted to partition Anatolia. This exercise in mutual ethno-religious cleansing received largely retroactive international sanction under the terms of the January 1923 Greco-Turkish Convention that was incorporated into the July 1923 Treaty of Lausanne between

Kemal's Turkish nationalist government on the one hand and the West European, Balkan, and Japanese members of the wartime Allied coalition on the other.[12]

The First World War also exacted a heavy toll on the empire's Turkish, Kurdish, Arab, and Jewish populations. In Mesopotamia (Iraq), the grinding war of attrition between the Ottoman army and the British-commanded (and largely Indian-manned) invading force made life very difficult for the population at large. In the western parts of the Fertile Crescent, Ottoman military requisitions and the Allied blockade contributed to a devastating famine that took hundreds of thousands of lives. Any possibility of a general uprising was ruthlessly preempted by Jemal Pasha, who took personal command of the region. His public hangings in Beirut and Damascus (in 1915 and 1916) of thirty-three Arab activists on charges of illicit communication with the enemy were to be commemorated in later years as a defining moment in the birth of Arab nationalism—a collective martyrdom from which subsequent generations of freedom fighters could draw inspiration. But at the time, Jemal's iron fist was very effective at deterring any kind of widespread revolt. There were some sporadic peasant uprisings, but the overwhelming majority of Arab notables, officials, and army officers either remained genuinely loyal to the Ottoman cause or dared not express their dissent throughout the bulk of the war years. Only a tiny minority defected across Allied lines to join the rebellion that had broken out in the Hejaz.

For it was here, on the empire's periphery, that trouble was brewing for the Ottomans. The Hejaz was a province running along the western coast of the Arabian Peninsula. Its significance in the Arab and Muslim worlds was out of proportion to its population and economic resources, for lying within its boundaries were the holy cities of Mecca and Medina. Its rulers had long been accustomed to functional autonomy within the Ottoman Empire. The CUP's centralizing policies had led to growing friction with the Hashemite Grand Sharif and Emir of Mecca, Hussein bin Ali (1852–1931). The outbreak of war between the British (based in Egypt) and the Ottomans created an opportunity for Hussein and his sons Feisal (1883–1933) and Abdullah (1882–1951) to try and break free from the Ottoman yoke.[13]

Feisal and Abdullah had been educated in Constantinople, where they had cultivated ties with the sons of notables from the empire's other Arabic-speaking regions. In 1915 and 1916, Feisal undertook trips to Damascus during which he made secret contact with members of al-Fatat and al-ʿAhd, and was sworn in as a member of the latter organization. A handful of Arab officers belonging to these two societies managed to desert from the Ottoman army and make their way to Cairo. Here they joined like-minded political exiles in meeting with British officials and talking up the potential for a massive Arab uprising against the Ottoman Empire if only the British provided a little aid.

The outgrowth of this nexus of communications was the famous 1915–16 correspondence between Sir Henry McMahon, British High Commissioner in Egypt, and Hussein, in which the former undertook to provide support for a general Arab uprising that would begin with the revolt of the Hejaz. The British further promised, in the event of success, to support Hussein's aspirations to become ruler of a state extending over a large, but imprecisely delineated, swath of territory comprising most of the Arabic-speaking regions east of Egypt.[14] Hussein duly raised the standard of rebellion in June 1916, declaring himself King of Arabia. With the help of British liaison officers such as T. E. Lawrence ('of Arabia'), Bedouin forces brought together under the command of Hussein's son Feisal began to lay siege to Ottoman military strongholds in the Hejaz and to sabotage recently built Ottoman railway lines.

It would be a stretch to call Hussein a nationalist. He tended to think in terms that were on the one hand provincial and on the other pan-Islamic. In his Arabic-language propaganda, he emphasized religious themes, denouncing the Young Turks as Godless secularists and promising to restore legitimate Islamic rule to the territories that came under his authority.[15] The Hashemites' military campaign played a largely ancillary role in support of the advance of British General Allenby's forces from Egypt, while in Mesopotamia, British-led forces from the Indian Raj continued to slog on unaided. It was more by the calculated courtesy of the British than by virtue of its independent force of arms that Feisal's Northern Army was able to claim credit for the 'liberation' of Damascus in October 1918.[16] Although the Druze of southern Syria provided some (profitable) logistical support to Feisal's forces along the way,[17] there was no coordinated, mass Arab uprising against the Ottomans. Use of the term Arab Revolt to describe these events is therefore misleading, and is best understood as part of a romanticized narrative co-authored after the event by a fledgling Arab nationalist movement, traditional Arab social elites in search of new bases for political legitimacy in the aftermath of Ottoman defeat, and imperial Britain's regional experts, eager to gain a long-term foothold in the region by acting as sponsors of Arab nationalism.[18]

In an ironic postscript to Sharif Hussein's successful rebellion and Britain's post-war installation of his sons Feisal and Abdullah as King of Iraq and Emir of Transjordan respectively (see below), by 1925 the Hashemites had been ousted from their home base of Hejaz by Ibn Saud (*c.*1880–1953), ruler of the central Arabian-Peninsula region of Najd. Ibn Saud came to power at the head of an Arabian tribal confederacy that derived its ideological cohesion, such as it was, from Wahhabi fundamentalist Islam rather than Arab nationalism. Saudi Arabia—as the united kingdom formed from the integration of Najd and Hejaz in 1932 was called—remains to this day the only country in the world whose people derive their 'national' designation from the name of their ruling family—not quite a ringing endorsement of self-determination doctrine.[19]

It is also a point worth emphasizing that, of the three multinational empires (Romanov, Habsburg, and Ottoman) that entered the First World War, the Ottoman Empire was the only one that did not shatter along ethnic fracture lines under the strain of total war, impending defeat, and/or internal revolution.[20] The fact that, in the wake of its Balkan losses, such a large majority of its population shared a common Sunni Muslim faith undoubtedly played an important role in this maintenance of internal cohesion, although certainly the sheer ruthlessness of the Young Turks should not be underestimated as a factor. In any case, the Ottoman Empire was slowly and painfully conquered by British-commanded forces; it did not collapse. The empire's Arab-populated lands found themselves on the apparent verge of independence in the wake of foreign occupation, not on the heels of a popular uprising.

That said, there is no question that an influential minority among urban Arab elites did take up the idea of national self-determination wholeheartedly and enthusiastically, eagerly embracing the possibilities that Wilsonian doctrine seemed to hold forth. The writings and teachings of Arabists such as Rashid Rida (see above) and the wartime political activism of the secret societies had helped lay the ideological and organizational foundations for an Arab nationalist movement. For their part, a number of Christian Arab exiles from the Levant (modern-day Syria and Lebanon) had articulated a Western-inflected, secular-nationalist vision in the pre-war years, a vision that suddenly seemed realizable with the collapse of the Ottoman 'caliphate' and the Allied and Associated Powers' apparent promotion of an enlightened new world order. Popular forces demanding empowerment also burst forth on the political scene, now that the old order had been summarily swept away.

The problem, here as among the peoples of the other former multinational empires, was that slogans such as freedom, nation, and self-determination could be associated with a diverse array of ideas and agendas—religious and secular, elitist and populist, territorially and demographically expansive/inclusive and reflexively regional and particularistic. A further complication was the occupation of most of the region by British forces and their French allies, who had been allowed by the British to establish a foothold in what was to become Lebanon and who had their eyes firmly set on Syria, where the British had promised them a sphere of influence in the secret 1916 Sykes-Picot agreement. Finally, the Zionist movement had gained the British government's public support in the November 1917 Balfour Declaration for '. . . the establishment in Palestine of a national home for the Jewish people . . . '.[21]

The result was a chaotic period in the Great War's aftermath during which a multiplicity of parties vied for power throughout the region. The disorder was further aggravated by the 1919 Paris Peace Conference's failure to apply the principle of national self-determination in any substantive or immediate sense to regions outside Europe and by Britain and France's apparent intention of giving precedence to the Sykes-Picot agreement over the terms of the Hussein-McMahon correspondence. A wave of resentment and unrest was triggered across the Middle East.

In Egypt, Britain had declared a protectorate following Ottoman entry into the war on Germany's side in November 1914. (The nominal Egyptian ruler was now titled sultan and later king, instead of khedive.) Here as elsewhere in the Middle East and the colonial world at large, the end of the war amidst Wilsonian proclamations raised expectations of national self-determination.[22] In spring 1919 a popular uprising in support of nationalist leader Sa'ad Zaghlul (1859–1927) convinced the British to allow him to lead a delegation (*wafd*—the kernel of Zaghlul's Wafd Party) to the Paris Peace Conference, where, however, the British succeeded in securing international recognition of their protectorate. Continued political turmoil induced the British in 1922 to renounce the protectorate and allow the Egyptian king to declare independence, subject to major restrictions. The 1936 Anglo-Egyptian treaty further formalized the country's technically sovereign status. Although Zaghlul held office as prime minister briefly in 1924, British concessions fell far short of the substantive and complete independence for which he and his supporters were holding out. It should be noted that, during much of this period, Egyptian nationalism did not emphasize its linguistic affinity with the other Arabic-speaking societies of the Middle East. Only towards the end of the interwar years did the potential advantages of mutual cooperation in the context of a pan-Arab nationalist movement become increasingly attractive to Egyptian nationalists.[23]

In Iraq, the British fought for several months in 1920 to suppress a popular uprising that featured cooperation between Shiʿites and Sunnis. Upon the suppression of the revolt, Britain's policy moved, here as in Egypt, towards the more flexible option of informal empire—in Iraq's case, under the facade of a League of Nations mandate. Feisal, Syria's deposed king (see below), was made king of Iraq in 1921 and the country's Sunni elites were temporarily appeased through a policy of cooptation that allowed them to reconsolidate the position of sociopolitical dominance they had been accustomed to enjoy under the Ottomans.[24] The 1930 Anglo-Iraqi treaty of alliance (implemented in 1932), which served as the model for the Anglo-Egyptian one of 1936, brought the League of Nations mandate to a formal close while leaving the British a large measure of effective control: they retained air bases in the now officially independent country as well as the right to use Iraqi territory and facilities for needs of military transit; their diplomats and advisors were assured special status vis-à-vis other foreign representatives. Iraqi oil production, begun in 1927, remained firmly in the hands of the misleadingly named Iraq Petroleum Company, which was jointly owned by British, French, Dutch, and American firms, to the exclusion of Iraqi participation.[25]

Case Study: Syria

In Syria, unrest and uncertainty reigned for the two years between Feisal's entry into Damascus in October 1918 and the French takeover in July 1920. The Syrian example can serve as a case study illustrative of the confusion surrounding the meaning and significance of Arab nationalism during its formative years.

In the aftermath of Feisal's entry into Damascus, the future status of the vaguely defined region of Syria remained undetermined. While the Syrian inland remained under temporary British military occupation, the British allowed the French to install themselves in Beirut, where they set about carving out a Lebanese state, extending the tiny Maronite Christian-dominated enclave of Mount Lebanon to encompass territories that included large Sunni, Shiʿite, Druze, and Greek Orthodox populations, whose members did not necessarily care for the new arrangement. As far as most Arab nationalists were concerned, the French had no business being there at all, and there were many who argued that the entire region including present-day Syria, Lebanon, Palestine/Israel, and Jordan rightfully belonged together in a Greater Syrian state.

Whether or not Iraq should be unified with Greater Syria in a centralized or federalized Arab super-state was a matter of controversy.

Within the territory roughly corresponding to present-day Syria, Feisal sought to establish his rule under the protection of British occupation forces and with the help of British subsidies. Yet on the domestic front alone, the challenges he faced were overwhelming. The urban notables who dominated much of Syrian society and local politics did not take kindly to the Hashemite claim to leadership of the Arab world. As far as most of them were concerned, these upstart Hejazis with their rag-tag Bedouin army had a less legitimate claim to power than the Ottomans they were seeking to replace. Some urban-notable clans were willing to climb onto the Hashemite bandwagon as a means of reconsolidating their local power.[26] Most of the urban notables looked askance at Feisal's improvised administration. Feisal's most trusted supporters were the Arab officers who had defected from Ottoman ranks or been recruited from British POW camps to help lead his Northern Army. Many of these were Iraqis, whose high profile in Feisal's administration only served to accentuate the alien character of his rule.

Feisal sought to legitimize his aspirations by arranging elections in 1919 to a Syrian National Congress. This functioned as little more than a talking-shop, where various schemes and plans for Syrian and/or Arab unity or federation were endlessly debated in the absence of any means to realize them. In the meantime, Feisal's attempt to introduce conscription led to widespread popular resistance in a land that had just gone through the hell of total war. Locally elected popular committees, loosely affiliated with a Higher National Committee in Damascus, constituted rival claimants to authority as the Syrian National Congress proved increasingly ineffectual.[27]

By March 1920, when Feisal was proclaimed King of Syria in the face of imminent British withdrawal and a mounting French threat, he had become little more than a figurehead leader. One month later, the Allied Supreme Council, meeting at San Remo, agreed on the final terms of a Middle Eastern territorial partition, confirming French control of Lebanon and Syria, while leaving Palestine (including what was soon to be carved out as Transjordan) and Iraq to the British. On 23 July, at the Battle of Maysalun, France's General Gouraud easily crushed a hastily assembled Syrian force consisting of several hundred regular troops plus zealous but untrained volunteers called out by the popular committees. Feisal, who had vainly opposed military resistance as futile, fled the country. The British soon compensated him by naming him King of Iraq, while his brother Abdullah became the Emir of Transjordan. The entire arrangement was given a fig leaf of legitimacy in the form of League of Nations mandates, which formally obliged the British and French to guide the populations of these territories towards eventual full independence (with some ambiguity in the case of Palestine). The mandatory authorities were officially accountable to the League, to which they were obliged to submit periodic progress reports.[28]

The fundamental hypocrisy of these arrangements notwithstanding, the Wilsonian facade took on a life of its own to the extent that it helped awaken expectations of national self-determination among the political elites and segments of the popular masses in these territories. Moreover, the lines of partition agreed at San Remo set in place the basic territorial-administrative foundation for what eventually became the region's independent 'nation states' in the aftermath of the Second World War.[29]

Again, however, terms such as 'nation state' and 'national self-determination' beg more questions than they answer. To return to our Syrian example, what nation was it that was seeking self-determination—a Syrian nation or the Syrian segment of a larger Arab whole? Were Christians and members of non-Sunni Muslim sects such as Druze and Alawites to be considered equal members of the nation or tolerated minorities? Who was to determine the answers to such questions—urban notables, religious authorities, urban masses, rural insurgents, Westernized intellectuals?

A burgeoning historiography has highlighted how hard it was then and remains today to provide clear-cut answers to any of these questions. Philip Khoury's work on urban notables suggests that, following a period of uncertainty, these city-based, landed elites were able to reconsolidate their sociopolitical dominance under the French mandate. At the same time, with the larger framework of the Ottoman-protected Islamic *ummah* gone, they had to find new sources of legitimacy. The rise of commercial classes that operated outside their traditional patronage networks increased the notables' incentive to establish novel rhetorical and ideological platforms that could appeal to a broader politicized public. Hence the emergence in the late 1920s of the National Bloc, a political coalition led by Muslim urban notables who claimed to speak for the Syrian nation in the face of French occupation. The National Bloc relied principally on its leaders' patronage networks and links to neighbourhood strongmen to mobilize support and assert its authority.[30] But its members also patronized secular nationalists like the French-educated, Christian Arab intellectual Edmond Rabbath, who articulated a more modern-sounding, socially inclusive, secular nationalism that held forth the promise of winning over non-Muslim minorities (in the face of French divide-and-rule tactics) while also appealing to the Syrian masses as a whole.[31]

In brief, the leaders of the National Bloc were ready to speak the democratic-populist language of nationalism and self-determination when it suited them, while continuing to wield power along lines of social segmentation and rigid hierarchy. They also proved ready and willing to reach a *modus vivendi* with the French on the model of Britain's arrangements in Iraq and Egypt. Such a deal was in fact negotiated with the National Bloc by France's left-wing Popular Front government in 1936, but the weakness of the Popular Front government stood in the way of the treaty's ratification, leaving Syria in political limbo on the eve of the Second World War.

Given the National Bloc's elitism and its willingness to negotiate at least a temporary *modus vivendi* with the French, some scholars have looked to other social and/or sectarian groups as the sources of full-fledged, modern nationalism in interwar Syria. James Gelvin has argued that the popular committees of 1918, which articulated an explicitly Islamicized conception of Syrian identity and organized a grass-roots movement of opposition to any form of French occupation in the face of Feisal's hedging, marked the birth of a truly popular Syrian nationalism.[32] For his part, in a case study of Aleppine politics during this period, Keith Watenpaugh has pointed to the largely

Christian middle classes of northern Syria's great city as the locus of an alternative, secular nationalism that embraced European values and was not altogether averse to the notion of French 'tutelage'. (It should be noted that such secular nationalists, even when of Christian background, tended to acknowledge the importance of Islam as a civilization in whose creation and cultural heritage Arabs of all faiths could take common pride.) Conversely, Aleppo's Muslim elite remained more strongly oriented towards its traditional economic hinterland in Anatolia than towards Damascene affairs. Watenpaugh argues that the true watershed moment in the evolution of a Syrian national identity was not 1918 but 1924, with the formal abolition of the caliphate by Mustafa Kemal's militantly secular, Turkish-national republic. Only when the last institutional vestige of the time-honoured pan-Islamic frame of reference had disappeared did nationalism remain as the only ready-to-hand source of legitimacy for those seeking to gain or retain power in Syria.[33]

Finally, Michael Provence looks neither to 1918 nor to 1924 but to Syria's Great Revolt of 1925 as the turning point in the emergence of modern Syrian nationalism. This uprising originated among the Druze sectarian minority in the south, but rapidly spread to other parts of the country. While most of the urban notables and their client networks sought to avoid getting dragged too deeply into the conflict, it struck a deep chord among disaffected peasants as well as among the commercial classes of relatively new urban quarters that lay outside the notables' webs of patronage and influence. Not until 1927 were the last embers of resistance stamped out by a ruthless French counter-insurgency campaign. Nonetheless, Provence concedes that the only common goal shared by the various sectarian, social, and regional elements of the uprising was the determination to oust the French from Syria.[34] What sort of regime a self-governing Syria would have, what territories it should encompass, what its relationship with other Arab countries would be, what role religion would have in defining its institutions and identity—all these remained (and arguably remain) open questions well after any alleged turning point in the crystallization of nationalist consciousness.

Pan-Arabism and State Patriotism

Nationalists in other Middle Eastern territories faced analogous dilemmas in the face of deep social, sectarian, ethnic, and tribal cleavages and in light of the tensions among pan-Islamism, pan-Arabism, and state patriotism. Even the terminology of nationalism reflected some of these ambiguities and uncertainties. The word most commonly used to denote 'nation' in Arab publications of the early post-1918 years was *ummah*.[35] This was simply a transposition of the term that traditionally referred to the borderless community of the Islamic faithful. It was ultimately displaced by a new vocabulary of nationalism that distinguished between *qawmiyyah* (nationalism with a pan-Arab frame of reference) and *wataniyyah* (nationalism directed towards one's particular state, such as Syria, Iraq, et cetera).

Qawmiyyah and *wataniyyah* were complementary in principle; in practice, reconciling the two was a tricky business at best. Members of the intelligentsia, political ideologues, and high-school and university students were initially among those most likely to embrace the vision of a grand political union of all the Arabic-speaking lands. Members of mercantile and industrial interest groups also tended to recognize a potential economic benefit in any lowering of political barriers to the movement of goods across the now fragmented territory of the former Ottoman Empire.[36] But the personnel of state apparatuses—governing elites, civil servants, military officers—had a strong vested interest in, and tendency to identify with, their respective political-territorial units (Syria, Iraq, Transjordan, et cetera). And yet these were countries whose borders had been defined by European powers and did not correspond to any clear-cut ethnic, religious, or historic lines of demarcation, whereas the doctrine that all Arabic-speakers were members of the same nation, irrespective of foreign-drawn frontiers, had the virtue of an obvious if superficial logic.

The result was an anomaly. There was an increasing tendency over the years (especially from the mid-twentieth century onward) for each Arab state's political elite to present itself as the selfless standard-bearer of pan-Arab nationalism while casting doubt on its neighbours' devotion to the cause and blaming them for the continued division of the Arab world. *Qawmiyyah* was thus a double-edged sword that called into question the political-territorial division of the Arab world while serving to perpetuate it. In the long run, the tension between *qawmiyyah* and *wataniyyah* contributed to a sustained crisis of political legitimacy in many Arab states.

As in the Syrian case, so too across the rest of the Arab world there was a wide gap between the modern rhetoric of political equality and national unity, and the vice-like grip on power (and the financial benefits associated with it) maintained by the governing strata. It should be noted that in interwar Iraq, given the country's formal independence as of 1932, ruling elites were able to go further than the Syrian National Bloc in propagating popular nationalism, at least among elements of the politically dominant Sunni Arab minority (the balance of the population consisting predominantly of ethnic Kurds and Shi'ite Arabs). Under the influence of European fascist examples, the Ministry of Education (under the rabidly extremist pan-Arab nationalist Sati' al-Husri and his successors) cultivated militant nationalism in school curricula and officially sponsored youth organizations. Yet the fundamental pattern was similar to that of the Syrian National Bloc: while seeking to affirm its nationalist credentials through the sound and fury of fascist-style speeches and spectacles, Iraq's Hashemite monarchy continued to govern through the cooptation of established tribal elders and Sunni notables rather than by embracing a populist-revolutionary transformation of the social order.[37] At the same time, the inauguration of an independent state dominated by members of the Sunni Arab elite heightened resentments among groups who felt disenfranchised (notably the Shi'ites), dispossessed (economically marginalized rural tribesmen and those tribal sheikhs whose authority was being undercut by the swelling power of centralized government), or who aspired to autonomy (the Kurds and members of the small Christian Assyrian minority). A confrontation with the

Assyrians escalated into an army massacre of hundreds of villagers in 1933. In 1936 a shaky coalition of social reformers and Iraqi-first nationalists led by the ethnically Kurdish general Bakr Sidqi (1890–1937) came to power briefly in a military coup, but the Arab nationalists and landowning elite staged a comeback following Sidqi's assassination just ten months later.[38]

The Origins of the Arab-Israeli Conflict

Beyond a common tendency to pay lip service to the ideal of pan-Arab unity, the one great point of convergence among most of the diverse manifestations of nationalism in the Arab world was hostility towards the *Yishuv* (the Zionist settlement) in Palestine. The Zionist movement was in many respects fundamentally different from Arab nationalisms. Most obviously, it did not arise among the contemporaneously indigenous population of Palestine. Conversely, the *Yishuv* enjoyed a degree of cohesion that eluded the Arabs in general and even the Palestinian Arabs in particular.

Jews had populated, and periodically established political independence in, the Land of Israel/Palestine in ancient times. Their evolving ethno-religious tradition had consistently kept alive the image of the Land of Israel as their ancestral and future homeland throughout the centuries since the Romans had laid waste to Judaea. The modern Zionist movement, which originated among East and Central European Jewry in the late nineteenth century and was officially founded in 1897 with Theodor Herzl's convening of the First Zionist Congress in Basel, Switzerland, sought to turn ethno-religious dreams into political reality. It challenged assimilated Jews and 'orthodox' Judaism alike. It rejected assimilation as a failure in light of the rise of modern racist anti-Semitism in countries such as Austria-Hungary, Germany, and France, where most Jews had sought to blend into the surrounding population in their dress, language, attire, and manners, and had gained official equality as citizens, yet found themselves increasingly targeted as an ethno-racially alien minority by radical nationalists. Zionism also rejected what it saw as the political passivity of traditional Jewry, looking instead to European nationalist movements as examples of what a resolute, well-run political endeavour could achieve in the way of mass mobilization and national unification and/or liberation. The mainstream of the Zionist movement was secular (and also predominantly socialist), although a religious Zionist organization was founded as early as 1902. Most orthodox Jews were initially suspicious of, or hostile to, Zionism's claims and ambitions.

But the most obvious complicating factor faced by the Zionists was that their ancestral homeland had to be repopulated by returnees from the Diaspora before there could be any thought of liberating it. Early settlement efforts on purchased lands did lead to the establishment of a roughly 60,000-strong Jewish presence in Palestine by 1914, at a time when the area's Arabs (Palestine did not exist as a formal administrative subdivision of the Ottoman Empire) numbered around ten times that figure. The *Yishuv* barely survived Jemal Pasha's wartime oppression, but then won a second life as the Balfour Declaration (see above) of November 1917, promising London's support for the creation of a Jewish national home in Palestine, was quickly followed by General Allenby's taking of Jerusalem in December.

The 1922 League of Nations mandate for Palestine enshrined the essence of the Balfour Declaration in international law. Under the terms of the League mandate, the Zionist Organization's Jewish Agency in Palestine enjoyed official standing in public law as an autonomous umbrella institution responsible for running many aspects of the *Yishuv*'s life. The leadership organizations formed by Palestinian Arab notables remained unrecognized *de jure* by the British authorities in light of their refusal to accept the terms of the League's mandate.[39] Over the first two decades of British mandatory rule, Jewish immigration to Palestine, chiefly from Eastern and Central Europe, led to a rapid increase in the *Yishuv*'s population, from the 60,000 of 1914 to almost half a million by 1939, while Palestine's Arab population grew to over one million.[40] In 1939, in the face of apparently imminent war with Germany—which made the British particularly eager to win over Arab public opinion—Whitehall issued a White Paper that limited further Jewish immigration to Palestine to a final cap of 75,000 over five years with a view to granting Palestine independence at the end of ten years.[41] This seemed to put paid to Zionist aspirations by setting the stage for the creation of an Arab-majority Palestinian state.

Relations between Arabs and Jews in Palestine had gone from bad to worse over the course of the interwar years. Under the British mandate, the Zionist movement's purchasing arm, the Jewish National Fund, acquired extensive tracts of land for the creation of Jewish agricultural settlements. Most of these properties were sold by absentee Arab landlords (many of them residing in Beirut). Thousands of Palestinian Arab tenant farmers were displaced in the process, and although they were normally paid compensation, uprooting them from the soil naturally provoked their enmity.[42]

As early as 1908, Palestinian Arab representatives in the Ottoman Parliament had begun to call for a crackdown on Jewish immigration into Palestine, a demand that was echoed by proto-nationalist[43] intellectuals from other parts of the Arab-speaking lands. Following the First World War, Palestine's sociopolitical and intellectual elites were not intrinsically averse to the idea of being incorporated into a Greater Syria, provided this led to a quashing of Zionist aspirations. But the failure of the 1920 General Syrian Congress, to which Palestinians had sent a delegation, reinforced a growing tendency to think of Palestine as a separate political-territorial entity whose elites had to take their people's fate into their own hands.[44]

Anti-Jewish disturbances in 1921 were followed by a much more serious outbreak of violence in August 1929. These week-long riots were incited by Haj Amin al-Husseini, Grand Mufti of Jerusalem, in the context of an escalating crisis over Jewish attempts to formalize their traditional prayer services at the Western ('Wailing') Wall.[45] Arab attacks culminated in the massacre of almost seventy Jews in Hebron, leading to the evacuation of the remaining members of that city's old, pre-Zionist Jewish community. From the perspective of mainstream Labor Zionists, the 1929 riots constituted a watershed event, in whose aftermath systematic military training and the cultivation of a self-sacrificing ethic among the *Yishuv*'s youth began to assume much greater importance than before.[46]

The militarization of the conflict was further catalyzed by the outbreak of the Arab Revolt in 1936. For Palestinian Arabs, the Revolt was, if not exactly a turning point, at least the object of romanticized nationalist mythmaking in the aftermath of its defeat. The Revolt was a peasant-based insurgency centred on what is today called the West Bank. It was directed against both British authority and the Jewish presence in Palestine, and targeted the British military and administrative apparatus and Jewish civilians alike. The British counter-insurgency campaign, which included the use of Jewish auxiliary forces, succeeded in gaining the upper hand by 1937, although widespread unrest continued to flare up until 1939. Military defeat was followed by apparent political victory for the Arabs with the issuing of the White Paper in May of that year (see above), although the Palestinian Arab leadership actually rejected its terms as insufficient. The Great Revolt also marked the entry onto the political scene of members of the rural underclass as not just actors in, but embodiments of, the Palestinian Arab national struggle. From this time on, the Palestinian male peasant's traditional headdress—the *kafiyyeh*—began to assume the symbolic status of national attire, even as substantive authority in the Palestinian Arab community remained in the hands of traditional notables.[47] The Great Revolt also galvanized anti-Zionist and pan-Arab sentiments in the broader Arab world to an unprecedented degree.[48]

Nonetheless, Palestinian society remained deeply divided both horizontally, along lines of class and education, and vertically, between feuding notable clans such as the radical-nationalist al-Husseinis and the more moderate Nashashibis. For its part, the *Yishuv* enjoyed a much higher degree of internal cohesion. That is not to say that suspicion and hostility did not run deep among rival Zionist movements. But among Jews, unlike Arabs, religious and secular definitions of communal membership were essentially congruent. That is, a socialist *kibbutznik* might labour on the Sabbath and eat pork on Yom Kippur just to flaunt his or her ardent secularism. But he or she would be doing so *as a Jewish nationalist*, and such actions would outrage an Orthodox Jew precisely because he or she would recognize the *kibbutznik* as a fellow Jew who was deliberately violating the Covenant. The furious ideological quarrels that raged among the various factions of the *Yishuv* centred, not on who was a Jew, but on what kind of individual and collective conduct being Jewish entailed.[49]

Moreover, leaving aside small communities of Orthodox Jews pre-dating Zionism, Palestine's Jewish population consisted overwhelmingly of immigrants and their descendants who were by definition a self-selected group with an ardent belief in the importance of rebuilding their nation. Many had come to the Land of Israel as part of a youth movement associated with one or another Zionist political party. Even those who had left their countries of birth more as a way of escaping persecution and economic marginalization than out of active ideological conviction became Zionists by default once they learned the revived language of Hebrew and joined the social and institutional framework of the *Yishuv*. The *Yishuv* also benefited from its effective organs of internal self-government that were legitimized by the terms of the mandate, even as the British began to turn a suspicious eye towards the *Yishuv*'s various military formations. Finally, the influx of highly educated Jewish immigrants from Eastern and Central Europe contributed to the development of a modernizing economy (and increasingly urban population) that Palestine's Arab population became either isolated from or dependent upon.

The obvious compromise solution to the Palestine question was a partition of some sort. The 1937 British Peel Commission's proposal of a future Jewish state on a relatively small patch of Palestine was rejected by Zionist representatives as an insufficient basis for the development of a viable polity. The Palestinian Arab leadership also said no: for Palestinian Arab nationalists, the notion of Jewish sovereignty on any portion of Palestine, no matter how tiny, was utterly unacceptable. (Ten years later, the Zionist leadership was reluctantly to accept a United Nations partition plan that was more generous to the Jews; Palestinian Arab leaders and neighbouring Arab states rejected it.)

The 1939 White Paper came as a terrible shock to the *Yishuv*, and appeared to many as a mortal threat to its long-term survival in any form. Within months, war had broken out in Europe. The war effectively validated the fundamental premise of Zionism—that, culturally assimilated or not, Jews could never achieve a life of dignity and security as a diasporic minority in Europe—on an utterly unimaginable scale. In the aftermath of the war, the crisis surrounding the quarter of a million Holocaust survivors crowding Displaced Persons camps in Europe, many of whom were eager to find their way to Palestine, combined with new American interest and influence in the Middle East, led to the British mandate's final crisis and the rapid escalation of the Palestine conflict into the first of several regional wars.

The Second World War and the Decline of the European Powers

The Second World War marked a decisive turning point for European empires across the globe, including the Middle East. In wartime Syria and Lebanon, British, Vichy French, and Gaullist forces played out a final, semi-farcical variation on the timeworn theme of Anglo-French imperial rivalry, which ended with Syria and Lebanon's full independence and the withdrawal of both wartime British occupation forces and the French military by 1946.[50]

Throughout the region, Nazi Germany's early military successes emboldened radical nationalists to try and seize the day. In Iraq, a pro-German military coup in 1941 led by Rashid Ali al-Kailani was forcibly reversed by the British, who were obliged to reoccupy the country. (It was Vichy French willingness to allow German planes to use air bases in Syria as staging grounds for supply missions in support of the Iraqi rebellion that had precipitated Britain's occupation of the French mandatory territories.) Jerusalem's Grand Mufti al-Husseini, who had found refuge in Baghdad from British forces during Palestine's Arab Revolt, had been involved with the Iraqi plotters and was now forced to flee again. He found refuge in Nazi-occupied Europe, where he proceeded to recruit Muslims into a special Waffen SS Division in Bosnia. In Egypt in February 1942, with the army of German General Rommel advancing from the west, the British resorted to the threat of force in order to compel King Farouk to appoint a cabinet (under the Wafd Party, ironically enough) with which they felt they could do business in the face of widespread pro-Axis sentiment among Egyptian elites and masses alike.[51]

Despite their wartime success at holding the lid down on the seething Middle Eastern cauldron, in planning for the post-war period the British realized that they would have to find ways of defusing the growing resentments of Arab nationalists by making their informal control of Iraq, Egypt, and Transjordan[52] less obtrusive. Yet His Majesty's Government continued to delude themselves into thinking that they could maintain their overall influence in the region by modifying their individual treaty relationships with client states and by acting as sponsors of pan-Arab nationalism. It was thus with British encouragement that the Arab League was formed in 1944–5.

The Arab League never evolved into much more than a forum for oratory, and in any event, the days of the established sociopolitical elites and their delicate balancing act between radical nationalist rhetoric and pragmatic political compromise were numbered in all of the countries we have discussed save Transjordan (later Jordan). Wartime political convulsions such as Rashid Ali's coup were not mere flashes in the pan; they were symptomatic of deeper forces of radicalization. By the 1930s if not earlier, many members of the growing middle classes, high-school and university students, and military officers in countries such as Iraq and Syria, had come to find that they shared common grievances against a Hashemite government and a National Bloc respectively, which seemed happy to talk of national self-determination and Arab unity, while in practice accommodating imperialism in exchange for the protection of their social, economic, and political preeminence. This perception helped fuel the rise of radically pan-Arabist, populist, secularist political movements such as the Ba'ath ('Rebirth') Party, established in Syria over the course of the 1940s. Meanwhile, others continued to look to pan-Islamism as a more attractive alternative to European-inspired secular nationalism, one that was rooted in the tradition of the caliphate and the dominant religious identity of Arab societies. The Muslim Brotherhood was founded in Egypt in 1928.

As the Second World War came to a close, the days of British and French predominance in the Middle East were numbered, while the shadow of American power loomed larger. But the end of European imperialism and the apparent triumph of Arab nationalism everywhere except for Palestine did not make it any easier to resolve the fundamental dilemmas surrounding the relationships among economic and political modernization, secularism, religious identity, ethnicity, and nationalism—dilemmas that had plagued the region since the beginning of the Ottoman reform efforts in the nineteenth century, that had both multiplied and intensified in the wake of Ottoman defeat, and that would lead to ever-escalating domestic and international conflicts in the decades to come.

Notes

1. For more on the development of nationalist movements in the Balkan possessions of the Ottoman Empire, see Miroslav Hroch's Chapter 9 on 'National Movements in the Habsburg and Ottoman Empires'.
2. This section, as well as similar narrative sections below, draws on E. J. Zürcher (1993) *Turkey: A Modern History*, London, chs. 6–7; B. Lewis, *The Emergence of Modern Turkey* (1968), 2nd edn., London, ch. 5.
3. P. J. Vatikiotis, *The History of Egypt* (1985), 3rd edn., London, ch. 4.
4. My discussions of Islamic modernism, Arabism, and Arab nationalism throughout this essay draw heavily on the following sources: E. Dawn (1973) *From Ottomanism to Arabism: Essays on the Origins of Arab Nationalism*, Urbana, IL; A. Hourani (1962) *Arabic Thought in the Liberal Age, 1798–1939*, London; R. Khalidi et al. (1991) *Origins of Arab Nationalism*, New York; P. Khoury (1983) *Urban Notables and Arab Nationalism: The Politics of Damascus 1860–1920*, Cambridge.
5. That is, they were educated in French and American schools based in the Middle East.
6. Hourani, *Arabic Thought*, 277–9.
7. G. Antonius (1938) *The Arab Awakening: The Story of the Arab National Movement*, London, chs. 3 and 5.
8. See the works cited in note 4 above.
9. E. Zürcher (1984) *The Unionist Factor: The Role of the Committee of Union and Progress in the Turkish National Movement, 1905–1926*, Leiden; M. Arai (1992) *Turkish Nationalism in the Young Turk Era*, Leiden, ch. 4. For a dissenting interpretation, see H. Kayali (1997) *Arabs and Young Turks: Ottomanism, Arabism, and Islamism in the Ottoman Empire, 1908–1918*, Berkeley and Los Angeles.
10. The full name was *Jam'iyyat al-ummah al-'arabiyyah al-fatat*—The Young Arab Nation Society.
11. Zürcher, *The Unionist Factor*, 76–7, 120–1; R. G. Suny (1993) *Looking Toward Ararat: Armenia in Modern History*, Bloomington and Indianapolis, IN.
12. P. B. Finney (1995) '"An Evil for All Concerned": Great Britain and Minority Protection after 1919', *Journal of Contemporary History*, 30, no. 3 (July), 533–51, esp. 542–3; N. M. Naimark (2001) *Fires of Hatred: Ethnic Cleansing in Twentieth-Century Europe*, Cambridge, MA, 54–5.
13. W. Ochsenwald (1991) 'Ironic Origins: Arab Nationalism in the Hejaz, 1882–1914', in Khalidi et al. (eds.) *Origins of Arab Nationalism*; Dawn, *From Ottomanism to Arabism*, chs. 1–4.
14. Whether or not the Hussein-McMahon correspondence explicitly or implicitly excluded Palestine from Hussein's prospective dominion remains a point of highly politicized, scholarly controversy—all of which merely serves to underline the vagueness and imprecision of the undertakings to begin with.
15. Ochsenwald, 'Ironic Origins'; Dawn, *Ottomanism to Arabism*, ch. 3; Z. N. Zeine (1977) *The Struggle for Arab Independence*, 2nd edn., Delmar, NY, ch. 1.

16. E. Kedourie (1984) 'The Capture of Damascus, 1 October 1918', in *The Chatham House Version and Other Middle Eastern Studies*, new edn., Hanover, NH.
17. M. Provence (2005) *The Great Syrian Revolt and the Rise of Arab Nationalism*, Austin, TX, 44. The Druze adhere to a Gnostic-like monotheistic religious doctrine (whose precise tenets are revealed only to a select group of initiates within the community) that evolved in the Middle Ages out of the Ismaili branch of Shi'ism. The main centres of Druze population are the Shuf mountains southeast of Beirut, southern Syria/Golan Heights, and Galilee.
18. K. D. Watenpaugh (2006) *Being Modern in the Middle East: Revolution, Nationalism, Colonialism, and the Arab Middle Class*, Princeton, NJ, ch. 5.
19. J. Kostiner (1993) *The Making of Saudi Arabia 1916–1936: From Chieftaincy to Monarchical State*, New York.
20. For comparative perspectives on the collapse of the Habsburg and Romanov Empires, see Miroslav Hroch's Chapter 9 on 'National Movements in the Habsburg and Ottoman Empires' and Theodore R. Weeks's Chapter 10 on 'Separatist Nationalism in the Romanov and Soviet Empires'.
21. As quoted in I. Friedman (1973) *The Question of Palestine, 1914–1918: British-Jewish-Arab Relations*, London, 279.
22. See E. Manela (2007) *The Wilsonian Moment: Self-Determination and the International Origins of Anticolonial Nationalism*, Cambridge, MA.
23. A. Dawisha (2003) *Arab Nationalism in the Twentieth Century: From Triumph to Despair*, Princeton, NJ, 103–6.
24. P. Marr (2004) *The Modern History of Iraq*, Boulder, CO, ch. 2.
25. D. Silverfarb (1986) *Britain's Informal Empire in the Middle East: A Case Study of Iraq 1929–1941*, New York, chs. 3 and 10; D. Yergin (1993) *The Prize: The Epic Quest for Oil, Money, and Power*, New York, ch. 10.
26. Watenpaugh, *Being Modern*, ch. 5.
27. J. L. Gelvin (1998) *Divided Loyalties: Nationalism and Mass Politics in Syria at the Close of Empire*, Berkeley, ch. 2.
28. H. M. Sachar (1969) *The Emergence of the Middle East, 1914–1924*, New York, ch. 9.
29. See L. Carl Brown (1984) *International Politics and the Middle East: Old Rules, Dangerous Game*, Princeton, NJ, 89.
30. P. Khoury (1987) *Syria and the French Mandate*, Princeton, NJ.
31. Watenpaugh, *Being Modern*, ch. 8.
32. Gelvin, *Divided Loyalties.*
33. Watenpaugh, *Being Modern.*
34. Provence, *Syrian Revolt.*
35. Gelvin, *Divided Loyalties*, ch. 6.
36. G. D. Schad (2006) 'Competing Forms of Globalization in the Middle East: From the Ottoman Empire to the Nation State, 1918–67', in A. G. Hopkins (ed.) *Global History: Interactions Between the Universal and the Local*, Houndmills, 205–6.
37. W. L. Cleveland (1971) *The Making of an Arab Nationalist: Ottomanism and Arabism in the Life and Thought of Sati' al-Husri*, Princeton, NJ, x–xi and 32–41, 62–3; R. S. Simon (1986) *Iraq between the Two World Wars: The Creation and Implementation of a Nationalist Ideology*, New York, 119–23, ch. 4 and *passim*; H. Batatu (1978) *The Old Social Classes and the Revolutionary Movements of Iraq*, Princeton, NJ, chs. 8 and 10.
38. Marr, *Modern History of Iraq*, ch. 2.

39. B. Wasserstein (1991) *The British in Palestine: The Mandatory Government and the Arab-Jewish Conflict 1917–1919*, 2nd edn., Oxford, 134–7.
40. J. McCarthy (1990) *The Population of Palestine: Population History and Statistics of the Late Ottoman Period and the Mandate*, New York, 10, 24, and 36.
41. The text of the White Paper can be found at <http://www.jewishvirtuallibrary.org/jsource/History/paper39.html>.
42. K. W. Stein (1984) *The Land Question in Palestine, 1917–1939*, Chapel Hill, NC.
43. I use the term 'proto-nationalist' in light of the fact that most advocates of Arab national interests at this time did not yet seek outright separation from the Ottoman Empire, but rather political autonomy and cultural and economic development within it.
44. R. Khalidi (1997) *Palestinian Identity: The Construction of Modern National Consciousness*, New York; M. Muslih (1988) *The Origins of Palestinian Nationalism*, New York; Y. Porath (1974) *The Emergence of the Palestinian-Arab National Movement, 1918–1929*, London.
45. B. Wasserstein (2002) *Divided Jerusalem: The Struggle for the Holy City*, 2nd ed., New Haven, CT, ch. 10; K. Armstrong (1996) *Jerusalem: One City, Three Faiths*, New York, 380–2.
46. The definitive study is A. Shapira (1992) *Land and Power: The Zionist Resort to Force, 1881–1948*, trans. W. Templer, New York.
47. Y. Porath (1977) *The Palestinian Arab National Movement: From Riots to Rebellion, Vol. II: 1929–1939*, London, 268; Provence, *Syrian Revolt*, 115.
48. Dawisha, *Arab Nationalism*, 107–16.
49. To be sure, in later years, the State of Israel was beset by controversies over 'who is a Jew?'. But until fairly recent immigration waves from Ethiopia and the former Soviet Union, this debate called into question the status of a tiny minority of the country's self-described Jewish population.
50. A. B. Gaunson (1987) *The Anglo-French Clash in Lebanon and Syria, 1940–45*, London; A. Roshwald (1990) *Estranged Bedfellows: Britain and France in the Middle East during the Second World War*, New York.
51. C. D. Smith (1979) '4 February 1942: Its Causes and its Influences on Egyptian Politics and on the Future of Anglo-Egyptian Relations, 1937–1945', *International Journal of Middle East Studies*, 10, no. 4 (November 1979), 453–79.
52. In 1946 the British granted Transjordan its formal independence, on the Egyptian and Iraqi models.

Suggested Further Reading

Dawisha, A. (2003) *Arab Nationalism in the Twentieth Century: From Triumph to Despair*, Princeton, NJ. Brings a twenty-first-century perspective to bear on the headier days of Arab nationalism.

Dawn, E. (1973) *From Ottomanism to Arabism: Essays on the Origins of Arab Nationalism*, Urbana, IL. A seminal collection of essays by the scholar who placed the rise of Arab nationalist ideologies in the context of changes and continuities in the sociocultural and geopolitical history of the Middle East.

Hourani, A. (1962) *Arabic Thought in the Liberal Age, 1798–1939*, London. A classic intellectual history of Arab political thought.

Khalidi, R. (1997) *Palestinian Identity: The Construction of Modern National Consciousness*, New York. An influential study that blends post-modern perspectives with nationalist apologetics.

Khoury, P. (1987) *Syria and the French Mandate*, Princeton, NJ. A pathbreaking study of how the persistence of old elites inflected Syrian responses to the collapse of Ottoman power and imposition of a French mandate.

Marr, P. (2004) *The Modern History of Iraq*, Boulder, CO.

Porath, Y. (1977) *The Palestinian Arab National Movement: From Riots to Rebellion, Vol. II: 1929–1939*, London.

Sachar, H. A. (2007) *A History of Israel: From the Rise of Zionism to Our Time*, 3rd edn., New York.

Shapira, A. (1992) *Land and Power: The Zionist Resort to Force, 1881–1948*, trans. W. Templer, New York. A penetrating, scholarly analysis of the Zionist movement's evolving struggle over how to reconcile political idealism with security needs and the dynamics of ethno-territorial conflict.

Simon, R. S. (1986) *Iraq between the Two World Wars: The Creation and Implementation of a Nationalist Ideology*, New York. A devastating look at the ideological origins of quasi-fascist, extremist nationalism in a major Arab state.

Vatikiotis, P. J. (1985) *The History of Egypt*, 3rd edn., London.

Wasserstein, B. (1991) *The British in Palestine: The Mandatory Government and the Arab-Jewish Conflict 1917–1919*, 2nd edn., Oxford.

Wilson, M. C. (1987) *King Abdullah, Britain, and the Making of Jordan*, Cambridge.

Yergin, D. (1993) *The Prize: The Epic Quest for Oil, Money, and Power*, New York. A classic in its own time on the role of oil in the Great Powers' relations with the Middle East.

Zamir, M. (2000) *Lebanon's Quest: The Road to Statehood, 1926–1939*, new edn., London.

Zürcher, Erik J. (1993) *Turkey: A Modern History*, London. An authoritative treatment that highlights the continuities as well as changes marking the transition from Ottoman Empire to Kemalist Republic.

CHAPTER 12

NATIONALISMS IN INDIA, 1857–1947*

JOYA CHATTERJI

INTRODUCTION

INDIAN nationalism, as it emerged in the later nineteenth century, has just enough features in common with European prototypes upon which most classical theories of nationalism are based to be deemed to belong to the same genus of political movement. Yet the differences are so significant that it may not be useful to analyse Indian nationalism from these perspectives. It was decidedly not a process by which a self-conscious national community sought to establish a state. Nor was it an archetype of 'state-sponsored' or 'top-down' nationalism described by Ernest Gellner. The British in India were not in the business of promoting nationhood amongst their subjects: indeed, when challenged by critics claiming to speak for an Indian nation, their line was to declare that India was nothing more than a 'geographical expression'. In the nineteenth century India's masses were not shepherded into state schools or conscripted into people's armies that turned 'peasants into Indians'. With fourteen major languages and more than two hundred dialects, India had no single culture based on language that could be deployed to create a sense of national identity. Nor had 'Indians' in the mid-nineteenth century experienced the wars against outsiders or the revolutions among themselves which, in other places and times, have been the crucible of modern nationalisms.

Indian nationalism possibly had more in common with some colonial nationalisms of the nineteenth and twentieth centuries that Benedict Anderson, among others, have discussed.[1] Indeed, it has often been seen as an exemplar of the nationalisms of colonial subjects struggling to be free[2]—just as the British Raj is often described as the *locus*

* J. Breuilly, T. Hochstrasser, A. Seal, and D. Washbrook read drafts of this essay, and I am grateful for their comments.

classicus of modern empires—but with one striking difference. The nationalisms of Creoles in Spanish America, of Czechs, Slavs, and Magyars against the Habsburg Empire (or indeed of Egyptians, Arabs, and Turks against Ottoman sultans) sought to break free and carve 'national' states of their own *out* of those empires. Indian nationalists alone aspired to take over an empire as a whole; not one part or the other, but *every* province and principality the British ruled directly and indirectly, and claim them all for the nation. It was, in this sense, a movement not only profoundly ambitious but also, in critically important ways, unique. Yet paradoxically, the very breadth of its scope circumscribed its modalities and constrained its programmes. Rather than seeking to explain why nationalism in India 'failed' to conform to other models, European or Latin American or Arab, or to speculate why other anti-colonial nationalisms did not subsequently emulate the 'norm' it might be thought to have established, this essay will map Indian nationalism's distinctive development until 1947.

Since this 'imperial' scope of all-India nationalism is what marks it out from other colonial nationalisms, the focus will be on explaining that scope as the product of several interrelated processes. First, the construction and development of a centralized state and political institutions that spanned the empire; second, the emergence—in a new public sphere—of the idea that all of India was one nation; third, the growth of the conviction among influential Indians that the interests of 'the people of India' could only be served if the unity of the imperial state were kept intact but was controlled by Indians; and finally, the political efforts by these leaders to capture that state.

This is not to suggest other local, regional, linguistic, or religious solidarities—indeed other *nationalisms*—did not develop in the subcontinent during this period. They did, and this essay will show why this is hugely significant. Nor will it deny processes that gave shape and substance to nationalisms with roots in earlier times. As Christopher Bayly has shown, 'traditional patriotisms' had emerged in some parts of the subcontinent in the eighteenth century, not least among the new states on the periphery of the Mughal Empire.[3] This essay will challenge the notion that all-India nationalism triumphed over these other solidarities and instead demonstrate how it engaged with these movements, on occasion content to coexist with them, at other times seeking to co-opt them to its cause, and when they threatened its core purposes, attempting to snuff them out.

Political Structures and Precursors: Imperial Governance in British India

The development of nationalism in India was closely linked with the new structures of governance that British India put in place in the aftermath of the revolt of 1857. In 1858 the Crown in Parliament replaced the rule of the East India Company. London dictated Indian policy through a Secretary of State, and its agent, the Government of India and the Viceroy, had a clear line of control over the governors of the presidencies and provinces, who in turn had more authority over the myriad localities under their charge. As it emerged from the ravages of the rebellion, the Raj took on some of the classic features of a bureaucratic and military empire. An elite corps of nine hundred Indian Civil Servants (sometimes known as 'the Guardians', with intended Platonic overtones) manned all key posts at the centre and in the provinces. They were supplemented—in clear subordinate roles—by a much larger body of uncovenanted civil servants (most of whom, after 1879, were Indians) and below them, thousands of lesser functionaries at the district and village level. This new apparatus of rule sought to recruit Indians in vast numbers into the service of a government capable of intervening more effectively than before in Indian life in areas that the East India Company—its reformist policies notwithstanding—had in practice left well alone.

As these interconnected structures of government became increasingly centralized, they also started to cost much more. So did the army—the search for greater security after the rebellion led to its reorganization, with more white troops permanently garrisoned in India, who were ten times costlier than their Indian counterparts. Railways had to be built, capable of transporting troops rapidly to places where they might be needed, and this demanded heavy investment. Canals were constructed to irrigate the Punjab, the main province from which the army recruited. Communications had to be made swifter and more secure, requiring expenditure on roads, posts, and telegraphs. Paying for it all placed a huge and growing fiscal burden on the Raj, which had to tax India more heavily and efficiently than before. Necessity (as much as the Victorian obsession with statistics) dictated that the government had to get information about its subjects and territories through censuses, cadastral and other surveys and gazetteers. Since it was a fundamental tenet of the Raj that India was not to be a charge on taxpayers at home, the government had to devise methods of squeezing more resources out of India without provoking its subjects into resistance. It also followed that London saw merit in actively seeking to stimulate and 'develop' the Indian economy, measures that historians have concluded had scant success. But the government brought larger numbers of 'non-official' Britons to India to participate—whether as planters, managing agents, commercial men, or even manufacturers—in an increasingly interconnected subcontinental economy.

It was this complex set of pressures—rather than any worthy scheme of political tutelage—that led to the first institutions of self-government in which Indians had a place. The 1870s reforms of the viceroy, Lord Mayo, established new local bodies, on which a few (hand-picked and reliable) Indians were invited to serve, to raise taxes. Their limited role in matters to do with local welfare and development, just as Viceroy Ripon's reforms of the early 1880s, was deemed to pose no threat to the wider purposes of British rule.

But these modest changes swiftly elicited novel Indian responses. The growing intervention of the state in their affairs gave Indians, powerful in the localities, an incentive to take part in these fledgling institutions of 'self-government', where, as they sought to influence policy on local issues, they had to learn new modes, forms, and languages of politics. They quickly recognized that real power no longer lay in the districts, but in provincial capitals, in the imperial headquarters in Calcutta, and ultimately in London itself. Consequently, they increasingly began to demand to be consulted on matters that went beyond limited local concerns, and be given a hearing at these higher echelons where policies affecting them were made.

Mayo's successors saw good political as well as fiscal arguments for bringing 'able and sensible natives', nominated by these local bodies, into the provincial Councils, since 'if [it] had a native party behind them, the Government of India would cease to stand up, as it does now, an isolated rock in the middle of a tempestuous sea'.[4] In 1892 the Indian Councils Act gave Indians a greater presence in the reformed and enlarged councils at the provincial and central level. In a development many historians accept was critically important to the growth of all-India nationalism, some of the Indian members of these councils were now drawn from the district and municipal boards by what was, in effect, a system of indirect elections. From now on, Indians who claimed to speak for their constituents and wanted to influence policy needed a mandate from their countrymen. Politicians with provincial ambitions had actively to solicit the backing of influential local politicians, mobilize wide networks, and be seen to 'represent' their interests and articulate their concerns. As historians of the 'Cambridge School'[5] have argued, the very structures of the British Empire unwittingly generated the motor force that drove Indians operating in these different arenas of politics to forge new linkages and alliances. These alliances were the crucial adhesive that came to bind the local, the provincial, and the all-India arenas into a single, interconnected field of politics, matching the interconnected structures of government with which it aimed to engage.

But the competition between Indians for the few, and much sought after, positions of influence was intense. As various of the Cambridge historians have argued, the dynamics of competition encouraged loose factions of 'outs' to adopt more critical postures towards authority and to try more populist modes in their efforts to dislodge the 'ins'. Their campaigns to get backing helped to induct new groups into these recently created domains of 'modern' politics in which they dared to criticize and challenge their rulers.

Yet there was much happening beyond these limited arenas and the self-interested jockeying for power within them; and some of the Cambridge historians have rightly been criticized for not giving these developments sufficient weight. As Anderson has pointed out, nations are cultural artefacts that generate passionate and sometimes selfless attachment (who—he asks—would willingly die for the COMECON or the EEC?); and analyses of the institutions and structures of the colonial state do not by themselves help us understand how the idea of India came to be one such 'cultural artefact'. Even if, just like many nationalists elsewhere, late nineteenth-century India's politicians were hungry for state power and justified their claims with nationalist arguments, it is nonetheless important to consider how such arguments were crafted and how they came to gain a wider purchase.

Nationalisms and the Colonial Public Sphere

Much less is known about the genesis of the idea that 'all-India' was a 'nation'.[6] The process had its roots in the earlier nineteenth century, a product more of an emerging civil society and public spheres than of the state (although developments in one arena, of course, had an impact on the other). Its main protagonists were, unsurprisingly, intellectuals. Most were drawn from the traditional literati—groups that in pre-colonial India had a monopoly on learning and saw themselves as the custodians of knowledge—religious, legal, or bureaucratic. Belonging in the main to families with long histories of service in the courts of earlier rulers, whether the Mughals, Nawabs, or Peshwas whom British rule had displaced, they sought to work for the new rulers as functionaries, scribes, petty officials, and 'native informants'. These groups observed the British conquest of India from a unique vantage point. Many learnt English and studied the religious and political ideas of their rulers. They were also in contact with European perceptions and histories of their own societies (which were mostly deeply disparaging), and they had to stomach unflattering accounts by British authors of how and why the old 'despotic' lineages and dynasties of the subcontinent had been so easily overthrown. Some began to reflect on the meaning and causes of these defeats. Raja Ram Mohun Roy, a leading Bengali intellectual; Sir Sayyid Ahmed Khan, scion of a north Indian Muslim family that for many generations had been part of the Mughal service elite; Delhi's *alim* (Muslim legal scholar), Shah Waliullah; the Parsi reformer Dadabhai Naoroji; the Hindu reformer Mahadev Govind Ranade of Bombay and Poona; Bengal's great essayist Bankimchandra Chattopadhyay: all in their different ways sought to understand the failure of their own societies to resist British domination. All found a common explanation, albeit in a variety of registers, in putative histories of moral and cultural decay, and called for programmes of cultural regeneration and renewal to reverse this process. Some, including Roy, Ranade, and Sayyid Ahmed Khan, believed that this renewal must come through modernization and reform, and they set up societies and associations to propagate their ideas. Significantly they looked to the British government in India for support: Roy, for instance, lobbied the East India Company to outlaw 'debased' practices such as polygamy and the immolation of widows, and Sayyid Ahmed Khan sought the government's backing for his new college at Aligarh that aimed to give Muslims a modern education. These campaigns were among the early expressions of an emerging Indian 'constitutional' liberalism[7] which insisted that the government had a duty to intervene for the 'common good', presaging later nationalist preoccupations with harnessing the power of the state for the welfare and uplift of the 'Indian people'.

Others, in contrast, believed that cultural renewal could only be achieved by a return to 'fundamentals'. For them, the moral decline had begun long ago with India's acquiescence to 'Muslim' conquest and rule, and they took the view that yet another alien government had no business interfering in their religious affairs and social customs. Roy's campaign to outlaw *sati* met with stout resistance among his fellow Bengalis: Radhakant Deb's Dharma Sabha was the first of many associations that championed a 'revived' (and in many senses invented) Hindu orthodoxy. Later, Bankimchandra Chattopadhyay developed his distinctive thesis about how the sources of its renewal should be found *within* Hindu society, where modern Hindus might 'recover' their physical strength and love of liberty to make them capable of resisting foreign domination. Ideas such as these stimulated political groupings different in style and content from the reforming societies and associations of would-be modernizers. Nabagopal 'National' Mitra's Hindu Mela, founded in Calcutta 1866, served as the model for physical culture clubs (*akharas*) which sprang up in their hundreds all over Bengal and western India in the late nineteenth century, whose aim was to train young men in traditional forms of exercise—sword- and stave-play and wrestling—to revive their cultural pride, to inculcate habits of self-assertion and to promote love of the motherland.[8] Bankimchandra, Ranade, Romesh Chandra Dutt, and many others turned to writing histories that lauded 'Hindu' resistance to 'Muslim' conquests and exalted 'national' heroes in plays, poetry, and song. Inherent in their writings was the claim, as Partha Chatterjee and others have pointed out, that in the realm of its internal spiritual life, the 'nation' already existed as an autonomous entity. The challenge, as these pioneers saw it, was to find ways to 'establish a strong central authority' grounded on the nation's 'immanent propensities'.[9]

A few intellectuals also began to construct geographies of imagined 'national' space,[10] but any conception of which specific territories constituted the Indian 'nation' or 'motherland' remained inchoate. When Bankimchandra used the terms 'we' and 'us', sometimes he meant 'we Bengalis' or 'we Hindus', and at other times an even wider constituency: 'we non-Europeans'. For him and his contemporaries, their main concern was with their regions: after all, Bankimchandra wrote of the plight of *The Bengal Peasantry* and Ranade chronicled *The Rise of Maratha Power*. Regional nationalisms, drawing on the themes of the 'traditional patriotisms' that Bayly has described, emerged more vigorously in the later nineteenth century than any idea of 'all-India'. Indeed Bal Gangadhar Tilak—the Marathi educationist and journalist regarded today as a seminal figure of 'extremist' Indian nationalism—rejected the idea of an overarching Indian nation, insisting 'it was only by accident that within the mantle of British rule the Hindus, Muslims, Sikhs, Parsis, Bengalis, Madrassis etc., all these peoples who once had different nationalities, have been brought together. *Therefore it is wrong to suppose from this that their nationality has become one.*'[11]

Subcontinental unities tended to be expressed mainly in terms of abstract religious identities. In the late nineteenth and early twentieth centuries more was written about 'the Hindoo race' than about 'India'; and those who did write about the nation, tended to see its distinctive cultural genius in Hindu spiritual traditions.[12] This was also the case with 'the Muslims of Hindustan' who, as Sayyid Ahmed Khan declared in the 1880s, constituted a 'nation'. In these arguments, 'nationhood' was conceived very differently from the territorially bounded nations of Europe. The 'Hindoo nation', and Sayyid Ahmed Khan's 'Muslim nation', were autonomous and self-regulating communities, each governed by shared culture, ethics, and values. But whereas the 'Hindoo nation' might broadly have been seen to be located in the sacred territories of 'Bharatvarsha' or 'Aryavarta', or have its origins in the *Arctic Home of the Vedas*,[13] the 'Muslim nation' remained divorced from any territorial definition.[14]

As the nineteenth century drew to a close, however, some protagonists began to assert that a nationalism built around a territorial conception of 'all-India' was a higher ideal. Speaking at Lahore in 1893, Dadabhai Naoroji firmly declared, 'I am an Indian and owe duty to my work and all my countrymen. Whether I am a Hindu or a Mahommedan, a Parsi, a Christian, or of any other creed, I am above all an Indian. Our country is India and our nationality is Indian.' Significantly, Naoroji was one of the founding fathers of the Indian National Congress, whose purpose was to influence government policy on issues that concerned educated Indians and their patrons, irrespective of region or religion. In this speech Naoroji had articulated the central tenet of the Congress.

By the time the Congress was established in 1885, nationalist ideas—to begin with confined to narrow, elitist, intellectual circles—had begun to be vigorously debated by much larger audiences. The interventionism of the rapidly expanding British administration, and the growing involvement of Indians with the state, played a critical role in these developments. The later nineteenth century saw a significant growth in English and vernacular education, largely financed by Indians themselves. Many new colleges were set up outside the presidency capitals and hundreds of English-medium schools sprang up in district towns,[15] processes that helped to create a 'secular intelligentsia'[16]—which was among the main forces driving all-India nationalism forward.

Government in India was the chief employer of the educated, and the ambition of the brightest students was to get better-paid jobs in the public sector. To do so, they had to master the English language, study the new curriculum and imbibe the ideas of western liberalism that underpinned it. After they entered service, however, they quickly had to face reality: the gulf between liberal theory and bigoted practice.[17] This was not only an age of new imperialism but also of high racism, not just in British India but throughout the world wherever the West interacted with other peoples and cultures. The Mutiny had signalled a growing racial divide between the rulers and the ruled; in its aftermath Britons segregated themselves from Indians in 'whites only' residential areas, cantonments, and clubs, putting as much distance between themselves and the 'Black Towns', which were now seen as hotbeds of vice and disease. Increasingly the British 'competition wallahs' treated the 'westernized oriental gentlemen' who worked under and alongside them with the contempt that the acronym 'wog' came to imply. The Ilbert Bill, by which the Viceroy, Lord Ripon, in 1883 tried to give Indian district magistrates and sessions judges the same powers as their European counterparts, sparked such a hysterical response among non-official whites that he was forced to drop this modest measure. This episode forced educated Indians to see just what whites thought of them, and indeed of the Viceroy's tempered liberalism and his whole 'd-d nigger party'.[18] As Rajat Ray and Sumit Sarkar[19] have pointed out, racial discrimination had much to do with politicizing many Western-educated Indians—

would-be collaborators who turned against the Raj. In this respect, they had much in common with the colonial intelligentsias described by Elie Kedourie who became radical critics of regimes with which they had tried to identify, but which instead of respecting the principles of liberal universalism they proclaimed, rejected and humiliated them.[20]

The bitterness of such Western-educated Indians came to be increasingly reflected in print. The number of presses owned by Indians grew by leaps and bounds, and by the turn of the century, 'there [was] . . . scarcely a town of importance which [did] not possess its printing-press or two'.[21] Out of these presses poured a flood of novels, play, and tracts both in English and in the vernacular, which gained wide circulation through newly established libraries and reading rooms. With the proliferation of newspapers and journals, a new kind of Indian journalism emerged that adopted a challenging stance towards government. High-handed attempts to censor and control this articulate press could not push back the tides of criticism: Lytton's Vernacular Press Act of 1878, which openly discriminated against Indian papers, met with sustained attacks for its double standards. The Indian reading public, whose numbers far exceeded the narrow circles of the formally educated, began to see themselves as participants in a shared public domain, a *vox populi* increasingly 'national' in scope, with an ever more critical relationship to government.

Increasingly the 'native press', as the British described it, saw as one of its prime duties to broadcast how whites treated 'natives', particularly of a humbler sort, who worked for them as coolies on their plantations or 'ayahs' and 'boys' in their homes. In 1861 the *Hindu Patriot* serialized Dinabandhu Mitra's play *Nil darpan* (*Mirror of Indigo*), which vividly depicted the brutality of white indigo planters against indentured peasants. After this pioneering venture, floggings of coolies by planters and tea-garden managers, the death of native servants whose spleens had burst as a result of being kicked by their masters, and 'shooting accidents' in which the sahibs 'bagged a native by mistake', made headlines, as did the scandalously light sentences the courts awarded to the few who were prosecuted for these crimes. There is no doubt that the indifference of the Raj to the behaviour of the white community provoked widespread outrage and fuelled nationalist sentiment.[22] Increasingly the press complained that 'the ordinary people' of India did not receive protection and justice from the state. The legal profession, which came into its own after Macaulay's Penal Code was implemented in 1862, became an important feature of this political milieu. It was no coincidence that of the seventy-two delegates who were at the first meeting of the Congress, thirty-nine were lawyers and fourteen were journalists.[23]

It is clear that print stimulated the spread of nationalism: as a British civilian remarked in 1878, 'within the [previous] . . . 20 years . . . a feeling of nationality, which formerly had no existence . . . [had] grown up, and the . . . Press [could] now, for the first time in the history of [British] rule, appeal to the whole Native Population of India against their foreign rulers'.[24] Indeed, it may not be too far-fetched to argue that in this period, 'all-India' nationalists adopted the British term 'native', stripped of its negative connotations, as the basis for a territorial definition of 'Indianness'. 'Indians', they began to insist, were all the *native* people who resided in territory under British rule. The concept of an inclusive, territorially defined India thus emerged alongside and simultaneously with other 'ethnic' ideas of nationhood and nationalism, which both enriched and challenged it. Yet, it was never inevitable that this 'civic' notion of nationalism would incorporate, subsume, and triumph over these other ideas of India.

Nationalist Organizations and Politics, 1885–1914

The Indian National Congress was a product of this milieu. It has often been characterized as self-interested, self-regarding, and mendicant in its early years. Most of its members were drawn from the English-educated intelligentsia, in the main lawyers, journalists, schoolmasters, and doctors. Not surprisingly its deliberations reflected their concerns: above all, the demand for greater 'native' representation, but also for more opportunities for educated Indians in government service, for freedom of the press, and for just and equal treatment for all Indians. This, and the stylized loyalism of their speeches and petitions, led their rulers (and some historians) to dismiss early Congressmen as a microscopic minority who 'represented nobody but themselves'. Yet it would be a mistake to brush them aside as the contribution of Congress to 'all-India' nationalism was of much greater significance than its low-key beginnings might suggest.

The plan to launch an 'all-India' Congress was first mooted in Bombay in 1884. Delegates of political associations from the three presidencies had gathered there to bid farewell to Lord Ripon, who was seen to be a liberal and a friend of India. They had in mind an annual conference of like-minded Indians to do what they could to ensure the Viceroy's departure did not mean the end of his reforming efforts to promote 'native representation' in government. By holding a conference or a 'Congress' in a different town or city each year, associations whose remit was provincial rather than 'national' would in this way join together to present government with a charter of common demands. 'Reception committees' appointed each year in the host towns were the immediate organizing arm, backed by more permanent provincial associations. In due course, these would evolve into the key structural component of the new organization, 'Provincial Congress Committees' charged with selecting and sending delegates to the annual all-India Congress meetings. Step by step, what began as a yearly get-together created connections between people in different regions, and gave the new peripatetic body a measure of organizational coherence and continuity, as well as a membership with a growing sense of solidarity.

Providing a forum and an organization for all-India nationalism was one of the major contributions of the early Congress. Another was the recognition of Congressmen that the political changes they sought could only be achieved if Government *at the centre* could be persuaded of their validity. Their strategy was to appeal, if necessary over the head of the Viceroy directly to Parliament in London, where they hoped to enlist the support of liberal opinion in Britain by drawing attention to 'the un-Britishness of British rule in India'. Integral to this strategy was the need to present themselves as imperial subjects and to articulate their demands in terms that would not alienate liberals in England.

Another crucial contribution of the early Congressmen was to fashion a secular critique of British rule. The Raj, they insisted, did not serve the interests of 'ordinary Indians'. Imports of Lancashire cotton had destroyed Indian manufactures, depriving millions of artisans of their livelihood. The revenue burden imposed by the British had impoverished India's peasantry,[25] and its 'home charges' had 'drained' away India's wealth to Britain.[26] This could only improve if Indians had a greater say in governing their own country. Today's historians might debate the validity of claims about the impact of British rule on India's economy; but in their time they provided the moral core of, and justification for, India's civic nationalism.[27] From the outset the Congress insisted that greater autonomy for Indians would bring about material improvement for Indian society, a vision that gave the movement—and in due course independent India—its most powerful claims to legitimacy.

Yet 'moderates' who led the early Congress, had to temper their liberal zeal to secure unity of purpose at an all-India level. 'All-India' was an arena of politics that could only be created by negotiation and compromise, and by all manner of self-denying ordinances. It followed that the plans and purposes of the Indian National Congress were marked by caution and gradualism, since demands for sweeping change of any sort could so easily have disrupted the fragile unities they were seeking to develop. Vexed questions of social and religious reform, and contentious regional or sectional claims, had to be firmly excluded. It was an explicit understanding of the early Congress that no proposition to which any religious group might object could be raised at its sessions.[28] Pragmatism, rather than principled or programmatic 'transcendent secularism', determined this stance.[29] It is clear why this central tenet, that 'the interests of the nation' had to stand above and outside religion and region, took such firm root in the historical context of a heterogeneous Indian Empire, and why the consensual style of politics the early leaders tried to achieve has survived as an ideal of national 'best practice'.

But from the start 'all-India nationalism' faced powerful challenges both within and outside the Congress *pandal*, or tent, in which the delegates gathered each year. As Gyandendra Pandey has observed, by denying legitimacy to the claims of communities, all-India nationalism often seemed to adopt its own 'statist perspective', not unlike the stance that 'colonialism had favoured and promoted for its own reasons'.[30] The reluctance of Congressmen to engage with the 'irrational' cultural politics of their fellow countrymen only strengthened these politics and encouraged its leaders to try to wrest the party from their control. In the 1890s, the Indian Nationalist leader Lokmanya Tilak (1856–1920) led a vociferous campaign against the state's interference in the 'private domain' of Hindu religious and family life when a Parsi social reformer introduced a bill seeking to raise the age of consent of Hindu girls, and when government officers, trying to stamp out the plague, entered the inner sanctums of Hindu homes and manhandled women. This encouraged an upsurge of an exclusively Hindu nationalism concerned to protect 'authentic' Indian cultural values preserved and embedded (or so it was claimed) in the Hindu family and personified by the Hindu wife.[31]

These regional, religious, and cultural nationalisms continued to grow in the twentieth century. Tamil 'language-devotion'[32] spread in southern India, and the piquant carryings-on of theosophists in Adyar captured many imaginations.[33] When the viceroy Lord Curzon partitioned Bengal in 1905, it sparked a widespread campaign to restore Bengali 'national unity'. The *swadeshi* movement pioneered new methods of mobilizing popular support, but it also deployed discourses of nationalism replete with regional and religious resonances.[34] Terrorist societies sprang up, chiefly in Bengal but also in western India and the Punjab, whose purpose was to drive the British out of India by gun and grenade, by assassinating key British officials. Particularly in Bengal, these terrorist groups conceived of India as the personification of a Hindu deity—the mother goddess. They saw it as their religious duty to defend and protect the motherland, and barred Muslims from joining them. By 1907 the Congress itself had split as a result of increasingly violent challenges from leaders of demotic movements determined to force it to adopt a more 'extremist' stance towards the Raj. For his part, Tilak struck up an unlikely alliance with the Irish theosophist leader, Annie Besant, to set up 'Home Rule Leagues', chiefly in western and southern India, to bring the two divided wings together under a more strident leadership.

In the same period, movements emerged that explicitly challenged the claim of the Congress to represent them. In western India, protest movements of lower castes were organized and gained strength.[35] In the United Provinces, already in 1888, Sayyid Ahmed Khan excoriated Congress as a party representing Bengal's Hindu service groups, and urged his North Indian Muslim supporters to steer well clear of it. This influential constituency, despite its small numbers, pressed the British to give Muslims special safeguards to ensure their jobs remained secure and their voices heard under the new regime. In 1906 the British granted Muslims separate representation in the councils. In the same year the Muslim League was created, claiming to speak for the 'Muslim nation'. But this claim was no sooner made than challenged: Muhammad and Shaukat Ali, alumni of the Aligarh College established by Sayyid Ahmed Khan, attacked his tactical loyalism and 'apologetic' modernism,[36] and in 1914 launched the 'Khilafat' campaign to save the caliphate and protect the holy places of Islam. And in the same period, the Justice Party in the south denounced the Congress as representing the self-interest of Brahmins.

All of this suggests an efflorescence of movements that defied the civic and territorial conception of India put forward by the moderate Congress. When the First World War broke out, it was hardly plausible to speak of the Congress as representing the 'mainstream' of Indian nationalism. Or if it was the mainstream, it was a rather narrow and shallow waterway.

Wars, Reforms, and Mass Politics: Nationalisms in the Age of Gandhi

India paid a heavy price for the Allied war effort, both in terms of men and money. After the war, peasants hit by wartime fluctuations in prices and interruptions in the supplies of essential commodities, demobilized soldiers sent home after service in European and other overseas theatres of war, heavily taxed traders and businessmen, and many others who had previously little to do with the politics of the Congress now began to look to it as a vehicle for expressing their discontent. The membership of the Home Rule League movement, absorbed into the Congress when Tilak wrested control over it in 1916, swelled to about 60,000. All over India there were sporadic outbreaks of political unrest. Particularly alarming to the British were signs that even the Punjab, a bastion of loyalism and the chief recruiting ground for the Indian army, was succumbing to the new mood. So instead of lifting draconian wartime controls, government extended the 'Defence of India Regulations' into peacetime, suspending indefinitely such rights to political expression as their Indian subjects had. When in April 1919, General Dyer ordered troops to fire upon peaceful protesters against these measures in the Punjabi city of Amritsar, it showed just how nervous the British had again become about their hold over India. This massacre at Jallianwalabagh, seen by British die-hards as the necessary whiff of grapeshot to quell a new rebellion, provoked revulsion among Indians all over the country.

Yet the idea of 'all-India' as a nation remained vulnerable. Unrest in town and countryside alarmed the big men of the localities on whom the British depended for control on the ground, and many now denounced extremist politics and distanced themselves from the Congress. With its usual tactic of combining carrot with stick, the government, with its Act of 1920, devised reforms intended to rally moderate Indian politicians into the provincial Councils—where under 'dyarchy' they would have a say in some aspects of local affairs—and undermine such fragile 'all-India' political unities as still survived.

This was the political scene to which Mahatma Gandhi returned from South Africa. His career is too complex, his impact too ambiguous, and his philosophy too elusive to be easily summarized: the more modest purpose here will be to touch upon his role in the development of all-India nationalism. Paradoxically, the Mahatma himself was not a nationalist, particularly if one accepts Breuilly's definition of nationalisms as political movements that seek state power. He had little faith in the power of the state to improve the lot of the people. He was no admirer of democracy and he was a profound critic of classical liberal ideas of economic development and social progress. He saw himself more as a social and religious reformer than a political leader. Yet there is no question that Gandhi contributed significantly to the growth of all-India nationalism.

That Gandhi encouraged the all-India Congress to demand full independence is well known, but he was not the first Indian to call for '*swaraj*', or self-rule. Just as the 'educator-intellectuals' of the nineteenth century before him, Gandhi too grappled with the conundrum of why the British had been able to conquer India. But his conclusion was radically different from theirs. In his seminal 1908 treatise, *Hind Swaraj*, he insisted that British rule in India rested not on conquest, but on the collusion and collaboration of Indians seduced by Western materialism and the false promise of modernity. If Indians withdrew their cooperation from the Raj—as they should, he later argued, when the Khilafat and Punjab 'wrongs' convinced him that it was both perfidious and morally bankrupt—it could not survive. In 1920, at the Congress session in Nagpur, he urged Indians not to cooperate with British rule, and non-violently refuse to obey its 'unjust' laws:

> If . . . the acts of . . . the Government be wrong . . . it is clear that we must refuse to submit to this official violence. Appeal to Parliament by all means if necessary, but if the parliament fails us and we are worthy to call ourselves a nation, we must refuse to uphold the Government by withdrawing cooperation from it.[37]

In a crucially important intervention, Gandhi urged Congressmen—and all Indians with political influence in the provinces—to boycott the new provincial Councils promised by the Government of India Act of 1920. At Nagpur, his 'non-cooperation' resolution was passed by a Congress session packed with angry Muslim Khilafatists, and backed by all manner of politicians who calculated that they would not do well in the elections, under the franchise carefully calibrated by the British, to the reformed Councils. By skilful and opportunistic tactics within a brilliant grand strategy, Gandhi captured Congress, outflanking many Congress leaders who were puzzled by his idiosyncracies, alarmed by his alliance with Muslim Khilafat supporters, and unconvinced of the merits of standing back from elected Councils in the provinces.

When he launched the non-cooperation movement a year later, Gandhi promised that it would achieve *swaraj* within twelve months. He was confident the ordinary people of India—who, in his view, had remained closer to the spiritual values of Indian civilization than the country's urban elites[38]—would quickly grasp his message of *satyagraha*[39] and non-violent resistance, and that British rule would simply collapse in the face of their resolve. He was wrong, of course. But the movement gained a far larger, more broad-based and disparate following than anything the Congress had achieved before. In part, as Judith Brown notes, this had to do with the fact that Gandhi had in certain regions enlisted powerful supporters (she describes them as 'sub-contractors')—rich peasants in Gujarat, prohibitionists in Karnataka, and Khilafatists in Bengal and North India- who were able to mobilize, albeit temporarily, networks of support behind impressive local campaigns.

But it would be a mistake to account for the successes of the movement—and indeed of the civil disobedience campaigns of the early 1930s—in terms of enlisting these networks. Gandhi couched his political message in a language—both symbolic and semantic—that ordinary people in India understood and could themselves deploy. In 1902, when the intellectual, civil servant, and politician Romesh Dutt (1848–1909) wrote of the destruction of Indian handicrafts, he did so in terms that could only be grasped by fellow intellectuals. When Gandhi stopped wearing suits woven on British looms and instead wore a strip of cloth he had himself made using a simple spinning wheel, he powerfully drew attention to the predicament of weavers and artisans under British rule. For many centuries in the traditions of subcontinental statecraft, the ideals of just rule had been to tax fairly, judiciously, and above all lightly, to patronize handicrafts, and to husband the wealth of the land. By his symbolic adoption of the spinning wheel and *khadi* (hand-woven cloth), Gandhi advertised to every Indian that British rule was amoral and illegitimate. So also when Gandhi urged Indians to break the government's monopoly over the production of salt, he drew attention symbolically (since the cess on salt was minuscule) to the unjustly high burden of taxation that British rule had placed on India. But since salt was also a metaphor for the symbiotic relations of obligation and loyalty that bound rulers and subjects, in urging the people to make their own salt, Gandhi sent out a highly charged signal that India's people should withdraw their fealty to their white overlords. As Rajnarayan Chandavarkar has suggested, India's working classes were often inspired by Gandhi's rhetoric because he was able to develop 'the blandest metaphor and the most platitudinous axiom in a distinctly subversive direction'.[40]

Ironically, however, Gandhi's very success in becoming the Mahatma of the masses compromised his hold over some sections of the Congress Party. Mass movements alarmed powerful elements in Indian society whose support was crucial for any political party seeking to capture and hold on to power in the subcontinent. 'Subaltern' movements against the establishment tended to follow moral and political imperatives quite different from those of their ostensible leaders,[41] as Shahid Amin showed in his study of Chauri Chaura.[42] In this hamlet in the obscure north Indian district of Gorakhpur, local villagers, believing Gandhi's victory would usher in a new utopia, burnt Indian policemen alive for standing in their way as they put their station to the torch in February 1922. This was only the most dramatic instance of widespread violence and disorder that prompted some monied men to rethink their support for Gandhi's campaign. But when Gandhi called off the movement because he could not control the growing tide of violence, it bewildered and disappointed some of his staunchest allies, most of whom did not subscribe to his religious views but had backed him because they believed that non-cooperation would drive the British out of India.[43]

The movement of 1921–2 thus ended in confusion. While Gandhi returned to his *ashram* to concentrate on his campaign against untouchability and for the 'reconstruction' of villages, most powerful provincial leaders ditched non-cooperation and elected for a different strategy—to join the Councils, ostensibly to wreck them from within, but in practice to exercise such power as they could inside the system. Provincial parties and provincial questions dominated the politics of the 1920s, much as the British had intended them to do. Until 1929, when Lord Simon's visit to India heralded a new round of reforms, politics at the all-India level seemed to have lost all momentum.

However, the Congress Party, and its all-India ambitions, survived these years of fragmentation and disillusionment, not least because of Gandhi's success in transforming its structures. At the Nagpur session of 1920, he had persuaded Congress to accept a new constitution that gave it a permanent all-India executive, a small Working Committee of fifteen leaders. The party, and its provincial and district committees with their much enlarged membership, were henceforth subordinated to the control of this new body, which until his death, Gandhi continued to dominate through his allies and disciples. Step by step, the Working Committee riveted its hold over the party. By reordering the party structure to fit linguistic (rather than British administrative) boundaries, it qualified the authority of regional leaders over their fiefdoms—particularly those of the large Bombay and Bengal presidencies. This did not put an end to regionalist pressures; on the contrary, these so-called 'linguistic provinces' opened up new fissures, dividing the Hindi-speaking north from the south and east. Nor did the central high command succeed in imposing even a semblance of ideological conformity over this growing party in which socialists, Hindu nationalists, and the supporters of innumerable regional and cultural causes, found fertile ground when its doors were opened to 'six-anna' members. Yet between 1920 and 1947, the Working Committee was able to exercise strong central authority and impose a measure of discipline and unity upon what was, by the very nature of Indian politics, a loosely organized, divided, and fractious party. The Congress high command spectacularly deployed its control in the elections of 1937, in pulling provincial ministries out of office in 1939, and in the negotiations for the transfer of power after the end of the Second World War.

So when the all-white Simon commission came to India in 1929 to take reforms in governance to the next stage, the Congress Party was quickly able to gear itself up for a new wave of civil disobedience under Gandhi in order to push for more power for Indians at the centre. Historians have sometimes drawn a misleading dichotomy between Gandhi's strategy of agitational politics and mass mobilization, and the commitment of other Congress politicians, including his closest allies, to the constitutional path to achieve the goals of all-India nationalism. In fact Gandhi's movements—whether 'non-cooperation' or 'civil disobedience' (or the 'quit India' movement of 1942)—strengthened the hand of the constitutionalists in their parleying with the British. Each wave of popular protest helped paper over their divisions and enabled Congress thereafter to successfully contest elections. The threat of mass action stepped up pressure on the British to make further concessions to the nationalists. In turn this boosted the Congress's portrayal of itself as an effective vehicle through which local leaders could have some political influence at the centre. Agitation and the politics of constitutionalism were thus two sides of a single Congress campaign to wrest control from the British Raj.

However in the 1930s Congress assaults upon the edifice of British power evoked serious challenges to its claim to speak for all India. In 1928, before the Simon Commission started its work, Congress in the Nehru Report had put forward its vision for a future constitution for India—a civic vision based on individual rights, universal franchise, and joint electorates. It also called for doing away with the safeguards for special interests that had been a feature of British India's reformed institutions. Mohammed Ali Jinnah, emerging now as the spokesman of Muslim interests, took issue with aspects of the Nehru Report in his famous Fourteen Points. A gulf began to open up between the Congress Party's unitarist vision of an independent India and those who feared that such a state would ride roughshod over the concerns of minority groups, chiefly Muslims. At the heart of this divide was the question of group rights: what rights, if any, would minority communities (whether defined by religion, caste, or region) exercise inside the larger India, and how would these be reconciled with principles of majority rule? Congress's response to this thorny question was not reassuring or clear-cut. Gandhi's proposed solution of good 'neighbourliness'[44] did not win credence even among his most amenable Hindu disciples, and his Muslim friends had long deserted him once the Khilafat-non-Cooperation alliance had broken down. Besides, Gandhi's religious politics were increasingly at odds with the rest of the Congress. The Congress high command found itself 'neither accepting nor rejecting' McDonald's Communal Award of 1932, which reserved fixed proportions of seats for minorities in the about-to-be reformed provincial assemblies. Much to the consternation of Dr B. R. Ambedkar, leader of the 'untouchables' or 'Scheduled Castes', Gandhi went on a fast unto death to prevent the implementation of plans to give them separate representation.

After the outbreak of the Second World War, when its rulers made India a combatant without even the pretence of consultation, the Congress, exploiting Britain's wartime troubles, demanded an immediate share of power at the centre. But Jinnah's ambiguous Lahore Resolution of 1940 calling for an ill-defined Pakistan gave Winston Churchill the excuse he wanted to put the question of India's future into cold storage. For the Congress leadership, Jinnah and his demands were an unwelcome distraction. Those on the left, Jawaharlal Nehru among them, tended to brush the League aside, dismissing it as unrepresentative and denouncing the Resolution as the self-serving, anti-democratic posturing of 'backward-looking' elites. Those on the right denounced Jinnah's demands as illegitimate—even treasonous—attacks on *Akhand Bharat* (the 'integrity of the nation'). While the British gave tacit encouragement to Jinnah and his implausible claims to speak for a united 'Muslim nation', Nehru and his fellow Congress leaders made the mistake of dismissing the Lahore Resolution as irrelevant. They ignored the growing movement for a Pakistan that appeared to stand for Muslim particularisms, provincialisms, and group rights, all threats to the unitary state these Congressmen were determined to capture in its entirety.

The Second World War shattered Britain's metropolitan economy and fundamentally altered the equations of profit and power that had for so long sustained the Raj in India. It destroyed its capacity and will to hold onto an empire ravaged by famine and by swelling tides of political unrest and communal violence. Another casualty of the war were the Conservatives in Britain who had wanted to hang onto India. After Labour won the elections in 1945, Clement Attlee's government declared its intent to transfer power to Indians as soon as possible, and the 'end game' had begun. But in that game, the power, priorities, and timetables of the players underwent a sea change. During the war, London had wanted to hang onto power in India and found Muslim demands a convenient bulwark against Congress. So it had made promises to Muslims and Indian princes that their concerns would be addressed in the final settlement of India's future. After the war, however, when London wanted to get out of India as quickly as possible, it could not ignore the 'Muslim question'. For its part, with the capture of the centralized apparatus of the British Raj almost within its grasp, the Congress leadership grew ever more inflexible about making any concessions to Muslims which might weaken that state and encourage particularist demands by others. Whereas the Congress had always insisted that India was indivisible, now it changed tack. In the complex tripartite negotiations for the transfer of power in 1946 and early 1947, the Congress high command settled for a limited partition that would cut out the troublesome Muslim-majority districts in the west and east and allow them to inherit the rest of British India with all its powers at the centre intact.

In arriving at this momentous decision, there was a rare unanimity between Congress leaders: liberals, socialists, and those of the Hindu Right all backed the high command's line. It also had the support of Hindu nationalists in Bengal, the largest Muslim-majority province—who refused to be subjected to 'Muslim rule' and demanded a partition (ironically not dissimilar to Curzon's partition of 1905) that would give them a homeland of their own inside a divided India.[45] The departing Viceroy, Lord Mountbatten, lacked the vision or the will to resist a solution that offered Britain a quick exit from a desperate and dangerous situation. With his particular combination of opportunism and vainglory, he persuaded London to accept the Congress's demand for a limited partition, pushed it through, and presented it to India and the world as his own idea.

Pakistan was thus the product as much of the Congress's long-term imperatives as the contingencies of the last years of British Rule. The Congress Party's single-minded unitarism forced a de-territorialized 'Muslim nation' into a 'moth-eaten and truncated' state, carved, as if by an inexpert butcher, out of those parts of the empire that its leaders no longer wanted nor could control.

And so we have the final paradox of all-India nationalism encapsulated by the Congress: its determination to inherit the mighty imperial state constructed by the British in India led to the division of that empire. That partition was the outcome of a curious and covert political entente between the weak and unprincipled Viceroy of a declining imperial power, 'civic' nationalists in a hurry to achieve independence with a strong centre, Hindu cultural nationalists in Bengal determined to protect its unique 'genius', and leaders of the Hindu right keen to purge Mother India of Muslim traitors. The consequence of partition was the creation of two warring nation states, both of whose membership was defined and vitiated, in crucial and complex ways, by religious identity.[46]

Conclusion

This essay has argued that all-India civic or territorial nationalism which the Indian National Congress represented did not defeat other rival solidarities—whatever its apologists might insist—and that these continued to multiply and flourish.

Nor did all-India nationalism decisively win victory over British imperialism. The British quit India in 1947 for a host of reasons, not least because their ability to hold on to it had been weakened by the war. Nationalist pressure was one among many factors that eroded Britain's will to hold on to India, but it did not drive the British out of India by mobilizing an irresistible mass movement. All-India nationalists did inherit control over a strong centralized state when the British left in 1947. But the India they achieved was not the prize for which they had striven for so long. Its inclusiveness had been fractured beyond repair by a partition based on religious identities that left millions stranded on the wrong side of frontiers of one or other of two (and later three) nation states, where they have failed to receive protection or achieve full citizenship.[47]

This essay has also sought to show that all-India nationalism did not follow a linear path. The complex circumstances in which it was born also produced a number of other competing allegiances and nationalisms that it never wholly subsumed. In the sixty years since the transfer of power, governments of independent India have in various ways worked to bring about 'the emotional integration of India', precisely because 'India' never was wholly united behind its nationalism, and because 'the nation' was imagined by its people in many contradictory ways. Pakistan too has struggled to produce unities between disparate regions and peoples, to manufacture a nation that could sustain an inherently weak state. It has not succeeded in this enterprise, as the subsequent secession of the majority of its population and the birth of Bangladesh in 1971 demonstrates. India has had a rather better record in nation building, not least because its government has deployed the attributes of sovereignty and the strong state it inherited to promote mass literacy and a 'national' curriculum within an increasingly integrated economy. New generations of nationalist intellectuals have lent India's leaders a hand by writing nationalist annals of 'all-India'. Yet at no stage in its history has independent India been free from serious challenges from rival 'national' claims. India has survived as a nation state through a process of continual renegotiation, but also, at critical junctures, through New Delhi's brutal suppression of movements deemed to be 'anti-national'. There are, therefore, many good reasons why the conventional teleology of Indian nationalism calls to be reassessed if its history, nature, and prospects are to be properly understood.

Notes

1. B. Anderson (1983) *Imagined Communities: Reflections on the Origins and Spread of Nationalism*, London.
2. J. Breuilly (1994) *Nationalism and the State*, Chicago, IL, 183.
3. C. A. Bayly (1998) *The Origins of Nationality in South Asia: Patriotism and Ethical Government in the Making of Modern India*, Oxford, 1998.
4. Dufferin to Kimberley, 26 April 1886, cited in A. Seal (1971) *The Emergence of Indian Nationalism: Competition and Collaboration in the Later Nineteenth Century*, Cambridge, 185.

5. The so-called 'school' includes J. Gallagher and A. Seal and their students: including D. Washbrook, (1976) *The Emergence of Provincial Politics: The Madras Presidency 1870–1920*, Cambridge; G. Johnson (1973) *Provincial Politics and Indian Nationalism: Bombay and the Indian National Congress 1880–1915*, Cambridge; C. Baker (1976) *The Politics of South India 1920–1937*, Cambridge; F. C. R. Robinson (1974) *Separatism among Indian Muslims: The Politics of the United Provinces' Muslims, 1860–1923*, Cambridge; B. R. Tomlinson (1976) *The Indian National Congress and the Raj, 1929–1942*, Cambridge; and J. Brown (1977) *Gandhi's Rise to Power*, Cambridge, and (1977) *Gandhi and Civil Disobedience*, Cambridge; and C. Bayly (1975) in his early work on the *Local Roots of India Politics: Allahabad 1880–1920*, Oxford. All these historians have made quite distinctive and individual contributions, but they began by sharing some common premises and their conclusions, in some respects, point in similar directions.
6. Recent works that have done something to restore the balance include P. Chatterjee (1986) *Nationalist Thought and the Colonial World: A Derivative Discourse*, London, and (1994) *The Nation and its Fragments*, Princeton; also see S. Khilnani (1997) *The Idea of India*, London.
7. C. A. Bayly (2007) 'Rammohun Roy and the Advent of Constitutional Liberalism in India, 1800–1830', *Modern Intellectual History*, 4, no. 1.
8. J. Rosselli (1980) 'The Self-Image of Effeteness: Physical Education and Nationalism in Nineteenth-Century Bengal', *Past and Present*, 86, February.
9. A. Sartori (2003) 'The Categorical Logic of a Colonial Nationalism: Swadeshi Bengal, 1904–1908', in *Comparative Studies of South Asia, Africa and the Middle East*, 23, no. 1, 275.
10. M. Goswami (2004) *Producing India: From Colonial Economy to National Space*, Chicago, IL; S. Ramaswamy (2008) 'Maps, Mother Goddesses and Martyrdom in Modern India', *Journal of Asian Studies*, 67, no. 3.
11. S. Wolpert (1989) *Tilak and Gokhale*, Oxford, 135–6. Emphasis added.
12. See for example, B. C. Pal (1916) *Nationality and Empire*, Calcutta and Simla, 47 and *passim*; and also Sartori, 'Swadeshi Bengal', 275–7.
13. See Tilak's work of the same name, published in 1903.
14. D. Gilmartin (1998) 'Partition, Pakistan and South Asian History: In Search of a Narrative', *Journal of Asian Studies*, 57, no. 4.
15. Schools and colleges were seedbeds of the new generations of nationalists: Surendranath Banerjea, a key figure in the early Congress, taught at the largest school on Calcutta and became 'the uncrowned king of students'. Seal, *Emergence*, 216.
16. Anthony Smith's distinction between 'educator-intellectuals' and 'secular intelligentsias' has relevance in the Indian context. A. D. Smith (1983) *Theories of Nationalism*, London, xxii–xxiii.
17. For the everyday humiliation of the Western-educated Indians employed in offices in early twentieth-century Bengal, see S. Sarkar (1992) '"Kaliyuga", "Chakri" and "Bhakti": Ramakrishna and his Times', *Economic and Political Weekly*, 26, no. 29.
18. Cited in Seal, *Emergence*, 165.
19. R. Ray (1984) *Social Conflict and Political Unrest in Bengal, 1875–1927*, New Delhi; S. Sarkar (2000) *Modern India 1885–1947*, New Delhi, 22–4.
20. E. Kedourie (1974) *Nationalism*, London.

21. G. Grierson (1889) *The Modern Vernacular Literature of Hindustan*, Calcutta, cited in C. A. Bayly (1999) *Empire and Information: Intelligence Gathering and Social Communication in India*, Cambridge, 343.
22. A typical reaction was that of Dinshaw Wacha, another Parsi founding father of the Congress, who wrote to Naoroji in 1891 expressing his horror at 'European murders of Natives'. Sarkar, *Modern India*, 22.
23. Seal, *Emergence*, 147, 278 n.
24. Cited in Seal, *Emergence*, 147.
25. R. C. Dutt (1900) *Open Letters to Curzon on Famines and Land Assessments in India*, London; see also his classic (1900) *Economic History of India under Early British Rule*, London.
26. D. Naoroji (1901) *Poverty and Un-British Rule in India*, London.
27. B. Chandra (1966) *The Rise and Growth of Economic Nationalism in India: Economic Policies of Indian National Leadership, 1880–1905*, New Delhi.
28. Resolution XIII of the Allahabad Congress of 1888 held that 'no subject shall be passed for discussion to any Congress by the president thereof if the introduction of which the Hindu or Muslim delegates object unanimously or nearly unanimously'.
29. A. Skaria (2002) 'Gandhi's Politics: Liberalism and the Question of the Ahram', *South Atlantic Quarterly*, 101, no. 4.
30. G. Pandey (1990) *The Construction of Communalism in Colonial North India*, Delhi, 253.
31. T. Sarkar (2001) *Hindu Wife, Hindu Nation: Community, Religion and Cultural Nationalism*, New Delhi.
32. S. Ramaswami (1997) *Passions of the Tongue: Language Devotion in Tamil India, 1891–1970*, Berkeley.
33. P. Van der Veer (2001) *Imperial Encounters*, Princeton, NJ.
34. See S. Sarkar (1973) *The Swadeshi Movement in Bengal, 1903–1908*, New Delhi; Sartori, 'Swadeshi Bengal'; and Goswami, *Producing India*.
35. R. O'Hanlon (1985) *Caste, Conflict and Ideology*, Cambridge.
36. F. Devji (2007) 'Apologetic Modernity', *Modern Intellectual History*, 4, no. 1.
37. Brown, *Gandhi's Rise to Power*, 245.
38. On Gandhi's notion of 'Indian civilization', see R. Fox (1989) *Gandhi's Utopia: Experiments with Culture*, Boston, MA.
39. Satyagraha is usually translated as 'truth force': for its subtler and broader meanings, from Gandhi's perpective, see Skaria, 'Gandhi's Politics'.
40. R. Chandavarkar (1998) *Imperial Power and Popular Politics*, Cambridge.
41. Inspired by Antonio Gramsci, members of the *Subaltern Studies* collective argue that 'subaltern' agency and consciousness remained 'relatively autonomous' from that of the elites who attempted to mobilize them in the name of the nation, and should thus not be subsumed within, or subordinated to, the history of 'the nation'. See Guha's introduction in R. Guha (ed.) (1982) *Subaltern Studies I*, Delhi.
42. S. Amin (1995) *Event, Metaphor, Memory: Chauri-Chaura 1922–1992*, Delhi.
43. See, for instance, Nehru's description of his 'amazement and consternation' at the suspension of the movement. J. Nehru (1936) *An Autobiography*, London, 80–1.
44. With 'neighbourly' good will and generosity on all sides, Gandhi believed that a righteous balance could be achieved between the legitimate claims of different sections of Indian society. Skaria, 'Gandhi's Politics'.

45. J. Chatterji (1994) *Bengal Divided: Hindu Communalism and Partition, 1932–1947*, Cambridge.
46. V. Zamindar (2007) *The Long Partition and the Making of Modern South Asia*, New York.
47. J. Chatterji (forthcoming) *Democracy and Disinheritance in India and Pakistan.*

Suggested Further Reading

Amin, S. (1995) *Event, Metaphor, Memory: Chauri-Chaura 1922–1992*, Berkeley, CA.
Baker, C. (1976) *The Politics of South India 1920–1937*, Cambridge.
Bayly, C. A. (1975) *Local Roots of India Politics, Allahabad 1880–1920*, Oxford.
Bayly, C. A. (1998) *The Origins of Nationality in South Asia: Patriotism and Ethical Government in the Making of Modern India*, Oxford.
Brown, J. (1972) *Gandhi's Rise to Power*, Cambridge.
Brown, J. (1977) *Gandhi and Civil Disobedience*, Cambridge.
Chandra, B (1966) *The Rise and Growth of Economic Nationalism in India: Economic Policies of Indian National Leadership, 1880–1905*, New Delhi.
Chatterjee, P. (1986) *Nationalist Thought and the Colonial World: A Derivative Discourse*, London.
Chatterjee, P. (1994) *The Nation and its Fragments*, Princeton, NJ.
Dutt, R. C., (1900) *Open Letters to Curzon on Famines and Land Assessments in India*, London.
Dutt, R. C., (1902) *Economic History of India under Early British Rule*, London.
Fox, R. (1989) *Gandhi's Utopia: Experiments with Culture*, Boston, MA.
Khilnani, S. (1997) *The Idea of India*, London.
Naoroji, D. (1901) *Poverty and Un-British Rule in India*, London.
Pal, B. C. (1916) *Nationality and Empire*, Calcutta and Simla.
Robinson, F. (1974) *Separatism among Indian Muslims: The Politics of the United Provinces' Muslims, 1860–1923*, Cambridge.
Sarkar, S. (1973) *The Swadeshi Movement in Bengal, 1903–1908*, New Delhi.
Seal, A. (1971) *The Emergence of Indian Nationalism: Competition and Collaboration in the Later Nineteenth Century*, Cambridge, 118–19.
Washbrook, D. (1976) *The Emergence of Provincial Politics: The Madras Presidency 1870–1920*, Cambridge.

CHAPTER 13

THE ORIGINS OF SOUTHEAST ASIAN NATIONS: A QUESTION OF TIMING

DAVID HENLEY

THE subject of this chapter is the history of nations and nationalism in Southeast Asia up to the end of the period of European colonialism in that region—that is, up to approximately 1950. Southeast Asia is the region east of India, south of China, north of Australia, and west of Papua New Guinea. In land area it is about half the size of Europe; in population, three quarters of the size (although this proportion was smaller in the past). Today it comprises the ten countries of ASEAN (Association of South East Asian Nations)—Myanmar (Burma), Thailand, Laos, Cambodia, Vietnam, Malaysia, Singapore, Indonesia, Brunei, and the Philippines—together with the new state (and aspiring ASEAN member) East Timor. A complex topography, combined with multiple prehistoric immigration streams, a polycentric pattern of indigenous state formation, a historic openness to foreign commerce and cultures, and more than four hundred years of competitive intervention by five European powers, have made Southeast Asia a region of intricate ethnic and political fragmentation. Partly for this reason it has proved—like eastern Europe, another complex, volatile, post-imperial region beloved of scholars of nationalism—a productive nursery for ideas about the nature and origins of nations, most notably in the work of Benedict Anderson.

This short chapter cannot claim comprehensive coverage of its topic. Nor does it aspire to balanced treatment of the various countries of the region, although each of the modern nations receives at least some attention. More complete factual accounts of the story of nationalism, particularly anticolonial nationalism, in Southeast Asia can be found elsewhere. (For fuller accounts, see Suggested Further Reading.) Here, instead, the origins of Southeast Asian nations are explored with particular reference to the two largest colonial states of the region, Dutch Indonesia and French Indochina, and in the context of two theoretical questions, one arising from a fundamental debate in the study of nationalism, the other from an influential theory of nationalism developed in a specifically Southeast Asian context.

The first question is the vexed one of antiquity: how old are nations? Specifically: do Southeast Asian nations pre-date the spread to Asia of the formal doctrine of political nationalism, developed in Europe in the eighteenth and nineteenth centuries, which holds that every nation has a right to its own sovereign state? The second, and closely related, question is this: why did one of the two giant colonial states of Southeast Asia, the Dutch East Indies, become a single independent nation (Indonesia) whereas the other, French Indochina, split upon independence into three nation states (Vietnam, Cambodia, and Laos)? Was it, as nationalists in all four countries usually claim, because both outcomes were predetermined by centuries of pre-colonial history? Or was it, as Anderson proposed in his seminal book *Imagined Communities*, because the decentralized structure of colonial institutions in Indochina made it difficult for Viet, Khmer (Cambodian), and Lao anticolonialists to see themselves as belonging to a single national community, as their Javanese, Malay, and Dayak counterparts did in Indonesia? Do the origins of today's Southeast Asian nations, in other words, lie in indigenous affinities and solidarities? Or are they to be found in the dynamics of Western expansion in the region, and the reaction against it?

Two Types of Southeast Asian Nation?

At first sight, the answer to both questions seems straightforward: it depends on which part of Southeast Asia we are looking at. In broad terms, the major modern nation states of *mainland* Southeast Asia—Burma, Thailand, Cambodia, and Vietnam—can all plausibly trace their origin to a major pre-colonial state that was, in turn, associated with a particular ethnicity and language: Bamar (Burmese), Thai, Khmer, Viet (Kinh). Only the 'residual' nation of Laos, consisting originally of that part of French Indochina which lay beyond, or at the margins of, the spheres of influence of pre-colonial Vietnam and Cambodia, and was culturally and sometimes politically closer to Siam (Thailand), is harder to see as the linear successor to an indigenous state. In one case, that of Thailand, the line of descent from pre-colonial kingdom to independent nation appears unbroken, since Thailand is the only country in the tropical world that never came under European rule. In the other cases there was a more or less lengthy colonial interlude (Burma: 1885–1947; Cambodia: 1863–1953; Vietnam: 1884–1954) during which the indigenous state was either abolished or reduced to the status of a powerless 'protectorate', but the memory of its independence continued to inspire and shape anticolonial movements.

By contrast, the major countries of *island* or *maritime* Southeast Asia—Malaysia, Indonesia, and the Philippines—all owe their borders to colonial states (respectively

British, Dutch, and Spanish) rather than pre-colonial kingdoms. West (peninsular) Malaysia became independent from Britain as the Federation of Malaya in 1957; East Malaysia, comprising the British territories in Borneo, joined it in 1963. Indonesian independence was declared in 1945, and recognized by the Dutch in 1949. In the Philippines a vigorous nationalist movement directed against Spanish rule developed before the end of the nineteenth century, and an attempt was made to form an independent republic in 1898. Soon afterward, however, the country came under American rule, which lasted until 1946.

In a pattern more reminiscent of India or Africa than of the Southeast Asian mainland, these three maritime states each incorporated a large number of indigenous political and cultural units, most of them very small. In one case, that of the Philippines, the independent successor state even retained, in African or Latin American style, its colonial name, while Malaysia and Indonesia both adopted names that were neologisms constructed from European languages. The island microstates of Singapore and East Timor are equally colonial in origin. In maritime Southeast Asia it is only the little sultanate of Brunei, being the remnant of an indigenous polity that fell under British control but refused, on decolonization, to join its neighbours in the Federation of Malaysia, which possesses a direct genealogical link with the pre-colonial past.

In the European context it is common to follow Hugh Seton-Watson by distinguishing between 'old nations' such as France, England, and Russia, which 'acquired national identity or national consciousness before the formation of the doctrine of nationalism', and 'new nations' such as Italy, Belgium, and Greece, where 'two processes developed simultaneously: the formation of national consciousness and the creation of nationalist movements'.[1] In mainland Southeast Asia a long process of political centralization, fuelled by interstate conflict, led over a period of centuries to a growing uniformity of language and culture within each state, akin to that of the 'old nations' of Europe. In island Southeast Asia, by contrast, political and cultural units remained much less connected with each other, and nation-building had to wait, as it did in the 'new nations' of Europe, until the imported doctrine of popular sovereignty provided (together with resentment of foreign rule) a basis for national solidarity other than cultural affinities and historic rivalries.

So far, so good: the countries of modern mainland Southeast Asia, with the possible exception of Laos, appear to be old, gradually evolved nations, whereas those of island Southeast Asia (except Brunei) are essentially new nations, constructed by nationalists to fill the arbitrary borders of the colonial states that they challenged and ultimately inherited. When the People's Council (*Volksraad*) of the Netherlands Indies debated the introduction of 'Indonesia' as an alternative name for the colony in 1921, one (European) member described it as 'a good name for a brand of cigar'.[2]

Closer inspection, however, casts doubt on the simplicity of the old nation/new nation dichotomy. In the first place, there is doubt about the degree to which the nations of mainland Southeast Asia really possessed, before the twentieth century, the 'national consciousness' that has been attributed to their counterparts in pre-Enlightenment Europe. Lower Burma, centred on Rangoon, was annexed by the British in 1852, and Upper Burma, including Mandalay, capital of the last independent Burmese dynasty, in 1885. Yet the rise of a Burmese nationalism, as opposed to royalist resistance or agrarian unrest, is usually said to have begun only with the foundation of a movement of religious revival, the Young Men's Buddhist Association, in Rangoon (not Mandalay) in 1906. It was not until the 1920s that explicitly nationalist political organizations appeared in Burma, and not until the 1930s that the call for independence from Britain became strong.

In Thailand (Siam), as noted, the indigenous state never lost its sovereignty, successfully manoeuvring between British and French threats under its great nineteenth-century kings Mongkut (r. 1851–68) and Chulalongkorn (r. 1868–1910). Nevertheless the idea of a Thai nation, consisting of citizens and territory as well as king and subjects, may be barely older than its Burmese counterpart. Nineteenth-century Siam, although loosely associated with the Thai ethnic group, was a dynastic polity based on personal hierarchy and supernatural legitimacy rather than territorial sovereignty or mass solidarity. It was not until 1902 that the king, previously the 'Lord of Life of Siam', was referred to as ruler of *prathet thai*, or 'Thai-land'.[3] And it was not until 1939 that this became the official name of the country.

Even in the 'old nations' of Europe, as Eugen Weber memorably demonstrated in *Peasants into Frenchmen*, the creation of nation states out of dynastic states was a slow process.[4] But if Thailand is really an old nation like France or England, then it still seems hard to understand why well into the twentieth century, the Western-educated Thai king Vajiravudh (r. 1910–25) had to wage a long propaganda campaign in order to convince his own people of that fact. And if Burma is an old nation, then the apparent acquiesence of the Burmese political elite in the first decades of British rule, and the subsequent detour through religious revival en route to the eventual 'national awakening', are almost equally puzzling. As Miroslav Hroch has shown, it is in new, not old nations that agitation for national sovereignty is characteristically preceded by a preparatory phase of heightened cultural awareness among the intelligentsia.[5] Even in mainland Southeast Asia, then, it seems that the period of high colonialism and anticolonial nationalism was more than just a passing hiatus in the history of a set of old, established nations.

Turning to maritime Southeast Asia, conversely, the absence of pre-colonial polities coterminous with the colonial and post-colonial states of Malaysia, Indonesia, and the Philippines should not blind us to the fact that these nations, although originating in the first place as daring figments of the anticolonial imagination, were in some ways also prefigured, and perhaps shaped, by other types of imagined community that had nothing to do with colonialism. The Malay (Melayu) ethnic group that gave Malaysia its name, and both Malaysia and Indonesia their national languages, was already a subjectively perceived community of sorts—sometimes referred to as the *alam Melayu*, or 'Malay world'—long before its members began to see it as a focus of national solidarity. Like Germans and Italians before German and Italian unification, pre-colonial Malays were widely aware of their shared language, culture, and institutions; in some contexts, they also recognized a common origin in the historic sultanates of Sriwijaya and Malacca.

Unlike the major ethnic identities of mainland Southeast Asia, that of the Malays was shaped more by their long history of commercial interaction—the Malacca Straits, where Malay ethnicity originated, being one of the world's great arteries of trade—than by warfare and state-formation. This helps to explain why a pre-colonial ideal of Malay political solidarity was not present. By the nineteenth century, however, the Malays did share a common religion, adherence to Islam having become an essential criterion, alongside the Malay language, of Malay identity. The idea of the indigenous population as a community of Islamic believers seems to have paved the way, at least in some degree, for the idea of a political nation both in Malaysia and in Indonesia.[6] Throughout Southeast Asia, from Buddhist Burma and Thailand to the Christian Philippines, nationalist movements have in fact been associated, especially in their early years, with religious beliefs, institutions, and communities.

It may therefore be too simple to say that the nations of island Southeast Asia are colonial in origin, and those of mainland Southeast Asia indigenous. Even in the Spanish Philippines, where the dominant religious institution, the Catholic Church, was as European in origin as the state, the elite constitutionalism and Enlightenment ideals of early nationalist leaders concealed, among their followers, solidarities based on indigenous Tagalog magic and millenarianism as well as folk Catholicism and freemasonry. In what follows, the diverse origins of Southeast Asian nations and nationalism—ancient and recent, indigenous and exogenous—are explored in greater depth with the help of a comparison between Indonesia and Indochina.

Ethnogeographic Integration and Exclusion in Anticolonial Nationalism

French Indochina and the Dutch East Indies were the two giant states of colonial Southeast Asia, accounting for 60 per cent of the region's land area and almost two-thirds of its population. Both produced strong anticolonial nationalist movements, culminating in almost simultaneous declarations of independence in 1945 following the surrender of the Japanese forces that had briefly occupied the region during the Second World War.[7] There was a major difference, however. In the Dutch East Indies, nationalists had sought to unite all of the regions and ethnic groups of the colony into a single nation, and it was as one nation that Indonesia became independent. In Indochina, by contrast, existing ethnogeographic divisions were not abridged by the common reaction against French colonialism, and the independence declared in Hanoi in 1945 was not that of Indochina as a whole, but of one part only, Vietnam. The remainder of Indochina was to follow its own paths to independence as two further nations, Cambodia and Laos. The Indonesian and Indochinese responses to colonialism represent examples of what may be called 'integrative' and 'exclusive' nationalism respectively.[8]

French Indochina has been described as 'an utterly anomalous entity that owed its existence entirely to French fiat'.[9] The construction of this 'anomaly' began with the French conquest of Saigon in 1859, and was completed in 1907 with the last of a series of territorial annexations at the expense of Siam. The resulting boundaries, determined essentially by the dynamics of Franco-British imperial rivalry, encompassed diverse cultures, and also divided singular ones. Both the Buddhist kingdom of Cambodia (a remnant of the medieval Khmer Empire of which Siam was also an offshoot) and its historic adversary Dai Viet (Vietnam), Southeast Asia's only Confucian state, were incorporated, as were dozens of smaller indigenous polities and ethnic groups. The colony's western border along the Mekong, meanwhile, split the ethnic Lao, historically the people of the Mekong Valley, arbitrarily between the control of France and that of Siam, which served as a buffer state between French Indochina and British Burma. When Laos became independent in 1954, consequently, most Laotians were not Lao, and most Lao lived in Thailand.

By the same token, however, Indonesia was no less a product of European fiat. (The term 'Indonesia', meaning 'Indian Archipelago', was first coined by two British scholars in 1850.) 'Netherlands India', approximately three times larger than Indochina in area and population, was also three times longer in the making, Dutch expansion in the archipelago dating back to the seventeenth century. But Java was the only major island to come under firm Dutch territorial control before 1850, and many areas, including Hindu Bali as well as the pagan interiors of Sumatra, Borneo, and Sulawesi, remained virtually independent until the early twentieth century. More than four hundred languages were spoken within the area that the colony eventually came to encompass, while in the north and west its borders with British Malaya divided the ethnic Malays, historically the people of the Malacca Strait, between the future states of Indonesia and Malaysia, just as Indochina divided the Lao between Thailand and Laos.

It is true that twentieth-century Indonesian nationalists found some useful historical material at their disposal when they sought to project the nation back into the pre-colonial period. They could, for instance, point to evidence that the fourteenth-century state of Majapahit had possessed dependencies in many parts of the archipelago. This knowledge, however, came from colonial scholarship rather than folk memory, and reflected a politically useful coincidence rather than a real historical continuity.[10] Ironically Majapahit, as a Javanese state, was probably more useful to Indonesian nationalism as a remote abstraction than it would have been as a recent memory. In Indochina, where the Vietnamese king Minh Mang made an unpopular attempt to rule Cambodia as a puppet state in the 1830s, the memory of this imperial expansion proved a positive impediment to Indochinese unity a century later.

The idea of an Indonesian nation, as already noted, was prefigured in some respects by that of a Southeast Asian Islamic ecumene. By the beginning of the twentieth century close to 90 per cent of the inhabitants of Netherlands India were Muslims, and increasing numbers of them were travelling as pilgrims or students to Arabia and Egypt, where they were collectively known as Jawi or 'Javanese', the Arabic term for anything originating from Southeast Asia. Michael Laffan argues that their intensifying interaction with the central lands of Islam, and with each other via local and international networks of Jawi *ulama* (men learned in Islam), gave rise to a new collective consciousness in rather the same way as did colonial education and travel to Europe, and perhaps with even greater potential to inspire anticolonial sentiments.[11]

Against this, however, it must be noted that Islamic Southeast Asia included parts of what would become Malaysia, Thailand, and the Philippines as well as Indonesia, and that whatever the contribution of Islamic ecumenicalism to the spirit of anticolonial nationalism in the region, it manifestly failed to transcend the borders of colonial states. Nor was it capable of mobilizing the non-Islamic minorities within the Dutch colony. As a specific, bounded community including both Muslims and non-Muslims, the Indonesian nation was in fact coeval with the Netherlands Indies, and was conceived only as that state reached its full development in the twentieth century. Majapahit was duly invoked to help legitimate it, and even inspired fleeting dreams of expansion into Malaya and Melanesia. But the success of Malaysia in creating a separate national identity for the Malay Muslims on the peninsular side of the Malacca Strait, like the story of East (until 1975, Portuguese) Timor and its long resistance to Indonesian annexation, confirms that if what is now Indonesia had been divided between many colonial states, it could just as well have become many separate nations.

The idea of Indonesia as a 'new nation', then, stands up after all to close inspection. And if Indonesia became a single new nation because it came under the control of a single colonial state, then it remains to be explained why Vietnam, Cambodia, and Laos became (or remained) separate nations *despite* coming under the control of a single colonial state. The discussion that follows begins by making a straightforward distinction between two broad approaches to this question. Explanations that locate the origins of Indochina's disintegration in the pre-colonial past, whatever their theoretical content, are referred to here as 'perennialist'. Theories that attribute the breakup to aspects of the situation under colonial rule, conversely, are referred to as 'modernist'. Both terms are borrowed from the work of Anthony Smith, although the meaning of 'perennialism' here, as explained below, is slightly different from the way Smith uses it.[12]

Explaining the Divergence: 1. Modernist Approaches

Nations, in the modernist view, are the products of a set of technological, social, and political changes—'modernization'—which began in Europe not much earlier than the eighteenth century. For Benedict Anderson, the most important of these changes concerned the development of new media of communication.[13] It was commercial printing and mass literacy that first made it possible for people to feel themselves part of the huge, anonymous 'imagined community' of a nation. Printed news media generated a sense of shared experience and fate that had no precedent in societies based on local and personal relationships. Mass publishing gave rise to national consciousness, and the geography of 'print-capitalism' therefore determined the geography of nations.[14]

When Europe exported commercial printing to its colonies, each colonial territory typically became a discrete publishing domain, most often with the imperial language serving as the main language of the printed media and therefore as the main vehicle for national consciousness.[15] In Indochina, however, the colonial government decided to concentrate upon promoting mass literacy in the main vernacular languages—Vietnamese, Khmer, and Lao—rather than in French, which consequently could not become a language of national unity. Instead, Vietnam, Cambodia, and Laos each acquired a separate reading public. Dutch educational policy in Indonesia also favoured indigenous languages, but here one particular language, Malay, was taught even in areas where it was not the local vernacular. Although already widely spoken in trade and diplomacy in pre-colonial times, Malay became the national language of Indonesia essentially because of its systematic promotion by the colonial state, and its consequent emergence as the medium of the nationalist press and literature.[16]

A supplementary argument concerns the geography of career trajectories for indigenous students and officials in each colony.[17] The comradeship of the classroom, Anderson notes, was perceived by Indonesian students as a microcosm of the emergent nation. In the secondary schools and colleges of Dutch Java, members of a multi-ethnic elite drawn from all over the archipelago learned to see themselves as natives of the single country marked out on their classroom maps. Initially a similar situation existed in Indochina, with the best Khmer and Lao students studying alongside Vietnamese classmates in Hanoi and Saigon. Later, however, such contacts became less common as educational facilities improved in Phnom Penh and Vientiane. The Indochinese administration also had a tendency to restrict Cambodian and Laotian officials to careers in their home territories, whereas outer islanders in Indonesia could and did seek state employment in Java. Recent research has expanded on Anderson's arguments by showing how the divisive effects of French language and administrative policy were enhanced by deliberate efforts on the part of the French to cultivate a sense of separate nationhood in both Cambodia and Laos.[18] Inspired partly by a desire to insulate their Khmer and Lao subjects from the political influence of neighbouring and culturally cognate Thailand, this project was pursued through the medium of officially sponsored Buddhist religious and cultural institutions as well as through the educational system.

While Anderson's model is convincing with regard to Indonesian integration, his explanation for Indochinese disintegration does not accord with the chronology of the exclusively Vietnamese nationalist movement. For a short time at the beginning of the twentieth century, according to Anderson, the Indochinese intellectual elite in Hanoi and Saigon did indeed understand its 'Indochinese-ness' in the same way as the students who converged on Batavia and Bandung understood their common Indonesian identity.[19] It was not until after 1917, when French education policy shifted toward decentralization and the vernacular languages, that this understanding broke down. The only direct evidence supplied by Anderson to support this assertion comes from the memoirs of a Laotian leader. But it was the Vietnamese, not the Lao, who pioneered anticolonial nationalism in Indochina; and well before 1917, nationalists in Vietnam had already determined that theirs was a Vietnamese rather than an Indochinese nation.

Dating the emergence of Vietnamese nationalism is difficult because of the gradual way in which it developed out of the royalist resistance movement of the late nineteenth century. After the annexation of central and northern Vietnam in 1885, supporters of the fugitive emperor Ham Nghi continued for a time to fight against the French. Their struggle, although in itself unsuccessful, shaped the experience of the first generation of explicitly nationalist intellectuals. Phan Boi Chau, who founded Vietnam's first modern political organization in 1904, had himself been involved as a youth in the resistance of 1885, as had the second most important nationalist of his generation, Phan Chu Trinh. Such men identified themselves as Vietnamese, not Indochinese, patriots, and while they did not themselves belong to the French-educated elite discussed by Anderson, they did have a strong influence on it. Insofar as nationalists in the first three decades of the twentieth century were interested in Indochina, they saw it mainly as a gratifyingly enlarged reincarnation of Vietnam (Annam): a 'remarkable confusion of two very different geopolitical entities, the first a traditional remembrance of a unified Annamese empire . . . and the new one being a French Indochinese space'.[20] After 1930, when dissenting voices in Cambodia and Laos began to highlight the contradiction between Vietnamese nationalism and Indochinese unity, this expansionist conceit was no longer tenable.

If Anderson sees the appearance of nations as a matter of technological and cultural transformation, most modernists have seen political change as a more important factor. For John Breuilly, nations are defined and created by the phenomenon of political nationalism.[21] There are two preconditions for the appearance of such nationalism: an undemocratic state claiming sovereignty over a given territory, and the presence of an ideal of popular sovereignty according to which that state should be controlled by 'the people'. Defining this 'people' in the racial terms suggested by the discriminatory behaviour of the colonizers, nationalists usually sought to mobilize the whole indigenous population of a colonial territory in order to depose the European rulers and appropriate their state. In some cases, however, special features of the colonial system caused the anticolonial response to be deflected to the regional level and diffracted into what Breuilly calls 'sub-nationalism'. This was likely to happen if the colonial state featured devolution of administrative and representative functions to regional sub-units, and if it discriminated not only against 'natives' in general, but also between indigenous ethnic groups.[22] In French Indochina, both diffracting features were present.

Indochina was not technically a single state, but a federation of five territories: Cochinchina, Annam, Tongkin, Cambodia, and Laos. In Cochinchina, which the French annexed outright in 1867, a direct system of colonial rule was applied. In

Annam and Tongkin the Vietnamese mandarinate, complete with its system of recruitment by examination in the Confucian classics, was preserved in modified form, and in Annam the emperor himself retained vestigial powers. The Cambodian monarchy, under French protection since 1863, also survived, as did the main Laotian principalities. Each territory, moreover, had its own rudimentary representative council with indigenous membership. A second divisive feature of French colonialism in Indochina was that it employed large numbers of Vietnamese civil servants in, and encouraged Vietnamese migration to, Cambodia and Laos. The result was that many Khmer and Lao felt, in the words of Bernard Fall, 'twice colonized'—first by the French, and then by the Vietnamese.[23]

Once again, however, a crucial point here is that it was Vietnam, not Cambodia or Laos, which first made the choice against an Indochinese identity—and this despite the fact that with 72 per cent of the Indochinese population, the Vietnamese had little to fear from Khmer or Lao competition. By contrast the ethnic Javanese, with only 47 per cent of the Indonesian population in 1930, took a bigger risk when they condemned themselves to minority status by choosing the integrative option. And if the political geography of colonial Indochina was not conducive to integrative nationalism, it was not obviously conducive to a specifically Vietnamese form of exclusive nationalism either, since the old empire of Vietnam was split into three territories, Cochinchina, Annam, and Tongkin. Modernist arguments, in short, may illuminate some aspects of the fragmentation of Indochina, but are not in themselves enough to explain why anticolonial nationalism in Vietnam took an exclusive form at the outset. Another factor, without doubt, was a sense of separate Vietnamese identity inherited from before the French conquest.

Explaining the Divergence: 2. Perennialist Approaches

Most historians of Indochina have assumed, implicitly or explicitly, that Vietnam already constituted a nation well before its colonization by the French.[24] Anthony Smith uses the term 'perennialism' to indicate the view that nations, although not necessarily 'primordial' or 'natural', have figured in human affairs throughout the historical record.[25] Most writers on Vietnam are perennialists insofar as they make two claims. The first is that both the sense of community described by Anderson, and the political solidarity emphasized by Breuilly, were already found in pre-colonial Vietnam despite the absence of either citizenship or print-capitalism. The second claim, always implicit rather than explicit, is that these characteristics predestined Vietnam to become a discrete modern nation state (rather than part of one, or a collection of several) once the political and ideological environment made this possible.

The first of these claims is assessed below with the aid of comparative observations from Java. The second will be dealt with more tentatively in the following section.

Before the French annexation, an independent state had existed in what is now North Vietnam since the tenth century. After a thousand years as a Chinese province, it broke away from China in 938 and became a separate kingdom. Over the succeeding centuries this kingdom was to bear several names, including Dai Viet, Dai Nam, and, between 1804 and 1820, Viet Nam. Wars with China, which periodically attempted to recapture its lost southern possession, gave rise to unmistakably patriotic sentiments. Following the expulsion of a Chinese occupation force in 1428, to take a much-cited example, the Viet scholar and statesman Nguyen Trai wrote a poetic proclamation celebrating his country's independence of, distinctiveness from, and equality with, its northern neighbour:[26]

> Now think upon this Dai Viet land of ours;
> Truly it is a cultured nation.
> As mountain and river make for various lands,
> so our Southern ways must differ from the North.
> It was the Trieu, Dinh, Ly and Tran
> who in succession built this country.[27]
> Even as the Han, the T'ang, and Sung and Yüan,
> each was sovereign in its own domain.[28]
> Sometimes strong, sometimes weak,
> yet never lacking heroes,
> we beat the ambitious Liu Kung
> and crushed Ch'ao Chie with his dreams of grandeur.[29]

Statements like this, however, tend to be selected by historians from a great volume of more ambiguous material precisely in order to demonstrate an anticipation of modern nationalism. At times of confrontation with China, Vietnamese mandarins could certainly view the customs of their own country in a positive light. But in general they had a deep admiration for classical Chinese civilization, and found many aspects of local culture 'barbaric'. Their education concentrated almost entirely on the literature, philosophy, history, and geography of China. Their system of government, with its officials selected by examination in the Chinese classics, was modelled on China's. The language of state was Mandarin Chinese, in comparison to which vernacular Vietnamese was thought 'vulgar and inadequate'.[30] 'Confucius and Mencius are my masters, the Han Dynasty is my fatherland', ran a motto of the Vietnamese mandarinate in the nineteenth century.[31] The theme of cultural distinctiveness and pride is present in Vietnamese history before the twentieth century, but its importance fluctuated considerably, and was particularly slight under the Sinophile emperors whose reigns immediately preceded the French invasion.

Within the Vietnamese Empire, the dominant ethnic group was the Viet or Kinh. These made up the majority of the population and virtually the whole of the official class. Originally a people of the Red River delta, over the centuries they expanded down the coastal lowlands, reaching the Mekong delta by the seventeenth century. At each stage, this southward expansion was accompanied by an equivalent extension of state power. Yet the relationship between ethnicity and political allegiance in pre-colonial Vietnam was neither explicit nor direct. The gulf between the Confucian official culture and the Viet vernacular culture was not the only reason for this. Another was that as a 'middle kingdom' in its own right, the empire included substantial numbers of Tay, Muong, Cham, and many other ethnic minority groups. The key to unity was not a common national culture, but a common set of political institutions, the most important of which was the monarchy. A 'son of heaven' like his Chinese model, the Vietnamese emperor personified the state and the country. The burst of anticolonial resistance that followed the French annexation of Annam and Tongkin in 1885 was known simply as the *can vuong* or 'save the king' movement.[32]

The existence of an ethic of loyalty (*trung*) to the king was no guarantee of stability or solidarity. For more than three centuries prior to the French conquest, the history of the country was one of almost continuous conflict between the followers of rival rulers and pretenders. From 1528 to 1592 the warring Le and Mac dynasties governed separate territories, both as hereditary crowns recognized by China. From 1600 to 1775 two great 'seigneurial' families, the Trinh and the Nguyen, ruled northern and southern Vietnam respectively as separate and mutually hostile states. A descendant of the Nguyen succeeded in reunifying the country, with Siamese and French help, in 1802, but the resulting state still proved no match for the colonial onslaught when it came. In 1863 Emperor Tu Duc ordered the defenders of Cochinchina to lay down their arms as part of his policy of conciliation toward the French. When the young king Ham Nghi fled his capital in 1885, the French were able to place his brother on the throne as the first in a series of puppet emperors. Preoccupied with Confucian ideals of personal virtue, most members of the mandarinate were prepared to accept the change once it became clear that under the new regime they would still be able to play their benevolent official roles.[33] Ham Nghi was captured in 1888, and by 1897 Governor General Doumer could report that 'the whole country seems to have come to accept our administration'.[34]

What nevertheless survived from this period to inform later political movements was a clear memory of Vietnam's past independence as a single state or 'country'—*quoc*, a term derived from the Chinese *kuo*—covering the territories which the French knew as Tongkin, Annam, and Cochinchina. In nineteenth-century texts the *quoc* is almost always mentioned in conjunction with the king, the two forming 'a dual concept, the twin elements of which were rarely differentiated'.[35] But the fact that the *quoc* had a territorial dimension, being a country as well as a polity, gave it the potential to be something more than an extension of the king. The conceptual breakthrough that heralded the rise of modern nationalism in Vietnam is associated with the Duy Tan Hoi or 'Reformation Society', a secret anticolonial organization founded in 1904. The essence of the breakthrough was that, in Phan Boi Chau's words: 'the people are in fact the country, the country is the people's'.[36] Out of this idea came a new term, *quoc dan*, 'country of people': the nation.

It was under the influence of European nationalist ideas—albeit mainly as interpreted by Chinese writers—that Phan Boi Chau and his contemporaries decided that the people, not the ruler, were the foundation of the state and the source of its legitimacy. They did so at a time when intellectuals all over Asia were reaching the same conclusion. The Vietnamese situation, however, differed from that of many other colonial countries in that indigenous institutions and conceptual categories already existed to which the new ideas could be applied. The framework for the new nation was provided by the *quoc* of Vietnam: Phan Boi Chau entitled his most important essay *Viet Nam vong quoc su*, 'A history of the loss of the country of Vietnam'.[37] This *quoc* was already established as an object of loyalty and emotional attachment, even if that attachment was initially inseparable from loyalty to the king. The new order could therefore be grafted so effectively onto the old that, in retrospect, the seam is barely noticeable.

Both the strengths and the weaknesses of the perennialist argument in the Vietnamese context can be illustrated by a comparison with the group that occupied the equivalent central position in Indonesia, the Javanese. Like the Viet, the Javanese are a clearly defined and relatively homogeneous ethnic group. They occupy the greater part of the island of Java, and until recently they were not found elsewhere. All speak the same language and all accept the same ethnic label, Jawa. The Javanese have long possessed an awareness of a common history and a common homeland. Their best-known traditional historical text is called simply *Babad Tanah Jawi*, 'History of the Land of Java'.[38] Because the Javanese courts ceased to imitate foreign cultural models (in their case, Indian models) after the ninth century, and because of the wide influence of popular art forms based closely upon royal prototypes, the distance between folk and court cultures was smaller in Java than in Vietnam.

Like the Viet, the Javanese possessed an ideal of political unity. Javanese political tradition after Majapahit, according to Merle Ricklefs, was 'predicated upon the assumption that there could only be a single sovereign in Java'.[39] More clearly than in Vietnam, the ruler's divine mandate appears to have been limited to a single ethnic community: it was accepted that a separate state should exist in the west of Java, where the population spoke Sundanese rather than Javanese. Beyond Java lay other islands that might become conquests or dependencies, but which always remained foreign countries: *tanah sabrang*, 'the lands across the sea'.

In practice, the political unity of Java was not often maintained for long periods. As in Vietnam, succession conflicts and regional rebellions repeatedly divided the country. But whereas the onset of French colonialism in Vietnam happened to fall during a period of unity, the slower growth of Dutch political pressure in Java coincided with a period of disintegration. In the early seventeenth century, Sultan Agung, the 'Great Sultan', unified Java under the kingdom of Mataram. But after Agung's death in 1646, his successor Amangkurat alienated his vassals and a civil war broke out. In 1677 the Dutch East India Company intervened to support Amangkurat's son, who was helped onto the throne in return for commercial privileges. In 1740 there began another series of wars that led first to the annexation by the Company of the north coast provinces, and then in 1755 to the division of Central Java between two separate courts, Yogyakarta and Surakarta. Further fragmentation produced two more even smaller polities, making four Javanese princely states (*vorstenlanden*) in all. This partition persisted until the balance of military power was decisively tipped toward Europe in the early nineteenth century. Whereas Vietnam faced the colonial onslaught as a single state, Java did so in a condition similar to that of Vietnam a century earlier: as a pair of regional kingdoms preoccupied by their own rivalry. And by the time the ideal of popular sovereignty spread among the intelligentsia in the early twentieth century, Javanese political unity was a dim memory. In French Indochina, by contrast, Vietnamese unity remained a living ideal, inadvertently nourished by the incorporation of the emperor and much of the old imperial bureaucracy into the colonial state.

Unlike Vietnam, Java had no strong pre-colonial tradition of patriotic resistance to foreign invasion that could inspire its response to the Dutch. However, there are signs that an explicitly defensive sense of Javanese solidarity was beginning to evolve during the eighteenth century as a result of prolonged interaction with the East India Company. In the *Serat Surya Raja*, a prophetic allegory written at the court of Yogyakarta in 1774, the Muslim Javanese battle together against the infidel armies of *tanah sabrang*, symbolizing the Dutch and their allies from the outer islands.[40]

Whatever the similarities and contrasts between Java and Vietnam before the twentieth century, the idea of a Javanese nation is less speculative than it sounds. An exclusive Javanese nationalism did exist for a time in late colonial Indonesia, and in the following section it provides a starting point for an approach to integration and exclusion in anticolonial nationalism that combines modernist and perennialist elements.

Nations that Might Have Been: Java and Indochina

The choice between integrative and exclusive forms of anticolonial nationalism was seldom an immediate or unanimous one. Successful integrative movements usually had to compete at some stage with exclusive ones, and vice versa. In India, for instance, the writings of Bombay intellectuals at the turn of the century reveal an exclusively Maharashtran regional nationalism that was later absorbed into the integrative Indian nationalist movement.[41] In this way, the 'nations that might have been' leave their mark on history in the form of ephemeral ideas and organizations. From the study of such organizations, it is possible to learn more about why the conceptions of the nation for which they stood did not ultimately prevail.

The beginnings of nationalism in Indonesia are conventionally traced to Budi Utomo, an association (and later political party) founded in 1908 by graduates of colonial schools and colleges in Java. But 'nationalism in Indonesia' is not synonymous with 'Indonesian nationalism', and Budi Utomo was an exclusively Javanese organization that consistently refused to include outer islanders either in its membership or in its vision of the nation.[42] When the idea of an *Indisch*, or 'Indies' nation—the term 'Indonesia' became popular only after 1920—was subsequently promoted by the *Indische Partij*, or Indies Party, a more radical group established in 1912 and led partly by Eurasians, the reaction of many in Java was to reject it as too artificial, indeed too colonial, a concept to serve as the basis for the national 'revival' that they sought. 'Our history will develop towards the unity of the Indisch people, but not towards an Indisch national unity,' wrote Soetatmo Soeriokoesoemo of the Committee for Javanese Nationalism, sponsored by the ruler of one of Java's princely states, in 1918. 'An Indies nation—could this be attained—would again fly into fragments'; the Javanese nation could not 'sacrifice itself' in this vain cause.[43]

In the end, integrative nationalism nevertheless gained the upper hand. Budi Utomo itself accepted the principle of Indonesian unity in 1928, and dissolved itself into the Indonesian nationalist party Parindra in 1935. As Anderson suggests, one reason for the eclipse of Javanese nationalism was that the predominance of the Malay over the Javanese language, particularly in the press, prevented Java from becoming a modern communication community in its own right.[44] The centralized structure of the colonial education system also supported integration. These factors, however, were fairly constant over time and can therefore explain neither why Javanese nationalism appeared in the first place, nor why it survived for as long as it did. Budi Utomo itself adopted the Malay language for meetings and publications almost immediately after its foundation, yet did not abandon its exclusively Javanese conception of the nation until almost two decades later.

The decline of Javanese nationalism was associated not so much with the emergence of an Indonesian communication community, as with the reorientation of the Javanese intelligentsia away from cultural and social issues toward the specific political goal of independence from the Netherlands. The founders of Budi Utomo belonged to the preparatory, cultural phase of nationalism identified by Hroch as a characteristic prelude to the birth of new nations.[45] They were nationalists in the sense that they strove to unify the Javanese in the pursuit of educational and economic progress on the basis of a rekindled pride in Java's cultural heritage and historical achievements. Gradually, however, the conviction developed, in Java as elsewhere, that neither economic development nor cultural pride was compatible with the continuation of Dutch colonial rule. At this point, to quote Anthony Reid, 'the problem of imperialism itself became more interesting to most Indonesian intellectuals than a continuing search for historical identity'.[46] Dutch imperialism was not limited to Java, and the most effective way to oppose it was to form what future president Sukarno called a 'brown front', comprising all the indigenous peoples of the Dutch East Indies. With the acceptance of this principle, cultural nationalism was turned in a new, inclusive direction, embracing ethnic diversity under the motto 'unity in diversity' while promoting Malay (renamed Indonesian) as a national lingua franca.

There are signs that if Javanese nationalism had been able to 'mesh' with political institutions corresponding more closely with the geography of the Javanese nation, it might have done so and avoided dissolution. 'Javanese nationalism—that means a restoration of independent Java and thus, destruction of foreign rule,' wrote the politician and educationalist Suwardi Suryaningrat in 1917. Suwardi was an *Indisch* nationalist, but also a Javanese patriot who looked for political as well as cultural inspiration to the princely states of Central Java, where the remnants of the Mataram empire survived. 'There in the *vorstenlanden*,' he declared, 'they know what Java was, how Java was feared by foreigners, but also how Java has suffered'.[47] Had Mataram survived as a single large princely state covering much of the island, it is probable that people like Suwardi would have been able to envisage Indonesia only in the same way as some contemporary Vietnamese nationalists envisaged the future of Indochina: as a federation of independent nations. And the indications are that it would not have been difficult to generate mass support for an exclusively Javanese nationalism on the basis of an existing state. The Pakempalan Kawulo Ngayogyakarta, a royalist party led by members of the Yogyakarta royal household, was still the largest political organization in Indonesia between 1930 and 1942 despite its very limited catchment area.

But Java had indeed suffered, and the tiny *vorstenlanden* could no longer provide a framework for Javanese independence. For the men who founded Budi Utomo, most of them young Javanese aristocrats or *priyayi*, the old ideal of a unified, sovereign Javanese state was perhaps still a living tradition despite the process of domestication and bureaucratization to which the *priyayi* had been subjected by the Dutch during the nineteenth century. But for Sukarno's generation of Javanese, born into an increasingly centralized Dutch colony at the beginning of the twentieth century, the only really important state was Hindia Belanda, the Dutch Indies, and it was this that they set out to conquer and make their own.[48]

In Indochina, where the Vietnamese equivalent of exclusive Javanese nationalism remained dominant to the last, the 'might have been' Indochinese equivalent of the Indonesian nation left only a fleeting mark on intellectual and political life.[49] Nevertheless, by the last few years of the colonial period the attraction of integrative nationalism was certainly being felt in some quarters. In 1930 the recently formed Vietnamese Communist Party renamed itself the Indochinese Communist Party (Dang Cong San Dong Duong) in order to carry the anticolonial struggle to Cambodia and Laos as well as Vietnam. The exponents of Indochinese communism talked in terms of proletarian solidarity rather than Indochinese *national* unity; at most they envisaged Indochina as a federation like the Soviet Union, comprising several 'nationalities'. But although their vocabulary was different, in substance their arguments closely resembled those used by Indonesian nationalists. The peoples of Indochina were natural allies against imperialism, and any hostility between them was to be blamed on the French: 'from the time Indochina was occupied, the imperialists have continued to carry out a policy of division and maintaining hatred of this people toward that people'.[50] A party periodical went so far as to state that 'although the three countries are made up of three different races, with different languages, different traditions, different behaviour patterns, in reality they form only one country'.[51] Here, surely, are the beginnings of an Indochinese 'unity in diversity' to match that of Indonesia.

A more explicit approach to Indochinese nationalism, meanwhile, was being made at the same period by an organization at the opposite end of the political spectrum: the Constitutionalist Party, a group of elite Viet politicians in Cochinchina who cooperated with the French regime. The Constitutionalists believed that Indochina as a whole should have dominion status within the French Empire, and in 1938 they began talking about the need to forge a single 'people' out of the various 'Indochinese peoples'. In 1939 one conservative Viet writer even looked forward explicitly to the creation of an 'Indochinese Nation'—albeit still in the ethnocentric form of 'a single country which Annamese blood will have fertilized', rather than as a fully multicultural project.[52]

If writers on Vietnam have tended to interpret Indochinese communism as a disingenuous combination of Vietnamese expansionism and proletarian internationalism, the Constitutionalist interest in Indochinese unity has been seen mainly as a symptom of excessive identification with the French *mission civilisatrice*.[53] Yet despite their deep differences, these two groups did also have something in common that helps to explain why they both approached an integrative position reminiscent of Indonesian nationalism: essentially, both were orientated in thought and action toward the colonial state rather than toward traditional institutions.

They shared this orientation partly for quite opposite ideological reasons: the communists saw French imperialism as the central issue and rejected the old Vietnamese institutions as reactionary, while the Constitutionalists believed in the continuing usefulness of French tutelage. But an element of common experience was also involved here. By the 1930s the traditional *quoc* that had inspired early Vietnamese nationalism was no longer the living institution that it had been for Phan Boi Chau. Most of its functions had been taken over by the colonial state, and this, for the young men who joined the Indochinese Communist Party, was the immediate reality. It was a government of Indochina that not only ruled and persecuted them, but had also educated and in many cases employed them; and so it was Indochina that they aimed to unify and liberate. The depiction of French Indochina in colonial school textbooks and maps, together with rapid improvements in transport and communications, had also given them a sense of personal familiarity and identification with the territory of the colony as a whole. The hegemony of colonial institutions and ideas was most complete in the homeland of the Constitutionalists, Cochinchina, where the French had exercised direct power for more than sixty years, where the Vietnamese Empire was no longer a living memory even for the old, and where the development of colonial education and representative councils had gone furthest.

In Indochina as in Indonesia, it is reasonable to suppose that the longer established and more intrusive the colonial state became, the greater the potential for integrative, as opposed to exclusive, nationalism. This is not to suggest that if the colonial period had gone on for longer, the existing ethnogeographically exclusive Vietnamese nationalism would have faded away.[54] By 1930 it already had too much momentum for that. But the timing of its birth, around the turn of the century, was critical.

Toward Synthesis: Chronology of Colonial Conquest as the Key to National Morphology

Whether or not Vietnam can be described as an 'old nation' is to some extent a matter of semantics. Both of the characteristics that modernist writers view as fundamental to nationhood—a sense of mass community and an ideal, if not always a reality, of political solidarity—were already present *in some degree* in pre-colonial Vietnam. But these features were only sometimes explicitly referred to in political discourse, and remained components of an ideological system that, as a whole, often worked against them. Not until they were selected, augmented, and combined, under the influence of Western rule and Western ideas about popular sovereignty, did they become defining features of the Vietnamese nation as it emerged in the early twentieth century.

The most important single aspect of the continuity between royalist and nationalist anticolonialism was the persistent notion of a *quoc*, a territorial state commanding—first as an extension of the emperor, later as an extension of the people—loyalty from its subjects. It was with *vong quoc*, the 'loss of country' to the French, that Phan Boi Chau began the intellectual and political journey that led to the *quoc dan* or nation. But this continuity was contingent on the coincidence that the idea that 'the people are the country' was disseminated close enough in time to the colonial conquest, while the independent *quoc* was still a recent memory, to ensure that *the country which was lost would also be the country which the nationalists sought to regain*. If all of Vietnam had been colonized early in the nineteenth century, and its administration incorporated into the colonial state as thoroughly as that of Java, such a conjuncture might not have occurred. And if the colonial conquest had coincided with a period of deep internal disunity, such as the north-south (Trinh-Nguyen) wars of the eighteenth century, then even the preservation of existing institutions within the colonial system might have militated *against* the emergence of a single nation—just as it did in divided Java—and ultimately strengthened the countervailing attraction of an integrative Indochinese nationalism.

It is of crucial importance here that the first generation of Vietnamese nationalists were brought up under the imperial system when the country was still independent. Phan Boi Chau and Phan Chu Trinh, both sons of imperial officials, had been involved in the 'save the king' movement and received classical Confucian education before they were exposed to the ideas of Jean-Jacques Rousseau and Thomas Paine. They were not rebel children of the colonial state, but loyal children of the old Vietnamese Empire, suddenly exposed to a transformed political situation and a new intellectual world. The late date of the colonial conquest in central and northern Vietnam meant that the transition from royalist anticolonialism to modern nationalism was made within a single generation.

The counter-example of Java shows that an ethnic community of sufficient coherence and historic stature can still generate the beginnings of a modern nationalist movement of the exclusive variety, even when it is no longer supported by an indigenous state. But by the same token, the eventual absorption of Javanese into Indonesian nationalism shows that without a strong inherited claim to political sovereignty over the ethnic homeland, such a movement is hard pressed to maintain its ethnic exclusivity once the capture of state power becomes the central nationalist issue. Vietnamese political nationalism, by contrast, was able to grow straight out of the framework of the indigenous state, without passing through a preliminary 'cultural' phase of identity politics and solidarity-building. Viet ethnic pride and linguistic homogeneity subsequently supported the political movement and were developed within it under the influence of 'print-capitalism'.

Finally, the federal system of administration in colonial Indochina, although it divided Vietnam into three, also supported Vietnamese nationalism insofar as it allowed the Vietnamese to avoid making a conscious choice *not* to integrate Laos and Cambodia into their own nation. If Indochina had been as centralized as Indonesia, with no separate administrations for Cambodia and Laos and no territorial boundaries between them and Vietnam, an exclusive Vietnamese nationalism would still have been problematic despite the memory of Cambodia and Laos as separate pre-colonial *quoc*. Even if such a situation were not enough to induce the Viet to opt for a multi-ethnic integrative nationalism like that of Indonesia, it might well have tempted them into the risky 'Burmese' gambit of claiming the whole colonial state, but still calling it Vietnam. That this is less than fantastic is illustrated by the fact that the first Vietnamese national flag, designed in 1912, featured five red stars, one for each of the provinces of French Indochina, including Cambodia and Laos. When Cambodia and Laos eventually became separate countries, they still did so in the forms given to them as federal substates by the French administration. Vietnamese nationalism, in other words, was only partly a rejection of the colonial administrative framework.

Both pre-colonial and colonial antecedents, to recapitulate, have shaped today's Southeast Asian nations. Some pre-colonial societies—including Vietnam and the other supposed 'old nations' of the mainland, but also Java in maritime Southeast Asia—had characteristics that predisposed them to serve as vehicles for modern nationalist movements: ethnic distinctiveness and homogeneity, and more importantly, a tradition or ideal of political unity and independence established over a long period. But whether or not this potential was realized also depended partly on the way in which the societies concerned were incorporated into their respective colonial states. Important variables here included the direction of colonial language policy, and the degree of political decentralization and ethnic favouritism within the colonial system.

Another factor, seldom discussed in the existing literature but of critical importance, was what happened to traditional political institutions during the colonization process, and *at what dates*. In pre-colonial times, ideals of political unity and independence were focused primarily on states and their rulers, and only to a much lesser extent on 'peoples'. When indigenous states were replaced by colonial institutions, the ideals associated with the former automatically began to decline in importance, especially in the eyes of the new generation of intellectuals and politicians nurtured by colonial education. Unless quickly revitalized by fusion with the imported doctrine of popular sovereignty on a national basis, those ideals could fade to the point where the modern nationalist movement, when it did arise, was shaped by the colonial state rather than by the memory of the pre-colonial kingdom. Whether anticolonial nationalism took an integrative or an exclusive form, then, depended heavily on *the time lag between the demise of the indigenous state and the onset of the ideological changes brought about by Western education.*

In this perspective Vietnam was not an 'old nation' that 'survived' colonialism, but rather a major pre-colonial state that was conquered almost intact and at a sufficiently *late date* to provide the most meaningful frame of reference for the inevitable anti-colonial nationalist reaction of the early twentieth century. Java, conversely, did not emerge as a discrete nation not because it had 'never been one', but because the Javanese state lost its unity and independence well before the era of nationalism, and was gradually absorbed into a highly centralized colonial polity that eventually evoked an integrated nationalist reaction from the whole of an indisputably new nation, Indonesia.

It is worth concluding by briefly considering the relevance of this model to the other countries of the region. In what is now Malaysia, the absence of a pre-colonial tradition of political unity among the ethnic Malays tended to preclude them, as a group, from developing a strong exclusive nationalism, so in their case the 'question of timing' does not really arise. Although sometimes exclusive with respect to the resident ethnic Chinese minority, Malay nationalism has seldom been inclined to reject colonial borders. The lateness and looseness of British control over the individual Malay sultanate of Brunei, however, was certainly a factor in Brunei's last-minute choice to opt out of Malaysia, ultimately following a separate path as an independent micro-state.[55] In the Philippines, as in Malaysia, the consistently integrative character of anticolonial nationalism reflected a lack of large, recently conquered indigenous states—although the relationship between the pre-colonial Muslim sultanates of the southern Philippines and the later Moro separatist movement there may well be worth re-examining in this context.[56]

On the mainland, the kingdom of Cambodia was incorporated into the French sphere both at a relatively late date—it became a protectorate in 1863—and in a relatively pristine form, its institutions surviving the colonial period more intact than those of Vietnam. Both circumstances would have predisposed it to an exclusive Cambodian nationalism even if Vietnam had not rejected the integrative (Indochinese) option. In Thailand the doctrine of popular sovereignty was grafted directly on to an unconquered indigenous state, without any sharp hiatus between royalism and nationalism. In Laos in the 1940s an indigenous principality preserved under French rule, Luang Phrabang, took a leading role in official nation-building, but it represented only part of the country and its leadership was short-lived. In Burma the core indigenous state remained independent until 1885—as late as in Vietnam. But it had already suffered serious territorial losses to the British well before its final conquest, and it was subsequently abolished rather than preserved as a protectorate. This discontinuity helps to explain why twentieth-century Burmese nationalism began more as a movement of cultural revival, as in Java, than as an ideologically reinvigorated movement of political resistance, as in Vietnam.

Here again we see that although it is a mistake to judge the antiquity of modern nations by the antiquity of the historic states from which they are keen to claim descent, the history of those precursor states—their rise, and more particularly their fall—may nevertheless greatly influence how new nations are imagined and constructed. In terms of the strength of this influence, the Southeast Asian nations represent a full spectrum. At one end of the spectrum lie Thailand, Cambodia, and Vietnam: whether or not these are old *nations* may be a matter of debate, but they are certainly countries where the morphogenetic link between an old *state* and a new nation is real and direct. In the centre of the spectrum are Burma and Laos, where traditions of indigenous statehood served alongside religious institutions as building blocks for national identity, but not as blueprints for national sovereignty. And at the other extreme lie Indonesia, Malaysia, and the Philippines, where, due to longer periods of colonial rule as well as weaker pre-colonial state formation, links between new nations and old states are either imaginary or absent.

Notes

1. H. Seton-Watson (1977) *Nations and States: An Enquiry into the Origins of Nations and the Politics of Nationalism*, London, 7.
2. H. van Miert (1995) *Een koel hoofd en een warm hart: nationalisme, Javanisme en jeugdbeweging in Nederlands-Indië, 1918–1930*, Amsterdam, 189.
3. D. Streckfuss (1993) 'The Mixed Colonial Legacy in Siam: Origins of Thai Racialist Thought, 1890–1910', in L. J. Sears (ed.) *Autonomous Histories, Particular Truths: Essays in Honour of John R. W. Smail*, Madison, WI, 140.
4. E. Weber (1976) *Peasants into Frenchmen: The Modernization of Rural France, 1870–1914*, Stanford, CA.
5. M. Hroch (1996) 'From National Movement to the Fully-Formed Nation: The Nation-Building Process in Europe', in G. Balakrishnan (ed.) *Mapping the Nation*, London, 78–97.
6. W. R. Roff (1967) *The Origins of Malay Nationalism*, Kuala Lumpur; M. F. Laffan (2003) *Islamic Nationhood and Colonial Indonesia: The* umma *below the Winds*, London.
7. In both cases, it took some years of conflict before the independence proclaimed in 1945 was recognized by the colonizing power.
8. Most anticolonial nationalist movements followed the integrative pattern. Apart from Vietnam, successful examples of the exclusive form include Pakistan, and in a sense Burma, which was also administered as part of British India until 1937.
9. M. F. Herz (1958) *A Short History of Cambodia*, London, 70.
10. A. Reid (1979) 'The Nationalist Quest for an Indonesian Past', in A. Reid and D. Marr (eds.) *Perceptions of the Past in Southeast Asia*, Singapore, 288.

11. Laffan, *Islamic Nationhood and Colonial Indonesia.*
12. A. D. Smith (1986) *The Ethnic Origins of Nations*, Oxford, and (2001) *Nationalism*, Cambridge.
13. This idea is prefigured, in a less sophisticated way, in K. W. Deutsch (1953) *Nationalism and Social Communication*, New York.
14. B. Anderson (2006) *Imagined Communities: Reflections on the Origin and Spread of Nationalism*, 3rd edn., London, 41–79.
15. See Chapter 6 by Don Doyle and Eric Van Young, and Chapter 12 by Joya Chatterji.
16. One author has even called Malay/Indonesian a 'foreign investment' in Indonesia: J. Hoffman (1979) 'A Foreign Investment: Indies Malay to 1901', *Indonesia*, 27, 65–92.
17. Anderson, *Imagined Communities*, 106–28.
18. P. Edwards (2007) *Cambodge: The Cultivation of a Nation, 1860–1945*, Honolulu; S. Ivarsson (2008) *Creating Laos*, Copenhagen.
19. Anderson, *Imagined Communities*, 116.
20. C. E. Goscha (1995) *Vietnam or Indochina? Contesting Concepts of Space in Vietnamese Nationalism, 1887–1954*, Copenhagen, 52.
21. J. Breuilly (1982) *Nationalism and the State*, Manchester; see also E. Kedourie (ed.) (1970) *Nationalism in Asia and Africa*, London.
22. Breuilly, *Nationalism and the State*, 167–85.
23. B. B. Fall (1963) *The Two Viet-Nams: A Political and Military Analysis*, London, 33.
24. Some also use the word 'nationalism' in relation to Vietnam before the twentieth century: for instance, Truong Buu Lam (1967) *Patterns of Vietnamese Response to Foreign Intervention, 1858–1900*, New Haven, CT, 29. Others, however, stop short of this, preferring 'protonationalism': Duiker, *The Rise of Nationalism in Vietnam*, 30, 287; C. A. Lockard (1994) 'The Unexplained Miracle: Reflections on Vietnamese National Identity and Survival', *Journal of Asian and African Studies*, 29, no. 1/2, 11; A. B. Woodside (1976) *Community and Revolution in Modern Vietnam*, Boston, MA, 29.
25. Smith, *The Ethnic Origins of Nations*, 12; Smith, *Nationalism*, 49–50.
26. The following translation is from S. O'Harrow (1979) 'Nguyen Trai's *Binh Ngo Dai Cao* of 1428: The Development of a Vietnamese National Identity', *Journal of Southeast Asian Studies*, 10–1, 168–70.
27. Trieu, Dinh, Ly, Tran: Vietnamese dynasties.
28. Han, T'ang, Sung, Yüan: Chinese dynasties.
29. Liu Kung: southern Chinese ruler who lost control over Vietnam in 938; Ch'ao Chie: second in command of a Chinese army that attempted to subjugate Vietnam in 1075–1077; Truong Buu Lam, *Patterns of Vietnamese Response to Foreign Intervention*, 61.
30. D. G. Marr (1981) *Vietnamese Tradition on Trial, 1920–1945*, Berkeley, CA, 136.
31. Huynh Kim Khanh (1982) *Vietnamese Communism, 1925–1945*, Ithaca, NY, 33.
32. Marr, *Vietnamese Anticolonialism, 1885–1925*, Berkeley, CA, 44–76.
33. 'Under the protectorate there will again be high mandarins', observed a member of the imperial court soon after its seizure by the French. 'Surely they will recover and govern us as in the past.' Quoted in A. B. Woodside (1971) *Vietnam and the Chinese Model: A Comparative Study of Nguyen and Ch'ing Government in the First Half of the Nineteenth Century*, Cambridge, MA, 111.
34. Quoted in Truong Buu Lam, *Patterns of Vietnamese Response to Foreign Intervention*, 27.
35. Lam, *Patterns of Vietnamese Response*, 68.
36. Marr, *Vietnamese Anticolonialism*, 129.

37. Marr, *Vietnamese Anticolonialism*, 114–19.
38. J. J. Ras (1987) 'The Genesis of the Babad Tanah Jawi: Origin and Function of the Javanese Court Chronicle', *Bijdragen tot de Taal-, Land- en Volkenkunde*, 143–2/3, 343–56. This chronicle was compiled in the seventeenth century; for older Javanese references to Java as a country or territory, see H. Kulke (1991) 'Epigraphical References to the "City" and the "State" in Early Indonesia', *Indonesia*, 52, 10, 18, 20.
39. M. C. Ricklefs (1974) *Jogjakarta under Sultan Mangkubumi, 1749–1792: A History of the Division of Java*, London, 416.
40. Ricklefs, *Jogjakarta under Sultan Mangkubumi*, 188–211.
41. J. C. Heesterman (1986) 'Unity and Diversity in India and Indonesia', *Itinerario: Bulletin of the Leiden Centre for the History of European Expansion*, 10–1, 85–7. See also Chapter 12 by Joya Chatterji.
42. The main academic study of Budi Utomo, by Nagazumi Akira, is entitled *The Dawn of Indonesian Nationalism: The Early Years of Budi Utomo, 1908–1918*, Tokyo. But even Nagazumi is obliged in places to describe the organization's standpoint as 'Javanese nationalism', and to regret its 'failure' to embrace the Indonesian ideal (54, 117).
43. Quoted in Reid, 'The Nationalist Quest for an Indonesian Past', 283.
44. Anderson, *Imagined Communities*, 121.
45. Hroch, 'From National Movement to the Fully-Formed Nation', 81.
46. Reid, 'The Nationalist Quest for an Indonesian Past', 289.
47. Reid, 'The Nationalist Quest for an Indonesian Past', 284.
48. Although in theory the colonial administration continued to depend partly on local aristocrats, in practice the hereditary principle was abandoned and the *priyayi* became an increasingly unified administrative corps. See H. Sutherland (1979) *The Making of a Bureaucratic Elite: The Colonial Transformation of the Javanese* priyayi, Singapore, 130–1.
49. Goscha, *Vietnam or Indochina?*, 75, as his use of quotation marks suggests, overstates his case when he claims that in the early twentieth century 'the idea of an "Indochinese nation" was quite "real"'. The expression was in very occasional use by Viet writers, but only in the sense of a Vietnamese nation ruling the whole of Indochina—an idea consistently rejected by Khmer and Lao intellectuals and politicians; Goscha, *Vietnam or Indochina?*, 52, 58.
50. From a party document of 1932, quoted in Porter (1981) 'Vietnamese Policy and the Indochina crisis', in D. W. P. Elliott (ed.) *The Third Indochina Conflict*, Boulder, CO, 123.
51. Quoted in Huynh Kim Khanh, *Vietnamese Communism*, 128. The party was not initially successful in recruiting Khmer and Lao members, and the ethnic emphasis in Vietnamese communism was reconfirmed with the formation of the Viet Minh (Viet Nam Doc Lap Dong Minh Hoi, 'League for the Independence of Vietnam') in 1941. But the Indochinese Communist Party continued to survive on a decentralized basis, laying the foundations for the 'special relationship' that existed between Hanoi and the communist regimes in Laos after 1975 and Cambodia after 1979, and which to some extent continues to exist today.
52. Tieu Vien, quoted in Goscha, *Vietnam or Indochina?*, 51.
53. Woodside, *Community and Revolution in Modern Vietnam*, 224–5; M. Cook (1977) *The Constitutionalist Party in Cochinchina: The Years of Decline, 1930–1942*, Clayton, Victoria, 125.
54. Again, Goscha (*Vietnam or Indochina?*, 75) probably overstates his case by making this argument. In the 1930s it was clear that Cambodia and Laos would never accept an

Indochinese nationality based on Vietnamese identity. Yet there was still almost nobody in Vietnam who could envisage an Indochinese nation based on anything else—and, in truth, probably not many who could envisage an Indochinese *nation* (as opposed to an Indochinese space, territory, state, or federation) at all.

55. Brunei became a British protectorate in 1888, but a British officer was not stationed there until 1906. A local movement for independence did not develop until after the Second World War, and independence was not proclaimed until 1983. See G. Saunders (2002) *A History of Brunei*, 2nd edn., London, 2002.
56. T. M. McKenna (1998) *Muslim Rulers and Rebels: Everyday Politics and Armed Separatism in the Southern Philippines*, Berkeley, CA, 25–68.

Suggestions for Further Reading

Anderson, B. (2006) *Imagined Communities: Reflections on the Origin and Spread of Nationalism*, 3rd edn., London, especially 116–31.

Edwards, P. (2007) *Cambodge: The Cultivation of a Nation, 1860–1945*, Honolulu.

Elson, R. E. (2008) *The Idea of Indonesia: A History*, Cambridge, esp. 1–97.

Goscha, C. E. (1995) *Vietnam or Indochina? Contesting Concepts of Space in Vietnamese Nationalism, 1887–1954*, Copenhagen.

Ivarsson, S. (2008) *Creating Laos: The Making of a Lao Space between Indochina and Siam, 1860–1945*, Copenhagen.

Laffan, M. F. (2003) *Islamic Nationhood and Colonial Indonesia: The* umma *below the Winds*, London.

Lieberman, V. (2003) *Strange Parallels: Southeast Asia in Global Context, c.800–1830. Volume 1: Integration on the Mainland*, Cambridge, esp. 37–44, 187–211, 313–37, 445–56.

Lockard, C. A. (1994) 'The Unexplained Miracle: Reflections on Vietnamese National Identity and Survival', *Journal of Asian and African Studies*, 29, no. 1/2, 10–35.

Reid, A. (2004) 'Understanding Melayu (Malay) as a Source of Diverse Modern Identities', in T. P. Barnard (ed.) *Contesting Malayness: Malay Identity across Boundaries*, Singapore, 1–24.

Tarling, N. (2004) *Nationalism in Southeast Asia: 'If the people are with us'*, London, 1–138.

Winichakul, T. (1994) *Siam Mapped: A History of the Geo-Body of a Nation*, Honolulu.

CHAPTER 14

NATIONALISM IN EAST ASIA, 1839–1945

RANA MITTER

The Origins of Nationalism in East Asia

Nationalism has perhaps been the single most powerful ideological force in the shaping of modern East Asia. In different ways, the societies of China, Japan, and Korea absorbed the idea of the nation into their political thought in the nineteenth century and used it to shape reform, revolution, and transformation in the twentieth. This essay examines the impact of nationalism in East Asia in four parts. First, it sketches the structure of premodern East Asia and analyses the arrival of nationalism in the region. It then discusses some of the ideological frameworks, such as Social Darwinism and pan-Asianism, which were so influential in shaping nationalism there. It then examines the period between the two World Wars when nationalism flourished and its different forms competed with one another. The chapter ends by analysing the fate of nationalism during World War II, when different models of the nation competed for hegemony.

Nationalism remains significant in the early part of the twenty-first century, particularly as China seeks to assert its power in the world. There is historical resonance in this new reality, as until the nineteenth century, China was at the centre of the East Asian world. The 'sinosphere' was a place in which norms of behaviour, ethics, and relationships were shaped by ideas that had developed in China.[1] Central to these ideas was traditional thought, and in particular, the philosophy associated with Confucius, the thinker who articulated the idea of a society that would be calm and harmonious, with a hierarchy that promoted both obedience to those in higher positions and concern for the welfare of those below.

Confucianism went through a variety of developments in its 2,500-year history, but its assumptions underpinned the development of state and society in East Asia just as much as Judeo-Christian and classical norms underpinned the development of Europe.

Confucianism was—and is—an ethical system, and it stresses factors such as the importance of correct behaviour and adherence to rituals as means of creating a society in balance; the necessity of hierarchies for social cohesion; of mutual obligations between superior and inferiors; and the drive for self-improvement through education and contemplation.

Yet although all three societies were shaped by Confucian norms, they were also culturally and linguistically distinct, with China, Japan, and Korea each possessing a strong sense of cultural unity, and a homogeneity that was largely fictive, but politically useful in the business of state-building. In each society, these norms had different consequences. In China, the stress on order and balance had led, for instance, around 1000 AD to the world's first entrance examinations for the civil service, and a system by which the emperor was expected to remit taxes and provide grain for disaster-stricken areas. In Japan, the hierarchical elements were brought more to the fore. Japan existed for most of the second millennium BCE as a military state; in the modern period, under the Tokugawa shogunate (regency) from 1600 to 1868, the social structure was rigidly arranged according to the system of *shinôkôshô* (samurai, peasant, artisan, and merchant) that came directly from the Confucian system of priorities; trade was always regarded as a less worthy life than that of the peasantry, even if both premodern China and Japan did develop a strong commercial culture. From 1392 until the modern era, Korea was under the control of the Chosôn dynasty. The five centuries of Chosôn rule saw the development of a more commercialized society, but one that also become very hierarchical, more rigid even than Japan. Yet by the early modern era, there was a move away from the classical Chinese language of the elite toward a more Korean-based intellectual and literary culture.

Nations base their unity on the idea of shared history, and both China and Japan gave the state a significant role in creating an official version of that history. Chinese courts sanctioned the writing of official histories of their predecessors, often biased toward explaining those predecessors' downfall, but at the same time giving legitimacy to the idea of a unified narrative of the people as a collective body. Japanese historians of the Tokugawa period developed the scholarly field of 'national studies', or *kokugaku*, a historical model that used as its basis the mythical origins of the Japanese imperial line as children of the gods. Nationalism—the ideology based on the nation as a self-aware citizen body drawing its legitimacy from an idea of 'the people'—arrived in East Asia as just one part of the wrenching impact of global modernity brought by imperialism in the nineteenth century. However, the major societies of East Asia—China, Japan, and Korea—all had characteristics which meant that nationalism, when it arrived, was not a wholly alien mode of political thought. The lessons that each society drew from the concept were different. Japan was only directly subjected to direct imperialism for a very short time compared to China. Yet its experience meant that for the Japanese, the conflict of empires was the most telling influence on their political development. The conviction that empire and strong nationhood went together led Japan on a heady but ultimately ruinous journey. Observation of the behaviour of European empires in East Asia had convinced the Japanese not only that they must keep out of the clutches of the imperialists but that they should create an empire of their own. In turn, the fate of Korea was shaped by the imperialism of Japan. For much of the modern era, Japan made use of nationalism on the basis of strength, China and Korea on the basis of weakness. And for China, the humiliations of imperial conquest by the West and Japan led not only to nationalist revolution but the embrace of a radical communist form of nationalism.

The Arrival of Nationalism in East Asia, 1840–1927

The Meiji Revolution in Ideology

Nationalism first emerged in Japan as a conscious ideological strategy during the period following the Meiji Restoration of 1868. Carol Gluck has described this period in terms of the creation of 'Japan's modern myths,' meaning the ceremonies and rituals that went to create a modern mass citizen culture in Japan.[2] Japan provided fertile conditions for the emergence of the nation state. It was relatively culturally homogeneous: aboriginal Ainu and Koreans were distinct, as were the *burakumin* (outcaste) grouping, but the majority population was more dominant than in China, where Tibetans, Manchus, and Mongols provided more prominent examples of ethnic difference. Japan was relatively small and self-contained, and the policy of official isolation from the outside world (*sakoku*) between the early seventeenth and mid-nineteenth century, while never absolute, had allowed a closely knit society to emerge.[3] However, many of the key elements of nationhood were still lacking. The legitimacy of the state was based on the rule of the shoguns, legitimated by the emperor, who was carefully locked away in a luxurious palace. The Japanese population were not citizens of a nation state, but subjects of a military hierarchy.

Incursions from the west in the 1850s weakened the position of the shogunate: between 1852 and 1855 the American Commodore Matthew Perry and the Russian commander Yevfimy Putyatin both made ever more insistent demands to enter Japanese ports and confront the policy of *sakoku*. The foreign incursions sparked rebellion against the shoguns, and in 1868 a short civil war ended with a new generation of aristocrats in charge. These oligarchs declared that a new imperial reign-period had begun, named Meiji ('brilliant rule'), a term that has come to describe the whole period of reform from 1868 to 1912. They decided very consciously to create a modernized state that would change the relationship between the elites and wider society. Hierarchies were still key: in many ways (for instance, the ability of women to inherit property), the Meiji period was even more restrictive than the preceding Tokugawa era. But the basis of the hierarchy drew on models from European nationalism. The rulers had found themselves suddenly in charge of an entire country that was in grave danger from the advancing forces of European empire, and looked to the reasons that Europe had been successful to draw up their own defensive plans.

Prussia was a particularly inspiring example for the oligarchs after 1871. The German state's rulers had taken a group of quarrelling central European polities and forced them together into a powerful nation state. A civil society had been created in which mass participatory politics and constitutionalism were central, but at the same time democracy was kept at bay by an elite ruling class and emperor. Prussia had pushed Germany into modern nation-statehood without having to democratize the state as much as in France or Britain. One of the most notable ways in which Japanese nationhood was created during the Meiji era was the public deployment of symbols. In 1889 a newly written constitution was proclaimed for Japan by the emperor, thereby combining political innovation with tradition. In addition, the traditional Japanese folk religion of Shinto ('the way of the gods') was reinvented as a full state-sponsored system of worship, designed to boost a sense of shared Japanese identity. But perhaps most central to the construction of nationhood was the person of the emperor himself. During the shogunate the emperor had been hidden away. Indeed, the term Meiji 'restoration' was meant to indicate that the oligarchs had given back to the emperor the direct prerogative of power that had been usurped by the shoguns. In reality, it did no such thing, but instead transferred executive power to the oligarchs. The role of the emperor did change significantly, however. In the entire Tokugawa period (1600–1868) emperors took just three official public visits. In his forty-five years on the throne (1867–1912), the Meiji emperor carried out 102 imperial excursions. Statements attributed to the emperor became central to the new polity, such as his reflection that 'the Constitution was necessary for the progress of our nation.' He also took up a new role as commander-in-chief of the army: during the war with China in 1894–5, it was stated in the media that he suffered alongside his troops, whereas during the Russo-Japanese War of 1904–5 he was portrayed more loftily, paying due attention to government decisions and conferences.[4]

The Japanese army was also central to the new nationalism. The role of the military in modern East Asia's two largest states differed greatly, making it ironic that both states nonetheless collapsed in the 1940s for military reasons. China's great problem in the late nineteenth and early twentieth century was that its army was too weak. Japan's path was shaped by the fact that its military was too strong. Military force in shogunate Japan had been heavily restricted, and firearms had been banned in the seventeenth century, largely because they democratized violence, allowing even the peasantry to command force. In contrast, the use of the classic samurai sword took years of patient training and practice, and its manufacture was an equally painstaking and secretive process. Now, the Meiji rulers reversed all these assumptions and created a conscription-based citizen army. Service was compulsory for men aged twenty: this 'blood tax' was highly unpopular, and conscription was met at first with rioting. But the induction of generation after generation of Japan's young men in a collective enterprise did a great deal to forge a new identity. The nature of Japanese military training also created a strong bond, although one that was heavily turned away from civic values, as recruits were trained to discount the value of their own lives in favour of service to the emperor.

Imperialism and Nationalism in China

The emergence of nationalism in East Asia is inseparable from another phenomenon: imperialism. For almost exactly a century, between 1842 and 1943, China was subjected to an internationally sanctioned regime that prevented it from being fully sovereign on its own territory. This reality underpinned every action taken by every Chinese political actor for a century: nationalist, communist, or collaborationist. It made post-World War I sentiments of 'national self-determination' expressed by the West sound hollow, and the memory of imperialist domination remains influential to this day. Most of China was not formally colonized through much of this period, although there were exceptions such as Hong Kong, and the foreign concession areas in cities such as Shanghai and Tianjin. However, imperialism was also manifested in impositions such as the principle of 'extraterritoriality', which granted immunity from Chinese law for foreigners who were citizens of the major Western powers (and Japan), even though they were on Chinese territory.

The Opium Wars opened up a crisis of governance in China, and by extension, in Japan. In 1839 China went to war with Britain over the latter's desire to trade opium on Chinese soil. China lost, and in 1842 had to sign the first of the 'unequal treaties' that forced the country to open up its territory and trade on terms defined by the Western imperial powers. This led to intense soul-searching among the Chinese literati of the era. The next few decades were marked by a search for a new Chinese identity that could combine the strengths of China's past with the modernity of the present. The 'self-strengthening' movement of the 1860s was just one part of this reformist thinking, in which reformers tried to combine Western techniques for practical technological development with a 'core' of Chinese thought. Among the first products of such thinking was Yan Fu, who was sent to England in 1877 to study at the Greenwich Naval College. Here he developed a particular interest in the new ideas of Social Darwinism, and translated many key works that would have a profound influence on Chinese reformers of the age, such as Thomas Huxley's *Evolution and Ethics*, John Stuart Mill's *On Liberty*, and Adam Smith's *The Wealth of Nations*. The idea of the nation as a 'body politic' was heavily influenced by Yan's argument that China needed a moral and physical revival as well as the adoption of modern forms of government such as constitutionalism and a national assembly.[5]

The civic form of Chinese nationalism was taken yet further by perhaps the single most significant figure of the late Qing nationalist movement, the thinker Liang Qichao. Liang drew heavily on the debates that had taken place in Japan after the Meiji coup, and one of his most powerful contributions was linguistic: the import into Chinese of Japanese neologisms that were used to translate terms such as 'nation', 'democracy', 'constitution', and so forth.[6] However, numerous other figures contributed to the debate. One who would become famous less for his theory of the nation than for his actions to develop it was Dr Sun Yatsen, a physician born in Hawaii who dedicated his life to the revolutionary overthrow of the Qing dynasty, and whose ideas were a mixture of the various theories, both civic and racial, that had shaped Chinese nationalism.[7]

The emergence of a nationalist consciousness in late nineteenth-century China turned out to be a source of profound crisis for the Qing dynasty. The period was one of intellectual ferment precisely because it was perceived that China was in political turmoil, but unlike in Japan, where the swift civil war of 1867–8 had set the country on a new path very fast, the death throes of the Qing would last for some seven decades. However, those decades proved to be fertile ones for the development of Chinese nationalism. The state itself became much more fragile after the bloody Taiping civil war of 1850–64, as a result of which military power ebbed away from the central authorities to the localities.[8] The result was political fragmentation, as the establishment of provincial armies set the stage for the warlordism that would mark the early twentieth century. In reaction to this, however, political thinkers and activists became more convinced that the establishment of a modern nation state was the only solution to China's problems. The most revolutionary of such thinkers saw a republic, rather than the traditional monarchy, as the most productive new form of government, among them Sun Yatsen, whose many failed attempts to overthrow the Qing dynasty gave him immense prestige among the emergent Chinese middle-class and diaspora communities who had lost faith in the Qing. Yet the dynasty's end was not in the end caused by the efforts of Sun and his fellow republican Nationalists, but followed the discovery of a bomb plot in the city of Wuhan in October 1911, which triggered a series of provincial revolts against the dynasty that ultimately led to the abdication of the last emperor in February 1912, and the formal declaration of the Republic of China.

Chinese Nationalisms in the Republic

Unlike in Japan, there was no one strong state in the Republic in early twentieth-century China (1912–49). One intellectual benefit that came from the political turmoil of the Republic, however, was the wide range of systems of thought that vied with each other during the period. Chinese nationalism was inflected by the other currents of thoughts that held sway at the time.

Nationalism in the early Republic is associated with two major events that have come to symbolize wider social changes. One was the demonstration by some three thousand students in central Beijing on 4 May 1919, protesting against the humiliating terms forced upon China at the Paris Peace Conference. The other was the widespread protests that followed the shooting dead of twelve unarmed workers by Shanghai police in front a Japanese-owned factory on 30 May 1925. 'May Fourth' and 'May Thirtieth' provided two touchstones for nationalism that still have immense resonance in the present day.

China's first independent participation in an international war was its entry into World War I. Although no Chinese soldiers fought in combat, some one hundred thousand labourers were sent to support the Allies on the Western Front, and three thousand of them died in the distant cold of northern Europe.[9] The popular understanding among the political classes of China's still-young republic was that China would be rewarded for its participation. However, the British and French had compromised themselves. Although they had solicited China's help, they had also signed secret treaties with Japan. In return for Japan holding back from assisting Germany in the Pacific, it was agreed that the German possessions in Shandong province (in north China) would not be restored to Chinese sovereignty, but awarded to Japan instead. US President Woodrow Wilson, initially sympathetic to the Chinese position, ultimately refused to help. On 30 April 1919 the telegraph transmitted the news about China's humiliation in a matter of hours from Paris to Beijing. It immediately sparked off anger among one of the most politically aware sections of society: the capital's university students. These students quickly organized a demonstration, which began with speeches in front of the Tiananmen (Gate of Heavenly Peace) at the centre of the city, and then proceeded to a march through the legation quarter. The peaceful events became rather more violent within hours, when students stormed the house of a Chinese minister perceived as close to Japan. The demonstration had dispersed by the early evening. Yet the 'May Fourth' event became so famous that even today any educated Chinese will understand its significance. For it symbolized a turn in the politics of modern China that has not been fully resolved: how Chinese nationalism could be made compatible with a role in a globalized world.[10]

The era of 'May Fourth' has become associated with the almost contemporaneous 'New Culture' movement. This started in 1915 as a reaction against the threat from the strongman president of the Republic, Yuan Shikai, to declare himself emperor and restore Confucianism as official doctrine. The political agenda of the era drew on the ideas of 'new culture' by trying to identify China's crisis and finding solutions for it, identifying the key problems as 'imperialism from without and warlordism from within'. The solution of thinkers such as the Peking University professor Chen Duxiu was in his phrasing, 'Mr Science and Mr Democracy'. There was a rather rosy-eyed faith among many that these concepts could reverse China's problems. At the same time, their effectiveness did mean that certain elements were stressed in the nationalism that developed in the period, in particular the rational ('science') and the civic ('democracy') that had emerged as part of the late Qing discussions on the meaning of Chinese nationalism. As Japanese nationalism moved further into the realms of the self-declaredly irrational in the 1930s, it was not a trivial achievement on the part of Chinese nationalists that their crisis, in many ways much greater than that of Japan, did not for the most part take refuge in the nostrums of blood and soil.

On 30 May 1925 a group of Chinese workers demonstrated outside a police station in Nanjing Road, in the British settler-controlled International Settlement of Shanghai.

Worried at the size and vociferousness of the crowd, the police fired into the crowd and killed four protesters on the spot (eight died later). The incident triggered a firestorm of protest. Within days, boycotts of foreign goods and businesses spread from Shanghai across the country. The Nationalist Party, still in exile in Guangdong and mourning the recent death of its leader, Sun Yatsen, seized the opportunity to promote its agenda of anti-imperialism. The Northern Expedition, a military campaign begun in 1926, saw the Nationalists install their government at the new capital of Nanjing in 1928, under the leadership of Chiang Kaishek, Sun Yatsen's eventual successor.

The conversion of China from empire to republic had not removed the special privileges that the Western powers and Japan enjoyed on Chinese soil. Imperialism, and opposition to it, remained at the heart of Chinese nationalism even during the Republican period. One particularly powerful site of confrontation was the city of Shanghai, which was split between a French Concession, an International Settlement largely run by British settlers, and the Chinese city. This split city was both an inspiration and a provocation. The imperial presence had brought industrial modernity to the city, and a new working class emerged as a result. The nature of links between rural and urban identity also changed. New cultural forms emerged and Chinese could experience aspects of the Western presence—advertising, cafes, books—without ever coming near Europe.

On the other hand, imperialism was a real and tangible assertion of foreign power on Chinese territory, and the modernity of the republican structure and constitution were severely compromised by the fact that China's sovereignty remained partial. One historian has referred to the ultimate case study of this phenomenon, the city of Tianjin, as being a 'hypercolony' because its urban territory was divided up between no fewer than eight colonial powers.[11] But it was perhaps in Shanghai that the clash between the foreign presence and Chinese nationalism became most vivid.

The events of 30 May 1925 crystallized wider currents in China at the time. The entire country was not suddenly seized by a longing for ideological nationalism. But the time was right for the Nationalist Party's march to power. Under Chiang Kaishek, the 'Northern Expedition' of 1926–8 saw the Nationalists finally thrust forward to seize control of much of China's heartland. It was an incomplete revolution: only China's eastern seaboard really ever came fully under Nationalist control, and the regime was heavily compromised by its financial woes and corruption. Yet its achievements should not be underestimated. From 1928, China had an internationally recognized government that had some genuine claim to popular support and ideological underpinnings. Chiang was accused by his enemies of being just another warlord, but this was far too crude a way to characterize a politician who was deeply flawed but much more subtle than his opponents acknowledged. To have a government that was explicitly tied to ideological anti-imperialist nationalism, and for that government to gain recognition from an unfriendly outside world, was no small achievement.[12]

The dominance of the Nationalist Party should not obscure the alternative models of the nation that emerged in early twentieth-century China. One was the move among some provincial leaders toward a more federal model of government in the 1910s and

1920s.[13] This partly made a virtue of necessity: the Republic had quickly split up into competing provincial fiefdoms. Another strain of thought that became stronger and ever more relevant was nationalism as advocated by the CCP (Chinese Communist Party). The most prominent early Communists, such as Mao Zedong and Cai Hesen, had also been shaped by the Social Darwinism of the late Qing, and their turn to Marxism in the early 1920s was likewise tinged with the May Fourth agenda of 'national salvation' through 'science and democracy.' The CCP's vision of the nation was predicated on a revolution based on class war; but it was a nationalist vision nonetheless. From 1923 the CCP and the Nationalists formed a united front under Soviet influence, although the alliance ended when in April 1927 Chiang turned on his former allies and had large numbers of them killed. Yet although this bloodshed sowed the seeds of rivalry, the CCP shared with the Nationalists a central ideological tenet: anti-imperialist nationalism.

Themes

Notions of Race and Social Darwinism

One particular philosophy informed nationalism in East Asia between the mid-nineteenth and mid-twentieth century: Social Darwinism, a concept that has come to be most closely associated with the Victorian British sociologist Herbert Spencer.[14] Yan Fu's analysis of China's crisis, while largely positing a civic model of nationalism for China, was heavily shaped by the influence of Social Darwinist thinkers. China had become weak and was now vulnerable to invasion. By strengthening individual bodies, a strong citizen body would be built up that would enable China to restore its position. Sun Yatsen went on to draw heavily on the idea of racial difference and potential conflict. He had no quarrel with the idea of different races, but believed that the 'yellow' races deserved a higher position than European hierarchies tended to accord them. He did not, however, believe in any necessary conflict between races. While Sun was opposed to the Manchu rulers of China, his vision of the Chinese Republic on its foundation in 1912 was of a combination of five 'races' (Han, Manchu, Mongol, Tibetan, and Muslims). Sun had first come to prominence in the late Qing as leader of the Tongmenghui, an anti-Qing revolutionary body, and after 1912, as the leader of the Nationalist (Kuomintang or Guomindang) Party that would shape so much of China's politics in the early twentieth century. Other revolutionaries of the time went further. Zou Rong and Zhang Binglin both believed in a more necessarily confrontational view of race, Zou arguing of the Manchus: 'Their land is foul land, they are of a furry race, their hearts are beast's hearts.'[15]

Although Yan Fu was the first Chinese to translate Spencer directly, most of the Social Darwinist texts that came to China after him came via Japan, and Japanese Social Darwinist thinkers such as Katô Hiroyuki became powerful influences on Chinese thinking. Yet in fact, it was Sun rather than Zou Rong's vision that became dominant during the Republic after 1912. There was relatively little violence during the 1911 revolution, although in some cities such as Nanjing acts of great brutality were committed against the Manchu inhabitants. However, the question of racial conflict within China quickly dissipated. Once the Manchus had been overthrown, there was little strong feeling from the population either in favour of restoring them or persecuting them.[16] Nonetheless, the Social Darwinist view of struggle continued to inform Chinese nationalist thought for much of the twentieth century, manifesting itself particularly in the desire for military reform.

The influence of Social Darwinism in Japan did have one malign effect that was less obvious in China: Japan developed a powerful form of exclusive racial discourse which demanded that Japan be considered superior to its neighbours in East Asia. In the Meiji era, this was marked by the phrase *datsu-A nyu-Ô*—'leaving Asia and entering Europe', a rather crude attempt to deny Japan's geographical position and class it instead with the western empires. This phase did not last long, being replaced by not only a 'return to Asia' but a new, powerful form of nationalist thought that drew its considerable power from its seeming ability to transcend nationalist boundaries: pan-Asianism.[17]

Pan-Asianism and Transnational Nationalism

In 1903 the Japanese artist and thinker Okakura Tenshin published *Ideals of the East*, in which he declared, 'Asia is one.' Okakura proposed a new version of one way of thinking about the relationship between the societies of Asia, in particular Japan, China, and India. There was a fundamental difference, he suggested, between the countries of the west and east: the former might be materially superior, but the Asian societies were joined by a spiritual bond. Of course, the idea of 'Asia' as a geobody uniting west, south, and east Asia was a product of the global mapping that had been forced upon the region by the arrival of imperialism. Nonetheless, the idea found significant purchase among intellectuals and politicians of the era. In India, the advocacy of the poet, artist, and public intellectual Rabindranath Tagore gave the idea great weight, and the concept also found many advocates in Japan. However, it had less purchase in China. Already by the late nineteenth century, Japan was perceived by many Chinese as an imperialist aggressor, and the message that China and Japan were spiritual allies seemed hollow in the wake of the Japanese capture of Taiwan (1895) and much of Manchuria (1905). But Sun Yatsen, who had been protected by Japanese while in exile from the Qing, always maintained an affection for the country, and made a well-known speech at Kobe in 1924 advocating 'greater Asianism' and referring to Japan as Asia's 'watchtower'.[18]

In the first four decades of the twentieth century, Pan-Asianism would mutate in form while maintaining its name. From being a gentle, rather artistic conception, it would become the basis for an ideological justification for Japanese imperialism. By the

1930s, the racial element of pan-Asianism would become much stronger than the cultural elements. The idea of Asian unity would metamorphose into a more sinister belief that Japan must provide the leadership role in the unification of Asia against the west. Even today in Japan there are significant voices that continue to argue that Japan's wartime role was to be the liberator of Asia, a continuity with the pan-Asian language of the 1920s and 1930s.

EAST ASIA, 1914–37

Confrontational Nationalisms: Japan and China

Unlike China, Japan had a good First World War. Japan had had to make relatively little military contribution, but it was able to use the conflict to establish its position as a major power in East Asia. It suffered defeats, such as the refusal by the Western powers to pass a racial equality clause at the Paris Peace Conference (something that united China and Japan in outrage), but overall, the war left Japan stronger. Subsequent treaties, such as the Washington Treaties of 1921–2, established that the Japanese navy could expand to 60 per cent of the size of the American or British navies. Japan gained a permanent seat on the council of the new League of Nations, and its economy grew and prospered.

Yet the tenor of Japanese nationalism during the interwar period went against the grain of these trends. Rather than reflecting a prosperous, outward-looking Japan, significant currents of thought instead portrayed the country as a nation under siege. The drive for empire was portrayed in zero-sum terms as a vital task to protect the Japanese nation as it sought to survive in a Social Darwinist world. The downturn in the economy at the end of the 1920s made matters worse. Japan suffered particularly badly from the Great Depression because of a disastrous year spent on the gold standard in 1929–30, and the subsequent collapse of its export markets. But the seeds of its inward turn had been there ever since the Meiji years.[19]

There was a liberal and constitutional aspect to Japanese nationalism. But that element came increasingly under attack. As Japanese politics moved away from electoral democracy toward militarism in the 1930s, an alternative vision of the nation became much more dominant, a strain of thought that located the heart of the Japanese nation not in imported and fragile civic rituals and laws, but in a less tangible sense of 'soul', located not in the fleshpots of the city but in the pure, if impoverished, countryside. This strain of thought centred on the mystical and hard-to-define concept of *kokutai*, sometimes translated as 'national polity', referring to the ineffable essence of Japaneseness that defined the nation without itself being clearly definable. There were few obvious equivalents in China, although there was a *guocui* ('National Essence' school) that had a minor influence within the political world.

The Japanese political system that emerged in the 1930s was shaped by a powerful form of militarized ultranationalism. Among the most prominent of the radical ultranationalists were Kita Ikki and Ôkawa Shumei, the latter of whom argued that 'Heaven has chosen Japan as the champion of the East.' Kita's position was somewhat different: as a socialist, albeit a nationalist rather than internationalist, he sought to define *kokutai* in more collective terms than some other thinkers, and also argued that the liberation of China from western imperialism was a worthwhile aim for Japan. As Japan became more radicalized, the role of *kokutai* also became more prominent, and the government circulated a booklet in 1937 entitled *Kokutai no hongi* (*Principles of the National Polity*), which defined Japan as 'a great family nation', and extolled the values of patriotism and *Bushidô* (a term that became popularized in the nineteenth century to describe a stylized version of the warrior code of honour that had been dominant in premodern Japan) at the expense of liberalism and democracy. The book was circulated nationwide until 1945.[20]

One source of great concern to Japanese ultranationalists was the growing consolidation of Chinese nationalism. This consolidation had emerged from the turmoil of the years 1925 to 1927, in which China had suffered two civil wars in tandem. The most obvious was the Northern Expedition, the campaign by the United Front of Nationalist and Communist forces, under Soviet advice, to conquer much of China's eastern seaboard, defeating militarist leaders or else persuading them to throw in their lot with the United Front. Under the surface, however, tensions were brewing between Chiang Kaishek, the new Nationalist leader, who had become increasingly suspicious of the Communists. In 1927, as Shanghai fell to the revolutionary forces, Chiang engineered a coup in which thousands of Communists in the city were slaughtered, ending the link between the two parties in the bloodiest way. However, within a year, Chiang had formally established his capital at Nanjing, and gained international recognition for his government. It was beset by multiple problems, including an unstable tax base, corruption, and very uncertain loyalties outside its greatest area of control in central China. Nonetheless, Chiang's government also made important advances in terms of regaining China's lost sovereignty, for instance, negotiating tariff autonomy in 1930. It also implemented ideological measures as a means of mobilizing the population. The most notable of these was the New Life Movement, initiated in 1934. Its simple homilies encouraged traditional virtues, loyalty to the government, and clean dress and personal habits; it never achieved deep penetration within society, but increasing use of New Life language did begin to spread in Chinese public life, particularly after the outbreak of the war with Japan in 1937. Meanwhile, the Chinese Communists continued to portray an alternative vision: while rarely using the overt language of nationalism, the language of thinkers such as Mao Zedong was heavily steeped in Chinese reality, providing an alternative vision of social change. However, the conflict between the Nationalists and Communists was abruptly suspended in 1937. In July of that year, war broke out between China and Japan, and as China fought for survival, both the Nationalists and Communists were forced to confront the greatest threat yet to the still inchoate nation: the war with Japan.

The Ambiguities of Imperial Collaboration: Korea

The most titanic clash of nationalisms in East Asia took place between China and Japan. But this should not obscure the development of complex nationalisms elsewhere within the region, in particular in Korea. Korean nationalism developed in the context of full colonization by Japan, making it in many ways more comparable with classic nationalist movements under colonialism (as in India or Kenya) than with China or Japan.

Korea spent much of the premodern period under Chinese influence; it was not a colony, but rather a state that paid tributary dues to China and in turn was left to develop autonomously. As a result, Korean society developed its own distinctive cultural and social forms over several centuries. This situation changed radically in the late nineteenth century. As Japan became more powerful, it became fixated on the Korean Peninsula as a buffer zone between itself and a weak China that the Western powers could use to attack Japan. In 1894–5 the first Sino-Japanese War was fought for influence in Korea; Japan won and Korea was removed from its centuries of allegiance to China. For a decade Korea retained an uneasy independence, engaged in discussions with powers such as Russia that seemed like possible protectors, but in 1910 the growing power of Japan led to full annexation, a truly colonial occupation that would last until 1945.

The Japanese colonial period in Korea is not remembered fondly by its victims. The colonial regime used the language of race to create a hierarchy in which the Koreans were inferior: this was particularly galling to educated Koreans who regarded their links to the motherlode of Chinese Confucian culture as more powerful than those of the Japanese. More than in China, Christianity emerged as a powerful shaping force in Korean nationhood (although prominent Chinese leaders such as Sun Yatsen and Chiang Kaishek had been Christians). The pivotal event of the colonial era was the March First Movement, a peaceful Korea-wide demonstration of over a million people against Japanese rule on 1 March 1919, which in turn influenced the May Fourth Movement in China just two months later. The movement was put down harshly. But the Japanese could not ignore the reality of an emergent Korean nationalism, and like other interwar colonial powers, sought to find areas by which they could allow a freer space for Korean identity to operate even while retaining overall control. The 1920s were a more liberal decade in Japan, and the colonial regime relaxed a little as well, allowing Korean-language newspapers such as the *Tonga ilbo* and *Chosôn ilbo* to be published. Some Nationalists also went into exile: Syngman Rhee (a Christian), later to be the president of South Korea, in 1919 took part in the establishment of a provisional government based in Shanghai, although he and his collaborators found it difficult to maintain significant links with the Peninsula. Another significant group turned leftward and formed the core of the Korean Communist Party, which was a significant partner for the CCP in occupied Manchuria after 1931. As Japanese politics became harsher in the years 1931–45, much of the earlier liberalization was reversed, and Koreans were forced to speak Japanese and brought more firmly into the Japanese war machine.[21]

The exploitation of Korea by Japan is not in doubt. However, the relationship between Korea and Japan did at times become more nuanced and broke down what might seem like monolithic nationalist categories. The official Japanese position was that Koreans were also citizens of the Japanese Empire, although this did not mean equality. However, this idea did have real consequences. For instance, in Japanese-occupied Manchuria, the colonial rulers prevented solidarity building up between the Chinese and the Koreans by giving the latter a higher status as Japanese citizens. Korean subjects in Manchuria were encouraged to invest in land and property and become indebted to agencies of the Japanese Empire. This alienated Koreans from the majority Han Chinese population who were not given such access. In Manchuria, therefore, the Koreans regarded the Japanese colonial state, if ambiguously, as its protector. The Chinese and Korean communist movements in occupied Manchuria were strongly bound by essentially contradictory nationalist projects, since the Koreans in Manchuria could hardly be expected both to be part of a Chinese nation state and a Korean homeland. The inability of the Chinese and Korean Communists to understand these ambiguities of identity, as well as the sheer pressure that both groups were under while on the run from the Japanese, led to horrific results: immense fratricidal purges that pulled apart both organizations for several years, until a new joint anti-Japanese campaign was begun in 1936.[22]

World War II

Rationality and Irrationality in East Asian Nationalism

By the late 1930s, Chinese and Japanese forms of nationalism were on a collision course. Within China, the Nationalists and Communists were deadly rivals between 1927 and 1937, and this enmity obscured the fact that their visions of nationhood had much in common, both drawing on a version of secular Enlightenment modernity and associated ideas of progress, although the Nationalists did not share the Communists' attachment to class war as a vehicle for that progression. In contrast, Japanese nationalism developed an ever-stronger attachment to the irrational that stemmed in part from forms of Buddhism historically more popular in Japan than China such as Zen and Nichiren, as well as the influence of European romanticism. That tendency became particularly prominent in 1942, as Japan was flushed with initial victory in the Pacific War, and the prominent nationalist philosophers who became known later as the Kyoto School held a conference whose title would become notorious: 'Overcoming Modernity' (*kindai no chôkoku*).

Chiang Kaishek, who set up a wartime government in exile in the southwestern Chinese city of Chongqing, did attack various aspects of modern politics (in particular the liberal aspirations of the May Fourth Movement) at around the same time, in his 1943 ghostwritten book *China's Destiny*. Yet neither he nor the Communists ever sought actively to define the national interest through a rejection of modernity's key assumptions. Instead, the debate took place over the shape of what a modern post-war China would look like. Chiang's Nationalists aimed for a China that would have sovereign authority, a significant role in the new world order, and a stable domestic consensus. The Communists offered their own alternative. In 1940, Mao, who was based in the northwestern town of Yan'an, crystallized his vision in a talk on 'new democracy' in which he argued that a cross-class alliance was needed as a first step in resistance to the Japanese invaders: While the eventual aim was revolution, the importance of bringing classes together within the nation was central to the policy: 'today is not yet the time to introduce socialism'.[23] As the war ground on, however, communist policy became much more oriented toward class conflict though it never lost its definition as part of a national struggle for survival against the Japanese invasion.

The war against Japan, which saw some 15–20 million Chinese deaths and 80–100 million refugees, was the crucial moment in the formation of Chinese nationalism in the twentieth century. No other event forced into focus so strongly the question of how the nation should be defined. The Nationalists and Communists offered rival visions of how the citizen body should be constituted and what defined the relationship between state and society that underpinned it. The Nationalist government proposed new schemes of welfare for their battered citizens in realization that the inevitable result of the war would be a nation in which state and society would have much greater obligations to one another. Communist policies of land reform were a yet more radical response to these efforts, envisioning a nation not only united against Japan but with a society radically overturned rather than merely reformed.[24]

The Nationalism of Wartime Collaboration

The encounter between Japan and China created another important variant of nationalism that is rarely discussed. In retrospect, it is clear that China and Japan would take separate paths as nation states that were confined within clearly defined borders. But that path was by no means as clear in the 1940s. Japan's empire was growing and showed no signs of collapse. China was split into a variety of factional regimes with the Nationalist regime looking increasingly hollow to many outside observers. In this context, it was natural that new forms of nationalism might emerge that would reflect the more complex reality of East Asia. Two particular experiments in nation-forming illustrate the complexities as well as the possibilities of the era.

The first experiment was the establishment of 'Manchukuo'. In 1931 the Kwantung Army, the Japanese garrison army stationed in Manchuria in the aftermath of the 1904–5 Russo-Japanese War, invaded and occupied the northeastern provinces of

China, then widely known as Manchuria. In doing so (without the Tokyo government's prior knowledge), the Army was forced to construct a narrative at short notice that explained their actions: since the Great War, all-out territorial seizures had gone out of fashion, even at the same time that the European empires retained control over large parts of the globe. The construction that emerged was one of rupture with the past. A new state, 'Manchukuo', was declared to have arisen, and was formally inaugurated in March 1932. The indigenous population (of which the Japanese settlers were held to be a part, along with Manchus and Mongols) was said to have revolted against the oppression of Chinese warlord rule, and had established a brand-new state whose name meant 'land of the Manchus.' To symbolize the Manchu link further, the deposed last emperor of China, Puyi, was wheeled out of exile in Tianjin, and placed upon the hastily invented throne of this new state. The state's narrative simultaneously sought to deny any links with the Chinese republic (and by implication, the modern Chinese state that had emerged in the early decades of the century) while seeking links with premodern ways of thought, reflecting the wider Japanese feeling of respect for ancient China's achievements and contempt for its modern weakness. Thus citizens of the new state were not to call themselves 'Chinese' but rather 'Manchukuoans'. The new state did not advocate nationalism, but rather a vague system of thought called Wangdao (the Kingly Way), a mishmash of Confucian pieties that was hastily articulated by theorists-for-hire.

In the end, it was not just Wangdao's vagueness that prevented it from serving as the basis of a deeply rooted 'Manchukuo nationalism'. Because it drew so heavily on Confucian tenets and was so consciously anti-modern, it was a very difficult vehicle to use to form an essentially modern identity. The universalistic elements of Wangdao prevented it from providing even a constructed genealogy for the Manchukuo nation state: vague references in hastily written textbooks to customs in the region being different from those in China provided the only attempts to provide some sort of specifically northeastern identity.

Nonetheless, it would be wrong to dismiss the Manchukuo experience as utterly lacking purchase among the wider Chinese population of the region. Notable in particular was the attempt by the Japanese to use local Buddhist Morality Societies in Manchukuo to engender support among middle-class women.[25] This was an astute move in at least two senses. First, it appealed to that significant proportion of the population which found Chinese nationalism alienating because it had so comprehensively rejected the social and religious context that had underpinned Chinese society for centuries and that was now being relentlessly secularized under the guise of terms such as 'anti-superstition'.[26] In addition, women found the discourse particularly powerful: again, modern nationalism has usually been expressed in highly masculine terms, and formations that sought out feminine spheres of existence many well have found some favour among the groups who were courted in this way.

The other, single best-known form of 'collaborationist nationalism' of the era was in stark contrast to Manchukuo. This was the regime of the defector Nationalist politician Wang Jingwei, which operated a Japanese-sponsored government based in Nanjing from 1940 to 1945 (Wang himself died in 1944). Unlike Manchukuo, Wang's regime did not seek to separate itself from Republican China, but rather used ideological sleight-of-hand to argue that it was the true inheritor of Sun Yatsen's revolution, and was a direct continuation of the Republic of China. It insisted that, in contrast, Chiang Kaishek's regime in exile in Chongqing was a Communist-influenced regime that was a client both of western imperialist and Soviet interests. Wang maintained to the end of his life that he was the only true Chinese Nationalist leader, and that both Chiang and Mao had sacrificed any right to that title.

Wang's position and the area that he nominally ruled was very different from Manchuria. Wang had been one of the earliest activists in the Nationalist Party, was associated with its progressive left, and had been close enough to Sun Yatsen to be considered his obvious heir by many in 1925. Yet his lack of influence within the party's military meant that Chiang, rather than Wang, seized power as the Northern Expedition unfolded. Wang held a string of important positions within the Nationalist government from 1928, including prime minister, but he never forgave Chiang for what he regarded as his usurpation. Ironically, Wang's views veered much closer to Chiang's during the decade that the Nationalists ruled from Nanjing: Wang came to share Chiang's virulent anti-communism, and while Wang was associated, unfairly, with being 'pro-Japanese,' he and Chiang were not very different in their views of the necessity of making tactical concessions to Japan while building up China's strength for a future confrontation.[27]

However, Chiang and Wang took radically different paths once war with Japan broke out in 1937. Chiang continued to resist all the way until 1945. Wang also joined the retreat, but became more and more convinced that a Chinese victory was unfeasible, and that to prevent further misery a Chinese leader would have to step in to negotiate peace with Japan. In November 1938 Wang slipped away to Hanoi, in French Indochina, and from there announced his desire to negotiate peace with Japan. Wang was permitted to inaugurate his regime in Nanjing on 30 March 1940, and it was officially recognized by Japan a few months later.[28]

Perhaps the most ideologically acrobatic aspect of this regime was the way in which Wang defined his collaboration with Japan as a form of nationalism. The Manchukuo experience had been very different: there, it was openly acknowledged that a new polity had come into being. The Japanese were not keen on Wang styling himself as the restorer of China's most notable nationalist administration. But Wang insisted that his government was a restoration of the pre-existing government that had had to retreat from eastern China in 1937–8. Its nomenclature did a great deal to support this story. It was called the 'reorganized' (*gaizu*) National government, and the newspaper coverage in Nanjing on 30 March 1940 referred to the *huandu*, the 'return to the capital' of the government, this time led by Wang Jingwei. Various aspects of the regime closely echoed the Nationalist government of Chiang: the use of the twelve-pointed star flag, and the establishment of a movements such as the New Citizen movement, an echo of Chiang's New Life movement.[29]

Yet reality was rather different. Nanjing, the capital to which Wang had 'restored' the government, had been the scene of a brutal Japanese massacre little more than two years previously. Even if he had a little leverage, Wang served essentially at the pleasure of the Japanese. How could Wang square this with his statement that his collaboration strengthened the Chinese nation, rather than reducing it? His answer was in part instrumental (that someone had to save China from the inevitable Japanese onslaught), but he also used two ideological tools, one negative and one positive. The negative one was anti-communism, an idea whose power Wang found so compelling that he made it one of the three key slogans of his regime (along with 'national reconstruction' and 'peace'). Wang's anti-communism was clearly deeply felt, but it also provided him with a powerful rhetorical tool to oppose two tenets of Chiang's argument that the exiled Chongqing regime was the truly Nationalist one. First, Wang could point to Chiang's accommodation, however uneasy, with the Communists in the United Front as a sign of his betrayal of China's fundamental interests. It also enabled him to make a politically useful comparison: by allying with the Communists, argued Wang, Chiang was selling China out to the USSR. In later years, Chinese communism was thought notable by external observers because of its indigenous roots and distinctiveness from the Soviet model, so it is worth recalling that before it took power, the common perception was that Mao's party was in thrall to the Soviets (and certainly the relationship was close). Making this accusation took some of the sting out of the argument that Wang's behaviour with regard to Japan was uniquely treacherous: furthermore, Wang pointed out that the Japanese were a reality that had to be dealt with in the here and now, whereas there was still time to prevent further Soviet influence in China. Wang also drew on one of the other positive threads in East Asian nationalism to cement his claim to power: pan-Asianism. Sun had, of course, been a strong advocate of the theory, and now Wang invoked Sun as a mentor in his quest to use pan-Asianism as the explanation for his actions.

Wang's attempt to create a collaborationist nationalism deserves more serious attention than it has achieved because of the defeat in World War II of the system that produced it. It was not an illogical response to what was clearly a major crisis of Chinese identity in the mid-twentieth century. Yet his experiment must ultimately be counted a failure. Above all, the reality of Wang's regime belied his rhetoric of partnership with Japan. Chiang's China had many flaws and did not enjoy full sovereignty. But it was much more powerful than Wang's regime, which in reality was dependent on Japan for its power and survival. When Japan was defeated, Wang's regime (by then led by Chen Gongbo) left behind few traces.[30]

Conclusion: Success and Failure

Looking at the nationalisms of East Asia in the century from 1839 to 1945, one could argue that Japan's was coherent and triumphant, whereas China's was weak and inchoate, and Korea's was suppressed and then liberated only by the *deus ex machina* of Japanese defeat in 1945. This is a superficially attractive interpretation, but it is also misleading.

Japan's nationalism, after all, led it to a self-destructive war. It is true that nationalism was not, by itself, the only cause of that war. It is also true that the Meiji revolution created, at breakneck speed, a modern nation state from a premodern military hierarchy. Japan before World War II enjoyed astonishing growth rates and became a highly sophisticated participant in the modern world. But it also succumbed to the worst aspects of nationalism. In particular, it drew on the anti-rational, romantic strain of nationalism that stressed the uniqueness of the Japanese nation, rather than its commonality with other such polities. Rather than primarily defining the nation in terms of civic values, it stressed primordial ones instead. Japanese nationalism sought to overcome modernity—by which it meant the rational, scientistic aspects of modernity—in a way that its Chinese counterpart never did.

Chinese nationalism has also generally been considered a failure, at least until its communist manifestation in the post-1949 era. Yet the journey from the Opium Wars to the end of World War II shows significant progress of the idea in the face of great difficulties. China did not have Japan's cohesion or prosperity at the time that Western imperialism arrived in force in the mid-nineteenth century. Following that was the experience of constant warfare through much of the early twentieth century. Despite the immense destruction that the war caused, spelling doom for the Nationalist Party, the idea of nationalism was boosted by the involvement of the wider population in the experience of total war, although the Communists were the beneficiaries. China maintained, in the face of powerful odds, a citizen-based nationalism that embraced more of the Enlightenment than it rejected. It took total defeat in wartime for the same to be true of Japan. And while half of Korea has also embraced civic nationalism, the other half still remains in thrall to a much less rational vision of the nation state, tied to the cult of one family. The formation of nationalism in East Asia that began in the mid-nineteenth century is not yet over.

NOTES

1. J. A. Fogel (2009) *Articulating the Sinosphere: Sino-Japanese Relations in Space and Time*, Cambridge, MA.
2. C. Gluck (1985) *Japan's Modern Myths: Ideology in the Late Meiji Period*, Princeton, NJ.
3. For a detailed examination of the period from 1600 to the late nineteenth century, see A. Gordon (2008) *A Modern History of Japan*, Oxford, chs. 1–3.
4. Gluck, *Japan's Modern Myths*, 74, 84, 89. N. Shimazu (2009) *Japanese Society at War: Death, Memory and the Russo-Japanese War*, Cambridge.
5. B. Schwartz (1964) *In Search of Wealth and Power: Yen Fu and the West*, Cambridge, MA.
6. L. Liu (1995) *Translingual Practice: Literature, National Culture, and Translated Modernity, China 1900–1937*, Stanford, CA.

7. M.-C. Bergère, trans. J. Lloyd (1998) *Sun Yatsen*, Stanford, CA.
8. P. A. Kuhn (1971) *Rebellion and its Enemies in Late Imperial China*, Cambridge, MA.
9. X. Guoqi (2005) *China and the Great War:* China's Pursuit of a New National Identity and Internationalization, Cambridge.
10. R. Mitter (2004) *A Bitter Revolution: China's Struggle with the Modern World*, Oxford.
11. R. Rogaski (2004) *Hygienic Modernity: Meanings of Health and Disease in Treaty-Port China*, Berkeley, CA.
12. J. Taylor (2009) *The Generalissimo: Chiang Kai-shek and the Struggle for Modern China*, Cambridge, MA.
13. P. Duara (1995) *Rescuing History from the Nation: Questioning Narratives of Modern China*, Chicago, IL, chs. 5 and 6.
14. J. R. Pusey (1983) *China and Charles Darwin*, Cambridge, MA.
15. F. Dikötter (1992) *The Discourse of Race in Modern China*, Stanford, CA, 118; for race in non-Western nationalist thought, see Chapter 4 by Andreas Eckert and on race in European fascist thought, see Chapter 29 by Roger Eatwell.
16. E. J. M. Rhoads (2003) *Manchus and Han: Ethnic Relations and Political Power in Late Qing and Early Republican China, 1861–1928*, Seattle, WA.
17. See also Chapter 34 by Cemil Aydin.
18. E. Hotta (2007) *Pan-Asianism and Japan's War, 1931–1945*, Basingstoke, 59.
19. J. B. Crowley (1966) *Japan's Quest for Autonomy: National Security and Foreign Policy, 1930–1938*, Princeton, NJ; R. Smethurst (1974) *A Social Basis for Prewar Japanese Militarism: The Army and the Rural Community*, Berkeley, CA.
20. M. Hane (1992) *Modern Japan: A Historical Survey*, Boulder, CO, 250, 262.
21. P. E. Tsurumi (1984) 'Colonial Education in Korea and Taiwan', and M. E. Robinson, 'Colonial Publication Policy and the Korean Nationalist Movement', in R. H. Myers and M. R. Peattie (eds.) *The Japanese Colonial Empire, 1895–1945*, Princeton, NJ.
22. H. O. Park (2005) *Two Dreams in One Bed: Empire, Social Life, and the Origins of the North Korean Revolution in Manchuria*, Durham, NC.
23. Mao Tse-tung [Mao Zedong] (1967) *Selected Writings*, Calcutta, 74.
24. See the essays in 'China in World War II', special edition of *Modern Asian Studies*, March 2011.
25. P. Duara (2003) *Sovereignty and Authenticity: Manchukuo and the East Asian Modern*, Lanham, MD.
26. R. Nedostup (2009) *Superstitious Regimes: Religion and the Politics of Chinese Modernity*, Cambridge, MA.
27. W. Ke-wen (2001) 'Wang Jingwei and the Policy Origins of the "Peace Movement", 1932–1937', in D. P. Barrett and L. N. Shyu (eds.) *Chinese Collaboration with Japan, 1932–1945: The Limits of Accommodation*, Stanford, CA.
28. J. H. Boyle (1972) *China and Japan at War, 1937–1945: The Politics of Collaboration*, Stanford, CA, 304.
29. D. P. Barrett (2001) 'The Wang Jingwei Regime, 1940–1945: Continuities and Discontinuities with Nationalist China', in Barrett and Shyu (eds.) *Chinese Collaboration*; F. Ferlanti (2010) 'The New Life Movement in Jiangxi Province, 1934–1938', *Modern Asian Studies*, 44.
30. But see M. Zanasi (2006) *Saving the Nation: Economic Modernity in Republican China*, Chicago, IL.

Suggested Further Reading

This list has been chosen to reflect texts that give greater academic depth on East Asian nationalism, but do not demand immensely detailed knowledge of the field.

Brook, T. and Schmid, A. (ed.) (2000) *Nation Work: Asian Elites and National Identities*, Ann Arbor, MI. Essays that show the interactions between various forms of East Asian nationalism.

Brownlee, J. S. (1997) *Japanese Historians and the National Myths, 1600–1945: The Age of the Gods and the National Myths, 1600–1945*, Vancouver. Examines the role of historians in shaping Japanese nationalism.

Duara, P. (1995) *Rescuing History from the Nation: Questioning Narratives of Modern China*, Chicago, IL. A theoretically rigorous examination of how nationalism can be a misleading way to understand modern China.

Eckert, C. J. et al. (1991) *Korea Old and New: A History*, Cambridge, MA. Essays by five key scholars on Korea, explaining the historical origins of contemporary Korean nationalism.

Fogel, J. A. (2009) *Articulating the Sinosphere: Sino-Japanese Relations in Space and Time*, Cambridge, MA. The first chapter in particular gives a thoughtful overview of the *longue durée* of two millennia of relations between China and Japan.

Gerth, K. (2003) *China Made: Consumer Culture and the Creation of the Nation*, Cambridge, MA. Shows that new social choices to do with consumption profoundly shaped modern Chinese identity.

Gluck, C. (1985) *Japan's Modern Myths: Ideology in the Late Meiji Period*, Princeton, NJ. A classic exposition of the way in which Japanese nationalism was created using 'invented traditions'.

Harrison, H. (2001) *China: Inventing the Nation*, London. Concise and accessible account of the way in which citizenship and symbolism contributed to the modernity of Chinese nationalism.

Mitter, R. (2004) *A Bitter Revolution: China's Struggle with the Modern World*, Oxford. Uses one crucial nationalist event, the May Fourth demonstration of 1919, to examine the formation of Chinese nationalism.

Narangoa, L. and Cribb, R. (eds.) (2003) *Imperial Japan and National Identities in Asia, 1895–1945*, London. Essays that use the Japanese Empire as a starting point to explore the rich range of anti-imperialist nationalisms in Asia.

Robinson, M. (1988) *Cultural Nationalism in Colonial Korea*, Seattle, WA. Important account of Korean nationalism as articulated by colonial intellectuals.

Smethurst, R. (1974) *A Social Basis for Prewar Japanese Militarism: The Army and the Rural Community*, Berkeley, CA. Detailed examination of the links between militarism and nationalism in pre-1945 Japan.

Shimazu, N. (2009) *Japanese Society at War: Death, Memory and the Russo-Japanese War*, Cambridge. An innovative account of how the public memory of war helped to shape Japanese nationalism.

Unger, J. (ed.) (1996) *Chinese Nationalism*, Armonk, NY. Essays by major scholars on the theory of Chinese nationalism.

Young, L. (1998) *Japan's Total Empire: Manchuria and the Culture of Wartime Imperialism*, Berkeley, CA. Shows that the expansion of empire in the 1930s helped to reshaped Japanese nationalism on the domestic front.

CHAPTER 15

NATIONALISM IN COLONIAL AND POST-COLONIAL AFRICA

BRUCE J. BERMAN AND JOHN M. LONSDALE

The Trapdoor of Historiography and the Errors of Conventional Wisdom

Students of nationalism rightly insist on their subject's diversity, but sub-Saharan Africa seems to offer one set of varieties too many. Its forty-odd states represent nearly one quarter of the United Nations, yet the ideas that first inspired them have fallen through the trapdoor of historiography and their subsequent histories have been misconstrued. General histories of nationalism often ignore the continent; it is as if Africa were not part of world history. For this neglect there are two connected reasons, imperial self-regard and Western conventional wisdom.

Imperial historians write of decolonization, not independence. This implies that, just as European rivalry had drawn Africa's political map, so too its freedom owed more to Western strategy than African effort. After the Second World War an exhausted Europe needed allies in the new Cold War. To satisfy nationalisms, once they became a threat, would foil a global communism. This Eurocentric view is valuable in noting different and changing contexts. Britain and France could apply in Africa lessons taught by nationalists elsewhere, which Belgium and Portugal, for example, had not shared. And Africans had to fight harder over time—as in the thirty-year wars of southern Africa. But imperial historians say little about African political ideas, beyond Western estimates of whether they were moderate or radical or, later, became a Chinese or Russian shade of red.

In the past half-century, moreover, the conventional understanding of Africa's nation states has recycled old stereotypes of the African 'other' in the new language of social science. The modern state, it is said, has failed to develop effectively in Africa because it was 'artificially' imposed by the colonial conquest that ruptured the 'natural' evolution of African societies. The primordial ties and identities of ancient tribal cultures have, in response, overwhelmed the weak national identities of post-colonial states. 'Tribalism', recently redubbed 'ethnicity' in more modern and ostensibly neutral usage, bears the brunt of the blame for Africa's supposed failure and regression into chaotic violence. As Leroy Vail noted, it has been treated 'as a cultural ghost... an atavistic residue... [that] should have evaporated with the passage of time [but] continues to refuse to obey the laws of social and political change'.[1]

Africa becomes an atavism, a throwback, a region of darkness and absence, the radical 'other', isolated and different from the rest of the world. It is where modernity has failed and ancient savagery reasserted itself in inhuman violence and ruthless plunder. The continent's history becomes a sequence of failures that have left it out of the globalized world. Economically, it has been marginalized and excluded. In James Ferguson's words, Africa has become 'a continent of failed states, faux nations and "basketcase" economies'.[2]

Our two chapters draw on recent African and Africanist scholarship to dispute this conventional view, and on three grounds, all rooted in an understanding of modern history as global and interconnected in which one cannot contrast the 'success' of some nations against the failure of others: first, the fact that Africa has long been shaped by rather than excluded from the global economy; second, that politicized ethnicity and nationalism are intertwined twins rather than polar opposites, both of them modern; and, finally, that comparisons between 'Western' and African nation states are more instructive than the contrasts too often drawn between an ideal type of the first and a dismissive caricature of the second.

First, conventional wisdom ignores the degree to which Africa has long been shaped by its connections with the rest of the world. Capitalism, nationalism, state-building, and globalization have affected Africa at least as much as other continents. Africa's post-colonial history, the subject of Bruce Berman's chapter (Chapter 18), sharpens this comparative perspective, since the possibilities of African nationhood were constrained by two very different phases of global political economy.

The new African states initially pursued nation-building with the state-centred 'development' strategies recommended by international economic institutions and the historical experience of most Western powers. But the economic context was now very different. Europe's new nation states were, by and large, industrializers. In the late twentieth century it was still Africa's primary products that attracted world commerce, and with declining terms of trade. Agriculture and mineral extraction widened the regional differentiation typical of the recent colonial past; unlike industry, they did not encourage the integration of new national economies. Nationalism and regionally based ethnicities, accordingly, competed to control state resources. Largely in consequence African states were marked by an increasing bureaucratic authoritarianism, both civil and military, and acquired their distinctive, two-faced character. The institutions and symbols of the modern nation state masked an underworld of personal power, clientelism, and patronage. Late and dependent entry to the modern global economy was Africa's problem, not its self-inflicted exclusion.

But then there came a sharp break in global economic history, when international institutions and Western states changed the rules of commerce in the 1980s; this was especially damaging to Africa. Neo-liberal 'structural adjustment' undermined the previous connections between state power and economic activity, weakening both. Widening gulfs between wealth and poverty, growing pauperization, and the diminution of state resources generated increasingly desperate attempts to grab what remained. New, extreme forms of violence, even when ethnic in character, were a response to this state failure, not its cause. Here was a 'crisis of governance' rather than a failure of nationhood; for it was internal as much as external pressure for democratization that opened the next phase in sub-Saharan Africa's history, a 'second liberation'.

This brings us to our second ground of dispute: our conviction that African ethnicity has much in common with nationalism, as in Europe. John Lonsdale's chapter (Chapter 16) traces long cultural, intellectual, economic, and social histories of African ethnicities, but their politicization is something new in its intensity. Ethnic awakening was contemporaneous with, sometimes opposed to, sometimes reinforcing, pan-ethnic movements of anti-colonial nationalism. Both political energies grew within colonial institutions before they turned against the colonial state. The social forces behind the imagining of Africa's ethnic and national communities are modern, not archaic.

The renewed democratization promised by the second liberation of the 1990s in fact gave birth to new forms of ethnic conflict. Paradoxically, these reinforce nationalism and demonstrate the enduring, if violently contested, reality of Africa's nation states. Insurgents have demanded from their states a parity of cultural respect, political influence, and economic entitlement. Africa's nation states are indeed struggling with their own versions of the same issues that threaten nation states across the world: mass migration, conflict between immigrants and 'natives', increasingly multi-ethnic societies and hybrid national identities—all in the shadow of a global crisis of capitalism that pits class against class, community against community, and nation against nation. Africa is comparable with other continents, not a different world.

We emphasize these global comparisons because—our final objection—Western political scientists tend to contrast what they suppose to be actual African experience with an ideal model of the Western nation state. The latter is assumed to be secular, industrial, capitalist, and democratic, resting on a strong, almost universal, national identity nurtured by a common history, language, and culture. Both dominant modernist paradigms, liberal and Marxist, see allegedly atavistic ethnicities as a threat to what they take to be this supposedly normal national story.

Agency and Contingency: The Creation of States, Classes, Ethnicities, and Nations

If, however, we focus on the conflicts in Western state-building rather than their fabricated myths 'of origins and national continuity... in which the imaginary singularity of national formation is constructed daily',[3] unhelpful contrast dissolves into useful comparison. There were roughly twenty-five European states in 1900, forty-odd colonial states in sub-Saharan Africa. If the latter were unnatural impositions, the same could be said of the former. In 1500 there had been five hundred European polities—dynastic empires, commercial leagues, principalities, clerical palatinates, city states, and, after prolonged civil war, a national monarchy in England. It took four centuries of conflict and violence, not natural evolution, to reduce them to twenty-five polities.

In the eighteenth century the rulers of most *ancien régimes* spoke the international language of civilization, French, and despised the vulgar vernaculars and cultures of their subjects, a common herd divided into local ethnic communities. Here was a cradle of nationhood no more promising than that of colonial Africa. But the historical contexts were very different, to appreciate which we have to distinguish between 'state building', the creation of an apparatus of control, and 'state formation', the outcome of a largely unconscious, contradictory process of conflict, negotiation, and compromise between diverse groups.[4] In Europe this process coincided with the growth of capitalist markets and class relations, especially the proletarianization of a national labour force. This freed people from 'feudal' relations, making them ready to demand citizenship. In Africa the two epochs of post-colonial history produced very different socioeconomic processes that formed sub-national regionalisms as much as states.

Nineteenth-century European nationalism was largely a response to the challenges of modernity from both state and market. The first brought people under greater state control; the latter sucked increasing numbers into the class conflicts of industrial capitalism, undermining the personal authority and patron-client reciprocities of pre-modern, largely agrarian, moral economies. For some, the new professional classes, modernity was an adventure and nationalism its ambition. For others, probably a majority, those who had been peasants and were becoming urban workers, modernity was an ordeal and nationalism a seeming protection. Nationalism, this contradictory sentiment, grew out of the conflicts and alliances within and between social classes, old and new, over how to redefine unprecedented capitalist inequalities within a new moral economy that might legitimate new state power. The answer to both ambition and anxiety was to make old states into new 'nations' in which members of all classes were deemed to be equal citizens, if often only after being forced into new definitions of identity and belonging.

Like all self-conscious human communities, nations are social constructions, imagined as timeless entities looming out of a distant past and sailing into an endless future. Such social imagination and political construction was well under way in Tudor

England. They powered both Spanish *reconquista* and Dutch republic, even the dynastic wars of Louis XIV.[5] Elsewhere in Europe it was the work of the long nineteenth century, from 1789 to 1914. A combination of the ideological subversions of secular enlightenment, the revolutionary adventure that converted French subjects into citizens, and the social ordeal of industrial capitalism—all evoked, especially in central Europe, a conservative, romantic reaction that seized on a concept of 'culture', the distinctive character of a people, or 'Volk', that would collect otherwise individual citizens into a unique 'nation'.

Much of nineteenth-century European cultural production, from linguistics and history to architecture and music, sought a return to the 'spirit' of the past by recovery of an 'authentic' national culture mythologized in a golden age of socially cohesive 'organic' communities. All this was an invention of tradition, 'the recycling—whether instrumental or unconscious—of fragments of a more or less phantasmal past in the service of social, cultural or political innovation'.[6]

The hybridity, malleability, and ambiguity of such constructions of nationhood produced a vigorous 'politics of authenticity' driven by internal conflict and external connections. With its overlapping imaginings of community—liberal, romantic, linguistic, and ethnic—nationalism's contradictions generated conflicts over national character and identity. After 1848 European nationalism became increasingly ethnicized, indeed racialized. Biological descent became the main criterion of belonging, as now in Africa, rather than choice and 'naturalization'. Intellectuals and the educated middle classes may have been the creators and consumers of invented national culture, but it was the state that took the lead in nationalizing society. Universal schooling and military conscription—as is not possible in Africa—fostered a fictive kinship and solidarity of national identity and patriotism.

Imagining an ethnic nation called for sharper boundaries between inclusion and exclusion. National citizenship required the marginalization of 'others' against whom the true nation could be rallied. The rise of modern anti-Semitism is the most emphatic example. Civic nationalism had first welcomed European Jews out of their ghettoes into the community of equal citizens, but a growing ethnic nationalism then sought to expel them from the nation as an alien intrusion and, ultimately, from the human race. Emancipated Jews came to embody the two main threats that secular modernity presented to supposedly organic national communities: the exploitation and class conflicts of capitalism and the cosmopolitan internationalism of socialism.

European nationalism's most distinctive political characteristic was its intimate ties with the state. Politics focused on winning state power. The state became the means to create and control the nation. It provided the framework of a new moral economy and it became the 'ultimate, impersonal, arbiter of secular dispute'.[7] State power supposedly protected the interests and integrity of the nation; its paternal trusteeship mitigated and legitimized capitalist inequalities between citizens. The disinterested authority of its institutions, serving the public interest with competence and probity, created an arena of civic trust. This displaced the personal, patron-client, ties of power and redistribution of pre-modern society, now redefined as corrupt intrusions into national governance.

The Colonial Origins of African States, Ethnicities, Classes, and Nations

The European officials who ruled Africa were among the finest products of the nation-forming process. Their nationalism, their bureaucratic culture, their support from the historical sense of white mission Christianity, all influenced the formation of African ethnicity and nationalism. Africans educated largely in mission schools—or, in anti-clerical French Africa, trained in bureaucracy at the École Normale William Ponty—absorbed both a sense of purposive history and a civic culture. This was the more true of those who went to metropolitan universities, perhaps especially to American ones, a disproportionate number of whom became nationalist leaders. They learned that the nation was the universal expression of successful modernity. Yet colonial officials were also convinced that ancient tradition must guide national community—as they themselves had been taught—and imagined similar models of authority and tradition for Africans.

Both the nationalism and the authoritarian paternalism of colonial officials influenced the redefinition of African ethnicity. While acting out before Africans a neo-traditional world dominated by the state, they were nonetheless ambivalent about African culture. Officials envied Africans their small, integrated, orderly 'organic' communities beloved of the European imagination. But 'tribes' were also seen as primitive, archaic, stagnant communities governed by rigid 'custom', survivals from an earlier stage of human evolution and bound to decay under Western impact, both cultural and capitalist. Africa's only defence against chaos was colonial state authority.[8] But officials (like political scientists later) also misunderstood. They thought tribal society to be natural to Africans, a nurse to social cohesion. John Lonsdale's chapter (Chapter 16) shows that Africans themselves had a more energetic, argued, sense of their ethnicity.

Colonial states acted ethnically, creating the strategic contexts in which ethnicity was or was not salient; they moulded the political choices that shaped ethnic politics in relation to other social cleavages. But officials had only a limited ability to control the social transformations over which they ruled. Their neo-traditional ideologies made them hesitant about encouraging the full-scale agrarian capitalism that would push peasants off their land. This caution resulted in a partial transformation-partial preservation of indigenous societies, in which most householders retained some rights to land while producing for the market and/or periodically entering into wage labour. This was not because such 'straddling' between self-mastery and wage employment was 'functional' for capitalism, but because colonial states were restrained both by limited resources and the fear of the political consequences of doing more.

While officials tried to cultivate a distant 'prestige' as the cheapest form of self-defence, their power was in reality interactive, drawing on collaborative alliances in which, as patrons, they attached client African elites to the state. These ties built upon existing African power relations, widening the inequalities previously negotiated within their moral economies. Access to the state became the key to wealth accumulation, controlled by local African officials in the interests of their kin and clients. Kin and clients with other resources were often their fiercest critics—like the growing literate intelligentsia employed elsewhere in the state apparatus, and the few wealthy farmers, cattle owners and traders who used their surplus to play their own patron-client politics in order to claim access to the wider patronage networks of the state. Chapter 16 shows how kings or chiefs were often involved in conflict they did not always win, especially when ownership of property became more attractive than wealth in people.

Colonial rulers could certainly not dictate the process of ethnic formation. Each administrative district ideally contained a single homogeneous 'tribe', with its taxpayers subjected to 'tribal discipline' by local authorities who supposedly drew their legitimacy from 'tradition'. It was not quite like that. Officials who thought they respected 'age-old custom' by clarifying its norms and sanctions often stirred up bitter, irresolvable, disputes about what custom had been or how it ought now to be reformed.[9]

Nor did the colonial desire to know who was who—principally to fix tax or labour obligations—work out as expected. Some administrative boundaries did, it is true, produce 'district tribes', or still larger provincial ones, that fleshed out colonial categories with a newly imagined African community, like the 'Luba' in the Congo. But this 'dual dynamic of assimilation and differentiation'[10] often fostered a cultural imagination that challenged colonial ideas about how society should work. Officials, missionaries, and anthropologists might combine to invent traditions, which, by defining tribal identities, would help preserve social stability and political control. But Africans had their own ideas, largely by recourse to redemptive histories—as in nineteenth-century Europe. Large, newly self-conscious ethnicities, substantial expansions of political scale like the Yoruba of Nigeria, the Kalenjin or Luyia of Kenya, the Zulu of South Africa, began to acquire a political awareness of their own to which colonial rule itself had to adjust—illustrations of unintended state formation. The emotive, self-reliant, images of kinship and 'home' infused larger social collectivities better able to cope with colonial power and wider markets.

For ethnicity provided people with their most easily assembled political assets in the competition for the scarce goods of modernity, for access to local resources of land and labour, and, perhaps above all, to protection against the costs of social differentiation. But how to use ethnicity, and to whose local advantage, whether to promote opportunity or protect survival, became a matter of internal debate over what, in new conditions, were the socially acceptable norms for allocating unequal obligation and entitlement in the allocation of values, summed up as 'moral economy'. This intimate arena of dispute we call *moral ethnicity*. Ethnicity is above all a relational concept, guiding how we relate to 'ourselves' as much as to 'others'. The obverse, external, side of this argumentative ethnic consciousness was the communal solidarity and political organization we call *political tribalism*, mobilized first against the alien colonial state and then against the competing interests of emerging rival ethnicities for access to the state and control of its patronage. It is this political tribalism that Western prejudice thinks natural to Africa, ignorant of the historical conflicts that have brought it into greater prominence than ever before.

One cannot understand post-colonial African nationalism, the subject of Bruce Berman's chapter (Chapter 18), without considering this legacy of the colonial state. The state and society linkages peculiar to colonial Africa—patron-client networks centred on the local African agents of colonial power and contained largely within emergent ethnic communities—created a plurality of communities of trust. Reputation, rights, and responsibilities were subject to social scrutiny within these communities, while between them there grew an increasingly intense, amoral, competition for access to the material resources of the state. There was little chance that Africans would develop, as in some European states, a systemic trust in the state as impersonal arbiter of conflict or disinterested distributor of public resources.

So African political languages are full of metaphors of 'eating' or 'devouring' opponents. Political ambition focuses on getting one's share of the state's resources. Politics bears a personal, material, and opportunistic character. It is also dangerous. Those who try to eat can also be eaten in the unscrupulous food-chain of power. This 'politics of the belly' originated in colonial institutions and social relations.[11] Dealing with the colonial state offered an opportunity for access to its resources, but courted the danger of running foul of its seemingly arbitrary sanctions. Survival in this capricious world required the support and protection that only patrons and clients could provide. Ethnicity provided a moral economy in which such protections could be negotiated.

Another colonial legacy was the lesson that 'development' was difficult. After 1945 the European powers tried to develop Africa, partly to regain a legitimacy bruised by American and Russian anti-imperialism, partly to earn the export dollars of post-war recovery. This 'second colonial occupation' brought an unprecedented expansion of the state's apparatus beyond the personalized relations of patronage. This deeper intrusion into indigenous societies was intended to improve economic productivity, provide a large increase in social services, and allow Africans to be taxed more heavily than before. But, to colonial consternation, development led to growing conflict on three levels: over the unequal distribution of benefits within African communities, to the discomfort of collaborating elites; over regional differentiations that fired up 'tribal' conflicts; and over the official efforts to control markets and wages, which aroused farmers and workers. At all three levels protest merged into a growing, mass, opposition, exploited or led by an intelligentsia employed largely by the state. Yet nationalism itself was nothing if not developmental and leaders were often uneasy at using popular resistance to schemes of which, in principle, they approved—once they were to the benefit of citizens, no longer subjects.

Kwame Nkrumah, prime minister of sub-Saharan Africa's first new nation, Ghana, famously advised nationalists: 'Seek ye first the political kingdom.' African nationalism was indeed, as in Europe, primarily an attempt to gain state power and control its collaborative networks and patronage sources, so as to domesticate modernity in the name of an imagined new community. But the rise of anti-colonial protest from such varied sources—from kings, chiefs, farmers, workers and, perhaps most alarmingly, women—and within such varied arenas as writing circles, the popular press, student societies, 'tribal welfare associations', and trades unions—some as determined to press their sectional interests as to unite to control the state—meant that the political kingdom was best left undefined. The Kenyan trade unionist and nationalist Tom Mboya argued that unity required simplification of aim, one which all could grasp 'without arguing about the details of policy or of government programmes after Independence. Everyone is taught to know the enemy—the colonial power—and the one goal—independence.'[12]

The definition of the nation, the entitlements of citizenship, the drive to 'develop' were all, as late-colonial history had shown and Mboya knew, deeply controversial matters. Africans now took on the tasks that colonial regimes had either blocked or in which they had failed. Their nationalism, like any other, was both a discourse of political legitimacy and an embodiment of popular sovereignty. But its colonial legacy made it protean in content, practices, and symbols. It made universal claims for the nation as a self-determining global actor; it also absorbed contradictory ethnic claims of cultural renewal and separate identity. The state power it inherited was one of authoritarian bureaucracy. Electoral democracy, parliamentary or presidential, was for the most part tacked on to hastily written independence constitutions. Nation-building was not going to be easy. And, as Berman's chapter shows, the international environment did not remain friendly for long.

Notes

1. L. Vail (ed.) (1989) 'Introduction: Ethnicity in Southern African History', in *The Creation of Tribalism in Southern Africa*, London, 1–3.
2. J. Ferguson (2006) *Global Shadows: Africa in the Neo-Liberal World Order*, Durham, NC, and London, 2–3, 8, 16.
3. E. Balibar (1991) 'The Nation Form: History and Ideology', in E. Balibar and I. Wallerstein (eds.) *Race, Nation, Class: Ambiguous Identities*, London, 87.
4. B. Berman and J. Lonsdale (1992) *Unhappy Valley: Conflict in Kenya and Africa*, London, Nairobi, and Athens, OH, 5 and ch. 2.
5. For England, Holland, France, and Spain (and Ethiopia) as pre-modern nations, see A. Hastings (1997) *The Construction of Nationhood: Ethnicity, Religion and Nationalism*, Cambridge.
6. J.-F. Bayart (2005) *The Illusion of Cultural Identity*, London, 35–6.
7. K. Silvert (ed.) (1963) 'The Strategy of the Study of Nationalism', *Expectant Peoples: Nationalism and Development*, New York, 21–4.
8. B. J. Berman (1990) *Control and Crisis in Colonial Kenya*, London, 106–8.
9. S. Berry (1993) *No Condition is Permanent*, Madison, WI.
10. S. Mozaffar (1995) 'The Institutional Logic of Ethnic Politics', in H. Glickman (ed.) *Ethnic Conflict and Democratization in Africa*, Atlanta, GA, 50–1.

11. J.-F. Bayart (1993) *The State in Africa: The Politics of the Belly*, London.
12. T. Mboya (1963) *Freedom and After*, London, 61.

Suggested Further Reading

Anderson, B. (1991) *Imagined Communities*, London and New York.

Hobsbawm, E. and Ranger, T. (eds.) (1983) *The Invention of Tradition*, Cambridge and New York; in which Ranger's chapter has been much qualified in T. Ranger and O. Vaughan (eds.) (1993) *Legitimacy and the State in Twentieth-Century Africa: Essays in Honour of A. H. M. Kirk-Greene*, London.

Iliffe, J. (1995, 2007) *Africans: The History of a Continent*, Cambridge.

Reid, R. (2009) *A History of Modern Africa: 1800 to the Present*, Chichester.

Seal, A. (1973) 'Imperialism and Nationalism in India', in J. Gallagher, G. Johnson, and A. Seal (eds.) *Locality, Province and Nation: Essays on Indian Politics 1870 to 1940*, Cambridge, 1–27 (an inspiration to Africanists and from where we take 'the trapdoor of historiography').

Spear, T. (2003) 'Neo-Traditionalism and the Limits of Invention in British Colonial Africa', *Journal of African History*, 44, 3–27.

Tilly, C. ed. (1975) *The Formation of National States in Western Europe*, Princeton, NJ.

CHAPTER 16

ANTI-COLONIAL NATIONALISM AND PATRIOTISM IN SUB-SAHARAN AFRICA[1]

JOHN M. LONSDALE

African Nationalism in World History

Thomas Hodgkin, an early analyst, never doubted that Africa belonged to world history. Discarding the preconceptions of imperial historiography and Western conventional wisdom, he saw African nationalism as 'the final stage of a chain-reaction' that the French Revolution had initiated by translating the rights of man into the rights of nations. African movements might be 'mixed up', with differing levels and aims—for workers' rights, peasant freedoms, religious liberty, tribal welfare, nation-statehood, or pan-African union—but so too were other nationalisms.[2] Hodgkin conceded that his views lacked historical perspective. We think we know more African history now. Paradoxically, this enables a still deeper global comparison. Our joint introduction argued that European nationalisms sought to tame modernity by recourse to an imagined history of a new community, the nation. Modernity was just as shocking to Africa; Africans had the same desire for instructive, often evasive, history, to restore in societies divided by new opportunities and dangers some sense of moral community.

When and how does one choose a vigilant history that entitles one to have a fabled moral economy restored? George Orwell answered both questions when, under aerial bombardment in 1941, he argued that England must turn socialist to survive. Class division was fatal in the crisis of war; revolution would also make the English 'more ourselves not less'; England would 'still be England'. Orwell thought patriotism stemmed from public concern for an honourable history under threat. But whose history did he choose? England's, not Britain's.[3] In old countries clustered memories of buried nations offer a choice of potential sovereignties to raise from the dead.[4] In new countries, as in Africa, these memories lie in shallower graves.

This chapter's argument depends on a distinction between patriotism and nationalism. By 'patriotism', a slippery term, I mean what Obafemi Awolowo called, in terms Orwell would recognize, a 'searching... self-examination' to ensure that self-rule respects the rights historically won by citizens, typically household heads in Africa.[5] Each sub-Saharan colony comprised many previously self-governing localities, what Léopold Senghor of Senegal called *patries*. Modern African patriotisms were bound to be local before 'national'. If, as Ernest Renan thought, nations need to get their history wrong, so too do Africa's localities, since they too, in a continent forever on the move, have plural pasts. Take Asante, built, like Europe's kingdoms, by war and migration. Its local chiefs promised self-restraint as a condition of justice: Not to chase women, nor get drunk, nor, crucially, to disclose the origins of their subjects, fearful of discrimination against strangers.[6] Patriotism is self-searching, nationalism seeks sovereignty. Nationalisms—coalitions of energized patriotisms or class-interests with disputed expectations of sovereignty—have good reason for imagined, inclusive, pasts.

When and how are patriotic pasts chosen south of the Sahara? Any old past will not do; to address crisis it has to convince. The African recourse to plausibly deserving or harrowing histories that Hodgkin could not know, born in the moral crisis of colonialism, may pull African nationalism back into scholarly examination, up through historiography's trapdoor. Orwell's thoughts on continuity, choice, and change are best focused, first, on Ethiopia, under alien rule for less than a decade. Its 1974 revolution, like the French, was a national adventure; it was also a patriotic ordeal, provoking ethnic awakenings in response, like later, nineteenth-century European nationalisms.

In 1963 the continent's new rulers founded the Organization of African Unity in Emperor Haile Selassie's capital, Addis Ababa. Some, when young, had made an equally quixotic pan-African gesture, condemning Italy's Ethiopian conquest. African Christianity had long been intrigued by the psalmist's vision of an Ethiopia reaching out to God. Some Ethiopians call their Christianity the oldest, conceived by the Queen of Sheba in Solomon's bed. When West Africans needed national histories they exhumed dead empires, Ghana and Mali. Liberation movements later resurrected the equally vanished glories of Zimbabwe or Azania. Ethiopia was an African exception, the real thing, a nation since antiquity and, with its sense of divine election as a second Israel, living proof of Africa's central place in world history.

Ethiopia is a nation by many criteria, with a continuous history since the fourth century CE; a line of 'Solomonic' dynasties chronicled in writing; a national Church with a common geography and calendar of pilgrimage; a peripatetic court that at times ruled its provinces while its aristocratic, Amharic, culture embraced ambitious provincials. By 1900 Ethiopia looked like an early-modern European kingdom. Its 'new monarchy' had defeated an earlier Italian invasion. Joining the African scramble, its Amharic core had won a polyglot empire. After 1945 Haile Selassie reinforced his central power against noble banditry and invited missionaries to expand provincial education. In 1974 he suffered the reforming despot's common fate, being deposed by the army, his autocracy's chosen servant, at a time of famine and peasant revolt. 'Trees that are planted,' he reflected, 'do not always bear the desired fruit.'[7]

Ethiopia's revolution was as terrible as any. But Orwell might well have observed that its Amharic core was still Ethiopia. The revolutionaries saw their Marxism as a patriotic path to global modernity, as messianic as the Orthodox Church, the more durable world-historical symbol they also co-opted. Ethiopia was changing nonetheless. Peasants found refuge from revolution in local patriotisms; Soviet nationality theory taught the regime, similarly, that Ethiopia was a multinational state. But the country's current 'ethnic federalism' also owes much to the emperor's earlier reforms. While the Orthodox Church had a national Bible, missionaries made vernacular translations. To non-Amhara the Bible was as modern as Karl Marx. If new nations elsewhere were imagined as moral narratives in a secularizing age, many Africans have found in the Bible an enchanted new gateway to political possibility.

Scripture has often served as a primer in nationhood; the groaning children of Israel, freed slaves, provide the global prototype. That image, previously confined to core Ethiopia, now multiplied in its provinces. Oromo, 40 per cent of the population, more numerous than Amhara, had not previously seen themselves as one people. In 1993 one of their Christians, Mathewos Ciibasa, remembered: 'When I was a young man my only ambition was to become an Amhara. But then I came across the Oromo Bible. Realizing that God talked to me in my own language surprised me with joy, and changed my ambition completely.'[8] Ethiopia ceased to be an exception, if not for that reason alone, joining the rest of Africa, and Britain, in possessing not one but several patriotisms, potential nationalisms.

Educated Oromo imagined a novel but credible past, history as a national ordeal. Their patriotism justified their strange new privilege, literacy. They taught that Ethiopian conquest, helped by turncoat Oromo who became Amhara, had brought tyranny; that their historic social ties, imagined as kinship and inscribed in land, had been broken by imperial and then revolutionary expropriations. They catalogued folk culture, disputed their language's orthography, and called for restoration of what they thought they had lost, a pastoral democracy disciplined by ritual observance, generational cycles of power, and egalitarian moral economy—unlike rapacious Amhara aristocracy.

Africa, then, has its place among nationalisms. Ethiopia's revolutionaries welcomed modernity's adventure, its provincial patriots resented history's ordeal. Yet we must still free ourselves from the teleology that foretells uniform nationhood, an increasing rarity. Contingency is a better guide. Oromo, like Europeans, asked how to protect household honour and unequal personal obligation against impersonal markets rigged by arbitrary rule. Their answer remains a work in progress. African nationalism deserves comparison not with idealized Western outcomes but with that universal response to crisis, the demand for a history to instruct the future.

In the 1960s Europeans thought colonial rule had imported such history to Africa—history as enlightened social change. Its private beneficiaries, the new elites, appeared to pursue modernity as public purpose. Patrice Lumumba, ill-fated first prime minister of the ex-Belgian Congo, agreed that political parties were extra-mural classes in citizenship.[9] Such shallow history continues to dismiss African nationalism as a modernizing project that failed. But there are deeper, African, histories to consider. Their patriotic potential has not yet failed. Africans continue to ask how the renewal of past moral economies might infuse their states with nationhood.

To substantiate that thesis I first recall the hopes thrice raised by African nationalism, then argue that colonial rule was widely experienced as an ordeal. In response, Africans often imagined historically argumentative, internal, moral ethnicities. Too often these became rival political tribalisms in the competition for state power. Such intrinsically African contradictions shaped nationalist visions of the future.

Times of Hope

African nationalism first raised realistic hope, not necessarily for nation states, after the Second World War. Modern African political thought had initially been Pan-African; in 1945 a fifth Pan-African Congress still looked to a cohesive continent.[10] Britain and France also believed in closer union for many of their colonies. Britain hoped that East and Central African federations would, upon their wider stage, heal the racial conflicts that separately baffled each colony of white and Asian settlement. Africans refused to solve Britain's settler problems in this way but francophone leaders, familiar with federations, were as keen as their rulers to dissolve colonialism into a multinational French Community, not into nation states. Shared citizenship and employment rights were preferable to separate pauper sovereignties.

Nation states resulted, all the same. Few officials imagined any alternative, for power shapes rulers and it was most visible in each colony, even in federal French Africa. It also shapes subjects; their local deals put paid to Pan-African dreams. Further, as Europeans tried to 'develop' their colonies, to pay for post-war recovery with African exports, African electoral competition developed faster still. For development demanded a new politics. Indirect rule through local chiefs had kept people quiet; 'partnership' with urban professionals would get things done. In French and British Africa, new universities proved the earnest gradualism of this hope, as did cautious increases in electorates and legislators. Anxious 'to stand well in the eyes of the world'—the interfering United Nations—and 'to deserve well of the colonial peoples' (better than the Soviet Union), Britain knew 'development from above' needed support 'from below'. Nationalism, the only apparent source of popular energy, must therefore be steered into 'constructive courses' short of independence.[11] But reform had its usual unintended outcome, creating 'legal channels for organizing the expulsion of the colonial power'.[12] Like Haile Selassie, colonial rulers were ousted by their favourite clients—or their clients' more impatient rivals.

So, in 1951, Kwame Nkrumah became 'leader of government business' in the Gold Coast (Ghana), British Africa's 'model colony', with a cocoa-funded prosperity apparently assured. Nkrumah had six years of dyarchy, shared power, ahead of him, a brief enough training in self-rule before independence. By 1961 the calendar was shorter still, when the British let Tanganyika (mainland Tanzania) go two years after Julius Nyerere won his first general election. Tanganyika had no better prospects than Ghana; to the contrary, London saw no point in clinging to a territory that would always be poor. Why antagonize a still-friendly nationalism and land Britain with costs better borne by Africans? The French and even the unbending Belgians had gone, and Britain recoiled from bearing the increasing odium of colonialism alone (Portugal did not seem to care).

Development planning had dwindled, in a decade, to an admission that to leave was better than to stay. Britain's hopes were always qualified by the prudent proviso, first stated of an earlier model colony, Ceylon (Sri Lanka), that 'giving too much and too soon' was 'wiser than giving too little and too late'.[13] Hopes were foiled and prudence fortified when development, far from attracting support, provoked protest against its intimate intrusions and social divisions. It was more like a second colonial occupation, with little to show for it. By 1960, too, Africa was no longer so useful; Europe had recovered from war; the Anglo-French Suez fiasco of 1956 shattered any illusion that empire was the answer to American or Soviet power. France also came to fear the costs of its worldwide Union, and reduced its commitments south of the Sahara in order to concentrate, vainly, on keeping Algeria French.

In the end, France and Britain had to trust to what a governor called the only guard dogs in their late-colonial kennels, the nationalists with most votes. Feeding them concessions would keep them friendly.[14] In 1960 the wreck of the Belgian Congo, abandoned in panic, showed the alternative. The least one could ask, to depart in good order, without 'scuttle', had become for Britain and France their highest aspiration.

Visiting scholars remained hopeful a little longer than departing rulers. While veering from David Apter's early enthusiasm to Aristide Zolberg's later concern, political scientists focused on elites for whom modernity was a voyage of discovery, nationalism the compass, and a 'mass' party their vessel. Social change, opening up closed tribal worlds, encouraged political daring. Riding history's tide, nationalists nevertheless still had work to do for few Africans were 'moderns'; most remained 'traditionals'. In between, pilgrim 'transitionals' looked for satisfactions that no supposedly decaying tribe could offer. As cultural brokers, nationalists must 'mobilize' and 'integrate' these transitionals politically, to defeat patron parties reliant on 'residual' tribal loyalties. Earlier protests had been riotously religious or tribally reactionary; mass parties, reassuringly rational, co-opted those voluntary associations and trade unions whose members had taken a first step in modernity by breaking their tribal bonds. A party's bravura, its press and rallies, inspired by a leader's charisma, could stamp progressive purpose on social flux. State patronage, finally, would discipline party machines.

This summary of the era's more buoyant analyses suggests that many scholars saw nationalism as a tribute to Europe's civilizing mission. Blindness to racial subjection could be startling. In 1922, as one might expect of a retired British proconsul, Lord Lugard had claimed that Egyptian and Indian nationalisms were inspired by their British tuition in freedom: 'Their very discontent [was] a measure of their progress.' But thirty years later a senior American scholar almost agreed: African nationalism was the 'inevitable end product of the impact of Western imperialism and modernity'. The historians Ronald Robinson and Jack Gallagher summed up: in jointly engineering a world revolution, nationalism was 'the continuation of imperialism by other means'.[15]

Radical scholars saw continuity as defeat. Frantz Fanon scorned colonialism's 'spoilt children', bartering freedom 'around a green baize table'.[16] Parties had created not citizens but middle classes who, as rulers, feared the masses they had roused but not fed. Without the colonial's security of a pensioned passage home, they bought insurance by splitting public goods with their ethnic clients. One-party regimes, coalitions in jobbery for a spineless class, the petite bourgeoisie, aspired to no more than neo-colonial dependence. Their citizens had no sturdier vision to offer. Largely self-employed, they lacked a class perspective. Where then was patriotic sinew to be found?

Armies seemed the next best bet. Officers seemed natural patriots, of many ethnicities but with one *esprit de corps*. It was not as simple as that. East Africa's armies entered politics as armed trade unionists; Nigeria's fell murderously apart along ethnic fault-lines widened by uneven access to colonial education. Only Ghana's soldiers lived up to expectations, marching back to barracks after reintroducing multi-party politics to a country tired of autocratic people's democracy. But they had unusually seasoned allies. An older generation of professionals and chiefs, roughly treated by Nkrumah, was there to revive an earlier, less plebeian, power. Other armies—which made, or attempted, over thirty coups in the 1960s—fell into the factions that divided their civil societies. Professional soldiers lost their shine.

In a third time of hope scholars turned to scruffier guerrillas preparing people's war against the Portuguese, Rhodesia, and South Africa. Fanon thought common struggle would hammer tribes into a nation, then nerve citizens to send their rulers 'to school with the people'.[17] Amilcar Cabral of Portuguese Guinea, agronomist turned guerrilla leader, was not so sure. Peasants were unlikely revolutionaries; political will, not class struggle, was the key. Basil Davidson, taught by his Yugoslav experience, agreed that partisan war did not inevitably liberate. The popular support guerrillas needed could be secured as well by terror as by argument. Intimidation of the unpersuaded was likely to mature into oppression when power was won. Until history decided that issue most scholars gave guerrilla nationalisms the benefit of the doubt. Their violence seemed justified by colonial rule, now seen less as an adventure, more as an ordeal.

Colonial Ordeals

If colonial rule was the crucible of nationalism, it was also a period of African history. Europeans counted Africans into named, taxable, 'tribes' with chargeable leaders. Africans fought this 'documentary bullying'[18] with history. This often set household honour, sustained by more or less unequal bargains with neighbours and patrons, against the unlawful, anti-social, violence of any greater power. Such patriotic thought, as constitutional as it was ethnic, could question its ideological contemporary, territorial nationalism, as much as their joint enemy, alien rule.

Before 1880 more Africans lived in small societies, more of the time, than under states. Few in population, they tolerated powers that protected household self-mastery within local moral economies of unequal reputation. Land was abundant; legitimate wealth lay in attracting people. By marriage, trade, and clientage, household clusters enlisted strangers with useful skills and connections, so that the 'House', a 'coalition of capacities'[19] assembled by a 'big man', was as much the basis of society as lineage. Africa's internal frontiers allowed this composite mobility; frontier authority was argued between first-comers, knowing the land, and later arrivals claiming military or judicial expertise. These ideological politics could generate ethnic communities; some 'tribal' names are centuries old. Other groups were as transient as their big-man leaders, and language use was generally too fluid to demarcate 'others'. However porous many of these past borders of belonging may once have been, later patriots, like Orwell, romanticized them as cradles of moral economy now in crisis.

Africans were scarce and slippery subjects; kings often had to enslave strangers to get work done. History could also be cruel. Famine, a regular visitor in some parts, could force the free to submit to the strong. Some strength seemed atrocious. Origin myths, disclosing political theory, portray drunken, incestuous, or inhuman kings who sacrificed children, practised sorcery or, in religious coups, sanctified patronage into prerogative. Often seen as cruelly protective leopards, kings might also be fathers, masters but providers who 'divided the leopard-skin'.[20] Africans understood this paradox of power: To exist, power must be greedy, eating its subjects' substance; to work, it must be generous, sharing its fruits with allies or conditionally with clients. Rulers try to build disciplined power but states also take vulgar forms, as personal ambition seeks political protection and public office serves private ends. These dynamics of state-building and formation troubled colonial governors as much as kings. Ghana's Akan peoples compare power to an egg. Held too tight, it breaks, as in Haile Selassie's grip in 1974; too loosely, and it drops, as from colonial fingers after 1945.

Colonial rule was in some ways as weak as earlier African states. But it could be revolutionary: literates found opportunity; new urban frontiers freed others from rural dependence. It was certainly disruptive: peace tempted households to cut their protective 'House' or lineage obligations; slaves worked out a less slavish dependence. And it was reactionary, building more intrusive states that allowed more predatory power to form. Such ambiguity spelt moral dilemmas, but whether more than before, who can say?

Africans looked not to residual loyalties for comfort but to demanding moral economies for guidance. To whom was duty now owed, at what cost, for whose benefit, in a situational calculus of new identities, religious, occupational, and political? In rethinking themselves as men and women few *remained* 'tribal'; most *became* more ethnically aware. Given other possible solidarities, the rights, duties, and protections of ethnicity had to be keenly argued, a moral ethnicity.[21] Literacy clarified the essentially constitutional issues. As among the Oromo, writers called up ethnic publics, often in return for the school fees their localities had paid for them as an investment in power. Since the 1850s pioneer literates have been, above all, historians. As Africans, they rebutted white assumptions of prehistoric savagery. As patriots, they showed 'their people' how past civic virtue could be undefeated by modernity. Print poured from writing circles which read their Bible or Qur'an, Racine or Shakespeare. This wordy history is central to our case. Of theories of imperialism the most relevant observes that whites ruled this least alluring, last invaded, continent 'on a shoestring'.[22] The price for Africans, in subjection, household conflict, and social unease, was not so cheap.

Subjection spelt dislocation, not reasoned modernization. Whites tried a succession of African agents in their seventy short years of rule. To build the power to change Africa, they first promoted the new men who emerged in the politics of conquest: Christian or Muslim literates, ex-sergeants, head porters. These pursued their own interests, sometimes provoking rebellion. Officials then tried alliance with 'traditional chiefs', thought to represent the cohesive tribes in which whites believed Africans to live. Conservative collaboration would build consent by borrowing 'the substance of ruling authority' from their subjects.[23] This 'indirect rule' failed too. Officials expected more energy than chiefs thought wise; chiefs exacted more profit than officials approved. The 1930s depression forced further reform; African poverty served no one. After 1945 governors tried to build a progressive partnership with lawyers and businessmen. These, vulgarizing power in turn, converted council membership into party leadership. In a dialectic of state-building and formation, sceptical officials had shuffled a series of insecure elites, each privately insuring against public removal in some future crisis.

Household conflict was broader than elite anxiety. Colonial 'gatekeeper states' did what little was needed to open the gates of export growth.[24] Until minimal welfare provision and trade-union rights were conceded after 1945, increasingly autonomous households bore all the costs of change. These could be unexpectedly intimate. In one region farming couples found they could not sleep together after officials tidied up seasonally shifting habitats.[25] To lower tax liability polygynists cut down on their huts and privacy. With men often absent, sometimes under coercion, working on the roads, on plantations or down the mine, women bore many of the burdens of export growth. Where farming prospered, land's rising value hurt its social ties. 'Cocoa', a Gold Coast grower complained, 'destroys kinship and divides blood.'[26] Migrant labour could seem equally pernicious. In return for filial duty young men had looked to fathers for their marriage portion. Now they could invest in a more individual adulthood by disloyal wage-labour for others. 'That plough is now his wife!', a Kikuyu father cried in disowning a returning son.[27] From the equator to the Cape, seniors accused lost youth of absconding from domestic discipline to the moral idleness of town.

Demographic change caused more unease. Never numerous, Africans lost millions to the disruption and plagues of conquest, an agonizing time that lasted until 'Spanish' influenza completed the Great War's imperial havoc. After 1920 population growth and urbanization were still more disturbing. Rising numbers of impatient youth made nationalism, in part, a generational revolt.

Social relations became more uncertain. Alliances between white officials and African patrons devalued clients. Market women made men anxious. Witchcraft fears flourished. These were not new, especially for women in polygynous households, but there were signs of a novel, capitalist, unease; urban elites began to fear rural envy. Jomo Kenyatta, who wrote instructive history for '[his] people of Gikuyu' before ruling all Kenya, mourned that 'in place of a unified tribal morality... a Gikuyu does not know what he may or may not, ought or ought not, to do or believe...'.[28] Moralized ethnicities entangled one in deeper pasts than a shared, trans-ethnic, history of colonial pain. Even educated elites were scarcely 'transitional' between tradition and modernity, a false dichotomy masking plural identities.

'Development' intensified intimate disquiet. Officials, keen to raise production but fearing ecological degradation, invaded the household domain. New rules of husbandry and land-tenure reforms threatened both self-mastery and the multiple rights of usage through which mutual obligation had been expressed. Commercial farmers found their export earnings creamed off in forced loans to support imperial currencies or diversify local economies. Late colonialism's crises were rural, not urban. In the 1950s urban and rural anger joined in armed insurgency only in Cameroun and Kenya. Elsewhere, legalized industrial relations appeased anger at wartime inflation; and cities acquired housing finance. Moreover, no colony had a national economy that might create national interests. Rural capitalism and agrarian regimentation, to the contrary, divided people. Politicians often had to catch up with rural discontents before using them. The 'masses' had often mobilized themselves, but behind a myriad local patriotisms.

Patriotism and Nationalism

'Become masters in your own home.' West African activists roused audiences with this call. To Kenya's trade-union leader, Tom Mboya, independence meant that 'it is we who can open or close the door'.[29] Who closes the door is master in his home. The boldest Tanganyikan newspaper in the 1940s was *Kwetu* [*Our Home*]. *Uhuru* meant a householder's freedom, distinct from slavery, *utumwa*, before it meant national independence. In southern Africa guerrillas killed witches and prostitutes, both threats to household fertility. Across Africa, nationalists promised to restore what patriotism demanded: masculine mastery over fertile wealth. Promise did not always meet demand.

Much depended on context, best differentiated by asking why, in 1957, Ghana (the Gold Coast) became the first new sub-Saharan nation. The answer lies in strategic geography, economy, education, historical continuity, the politics of conquest, religious regionalism, and imperial policy. In West Africa, not the settler-dominated East, Ghana's petty-capitalist (not 'peasant') economy profited African households. Its educated elites pre-dated colonialism as also, to an unusual extent, did its borders. Its largest kingdom was a conquered country. Its Muslim interior was small. It was British.

Ghana had neither settlers nor a port 'east of Suez'; imperial strategists could rest easy. Conversely, as the world's leading cocoa growers, its commoners could afford to pay for politics, attacking chiefs' privileges and European monopolies. Inland French Africa was poorer; eastern Africa's profits went to immigrant employers. The pre-colonial origins of Ghana's educated elites also meant, as in Senegal, Nigeria, and South Africa, that conquest came as a racial insult; their pained self-interest created a single, potentially national, public sphere early enough for a younger generation to outflank their seniors' moderation. Ghana's Convention People's Party (CPP) was the pushy plebeian prototype. In East Africa schooling had barely preceded conquest; nationalist leaders, often pioneer literates to whom alien rule had brought opportunity, saw in popular unrest a fissile threat as much as a unifying spur.

Ghana also enjoyed a rare degree of cultural commonality. Its borders encased similar Akan kingdoms, of which the strongest, Asante, enjoyed little of the official favour that elsewhere fractured national politics; the British had fought Asante too often. The Muslim interior was too small to delay independence, to catch up with the mission-schooled south, unlike Nigeria's 'big North'. Finally, while urban Senegalese, French citizens since the 1870s, had sent a black deputy to Paris in 1914, British colonies were autonomous. Africans first entered the Gold Coast legislature in 1850 but never Westminster. They fought their first, limited, elections in 1928; and from 1946 enjoyed an African majority. Once decolonization was on the cards nationhood was trumps. Nkrumah's pan-Africanism was fantasy; no French-style wider Union was on offer. The British were less centralized than the French, not more liberal. In settler-dominated British East Africa the first African legislator was nominated, not yet elected, as late as 1944. Belgium and Portugal permitted still fewer freedoms, while white minorities had ruled South Africa since 1910 and Southern Rhodesia since 1923.

Local patriotisms affected territorial nationalisms still more than imperial policy and in three different ways. Old kingdoms competed, variously, with new nationhoods. 'Republican' discontents in stateless societies alarmed some nationalisms and inspired others. Southern liberation movements could suppress or respect ethnic or regional difference.

The colonial politics of monarchy reinterpreted past constitutional relations between royal, religious, noble, and commoner 'estates'. In a rising scale of harm to nation-statehood, Nigeria's emirates have held sway, but in a country few ever saw as one nation; Zulu history was less dangerous to South Africa than Asante's to Ghana; Buganda's populism denied peace to Uganda; Rwanda's kingdom was consumed in fire, blood, and referendum. Colonial histories certainly mattered: Nigeria's emirs had joined with the British against a more militant Islam that endangered both; Zulu and Asante were both conquered and had had rebellions crushed; Buganda was Britain's strongest local ally; Rwanda's aristocracy enjoyed most colonial support. But for anxious householders their own imagined constitutional history could weigh still more.

There were over 30 million Nigerians in 1960; their nationalism was inevitably plural. The British feared secession by the northern region, 60 per cent of the population, but its aristocratic Islam was not Nigeria's most incisive patriotism. Cultural stereotypes, shaping householder hopes, will have to do. In the west the Yoruba expected much of patrons: 'the elder who eats all his food [not considering his dependants] will carry his load by himself'. Inequality was starker in the north, not only for women, but brides were warned, 'Resign yourself, patient girl. Marriage is an ill you can't revenge. Only death will bring relief.' The chiefless Igbo of the east valued equality of honour above all: a tortoise in a folk tale persuades a leopard to let him scratch up the ground before being killed, so that passers-by may later say, 'yes, a fellow and his match struggled here'. To explain Nigeria's federated political vigour one must appreciate not only elite Islamic hegemony over the northern poor but also Yoruba 'big man' competition for prosperous dependants and the republican energy of Igbo 'fighting each other with schools',[30] whose educated young, like the Scots, left their poor soils to seek the waged road to adulthood all over Nigeria, to others' growing alarm.

Leaders personified regions. The Yoruba Obafemi Awolowo financed his legal studies in London as a businessman. Ahmadu Bello, lordly war-captain to the Sultan of Sokoto, shared northern leadership with Abukakr Tafawa Balewa, son of a slave who, in this most bureaucratic case of indirect rule, had profited from the education given to able servants. Nnamdi Azikiwe, typically Igbo, culturally Nigerian, followed his civil servant father's career around the colony, gained confidence at an American university and then a journalist's wider vision. Contrasting histories informed their politics. Awolowo had read Samuel Johnson, Christian historian of a redeemed Yoruba nation, and entered Nigerian politics by founding an ethnic cultural association. Global, not national, history reminded Bello and Balewa that faithful Muslims had survived infidel conquest ever since the Mongols entered Baghdad; northern workers similarly trusted in Islamic rather than Nigerian or proletarian rights. Azikiwe's Igbo, unable to agree on a standard vernacular, wrote history as a multiple 'hometown' contest in modernity, not as an ethnic saga. Awolowo, by contrast, hoped federalism would protect the local accountability proper to ethnic patriotism.[31] In the event, each regional government suppressed minority voices, to strengthen its hand at the centre. The northern emirates have merely been the most ruthless in this regional competition.

Thirty years after Nigeria's independence the Zulu people, heirs to a kingdom and South Africa's largest language group, seemed ready to outdo Nigeria's northern separatism. The threat vanished in 1994 when Nelson Mandela became South Africa's first black president, not because Zulu lacked 'residual tribal loyalty' but because how to become Zulu was so hotly argued. In the 1820s Shaka Zulu had defeated other Nguni-speakers to build his kingdom. Modernity was just as divisive as this memory. White domination raised hard questions. Zulu Christianity, fount of patriotic debate, offered different answers, divided between a royal establishment, Africanist intellectuals, and a popular 'independency', in which a prophetic Church saw white rule as punishment for past royal violence, as sinful as that of Israel's King Saul. Migrant labour weakened households to similarly divisive effect. An emergent middle class sponsored football, not chieftaincy; workers retained respect for monarchy when learning class solidarity. White policy had reduced Zulu kingship to a cipher by the 1950s, but it was apartheid's separation of rural local government from the fragile privileges of townspeople that finally split Zulus between the hierarchical Inkatha Freedom Party and the urban, more democratic, African National Congress (ANC). Conservative and progressive patriotisms can be the bitterest enemies.

This was true of all South Africans as apartheid fought to survive. In the 1940s Afrikaner nationalists had hoped to unify their *volk*, against English-speakers as much as Africans, through the disciplines of rule and privileges of apartheid. By the 1970s the 'loyal resistance' among intellectuals, churchmen, and big businessmen believed, after searching self-examination (to recall Awolowo) that the *volk* could survive with justice only by replacing apartheid's separate freedoms with freedom for all in a plural society. Afrikaners debated political morality in print; Africans had to settle their differences on the streets. Zulu fought Zulu as well as strangers, in part over how to practise true manhood at a time of trial. Argument between Xhosa-speakers also intensified, following two centuries of mutual disdain between 'reds' who herded the household cattle and 'schools' who absconded to town. Those yet to achieve adult responsibility now felt their elders had betrayed it. Complaining that the latter preferred beer to freedom, 'comrades' washed out drinkers' mouths with soap.[32] Outraged moral ethnicity can provoke more intimate violence than political tribalism.

The conflict between Nkrumah's CPP, strongest in Ghana's southern kingdoms and Atlantic ports, and the inland Asante's National Liberation Movement (NLM), shows, similarly, how history can divide those with customs more or less in common. In 1956 the NLM's federal demand made the British hesitate over Ghana's unitary future. Yet party and movement had similar leaders, second- or third-generation professionals, critical of their gentlemanly elders; CPP defectors had created the NLM. Both attracted urban crowds, cocoa-growers, and businessmen for whom politics was an investment. Both engaged with similar chieftaincy politics, in which chiefly houses competed to protect ancestral mysteries and communal property, advised by rich, high-born, elders. Well-connected commoners, 'youngmen' or *nkwankwaa*, could press for unpopular chiefs to be 'destooled'; in Asante they had led 'republican' revolt against a tyrannous *Asantehene*, their king, in 1883. Christianity and cocoa added to their discontents. Some came to deplore their chiefs' mysteries; more resented their market prerogatives. 'Destoolment' became as common in Asante as elsewhere, and Asantes supported the CPP's drive to end 'tribal feudalism', a radicalization of British plans for local government reform. So why did Asante's 'youngmen' turn against the party? In short, cocoa and citizenship.

Producing the most cocoa, Asante became a resentful region, over-taxed by the state's monopoly cocoa marketing board and under-represented. But what made region a nation? Asantes would say they had always been a nation. A manifesto exclaimed: 'Save the Ashanti Nation for it has History.'[33] This history forced commoners to fight for self-mastery. In the past, belonging to one of the kingdom's matrilineal clans had made them citizens, not slaves. The NLM now contrasted a citizen's fruitful toil with the new slavery, subjection to Nkrumah's dictatorship. But citizenship needed constant assertion in 'a dynamic of participatory inequality', within 'a relational web of lives' rooted in Asante's past, not in the Ghanaian party. Arguments about status could reach two centuries back, to Asante's origins; 'the past remain[ed] in the ears'. In the 'marketplace of power' one traded history, the coin of reputation, for the ear of the king.[34] In 1957, caught between attacks on chieftaincy from above and *nkwankwaa* uproar below, the *Asantehene* made his peace with the CPP government. Asante's market in patriotism collapsed into the confederacy of intrigue out of which the kingdom had first been built. The CPP's cocoa-fuelled party machine, freed from the frustration of trimming chieftaincy under British eyes, set about building a people's developmental democracy with the familiar tools of enticement and intimidation of its opponents, supposedly the people's enemies.[35]

Buganda's relations with the rest of Uganda might well have been similar, but for a crucial difference. Britain had conquered Asante; Buganda helped Britain conquer Uganda. The kingdom's high politics, distributing land to support office, had earlier been sharpened by its chiefs' competition for imported guns and luxuries, and its commoners' fears of new burdens when domestic slaves were exported in exchange. Islam and competing Christianities, French Catholic and British Protestant, aided faction-formation. Britain got control, first over Buganda, by backing the winning, Protestant, side in a civil war, and then the rest of Uganda with the aid of Ganda guns and political agents. In 1900, during a royal minority, the ruling chiefs cemented this alliance with an agreement that granted them land by the square mile (*mailo*). Secure in property and British support, they could ignore the market for royal favour in which they had staked the loyalty of their followers, historically entitled to switch allegiance. Client householders now had to pay their protectors in forced labour on export crops. Property had trumped people.

In the 1920s a coalition of commoners and displaced office-holders called on their king, the *Kabaka*, now adult, to restore their ancient constitution. A single layer of British-backed chiefs had, they said, suppressed the competition in power that, as in Asante, had once allowed free Ganda a voice. Simply to be heard was colonial Africa's deepest cry. The *Kabaka* met some of his petitioners' demands. Loyal populists, encouraged, later looked to him for further defence against over-mighty chiefs, Asian traders, and British rule. The constitutional battle inspired a prolific vernacular historiography. A patriot wrote to the London *Times* with a comparative eye: 'We are a nation. We are not a tribe, like the Welsh or the Scots.'[36] In the 1950s Ganda constitutionalism was more passionate than any Ugandan nationalism. The British made the *Kabaka* a hero by deporting him for opposing a unitary post-colonial state. On his return the old generation of chiefs was swept away and his *lukiiko*, or parliament, (fruitlessly) declared Buganda independent. Uganda's nationalism returned the compliment, anti-Buganda as well as anti-colonial. The British departed, leaving Ugandans to settle, in blood, the outstanding conflicts between Buganda and the rest. Popular royalism, asserting household rights against a bureaucratic baronage, faced a nationalism now armed with state power, determined to undo the regional inequalities of conquest. Ghana was fortunate that Asante was never Britain's friend.

Rwanda's history has been still more tragic than Uganda's. Here, a violent monarchy, European racial theory, colonial exactions, and changing missionary theology joined to nourish, first, aristocratic privilege, and then householder hope, a combustible contradiction that the colonial regime lacked the will to arbitrate until too late. By the 1950s it was widely believed that Tutsi military elite and Hutu peasantry had separate migrant origins. Historians now question that; nonetheless, the last independent king, Rwabugiri, had imposed new labour duties, seemingly on Hutu alone. German and then Belgian rulers were entranced by Tutsi elegance (thin-nosed like themselves), as also, initially, were Catholic missionaries. While the Belgians thought to lighten peasant duty owed to Tutsi patrons, still heavier colonial tax and labour demands were appropriated by Tutsi chiefs. The young deserted peasant households, preferring migrant labour to subjugation. After 1945 fresh missionaries, imbued with the new Catholic concern for the poor, encouraged a clerical Hutu counter-elite. Impending decolonization lit the tinder of revolution. The Tutsi minority (like Zanzibari Arabs or white Rhodesians) tried to lead Rwanda's nationalism in order to defuse its democratic potential, only to alert Hutu clerics to that very danger. Peasant jacqueries, especially in border areas, torched Tutsi dwellings; the king tried a counter-attack; the Belgians belatedly tried to douse the flames by overseeing the Hutu-ization of public life. A referendum finished the monarchy, doomed by its association with householder oppression in an era of promised freedom.

Elsewhere 'republican' patriotisms, fired by new conflicts within already unequal moral economies, could have similarly marked effects on visions of national citizenship. To take two pairs of contrasting nationalisms, in French West and British East Africa: the Ivory Coast and Kenya were 'conservative', their neighbours Guinea and Tanganyika were 'radical'. One could argue that class interest, not fear of fired-up patriotism, was sufficient cause for nationalists to be conservative, and more Ivoirians and Kenyans had started in rural capitalism than Guineans or Tanganyikans. Moreover, powerful settler minorities in the first two cases demanded harsher repression of African hopes after 1945, another reason for elites to control the unruly poor. But there was no inevitability here. Guinea's ruling party, Sékou Touré's Parti Démocratique de Guinée (PDG), was also persecuted by the French for many years, and Nyerere's Tanganyika African National Union (TANU) was as alarmed as the British by popular protest against the second colonial occupation. The socialism both these leaders adopted was an ideology of control as much as progress, just like their neighbours' capitalism.

Nonetheless, fear of the anger aroused by the betrayal of moral economy certainly drove Kenya's conservatism. The terrorism of 'Mau Mau', 'famished eaters [of elders' authority]' among Kikuyu, 20 per cent of the population, stunned Kenya's nationalists, as did British counter-terror. Kikuyu dominated Nairobi's markets in skilled labour, slum housing, transport, food, fuel, and criminal opportunity. As in Buganda, property began to trump people. For senior Kikuyu, unfettered control of land became more politically profitable than client followings. In the late 1940s white settlers, similarly, revoked their 'squatter' tenancies, held largely by Kikuyu, in order to intensify their farming. Kikuyu juniors were gripped by fear of social extinction, unable to establish even client households, betrayed by patrons white and black. Redundant dependants, their claims on moral ethnicity were ignored. Lacking Buganda's constitutional remedy they turned to violence. Kikuyu split (like Zulu) between radical and conservative patriots—Mau Mau and the 'loyalists' who backed the British and inherited their power. Both agreed that ethnic citizenship rested on sweated self-mastery. Each blamed the other for loss of trust between patron and client. At independence Kikuyu leaders used state power to create a multi-ethnic alliance united only by a determination to ensure that the means to self-reliance, in property or employment, would answer to elite patronage, not client demand.

A less bloody, more complex, history lay behind Ivoirian conservatism. The coffee-planter patrons of the Parti Démocratique du Côte d'Ivoire (PDCI) were shaken by the ethnic violence and youthful anarchy aroused by *la repression* of the late 1940s, when the French coerced the PDCI—with other West African parties—into breaking with the communists after the latter left the French coalition government in 1947. Guinea suffered still more than the Ivory Coast, yet the PDG held to a radical course, ending in 1958 as the only party to vote 'Non' to Charles de Gaulle's offer of autonomy within a French Community. The explanation lies in contrasts between societies rather than in ideological differences between leaders. Sékou Touré's conversion to the 'Non' was pressed on him by his party branches, dominated by trades unionists, memories of indigenous slavery, and educated criticism of local Islamic practices, not least with regard to women, who at times had led their men in protecting household survival. The Ivory Coast, by contrast, was a classic frontier zone in which big planters could still relieve popular anger by sponsoring forest clearance for cultivation. Here, class formation helped rather than hindered youthful household ambition; Ivoirian conservatives could enjoy a legitimacy that their Kenyan counterparts had forfeited.

But one cannot explain the benevolent despotism of Tanganyikan (Tanzanian) nationalism without considering its leader's thought. Looking to history for instruction, Nyerere misread it, romanticizing past moral economies as a chain of communalisms. As elsewhere, they had in truth embodied attempts to socialize inequality with vertical ties of obligation. Tanganyikans argued about how to modernize these obligations, more than was tolerable to TANU, an unusually bureaucratic party, thanks to its origins in the Swahili-speaking lingua franca of towns. TANU's unitary, uniform, vision of nationhood was disputed by some in wealthier regions who, like Awolowo, favoured an ethnic confederation, while others in isolated areas hoped freedom meant tax-free statelessness. Some wanted to confine citizenship to propertied householders; more thought it should be unconditional for Africans but denied to South Asians, traders too easily portrayed as bloodsuckers. Men in particular worried about how to control power. Rural clans had had a known responsibility for their members' actions, and chiefs could be challenged if they failed to 'heal the land' or make rain, but TANU's officials had an institutional self-belief difficult to question. In towns women were shockingly prominent in the political theatre of protest. Such argumentative untidiness was what perhaps persuaded Nyerere to abolish chiefly hierarchy, as in Guinea, and to see the regimented modernity of *ujamaa*—resettled village socialism with public services—as the best means to restore to Tanzanian citizenship its communal virtue.

One can scarcely doubt, to consider a final set of relations between patriotism and nationalism, that personal commitment to the perils of guerrilla war must come mainly from a sense of duty to free one's *patrie*—to quote Senghor—from the shame and disorder of alien rule. However, contrary to Fanon's hopes, liberation war proved to be Africa's most divisive form of anti-colonial nationalism. Its military elites could become as distant as political party leaders. It was never a unifying experience, even in tiny Portuguese Guinea where Amilcar Cabral showed a practical concern for social democracy even during the struggle. Other movements, led with less care, made enemies as much as friends, not only because their supporters could suffer terrible retribution from incumbent regimes. Guerrilla loyalties in any case tended to be ethnic rather than 'national'. In a vast country Angola's fighters set out from three regional bases and never escaped their ethnic origins; civil war continued long after independence. The two main Zimbabwean movements became more 'tribal' over time. FRELIMO in Mozambique was more successful in generating territorial unity perhaps because, unusually, it despised African history, but it paid heavily for its modernist 'commandism' in peasant resistance after independence. Under the pretext of defending western Christianity against savagery and Soviets, the Portuguese, white Rhodesians and, striking beyond their borders, the South Africans were not slow to exploit these divisions but did not create them.

Guerrilla armies tended to become less politically sensitive, more militarily self-contained, as they neared the seizure of power. Local patriotisms, fortified by the histories of social and environmental healing voiced by the spirit mediums of past rulers, lost control over the boys in the bush. Many found warfare became so 'hot'—with increasing demands on labour and loyalty, but decreasing safety—that they became worthless slaves, denied the dignity of household autonomy, no matter who was for the moment in control. In Zimbabwe neither guerrilla army seized the state; independence was negotiated. The subsequent power struggle brought more systematic violence than the war for freedom. One guerrilla veteran, punished as a dissident, complained, 'We'd done our duty, we wanted to build our homes, what had we done wrong?'[37]

Earlier, in the 1960s, Sketchley Samkange, a middle-class Methodist, had enjoyed a liberal Zimbabwean nationalism that respected freedom of association and accommodated differences of view. Partisan war is different, for it has to impose absolute loyalty. South Africa was fortunate therefore that, by contrast with its contemporaries in Zimbabwe, Portuguese Africa and Namibia, the *Umkhonto weSizwe* armed wing of South Africa's exile ANC was scarcely able to enter the country until after internal resistance had weakened the hold of apartheid and established a violent street democracy. The township wars of the 1980s, conducted under the multiracial umbrella of the United Democratic Front, toughened a citizenry against any threat of liberationist dictatorship, as did Africa's strongest trades unions in Africa's most industrialized economy. That was one assurance of post-apartheid democracy. The other belonged, unexpectedly, to the opposite end of the political spectrum, a 'politics of notables' that originated with the formation of the ANC in 1912; had always distrusted mass action, even in the 1950s Defiance Campaign; had turned Bantustan 'self-government' into an African political resource under its white alibi for domination; and provided Nelson Mandela, member of a chiefly house, with a network of family, school, and professional links with which to weave a governing alliance of local patriotisms. The ANC encouraged that diversity. Least remarked upon in the negotiations that led to majority rule in 1994 was the adoption of proportional representation with a party 'list' system, the electoral system most conducive to plural democracy in a 'rainbow nation' of many voices.

Conclusion

In such contrasting circumstances did African patriotisms and nationalisms fight their own battles, informed by African history, to take over externally derived states. Nationalists saw their vocation as modernization, one word summarizing the fight against poverty, ignorance and disease. The unity needed for that daunting task appeared to require tight control when independence was won. All opposition was blamed on 'tribalism'. Political tribalism, a collective solidarity that silenced the patriotic self-examination of moral ethnicity, was indeed the surest means to assemble a vote-bank large enough to secure a share of the national cake. No wonder Samora Machel, president of FRELIMO's Mozambique, believed that 'for the nation to live, the tribe must die'.[38] But there were huge costs in gagging the constitutional debates that had informed local patriotisms; as a Shambaa proverb from Tanzania warns: 'All healers draw blood.'[39] As Awolowo forecast, and Samkange would sadly agree: '[N]ationalism knows no moderation: when it is in the saddle it rides hard.'[40]

African history has yet to make its own the states which hard-riding nationalists inherited. So far that history has been contradictory. Mandela, who observed thirty years of African independence before taking power himself, learned that respect for historically informed patriotic diversity was the road to national unity. Jomo Kenyatta, conservative believer in ethnic self-discipline, once called his country 'a kind of United Nations in miniature', but Kenya has not been spared the ravages of political tribalism.[41]

Notes

1. I thank but exculpate those colleagues who have helped me: David Anderson, Gareth Austin, Bruce Berman, John Breuilly, Joel Cabrita, Holly Hanson, Emma Hunter, Paul la Hausse, Tom McCaskie, Derek Peterson, and Richard Waller.
2. T. Hodgkin (1956) *Nationalism in Colonial Africa*, London, 17, 24.
3. G. Orwell (1941) *The Lion and the Unicorn: Socialism and the English Genius*, London, 111, 126, 89.
4. R. Rathbone (2000) *Nkrumah and the Chiefs: The Politics of Chieftaincy in Ghana 1951–60*, Accra, 7, for clustered histories.
5. O. Awolowo (1966; 1947) *The Path to Nigerian Freedom*, London, 34.
6. K. A. Busia (1958; 1951) *The Position of the Chief in the Modern Political System of Ashanti*, London, 12.
7. R. Hess (1970) *Ethiopia, the Modernization of Autocracy*, Ithaca, NY, 141.
8. Ø. Eide (2000) *Revolution and Religion in Ethiopia 1974–85*, Oxford, 74.
9. P. Lumumba (1962) *Congo my Country*, London, 177.
10. See Cemil Aydin's Chapter 35 on pan-nationalisms.
11. A. C. Jones (1948) *Colonial Office Summer Conference on African Education: The Encouragement of Initiative in African Society*, London, Colonial Office, African No. 1174 'not for publication', quotes from 10, 14, 19.
12. R. S. Morgenthau (1964) *Political Parties in French-Speaking West Africa*, Oxford, 334.
13. Lord Soulbury (1944) in R. Hyam (2006) *Britain's Declining Empire: The Road to Decolonization 1918–1968*, Cambridge, 120.
14. Arden-Clarke to Cohen, 1951, in R. Rathbone (ed.) (1992) *Ghana*, Part I, London, HMSO [*British Documents on the End of Empire*], 324.
15. Lord Lugard (1922, 1965) *The Dual Mandate in British Tropical Africa*, London, 618; J. S. Coleman (1954) 'Nationalism in Tropical Africa', *American Political Science Review*, 48, 426; R. E. Robinson and J. Gallagher (1962) 'The Partition of Africa', ch. XXII in *The New Cambridge Modern History, vol. XI*, ed. F. H. Hinsley, Cambridge, 640.
16. F. Fanon (1961, 1967) *The Wretched of the Earth*, Harmondsworth, 37, 47, 48.
17. Fanon, *Wretched*, 56–8, 73–4, 120.
18. D. R. Peterson and G. Macola (eds.) (2009) 'Homespun Historiography and the Academic Profession', *Recasting the Past: History Writing and Political Work in Modern Africa*, Athens, OH, 8.
19. H. Hanson (2003) *Landed Obligation: The Practice of Power in Buganda*, Portsmouth, NH, 27.
20. J. Vansina (1990) *Paths in the Rainforest: Toward a History of Political Tradition in Equatorial Africa*, Madison, WI, 119–20.
21. J. Lonsdale, 'The Moral Economy of Mau Mau', in B. Berman and J. Lonsdale (eds.) (1992) *Unhappy Valley*, London, 267–9, 316–17, 326–67, 402–5, 461–8.

22. S. Berry (1993) *No Condition is Permanent: The Social Dynamics of Agrarian Change in Sub-Saharan Africa*, Madison, WI, 1993.
23. R. Robinson (1972) 'Non-European Foundations of European Imperialism: Sketch for a Theory of Collaboration', in R. Owen and B. Sutcliffe (eds.) *Studies in the Theory of Imperialism*, London, 117–40, quote from 133.
24. F. Cooper (2002) *Africa since 1940: The Past of the Present*, Cambridge.
25. H. L. Moore and M. Vaughan (1994) *Cutting down Trees: Gender, Nutrition and Agricultural Change in the Northern Province of Zambia, 1890–1990*, Portsmouth, NH, 13–15.
26. Busia, *The Position of the Chief*, 127.
27. P. K. Mugo to editor, *Muigwithania*, vol. I, ii (April 1929), 3, in Kenya National Archives, file DC/MKS. 10B/13/1.
28. J. Kenyatta (1938) *Facing Mount Kenya: The Tribal Life of the Gikuyu*, London, 251.
29. Morgenthau, *Political Parties*, xix; Mboya reported in *Time*, 7 March 1960.
30. E. Amadi (1982) *Ethics in Nigerian Culture*, Ibadan, 53; M. F. Smith (1954) *Baba of Karo, a Woman of the Muslim Hausa*, London, 91; E. Isichei (2002) *Voices of the Poor in Africa*, Rochester, NY, 253–4, and *The Ibo People and the Europeans: The Genesis of a Relationship—to 1906*, London, 176, rephrased.
31. Awolowo, *Path*, 53.
32. *Report of the Commission of Enquiry into the Riots at Soweto and Elsewhere from 16 June 1976 to 28 February 1977* (Government Printer, Pretoria, 1980), vol. I, 309–31.
33. J. M. Allman (1993) *The Quills of the Porcupine: Asante Nationalism in an Emergent Ghana*, Madison, WI, 3.
34. S. Berry (2001) *Chiefs Know their Boundaries: Essays on Property, Power, and the Past in Asante, 1896–1996*, Portsmouth, NH, 198; T. C. McCaskie (2000) *Asante Identities: History and Modernity in an African Village 1850–1950*, Edinburgh, 236, and (1984) '*Ahiyamu*—a "place of meeting": An Essay on Process and Event in the History of the Asante State', *Journal of African History*, 25, 176.
35. Rathbone, *Nkrumah*, 59–149.
36. A. Sempa, in C. Pratt (1961) 'East Africa: The Pattern of Political Development', in M. Maclure and D. G. Anglin (eds.) *Africa: The Political Pattern*, Toronto, 113.
37. J. Alexander, J. McGregor, and T. Ranger (2000) *Violence and Memory: One Hundred Years in the 'Dark Forests' of Matabeleland*, Oxford, 192.
38. M. Mamdani (1996) *Citizen and Subject: Contemporary Africa and the Legacy of Late Colonialism*, Princeton, NY, 135.
39. S. Feierman (1990) *Peasant Intellectuals: Anthropology and History in Tanzania*, Madison, WI, 237.
40. Awolowo, *Path*, 134.
41. J. Kenyatta (1968) *Suffering without Bitterness*, Nairobi, 247.

Suggested Further Reading

Branch, D. (2009) *Defeating Mau Mau, Creating Kenya: Counterinsurgency, Civil War, and Decolonization*, Cambridge.

Davidson, B. (1981) *The People's Cause: A History of Guerrillas in Africa*, London.

Donham, D. (1999) *Marxist Modern: An Ethnographic History of the Ethiopian Revolution*, Berkeley, CA.
Giliomee, H. (2003) *The Afrikaners: Biography of a People*, London.
Iliffe, J. (1988) *Honour in African History*, Cambridge.
Newbury, C. (1988) *The Cohesion of Oppression: Clientship and Ethnicity in Rwanda, 1860–1960*, New York.
Peel, J. D. Y. (2000) *Religious Encounter and the Making of the Yoruba*, Bloomington, IN.
Ranger, T. (1995) *Are We Not Also Men? The Samkange Family and African Politics in Zimbabwe 1920–64*, Harare.
Schmidt, E. (2005) *Mobilizing the Masses: Gender, Ethnicity, and Class in the Nationalist Movement in Guinea, 1939–1958*, Portsmouth, NH.
Zolberg, A. (1966) *Creating Political Order: The Party-States of West Africa*, Chicago, IL.

PART III

NATIONALISM IN A WORLD OF NATION STATES: POLITICS AND POWER

CHAPTER 17

NATIONALISM AND IMPERIALISM, *c*.1880–1940

JOHN DARWIN

Explaining Imperialism

The extraordinary expansion of colonial empires in the second half of the nineteenth century is one of the most familiar chapters in the history of the modern world. Although historians make much of the partition of Africa, carried out for the most part between 1885 and 1904 (the second date is when Britain and France agreed upon their respective positions in Egypt and Morocco), partitions also occurred in Southeast Asia, with the parcelling out of Burma, Malaya, Vietnam, Cambodia, and the Indonesian archipelago; in Central Asia (where Russia scooped the pool); and in the Pacific, whose island groups and archipelagos were divided between Britain, France, Germany, Japan (which took the Kuriles, Ryukyus, and Taiwan), and the United States. But this dramatic (and dramatically rapid) division of the imperial spoils is only part of a larger and longer story.

A longer story because in some ways at least the late nineteenth-century share-out of Africa and elsewhere can be readily seen as the grudging last act of a much longer process. After all, before the Europeans came to partition Africa, they had already divided and re-divided North and South America, the Caribbean, and much of South Asia, while in an act of pre-emptive partition, the British had laid claim to the whole of Australia by 1824. The 'independence' of the United States and Latin America loom large in their provincial histories, but from the point of view of indigenous peoples it meant little more than a change from one variety of European colonialism to another, and usually more aggressive, version. Indeed, a vigorous case has been made that in the partition of Africa, the European imperialists were 'scraping the bottom of the barrel':

all the best prizes (to be found in the Americas and Asia) had long since been snapped up.[1] Far from approaching their tropical African colonies with a gleeful rubbing of hands, the European governments viewed their new responsibilities with a mixture of resignation and gloom. Whether this was true of all their new acquisitions, we shall see later on. But it was certainly true that on any long view the regions colonized by Europe in the late nineteenth century were also those where its cultural and demographic impress was to prove much less durable than in earlier spheres of expansion.

This is a larger story because, from another point of view, the partitions and annexations that loom so large on the map were merely the outward and visible sign of a vaster movement of Western expansion. The European powers and (after 1898) the United States may have been piling up a set of possessions where they governed, or claimed to govern. But they were also engaged in the headlong extension of their cultural, economic, and diplomatic influence over many parts of the world that remained technically sovereign. This was true in ex-colonies in Latin America like Argentina or Uruguay.[2] It was true of the Middle East where both the Ottoman and Iranian empires were subjected to more and more external interference. It was true of China, where the scale of European and American extra-territorial rights (most strikingly seen in the treaty port enclaves) was growing by leaps and bounds in the closing decades of the century.[3] Then the political, military, economic, and cultural power of the West in the non-Western world seemed to be reaching its peak. The fate of those states that had escaped Western rule was widely expected (both in the West and outside it) to be a form of tutelage at best.

Historians of European (or more broadly Western) imperialism up to 1914 have thus been faced with a double problem. They have to explain why the European states (including Russia, Germany, France, Italy, the Netherlands, Portugal, and Britain—the 'Belgian' Congo was from 1879 to 1908 the private estate of the Belgian king) entered so enthusiastically into a scramble for territory often in places whose economic resources were scarcely a gleam in the speculator's eye. This requires an explanation in terms of the political process whereby the state and its government assumed the burdens of sovereignty. Acquiring 'formal' empire was after all a formal act that needed (sometimes) parliamentary approval, an international treaty, or an explicit declaration of geographical boundaries. But historians also have to explain the much less visible forward movement of commercial, missionary, and diplomatic interests, the makers and agents of 'informal empire', who deliberately chose to veil their activities (or were forced to do so) to avoid provoking either local resistance or the jealous resentment of other great powers.[4] To complicate matters, some kinds of 'informal empire' seemed to depend very little upon the power and influence of a European *state*. Some could scarcely survive without it. Yet others (the obvious case is Egypt after 1882) could best be described (as Egypt often was) as 'veiled protectorates'—colonies in all but name.[5]

The historiography of imperialism reflects this difficulty. Thus much of the older literature is preoccupied with explaining why European governments seemed so willing to amass new territories in the tropical world and risk disputes with other great powers to make good their claim. Three main schools of thought emerged. The first insisted that territorial expansion was the response of governments pursuing the national economic interest as they (or those with most influence upon them) interpreted it. The race for markets, supplies, or fields of investment was seen as part of the struggle for national survival: colony-grabbing was nationalist economics.[6] The second saw empire-building as political theatre, or perhaps political circus. When the masses arrived in national politics, it was necessary to appease their crude jingo mentality, or expedient to do so. This was especially true for old or unprogressive elites who feared that without this distraction mass politics might turn inconveniently radical. In ideological terms, acquiring some (or more) empire could be held up as evidence of national vitality, a vindication of the 'national' project, and (if scope for emigration existed) as a physical strengthening of the national community. This was imperialism as the outgrowth of (European) nationalism.[7] The third saw the competition for colonies as the unavoidable by-product of European rivalry within Europe, perhaps even an effort to displace European tensions into less dangerous places where less was at stake. This was imperialism as nationalist diplomacy.[8] The volatile mood of late nineteenth-century Europe, stoked up by the state-strengthening rhetoric of governments and intellectuals, had created a tinder-box atmosphere in European politics. Rivalry outside Europe could not be avoided and an appearance of weakness might be fatal to political ambition at home. But dividing the property of powerless third parties was easier than adjusting borders within Europe itself, or reversing the verdict of previous wars.

It is obvious enough that explanations like these have little to say about the broader context of the West's encroachment on the non-Western world, and nothing at all about non-territorial forms of imperial expansion. Each suffers from the difficulty that while it might fit (at best) one case of European empire-building, it breaks down completely when applied to the next. It might be argued, for example, that appeasing the masses was an urgent priority in Wilhemine Germany, but this was hardly the case before 1905 in Romanov Russia.[9] Extending the national economy by acquiring new colonial monopolies might make some sense when the home economy was heavily defended by tariffs (as was the case with Russia), but what about Britain which maintained free trade until 1931? It might have been true that strong nationalist passions influenced the diplomacy of the continental great powers, but (again) what about Britain?[10] We might be tempted to think that explaining imperialism in ways that exclude the premier case is not very profitable. Histories of European imperialism that leave Britain out have only limited value.

It is easy to see why for many years now historians have been attracted to a looser and more flexible understanding of imperialism, one that leaves room for a wider variety of 'imperial' relationships than the enforcement of rule. Indeed, more than fifty years ago, the most brilliant and original of the historians of modern imperialism proposed to define it as 'a function of [the] process of integrating new regions into the expanding economy'.[11] What John Gallagher and Ronald Robinson meant by this (and they were thinking primarily of Britain) was that the fundamental motive behind British expansion was to open new markets in the world beyond Europe. But they went on to insist that 'imperialism', by which they meant the *political* input needed to achieve this objective, varied widely from place to place according to circumstance. Where local interests cooperated willingly in removing trade barriers, it merely required a forceful diplomacy to ensure that British interests were not treated unfairly. But where they proved more resistant (the classic case was in China), gunboats, garrisons, and treaty port privileges might be needed to secure access for British trade and protection for British persons and property. In a third case, the full-blown exertion of British control (in other words formal rule) might be needed to reap the harvest of trade. There was an important proviso in the Gallagher-Robinson model: formal rule might be imposed in places of no commercial importance at all. But this was because they held a strategic significance, guarding the routes or overlooking the sea lanes connecting Britain to regions that were economically vital.

If we follow this lead, we might define imperialism as one state's attempt to impose its predominance over other societies by drawing them into its political, cultural, and economic system. This might be done by direct political control in the zone of expansion. But it was sometimes convenient to leave in place a notionally sovereign government. Often the motive was to delimit a sphere of economic exclusion, reserving trade and investment to the imperial power—but not invariably. Usually, the assertion of dominance was based on an ideological claim—the so-called 'civilizing mission'—and an appeal to the idea of a cultural hierarchy in which the 'progressive' energy of the West was contrasted with the sloth, regression, or barbarism of the non-Western world.[12] But imperialism was also a competitive activity and the states that cherished imperial ambitions varied considerably in their expansive capacities. Some were held back by the fear that a reverse overseas would damage their domestic regime. Most were concerned to prevent their imperial activities from igniting a major explosion in the cockpits of Europe. Those that lacked capital and geopolitical leverage hoped to exploit the divisions between the richer and stronger but could not always do so. Those that came late to the race found the best pickings had gone. And in a number of cases, the local resistance was just strong enough to make the risks of partition too high to court. A partition-by-war in which several powers were involved might well light the fuse for a European war. Hence the advance of the West into the non-Western world in the 'age of imperialism' between 1880 and 1914 was a curiously tepid affair in which no blood was spilt between the European powers (they made up the deficit with that of Asians and Africans). Its impact was patchy and quite often shallow. And in the regions where all the great powers had large interests at stake, it remained, ironically, at its most incomplete.

Western Expansion

But what led Europeans (and sometimes their governments) to think that the domination of the non-Western world was remotely practicable, let alone in their interests? By the 1820s and 1830s the British and Dutch had acquired extensive eastern empires.

The British had used their great base in India as a springboard for the commercial penetration of China, and then in 1840 for the military onslaught that forced on the Qing the first of the 'unequal treaties'. To guard their sea routes to India the British had seized control over the Cape and asserted a naval protectorate in the Persian Gulf.[13] They were also determined to let no other great power rule over the isthmus of Suez or command the Red Sea, and watched both ends of this maritime corridor from bases in Malta and Aden. The French had acquired two African bridgeheads: in the old Muslim state of Algiers and (in the 1840s) at the mouth of the Senegal river. The Russians were locked in their struggle with the Caucasus Muslims, the costly sideshow in their slow southward expansion into the Iranian borderlands.[14] But over most of Afro-Asia in the first half of the nineteenth century, European influence was conspicuously lacking and the imposition of European rule the dimmest of prospects.

There were several reasons for this. Firstly, it was far from clear that the European powers could manage successfully the territories they already controlled. British expansion in India had been frowned on in London as a costly and reckless experiment only permissible because the East India Company government could meet its military bills. The Dutch had made Java an enviably profitable venture, but lacked the military means to expand their control over the surrounding archipelago. Across much of Russian North Asia, Tsarist authority was the faintest of rumours. Secondly, except along coasts or inland waterways, European access to the continental interior of Asia and Africa remained expensive and difficult. Indeed, despite the efforts of European travellers, much of that interior was still little known. Thirdly, far from existing in a political vacuum, much of Afro-Asia was governed by relatively organized states that seemed for the most part perfectly capable of controlling their territories and excluding or containing unwelcome outsiders. China and Japan were the most striking examples of this. But even the riverine statelets of the Niger delta were strong enough to prevent European interlopers from breaking their grip on the inland trade of the region.[15] Fourthly, with such limited access to the Afro-Asian economies (scarcely a mile of railway had been built in India before 1850),[16] and with little prospect, as it seemed, of enlarging it greatly, colonizing Afro-Asia through trade, let alone by rule, held little appeal and promised few fortunes.

By the 1860s, however, Europe's hesitant advance into Afro-Asia had begun to speed up. The caution that Europeans had shown hitherto in their dealings with its states began to give way to an aggressive self-confidence. The mid-century world in which so much of the Afro-Asian interior seemed beyond the reach of the European powers was replaced by one in which, by the end of the century, global connectedness was all but complete. Why had this happened? Perhaps the critical fact was the expansion of the Euro-Atlantic economy, which was now strong enough to absorb Europe's commercial relations with the rest of the world.[17] One obvious symptom of this was the increased flow of investment to fund the production of commodities like cotton, coffee, and sugar, and to pay for costly agricultural improvements like the draining of the Nile delta and the irrigation works in North India. But much the most striking was the huge flow of capital into systems of transport. The Suez Canal (completed November 1869) not only drastically shortened the voyage from Europe to India. It also made it worthwhile to extend the revolution in maritime transport brought by the iron-hulled steamship to the world East of Suez.[18] Above all, it was the building of railways that promised to galvanize the Afro-Asian interior. By cutting the cost of carrying bulk goods by three quarters or more, they would drag vast inland regions into the orbit of the commercial economy, multiplying consumers and producers at a stroke. Nor were these the only technological innovations to reduce the tyranny of distance. The spread of the telegraph across Asia (an undersea cable reached northern Australia in 1872) cut the time taken to transmit news and commercial information from weeks to minutes. Within Asia, the political and military value of the telegraph had already been demonstrated. Advance warning by telegraph allowed the British to prevent the spread of the 1857 Mutiny into the Punjab and to use the province as the base for the recapture of Delhi—the critical first step in regaining control of north India.[19]

The emergence of a global economy in which ordinary bulk goods as well as high-value luxuries were traded round the world with little price variation promised the spread of commercial prosperity to previously 'remote' or inaccessible regions, as well as new commercial opportunities to merchants, shippers, financiers, and industrialists in Europe. It also had huge implications for the geopolitical matrix that governed the relations of the main European states and their transatlantic offshoot in the United States. Before the transport revolution was exported to Afro-Asia, it was reasonable to expect that the growth of European influence there would be slow, patchy, and piecemeal. Even in China, where the European powers extracted a second round of unequal treaties in 1858–60, foreign businessmen found commercial conditions demanding, and the toll of failure was high.[20] The interior of Africa, except in a few favoured footholds like the Cape diamond district or the cotton fields of the Nile delta, had been a graveyard of commercial ambition once the slow throttling of the Atlantic slave trade set in following the British Slave Trade Act of 1807. Of course, none of this had prevented the spasms of mutual paranoia that punctuated Anglo-Russian relations as the agents of both powers schemed and intrigued in the vast borderlands of Central Asia. But the capacity of either to do the other much harm was in practice quite limited, and a decisive success in their 'battle for Asia' was absurdly improbable.[21] The geopolitical implications of the new world economy changed all that.

Their impact could be seen in four different ways. Firstly, and most alarmingly, railway technology had the power to reorient the external relations of regions and states with sensational rapidity. Once a railway was built into an interior tract, its trade would flow along the new iron conduit and its prosperity depend on its new outside connection. Those who owned or controlled the main line and its branches would acquire overnight a position of economic and political dominance powerful enough to obliterate all rival influence. The local elite would now be their clients. To make matters worse, the new railway line from the coast to the interior allowed a foreign government to deploy its armed forces in the depths of a continent at the behest of its commercial 'men-on-the-spot', and turn yesterday's market into tomorrow's protectorate in the twinkling of an eye. Partitioning the world was no longer a fantasy. Secondly, the extensive mobilization of capital for investment in Afro-Asia (made possible by the growth of the Euro-Atlantic economy) hugely raised the stakes in the Afro-Asian diplomacy of the European powers. Once large financial interests (and perhaps the stability of Europe's domestic finances) turned on the safety of overseas property in Asian and African states, the pressures to interfere in their local affairs—to promote 'reform', 'discourage' default, or demand a 'concession'—became enormously greater. The likelihood was that such a 'financial protectorate' would graduate quickly into commercial annexation or its political analogue. Thirdly, what had hitherto been the preserve of the interested few, mad or bad enough to seek their fortunes in the chance-ridden corners of Asian or African commerce, would now broaden out (as the volume of trade and investment expanded) into a great 'national interest'. It would attract the attention of newspapers and pundits, politicians and publicists, and sooner or later the unpredictable force labelled 'public opinion'. Once this had happened, there would be much less scope for 'old' diplomacy to square the disputes between the 'men-on-the-spot', and muffle their screams with chancery flannel. The pressure to take up a belligerent stance—'to run before the jingo hurricane with bare poles' in Lord Salisbury's evocative phrase—would be all the greater.

Fourthly, the increasing leverage that European interests could now bring to bear in the autonomous states of Asia and Africa had 'collateral' implications that were even more startling. At bottom, the continued independence of those states rested on the ability to contain or control foreign business activity. Afro-Asian regimes had to tread the fine line between opening the door to commercial outsiders (in case, as in China, they simply kicked it in) and allowing them to unsettle their domestic politics. This could happen in a number of ways. Foreign merchants, after all, might displace the home-grown commercial elite. The imports they brought in might throw local artisans out of work. If they established direct relations with local producers, they might disrupt the existing pattern of credit and clientage. If they encouraged the landholding elite to convert their broad acres to cash crops and commodities, the result might be the proletarianization of the rural poor, the loss of customary rights, and even immiseration. Opening the door to commercial outsiders might enrich a minority but open the way to social unrest. Secondly, it was almost inevitable that foreign influence would spill over from commerce into cultural life. The design and appearance of foreign-made fabrics, the habits and values of foreign merchants, their dress and deportment and their patterns of leisure, were bound to exert a powerful attraction. If foreign technical skill became the obvious means to increase local wealth (for example, by draining or improving the land), the urge to acquire it would reduce the appeal of 'traditional' education, and the social authority of those who supplied it. If opening the door meant the admission of missionaries (a missionary, remarked Lord Salisbury, was a 'religious Englishman with a mission to offend the religious feelings of the natives'),[22] then the cultural assault might soon become frontal. Before things had gone very far, the local cultural elite whose influence was at stake might be up in arms. Thirdly, those Afro-Asian states that tried to restrict the activity of commercial outsiders might find that those same outsiders already enjoyed the local backing of those who had profited from the new channels of trade or expected to do so.[23] Lastly, the bitterest of twists, those states that had embraced the new commercial future with the greatest enthusiasm, borrowing to improve the infrastructure of transport or their agrarian productivity, might discover too late that the scale of their debts, far from making them stronger, had exposed them much more to outside interference, and perhaps even bankruptcy. In short, entering the new global economy, like entering the earth's atmosphere, was a highly dangerous manoeuvre. Without a large dose of luck, or very fine judgement, those who tried it might 'burn up' on entry. At the least, it was likely to lead to a crisis.

This, then, was the global scenario that began to take shape in the last quarter of the nineteenth century. The means to expand into the Afro-Asian interior were ready at last. The speculative motive was strong. The private interests were gathering. Public interest was growing. Information—often partisan, unreliable, self-interested, and crude—flowed more freely. The lobbies howled more loudly. But at the same time, the non-Western states at which all this was directed seemed less and less able to control their own local politics, or to strengthen their hold over their external defences. Far from being able to manage the Western intruders, they now seemed too weak to prevent a disorderly scramble between them. Viewed from the West, this new situation was both enticing and alarming. The weakness of Afro-Asian polities meant that Western business would be free to refashion their economies, or at least to exploit them. But it raised the worrying prospect that governments at home would soon be drawn into the struggles of their commercial adventurers or be pressed to protect the 'national interest' against the threat of commercial exclusion. Indeed, by the end of the century, it was widely assumed in the West that the non-Western world would soon be partitioned between a half-dozen (Western) 'world states',[24] and that those states failing to lay claim to their share would enter the age of 'world politics' in a fatally weakened position.

The Imperialism of Coexistence, 1880–1914

It was thus hardly surprising that in the main Western states lobbies and movements sprang up to argue that national survival required imperial expansion. In fact this opinion was also felt strongly in those smaller powers, like the Netherlands and Portugal, whose imperial claims now faced a challenge from rival men on the spot—French, British, or German. It was nourished by three domestic developments that converged towards the end of the century. The first was the growth of a popular press to meet the demands of new urban populations.[25] This was a platform from which the demand for expansion could be trumpeted, embellished by tales of heroic white men bringing light to regions of African darkness or Asian intrigue. While European governments varied considerably in their deference to the press (French ministries were thought especially susceptible to what British diplomats called France's 'reptile press'), few could ignore an orchestrated bellow of patriotism, however bogus its source. The second was the rapid expansion of financial institutions to channel domestic savings abroad—the process by which Europe had become the 'world's banker'.[26] The concerns that emerged to gull the investor with hopes of quick profit portrayed jungles and deserts (as well as more promising regions) as new Eldorados. The late-century gold rushes played into their hands, and they could often rely on a venal financial press to whip up a speculative frenzy.[27] The third was the widely held belief that now was the time to strengthen the grip of the 'nation' on the mind of the masses. In part this reflected the fear of political elites that new working-class voters, if left to themselves, would refuse to support the costly apparatus of naval and military power and weaken the state against its predatory neighbours. But it also arose from the prosaic concerns of social and economic state-building. State education, welfare entitlements, and the policing of borders all emphasized the new ways in which a 'national' identity—assumed or imposed—was now fundamental to the functions of a modern society. The cry was taken up by a medley of those staking a claim to public attention, not least the purveyors of mass-consumption products and 'popular' culture. None of this meant the sudden conversion of mass public opinion to 'imperialist' expansion. But it greatly widened the circle of those with an interest in winning state backing for their far-flung adventures, and gave them a much louder 'echo-chamber' through which to bring pressure on hesitant governments.

It is thus easy to see why it became an historical cliché that the era between the Franco-Prussian War of 1870–1 and the First World War was one of unrestrained rivalry between the European powers for colonial possessions or their commercial equivalent in the form of concessions and spheres; and why immediately after 1918, and for much of the time since, it became usual to blame the anarchic pursuit of imperialist gain for the catastrophic explosion of European conflict.[28] But if we inspect the competition of the European states more closely, it is the caution with which they dealt with each other, not their hunger for territory no matter the cost, that really stands out. This pattern becomes clear if we trace the course of events in the three epicentres of geopolitical turbulence that preoccupied European governments (and eventually the United States) in the three decades before 1914.

The first of these lay closest to Europe in the 'Near' or 'Middle' East.[29] In the mid-nineteenth century, the Ottoman Empire still ruled over much of southeastern Europe, including modern Bosnia, Albania, Macedonia, and Bulgaria, as well as parts of modern Romania, Serbia, and Greece. Today's Turkish Republic, Iraq, Syria, Lebanon, Jordan, Israel, Palestine, Cyprus, and Crete formed parts of Ottoman provinces, and the Ottoman government also administered what is now western Saudi Arabia (the Hedjaz) and the Holy Places at Mecca and Medina. The Ottoman sultan regarded the *khedive* (or viceroy) of Egypt as his vassal, and made similar claims over Libya and Tunis. The break-up of this sprawling political system was regarded in Europe with a mixture of anticipation and alarm. Those eager to liberate its Christian communities (Orthodox, Catholic, Armenian, and others) from what they saw as Muslim oppression urged the expulsion of Ottoman power from Europe 'bag and baggage'. In Russia, the recent growth of 'pan-Slav' identity, a longer tradition of religious solidarity with the

Orthodox Church in its 'Turkish captivity', and a Tsarist *Machtpolitik* at least as old as Peter the Great, made control of the Straits and Constantinople and the destruction of the Ottoman Empire an object of almost obsessive ambition.[30] But in London, Paris, Vienna, and (later) Berlin, such a massive extension of Russian imperial power into southeastern Europe and the Mediterranean was quite unacceptable. For the British especially, Russian control of the Straits, combined with what seemed a slow grinding advance south from the Caucasus, threatened their short route to India and perhaps Russia's arrival at the head of the Gulf. Everything turned, so it seemed, on the Ottomans' success in reinvigorating their state, modernizing their army, and increasing their revenues: the vital ingredients of what the West called 'reform'. An improved Ottoman state would be less offensive to Christian feeling in the West and deny Russia the excuse for interference. But in the mid-1870s, everything went wrong. The Ottomans plunged into default on their loans and then into bankruptcy. Amid the political chaos, the repression of Christians (the 'Bulgarian Horrors') provoked a furious Western reaction and offered the Russians the excuse that they needed for armed intervention. The prospect of Russian control of the Straits and of a Russian client-state on the shores of the Mediterranean loomed large. At much the same time, Egypt, the most dynamic economy in the Near East, also collapsed into bankruptcy. By 1880, the attempt to impose external control over its public finances in the interests of foreign bondholders had brought its politics to the brink of revolution.

The geopolitical implications of this double disaster were staggering. No other great power was willing to see such a colossal enlargement of Russia's imperium. No one could be sure that the loss of so much of its territory would not lead to the general collapse of the Ottoman Empire, in Asia as well as Europe—thus spreading still wider the zone of political chaos. In Britain and France, the rise of what was seen as a populist anti-Christian regime in Egypt by 1881 threatened financial loss (to the bondholders), political embarrassment (both ruled large Muslim populations), and (to the British particularly) strategic uncertainty, since the Suez Canal had become the express route to India. Yet the risks of a 'forward policy' to safeguard 'national interests' were dauntingly high. For all European governments, the danger that nationalist or xenophobic feeling (like the Russophobic 'jingoism' in Britain in the late 1870s) might push them into unwanted confrontations was a constant threat. Faced with the chance of a general war, the European governments muddled their way to an untidy compromise that preserved Ottoman rule across the southern Balkans, denied the Russians a Mediterranean client-state, and created a financial regime—the Ottoman Public Debt Administration—to pay off the Ottomans' debts. The outcome in Egypt was just as untidy. There the British did intervene to smash the Arabi government in September 1882 and impose a client-regime. But they insisted that their presence was 'temporary' and carefully preserved the privileged status of other Europeans. Far from annexing the country or declaring a protectorate, they did all they could to conceal the scale of their influence even after deciding by the late 1880s that they could not withdraw. The omnipotent Lord Cromer, the 'whisper' behind the Egyptian throne, remained a mere 'consul-general' to soothe diplomatic outrage in Europe.[31]

Perhaps the British were lucky that their occupation of Egypt was not generally seen as upsetting the balance on the European continent, and that no other power was prepared to join France to enforce their withdrawal. But their uneasy position and the need to conciliate their European neighbours weakened their claims in the second great zone of Afro-Asian instability that now opened up. By the late 1870s, the prospect of exploiting the African interior commercially had become much more attractive, and seemingly more practicable. The steamer and railway would open it up. Henry Morton Stanley's descent of the Congo (1876–7) revealed a huge river system, navigable above Stanley Pool (modern Kinshasa). The Suez Canal brought Zanzibar and its East African trade network closer to the trunk route between Europe and India. The French in West Africa dreamt of a Trans-Saharan railway. The discovery of gold in the eastern Transvaal (but not yet on the Rand) encouraged the hope of finding still more in what is now Zimbabwe. Although the European powers agreed (at the Berlin West African conference in 1884–5) that 'effective occupation' should be the test of territorial claims, the British found it expedient to agree that the filibuster-king of the Belgians Leopold II should take as his prize the whole Congo basin, while the German chancellor Otto von Bismarck was appeased with the offer of modern Tanzania (but not Zanzibar), Namibia, and Cameroon.[32] As it turned out, these lines on the African map preceded anything that resembled 'effective occupation'. They signalled instead the onset of struggle by the states and polities of the African interior against the wasting effects of European influence and firepower. The competition for treaties and trade between rival European men-on the-spot, their appeal for support to their backers at home, and the rousing of 'jingo' emotion in popular politics, made the partition diplomacy of the 1890s an ill-tempered, sabre-rattling affair. It climaxed at Fashoda in late 1898 when a handful of Frenchmen gave up the attempt to claim the Upper Nile in the face of Lord Kitchener's army, fresh from defeating the Mahdist state at Omdurman in September.

The 'scramble' for Africa has often been treated as proof of the ruthless aggression of the European states and their willingness to go to any lengths to acquire supposedly valuable colonies. The truth is more subtle. The predation and violence that the Europeans inflicted on Africans is undeniable. So is the contempt with which they treated Africans' property rights (including the right to their own labour). But except in the special circumstances of the South African War of 1899–1902, no blood was shed *between* Europeans. For all the jostling of the men-on-the-spot and sound and fury of their sponsors at home, European governments (with the partial exception of Italy)[33] showed no inclination to fight each other on behalf of their African claims.[34]

The same was true of the third epicentre of geopolitical turmoil that appeared in East Asia after 1895, when China's defeat at the hands of Japan (the dispute was over Korea), and its recourse to European loans to pay an indemnity, raised the spectre of the rapid implosion of the Qing imperial state, and a division of spoils, if not of spheres, among the Western powers and Japan. The race for concessions and bases, the abortive rush to reform by the court in Beijing, the Boxer rebellion and the occupation of North China, largely by Russian and Japanese troops, all seemed to be driving towards the break-up of China, and its fractious division between multiple claimants.[35] And unlike tropical Africa, the economic and geopolitical stakes in China were thought to be high. China possessed a commercial economy that was ripe for the plucking by foreign-owned railways; and political control over its vast interior was bound to shift the balance of power not just in Asia, but across the whole of Eurasia. In London, the threat of a 'scramble for China' at a time when Britain was still in the toils of its South African war was acutely alarming. With Russian troops in Manchuria, a German sphere in Shandong, and French designs on South China, the idea of proclaiming a 'Yangtse protectorate' to guard British interests in the huge riverine hinterland stretching back from Shanghai was considered and rejected as too risky a move. Instead the British concluded an alliance with Japan against the danger that Russia and France (already allies in Europe) might try a joint squeeze on their (or Japan's) East Asian interests.[36]

Fear of China's partition was in fact premature. Among the banks and finance houses with interests in China, international cooperation was greatly preferred to cut-throat competition. Moreover, the easy assumption that the Chinese authorities would simply cave in before the face of foreign demands turned out to be wrong. Instead, provincial administrations pursued 'rights recovery' and China's 'self-strengthening' against foreign attempts to control the construction of railways. When friction between Russia and Japan over Korea and Manchuria burst out into war in 1904, it was the Russians who suffered a crushing defeat on land and sea. The balance of power in East Asia now seemed to rest with those who disliked the break-up of China since Japan was unlikely to challenge the combined opposition of Britain and the United States, both of which favoured an 'open door' policy over one of partition. The real danger in China on the eve of the First World War was less an agreement by the great powers to divide up its assets, or a military struggle for concessions and spheres, than the failure of the new post-revolution regime to impose its authority over the provincial authorities.

Looked at more closely, the age of Europe's 'high imperialism', when the clash of ambition was supposedly reaching its climax, was a patchy affair. It was true that the Europeans had divided up Africa (almost completely) to the crowing and wailing of the interested parties. But except in South Africa and perhaps also in Egypt, the stakes had been low and compromise easy. In China where the stakes were certainly larger, the rival contenders found that they had to cooperate against Chinese resistance at the time of the Boxer rebellion. No European power contemplated fighting another to force a Chinese partition: none had the strength to impose its will on the region. In the Near and Middle East much the same picture emerged. The Ottoman Empire showed a surprising resilience.[37] Despite their mutual fears and suspicions, or perhaps because of them, the European powers preferred to keep it in being rather than face the dilemmas of dividing it up. Nor should we be surprised at the general timidity of European statecraft. It is easy to exaggerate the scale of European interests in the non-European world: only Great Britain had important foreign investments outside the home continent. While most European statesmen (and Americans as well) believed themselves living in the age of 'world states', 'competitive coexistence', not a war to the death, was the motto they followed. That meant much puffing and croaking in the manner of bullfrogs, not a fight to the finish. It's not hard to see why. Britain and France had little to gain. In Russia, Austria-Hungary, and Germany, the ruling elites might have fingered their swords, but they knew very well that a general war over China or Africa would inflict terrible strains on their multi-ethnic empires at home. Here the 'logic' of nationalism was not the pursuit of imperial ambition in the world beyond Europe but its careful restraint. For the nationalisms that mattered were those of Czechs and Poles, South Slavs and Ruthenians. Keeping them quiet required a conservative policy, not rocking the boat of Europe's balance of power. It was the reckless desertion of this long-standing policy amid the chaos that followed the two Balkan wars of 1912–14 that brought Europe's house down in July 1914. Nationalism not imperialism set off Armageddon.

The New Imperialism of the Inter-War Years

It used to be argued that the end was in sight for Europe's overseas empires after 1918. With their moral credentials in tatters, their wealth and manpower depleted, and their rule under siege by discontented colonials, they could hardly resist the new global doctrine of national self-determination. The defeated 'Central Powers'—the Germans, Habsburgs, and Ottomans—had their empires broken up. Bolshevik Russia, defeated by Germany in March 1918, lost control of its 'Romanov' Empire in the Caucasus and Central Asia, as well as in Europe. In the Middle East and East Asia, Arab, Turkish, Iranian, and Chinese nationalisms asserted the claims of new nation states against the undeclared empires and 'veiled protectorates' of the European powers. The Washington treaties of 1921–2 guaranteed China's integrity. The age of partitions was over: the world of nations was on the march. Or so it seemed.

But when the dust had settled, much of the old imperial order remained in place, even if in a new guise. In the Caucasus, Central Asia, and the Pacific 'Far East', Russian power was restored. Federal union was the form, the Communist Party the glue, but empire the reality. Germany's lost colonies were shared out as 'mandates' under League supervision, but for all practical purposes they were governed as colonies. The same was true of Ottoman Syria and Lebanon, awarded to France as the mandatory power.[38] The British were keen to lay down their mandate for Iraq, which became independent in 1932. But only because they could use it more cheaply as a pensioner state on their air route to India.[39] In face of nationalist movements in Egypt and India, the British conceded degrees of self-government in the byzantine endeavour to divide and confuse their opponents.[40] They were largely successful. In tropical Africa, 'indirect rule' through 'traditional' chiefs and 'customary' law reduced political life to a strictly local activity. Perhaps only in China, where the West had been weakest, was the promise of nationalism sustained through the post-war decade. But that too was about to change.

The catalyst was the Great Depression. The sudden implosion of the global economy in 1929–31 wrecked the half-liberal, half-imperial order over which Britain and France, Europe's two victor powers, had hoped to preside with American help, and through which they meant to restrain both German resurgence and the unruly ambitions of Russia and Japan. Depression destroyed the authority of liberal politicians in Tokyo and Berlin and drove a deep wedge between London and Washington.[41] As its impact sank in, a new kind of world order swam into view. As trade contracted, the 'open' global economy began to break up into a series of blocs, guarded by tariffs or currency rules. Economic survival now seemed to depend upon the control of the zone from which imports were drawn and to which they were sent. For industrial states without a massive home market (the American pattern) or a vast trading empire (the British), the implications were dire. They spelled out the need for a new and more ruthless form of economic imperialism, far more thorough and real than the slash-and-burn colonialism of Leopold's Congo Free State. What made this more urgent was the far stronger sense of domestic political danger than Europe's ruling elites had felt before 1914. The spectre of Bolshevism loomed over the battered economies of Europe and Asia. Indeed, to many observers in different parts of the world, the crisis of capitalism seemed to confirm that Marx and Lenin had been right all along: the capitalists had delayed but could not evade their ultimate fate. But if this was a message of cheer to leaders and led on the Left, it convinced many others that they faced a supreme emergency: drastic measures were needed to escape economic collapse, intense social conflict, and the politics of class war.

For the 'have' powers, the solution was straightforward. Those with empires or (like the British) with additional zones of informal pre-eminence, could secure them by tariffs or bilateral agreements (as the British did with Argentina, Denmark, and elsewhere).[42] Those with a home market could rely on protection—the American model. Those without either—the 'have-nots'—faced exclusion from world markets, and the wreck of their own. This was the context in which Tokyo abandoned the indirect form of expansion it had practised in China for much of the 1920s and sanctioned first the forward movement of the Kwantung army in Manchuria in 1931 and then (from 1937) the all-out war to control maritime China. The 'Great East Asian Co-Prosperity Sphere'—the doctrine invented to dignify Tokyo's actions—invoked the common interest of East Asians in resisting exploitation by the West in an artful fusion of imperialism and nationalism.[43] In Hitler's Germany, which took refuge in exchange control and barter trade,[44] the economic domination of an East European hinterland was soon supercharged in Nazi ambitions by the colonization of the 'East'—the vast realm of southern Russia and Ukraine to be cleared of their 'backward' inhabitants. If the pre-1914 imperialists had followed a 'gentlemanly' code of honour among thieves, as they stole the land and freedom of non-European peoples, this was imperialism without limits and with no holds barred.

What made it more deadly was the apparent indifference of the new imperialists to the crucial constraints felt before 1914. Then, as we have seen, it was fear of a European war, and the damage it might do to the brittle empires 'at home', that discouraged too much aggression on the Afro-Asian 'periphery'. But though the new rulers in Tokyo and Berlin were not without fears, they were deeply opposed to the existing world order, had little incentive to prop up its weakness, and were increasingly sure that it could and must be pulled down. In their geopolitical thinking, as well as their ideology, they had nothing in common with Britain and France, the two jaded custodians of the 'liberal-imperial' order. To make matters worse, the new Soviet state, whose geostrategic potential was a critical factor in the imperial ambitions of both Tokyo and Berlin, was no less hostile than they were to the global regime favoured by Britain and France—and thus willing to sup with the devil in August 1939.[45] American alienation did not run so deep. But the breach between London and Washington that ruled out joint action until after war had begun was at least partly a consequence of American feeling that they had little to gain from a global regime that locked up so much of the world in the trading and currency blocs managed from London and (in a much smaller way) from Paris, Brussels, and The Hague. With the fall of France in June 1940, the trigger was pulled. The imperialism by coexistence, which had allowed Europeans to share out the globe before 1914, had run out of backers. It was about to be pulled down not by the revolt of its subjects but by the economic nationalism of those who aspired to build new forms of empire on the ruins of the old.

Notes

1. For a brilliant expression of this view, R. Robinson and J. Gallagher (1961) *Africa and the Victorians*. 'European' includes British.
2. See J. Gallagher and R. Robinson (1953) 'The Imperialism of Free Trade', *Economic History Review*, New Series, VI, no. 1, 1–14. For informal empire in Argentina, H. S. Ferns (1960) *Britain and Argentina in the Nineteenth Century*, Oxford; for Uruguay, P. Winn (1976) 'British Informal Empire in Uruguay in the Nineteenth Century', *Past and Present*, 73, 100–26.
3. For the treaty port system in China, H. B. Morse (1908) *The Trade and Administration of the Chinese Empire*. For a modern survey, J. Osterhammel (1999) 'Britain and China 1842–1914', in A. Porter (ed.) *Oxford History of the British Empire: The Nineteenth Century*, Oxford, 146–69.
4. For this argument, J. Darwin (1997) 'Imperialism and the Victorians', *English Historical Review*, 112, no. 447, 614–42.
5. For all its importance, there is yet to be a full scholarly study of the British regime in Egypt 1882–1954. For the Cromer period, the best recent account is R. Owen (2004) *Lord Cromer*, Oxford.
6. The theory of economic imperialism found its classic expression in J. A. Hobson (1902) *Imperialism: A Study*, London, although Hobson stressed above all the role of surplus

capital. For a close but critical examination of the theory, D. K. Fieldhouse (1973) *Economics and Empire 1830–1914*, London.

7. An early scholarly version of this argument was W. L. Langer (1935) *The Diplomacy of Imperialism*, New York, 2 vols., vol. 1, ch. 3. For a German version, H. Pogge von Strandmann (1969) 'Domestic Origins of Germany's Colonial Expansion under Bismarck', *Past and Present*, 42. For Italy, C. Duggan (2002) *Francesco Crispi 1818–1901*, Oxford, 411–15, 670–709.
8. An influential statement of this thesis was A. J. P. Taylor (1938) *Germany's First Bid for Colonies*, London. The date of publication is not insignificant.
9. For Russian imperialism, the best introduction is now D. Lieven (2002) *Empire: the Russian Empire and its Rivals from the Sixteenth Century to the Present*, London, which has an excellent bibliography.
10. Although it has been persuasively argued that support for empire became embedded in British opinion, this is not the same as popular enthusiasm for imperial *expansion*. See J. MacKenzie (1984) *Propaganda and Empire: The Manipulation of British Public Opinion 1880–1960*, Manchester.
11. Robinson and Gallagher, 'The Imperialism of Free Trade'.
12. See E. T. Stokes (1959) *The English Utilitarians and India*, Oxford; and T. R. Metcalf (1995) *Ideologies of the Raj*, Cambridge, for the classic case of the British in India.
13. J. B. Kelly (1968) *Britain and the Persian Gulf 1795–1880*, Oxford, is the authoritative study.
14. See A. Kappeler (2001) *The Russian Empire: A Multiethnic History*, Harlow; F. Kazemzadeh (1968) *Russia and Britain in Persia 1864–1914*, New Haven.
15. See K. Dike (1956) *Trade and Politics in the Niger Delta 1830–1885*, Oxford; M. Lynn (1986) 'The Imperialism of Free Trade and the Case of West Africa', *Journal of Imperial and Commonwealth History*, 15, 22–40.
16. The dissatisfaction of British merchants with the slowness of the East India Company government to 'open up' India with railways and roads occasioned a parliamentary inquiry in the late 1840s. See A. W. Silver (1966) *Manchester Men and Indian Cotton 1847–1872*, Manchester.
17. See K. H. O'Rourke and J. G. Williamson (1999) *Globalization and History: The Evolution of a Nineteenth-Century Atlantic Economy*, Cambridge, MA; for the larger picture, A. G. Kenwood and A. L. Lougheed (1983) *The Growth of the International Economy 1820–1980*, London.
18. See D. A. Farnie (1969) *East and West of Suez: The Suez Canal in History, 1854–1956*, Oxford; J. Forbes Munro (2003) *Maritime Enterprise and Empire: Sir William Mackinnon and his Business Network 1823–1893*, Woodbridge.
19. See C. A. Bayly (1996) *Empire and Information*, Cambridge, ch. 9; generally D. Headrick (1981) *The Tools of Empire: Technology and European Imperialism in the Nineteenth Century*, Oxford.
20. For European commercial difficulty in China, F. E. Hyde (1973) *Far-Eastern Trade 1860–1914*, London, ch. 5.
21. See D. Gillard (1977) *The Struggle for Asia 1828–1914: A Study in British and Russian Imperialism*, London.
22. A. Roberts (1999) *Salisbury: Victorian Titan*, London, 42.
23. An early case was the desertion of the Bengal subahdar, Suraja Daula, by many of his leading supporters before his battle with Clive at Plassey in 1757.

24. This phrase was used, and may have been coined, by Sir John Seeley in his *Expansion of England* (1883).
25. For the French popular press and empire, W. H. Schneider (1982) *An Empire for the Masses: The French Popular Image of Africa, 1870–1900*, Westport, CT.
26. The scale and direction of European lending is laid out in H. Feis (1930) *Europe the World's Banker*, New York.
27. For this view of the City of London, see I. R. Phimister (2000) 'Corners and Company-mongering: Nigerian Tin and the City of London', *Journal of Imperial and Commonwealth History*, 28.
28. A forceful statement of this was G. Lowes Dickinson (1926) *The International Anarchy*, London.
29. The term 'Middle East' seems to have become current during the First World War. For treatments of these regions and the role of other powers from different perspectives, see the chapters in this book by Aviel Roshwald (11), Miroslav Hroch (9), and Theodore Weeks (10).
30. See B. H. Sumner (1937) *Russia and the Balkans 1870–1880*, Oxford.
31. See A. Schölch (Eng. trans. 1981) *'Egypt for the Egyptians': The Socio-Political Crisis in Egypt 1879–1882*, London.
32. For the Berlin Conference of 1884–5, S. Forster et al. (eds.) (1988) *Bismarck, Europe and Africa*, Oxford; J.-L. Vellut (1992) *Un centenaire 1885–1985. Les relations Europe-Afrique au crible d'un commemoration*, Leiden.
33. Duggan, *Crispi*, 670–709.
34. From a different perspective, see Chapter 16 by John Lonsdale.
35. For a recent scholarly treatment, T. Otte (2007) *The China Question*, Oxford.
36. See I. H. Nish (1966) *The Anglo-Japanese Alliance*, London.
37. For Ottoman reform, S. Deringil (1998) *The Well-Protected Domains: Ideology and the Legitimation of Power in the Ottoman Empire, 1876–1909*, London; E. Rogan (1999) *Frontiers of the State in the Late Ottoman Empire: Trans-Jordan 1850–1921*, Cambridge.
38. The authoritative account is P. S. Khoury (1987) *Syria and the French Mandate: The Politics of Arab Nationalism 1920–1945*, Princeton, NJ.
39. See D. Silverfarb (1986) *Britain's Informal Empire in the Middle East: A Case Study of Iraq 1929–41*, Oxford.
40. J. Darwin (1981) *Britain, Egypt and the Middle East: Imperial Policy in the Aftermath of War 1918–1922*, London; D. Page (1982) *Prelude to Partition: The Indian Muslims and the Imperial System of Control 1920–1932*, Delhi.
41. M. Metzler (2006) *Lever of Empire: The International Gold Standard and the Crisis of Liberalism in Pre-war Japan*, Berkeley; Generally, H. James (2001) *The End of Globalization*, Cambridge, MA.
42. The best account of the British case is T. Rooth (2002) *British Protectionism and the International Economy: Overseas Commercial Policy in the 1930s*, Cambridge.
43. For the persistence of economic complementarity between Japan and the British Empire until 1937, see S. Akita and N. Kagotani (2002) 'The International Order of Asia in the 1930s', and Y. Kibata (2002) 'Reasserting Imperial Power? Britain and East Asia in the 1930s', both in S. Akita (ed.) *Gentlemanly Capitalism, Imperialism and Global History*, Basingstoke. For the thinking in the military clique that dominated the Tokyo government, A. Iriye (1998) 'The Failure of Military Expansionism', in S. Large (ed.) *Showa Japan: Political, Economic and Social History 1926–1989, vol. 1: 1926–1941*, London, 213–15,

223, 226–7. For an older discussion, F. C. Jones (1954) *Japan's New Order in Asia: its Rise and Fall*, Oxford.

44. For an outstanding account, A. Tooze (2006) *Wages of Destruction: The Making and Breaking of the Nazi Economy*, London.
45. The best study of Stalin's diplomacy in 1939–41 is now G. Gorodetsky (1999) *Grand Delusion: Stalin and the German Invasion of Russia*, New Haven.

Suggested Further Reading

Three master-writings by R. E. Robinson and J. Gallagher, 'The Imperialism of Free Trade', *Economic History Review*, new series VI, 1 (1953); *Africa and the Victorians* (Cambridge, 1961); and 'The Partition of Africa', in *New Cambridge Modern History*, vol. 11: *Material Progress and World Wide Problems* (Cambridge, 1962), provide what remains the most powerful overall interpretation of the nineteenth-century encounter of imperialism and nationalism. Many of these insights are marshalled in Gallagher's posthumous (1982) *Decline, Rise and Fall of the British Empire*, Cambridge. See also D. Lieven (2002) *Empire: the Russian Empire and its Rivals*; some of its key ideas are brilliantly summarized in his (1999) 'Dilemmas of Empire: Power, Territory and Identity 1850–1918', *Journal of Contemporary History*, 34, no. 2, 163–200.

On economic aspects of imperial expansion, D. K. Fieldhouse (1973) *Economics and Empire 1830–1914* has yet be superseded. But see also K. H. O'Rourke and J. G. Williamson (1999) *Globalization and History: The Evolution of a Nineteenth-Century Atlantic Economy*, Cambridge, MA.

The response of non-Western societies can be followed in: J. Lonsdale (1985) 'The Race Against Time', in R. Oliver and G. N. Sanderson (eds.) *Cambridge History of Africa, vol. 6: 1870–1905*, Cambridge; A. Hourani (1962) *Arabic Thought in the Liberal Age*, Cambridge; M. Aksakal (2008) *The Ottoman Road to War in 1914*, Cambridge; T. Raychaudhuri (1989) *Europe Reconsidered: Perceptions of the West in Nineteenth-Century Bengal*, Delhi; A. Seal (1973) 'Imperialism and Nationalism in India', in J. Gallagher, G. Johnson, and A. Seal (eds.) *Locality, Province and Nation*, Cambridge; R. Bin Wong (1997) *China Transformed: Historical Change and the Limits of European Experience*, Ithaca, NY; H. van der Ven (2003) *War and Nationalism in China 1925–1945*. A neglected classic is E. H. Norman (1940) *Japan's Emergence as a Modern State*, New York. A panoptic view of the period is C. A. Bayly (2004) *The Birth of the Modern World 1780–1914: Global Connections and Comparisons*, Oxford.

CHAPTER 18

NATIONALISM IN POST-COLONIAL AFRICA

BRUCE J. BERMAN

Development and Nation-Building in the 1960s and 1970s

At independence, states and nations, ethnic groups and classes, were all in flux, processes of active social construction and political contest rather than stable entities. They continue to be so today. In the first decades of independence most African states pursued nation-building as a conscious strategy and objective, believing national unity to be a prerequisite of socioeconomic development. They were also pressured by international and bilateral national aid organizations that both saw the secular industrial nation state as the sole embodiment of modernity and development, and feared that the weak 'new nations' of Africa would be torn apart by 'atavistic' tribalism. Even before independence tenuous ethnic and class coalitions had begun to unravel into competing factions struggling for control over the material rewards of state power. In several states, minority, ethnically based, parties challenged dominant nationalist movements. At independence, competitive elections and the Africanization of the state apparatus made ethnicity increasingly important as a basis of political support and access to higher levels of the state apparatus.[1]

In a Cold War international environment in which both sides were hostile to the break-up of states, state-focused development strategies and national development plans became the order of the day. The Keynesian/social democratic moral economy of the post-war West was the hegemonic paradigm for a state-regulated capitalist national development. Ideologically, nationalism guided and promoted economic development by appeal to national rather than class or regional ethnic interests. A variety of nationalist discourse was expressed in different, if ostensibly inclusive, nation-building strategies. These ranged from the neo-traditionalism of Julius Nyerere's Tanzania that sought to revive supposedly collectivist African tradition, yet was forcefully state-centric and suppressed expressions of ethnic politics; to the multi-ethnic national commonwealth of Jomo Kenyatta's Kenya, firmly grounded in the ethnic patronage networks of colonialism; the secular modernism of Kwame Nkrumah's Ghana, which subdued the country's powerful chiefs; and the radically modernist 'scientific socialism' of Samora Machel in Mozambique, who proclaimed 'For the nation to live, the tribe must die.'[2]

Beyond nationalism as the promotion of economic development by appeal to national rather than ethnic or class interests, as in Kenyatta's declaration that in the nationalist struggle 'We all fought for freedom' and his call for 'Harambee' ('All pull together'), nation-building tried both to create a discourse of legitimacy for the state and a doctrine of popular sovereignty and citizenship. It focused on education for the masses, including propagation of a legitimating charter, a national historical epic of struggle for anti-colonial liberation. It also pursued the cultural and symbolic dimensions of the national project, from the newly created 'national' flags and anthems to a focus on popular culture and sport, making heroes out of performers and captains of national teams.[3] However, nationalism as a development ideology or nation-building through cultural engineering proved to be of only limited effectiveness in either state formation or national integration. All the nationalist ideologies of post-colonial Africa ultimately failed to reconstruct an effectively hegemonic 'national' moral economy attached to a legitimate, widely trusted arena of civic politics in the state.

Instead, behind the facade of ostensibly modern state institutions, the politics of the belly spread through ethnic patronage networks to the centre of the state apparatus, with ramifying linkages reaching from cabinet to village, to produce what J.-F. Bayart graphically described as the 'rhizome state'.[4] So-called 'neo-patrimonialism' was grounded in ethnic patronage networks. At the grass roots, ethnic identity and communal membership were reinforced as the basis for access to the state and its resources. There were also repeated attempts, with varying degrees of success, to co-opt or force into the patron/client nexus such diverse social groups as religious congregations that represented a non- or trans-ethnic moral community and ideology; or trade unions, professional associations, and non-governmental organizations that spoke for class or interest-based expressions of a more secular modernity. African heads of state themselves became clients of both international capital and of external powers such as the US and, in particular, France.

The two faces of the African post-colonial state have been vividly described by Emmanuel Terray as '*le climatiseur et la veranda*', the air conditioner and the verandah. The first is the face of modern state power, bureaucratic authority, and technical expertise; the second where the real business of government is conducted, handing out patronage.[5] The facade of state power was expressed in an obsession with the symbolic pomp and theatrical ritual of the 'nation', and an opaque and arbitrary decision-making process that masked the vulgar reality of power from its subjects. Moreover, in state after state, the political and cultural construction of the 'nation' turned into a cult of personality around the president or leader as the embodiment of the nation and father of his people. The charisma of leadership[6] undermined nationalism and reinforced the political culture of personal leadership and patronage, including the taking of traditional, or traditional-sounding, titles such as Mobutu Sese Seko or Osagyefo Kwame Nkrumah.

The rule of Africa's big men was linked to the growing suppression of political expression and competition, and an increasing authoritarian cast to the state and ruling parties. Increasingly, de facto and de jure 'one-party democracies' declared the ruling party to be the essential carapace of national unity. Competing parties, especially any based on ethnic loyalty, were suppressed, with their leaders incorporated into the single party led by the great national leader. As Angelique Haugerud notes, 'both colonial and post-colonial states emphasized that politics were dangerous, and that political activity had to be curbed in order to preserve civil order.... The state's capacity to convince citizens that restrictions on political expression are needed to preserve order (or to prevent chaos) depends in part on delivering to the populace some of the material benefits of "progress" and "modernity".'[7] Increasingly authoritarian rule eliminated the political meaning of citizenship and offered instead an implicit, tenuous moral contract of material benefits in return for political quiescence. The single-party state permitted the distribution of material resources between ethnic communities to be negotiated between their leaders, without resort to the public mobilization of their supporters. The politics of political tribalism and moral ethnicity became linked to the ability of the 'big men' with state office to obtain for their communities a significant share of the collective benefits of 'development', as well as the more individual rewards apportioned on the verandah.

The wave of coups that began in January 1963 with Togo's 250-man army killing the president, Sylvanus Olympio, brought to power military regimes in many African states. In spite of their extravagant claims to be agents of national unity and their suppression of 'divisive' parties and organizations, military regimes did little to change state-focused patronage systems. Instead, the military magnates incorporated themselves into a dominant position within the patrimonial networks of patronage and appropriation of state resources. Ramshackle armies were lavishly rearmed, claiming larger and larger portions of national budgets, and the military 'big men' were amongst the most enduring and profligately corrupt of Africa's rulers.

Neo-Liberal 'Reform' and State and Nation in Africa in the 1980s

The rise of neo-liberal hegemony in the dominant capitalist nations and international financial institutions in the 1980s caused a stunning reversal of the idea of 'development' as conceived in the first decades of independence with its state-centred strategies of economic development and nation-building. Instead, the focus was radically narrowed to the market alone. The irremediably corrupt and 'predatory' state in Africa was now the enemy of 'development'. Neo-liberal doctrine rejected the legitimacy of politics and sought to remove state 'interventions' that distorted the free play of market forces and, it was asserted, retarded growth. Access to aid and finance became dependent on the implementation of 'reforms' contained in Structural Adjustment Programmes (SAPs), uniform for each country that accepted the conditions for receiving aid: currency devaluation, imposition of fees for basic public services like health and education, removal of price subsidies for food, elimination of budget deficits, removal of barriers to 'free' trade, and privatization of public corporations and other state-owned economic assets.

The painfully won gains of national development of the 1960s and 1970s were dismissed as restraints on market-driven growth. Instead, SAPs were economically and scientifically 'correct' in a way that tolerated no dissent. From the Berg Report (1981) onwards, 'extremely controversial and widely disputed claims [were] blandly asserted as simple, incontestable, scientific facts'. Efforts at industrialization and economic diversification had to be abandoned because 'it was not economically correct for African countries to seek to escape the niche the world market had provided for them'; they had therefore to concentrate on their areas of 'comparative advantage' in producing cash crops, so pushing them back into the structures of the colonial political economy. 'The effectiveness of the whole package of prescribed policy [was] definitively demonstrated through a "simulation" projecting, with the Bank's usual fraudulent pseudo-precision ... the exact percentage increases that the specific reforms [would] bring in GDP, agriculture, exports, and imports. What is there to argue about, after all? It's right there in the numbers.'[8] Politics could only be a corrupt intrusion into the pursuit of the scientifically determined result.

Neo-liberal structural adjustment programmes, part of a conscious effort to 'globalize' the capitalist system, represented the most rigorous and coercive effort to impose the self-regulating market since the early nineteenth century. In Ghana, the international financial institutions disciplined the 'revolutionary' populism of the second Rawlings regime into accepting a neo-liberal reform package in return for aid to rescue it from imminent economic collapse in 1983–4. In South Africa, the new ANC government was pressured by the World Bank and IMF to implement the 'technical' and 'scientific' policies that would preserve South African capitalism and bring the country back into the global economy from the isolation of the apartheid regime.[9]

The common result of globalization and structural adjustment for Africa, while producing periods of economic growth in some countries, has been general economic decline, social decay, and disorder. Africa has been brought into the global economy in segmentary fashion that has marginalized large portions of each nation and the continent as a whole. In 1976 the per-capita GNP of sub-Saharan Africa was 17.6 per cent of the world average, but had dropped to 10.5 per cent by 1999. The average country's GNP per capita shrank by almost 10 per cent between 1970 and 1998, and the continent's share of global economic activity was only 1.1 per cent, despite having more than 10 per cent of the world's population. Rather than neo-liberal reform bringing the predicted increased foreign investment, Africa received only 0.6 per cent of the world total.[10] By the 1980s, even the economic miracle in the Côte d'Ivoire was in radical decline; while in Ghana the World Bank implemented its Program of Assistance to Mitigate the Social Costs of Adjustment (PAMSCAD), a tacit admission of the failure of market reform.[11] Rather than development, neo-liberalism brought 'the steepest economic inequalities seen in human history to date',[12] with corresponding declines in literacy and life expectancy and unprecedented growth in the proportion of African populations living in absolute poverty. This was correlated with rural decline, runaway urbanization, and the growth of metastasizing slums housing the 'shadow economy' of the informal sector.

The impact of structural adjustment and globalization on African states was severe. Cuts in personnel and services 'hollowed out' most states, reducing their administrative capacity and limiting their effective authority to a radius of a few miles around the capital city and other major towns, often with little effective presence beyond the police in the festering slums. The undermining of state capacity and loss of direct developmental functions and services made space not for markets to produce rapid growth, but for increased 'corruption and rent seeking'.[13] Equally important was the effective loss of state sovereignty, weak to begin with, ceding control over macroeconomic policy to international financial institutions and of vast tracts of territory to private corporations and NGOs.

Africa experiences globalization, with its combination of linkage and marginalization, as highly capitalized enclaves, particularly for natural resource extraction, with little connection to the marginalized tracts around them. As James Ferguson notes, 'usable Africa gets secure enclaves—non-contiguous "useful" bits that are secured, policed, and, in a minimal sense, governed through private or semiprivate means. These enclaves are increasingly linked up, not in a national grid, but in transnational networks that connect economically valued spaces dispersed around the world in a point-to-point fashion.'[14] The growth of such enclaves with their private security of hired mercenaries means that many states have lost the key monopoly of legal organized force. Delivery of public services and 'development' programmes has also been taken over by a wide range of non-governmental organizations—local, international, and transnational—exercising state-like functions according to their own political, economic, and religious agendas. Often these dominant components of what is called 'civil society' constitute 'integral parts of a new, transnational apparatus of governmentality [that] does not *replace* the older system of nation-states, but overlays and coexists with it'.[15]

This undermining of the state threatened established structures of political and economic power and the politics of patronage. Political elites dependent on state patronage periodically clashed with international financial institutions over the terms of adjustment programmes, as both the civilian Moi regime in Kenya and the military magnates of Nigeria did in the early 1990s. State deregulation and investment did not so much free markets as extend political struggles to control key sectors of the national economy from the state into the private sector. Political elites often used their declining state power to gain a hold over portions of the rapidly growing international criminal economy, especially drugs and arms trafficking, that accompanied globalization; and increasingly relied on fraud, trickery, and deception in dealing with external political and economic forces.[16]

The decay of the state and the resulting intensified struggle to control resources and accumulate wealth amid the growing poverty and uncertainty of the mass of the population increased the conflicts of moral ethnicity and political tribalism. Contracting states cannot create new programmes and positions or even pay the salaries of existing officials, while patrons with declining or threatened resources are unwilling and unable to sustain distributions to their clients. The increasingly materialistic and opportunistic appropriation of state resources for private gain undermines the relations of trust underpinning patronage networks with growing cynicism and corruption over the failure of 'big men' to meet their obligations of reciprocity and redistribution to the poor. The ambivalence of the relationship between the classes finds expression in the fraught idioms of kinship in which the relations between leaders and masses are expressed: 'Nothing is more confused and volatile than the tales of "love" between rulers and the ruled, and current reality is full of sudden reversals in which people move from fervent expressions of allegiance to the most violent kind of rejection.'[17] From aiding their followers to a share of the 'national cake', elites, in a profound reversal, are seen to 'eat' their people by failing to protect them from the ravages of neo-liberal 'adjustment'. Big men are seen as agents of sorcery and witchcraft, their occult powers sucking life from the poor. While the poor place greater demands on the wealthier kin for aid and families bitterly divide over the inheritance of land and property, the broader conflict between rich and poor is also expressed in acts of resistance and escape, as in the growth of parallel economies beyond the grasp of decayed states.

The increasing conflict between ethnic communities for the decreasing resources of the state has not undermined nationalism but, rather, reinforces it by making ethnicity increasingly the criterion of citizenship. Where ethnic identities and communities have historically been ambiguous, fungible, and hybrid in their construction, modern population movements along with 'weakened states, refugees, economic deregulation, and systematic new forms of pauperization and criminalization' have introduced new sources of uncertainty about who are legitimate members of the nation.[18] The ability to control those states that have played a central role in the official recognition of ethnic communities, their numbers and territory, becomes the means to resolve the uncertainties of the sociopolitical boundaries of the nation and defining which groups legitimately belong to it and, emphatically, those that do not.

Rural land tenure has become a major source of ethnic conflict. The international aid agencies have inconsistently promoted both commodification of land and legal titles for individual holdings to stimulate commercial agriculture and preservation of traditional 'communal' tenure systems as part of the efforts to 'decentralize' development to local communities. Where accurate surveys are often lacking and there is ambiguity and confusion over the legal status of landholdings and transactions, the situation is further complicated by the development of 'vernacular' land markets in which elites buy and sell tracts, often to 'strangers', and displace poor kin and dependents reliant on them for access to land. Undermining of the traditional agrarian moral economy has made land disputes the most important source of conflict and social violence both within and between ethnic communities, and intensified social cleavages and class formation. In Ghana and Kenya, as well, elite appropriation of ostensibly state-owned 'public land' has become a major component of corruption and patronage. Confrontations over land are linked to the increasing ethnicization of citizenship and explosive conflicts of 'autochthony' that have developed since the 1990s over clashing claims of belonging and exclusion over ethnic territory and landholdings.[19]

Social Violence, Contested Nations, Persistent States

Since the late 1980s the erosion of state capacity in Africa has been accompanied by a widespread increase of social violence. With the withdrawal of social services and the decline of patronage networks, disorder, crime, and insecurity took their place. Still more disturbing was the increasingly savage nature of the violence carried out by organized groups, whether criminal gangs, national armies, and police, or insurgent movements and private 'war lord' armies, involving mass murder, mutilation, and rape of mostly civilian populations, especially women and children. Such violence was highlighted in the Western news media, which often covered little else about Africa, as 'senseless', 'irrational', an 'end in itself'. This emphasis constructed African 'difference' and 'darkness' as a reversion to primordial savagery, or, in Robert Kaplan's influential characterization, as a harbinger of the collapse of civilization.[20] The leading explanation of African 'civil wars' by the economist Paul Collier and his colleagues, sponsored by the World Bank, depicted them as driven not by political grievance but by greed, that is, a rational calculation of the economic returns to violence made by predatory insurgent groups and warlords who fought for control over natural resources ('conflict diamonds'), drug trafficking, and ruthless exploitation of local populations.[21]

The problem with such simplistic stereotypes is that it obscures a complex reality and makes the relationship between social violence and the nation state in Africa impossible to understand. Compared to the rest of the world in the sanguinary twentieth century, as Tiyambe Zeleza notes, 'Africa has been no more prone to violent conflicts than other regions. Indeed, Africa's share of the more than 180 million people who died from conflicts and atrocities during the twentieth century is relatively modest.'[22] The horrific genocides of Rwanda and Darfur do not place Africa outside 'civilization', but include it in the grim global record of state-sponsored and organized slaughter that is the evil legacy of modernity, including the bloody ethnic confrontations in the Balkans and the Caucasus occasioned by the collapse of Yugoslavia and the Soviet Union.

Second, not only are most of Africa's worst civil conflicts, including its most violent ethnic clashes, grounded in the political and economic experience of the colonial era, but the 'law and order' of the colonial 'civilizing mission' was itself marked by the routinely harsh coercion of subject populations. The paternalistic agents of the colonial state customarily applied corporal punishment, including flogging, to their African charges.[23] The hide whip became the evil symbol of how one could be 'eaten' by the state and made subject to its harsh sanctions, making protective patrons necessary. State violence remains an ever-present threat in Africa in any encounter with its security forces. In short, the level of social violence in Africa rose dramatically from an already violent historical base, whether carried out by state or non-state actors, organized groups or in interpersonal assaults, with the line between criminal and political agents increasingly porous, all facilitated by the ready availability of small arms, especially automatic weapons, in the post-Cold War global arms bazaar.

Third, narrowly economistic and reductionist explanations of African 'civil wars' must be rejected. Based on rational choice models of individual actors motivated solely by maximization of material rewards ('looting'), for which no empirical evidence of its existence in any African context is offered, it offers correlations rather than explanations for the occurrences of violence based on dubious evidence of often poorly understood and mischaracterized cases.[24] What is missing is any conception of the sociocultural and political factors that shape the historical context of conflict and the motivation and meaning for both individual actors and insurgent movements ('grievance'). Analysis of the new civil conflicts of the 1990s and 2000s must focus on their complex internal and external origins including 'the interplay of historical and contemporary processes, the intersections of politics, economy and culture, the connections between local, regional and global systems, the role played by national and transnational formations, by the state, capital and civil society, and how material forces and popular discourses, institutional conditions and symbolic constructs structure and reproduce conflicts'.[25] Intersections of shared and idiosyncratic factors shape each case. Compared with the largely secular nationalist movements of the late colonial period, the ethno-national movements of the end of the twentieth century have become increasingly religious in expression and motive, although the interplay of religious ideology and institutions varies in each state.[26]

Fourth, given the ostensible artificiality and fragility of African nation states, they have proven remarkably durable during the first half-century of independence, and especially during more than a quarter-century of escalating violence. Internal wars have largely focused on controlling the state within established territorial boundaries or gaining some degree of regional autonomy and more equitable division of resources within it. In only 'nine instances (Ethiopia, Somalia, Uganda, Rwanda, both Congos, Chad, Liberia, and Sierra Leone) have insurgents from the periphery destroyed an incumbent regime, resulting in the dissolution or dispersal of existing security forces, rather than their switch of loyalty to new rulers which occurred in an earlier period when regime change occurred by coup'.[27] In only two instances, the separation of

Eritrea from Ethiopia and of South Sudan from Sudan, have divisions of an existing state occurred and been internationally recognized.

The issue of 'state collapse', a major focus of recent political research on Africa, is a matter of some controversy as to whether and how often it has actually occurred. Even where there has been a dramatic recession of state authority and control over wide parts of its national territory, as in Zaire in 1996–7 and a few years earlier in Somalia, national boundaries have remained largely intact and internationally recognized. Indeed, the reconstitution of a functioning state in the portion of Somalia that was the former British colony of Somaliland has thus far failed to gain international recognition. Bayart notes, 'Africa's globalization has greatly magnified the place taken by coercion in the whole repertoire of political action, because the practice of coercion has been embroiled with the imposition of central control and with a precise marking of territorial boundaries on a scale previously unknown.'[28] Even where the civil administrative apparatus of African states has evaporated in the countryside, the military and police have remained to contest insurgent movements for control of the national territory. And the criminalization of the state may actually indicate a consolidation and expansion of state resources in a manner 'not dissimilar to the ways in which wars, piracy and gangsterism contributed to state building in early modern Europe'.[29]

In states weakened by globalization and neo-liberal reforms the focus of conflict has been of contested nationalisms and 'battles over state-formation (and reformation) and the morphology of the nation'.[30] This suggests not only the degree to which nationhood and nationalism have become powerfully rooted in the political and cultural imaginary of even small and weak African states,[31] but also the increasing intertwining of nationalism and mobilized ethnicity in the complex motivations underlying political violence. Indeed, rather than an artificially imposed conception, the nation, despite the general failure of earlier efforts at 'nation-building', has become part of popular consciousness, 'as one of the un-reflected, assumed givens of social life'.[32] The socio-cultural boundaries of the nation and individual citizenship have become increasingly ethnicized and link together the efforts at democratization and the intense civil conflicts of the last decade of the twentieth and first decade of the twenty-first century.

Democracy and Disorder: African Nations and Conflicts of Autochthony

In 1989, of the forty-seven states of sub-Saharan Africa, only five possessed competitive multi-party systems, eleven were military oligarchies, twenty-nine were civilian one-party states with varying degrees of permitted internal political competition, and two (Namibia and South Africa) were white settler regimes. The 1990s came with a wave of 'democratization', as popular protests and foreign pressures pressed authoritarian regimes for political reforms and multi-party elections. By the middle of the decade, sixteen countries had newly elected governments, although in twenty-four others incumbent regimes had successfully blocked reforms or were able to manipulate them and win an electoral mandate, often through deeply flawed elections.[33] The decade ended with the development of particularly vicious civil conflicts in several of the most important newly democratized states that extended into the new century. 'Democracy' itself, moreover, appeared to be a source of social disorder.

Pressure for the establishment or restoration of democracy in African states came from both external and internal sources. Externally, the international financial institutions and major Western powers, especially the United States, alarmed at the decay of African states, their obvious loss of popular legitimacy, and the resulting crisis of governance from the efforts to implement neo-liberal reform programmes, pushed for the restoration of multi-party politics, free elections, and the open development of civil society institutions. The end of the Cold War also removed any strategic reason for continuing support of authoritarian regimes like that of Mobutu Sese Seko in Zaire. The sort of democracy endorsed by the Western powers was, however, highly elitist and narrowly procedurally focused. The intent was to provide a process to legitimate ruling groups and entrench neo-liberal reforms and the 'free market' as the untouchable bases of 'democracy'. The liberal democracy promoted was a disciplined one in which capitalism was sacrosanct and there was not 'too much' democracy over issues of distributional inequality.[34]

Internal pressures, by contrast, emerged from a growing wave of popular protest between 1988 and 1992 challenging, in circumstances of increasing poverty and insecurity, patrimonial autocracies, both civilian and military. Largely urban based, at least initially, these protests were led by trade unions, students, civil servants, professional organizations and, in some instances, religious institutions. Often economically motivated, they were quickly politicized, demanding political reform and civil liberties. In eleven francophone countries reform movements led to national conferences and new constitutions, while constitutional change also marked reforms in other countries. Common elements included legalization of political parties, the separation of powers, and multi-party legislative and presidential elections. Space was also provided for the press outside of government control and a new range of civil-society organizations.[35] These reform movements testified to the value that popular consciousness attached both to the nation and to the state as its political expression.

By the end of the 1990s, the tide of democratization was ebbing and many governments were receding back into 'semi-democracies' and a reassertion of elite control that revealed the serious limits of the democratization process. Newly elected regimes were unable, under heavy pressure from international financial institutions and Western governments, to depart from neo-liberal policy prescriptions, compromising their ability to address local issues of poverty and redistribution.[36] Moreover, little effort was made to reform African states' bureaucratic apparatus, the fundamental focus of the patron-client system and appropriation of state resources, to provide the competence and probity that would inspire public trust.

The narrowly restricted 'democracy' exacerbated ethnic conflicts and political mobilization. First, the competition between ethnically based patronage networks for access to state resources was intensified by electoral competition. Despite efforts in some countries to limit the expression of ethnic conflict by banning explicitly ethnic parties and requiring presidential candidates to achieve a minimal level of at least minority support in all regions of the country, militant ethnic politics increased from the mid-1990s. Rather than discreetly bargaining between themselves within the carapace of the single ruling party or behind the opaque shield of a military autocracy, elites now had to compete publicly for electoral support. The hegemony of neo-liberal policies allowed for little if any variation of ideology between parties and left little but their ethnic base to appeal to. And patron-client politics worked effectively within the electoral process, as it has in many countries outside Africa, by turning votes into what clients could provide for their patron/leaders in return for the redistribution of material benefits.

At the same time, the winner-take-all outcome of elections, especially in first-past-the-post systems without proportional representation, increased smaller communities' fear of domination by larger groups, the increasingly inequitable distribution of wealth, and ultimate exclusion from access to the state. Such fears grew not only during economic crisis and decline, when the competition of political tribalism grew over a shrinking pool of resources, but also in periods of rapid economic growth, when ethnic elites competed for their 'fair' share of a growing pool of wealth. Democratization did not reduce political corruption, but allowed it to reach gaudy new heights, and the politics of the belly, the intense struggle for 'our turn to eat', revealed the personal, materialistic, and opportunistic character of African politics, and the relative unimportance, if not irrelevance, of ideology or principle outside of ethnic solidarity. Moreover, Western expectations that the growth of 'civil society' would serve as a force for social and political renewal in Africa proved illusory. The focus on the sociocultural forms borrowed from the West—churches, professional organizations, trade unions, universities, et cetera—ignored the dense networks of indigenous institutions that surround and pervade them, in other words, precisely those features of historical experience and the social landscape that are idiosyncratically African. Civil society in the form in which it ostensibly exists in Western liberal democracies does not exist in Africa. It is neither a democratic *deus ex machina* nor movement of popular empowerment, but a 'disorganized pluralism of mutually exclusive projects that are not necessarily democratic', and is traversed by inequalities and clashing interests of ethnicity, class, and gender revealing deep and potentially violent conflicts.[37]

The most intense of these conflicts increasingly focused on the meaning of citizenship and national belonging. Citizenship was increasingly 'ethnicized'; it must be derived solely from birth into one of the original ethnic communities of the nation. The sociocultural boundaries of ethnic groups and their claims to being the native inhabitants of national territory became objects of growing conflict with regards to both political participation and access to material benefits. As Bambi Ceuppens and Peter Geschiere note, 'the reintroduction of multipartyism inevitably turned into red buttons such questions as "who can vote where?" or, more important "who can stand [as] candidate where?"—that is, questions where one belongs', and locals' fear of being outvoted by more numerous 'strangers'. Furthermore, the switch to development policies bypassing the state, focusing on decentralization, and reaching out to civil society and NGOs 'almost inevitably triggered fierce debates about belonging, i.e., over who could or could not participate in a project'.[38]

The conflicts over the ethnic definition of national citizenship brought a new intensity to the politics of authenticity that combined the internal conflicts of moral ethnicity and the external confrontations of political tribalism. As the twenty-first century began, these found expression in conflicts over 'autochthony', of literally being 'sons of the soil', which began in Francophone countries and then emerged in varying, but no less violent circumstances, in countries of Anglophone Africa as well. It is a flip side of globalization that produces a vigorous 'production of locality' and territorial attachment. While 'belonging promises safety, . . . in practice it raises fierce disagreement over who "really" belongs—over whose claims are authentic and whose are not'. It involves a political struggle over belonging to the nation, in circumstance of economic distress and uncertainty that addressed real material issues of access to land and work. 'What is at stake is often less a closer definition of the local than a struggle over excluding others from access to new avenues of riches and power.'[39]

These conflicts of autochthony involve, however, efforts to define fixed criteria of identity and discourses of exclusion to define group boundaries in circumstances where mobility, immigration, and urbanization have produced mixed ancestries in increasingly diverse populations. These efforts to rehabilitate 'authentic' origins entail a 'reinchantment' if not an invention or appropriation of 'tradition'.[40] They are linked as well, as Achille Mbembe, notes, to a 'neurosis of victimization' and the 'urge of difference' and develops 'a negative, circular and xenophobic thought' that defines the enemy, the interloping stranger, and his innocent autochthonous victim.[41] The righteous imagery of victimhood amid the reality of the contested ambiguity of identities, as Arjun Appadurai notes, gives the violence of the conflicts a particularly vicious quality, as the 'other' is definitively eliminated by murder and atrocity.[42]

In the context of democratization and economic crisis, the violent conflicts that exploded in the Côte d'Ivoire in 2002 pitted 'autochthonous' communities in the south against 'allogenes', including both foreign immigrants from Burkina Faso and Mali, and internal migrants from the north of the country. It was both a struggle over land and over the definition of citizenship of true Ivoirians (*ivoirité*) as opposed to foreigners or strangers. 'The exacerbation of ethnicity as a form of political self-identification and contestation goes hand in hand with the revitalization of autochthony as the grounds of national belonging.' This 'war of who is who' in real world circumstances of ambiguity and hybridity focused on grasping control of the state and its historic role in defining group identities. As Ruth Marshall-Fratani notes, 'the Ivoirian case seems to show the continued vitality of the nation-state, not only as the principal space in terms of which the discourses of autochthony are constructed and make sense (*fait sense*), but also in terms of the techniques and categories which the political practice of autochthony puts into play'.[43]

In the northeast corner of the Democratic Republic of the Congo, bordering Rwanda and Burundi, the outbreak of ethnic violence in 1997–8 was focused on issues of autochthony and national citizenship, and the role of the state in effectively defining both in a region that is 'a dazzling vortex of identities with ever-changing names and historical claims'.[44] The issue was the authenticity of the citizenship of the 'Banyarwanda', itself a composite group of the Banyamulenge or 'Congolese Tutsi' who had settled in the area shortly before the territorial divisions of 1885 had placed them under Belgian rule, and later Tutsi and Hutu immigrants, including Tutsi refugees from the first pogroms in Rwanda in 1959 and Hutu refugees fleeing the victorious Tutsi army at the end of the Rwandan genocide of 1994. President Mobutu first granted citizenship to the Banyamulenge when he depended on their support and reneged on it when he needed support from other groups. Between 1992 and 1996 Mobutu used the citizenship issue to destabilize the democracy movement and made people of Rwandan origin the first target. When the Banyamulenge resisted, it provided the pretext for the interventions of Rwanda and Uganda to 'prevent another genocide'.[45]

While the concept of 'autochthony' is rarely invoked in Anglophone African countries, clashes over conflicting claims to land and citizenship and efforts to exclude strangers or foreigners from the nation are becoming more frequent. Two outbreaks in early 2008 were particularly striking. In January and February a major element of the violence following on the contested outcome of the Kenya election of December 2007, like those following the earlier multi-party elections in 1992 and 1997, were attacks by Kalenjin 'warriors' on Kikuyu farmers in the Western Rift Valley. An act of blunt ethnic cleansing, later found to have been planned and paid for by senior political figures from the area, it was an attempt by earlier migrants to the area to rid it of latecoming 'strangers', with likely actual autochthonous inhabitants, the Okiek, too small in numbers or power to be an issue. The Kikuyu were descendants of landless peasants settled on former white-settler estates at the end of the colonial period, but on land that the local Kalenjin believed should have become once again their own. For the British, who believed Kikuyu landlessness was a cause of the Mau Mau uprising in the 1950s, it was a solution to a problem, but it created another in its stead. The Kikuyu established their claim by their productive labour and creation of wealth; the Kalenjin rejected not their citizenship but their presence in the wrong place and what they perceived as Kikuyu arrogance and dominance.[46]

Finally, in the multi-ethnic and multi-racial nation of South Africa, in May 2008 violence broke out in the townships surrounding Johannesburg as black South Africans attacked immigrants and refugees, especially those from Mozambique and the increasing numbers fleeing the political and social collapse in Zimbabwe. In a nation that officially prides itself on being a beacon of democracy and human rights, Jonathan Crush and other researchers have revealed a powerful undercurrent of xenophobia among all South African racial and ethnic communities, directed in particular against the *makwere-kwere*, or African immigrants from across the Limpopo river. Stigmatized as sources of crime and disease and stealers of jobs from real citizens, immigrants were thought by most South Africans to be undeserving of basic human rights, let alone those of citizenship. As Crush notes, 'the rise of xenophobia cannot be divorced from the ideology and practice of new nation-building... xenophobia is the underside of democratic nationalism'.[47]

The African Nation State as Shadow and Portent

Once we move beyond the distorting myths of the 'artificiality' of the nation state in Africa, the supposed disruption of its development by the ancient primordial sentiments of primitive tribes, and the consequent relegation of sub-Saharan Africa to the dark and alien 'other' beyond the experience of the rest of the world, we find that, as elsewhere, the nation state in Africa is a continuously unfinished project, a contingent outcome of the universalized social forces of globalized modernity and its own distinctive cultural diversity, mediated by the idiosyncrasies of the colonial experience of Western domination. African nations both shadow the development of Western nation states, the real historical nation states, rather than the idealized forms too many scholars use as the template for assessing the failures of non-Western nations; and are a portent of the challenges posed to all nations by contemporary globalization.

In Africa both nationalism and ethnicity emerged from the encounter with the colonial state and the market structures it imposed. Ethnic communities were open-ended and often ambiguous social constructions shaped by state policies of recognition and classification and by internal conflicts of class, generation, and gender, as well as by external confrontations and competition for access to the state and its resources. The nationalist movements after 1945 were trans-ethnic and often trans-class coalitions struggling to control late-colonial states as the tide of European imperialism receded. Post-colonial nationalism was based on increasingly authoritarian military and civilian regimes that radically reduced the sphere of open competitive politics in the name of national unity, and an underlying reality of largely ethnic-based patron-client networks competing for control of state resources. State-focused programmes of nation-building and development, modelled after the dominant forms of state-managed capitalism in the West, or, less frequently, state socialism of the East, provided for a dramatic increase in such resources and competitive investment in social capital and productivity. The Cold War gave international support to the territorial integrity and formal sovereignty of African nations and handsomely rewarded their allegiance to one side or the other.

While deliberate efforts at nation-building rarely worked out as intended, as they have rarely done elsewhere, the first decades of independence appear to have produced throughout sub-Saharan Africa a popular sense of both nationhood and of the need to eat from and avoid being eaten by the nation's state. African states have, with some tragic exceptions, endured with striking tenacity the recent depredations of neo-liberal globalization. Although state administrative apparatuses have been seriously undermined and state control, particularly of large areas of the countryside, has receded and sometimes disappeared for considerable periods of time in some of the weaker states, 'state collapse or state failure' has been significantly exaggerated, often to conceal the failures of neo-liberal structural adjustment and turn the state from victim to predator.

While the civil conflicts of sub-Saharan Africa at the end of the twentieth and beginning of the twenty-first century have been as violent and vicious as in other parts of the world, they are not unique examples of atavistic savagery. Most of the violence has been focused on defending or gaining control of the state within a nation and redolent of the earlier struggles of blood and fire in the construction of European nation states, although in a strikingly different global context. The movements of democratization, propelled by both internal and external pressures, attest to the continuing reality of African nations and nationalism both internally for citizens struggling to reconstruct the state and externally for an international community loathe to recognize any nations in Africa other than those that already exist. Repeated efforts to rewrite national constitutions, both successful and failed, attest to the continuing political energy of nationalism and the popular consciousness of the nation on the continent. At the same time, the disturbing connection between democratization and civil violence, increasingly expressed in the bitter conflicts of autochthony, reveals the growing ethnicization of nationalism and more narrowly bounded notions of citizenship in African countries. The link between nation and ethnicity bears interesting comparison to the development of ethnic nationalism in European nations from the mid-nineteenth century and the increasingly violent distinctions between 'us' and alien 'others'.

While aspects of African nationalism may reflect at some historical distance the experience of Western states, the context in which this takes place makes Africa the embodiment of the challenges increasingly facing all nation states in a globalized world. In Africa, ethnicized nationalism and citizenship occurs in a diverse, multi-ethnic world embracing both the local sons of the soil and the alien others. Social diversity and the challenges of multiculturalism are increasingly global, thanks to massive and unprecedented movements of people from the southern hemisphere to the north, many of them from sub-Saharan Africa to Western Europe. Most recently, globalization has brought, in the context of an emerging global food crisis, the purchase or leasing of vast tracts of farmland in Africa by foreign countries and firms, starting with China and now including Libya, Saudi Arabia, Canada, Belgium, France, South Korea, and India, amounting to more than 70 million acres in 2009 alone, to produce food for their own populations, and involving the removal of the indigenous farming populations. Hundreds of thousands of peasants are being displaced in countries like Ethiopia, Uganda, Liberia, Zambia, and the Democratic Republic of Congo, laying the basis for potentially explosive unrest in the future.[48]

Meanwhile, Western nation states have been challenged from within by the political mobilization of minority ethnic communities hitherto submerged beneath the juggernaut of earlier nation-building, and, in North America and other colonies of settlement, by versions of conflicts of autochthony in the demands of suppressed and dispossessed indigenous peoples. All nations now confront the challenges of the meaning of the nation and identity, democratic development and accountability, citizen and communal rights, and the balancing of multicultural mosaics versus integrationist melting pots amid intensifying conflicts of cultures, classes, and genders. And they do so in the context of the greatest global crisis of capitalism since the 1930s and looming environmental collapse after being undermined by a generation of reckless neo-liberal 'globalization'. In the twenty-first century all communities are being reimagined and the future of nationalism and all nation states is in doubt.

Notes

1. C. Young (1986) 'Nationalism, Ethnicity and Class in Africa: A Retrospective', *Cahiers d'études africaines*, 103, XXVI-3, 82–5.
2. A. Coulson (1982) *Tanzania: A Political Economy*, Oxford; B. Berman and J. Lonsdale (forthcoming) *The House of Custom: Jomo Kenyatta, Louis Leakey and the Kikuyu*; R. Rathbone (2000) *Nkrumah and the Chiefs: The Politics of Chieftaincy in Ghana, 1951–60*, Oxford; and Machel quoted in M. Mamdani (1996) *Citizen and Subject: Contemporary Africa and the Legacy of Late Colonialism*, Princeton, NJ, 135.
3. C. Young (2007) 'Nation, Ethnicity and Citizenship', in S. Dorman et al. (eds.) *Making Nations, Creating Strangers*, Boston and Leiden, 248–50.
4. J.-F. Bayart (1993) *The State in Africa: The Politics of the Belly*, London, 218–27.
5. Quoted in D. Cruise O'Brien (1991) 'The Show of State in a Neo-Colonial Twilight: Francophone Africa', in J. Manor (ed.) *Rethinking Third World Politics*, London and New York, 151–2.
6. As reflected in many of the early studies of colonial nationalism and independence such as D. Apter (1955) *The Gold Coast in Transition*, Princeton, NJ; and A. W. Singham (1968) *The Hero and the Crowd in a Colonial Polity*, New Haven, CT.
7. A. Haugerud (1995) *The Culture of Politics in Modern Kenya*, Cambridge, 76 and 106.
8. All quotations in this paragraph are from J. Ferguson (2006) *Global Shadows: Africa in the Neo-Liberal World Order*, Durham, NC, and London, 78–9.
9. P. Nugent (1996) *Big Men and Small Boys and Politics in Ghana*, Accra, ch. 3; N. Klein (2007) *The Shock Doctrine: The Rise of Disaster Capitalism*, Toronto, ch. 10.
10. G. Arrighi (2002) 'The African Crisis: World Systemic and Regional Aspects', *New Left Review*, vol. 15, 17; N. van de Walle (2001) *African Economies and the Politics of Permanent Crisis, 1979–1999*, New York, 5–6, 277.
11. R. Marshall-Fratani (2007) 'The War of "Who is Who": Autochthony, Nationalism and Citizenship in the Ivoirian Crisis', in S. Dorman et al. (eds.) *Making Nations, Creating Strangers*, Leiden and Boston, MA, 44; E. Hutchful (1994) '"Smoke and Mirrors": The World Bank's Social Dimensions of Adjustment (SDA) Programme', *Review of African Political Economy*, 21, 62.

12. Ferguson, *Global Shadows*, 48.
13. Van de Walle, *African Economies*, 275–6.
14. Ferguson, *Global Shadows*, 39–40.
15. Ferguson, *Global Shadows*, 103.
16. J.-F. Bayart and Stephen Ellis (2000), 'Africa in the World: A History of Extraversion', *African Affairs*, 99, no. 395 (April), 259–60; J.-F. Bayart, S. Ellis, and B. Hibou (eds.) (1999) *The Criminalization of the State in Africa*, Oxford.
17. J.-F. Bayart, *The Illusion of Cultural Identity*, London, 168–76.
18. A. Appadurai, 'Dead Certainty: Ethnic Violence in the Era of Globalization', in B. Meyer and P. Geschiere (eds.) (1999) *Globalization and Identity: Dialectics of Flow and Change*, Malden, MA, 306.
19. W. Tettey, B. Gebe, and K. Ansah-Koi (2008) *The Politics of Land and Land-Related Conflicts in Ghana*, Legon; K. Kanyinga (2009) 'The Legacy of the White Highlands: Land Rights, Ethnicity and the Post-2007 Election Violence in Kenya', *Journal of Contemporary African Studies*, 27, no. 3, 325–44.
20. R. Kaplan (1994) 'The Coming Anarchy: How Scarcity, Crime, Overpopulation and Disease are Rapidly Destroying the Social Fabric of our Planet', *Atlantic Monthly*, February.
21. P. Collier (2000) *Economic Causes of Civil Conflict and Their Implications for Policy* Washington, DC; P. Collier and A. Hoeffler (2001) *Greed and Grievance in Civil War* Washington, DC.
22. P. Tiyambe Zeleza (2008) 'Introduction: The Causes and Costs of War in Africa', in A. Nhema and P. Tiyambe Zeleza (eds.) *The Roots of African Conflicts: The Causes and Costs*, Addis Ababa and Oxford, 1–2.
23. J.-F. Bayart (2000) 'Africa in the World: A History of Extraversion', *African Affairs*, vol. 99, 255–7.
24. T. Mkandawire (2008) 'The Terrible Toll of Postcolonial Rebel Movements: Towards an Explanation of Violence Against the Peasantry', in Nhema and Zeleza (eds.) *Roots*, 109–13.
25. Zeleza, 'Introduction', 16.
26. J. Fox (2004) 'The Rise of Religious Nationalism and Conflict: Ethnic Conflict and Revolutionary Wars, 1945–2001', *Journal of Peace Research*, 1, 41.
27. Young, 'Nation, Ethnicity and Citizenship', 260.
28. Bayart, 'Africa in the World', 255.
29. P. Kaarsholm (2006) 'Introduction', *Violence, Political Culture and Development in Africa*, Oxford, 7. For Europe, see C. Tilly (1990) *Coercion, Capital and European States, A.D. 990–1990*, Oxford.
30. Dorman et al., 'Introduction', *Making Nations*, 22.
31. Kaarsholm, 'Introduction,' *Violence, Political Culture and Development in Africa*, 8.
32. Young, 'Nation, Ethnicity and Citizenship', 262.
33. M. Bratton and N. van de Walle (1997) *Democratic Experiments in Africa*, Cambridge, 79, 119–22.
34. R. Abrahamsen (2000) *Disciplining Democracy: Development Discourse and Good Governance in Africa*, London.
35. Bratton and van de Walle, *Democratic Experiments in Africa*, ch. 3; Young, 'Nation, Ethnicity and Citizenship', 256–8.
36. Abrahamsen, *Disciplining* Democracy, chs. 5–6.

37. R. Fatton (1995) 'Africa in the Age of Democratization: The Civic Limitations of Civil Society', *African Studies Review*, 38, no. 2, 75, 72–7.
38. B. Ceuppens and P. Geschiere (2005) 'Autochthony: Local or Global? New Modes in the Struggle over Citizenship and Belonging in Africa and Europe', *Annual Review of Anthropology*, vol. 34, 389.
39. Quotations from Ceuppens and Geschiere, 'Autochthony' 387.
40. Marshall-Fratani, 'The War of "Who is Who"', 32, 51–2, 57–9.
41. A. Mbembe (2000) 'A propos des écritures africaines de soi', *Politique africaine*, 77, 25.
42. Appadurai, 'Dead Certainty'. The similarities to the discourse of anti-Semitism in European nationalism are striking.
43. Quotes from Marshall-Fratani, 'The War of "Who is Who"', 31, 45, and 32.
44. Ceuppens and Geschiere, 'Autochthony: Local or Global', 395.
45. G. Nzongola-Ntalaja (2007) 'The Politics of Citizenship in the Democratic Republic of Congo,' in Dorman et al. (eds.) *Making Nations*, 70–6.
46. J. Lonsdale (2008) 'Soil, Work, Civilization and Citizenship in Kenya', *Journal of Eastern African Studies*, 2, no. 2, July 2008.
47. J. Crush (2000) 'The Dark Side of Democracy: Migration, Xenophobia and Human Rights in South Africa', *International Migration*, 38, no. 6/2, 118.
48. N. MacFarquhar (2010) 'African Farmers Displaced as Investors Move In', *The New York Times*, 21 December.

Suggested Further Reading

Appadurai, A. (2006) *Fear of Small Numbers: An Essay on the Geography of Anger*, Durham, NC, and London.

Bayart, J.-F., Ellis, S., and Hibou, B. (eds.) (1999) *The Criminalization of the State in Africa*, London and Bloomington, IN.

Branch, D. (2011) *Kenya between Hope and Despair, 1963–2011*, New Haven, CT, and London.

Davis, M. (2006) *Planet of Slums*, London and New York.

Dorman, S., Hamett, D., and Nugent, P. (eds.) (2007) *Making Nations, Creating Strangers: States and Citizenship in Africa*, Leiden and Boston, MA.

Eisenberg, A. and Kymlicka, W. (2011) *Identity Politics in the Public Realm: Bringing Institutions Back In*, Vancouver and Toronto.

Ferguson, J. (2006) *Global Shadows: Africa in the Neo-Liberal World Order*, Durham, NC, and London.

Geschiere, P. (2009) *The Perils of Belonging: Autochthony, Citizenship and Exclusion in Africa and Europe*, Chicago, IL, and London.

Kaarsholm, P. (ed.) (2006) *Violence, Political Culture and Development in Africa*, Oxford and Athens, OH.

Kertzer, D. and Arel, D. (eds.) (2002) *Census and Identity: The Politics of Race, Ethnicity, and Language in National Censuses*, Cambridge.

Klein, N. (2008) *The Shock Doctrine: The Rise of Disaster Capitalism*, London.

Lentz, C. (2006) *Ethnicity and the Making of History in Northern Ghana*, Edinburgh.

Lynch, G. (2011) *I Say to You: Ethnic Politics and the Kalenjin in Kenya*, Chicago, IL, and London.

CHAPTER 19

LATIN AMERICA: STATE-BUILDING AND NATIONALISM

NICOLA MILLER

Introduction

The newly independent states of Latin America started out in the 1820s with none of the differentiating features usually specified as the basis for nationhood (namely, ethnicity, culture, language, or religion). In this sense they were, as Benedict Anderson famously argued, 'pioneer nations',[1] optimistically aiming to mould ex-colonial societies, which had been legally divided along racial lines, into modern republics based on concepts of individual liberty and popular sovereignty. With economic activity significantly interrupted by the wars of independence, these aspiring nation states manifestly lacked what Antonio Gramsci called an 'efficient Jacobin force' to articulate a popular collective will and break the barely diminished power of the corporate institutions of Church, military, and large landed estate.[2] From such unpromising beginnings, nationalism developed into a surprisingly persistent and pervasive force throughout the region.[3] By the end of the nineteenth century, notwithstanding political instability, wars (both within and between Latin American states), foreign interventions, and economic uncertainty, there had been notable achievements: territories had been defined and diverse regions brought together under federal states; infrastructure was being built; and capital cities were being modernized as showcases of national potential. During the twentieth century, not only social revolutions (Mexico, Guatemala, Bolivia, Cuba, Nicaragua) but also military coups (Brazil, Peru, Ecuador, Bolivia, Argentina, Chile, Uruguay, and others) were carried out in the name of national redemption. The prevalence of populism across the region during the mid-twentieth century was at least partly symptomatic of the fact that the only political ideology with the potential to command widespread support in Latin American societies was nationalism.

Even in the contemporary era of globalization, when nationalism has been widely thought to be under threat from transnational forces, in Latin America nationalism has not only experienced a revival but also reassumed the specifically economic guise that neo-liberals had long thought safely banished. The new revolutionary leaders who emerged during the 1990s—Comandante Marcos of the Mexican Zapatistas, Evo Morales in Bolivia, Hugo Chávez in Venezuela—portrayed themselves not as going beyond the nation but as going *back* to it: 'we were able to recover words that had been completely prostituted: patria, nation, flag, country'.[4] As has often been noted, separatist movements have been rare in Latin America; sectarian violence has not been a significant feature of the region's history; Latin American states have fought each other over resources but not over matters of religion or race. The aggression often associated with nationalism has been turned inwards rather than outwards in Latin America, where nationalism and internationalism have usually been seen as complementary rather than conflictual.

Within national borders, there has been recurrent state repression of people deemed unfit for membership of the national community. Wars were fought against indigenous peoples during the nineteenth century, especially in Argentina, Chile, and Mexico, and there are many other instances of state-condoned violence against indigenous peoples and Afro-Latin Americans. Furthermore, the wider human rights violations carried out by military regimes during the Cold War in the name of national security testified that nationalism in Latin America could assume a deeply authoritarian form. Even so, however, nationalism in this part of the world never entirely lost its early-nineteenth century connotations of emancipation and self-determination, which were revived in the 1960s after the Cuban Revolution and articulated in the widely disseminated works of Che Guevara. Many Latin Americans would probably agree with one Brazilian writer's view that 'nationalism is [. . .] an indispensable strategy of defence, because it is on the scale of the nation that we have to struggle against economic absorption by imperialism'.[5]

In the enduring debate about whether nationalism is invented or innate, it has long been maintained that there is little scope for seeing Latin American nationalisms in anything other than constructivist terms. Indeed, in many respects Latin American experiences are a dream for historians who wish to highlight the importance of social engineering, invention, and imagining. The state, capitalism, and the mass media all undeniably played their part in creating the conditions for nationalism in Latin America, and it would be impossible to understand its varied history without taking them into account. The mass media, in particular, played a major role in bringing the majority of the population into the national political arena (radio—in many ways more important than television—was used to great effect by, for example, Juan Perón in Argentina and the revolutionaries in Cuba). Increasingly, however, evidence has been coming to light that shows the overall picture to be more complicated. While Latin American history duly confirms the modernists' contention that it is perfectly possible for nationalism to develop without positing identities that are primordial or even perennial, the region's experiences also lend support to Geoff Eley's welcome suggestion that nationalism always involves a 'complicated dialectic of political innovation and actually existing cultures'.[6] Moreover, a variety of forces were at work, by no means all of them deriving from the elites. Cultural producers (not only the writers and intellectuals who have attracted so much attention, but also musicians, cartoonists, photographers) and, to a surprising extent, popular leaders and organizations, have also been significant agents in the history of nationalism in Latin America. In general, the political Left, in all its various manifestations, has been a vociferous champion of nationalism because US interventionism, often carried out with the tacit support of Latin American elites, enabled the Left triumphantly to play the anti-imperialist card. The people, it was claimed even by quite moderate reformists (let alone by revolutionaries), had been robbed of their historic entitlement to national sovereignty by the imperialists and their local lackeys. Public opinion has in fact radicalized official nationalism at certain times and places, one notable example being the nationalization of oil in Mexico in 1938. Moreover, evidence is accumulating that even in the nineteenth century, nationalism was present beyond the elites, at least among some identifiable sectors of the masses.

This essay covers the period from the late nineteenth until the late twentieth century. Two factors that had a significant impact on both state-building and nationalism came to the fore towards the end of the nineteenth century: first, the cumulative effects of modernization from the 1870s onwards, which led to the strengthening of a central state and the rise of mass politics; and second, the rise of US interventionism on all fronts—economic, cultural, military, and political—particularly after the Spanish-American War of 1898. The effects of modernization compelled ruling elites to confront the problem of the exclusion of large sectors of their populations not only from the body politic but—far more significantly—from what were increasingly becoming national economies. By the 1920s, most Latin American states had switched away from Social Darwinist policies to eliminate their indigenous, black, and mixed-race people (by war, repression, or European immigration) towards ideologies to assimilate them as modern worker-citizens (although violence recurred, especially against indigenous peoples, in some countries). The increased US presence in the region, both from the private sector (entrepreneurs, engineers, and managers from US mining and agri-business) and in an official capacity (military personnel, diplomats, and economic advisers), meant that the United States became the most significant 'other' in Latin American debates about identity. Hitherto, Latin Americans had defined themselves mainly in relation to the former colonial powers of Spain and Portugal, Britain as the neo-colonial power, or each other (neighbours and rivals such as Chile and Argentina or Colombia and Venezuela).

The cumulative effect of all these developments was to bring the dominant ideology of liberalism to crisis point, by making unacceptable its continual deferral of citizenship rights for the majority of the population. For all these reasons it is widely agreed among historians that the character of Latin American nationalisms changed during this time, but there is little consensus as to the nature of that change. This dispute touches upon most of the main differences of opinion about the history of nationalism in Latin America and so is worth discussing here in some depth.

One widely expressed view is that nationalism in the region was mainly civic before the late nineteenth century and mainly ethnic thereafter. Or, to put it another way, Latin American countries engaged first in state-building and then moved on to nation-building. Or, in different terms again, Latin America experienced only republicanism or patriotism for several decades after independence and the term 'nationalism' was not relevant until the twentieth century. The argument of this chapter is that all these interpretations, which are very close to each other, underestimate both the role of ethnic factors during the earlier nineteenth century and the role of civic factors during the twentieth century. Moreover, what the history of nationalism in Latin America shows us, above all, is the importance of exploring the interrelatedness of processes that are still too often analysed separately: state-building and nation-formation. In what follows, I will illustrate this argument briefly for the nineteenth century and more fully for the twentieth.

The Nineteenth Century: Nationalism or Patriotism?

A flurry of debate was provoked by Benedict Anderson's claim, in *Imagined Communities* (1983), that the Latin American wars of independence were nationalist. Anderson's case was widely challenged by Latin Americanists, who now tend to concur that there are no good grounds even for characterizing the independence movements as nationalist, let alone explaining them as such. It does seem to be clear that the wish for political independence did not necessarily imply any desire for cultural unity on the part of those who led the fight for it.[7] Furthermore, the states conceived in the founding constitutions of Latin America (which were drawn with varying emphases from the Spanish Liberal constitutions of 1812 and 1820, the US Constitution of 1787, and French documents, especially the *Declaration of the Rights of Man and Citizen* of 1789 and the Constitution of 1795) were based on rights that were theoretically open to all, not on any sense of unique identity. The United States was not the only former colony in the Americas to develop a sense of manifest destiny (see Chapter 20 by Susan-Mary Grant): the founding dream of the emancipated Spanish American countries was to redeem the world from the despotic, self-interested rivalries of Europe and establish a new international politics based on the idea of the whole of humanity as a nation, 'in which nationalities would be merely large municipalities'.[8] Well into the nineteenth century, Liberal Latin American statesmen continued to make declarations about their nations being the bearers of universal values. Does it follow, then, that we should see this period as one of republicanism and elite patriotism?

I would say not—at least, certainly not from the 1830s, when the circulation of French and German Romantic ideas fed into the emerging interest of Latin American intellectuals in studying 'ethnic groups [*razas*], national characteristics and customs, historical antecedents' in order to design the most appropriate institutions and laws to promote national development.[9] Even for the 1820s, 'nationalism' is probably the most appropriate term to capture the political discourse that by then had come to prevail. Within the cultural field in which Latin American statesmen and intellectuals operated, namely the Americas and Europe, by the start of the wars of independence terms such as 'nation', 'state', and 'people' had already become permanently charged with an ideological significance that they had lacked before the American and French Revolutions. The Enlightenment thinkers had hoped that political association would henceforth be based on choice rather than compulsion; it followed—as argued by Jean-Jacques Rousseau and Johann Gottfried von Herder (both of whom were widely read in Latin America)—that such choices were unlikely to be based on political criteria alone. Once it had been declared that 'Le principe de toute souveraineté réside essentiellement dans la nation' (article 3 of the *Declaration of the Rights of Man*)—a stipulation that was included in most of Latin America's founding constitutions—then it became an overwhelming political imperative, if not an absolute logical necessity, to endow the abstract concept of 'the nation' with a human face. The independence movements may not have started out as self-consciously nationalist, but by the end of the wars—which were lengthy—they had been compelled to become so. In turn, this meant that if monarchy was rejected, as it was throughout Latin America except in Mexico (briefly, 1821–4) and Brazil (until 1889), and liberal republican democracy accepted as the ideal, then visualizing the nation meant depicting 'the people' who were to be the 'porte-parole de la nation' ['bearers of the word "nation"'].[10] The strength of the concept of 'nation' lies in its very abstractness, which, as Charles de Gaulle famously remarked, enables it to bear the weight of 'past, present and future'. But precisely because it is abstract, 'the nation' cannot actually exercise the sovereignty so rudely wrested in its name from absolutist monarchy; in consequence, a concept of 'the people', willing to live together, is needed to supply the nation's delegated agent of sovereignty. And in the necessarily continuous creation of such a collective will (Joseph-Ernest Renan was right that a nation is 'a daily plebiscite') it is likely, albeit not inevitable, that not only political rights but also cultural factors will come to matter.

In this connection, it is also worth noting that the Spanish word *nación* was associated with the racial divisions under colonialism—the *nación* of the Spaniards, which included both those native to the Peninsula and those born in the Americas, and the separate *nación* of the indigenous peoples. For these reasons, *patria* was the term usually used by independence leaders to invoke the would-be nation states that they sought to found, which they envisaged as bringing together the hitherto separate groups of European and indigenous descendants into a unified, bounded community. In time, *nación* acquired the sense of nation state, and by the late nineteenth century it had gained common currency—for example in the titles of newspapers and periodicals—although the term *patria* (which is difficult to translate precisely because it means something in between 'native land' and 'nation state') continued to be in wide usage during the twentieth century.

Moreover, the founding documents of the new nations exhibit at least a nascent sense of cultural distinctiveness, in claims that these nations had been founded not only for the peoples of the region to 'reclaim their rights' but also for them to 'fulfil the high destiny to which they are called'.[11] In Mexico, the importance of *federation* was emphasized as a means of reconciling the necessary notion of a collective will of Mexicans with manifest regional differences. The manifesto distributed by the Constituent Congress that drafted the 1824 Constitution argued that only 'the calculated tyranny of Spanish mandarins' could have aspired to govern such a 'huge territory' as Mexico by the same laws, in sublime disregard of 'the enormous differences in climate and temperament'; a federal state, in contrast, would 'give each of the peoples laws appropriate to their customs, localities and other circumstances' so that each region could develop at its own pace.[12] Leaders of the new nations seemed to be perfectly well aware of the difficulties entailed in what they envisaged. The drafters of Mexico's 1824 Constitution noted that it was 'a very arduous task to obtain through enlightenment and patriotism that which is only the work of time and experience', but they were reassured by the fact that they had the advantages of not being 'contaminated' by the vices of Europe; of having the models of 'the modern peoples' to follow; of being able to learn from 'the lessons the world has received since the happy discovery of social science has shaken the foundations of tyranny'.[13]

Debates about cultural distinctiveness in the different states of the region began shortly after independence. Initially, the main vehicle, in which civic and ethnic elements came together, was the writing of national histories. The wars of independence were seen by some historians as an extraordinarily intense period—'we ourselves have experienced three centuries worth of history in fourteen years'—which constituted a foundational moment comparable to the French Revolution.[14] Commemorations of declarations of independence began very soon after they had taken place. Throughout the nineteenth century, state-sponsored independence days, involving 'fireworks, raffles, religious services, distribution of alms, and patriotic speeches' drew both on colonial traditions and religious practices to create national festivals that celebrated the indigenous past, replacing the colonial figure of the catechized Indian with the insurgent Indian and then later the Indian as noble savage, the wars of independence being represented as the avenging of the great indigenous civilizations defeated by the conquerors.[15] In fact, there was little consensus among creoles (people of Spanish descent born in the Americas) about what constituted a usable past—some liberals saw the beginnings of the nation in the wars of independence; others preferred to go back to the pre-conquest civilizations; conservatives held fast to 1492 as their origin myth. What is fascinating is that aspects of the indigenous were prominent in most of the versions in play, with even the conservatives bringing them in as evidence that the conquerors had been a great civilizing force.[16] Even in Argentina, notorious for the insistence of its elites on being 'white and European', the national anthem refers to its citizens as sons of the Inca. It is hard to understand any of this evidence in terms of republicanism alone.

Works by Rousseau and Herder circulated among the educated minority, and it is worth noting that these thinkers were received in Latin America not as advocates of one nation/one culture, but rather as a way of reconciling an appreciation that peoples and cultures were different in different parts of the world with the universalist promise of the Enlightenment.[17] By mid-century, in a second wave of liberalism, new generations of nation-builders across the region were starting to accept the conservative view that local specificities had to be taken into account, in a searching critique of the abstract rationalist blueprints of the independence generation, which, it was claimed, had led to the subsequent civil wars. A wide range of essays, novels, and poetry depicting and analysing local landscapes, customs, and modes of sociability helped to create and sustain imagined communities throughout Latin America.

Liberals were by no means hegemonic until the late nineteenth century, by which time their versions of liberalism had been adapted so much to achieve that very dominance that they bore little resemblance to the Lockean original. There was in fact a variety of liberalisms that developed in Latin America during the course of the nineteenth century, although there is a tendency in the historiography to see them all as one. From the 1830s to the 1850s, liberals in most Latin American countries tended to focus on anti-clericalism and/or institution-building. Later, however, particularly in Mexico (but also elsewhere), more socially radical approaches gained ground. The European revolutions of 1848 had their impact in Latin America—in some places, at least, dovetailing with local events to stimulate moves towards fulfilling the liberal promise of inclusivity. The leaders of the Mexican Reform Movement all developed this approach: Benito Juárez, first Mexican president of indigenous—Zapotec—birth (1806–72; president 1861–72); Ignacio Altamirano (1834–93), pioneer of cultural nationalism who called for a Mexican cultural renaissance; and Ignacio Ramírez (1818–79), who advocated education for the indigenous peoples. Around the mid-nineteenth century, then, at least some of Latin America's rulers were publicly committed to the idea that ultimately all the people living within their territory would be brought into the nation state, through education and other civilizing measures. It was later in the century, when competition for land and resources led to violent clashes between creole elites and indigenous groups, that denials of the potential of indigenous, black, and mixed-race people for citizenship were routinely expressed by political leaders. The elites appropriated Social Darwinism and (crude accounts of) positivism to justify their continuing exclusion of the majority of the population in the name of the positivist promise of 'order and progress'. The liberals of the late nineteenth century, as manifest in the dictatorship of Porfírio Díaz in Mexico (1876–1911) or the oligarchic rule of the PAN (National Action Party) in Argentina (1880–1916), were liberal only in their economic policies. Politically and socially, they were highly repressive, which partly explains why liberalism entered into crisis in the early twentieth century as mass politics emerged. From a variety of perspectives, others then began to do what Juárez had recognized as necessary, namely to introduce ethnic elements into primarily civic conceptions of nationalism, on the grounds that only by doing so would the extension of liberal rights become meaningful to large sectors of the population.

State-building and nation-building happened alongside each other in many modern nation states, including most of Europe;[18] in this respect Latin America is unusual only in degree, not in kind. It was not only nations that were incipient in the aftermath of independence, but also states. Ideas about how to create a nation and who should be included or excluded themselves became factors in the formation and functioning of state institutions. Governments could strengthen their claims to legitimacy by demonstrating that they were acting in the national interest. There is also a growing body of evidence that the liberal version of nationalism did permeate more widely in society than used to be thought. The idea of equality before the law was used, with some success, by poor, ill-educated people to claim rights to land or fairer treatment at work. During the course of the nineteenth century, Latin American elites 'constructed both national images and stable states by political bargaining and negotiation in which democratic representation was used or abused according to the balance of power'.[19]

For all these reasons, I do not see a major shift from patriotism or republicanism in the nineteenth century to nationalism in the twentieth century, as has been proposed by several observers. The project was nationalist from the outset and inseparable from the vision of becoming modern, which was a founding aspiration of Latin American countries, even if the economic conditions for it did not attain critical mass until late in the nineteenth century.

The Twentieth Century: The Eclipse of Civic Nationalism?

The early twentieth century was a period of optimism in Latin America. Even those intellectuals and politicians imbued with racial pessimism tended to see their nations as potentially great, if only they could eliminate the allegedly bad blood of indigenous and black people by a process of whitening through European immigration. There was a widespread desire among Latin American elites to attract supposedly sober and industrious (north) Europeans, imbued with the Protestant work ethic, to meet their need for a skilled labour force. However, it is worth bearing in mind that European immigration was only a major feature in Argentina, Brazil, Chile, and Uruguay—and even there, the immigrants mostly came from Italy, Portugal, and Spain, and were rapidly cast in a negative light as lazy and/or tempestuous and violent. The otherwise positive trend of recent historiography towards thinking comparatively about the whole of the Americas has had one drawback, namely a tendency to categorize all American nations as 'immigrant nations' in the mode of the United States or Canada.[20] While Latin American nations did indeed all experience some immigration, mainly between about 1880 and 1920, none of them have defined themselves as immigrant nations, not even Argentina where the phenomenon was most pronounced. Indeed, a surprisingly strong and adaptable creole cultural identity dug in its heels against any notion analogous to the melting pot. Recent research has confirmed how difficult it was historically for any of the immigrant communities to achieve recognition as members of the nation. In order to *hacer la América*, immigrants to South America had to assimilate *culturally* (especially linguistically) to a far greater extent than in the United States, where political loyalty and compliance with the law sufficed. It does not strike me as persuasive to talk about 'plural ethnic identities' in Latin America.[21]

Although the European model of one nation/one culture was manifestly unworkable in Latin America, the region's elites—confronted by an increasingly militant labour movement, peasant mobilization, and general social unrest, some of which was led by radical immigrant workers—elaborated a modified version of the European model of ethnic homogeneity in the ideology of *mestizaje* (racial and cultural mixing). This positive re-evaluation of racial mixing originated in a refutation by Latin American intellectuals of the low status attached to the mixed races in the Social Darwinist hierarchy; they began to argue that, to the contrary, mixing could be a source of superiority because it combined the talents of all races into a glorious new whole—the 'cosmic race'—that was greater than the sum of its parts.[22] Politicians appropriated this idea, which enabled them to contain the challenge from increasingly mobilized popular forces. First in Brazil, then in most other Latin American countries, governments claimed that they presided over 'racial democracies', in which class, not race, determined an individual's life prospects. Such claims did not come under serious scrutiny until the 1970s and 1980s, when social-science analysis showed that there was an undeniable overlap between class and race.[23]

It is hard to overstate the complexity of the phenomenon of *mestizaje*, which assumed a range of meanings that differed according to time and place. Often, it was effectively synonymous with Hispanicization and encouragement of the suppression of indigenous and/or black identities. At other times, in other countries (examples would be Mexico in the 1930s and Bolivia after the Revolution of 1952), it was complemented by pro-indigenous policies (*indigenismo*) that went some way towards creating a place in the national polity for indigenous ways of life. Those relatively short-lived policies have been the object of criticism on the grounds that they, too, were premised on the assumption that everyone would ultimately succumb to the allure of modern goods and modern conveniences. There is a wealth of evidence that an ideology (and sometimes a practice) of racial mixing has long coexisted with racialized states and societies. After all, it was not until the 1990s that Latin American countries reformed their constitutions to grant recognition and rights to indigenous peoples. However, it is at least arguable that, even when it was overtly assimilationist, the ideology of *mestizaje* still created symbolic space for indigenous and Afro-Latin Americans in national narratives, especially when linked to *indigenista* or *negrista* movements, which, however romanticized and prejudicial, made it impossible to tell any story but one of heterogeneity.

Thus, the idea that nationalism was inevitably a project requiring the repression of difference (a view vehemently rejected by progressive Latin American nationalists who see it as a European assumption) has historically existed in Latin America alongside a variety of pressures for the recognition of difference. Indeed, it was claimed that one feature common to the various Latin American cultures was their limitless capacity to integrate whatever they found. Thus, mixing in its most radical sense was not seen as a one-way process of assimilation, but rather as a continually creative flux of encounter, borrowing, and exchange, an expression of the shared Latin American values of openness and hospitality that constituted a genuine universalism: 'There are European cultures far more "developed" than ours, but they are closed in on themselves (rather than "developed" it would be better to say "elaborated").'[24] Such a claim does capture a widely articulated element of Latin America's collective self-image, one that is endowed with its own particular nationalist history and aspect in the various different countries.

Cultural nationalism was a major feature of the first half of the twentieth century in Latin America and its manifestations were by no means dominated by the modernizing states—indeed, they often had to catch up with developments in society. A significant impetus was the wish to achieve clear differentiation from the United States, which was no longer seen as the embodiment of ideals of democracy and freedom that also animated Latin American republics, but rather as the manifestation of how those ideals could become corrupted by aggression, materialism, and sheer vulgarity. The newly imperialist United States was caricatured as 'a buffalo with silver-plated teeth', as the leading Nicaraguan poet Rubén Darío put it, or—most influentially—as Caliban, the brutish barbarian from Shakespeare's *The Tempest*. Many intellectuals, following the lead of the Uruguayan essayist José Enrique Rodó, posited an opposition between Latin 'spirituality' (which referred to a commitment to ethics and an appreciation of culture and ideas rather than to religiosity) and Anglo-Saxon materialism. Again, this Latin-America-wide identity was reworked into specific manifestations at national levels, where political values—an innate capacity for liberty, democracy, and heroism—were attributed to popular cultural archetypes—in Argentina, the gaucho; in Mexico, the mestizo (of mixed indigenous and Spanish descent) peasant. The increased presence of the masses in politics fed through into a modification of the national imaginary, as the ruling elites were compelled to make some concessions to popular values. The Argentine modernist poet Leopoldo Lugones could never have persuaded the chattering classes of Buenos Aires that gauchos were chic had it not been for the genuinely popular success in the 1880s of the epic ballad depicting life on the pampa, José Hernández's *Martín Fierro*. Similarly, in Mexico City after the revolution murals depicting indigenous peasants as the stoic heroes of Mexican history would probably not have become so fashionable among the new bourgeoisie had it not been for the forcefully demonstrated and widely admired—not least by foreigners—capacity of peasant leader Emiliano Zapata and his followers to fight for their demands for land.

Just as ethnic factors were far from absent during the nineteenth century, however, so were civic factors very much present during the twentieth. States became powerful enough to start implementing policies on infrastructure, institution-building, and services. In societies still lacking an entrepreneurial class, the state was accepted as the champion of development. Their capacities were limited in comparison to West European states of the time: they could conscript (which they began to do in the

1930s) and they could educate, at least at primary level (mainly a post-1945 policy, apart from in Mexico), but their ability to tax effectively was weak. Correspondingly, their service provision was limited and targeted at certain strategic groups (usually key labour sectors such as railway or port workers).[25]

On the face of it, these states did not offer their populations a great deal in terms of political rights. There was relatively little of the pluralist liberal democracy specified in the constitutions. Suffrage was extended very slowly. Most of the revised constitutions of the first half of the twentieth century removed any qualification for literacy, although notably Chile kept it until 1970 and Brazil until 1988. Ecuador pioneered votes for women in 1929 and most countries followed suit in the 1930s and 1940s, but the process was not completed until the early 1960s. The separation of Church and State had taken place in most Latin American countries by 1930, but the enduring power of the Church, at least in some countries, was graphically illustrated by the role it played in undermining the socialist revolution in Nicaragua in the 1980s. Land reform was slow to occur (apart from Mexico, it was not implemented in most of the continent until the 1960s at the earliest), and the military grew in strength as it became more modern and professional during the early to mid-twentieth century. Thus powerful corporate institutions continued to coexist uneasily with constitutions championing the rights of the individual. The paternalist populists or more overtly authoritarian military leaders who mainly controlled the state from the 1930s until the 1980s all routinely invoked the virtues of democracy but did little to create the conditions for its effective operation.[26]

Nationalism was strongly promoted by all these regimes, in the absence of other policies to command consensus or legitimacy, and it was the main vehicle for incorporating the masses into politics. The role states assigned themselves in promoting the new popular nationalism that was to dominate Latin American politics for much of the twentieth century was explicitly set out in the Mexican Constitution of 1917. This was a lengthy document, drafted while the revolution was still in process, the unwieldiness and inconsistency of which testified to the varied and conflicting interests that lay behind ten years of civil unrest. It presaged the region-wide shift from exclusion to inclusion of the masses. Right at the beginning, in a signal that mass citizenship could no longer be indefinitely postponed, there was a commitment to public education, which, it was stated, would be both 'democratic' and 'national, in as much as it will – without hostility or exclusivism—attend to the understanding of our problems, the advantageous use of our resources, the defence of our political independence, the securing of our economic independence and the continuity and growth of our culture'.[27] In its notorious Article 27 the Mexican Constitution laid down the founding statement of economic nationalism in Latin America, declaring the right of 'La Nación' [*sic*] to administer natural resources and private property—native- or foreign-owned—in 'the public interest'.

In countries where both race and class divisions were acute, it is hard to overstate the importance of economic nationalism, which became a major feature of all Latin American nationalisms during the mid-twentieth century and is one powerful example of the continuing role of civic nationalism. It is linked to the widespread sense that political independence did not enable the full exercise of sovereignty, which entails not only the right but also the power to take decisions about the resources that determine prosperity.

Economic nationalists habitually referred back to the wars of independence: for example, Perón's Declaration of Economic Independence on 9 July 1947 was made in the same house in Tucumán where Argentine independence had been declared on the same date in 1816;[28] the Cuban revolutionaries' talk of a Second Independence of Latin America articulated a demand with resonance throughout the region; when President Carlos Andrés Pérez nationalized Venezuelan oil in 1976 he invoked the Liberator Simón Bolívar leading the nation to freedom from Spain at the Battle of Carabobo in 1821. An assertion of sovereignty over natural resources is also one very obvious way in which the state can assert itself as the concrete manifestation of the national interest. Fernando Coronil has described how the Venezuelan state succeeded in acquiring a high level of legitimacy through its role as mediator between 'the nation' and foreign oil companies during the early twentieth century. By representing itself as the sole means of unifying the 'body politic' of the nation (its citizens) with its natural body (subsoil resources), the Venezuelan state assumed 'a providential hue' by '[providing] the material foundation for the institutionalization of popular sovereignty'.[29] Economic nationalism enables governments to claim that they have made the nation manifest through the transcendent power of the state to mould nature in a physical, visible reconfiguration of its territory—an example would be the Brazilian military's opening up of Amazonia during the 1960s and 1970s. The idea of nations as *construction* thereby takes on a literal sense and a particular significance in Latin America, where the relative absence of any common culture has often been compensated for by a highly assertive act of domination over nature. After Benedict Anderson's famous definition of the nation as 'an imagined political community—and imagined as both inherently limited and sovereign',[30] historians have paid a great deal of attention to the terms 'imagined' and 'community'. Latin America's history reminds us both of the need to focus on the nation's *political* character and of the importance of sovereignty.

Other elements of civic nationalism continued to be salient throughout the twentieth century in Latin America. Revisions to constitutions, which occurred quite often in most countries, tended to attract a great deal of public interest and controversy. Moreover, constitutions were invoked as sources of legitimacy by a wide variety of political actors (from Fidel Castro's emphasis on the Constitution of 1940, introduced during the elected presidency of Fulgencio Batista, the dictator overthrown by the revolution, to Augusto Pinochet's surprisingly successful claim that the revised Constitution of 1980 gave him a mandate to rule). Likewise, democracy was continually invoked in the rhetoric of Latin American leaders across the political spectrum, particularly those who had suspended it, from the claim by the military authoritarian leaders in Brazil that they were only in power in order to take the steps necessary to make their nation ready for democracy to the insistence by Cuban or Nicaraguan revolutionaries that participation, not pluralism, was the benchmark of genuine democratic practice. Furthermore, particularly during the 1990s, after procedural democracy had become the norm everywhere except in Cuba, major struggles erupted over citizenship rights and over the legacy of human-rights violations. All these are civic matters, debates about all of them are cast in terms of nationalism and national identity, and even though some of them—particularly citizenship—also raise ethnic concerns, their significance arises from the interrelatedness of civic and ethnic. This is illustrated most vividly by the debates around what is meant by being indigenous: slogans of the protest movements against the presence of TNCs (transnational corporations) in Bolivia proclaimed 'We are all indigenous now!', that is, all non-elite Bolivians, not only those of indigenous birth, were excluded from the benefits of globalized capitalism supported by the sell-out elites. Thus a term denoting ethnic identity acquired a civic referent.

What Latin American history shows, above all, is that the most successful nationalisms have brought together civic and ethnic elements. Revolutionary governments, especially in Mexico and Cuba, were particularly good at integrating foundation myths, official histories of national redemption that cast the revolution as the catalyst for true national self-realization, anti-imperialism, economic nationalism, and an emphasis on popular participation. In all Latin American countries, heroes play a major role in generating popular allegiance to nationalism: with their exemplary lives, they are represented as incarnations of popular values, endowed with the national virtues and portrayed as men of the people. Most Latin American countries include people of mixed race in their pantheon; black or indigenous leaders are rarer, although not absent. Images of super-heroes, such as Liberator Simón Bolívar, convey an extraordinary range of racial representations of him, from absolutely white to almost indigenous, depending on the context in which his name was being invoked. The comparative history of Latin America's heroes and the political appropriation of their images is as yet relatively little studied, but would probably be very revealing about the entwining of civic and ethnic components of nationalism.

Conclusion

Latin American experiences invite revision of a series of generalizations that have been made about nationalism, based mainly upon European examples. What makes Latin America particularly interesting in the history of nationalism is its ambivalent relationship to European models: unlike in many of the other post-colonial nations that achieved independence in the mid-twentieth century, nationalism in Latin America was initially shaped not so much by opposition to European powers as by a desire to avoid their mistakes. In taking a stand for democracy against despotism, the Latin American nations were founded in the hope that they could enact the European Enlightenment project that had not been fully realized in Europe. Latin Americans envisaged their nations as being both *different from* and *better than* the European; they differentiated between what they wished to emulate (economic success), what they wished to do differently (politics), and what they wished to transcend (culture). Being constituted as modern republics, committed to liberal principles of democracy and the separation of powers, has remained fundamental to Latin American nations' sense of identity. Thus European models and ideas were far from irrelevant, but, as Partha Chatterjee and others have long since pointed out,[31] the process of adaptation to circumstances was far more complex than can be captured by any notions of imitation or passive consumption. This can be seen in a series of shared features of Latin American nationalism that suggest the need for revision or qualification of certain widely held assumptions about nationalism in general. I will briefly outline these below.

In Latin American nations there certainly was an elite-led drive towards homogeneity around the ideology of *mestizaje*, with its latent agenda of whitening—but even that was posited on a claim that what is unifying is the shared experience of difference, of mixing. In practice, there has been a constant set of pressures to accommodate difference, not least in the idea that the capacity to do so is a distinctive feature of being Latin American, particularly in contrast to the racially segregated United States. There has been a recurrent tendency to make a virtue out of difference, representing it as abundance: Brazil is *all* of this. Nationalism in Latin America has rarely been conceptualized as an exclusive identity, precluding the possibility of local, regional, or continental identifications. The latter, known first as Hispano-Americanism, later as Latin Americanism, have functioned as a pool of values to draw upon, from which distinctively national variations can be marked out.[32] In a range of ways, Latin American processes of identity creation have worked not within a self-other dichotomy, but rather within a looser framework of multiple selves and multiple others. From the outset, it is possible to trace a series of transnational routes to creating national identities in Latin America, in a three-way relationship between Latin America, Anglo-Saxon America, and the various European countries (really, we should disaggregate further, particularly between the Iberian former colonial powers and the models of Britain, France, Germany, and Italy). Relationships within Latin America also played their part in the process of self-differentiation: Argentina and Brazil have long defined themselves in terms of not being what the other is thought to be; Mexico sees itself not only as not the United States, but as not Guatemala either. Within the borders, as Claudio Lomnitz argued in a critique of Benedict Anderson, the nation has not necessarily been envisaged as dependent upon horizontal bonds, assuming equality in community; instead, one route towards national integration has been through vertical connections of patronage and clientelism.[33]

The relationship between religion and nationalism in Latin America is an area that is still under-researched, but it is evident that the claim of Anderson and others that nationalism functions as a replacement for organized religion is not borne out by Latin American histories. Religious symbols are prominent in the iconography of Latin American nations. The Mexican Virgin of Guadalupe is the most famous, and the most studied, but most Latin American countries have their own particular manifestation of the Virgin Mary, which has acquired status as a national symbol. Latin American liberal nation-builders were often vehemently anti-clerical (although this varied according to country) but most of them argued that spirituality should have a place in modern life. As noted above, many of the civic festivals organized to promote identification with the nation drew upon religious symbols and practices. The Mexican reformist intellectual Ignacio Altamirano evidently regretted the fact that 'the only bond' that united Mexicans was adoration of the Virgin of Guadalupe,[34] yet the enduring power of this cult was not only testament to the limitations of the liberal secularizing project but also to the capacity of religious symbols to generate nationalist sentiments.

Conceptions of time are manifestly crucial to nationalism, although Latin America offers fascinating evidence that it is not only Anderson's homogeneous empty time that matters, or indeed the linear sequence of past, present, and future. Latin American literature, social commentary, and philosophy explore the concept that time can be experienced not only sequentially but also simultaneously. This idea connects to the main point to highlight here, which is that—as Anderson himself noted in the revised edition of *Imagined Communities* (1991)—ideas about space are also crucial to nation-building. This was particularly so in Latin America where, as discussed above, history was so problematic. Thus, geographies of nationalism are important and quite a lot of research has been done on the initiatives undertaken by states throughout the nineteenth century to map their countries and to chart the flora and fauna of the landscape. If neither history nor culture could provide a unifying nationalist theme, the land potentially could and it became a primary object of attention initially for poets, then later for essayists and novelists. Later, towards the start of the twentieth century, archaeology and anthropology began to modify conceptions of the relationship between history and the land.

Analogously, while Latin America does provide some evidence for Anderson's emphasis on textuality—from the mid-nineteenth century onwards Romantic novels played a role in creating a national imaginary in which people of different races were present, and poets and essayists have been important throughout—what I would emphasize here is the evidence Latin America offers that visual culture is a crucial part of nationalism. National identity becomes embodied: the 'face, expression, look' of a particular nation matters,[35] and can be studied in visual images of all kinds from cartoons to photographs to public monuments, posters, dress codes, public spectacles, film, and murals. This point connects also to the importance of everyday practices, which are increasingly being studied, particularly the place of food in self-differentiation, for example, the Peronist campaign to make everyone 'eat Argentine'. We also know a lot more about the role of sport—notoriously, soccer, but also baseball and basketball, have been vehicles for nationalism, both at national state and local levels—and music. Both state and local environments can be seen as microcosms of how nationalism works in Latin America: the state plays a role, as do transnational market forces, but the popular input is crucial and remarkably resistant to manipulation.

In sum, if historians take Latin American experiences into account, it is no longer possible to sustain the arguments that nationalism requires homogeneity; seeks to displace other sources of loyalty, especially local and continental identities; is necessarily secular; is primarily shaped by conceptions of time; is shaped primarily by textual practices; or is mainly about high politics and/or revanchist projects. Above all, the history of Latin American nationalism indicates that successful nationalist projects entail *both* a commitment to popular sovereignty (even if delegated) *and* a sense of cultural uniqueness. Nationalists can choose to emphasize either civic or ethnic sources of identity, but in order to succeed they usually have to offer elements of both. To put it another way, returning to Rousseau—where many of the Latin American nation-builders started—the need is to find a balance between autonomy and authenticity, each of which is, to a significant degree, dependent upon the other.

Notes

1. B. Anderson (1991, 1983) *Imagined Communities: Reflections on the Origins and Spread of Nationalism*, London, 47–67.
2. A. Gramsci (1957) *The Modern Prince and Other Writings*, London, 139.
3. For the colonial period, see Chapter 6 by Don Doyle and Eric van Young.
4. Comandante Marcos, interviewed by Carlos Monsiváis and Hermann Bellinghausen, in *La Jornada* (Mexico City), 8 January 2001.
5. Brazilian critic and commentator Antônio Cândido, cited in A. Castillo, E. Muzzopappa, A. Salomone, B. Urrejola, and C. Zapata (eds.) (2003) *Nación, estado y cultura en América Latina*, Santiago.
6. G. Eley (2000) 'Culture, Nation and Gender', in I. Blom, K. Hagemaan, and C. Hall (eds.) *Gendered Nations: Nationalisms and Gender Order in the Long Nineteenth Century*, Oxford and New York, 31.
7. D. H. Doyle and M. A. Pamplona (eds.) (2006) *Nationalism in the New World*, Athens, GA, 4. See also Chapter 6 in this book by Don Doyle and Eric van Young.
8. F. Bilbao (1866) *Obras completas*, Buenos Aires, 2 vols., II, 483.
9. D. F. Sarmiento, cited (without reference) in R. Orgaz (1937) *Alberdi y el historicismo*, Córdoba, iv.
10. *La déclaration des droits de l'homme et du citoyen de 1789. Histoire, analyse et commentaires sous la direction de Gérard Conac, Marc Debens, Gérard Teboul*, Paris (1993), 91.
11. 'Acta de la independencia' [de Chile], 1810, in J. B. Espinosa (ed.) (1889) *Constituciones de Chile*, Santiago, 37. Similar examples can be found throughout the region.
12. 'Manifiesto del congreso social general constituyente á los habitantes de la federación [de los Estados Unidos Mexicanos]', 1824, in *Colección de constituciones de los Estados Unidos Mexicanos*, Mexico (1828), 3 vols., vol. I, 16–32, 22–3.
13. 'Manifesto del congreso', 23–4.
14. 'Manifesto del congreso', 24.
15. R. Earle (2002) '"Padres de la Patria" and the Ancestral Past: Commemorations of Independence in Nineteenth-Century Spanish America', *Journal of Latin American Studies*, 34, no. 4 (November), 775–805, esp. 782–4.

16. R. Earle (2007) *The Return of the Native*, Durham, NC, and London.
17. As Ernest Gellner valuably reminds us, Herder's critique of universalism 'was relatively modest, almost humble, rather than vicious and lethal'. See E. Gellner (1997) *Nationalism*, London, 69.
18. G. Eley (2000) 'Culture, Nation and Gender', in Blom, Hagemaan, and Hall (eds.), *Gendered Nations*, 30. The classic study for Europe remains E. Weber (1976) *Peasants into Frenchmen: The Modernization of Rural France*, London. See also A. Knight (1994) 'Peasants into Patriots: Thoughts on the Making of the Mexican Nation', *Mexican Studies/Estudios Mexicanos*, 10, no. 1 (Winter), 135–61, which cites Weber.
19. M. Tenorio-Trillo (1999) 'Essaying the History of National Images', in M. Thurner and A. Guerrero (eds.) *After Spanish Rule*, Durham, NC, 59–86, 64.
20. Doyle and Pamplona, *Nationalism in the New World*, 2.
21. Doyle and Pamplona, *Nationalism in the New World*. Statistics on immigration to Latin America are difficult to pin down, not least because many immigrants were seasonal, or did not settle permanently. The best-documented case is Argentina, where foreigners constituted 12 per cent of the population in 1869 and 30 per cent in 1914. For a survey of the debates, see N. Sánchez-Albornoz, 'Population', in L. Bethell (ed.) (1989) *Latin America: Economy and Society, 1870–1930*, Cambridge, 83–114, esp. 88–101.
22. The classic text is J. Vasconcelos (1925, 1997) *The Cosmic Race: A Bilingual Edition*, trans. D. T. Jaén, Baltimore, MD.
23. The literature is well reviewed in T. Skidmore (1993) 'Bi-Racial USA vs. Multi-Racial Brazil: Is the Contrast Still Valid?', *Journal of Latin American Studies*, 25, 373–86.
24. 'Mesa redonda: Nacionalismo, patriotismo y emancipación', *Contracorriente. Una revista cubana del pensamiento* (Havana), 3, no. 9 (1997), 122.
25. L. Whitehead (1994) 'State Organization in Latin America since 1930', *The Cambridge History of Latin America Economy, Society, and Politics. Vol. 6, Part 1: Latin America since 1930: Economy and Society*, ed. L. Bethell, Cambridge, 3–95.
26. For a good survey, see E. Williamson (1992) *The Penguin History of Latin America*, London, esp. ch. 9, 'Nationalism and Development: An Overview', 436–58.
27. L. L. Guerra and L. Aguiar de Luque (eds.) (1992) *Las constituciones de Iberoamérica*, Madrid, 573.
28. M. E. Rein (1998) *Politics and Education in Argentina, 1946–1962*, Armonk, NY, and London, 65.
29. F. Coronil (1997) *The Magical State: Nature, Money and Modernity in Venezuela*, Chicago, IL, 168 and 1.
30. Anderson (1991 edn.) *Imagined Communities*, 6.
31. P. Chatterjee (1996) 'Whose Imagined Community?', in G. Balakrishnan (ed.) *Mapping the Nation*, London, 214–25. Many of Chatterjee's points about the reception of the national idea in Asia and Africa strike me as relevant to Latin America, although he categorizes 'the Americas' together with 'Europe' as 'Western models' that condemn the rest of the world to immiserated mimesis.
32. There are affinities here with the cases of pan-nationalism in other parts of the world considered by Cemil Aydin in Chapter 34 of this book.
33. C. Lomnitz (2001) 'Nationalism as a Practical System: Benedict Anderson's Theory of Nationalism from the Vantage Point of Spanish America', in M. A. Centeno and F. López-Alves (eds.) *The Other Mirror: Grand Theory Through the Lens of Latin America*, Princeton, NJ, 329–49.

34. D. A. Brading (2001) *Mexican Phoenix. Our Lady of Guadalupe: Image and Tradition Across Five Centuries*, Cambridge, 256.
35. Tenorio-Trillo, 'Essaying', 59.

Suggested Further Reading

Appelbaum, N. P., Macpherson, A. S., and Rosemblatt, K. A. (eds.) (2003) *Race and Nation in Modern Latin America*, Chapel Hill, NC.

Brading, D. (1991) *The First America*, Cambridge.

Castro-Klarén, S. and Chasteen, J. C. (eds.) (2003) *Beyond Imagined Communities: Reading and Writing the Nation in Nineteenth-Century Latin America*, Washington DC.

Doyle, D. H. and Pamplona, M. A. (eds.) (2006) *Nationalism in the New World*, Athens, GA.

Dunkerley, J. (ed.) (2002) *Studies in the Formation of the Nation State in Latin America*, London.

Earle, R. (2007) *The Return of the Native: Indians and Myth-Making in Spanish America, 1810–1930*, Durham, NC, and London.

Lomnitz, C. (2001) 'Nationalism as a Practical System: Benedict Anderson's Theory of Nationalism from the Vantage Point of Spanish America', in M. A. Centeno and F. López-Alves (eds.) *The Other Mirror: Grand Theory Through the Lens of Latin America*, Princeton, NJ, 329–49.

Mallon, F. (1994) *Peasant and Nation: The Making of Postcolonial Mexico and Peru*, Berkeley, CA.

Miller, N. (1999) *In the Shadow of the State: Intellectuals and the Quest for National Identity in Twentieth-Century Spanish America*, London.

Roniger, L. and Sznajder, M. (eds.) (1998) *Constructing Collective Identities and Shaping Public Spheres*, Brighton.

Thurner, M. and Guerrero, A. (eds.) (2003) *After Spanish Rule: Postcolonial Predicaments of the Americas*, Durham, NC, and London.

Wade, P. (2000) *Music, Race and Nation: Música tropical in Colombia*, Chicago, IL.

CHAPTER 20

STATE-BUILDING AND NATIONALISM IN NINETEENTH-CENTURY USA

SUSAN-MARY GRANT

This Country must be united. If persuasion does not unite it, the sword will.

(Gouverneur Morris to the Federal Convention, 1787)[1]

During my short sojourn in this country I have never yet met any person who could show me where the sovereignty of the Union resides. General Prentiss, however, and his Illinois volunteers are quite ready to fight for it.

(William Howard Russell, *My Diary North and South*, 1863)[2]

Introduction

In his contemplation of *The Future in America*, published in 1906, H. G. Wells famously asserted that 'the typical American has no "sense of the state". I do not mean that he is not passionately and vigorously patriotic,' Wells continued, but 'that he has no perception that his business activities, his private employments, are constituents in a large collective process . . . he sees the world in fragments . . . . The American . . . has yet to achieve the conception of a whole to which all individual acts and happenings are subordinate and contributory.' America as a unified entity, Wells concluded, found expression only through 'the flag', but beneath it 'America is lost among constituent States and cities.' Wells was an outsider looking in, but he had identified something of a perennial theme in this case, one that had engaged both foreign observers and Americans alike since the nation's inception. 'State attachments and State importance have been the bane of this country,' Gouverneur Morris had announced to the Federal (or Constitutional) Convention of 1787 that drafted the American Constitution. At this point, of course, the country in question had barely been a decade in existence, assuming one measures its inception from the Declaration of Independence of 1776; if one measures instead from the Treaty of Paris (1783), which formally ended the War for Independence, then America, when Morris made his pronouncement, was a rather youthful four years old.[3]

The nation had survived its awkward teenage years by the time French aristocrat Alexis de Tocqueville arrived in 1831 to interrogate the political constructions of the new nation, but his assessment, published in 1835, both echoed Morris and presaged Wells: the American Union, he observed, 'is a vast body, which presents no definite object to patriotic feeling'. The individual States, by contrast, were 'identified with the soil; with the right of property and the domestic affections; with the recollections of the past, the labours of the present, and the hopes of the future'. Americans themselves were hardly unaware of the fact; when the Southern States selected to remove themselves from the Union in 1860–1, it simply confirmed New York lawyer George Templeton Strong's gloomy verdict that America was little more than 'an aggregate of communities, ready to fall apart at the first serious shock... without a center of vigorous national life to keep us together'. By the war's conclusion, however, it was a different matter. With the Union triumphant, it seemed both to contemporary observers and to many scholars since that in the defeat of secession, a nation had been born, a state—a truly national, modern state—created. 'Even if among us in the earlier day there was no occasion for the word Nation,' Republican senator Charles Sumner observed in 1867, 'there is now. A Nation,' he confidently asserted, 'is born.'[4]

Modern studies of American state formation frequently echo Sumner's perspective. They highlight the absence of a strong central state prior to the Civil War of 1861–5 and date the emergence of the modern state from 1877, the year when Reconstruction (1865–77) formally ended and federal troops were finally removed from the Southern States. Shifting attention away from the specifics of conflict toward wider social, demographic, environmental, and administrative forces at work in late nineteenth-century America, Stephen Skowronek suggests that the impetus for the emergence of the modern state arose from the 'combined impact of *crisis*, *class conflict*, and *complexity*' between 1877 and 1920; in short, it is in the traditional triumvirate of later nineteenth-century industrialization, urbanization, and immigration that he locates the origins of the modern American state.[5]

There is a distinction, however, between American state-building and the process of the construction of American nationalism; there is also a link between the formation of the modern American state—whether one dates that from the Civil War or from 1877—and the overt expression of nationalism in the United States.[6] The link, however, is more complex than it at first appears, more grounded in the antebellum era (*c*.1830–60) than is usually assumed, and more multilayered than studies of late nineteenth-century state-formation allow. What follows seeks to position the evolution of American nationalism within the broader parameters of American state-formation in the nineteenth century; first, however, some discussion of definition is in order.

The state, Michael Mann observes, 'is undeniably a messy concept'. Nationalism, of course, is hardly a tidier one, but John Breuilly cuts through much of the confusion in his insistence 'that nationalism is, above all else, about politics and that politics is about power . . . principally about control of the state'. Yet if nationalism relates 'to political movements seeking or exercising state power and justifying such action with nationalist arguments', America appears to be excluded on the grounds that colonial Americans justified their demands for independence from Great Britain on universal grounds rather than by invoking any specific ethnic or cultural identity that rendered them unique. Politically, theirs was very much 'a resistance in favor of the liberties of England'. Yet it was also a resistance based on a substantial set of specific grievances against the British Crown, and there was a greater focus on this than subsequent scholarship, voluminous though it is, has allowed. The leadership who formed, and the populace that acknowledged the authority that was the Continental Congress, constituted at the very least a fledgling people, a proto-nation with both cultural and political bonds. It was those bonds that held the Revolutionary impulse together, gave it direction, and justified the existence of the new nation; in short, it was those bonds that made the universal particular, and laid the groundwork for the American state. The resurgence of antagonism between the former colonies and Great Britain in the War of 1812, further, reinforced these bonds, and the nationalism they both implied and inculcated.[7]

Definitions of the state, according to Mann, 'contain two different levels of analysis, the "institutional" and the "functional" . . . the state can be defined in terms of what it looks like, institutionally, or what it does, its functions'. Definitions of nationalism, however, involve multiple layers of analysis: political—relating to the state—but also cultural and ideological, and within these parameters we might include the specific components of class, identity, localism, gender, and ethnicity. Nationalism can, therefore, also be described institutionally—those aspects of nationalism that support the state—and functionally—the ways in which nationalist ideology is invoked by the state-ruling elites and, beyond them, understood and expressed by the populace as a whole. In short, and to paraphrase Mann, in the American case we might ask what is the nature of the nationalism utilized by individual States and state elites in the Civil War era? American state-formation cannot be understood without reference to that most elusive concept, American nationalism. Relative to many other examples in western Europe and elsewhere, both nationalism and state-formation in America happened in reverse order. European societies approached modernization in three stages: 'first, the extension and consolidation of central state power; second, bureaucratic specialisation; and, last, popular political participation', whereas in the United States the political structure, and by the early 1830s the popular political participation along with it, preceded the development both of a national culture and the accoutrements of state power that might have directed that culture. Americans, it has been argued, 'practiced nationalism before they had a fully developed national state', or, in John Murrin's memorable phrase, 'erected their constitutional roof before they put up the national walls'. Any discussion of American nationalism or American state-formation must explore the implications of this reversal of traditional nationalist fortunes; it must also begin with the nation's founding documents: the Declaration of Independence and the Constitution.[8]

Constitution and Covenant

The American nation, it has been asserted, 'was explicitly formed in the covenant of its constitution'. Naturally, when devised the Constitution was not imbued with the sacred authority it later acquired; a necessary revision to the Articles of Confederation, the Constitution expressed the desire of 'the people... to form a more perfect union, establish justice, ensure domestic tranquility, provide for the common defence, promote the general welfare, and secure the blessings of liberty to ourselves and our posterity'. The more revolutionary document—without which there could have been no Constitution and no nation—was the Declaration of Independence, the originating 'American scripture' and the one fixed point in the midst of the nineteenth-century conflict over the interpretation of the Constitution's legality, the American state's validity. Rooted in the English tradition of justifying the removal of incompetent monarchs (*rex inutilis*), the Declaration followed a frequently tortuous and sometimes hesitant path to publication, in part because its authors realized that 'in announcing their separate nationhood' the new Americans had 'to link their cause with a purpose beyond survival alone, to raise the vision of a better future so compelling that in its name men would sacrifice even life itself'.[9]

The Declaration of Independence, therefore, invoked specific grievances alongside universal principles to justify the separation of one people from another. It can be read, it has been argued, as a rejection of 'the organisational qualities of the state as they had been evolving in Europe.... Standing armies, centralized taxing authorities, the denial of local prerogatives, burgeoning costs of administrators—these were the focus against which a new political culture found definition.' It was in no sense, however, a document of government. Government derived from the new constitutions drawn up by all States bar Connecticut and Rhode Island (which simply revised their colonial governing charters). Although most of these evinced a suspicion of executive power and were consequently more restrictive in the degrees of authority they allowed their State governors, they did not, on the whole, vary greatly from the colonial pattern, nor did they, neither in their individual declarations of the causes of separation from Britain nor their bills of rights, reiterate directly the assertion that 'all men are created equal'. None of these documents, in fact, invoked the Declaration 'as a classic statement of American political principles'. Having performed its 'constitutional function in formally closing the previous regime', its work was done once it had been disseminated, and it was all but forgotten as Americans turned to the pressing issue of establishing a functioning central state.[10]

The 'idea' at the heart of American nationalism, frequently ascribed by a later age to the Declaration of Independence, in the late eighteenth and early nineteenth century resided in the Constitution and the Bill of Rights, the documents of both nation and nationalism, but their touch, in state terms, was a light one; perhaps too light, since the post-Revolutionary era has been summed up, with accuracy, as one 'overcast by a federal vagueness'.[11] This vagueness worried some members of the Revolutionary elite; the desire to create, in the words of the Constitution, 'a more perfect union', derived from the fear, succinctly expressed by George Washington's former aide, Alexander Hamilton, on 4 July 1782, that there was:

> ... something noble and magnificent in the perspective of a great Federal Republic, closely linked in the pursuit of a common interest, tranquil and prosperous at home, respectable abroad; but there is something proportionally diminutive and contemptible in the prospect of a *number* of *petty States*, with the appearance only of union, jarring, jealous, and perverse, without any determined direction, fluctuating and unhappy at home, weak and insignificant by their dissensions in the eyes of other nations.[12]

The Articles of Confederation, drawn up as the governing legislation between the thirteen states in 1776 but not ratified until 1781, treated each State as a discrete entity, and the relationship between them as no more than, in John Dickinson's words, 'a firm league of friendship', voluntarily entered into and respectful of the sovereign rights, freedom, and independence of the individual State. As a legislative tool, Hamilton believed, they were 'neither fit for war nor peace. The idea of an uncontrollable sovereignty in each State,' he warned, 'will defeat the other powers given to Congress, and make our union feeble and precarious.' Since the debates between the various 'Founding Fathers' of the American nation took place against the backdrop of the Revolutionary war, it was the behaviour of the individual States in that conflict that gave Hamilton pause. 'In the midst of a war for our existence as a nation—in the midst of dangers too serious to be trifled with,' he pointed out, 'some of the *States* have evaded or refused compliance with the demands of Congress in points of the greatest moment to the common safety. If they act such a part at this perilous juncture, what are we to expect in a time of peace and security?'[13]

Not everyone was so pessimistic. Gouverneur Morris, although he was later to decry State attachments, believed that the kind of national unity Hamilton called for would develop in time. 'A national spirit is the result of national existence,' he asserted, 'and although some of the present generation may feel colonial opposition of opinion, yet this generation will die away and give place to a race of Americans.' Hamilton, however, did not believe 'that time was on the side of nationalism in the United States', and believed that inaction on the part of the Revolutionary generation 'in the work of building a nation' would leave 'no nation for the next generation to cling to'. The issues would be debated at length in the Constitutional Convention of 1787, out of which the

American Constitution, constructed by 'a nationally conscious political elite', eventually emerged, but the tension between those who called for a strong central state (Federalists) and those who favoured individualism, or in its legislative form, States' rights (anti-Federalists), persisted through the Early Republic and into the antebellum era.[14]

The debates between Federalists and Anti-Federalists were, however, 'over the meaning of the Constitution, not its legitimacy', and the Constitution did represent a turning point for America, as leading British historian and statesman James Bryce noted. 'The acceptance of the Constitution of 1789,' he observed, 'made the American people into a nation.' That it was an unusual nation he fully accepted: neither like the Hanseatic League of medieval Germany nor the Germanic Confederation (1815–66), nor like the modern nations of Europe, he concluded that the American Federal Republic represented a kind of national middle-ground, and described it as 'a large building and a set of smaller buildings standing on the same ground', as 'a Commonwealth of commonwealths, a Republic of republics, a State which, while one, is nevertheless composed of other States, even more essential to its existence than it is to theirs'. At the heart of both the national state and the individual States, Bryce perceived, lay the Constitution. His assessment, originally made in 1893, has attracted little dissension. The Constitution's effectiveness as the legislative document of the American nation lies partly in its immediate and near universal acceptance but also in the fact that it faced no serious challenges—only three amendments, all deriving from the Civil War of the mid-nineteenth century, were added to it between 1804 and 1913—for over a century.[15]

Yet while the Constitution, and constitutionalism, may have held the nation together, its essential function as not just the instrument of government but as a brake on excess government produced a weak, almost superfluous, central state, and positioned Washington as 'a capital without a country'. The impact of the state on its citizens was low. There was, for example, no direct taxation; there was no need, since at federal level the revenue acquired through land offices, post offices, and customhouses—the three main tangible instruments of the state—produced, for the 1830s and 1840s, a surplus. Law and order were matters for the individual States, and the nation as a whole, separated as it was by three thousand miles of ocean from the European entanglements that George Washington had warned it against, experienced no perceptible foreign threat to its stability. By the mid-nineteenth century, out of a population in excess of 30 million, the federal government only had around 36,700 employees, and of those, 30,000 were local postmasters. In these circumstances, it is hardly surprising that Thomas Carlyle concluded that the American federal system was 'anarchy plus a street constable'.[16]

Even a brief perusal of the *Congressional Record* for the antebellum period reveals that the American government's main functions 'were virtually all promotional, distributive, and developmental, and not regulatory or restrictive' at this time. The public lands, railways, harbour improvements, and the construction of canals were the main subjects of debate: however, even out of such apparently innocuous material, sectional tensions could and did arise. Sectional antagonism, sometimes even fully blown separatist impulses, in the early American state did not necessarily imply a lack of nationalist sentiment. In the absence of a strong central state—by European standards—the development of a 'state of courts and parties' in the form of the judiciary and the two-party system worked both to contain as well as express sectional—predominantly North/South—divisions in the decades before the Civil War. Constitutional federalism may have restricted the development of central authority, leaving 'the most practical questions of state operations shrouded in ambiguity', but what was unambiguous, what flourished uninhibited, was a strong and growing sense of nationalism. This nationalism found its most obvious, public expression through the flag, the Great Seal with its declaration '*Incipit Novus Ordo Saeclorum*', taken from Virgil and emphasizing America's role as the earth's new 'chosen nation', and, by the antebellum period, the Declaration of Independence. This was very much the product of a politically conscious elite who, aware of the absence of, in George Templeton Strong's words, 'centuries of achievement and calamities to look back on', perceived the need to construct a '*record* of Americanism', and did so, remarkably effectively, given the circumstances.[17]

Antebellum publications, political parties, and the pulpit all functioned together to create a sense of Americanism, a cultural, political, and religious nationalism, and disseminated this vigorously throughout a population that, it must be remembered, was growing at a remarkable rate; from just over 7 million in 1810, it had reached 31 million by 1860, by which point, too, the original thirteen States that had separated from Britain had become thirty-three. Heeding Noah Webster's call to 'act like independent beings . . . you have an empire to raise and support by your exertions—and a national character to establish and extend', Americans showed little hesitation. Via the overt patriotic ceremonies on 4 July, the lessons of the history books, disseminated nationally, that revered the Revolution and reminded Americans of the personal sacrifices made during that conflict, the constant references to the political debt they owed the Founding Fathers, and the religious as well as the political declarations of America's 'Manifest Destiny' to expand westwards, this nationalism expressed itself over an increasingly wide geographical area.[18]

Anthony Smith notes how, over time 'the belief in a providential and manifest destiny was extended from the chosen people to the land and landscapes of America', as the nation expanded westward beyond the Allegheny Mountains. Yet two points need to be stressed in regard to this process. The first is a practical, Constitutional one: although scholars frequently emphasize the religious, literary, cultural, and ideological roots of American nationalism, it must be remembered that only the federal government could make the nation tangible, acquire the land on which it could build, over which it would spread. The Louisiana Purchase of 1803, which added some 828,000 square miles to the national territory at a cost of $15 million, or the removal of the Cherokee Nation from Georgia in the early nineteenth century, were the result of the actions—constitutionally defended though not in the strictest sense constitutional in either case—of the federal government; no individual State, no matter how sovereign, could have established the territory across which America would make manifest her destiny. Government of the Western Territories, as stipulated by the Northwest Ordinance of 1787 was the responsibility of the national state until the population reached five thousand—at which point a separate legislature could be formed—or sixty thousand—at which point the territory could apply for statehood on the same terms as the original thirteen States.[19]

The second point relates to the national resonance of the idea of Manifest Destiny or, more specifically, to the belief in Americans as a chosen people, defined and determined by both a secular—the Constitution—and a religious covenant. This belief was not shared equally by North and South; indeed the very 'notion of the redeemer nation was essentially a Yankee idea', which spread across the North and, via migration, the West, gaining momentum in the years leading up to the Civil War. It was only a part, but an increasingly influential one, of a more widespread sense of the significance of what was frequently referred to as the 'universal Yankee nation', a concept linked to American nationalism, from a Northern perspective. A meditation on Thanksgiving Day that appeared in a leading New England magazine summed it up:

> The Union of these States is not consummated by appeals to national loyalty, nor to that national pride expressed in our motto, that union is strength. In short, all theoretical and abstract appeals to the Union are without root, and consequently without fruit. What makes the Union more than a mere word for poets or politicians, what makes it a blessing to be prayed for and preserved at any hazard, is quite on other grounds than pride. An angry man hesitates to get his house on fire, because in every room is one of his own sleeping children. In these United States are scattered broadcast, growing up side by side with the natural productions, or else grafted on the ancient trees, the universal Yankee nation.

This universal Yankee nation came at a price; one paid by the indigenous peoples inhabiting the Western Territories, who were not the 'natural productions' this New England author had in mind. Increasingly, too, the South became excluded from this nationalist impulse. In sermons, literature, and, above all, in Congress, between 1830 and 1860 a nationalism arose that carried the nation westward toward its 'Manifest Destiny', but it was a white 'northern nation', ethnically defined against both Native and African Americans and, increasingly, culturally defined against the white South. Before the Civil War, geographic but also ideological expansion was the most obvious outward expression both of federal authority and of American nationalism; its Northern aspect, however, became the fulcrum for the secession of the South in 1861, the breaking, albeit temporarily, of the covenant represented by the Constitution.[20]

Northern Nationalism, Southern Nation

'Any study of the American state,' it has been stressed, 'must address two questions posed by the Civil War: Why did the South secede from the Union? and why did the North resist secession?' The answer to both lies in the nature of American nationalism as this developed in the antebellum era. The nationalism of the earlier period cohered around the Constitution. In many ways, the Constitution was an extremely effective tool of government, and its efficacy did not diminish even as the nation itself expanded, political parties—which the Founding Fathers had not anticipated—emerged, and the franchise broadened in the early nineteenth century. That was its greatest success; the outbreak of Civil War in 1861, however, represented its greatest failure. It was not simply a failure to resolve the slavery issue—the greatest divide between North and South—but a more fundamental failure to resolve internal conflict and balance the federal with the local, the national with the sectional. The fault lines in America's federal fabric ran in the direction they did in part because of the nature of the Constitution itself and the division of sovereignty, but mainly because of the nature of the 'state of courts and parties' that developed to interpret it for a fast-changing nation. The emergence in the 1850s of the Republican Party, a sectional party that wrapped itself in the flag of American nationalism, changed the rules of engagement between sectionalism and nationalism, and brought to a head the conjoined issues of slavery, westward expansion, and States' rights within the federal system.[21]

The weakness of the central state in antebellum America has obscured the extra-governmental routes taken in the formation of American nationalism. A decentralized state, with little impact on its population, did not translate into a weakened sense of nationalism; quite the opposite. Localism functioned as a means of offering the American people a direct stake in the nation, strengthening ties that, from a purely state-building perspective, may seem to have been flimsy, or indeed non-existent. Politics was the strongest national tie, with voter turnout in the North reaching 90 per cent at times; in 1860 it was 81 per cent; through politics the balance between State and national authority was continuously renegotiated. Each State was sovereign, yet each State, to paraphrase John Donne's famous poem, was not an island, but part of the whole. So long as no issue arose around which particular group of States might cohere, federalism functioned effectively. Such an issue did arise in the form of slavery's further expansion, but it was not the case that 'Southern nationalism' emerged in isolation, that of the South from the North, of the South from the Union. Southern nationalism emerged in the context of a very specific Northern nationalism against which it found definition. 'Northern nationalism' remains a less familiar concept than 'Southern nationalism' since, as a perceived 'successful' nationalism, it seemed to have no existence at all. Much of the literature on American nationalism, in this sense, follows Breuilly's observation that nationalism 'remains distinctive only for so long as it is unsuccessful. Nationalism is one particular response to the distinction, peculiar to the modern world, between state and society. It seeks to abolish that distinction. In so far as it succeeds in doing so it abolishes its own foundations.' The nationalism of the North appeared to be successful, to be neither more nor less than American nationalism; it therefore rendered itself, to all intents and purposes, invisible. Southern nationalism, by contrast, apparently solely the product of a crisis that threatened the status quo and sought the establishment of a new nation, is more obviously a recognized 'nationalism'. American nationalism, by the antebellum period, however, no longer represented a national consensus, but was, increasingly, sectionally defined.[22]

In the face of sectional threat, which came mainly—but not exclusively—from the South, Northern elites developed a nationalist defence that juxtaposed North and South, free labour with slave, democracy with aristocracy, and the future with the past. Effectively, the North 'hijacked' American cultural nationalism, but its methods 'were not so much official, public, or governmental as unofficial, private, and extra-governmental', and its origins lay in New England. Antagonism between New England and the South had long been a feature of the nation's development, both culturally and politically. It was from New England pulpits that the loudest denunciations of the 'Slave Power' issued, in New England papers and periodicals that the Southern threat was debated and the region increasingly denounced, and from New England pens that the most damning indictments of slavery poured—the most obvious example being, of course, Harriet Beecher Stowe's *Uncle Tom's Cabin*. The negative portrayal of the South had a resonance far beyond New England, however, and achieved it in three main ways: first, via the vast New England diaspora that spread out across the West in the nineteenth century; second, through the many and various evangelical bodies, private organizations, trusts, voluntary associations, reform societies, and missionary groups produced by the northeast, in particular, in this period; and finally, through the rise of the professions.[23]

The reform groups of the antebellum era acted almost as a kind of shadow state; distinct from both the national state and the state of courts and parties, they nevertheless paralleled developments in both. The South offered less fertile ground for reform associations, since slavery, and the society predicated on it, was increasingly the focus of antebellum activist concerns. Further, as far as private institutions were concerned, after 1800 a clear division of authority in the United States emerged between 'the people' dominating the political sphere, and the elites, in the form of New England private corporations driving 'the economic and intellectual sphere'. From a Southern perspective, however, this division was of less consequence than was the fact that in both spheres—the political and the cultural—the ground on which American nationalism had been predicated was shifting, away from the South and toward a distinctive Northern interpretation of the nation, of American nationalism, one that found political expression in the new Republican Party.[24]

At the centre of this new definition of the nation lay the concept of the activist central state, one committed to improvement, to 'free soil, free labor, free men', a state open to all; it was less about the preservation of the legacy of the Founding Fathers than it was about building on that legacy to create future national purpose and opportunity.

Here northerners could build on the notion of culturally contrasting sections, of the southern 'Cavalier' and the northern 'Yankee' having separate, distinctive ethnic, origins, and divert attention from slavery's national significance by making it a sectional issue, an institution 'peculiar' to the South. The belief in a 'Slave Power' of Southern politicians controlling the federal government gained momentum, and allowed the convergence of cultural, political, economic, and ideological opposition to the South to coalesce.[25]

The rise of the Republicans represented the political expression of a more aggressive form of American nationalism than had existed before; less concerned with the sacred inheritance of the Revolution than it was with the need to develop a form of nationalism capable of acting as a cohesive force in a nation expanding, geographically and demographically. Although this nationalism functioned within the constitutional system, it contained a moral as well as a practical dimension that challenged the status quo in the South, even though it was not the slave system itself, but rather its potential westward expansion, that formed the context of political debate and, increasingly, disagreement during the political crisis of the 1850s. The Republican version of American nationalism, although expressed in the context of partisan politics, derived from much broader national and sectional forces at play in the American nation, forces that increasingly drew North and South apart. With the emergence of the Republicans, a distinct 'northern nationalism' found expression; in part predicated on opposition to the South, in part the product of the perceived need to shift the nationalist ground on which a nation of immigrants was constructed, this northern nationalism held out a vision for the nation, and for American nationalism, that many in the South did not share.

It was in this context that the Declaration of Independence really found its resonance, as it was in the justification for the Revolution of the eighteenth century that both North and South found support for their respective positions, their contrasting, and ultimately clashing, versions of American nationalism. 'Our republican robe is soiled, and trailed in the dust,' Abraham Lincoln had declared in 1854:

> Let us repurify it. Let us turn and wash it white, in the spirit if not the blood of the Revolution. Let us turn slavery away from its claims of 'moral right'. . . . Let us return it to the position our fathers gave it; and there let it rest in peace. Let us readopt the Declaration of Independence, and with it the practices and policy which harmonise with it.[26]

The Declaration of Independence was central to Lincoln's understanding of how American nationalism functioned in a nation of immigrants. Reflecting on the importance of 4 July to Americans whose ancestors had won American independence, he noted that many Americans could not trace their blood lineage back to the Revolutionary generation. Nevertheless, Lincoln asserted, the moral sentiment of the Declaration 'is the father of all moral principle in them, and . . . they have a right to claim it as though they were blood of the blood, and flesh of the flesh of the men who wrote that Declaration'. With his emphasis on the 'moral sentiment' of the Declaration, Lincoln was effectively interpreting it as a national mission statement. For the South, however, the Declaration of Independence was less a mission statement than an insurance policy against the encroachments of centralized power, and its assertion that a people had the right to 'alter or abolish' a government which no longer guaranteed their 'safety and happiness' became more important to southerners than the 'life, liberty, and the pursuit of happiness' philosophy that, Lincoln argued, informed America's national doctrine. As the Republicans 'fused Jeffersonian universalism into a new nationalism the key words of which were equal liberty, equality of opportunity, and the maintenance of a national government to support those ideals', many southerners concluded that their constitutional rights—absolute State sovereignty, as they interpreted it, the sovereignty of the slave system—would be better preserved out of the Union than in it.[27]

Northern—at least, Republican—constructions of American nationalism left no room for the right of secession in 1860–1. Although secession had become a perennial threat in American politics since the 1830s, one that northerners had periodically called the South's bluff on, when the Confederacy became a reality, there was no question of permitting one nation to become two. In his First Inaugural, Lincoln made that clear: 'the Union of these States is perpetual. Perpetuity is implied, if not expressed, in the fundamental law of all national governments,' he argued, 'no State, upon its own mere motion, can lawfully get out of the Union'. This was a point echoed in the Northern press; after South Carolina had announced her withdrawal from the Union on 20 December 1860, *The New York Times* observed that 'even if the Union . . . be only a treaty—a compact between the States—it is nevertheless binding upon them all'. All States, the paper insisted, 'parted with a portion of their sovereignty' when they 'agreed to accept a common arbiter'. Secession was a misnomer, the *Times* suggested; the actions of South Carolina were neither more nor less than illegal and insurrectionary. For Lincoln, too, secession was 'the essence of anarchy', an attack on the people, and on their institutions. 'Must a government,' he inquired a few months later, 'of necessity be too strong for the liberties of its own people, or too weak to maintain its own existence?' This, for Lincoln, was a question that involved 'more than the fate of these United States. It presents to the whole family of man, the question whether a constitutional republic, or a democracy—a government of the people, by the same people—can, or cannot, maintain its territorial integrity, against its own domestic foes'.[28] Yet it was more than a merely constitutional question of who 'the people' actually were and whether they could defend themselves; it also involved what the people might expect from government. From this perspective, as Lincoln saw it, the Civil War was:

> . . . essentially a People's contest. On the side of the Union, it is a struggle for maintaining in the world, that form, and substance of government, whose leading object is, to elevate the condition of men—to lift artificial weights from all shoulders—to clear the paths of laudable pursuit for all—to afford all, an unfettered start, and a fair chance, in the race of life.[29]

On the side of the South it was a different matter. Southern cultural nationalism, for so long defined against the North's free labour society, took military rather than purely political form in 1860–1. 'States' rights' within the federal system was the South's rallying cry, but the sole right under threat was slavery. For many in the North, slavery was not the issue in 1860; the Civil War was a test of republican government; only in time did its moral dimension emerge, and with Northern victory came the opportunity to transform America into a truly 'universal Yankee nation'.[30]

Compromise and Consolidation

The Civil War has been termed the 'second American Revolution', and certainly many southerners saw it in those terms. As Southern spokesman, William Lowdes Yancy, explained it, Lincoln's election promised 'just such a government as incited the Revolutionary patriots to throw off British allegiance. They denied the right of a foreign people, of the same blood, language, religion and government, to legislate for them.' This was 'the essence of Southern nationalism', one that, in effect, sought 'revolutionary legitimacy'. The parallels with the Revolution were not only on the Southern side. Just as the colonists in the eighteenth century had to invoke universal principles in the service of a nation worth fighting for, so northerners—but especially Abraham Lincoln—had to defend their denial of secession on grounds broader than the simple defence of the status quo: this was the main point of divergence between the Republicans and the Democrats during the war; while the latter looked for a re-establishment of, as their slogan in the 1864 election put it, 'The Constitution as it is, the Union as it was', the former had to keep reinforcing the message that the conflict was not just about defending the state, but establishing a state worth defending. As a 'people's contest' in the sense that volunteer armies, on both sides, were the combatants, the Civil War from a Northern perspective was about more than the Union as it was; it became a conflict for the Union as it ought to be. The most obvious revolutionary outcome, from the perspective of both North and South, was of course the emancipation of some four million slaves; in practice, however, it was a revolution with limits.[31]

That the Civil War strengthened American state-formation is on one level undeniable, not least in the utilization of war powers by the executive and the concomitant 'shift of authority and leadership from the states to Washington'. A raft of legislation was passed by the Union during the war, much of it of lasting significance: the Homestead Act, the Pacific Railroad Act, and the National Banking Act are just some examples. Administrative components of the modern American state were also established or expanded during the war; the office of the Commissioner of Internal Revenue and the Government Printing Office, and the Treasury, grew in size from some four thousand employees in 1861 to over ten thousand by 1865, an increased staff reflecting a greatly expanded remit, including the survey of over fifteen hundred national banks, the implementation of the income tax, control of currency and inflation during the war, and the administration of a national debt that had, for obvious reasons, grown considerably between 1861 and 1865. The number of civilians employed by the federal government rose, too; from around 36,700 in 1861, by 1865 it was closer to 195,000.[32]

Beyond the practical extension of both the government and the military during the Civil War—an extension that was, for the military at least, short-lived—and in the context of American nationalism and its relationship to state-building, lay the larger question of what the war had achieved, in terms of state-formation and in terms of nationalism. On his visit in 1831, de Tocqueville had concluded that the American government was 'artificial' and not 'organic', and the Civil War thirty years later seemed to bear him out, representing as it did not just the failure of federalism, but 'the incomplete nature of American nationalism'. From this perspective, the Reconstruction (1865–77) of the nation implied not solely the reconstruction of a political system, a single state, but the removal of those elements of cultural and economic nationalism, most notably slavery as both a labour and social system that had set the South apart from the North. In that respect, the changes to the American state and to American nationalism had been significant. Out of emancipation arose the first definition of American citizenship, via the Fourteenth Amendment, a citizenship based on the nation, not on the State, referring as it does to all 'persons born or naturalised in the United States'. For modern sensibilities this seems a fairly obvious statement, yet only a decade earlier the Supreme Court had ruled—in *Dred Scott v. Sandford* (1857)—that African Americans could never be citizens, that 'they had no rights that the white man was bound to respect'. The extent to which the war was productive of a new nationalism, one incorporating both African Americans and the defeated South, however, was rather more limited. The 'amount of permanent consolidation produced by the war', it has been argued, was 'neither small enough to be called unimportant nor large enough to be called revolutionary. The principal achievement for American nationalism under Lincoln's leadership was the negative one of arresting a drift toward decentralisation that had become a plunge into disintegration.'[33]

Conclusion

The American state obviously survived the Civil War, but the extent to which it was transformed in the process was perhaps less revolutionary than was once thought and the degree to which it witnessed a shift from a Union into a nation rather less successful, from certain perspectives, than some scholars would have it. Certainly in the course of the war, and for the period of Reconstruction after it, when federal troops were stationed in the South, 'the American state and the Republican party were essentially the same thing', and central state authority was exercised 'in the name of northern-led nationalism'. Yet with the return of the South to the political system in 1877, the Republicans were forced to relinquish at least some of the consolidated authority they had built up, to abandon at least part of the dream of the universal

Yankee nation, not least its promise of full civic equality for all those who had, briefly, dominated the American wartime state, and informed the ideal of post-war American nationalism.[34]

The universal Yankee nation of the post-Civil War era was certainly rooted in a stable state structure, but the Reconstruction amendments, designed to secure the rights of African Americans in the nation, 'were not self-enforcing'. A more secure state, one no longer susceptible to secession, did not automatically translate into the achievement of the moral revolution that the Republicans, that Lincoln, that many northerners by 1863 had anticipated. For E. L. Godkin, the editor of *The Nation*, the American state after the Civil War was in much the same position as before it, the position in which H. G. Wells found it; it represented 'sovereignty without centralisation'. An expanded federal bureaucratic structure represented the increased power of the state, but the cultural supports for that structure did not automatically inculcate a stronger and more inclusive nationalism. The 'emergent intelligentsia' who dominated the post-war nation and established the institutions of the modern American state did not differ from their antebellum counterparts as much as scholars seem to suppose. Most of those publications through which the new American nationalism was promulgated—the *Atlantic Monthly*, *Harper's Weekly*, *The Nation*, and the *North American Review*—preceded the Civil War, and their reform message, as far as American nationalism was concerned, had hardly changed.[35]

If the war finally gave America's intellectual reformers 'a government they could respect, a cause that they could serve, and a popular audience that they had never before enjoyed', their voice was hardly mute before the war broke out; indeed, in many ways it was the voice of sectionalism as much as of nationalism, and contributed to the chorus of disapproval of the South that had, in some ways, led to the outbreak of war in the first place.[36] In its aftermath, the rights of African Americans were allowed to drift—legally secured in theory, in practice they were too readily abandoned—and the South became America's 'problem' region; economically blighted, socially suspect, politically reactionary. In this respect, the American state after the Civil War effected a fairly rapid return to the status quo antebellum, certainly in the matter of race relations in the South. American nationalism in general, in its outward, imperial dimensions as the nation moved onto the world stage toward the end of the nineteenth century, remained blighted by the ethnic reality of its civic ideal, too often defined by exclusionary policies that affected native born and foreign, black and white alike. In internal, political terms, the 'state of courts and parties' did not dissipate, but continued to fill the void left by the demise of wartime centralization. Yet, crucially, this state of courts and parties included new players; the universal Yankee nation was no longer entirely a white one and, in the long run, from the perspective both of state-building and American nationalism, that would make all the difference.

Notes

1. Gouverneur Morris, 5 July 1787, in M. Farrand (1911) *The Records of the Federal Convention of 1787*, New Haven, CT, 4 vols., I, 531.
2. W. H. Russell (1863) *My Diary North and South*, New York and Boston, MA, 338.
3. H. G. Wells (1906) *The Future in America: A Search After Realities*, New York and London, 153–4, 205; Morris to the Federal Convention, 5 July 1787, in Farrand, Records, I, 530.
4. A. de Tocqueville (1945; 1840; 1835) *Democracy in America*, trans. H. Reeve, ed. P. Bradley, New York, 2 vols., I, 401–2; George Templeton Strong diary entries for 11 and 12 March 1861 in A. Nevins and M. Hasley Thomas (eds.) (1952) *The Diary of George Templeton Strong*, New York, 4 vols., III, *The Civil War, 1860–1865*, 109; C. Sumner (1867) '*Are We a Nation?*', New York, 4–5.
5. R. F. Bensel (1990) *Yankee Leviathan: The Origins of Central State Authority in America, 1859–1877*, New York and Cambridge, ix; S. Skowronek (1982) *Building a New American State: The Expansion of National Administrative Capacities, 1877–1920*, New York and Cambridge, 9–10.
6. S. P. Huntington (2005; 2004) *Who Are We? America's Great Debate*, London, 126–39; W. Zelinsky (1988) *Nation into State: The Shifting Symbolic Foundations of American Nationalism*, Chapel Hill, NC, and London, 15–18.
7. M. Mann (1984) 'The Autonomous Power of the State: Its Origins, Mechanisms and Results', *Archives européennes de sociologies*, 25, 185–213, 112; J. Breuilly (1993) *Nationalism and the State*, 2nd edn., Manchester, 1–2; H. Kohn (1957, 1961) *American Nationalism: An Interpretative Essay*, New York, 19; P. Maier (1999; 1997) *American Scripture: How America Declared its Independence from Britain*, London, 92–6, 133.
8. Mann, 'Autonomous Power of the State', 112; Bensel, *Yankee Leviathan*, 4–5; D. Waldstreicher (1997) *In the Midst of Perpetual Fetes: The Making of American Nationalism, 1776–1820*, Chapel Hill, NC, and London, 112–13; J. Murrin (1987) 'A Roof Without Walls: The Dilemma of American National Identity', in R. Beeman, S. Botein, and E. C. Carter II (eds.) *Beyond Confederation: Origins of the Constitution and American National Identity*, Chapel Hill, NC, 333–48.
9. R. Niebuhr and A. Heimert (1963) *A Nation So Conceived: Reflections on the History of America from its Early Visions to its Present Power*, London, 15; Maier, *American Scripture*, 50–5, 95–6.
10. Skowronek, *Building a New American State*, 20; Maier, *American Scripture*, 162, 154, 167.
11. Kohn, *American Nationalism*, 20; Skowronek, *Building a New American State*, 5; D. J. Boorstin (1988; 1965) *The Americans: The National Experience*, New York and London, 401.
12. A. Hamilton (1904) *The Works of Alexander Hamilton*, ed. Henry Cabot Lodge, New York, 12 vols., I, 30–1.
13. Hamilton, 3 September 1780 and 9 August 1781, *The Works of Alexander Hamilton*, I, 45.
14. Morris quoted in J. C. Miller (1959) *Alexander Hamilton: Portrait in Paradox*, New York, 119; D. Ratcliffe (2000) 'The State of the Union, 1776–1860', in S.-M. Grant and B. Holden Reid (eds.) *The American Civil War: Explorations and Reconsiderations*, Harlow, Essex, 3–38, 7.

15. Ratcliffe, 'State of the Union', 8; J. Bryce (1922) *The American Commonwealth*, New York, 2 vols., I, 32, 16–17, 15; P. J. Parish (2003) 'Nationalism and the Constitution', *The North and the Nation in the Era of the Civil War*, ed. A. I. P. Smith and S.-M. Grant, New York, 71–91.
16. R. H. Wiebe (1986) 'Lincoln's Fraternal Democracy', in J. L. Thomas (ed.) *Abraham Lincoln and the American Political Tradition*, Amherst, MA, 14; Parish, 'The Importance of Federalism', *The North and the Nation*, 93; Skowronek, *Building a New American State*, 23; Carlyle quoted in Parish, 'The Importance of Federalism', 96.
17. Parish, 'The Importance of Federalism', 96; Skowronek, *Building a New American State*, 22, 21–2; Strong, Diary entry for 8 November 1854, in Nevins and Hasley Thomas, *Diary of George Templeton Strong*, II, *The Turbulent Fifties*, 196–7.
18. S.-M. Grant (2006) *The War for a Nation: The American Civil War*, New York, 3; Noah Webster quoted in Kohn, *American Nationalism*, 57.
19. A. D. Smith (2003) *Chosen Peoples: Sacred Sources of National Identity*, Oxford, 140.
20. Parish, 'The North, the Nation, and the Southern Response', *The North and the Nation*, 139; *Godey's Lady's Book*, vol. LIX (November 1859), 466.
21. Bensel, *Yankee Leviathan*, 18; Parish, 'Nationalism and the Constitution', 73–9, 80.
22. Breuilly, *Nationalism and the State*, 390; P. Paludan (1994) *The Presidency of Abraham Lincoln*, Lawrence, KS, 13.
23. Parish, 'The North, the Nation, and the Southern Response', 130, 139.
24. A. M. Schlesinger (1944) 'Biography of a Nation of Joiners', *The American Historical Review*, 50, 1 (October), 1–25, esp. 11–12; P. D. Hall (1984) *The Organisation of American Culture, 1700–1900: Private Institutions, Elites, and the Origins of American Nationality*, New York, 89; Y. Arieli (1964) *Individualism and Nationalism in American Ideology*, Cambridge, MA, 309–10.
25. Bensel, *Yankee Leviathan*, ix and, on Southern political power, 19; Arieli, *Individualism and Nationalism in American Ideology*, 308; L. L. Richards (2000) *The Slave Power: The Free North and Southern Domination, 1780–1860*, Baton Rouge, LO, 58; W. R. Taylor (1957, 1979) *Cavalier and Yankee: The Old South and American National Character*, Cambridge, MA; S.-M. Grant (2000) *North Over South: Northern Nationalism and American Identity in the Antebellum Era*, Lawrence, KS, 144–50.
26. Abraham Lincoln, 'Speech at Peoria', 16 October 1854, in R. Basler (ed.) *The Collected Works of Abraham Lincoln*, New Brunswick, NJ., 11 vols., II, 276.
27. Abraham Lincoln, 'Speech at Chicago', 10 July 1858, in Basler (ed.) *The Collected Works of Abraham Lincoln*, II, 499–500; Arieli, *Individualism and Nationalism in American Ideology*, 315.
28. Abraham Lincoln (1861) 'First Inaugural', 4 March, in Basler (ed.) *The Collected Works of Abraham Lincoln*, IV, 265, 268; *The New York Times*, 13 December 1860; Abraham Lincoln (1861) 'Message to Congress in Special Session', 4 July, in Basler (ed.) *The Collected Works of Abraham Lincoln*, IV, 426.
29. Lincoln, 'Message to Congress in Special Session', 438.
30. Hall, *Organisation of American Culture*, 221.
31. C. A. Beard and M. R. Beard (1927) *The Rise of American Civilisation*, New York, 2 vols., II, 53–4; B. Moore, Jr (1966) *Social Origins of Dictatorship and Democracy: Lord and Peasant in the Making of the Modern World*, Boston, MA, 112; Yancey quoted in J. McCardell (1979) *The Idea of a Southern Nation: Southern Nationalists and Southern*

Nationalism, 1830–1860, New York and London, 331; J. M. McPherson (1990) *Abraham Lincoln and the Second American Revolution*, New York and Oxford, 26.

32. Parish, 'The Importance of Federalism', 101–2; W. R. Brock (1973, 1978) *Conflict and Transformation: The United States, 1844–1877*, London, 283, 284.
33. De Tocqueville quoted in C. N. Degler (1992) 'The United States and National Unification', in G. S. Boritt (ed.) *Lincoln: The War President*, New York, 91–119, 96, 101; R. T. H. Wiebe (2002) *Who We Are: A History of Popular Nationalism*, Princeton, NJ, and Oxford, 78–9; D. E. Fehrenbacher (1979) 'Lincoln and the Constitution', in C. Davis et al. (eds.) *The Public and Private Lincoln: Contemporary Perspectives*, Carbondale, IL, 127; Parish, 'The Importance of Federalism', 104.
34. Bensel, *Yankee Leviathan*, 2, 3–4, x.
35. Skowronek, *Building a New American State*, 43–4; Parish, 'The Importance of Federalism', 105.
36. Brock, *Conflict and Transformation*, 316.

Suggestions for Further Reading

Arieli, Y. (1964) *Individualism and Nationalism in American Ideology*, Cambridge, MA.

Bensel, R. F. (1990) *Yankee Leviathan: The Origins of Central State Authority in America, 1859–1877*, New York and Cambridge.

Degler, C. N. (1992) 'The United States and National Unification', in G. S. Boritt (ed.) *Lincoln: The War President*, New York.

Grant, S.-M. (2000) *North Over South: Northern Nationalism and American Identity in the Antebellum Era*, Lawrence, KS.

Grant, S.-M. (2005) 'When was the First New Nation? Locating America in a National Context', in A. Ichijo and G. Uzelac (eds.) *When is the Nation? Towards an Understanding of Theories of Nationalism*, London, 157–76.

Grant, S.-M. (2006) *The War for a Nation: The American Civil War*, New York.

Hall, P. D. (1984) *The Organisation of American Culture, 1700–1900: Private Institutions, Elites, and the Origins of American Nationality*, New York.

Huntington, S. P. (2004, 2005) *Who Are We? America's Great Debate*, London.

Maier, P. (1997, 1999) *American Scripture: How America Declared its Independence from Britain*, London.

McCardell, J. (1979) *The Idea of a Southern Nation: Southern Nationalists and Southern Nationalism, 1830–1860*, New York and London.

McPherson, J. M. (1990) *Abraham Lincoln and the Second American Revolution*, New York and Oxford.

Niebuhr, R. and Heimert, A. (1963) *A Nation So Conceived: Reflections on the History of America from its Early Visions to its Present Power*, London.

Parish, P. J. (2003) *The North and the Nation in the Era of the Civil War*, ed. A. I. P. Smith and S.-M. Grant, New York.

Skowronek, S. (1982) *Building a New American State: The Expansion of National Administrative Capacities, 1877–1920*, New York and Cambridge.

Taylor, W. R. (1979; 1957) *Cavalier and Yankee: The Old South and American National Character*, Cambridge, MA.

Tuveson, E. L. (1968) *Redeemer Nation: The Idea of America's Millennial Role*, Chicago, IL, and London.

Waldstreicher, D. (1997) *In the Midst of Perpetual Fetes: The Making of American Nationalism, 1776–1820*, Chapel Hill, NC, and London.

Wiebe, R. H. (2002) *Who We Are: A History of Popular Nationalism*, Princeton, NJ, and Oxford.

Zelinsky, W. (1988) *Nation into State: The Shifting Symbolic Foundations of American Nationalism*, Chapel Hill, NC, and London.

CHAPTER 21

NATIONALISM IN EUROPE, 1918–45

OLIVER ZIMMER

One cannot live here. We must leave. We are going to Africa. It is our last trick in the bag.

Carlo Levi, *Cristo si è fermato a Eboli* (Turin: Einaudi, 2010 [1945], 25)

We have to inspire Romanians with hatred against the enemies of the nation. This is how I grew up, with hatred against the Turks, the kikes and the Hungarians.

General Antonescu (April 1941)

What drew people [to us]? The national idea*!*

Adolf Hitler (14 September 1930)

Introduction

Never has nationalism's destructive potential been more fully revealed than during the period encompassing the two World Wars. Equally, however, there is perhaps no other historical era that brings into sharper relief the limitations of employing a generalized concept of nationalism. This usage of nationalism—Nationalism with a 'capital N'—has often served as a pejorative label, sometimes to the extent where it becomes just another word for fascism. The frequency with which the word 'nationalism' is employed in this way in political debate testifies to the moral force the term acquired after 1945. Yet historians and social scientists should be more discriminating. What part nationalist ideology and practice have played in the ascendancy of European fascism, the unleashing of large-scale military conflict, and in the discrimination against, and persecution and murder of, ethnic minorities—these are questions that need analysing. They should not be taken as foregone conclusions.

This chapter discusses two phenomena that played a pivotal role in the history of interwar Europe. The first part looks at the nationalism practised by and within the so-called successor states of Romania, Poland, and Czechoslovakia, particularly towards the minority populations living in these states. This nationalism, which is the product of the territorial and demographic upheavals wrought by the war, partly reflects an attempt to counter the revisionist nationalism of the defeated states. The second, more extensive part, investigates the relationship between nationalism and fascism. I shall argue that pre-existing forms of nationalism, usually in radicalized form, could play a central role in fascist mobilization and the genesis of fascist movements.

The Nationalism of the Successor States

While the prevalent nationalist doctrines varied from one society to another, nationalists everywhere fostered cultural communities by supplying criteria for the definition of members as well as non-members. Whether they endorsed a more liberal, 'Western'-type of nationalism, where minorities are expected to assimilate to the culture of the majority, or a more exclusivist, 'organic' or 'integral' variety, where cultural assimilation is considered difficult or even impossible: each version presupposes a core group that is regarded as constitutive of the putative national community that nationalists claim to represent. In practice nationalists often combined these different elements. While drawing on established cultural traditions, their choices were in important ways shaped by the political and geopolitical contexts in which they had to operate.[1]

From the middle of the nineteenth century, nationalism began to change the ways in which minority populations and imperial states were perceived. It transformed, in the words of Rogers Brubaker, 'ethnic groups' with no claim to independent statehood into 'nationalities' that harboured such claims. When it comes to explaining the fate of minority populations during the interwar period, it is therefore useful to draw a distinction between 'ethnic' and 'national' minorities. Ethnic minorities did not possess a 'national homeland', as opposed to national minorities, whose members, at least theoretically, could migrate to, and expect protection from, their 'home' state. Examples of large national minorities in interwar Europe are the Hungarians in Romania and Czechoslovakia, the Germans in Poland and Czechoslovakia, and the Ukranians and Belarusians in Poland. The classic example of an ethnic minority in interwar Europe are the Jews, who, although they shared a sense of ethnocultural belonging, lived dispersed over several countries, including Poland, Russia, Germany, Hungary, Romania, and Czechoslovakia.[2]

The First World War and the destruction of the German, Austro-Hungarian, Ottoman, and Russian empires that it brought in its wake shifted the minority question to the centre of political attention. Numerous new states, built on the principle of national self-determination, dramatically increased the proportion of minorities in central and eastern Europe. Many of these states were as multi-ethnic or multinational as the empires they had succeeded. Of the approximately 35 million minority inhabitants in interwar Europe, only about one-quarter lived in western Europe. More than 25 million lived in central and eastern Europe.[3]

Most of the numerically dominant groups subscribed to a hegemonic brand of state-building nationalism that either showed little regard for minorities or (which was more common) even regarded them as a threat to the cultural coherence and territorial integrity of the nation state. In this nationalist vision, the state had to be identical with the culture of the dominant group, which was defined mainly in linguistic terms. This explains why all of the successor states, if to varying degrees, promoted cultural initiatives designed to spread the dominant cultural idiom.

These nationalist projects were fuelled, at least in part, by the irredentist nationalism of the defeated states. Thus the biggest benefactors of the post-war settlement—Poland, Czechoslovakia, and Romania—came immediately under pressure from those states—particularly Germany and Hungary, but also Russia—which sought to revise the territorial status quo. The armed clashes that followed the Armistice in 1918 and in some instances lasted until the early 1920s (among Poles, Ukrainians, and Russians in Galicia; between Germans and Poles in Upper Silesia; Romanians and Ukrainians in the Bukovina; and between the Hungarian Red Army and the troops of the new Czechoslovak Republic and of Romania) provided early manifestations of the vicious circle unleashed by geopolitical turmoil, the nationalism of the new states, and the revisionist ambitions of the states whose territory had been reduced. This 'generalised Central European civil war of the immediate post-war years' offered a foretaste of the 'barely controlled enmities of the interwar period'.[4]

Admittedly, there were attempts after the war to protect the rights of minorities. All in all, fourteen agreements regulating the treatment of national and ethnic minorities were concluded from 1919 to 1923 between the Allied and Associated Powers and the states that included substantial minority populations. These were Poland, Czechoslovakia, Yugoslavia, Romania, Greece, Austria, Hungary, Bulgaria, Turkey, Finland, Albania, Lithuania, Latvia, and Estonia.[5] However, apart from stateless minorities such as the Jews, most self-declared champions of minority rights were motivated by an ill-disguised revisionist agenda. This holds true in particular for the defeated states: Germany, which had lost Alsace-Lorraine, Poznania, Upper Silesia, and Northern Schleswig; Russia, which had lost Congress Poland; and Hungary, which had lost 70 per cent of its territory and 60 per cent of its population, mostly to Greater Romania. Weimar Germany under Foreign Minister Gustav Stresemann, for example, sought to prevent the loss of ethnic Germans living as minorities in Poland and Czechoslovakia as a result of either emigration or assimilation to the dominant culture of those states.

It was thus the fateful dialectic between the nationalizing policy of states such as Poland and Romania on the one hand, and the homeland nationalism of revisionist states like Germany and Hungary on the other, that created the vicious circle of nationalist resentment which became such a characteristic feature of the interwar period.

When it comes to understanding these dynamics, Poland offers a particularly instructive example. Throughout the 1920s Poles comprised some 69 per cent of the total population, with Ukrainians, Jews, Germans, Lithuanians, and Belorussians providing substantial minority populations. The Germans lived mainly in the western regions, while the Belorussians and Ukrainians were concentrated in the east. The Jews, although they lacked a clear regional concentration, played an important part in the urban economy. In terms of their occupational position, the Belorussians and Ukrainians were overwhelmingly agricultural, the Jews commercial and artisan, while the Germans were mixed.[6]

In spite of these substantial minority populations, however, the new Polish state was officially construed as the state of and for the ethnolinguistically defined Polish nation. Not only were the minorities excluded from the constitution-drafting process, the Constitution was also highly centralist and insisted on the need for minorities to assimilate. This applied especially to the German minority. The Polish government viewed the Germans as a 'fifth column' whose primary loyalty was to Germany. In line with this perception of the situation, from the mid-1920s onwards, the Polish authorities pursued a strategy of more or less open exclusion. The measures adopted included the Polonization of the civil service, the staging of anti-German demonstrations in the larger towns, the expropriation of German landlords, ethnic discrimination in business and the professions, and, increasingly, the implementation of strict monolingualism in public institutions, and particularly in primary education. Partly as a result of these measures, some two-thirds of the roughly 1.1 million ethnic Germans had left Poland by the mid-1920s, including 85 per cent of the urban population and 55 per cent of those employed in agriculture or related sectors. Those who remained in the ex-Prussian provinces of Poland well into the 1930s despite these discriminatory policies divided politically into Nazi supporters (the majority), bourgeois-nationalist, Catholic, and socialist groups.[7]

Similar tendencies can be observed in interwar Romania. Greater Romania was more than twice the size of the old kingdom that had existed since 1881. With a population of around 18 million in 1930, Romania had become the second most populous state in east-central Europe after Poland. It had acquired southern Dobrina (from Bulgaria), Bukovina (from Austria), Bessarabia (which had been under Russian rule since 1812), and Transylvania (part of historic Hungary). Ethnic Romanians constituted about 70 per cent of the population. The three largest of the minorities—Hungarians, Germans, and Jews—lived in the newly acquired provinces. In the Bukovina, for example, Ukrainians had formed a majority in 1910 (38.4 per cent), followed by Romanians (34.4 per cent), Jews (12 per cent), and Germans (9.3 per cent); and in the important province of Transylvania, Magyars supplied a substantial minority.[8]

However, in the official nationalist perspective the minority populations in the newly acquired territories—particularly Magyars and Jews—were perceived as 'foreigners'. Magyars in Romania can be compared to Germans in interwar Poland. As a former ruling group retaining their loyalty to 'Lesser Hungary', the approximately 1.6 million-strong Magyar population was seen as a constant threat to the stability of the Romanian nation state. Similar to the Jews, albeit for different reasons, they tended to be resented for the important role they played in the economy, the free professions and education in a country that even by eastern European standards was extremely backward. As in Poland, official Romanian nationalism manifested itself above all in the field of education. The number of primary schools and teachers more than doubled between 1918 and the end of the 1930s. In terms of educational content, there was an increased emphasis on the Romanian language, Romanian history, geography, and civics. Although Romania's official, secular nationalism was also directed against the strong regional identities of ethnic Romanians—most obviously in Transylvania, where the Orthodox and Uniate Churches provided alternative sources of identification to the secular state—its main concern was the Romanization of minority cultures. In the Bukovina, for example, the number of Romanian schools increased dramatically at the expense of Ukranian and German ones. The policy of Romanization was even more marked in newly acquired Transylvania, where Hungarians made up close to 30 per cent of the populations, with Germans (10.7 per cent) and Jews (3.5 per cent) also constituting significant minorities.[9]

Czechoslovakia, the most obviously manufactured of the successor states besides Yugoslavia, displays a slightly different pattern. As well as being the only functioning democracy in eastern Europe between the wars, Czechoslovakia was also the most industrialized and urbanized state in the region. The percentage of the population employed in the agricultural, industrial, and commercial sectors was respectively 39.5, 33.8, and 5.78 percent in 1921, and 34.6, 34.9, and 7.43 percent in 1930. Of course, there was considerable regional variation. Bohemia was Czechoslovakia's most advanced economic region, followed by Moravia-Silesia, while Slovakia (whose population had been subjected to Hungarian rule and its Magyarization policies since 1867) and Ruthenia remained heavily agricultural during the entire period.[10]

In ethnic terms, too, Czechoslovakia was highly diverse, which in the nationally charged climate of interwar Europe caused problems both domestically and with respect to foreign relations. The inclusion of substantial national minorities living along its borders—over 3 million ethnic Germans in the Sudentenland, 2.5 million Slovaks (although the Slovaks were not recognized as a minority in official censuses but rather amalgamated into the hybrid nationality of the 'Czecho-Slovaks'), 700,000 Hungarians in the south of Slovakia, 75,000 Poles in the economically important and fiercely contested region of Cieszyn in Silesia—meant that most of its neighbours harboured irredentist claims against Czechoslovakia from the moment its independence was proclaimed on 28 November 1918. Throughout the interwar period, relations with Hungary, Poland, and Germany remained marked by deep distrust and open hostility.[11]

Although the government's official stance towards the aspirations of national minorities was less repressive than that of its neighbours, the Czechs dominated the new state both politically and culturally. The 'Pittsburgh Agreement', signed in May 1918 between the leading Czech nationalist Tomás Masaryk and Slovak émigrés in the United States, in which the Slovaks (who at the end of the First World War constituted

16 per cent of the state's population, with Czechs making up 48 per cent) had been guaranteed autonomy within the future Czecho-Slovak state, was never implemented. Czech officials had a strong presence in Slovakia, regarding themselves as colonizers of a backward region. These measures often provoked the opposite of what their proponents had set out to achieve, however, and by the 1930s Slovak nationalism had developed into a recognizable force.[12]

But the fiercest conflict in interwar Czechoslovakia, one that would pose the most serious threat to the new state's existence, was the one between Czechs and Sudeten Germans. At the Paris peace negotiations, the Czechoslovak Foreign Minister Edvard Beneš declared his government's intention to create a Czechoslovak state on the Swiss federalist model, provided such a solution was commensurate with the conditions in the Czech and Slovak lands. In his much-noted speech before the National Assembly in Prague in December 1918, however, Masaryk chose a different tone. Reminding the Sudeten Germans that they had once come as immigrants and colonists, he insisted that the new Czechoslovak government would not allow them to challenge the state's territorial integrity. Masaryk's statement must be placed in the context of the events that had accompanied the declaration of Czechoslovak independence. After the republic had been proclaimed on 28 November 1918, the Sudeten Germans refused to accept its jurisdictional authority by declaring Deutschböhmen and the Sudetenland as independent provinces of Austria. When it became clear that neither Austria nor Germany was in a position to lend active support to these claims, the Czech Legion troops occupied these regions in December.[13]

Nationalism and Fascism

The gravest threat to the principles of democracy and cultural pluralism would emanate not from nationalism, however, but from the rise of fascism from the late 1920s onwards. Nationalism provided but one of several factors that proved conducive to fascist mobilization, though one that has rarely been explored systematically by students of either nationalism or fascism.

Much of the current scholarly debate about the origins of fascism centres on the question of whether the phenomenon is best explained by reference to cultural and ideological traditions, domestic politics and institutional breakdowns, geopolitical challenges, or economic crisis and class conflict. Cultural interpretations of fascism have tended to emphasize the role of established ideas and ideologies. These include political romanticism, direct democracy, corporatism, millenarianism, notions of national rebirth, as well as Social Darwinism and racism. To this are added elements that had grown out of the experience of the First World War, including masculine aestheticism, the glorification of youth, and the veneration of violence and war not as a means to an end but as an end in itself. The fact that fascist organizations worked with cultural idioms that were either well established or rooted in the personal experience of contemporaries goes some way to explaining, from this perspective, why their message found resonance in certain societies.[14]

The cultural approach to fascism has not remained unchallenged, however. In a powerful critique, Robert Paxton has argued that the causal link between doctrine and action—and more specifically between fascists' ideology and their ability to gain state power—is notoriously difficult to ascertain. Paxton has urged historians to concentrate instead on 'fascism in action' by examining the processes and contexts in which fascist movements took shape and developed. Fascist movements were most likely to gain power, Paxton tells us, where existing conservative elites were willing 'to work with the fascists' who offered their own solution to a crisis.[15] However, making little allowance for ideology creates its own problems, even for an explanation that concentrates on power and fascist agency. In particular, it makes it difficult to explain why coalitions between conservatives and fascists could be forged in the first place, and why certain fascist movements managed to capture the imagination of wider sections of a given population.

Could nationalism provide part of the answer? Not a few scholars seem to think that it does. Thus, according to Juan J. Linz, fascism is 'above all a nationalist movement', and the prominence of nationalism in a particular society therefore 'probably accounts for the relative strength of fascism more than any other variable'.[16] Geoff Eley links fascism to the emergence of 'radical nationalism' in the decades before the First World War, while Eugen Weber notes fascists' violent obsession with national unity.[17] George L. Mosse has described nationalism as a 'belief-system which provided the foundation for all fascist movements', while Michael Mann has termed it 'a distinctively paramilitary extreme version of nation-statism'.[18]

In spite of this seeming agreement on the centrality of nationalism, however, its specific links with fascism remain little understood. What seems beyond doubt is the crucial significance of the First World War. Without the severe political crisis of the interwar period, it is unlikely that the fascists would have crossed the threshold of power in Germany and Italy and enjoyed considerable success in Romania, Hungary, and a few other societies.[19] Not only did the First World War produce the kind of institutional instability on which political extremism of various kinds could grow, but the war itself was also the formative experience in the lives of many who would later join fascist movements and organizations, or even played a dominant part in their creation. Juan Linz estimates that 19 per cent of fascist leaders in interwar Europe had a military career background of some sort; many, including Adolf Hitler, had even served at the front.[20] What deserves even greater attention is geopolitics, or rather the relationship between shifting national boundaries, ethnonationalist campaigns in mixed-border areas, and the appeal of fascist movements promoting irredentist forms of nationalism. As Brubaker has written on these fateful dynamics: 'In interwar Europe, one of the most dangerous fault lines was that along which domestic nationalism of ethnically heterogeneous nationalizing states collided with the trans-border nationalism of neighbouring "homeland" states, oriented to co-ethnics living as minorities in the nationalizing states.'[21]

Brubaker's argument has been confirmed by the comparative accounts of fascism by Michael Mann and MacGregor Knox.[22] Significantly, however, both Mann and Knox have shown that the First World War did not produce nationalisms obsessed with domestic 'aliens' and 'co-ethnics' living outside a given nation state. Its effect, rather, was to radicalize established nationalist idioms. Both the acquisition of substantial minority populations (the Romanian scenario) or the contraction through the loss of both territory and perceived co-ethnics or *Volksgenossen* (the Hungarian and German scenarios) favoured this process of nationalist radicalization. It was in this context that fascist ideologues would draw on nationalist arguments to increase the internal coherence and external appeal of their movement. The remainder of this chapter tries to assess the validity of this argument using Germany, Hungary, Romania, and Italy as examples.[23]

Yet before turning to cases of successful fascist mass mobilization, let us look at two examples of stalled fascist movements: Switzerland and France. In Switzerland, the two conditions that proved conducive to fascist mobilization in Hungary, Romania, Germany, and Italy—a tradition of strong organic nationalism and geopolitical turmoil as a result of the First World War—were either weakly developed or absent. In France, organic nationalism had clearly been present at the intellectual level from the late nineteenth century, but it had on the whole been kept in check by a strong current of republican nationalism that was rooted in the country's institutions, particularly in elementary education. Besides, France saw its former territory restored after the First World War.

In Switzerland from the late 1920s, developments in Germany and Italy lent legitimacy to existing and encouraged novel forms of right-wing political mobilization. The ascendancy of the National Socialists in the early 1930s produced a mushrooming of political protest groups, most of them situated on the radical Right. The most successful were the *Nationale Front* and the *Neue Front*. Founded in 1930, the two movements fused in April 1933 to become the most popular fascist organization in Switzerland. Possessing strongholds in Zürich, Schaffhausen, Aargau, and St Gallen (with branches in Neuchâtel, Geneva, and Lausanne), the Nationale Front displayed the classic features of proto-fascist organization: it was committed to an anti-liberal, anti-democratic, anti-socialist, and anti-Semitic agenda, and called for a cultural and spiritual regeneration of the nation through a strong charismatic leader. A number of lower middle-class protest movements constituted the second current within the right-wing mobilization of the early 1930s.[24]

In 1934 these proto-fascist organizations, middle-class protest movements, as well as a few established conservative parties (including the Catholic Conservatives), joined forces in an attempt to reorganize Swiss society along corporatist lines. These aims found expression in a plebiscite for the total revision of the Swiss Constitution. Its demands included the abolition of proportional representation and the transfer of power from Parliament to professional organizations and the state executive. While the initiative's appeal clearly went beyond the fascist right to include the Young Liberals, the Catholic *Schweizerisch Konservative Volkspartei*, and the conservative *Liberale*

Partei der Schweiz, 72 per cent of those who went to the polls on 8 November 1935 opposed it. Although some of the radical protest movements survived this political defeat, it nonetheless marked a turning point. By the end of 1935, the right-wing movement for national regeneration had run out of steam, with its most radical exponents finding themselves increasingly isolated and stigmatized. The cooperation of the fascist right with members of the conservative political establishment, which Paxton sees as the key to fascism's success, had broken down.[25]

But the breakdown of the strategic cooperation between conservatives, radical nationalists, and proto-fascist organizations after their collective defeat in 1935 requires an explanation. To single out the strength of Switzerland's liberal and democratic traditions and institutions does not offer a sufficient explanation. The limited appeal of National Socialism was in important respects a consequence of the fact that the Nazi doctrine of the *Einheit von Volk und Rasse* posed a direct threat to Switzerland's territorial integrity as a polyethnic state. Ever since the foundation of the federal state in 1848, a distinctive Swiss nationalism had developed in explicit opposition to the ethnic nationalisms emanating from both Italy and Germany; the 1930s in particular saw the emergence of a distinctive brand of popular nationalism, one that centred on the concept of a distinctive Swiss *Volksgemeinschaft*, which was defined in cultural rather than ethnic, let alone racial, terms. This defensive nationalism partly explains the limited success of fascist groups at the ballot box.[26]

France provides a more prominent example of stalled fascism. Although fascism eventually failed in France, the country produced many of the movement's leading thinkers and witnessed the formation of several proto-fascist movements before the First World War. It was only in the second part of the 1920s that the fascist threat visibly receded, only to experience a revival of sorts during the German occupation from the summer of 1940. Its marked anti-Semitic policies notwithstanding, however, the Vichy government was a regime of right authoritarianism rather than fascism. Genuine French fascists and proto-fascists for the most part remained in the occupied north.[27]

Many of France's most influential proto-fascist writers emerged before the First World War. The Third Republic had been born out of defeat in the war against Prussian-led Germany in 1870, a defeat that resulted in the loss of Alsace-Lorraine. Paul Déroulède's League of Patriots (founded in 1882), the Boulangist movement of 1886–9, and the Action Française (founded in 1899) were all impregnated with a revolutionary nationalism and a rhetoric of national vengeance directed against Germany. Although in the wake of the French defeat at Sedan this revisionist nationalism cut across classes and political affiliations—a nationalism that had its powerful symbol in the 'lost province' of Alsace-Lorraine—its fiercest exponents were on the right. It is therefore hardly an accident that, apart from Paris, right-wing and proto-fascist candidates were particularly successful in France's eastern departments.[28]

During the Dreyfus affair (1898–1900) this radical and revisionist nationalism clashed head-on with bourgeois-democratic and socialist defenders of the Republic. Their defence of the republican order was not based on cosmopolitan rhetoric but drew inspiration from a nationalist idiom that had established itself in post-Revolutionary France. The French republican counter-nationalism of the late nineteenth century defined national belonging in voluntarist rather than organic terms and was uncompromising in its demand for assimilation as a precondition for civil rights.[29]

But the reference to political culture and institutions can only be part of an explanation of why right-wing movements were incapable of crossing the threshold to power in France. Geopolitical factors need also be considered. Thus, despite her defeat in 1870, France was spectacularly successful as an imperial power. Not that by 1900 the champions of French imperialism had become saturated and tame in their ambitions. But the Entente Cordiale (1903) put an end to the competition between France and Britain in Africa. More important still, France, albeit at an enormous loss of human life (1.35 million died and 3.5 million were wounded) was among the victors of the First World War; France saw her territory restored through the incorporation of Alsace and Lorraine. If we remind ourselves that the two provinces had been a focal point of radical nationalist mobilization for more than three decades, it seems plausible to assume that the outcome of the war helped reduce the potential for fascist-style mobilization in interwar France.[30]

In Germany, Hungary, Romania, and Italy fascist movements succeeded in mobilizing mass support. Success here is not defined in terms of fascist movements acquiring state power. Only in Germany and Italy were fascists truly successful in this respect, while in Hungary and Romania their position was more ambivalent and depended considerably on external support, or even active interference by a major fascist power. However, in both Hungary and Romania fascist movements were successful in mobilizing large sections of the public in national elections.

In Romania, organic nationalism, underpinned by a tradition of popular anti-Semitism, was well established in core Romania even before the First World War.[31] Although the country's nationalist imperialists welcomed the transition of the old kingdom into Greater Romania, this also created considerable problems in a society as poor and backward as interwar Romania. In particular, the acquisition of substantive minority populations clashed with the organic vision of a state dominated by ethnic Romanians. The Romanian authorities, eager to fight economic backwardness and catch up with the West, saw their ambitions undermined by the predominance of non-Romanians (Jews, Germans, and ethnic Hungarians) in important sectors of the economy, education, and cultural life more generally. Thus while Romania no doubt benefited from the peace settlement, the new multi-ethnic reality was widely seen as a threat to the nation's unity, integrity, and prosperity.

Unlike in late nineteenth-century France, however, where the radical and proto-fascist right was challenged and defeated by a republican nationalist movement, in Romania official and popular radical nationalism tended to feed off each other. The state sought to strengthen the position of ethnic Romanians among the middle classes, in the key public services, and in the economy. Given the prominent position of minorities in Romania's economic and cultural life, this project involved active discrimination against these groups. In the nationalist perspective, these were legitimate tactics in a struggle against the alleged domination of the Romanian people by 'foreigners'. The emancipation of the Jews, for example, supported before 1914 by King Carol and other members of the Romanian establishment, had no chance of success in Romania's Parliament. When Jews were finally granted equal rights in 1919 as a result of external pressure, this was seen as an act of interference in Romania's national affairs and caused considerable resentment.[32]

What kept nationalist resentments on the boil was the fact that the state's official nationalist mission was difficult to accomplish in practice. For one thing, Romanian state nationalism triggered irredentist counter-nationalisms from the revisionist states, particularly Hungary, targeting the national minorities that had fallen under Romanian control. Romanian dominance was impossible where minority populations dominated important sections of the economy. The inevitable setbacks and failures only served to reinforce existing nationalist resentment. Fascists like Alexandru Cuza and Corneliu Codreanu began to liken Romania to a potentially healthy body that had been infected by foreign mores and customs, selecting the Jews as their prime scapegoats.[33]

Once accepted as the new common sense, this nationalism lowered the threshold for violent action against the declared 'enemies'. Codreanu was acquitted of murdering the Jassy police prefect in 1924, as were many of those who had organized and taken part in riots against Jews. The trials, as well as the conspicuous lack of intervention by local police, suggests that fascists who used violence against Jews enjoyed wide support. From the mid-1920s, it seems, the radical nationalists around the League of National Christian Defence and the later Legion of the Archangel Michael, or Iron Guard, rather than the ruling National Liberals, were calling the shots in the provinces. The power struggle between King Carol II and the Iron Guard in the late 1930s provides testimony of the appeal that fascists had come to enjoy by the outbreak of the Second World War. For although General Antonescu turned decisively against the Iron Guard as that movement threatened to get out of control in the autumn/winter of 1940, the regime he established in January 1941 was still a 'fascist military dictatorship'.[34]

Hungary presents us with the virtual inversion of the Romanian scenario. If the states of Czechoslovakia and Poland were created after the First World War, and Romania emerged from it much enlarged, Hungary was the biggest loser in the peace settlement apart from Germany. Whereas the Compromise of 1867 had elevated Hungary to the status of the second partner within a large multinational empire, defeat in the war relegated her to a small nation state. As a result of the Treaty of Trianon (4 June 1920), three-fifths of Hungary's population, including 28 per cent of the Hungarian speakers, were 'lost' to other states. While pre-war Hungary had had a population of close to 21 million, post-Trianon Hungary contained just 7.5 million people. Over 3 million ethnic Hungarians had been transferred to neighbouring states, including Romania, Czechoslovakia, and what would later be called Yugoslavia. Transylvanian Hungarians in Romania emerged as the largest national minority in Europe. In economic terms, too, the loss was devastating: Hungary lost 58 per cent of her railroad lines, 60 per cent of her road mileage, 84 per cent of her timber resources, and 83 per cent of her iron ore.[35]

The psychological effects of the peace settlements on Hungary were profound. As well as standing for national humiliation, Trianon became a hated symbol of defeat and the focal point of a revisionist nationalism that was popular and state-sponsored. Hungarian schoolchildren were brought up reciting the revisionist slogan 'No, no, never' during the entire interwar period. The rise of Hungarism, a doctrine demanding the creation of a Greater Hungary, was perhaps the inevitable consequence of this experience of collective humiliation. In 1928 Count Kunó Klebelsberg insisted that Trianon had rendered obsolete the traditional aim of Hungarian nationalism. Hungarians, Klebelsberg suggested, should 'find new aims for old feelings' by striving to become culturally and economically superior to their neighbours. They should, so he continued, endeavour to become 'a racially more important nation' than the people living around them.[36] Even though Klebelsberg did not openly advocate a revisionist policy, his argument implied precisely that. How else was rump Hungary to accomplish the regional hegemony that he envisaged for her?

Yet in Hungary too, right-wing nationalists and fascists could build on the central premise of the policy of Magyarization that had been government policy between 1880 and 1914: that the Hungarian state was the property of the ethnic Hungarians and that Hungary was one and indivisible.[37] Given the new situation of post-Trianon Hungary, this nationalism was transformed in two directions. First, and reflecting the fact that interwar Hungary had become much more homogenous in ethnic terms, the Jews became the preferred domestic target of radical nationalist agitation. Second, given the fact that millions of ethnic Hungarians had come under 'foreign rule'—above all in Greater Romania and in the newly created Czechoslovakia—organic Hungarian nationalism became expansionist and aggressive. This new nationalism proved conducive to the rise of Hungarian fascism, which had its most powerful champion in the Arrow Cross.[38] Based on an agenda of anti-capitalism, anti-socialism, anti-Semitism, and racism, the Arrow Cross recruited its leadership above all from army officers and civil servants. By the end of 1938 the movement, no doubt benefiting from German financial assistance and encouraged by the success of Nazi foreign policy (the *Anschluss* of Austria was immediately followed by the occupation of Czechoslovakia), had become a real political force with a membership of approximately three hundred thousand. It derived its main support from students, unskilled workers, and sections of the industrial proletariat, the lower middle classes of the towns and villages, and from agricultural labourers. In the 1939 parliamentary elections the movement received a quarter of the vote polled nationally, which was double the socialist vote and relatively close to the vote of the Government Party.[39]

To be sure, Hungarian fascism's success at the regime level was short-lived. The Government Party remained in office until 1944, by which time the Arrow Cross was divided and in serious decline. It was only German interference that allowed it a brief tenure of power in 1944 because Hitler felt that Miklós Horthy, Regent of Hungary, had betrayed him and installed the Arrow Cross in office. Even so, the electoral appeal of fascism in Hungary was considerable throughout the 1930s. It was also closely linked to a revisionist nationalism that proved highly popular. Hungarian nationalists felt an elective affinity with the revisionist powers of Italy and Germany that went beyond strategic considerations. Hungary's leadership concluded treaties with Benito Mussolini's fascist Italy in 1927, followed by an agreement with Nazi Germany in the summer of 1933. In 1935, moreover, the Hungarian prime minister Gyula Gömbös signed a secret agreement with the leading Nazi Hermann Goering in which he promised to establish in Hungary a political system modelled on the Third Reich. After the *Anschluss* in 1938, Hungary introduced anti-Semitic laws along National Socialist lines, although the Government Party was extremely reluctant to implement them in spite of considerable German pressure. It was only in March 1944, when Germany established a puppet government of the extreme right in Hungary, that the concentration of Jews in ghettos and camps occurred that prepared the ground for their systematic deportation to Nazi extermination camps. The return of southern Slovakia and Ruthenia in 1938 (then part of Czechoslovakia) and part of Transylvania in 1940 (then part of Romania) was the reward for Hungary's alliance with the Axis powers. But these gains would be eradicated when the German offensive in the East came to a halt and the offensive of the Red Army began in 1943.[40]

In interwar Germany, the success of National Socialism in the election on 5 March 1933 dealt the final blow to the besieged Weimar Republic. But even in this most prominent of fascist takeovers there was continuity amidst the discontinuity. The outcome of the First World War and the consequences of defeat no doubt radicalized established nationalist ideologies. These events did not produce these ideologies ex nihilo.

The debate and practice surrounding German national citizenship is revealing in this respect.[41] A conspicuous shift occurred after German unification. From the 1880s, naturalization was increasingly denied on ethnic grounds. In 1885 the Prussian Minister of the Interior, Robert von Puttkammer, introduced a new law, along with a series of other legislative changes concerning the minorities in eastern Prussia, that was clearly directed against Poles and Polish Jews. The law helped to ensure that applications to citizenship, especially by Jews from eastern Europe, had virtually no chance of success. While Prussia was leading the way in this respect, from the 1890s the Prussian practice was being adopted by other states within the second German Empire. The introduction of *jus sanguinis* at national level in the *Reichs- und Staatsangehörigkeitsgesetz* of 1913 found the support of all the major political parties except the Social Democrats and the Progressives who favoured a qualified version of *jus soli* along French lines. Speaking in the Reichstag before the final vote took place, the conservative delegate Ernst Giese expressed his satisfaction about the legislation thus: 'We welcome the fact that... ethnic descent and affiliation of blood form the guiding principles when it comes to granting citizenship rights. This principle is best suited to maintaining and conserving the German *völkisch* character.'[42]

Recent research on popular associations in the late nineteenth century suggests such an organic understanding of nationhood was neither confined to the political class nor the conservative fringes of society. The German choral societies, for example, explicitly emphasized that the German *Volk* reached beyond the territorial borders of the nation state. The choral societies, too, were very concerned with the question of Germans living abroad. The Austrian, the Sudeten German, even the Swiss choral societies, received invitations to take part in the annual festival because the organizers saw them as part of one German *Volk*. The evidence suggesting that irredentism began to permeate the German folk song movement several decades before the outbreak of the First World War is overwhelming. A recent study of German gymnast societies identifies a shift towards an ethnic conception of German nationhood, manifesting itself in a preoccupation with Austria, which occurred after the small-German unification of 1871. The result was an increasingly common differentiation between 'nation' and *Volk:* While the former concept was associated with the newly created nation state, the latter stood for a community of German co-ethnics that transcended state boundaries.[43]

This understanding of nationhood was politicized and radicalized around the turn of the nineteenth century. Geoff Eley distinguishes two phases in the formation of a radical nationalism before the First World War. In a first phase, stretching roughly from 1890 to 1908, we witness the genesis of a 'dissident and largely anti-parliamentary radical nationalist public'. The nationalism underpinning this movement showed a strong concern with the fate of ethnic Germans abroad—with the German national minorities in Austria, in Bohemia, in the Baltic, and in Hungary—who were portrayed as under threat. This portrayal of the fate of German minorities served as the justification for the larger demand to consolidate the entire German *Volk* within a Greater Germany yet to be created. Among the nationalist pressure groups promoting this agenda were the Pan-German League (1891), the Society for the Eastern Marches (1894), the Navy League (1898), the Imperial League against Social Democracy (1904), and the Army League (1912). Although most of these movements remained relatively small in terms of their membership, some managed to attract a considerable following. The Navy League, for example, had a total membership of 331,000 on the eve of the First World War, and its links with government secured it a degree of influence that was not reflected in its size.[44]

After the outbreak of the First World War, this radical right was reintegrated into the 'right-wing mainstream', which after the Second Moroccan Crisis (1911) adopted an increasingly expansionist and imperialist orientation. According to Eley, during the radicalization that occurred between 1912 and 1920, 'the Pan-German panacea—the idea of a unified race-people mobilized for battle with internal and external foes, obliterating the divisiveness of class-sectional, particularist and confessional loyalties via the fanatical pursuit of German aggrandizement—entered the discourse of the right as a whole'. The outbreak of the war offered an opportunity to put this programme into practice, particularly after the initial victories in the East, only to be frustrated by the final defeat in 1918. The profound sociopolitical turmoil that followed—embodied in the Kaiser's abdication, the revolutionary threat, the gains of the left in national elections, and the extensive territorial losses—meant that, for large sections of the German public, the Pan-German and radical nationalists seemed to offer a more appealing political vision than the traditional Conservatives.[45]

Whereas up to 1918 the imperial authorities had managed to contain 'homeland nationalism', after the First World War, as millions of Germans became members of national minorities and found themselves exposed to the nationalizing pressures of the successor states—the Baltic German Ewald Ammende estimated the number of ethnic German living outside the German state at approximately 9 million—this proved increasingly difficult. Thus one of the reasons why the Weimar Republic lacked legitimacy in the eyes of many Germans was its association with a weakened German nation state allegedly incapable of protecting the German *Volk*. Both Austrians and the majority of Germans desired the *Anschluss* of Austria to Germany after the war. The Weimar National Assembly voted unanimously in favour of incorporating the Austrians into the German *Reich*. The French government, fearful of an enlarged and invigorated Germany, prevented this from happening. The German government had no alternative but to comply, adding yet more fuel to German nationalist resentment. It also favoured the proliferation of new pressure groups devoted to an expansionist nationalist agenda during the Weimer period. These included the Association of Germandom Abroad (2 million members), the German Protective League for Border and Foreign Germandom, the Organization of German Ethnonational Groups in Europe, as well as various youth and church associations advocating the same cause.[46]

A flood of literature on the subject of *Ostforschung* (research on the East) was published at academic and pseudo-academic levels. All these groups and individuals regarded the German national minorities abroad as ethnic frontier groups whose resettlement was to be opposed and prevented at all cost. But even where this failed it was not necessarily detrimental to the revisionist cause. Resettlers from Poland played a key role in the *Deutschtumspolitik* of the Weimar era and supplied an important contingent of Nazi supporters. To some extent, this also applies to resettlers from the Baltic states, the Sudetenland, and the formerly Russian and Austro-Hungarian territories. Following the *Anschluss* of Austria in 1938, most Habsburg officers served Nazi Germany, and 'more than 300 former Habsburg career officers reached the rank of general in the Wehrmacht or the Waffen SS'.[47]

In an important sense, then, the National Socialists were the true beneficiaries of Weimar homeland nationalism, a nationalism they had actively promoted ever since their organization had been founded. As Brubaker has argued, they appropriated its *völkisch* idioms and its notion of *Lebensraum*, its network of official and semi-official agencies and organizations. The Nazis also used the staunchest advocates of such nationalist convictions among the German frontier groups to destroy the Polish and Czechoslovak states. The German ambassador in Czechoslovakia estimated that by the end of 1933 about 2 million of the 3 million Sudeten Germans were Nazi sympathizers.[48]

Domestically, too, there is reason to assume that the Nazis' expansive nationalist rhetoric paid some political dividends, particularly in borderland areas. Thus a glance at the ten districts most supportive of the National Socialists in the Reichstag elections between 1930 and 1933 reveals that more than half represented such geographic areas. Districts like East Prussia, Pomerania, Schleswig-Holstein, Chemitz Zwickau, and Frankfurt Oder were consistently among the National Socialists' strongest backers.

Even within predominantly Catholic regions, which normally tended to favour the Catholic Centre Party over the National Socialists, the border districts reveal a certain degree of deviation from this pattern. The two districts of Breslau and Liegnitz, for example, located in the predominantly Catholic yet industrialized region of Silesia with its legacy of anti-Polish agitation, displayed much stronger support for the Nazis than other Catholic regions. The same applies to the denominationally mixed Palatinate, which experienced a wave of nationalist revival in the 1920s in the wake of the French occupation of the Ruhr.[49]

What about Italy, where in 1922 the fascists joined the government and, a mere three years later, succeeded in establishing a dictatorship? The Italian peninsula, which in Mussolini produced the first important fascist leader and inaugurated fascism as a mass movement, seems to contradict the argument that the path to fascism often led via a radicalized brand of homeland nationalism. Italy, one might argue, was among the victors of the First World War, its territorial boundaries were not contested, and the number of Italians living outside Italy was relatively small. One might therefore assume that expansionist nationalism must have played a rather marginal role in the emergence of Italian fascism as a movement, let alone its installation at regime level. Other factors—the divisive debates of the liberal era, uneven development, and the socio-economic hardship and grievances they produce, political instability—were much more important.

There is indeed much to be said for an explanation that centres on the crisis of social order and political system in the period 1918–21. Italy's entry into the First World War at the side of the Entente in 1915 had itself been extremely controversial, prompting mass demonstrations and open conflict between supporters and opponents of the war effort. At the political level, Italy's transition from liberal parliamentarianism to full democracy (a significant extension of the male suffrage occurred in 1918, followed, in 1919, by the introduction of proportional representation) was both sudden and conflict-ridden, resulting in deep divisions within political liberalism. The traditionally dominant liberal and democratic parties emerged as the big losers from the election of 16 November 1919, while the Catholic PPI and the socialist PSI made big gains. Northern and southern Italy, the traditional strongholds of Risorgimento liberalism, had been captured by socialist and Catholic mass parties. As political liberalism was declining, the potential for (violent forms of) mass mobilization was increasing: the protracted demobilization of Italy's 4 million-strong army from November 1918 coincided with a period of political radicalization that affected both the towns and the agricultural areas. The latter in particular experienced an intense and often violent class struggle between rural workers and landlords. It was in this climate that fascist paramilitaries began to assume the mantle of defenders of social order in their fierce and increasingly well-organized struggle against radical socialists. Following the strikes of 1918–19, fascist gangs succeeded in portraying themselves as the most potent weapon against a left-wing revolution, despite the fact that Prime Minister Giovanni Giolitti, by refusing to use the army against socialist radicals, had done most to alleviate the situation by November 1920.[50]

But while social and political instability in the immediate aftermath of the war was a precondition for the fascists' ability to conquer state power, revisionist nationalism did play an important role as well. It did so because its essential message of territorial expansion resonated with a sizeable section of the Italian public. What added credence and mobilizing drive to this kind of nationalism was the fact that Italy's liberal regime proved unable to satisfy existing expectations of territorial aggrandizement after the war had ended; that the benefits Italy was able to reap by ending the war on the winning side were much less extensive than many Italians—irrespective of whether they sympathized with right-wing radicalism or subscribed to the established creed of liberal nationalism—had hoped. The 'compendium of united Italy's great-power fantasy',[51] agreed between leading politicians and the army and navy before Italy's entering the war in 1915, was equally voluminous: the Brenner frontier; Dalmatia and Fiume; several mandates and colonies in Africa and Asia Minor; a protectorate over Albania; control over the Adriatic through the demilitarization of Yugoslavia's remaining coastline. But at Paris the British and French made it quite clear that they did not think Italy's contribution to the war effort justified such excessive rewards. Besides, President Woodrow Wilson's support for national self-determination, while buttressing the national aspirations of the Yugoslavs, dealt a further blow to Italy's most immediate territorial ambitions in the Adriatic. Thus when in June 1919 Italy's prime minister Vittorio Orlando had to admit before Parliament that Italian hopes had been dashed, many Italians saw this as a national defeat. The result was a widespread perception that future revenge would be justified, certainly as far as Italy's more immediate concerns in the Adriatic were concerned.

There is some evidence that the support for Mussolini's fascist movement, founded in March 1919, was particularly strong in Italy's border regions of Trieste and the South Tyrol. While Italy was composed of seventy-one provinces, these two provinces supplied 20 per cent of fascist members in 1921.[52] These were also the two regions in which fascists supported ethnic politics and violence against minorities.[53] There at least, it seems, an organic nationalism preoccupied with foreign policy and imperialist revisionism fell on fertile soil. As Michael Mann has emphasized, Mussolini and other fascists kept insisting that Italy should expect a fairer deal from Britain and France. While it is difficult to establish which sections of the Italian public were particularly receptive to this kind of rhetoric, it is clear that 'fascism attained easily its highest recruitment rates in the northern border provinces'. But, beyond that, there is also evidence to suggest that Italy's educated classes supported an expanding agenda that challenged the post-war agreement.[54] An even stronger case for the centrality of nationalist revisionism has been made by MacGregor Knox, who has argued that the myth of Italy's incompleteness as a powerful nation state—'Italy's unfulfilled great-power destiny'—had been 'well established by 1890'. The only shortcut to realizing these ambitions of national grandeur was war, which the fascists, in the post-1918 climate, were ready to contemplate.[55]

Conclusion

Interwar Europe, and particularly its central and eastern regions, witnessed a clash between the nationalizing nationalisms of states such as Poland, Romania, and Czechoslovakia, and the homeland nationalism of defeated states like Hungary and Germany. The so-called successor states interpreted the Wilsonian principle of national self-determination as the right of the dominant nationality to impose its culture on the minority populations living within a particular state territory. While this fateful dynamic could build on pre-war traditions of organic and expansionist nationalism, it was the radicalization they experienced after 1918 in a number of societies—above all Germany and Italy, but also Hungary and Romania—that rendered them a powerful device for fascist mobilization. For the leaders and supporters of fascist regimes, open threats and expansionist warfare were equally legitimate means to realize revisionist and expansionist goals. It is worth recalling, for example, that the first states to be annexed by Nazi Germany—Czechoslovakia, Austria, Poland, and France—had been explicit targets of German homeland nationalism ever since the peace treaties had been signed.

Notes

1. M. Mann (2004) *Fascists*, New York, 2. See also R. Brubaker (2004) *Ethnicity without Groups*, Cambridge, MA, 24. See also O. Zimmer (2003) 'Boundary Mechanisms and Symbolic Resources: Towards a Process-Oriented Approach to National Identity', *Nations and Nationalism*, 9, no. 2 (April), 173–93.
2. R. Brubaker (1996) *Nationalism Reframed: Nationhood and the National Question in the New Europe*, Cambridge, 3.
3. M. Mazower (1998) *Dark Continent: Europe's Twentieth Century*, Harmondsworth, 55–6.
4. I. Deák (1997) 'The Habsburg Empire', in K. Barkey and M. von Hagen (eds.) *After Empire: Multiechnic Societies and Nation-Building: The Soviet Union and the Russian, Ottoman, and Habsburg Empires*, Boulder, CO, and Oxford, 132–3.
5. C. Fink (1972) 'Defender of Minorities: Germany in the League of Nations, 1926–1933', *Central European History*, 4, 330–2.
6. J. Rothschild (1974) *East Central Europe between the Two World Wars*, Seattle, WA, and London, 35–8; R. Pearson (1983) *National Minorities in Eastern Europe, 1848–1945*, Basingstoke, 160–6.
7. Brubaker, *Nationalism Reframed*, ch. 4; Rothschild, *East Central Europe*, 34, 41–2.
8. I. Livezeanu (1995) *Cultural Politics in Greater Romania: Regionalism, Nation Building, & Ethnic Struggle, 1918–1930*, Ithaca, NY, 49.
9. Livezeanu, *Cultural Politics*, 35, 135, 143.
10. Rothschild, *East Central Europe*, 91–2, 117–18; P. Wandycz (1992) *The Price of Freedom: A History of East Central Europe from the Middle Ages to the Present*, London, 171–2.
11. Rothschild, *East Central Europe*, 78, 85–7; Deák, 'The Habsburg Empire', 132–4.

12. Pearson, *National Minorities*, 149–54.
13. Rothschild, *East Central Europe*, 79; Pearson, *National Minorities*, 151–3.
14. G. L. Mosse (1999) *The Fascist Revolution: Toward a General Theory of Fascism*, New York; Z. Sternhell (1994) *The Birth of Fascist Ideology*, Princeton, NJ; R. Griffin (2002) 'The Primacy of Culture: The Current Growth (or Manufacture) of Consensus within Fascist Studies', *Journal of Contemporary History*, 37, no. 3, 21–43.
15. R. O. Paxton (2004) *The Anatomy of Fascism*, London, and (1998) 'Five Stages of Fascism', *Journal of Modern History*, vol. 70, 1–23.
16. J. J. Linz, 'Some Notes Toward a Comparative Study of Fascism in Sociological Historical Perspective', in W. Laquer (ed.) (1976) *Fascism: A Reader's Guide*, New York, 15.
17. G. Eley (1986) *From Unification to Nazism: Reinterpreting the German Past*, Boston, MA, and London, 266; E. Weber (1991) *My France: Politics, Culture, Myth*, Cambridge, MA, 274.
18. Mosse, *The Fascist Revolution*, 158; Mann, *Fascists*, 2.
19. See, for example, G. Eley (1990) 'Conservatives and Radical Nationalists in Germany: The Production of Fascist Potentials, 1912–28', in M. Blinkhorn (ed.) *Fascists and Conservatives: The Radical Right and the Establishment of Twentieth-Century Europe*, London, 50–70; S. Payne (1995) *A History of Fascism, 1914–1945*, London, 71–9.
20. Linz, 'Some Notes Toward a Comparative Study of Fascism', 55. On the role of the front soldier in fascist mythology and politics, see G. L. Mosse (1990) *Fallen Soldiers: Reshaping the Memory of the World Wars*, Oxford.
21. Brubaker, *Nationalism Reframed*, 107.
22. Mann, *Fascists*, ch. 1; M. Knox (2007) *The Origins and Dynamics of the Fascist and National Socialist Dictatorships, vol. I: To the Threshold of Power, 1922/33*, New York, Introduction.
23. An earlier formulation of the argument can be found in O. Zimmer (2003) *Nationalism in Europe 1890–1940*, Basingstoke, ch. 4; see also A. A. Kallis (2003) 'To Expand or not to Expand? Territory, Generic Fascism and the Quest for an "Ideal Fatherland"', *Journal of Contemporary History*, 38, no. 2, 237–60.
24. P. Gilg and E. Gruner (1996) 'Nationale Erneuerungsbewegungen in der Schweiz, 1925–1940', *Vierteljahreshefte für Zeitgeschichte*, 14, 1–25. P. Gilg and E. Gruner, *Nationale Erneuerungsbewegungen*. B. Glaus (1969) *Die Nationale Front: Eine Schweizer Faschistische Bewegung, 1930–1940*, Zürich, 71, 359.
25. O. Sigg, *Die eidgenössischen Volksinitiativen, 1892–1939*; O. Zimmer (2004) '"A Unique Fusion of the Natural and the Man-Made": The Trajectory of Swiss Nationalism, 1933–1939', *Journal of Contemporary History*, 39, no. 1, 5–24.
26. O. Zimmer (2003) *A Contested Nation: History, Memory and Nationalism in Switzerland, 1761–1891*, Cambridge, chs. 4–5; Zimmer, *A Unique Fusion*.
27. Payne, *A History of Fascism*, 398–9.
28. Weber, *My France*, ch. 9.
29. R. Brubaker (1992) *Citizenship and Nationhood in France and Germany*, Cambridge, MA, 85–6.
30. Payne, *A History of Fascism*, 41–8.
31. S. Fischer-Galati, 'Fascism in Romania', in P. F. Sugar (ed.) (1971) *Native Fascism in the Successor States, 1918–1945*, Santa Barbara, CA, 114. Mann, *Fascists*, 261–96.

32. Livezeanu in Blinkhorn, *Fascists and Conservatives*, 219–22; E. Turczynski (1971) 'The Background of Romanian Fascism', in P. F. Sugar (ed.) *Native Fascism in the Successor States*, 105.
33. Livezeanu in Blinkhorn, *Fascists and Conservatives*, 223; Mann, *Fascists*, 272–81.
34. Fischer-Galati, *Fascism in Romania*, 119.
35. Rothschild, *East Central Europe*, 156.
36. Cited in Frank in P. F. Sugar (ed.) (1995) *Eastern European Nationalism in the 20th Century*, Washington, DC, 209–10.
37. Ibid., 223. See also E. Loránd (2003) '"The Magyars: A Ruling Race": The Idea of National Superiority in Fin-de-Siècle Hungary', *European Review of History*, 10, no. 2, 5–33.
38. Rothschild, *East Central Europe*, 171–7.
39. Lacko in S. U. Larsen, B. Hagtvet, and J. P. Myklebust (eds.) (1980) *Who were the Fascists? Social Roots of European Fascism*, Oslo and Bergen, 395. Rothschild, *East Central Europe*, 180–2; Lackon in Larsen et al., *Who were the Fascists*, 395–7; Ranki in Larsen et al., *Who were the Fascists.*
40. Tilkovszky in P. F. Sugar (ed.) (1990) *A History of Hungary*, Bloomington, IN; Frank in Sugar, *Eastern European Nationalism*, 230; Rothschild, *East Central Europe*, 179, 183–4.
41. See D. Gosewinkel (2001) *Einbürgern und Ausschliessen: Die Nationalisierung der Staatsangehörigkeit vom Deutschen Bund bis zur Bundesrepublik Deutschland*, Göttingen; A. K. Fahrmeier (1997) 'Nineteenth-Century German Citizenships: A Reconsideration', *Historical Journal*, 40, no. 3, 721–52.
42. Cited in W. J. Mommsen (1996) 'Nationalität im Zeichen offensiver Weltpolitik: Das Reichs- und Staatsangehörigkeitsgesetz des Deutschen Reiches vom 22. Juni 1913', in M. Hettling and P. Nolte (eds.) *Nation und Gesellschaft in Deutschland: Historische Essays*, Munich, 134.
43. G. L. Mosse (1991) *The Nationalization of the Masses: Political Symbolism and Mass Movements in Germany from the Napoleonic Wars through the Third Reich*, new edn., Ithaca, NY, 143; S. Goltermann (1998) *Körper der Nation: Habitusformierung und die Politik des Turnens, 1860–1890*, Göttingen, 222–4. The aggressive and expansionist tendencies within German middle-class nationalism are also stressed by H.-U. Wehler (2003) *Deutsche Gesellschaftsgeschichete. Vierter Band: 1914–1949*, Munich, 18–21, 548–50.
44. Eley, 'Conservatives and Radical Nationalists'; Wehler, *Deutsche Gesellschaftsgeschichte*, 543–5; J. Retallack (2006) *The German Right 1860–1920: The Political Limits of the Authoritarian Imagination*, Toronto.
45. Eley, *Conservatives and Radical Nationalists*, 61, 64–5; Wehler, *Deutsche Gesellschaftsgeschichte*, 545–6.
46. M. Housden (2000) 'Ewald Ammende and the Organization of National Minorities in Inter-war Europe', *German History*, 18, no. 4, 448; M. John (1999) '"We Do Not Even Possess Our Selves": On Identity and Ethnicity in Austria, 1880–1937', *Austrian History Yearbook*, 30, 61–2. Brubaker, *Nationalism Reframed*, 119.
47. Deák, 'The Habsburg Empire', 134. Brubaker, *Nationalism Reframed*, 117–36.
48. M. Kitchen (1988) *Europe between the Wars: A Political History*, London, 128–9.
49. For detailed statistics and comments on these elections, see J. Noakes and G. Pridham (eds.) (1983) *Nazism, 1919–1945: A Documentary Reader*, Exeter, 4 vols., 1, 83. Nazi support was particularly strong in areas that were both Protestant and located in 'threatened border' areas. See Mann, *Fascists*, 189.
50. Mann, *Fascists*, 119–26; Knox, *Origins and Dynamics*, 247–53, 268–81.

51. Knox, *Origins and Dynamics*, 241–3.
52. Renzo de Felice (1977) *Interpretations of Fascism*, Cambridge, MA, 8; Linz, 'Some Notes', 82–4.
53. Mann, *Fascists*, 106–7.
54. Mann, *Fascists*, 131.
55. Knox, *Origins and Dynamics*, 110–12.

Suggested Further Reading

Blinkhorn, M. (ed.) (1990) *Fascists and Conservatives: The Radical Right and the Establishment of Twentieth-Century Europe*, London.
Bosworth, R. J. B. (1998) *The Italian Dictatorship: Problems and Perspectives in the Interpretation of Mussolini and Fascism*, London, ch. 4.
Brubaker, R. (1992) *Citizenship and Nationhood in France and Germany*, Cambridge, MA.
Brubaker, R. (1996) *Nationalism Reframed: Nationhood and the National Question in the New Europe*, Cambridge.
Brubaker, R. (2004) *Ethnicity without Groups*, Cambridge, MA.
Eley, G. (1986) *From Unification to Nazism: Reinterpreting the German Past*, Boston, MA, and London.
Griffin, R. (1998) *International Fascism: Theories, Causes and the New Consensus*, London.
Knox, M. (2007) *Origins and Dynamics of the Fascist and National Socialist Dictatorships, vol. I: To the Threshold of Power, 1922/33*, New York.
Laquer, W. (ed.) (1996) *Fascism: A Reader's Guide*, New York.
Larsen, S. U., Hagtvet, B., and Myklebust, J. P. (eds.) (1980) *Who Were the Fascists? Social Roots of European Fascism*, Oslo and Bergen.
Livezeanu, I. (1995) *Cultural Politics in Greater Romania: Regionalism, Nation Building, and Ethnic Struggle, 1918–1930*, Ithaca, NY.
Mann, M. (2004) *Fascists*, Cambridge.
Mazower, M. (1998) *Dark Continent: Europe's Twentieth Century*, Harmondsworth.
Mosse, G. L. (1991) *The Nationalization of the Masses: Political Symbolism and Mass Movements in Germany from the Napoleonic Wars through the Third Reich*, new edn., Ithaca, NY.
Mosse, G. L. (1999) *The Fascist Revolution: Toward a General Theory of Fascism*, New York.
Paxton, R. O. (2004) *The Anatomy of Fascism*, London.
Payne, S. (1995) *A History of Fascism, 1914–1945*, London.
Pearson, R. (1983) *National Minorities in Eastern Europe, 1848–1945*, Basingstoke.
Rothschild, J. (1974) *East Central Europe between the Two World Wars*, Seattle, WA, and London.
Sternhell, Z. (1994) *The Birth of Fascist Ideology*, Princeton, NJ.
Sugar, P. F. (ed.) (1971) *Native Fascism in the Successor States, 1918–1945*, Santa Barbara, CA.
Sugar, P. F. (ed.) (1990) *A History of Hungary*, Bloomington, IN.
Sugar, P. F. (ed.) (1995) *Eastern European Nationalism in the 20th Century*, Washington, DC.
Von Hagen, M. (ed.) (1997) *After Empire: Multiethnic Societies and Nation-Building: The Soviet Union and the Russian, Ottoman, and Habsburg Empires*, Boulder, CO, and Oxford.
Zimmer, O. (2003) *Nationalism in Europe, 1890–1940*, Basingstoke.

CHAPTER 22

NATIONALISM IN THE ARAB WORLD SINCE 1945

FRED HALLIDAY†

Introduction: Ideological Turmoil, State Endurance

In the half-century and more since the end of World War II, the Arab world has gone through multiple upheavals and changes, some born of conflicts and events within the region, some as a result of those global processes—the end of European colonialism, Cold War, globalization—that have affected its component states as much as the rest of the world. In regard to nationalism, its associated ideologies and political movements, the record is two-sided. On the one hand, there has been a rapid shift from one form of nationalist orientation to another, liberal ideas in the 1940s being displaced by radical socialist and revolutionary pan-Arab perspectives in the 1950s and 1960s, these themselves gradually yielding to nationalisms characterized more and more by reference to Islam, and defined in relation to particular Arab states (Egypt, Syria, Palestine, Saudi Arabia, Iraq, et cetera). On the other hand, the underlying ideas, and intrinsic uncertainties, of Arab nationalism have remained remarkably constant, with an aspiration to unity, opposition to foreign intervention, and a concern for Palestine being constants. At the same time, and in contrast to other regions of the world marked by interstate conflict and nationalist upsurge, for example in formerly communist Europe, the Horn of Africa, and South Asia, the map of states characterizing the Middle East, and indeed the Arab world as a whole, has remained constant. For all the talk of state unification and/or fragmentation, of the artificiality of borders, and of the vagueness of 'Arab' identities, whether pan-Arab or state specific, this map of the region, forged by colonialism and war in the early part of the twentieth century, has endured.

The Arab World Since 1945

Decolonization

At the end of World War II, few Arab states were, in both a formal and real sense, independent entities. Two countries had been in effect independent since their creation in the wake of the Turkish withdrawal after 1918: Saudi Arabia, created by conquest in 1926, and the Imamate of Yemen, successor to the Ottoman-ruled provinces of North Yemen, separated from the region of South Yemen (known at the time as Aden and South Arabia and ruled by Britain) by an Anglo-Ottoman boundary agreement of 1913. Neither of these two states played, however, a significant role in intra-Arab or Arab nationalist politics, this role being assumed by larger states that were, at least in practical terms, still under strong foreign influence, namely Egypt and Iraq, rivals but under British tutelage, and Syria, ruled until 1946 by France. Britain had indeed formally granted independence to Egypt in 1922, and to Iraq in 1932, but the ruling families of these two states remained dependent on British force, a control that had, if anything, been made stronger and more overt by World War II and by the assertion of British authority against nationalist sentiment in both states.

For the first decade and more after 1945 the dominant issue in the politics, and nationalism, of the Arab world, was the struggle against colonial rule. The ending of World War II, with the exhaustion of the colonial powers, the rise of nationalist sentiment in the colonial world, and pressure for decolonization from both the USA and the USSR, meant, however, that the British and French imperial systems in the Middle East had to come to an end. France departed from Lebanon and Syria in 1946, and the British, while maintaining informal military control, granted independence to Jordan in the same year.

Much more controversial, however, were developments in the other colonies that France and Britain had acquired before and after World War I, in the case of the former in North Africa, in the case of the latter in the former Ottoman colonies of Egypt and the Arab 'East'. In North Africa there were strong nationalist mobilizations in Tunisia and Morocco, preceding independence for each in 1956; and in Algeria, which due to its three million European settlers the French government had intended, as *Algérie Française*, to retain permanently as part of French territory, a nationalist insurrection broke out in 1954: by the time it ended, in 1962, a million Algerians had died. In the British colonies, the pattern was equally varied, even if each individual state, and the attendant crises, were merged into a broad suspicion and critique of British policy in the region. In Palestine, an entity created by the British after World War I, attempts by the colonial power to control the growing conflict between the Arab Palestinian population and the expanding Jewish community failed and in May 1948 the British unilaterally departed: the result was the First Arab-Israeli War, out of which Israel acquired a state of its own, while the remaining territories were occupied by Jordan and

Egypt. It was to be another twenty years before an identifiable, and organizationally distinct, Palestinian nationalist movement was to emerge again, but neither this, nor the many attempts made by Arab states to resolve the issue by force of arms, or negotiations, resolved the Palestine issue. Thus, throughout the post-1945 period, the Palestine question remained not the only, but indubitably the single most important source of anti-Western, nationalist sentiment across the Arab world.

Britain's scuttling from Palestine was not, initially, replicated elsewhere. However, the pro-Western monarchies established and consolidated before and during World War II were not to last long: that of Egypt was overthrown in July 1952, that of Iraq in July 1958, those of South Arabia in 1967, that of Libya in 1969. In these cases nationalist military regimes, of an increasingly 'anti-imperialist' and 'socialist' orientation, took their place, denouncing the West and, to varying degrees, allying with the Soviet Union, even as they competed with each other. In the case of Egypt the British withdrawal was complicated by lack of agreement on two major issues: Sudan and the Suez Canal.

Egyptian nationalism claimed Sudan as part of Egypt, but the Sudanese political leaders, supported by Britain, opposed this, and in 1956 Sudan became independent in its own right. The Suez Canal crisis of October–November 1956 came in two parts: first, opposition by Egypt to the retention by Britain of a military zone along the canal, and a rising incidence of guerrilla attacks on British installations there; secondly, strong French and British opposition to the Egyptian claim to ownership of the Canal, operated since its opening in 1869 by the Anglo-French Suez Canal Company. The dispute over the Canal Zone itself was resolved by 1954 and British forces withdrew from the areas, and bases, they controlled. In July 1956, however, a more serious crisis broke out when Egypt nationalized the Canal and took immediate control of the running of the waterway. Britain and France refused to accept the nationalization and, seeing Egypt's action as part of a broader challenge to their remaining positions in the region (the British in South Arabia, Iraq and the Gulf, the French in Algeria), came to a secret agreement with Israel to attack Egypt at the end of October. A brief conflict, the 'Suez War', followed: but while the invading forces were militarily successful, international pressure, including joint opposition from both Washington and Moscow, forced a speedy and humiliating withdrawal.

The Suez Crisis of 1956 marked a watershed, if not a final conclusion, of European colonial influence within the Arab world. Egypt, under the leadership of President Nasser, emerged as a hero of Arab opinion, and Britain appeared to be in retreat: its monarchical ally in Iraq was to be overthrown two years later, in July 1958, and its political position in the and around the region was further undermined by the independence of two states that, albeit politically marginal, were strategically important, Cyprus, in 1960, and South Yemen, in 1967, both after several years of nationalist guerrilla war.[1] Almost miraculously Britain was able to preserve its other monarchical-military allies, even if the regimes in question had themselves to resort more and more to nationalist gestures: in Jordan, where British troops intervened in 1958 to control dissent; in Kuwait, where Britain had to rush troops to fend off an Iraqi claim that followed independence in 1961; and in Oman, scene of two guerrilla uprisings (in 1957–9 in the Omani interior, in 1965–75 in the southern province of Dhofar). Independence for the remaining Gulf colonies, Bahrain, Qatar, and the Emirates, came more smoothly in 1971.[2]

The Arab-Israeli Conflict

All of these decolonizations, and the disputes, delays, and attempted reversals associated with them, served to fuel a broad sense of nationalism in the Arab world, be it at the pan-Arab or nation-specific level. The most unresolved, and bitter, legacy of colonialism, the one that more than any other, more indeed than Suez or Algeria, was to affect Arab opinion, was that of Palestine. The political and administrative entity of 'Palestine' itself was a consequence of World War I, the projection and imposition onto what had hitherto been three unconnected administrative entities within the Ottoman Empire of, in effect, a Christian imaginary territory, fostered by the nineteenth-century biblical and romantic imagination. Prior to 1918, the inhabitants of this territory, 80 per cent Muslim, 20 per cent Christian, with a tiny minority of Jews, considered themselves more 'Syrian' (in Arabic *shami*) than anything else: however, they, and the increasingly influential Zionist movement, which on the model of European nationalism had, since its founding in 1897, aspired to create a Jewish state in what it postulated as ancestral territory, had no difficulty in adjusting to the newly invented territory and claiming it as their historic and 'God-given' object of struggle. The establishment of this 'Palestine', with Jerusalem as its capital, also gave that city, which had always enjoyed symbolic importance, a new political prominence: a marginal municipal unit in Ottoman times, but not the capital of a larger area, Jerusalem had been of little practical importance, economic or political, in the immediately preceding centuries. Given later claims about its importance to both religions, it is worth recalling that for the centuries preceding neither Muslims nor Jews had treated it as a major pilgrimage site, nor had Jews, who formed significant communities in many other cities of the Ottoman Empire, sought to settle there.

Three simultaneous processes were to alter all this. First, the delineation of an entity called 'Palestine', as in other invented colonial units, including Iraq, Lebanon, and Syria, had now created the administrative and political space, the nationalist 'box' or frame, within which political movements, new identities, and new competitions for power could develop. Secondly, while the Arab inhabitants of Palestine came, over one or two generations, to define their identity and aspirations in terms of this entity, they were also affected by, and incorporated into, the broader political and ideological movement of pan-Arab nationalism. Finally, while the Arab inhabitants of Palestine were like those of other colonial entities in the region dealing with, and resisting, colonial authorities, in this case the British, they were simultaneously and increasingly in conflict with the Jewish community that was, as a result of the promotion of immigration by Zionism, growing within the country. That *both* the Arab Palestinian population *and* the Hebrew-speaking Jewish, later Israeli, community were, in effect, modern creations, a result of the delineation of the Palestinian state boundaries after 1918 and of the growing triangular conflict therein, did not detract from the passions, and atavistic associations that this conflict aroused (see also Chapter 11).

The history of the Palestinian conflict since 1945 is, in essence, that of a succession of wars, and attempted negotiated settlements, which, six decades later, have left the problem very much where it had been in the mid-1940s. After various initiatives by the British in the interwar period to resolve the issue, tilting to one side or the other, a final attempt was made to avoid war by the UN, which voted in 1947 to partition the pre-war 'Palestine' into Arab and Jewish zones. The Arab world, acting at the UN in some concert, and mobilizing protest in the Middle East itself, rejected this plan, fighting within the communities in Palestine increased, and in May 1948 the British abandoned the territory. The result of the first war, that of 1948–9, was indeed to partition the territory, but into an independent Jewish Israel, proclaimed in May 1948, and two areas occupied by Arab states, the West Bank by Jordan, and the Gaza Strip by Egypt. The second war, that of Suez in 1956, for all that it transformed the Arab world as a whole, did not substantially affect the situation in pre-1948 Palestine itself. On the other hand, that of June 1967 did, with Israel conquering both the West Bank and Gaza and, in effect, restoring the territorial and political status quo ante: from June 1967 onwards, the Arab-Israeli conflict has returned to being what it was before 1948, a civil war, within one territory, 'Palestine'/Israel, between two communities.

None of the subsequent wars: that of 1973, which Egypt launched to win back the Sinai Peninsula, that of 1982, which Israel waged to destroy its enemies in Lebanon, and that of 2006, which repeated, on a limited scale, that of 1982, affected the situation on the ground in Palestine/Israel. At the same time, and despite many attempts by regional actors, and outside powers, to broker a settlement, most noticeably that signed in Oslo in 1993, no solution was attained. This apparent paralysis and endless, unresolved, conflict were, however, accompanied by other changes, three in particular, which affected and in some measure transformed the Palestine issue.

First, the complete elimination of independent Palestinian parties and voices after the 1948–9 war, in which both Israel and the Arab states participated, was decisively ended by the war of 1967. As a result of the Israeli occupation of large Arab populations in the West Bank and Gaza, and of the freedom of manoeuvre enjoyed by Palestinian organizations, most prominently the PLO and Al Fatah, in the Arab world, the Palestinian movement, at once political, diplomatic, and military, re-emerged, and, now an autonomous force, came to play an important role within the areas occupied by Israel, and also in the politics of neighbouring states, namely Jordan and Lebanon.[3] In effect, this too restored a certain 'normality' to Palestinian nationalism, so that it, as much as others, reasserted its duality as both country-specific and pan-Arab: it operated on both the local state level and at the pan-Arab level, using the resources it had, the shifting alliances it enjoyed with Arab states, and the prestige of the 'Palestinian revolution' within the Arab world, to promote its interests. To a degree greater than with most other modern nationalist guerrillas, the Palestinian movement was marked by fragmentation: between those under Israeli rule and those in Arab lands; between refugees and those still living on Palestinian land; between the allies and clients of different Arab states. Ideological, leadership, and organizational divisions all played a significant role; those of class, religious, or regional origin much less so.[4] Although the PLO, its main component Al Fatah, and the other smaller, more radical, groups, were not able to maintain their armed organizational presence in Jordan or Lebanon, and were never allowed to do so in Egypt and Syria, they established and maintained after 1967 a prominent place in the Arab world that had been denied to Palestinian political representatives between 1948 and 1967.

The second important change after 1967 was shifting Arab involvement in the Palestinian question itself. As early as the 1940s, support by Arab states for the Palestinian cause was combined with tactical, interstate, calculations, above all by Cairo, Amman, Damascus, and Baghdad. As a result of the 1967 war, a common Arab front was created, rejecting negotiations and 'surrender', but this was to change after the war of 1973. Egypt's goal in this war had been not to 'liberate' Palestine, but to win back its national territory, something it did, via US diplomacy, in the Camp David Accords of 1978. Egyptian President Sadat himself visited Jerusalem in October 1977, to the consternation of many in the Arab world.

The Sadat visit divided the Arab world as no war with Israel had done. Egypt's initiatives, and its recognition of Israel under the Camp David Accords, led to its expulsion from the Arab League, of which it was the host country, and to a bitter conflict that lasted through the 1980s, between the minority of Arab states that, while still giving support to a Palestinian cause, wanted compromise with Israel, and the majority, led by Syria and Iraq, themselves both in competition, who opposed any contact with 'the Zionist entity'. At the same time, in those countries that were prepared to negotiate with Israel, there was a noted falling off in support for the Palestinian cause, something compounded by the factional role played by the PLO in the onset and development of the Lebanese civil war from 1975. That the conservative oil producers, led by Saudi Arabia, were unable to articulate a clear, let alone influential, stance of their own only served to prolong the fissures in the Arab world. The support given by the Palestinian leader Yasser Arafat and, by all indices, by Palestinian public opinion as a whole to the Iraqi occupation of Kuwait in August 1990 (leading to the First Iraq War) only served further to alienate elite sentiment in the Gulf states, even as, by all accounts, it antagonized much of opinion within Iraq itself, where the Palestinians were seen as complicit with the dictatorship of the Iraqi leader Saddam Hussein. The corruption and inefficiency shown by the Palestinian parties when they returned to Gaza and the West Bank in 1994, as a result of the Oslo Accords, only enhanced this alienation.

The third important process that took place from 1967 onwards, and which became much more evident from the second half of the 1980s, was the shift in the ideological character of the Palestinian movement, from the secular nationalism, and various forms of radical and Marxist ideology, that had dominated in the 1960s and 1970s, to the domination of Islamist ideas, associated with the establishment in 1987 of Hamas[5] (the Palestinian branch of the Muslim Brotherhood) and of Islamic Jihad. At first, up to the mid-1980s, with the Israelis and foreign states focused on the dominance of the secular parties, this religious sentiment was not given due attention, but by the late 1980s, when it was Hamas that led the first Palestinian uprising, or *intifadha*, the monopoly of the PLO and the dominance of Al Fatah had come under threat. The Oslo Accords of 1993 were, from the start, denounced by Hamas and other Islamist groups, and with the outbreak of the second *intifadha* in 2000, this challenge was even more evident. Increasingly bitter relations between the two trends came to a head in 2006, when Hamas for the first time won a majority in the Palestinian Parliament. With the PLO supported by Israel and the USA, and Hamas receiving support from Iran and Syria, an open split occurred, culminating in the seizure of control in Gaza by Hamas in June 2007, thereby confirming a further partition of Palestine, this time between the two components of the designated Palestinian territory. This displacement of secular by religious sentiment was, of course, part of a broader regional trend: the rise of Islamism was evident across the Arab world (see below), and as in the case of countries ruled by increasingly corrupt and ineffective secular rulers, Algeria, Syria, Egypt to name but three, the crisis of legitimacy, and of administrative delivery, associated with these regimes of the 1950s and 1960s, was evident.[6]

Revolution and Unity

If the period after 1945 began with Arab nationalism being defined in predominantly 'liberal' terms, aspiring to independence, parliamentary democracy, civilian rule, secularism, and cultural pluralism, this was soon to change, under the impact of the post-independence crises in many states, above all involving military coups, the rising anger in the Arab world over the Israeli victory in 1948–9, and, from without the region but with major political and ideological impact on Arab state and mass politics, the Cold War and the rising influence of the USSR and China on a significant part of Arab intellectual life. The 'failure' of liberalism, not unlike that which had taken place earlier in the century in parts of Europe and Latin America, had, in the 1930s led some groups (the Lebanese Phalangist Party, early components of the Ba'th Party) to admire European fascism. However, in the post-war epoch this weakness of liberalism gave the initiative to the more militant, authoritarian, and 'socialist' regimes comprised by the military rulers of Syria (from 1949), Egypt (from 1952), Iraq (from 1958), Yemen (from 1962), Libya (from 1969), Sudan (from 1969), and by the triumph in nationalist guerrilla movements of left-wing, radical if not communist, parties in Algeria (1962) and South Yemen (1967). The fact that in other countries, ones that eschewed socialism, the regimes relied equally on the military (Jordan, Morocco) or on authoritarian oil-producing oligarchies (Saudi Arabia and the smaller Gulf states), provided a convenient regional opponent for the radical regimes, but not an alternative model. Only Lebanon, despite being driven by communal tensions since independence in 1943, appeared, in the years up to 1975, to resist this pattern.

The fashion for 'Arab socialism', in its comparatively milder 'Nasserist' version and in the harsher Ba'thist version that took power in Syria and Iraq, ran from the mid-1950s, with the consolidation of the regime in Egypt and the Suez war, through revolutions in Iraq, Yemen, Algeria, and elsewhere, to the early 1970s.[7] At first, it appeared as if the Egyptian model, espoused by Nasser, would sweep the region and, in so doing, establish not only a distinctive model of political and economic development, but also achieve the core nationalist goal of unity, *wahda*. The high point of this unificatory project came in 1958 when the leaders of Syria, Arab nationalists fearful of a communist takeover with support from their rival, Iraq, appealed to Egypt for union: the result was the birth of the United Arab Republic. In 1961, however, the Syrians broke away, on the grounds of excessive Egyptian interference, and with this a body blow was given to the goal of 'unity': intermittent attempts by Egypt in 1962–3 to restart the UAR project with Syria, Iraq, and Yemen, and later initiatives involving Libya, came to nothing. Later, as the banner of anti-imperialist Arab unity shifted to Syria and Iraq, the former claiming to be the 'Beating Heart of Arabism', the latter 'The Citadel of Arabism', Egypt went more and more its own way, culminating in the reconciliation with Israel in 1978–9 and the expulsion of Egypt from the very Arab League it had helped to found in 1945. Saddam Hussein's interpretation of Arab unity was more coercive, culminating in the occupation of Kuwait in August 1990: but this was reversed, within a matter of months, by the US-led military campaign to re-establish Kuwaiti independence. Only in one remote, and unrepresentative, corner of the Arab world was a lasting, if itself later violent, fusion of two states to occur, that of North and South Yemen, formerly 'The Arab Republic of Yemen' and the 'People's Democratic Republic of Yemen', in May 1990.[8]

From this failure of Arab socialism and of Arab unity, some observers then drew the conclusion that the very idea of Arab unity had died. Not only had the state-unification projects failed, but in the rhetoric of many Arab leaders, notably in Egypt and Libya, there was a growing rejection of the commitment to an 'Arab' identity, and a greater stress on the national, state-centric, element in politics and ideology. Nonetheless, as with so many questions in the study of nationalism, the story may not be as one-dimensional as it appears. Indeed, and in comparative perspective (Africa, Latin America, the European Union), the failure of established states to combine and fuse should come as no surprise. Not only did pre-twentieth-century geographical and cultural differences retain their vitality, now recycled, not least by state educational systems, in 'national' form, but the very administrative, security, and economic interests created by the plurality of states militated against sharing with others.[9] This did not entail, however, that a sense of shared Arab identity, and a set of consequent political attitudes, had ceased to exist. In particular a sense of solidarity with Arab peoples felt to be objects of foreign occupation or maltreatment, notably Palestine and, from the 1990s onwards, Iraq, the sense of being an embattled community fostered by the impact of new satellite TV stations and by the Internet, were an important factor in Arab politics, one to which regional states, and indeed external ones such as Britain and the USA, could not be indifferent. The reluctance of nearly all Arab states, despite Western pressure, to normalize relations with Israel, the hostility evident across the region to US policy, and the sympathy, qualified as it may have been but attested to by a variety of sources, with those who resisted the West, be they Yasser Arafat, Saddam Hussein, or Osama bin Laden, illustrated this point.[10]

Nationalism Theory and the Arab World

Against this background, it may be possible to examine the historical record of Arab nationalism in a more analytic and comparative context. In the Arab world as elsewhere, there can be no such thing as a theoretically innocent, or purely narrative, account of any nationalism. The study of Arab nationalism, and indeed of all nationalisms, is beset with problems that arise as much from the general character of the topic as from the analytic uncertainties of any particular case. First, the very imprecision, lack of theoretical or definitional clarity, of the main concepts involved, starting with the definition of the word 'nation' itself. Secondly, the confusion, inherent in the very word, between two quite different objects of study—nationalism *as a movement*, as a social and political force, whether this be in the hands of states or those who challenge them, and nationalism *as an ideology*: the first allows of objective, historical, analysis, of how a particular movement arose and developed in a determinate country, of the social groups that supported and/or opposed it and, not least, of how states have sought to define and utilize it; the second is an aspiration, an ideological and normative claim, one with a strong tendency to control and distort public debate, and with, in particular, an inherent tendency to distort the history of the supposed 'nation'. Thirdly, while modern history has yielded hundreds of cases of nationalism, as movement and ideology, nationalism, by virtue of the special claims nationalists make for their particular nation, almost always occasions analysis that is singular, treating the 'nation' or country in question as unique, avoiding comparison. This pervasive difficulty with the study of nationalism has, in recent decades, begun to allow of some resolution, even if the resolutions offered by some writers are ones that virtually all nationalists, in other words 99 per cent of humanity, at least reject.[11]

All of this should fall like a cascade of very cold, if long overdue, water onto the often heated, partisan, and also intellectually and analytically parochial debates about Middle Eastern, and not least Arab, nationalism. First of all, comparison: virtually all literature on the nationalism of the Arab world, whether partisan or academic, treats it as unique, or at least very different. Yet many, if not all, of the major features attributed to its modern history can be found elsewhere. Ditto Israeli, Turkish, and Iranian nationalism. The supposed 'failure' of the Arabs to unite into one state is not really that different from that of the other post-colonial continents—Latin America, Africa, and South Asia—that aspired to, or once enjoyed, unity. The reason is, in essence, very simple: once distinct state, and economic, interests are established, it is very difficult to merge them. This is also, evidently, the case in the European Union. Instead of asking why the Arabs 'failed' to unite, it would be more appropriate to why they *should*.

Secondly and similarly, the apparent 'inconsistency' of identity in the Arab world, between pan-Arab (*qaumi*) and state-specific (*qutri, watani*) identification, and the slipping of Arab states and politicians back and forth between them, is explicable within a conception, such as that developed by Amartya Sen, of multiple identities. This is something that to anyone who is American (with the variations of, as it were 'pan-American' and other hyphenated '-American' identities), or the espousal of Englishness and Britishness by most inhabitants of the United Kingdom, not to mention the slippages between Turkish, Turkic, and Ottoman identities, should come as no surprise. The supposed addiction of the Arabs to utopian projects, to 'dreams' and illusions, about nationalism, for which recent writers so complacently castigate them, can be found in many other countries in the world, for example Serbia.

Thirdly, the relationship of Arab nationalism to Islam is neither as mysterious, nor unique, as some commentators allege, or, in nationalist-Islamic vein, claim. Throughout its history, Arab nationalism, in both forms, has had a close, if shifting, relation to the religious, in this case Islamic, legacy of the Arab world. This is in part because of the political and historical importance of Islam as the ideological form, and in some respects organizing principle, of the major states and empires to which the Arabs have belonged; in part also because the very rise of interest in Arab culture, literature, and, above all, language from the mid-nineteenth century onwards, necessitated a close engagement with, and respect for, the language of the Koran, for Muslims the word of Allah or God.

While one of the distinctive contributions of the nineteenth-century revival was to draw attention to the poetry of the pre-Islamic *Jahiliya*, 'Period of Ignorance', and while all Arab states, Saudi Arabia partially excepted, have no difficulties on conventional nationalist grounds in celebrating their pre-Islamic pasts, even those Arabs who were Christians tended to accord a special place to Islam in the definition of Arab culture and history. Even in the decades of strongest secularism within Arab nationalism, it was evident that the Islamic legacy was present, if only in the usage for modern, patriotic, purposes of a vocabulary that had Qur'anic origins and resonances: words like *umma* ('national community/nation'), *watan* ('homeland'), *shahid* ('martyr'), *jihad* ('struggle'), *mujahid* ('fighter'), and *risala* ('mission/message'), modular components of nationalist ideology and self-definition across the world, were in Arabic taken from the religious lexicon. The same, of course, applied to much of the, in origin, Christian vocabulary of European nationalism—'sacred' territory and duty, 'martyrs' and 'sacrifice', et cetera. Consequently, that nearly all writers on the ideas, origin, identity of Arab nationalism mention a link to Islam is hardly surprising, given the importance of the Qur'an in the formation of the Arabic language, the predominance of Islam as a religion among Arabs, and the role of 'Islamic' states in the Arab history.

To go from this use of Islamic heritage to regarding all Arab nationalism as somehow inherently *Islamic* and, by extension, not really conforming to an international model of nationalism is, however, unfounded. The reality for several decades was, indeed, that the new secular states, before and after independence, for all their invocation of Islamic symbols and forms of legitimacy, were in contradiction with the religious establishment, as they sought to control education, the law, land ownership and, in a more general way, the definition of power, authority, and legitimacy in twentieth-century society. Equally illustrative of the distinction between Arab nationalism in its earlier phases and the later Islamist tendencies, ones that came to the fore in the 1970s, is the fact that these groups themselves, be they in Egypt, Palestine, Syria, Jordan, Iraq, or Algeria, saw the established states as their enemy and sought to replace or, in several cases, overthrow them. In many ways, the Islamist currents that emerged in the Arab world, comparable to those that emerged in Iran, Afghanistan, and Pakistan, and which to some degree influenced them, were a reaction to, not a continuation of, the earlier nationalist, and in their core ideas and interests, secular regimes.

Arab nationalism was not, therefore, inherently, or essentially, 'religious': if anything, it was the other way around: the national captured the religious. For it was the failure of the secular state, in its economic, social, and state-building roles, as well as in foreign policies, that led to the rejection of nationalism, and associated ideas of socialism and revolution, in much of the Arab world. This was true for the rise of Hamas in Palestine from the late 1980s onwards, as it was for the popularity of the Muslim Brotherhood in Egypt, or of the FIS in Algeria. For all the ideological and cultural overlap there may have been, for all the use by some monarchies of a supposedly religious legitimacy,[12] in terms of political power, and of the competition for control of states and economic resources, there was a clear distinction between secular nationalist regimes, of left and rights, and Islamist movement. This was evident from the 1950s onwards in Egypt, Syria, Iraq, and later in the bloody conflicts that affected Syria in the 1980s, and Algeria and Egypt in the 1990s, not to mention Palestine from 2006 onwards. In effect the Islamist movements were political parties, and groups, which argued that a political and social programme for the modern world in general, and for their societies in particular, could be derived from religious tradition and text.

Hence the paradox, one that for much of the time neither Islamists nor their opponents were willing to acknowledge, namely that, while in appearance the ideologies and goals of Islamist movements were opposed, many of the ideas they espoused, and the broad goals they set themselves, including the character of the state they sought to establish, were very similar to, and derived from, the programmes of the earlier, secular, nationalist, populist, and radical movements.[13] Thus, for all the rivalry and often violence involved, the Islamist movements were beneficiaries and inheritors of the secular nationalist agenda, as much if not more than the secular parties and states that had religious elements. For the political programmes, and indeed the ideology, of the Islamist groups, be they peaceful or violent, nation-specific or pan-Muslim, borrowed heavily from the radical and nationalist secular ideologies of the twentieth century: a concept of the oppressed community, an economic and political critique of imperialism, an emphasis on the corruption of culture by imported ideas, the denunciation of rulers and elites for their ties to the 'corrupt' West. Many of the issues on which

Islamists made most ground were, in essence, national ones, prime among these being the 'occupation' of Muslim lands by foreign peoples and states. In the 1990s Palestine, the classic Arab case, was joined to Kashmir, Bosnia, and Chechnya, and, in the aftermath of 9/11 (2001), to Afghanistan and Iraq. For example, Hamas in its Charter of 1989 had no difficulty in accepting the entirely secular concept of 'Palestine' as its frame of reference. Indeed, although without attribution and in Islamic terms, it even used the Christian category of a 'Holy Land' to refer to this territory. For all the eccentricity of organization and rhetoric, even the propaganda statements of Al Qaida could be analysed as, in larger measure, a recycling of Arab nationalist and Third World populist themes in a Qur'anic and mystical language.[14] In a comparative and rigorous perspective, therefore, the argument about the religious character of Arab nationalism may be turned on its head, drawing attention to the nationalist, and, in historical terms, secular, provenance of much of the political appeal of the Islamist movements.

Finally, the interrelationship of Arab nationalism with outside, colonial and anti-colonial, powers—often treated in terms of some 'special', either sympathetic and affiliated, or hostile, 'Orientalist', 'Eurocentric', or 'Islamophobic' cultural substratum, defining a peculiar form of Western attitude, and hence policy, towards the region—is, on closer inspection, not so specific: in particular there is no special hatred of 'Islam', more a general disdain for, and reification of, other peoples. The attitudes of Western writers towards the Middle East, or towards Arab and Muslim immigrants in Europe, are, for all the literature on some supposedly separate 'Orientalism', more or less those found in relation to other parts of the non-European world: romanticization and idealization coincide with denigration; cultural and religious tropes intersect with economic interest; alleged 'historic' friendships and shared interests regularly succumb to national interests, sometimes slowly as in periods of epochal conflict (colonialism, Cold War), at other times rapidly and with sudden reversals (as in World Wars I and II). As for the common Middle Eastern, especially Arab, claim of imperial and Western 'betrayal', in the Arab case especially said to have taken place during World War I and its aftermath, the fate of the Arabs bears comparison with other 'betrayals', say, of the Armenians or, further afield, the Vietnamese.[15]

Issues in Historical Sociology: State Formation, History, and Modernity

There are now, with the inclusion of Palestine, twenty-two independent political entities that lay a claim to be 'Arab'. All of these states claim ancient origins, and seek to derive legitimacy from this. This issue of how nations and nationalisms, including those of the Arab world, have been and are being formed can, however, be dealt with critically via the application of a modernist, non-deterministic, account of history. The starting point for such an analysis and history is not where nationalists themselves begin, namely a mythical and ancient 'nation', long oppressed or obscured and now emerging, but with the formation of modern states, distinct entities of coercion, administration, and territorial delimitation within which distinct and often newly defined peoples are contained, ruled, and governed. This involves looking at the origins of states and state formation, and, in particular, at the questions of how this map of states came about, and what the formative historical forces determining the outcome were.

A brisk, and unflinching, application of the historical sociological knife may tell a different story to that of most nationalists. First, for all of the talk of ancient peoples, times, and so forth, no state in the Arab world is more than five hundred years, half a millennium, old, and none has any plausible derivation from, or continuous association with, the historic or ancient states—the Egypt of the Pharoahs, the Yemen of Himyar and Saba, the Mesopotamia of Hamurrabi, the North Africa of Phoenicia and/or Rome—from which many claim legitimacy or descent. Equally for all the claims as to legitimacy or systems of government and law descended from the original years of Islam, in the seventh century AD, these are convenient inventions. Even those states that have been distinct and recognizable continuous entities over recent centuries—Oman, Yemen, Tunisia, Morocco—they, like the non-Arab state of the region that might claim similar ancestry in the sixteenth century, have been so transformed by modernity, in military, economic, administrative, and ideological terms that they bear only remote, and analytically nugatory, relations to their ancestors.

Rather, what we see is the emergence, or rather the forcible, coercive, bloody, and contingent creation of blocs of states over the past centuries, above all as a result of three formative phases: dynastic state formation in the sixteenth century, which produced Morocco, Yemen, and Oman, as it did Spain, France, Turkey; colonial occupation and delineation in the nineteenth and early twentieth centuries, out of which emerged the map of Arab states from Syria to Morocco, together with Malta and Cyprus; and inter-ethnic conflict in the twentieth century, shaping the Balkans and Israel/Palestine. Whatever else, there is little that is ancient, cultural, 'natural', let alone 'God-given' in this outcome. Strategic interest and military power, be they internally generated or imposed, as with colonialism, from without, were the dominant factors. The consolidation of elite power, military backing from outside, and a flow of income in various forms of rent, has continued the job.

Against this background, it becomes possible to address the question, inherent in the history of every nationalism in the world, of the relation between the formation and development of states, as entities of administration and coercion, and the emergence, or creation, of communities termed 'nations'. If nationalisms always claim that it is nations that come first, with states expressing or representing these already existing and self-conscious entities, historical sociological realism would suggest a more complex answer, if not one that in almost all cases directly contradicts the 'nations into states' narrative. Studies of specific Arab states, and of the dual nationalism present in each, indicates how it was within the administrative territories, 'boxes' created by modern war, occupation, and colonialism before and after World War I, that the nationalism of these states was formed, developed, and defined itself. The role of post-independence states in forging and fomenting, as well as giving particular ideological colour to, these nationalisms, is equally evident. In the Arab world as in so many other parts of the world, it was the state, first the colonial state by administrative definition and ideological provocation, then the post-independent state by socialization and imposition, that forged the nationalism, local and pan-Arab, of these entities.[16]

A brisk, and ideologically unflinching, application of modernist theory to the Middle East should serve other, more critical, and potentially educative and emancipatory purposes, in particular to undercut the claims to ancient origins, God-given particularity, cultural superiority, and general nationalist propaganda that beset all the peoples of the region, Arabs and Israelis, Turks and Iranians, Kurds and Armenians, alike. While some regional states can indeed claim centuries of existence as distinct institutional entities, the state systems now controlling this region are all modern creations, to an almost complete extent products of the post-World War I settlement and the international pressures affecting the region, and the political communities they claim to represent, 'nations', even more so. A modernist approach should also serve to inject some scepticism into the recent debate on the 'failure' of Arab nationalism: the feeling of belonging to an Arab political and cultural community is probably just as strong now as it was decades ago, and with modern communications, and many an unresolved regional conflict, this feeling is likely to continue.

As for claims, bloodily and tenaciously proclaimed, to one or other piece of territory, on the grounds of historic primacy or divine allocation, these should be questioned, and practical, and reasonable, solutions adopted. That this is most unlikely to happen, in Palestine or Kurdistan, in Nagorno-Karabagh or Kashmir, only goes to underline the immense, and pernicious, influence of the traditional 'atavistic' conception of nationalism and of the interests served by proclaiming, inculcating, and implementing policies based on such ideas.[17]

Conclusion: The Costs of Nation

The history of Arab nationalism since 1945, indeed since the emergence of ideas and movements claiming allegiance to it in the latter part of the nineteenth century, therefore shares much in common with that of other nationalist movements, in Europe and in other parts of the Third World. This is as true of the modular components of the ideology itself—nation, land, history, identity, symbols, et cetera—as it is of the actual development, at the level of political system and state, of nationalism as a movement. The process of state formation and of state promotion of national identities, for domestic and regional ends, is also parallel to that seen in other parts of the world. None of the features supposedly 'unique' to Arab nationalism—its multidimensional identity, its invocation of religion, its opposition to imposed boundaries and administrative systems, its successes and its 'failures', above all in regard to unity—are themselves particular or unique to the Arab world. The Arabs, taken as a people in general, and in each of the more than twenty states and particular identities associated with them, have for sure individual histories, geographical endowments and locations, cultural traits, not to mention aspirations and defeats, but this too has been very much the fate of nationalisms the world over.

In one other respect too, nationalism in the Arab world bears comparison with that in other parts of the world, namely in the costs that the pursuit of nationalist goals, domestically and internationally, have entailed. First is the very cost of pursuing a nationally based, more or less autarchic, economic model, something shared by many developing states, of left and right persuasions, in the twentieth century, but which, it can be argued, has cost many of these states dear in terms of the longer-run attainment of political, social, and economic goals. Given the large amount of oil rent paid since the early 1970s, the Arab world as a whole has not lacked capital, deemed by many to be the most important precondition for economic development: yet it has used this capital badly, in the main, and has failed to develop any meaningful inter-Arab or more broadly regional forms of cooperation. There is no real economic cooperation between Arab states and attempts to promote it have, in the main, failed: the Arab Maghrib Union has been stymied by the political conflict between Algeria and Morocco over Western Sahara (their land border has been closed since 1993), while the apparently more successful Gulf Cooperation Council, set up in 1981, is little more than a diplomatic and security coordination body.[18]

A second area that might benefit from critical reassessment is the use of nationalist legitimacy, ideology, and resulting power by regimes to suppress and brutalize their own populations, all in the name of 'anti-imperialism' and the defence of national interests: Iraq, Syria, Libya all gave plenty of examples of this. Nationalism in the Arab world has also been associated, as elsewhere, with a sense of ethnic and cultural exclusion and a restrictive, when not bigoted, cultural nationalism: on the one hand, a rejection, as 'alien' to the new, independent, nation, of those inhabitants, above all of major trading cities and political centres, who were deemed, by dint of religion, origin, or language not to be part of the new 'national' community; and on the other hand, the use by politicians of left and right, secular and religious, of the tropes of cultural nationalism, whereby all ideas and practices, ancient or modern, that are deemed to come from elsewhere are thereby devalued, or rejected. The impact of the former can be seen in the emptying, with varying degrees of coercion, of the hitherto cosmopolitan and culturally rich cities of the Arab world, be they Baghdad, Cairo, Alexandria, Tripoli, Algiers, Tangiers, of communities of earlier centuries which had migrated and settled there; the systematic expulsion, especially from 1948, and with some considerable connivance from Israel itself, of long-established Jewish inhabitants of these countries, hitherto considered to be 'Arabs'; and, in the latter part of the twentieth and early years of the twenty-first century, the gradual driving out of the Arab Christian communities from Palestine, Iraq, and Syria, descendants of those who lived in these countries before the coming of Islam.

Finally, the emphasis of nationalism on struggle, combat, and, in much rhetoric derived from modern European history, war, has led to a validation of various wars, with all their costs, in much of modern Arab history, which have ill served the inhabitants of the countries concerned, let alone the building of a secure Middle East more generally. The causes of these wars do not lie in the ideology itself, but in the character of the states involved and of their relations with each other: but nationalist ideology, and the uses to which it is capable of being put, in the Arab world as in early twentieth-century East Asia or Europe, has been well suited to this violence and to the hatreds, casualties, and permanence of conflict so associated with the region. In the end, of course, the balance sheet of nationalism in the Middle East resembles that of nationalism elsewhere: a final judgement must, therefore, be made in a comparative context and in the light of the alternatives, ideological and political, that can reasonably be argued to have existed in recent times.

Notes

1. Britain kept two bases, as 'Sovereign Areas', within independent Cyprus, but was unable to use them for anything except training, transit, and electronic surveillance of the Middle East.
2. For a comprehensive overview of this period, see M. Yapp (1991) *The Near East Since the First World War*, London; and A. Hourani (1991) *A History of the Arab Peoples*, London.
3. The PLO was in fact set up in 1964, prior to the 1967 war, and was initially entirely controlled by Egypt, a tool in its rivalry with Syria. However, after the Egyptian and Syrian defeats in 1967, and the changed political and military demography of the region, both the PLO and the hitherto underground nationalist Al Fatah were able to cast off these state controls and play an autonomous political and military role.
4. In the 1960s and 1970s much was made, by Palestinian left-wing groups and by Marxist analysts internationally, of supposed class correlations—'proletarian', 'bourgeois', even 'feudal'—of different Palestinian groups, but this was almost all rhetoric. The very fragmentation of Palestinian society, the autonomy and factionalism of armed groups and, not least, interpersonal rivalries within the elite were of more importance.
5. Abbreviation of *harakat al muqawama al islamia*, 'The Islamic Resistance Movement', itself an implicit critique of its main rival, Al Fatah, where the word *fatah* is a reverse acronym for *harakat al tahrir al filastini*, 'The Palestinian Liberation Movement'. Note the contrast between the secular 'Palestinian' and the term 'Islamic', the latter proposing a different form of identity, and programme. Hamas and Fatah are also Arabic political terms in their own right, meaning 'effort' and 'conquest' respectively.
6. The most authoritative works on Palestinian nationalism are Y. Sayigh (1997) *Armed Struggle and the Search for a State*, Oxford; and R. Khalidi (1997) *Palestinian Identity*, New York.
7. The Arab Ba'th Socialist Party, founded in the 1940s with a mélange of right-wing European nationalist and semi-fascist ideas with models of organization and hierarchy taken from communism, aimed at the revival, in Arabic *ba'th*, of the Arab world. Its main

slogan was 'Unity, Freedom, Socialism', where 'freedom' denoted not individual freedoms but freedom of the nation from external oppression.

8. In May 1990 North and South Yemen, respectively pro-Western and pro-Soviet, entered a loose, in effect 'confederal', unity, each retaining separate armies, administrations, and political parties. The understandings on which this agreement were based soon broke down and at the end of April 1994 the North launched an invasion of the South to bring it under its control. As much as East Germany, South Yemen, or 'the People's Democratic Republic of Yemen' as it was known, was eliminated by its stronger opponent.
9. Of course, the major explanation given in the Arab world for this 'failure' was that the Western states were opposed to it. There is little evidence of this, unless where such states feared that 'unity' would give advantage to the USSR. If there was an enduring bias in the international system it was against the *fragmentation* and *secession* of states, not their fusion. Britain's patronage of the founding of the Arab League in 1945 was, if anything, a sign of favour towards Arab unity.
10. For critical accounts of Arab nationalism, see A. Dawisha (2003) *Arab Nationalism in the Twentieth Century: From Triumph to Despair*, Princeton, NJ; F. Ajami (1981) *The Arab Predicament: Arab Political Thought and Practice Since 1967*, Cambridge; B. Tibi (1981) *Arab Nationalism: A Critical Enquiry*, New York.
11. Here I would refer, in particular, to the work of 'modernist' writers on nationalism in general (Ernest Gellner, Tom Nairn, Benedict Anderson, John Breuilly, Eric Hobsbawm, and Umut Özkirimli among others) as well as to those, such as Amartya Sen, who have redefined the debate on identity, by critiquing the hitherto static, monist, inevitable meanings attached to such affiliations.
12. Of the eight Arab monarchies two, Jordan and Morocco, claim descent from the Bani Hashim, the family of the Prophet. The Saudi monarch also attributes to itself the title 'Guardian of the Two Holy Places'.
13. For general arguments on the 'modernity' of Islamist ideas, see A. al Azmeh (1993) *Islam and Modernities*, London; E. Abrahamian (1993) *Khomeinism: Essays on the Islamic State*, London. See also the perceptive article by D. McAuley (2005) 'The ideology of Osama Bin Laden: Nation, Tribe and World Economy', *Journal of Political Ideologies*, 10, no. 3 (October), 269–87.
14. Bruce Lawrence (ed.) (2005) *Messages to the World: The Statements of Osama Bin Laden*, London.
15. Very little of the literature on Arab nationalism includes a comparative or theoretical dimension. For discussion that does address some of these issues, see J. Jankowski and I. Gershoni (eds.) (1997) *Rethinking Nationalism in the Middle East*, New York; F. Halliday (2000) *Nation and Religion in the Middle East*, London; Tibi, *Arab Nationalism: A Critical Enquiry.*
16. E.g. citing works in the bibliography to this entry, on Egypt, see Jankowski and Gershoni, *Rethinking Nationalism in the Middle East*; on Iraq, A. Baram (1991) *Culture, History and Ideology in the Formation of Modern Iraq (1968–1989)*, London; on Palestine, Khalidi, *Palestinian Identity: The Construction of Modern National Consciouness*, and Y. Sayigh (1997) *Armed Struggle and the Search for a State: The Palestinian National Movement, 1949–1993*, Oxford; on Yemen, Halliday, *Nation and Religion in the Middle East.*
17. The best introductions to the historical sociology of the Middle East remains S. Bromley (1994) *Rethinking Middle East Politics*, Cambridge; M. Kamrava (2005) *The Modern*

Middle East, Berkeley, CA; R. Owen (2007) *State, Power and Politics in the Making of the Modern Middle East*, 3rd edn., London.

18. For some time, after the mid-1980s, it was claimed that one inter-Arab Project, the initially multi-state Gulf Airways, was an example of such cooperation, serving the small Gulf states of Bahrain, Qatar, Oman, and the seven United Arab Emirates. Over time, however, this proved to be impossible and, one by one, different states broke away to form Qatar Airways, Emirates (i.e. Dubai) Airways, Etehad (i.e. Abu Dhabi) Airways, and Oman Airways. Gulf Airways remained as the, impoverished, airline of the state of Bahrain.

Suggested Further References

Ajami, F. (1978–9) 'The End of Pan-Arabism', *Foreign Affairs*, 57, no. 2 (Winter), 355–73.

Ajami, F. (1981) *The Arab Predicament: Arab Political Thought and Practice Since 1967*, Cambridge.

Baram, A. (1991) *Culture, History and Ideology in the Formation of Modern Iraq (1968–1989)*, London.

Bin Laden, O. (2005) *Messages from Afar: The Statements of Osama Bin Laden*, ed. and intro. B. Lawrence, London.

Choueiri, Y. (2000) *Arab Nationalism: A History*, Oxford.

Dawisha, A. (2003) *Arab Nationalism in the Twentieth Century: From Triumph to Despair*, Princeton, NJ.

Halliday, F. (2000) *Nation and Religion in the Middle East*, London, ch. 2, 'The Middle East and the Nationalism Debate', ch. 3, 'History and Modernity in the Formation of Nationalism: The Case of Yemen'.

Jankowski, J. and Gershoni, I. (eds.) (1997) *Rethinking Nationalism in the Middle East*, New York.

Khalidi, R. (1997) *Palestinian Identity: The Construction of Modern National Consciousness*, New York.

Sayigh, Y. (1997) *Armed Struggle and the Search for a State: The Palestinian National Movement, 1949–1993*, Oxford.

Tibi, B. (1981) *Arab Nationalism: A Critical Enquiry*, New York.

CHAPTER 23

NATIONALISM IN NORTHEAST ASIA SINCE 1945

AARON WILLIAM MOORE

THIS chapter will introduce some of the major themes in the evolution of nationalist discourse in post-war East Asia, with special attention to the effects of Soviet and American Cold War rivalries. It is important, however, not to allow Cold War history to fully consume East Asian nationalism, for such an approach would leave many events, such as the grass-roots pacifist movement in Japan and minority nationalism in China, difficult to explain; it also encourages a form of intellectual myopia, which centres its gaze on 'the West' (however defined) as the paramount force in political change. Nevertheless, the shifting relationship between East Asian governments and the two Cold War superpowers left an unmistakable imprint on how nationalism was expressed, from Mao's cries of 'big-power chauvinism' to Ishihara Shintarō's 'Japan that can say "no"'. Being such a short introduction, this chapter will eschew many important topics and focus on 'anti-imperialism', supporting economic growth as patriotism, 'minority nations', and the foreign-policy crises that have shaped domestic politics in China and Japan, followed by a short comparison with the emergence of vigorous patriotic rhetoric from the Korean Peninsula. The primary argument presented here will be that, even in the post-colonial era in East Asia, strong articulations of nationalism proceed primarily from the inherent contradictions within that discourse.

LAYING CLAIM TO THE 'REAL CHINA': AN ONTOLOGICAL ADVENTURE

Discourse on nationalism in post-war China was arguably the primary space in which the Chinese Nationalist Party (*Guomindang*, or GMD) and the Chinese Communist

Party (CCP) conducted their ideological struggle. It is important to decouple Chinese nationalism from *post-war* single-party states (the People's Republic of China [PRC], Singapore, and, until the 1990s, the Republic of China [ROC] in Taiwan) by rooting the emergence of nationalist discourse in the events of the highly divided, tumultuous *pre-war* period. Like Korea today, mainland China was a 'nation' of many states until 1949; after the CCP victory, the 'Chinese nation' was still divided: the large non-mainland community lived under different 'Chinese' states (Singapore, the ROC, and, until 1997, Hong Kong), as well as states in which the Chinese were a significant minority, such as Malaysia. A common language of nationalism was defined in the early twentieth century, and merits a quick review before moving on to post-war history. Early twentieth-century anti-imperialism (first articulated primarily against Japan) particularly shaped the discourse on mainland China, especially after 1949. Whilst the GMD adopted the rhetoric of 'freedom and democracy' and traditional Chinese cultural heritage, mainland Chinese nationalist discourse was in conflict with the CCP's views on class. The difficulty of the CCP's minority policy in a discourse otherwise dominated by Han Chinese concerns will also be addressed.

Although the Cold War was an important factor in post-war Chinese nationalism, it is erroneous to assume that it was solely the rivalries of the 'superpowers' that generated the battles and rhetoric of the GMD and the CCP; even before total war in 1937, foreign powers including (but not limited to) Japan, the United States, France, imperial Russia, and later the Soviet Union had interfered with and given aid to various Chinese political movements (and warlords). Most of these Chinese domestic forces had offered their own plans for national unification and 'revitalization', and the most important of all of the pre-war foreign influences would come to be the Soviet Union and imperial Japan. The language that the CCP and the GMD respectively adopted was primarily forged in the violent dynamic that existed between them, within pre-war and wartime China, rather than as a consequence of foreign meddling. This could be quite confusing to foreign observers, because whilst Chinese leaders might speak to their supporters abroad with one voice, they would conduct their campaigns for national unification in China with a different one. The 'resistance' rhetoric that would come to characterize GMD and CCP nationalist discourse after 1945 was largely, as Rana Mitter points out in this volume (Chapter 14), a consequence of their pre-war and wartime experiences. In that sense, China's 'Cold War' was a long one, going back to, at the very least, the Comintern sponsorship of the GMD against the interests of imperial powers such as Britain and the United States in the 1920s. The GMD-CCP civil conflict over the leadership of Chinese nationalism is therefore a 'trans-war' phenomenon.

For the GMD, nationalist discourse went through three distinct phases: revolutionary, authoritarian, and 'democratic.' The party had always been anti-imperialist and, until democratization during the late 1980s and 1990s, it had also adhered to Sun Yat-sen's theory of 'political tutelage.'[1] Simply put, political tutelage stated that citizens of an emerging nation required a period of state-directed social discipline in order to become responsible enough for enfranchisement. Early GMD efforts, funded in part by the Comintern, were genuinely 'revolutionary': they aimed, in the spirit of Chinese reformers since the end of the Qing dynasty, to transform Chinese political, cultural, and social institutions. After Chiang Kai-shek's Northern Expedition of 1926–8, GMD nationalism entered a distinctly 'authoritarian' phase, when 'political tutelage' meant the elimination of political rivals and the subjugation of citizens to the dictates of the party. Finally, in the GMD's 'democratic' phase, Chiang Kai-shek, whilst in fact continuing Sun's policy of 'political tutelage', used the language of 'freedom and democracy' to placate foreign allies. Throughout this period, the GMD maintained a few consistent positions on nationalism: the concept of political tutelage; the goal of the unification, or restoration, of all sovereign Chinese territory; and, despite the authoritarianism following 1927, the promotion of revolutionary nationalism, intended to lead to democracy through the transformative powers of military-style discipline.

By contrast, following the collapse of the First United Front in 1927, emerging leaders within the CCP, including Mao Zedong, criticized the idea that national revitalization could be achieved by the GMD because of its relationships with foreign powers. Mao insisted that the GMD's links to the financial resources of China's capitalists, landlords, and petty bourgeoisie made it *inherently antagonistic* to national unification, because the propertied class was reliant on international finance—in other words imperialism.[2] Consequently, Mao and his supporters in the CCP advised against cooperating with the GMD for national liberation. Initially, this viewpoint was one of many within the party, vigorously challenged by Russian-trained Chinese communists.[3] The military failure leading to the collapse of the Jiangxi Soviet in 1935, however, followed by violent clashes such as the 1940 New Fourth Army Incident, delegitimized CCP members who advocated cooperation with the GMD. This set the stage for the Yan'an Rectification Campaign (1942–4), where Mao's views of national unification (and Marxism) became orthodox. Thereafter, the CCP's ideology, as crafted by Mao and his supporters, rejected Trotskyism and emphasized the use of 'the people' to secure national interests (in the language of anti-imperialism). Consequently, post-war Maoists would regularly engage in mass-mobilization campaigns that emphasized organization 'from below' (albeit with the imprimatur of the central leadership). Because nationalism had always been part of Mao's 'sinification of Marxism', these campaigns often took on a narrowly sinocentric character. After the CCP's victory in 1949, the party (under Mao's leadership) proclaimed the restoration of 'China' through party leadership; building communism was equivalent to (re-)constructing the nation, Chinese identity, and finally resolving the problems of the past such as prostitution, gambling, banditry, and opium.[4]

The importance of nationalism in Chinese communist discourse is demonstrated by the fact that arguably the first major mass campaign of the PRC was directed against the United States during the Korean War (1950–3). Mao's 'military romanticism' involved guerrilla-style mobilization to confront the expansion of US interests along China's border. Sold to the newly minted citizens of a communist state as an 'anti-imperialist' war of liberation conducted by a 'volunteer army', the conflict carried echoes of CCP rhetoric developed during the War of Resistance against Japan (1937–45). Peng Dehuai, who was given the thankless task of leading Chinese forces, declared that the United States was 'fighting for imperialism', and that China's presence in Korea was 'a just war and a struggle for national liberation'.[5] Nationalism's continuing importance in Maoism was exposed again during the Great Leap Forward (1958–61). Always articulated as a symbol of Chinese greatness vis-à-vis foreign powers, whenever local cadres set impossibly high target figures for agricultural output, they proclaimed to have 'launched a sputnik' against foreign enemies. While conducting widespread language reforms, party leaders lauded the importance of the Chinese language in expressing *uniquely* Chinese sentiments—therefore, a proposal to Romanize Chinese was considered treasonous. Even movements that seem utterly dominated by domestic political concerns, such as the Three Antis, Five Antis, and the Anti-Rightist Campaigns (1951–2)[6] harkened back to the wartime days of Yan'an, when the CCP preached national liberation through party leadership. CCP efforts to transform 'China', then, were also aimed at creating it: language reform was simultaneous with calls for 'liberating' Taiwan, the suppression of Tibetan independence movements was followed by attacks on the Chinese 'bourgeoisie', and PRC films both lauded the new socialist citizen and dramatized the suppression of borderland 'bandits'. In this sense, making a sharp division between Maoism as ideology and 'national interest' does not help in the analysis of nationalism. Even after unification under CCP rule, 'imperialist' threats to national sovereignty continued without any end in sight. Thus, as in the non-communist world, the 'threat' to *ideological* ideals was often also seen as perilous to *national* interest.

Nevertheless, one of the enduring contradictions of CCP nationalist discourse was that it also expressed itself as part of a global socialist movement; these disputes over how to combat imperialism and achieve national sovereignty resulted in serious conflicts with its 'big brother', the Soviet Union. While the PRC relied heavily on the USSR for technology transfers, trade, and equipment (especially during the Great Leap Forward, 1958–61), Mao and his supporters meanwhile attempted to adopt a position of leadership vis-à-vis the USSR in inspiring global 'anti-imperialist' movements. Tensions between the USSR and the PRC were exacerbated by the 'Sino-Soviet Split' during the 1950s, when Stalin's death (1953) triggered a re-evaluation of his system of governance under his successor, Nikita Khrushchev. These conflicts were sustained abroad by the PRC foreign ministry, headed by Chen Yi, who had sent aid to 'national liberation' movements in countries such as Indonesia in the 1960s. This was particularly infuriating for Soviet leadership, which was already expending tremendous resources around the world in order to fend off NATO; for CCP leadership, then, the USSR represented a threat to emerging socialist nations' independence, and the growth of Soviet influence was a threat to national sovereignty worldwide. Accusations of 'big-power chauvinism' were not a 1960s Maoist invention; they were not far off, in terms of rhetorical effect, from the old anti-imperialist invective developed by the GMD during the War of Resistance. In 1958, whilst the CCP was criticizing the USSR, in fact, it was also preparing to shell GMD-controlled islands near mainland Chinese shores. Although Mao seems to have entertained rather Orwellian ambitions of keeping the populace in a state of constant mobilization leading up to the Great Leap Forward (GLF),[7] these moves, which greatly imperilled China's relationship with the USSR, were heavily reliant on the language of national unification and liberation. Also, the anti-Soviet rhetoric of the CCP was not restricted to Mao or his supporters; in general, the PRC leadership viewed any sort of US-Soviet détente as a form of capitulation to imperialism. After the GLF, in 1963, Chinese leaders referred to the USSR-UK-US Test Ban Treaty as a 'dirty fraud' aimed at maintaining a nuclear monopoly, and this came under the leadership of (then President) Liu Shaoqi while Mao had temporarily 'retired' from politics.[8] This sort of antagonism between socialist powers (including serious border clashes in 1969), couched in the terms of national liberation, continued until the 1970s, when Sino-American rapprochement in part made possible Deng Xiaoping's reforms.

The PRC rivalry with foreign powers, in the name of defending its sovereignty, put undue pressure on many of China's 'minorities' in the borderlands—exemplified by the crisis over the 1962 flight of thousands of Uighurs to the USSR. As Michael Szonyi demonstrated, competing states with the same claims of 'liberation' turned heretofore geographically insignificant places into spaces of extraordinary importance, effectively 'geopoliticizing' nearly every aspect of their society, economy, and even daily life.[9] The preoccupation with liminal spaces (geographically speaking) and liminal people (ethnically speaking, with the Han at the epicentre of Chinese nationalism) is a reflection of the profound insecurity of Chinese nationalism.[10] It was not merely insecure due to divisions of state (PRC versus ROC), however, but also due to the immense non-Chinese population in the heart of 'China' itself. China's 'minorities', particularly in sensitive borderlands, were increasingly important in the reification of the nation's geographical boundaries during the post-war period. While this process began earlier, during the expansion of Chinese anthropology as part of the war effort,[11] it became sharply amplified during the period of PRC national integration. In fact, the ambiguous space that non-Han groups occupy in post-war China reflected the late-Qing and early Republican vacillations between anti-Manchu Han nationalism and calls for the 'harmony of the five races'. The PRC, although operating with much greater ideological conformity in its political discourse, still wavered between assimilation and, for want of a better term, multiculturalism. Assimilation discourse has been influential throughout the Sinophone world: in 1957 Zhou Enlai quipped that 'The Han are so numerous because they have assimilated other nationalities',[12] the historical concept of 'Sinicization' came back into vogue both on the mainland and in Taiwan,[13] and scholars explained the 'unification' of nationalities with the Han as a consequence of Chinese cultural and technological superiority.[14] Nevertheless, the early PRC state also adopted Stalinist practices, including defining minority groups as 'nationalities' (*minzu*), and fifty-five such 'nations' within the PRC had been accepted by the state by 1955. In this context, the ontological project of Chinese nationalism contained within it several contradictions that were (and are) readily apparent to those who are not 'Han'. Within the PRC, then, in 'autonomous zones' (*zizhiqu*) that are 'self-governed' by ethnic groups including Tibetans, Uyghurs, Mongolians, Hui, and Yi, independent nationalisms evolved in dialogue with an ideological state apparatus that has consistently promoted 'national unification' (*minzu tuanjie*).[15] Since the late nineteenth century, then, the inheritance of the Qing Empire, built in an age before nationalism, has presented post-war China with significant structural and demographic problems.

Still, perhaps the largest contradiction here is that, while minority groups were encouraged to don the trappings of difference, the Han themselves went through a tumultuous period of attacking markers of their shared cultural heritage—even if some took limited measures to defend China's treasures from the Cultural Revolution (1966–76).[16] Throughout the period of the Cultural Revolution, radicals not only destroyed symbols of 'Chineseness', they also frequently disrupted China's relations with its neighbours (most importantly, the USA and the USSR) by attacking foreign embassies and promoting a global, transnational, Maoist revolution in countries such as Indonesia, Cambodia, Korea, and Vietnam; this violence and instability was, in fact, a rearticulation of the principles of Maoism itself: not just the 1954 and 1958 'crises' over Taiwan, but even as far back as the rhetoric of an anti-imperialist struggle for national sovereignty conducted through socialist means. The consequences of this form of continual national 'liberation' were serious for China's political stability, foreign relations, economic development, and culture. Indeed, the end of Maoism may have been a victory for Chinese nationalism, for, even with 'Red Tourism', the state is no longer strongly committed to the divisive class conflict through which the party formerly legitimized its control;[17] nevertheless, many of the normal tools used to reify nationhood, including the transmission of art forms, material culture, and religious traditions, have been damaged or lost as a result of Maoism. Trying to (re-) constitute the roots of Chinese national identity after the Maoist period continues to be a highly problematic project.

Throughout the Maoist period, the CCP tried to claim the mantle of Chinese nationalism from Sun Yat-sen; meanwhile, Sun's party, the GMD, was still active on Taiwan. The ROC government also claimed that its mission was national unification and liberation of the Chinese people, and Chiang Kai-shek, throughout the 1950s, insisted that the PRC government was controlled by its puppet masters in Moscow. The ROC government intensified its 'cultural education' during this period, which emphasized mainland 'Chinese' civilization; by making the Taiwanese more Chinese than the mainlanders, Chiang's government was creating a 'real' China outside of the Maoist state.[18] In this way, the language of Chinese nationalism had become inextricably linked with Cold War ideological divisions, with each side claiming to be saving the 'real China'.

Chinese nationalism in the post-war period is thus stridently expressed not only because of the diverse ethnic groups within the PRC or the ongoing 'crisis' with Taiwan, but also because of the contradictions within the discourse of national identity itself. The PRC state tries desperately, on the one hand, to show how it can encompass many 'nations' (*minzu*), even a 'greater China' (*dazhongguo*) beyond its borders,[19] but its symbolism rests almost exclusively on Han Chinese cultural examples; indeed, in some cases, mobilization of patriotic sentiment is rooted in the retelling of premodern Han Chinese narratives of 'barbarian suppression', which include violent confrontations with peoples who are now ostensibly part of the polity (for example, Mongols and 'Manchurians'). This contradiction—between a multi-ethnic state and a unified 'Chinese' nation—was further exposed by the PRC's nationality policy in 1980 concerning the residents of the soon-to-be-returned city of Hong Kong: the state maintained there was room for non-Han people in 'China', but non-'Chinese' residents of Hong Kong were not permitted to become citizens. This sort of confusing government policy is strongly reminiscent of the muddled 'harmony of the five races', wherein a Mongol or a Tibetan can somehow be quintessentially 'Chinese', but an Indian or a white Englishman cannot. Territorial disputes will continue to add fuel to the fire of modern Chinese nationalism, but the most powerful anxieties are born out of its inherent contradictions.

Japan: The Trouble with Being 'Normal'

When compared superficially with China, Japanese nationalism has contended with radically different historical factors: 'blessed' with natural geographical boundaries that were accepted by the imperial powers of the nineteenth century, sorting out who was Japanese could be resolved by simple reference to a map. As Rana Mitter has shown in this volume (Chapter 14), however, the legacy of the empire and nation-building project had left Japan, as it did in China, with a state presiding over many ethnic groups,[20] despite the state's attempts to promote what Oguma Eiji has referred to as 'the myth of Japanese homogeneity'.[21] To further complicate the matter, the boundaries of Japan after World War II were ultimately a decision made by the victorious Allies, and this has greatly affected Japanese nationalism. On the political front, Japan's post-war nationalism has been, to a large degree, shaped by its relationship with the United States and the Cold War. Even beyond the US occupation (1946–52), Japan continued to be a junior partner in American global ambitions. Domestically, nationalism was influenced by the actions of the US, but, on the cultural front, pre-war and wartime nationalist discourse was also enduring. Thus, in order to make sense of the continuance of Japanese imperial discourse, changes in the political environment after 1945 must first be considered.

During the Allied occupation, for a brief period between the time American forces first arrived and the so-called 'reverse course' of the early 1950s,[22] it seemed possible that Japanese politics, society, and nationalism might be radically transformed from its wartime past. First, the new pro-American prime minister, Shidehara Kijūrō, supported the development of a new 'pacifist' constitution that rejected the nation's right to send its army abroad, and severely restricted defence spending (under the famous Article 9). Directly after this, the Japanese Socialist Party (JSP), led by Katayama Tetsu, rode on a wave of criticism (of the wartime state) and protest (against the USA and Japanese conservatives) to government in May 1947. Embittered veterans, demobilized university students, and long-suppressed political activists felt that the time to re-define 'Japan' and its national system had come. In a bid to win a broad base of support, the JSP and the Japanese Communist Party (JCP) made a significant effort to tie their political platforms to Japanese nationalism, which was seen as a model that the Chinese communists were using with considerable success.[23] Nevertheless, although they would carry on as important parliamentary opposition, Katayama's government failed almost immediately due, in part, to internal squabbling over appointments; it also demonstrated, however, what would become a fundamental characteristic of the post-war system: the continuing dominance of an unelected civilian bureaucracy that was particularly strong in economic affairs.[24] The efforts of occupation forces to purge the government were largely feckless: the Far Eastern Military Tribunal removed only the most visible and influential military leaders, leaving intact most of the civilian bureaucracy, including those who had supported expansionism and ultra-nationalism (but not domestic military rule). One of these individuals was the conservative politician Yoshida Shigeru, whose 'Yoshida Doctrine', put simply, stated that the Japanese government would not seek rearmament until it had sufficiently recovered from the war. In the meantime, Japan would serve as America's ally in the containment of global communism.[25] Professional bureaucrats, once in league with a dominant political party (see below), would help revive Japanese anti-communism, and define Japanese nationalism as being primarily committed to economic development.

It is not fully accurate, however, to see the economically minded bureaucrats as happy supplicants in the expansion of US power. Even Yoshida was displeased with the subordination of Japan to US military and strategic interests, and many conservatives agreed with him.[26] Japanese post-war politicians were frequently tied to industrialists and bankers by descent and marriage, but not militarists; they were not the 'go fast' imperialists of the wartime era.[27] Thus, the removal of the military leadership by the leadership of the Allied occupation refocused Japanese state efforts towards the accumulation of wealth through state-supported capitalist expansion, for which the Bretton Woods system and the US-Japan relationship was ideally suited. As a consequence, post-war Japanese nationalism found itself articulated in terms of economic achievements. Development (or 'modernization') as patriotism was not entirely new in Japan,[28] but national power was no longer promoted (or defined) by the gun, and, certainly by the 1950s, the dominant justification for government policy was, in a single word, 'growth'.

Thus, Japanese nationalism lost its military character[29] and became inextricably linked with industrialization, capital accumulation, and export-led development. This is also the history of Japan's most successful political party, the Liberal Democratic Party (LDP), which built its nearly uninterrupted half-century of dominance not only on rural pork-barrel politics but on 'growth nationalism'—albeit one that would require sacrifices from Japan's working classes.[30] Pursuant to an agreement amongst Japanese conservatives in the early post-war period, the 1955 formation of the LDP was largely achieved through the leadership of Prime Minister Hatoyama Ichirō with three major policies: oppose trade-union power, boost foreign exports (which included the normalization of relations with Asian neighbours), and defend security agreements with the United States (the Yoshida Doctrine). 'Growth nationalism' would not only steal thunder from unions (as well as the JSP and JCP) seeking to exploit enduring class divisions, but also place Japan within an increasingly tightly knit, global, capitalist 'Pax Americana'. For many Japanese citizens, this was symbolized in 1959 by the selection of Tokyo as the site for the 1964 Summer Olympics. The primacy of 'growth' reached its zenith with Prime Minister Ikeda Hayato's 1960 'Income Doubling Plan', which aimed to secure LDP dominance and weaken opposition from the left. This model became so successful that it has been emulated by Japan's neighbours, including Malaysia, Indonesia, the Republic of Korea, the Republic of China (Taiwan), Singapore, and even the contemporary PRC.[31]

Hitching Japan's wagon to the star of 'Pax Americana', and thereby legitimizing their patriotism in the public eye, might have seemed an astute manoeuvre on the part of the LDP, but unpredictable shifts in US policy created tremendous instability in Japan. First, the emergence of the nuclear arms race between the United States and Japan's nearby neighbour, the Soviet Union, caused considerable anxiety. When occupation-period security agreements approached expiration in the late 1950s, many Japanese citizens aggressively protested Prime Minister Hatoyama's attempt to rally Diet support for ratification of the 'Treaty of Mutual Cooperation and Security between the United States and Japan' (commonly referred to as 'Ampō') by 1960. The vision of Japan embraced by opponents of the Security Treaty was of a peaceful, non-aligned country, but was still a form of patriotism. Second, being America's 'unsinkable battleship' in a war to contain communism was never an equal partnership, and this regularly generated political crises and catastrophes for Japanese governments. These moments of instability would open pathways for alternative views on Japan's future, particularly for rival factions within the LDP. For example, Richard Nixon's erratic behaviour (often referred to as 'Nixon Shock'), as well as calculated pressure from Chinese Foreign Minister Zhou Enlai, helped to bring down the government of Prime Minister Satō Eisaku in 1972, much to the delight of his rivals.

In fact, the 1960 Ampō crisis and the normalization of relations with the PRC in 1972 were the defining moments for Japanese post-war nationalism across the spectrum. First, to the extent that an individual Japanese citizen had strong feelings about the nation, they would have an equally strong opinion about the Security Treaty—whether for or against. On the left, resistance to the Treaty galvanized what would otherwise have been a political community divided by views on Russian and Chinese communism, non-violent resistance or armed confrontation with the Japanese government, and whether or not to work with American 'democracy' in Japan.[32] The far right was emboldened by US anti-communism to attack their enemies in the 'peace movement' and the far left, perceiving them to be a fifth column. Several incidents of right-wing violence against labour unions and pacifists demonstrated that the putative threat of communist insurgency had rejuvenated militarism, imperialism, and ultra-nationalism amongst some elements of Japan's wartime generation; these pro-military, 'patriotic', and highly nationalistic individuals and groups had, since 1917, consistently placed international communism as the chief threat to Japanese interests and sovereignty.

In this sense, the strong presence of US strategy in Japanese politics helped shape the kinds of nationalism expressed, and at the heart of this debate was what kind of 'nation' Japan should be: peaceful or strong, pro-PRC or pro-containment, subordinate to US foreign policy or independent, supportive of Taiwanese independence or dismissive of the ROC. Ultranationalist groups within the LDP, such as the 'Cold Front Group' (*Seirankai*), vigorously attacked any attempt to normalize relations with the PRC on Zhou Enlai's terms, while other LDP conservatives saw trade relations with China to be an immensely important step towards establishing Japanese economic independence from the United States. Those on the left perceived that the Japanese would continue suffering from a pathological national chauvinism until it confronted its crimes against China, which necessitated working with the PRC, and not just Chiang Kai-shek's government. Inevitably, perhaps, these disputes spilled over into education. In the well-known 1980s textbook controversy, Sino-Japanese relations were imperilled by the (alleged) attempts of the Ministry of Education to change the description of Japanese 1937 'invasion' (*shinryaku*) to a mere 'advance' (*shinshutsu*) into Chinese territory. Pitting the JCP-backed Teachers' Union (*Nikkyōso*) against the conservative Ministry bureaucrats, struggles over how young Japanese should learn modern history was a reflection of diverging discourses on the nation.

Indeed, nostalgia for the imperial past has been a significant influence over expressions of post-war Japanese nationalism; disaggregating the constructed historical memory of this past from the actual discursive influences from that bygone era is complicated. First, the pre-war origins of national myth-making were still powerful in the post-war period. In terms of promoting nationalist support for the armed forces, history museums such as those of the Self-Defence Forces still draw on the rhetoric of state Shintō and wartime patriotism to inspire their recruits. Second, the concept of 'Japanese culture', as a *national* culture, was itself a product of government efforts. Though grounded in early modern philosophy,[33] 'national culture', as such, was a modern state-led enterprise, even if it also drew heavily on civilian participation. Once the definition of 'Japaneseness' became a preoccupation amongst scholars in interwar Japan, 'uniqueness' was to be a continual fixture in Japanese nationalist discourse, culminating in the 'theory of the Japanese people', or Nihonjinron, that became popular in the 1970s.[34] Thus, discussing 'what Japan is' reified 'Japan' itself and, as Japanese Zen Buddhism and 'wabi-sabi' aesthetics became popular in America and Western Europe, foreign admirers reaffirmed claims of 'uniqueness' for Japanese nationalists. Third, ethnology and anthropology played an important role in this process. The Tokyo Anthropological Society (formed 1884) became one of the first non-Western anthropological groups and, significantly, began with studying the origins and character of the members' own 'ethnos'—the Japanese themselves. By the time the famous folklorist Yanagita Kunio emerged on the scene in the 1930s, Japanese ethnology, anthropology, and archaeology had already produced reams of scholarship on what it meant to be 'Japanese'. Yanagita is significant, however, as a transitional figure: in 1946 he communicated to the next generation of scholars that, in the perilous post-war period, their study of national uniqueness would be even *more* important than when they had travelled far and wide in service of the empire.[35] In the 1950s many scholars continued to accept that the social sciences would concern themselves with the task of defining 'Japaneseness'. Thus, 'Japanese civilization' and 'Japaneseness' were already fixed (and largely accepted) within the post-war discourse on identity and culture in Japan, largely due to the success of the interwar ontological project of defining 'Japanese civilization' as a monolithic entity.

Changes in the political system have, however, affected the nature of post-war Japanese nationalism. The 1994 electoral reform, combined with administrative reforms in 2001, greatly weakened the LDP's '1955 System', and television and other forms of mass media have also played a role. Consequently, a broader, often nationalistic rhetoric has emerged, particularly amongst conservatives, in order to rally support during Diet elections; on the far right, this can involve a specious romanticization and troubling nostalgia for the wartime past, as seen in cultural spaces such as Yasukuni Shrine and its museum Yūshūkan in Tokyo. Thus, since the 1980s, a 'new nationalism' has emerged in Japanese electoral rhetoric, especially symbolized by politicians such as Nakasone Yasuhiro. Nevertheless, given the failure of the recent Hatoyama government (only the second non-LDP government since 1955) to remove the US military base at Futenma, it would appear that the major parameters of the US-Japan relationship, created through the Yoshida Doctrine, remain strong. The US-Japan relationship continues to have a profound influence over how the Japanese express their nationalism in the post-war period, producing several distinct discourses on 'Japan'. Despite the fact that Japanese politics have changed significantly since the 1980s, newer discourses of the ideal nation still have deep roots in the Cold War, the Sino-Japanese relationship, and the vestiges of Japan's former empire.

First, beginning in the 1980s, the US-Japan relationship produced a stridently conservative nationalism that continues to seek to free Japanese foreign policy from US dominance. These headline-grabbing members of Japan's far-right above all desire the re-establishment of a fervently patriotic and pro-military culture that would greatly resemble, perhaps unsurprisingly, the ideals of American neoconservatives. Like American 'neocons', not only are they anti-union and anti-socialist, they also envision a Japan that would promote its national interests through the UN Security Council and even direct military intervention. As in the pre-war period, there appears to be some connection between these groups and criminal organizations (smuggling, corruption, and, of course, the Japanese mafia), although not all 'grass-roots' supporters of the new Japanese right-wing nationalism are engaged in illegal activities, sympathetic with them, or even aware of them. It is also erroneous simply to equate this brand of Japanese neoconservatism with the LDP, since some of the targets of the *uyokudan* (right-wing domestic terror groups) include LDP members such as Katō Kōichi. These are the Japanese nationalists who want to create a 'Japan that can say "no"' (to the USA), and they fully embrace the 'myth of Japanese homogeneity'. Domestically and abroad, they promote an exotic Japan with timeless traditions that must be preserved from foreign (formerly American, but increasingly Chinese and Korean) influence. Like the British National Party, the Japanese right wing is unlikely ever to gain a majority in the Diet (or even be a majority within a coalition government); nevertheless, like the American 'Tea Party Caucus', it can influence the policies of larger conservative parties such as the LDP in a manner out of step with its actual electoral support, and thus poses a continual risk to Japanese domestic and foreign policy.

Second, 'pacifist nationalism' shows remarkable durability, even as it responds to new forms of political and social organization. Its most visible incarnation is the 'peace movement' (*heiwa undō*), which has seized the post-war Constitution as an opportunity resolutely to oppose any form of rearmament. This movement is a loose coalition including members of the Teachers' Union, the JSP, and JCP, various 'peace museums', and even ordinary 'bicycle citizens' who organize within the local food cooperatives.[36] Despite their shared opposition to the subordination of Japanese foreign policy, they are bitter enemies of the new right-wing movements because of domestic issues. The relative strength of the 'pacifist nationalists' vis-à-vis the 'patriotic nationalists' is due largely to the former's broader base of support; the latter relies on a narrow, if very active, group on the far right, whereas the former draws in housewives, students, pensioners, and, of course, the far left. Here is one of Japan's strongest post-war contradictions: Yoshida's plan for 'restoring' pre-war Japan produced a voting block of citizens who have locked on to the view that their country is a non-aligned 'peaceful nation'. Also ironically, the movement has vigorously attacked US-Japan security treaties, US foreign policy (particularly in Vietnam), and Japan's position within the US 'nuclear umbrella'—in other words, all of the conditions that arguably made Japan's 'pacifist' Constitution possible in the first place. Whether the Constitution could survive the collapse of US-Japan security agreements is unclear and often debated passionately.

Third, a far subtler form of post-war Japanese nationalism has developed, which employs terms such as 'normative' and 'globalized'. When Japan was criticized for not sending troops in support of the First Gulf War (1990–1), the perceived need to 'become a normal nation' arguably became mainstream political discourse. It appears that, whenever descriptions of 'Japan' make reference to idealized claims of 'normal' nationhood, this notion of 'nation' is apparently defined by some sort of (imagined) international standard. In this discourse, Japan is an 'outnation', or an abnormality, and its political, social, and/or cultural systems must be realigned with the world's. This is not merely an invention of pundits or the state; Japanese industry's vigorous embrace of the International Standards Organization (ISO), the ubiquitous presence of citizens in nearly every major international NGO/NPO group, and the advocacy of 'international' issues in the domestic context (for example, environmentalism and human rights) show us that, above all, the Japanese 'nation' is most popularly desired to be 'normal'. Although 'normative, globalized nationalism' has become a stronger force in post-war Japanese politics, preoccupation with 'normal' nationhood has always been part of political speech in Japan.[37] Political figures in pre-war Japan described their expansionist policies as a 'normal' part of global power politics and, when Japanese expansion encountered resistance after World War I, powerful, state-sanctioned cries of Japanese exceptionalism emerged. There is little that is less 'exceptional' than claims of national uniqueness, but the post-war return to 'normalcy' and belonging to a 'global community' can be interpreted as Japanese efforts to distinguish two things: 1. attempts to achieve independence from the US-Japan relationship; and 2. Japan's 'rogue nation' status after leaving the League of Nations in 1933.

Nevertheless, Japan's 'normative nationalism' is rife with contradictions, including the fact that both the 'patriotic' far right and the 'pacifist' left employ the rhetoric extensively. First, the 'patriotic' nationalists see the use of military power in defence of national interests as entirely 'normal', and it is not difficult to see how they might adopt this view. Prime Minister Koizumi Junichirō did not see the difference between a US president's prayer of thanksgiving for Vietnam veterans' sacrifices and his 'personal' worship of Japan's war dead at Yasukuni Shrine. In the view of Japan's 'neoconservatives', it is only through the hypocrisy of 'victor's justice' (in other words the Tokyo War Crimes trials) that Japan is kept out of the realm of 'normality', where it could participate in, for example, a UN-mandated 'coalition of the willing'. The right's adoption of the rhetoric of 'normality' should not be seen as transparent realpolitik, because, among other reasons, the dedication of right-wing nationalists in Japan to this discourse has built bridges with their comrades in Western Europe—exemplified by the visit of the French far-right leader Jean-Marie Le Pen to Yasukuni in August 2010. As a testament to the allure of this rhetoric, the language of the 'peace movement', populated as it is by both moderate liberals and the far left, mirrors what Japan's neoconservatives are claiming, but on different issues. Why must Japan be continually occupied by the USA, they claim, when it has not invaded a foreign country in decades? It is only the cruel reality of the post-war Security Treaty that has rendered Japan 'abnormal' and unable fully to exorcize the spectre of US 'neo-imperialism' and nuclear weaponry. Japan should be free to *oppose* the United States, through the UN Security Council. Thus, both sides want a 'Japan that can say "no"' to the USA, but they are utterly incapable of agreeing on what exactly Japan should oppose.

In the 1990s the nationalistic, right-wing *manga* (graphic novels) of Kobayashi Yoshinori attracted the attention of observers of Japanese politics.[38] Because of his apparent popularity, Kobayashi's views—including the sacrifice of one's body for the nation, military might, and historical revisionism—might seem alarmingly mainstream in Japan today, but one should not immediately conflate high sales with political consensus. Most Japanese citizens embrace 'normative nationalism' as an expression of their fundamental political moderation. In other words, Japan should not aggressively defend its interests through military might, nor should it continue to be subordinate to US interests in the name of domestic pacifism. The ultimate impossibility of defining what course the Japanese government should take is reflective of the extraordinary plurality of political opinion in democratic post-war Japan, even if its inherent contradictions produce anxiety (and poorly written *manga*).

Conclusion (and a Short Note about Korea)

In many respects, Korea is the real 'outnation' of post-war East Asian nationalism (along with Taiwan's ROC after the end of GMD dominance), and here the contradictions of Korea's historical experience have generated what might be the strongest nationalism in the entire region. First, while most Koreans identify the entire Peninsula as a single 'nation', it has been divided into two states since the conclusion of the Korean War in 1953: the Democratic People's Republic of Korea (DPRK) in the North and the Republic of Korea (ROK) in the South. Like the long civil war between the GMD and the CCP, the ideological warfare conducted between the two states is often fought in the arena of claims to monopolize legitimate nationalism.[39] The DPRK continues to draw from its history of resistance against foreign aggression, whilst the ROK emulates both the ROC and Japan in its reliance on export-led economic growth for its appeal. Second, Korea has an imperial legacy that is radically different from that of its neighbours (again, apart from the ROC). From 1905 it was subject to protectorate status under the Japanese Empire, and then from 1910 to 1945 it simply ceased to exist as a sovereign nation. Accusations of familial collaboration with the Japanese Empire can be a stinging form of insult, even though most Koreans of any means (including former president Park Chung Hee) had done so. Whether the Japanese development of Korea was on balance positive or negative is something Korean historians have vigorously debated in the past, and continue to do so. Still, despite strong claims of uniqueness, the Korean case bears some similarity to that of its post-war neighbours.

Korean nationalism relied on spurious or politically motivated research in anthropology and archaeology;[40] featured communism that is made to fit patriotic discourse;[41] adopted the image of suffering women as a symbol of national humiliation;[42] bore witness to conflict between left-leaning, pacifist movements (usually involving university students) and pro-government right- wing groups; and, perhaps most importantly, has been structured by the ROK's ongoing relationship with the United States and its changing regional strategies. In the last case, the beginnings of the Republic of Korea's independence from Japan were characterized by the corrupt politics of President Syngman Rhee, who was supported by the United States. Rhee's fall (following massive student protests) in 1961 led to the emergence of military leaders who dominated Korean politics until the 1990s—once again as a result of cooperation with American strategy in Northeast Asia. Unlike Japan, citizens of the ROK were not able to voice their discontent through a properly representational government, and thus had to resort to acts of protest. For many citizens of the ROK, then, the obstacle to national unification was American military power, which was symbolized by the ubiquitous GIs who roamed (and sometimes menaced) Korean streets. Nevertheless, the projection of US power resulted in Korea's own form of 'growth nationalism'. Like Japan, the state asked individuals to defer personal 'luxury' consumption in favour of national development, leading to an era of high growth and eventually prosperity by the 1980s.[43] Although it suffers more from contradictions due to its ongoing division and experience of imperialism, the ROK has largely aligned itself with the 'growth nationalism' of Japan and the post-Reform Era PRC.

Meanwhile, China and Japan continue to struggle with the vestiges of their imperial past, which even the conflagration and widespread suffering of World War II failed to resolve. Discourses of uniqueness—which, ironically, make them appear more similar to each other than different—were carried over from the pre-war into the post-war period, handily surviving attacks by scholars, public intellectuals, and educators armed with a postmodernist scepticism regarding national identity.[44] China's internal divisions are far more serious than those of Japan, in part because Japan's empire was largely destroyed, whilst the PRC struggles to preserve the boundaries of the Qing dynasty. Nevertheless, Japan's internal political factions are serious, and may grow even more so when and if the US-Japan Alliance ceases to have a reason for its existence. When that happens, and the perilous domestic struggle over Japan's future role in Asia comes to the forefront of politics, stronger articulations of nationalism, like those in the PRC and Korea, are sure to follow.

Notes

1. Sun Yat-sen's 'Three Principles of the People' (*Sanminzhuyi*) was the early GMD's primary text of political philosophy, but it was also used later by Chiang Kai-shek. M.-C. Bergère (1998) *Sun Yat-sen*, trans. Janet Lloyd, Stanford, CA; and J. Taylor (2009) *The Generalissimo: Chiang Kai-shek and the Struggle for Modern China*, Cambridge, MA.
2. For the clearest articulation, see Mao's famous speech, 'On New Democracy', in T. Cheek (1996) *Mao Zedong and China's Revolutions*, Armonk, NY, 76–112. See also D. Apter and T. Saich (eds.) (1996) *The Rise to Power of the Chinese Communist Party*, Armonk, NY, 316–17; J. K. S. Yick (1995) *Making Urban Revolution in China: The CCP-GMD Struggle for Beiping-Tianjin, 1945–1949*, Armonk, NY, 20–33.
3. Some of these debates are summarized in W. T. de Bary (ed.) (2000) *Sources of Chinese Tradition*, vol. 2, New York, NY, 426–49. Also see essays in T. Saich and H. van de Ven (eds.) (1995) *New Perspectives on the Chinese Communist Revolution*, Armonk, NY.
4. Zhou Yongming, 'Nationalism, Identity, and State-Building: The Antidrug Crusade in the People's Republic, 1949–1952', in T. Brook and B. Wakabayashi (eds.) (2000) *Opium Regimes: China, Britain, and Japan, 1839–1952*, Berkeley, CA.
5. Quoted in S. G. Zhang (1995) *Mao's Military Romanticism: China and the Korean War, 1950–1953*, Lawrence, KS, 190.
6. Although the Three Antis and Five Antis Campaigns (1951–2) were mainly aimed at domestic issues such as corruption, tax evasion, and waste, they were part of the party's attempt to discipline its ranks and achieve unity. Similarly, the Anti-Rightist Campaign (1957–62) was an effort both to silence dissent and achieve ideological conformity within the party.

7. C. C. Jian and Y. Y. Kuisong (1998) 'Chinese Politics and the Collapse of the Sino-Soviet Alliance', in O. A. Westad (ed.) *Brothers in Arms: The Rise and Fall of the Sino-Soviet Alliance*, Stanford, CA, 270–1.
8. C. Pleshakov (1998) 'Nikita Khrushchev and Sino-Soviet Relations', in Westad (ed.) *Brothers in Arms*, 226; and L. M. Lüthi (2008) *The Sino-Soviet Split: Cold War in the Communist World*, Princeton, NJ, 260–72. 'Moderates' such as Zhou Enlai, Deng Xiaoping, and Liu Shaoqi participated in criticizing the Treaty.
9. M. Szonyi (2008) *Cold War Island: Quemoy on the Front Line*, Cambridge.
10. J. A Fogel (2000) 'Introduction: The Nanjing Massacre as History', in Fogel (ed.) *The Nanjing Massacre in History and Historiography*, Berkeley, CA.
11. A. Rodriguez (2010) 'Building the Nation, Serving the Frontier: Mobilizing and Reconstructing China's Borderlands during the War of Resistance (1937–1945)', *Modern Asian Studies*, 45, no. 2 (March), 345–76, and G. E. Guldin (1994) *The Saga of Anthropology in China: From Malinowski to Mao*, Armonk, NY.
12. E. Friedman (1994) 'Reconstructing China's National Identity: A Southern Alternative to Mao-Era Nationalism', *Journal of Asian Studies*, 53, no. 1 (February), 67–91.
13. A. Chun (1994) 'From Nationalism to Nationalizing: Cultural Imagination and State Formation in Postwar Taiwan', *The Australian Journal of Chinese Affairs*, 31.
14. D. C. Gladney's discussion of Fei Xiaotong: Gladney (1991) *Muslim Chinese: Ethnic Nationalism in the People's Republic*, Cambridge, MA, 72–4; and B. Sautman (2001) 'Peking Man and the Politics of Paleoanthropological Nationalism in China', *The Journal of Asian Studies*, 60, no. 1 (February), 95–124.
15. Regarding 'assimilation' and the emergence of 'minority' politics, see J. Dreyer (1971) *China's Forty Millions: Minority Nationalities and National Integration in the People's Republic of China*, Cambridge, MA; and D. Y. H. Wu (1990) 'Chinese Minority Policy and the Meaning of Minority Culture: The Example of Bai in Yunnan, China', *Human Organization*, 49, no. 1, 1–13.
16. D. D. Ho (2006) 'To Protect and Preserve: Resisting the "Destroy the Four Olds" Campaign, 1966–1967', in J. W. Esherick, P. G. Pickowicz, and A. G. Walder (eds.) *The Chinese Cultural Revolution as History*, Stanford, CA.
17. For more on Yan'an in history and memory, see D. Apter and T. Saich (1994) *Revolutionary Discourse in Mao's Republic*, Cambridge, MA, particularly chs. 5 and 7.
18. Chun, 'From Nationalism to Nationalizing', 49–69; S. E. Phillips (2003) *Between Assimilation and Independence: The Taiwanese Encounter Nationalist China, 1945–1950*, Stanford, CA; and Taylor on Chiang's 'final victory' in *Generalissimo*, 533–5.
19. H. Harding (1993) 'The Concept of Greater China: Themes, Variations, and Reservations', *China Quarterly*, 136, 660–86.
20. M. Wiener (1994) *Race and Migration in Imperial Japan*, New York, NY; S. Ryang (1997) *North Koreans in Japan: Language, Ideology and Identity*, Boulder, CO, Part 2: 'The History'; and, of course, many Japanese were also displaced in the empire, subsequently uprooted by SCAP policy: L. Watt (2009) *When Empire Comes Home: Repatriation and Reintegration in Postwar Japan*, Cambridge, MA.
21. O. Eiji (1995) *Tan'itsu minzoku shinwa no kigen—'Nihonjin' no jigazō no keifu*, Tokyo; trans. D. Askew (2002) *A Genealogy of Japanese Self-Images*, Melbourne.
22. The 'reverse course' refers to the Allied Occupation's hardened attitude towards leftists in Japanese politics following the 'fall of China' to the CCP and the acceleration of the civil war in Korea.

23. R. A. Scalapino (1967) *The Japanese Communist Movement, 1920–1966*, Berkeley, CA, 53.
24. C. Johnson (1982) *MITI and the Japanese Miracle: The Growth of Industrial Policy, 1925–1975*, Stanford, CA.
25. J. Dower (1988) *Empire and Aftermath: Yoshida Shigeru and the Japanese Experience, 1878–1954*, Cambridge, MA.
26. See discussion in C. Johnson (1986) 'The Patterns of Japanese Relations with China, 1952–1982', *Pacific Affairs*, 52, no. 3 (Autumn), 402–28.
27. On 'go fast' versus 'go slow' imperialists, see Dower, *Empire and Aftermath*, 85. On the complex relationship between the *zaibatsu* and the military: M. Barnhart (1987) *Japan Prepares for Total War: The Search for Economic Security, 1919–1941*, Ithaca, NY; and L. Young (1998) *Japan's Total Empire: Manchuria and the Culture of Wartime Imperialism*, Berkeley, CA, particularly ch. 4.
28. The historical scholarship in this field is extensive. J. B. Crowley (1966) *Japan's Quest for Autonomy: National Security and Foreign Policy, 1930–1938*, Princeton, NJ; M. Peattie (1975) *Ishiwara Kanji and Japan's Confrontation with the West*, Princeton, NJ; and P. Duus (1955) *The Abacus and the Sword: The Japanese Penetration of Korea, 1895–1910*, Berkeley, CA.
29. For the military character of the period, see R. Smethurst (1974) *A Social Basis for Prewar Japanese Militarism: The Army and the Rural Community*, Berkeley, CA; Young, *Japan's Total Empire*; and especially the new study by K. J. Ruoff (2010) *Imperial Japan at its Zenith: The Wartime Celebration of the Empire's 2,600th Anniversary*, Ithaca, NY.
30. A. Gordon (2001) *The Wages of Affluence: Labor and Management in Postwar Japan*, Cambridge, MA; and G. McCormack (2001) *The Emptiness of Japanese Affluence*, Armonk, NY.
31. S. Garon (2006) 'The Transnational Promotion of Saving in Asia: "Asian Values" or the "Japanese Model"?', in S. Garon and P. L. Maclachlan (eds.) *The Ambivalent Consumer: Questioning Consumption in East Asia and the West*, Ithaca, NY, and (2002) 'Saving for "My Own Good and the Good of the Nation": Economic Nationalism in Modern Japan', in S. Wilson (ed.) *Nation and Nationalism in Modern Japan*, New York. The economic policies of the so-called 'four tigers' (ROC, ROK, Singapore, and Hong Kong) closely followed Japan's: Li-min Hsueh, Chen-kuo Hsu, and D. Perkins (2001) *Industrialisation and the State: The Changing Role of the Taiwan Government in the Economy, 1945–1998*, Cambridge, MA.
32. F. Seraphim (2008) *War Memory and Social Politics in Japan, 1945–2005*, Cambridge, MA. See also L. Hoaglund's (2010) recent documentary, *Anpo*.
33. K. Wigen (1995) *The Making of a Japanese Periphery, 1750–1920*, Berkeley, CA; L. Roberts (1998) *Mercantilism in a Japanese Domain: The Merchant Origins of Economic Nationalism in 18th-Century Tosa*, Cambridge; and D. Howell (2005) *Geographies of Identity in Nineteenth-Century Japan*, Berkeley, CA.
34. For more information, see H. Befu (2001) *Hegemony of Homogeneity: An Anthropological Analysis of 'Nihonjinron'*, Melbourne.
35. T. Morris-Suzuki (1995) 'The Invention and Reinvention of "Japanese Culture"', *The Journal of Asian Studies*, 54, no. 3 (August), 768.
36. R. M. Leblanc (1999) *Bicycle Citizens: The Political World of the Japanese Housewife*, Berkeley, CA.
37. M. Ravina (2005) 'State-Making in Global Context: Japan in a World of Nation-States', in J. Fogel (ed.) (2005) *The Teleology of the Modern Nation State*, Philadelphia, PA.

38. See De Bary, *Sources of Chinese Tradition*, 565–7.
39. Gi-Wook Shin (2006) 'Ilmin Chuŭi and "Modernisation of the Fatherland"', *Ethnic Nationalism in Korea: Genealogy, Politics, and Legacy*, Stanford, CA, ch. 5, 96–110.
40. Hyung Il-Pai (2000) *Constructing 'Korean Origins': Archaeology, Historiography, and Racial Myth*, Cambridge, MA.
41. M. Robinson (1984) 'National Identity and the Thought of Sin Ch'ae-ho: *Sadaejuŭi* and *Chuch'e* in History and Politics', *The Journal of Korean Studies*, 5, 121–42.
42. S. M. Jager (1996) 'Women, Resistance, and the Divided Nation: The Romantic Rhetoric of Korean Reunification', *The Journal of Asian Studies*, 55, no. 1 (February), 3–21.
43. L. C. Nelson (2005) 'South Korean Consumer Nationalism: Women, Children, Credit, and Other Perils', in S. Garon (ed.) *The Ambivalent Consumer: Questioning Consumption in East Asia and the West*, Ithaca, NY, 188–207. See also L. C. Nelson (2000) *Measured Excess: Status, Gender, and Consumer Nationalism in South Korea*, New York.
44. For recent attacks on the coherency of 'nations' in East Asia, see P. Duara (1995) *Rescuing History from the Nation: Questioning Narratives of Modern China*, Chicago, IL; and S. Tanaka (1995) *Japan's Orient: Rendering Pasts into History*, Berkeley, CA, as well as O. Eiji's work (see note 21).

Suggested Further Reading

English-Language Primary Sources

Cheek, T. (ed.) (2002) *Mao Zedong and China's Revolutions: A Brief History with Documents*, New York. A brief introduction with key primary sources, ideal for those encountering Maoism for the first time.

De Bary, W. T., Gluck, C., and Tiedemann, A. E. (eds.) (2000) *Sources of Japanese Tradition, Volume Two: 1600–2000, Part 2: 1868 to 2000*, 2nd edn., New York; De Bary, W. T. and Lufrano, R. (eds.) (2000) *Sources of Chinese Tradition, Volume Two: From 1600 through the Twentieth Century*, 2nd edn., New York. This is an invaluable series with a collection of primary sources covering a broad range of topics in modern Chinese and Japanese history, although it is heavily weighted towards intellectual and political history.

Frolic, B. M. (1980) *Mao's People: Sixteen Portraits of Life in Revolutionary China*, Cambridge, MA. A collection of sixteen biographies, Frolic's book is a useful and readable sourcebook for students interested in the social history of China during the Maoist period.

Secondary Sources

Befu, H. (ed.) (1993) *Cultural Nationalism in East Asia: Representation and Identity*, Berkeley, CA.

Dittmer, L. and Kim, S. S. (eds.) (1993) *China's Quest for National Identity*, Ithaca, NY.

Gladney, D. (1991) *Muslim Chinese: Ethnic Nationalism in the People's Republic*, Cambridge, MA. Gladney's study of China's Muslim population is one of the most useful for understanding the dynamics of ethnic nationalism and minority politics within the boundaries of the PRC.

Vlastos, S. (ed.) (1998) *Mirror of Modernity: Invented Traditions of Modern Japan*, Berkeley, CA. The articles in Vlastos's volume are very useful for disabusing undergraduates of essentialist notions of 'timeless tradition' in Japan; it is occasionally useful for colleagues, as well.

Wilson, S. ed. (2002) *Nation and Nationalism in Modern Japan*, New York.

Zhang, S. G. (1995) *Mao's Military Romanticism: China and the Korean War, 1950–1953*, Lawrence, KS. One of the most interesting studies of Maoist discourse, this monograph exposes how Mao's thought and anti-imperialist nationalism were closely tied.

CHAPTER 24

NATIONALISM IN POST-INDEPENDENCE SOUTHEAST ASIA: A COMPARATIVE ANALYSIS

JOHN T. SIDEL

INTRODUCTION

WHILE the rise and triumph of nationalist movements in Southeast Asia have been discussed and debated by scholars for more than half a century, the trajectories of post-independence nationalism across the region have attracted less academic attention and analysis. Yet the past two decades have witnessed a belated boom in the study of post-independence nationalism in Southeast Asia. This growing body of literature is notable for two distinctive features. First, as with much scholarship on Southeast Asia, the study of post-independence nationalism is dominated by single-country studies, with broader attempts to cover the region as a whole both rare and almost entirely restricted to description rather than analysis. Second, as with much scholarship on nationalism, the treatment of Southeast Asia focuses largely on what is often termed the 'management of diversity', with the primary challenges facing the new nation states of the region seen as those stemming from cultural, ethnic, linguistic, regional, and religious pluralism. This essay, by contrast, departs from these dominant features of the literature on post-independence nationalism in Southeast Asia, offering comparative analysis within the region, and arguing that the primary challenges for nationalism in Southeast Asia lay in the conflicts and compromises, difficulties and disappointments, accompanying the reincorporation of new nation states into the Cold War geopolitical order and the world capitalist economy in the second half of the twentieth century.

Nationalism Without Struggle: Thailand and the Philippines

Thailand and the Philippines entered the post-independence era without the tumultuous patterns of mass mobilization and tortuous processes of transition to independence seen in other parts of Southeast Asia. Thailand escaped direct colonization by the Western powers, and the country was likewise spared Japanese invasion and occupation during World War II. The Philippines, colonized by the Spanish, the Americans, and the Japanese, and devastated by war in 1942–5, won independence in 1946 not through nationalist struggle but as part of a gradual phasing-out of American colonial rule that began in the interwar era. Thus in both countries, nationalism was associated not with disruptive early post-war mass mobilization, but rather the restoration of the status quo *ante bellum*.

Against this backdrop, Thailand and the Philippines established close ties with the new imperial power, the United States, and were quickly incorporated into its geopolitical orbit in the context of the Cold War. By the late 1940s, the Thai and Philippine military establishments were closely linked to the Pentagon, and both countries enjoyed generous American counter-insurgency training, military assistance, and security guarantees against external threats. Both countries, moreover, hosted important US military installations, with the Philippines the home of the single largest American naval base at Subic Bay, and Thailand serving as what was famously described as a vast 'aircraft carrier' for US bombing missions in Indochina and a base for tens of thousands of American troops in Vietnam from the mid-1960s up into the early 1970s.[1]

At the same time, the early and virtually uninterrupted integration of Thailand and the Philippines into the world capitalist economy from the mid-nineteenth century prefigured limitations on early post-war 'economic nationalism' in the two countries. Colonial-era state policies promoting the assimilation and integration of Chinese immigrants had produced Sino-Thai and Chinese-*mestizo* business classes in Thailand and the Philippines, respectively, thus limiting the appeal of early post-war schemes to promote 'national capital' against 'foreign' Chinese competition and control through state intervention and affirmative intervention, which enjoyed far greater popularity elsewhere in the region. In both countries, openness to foreign trade, investment, and ownership remained largely unimpeded by the restrictions imposed by more 'nationalist' governments elsewhere in Southeast Asia. Overall, in both political and economic terms, nationalism in Thailand and the Philippines in the latter half of the twentieth century remained strikingly conservative in terms of welcoming external—'imperialist'—intervention in the political realm and foreign control in the economy, in sharp contrast with patterns elsewhere in Southeast Asia.

Alongside these broad similarities in the fate of nationalism in Thailand and the Philippines, important differences are also discernible and worthy of note. In Thailand, new efforts to promote Thai national identity began to crystallize by the late 1950s under conditions quite different from those obtaining in the Philippines. Thailand, after all, remained under centralized military rule until the early 1970s, and the preceding pattern of state formation under the absolutizing Chakkri dynasty facilitated the top-down imposition of coherent conservative notions of Thai nationhood under authoritarian auspices during the early post-war era. As the school system steadily expanded to incorporate more and more pupils and extended into mass university education during this period, and as national newspapers, radio channels, and television stations incorporated an increasingly broad audience into their orbit, government ministries in Bangkok worked through censorship and control to bring coherence to the meaning of the Thai nation. The Central Thai dialect was promoted as the standardized form of the Thai language at the expense of other linguistic forms, and the map of a timeless Thailand was established as the basis for the geo-body of the Thai nation. A strikingly state-centred account of modern Thai history was inculcated among schoolchildren and university students across the country, lionizing the Chakkri dynasty for its putative defence of the Thai realm against foreign encroachment, preservation of Thai culture, and modernization of the country, even as 'the Thai people' remained inert and invisible in the making of Thailand.[2] The same early post-war decades, moreover, witnessed a broader restoration of the monarchy in public life to a position of centrality in national identity, with the young king Bhumibol Adulyadej positioned by the military dictator General Sarit and his successors as the embodiment of the Thai nation through his central role in an ever-widening range of official duties and state rituals, his long service as Head of State and titular chief of the armed forces, and his tireless efforts as patron of rural development programs and diverse philanthropic activities.[3] Over successive decades, in these capacities and in his episodic interventions in Thai politics, the King thus came to occupy an authoritative—indeed, authoritarian—position in the strikingly hierarchical and conservative 'imagining' of the Thai nation. Challenges to royalist nationalism have been suppressed, through legal and extra-legal means (including *lèse majesté* laws), and through violence. Left-wing and anti-imperialist nationalism in the mid-1970s was extinguished through a campaign of anti-communist persecution, extensive counter-insurgency operations, and a military coup in 1976, all actively supported by the King. The election of a powerful populist prime minister, Thaksin Shinawatra, in 2001, and his unprecedented re-election in 2005, led to large-scale Palace-backed protests and a royalist military coup in 2006. But subsequent elections reaffirmed the continuing popularity of Thaksin, thus attesting to the emergence and endurance of forms of Thai identity not fully captured by royalist official nationalism.

Meanwhile, in stark contrast with the strikingly centralized, consolidated, and conservative form of official nationalism perpetuated and preserved over the past sixty years in Thailand, nationalism in the Philippines from independence in 1946 has been much less firmly lodged in the institutions and symbols of state power and much more available for popular forms of appropriation, representation, and mobilization. With its highly decentralized, American-style presidential democracy, after all, the Philippines was always conspicuously lacking in the kind of Archimedean point from which an avowedly neutral institutionalized embodiment of the national interest could be articulated and asserted. Instead of a strongly state-centred national identity imposed top-down from the national capital as in Thailand, something much less defined and didactic, and much more diffuse and demotic, began to emerge 'from below' in the Philippines through popular representations and struggles styled as 'Filipino'. The first signs of this nascent popular nationalism arose in the late 1960s and early 1970s with the emergence of a lively student movement in the universities of Metro Manila and other Philippine cities, protesting, inter alia, the ongoing use of American military bases in the Philippines in the war in Indochina and the 'parity rights' enjoyed by US companies in the exploitation of natural resources in the archipelago.

With the declaration of martial law in 1972 by then President Ferdinand Marcos, the Philippines experienced its version of Thailand's coup of 1976, but without corresponding success in imposing a hegemonic state-based official nationalism. Indeed, forced underground and further radicalized by martial-law rule, student activists revived the moribund Communist Party of the Philippines (CPP) and built up the New People's Army (NPA) in the 1970s, while organizing a number of closely affiliated 'cause-oriented groups' which by the early 1980s had mobilized hundreds of thousands if not millions of peasants, workers, and urban poor folk against a common national target, the so-called 'US-Marcos Dictatorship'. By the mid-1980s, through strikes, street demonstrations, semi-clandestine meetings, and protest literature, this movement had swelled in tandem with the growth of the NPA in many provinces, creating a nationwide, popular nationalist, counter-hegemonic language and culture of protest—largely in Tagalog (now styled as Pilipino)—with the New Nationalist Alliance (Bagong Alyansang Makabayan or BAYAN) as the leading leftist umbrella group and the folk singer Freddie Aguilar's ballad 'Bayan Ko' ('My Country') as the theme song of the opposition campaign that finally toppled the Marcos regime in 1986. This pattern of sustained popular nationalist mobilization in the Philippines of the 1980s was unparalleled in its breadth, depth, and duration elsewhere in Southeast Asia during the same period.

While popular mobilization in the Philippines peaked and subsided in the 1980s, notions of Filipino national identity have continued to circulate and to cohere in distinctively popular form. Already by the 1970s, the expanding circuitries of the national media industry had, through Tagalog movies and television shows, succeeded in connecting millions of Filipinos to a common 'imagined community' in Tagalog—or 'Pilipino'—reinforced by analogous trends in the production and distribution of consumer goods for a truly *national* market.[4] Meanwhile, the increasing circulation of Filipino labourers, both within the Philippines and internationally, has also worked both to enhance and to define the representation and celebration of the Filipino experience. Aside from complex patterns of internal migration in the archipelago, the growing numbers of Filipino overseas contract workers (OCWs)—working as construction labourers, domestic servants, merchant seamen, nurses, prostitutes, and in a variety of other occupations in Asia, Australia, Europe, the Middle East, and North America—have helped to promote a new kind of 'long-distance nationalism' that stretches far beyond the map of the Philippine islands. With millions of OCWs (and millions more emigrants residing permanently abroad, mostly in the United States) clustering in Filipino labour niches and enclaves, and sending billions of pesos a year home to their loved ones in the Philippines, it could hardly be otherwise.

Indeed, the shared hardships of OCWs from the Philippines have worked to generate new solidarities and forms of consciousness among Filipinos. On construction sites in Saudi Arabia or Japan, at housemaids' day-off meeting places in Abu Dhabi, Hong Kong, Rome, and Singapore, in the basements of hotels and hospitals in London and New York, and on the lower decks of ocean-going freighters, Filipinos regularly congregate to eat, swap stories, and share news from the Philippines. In such venues, and increasingly among concerned friends and relatives back home, the shared lived experience of Filipino OCWs is understood as that of subalterns, as overworked and underpaid, as exploited and ill-treated *Filipinos*. Thus in recent years the abuses suffered by Filipino OCWs—murders in Tokyo, executions in Singapore, imprisonments in Abu Dhabi—have led to widespread *nationalist* outrage, as seen in countless newspaper articles, television shows, and demonstrations in front of foreign embassies in Manila.[5] Thus, in sharp contrast with the conservative, hierarchical, monarchical, official nationalism found in Thailand, the Philippines has come to boast a distinctively popular form of nationalism. This popular nationalism owes much to the experience of anti-Marcos struggles in the 1970s and 1980s, to the enjoyment of Philippine movies, television, and pop music, and to the everyday struggles of Filipino OCWs around the world. Rooted firmly in the lived experience of millions of ordinary Filipinos, popular nationalism in the Philippines has been stimulated and sustained not by 'official nationalism' but by the creative energies of Filipinos labouring outside—and often against—the Philippine state. The contrast between this kind of nationalism in the Philippines and the version found in Thailand could not be sharper.

Nationalists Without National Bourgeoisies?: Burma and Indonesia

In contrast with Thailand and the Philippines, Burma and Indonesia emerged as independent new nation states with a very different kind of early post-independence nationalism. In the colonial era, the emerging market economies of the core zones of British Burma and the Netherlands East Indies were strictly segmented along ethnic lines, with segregated and stigmatized immigrant minority groups—Chettiar 'Indians' in Burma, Hokkien-speaking 'Chinese' in the Indies—serving as 'pariah capitalist' merchants, moneylenders, and middlemen between Western firms and the indigenous peasantry.[6] Against this shared backdrop, nationalist movements in Burma and the

Indies emerged among urban educated youth on the fringes of the state in the core, commercialized zones of colonial rule during the interwar era.[7] In both countries, these nationalist movements were enlisted and in some measure empowered by the Japanese occupying forces during World War II, with the leaders of Burma and the Indies given important symbolic positions of authority and unprecedented opportunities to communicate with the population at large, even as tens of thousands of nationalist youth were mobilized in military or paramilitary units—the Burma National Army (BNA), the *Pembela Tanah Air* (PETA, or Defenders of the Homeland)—in advance of anticipated Allied attacks.[8] In this context, attempts to restore Western colonial rule in both Burma and Indonesia in the early aftermath of World War II ran aground in the face of mounting popular mobilization, forcing the British and Dutch governments to cede independence to nationalist leaders in their former colonies in 1947 and 1949, respectively.

Thus nationalism in the new nation states of Burma and Indonesia shared a common point of departure at independence. Unlike Thailand and the Philippines, nationalism entailed large-scale popular mobilization in the period leading up to independence and involved considerable dislocation and destruction of the institutions of the state. Unlike Thailand and the Philippines, moreover, anti-colonial struggle and problematically 'foreign' immigrant mercantile minorities under colonial rule prefigured strong support for economic nationalism and state intervention to prevent the 'free hand' of the market from perpetuating control by 'foreign' (i.e. Indian, Chinese, and European) capital. Unlike Thailand and the Philippines, furthermore, the combination of indirect and direct colonial rule in British Burma and the Netherlands East Indies, the dislocations and difficulties of World War II, and the struggle for independence left the processes of state formation and national integration markedly incomplete.

Against this backdrop, the first decade and a half following independence saw striking parallels in the fate of nationalism in the new nation states of Burma and Indonesia. In both countries, parliamentary democracy helped to absorb forces and energies mobilized in World War II and the struggle for independence, with demobilization achieved through incorporation into the rapidly expanding agencies of the two post-colonial states. In both Burma and Indonesia, moreover, the reconstitution of state authority along national lines was enabled by the expansion of the state's role in the economy in pursuit of economic nationalism and the hopes for social redistribution were raised by popular participation in the struggle for independence. In both Burma and Indonesia, however, this pattern of state expansion, absorption, and inclusiveness was soon tempered by a notable trend towards the centralization and insulation of state power. Signs of this trend were already evident in the first months and years of independence with the rapid abandonment or undermining of the federal state structures imposed by the outgoing British and Dutch colonial governments on both Burmese and Indonesian nationalist leaders.[9]

Such reversals helped to stimulate armed mobilization by forces claiming to represent those minorities disenfranchised or otherwise disadvantaged by the centralization of power in Rangoon and Jakarta, with a welter of ethnic insurgencies in Burma soon fairly matched by a series of regional rebellions in Indonesia.[10] These challenges, alongside those mounted by armed guerrilla forces—Communist in Burma, Islamist in Indonesia—whose ranks had mobilized in the struggle for independence but found themselves marginalized by nationalist leaders, represented a major menace to the fragile authority of the new nation states. At the same time, the Cold War brought dramatic new forms of foreign intervention—in Burma, the US-backed flight and encampment of Kuomintang forces fleeing Communist rule in China in 1949–51; in Indonesia, US covert and military support for the regional rebellions in 1957–9—which seriously threatened to compromise both countries' newly established national sovereignty.[11]

It was in this shared context that the 1950s and early to mid-1960s saw parallel processes of deepening militarization, as embryonic national armed forces engaged in violent 'pacification' and internal colonization to preserve and enhance national sovereignty and state power in both Burma and Indonesia. Thus by the late 1950s, experiments with martial law and the expansion of military powers in outlying regions of conflict had vastly increased the prerogatives of the armed forces in Rangoon and Jakarta. Against this backdrop, the early to mid-1960s witnessed the onset of full-blown military rule in both Burma and Indonesia, precipitated by a coup in Rangoon in 1962 and a coup and counter-coup in Jakarta in late 1965. If the new nation states of Burma and Indonesia entered the 1950s with the fate of nationalism seemingly dispersed among the highly mobilized, if fractious, Burmese and Indonesian peoples, by the mid to late 1960s the fate of nationalism in both countries had fallen into the hands of increasingly insulated and narrowly centralized authoritarian regimes.

Despite these striking similarities in the early post-independence trajectory of nationalism in the new nation states of Burma and Indonesia, by the mid to late 1960s the fate of nationalism in the two countries had already begun to show signs of marked divergence, with the differences widening dramatically over the succeeding decades. In Burma, the 1962 coup was not accompanied by a rightward shift in economic policy or geopolitical orientation; instead, the Army committed itself to the 'Burmese Road to Socialism', enforcing an unusual extent of economic autarchy while maintaining neutrality in the face of the Cold War and deepening American intervention in Indochina. At the same time, the years following the coup saw a dramatic exodus of Burma's residual Indian immigrant population, as the military regime tightened restrictions on private economic activity and on citizenship.[12]

This continuing—indeed, deepening—pursuit of economic nationalism through autarchy and anti-immigrant policies combined with the established pattern of ethnic exclusiveness to constrain the possibilities for nation-building in Burma under military rule from the early 1960s onwards.[13] Burmese nationalism had been narrowly Burman since its emergence in the 1930s, drawn from the commercialized rice-bowl areas of directly ruled British Ministerial Burma. Its ethnic, linguistic, and religious identity and orientation largely excluded the minorities populating the indirectly ruled areas of British Burma, as well as minorities such as the Karens in Ministerial Burma itself.

With the Japanese invasion and occupation of Burma during World War II, moreover, the narrowly ethnic-Burman complexion of Burmese nationalism had deepened, as the Japanese armed and empowered—ethnic-Burman—Burmese nationalist leaders to fight the British colonial army with its overwhelmingly Indian, Chin, Kachin, Karen, and otherwise non-Burman regiments. Even as leading Burmese nationalist leaders belatedly betrayed their Japanese sponsors towards the end of the war and founded the Anti-Fascist People's Freedom League (AFPFL), they continued to draw on the narrowly ethnic-Burman organizational resources and identities established under Japanese tutelage, and to view representatives of Burma's minorities as stooges for the restoration of British rule.[14] Thus when early post-war anti-colonial mobilization championed by nationalist leaders spurred the British government to grant independence in early 1948, the non-Burman minorities were weakly represented in the government of the newly founded Union of Burma, with federal provisions for the representation and autonomy of minorities ill-defined and, over time, increasingly unenforced. In this context, the years following independence saw the emergence and expansion of a number of separatist movements within Burma, demanding independent homelands for the sizeable Chin, Karen, Kachin, Mon, and Shan minorities in the country.[15]

Since the onset of military rule in 1962, this decidedly unpropitious backdrop has combined with the abiding ethnic narrowness and international vulnerability of the regime in Rangoon to constrain the possibilities for effective national integration in Burma. Given the economic autarchy and political isolationism of the regime, its efforts to impose military rule over all of Burma soon foundered, with armed separatist insurgencies enjoying effective control over large swathes of minority-populated areas of the country. The poverty of Rangoon severely limited its ability to defeat the insurgencies, or to construct a serious infrastructure—in terms of communications, education, and transportation—of national integration.[16]

As already evident with the invasion of Burma by tens of thousands of Kuomintang troops in the early 1950s, moreover, the country's location and the porousness of its borders rendered effective enforcement of its national sovereignty especially difficult. With the neighbouring People's Republic of China sponsoring the Burmese Communist Party's armed insurgency until the late 1980s and neighbouring Thailand aiding and abetting the Karen and Shan struggles for independence, and with the international narcotics trade in the so-called 'Golden Triangle' providing additional fiscal bases for effective autonomy if not independence from Rangoon, manifold forms of stalemate persisted over the decades since independence and the onset of military rule. Due to Rangoon's rapprochement with both Beijing and Bangkok since the late 1980s, and the consequent elimination of external support for various armed separatist insurgencies, the externally strengthened Burmese military regime succeeded in clawing back some of its sovereignty over its territory. But even today, instead of effective national integration in Burma, there persists a patchwork form of parcellized sovereignty, based on a complex welter of ceasefire agreements and live-and-let-live arrangements outside the core ethnic-Burman areas of Burma.[17]

In contrast with Burma, a very different pattern of nation-building has unfolded since the onset of military rule in Indonesia. Unlike in Burma, the consolidation of military rule in Indonesia in the 1960s was accompanied by a sharp reduction in economic nationalism, by a dramatic opening of the country's economy to foreign direct investment, and by a shift to heavy reliance on loans from foreign governments and international financial institutions, in exchange for a commitment to liberalization, privatization, and deregulation. Against this backdrop, and in the context of Indonesia's enjoyment of considerable oil and natural gas reserves, the 1970s and 1980s witnessed a phase of sustained import-substitution industrialization, followed by a decisive shift in the mid-1980s into export-oriented industrialization, with foreign companies overwhelmingly dominating the export sector.[18]

Accompanying this diminution of economic nationalism in Indonesia in the mid to late 1960s, moreover, was a commensurate abandonment of anti-imperialist nationalism in the political realm. Even as the former Army general Suharto was manoeuvring to replace Sukarno as president in late 1965 and early 1966, his emissaries were engineering the de-escalation of *Konfrontasi* with neighbouring Malaysia, which Sukarno had derided as a British-controlled 'neo-colony', and by 1967 then President Suharto's diplomats had helped to create the Association for Southeast Asian Nations (ASEAN) to establish Indonesia's newly found eagerness to strengthen its relations with neighbouring countries like Malaysia and Singapore (with its British military bases), as well as the Philippines and Thailand, both deeply involved in the American war effort in nearby Vietnam, Cambodia, and Laos. Meanwhile, even as Suharto's lieutenants were orchestrating large-scale anti-Communist pogroms in late 1965 and early 1966, he was forging a close Cold War alliance with the United States that would last well into the final years of the twentieth century. Thus, in sharp contrast with Burma, the fate of nationalism in Indonesia from the mid-1960s was one in which hopes and dreams of achieving greater independence from foreign economic control and efforts to confront and oppose imperialist meddling in Indonesia and elsewhere in Southeast Asia were essentially abandoned in favour of integration into the world capitalist economy and a global political order dominated by the United States.[19]

The advantages accruing to the national government in Jakarta from its opening to foreign investment and finance, its embrace of the United States, and its access to considerable oil and natural gas reserves from the mid to late 1960s, combined with the earlier, formative history of Indonesian nationalism to make for far easier, more extensive, and more fully internalized national integration across the sprawling archipelago since the late 1960s than witnessed in autarchic, 'isolationist' Burma during the same period. Compared with Burma, after all, Indonesian nationalism had, from the outset, been much more open and inclusive, with a dialect of Malay—rather than Javanese—adopted and adapted as the national language (*Bahasa Indonesia*), Communist and Islamic organizations, ideologies, and idioms incorporated into the national struggle, and prominent figures from beyond Java included in the leadership of the nationalist struggle. During the *Revolusi* of 1945–9, armed guerrilla-style struggle by the fledgling *Republik Indonesia* against Dutch efforts to restore colonial rule was highly localized in terms of recruitment, leadership, and command structure. Yet the commitment to a broader 'Indonesia' was famously strong enough to inspire nationalist forces in the northernmost Sumatran province of Aceh, where a small-scale 'social revolution' had decimated the local aristocracy and deterred the Dutch from even attempting to return, to raise funds to purchase the sole airplane in the Republican air force. The Republican leadership's commitment to a broadly conceived 'Indonesia', in turn, was signalled by its jettisoning of provisions for Islamic law in the Indonesian Constitution in favour of more ambiguously worded references to religious faith, and by the adoption of the celebrated multicultural slogan *Bhinneka Tunggal Ika*—Unity in Diversity. Thus even the major 'regional rebellions' of the 1950s—*Darul Islam Indonesia, Pemerintah Revolusioner Republik Indonesia*—were framed in terms of aspirations for a different kind of *Indonesia*, rather than for new nation states per se.[20]

The legacies of this preceding pattern of inclusive nationalism, moreover, combined with the aforementioned advantages of Indonesia's mode of reincorporation into the world capitalist economy and the Cold War geopolitical order from the mid-1960s to promote a discernible intensification of national integration across the archipelago. Thanks to the windfall revenues from the oil boom, and the flows of foreign loans and investments, the 1970s, 1980s, and early to mid-1990s witnessed the unprecedented creation of a genuinely national market, the dramatic expansion of a national bureaucracy, the tremendous extension of the national educational system, along with parallel trends in terms of media—national television, radio, newspapers, and magazines—in the national language, *Bahasa Indonesia*. Under Suharto's highly insulated and repressive authoritarian rule (1966–98), Jakarta enjoyed three decades of unimpeded centralized control over the provinces, managing a wide range of national state enterprises, implementing diverse national policies and programs, and rotating civilian and military officials across the sprawling archipelago with great ease and with lasting effects on Indonesians' sense of connectedness and shared experience with their fellow countrymen.[21]

Given the Suharto regime's close Cold War alliance with the United States, moreover, Jakarta was able to consolidate—and extend—Indonesian national sovereignty without the kinds of complications and compromises suffered by Rangoon. By the end of the 1960s, the United Nations' transitional stewardship in the former Dutch territory of West Papua gave way to incorporation of a renamed 'Irian Jaya' into Indonesia, with a dubious 'viva voce' referendum masterminded by Indonesian military intelligence accepted with a wink and a nod in Washington, DC, and at UN headquarters in New York.[22] When, moreover, in late 1975 the national liberation movement Fretilin (*Frente Revolucionária de Timor-Leste Independente*) declared independence in the former Portuguese colony of East Timor, Indonesia invaded and forcibly occupied the country, imposing harsh direct military rule that lasted until 1999. Here too, despite egregious human-rights abuses and sustained violation of international law, Indonesia enjoyed the effective support of the United States and its major Cold War allies against the threat of the left-wing Fretilin in the tiny former Portuguese colony. As in West Papua and Aceh (where a separatist movement emerged in the late 1970s), popular armed struggle for independence ran aground in the face of a highly militarized Indonesian state whose enjoyment of oil wealth, sustained industrial growth, and foreign support made for far, far greater strength than its Burmese counterpart.[23]

Although, as in Burma, the early post-independence era witnessed the inexorable reconstitution and reassertion of state power in national terms and the 'fossilization' and forced encapsulation of the diverse energies and social forces—'the People' (*Rakyat*)—mobilized in the *Revolusi*, the three subsequent decades of sustained industrialization and the accompanying social and political transformations made for a different fate for Indonesian nationalism by the end of the twentieth century.[24] Under Suharto, for example, Indonesians of Chinese ancestry suffered from stigmatization, discrimination in terms of state employment and educational opportunities, and restrictions on cultural expression and activity, and they were subjected to extortion, harassment, and, at times, attacks on their property.[25] Yet unlike their 'Indian' counterparts in Burma, Indonesians of Chinese ancestry had in various ways contributed to the nationalist struggle—and to the making of the national language—and instead of expropriation and expulsion, they were afforded greater opportunities for citizenship and, crucially, for resuming their role as 'pariah entrepreneurs' in the rapidly industrializing and expanding Indonesian economy.[26]

Under Suharto, avowedly authentic 'indigenous' mechanisms of authoritarian control were woven out of the rich tapestry of cultural and ethnic diversity of the Indonesian archipelago: the proud slogan *Bhinneka Tunggal Ika* was replaced by the implicit strategy of *divide et impera*. The Indonesian state was restyled as the protector and promoter of diverse cultures and traditions, and as embodying notions of legitimate authority deeply rooted in traditional culture.[27] The supra-parliamentary body stacked with regime loyalists that '(re)elected' a sole candidate—Suharto—to the presidency every five years, for example, was called the People's Consultative Assembly (*Majelis Permusyawaratan Rakyat*), with the notion of *musyawarah*—consultation, consensus—celebrated as enjoying a genuine legitimacy among Indonesians that competition between rival candidates, parties, ideologies, and social forces—i.e. liberal democracy—allegedly could not claim. By the 1990s, the regime also began to expend considerable energies to celebrate—and to appropriate—the majority faith of the archipelago, Islam, as seen in Suharto's sponsorship of the All-Indonesian Association of Islamic Intellectuals (ICMI).[28] Overall, the Indonesian state under Suharto was repositioned as both the authentic embodiment of the Indonesian nation and as the sole guarantor of national integrity in the face of potentially fractious cultural, ethnic, regional, and religious diversity.

Yet in contrast with Burmese nationalism in the context of economic stagnation and social stasis, the dramatic social transformations accompanying three decades of rapid, sustained industrialization and economic growth generated new possibilities for 're-imagining' the Indonesian nation. By the 1990s, the national market had given rise to a renewed visibility for the *Rakyat* in a vibrant urbanizing society rapidly outgrowing centralized authoritarian rule. When, in mid-1998, the aging dictator Suharto was forced to resign in the face of deepening economic crisis and mounting popular protests, a decisive reconfiguration of the Indonesian nation state rapidly unfolded, coloured by considerable contestation and violent conflict.[29]

As the shift from centralized authoritarian rule to competitive elections and decentralization began to unfold in 1999, the tremendous ethnic, religious, and regional diversity of the archipelago seemed to threaten the violent disintegration of the Indonesian nation state, much as the discourse of Suharto's regime had long foretold. Large-scale riots in Jakarta and other major cities had seen unprecedented attacks on Indonesia's ethnic-Chinese minority in 1998, inter-ethnic violence in West and Central Kalimantan and inter-religious conflict in Maluku and parts of Central Sulawesi unfolded in 1999–2001, and paramilitary mobilization and terrorist bombings raised the spectre of Islamist *jihad*. A UN-supervised referendum in East Timor in August 1999, moreover, led to an overwhelming vote in favour of independence and, despite violent Indonesian military-led resistance, the onset of a forced termination of the long-standing Indonesian occupation of the territory. These events in East Timor, as well as the ongoing processes of democratization across the Indonesian archipelago, helped to encourage a renewal of popular mobilization in support of independence struggles in Aceh and West Papua. Indonesia, it appeared, was destined to go the way of Yugoslavia, as Suharto's Army generals—much like their Burmese counterparts—had been warning for many years.[30]

This scenario was both descriptively and predictively false. The 'anti-Chinese' riots of May 1998, after all, had been instigated and orchestrated by Army generals themselves, and, with the departure of Suharto, violence against the ethnic-Chinese minority effectively ceased. Indonesians of Chinese ancestry soon saw a dramatic easing of restrictions on their cultural, political, and religious freedom, along with a reduction of impediments to naturalization for those still lacking Indonesian citizenship. Meanwhile, large-scale inter-ethnic and inter-religious violence—even in 1999–2001 confined to a small number of localities across the sprawling archipelago—faded from view.[31]

At the same time, the putative threat of territorial dismemberment of the Indonesian nation state also dramatically diminished from the much-inflated panic of 1999. East Timor, after all, had never been a part of the Netherlands East Indies territories which comprised the hopes and dreams of Soekarno and his fellow colonial-era nationalists for an independent Indonesia. The Indonesian occupation of East Timor, moreover, had always remained illegal under international law and largely been denied formal recognition; in practice, the territory remained a fiefdom of the Indonesian military establishment, even after its formal incorporation as a province of the country.[32] Much to the disappointment of activists in Aceh and West Papua, the transition process in East Timor did not constitute a precedent for further breakaway new nations, given the weaker basis of mobilization on the ground and much more limited foreign sympathy enjoyed overseas for the cause of Acehnese or West Papuan independence. Instead, as Indonesia had embarked on comprehensive decentralization in 1999, with locally elected parliaments and local executives enjoying unprecedented powers over local state agencies, 'special autonomy' packages were extended to West Papua and Aceh, and, in the latter case, proved sufficiently attractive to spur the Free Aceh Movement

(*Gerakan Aceh Merdeka*, or GAM) to abandon armed struggle in favour of participation in parliamentary politics.[33] Thus, overall, in stark contrast to the as yet unresolved problems of national integration in authoritarian Burma, the first decade of the twenty-first century saw nationalism re-emerge not only intact but arguably in more inclusive and elastic form under conditions of democratization and decentralization in Indonesia.

Cold-War Federalisms Forced, Failed, and Fudged: Indochina and Malaysia

As in Burma and Indonesia, the impact of the Cold War international context on the making of the three new nation states of Indochina—Cambodia, Laos, and Vietnam—on the one hand, and the formation of Malaysia, on the other, in the post-independence era was likewise demonstrably decisive. The division of Indochina into the three separate nation states of Cambodia, Laos, and Vietnam amidst anti-colonial and anti-imperialist revolution, and the creation of the Federation of Malaysia under British 'neo-colonial' auspices, provide the basis for a final paired comparison worthy of consideration.

As Christopher Goscha has demonstrated, French colonial rule from the mid-nineteenth century up through the mid-1940s had created—however imperfectly, incompletely, and unevenly—the possibilities for the imagining of an 'Indochine' across the territories of what today constitutes Cambodia, Laos, and Vietnam (for an alternative view, see David Henley's Chapter 13 in this volume). French officials as well as 'native' Annamese and Tonkinese clerks circulated for decades across the full extent of French colonial Indochine; Khmer-, Lao-, and Vietnamese-speakers were, in small numbers, classmates in French schools, most notably the Université de l'Indochine. The colonial economy drew Tonkinese and Annamese labourers onto French rubber plantations in eastern Cambodge, even as the burgeoning trade along the Mekong saw the tightening of connections between Saigon in the fertile river delta and thousands of Lao- and Khmer-speaking rice farmers in the hinterlands of this entrepôt at the heart of the multi-ethnic Cochinchinese frontier zone. Small wonder, Goscha notes, that Ngyuen Ai Quoc, alias Ho Chi Minh, and his fellow revolutionaries had founded the *Indochinese* Communist Party in 1930, and that as late as 1945 there was still considerable debate over alternative—Indochinese versus Vietnamese—understandings of the ultimate goals of the struggle for independence.[34]

Yet, as Goscha and other scholars have shown, hopes and dreams for an independent, unified Indochine began to run aground by the 1950s, constrained both by the legacies of French colonial-era state formation, on the one hand, and the exigencies of the Cold War in the region, on the other. Petty clerks, plantation workers, small-scale rice traders, and other émigrés from Annam and Tonkin had headed west into

Cambodge and Laos under colonial rule, but flows eastwards consisted largely of rice and other agricultural commodities, rather than Khmer- and Lao-speakers, thus limiting the imagination and allure of a unified Indochine largely to the Vietnamese-speaking circuitries of the colonial state and economy. Meanwhile, the French in their concern to shore up the problematic, porous borders of their protectorates in Laos and Cambodge in the face of enduring close connections to, and territorial claims by, Siam (and, by the 1930s, an irredentist 'Thailand'), began to encourage the reinforcement and reinvention of distinctly Lao and Cambodian conceptions of cultural, religious, and ethnic identity. These policies rendered their potential incorporation into a unified independent Indochine dominated by Annamese and Tonkinese increasingly problematic.

Whatever possibilities there might have been for an independent Indochine of some kind, they were largely foreclosed by external pressures in the early Cold War era. Under Soviet pressure, the Indochinese Communist Party was formally dissolved, with separate parties for Cambodia, Laos, and Vietnam formally constituted in 1951, albeit with Cambodian and Laotian comrades taking guidance from their Vietnamese counterparts in Hanoi as they waged armed revolutionary struggle against the French colonial army. In their efforts to confine the revolutionary struggle for independence within Vietnam, moreover, the French colonial regime enhanced the formal status of Laos and Cambodia within the French Indochinese Union in the early 1950s. Laos and Cambodia were then granted formal independence as part of the 1954 Geneva Accords, which recognized the sovereignty of the three new nation states, while forestalling the unification of Vietnam. As seen in Soviet and Chinese pressures on the Vietnamese Communist leadership in the 1950s to accept the formation of separate Communist parties in 1951 and then to sign the Geneva Accords in 1954, international support for a unified independent Indochine was essentially non-existent.[35]

Yet the legacies of state formation from the era of French colonial Indochine lived on in subsequent decades, decisively colouring relations between the three new nation states for years to come. From the mid-1950s up through the Communist victories of 1975, the Vietnamese Communist Party leadership in Hanoi enjoyed considerable influence among the Pathet Lao forces in neighbouring Laos and the Khmer People's Revolutionary Party in neighbouring Cambodia.[36] Access to areas of Laos and Cambodia allowed Vietnamese forces to infiltrate guerrilla units, arms, and logistical support to aid the fight against successive American-backed governments in southern Vietnam, thus spurring the United States to widen its counter-insurgency and bombing campaigns to cover much of the breadth of Indochina.[37] Thus when Communist forces seized control of Phnom Penh, Saigon, and Vientiane in the spring of 1975, they did so as part of an effort driven if not directly dictated by Hanoi.[38]

It was against this backdrop that belated processes of national integration began to unfold across the three new nation states of former French Indochina in the mid-1970s. With 'Reunification' in Vietnam, the complicated history of attenuated imperial control of the Cochinchinese frontier from Hué and the hybrid cultural, ethnic, and religious complexion of the Mekong Delta were obscured in favour of an official nationalist narrative stressing the restoration of an integral part of a timeless Vietnam long besieged by external enemies. Differences between the two parts of Vietnam separated by war from 1954 through 1975 were ascribed to residual neocolonial American influences and attacked as foreign pathologies to be eradicated in the process of extending Communist control over southern society.[39] Meanwhile, in neighbouring Laos, the effective consolidation of fragile Communist control and the daunting tasks of socialist transformation required considerable external assistance, with Vietnamese advisors overseeing efforts to construct a coherent party-state and to collectivize agriculture across the country.[40]

In Cambodia, by contrast, the impulse to assert national independence was much greater, and thus necessitated resistance to Vietnamese hegemony. Under the leadership of Pol Pot, the renamed Communist Party of Kampuchea undertook drastic purges of its ranks to eliminate Vietnamese influence, embarked on a desperate, genocidal drive to achieve economic autonomy and political control over the countryside (a 'Super Great Leap Forward'), and provoked border disputes with Vietnam.[41] By late 1978, Cambodia and Vietnam were at war, and in early 1979 Vietnam invaded Cambodia, occupying and essentially running the country in the face of enduring opposition from the United States, Thailand, and other US allies in Southeast Asia, as well as the People's Republic of China, which fought brief border wars with Vietnam in 1979 and again in 1981.[42]

Overall, in the former French Union of Indochina the effective independence and integration of the three new nation states unfolded with considerable violence. Although colonial-era state formation had made an independent Indochina imaginable as an object of nationalist struggle and plausible as a unified—if perhaps federalized—new nation state, Cold War circumstances dictated otherwise, with French manoeuvres to forestall decolonization, and American, Soviet, and Chinese policies encouraging the creation of separate national states, Communist parties, and, in due course, party states in Cambodia, Laos, and Vietnam. But, as Goscha and other scholars have shown, the struggle for the 'reunification' of Vietnam up through 1975 spilled over into neighbouring Cambodia and Laos, and the processes of post-1975 national integration in Cambodia entailed efforts to assert the embryonic party-state's national independence from Vietnamese hegemony, which led to considerable violence and, in short order, Vietnamese invasion and occupation.

This pattern of nation-state formation in former French Indochina stands in stark contrast with the fate of nationalism across the various British colonial territories that emerged as the Federation of Malaysia (and Singapore) over the course of the 1950s and early to mid-1960s. As the British began to consolidate their power in the Malay Peninsula and the northern shelf of Borneo from the late eighteenth century onwards, they did so in a patchwork fashion, establishing directly ruled Straits Settlements in Malacca, Penang, and Singapore in 1826 (redesignated as a Crown Colony in 1867), and then imposing Residents in the Federated Malay States of Selangor, Perak, Negeri Sembilan, and Pahang in 1874, and in the Unfederated Malay States of Johor, Kedah, Kelantan, Perlis, and Terengganu in 1909. Meanwhile, the Sultanate of Brunei, the

British North Borneo Company's territory in Sabah, and the Brooke dynasty's empire in Sarawak, enjoyed separate protected status rather than any form of direct British colonial rule. Thus the pattern of state formation across the disparate, vast, sprawling hodgepodge of territories that would come together in the early to mid-1960s as the Federation of Malaysia provided an extremely weak and fragile historical basis for the making of a new nation state, arguably much weaker than the Indochinese prospects of what would become Cambodia, Laos, and Vietnam.[43]

At the same time, moreover, the unparalleled nature and extent of immigration into the Malay Peninsula, northern Borneo, Penang, and Singapore also threw up other seemingly self-evident obstacles to nation-building. From the late eighteenth century onwards, migration from the southern coastal provinces of China had created sizeable communities around rich mining areas of the Malay Peninsula and northern Borneo, with the harbours, mills, and sweatshops of various port towns and cities swelling with additional Hokkien- and Teochiu-speaking labourers over the subsequent century and a half of deepening integration into the British imperial economy.[44] Thus, combined with the thousands and thousands of rubber plantation labourers recruited in the late colonial era from various parts of the Indian subcontinent, these immigrants comprised the working class of the territories that would come to be known as Malaysia, fairly matching and in some places greatly exceeding the sparsely scattered Malay-speaking peasant population, as seen most dramatically in overwhelmingly 'Chinese' Singapore. At the same time, the so-called 'Malay' population of the Malay Peninsula increased considerably during this time, through steady streams of migration from nearby Sumatra, Sulawesi, and other parts of the Netherlands East Indies. Overall, these huge immigrant populations thus combined with the patchwork pattern of state formation to make for a seemingly very fragile basis for nationalism in a unified 'Malaysia'.[45]

Yet Cold War circumstances conspired, both literally and figuratively, to make possible an agglomeration of these disparate territories into what would prove to be—with the exception of Singapore—the basis for an enduring federalized nation state. By the time of the Japanese surrender in August 1945, the armed guerrilla units of the Communist-controlled Malayan People's Anti-Japanese Army were in effective control of many towns and cities across the Malay Peninsula, and the restoration and reconstitution of British colonial rule—under the Malayan Union in 1946–8, then under the Federation of Malaya in 1948–63—ran up against strong resistance from the Malayan Communist Party (MCP), which also enjoyed considerable strength in the 'Red City' of Singapore. On the Malay Peninsula, the British defeated an armed insurgency waged by the MCP, through counter-insurgency operations under what was termed 'The Emergency', through the hamletting of rural communities in 'New Villages' policed by so-called Home Guards, and through the creation of the Malayan Chinese Association (MCA) as a British and Chinese business-backed patronage network to counter the—overwhelmingly ethnic-Chinese—MCP. At the same time, moreover, a carefully stage-managed decolonization was effected on the Malay Peninsula, with the British gradually handing over power to a coalition representing the ethnic-Chinese business elite (the MCA) and the Malay aristocracy, now mobilized as the United Malays' National Organization (UMNO). In 1957, more than a decade after Aung San, Ho Chi Minh, and Sukarno had declared independence in Burma, Vietnam, and Indonesia, respectively, a 'National Alliance' government of UMNO, MCA, and the Malaysian Indian Congress (MIC) was handed power, as a Singaporean observer named Lee Kuan Yew famously noted, 'on a silver platter with red ribbons by British royalty in uniform'.[46]

Yet if transfer of power to a conservative, compliant, 'neo-colonial' government, fervently anti-Communist and fully open to foreign capital, was effectively achieved on the Malay Peninsula in 1957, Cold War tensions and uncertainties persisted well into the 1960s in Singapore and the northern shelf of Borneo. The MCP remained a dominant force within the dominant People's Action Party (PAP) in Singapore, which was granted formal independence in 1959 but compelled to accept a continuing British military presence and involvement in the city state's internal security. Meanwhile, left-wing mobilization among ethnic-Chinese mining communities in Sarawak, among the local population on Brunei, and in parts of Sabah enjoyed sympathy and support from the Sukarno regime in neighbouring Indonesia, with the goal of an independent federation of North Kalimantan actively encouraged by Jakarta in the early to mid-1960s. Thus the prospects for a Communist takeover in Singapore, and for the spread of left-wing Sukarnoist anti-imperialism into a new nation state in the remaining territories of the former British empire in Southeast Asia, loomed large on the horizon at the time.

Against this backdrop, 1962–3 saw London-led movement towards the formation of a broadly based Malaysia that would subsume these disparate hotbeds of left-wing activism within the folds of a federation dominated by the effectively pacified, politically conservative heartlands of the Malay Peninsula. In 1962 the leading party in Brunei, the left-wing Partai Rakyat Brunei, was suppressed and forcibly disbanded amidst a failed popular rebellion, and in the following year, moves towards the formation of the Federation of Malaysia were advanced by British officials in London, the Federation of Malaya government in Kuala Lumpur, and conservative elements within the PAP in Singapore led by Prime Minister Lee Kuan Yew. In May 1963 a Federation of Malaysia expanded to include Sabah, Sarawak, and Singapore was proclaimed in the face of resistance by the left-wing Sarawak United People's Party (SUPP) and, in Sabah, by the Pasok Momogun (Indigenous Peoples') Party, even as MCP cadres were being rounded up by the security services under 'Operation Cold Storm' in Singapore. The formation of this 'neo-colony' was bitterly opposed by the Sukarno government in neighbouring Indonesia, leading to a two-year period of armed hostilities on Borneo—known as *Konfrontasi*. The overthrow of Sukarno and the decimation of the PKI in late 1965, however, spelled Indonesian acquiescence in the incorporation of Sabah and Sarawak into Malaysia, with the Indonesian Army violently eliminating sources of refuge and support for residual SUPP resistance to Malaysia in Sarawak in 1967. With the exit of a now effectively MCP-free Singapore from the Federation in 1965 due to frictions between the PAP and the UMNO-led government in Kuala Lumpur, the contours of the new nation state of Malaysia were now firmly fixed.[47]

Given the shallow historical roots—and marked ethnic diversity—of this new nation state, the prospects for post-independence nationalism in Malaysia would seem to have been highly problematic. Indeed, the mid to late 1960s saw a dramatic decline in the strength of the ruling 'National Front' coalition between UMNO and the MCA in Kuala Lumpur, with the May 1969 elections threatening to permit the political turnover not seen since independence in 1957. But violence in the early aftermath of the elections provided a convenient excuse for the proclamation of emergency rule in Malaysia, and for the elaboration of a New Economic Policy the following year as the basis for a new strategy managing the 'plural society' inherited from colonial rule. The British colonial government had classified the population of the Malay Peninsula as 'Chinese', 'Indian', or 'Malay', the latter category incorporating recent migrants from the neighbouring Netherlands East Indies and offering special 'protection' to such supposed 'natives' in the face of steady (British-induced) flows of immigrant labour.[48] This protected status for 'Malays' was noted in the 1957 Constitution, and, under the New Economic Policy (NEP) from 1970 onwards, belatedly extended to serve as the basis for affirmative action (via quotas. preferential loans, and hiring schemes) in favour of those henceforth described 'Sons of the Soil', or *Bumiputra*.[49] Under the NEP, the avowed aim of creating a *Bumiputra* business class through vastly expanded forms of state intervention and ownership in the economy served to strengthen both the federal government's powers across Malaysia and UMNO's political position in Malaysian politics, achieving unbroken hegemony well into the twenty-first century, without any turnover in national politics.[50] Against this backdrop, Malaysia's federal system drew state-level elites in distant Sabah and Sarawak into alliances with the UMNO assemblymen, even as the growing reach of the federal government made inclusion in Malaysia increasingly meaningful and materially rewarding for those 'native sons' in far-flung northern Borneo who conveniently qualified as *Bumiputra*.[51] Thus the hodgepodge of largely unconnected former British territories that came to comprise 'Malaysia' muddled through the first decades since the formation of this new nation state, with the construction and promotion of an 'indigenous' and thus genuinely *national* bourgeoisie serving as an attractive basis for inclusion within the new nation state and an effective rubric for expanding national state power.

Conclusions

As suggested in the preceding pages, the diverging trajectories of nationalism in the countries of Southeast Asia over the past six decades defy the conventional arguments of mainstream scholars of nationalism. The variegated patterns of post-independence nationalism, after all, are not explicable in terms of the constellations of cultural, ethnic, religious, and regional diversity and their variously enabling or impeding impact on the imperative of national integration. Apparently improbable new nation states—Indonesia, Malaysia, or Laos, for that matter—have seemingly settled quite comfortably into nationhood over the years, with little remaining plausible fear of dissolution. Even in Burma, the threat posed by various ethnic separatist—or nationalist—movements remains weak, with the regime in Rangoon arguably exercising more effective national sovereignty over its territory today than ever before, and the ongoing experiment with civilian parliamentary institutions offering a rubric for further co-optation and demobilization of ethnic insurgencies. For better and for worse (just ask around in Pattani or West Papua, Mae Sot or Maguindanao), the fate of various nationalisms across Southeast Asia now appear to be firmly fixed. East Timor's independence is the sole exception that proves this impressively unfalsified Andersonian rule: nation states, however seemingly problematic, 'do not go gentle into that good night'.

How, then, can we explain the variations observed across Southeast Asia in the trajectories of nationalism over the past several decades since the transitions to independence in the 1940s and 1950s? As highlighted in the three successive paired comparisons in the pages above, the crucial questions, challenges, cleavages, and conflicts facing the new nation states of Southeast Asia were not those of 'national integration' in the face of 'internal' cultural, ethnic, religious, and regional diversity, but those concerning (re)integration into the world capitalist economy and the Cold War geopolitical order. Whether cast in terms of imposed constraints or ideological choices, the ways in which various nation states in Southeast Asia negotiated their international relations served as critical determinants of nationalist (de)mobilization, nation-building, and nationhood. How else to understand the strangely striking similarities between Thailand and the Philippines, the belated divergence between Burmese and Indonesian nationalism, or the contrast between successful federation-making in Malaysia and federation-breaking in Indochina? The consequences of capitalist development and the circumstances of the Cold War era smiled far more favourably on some nationalisms than on others.

What light does this account of the varying fate of nationalism in the new states of Southeast Asia shed on the broader study of nationalism, especially in the post-colonial world? On the one hand, the argument above has demonstrated the possibilities—as well as the limitations—of comparative analysis of nationalism within a given region of the world. On the other hand, this analysis of post-independence nationalism in Southeast Asia has also pointed to the significance of the broader international economic and political context within which the crystallization and consolidation of new nation states unfolded. In contrast with mainstream scholars' stress on the challenges of managing cultural diversity and the existential problems inherent in the formation of national identity, this essay has offered a reminder of the importance of state institutions, economic power, and international relations in shaping the fate of nationalism in the post-colonial world.

Notes

1. See W. S. Thompson (1975) *Unequal Partners: Philippine and Thai Relations with the United States, 1965–1975*, Lexington, MA; S. R. Shalom (1981) *The United States and the Philippines: A Study of Neo-Colonialism*, Philadelphia; R. Bonner (1987) *Waltzing with a Dictator: The Marcoses and the Making of US Policy*, New York; and D. Fineman (1997) *A Special Relationship: The United States and Military Government in Thailand, 1947–1958*, Honolulu.
2. For a path-breaking, penetrating critique of this historiographical tradition, see B. Anderson (1978) 'Studies of the Thai State: The State of Thai Studies', in E. B. Ayal (ed.) *The Study of Thailand: Analyses of Knowledge, Approaches, and Prospects in Anthropology, Art History, Economics, History, and Political Science*, Athens, OH, 193–233.
3. P. M. Handley (2006) *The King Never Smiles: A Biography of Thailand's Bhumibol Adulyadej*, New Haven, CT, 139–79. See also T. Chaloemtiarana (2007) *The Politics of Despotic Paternalism*, Ithaca, NY.
4. See E. Reyes (1989) *Notes on Philippine Cinema*, Manila; and E.-L. E. Hedman (2001) 'The Spectre of Populism in Philippine Politics and Society: *Artista, Masa, Eraption!*', *South East Asia Research*, 9, no. 1 (March), 5–44.
5. V. Rafael (1997) 'Your Grief Is Our Gossip: Overseas Filipinos and Other Spectral Presences', *Public Culture*, 9, no. 2 (Winter), 267–91.
6. J. S. Furnivall (1948) *Colonial Policy and Practice: A Comparative Study of Burma and Netherlands India*, Cambridge.
7. M. Maung (1980) *From Sangha to Laity: Nationalist Movements of Burma, 1920–1940*, New Delhi; Daw Khin Yi (1988) *The Dobama Movement in Burma (1930–1938)*, Ithaca, NY; G. McT. Kahin (2003) *Nationalism and Revolution in Indonesia*, Ithaca, NY.
8. D. H. Guyot (1966) 'The Political Impact of the Japanese Occupation of Burma', Ph.D. dissertation, Yale University, New Haven, CT; B. Anderson (1972) *Java in a Time of Revolution: Occupation and Resistance, 1944–1946*, Ithaca, NY.
9. R. H. Taylor (1987) *The State in Burma*, London, 217–90; B. Anderson (1990) *Language and Power: Exploring Political Cultures in Indonesia*, Ithaca, NY, 99–109.
10. B. Lintner (1994) *Burma in Revolt: Opium and Insurgency since 1948*, Boulder, CO; M. T. Smith (1999) *Burma: Insurgency and the Politics of Ethnicity*, London; B. S. Harvey (1977) *Permesta: Half a Rebellion*, Ithaca, NY; C. van Dijk (1981) *Rebellion Under the Banner of Islam: The Darul Islam in Indonesia*, The Hague.
11. R. H. Taylor (1973) *Foreign and Domestic Consequences of the KMT Intervention in Burma*, Ithaca, NY; A. R. Kahin and G. McT. Kahin (1995) *Subversion as Foreign Policy: The Secret Eisenhower and Dulles Debacle in Indonesia*, New York.
12. N. R. Chakravarti (1971) *The Indian Minority in Burma: The Rise and Decline of an Immigrant Community*, London.
13. R. H. Taylor (1982) 'Perceptions of Ethnicity in the Politics of Burma', *Southeast Asian Journal of Social Science*, 10, no. 1, 7–22.
14. A. Selth (1986) 'Race and Resistance in Burma, 1942–1945', *Modern Asian Studies*, 20, no. 3, 483–507.
15. J. Silverstein (1980) *Burmese Politics: The Dilemma of National Unity*, New Brunswick; M. Gravers, 'The Karen Making of a Nation', in S. Tønnesson and H. Antlöv (eds.) (1996)

Asian Forms of the Nation, London, 237–69; A. South (2003) *Mon Nationalism and Civil War in Burma: The Golden Sheldrake*, London.

16. J. Silverstein (1977) *Burma: Military Rule and the Politics of Stagnation*, Ithaca, NY.
17. M. P. Callahan (2007) *Political Authority in Burma's Ethnic Minority States: Devolution, Occupation and Coexistence*, Washington, DC; A. South (2008) *Ethnic Politics in Burma: States of Conflict*, London.
18. J. A. Winters (1996) *Power in Motion: Capital Mobility and the Indonesian State*, Ithaca, NY.
19. J. Roosa (2006) *Pretext for Mass Murder: The September 30th Movement and Suharto's Coup d'état in Indonesia*, Madison, WI; B. R. Simpson (2008) *Economists with Guns: Authoritarian Development and U.S.-Indonesian Relations, 1960–1968*, Stanford, CA.
20. On these points, see Anderson, *Language and Power*, esp. 123–51; and B. Anderson (1983) *Imagined Communities: Reflections on the Origin and Spread of Nationalism*, London, 120–2.
21. J. A. MacDougall (1982) 'Patterns of Military Control in the Indonesian Higher Central Bureaucracy', *Indonesia*, 33 (April), 89–121; R. Robison (1986) *Indonesia: The Rise of Capital*, Sydney; D. Dhakidae (1991) 'The State, the Rise of Capital, and the Fall of Political Journalism: Political Economy of Indonesian News Industry', Ph.D. dissertation, Cornell University; M. S. Malley (1999) 'Resource Distribution, State Coherence, and Political Centralization in Indonesia, 1950–1997', Ph.D. dissertation, University of Wisconsin at Madison.
22. J. Saltford (2002) *The United Nations and the Indonesian Takeover of West Papua, 1962–1969: The Anatomy of a Betrayal*, London.
23. See the various fine essays in B. Anderson (ed.) (2001) *Violence and the State in Suharto's Indonesia*, Ithaca, NY.
24. B. Anderson (2002) 'Bung Karno and the Fossilization of Soekarno's Thought', *Indonesia*, 74 (October), 1–19.
25. M. G. Tan (1991) 'The Social and Cultural Dimensions of the Role of the Ethnic Chinese in Indonesiam Society', *Indonesia*, 51 (April), 113–25.
26. D. Oetomo (1991) 'The Chinese of Indonesia and the Development of the Indonesian Language', *Indonesia*, 51 (April), 53–66; Yoon Hwan Shin (1991) 'The Role of Elites in Creating Capitalist Hegemony in Post-Oil Boom Indonesia', *Indonesia*, 51 (April), 127–43.
27. J. Pemberton (1994) *On the Subject of 'Java'*, Ithaca, NY.
28. R. W. Hefner (1993) 'Islam, State, and Civil Society: ICMI and the Struggle for the Indonesian Middle Class', *Indonesia*, 56 (October), 1–35.
29. J. T. Sidel (1998) '*Macet Total:* Logics of Circulation and Accumulation in the Demise of Indonesia's New Order', *Indonesia*, 66 (October), 159–85.
30. For a fine overview of these developments, see J. Bertrand (2004) *Nationalism and Ethnic Conflict in Indonesia*, Cambridge.
31. J. T. Sidel (2007) *Indonesia: Migrants, Migrant Workers, Refugees, and the New Citizenship Law*, Geneva; J. T. Sidel (2006) *Riots, Pogroms, Jihad: Religious Violence in Indonesia*, Ithaca, NY.
32. B. Anderson (1998) 'Gravel in Jakarta's Shoes', *The Spectre of Comparisons: Nationalism, Southeast Asia and the World*, London, 131–8.
33. E. Aspinall (2005) *The Helsinki Agreement: A More Promising Basis for Peace in Aceh?*, Washington, DC; T. Kivimaki (2006) *Initiating a Peace Process in Papua: Actors, Issues, Process, and the Role of the International Community*, Washington, DC.

34. C. E. Goscha (1995) *Vietnam or Indochina? Contesting Concepts of Space in Vietnamese Nationalism, 1887–1954*, Copenhagen, 13–95.
35. Goscha, *Vietnam or Indochina?*, 96–146.
36. C. E. Goscha (2004) 'Vietnam and the World Outside: The Case of Vietnamese Advisers in Laos (1948–62)', *South East Asia Research*, 12, no. 2 (July), 141–85: S. Heder (2004) *Cambodian Communism and the Vietnamese Model, Volume 1: Imitation and Independence, 1930–1975*, Bangkok.
37. T. Castle (1993) *At War in the Shadow of Vietnam: U.S. Military Aid to the Royal Lao Government, 1955–1975*, New York.
38. C. E. Goscha and T. Engelbert (1995) *Falling Out of Touch: Vietnamese Communist Policy towards an Emerging Cambodian Communist Movement (1930–1975)*, Clayton, Victoria.
39. P. Taylor (2000) *Fragments of the Present: Searching for Modernity in Vietnam's South*, Honolulu; P. M. Pelley (2002) *Postcolonial Vietnam: New Histories of the National Past*, Durham, NC.
40. G. Evans (1990) *Lao Peasants Under Socialism*, New Haven, CT; V. Pholsena (2006) *Post-War Laos: The Politics of Culture, History, and Identity*, Ithaca, NY.
41. D. P. Chandler (1993) *The Tragedy of Cambodian History: Politics, War, and Revolution Since 1945*, New Haven, CT.
42. E. R. Gottesman (2004) *Cambodia After the Khmer Rouge: Inside the Politics of Nation Building*, New Haven, CT.
43. W. R. Roff (1967) *The Origins of Malay Nationalism*, New Haven, CT.
44. C. A. Trocki (1990) *Opium and Empire: Chinese Society in Colonial Singapore, 1800–1910*, Ithaca, NY.
45. C. Hirschman (1987) 'The Meaning and Measurement of Ethnicity in Malaysia: An Analysis of Census Classifications', *Journal of Asian Studies*, 46, no. 3 (August), 555–82.
46. On this period, see T. N. Harper (1999) *The End of Empire and the Making of Malaya*, Cambridge.
47. On this formative period in the making of Malaysia, see M. Jones (2002) *Conflict and Confrontation in South East Asia, 1961–1965*, Cambridge; and G. Poulgrain (1998) *The Genesis of Konfrontasi: Malaysia, Brunei, Indonesia 1945–1965*, London.
48. M. Freedman (1960) 'The Growth of a Plural Society in Malaya', *Pacific Affairs*, 33, no. 2, 158–68; C. Hirschman (1986) 'The Making of Race in Colonial Malaya: Political Economy and Racial Ideology', *Sociological Forum*, 1, no. 2 (1986), 330–61.
49. G. P. Means (1972) '"Special Rights" as a Strategy for Development', *Comparative Politics* (October), 29–61.
50. J. K. Sundaram (1988) *A Question of Class: Capital, the State, and Uneven Development in Malaya*, New York; J. V. Jesudason (1990) *Ethnicity and the Economy: The State, Chinese, Business, and Multinationals in Malaysia*, Singapore; E. T. Gomez and K. S. Jomo (1997) *Malaysia's Political Economy: Politics, Patronage and Profits*, Cambridge.
51. See the various fine essays by Francis Loh Kok Wah, Lim Hong Hai, and Andrew Aeria in the Special Issue on 'Sabah and Sarawak: The Politics of Development and Federalism', *Kajian Malaysia*, 15, nos. 1 and 2 (January/December 1997).

Suggested Further Reading

Anderson, B. (1990) *Language and Power: Exploring Political Cultures in Indonesia*, Ithaca.

Anderson, B. (1998) *The Spectre of Comparisons: Nationalism, Southeast Asia and the World*, London.

Bertrand, J. (2004) *Nationalism and Ethnic Conflict in Indonesia*, Cambridge.

Chandler, D. P. (1993) *The Tragedy of Cambodian History: Politics, War, and Revolution Since 1945*, New Haven, CT.

Handley, P. M. (2006) *The King Never Smiles: A Biography of Thailand's Bhumibol Adulyadej*, New Haven, CT.

Hedman, E.-L. E., and Sidel, J. T. (2000) *Philippine Politics and Society in the Twentieth Century: Colonial Legacies, Postcolonial Trajectories*, London.

Pholsena, V. (2006) *Post-War Laos: The Politics of Culture, History, and Identity*, Ithaca, NY.

South, A. (2008) *Ethnic Politics in Burma: States of Conflict*, London.

Taylor, P. (2001) *Fragments of the Present: Searching for Modernity in Vietnam's South*, Honolulu.

Taylor, R. H. (2008) *The State in Myanmar*, London.

Tønnesson, S., and Antlöv, H. (eds.) (1996) *Asian Forms of the Nation*, London.

CHAPTER 25

NATION-BUILDING AND NATIONALISM: SOUTH ASIA, 1947–90

CHRISTOPHE JAFFRELOT

South Asia has been a real laboratory for the students of nation-building and nationalism over the last sixty years. No region has experienced two Partitions of this magnitude—the one in 1947, which gave birth to India and Pakistan through a massive exercise in ethnic cleansing (10 million refugees and 1 million casualties), and the one in 1971, which resulted in the creation of Bangladesh.

Such a chaotic history may stem from the unique religious and linguistic diversity of the Indian subcontinent. But such an interpretation would be too simplistic—or 'primordialist' to use the jargon of the specialists of nationalism. In fact, one needs to analyse ideologies and strategies of the relevant political actors to understand the trajectories of the nationalisms of India and Pakistan.

India's 'Unity in Diversity'?

The Legacy of the Colonial Era: Two Types of Nationalism

The Indian nationalist movement, embodied since 1885 by the Indian National Congress, rapidly split into two currents, moderates and extremists during the 1890s: the former conceived of the nation in a universalistic perspective, free from any reference to ethnicity, while the latter lay ready claim to a prime status for the Hindu community (see Chapter 12 by Joya Chatterji).

After the 1920s, however, there was a subdivision of the first school of thought. Mahatma Gandhi advocated a form of multiculturalism that recognized the right of existence of all religious communities in public life. In fact, in his eyes, the Indian nation was a collection of religious communities, all on an equal footing. The progressive intelligentsia, epitomized by Jawaharlal Nehru, attempted to prune the role of religious communities in political life, advocating that the individual was the basic unit of the nation.[1] Nevertheless, Gandhi and Nehru represented two faces of the same coin.

Heirs of the extremists, the Hindu nationalists and the Hindu traditionalist wing of the Congress Party, opposed this twofold current. Although less extreme than the Hindu nationalists, the position of Hindu traditionalists was characterized by the fact that it sought to protect Hindu culture in the widest sense of the term. Ayurvedic medicine, Sanskrit, et cetera, were thus viewed as elements of a legacy to be preserved.[2]

This trend further strengthened its position as the voice of separatism gained ground amongst an increasing number of Muslims. Indeed in the years following 1906, yet another pole was formed in the interplay of Indian politics embodied, this time, by the Muslim League. This political grouping first succeeded in acquiring a separate electorate for the Muslims just before the progressively elected provincial assemblies were set up in 1909. The Muslim League further propounded the theory according to which Hindus and Muslims constituted 'two nations'. It was by virtue of this theory that the group, arousing interest amongst an increasing number of people, demanded the formation of Pakistan in the 1940s.

The Constitutional Moment[3]

The Constituent Assembly elected in 1946 comprised mostly congressmen who, however, belonged to two different schools of thought, the Gandhi/Nehru one, and the Hindu traditionalist one. Gandhi died in January 1948—killed by a Hindu nationalist—more than one year before the assembly finalized the text of the Constitution, but Nehru actively represented the secular viewpoint there. He wanted to build a multifaceted nation by combining the need for unity and respect for pluralism. For him the genius of the Indian nation lay in its capacity for melting together Hindu culture and successive waves of invaders or migrants.[4] On the other hand, the Hindu traditionalists who suspected the Muslims of harbouring separatist tendencies wanted a standardized, Hindu-dominated culture for the country. Leading figures amongst them included Vallabhbhai Patel, the deputy prime minister and home minister, and Rajendra Prasad, the president of the Assembly.

Nehru's position prevailed most of the time during the three years over which the Constituent Assembly debates were held. Secularism, as a result, became the official doctrine of the Republic, Hindu nationalists, the only proponents of some Hindu State, being almost totally absent from the Assembly anyway. The Indian version of secularism did not equate with the French concept of *laïcité*, which did not recognize religious or other cultural differences in the public sphere; instead the State recognized all religious communities on an equal footing. Consequently, Article 30 of the Constitution considered religious and linguistic minorities' schools as legal and allowed them to apply for public funding.

Not only did the Indian Constitution acknowledge the role of religions in the public sphere, but it also made special concessions to some minorities, including the Muslims whom Nehru was keen to reassure since they had chosen to stay in India instead of joining Pakistan and were now only one-tenth of the population.[5] While they lost the separate electorate the British had granted them, Muslims retained the right to use the Shariat as a personal law. Muslims had, in fact, expressed their attachment to the Shariat quite early in the Constituent Assembly debates. Hindu traditionalists such as K. M. Munshi were, however, in favour of a Uniform Civil Code and invoked the need to 'consolidate and unify our personal law in such a way that the way of life of the whole country may in course of time be unified and secular'.[6] Nehru objected that Muslims should themselves freely choose the path of reform. Eventually, Article 44 of the Constitution merely stated: 'The State shall endeavour to secure for the citizens a uniform civil code throughout the territory of India.' Similarly, while Hindu traditionalists objected that freedom to profess one's religion would result in a huge number of conversions to the detriment of Hinduism, given the organizational strength and missionary zeal of the Muslim clerics and the Catholic Church, freedom of religious practice and to propagate one's faith was officially recognized in Article 25 of the Fundamental Rights.

Multilingualism was achieved with greater difficulties. Soon after the Assembly met for the first time, Hindu traditionalist members raised the question of the language in which the Constitution would be written and they spoke in favour of Hindi, the language they equated with the Hindu civilization, Urdu now being regarded by them as the language of Pakistan (and the Muslims).[7] Members from South India objected that Hindi was hardly spoken in their area and declared that English seemed to be the most suitable language at the national level. Nehru agreed that there should be a Hindi version of the Constitution but he preferred that an English version should be first voted on. He strongly opposed Rajendra Prasad on this issue.[8]

The controversy bounced back when the question of choosing the official language of the country arose. G. Ayyangar, an eminent Congress Party member of the Constitution Drafting Committee, proposed a compromise formula: while the official language must be Hindi in Devanagari script, English would be used at the same time at the national level for a period of fifteen years after the promulgation of the Constitution in 1950, a period that could be extended by the Parliament. A list of thirteen vernacular languages concluded Ayyangar's amendment, a sure sign of respect towards regional languages that were to be used at the province level for administrative purpose and as languages of instruction.[9] Nehru supported this proposition forcefully against Hindu traditionalists who lost by one vote.

In 1963, with the 1965 deadline approaching, the Parliament reviewed the issue and the Official Languages Act upheld the situation prevailing since 1950, with English becoming the 'associate official language'. After a final attempt by supporters of Hindi, which spurred a number of demonstrations in South India, a 1967 amendment dispelled the fears of non-Hindi-speaking states by clarifying that this arrangement would not be challenged as long as even one of them remained attached to it. Last but not least, as mentioned above, Article 30 of the Constitution allowed not only religious communities but also linguistic groups to establish their own educational institutions, and to seek State subsidies to help them function.

Linguistic Federalism

The Constitution of 1950 recognized fifteen official languages. With the exception of English, these were regional languages to which the local populations were very attached. Language-linked patriotism fed authentic ethnic regionalisms in certain provinces of the Dravidian South, for example in the Tamil lands. These movements penetrated the Congress Party and influenced it from within. They managed in this way to contest the all-powerful nature of the central State inherited from the British, and served as a source of support for political pluralism without putting the nation's integrity into question, as illustrated by the decisive episode of the reordering of the states of the Indian Union along linguistic lines.

Within the Constituent Assembly, partisans of such a reorganization had argued sporadically in the years 1946–50 that the administrative borders inherited from the British were artificial as they did not correspond to any linguistic reality.[10] Nehru was hostile to these claims because he feared that a recognition of regionalisms would hinder the process of nation-building.[11] He was also particularly concerned with keeping a strong State, not just because the British had bequeathed him one and no one lightly reduces his own power, but also because his brand of socialism required that he have a powerful administration at his disposal. However, the idea of 'linguistic states' gained ground within the local branches of his Congress Party, because regional identities, to which language was often the key, were taking hold throughout India on the rubble of the 'all English' system imposed by the British. On 15 December 1952 a former disciple of Gandhi, Potti Srisamullu, who had called for the formation of a province, 'Andhra', to be constituted from the division of Madras Province, died as a result of a hunger strike. His death aroused such emotion that Nehru resigned himself to announcing the formation of Andhra Pradesh, whose frontiers coincided with the extent of the Telugu language. This new entity was to be followed by several other linguistic states. The prime minister decreed on 22 December 1953 the creation of a commission charged with setting out 'the broad lines according to which states should be reorganized.'[12] He received the report of the States Reorganization Commission on 30 September 1955. This text recommended the replacement of the twenty-seven existing states by three Union Territories administered by New Delhi and sixteen states, of which only three would be created along linguistic lines. This provoked violent demonstrations, notably in Maharashtra, where Marathi-speakers sought to free themselves from the domination of the Gujaratis to whom they found themselves bound, artificially in their eyes, within the Bombay Presidency. The reorganization of the majority of states on a linguistic basis was agreed to in 1956. Maharashtra and Gujarat were created in 1960.

The debate around linguistic states, and its outcomes, reveal the importance of regional linguistic identity and the capacity of an accommodating federal system to defuse these centrifugal forces. This dynamic acquired an even greater significance when the political parties playing the federal game articulated the interests of linguistic groups. The Dravida Munnetra Kazhagam (DMK)—a Dravidian Party in Tamil Nadu—was a case in point. After having been tempted by separatism, the DMK decided to play the electoral game, recognizing that the federal framework allowed them to manage their province themselves. Far from wrapping themselves up in nationalism and rejecting the system, these groups went into politics and fought in elections from the 1950s on.

Similarly, the Sikh people of Punjab who had asked for a separate Sikhistan in 1947 eventually decided to play the constitutional game fully when it occurred to them that they might benefit from the linguistic logic of the Indian federal system. Their main party, the Akali Dal, asked for a redrawing of the frontier of the province according to the linguistic criterion—Sikhs speaking Punjabi while Hindus spoke Hindi. Such a reform was bound to transform Sikhs into a majority in Punjab. Their movement for a Punjabi *suba* (that is, a Punjabi-speaking 'province') succeeded in 1966, the central government having displayed a great deal of pragmatism, eventually overcoming its initial strong reluctance due to the opposition of the Hindi-speaking community .

The same kind of flexibility was observed in the case of the North-East where Assam shrunk as new states and Union Territories—an administrative status giving less autonomy than that of a state—were created in order to give to ethnic groups a land they could call their own. In 1963 the Nagas, a Christianized tribe, obtained Nagaland. In 1966 it was the turn of the Mizos who got a Union territory. In 1972 Meghalaya became a state. Then, the demand for a Gorkhaland gained momentum among the Gorkhas of Darjeeling district. Eventually in the 1980s, they gained a relatively autonomous status within the state of West Bengal, with the creation of a Hill Council.

The Rise of Communalism

The Indian Constituent Assembly debates had echoed the old ideological cleavage within the Congress Party, so far as the conception of the nation was concerned, and it seemed that Nehru had won against Hindu traditionalists. Because of his concerns over religious impartiality, and most certainly, over avoiding giving the regime too many Hindu features, the Indian Republic drew upon Buddhism to adorn itself with symbols that could be both Indian and neutral: the official emblem replicates the lions of Ashoka, the great Buddhist emperor, for instance.

India's multiculturalism was affected from below, and then from above, within the Congress Party: first, the local leaders were mostly Hindu traditionalists, and second, Nehru's successors did not maintain his secular attitude. Such an attitude prepared the ground for the Hindu nationalist backlash of the 1980s.

Hindu traditionalists remained in control of the Congress Party at the local and state levels after the vote of India's Constitution, so much so that its provisions could not be fully implemented. In Uttar Pradesh, the largest state of the Indian Union, G. B. Pant, the chief minister, declared Hindi as the official language. Urdu speakers, who were in large numbers in this stronghold of the Indo-Persian culture, petitioned the President of the Republic in 1954 in order, at least, that Urdu school classes be set up. The central government reiterated this recommendation twice, which led the government of Lucknow to open Urdu classes in only six districts where more than one fifth of the population was Muslim.[13] Urdu was not recognized as an official language of Uttar Pradesh before 1989.

Similar scenarios unfolded themselves in Madhya Pradesh, Rajasthan, and most of the states where Hindu traditionalist chief ministers were so strongly entrenched that they could resist the injunctions of Nehru and his progressive colleagues. They not only refused to recognize Urdu as much as they should but also patronized Hindi through associations like the Hindi *sahitya* academy (Hindi literature academy), supported Ayurvedic medicine, prohibited the slaughter of cows, and passed laws in defence of Hinduism to forbid 'fraudulent conversions'. In addition to losing ground in terms of education, Muslims were also victims of recurrent violence in places like Aligarh, Varanasi, Jabalpur, and Ahmedabad.

However, the communalization of the Congress Party leadership affected more radically the secular fabric of India's society from the 1980s onwards. Under Nehru, the government had treated all religious communities equally; under Indira Gandhi, the same arrangement prevailed till the 1980s, but things changed during her third term: now, the ruling party attempted to exploit communal feelings. As early as 1980, the Congress government introduced a bill seeking to revise the constitution of Aligarh University—the matrix of the Muslim League and then of the movement for Pakistan—in order to reaffirm its Muslim identity and to accord it more autonomy.

Soon after, Indira Gandhi secretly supported Sant Bhindranwale, a Sikh nationalist who had initiated a rather radical but popular mobilization in favour of a separate state for his community in Punjab. The prime minister obviously believed that this extremist leader would help her to destabilize the Akali Dal, a Sikh moderate party that was ruling a state she coveted for the Congress Party.

Last but not least, in 1983 Indira Gandhi attended the inauguration of the Bharat Mata Mandir (Temple of Mother India), a Hindu nationalist temple, and took part in the ceremonies marking the centenary of the death of the founder of the Arya Samaj, a socio-religious reform movement founded in 1875 that has been one of the crucibles of the Hindu nationalist movement.

Rajiv Gandhi, who took over from his mother after she was assassinated by her Sikh bodyguards in 1984, went even further in the communalization of the Congress Party.

In 1985 he ensured that the Shariat remained the source of Muslim Civil Law by getting an Act passed in Parliament that removed the Muslim community from the ambit of the Penal Code clause relating to divorce. He did so under pressure from conservative Muslim leaders who were supposed to control the 'Muslim vote'—which the Congress Party most obviously coveted—and who protested against the Supreme Court ruling in the Shah Bano case. This woman, Shah Bano, having been divorced by her husband according to the Shariat's procedure, had filed a case in the High Court and won. She won again when her husband went to the Supreme Court on appeal. Thus, Rajiv Gandhi had disowned the judges in order to please a handful of Muslim opinion leaders. This decision prepared the ground for the Hindu backlash that Hindu nationalist movements articulated immediately by claiming that Hindus were second class citizens in their own country.

The Hindu nationalist movement posed the biggest threat to secularism and the Nehruvian multicultural nation-building process. As an ideology Hindu nationalism is heir to a long tradition harking back to the Arya Samaj. It looks at Hindu civilization as the most ancient and perfect one and as the embodiment of Indian culture. Consequently it expects from the religious minorities that they practise their faith privately but pay allegiance to Hindu symbols and beliefs in the public sphere. The main incarnation of Hindu nationalism today, the Rashtriya Swayamsevak Sangh (National Volunteer Corps), was founded in 1925 and developed from its birthplace, Nagpur, all over India. With about 37,000 local branches and more than 2 million members, it has become one of the largest organizations in India.

After setting up its own network, the RSS started to develop front organizations in different directions. In 1948 RSS cadres based in Delhi founded the Akhil Bharatiya Vidyarthi Parishad (ABVP, the Indian Student Association), a student union whose primary aim was to combat communist influence on university campuses and that currently ranks among the first student unions in terms of membership. In 1955 the RSS created a worker union, the Bharatiya Mazdoor Sangh (BMS—Indian Workers' Association), whose primary mission was also to counter the 'red unions' in the name of Hindu nationalist ideology, promoting a doctrine of social cohesion over class struggle. In the 1990s the BMS became India's largest trade union.

In addition to these unions, the RSS developed more focused organizations. In 1952 it founded a tribal movement, the Vanavasi Kalyan Ashram (VKA, an Ashram for the welfare of the tribals),[14] which above all aimed to counter the influence of Christian movements among the aboriginals of India where proselytism and the social work of priests have resulted in numerous conversions. The VKA applied itself to imitating the methods of missionaries and thus achieved numbers of 'reconversions'.

In 1964, in association with Hindu clerics, the RSS set up the Vishva Hindu Parishad (VHP—World Council of Hindus), a movement responsible for grouping together the heads of the various Hindu sects in order to give this rather unorganized religion a sort of centralized structure.[15] Another subsidiary, Vidya Bharati (Indian Knowledge), was established in 1977 to coordinate a network of schools developed by the RSS, which started in the 1950s on the basis of local initiatives. Lastly, in 1979, the RSS founded

Seva Bharati (Indian Service), to penetrate the slums through social activities (free schools, low-cost medicines, et cetera).

Taken together, these bridgeheads are presented by the mother organization as forming the 'Sangh Parivar', 'the family of the Sangh', that is of the RSS.[16] Their action plans, each in its own field, have naturally weakened the secular fabric of India's society, and developed anti-Muslim feelings.

The Political Influence of Hindu Nationalism

Among the most important members of the 'RSS family' figures a political party, the Jana Sangh, which was founded in 1951 for the first general election and that Nehru immediately identified as the chief enemy of the Congress Party. This party has always wavered between two strategies. One, moderate, involved positioning itself as a patriotic party on behalf of national unity and as the protector of both the poor and small privately owned businesses in a populist vein that nevertheless stopped short of including the non-Hindus. The other line, more militant, was based on the promotion of an aggressive form of 'Hinduness', symbolized by vigorous campaigns in the defence of the cow, a sacred animal for the Hindus but not for the Muslims. The latter were the implicit target of a fight against slaughtering cows initiated in 1966 in the context of the fourth general election campaign.

Although the militant strategy was more in keeping with the wishes of the RSS and the feelings of its activists, it ran up against India's rules of secularism and kept the Jana Sangh isolated by preventing it from striking up alliances with other parties, except the very few ones that accepted its communal discourse. This strategy changed in the 1970s. In 1977, after the state of emergency declared by Indira Gandhi was lifted, the Jana Sangh—which had resigned itself to following a moderate line—merged with the Janata Party. This party won the sixth general election in March 1977 against the Congress Party. However, the former Jana Sangh had not broken with the RSS, to the great displeasure of some of its partners in power, particularly the socialists. This group, associated with the government's second in command, Charan Singh, who sought to destabilize Prime Minister Morarji Desai all the better to take his place, drew their argument from an upsurge in Hindu-Muslim riots in which RSS activists were involved, to demand that the former Jana Sanghis break with this movement. Their refusal precipitated the dissolution of the Janata Party, paving the way for Indira Gandhi's return.

In 1980 the former Jana Sangh leaders started a new party, the Bharatiya Janata Party (BJP), which remained faithful to the moderate strategy. The BJP, which had Atal Bihari Vajpayee as its first president, diluted the original ideology of the Jana Sangh in order to become more acceptable in the Indian party system and to find allies in this arena. This more moderate approach to politics was very much resented by the rest of the Sangh Parivar.

The RSS, in irritation, adopted some distance and made greater use of the VHP to rekindle its militant strategy. This strategy found its main expression in the launching of the Ayodhya movement in the mid-1980s. Ayodhya, a town in Uttar Pradesh, is described in the Hindu tradition as the birthplace and capital of the god-king Lord Ram. The site was supposedly once occupied by a Ram temple until it was destroyed in the sixteenth century on the orders of Babur, the first Mughal emperor, in order to build a mosque. In 1984 the VHP called for this site to be returned to the Hindus. In 1989, throughout the entire summer, with the logistical support of the RSS, it organized *Ram Shila Pujan* festivals, which involved worshipping bricks (*shila*) printed with Ram's name. These holy bricks were to be used to build the Ayodhya temple.

The BJP then rallied to the ethno-religious mobilization strategy and even participated in these processions, which took place all over India: the agitation contributed to its success at the polls, taking it from two seats in 1984 to eighty-eight seats in 1989. In 1990, while the party was a major component of the coalition in power that had just ousted the Congress Party, its president, L. K. Advani, headed a 10,000-kilometre 'chariot-journey' (*Rath Yatra*) that was to end with the construction of the Ayodhya temple. Advani was stopped before entering Uttar Pradesh and the repression of activists who attacked the mosque left some dozen dead. This episode reinforced the image that the BJP was trying to acquire among the majority community, of being a champion of Hinduism. The 1991 general elections actually enabled the party to win 20.08 per cent of the vote and 120 seats in the Lok Sabha, but its success in Uttar Pradesh, where the BJP was able to form the government, did not enable it to solve the issue of Ayodhya.

Hindu nationalist militants tried to put an end to this deadlock by demolishing the mosque on 6 December 1992. This operation and the ensuing Hindu-Muslim riots—around twelve hundred dead in a few days—prompted the Congress government that had been formed in 1991 to take a number of repressive measures, including the dissolution of the assemblies in states where the BJP was in power (Uttar Pradesh, Madhya Pradesh, Himachal Pradesh, and Rajasthan) and the ban of the RSS and the VHP—a temporary measure that did not affect the Sangh Parivar.

From the Nehru era to the rise of the Hindu nationalist movement the centre of gravity of Indian politics has moved from a secular (in other words multicultural) brand of nationalism to a clearly ethno-religious one. The minorities are the losers to the growing Hindu-oriented xenophobia that started in the 1980s, partly as a reaction to the communalization of politics by the Congress Party: while Nehru and Indira Gandhi during her two first terms had made a point of excluding communal forces from the legitimate political space, Indira Gandhi and then her son Rajiv prepared the ground for a Hindu backlash by playing one community against another in the 1980s. At the same time, India has maintained the initial multilinguistic option and thereby defused ethno-linguistic centrifugal forces that had manifested themselves, especially in South India, as early as the 1940s. In contrast, Pakistan has never been able to use Islam as a cementing force transcending ethno-linguistic identities.

Islam is Not Enough in Pakistan

When the word 'Pakistan' was introduced in the 1930s, 'P' stood for Punjab, 'A' for the Afghans (the Pathans of the North-West Frontier Province, NWFP), 'K' for Kashmir, and 'S' for Sindh. Interestingly, no reference was made to the Bengalis. The resolution of Lahore in which the Muslim League asked for the creation of Pakistan for the first time in 1940, regarded the Pakistan claim as a means to give a country to the Muslims of British India since Hindus and Muslims represented, according to the League, much more than religious communities: they form 'two nations'. After 1947, Mohammed Ali Jinnah, the first governor general of Pakistan, looked to Islam as a cementing force that would be able to surmount the regional cleavages.[17] General Ayub Khan, who ruled Pakistan between 1958 and 1969, also made use of Islam—certainly in a modernized and reformist form—and the Constitution of 1962 stipulated that the laws of the State could not contradict the precepts of the religion. Prime Minister Zulfikar Ali Bhutto inscribed the notion of an Islamic Pakistan in the Constitution of 1973 and went one step further: he declared the Ahmadis[18] non-Muslims. General Zia reasserted this approach forcefully in the late 1970s, stating: 'The basis of Pakistan was Islam. The basis of Pakistan was that the Muslims of the subcontinent are a separate culture.'[19]

Parallel to their effort to make Islam the ideological cement of the Pakistani nation, the establishment opted early for a centralized authoritarian pattern of state-building. One of Jinnah's first gestures was to dismiss the government of the North-West Frontier Province, a forewarning of the coming power relations between the centre and the provinces.

In fact none of the Constitutions of Pakistan have really been respectful of federalism. That of 1956 and of 1962, for instance, gave to the centre the task of collecting the most lucrative taxes as well as dispatching the fiscal resources and enabled the president to veto the laws voted by the provincial assemblies. The Constitution of 1973 gave representation to the provinces in the Council of Common Interests and the National Finance Commission, two new bodies in charge of allocating State resources. But the State remained very much centralized. The laws passed by the provincial assemblies could be declared null and void by the federal Parliament, for instance.

The dialectical tension between an Islamic, centralized (even authoritarian) State and ethno-linguistic groups forms the framework of what may be called the Pakistan pattern of nation-(un)making.

The Punjabization of the State

In contrast to India, Pakistan is inhabited by a clearly identified small number of linguistic groups whose elites have been gradually tightening control. The 'Mohajirs' were the initial architects of Pakistan. This term applies to all 'those who migrated' from what became India in August 1947 but it has come to define more especially those who came from the provinces of India where the Muslims were in a minority (Uttar Pradesh, Bihar, Bombay Presidency). It is in this social milieu, which shares a common language, Urdu (except for those who spoke Gujarati), that the Muslim League, and then the idea of Pakistan, found their first support, in particular, amongst a literary elite that was more and more threatened by the Hindu majority and hence anxious to find a base into which to withdraw, or even a state to govern. In 1947, one hundred thousand Urdu-speaking Biharis opted for eastern Pakistan and one million Muslims of Uttar Pradesh and Gujarat migrated to western Pakistan. They settled down above all in the cities of Sindh, in particular Karachi, the big industrial, commercial, and administrative centre of the new country that was then its capital.

The Mohajirs then dominated the State through the Muslim League, 'their' party, and its two chiefs, Governor General Jinnah (initially from the province of Bombay), and Prime Minister Liaqat Ali Khan (initially from Uttar Pradesh) whose government had a majority of Mohajirs.[20] These men made Urdu the official language of Pakistan. The Mohajirs were also over-represented in the administration: out of 101 Muslim members of the Indian Civil Service, 95 opted for Pakistan. Whereas they represented only 3.5 per cent of the population, in the early years of the new State, Mohajirs occupied 21 per cent of the posts of the Pakistan Civil Service.[21]

Mohajirs started to lose ground quickly though. Jinnah died in 1948, Liaqat Ali Khan in 1951, and the Muslim League rapidly lost its influence due to the weakness of its organization. Besides, the Mohajirs were ill-accepted in Sindh. Even though they were in a small minority, businessmen—mainly from Gujarat—were also influential and their quick recovery was resented by the 'locals'.[22]

From the beginning the Punjabis shared a dominant position with the Mohajirs because of their former status as the 'martial race': in British India they had provided 80 per cent of the armed forces.[23] The authoritarian reign of General Ayub Khan (1958–69) reinforced the rise of the Punjabis at the expense of the Mohajirs.

The rise of the Punjabis went on a par with the centralization of the State and the establishment of authoritarian regimes in the successive Constitutions. In 1959 Ayub Khan instituted the regime of 'Basic Democracies' that banned the political parties and relied on local notables who formed an ad hoc electorate for designating the president. This scheme was a good means to avoid the verdict of free elections, which would have placed the Punjabis at a disadvantage since they were in a minority. In fact, the law of numbers would have benefited the Bengalis of East Pakistan.

Bengali Separatism and the Making of Bangladesh

After 1947 the Bengalis were more numerous than the inhabitants of West Pakistan, 41.9 million as against 33.7 million, and on this basis demanded a representation superior to that of the 'western wing' in the institutions that the Constituent Assembly was responsible for establishing. This demand, which annoyed the Punjabis and the Mohajirs, paralyzed the Constituent Assembly.

The Bengalis also protested against the elevation of Urdu to the status of the national language at the expense of their language. After violent protests, Bengali was also recognized as a state language. But the Bengalis increasingly complained of economic exploitation by West Pakistan which, in fact, paid for many of its imports with the excess commercial balance of East Pakistan.[24] The Awami League that orchestrated their protest was subjected to severe repression. Its leader, Mujibhar Rahman, radicalized the movement and advanced in 1966 an openly autonomist programme. Ayub Khan replied with more repression but had to retire in 1969. His successor, General Yahya Khan, organized free elections in December 1970: it was a triumph for the Awami League, which got 160 seats against 81 for the Pakistan People's Party (PPP) of Ali Bhutto, for which the Sindh and Punjab voted massively. The new Pakistani establishment refused the verdict of the ballot box and sent thousands of soldiers to East Bengal. The repression that followed resulted in innumerable victims and provoked an exodus of 10 million Bengalis into India. New Delhi then launched a military operation that obliged Islamabad to release their hold over East Pakistan. This resulted in outright secession and the creation of Bangladesh in December 1971.

Sindhi Nationalism: On the Decline or Cyclical?

The Sindhis are possibly the only ethnic minority whose nationalism has declined in the course of time. There is one good reason for that: even though, after the Bengali secession of December 1971, the Punjabis represented about 60 per cent of the population of Pakistan and occupied 70 per cent of jobs in the armed forces,[25] for the first time a Sindhi, Zulfikar Ali Bhutto, took over from Yahya Khan as Head of State.

In 1972 the PPP also won the elections in Sindh and formed the government in Karachi. The state government made Sindhi compulsory in school for those who had another mother tongue and even forced bureaucrats to use Sindhi as an official language. These decisions triggered violent resistance from the Mohajirs. Bhutto, who had supported the initial measures, intervened and persuaded the government of Sindh to give bureaucrats twelve years to learn Sindhi. However, a quota of 11.4 per cent was established in favour of rural Sindh—where most of the local Sindhis lived—in the central administration, as a way of redressing the imbalance of which the Mohajirs were the principal beneficiaries: in 1973 they still occupied 33.5 per cent of the posts in public administration whereas they only represented 8 per cent of the total population; the rural Sindhis themselves occupied only 2.7 per cent of the posts of employees and 4.3 per cent of the posts of the officer grade.[26] In the army, Sindhis represented only

2.2 per cent of the total in 1947 (as against 80 per cent of Punjabis), and according to S. P. Cohen these proportions have remained more or less the same ever since.[27]

In the late 1970s Sindhi nationalism found itself exacerbated by the dismissal of Bhutto from power by General Zia-ul-Haq, a Punjabi. Bhutto's condemnation (by a tribunal consisting of a Punjabi majority)[28] and later his execution in April 1979 made him a martyr in the opinion of many Sindhis. Zia then favoured Punjabis at the expense of Sindhis. Some of them were evicted from the provincial administration. In the mid-1980s, the central administration was over-dominated by the Punjabis, who retained 56 per cent of the jobs, whereas the rural Sindhis got only 3 per cent (almost as little as the Balochs, 2.5 per cent, and much less than the Mohajirs, 25 per cent, and the people from the NWFP, 11 per cent).

Not surprisingly, the Movement for the Restoration of Democracy, a PPP- sponsored alliance of opposition parties, which organized a series of demonstrations against Zia in 1983, was especially successful in Sindh. Some 45,000 soldiers were deployed for a repression that lasted six months, which resulted in 300 deaths and 100,000 arrests. The charter of the movement demanded the establishment of a confederation where Sindh would enjoy the maximum autonomy.

The movement was not well structured but it got demobilized and lost its Sindhi nationalist overtone for another reason: the electoral successes of the PPP and the appointment of Benazir Bhutto as Prime Minister in 1988. The PPP, in fact, appeared as a Sindhi Party winning all the electoral seats in the constituencies of rural Sindh, and that a Sindhi could be at the helm of power militated in favour of a renewed loyalty of its 'compatriots' to the notion of a Pakistani nation, even in the form of a centralized State. This fluctuating identification with the State as a function of the ethnic affiliations of those in power shows that the State does not transcend social conflicts but rather represents a stake in the competition between different communities. Such a pendulum-like oscillation according to who is in power is also obvious in the case of the Mohajirs.

The Mohajir Backlash

The Mohajirs are, indeed, very revealing of the malleability of political identity according to the interests one pursues. To begin with, they identified themselves with the new State of Pakistan which was largely their creation. However, the more they felt threatened, the more they projected themselves as an oppressed minority with a distinct identity.

The Mohajirs were affected by long-term sociological trends. On the one hand the Green Revolution, of which Punjab was the first beneficiary, since the end of the 1970s reinforced the domination of this province and permitted its natives to invest in industry, including in Karachi. On the other hand, migrants poured into this city and benefited from its dynamism: in 1984 the city accounted for 3.3 million Mohajirs compared with 1 million Punjabis, 1.1 million Balochis, 700,000 Pakhtuns—a good number of them refugees from Afghanistan—and a few hundred thousand Sindhis.

The Mohajir Qaumi Mahaz (Mohajir National Movement) was created in this context in 1984. Its cadre and even its chief, Altaf Hussain, came from the middle class and above all recruited its members from amongst students frustrated in their aspirations of social mobility. The MQM demanded that only persons settled for a minimum of twenty years in Sindh should be considered as residents and enjoy the right to vote; that foreigners could not acquire properties in Sindh; that the Mohajirs should be recognized as the fifth 'nationality' of Pakistan; finally, that Karachi, the first city of the country, should be named a province (Karachi suba), which would in fact be a Mohajir province.[29] Altaf Hussain occasionally claimed that he wished to partition Sindh in the same way that Bangladesh was carved out, if Islamabad continued to ignore his demands.[30] Yet, his strategies of contesting elections and allying the MQM with other national parties suggested that he was still more interested in exerting power within the institutional framework of Pakistan than anything else.

Yet, the MQM also resorted to violent methods, so much so that in June 1992 the army was deployed in Karachi for 'Operation Clean Up'. The leaders of the MQM went into hiding or abroad. (Altaf Hussain had already established himself in London.) 'Operation Clean Up' only radicalized the population in favour of the MQM, and the military implicitly admitted this before leaving Karachi in November 1994.

'Balochistan to the Balochs!'

Balochistan contains only about 3 per cent of the population of Pakistan, but it represents 42 per cent of the country's territory. In 1947 the ruler of Kalat, the largest Baloch princely state, opted for independence, but the Pakistani army broke his resistance in a few months. The government then succeeded in co-opting influential local notables (Sardars) and even their chief, the Khan of Kalat. The national movement, inhibited by rivalries, did not survive, except through guerrilla warfare of low intensity that persisted under the rule of Ayub Khan (1958–69). It really crystallized rather late as a reaction to the centralization of the Pakistani state.

In 1972, an alliance of the Awami Party and the Jamiat-Ulema-Islam (a conservative Islamic party supported by the Sardars) won the elections in Balochistan, as well as in the NWFP. One of the first decisions of the new government was to make the administration more indigenous by replacing officers from other provinces, mainly from the Punjab, with 'sons of the soil'. The central government denounced this spoils system, which would have deprived the members of the national elite (above all, Punjabis) of coveted posts. The direction of industrial investments constituted another bone of contention. Balochistan and the NWFP blamed Islamabad for failing to advance the economic development of their territory and demanded control over the industrialization process.

Zulfikar Ali Bhutto dismissed the government of Balochistan in 1973, justifying this by invoking separatist activities. The Balochi Peoples' Liberation Front (BPLF) and the Baloch Students' Organization (BSO) then initiated an uprising that mobilized some 55,000 militants (including 11,500 regular combatants) over four years. The Pakistani army deployed some 88,000 men for a war that resulted in about 5,300 deaths in the ranks of the Balochs and 3,300 amongst the soldiers.[31]

General Zia appeased a section of the Baloch nationalists by liberating thousands of prisoners in the late 1970s and pardoning those who had taken refuge in Afghanistan. Some nationalists chose exile, like Attaullah Khan Mengal, who left for London to found the Sindh Baloch and Pakhtun Front with the help of Mumtaz Bhutto (first cousin of Zulfikar Ali Bhutto). Mengal still did not want anything short of a confederal Pakistan, enabling Balochistan to become an independent country. But most of the other Baloch leaders showed greater moderation, partly because of Zia's ability to co-opt them.

The democratization process that commenced in 1988 did not result in the re-emergence of regionalist forces, since the Sardars preferred to form alliances with parties in power in Islamabad, either the PPP or the PML(N).

From Pakhtunistan to Pakhtunkwa

The Pakhtuns live in the only province of Pakistan, the NWFP, with a name that, until 2010, did not reflect any ethnic feature, even though the province contains most of the 16 per cent of the Pashto speakers who live in the country. In 1947 the Pakhtuns engaged in an anti-British struggle that had been organized inside a movement called the Red Shirts, which was opposed to integration into Pakistan and instead demanded, through its main leader, Khan Ghaffar Khan, the formation of a Pakhtunistan that would cover the Afhgan Pakhtun and the Pakhtuns (or Pathans) of the NWFP. Ghaffar Khan and his supporters boycotted the referendum by which NWFP was finally integrated into Pakistan and later demanded at the Constituent Assembly of which he was a member that the Province be named Pakhtunistan. He was arrested soon after and his brother, Dr Khan Sahib Zada, the then chief minister of the NWFP, was dismissed by Jinnah.

Yet, the heirs of the Red Shirts movement were integrated into the new regime. In 1956 the son of Ghaffar Khan, Wali Khan, founded the National Awami Party (NAP), which became part of the political system. This sign of moderation can partly be explained by socioeconomic factors. The Pakhtuns were already well represented inside the Pakistani state because of their place in the army (a legacy of the colonial period, the British having classified them among the martial races), of which they composed 19.5 per cent of the personnel in 1948.[32] In 1968 they constituted almost 40 per cent of the 48 top military elite—a bigger share than the Punjabis (35.4 per cent). Right from the beginning, the intensity of Pakhtun nationalism declined in proportion to the possibilities of upward mobility opened by the new state. For all these reasons the

NAP obtained less than 20 per cent of the valid votes in the general as well as provincial elections of 1970, a strong incentive for the NAP to dilute its programme, which had already accepted the borders of Balochistan and the NWFP in 1969.

The fact that the Pakhtuns had close contacts with their Afghan counterparts favoured a form of irredentism. Kabul had always had designs on part of the NWFP, so much so that it has been a bone of contention going back at least to the drawing of the Durand line which, in 1893, partitioned the territory of this ethnic group into two almost equal halves. In 1947 the Afghan government asked the British to give the Pakhtuns two other choices, in addition to the possibilities of acceding to Pakistan or India: to merge with Afghanistan or to form an independent Pashtunistan. Subsequently, this question poisoned the diplomatic relations between Britain and Afghanistan to the point of provoking their break in 1961–2. This thaw in their relations did not last long. However, tension remained, especially after the rise to power of Mohammed Daoud Khan, one of the staunchest partisans of Pashtunistan in Kabul. In his first speech and in his official position, he singled out Pakistan as the only country with which Afghanistan had unresolved problems and mentioned Pashtunistan in this respect. Daoud was then helping Ajmal Khattak, the General Secretary of the NAP, who was self-exiled in Kabul where he declared in 1973 that his aim was to carve out an independent Pashtunistan on the model of Bangladesh. The irredentist dimension of the Pathan movement thus helped the NAP by providing its self-exiled leaders with some logistics and support.

However, this external factor would not have played a major role if, at the same time, the Pakistani Pakhtuns had not been alienated by the centralized authoritarianism of Ali Bhutto. When Bhutto dismissed the Awami Party-led government of Balochistan in 1973, the government of the NWFP resigned immediately as a sign of solidarity. Two years later Bhutto had Wali Khan arrested under the pretext of his implication in the murder of a minister of the NWFP, and he dissolved the Awami Party. The trial of Wali Khan lasted right up till the dismissal of Bhutto in 1977 by General Zia, when the accusations were withdrawn. After his release from prison in 1978, Wali Khan decisively downplayed his Pakhtun nationalism.

The Afghan War from 1979 to 1989, between the USSR and those it supported on the one hand and the Mujahideen on the other hand, revived the Pakistani fears of an eventual revival of Pakhtun irredentism as a result of the massive influx of refugees. Between 1979 and 1981, 2.4 million Afghans settled in the NWFP, which now had 16 million inhabitants, as compared to Afghanistan's 14 million. However, Islamabad was not under the threat of a Pakhtun mobilization, and again there were good socioeconomic reasons for this. The NWFP saw its economic situation improving from the end of the 1970s. The Pakhtuns joined the army and the bureaucracy in great numbers and those who did so came primarily from those districts that had traditionally been strongholds of the Pakhtunistan movement. Secondly, after Punjab, it was the NWFP that profited most from the rural exodus towards Karachi and the emigration to the Gulf countries: the Pakhtuns represented 35 per cent of the Pakistanis who went abroad between 1976 and 1981. For all these reasons, the ANP of Wali Khan showed some solidarity with Zia (during the Movement for the Restoration of Democracy

[MRD] of 1981, for example). The Pakhtun leaders who were still exiled in Afghanistan returned to Pakistan in 1986.

The process of democratization that began in 1988 did not result in the revival of Pakhtun nationalism. The collaboration between Pakhtun notables and the national elite remained the rule at the moment of the elections to the provincial assembly. After the 1988 elections the ANP made an unprecedented alliance with the PPP, and then in 1990 formed part of a coalition government led by the Muslim League.

Conclusion

Two interrelated conclusions may be drawn from the comparison between India and Pakistan in terms of nation-building and nationalism.

So far as the nation-building process is concerned, the Indian pattern relies on an accommodating linguistic federalism reflected in the official multilingualism already established in 1950 and the creation of linguistic states as early as the 1950s. India continued to create new states in order to defuse centrifugal forces after 1990: in 2000 Uttaranchal was carved out of Uttar Pradesh, Chhattisgarh out of Madhya Pradesh, and Jharkhand out of Bihar. By contrast, though it designed official regions according to linguistic criteria, the Pakistani State remained highly centralized and suspicious vis-à-vis the provinces to which it gave little autonomy until the 2010 18th amendment. State governments were repeatedly dismissed by the centre and their prerogatives limited, something that occurred only occasionally in India during the third term of Indira Gandhi—or more generally in relation to Jammu and Kashmir. As a result, whereas New Delhi has been able to defuse ethno-nationalist separatisms—except in a few cases such as Kashmir, Nagaland and Assam—Islamabad has radicalized the centrifugal forces it wanted to suppress. These movements either succeeded in creating a new nation state—like Bangladesh in 1971—or developed resilient guerrillas—as in Balochistan, where separatist groups have once again been active since the late 1990s, still in reaction to the exploitation of the region's resources by outsiders from Punjab and Karachi.

The second conclusion one can draw from the India/Pakistan comparison concerns the roots and trajectories of different forms of nationalism. Certainly, ideological motivations play a key part in most of the nationalist movements mentioned above. This is why the term 'schools of thought' has been used so often. Indian activists belonging to the Gandhian, Nehruvian, and Hindu nationalist traditions did refer to competing world views. However, South African trajectories of nationalism show that one cannot ignore the political and socioeconomic dimensions of this 'ism'. Ideologues are also political entrepreneurs exercising cultural identities in order to mobilize supporters and voters. The Muslim League leaders were a case in point in the 1940s when they launched the Pakistan movement in order to get a separate State to administer, and the BJP has become an adept at manipulating Hindu symbols of identity for electoral gain. Socioeconomic factors are also prominent at times: ethnic groups may become nationalist—and 'discover' (that is, construct) a separate political identity—because they suffer from socioeconomic discrimination. Interestingly, this state of affairs was more prominent in Pakistan, largely because of the centralization and punjabization of the State, which caused a lot of resentment.

The political and socioeconomic dimensions of nationalism help explain its varying forms, but this cannot be divorced from the previous variable, namely, the degree of centralization of the State. The militancy of the Mohajir, Sindhi, and even Pakhtun leaders varied according to their access to state power, which had much to do with the absence or resurgence of federalism. Bengali separatism derived largely from the excessive centralization of the State and Baloch nationalism really crystallized in reaction to the reduction of provincial autonomy granted by Islamabad. Atul Kohli argues that in contrast to India, Pakistan cannot accommodate centrifugal movements (as in Tamil Nadu and Punjab in India) because it does not have a federal framework and the democratic culture to do so.[33] These two characteristics enable—or oblige—India to make concessions in such a way that eventually ethnic movements recede; hence the metaphor of the inverted 'U' curve that Kohli applies to movements such as that of the Tamils asking for a Dravidistan in the 1940s–1960s and the Sikhs demanding a separate Khalistan in the 1980s and then contenting themselves with more autonomy. One could object that in Pakistan, too, some ethnic movements followed the shape of an inverted 'U' curve: in the NWFP the tensions were much less in 1990 than in the 1970s. However, this may not be because the state granted the province more autonomy but rather because of the co-option of local leaders and economic development that led to the formation of a bourgeoisie.

Notes

1. This typology draws inspiration from the one established by G. Pandey (1990) *The Construction of Communalism in Colonial North India*, Delhi.
2. I have borrowed this definition of Hindu traditionalism from B. Graham (1990) *Hindu Nationalism and Indian Politics*, Cambridge.
3. For more details, see C. Jaffrelot (2004) 'Composite Culture is not Multiculturalism: A Study of the Indian Constituent Assembly Debates', in A. Varshney (ed.) *India and the Politics of Developing Countries: Essays in Memory of Myron Weiner*, New Delhi.
4. See J. Nehru (1946, 1989) *The Discovery of India*, New Delhi, 50ff.
5. S. Gopal (1984) *Jawaharlal Nehru*, London, 3, 172.
6. *Constituent Assembly Debates [hereafter CAD]* (1989) New Delhi, Lok Sabha Secretariat, I, 547.
7. G. Austin (1972) *The Indian Constitution: Cornerstone of a Nation*, Bombay, 297.
8. Austin, *The Indian Constitution*, 285.
9. *CAD*, vol. IX, 1,323.
10. Such was, for example, the case of N. G. Ranga. *CAD*, VII. 351—debate of 9 November 1948.
11. Gopal, *Jawaharlal Nehru*, 262.

12. Gopal, *Jawaharlal Nehru*, 373. However, he let his worries be known to the provincial heads of government. Letter dated 24 December 1954, in G. Parthasarathi (ed.) (1988) *Jawaharlal Nehru: Letters to Chief Ministers vol. 4 (1951–1957)*, Delhi, 116. See also the letters of 20 May 1955 (p. 181) and 2 August 1959 (p. 224).
13. B. D. Graham (1990) *Hindu Nationalism and Indian Politics: The Origins and Development of the Bharatiya Jana Sangh*, Cambridge, 113ff.
14. Hindu nationalists translate 'indigenous peoples' as *vanavasi*, literally, 'those who live in the forest' instead of the more commonly used term throughout India, *adivasi*, in other words, 'those who were there first', because from their very ideological standpoint the initial inhabitants of the country were 'Aryans' and not the aboriginals, driven away or conquered by Aryan invasions, from which the tribes today descend.
15. C. Jaffrelot (2001) 'The Vishva Hindu Parishad: A Nationalist but Mimetic Attempt at Federating the Hindu Sects', in V. Dalmia, A. Malinar, and M. Christof (eds.) *Charisma and Canon: Essays on the Religious History of the Indian Subcontinent*, Delhi.
16. For more details, see C. Jaffrelot (ed.) (2005) *The Sangh Parivar: A Reader*, Delhi.
17. A. Jalal (1990) *The State of the Martial Rule*, Cambridge, 280.
18. The sect of the Ahmadis was founded in 1889 by Mirza Ghulam Ahmed. He is venerated equal to the Prophet by the members of the community and this heresy very early drove the most orthodox guardians of Islamic law to demand that the Ahmadis should not be recognized as Muslims.
19. Cited in T. Amin (1993) *Ethno-National Movements of Pakistan: Domestic and International Factors?*, Islamabad, 171.
20. L. Binder (1961) *Religion and Politics in Pakistan*, Berkeley, CA, 205.
21. K. B. Sayeed (1967) *The Political System of Pakistan*, Boston, MA, 132.
22. F. Ahmed (1998) *Ethnicity and Politics in Pakistan*, Karachi, 95–7.
23. S. P. Cohen (1987) 'State Building in Pakistan', in A. Bannazizi and M.Weiner (eds.) *The State, Religion and Ethnic Politics: Pakistan, Iran and Afghanistan*, Lahore, 318. They represented about 55 per cent of the administration (C. H. Kennedy [1987] *Bureaucracy in Pakistan*, Karachi, 194).
24. M. Rashiduzzaman (1982) 'East-West Conflicts in Pakistan: Bengali Regionalism, 1947–1970', in A. J. Wilson and D. Dalton (eds.) *The States of South Asia: Problems of National Integration*, London, 117.
25. A. Jajal (1995) *Democracy and Authoritarianism in South Asia*, Cambridge.
26. C. H. Kennedy (1991) 'The Politics of Ethnicity in Sindh', *Asian Survey*, 31, no. 10 (October), 938–55.
27. S. P. Cohen (1998) *The Pakistan Army*, Karachi, 44.
28. The four Punjabi judges considered he was guilty whereas all the others, who came from other provinces, were in favour of acquitting him (O. Noman [1992] *Pakistan: Political and Economic History since 1947*, London, 193).
29. J. Rehman (1994) 'Self-Determination, State-Building and the Mohajirs: An International Legal Perspective of the Role of the Indian Muslim Refugees in the Constitutional Development of Pakistan', *Contemporary South Asia*, 3, no. 2, 122–3.
30. Interview in *India Today*, 15 July 1995, 42.
31. K. B. Sayeed (1980) *Politics in Pakistan: The Nature and Direction of Change*, New York. See ch. 6 entitled 'Pakistan's Central Government versus Balochi and Pashtun Aspirations', 113–38.
32. Cohen, *The Pakistan Army*, 44.

33. A. Kohli (1997) 'Can Democracies Accommodate Ethnic Nationalism? The Rise and Decline of Self-Determination Movements in India', *Journal of Asian Studies*, 56, no. 2 (May), 325–44.

Suggested Further Reading

Ahmed, F. (1998) *Ethnicity and Politics in Pakistan*, Karachi and Oxford.
Austin, G. (1972) *The Indian Constitution: Cornerstone of a Nation*, Bombay.
Brass, P. (1974) *Language, Religion and Politics in North India*, Cambridge.
Cohen, S. (2005) *The Idea of Pakistan*, Lahore.
Gandhi, M. K. (1922) *India Home Rule*, Madras.
Gould, W. (2004) *Hindu Nationalism and the Language of Politics in Late Colonial India*, Cambridge.
Graham, B. (1990) *Hindu Nationalism and Indian Politics*, Cambridge.
Hardy, P. (1972) *The Muslims of British India*, Cambridge.
Jaffrelot, C. (1996) *Hindu Nationalism and Indian Politics*, London.
Jaffrelot, C. (ed.) (2004) *Pakistan, Nationalism without a Nation?*, London and New York.
Khilnani, J. (2004) *The Idea of India*, Delhi.
Nehru, J. (1945, 1985) *The Discovery of India*, Delhi.
Pandey, G. (1990) *The Construction of Communalism in Colonial North India*, Delhi.
Rahman, T. (1998) *Language and Politics in Pakistan*, Karachi.
Robinson, F. (1975) *Separatism among Indian Muslims: The Politics of the United Provinces Muslims, 1860–1923*, Cambridge.
Sisson, R. and Wolpert, S. (eds.) (1988) *Congress and Indian Nationalism—The Pre-Independence Phase*, Delhi.
Zavos, J. (2000) *The Emergence of Hindu Nationalism in India*, Delhi.

CHAPTER 26

NATIONALISM IN SOUTHEASTERN EUROPE, 1970–2000*

SABINE RUTAR

INTRODUCTION

FEW scholarly works share the fate of Katherine Verdery's *National Ideology Under Socialism: Identity and Cultural Politics in Ceaușescu's Romania*, sent to press on 8 November 1989 and turning literally overnight from an open-ended analysis into a self-contained event: 'From being an analysis of how cultural production and national ideology are intertwined in a socialist society, it became a recent history of a now-very-different future cultural and national politics, in the transition from socialism to whatever will come after it.'[1] This 'whatever will come after it' has, unsurprisingly, influenced many recent interpretations of and attitudes towards communism. Research has tended to formulate questions in an ex-post facto manner or in the search for explanations for what came after the systemic break.[2] The social scientists' analytical grid has often been conditioned by the expectation that a Western-type democracy and market economy stand at the end of what is called *transition*. This chapter historicizes 1989, seeking to understand the *given* society of late socialism, the one that collapsed and then *changed* into something new. Absorbing the expectations of the West has certainly been part and parcel of this *transition*, but such absorption did not happen on a *tabula rasa*. With regard to Yugoslavia, the question why so much *violence* was generated in the course of its break-up has been the most pressing one, and too often explanations have implied that this multinational state was doomed from its beginnings, approaching

* I thank Ulf Brunnbauer and Heike Karge for their valuable comments on earlier drafts of this chapter.

it thus with yet another pre-set analytical grid.[3] Indeed we need to overcome a disciplinary divide between those who study the 'before' (historians) and those who study the 'after' (political and social scientists) of the systemic change.[4]

The politicization of both social/class and ethnic/national consciousness originated in the nineteenth century. In the twentieth, both took on radicalized forms associated with crimes that rank among the most gruesome in history. Whereas scholars ceased decades ago to treat *class* as a given entity, they generally continue to perceive *nation* as such, in spite of all deconstructivist efforts.[5] Recent scholarship on nationalism has produced various canonical conventions: traditions are invented, national communities imagined, the nation gendered. Even so, the question about what makes appeals to the national more or less effective, what turns them into something integrating or, to the contrary, disintegrating, if not violent, still awaits a satisfactory answer.[6] Analogous to what has become consensual when referring to social identities (*class*), the definition proposed here conceptualizes the nation as a process, an institutionalized form, practical category, a contingent and context-dependent event.[7] *Nationalism* thus is a discursive strategy, an ideology that seeks to instrumentalize the nation politically, that aims to construct, foster, mobilize, and make use of feelings of belonging oriented to the nation. The constructions (and deconstructions) of state socialism were inextricably intertwined with nationalism, leading to differing national histories of communism, and, after 1989, to differing transitions. Defining both *class* and *national* identities as practical categories is a prerequisite for a better understanding of how the national is deeply embedded in social contexts, and how this can work in either integrative or disintegrative ways.

The period chosen, 1970 to 2000, is indicative. The date of 1970 encompasses the general turmoil of 1968, the 'Prague Spring' of that year, the 'Croatian Spring' of 1971, as well as the 'watershed'[8] of the Cold War in 1975, the Helsinki Accords.[9] State socialist economic crises in southeastern Europe began about this time, contributing to the growing importance of nationalism. The date of 2000 not only comprises the end of 'that dreamlike era from 11/9 to 9/11', 'the historical hiatus between the Cold War and the war on terror',[10] but points to a specific watershed for southeastern Europe. Bulgaria, Romania, and Albania saw the end of their first decade of transformation which had been characterized, to varying degrees, by power continuums from socialist times rather than by decisive breaks. Albania's state collapse in 1997 is only the clearest expression of this. The Kosovo war of 1998–9, the death of Croatia's president Franjo Tuđman in December 1999, and the end of Slobodan Milošević's regime in what remained of Yugoslavia in October 2000 signalled the end of a decade of wars.

It has been said of southeastern Europe since 1989 that it produces more nationally saturated history per square metre than it can possibly digest.[11] The national, or better, nation-state master narrative continues to exercise a powerful influence. Attempts at deconstructing such narratives—interestingly often by foreign scholars—have stimulated aggressive reactions, including personal insults and even threats of violence. The battle is about myth; those pieces of national history claimed to be constitutive for the nation. The myths shape the politics of identity, the Serb myth of the 1389 Battle of Kosovo being just the best-known case. The fierceness of the polemics against the historians who debunk such myths points to the continued importance of the primordialist view of the nation, especially amongst nation-state elites. At the same time, it suggests just how vulnerable, self-conscious, and transformative such identities are, and therefore how much in need of simple truths.[12]

The Communist Modernization Project

As elsewhere in eastern Europe, so with communist state-building efforts in the Balkans, the pretension was to build society anew. Yet legacies from the interwar period and the Second World War conditioned the establishment of state socialist regimes, and not only because the nation state continued to be the dominant framework in which political entities were fostered. The view of the nation as an ethnic rather than civic concept, as practised after the First World War, ideologically mingled with and was complemented by Soviet nationality theory, providing nationalist legitimation under radically changed circumstances.

At the end of the Second World War, those associated with the Axis powers and occupying forces found themselves in a difficult position or would not accept the new circumstances. Among these were the approximately 250,000 Germans who fled Romania after the war and the 125,000 Hungarians who left Transylvania, when it was returned to Romania in 1945–6. In Yugoslavia, during the last months of the war, about 300,000 ethnic Germans were expelled, and another 80,000 left the country in the 1950s, reducing this minority to a tiny remnant. The majority of Italians—up to an estimated 250,000 people—left Yugoslavia (Istria) between 1943 and 1960, as a consequence of the general political climate evoked by the 'Trieste question'. Such purges, however, were directed against anti-communists rather than particular national groups, even if, as with the Germans, such categories overlapped. Also purged were thousands of Serbs, Croats, and Slovenes in Yugoslavia, as well as Bulgarians, Romanians, and Albanians who were expelled or executed because they had allegedly fought against the communists, often collaborating with the occupying forces.

The year 1948 brought a first break in southeastern Europe's post-war history: Yugoslavia's conflict with the Soviet Union and the other communist countries. A second break occurred in the years 1953 to 1956, introducing de-Stalinization but also marking the limits of independence with the bloody crushing of the Hungarian revolution of 1956. Yet the crises shaking the Eastern bloc, as well as Nikita Khrushchev's denunciation of Stalin's crimes and cult of personality, pointed to the fragility of authority and the need for all regimes to find new sources of legitimacy. The various reforms led to considerable differences in the (nation-)state socialisms of the region by the beginning of the 1960s.

The communists embarked on their project with a radical change of elites, helped by the fact that many members of the former ruling strata—if they had survived the war—had left the country. Those remaining often experienced humiliation and expropriation. Consequently the first two decades of communist rule were characterized by strong social mobility, with opportunities for the children of workers and peasants.

This constituted a core element of legitimacy for state socialism. From the 1970s onwards, however, social groups—including the elites—increasingly reproduced from within. Furthermore the younger generations harboured expectations different from those of their parents and grandparents; they did not compare their lives to the poverty of the 1950s but to the living standard of their peers in the West.

In Bulgaria and Romania, the regimes co-opted most intellectuals by coercion, but also by granting privileges and making 'patriotic' issues a communist cause. Whereas censorship in Albania was even more severe, in Yugoslavia it was officially abolished. The emblem of Yugoslavia's literary excellence was the 1961 Nobel Prize for Ivo Andrić. Yet, even in non-censoring Yugoslavia creative writers and academics knew their boundaries. Certain taboos prevailed, such as any discussion of communist crimes, as did compulsory interpretative schemes, such as for the partisan war. Though disputed earlier, only in the 1980s were challenges to the party line increasingly articulated in public.

The challenge of integrating the masses had to be mastered by political elites in all countries. Even though social outcomes in many respects did not correspond to regime intentions, one should not underestimate the significance of social policies. As in the rest of the Eastern bloc, this was an unprecedented project to reorganize society according to ideological objectives. The project confronted pre-communist political culture, patron-client networks, corruption, and the destructive legacy of the Second World War. Charismatic leadership and nationalism remained central.

The region experienced, in varying intensities, significant social change: agrarian decline, urbanization, the growth of social mobility, increases in living standards, modernization of material culture and education as well as improvements in the position of women, along with changes in gender and family relationships. State policies included violence and coercion, propaganda and indoctrination, yet also manifold social incentives. Inspired by the Soviet model, the aim was the establishment of a classless, modern collective, understood as an irrevocable break with 'backwardness', by which was meant patriarchy, religion, ignorance, capitalism, and, not least, the 'wrong' political attitude.[13]

Albania: From Heroic Self-Defence to State Failure

Albania's state socialism was dominated by extreme fears of dependency and remained Stalinist until well into the 1980s. Its isolation took place in stages. In 1948 it broke with Yugoslavia, supporting the USSR. In 1961 it broke with the USSR, rejecting Khrushchev's de-Stalinization. For a decade, China compensated for lack of Soviet support. In 1972, this relationship deteriorated following US president Richard Nixon's visit to China and the ensuing detente between the two countries. In 1978 Albania broke with China and continued in isolation, with a very small export economy. Hundreds of thousands of small bunkers scattered over the whole country vividly symbolized the siege mentality of the Albanian communists.

Enver Hoxha's China-inspired cultural revolution wanted both to modernize the country and complete the Albanian nation-building project. He intended to do away with tribal structures, and in 1967 declared Albania the world's first atheist country, as religion was deemed the main contributor to the country's backwardness.[14] Increased attention was paid to national history, especially from the beginnings of the national movement in the late nineteenth century, leading to independence from the Ottoman Empire in 1912. The master narrative focused on Albanian heroism in defending freedom against more powerful foes. The medieval national hero George Kastrioti Skanderbeg was intensely mythologized by communist historians. It was claimed that the Albanians descended from the Illyrians, making them the one and only autochthonous nation in the region. Such nationalist propaganda and siege identity politics sought to legitimize repressive domestic and isolationist foreign policies.[15]

Only with Hoxha's death in 1985 did his successor Ramiz Alia begin a gradual opening-up, establishing diplomatic relations with Germany in 1987 and participating in the 1988 meeting of Balkan foreign ministers in Belgrade. In July 1990 diplomatic relations with the Soviet Union were established (with the USA only in March 1991). The border with Greece was gradually opened, after Greece in 1987 declared an end to the formal state of war with Albania. In 1989–90 critical voices began to be heard, some political inmates were released and public protests increased, though still suppressed by Albania's secret service *Sigurimi*. In July 1990 Albanians stormed foreign embassies in Tirana, pressing for measures such as freedom to practice a religion, the restoration of a Ministry of Justice, and reform of penal law. The government removed Stalin's monument in Tirana. At the beginning of 1991 new demonstrations occurred, with Tirana's students in the lead, obtaining the release of all remaining political prisoners. The images of tens of thousands of Albanians fleeing their country on rusty ships to Italy in March 1991 went around the world. Over the following years the authoritarian governing style did not change, nor the polarization between the Socialist Party and the Democratic Party, nor the fostering of administrative clientelism. At the beginning of 1997 the collapse of financial pyramid schemes destroyed the savings of many Albanians, creating political instability. Protests, riots, and de facto lawless areas, especially in the country's southern part, indicated state failure, something unique in Europe's twentieth-century history. Albania had to start over again.

Bulgaria: Nationalizing the Socialist Way of Life and Afterlife

Bulgaria pursued a distinctively steady pro-Soviet course, including de-Stalinization, which saw the replacement of party leader Vălko Červenkov in 1954 by Todor Živkov.

The Bulgarian socialist vision consisted principally of two goals: the establishment of a large capital-goods sector and a homogeneous socialist nation, both of which seemed indispensable for modernization. Given the absence of a specifically anti-Soviet position, the legitimatory function of nationalism was even more obvious than in the other three countries. Intensive propaganda for the 'socialist way of life'[16] was carried out by the 'Patriotic Front', the country's largest mass organization, whose activities increasingly shaped socialist everyday culture as a national Bulgarian endeavour. Rehabilitating nationhood through officially supported 'socialist patriotism' proved a relatively successful instrument for the legitimation of authority.

Such nationalization required the compliance of national minorites, especially the Muslims whose way of life was considered as backwards, 'the Orient within'.[17] Indeed, conflating religion with national identity legitimated many of the religious and minority policies of communist regimes. Suppression, if not abolition of religion was a core constituent of the communist ideological package.[18] The Bulgarian Turks, for example, remained a bothersome minority for Bulgaria. Pushed by collectivization, bad living conditions, the suppression of religious freedom, the forced unveiling of women, as well as political pressures, about 155,000 Turks emigrated from Bulgaria in the 1950s, under the terms of a treaty with Turkey. Advocating a unitary socialist nation in both national and religious terms, Bulgaria's constitution of 1971 no longer mentioned Turks or Roma or Pomaks (Bulgarian-speaking Muslims). In 1973–4 some 250,000 Pomaks were forced to change their Turkish-Arabic names for Bulgarian ones. Any resistance was brutally supressed. This 'rebirth' was based on the premise that the Pomaks were ethnic Bulgarians who had been forcibly converted to Islam in Ottoman times and were now to be 'reborn' with the help of state and party. In 1984 this policy was applied to the remaining 800,000 Turks who were officially regarded as Islamicized and Turkified Bulgarians. The public use of Turkish was prohibited, as were all traditional Muslim garments; many cemeteries and mosques were devastated. Resistance to this forced assimilation considerably undermined communist authority in Bulgaria.[19]

Apart from economically motivated unrest, it was the mass exodus of about 350,000 Turks between May and August 1989, after Bulgaria had opened its borders with Turkey, which decisively contributed to destabilizing the regime. In June 1990 Bulgaria saw the first free elections since 1946, with the successor to the Communist Party, the Bulgarian Socialist Party, gaining an absolute majority of votes. For just a decade, political power was contested between reformist and old-style communists on the one hand and the democratic opposition on the other, while the country experienced one of the most serious economic crises of its recent history. The Turkish-led Movement for Rights and Freedom came to hold the balance of power; it had indeed been the first serious opposition party, from its beginnings as an underground movement in 1985 to its official establishment in January 1990.

Romania: Ceauşescuism and its Legacy

Reacting to Khrushchev's new course, at the seventh party congress in 1954, the prime minister Gheorghe Gheorgiu-Dej declared Romania to be an independent and sovereign state, subsequently underlining this stance by harsh criticism of the Soviet intervention in Hungary. Differences over economic policies played a central role in this Romanian assertion of independence. In the framework of Soviet attempts to establish a division of labour among its satellites in service of Soviet needs, Romania's function was to deliver agricultural produce and raw materials. The Romanian communists were not prepared to renounce their vision of (heavy) industrialization, and this led to promulgating an ideology of national communism.

Nicolae Ceauşescu, taking office after Gheorghiu-Dej's death in 1965, enforced this course: Romania did not participate in the Warsaw Pact intervention in Czechoslovakia in 1968, and maintained friendly relations with China, despite the Sino-Soviet conflict. At the same time, Ceauşescu consolidated his relations to Western states. The promotion of national heritage took on grotesque features in the 1970s and 1980s, when the historical roots of the Romanians were identified with the ancient Dacians, and the Romanians presented as one of the greatest peoples of all times—with Ceauşescu as their wise father figure and architect of their historical mission. Artists and scholars came under enormous pressure, as they were expected to support such views.[20] The rest of the population came to experience national megalomania in a palpable manner. Apart from a close-meshed control carried out by the secret service *Securitate*, strikes were mercilessly crushed, and in 1988 Ceauşescu declared a plan to 'systematize' the countryside. Almost half of the villages were to be replaced by buildings made from prefabricated slabs. This was only realized to a limited degree, whereas in Bucharest the demolition of the old city centre did happen. A whole quarter was razed to make way for the Palace of the Republic, one of the largest buildings in the world, completed only after Ceauşescu's demise.

In Romania, the national discourse had become ideologically powerful in the interwar period; for the communists, it was an easy and convincing reference to adopt.[21] The fate of the ethnic Germans in Romania illustrates the persistence of such practices. In interwar Romania the Transylvanian Saxons had experienced a substantial loss of property, as a consequence of a radical agricultural reform. After massive emigration in the immediate post-war period, they experienced further blows to their formerly solid socioeconomic self-confidence with communist collectivization. This marginalization of ethnic Germans that began in 1918 found a unique and cynical finale under communism. Between 1967, following the establishment of diplomatic relations with the Federal Republic of Germany, and 1978 some 69,000 Transylvanian Saxons left Romania. In that year Germany and Romania concluded a treaty that allowed another 10,000 Romanian Germans to emigrate, with the Federal Republic paying 8,000 Deutschmarks per person to Ceauşescu's regime, literally a head tax. Like Bulgaria,

Romania carried out the nationalization of communism at the expense of its national minorities.

The degree of coercion and megalomania in Romania came closest to the Albanian experience. While Albanians after 1989 expressed their despair in mass emigration, the Romanians staged a bloody end. The population was intimidated and atomized by the omnipresence of the *Securitate*, and also preoccupied with sheer survival, lacking the bare necessities of life. In mid-December 1989 protests spread from Timişoara to Bucharest and other cities, encountering brutal violence as the regime sought to crush the revolt. Yet, when the army and police disobeyed the order to shoot, leaving the *Securitate* the only prop of the regime, the police quickly managed to arrest Ceauşescu and his wife, handing them over to the army. After a quick and improvised military tribunal, both were executed on 25 December 1989. As in Albania and Bulgaria, power was seized by the reform-oriented group of communists led by Ion Iliescu's newly founded 'Front of National Salvation', which in May 1990 won in Romania's first free multi-party elections. Also here, the first post-communist decade was characterized by the weakness of the opposition and the revolutionary aura claimed by the 'Front of National Salvation'.[22] As in Bulgaria, an ethnic minority alliance—the Democratic Union of Hungarians in Romania—came to hold the balance of power.

Yugoslavia: From Titoist *Sonderweg* to Threefold Transformation

The Yugoslav communists, led by Josip Broz Tito (1892–1980), wishing to avoid the mistakes of centralized, Serb-dominated interwar Yugoslavia, constructed a federal state based on the principle of equality among its constitutive nations (*narodi*): Croats, Macedonians, Montenegrins, Serbs, and Slovenes. The census of 1971 recognized 'Muslims', meaning the Slav Muslims of Bosnia and Herzegovina, as the sixth constitutive nation, following a decade-long debate on the issue. The Yugoslav communists also identified nationalities (*narodnosti*), to which they granted extensive minority rights. However, Yugoslavia's *narodnosti* were defined not by their number—there were approximately as many Albanians as Slovenes and Macedonians—but by the fact that they were part of a nation that possessed a nation state. Consequently, it was assumed, the *narodnosti* could not exercise their self-determination in the form of a republic within the Yugoslav federation. Again we see as the strongest legacy from the interwar period the dominance of the idea of the nation state being the ultimate political organization. What is more, post-war policies of massive ethnic population exchange, particularly in eastern and southern Europe, affirmed the goal of building homogenous nation states. In this perspective, communist Yugoslav nationality policies attempted something innovative, a federation of nationally defined republics.

Unlike interwar Yugoslavia, the socialist state did not claim to be ethnically homogeneous and did not profess that as an aim.

Following the split with the Soviet Union in 1948, Yugoslavia made substantial changes to the Stalinist model, developing a state socialism *sui generis* in the face of many challenges. The regime redirected both its foreign and domestic policies; it incorporated the liberalizing developments of the 1960s; it envisaged, in a federal system, a balance between the central government and the republics; it sought answers to the challenge of enormous regional disparities. The result was the Yugoslav socialist *Sonderweg*.[23] The keywords of this project are: workers' self-managment, decentralization, freedom to travel, labour migration, non-alignment, liberalization, socialist market economy. On the one hand, the changes were due to the need to approach the West, on whose (financial) support Yugoslavia depended; on the other hand, they should be read as a genuine attempt to construct a socialist society within the specific Yugoslav framework. Ideology as a reference point for political decisions has to be taken seriously.

Within this ideological framework, as from 1950 the new Yugoslav identity was closely linked to anti-Stalinism. To be a good Yugoslav meant to be loyal to the ideology of socialist self-management and non-alignment as alternatives to Soviet socialism. Subsequently, once the Soviet Other began to crumble, it threatened the very essence of what it meant to be a good Yugoslav. Unlike the countries that hovered in the Soviet sphere of power, the Yugoslavs had no one but themselves to blame for the failure of their communist project. Thus anti-communism in Yugoslavia was to a large extent organized in opposition to the concept of good Yugoslavism, as imagined by Yugoslav communists.[24]

In their economic policies the Yugoslav communists turned away from the Stalinist model of enforced heavy industrialization, giving priority to consumer goods industries and the tertiary sector, especially tourism. Decision-making processes were steadily decentralized, market mechanisms given room, in spite of also devising development plans and making politically motivated investments. The Yugoslav economy was increasingly integrated into the global one, including massive labour migration from the 1960s onwards. At the same time, Yugoslavia experienced a phenomenon unique within the state socialist planned economies: unemployment. This contributed considerably towards the delegitimization of the system; in 1988 the unemployment rate averaged 18 per cent. At the same time, it proved impossible to reduce regional disparities in living standards. In spite of the creation of a special fund for promoting the poorer regions in 1963, disparities grew. Unemployment was just 2.5 per cent in Slovenia but a massive 58 per cent in Kosovo.

A second core field of political reforms was the division of authority between the centre and the republics. The result of Yugoslav constitutional development was far-reaching state decentralization, which, from 1974 onwards, contained elements of a confederation. This was in part due to the politics of interest pursued by the republics but was also ideologically motivated. Tito's chief ideologue Edvard Kardelj, *spiritus rector* of the Yugoslav constitutions, pursued a policy of the withering away of the state.

The second constitution of 1953 anticipated the subsequent trend of devolving decision processes from the centre to the republics. The third, of 1963, granted the republics the right of secession. The constitution of 1974 was the longest in the world (over four hundred articles) and in some respect incomprehensible, especially with regard to the modalities of electing the National Assembly. It again strengthened the federalization of the country, granting the two autonomous provinces within Serbia, Kosovo and Vojvodina, almost the same rights as the republics. Even in defence policy, the centre was not the only decision taker as, in the wake of the Prague Spring and a perceived strong Soviet threat in 1968, the state introduced 'territorial defence', to be administered by the republics and two autonomous provinces.

These defence units have been ascribed a key role in explaining the violence accompanying state collapse. 'Territorial defence' included military education from elementary school upwards, motivated by the determination to be prepared for conflict with any external enemy. Contrary to its intention, this essential militarization of society would become an implosive force. It went hand in hand with the massive exposure of younger people to an increasingly violent (and colourful) imagery designed in a sensational way to secure their consent to Yugoslavia's core founding myth: the partisan war. It has been argued that this increasing militarization of education, media, institutions, and young minds was crucial in lowering the barrier against the use of violence.[25]

A far-reaching liberalization of social life after the removal of the hardline minister of the interior Aleksandar Ranković in 1966—from the abolition of censorship to substantial freedom of travel—was accompanied by similar developments in the political realm. In Slovenia, Croatia, Serbia, and Macedonia the party leaderships were labelled 'liberal', claiming to continue both economic and political reforms. However, the central party committee reacted to the crises of the late 1960s with restrictive measures. The core claim of the 1968 student protests in Belgrade and other cities, together with Marxist intellectuals around the journal *Praxis*, was that the central party had betrayed the ideals of communism. In Kosovo the same year saw massive Albanian protests for recognition as a Yugoslav nation (rather than nationality). In Croatia the Liberal Party leaders tolerated a movement initiated by intellectuals that demanded Croatian-national reforms in realms like language and economy, giving rise by 1970 to mass protest.

The central party perceived this 'Croatian spring' as especially threatening, for it seemed to endanger the delicate balance of nationality politics and the central party's power monopoly. When demands were made that would in effect have led to the independence of the Croatian Republic, Tito in December 1971 decided to purge the Croatian party leadership and suppress the mass movement. About 50,000 Croatian members were expelled from the League of Communists. In 1972 the Liberal Party leaderships in Serbia, Slovenia, Macedonia, and Vojvodina were also purged. One needs to be clear about the purpose of these measures. It was not about reintroducing centralization, but about re-establishing power balance. Indeed, the constitution of 1974 actually realized some Croatian demands for more autonomy. The 1974 constitution was accepted because the communist leaders of the republics saw it as another step toward that vision of a self-managing and socialist Yugoslavia that allowed for the free development of its nations and nationalities.

A key to understanding the dynamics of nationalism in socialist Yugoslavia lies in the acceptance of the 1974 constitution by the constituent republics. As Dejan Jović notes, 'one should never forget that leaders of Yugoslav republics and provinces at that time were communists—not nationalists'.[26] However, the communists fought nationalism primarily in their own republic. Serbian communists acted against Serb nationalism, Croatians against Croat nationalism, and so on. In the face of the 'Croatian spring' of 1971, the Serbian public reckoned that the danger of Serb nationalism was exaggerated by the Serbian communists, while other nationalisms, especially Croatian and Albanian, were underestimated. The communists found themselves accused of overly chastising their own nation, which fuelled the arguments of nationalists about 'treacherous' communists. Especially for the Serbian communists, who were keen to counteract the historical burden of great-Serbian domination in interwar Yugoslavia, compromise with nationalism was unacceptable. Consequently, they were caught between being perceived as accepting of nationalism in other republics and the provinces and the need to show that they were not nationalists. This tension between principles and practice was a source of permanent political crisis in Serbia and Yugoslavia throughout the 1970s and 1980s.

As long as Tito was alive, the flaws of this increasingly complex system surfaced only softly and occasionally, as his charismatic leadership and capacity to act as ultimate arbiter counterbalanced many decision-finding stalemates. After his death in 1980, any coherent central answer to the manifold problems of the 1980s proved impossible. The party could not act in place of the 'state that withered away' (the subtitle of Jović's book), as already in 1953 it had transformed from centralized organization into a republican-based League of Communists. The ideological narrative of self-management was also anti-statist, and with the communists being anti-nationalist as well, it comes as no surprise that their opponents would often be just the opposite: ultra-statist and ultra-nationalist.

After Kardelj's death in 1979 and that of Tito the following year, the Kosovo crisis of 1981 was symptomatic of the by then fully fledged paradoxical peculiarities of Yugoslav politics. For example, six months after Tito's death, the president of Serbia's constitutional court, Najdan Pašić, demanded changes to the constitution. Six months later protesting Albanian students demanded the same. Even with Kosovo's extensive autonomy, granted by the 1974 constitution, the Albanians felt subordinate. Given that numerically they ranked fourth behind Serbs, Croats, and (just) Slovenes, they felt that only if Kosovo became a republic could they overcome economic, political, and ethnic inequality. By contrast, Serbs saw their position impaired not only by the fact that they harboured two autonomous provinces within their republic but also by the way federal boundaries were drawn so that there were approximately twice as many Serbs outside the Serbian republic than there were Slovenes in Slovenia or Albanians in

Kosovo. Hence, a sense of inequality was the main motive of both the Kosovar protests of 1981 and the Serbian reaction to them.

The end of Yugoslav socialism was overshadowed by the demise of the compound state. Considering that the two other socialist federations—the Soviet Union and Czechoslovakia—also did not survive the end of socialism, it seems easier to explain the dissolution of Yugoslavia than its bloody aftermath. While the transition to multi-party systems at the republican level happened rather smoothly, the dissolution of the federation had dramatic consequences: nearly a decade of wars with more than 100,000 dead and millions of displaced persons and refugees. Both processes—the end of socialism and the dissolution of the state—were deeply intertwined. The desire for more autonomy and more control over the distribution of resources were important motors for opposition within individual republics and provinces. If Serbia had originally accepted the confederal model of 1974 in order to secure more autonomy in its internal affairs, it quickly complained about being restricted on precisely this point. Because the provinces—Kosovo and Vojvodina—understood themselves as being equal to the republics, they frequently prevented Serbia from exercising full control over their territories. Serbia, her leaders felt, remained the only Yugoslav republic that did not achieve statehood with the constitutional changes of 1974.

Dejan Jović has provided a good critical assessment of existing analyses of the disintegration of Yugoslavia, enumerating them as '(1) the economic argument, (2) the ancient ethnic hatred argument, (3) the nationalism argument, (4) the cultural argument, (5) the international politics argument, (6) the role of personality argument, (7) the fall of the Empires argument, and (8) the constitutional and institutional reasons argument', dismissing only the ancient ethnic hatred argument in its entirety.[27] In fact, while antagonistic representations of the ethno-national past indeed were heavily (mis-)used during the Yugoslav wars as a source of rhetoric and persuasion that fuelled the conflict, one must be careful not to turn these forceful categories of practice into categories of historical analysis, in other words into an essentialized approach to the nation.[28]

By 1990 no narrative remained that could keep Yugoslavia together. Although the common beliefs of the communist elite had made very difficult compromises viable—such as that of the 1974 constitution—the absence of common beliefs now made much more apparently viable options impossible.[29] Almost all parties that had been established in the individual republics as an expression of the new pluralism were oriented to the republican level or a particular ethnic category. In 1991 and 1992 four republics (Slovenia, Croatia, Macedonia, and Bosnia and Herzegovina) declared their secession from the federation, while the Serbs were busy fostering re-centralization plans.

With these secessions, the point of no return in the nationalization of politics had been reached and soon escalated into war. So far as Slovenia was concerned, the central government in Belgrade had little power to stop the movement for independence and democratization. In Croatia, the ethnicization of the nation state as well as Milošević's pouring oil onto the fire drove Serbs in towns like Knin and in the Krajina to violent protests. Their unofficial referendum of August 1990 against planned Croatian constitutional changes further aggravated the situation, especially when intervention by Zagreb's police forces was blocked by the Yugoslav People's Army. After the Slovene and Croatian declarations of independence in December 1990 and June 1991, Belgrade justified its military intervention by claiming that it needed to protect Serb and other national minorities. Following the ten-day war in the summer of 1991 when Belgrade realized it could not retain Slovenia, the conflict in Croatia escalated. The siege of Vukovar and the bombardment of Dubrovnik mark the most ruthless moments of that war. In December the Serbs in Krajina and western Slavonia united to form the Republic of Serb Krajina with Knin as its capital, controlling a third of Croatian territory. As Bosnia and Herzegovina became the main arena of war, the Croatian army grew stronger, and the European Union recognized Slovenia and Croatia (15 January 1992), the Yugoslav People's Army gradually withdrew, leaving paramilitary local units to control much of the country. As a reaction, and despite international pressure and the presence of United Nations Missions, Zagreb, in what became known as 'Operation Storm' (August 1995), employed ethnic cleansing against Serbs in western Slavonia, Krajina, and eastern Slavonia.

Croatia pursued a politically ambiguous course in the first decade of independence. A radical exchange of elites was implemented as communist organizations were prohibited. The Croatian Democratic Union (CDU) led by Franjo Tuđman dominated the nationalist movement, mobilizing the population by appealing to a Croat-Serb hereditary enmity. CDU dominance only ceased with the Dayton Agreement/Accords (signed December 1995) at the US airbase in Ohio, the end of 'Operation Storm', and an increasing desire for reforms, which became more realistic with Tuđman's death (December 1999). In 2000 the first oppositional president to be elected, Stjepan Mesić, initiated a process of political democratization, moderating blatant Croatian ethnonationalism. The commander of 'Operation Storm', General Ante Gotovina, was sentenced to twenty-four years of imprisonment in April 2011 by the International Criminal Tribunal for the formerYugoslavia (ICTY) in The Hague. While his extradition to the ICTY in 2005 had decisively increased Croatia's EU prospects, Croatians perceived the sentence as an affront against their very state; for the large majority of the population 'Operation Storm' remains the decisive battle of Croatia's war for independence, and Gotovina its hero.

The rest of Yugoslavia, also called the 'third Yugoslavia', witnessed a rapid polarization between the authoritarian Milošević regime and the democratic opposition. Milošević's Socialist Party of Serbia (founded in mid-1990), successor to the Serbian Communist Party, in 1992 entered into a coalition with the nationalist Serbian Radical Party and with the 'Yugoslav Left' of Milošević's wife Mirjana Marković. With these two parties appealing to radical nationalists and old communists respectively, Milošević could present his party as the moderate peoples' party in between. Even though his regime clearly did not shy away from repressive measures and ballot-rigging, he enjoyed broad popular support. This support began to wane from mid-1996 due to the effects of war, deprivation, corruption, and international isolation, culminating in the Kosovo war and NATO bombing of Serbia from March to June 1999, which led to Serbia's loss of the province. On 5 October 2000, after massively manipulating the elections two weeks earlier, Milošević was ousted from power by the opposition and popular street protests. Half a year later the new prime minister, Zoran Đinđić, extradited him to the ICTY, where he died in March 2006, without being sentenced.

The bloodiest war took place in Bosnia and Herzegovina. Three ethnically defined parties dominated the elections of November and December 1990, ousting from power the republic's Communist Party. When the Bosnian Parliament declared Bosnia and Herzegovina sovereign in October 1991, the Serb Party, which had become the long arm of Belgrade, withdrew from the common institutions and founded an entity of its own. When the Parliament in Sarajevo, or rather its Croat and Bosnian Muslim (Bosniak) members with the Serbs boycotting, declared Bosnia and Herzegovina independent in March 1992, the conflict escalated into open war, involving massive ethnic cleansing, mass murder, mass rape, the four-year siege of Sarajevo, the destruction of the Ottoman bridge in Mostar, and genocide against the Bosnian Muslims in Srebrenica. This last outrage finally led to a more resolute international intervention. By means of air strikes on Serb positions, NATO forced the Serb side into negotiations, which took place at the US airbase in Dayton, Ohio, and in Paris in November and December 1995. Milošević succeeded in presenting himself as the peace-seeking mediator with regard to the Serb militias. The much-criticized terms of the agreement were dictated by Washington; its underlying principle was the territorialization of ethnicity and the acceptance of the outcome of ethnic cleansing. Alternative solutions seemed to offer little hope for ending the fighting. The Dayton Peace Accords divided Bosnia and Herzegovina into a state with three constitutive nations (Bosniaks, Serbs, Croats) and two entities—the Serb Republic (*Republika Srpska*) and the Federation of Bosnia and Hercegovina, which consists of ten cantons. Both for the Federation between Bosniaks and Croats and for the compound state of Bosniaks, Croats, and Serbs the principle of ethnic proportional representation was entrenched. This led to a unique ethnic stalemate, rewarding those politicians who rejected responsibility for the compound state, and punishing those who sought compromise rather than nationalist maximalist goals. Inter-ethnic political cooperation was virtually impossible, and so was a gradual transfer of competences to the central state. As a consequence, gradually removing the powers of the Office of the High Representative proved very difficult. Indeed, in 1997, his authority was even strengthened, in order to prevent the collapse of the state.[30] After the three most sought-after war criminals of the Bosnian war—Radovan Karadžić, Ratko Mladić, and Goran Hadžić—were arrested and extradited to the ICTY in July 2008, May 2011, and July 2011, respectively, the ICTY had completed its mandate.

The withdrawal of its autonomous status, Milošević's aggressive rhetoric, and the removal of Albanians from key positions led to the establishment of an Albanian parallel society in Kosovo. Education, politics, social and medical care were transferred to underground movements. This strategy of retreat into the private sphere and non-violent protest was led by Ibrahim Rugova and his Kosovo League. Little space was left for the old communist cadres; the new parties, the League and the Democratic Party of Kosovo, came from civil society. In 1992 Rugova was elected president, but his popularity was undermined both by his readiness to negotiate with Milošević after the Dayton Accords of 1995 and the increasing activities of the armed underground organization *Ushtria Çlirimtare e Kosovës* (UÇK). In 1998 three factors helped turn non-violent resistance into open war. First, Kosovars' frustration over their exclusion from the Dayton Accords had led them to believe that only violent resistance would bring international attention, as it had in Bosnia. Second, state collapse in neighbouring Albania in 1997 made possible the import of armaments, including heavy weapons. Third, leaders of the UÇK and the Democratic Party of Kosovo carried out guerrilla attacks in order to provoke the Serbs, who responded with atrocities against the civilian population. All this engaged the attention of the international media and the UN. Determined to prevent an escalation of the Bosnian type, the USA and the European Union pressed for negotiations over Kosovo's status. Despite the threat of a NATO military strike, the Serbian delegation refused to sign the peace treaty drafted at Rambouillet. When the Kosovar delegation did sign, NATO launched an airstrike on Serbian targets that lasted three months, a controversial operation due to its lack of backing by the UN Security Council where Russia used its veto. After Belgrade's capitulation a ceasefire agreement was signed at Kumanovo on 3 June 1999. The UN Security Resolution 1244 of 10 June stipulated that Kosovo *de iure* remained under Yugoslav sovereignty but that this sovereignty was to be *de facto* exercised by a UN Mission, until a solution was found that both Belgrade and Prishtina would find acceptable. On 17 February 2008 the Kosovar Albanians unilaterally declared independence. Kosovo today is a contested and weak state, where many different domestic and foreign actors exercise a myriad often overlapping state institutional and political functions.

Conclusion: The Persistence of the National

Between 1970 and 2000 the socialist states of southeastern Europe experienced growing economic problems, a stalling of political reform, the collapse of the political system, and the transition to a market economy and multi-party politics. All pervasive were appeals to nationhood that aimed at legitimizing power structures and holding together the social fabric. The weaker the system and the more insecure the social vision and reality, the more successful was the appeal of nationalism. More than any other ideology, nationalism successfully mobilizes feelings of belonging. The flexibility with which national identity can combine with other identities, such as class and religious ones, can contribute much to establishing a solid and lively polity. However, that same flexibility readily lends itself to abuse and instrumentalization, extending to inciting violence and war. This is especially true when nationalism pursues the project of homogeneous nation states, with the exclusive mechanisms this involves.

Key elements in the demise of state socialism were the economic crises and the subsequent lowering of living standards that began in the 1970s. Reforms of the planned economy, whether far-reaching as in Yugoslavia or very limited as in Albania, proved unable to generate sufficient growth. After attaining a certain level of industrialization, there was a failure to switch from an extensive to an intensive economy, thereby increasing technological and material deficiencies, especially when compared with the West. Another key element was the reduction of upward social mobility; by the 1970s and 1980s, all social strata increasingly reproduced from within. Well-educated young people encountered difficulties in finding a satisfactory social position. A third problem was the systemic incapacity for genuine reform; the party-state was not willing to risk its authority. Reacting with violence and coercion to protests, it only produced more unrest and, consequently, violence, further diminishing the base for governing by consent. The deficits inherent in the political system were, however, for a considerable time camouflaged by the charisma of the leaders. A contradiction became increasingly apparent between the leaders' claim to govern according to democratic and rational principles and the personal cult in which they engaged. And charisma waned, through death or loss of appeal. Younger people did not feel particularly attracted to the communist founding myths and their ageing protagonists. Finally, the dominance of the party made it easy to find the culprit for everything that had gone wrong. Yet, despite their authoritarian appearance, these states were actually weak. An inability to get things done while denying power to any other social force conduces to a state that crumbles the instant an effective challenge arises.[31]

This gradual, multilayered loss of legitimacy happened interdependently with *perestrojka* and *glasnost* in the Soviet Union and the end of the Cold War, finally leading to a simultaneously precipitous end. While transformation research has applied the term 'double transformation' to post-communist states that had to master the transition both to market economies and to pluralist democracy, for the successor states of Yugoslavia a third dimension must be added. This is the need to come to terms with the consequences of war, to make the change from violent conflict to peaceful competition, both within and between the states that had formerly been one state.

Hardly anywhere was the collapse of state socialism followed by a radical change of who ruled. Only in some Yugoslav republics and provinces was there such change, demonstrating continuity between a comparatively liberal socialist society and a pluralist one. Mostly however, the continuity was an authoritarian one and the reformist elements of the old establishment took over, taking on a democratic appearance, yet often governing as they had done in the previous regime. The social cracks left by the old political system were filled with the same glue that had previously proven successful in terms of legitimization: nationalism. Both during profound social transition and the previous epoch of a weak state (socialism), nationalism has been successful in suggesting continuity and security, and legitimizing new identities.

The story of recent nationalism in southeastern Europe points to another set of challenges. After the Second World War, the consolidation of the Western-type democratic state based on the liberal idea of individual rights treated the problem of national minorities as one of ensuring basic individual rights. As a result, the relationship between the state and national minorities was often neglected, especially when it came to processes of majoritarian decision-making. In the transitions of the formerly socialist states of southeastern Europe, a key political question is how to make democracy compatible with culturally plural societies, in other words how to entrench group-sensitive citizenship rights as an alternative to the classic nationalist project of a homogeneous nation state.[32] The way in which national minority parties politically tipped the scales in both Bulgaria and Romania after the demise of state socialism presents a telling story about such (in)compatibility. The political stalemates and desperation in Bosnia and Herzegovina as well as Kosovo tell another story. However, such problems appear less intractable if we recognize, as this chapter has argued, that nationalism is not engendered by nations but rather induced by political, cultural, and economic fields of particular kinds. Its dynamics are governed by the properties of these fields, not by the alleged properties of collectivities called nations.[33]

Notes

1. K. Verdery (1991) *National Ideology under Socialism: Identity and Cultural Politics in Ceauşescu's Romania*, Berkeley, CA, XI. The extension of this publishing experience is Verdery's (1996) *What Was Socialism, and What Comes Next?*, Princeton, NJ, expressing deep scepticism with scholarly transitologist writings and their tendency both to disregard the socialist era and to impose Western concepts on post-socialist societies.
2. C. King (2010) *Extreme Politics: Nationalism, Violence, and the End of Europe*, Oxford, 59.
3. In hindsight, a core feature of Yugoslav statehood from 1918 may appear to be its failure to create sustainable legitimacy, suggesting it was doomed from the beginning. Yet such an assessment disregards the intentions of generations of state engineers who certainly did not feel their project to be doomed. S. P. Ramet (2006) *The Three Yugoslavias: State-Building and Legitimation, 1918–2005*, Washington, DC, is a sophisticated analysis that nevertheless proceeds from this analytical flaw. By flatly declaring the state to be illegitimate, Ramet dispenses with the need to consider its legitimizing efforts. However, she also insists on the emergence of a crisis of legitimacy, thus producing both a paradox and a circular argument.
4. Cf. King, *Extreme Politics*, 181–3, for a nice synthesis of the unproductive 'quiet derision' dominating the intellectual rivalry between history as a discipline and political science.
5. Examples are Verdery, *National Ideology under Socialism*, as well as Ramet, *The Three Yugoslavias*.
6. King, *Extreme Politics*, 22–36, offers a good overview of the difficulties of making the concepts connected to the *nation* universally operable.
7. R. Brubaker (1999) *Nationalism Reframed: Nationhood and the National Question in the New Europe*, Cambridge, 13–22.
8. E. J. Hobsbawm (1994) *Age of Extremes: The Short Twentieth Century, 1914–1991*, London and New York, 285.

9. Cf. C. M. Rostagni (ed.) (2005) *The Helsinki Process. A Historical Reappraisal: Proceedings of the Workshop Held in Padua, 7 June 2004*, Padua, herein: J. Pirjevec, 'Yugoslavia and the Helsinki Process'; and C. Vlad, 'Romania and the CSCE Process, 1960–1975.'
10. King, *Extreme Politics*, 4 and 5.
11. A fascinating demonstration of this is provided by S. M. Weine (1999) *When History Is a Nightmare: Lives and Memory of Ethnic Cleansing in Bosnia and Herzegovina*, New Brunswick, NJ.
12. For a good overview of the crucial role that state official historiography played in constructing national master narratives, see U. Brunnbauer (2011) 'Historical Writing in the Balkans', in A. Schneider and D. Woolf (eds.) *Historical Writing since 1945 (The Oxford History of Historical Writing, 5)*, Oxford, 353–75. Cf. the case studies on Bulgaria, Albania, and Serbia in *Südosteuropa: A Journal for Politics and Society*, 58, no. 2 (2010). Generally, see M. Todorova (ed.) (2004) *Balkan Identities: Nation and Memory*, London.
13. Cf. the excellent syntheses by U. Brunnbauer (2011) 'Politische Entwicklung Südosteuropas von 1945 bis 1989/1991', and (2011) 'Gesellschaft und gesellschaftlicher Wandel in Südosteuropa nach 1945', in K. Clewing and O. J. Schmitt (eds.) *Geschichte Südosteuropas. Vom frühen Mittelalter bis zur Gegenwart*, Regensburg, 597–707.
14. A. M. Basha, 'Muslim Communities under the Anti-Religious Regime in Albania (1945–1990)', 163–72, M. W. E. Peters, 'Die Römisch-Katholische Kirche in Albanien nach 1944', 173–214, and E. Ceka, 'Atheismus und Religionspolitik im kommunistischen Albanien', 215–32, all in O. J. Schmitt (ed.) (2010) *Religion und Kultur im albanischsprachigen Südosteuropa*, Frankfurt an Main.
15. O. J. Schmitt (2005) 'Genosse Aleks und seine Partei oder: Zu Politik und Geschichtswissenschaft im kommunistischen Albanien (1945–1991)', in M. Krzoska and H.-C. Maner (eds.) *Beruf und Berufung. Geschichtswissenschaft und Nationsbildung in Ostmittel- und Südosteuropa im 19. und 20. Jahrhundert*, Münster, 143–66; cf. S. Schwandner-Sievers and B. J. Fischer (eds.) (2002) *Albanian Identities: Myth and History*, London.
16. U. Brunnbauer (2007) *'Die sozialistische Lebensweise'. Ideologie, Gesellschaft, Familie und Politik in Bulgarien (1944–1989)*, Vienna.
17. M. Neuburger (2004) *The Orient Within: Muslim Minorities and the Negotiation of Nationhood in Modern Bulgaria*, Ithaca and London.
18. C. Riis (2002) *Religion, Politics and Historiography in Bulgaria*, New York.
19. Riis, *Religion, Politics and Historiography*; Vassil Vassilev (2008) *Nationalismus unterm Roten Stern. Vorgeschichte, Durchführung und Auswirkungen der Namensänderungskampagne 1984–89 gegenüber der türkischen Minderheit in Bulgarien*, Vienna.
20. Verdery, *National Ideology under Socialism*, 101–34.
21. Verdery, *National Ideology under Socialism*, 99.
22. T. Gilberg (1990) *Nationalism and Communism in Romania: The Rise and Fall of Ceausescu's Personal Dictatorship*, Boulder, CO, 271–8. Written in the midst of events, Gilberg offers an interesting and, in hindsight, apt prophecy of what the legacies of Ceauşescuism would mean for Romania's transition.
23. H. Sundhaussen (2007) *Geschichte Serbiens: 19.–21. Jahrhundert*, Vienna, 349–54. 'Sonderweg' means 'special path' and was originally coined as a name for the peculiar trajectory of modern German history. Here the term has been transferred to the case of Yugoslavia.
24. D. Jović (2009) *Yugoslavia: A State that Withered Away*, West Lafayette, IN, 4. The following section refers to several more works arguing along analogous lines: J. Dragović-Soso (2002) *'Saviours of the Nation': Serbia's Intellectual Opposition and the Revival of*

Nationalism, London; A. B. Wachtel (1998) *Making a Nation, Breaking a Nation: Literature and Cultural Politics in Yugoslavia*, Stanford, CA; J. M. Halpern and David A. Kideckel (eds.) (2000) *Neighbors at War: Anthropological Perspectives on Yugoslav Ethnicity, Culture, and History*, Pennsylvania, PA. Jović's book stands out for its admirable clarity of argument.

25. N. Bašić (2004) *Krieg als Abenteuer. Feindbilder und Gewalt aus der Perspektive ex-jugoslawischer Soldaten 1991–1995*, Gießen.
26. Jović, *Yugoslavia*, 96.
27. Jović, *Yugoslavia*, 13–40.
28. King, *Extreme Politics*, 180, labels such attitudes as 'cliophilia'.
29. Jović, *Yugoslavia*, 363.
30. X. Bougarel, E. Helms, and G. Duijzings (eds.) (2007) *The New Bosnian Mosaic: Identities, Memories and Moral Claims in a Post-War Society*, Aldershot.
31. N. Caspersen (2010) *Contested Nationalism: Serb Elite Rivalry in Croatia and Bosnia in the 1990s*, New York and Oxford, 39ff; cf. Verdery, *National Ideology under Socialism*, 83–7.
32. Cf. on this issue G. Krasniqi (2010) 'The International Community's Modus Operandi in Postwar Bosnia and Herzegovina and in Kosovo: A Critical Assessment', *Südosteuropa: A Journal for Politics and Society*, 58, no. 4 (2010), 520–41.
33. Brubaker, *Nationalism Reframed*, 17.

Suggested Further Reading

Gilberg, T. (1990) *Nationalism and Communism in Romania: The Rise and Fall of Ceausescu's Personal Dictatorship*, Boulder, CO. Written in the midst of state dissolution, the book convinces with its sharp analytical capacity.

King, C. (2010) *Extreme Politics: Nationalism, Violence, and the End of Europe*, Oxford. A sharply analytical and convincing argument.

Neuburger, M. (2004) *The Orient Within: Muslim Minorities and the Negotiation of Nationhood in Modern Bulgaria*, Ithaca, NY, and London. An account from the perspective of minorities, providing key insights in the overall Bulgarian framework.

Schwandner-Sievers, S. and Fischer, B. J. (eds.) (2002) *Albanian Identities: Myth and History*, London. Two of the most authoritative scholars on the Albanian-inhabited regions provide an overview of the intricacies of Albanian history and the sometimes paradoxical processes of identity formation.

Verdery, K. (1991) *National Ideology under Socialism: Identity and Cultural Politics in Ceaușescu's Romania*, Berkeley, CA. Excellent reading for all those interested in the dynamics of socialist Romania.

On Yugoslavia, the following books provide illuminating accounts of the dynamics of dissolution and war, as well as of coming to terms with both:

Bougarel, X., Helms, E., and Duijzings, G. (eds.) (2007) *The New Bosnian Mosaic: Identities, Memories and Moral Claims in a Post-War Society*, Aldershot. The contributors to this volume offer innovative research that helps understanding the Bosnian dilemma.

Caspersen, N. (2010) *Contested Nationalism: Serb Elite Rivalry in Croatia and Bosnia in the 1990s*, New York and Oxford. Gives excellent insights into the mechanisms of nationalist mobilization.

Dragović-Soso, J. (2002) *'Saviours of the Nation': Serbia's Intellectual Opposition and the Revival of Nationalism*, London.

Gagnon Jr., V. P. (2004) *The Myth of Ethnic War: Serbia and Croatia in the 1990s*, Ithaca, NY, and London.

Halpern, J. M. and Kideckel, D. A. (eds.) (2000) *Neighbors at War: Anthropological Perspectives on Yugoslav Ethnicity, Culture, and History*, Pennsylvania, PA.

Jović, D. (2009) *Yugoslavia: A State that Withered Away*, West Lafayette, IN. A very acute assessment of socialist Yugoslavia and the mechanisms behind its demise.

Wachtel, A. B. (1998) *Making a Nation, Breaking a Nation: Literature and Cultural Politics in Yugoslavia*, Stanford, CA.

PART IV

NATIONALISM IN A WORLD OF NATION STATES: IDEAS, SENTIMENTS, AND INTERNATIONAL RELATIONS

CHAPTER 27

INTERNATIONAL SOCIETY, STATE SOVEREIGNTY, AND NATIONAL SELF-DETERMINATION

JAMES MAYALL

INTRODUCTION

IT is an irony that the legal, diplomatic, and political principles and practices that define international society historically pre-date the age of nationalism, let alone the elevation of the principle of the self-determination of peoples to its present position as an inalienable right inscribed in the United Nations Charter. Originally sovereignty, the principle of supreme power and authority, was an attribute of Princes, and international law, diplomatic practice, and even the regulation of their conflicts and consolidation of their conquests through treaties and marriage settlements was essentially a personal not a collective matter, a society of states but definitely not of peoples. Only with the French and American revolutions did the concept of national self-determination enter the political lexicon. The purpose of this chapter is to explore, first, how the nationalization of the sovereignty principle both challenged and was accommodated within traditional international society during the twentieth century, and second, the extent to which this accommodation has been modified since the end of the Cold War.

INTERNATIONAL SOCIETY

Politicians—and indeed the general public—are more likely to refer to the international community than to international society, presumably because 'community' signifies human solidarity without specifying any particular rights and obligations that attach to membership. It sounds warm and offers no hostages to fortune. The most influential account of international society, on the other hand, was entitled *The Anarchical Society*,[1] introducing at the outset the essential paradox of international relations—that they are indeed social, and therefore governed by moral reasoning, whether the issue is cooperation, commercial and cultural exchange, or war, but at the same time international relations take place under conditions of anarchy in that they are between sovereigns rather than under government. It is this absence of coercive authority that has led some realists to deny the reality of any normative framework for international relations, invoking Thomas Hobbes's dictum, 'Covenants without the sword are but words.'[2]

This bleak vision does not bear scrutiny. If a Hobbesian war of all against all was all that was to be said on the matter, we could not explain, for example, the sustained growth of international organization from the end of the nineteenth century onwards, nor indeed the exponential development of public and more specialized forms of international law. The original conception of international society was what the German sociologist Ferdinand Tönnies described as a *Gesellschaft*, that is, an association primarily held together by collective self-interest, rather than the more solidarist *Gemeinschaft*, whose members share a wide range of collective mores and substantive values.[3] One immediate consequence of the nationalization of the sovereignty principle was to raise a question as to whether a *Gesellschaft* could mutate into a *Gemeinschaft*, and if so under what circumstances.

I shall return to this question in the final section of this chapter. For the moment, the point to note is that the ancestor of contemporary international society emerged from a specific historical context in one part of the world. In the sixteenth and seventeenth centuries the Christian West was shaken by two developments: the rise of several strong centralized states and a religious schism, which created a fault line between Catholic and Protestant Europe and provided a convenient *casus belli* for the rival Princes. What is today conventionally described as the Westphalian system refers to the peace settlement that brought the European wars of religion to an end in 1648. The principles on which the Peace of Westphalia was based were not new, but they were codified in a way that was to lay the foundations for modern international society. By a negotiated consensus it was agreed that henceforth the sovereign would be accepted as the final source of authority within his or her domain. The formula *cuius regio eius religio*, roughly 'to each prince his own religion', was the ancestor of the modern principle of non-intervention, without which a system of international cooperation could not have developed.[4] It also had the desirable outcome of proscribing wars over religious faith, of raising the role of prudence, rationality, and interest in human affairs, and reducing the role of passion.

The relative stability in Europe brought about by the Treaty of Westphalia allowed the institutions of international society to take shape. The two most important were international law and the diplomatic system, which increasingly involved the establishment of resident embassies and the codification of diplomatic practice and privilege, the former to allow international negotiations to be conducted in a reasonably orderly fashion, the latter to bring to an end disputes over protocol and precedence amongst those granted plenipotentiary powers by their sovereigns.

The remaining three institutions commanded less than universal consent. Compared with the hierarchical structure of feudal Europe, the Westphalian system was egalitarian, since sovereigns by definition were all supreme within their own territory. They were not all equal in terms of power, so the question remained as to how the rivalries of the Princes were to be constrained in the interests of order. Religious war had been outlawed but not war itself. Indeed, sovereigns could go to war (and frequently did) for any other reason up to and including territorial conquest. The solution to this problem that was most frequently advanced in the eighteenth century was the balance of power. This concept has attracted ferocious criticism over the years, but is still accepted by most political theorists and historians as the ordering institution of international society. Since at times it required the Great Powers to partition countries or continents—for example, Poland in the eighteenth and Africa in the nineteenth centuries—in the interests of order, unsurprisingly, the principle appealed more to the strong than the weak.

The institutional status of the Great Powers considered as a collective, with special rights to correspond to their responsibilities for managing the balance of power, was also never wholeheartedly endorsed by the smaller and weaker states—the involuntary consumers of Great Power order—although it has lived on into the contemporary period in terms of the veto-wielding Permanent Five members (P5) of the UN Security Council. Finally, war itself was not considered to be a breakdown of international society, which is how we would tend to see it today, but as an institution, the mechanism to be employed for bringing about change after all legal and diplomatic efforts had been exhausted. The theoretical justification for this view is to be found in the logic of sovereignty. In most societies there are legal and customary ways of settling disputes, but where existential interests are involved, which affect the honour of the disputants, the law will not suffice. In such cases the duel, a trial of physical strength, was originally used within European society to settle the matter, the right going to the victor. And since sovereigns were originally individuals, even though they could command armies, the same logic applied within international society.

The Impact of Nationalism

The spread of nationalism after the French and American revolutions challenged this traditional conception of international society in three respects. First, the nationalists challenged the hierarchical notion that had supported both absolute monarchy and the right of a privileged aristocratic class to rule. The idea of popular sovereignty implied that the state belonged to the people, even if most early nationalist intellectuals had a fairly restricted idea of who they meant by people. Second, it followed that nationalists opposed the special privileges that the Great Powers arrogated to themselves. Dynasticism, the governing principle in most European states before the revolutions, might accidentally reflect national identity but it often did not. Third, the idea that territory, which nationalists regarded as the sacred national patrimony, could be traded or regarded as one of the legitimate spoils of war, was anathema to the nationalist spirit. But these early challenges were largely defeated after the fall of Napoleon Bonaparte. At the Congress of Vienna in 1815 the old order was restored. The nationalist challenge went underground for a time, resurfaced in the form of the southeast European revolt against the Ottoman Empire from the 1820s, was taken over by the *ancien régime* at the time of Italian and German unification ending in 1870–1, and finally returned to centre stage in the form of demands for a fundamental makeover of international society at the Versailles Conference following the First World War.

The story of what happened next has been told many times, but by no one better than the historian Alfred Cobban, whose *National Self-Determination* was first published in 1945.[5] President Woodrow Wilson had taken the United States into the First World War in April 1917 in order that 'the world be made safe for democracy'. The following January he delivered the speech to the United States Congress in which he outlined the 'Fourteen Points' on which he believed the post-war settlement should be based. These principles are in fact less vague than they are frequently represented as being—they did not for example offer the principle of national self-determination as a universal human right—but they nonetheless were widely accepted by nationalists beyond Europe as applying in principle to themselves as well as to the citizens of the Hapsburg and Ottoman Empires whose dynastic rulers were about to be overthrown.[6] Even the European states, to which they were immediately addressed, were unable to implement them, and, in Cobban's view, the liberal doctrine of national self-determination, which implied freedom of choice, was transformed into an illiberal doctrine of national determinism under which political identity was determined by nationality. Even more worrying, it proved impossible to redraw the political map so that each national group would have its own state. The reason was simple: the long period of European dynasticism, in which both boundaries and populations shifted many times, meant that however the map was redrawn the new states were likely to include minorities, most of whom would view the new dispensation with suspicion, and might actively seek to break away and join a neighbouring state in which they would be part of the majority. This problem was most intense in the successor states to the Hapsburg empire.

The solution that eventually emerged was to make entry into the new League of Nations—the creation of which was Wilson's fourteenth point—dependent on the governments of the new states, providing guarantees that minority rights would be respected.[7] This solution was always unpopular in eastern Europe, since it seemed to create a kind of second-class international citizenship: neither Britain nor France were ethnically homogenous, yet there was never any question of them being required to provide guarantees to the Welsh, Scots, Bretons, or Basques. The governments of both countries could quite reasonably insist that there was a difference; that

British and French nationality was defined by citizenship rather than by ethnic origin, but while true, this was not an argument that was likely to cut much ice with Czechs, Slovaks, or Hungarians. So they tried to avoid their obligations whenever it was convenient for them to do so, and when the Third Reich used alleged discrimination of ethnic Germans as a justification for its eastern expansion, the principle of collective minority rights fell into disrepute.

Since the US Senate refused to ratify the Versailles Treaty and the Bolsheviks also refused to join the new world body, the League did not in any case establish the central authority over the course of world politics that Woodrow Wilson, its chief architect, had intended. It was the war that destroyed the old international order, not Wilson's dream of what should replace it. But not even his harshest critics could deny that as a mobilizing inspiration, Wilson's vision of a national, democratic world order was a triumphant success. Although dynasticism survives here and there—as in Saudi Arabia, Morocco, Bhutan, Swaziland, and until recently Nepal—the legitimacy of hereditary rule ended in 1919. From then on the nation state rather than the multicultural empire was to be the dominant political form. The European powers with overseas empires would refuse to accept this conclusion for as long as they could, but since they were constitutional democracies that claimed the right of self- determination for themselves, their leaders recognized that the writing was on the wall and that all they could do was to play for time.[8]

Self-Determination as Decolonization

The United States again played the lead role in shaping the new world order after 1945. Indeed, its war aims—including the opening of world markets, support for democracy, and an end to European imperialism, set out in both the Atlantic Charter of 1942 and the Lend Lease Agreements—bore a striking resemblance to the Wilsonian scheme. The most obvious difference lay in the American resolve to use its power in support of these values. The failure to pay proper attention to enduring realities of power politics had been ruthlessly exposed in 1939 in E. H. Carr's *Twenty Years' Crisis*, one of the most influential books of the period.[9] When representatives of fifty-one states met in San Francisco in 1945 to draw up the Charter of the United Nations Organization, they were faced therefore with the need to balance the requirements of order, as the concept was understood by the victorious grand alliance, and the demands of justice in which the US for the most part made common cause with the small states and those who wanted an end to empire, sometimes against the more conservative interests of the European imperial powers.

Order generally triumphed over justice, when the two principles came into conflict, most notably in the lead role given to the Security Council in matters of war and peace, and more particularly by the decision to have permanent members, with the power of veto, in addition to those who would be elected to serve a two-year term. But from very early on the question of who was to have the right to self-determination arose as a major political and legal problem within the world body. There was at this stage no agreed consensus on this question, but one would have to be reached as the newly established Trusteeship Council required the administering powers of the territories for which they had been given responsibility under the League Mandate system, not merely to account for their stewardship to the UN but also to prepare the territories for independence.[10] The assumption that these trusteeships were temporary and had been earmarked for sovereign status had an inevitable spillover effect within the wider colonial world, even though the European powers refused to acknowledge that the UN had any rights or influence over their colonial policies.

The UN Charter affirms twice (Articles 1.2 and 55) the support for the principle of 'equal rights and self-determination of peoples'. But who exactly were these peoples? This was a new question. It is true that the majority of South American countries had achieved independence from Spain and Portugal in the early 1800s, that Greece seceded from the Ottoman Empire in 1829 and Bulgaria did so in 1908, but although outside powers were involved directly or indirectly in these events, they did not lead to any multilateral attempt to revise international law, let alone to establish the right of self-determination as a constitutive principle of international society. The logic of the duel, to which I referred earlier, continued to apply: international recognition followed the successful assertion of sovereignty and the ability of the new rulers to demonstrate empirically their territorial and juridical control. By asserting a right of self-determination it became necessary, at least in theory, to identify the right holders in advance of the fact.

The original Wilsonian solution to the problem was the plebiscite. It failed, not merely because of the irreconcilable national and territorial claims in central and eastern Europe after the First World War, nor because the Great Powers had no intention of testing their legitimate title in their own possessions by this method, but also because it regarded the identity of the population to be polled as self-evident. As Ivor Jennings, a British judge on the World Court, famously put it in 1956: 'on the surface it seemed reasonable: let the people decide. It was in practice ridiculous because the people cannot decide until someone decides who are the people.'[11] Plebiscites were nonetheless used in two UN Trusteeship territories—Togo (1956) and Cameroon (1961)—where the former German colonies had been divided between France and Britain under the League Mandate system. In the case of the Cameroons this led to the reunification of the country with the part that had been administered by the British within eastern Nigeria.

It seems likely that the use of the word 'peoples' rather than 'nation' in the UN Charter was chosen deliberately to avoid the claims and counter-claims that had bedevilled interwar politics in Europe and to make it clear that the reference was to the entire population of a discrete and already existing territory. It was not a great improvement. If it is impossible, objectively, to establish the identity of a nation, it is not immediately obvious that the problem can be solved by a change of language.

At the end of the Second World War it was still not clear how the problem would be resolved. In Asia in particular there was a fair amount of post-colonial tidying up and territorial consolidation. No one paid much attention to theories of self-determination at this time.[12] In India the formula agreed with the British for partitioning the subcontinent and deciding the fate of the Princely states came unstuck, first in Kashmir when Pakistan attempted to reverse the Maharajah's decision to join India, and then when India mounted a police action to reverse the Nizam's decision to join Hyderabad to Pakistan. India also subsequently 'liberated' Goa from Portuguese rule in 1961. In West Irian the Dutch had to be pressured by the Americans into surrendering the territory to the Indonesians, and even in Africa Julius Nyerere flirted with the idea of forging a union with Katanga after the province had unilaterally seceded from the Congo in 1960, but before he had become president of an independent Tanganyika.

Territorial revisionism was not widely advocated by the leaders of new states. Indeed, it was in Africa during the 1960s that a conventional interpretation of the political meaning of the principle of self-determination emerged. The subversive potential of the principle—the implied invitation to aggrieved minorities to rebel—quickly became as evident to new states as to those long established. The difficulty in Africa was that prior to independence African nationalists had frequently complained about the 'Balkanization' of the continent at the time of the Berlin Conference and the need for rebuilding it in line with African interests and identities after independence.

The most vocal advocate of this wholesale rejection of the colonial legacy was Kwame Nkrumah, the first president of Ghana. His proposals for Pan-African political unification alarmed most African leaders and fuelled the political warfare that dominated West African politics in the early 1960s. The bickering over the meaning of African Unity, a principle to which all African leaders professed to be committed, only ended with the establishment of the Organization of African Unity (OAU) in 1963. The OAU Charter was influenced by Latin American legal experts who were brought in to advise on the drafting and revived the principle of *uti possidetis juris* (roughly 'you hold what you possess') to secure the agreement of all African governments to the territorial boundaries bequeathed to them at independence, and to put an end to the threat of secessionist and irredentist claims.[13]

Although it was never the subject of a UN Resolution, the African solution to the self-determination problem quickly established itself as the conventional interpretation within the wider international society. The peoples who were to enjoy 'equal rights and self-determination' were the undifferentiated populations of existing colonies; in other words no attention was to be paid to ethnic or religious affiliations. State succession was a once and for all event tied in time and space to European decolonization. No further secessions would be countenanced, unless of course they were freely agreed in negotiations between a sovereign government and a separatist movement or subordinate government. In this latter case the matter would be regarded as falling solely within the internal affairs of the country in question and the world body would have no role to play prior to admitting the new state as a member.

The Impact of the Cold War

The conventional interpretation suited the vast majority of governments, regardless of their ideological colouring. A few revisionist governments were unreconciled. Irredentist claims were seldom abandoned during the Cold War, but the ambitions of the governments that harboured them—such as Spain to Gibralter, the Phillipines to Sabah, Morocco to Mauretania, the Republic of Ireland to Ulster, the Argentine to the Falkland Islands—faced formidable practical obstacles. They were prohibited under international law from using force as an instrument of foreign policy to redeem their 'lost' territories; it was virtually impossible to generate diplomatic support for their cause within the General Assembly or other international organizations; they were unable to gain support from either superpower. Somalia, whose Constitution pledged the state to reunite all five centres of Somali population (in other words the Ogaden region of Ethiopia, Djibouti, and the North East Province of Kenya, in addition to the former Italian colony and British Protectorate, which had united to form the Somali Republic in 1960) tried to achieve this objective by allying itself in turn with the Soviet Union and the United States, but failed each time.[14]

There is also something anachronistic about irredentist claims since they generally invoke ancient land rights, or claims of suzerainty and the right to exact tribute.[15] These relate more to an age when social relations were organized on a hierarchical basis rather than according to the theoretically egalitarian principle of popular sovereignty. Opposition to irredentism preceded the Cold War and indeed survived its end. It is difficult to think of an irredentist claim that is likely to challenge the international order seriously unless it is the Chinese claim to Taiwan. This is a special case, however, since the KMT (Kuomintang—the Nationalist Party expelled by the Chinese communists from the mainland in 1949), which for most of the Cold War period was in power in Taiwan, claimed to be the legitimate authority within mainland China. The People's Republic itself claimed that Taiwan was an integral part of China, and in the face of US support for Taiwan, a tacit acceptance of the status quo emerged on both sides of the Straits under which Taiwan enjoyed de facto but not de jure independence. This situation survived the Cold War. Were it to break down it would almost certainly be because of a victory at the polls by the Democratic Progressive Party (DPP) followed by a unilateral declaration of independence. The risks involved in such a policy would be very great and it is unclear under what circumstances the DPP would be prepared to take them.

The main challenge to the interpretation of self-determination as decolonization during the Cold War came from secessionist movements. They were, after all, precisely those who took the principle seriously and who understandably drew the conclusion that if self-determination was an inalienable human right, it should apply to them. Of the three Cold War secessionist crises that boiled over onto the world stage—Katanga (1960–3), Biafra (1967–70), and Bangladesh (1971)—only the Biafran case was seriously debated in terms of the substantive meaning of self-determination. The reintegration of the Katanga into the Congo was the price that the Kennedy Administration in the US was prepared to pay to marginalize the influence of the Soviet Union in the UN peacekeeping operation in the Congo. Bangladesh gained its independence at the hands of the Indian army, which defeated and expelled the Pakistan army, so its admission into international society followed the traditional pattern of recognizing a fait accompli rather than any acknowledgement of a right of secessionist self-determination. Indian intervention in the crisis followed a period of intense diplomatic activity, the climax of which was the signing of an Indo-Soviet Treaty of Friendship and Cooperation. This had the intended consequence of forestalling any chance of the Americans coming to the aid of Pakistan, with whom they were officially allied.

Biafra's bid for independence collapsed because the Biafrans failed to secure a powerful external patron who was prepared to defy the international consensus in favour of the territorial status quo. France came close but in the end President Charles de Gaulle indicated that he would be guided by African opinion. By 1969 four African states—Ivory Coast, Gabon, Tanzania, and Zambia—had recognized Biafra, and several others were rumoured to be sympathetic to its cause. At the annual OAU summit in 1969, President Nyerere of Tanzania circulated a memorandum to his fellow Heads of State arguing the case for recognition.[16]

Nyerere's argument was straightforward. Colonial borders, he suggested, had been accepted for practical reasons—to facilitate interstate cooperation, minimize opportunities for conflict, and release energies that could more fruitfully be devoted to development. Nonetheless the right of governments to rule rested on their ability to serve the population as a whole. When a government could no longer protect the lives of all its citizens, and when a particular group believed itself to be threatened by genocide, that government forfeited its legitimacy. The same political considerations that had led Nyerere to accept existing territorial arrangements could now (and in his view should) be advanced in support of Biafra's secession.

This attempt to establish internal standards of accountability and good government as criteria for international recognition in a conflict over self-determination failed. Not only did the presidents for life and military dictators who headed the majority of African governments in the 1960s have no interest in lowering their sovereign guard to accommodate international criticism, but the Biafrans could neither appeal to international law nor dent the recognized government's monopoly of the symbols of nationalism at the United Nations. The Cold War exercised only a minimal influence on the Nigerian civil war. As the former colonial power the British government faced intense pressure at home from supporters of both the secessionists and the Federal government, primarily over the issue of arms supplies. Its solution was to suspend arms sales to both sides, a policy that led the Lagos authorities to turn to the Soviet Union. Moscow prevaricated until such time that the Americans had made it clear that they regarded the conflict as a West African civil war, in which they would remain neutral, after which the USSR did indeed sell arms to the Federal Nigerian government.

The lasting significance of Nyerere's failure is that in the argument over the exercise of the right to self-determination and international recognition the Cold War was irrelevant. As we shall see, his essential point—that sovereignty is conditional on the ability of the government to protect the population as a whole and promote its welfare—has been revived in the post-Cold War world by both lawyers and diplomats in their efforts to reconstruct international society after the collapse of communism. The fact that Cold War considerations did not determine the outcome in the 1960s, however, should perhaps have been taken as a warning that attempts to redraw the international map on the basis of 'genuine' self-determination would face formidable obstacles under any circumstances.

International Society Revisited

The warning was not heeded. In the euphoria that accompanied the collapse of the communist regimes of Eastern Europe and then the disintegration of the Soviet Union, there was an understandable tendency for minority leaders and other would-be revisionists to fantasize that an open season had been declared for secessionist self-determination. It did not take long for the major powers to construct a road block against any such radical development. When, in March 1990, the Lithuanian Parliament voted democratically to seek independence from the Soviet Union, Western governments withheld recognition and urged the nationalists to reach an accommodation with Moscow. As Misha Glenny noted at the time, initially, the West 'understood self-determination to mean the right of east European countries to leave the Soviet bloc', not the right of the Soviet Republics to secede from the Union itself.[17] When it eventually became clear that the centre could not hold, both the Soviet government and the major outside powers treated the disintegration of the USSR into its constituent parts as a case of decolonization, thus leaving the conventional interpretation of self-determination intact. The Russians then established the Commonwealth of Independent States (CIS) to maintain their influence in their 'near abroad', and perhaps also to cope with the psychological shock of the loss of empire, rather as the British had done in the then British Commonwealth when its own empire began to break up with its withdrawal from South Asia, in 1947.

Even if the West had won the Cold War by default, it had still won. In the aftermath of this largely unexpected victory there was a mood of triumphalism and a temptation to conflate Western ideology with international society. It is worth reiterating, therefore, that this conflation was invalid. The East-West confrontation had often strained the institutions of international society to near breaking point, but the value of a minimal framework of coexistence proved too valuable for either side to abandon it. Even during the long period when the United States kept the People's Republic of China (PRC) out of the United Nations, lines of communication were kept open through the US Embassy in Warsaw. The periodic frustration of both superpowers with the UN also did not stop them using it, both to deal with otherwise unsolvable problems, where Soviet and Western interests conflicted, at the start of the Cold War, such as the disposal of the Italian colonies, and later as a mechanism for bringing the Cold War to a close. In other words, the essential characteristic of international society was pluralist, an association based on the self-interest of its member states, not on any particular formulation of the good life.

A counter-argument has existed, at least since the Versailles Peace Conference of 1919, that international society should be reformed to reflect human solidarity rather than to protect the interests of governments. As noted at the beginning of this chapter, the nationalization of sovereignty gave a strong impetus to this wish to transform international society, first through the League and then the UN, into a genuine *Gemeinschaft*. On this view, first the rise of fascism and Nazism in Europe, and then the Cold War, delayed the realization of this vision rather than proving it unrealizable. Indeed the success of the first Gulf War in 1991—and even more its aftermath—encouraged solidarists in their conviction that a structural reform of international society was not only necessary but imminent. Operation Desert Storm was mounted to end Iraq's occupation of Kuwait on the basis of a Chapter VII Resolution of the Security Council, with the full support of all five permanent members and of all but one of Iraq's regional neighbours (Jordan). It was the nearest thing to the Security Council operating in the way and for the purposes for which it had been designed.[18]

Shortly after achieving victory in the Gulf, President George Bush (Sr.) made a speech in which he called for a New World Order (NWO), under which there would be respect for the rule of law and the weak would be protected as much as the strong. For the first time the Security Council convened at the summit and the then Secretary General, Boutros Boutros-Ghali, was commissioned to write a report on the role of the UN system in delivering the NWO. Operation Desert Storm was not the result of a dispute over self-determination, nor was it a humanitarian intervention. Although Saddam Hussein used a border dispute as a pretext for his annexation of Kuwait, the UN was reversing an aggression by one member of the Organization against another.

Nonetheless, Boutros-Ghali's *Agenda for Peace*[19] acknowledged that the issue of self-determination could not be ignored altogether. The immediate background was the humanitarian intervention by the Western powers to support the Kurds, whose rebellion following the war had been brutally suppressed by Saddam Hussein. The Kurds—divided between Iran, Iraq, Turkey, and Russia—are the largest stateless nation in the world. Their national aspirations had been recognized by the victorious Allies after the First World War, but the French and British then reneged on their promise of a homeland for the Kurds when Kemal Ataturk refused to surrender any territory following the Turkish Revolution. Since then there has never been any question of Kurdish independence, partly because the Kurds themselves have always been divided but mainly because the states in which they reside as a minority would not countenance it. None of the outside powers involved in the Iraq crisis favoured partition, but the result of the humanitarian catastrophe in northern Iraq was nonetheless the creation of an autonomous Kurdistan, protected from Saddam Hussein's forces from the air.

Implicitly, the oppression of the Kurds also raised the kind of question about the right of tyrannical governments to claim sovereignty over those they oppress, which Julius Nyerere had raised in his memorandum to the OAU summit in 1969.

The *Agenda for Peace* did not endorse what international lawyers refer to as the theory of constitutional self-determination,[20] but it shuffled in that direction, mindful as always to balance the conflicting demands of order and justice. In his discussion of the new international context Boutros-Ghali made three statements that seemed to hint at a process of managed constitutional reform for international society. First he argued that while the state must remain as the foundation stone, its authority was not absolute. 'Respect for its fundamental sovereignty and integrity are crucial to any common international progress. The time of absolute and exclusive sovereignty, however, has passed; its theory was never matched by reality.' Second, he insisted that the United Nations had not closed its doors to new members but that 'if every ethnic, religious or linguistic group claimed state-hood, there would be no limit to fragmentation, and peace, security and economic well-being for all would become ever more difficult to achieve'. Finally, he suggested that the way to resolve the rival claims of sovereignty and self-determination was through respect for human rights, particularly the rights of minorities, on the one hand, and democratization on the other. 'Respect for democratic principles at all levels of social existence is crucial: in communities, within states and within the community of states.'[21]

This rather bland attempt to reformulate the criteria for the exercise of self- determination and state recognition has been tested on at least ten occasions. It would be difficult to claim that either international law or state practice have established a new interpretation to replace the conventional interpretation of self-determination, but nor is it clear that the conventional interpretation has survived unscathed.

Test Cases and New Theories

That nationalism continues to exercise a major influence on world politics is indicated by the admission of thirty-six new members to the United Nations between 1989 and 2006. Of these no fewer than twenty were successor states of the Soviet Union and Yugoslavia, and a further ten were ex-European colonies. A review of these cases points to three broad conclusions. The first is that most governments shared Boutros-Ghali's fear of runaway fragmentation. More particularly they remained deeply attached to territorial integrity as an attribute of sovereignty, and consequently opposed to the idea of secessionist self-determination. Second, they continued to support the principle of *uti possidetis* or some analogue of it. Third, in cases where the establishment of a new state reflected the outcome of a conflict over self-determination, they would only contemplate recognition after there had been some sort of democratic test to establish its legitimacy. Let us consider each of these conclusions in turn.

Territorial Integrity

The insistence in the UN Charter on territorial integrity as an entailment of sovereignty reflects the proscription in international society of unilateral secession, not secession per se. There has never been any objection, in principle, to the break-up of existing states, providing the divorce is consensual and the result of negotiation, as it was between Norway and Sweden in 1905, the Irish Free State and the United Kingdom in 1921, Malaysia and Singapore in 1965, the Czech and Slovak Republics in 1993, and Serbia and Montenegro in 1996. Nonetheless, while such negotiation may open a pathway to international recognition, even democratic governments are reluctant to invite peaceful territorial challenges to their authority.

The one major change in the debate about self-determination since the end of the Cold War is that it is no longer plausible to argue that strategic necessity rules out territorial change. This may seem a small change but it opens the floodgates, an illusion of stability giving way to an equally illusory sense of almost infinite flux and possibility. It was against this background that in 1996 the Canadian government sought to head off at the pass the secessionist challenge that has been periodically advanced by the Parti Quebecois (PQ). It asked the Supreme Court for a ruling on whether there was anything in the Canadian Constitution or international law that would permit Quebec to secede unilaterally, and second, in the event of a conflict between the Constitution and international law on this issue, which should take precedence. The Supreme Court endorsed the view of the two international experts whom the Federal government had consulted. They had concluded that 'outside the colonial context, there is no recognition of a right to unilateral secession based on a majority vote of a sub-division or territory, whether or not that population constitutes one or more "peoples" in the ordinary sense of that word'. It is true that both experts hedged their bets by suggesting 'that there may be developments in the principle of self-determination according to which not only colonialism but also flagrant violations of human rights or undemocratic regimes could lead to a right of unilateral secession', although they made it clear that none of these developments applied to Quebec.[22]

This opinion remains the most authoritative statement on self-determination. It has not been put to the test in an established democracy but, as we shall see, the qualification with which the Opinion concludes, and the possibility of remedial and constitutional self-determination, at which it hints, have featured in a number of disputes over self-determination in the Balkans and elsewhere.

Uti Possidetis

The conservative bias of international society was illustrated by the preference of the major powers in the early post-Cold War period for the territorial status quo in Yugoslavia as well as in the Soviet Union. When it became clear that disintegration was inevitable, the solution that was adopted was to recognize the existing borders of the Federal and Soviet Republics as the new international borders. In terms of the clear purpose of this strategy, in other words to preserve the conventional interpretation of the principle of self-determination, it was only partially successful. This was because it had the unintended consequence of reinforcing the ethnic definition of the nation rather than the civic version implied in the view that it is the entire population of a territory that enjoys the right to self-determination. Joseph Stalin's nationalities policy had resulted in the creation of predominantly ethnic Republics in the territories that the Bolsheviks had taken over from the Tsarist Empire, so that the transition was reasonably smooth in most of them, although the presence of Russian minorities, the result of Soviet-era migrations, represented a continuing hostage to fortune.

The first international involvement in the break-up of Yugoslavia was by the European Union (EU), acting through and alongside UN peacekeeping forces. The Badinter Commission was appointed to ensure that democratic practices had been put in place prior to the recognition of the successor Republics and that they should be defined in the same way, and with the same boundaries, as had existed before the break-up. The EU proved powerless to prevent the ethnic cleansing that dominated the wars of Yugoslav succession. In the end the Bosnian crisis was only ended when the Americans intervened forcefully to change the balance of power on the ground between the Serb, Croat, and Bosniak armies, and force them to the negotiating table at Dayton, Ohio, in 1995. The Americans had no wish to endorse a new principle of ethnic self-determination and were determined to maintain, however fictitiously, the twin myths that force could not be used to change the political map and that Bosnia must remain a multi-ethnic country. They were also prepared to invest heavily, both financially and in terms of diplomatic effort, to secure this outcome. From this point of view, the Dayton Accords of 1995 could be seen as a victory for the conventional interpretation since they preserved the pre-existing borders of Bosnia, recreating the country as a confederation and skating over the fact that the political geography of the country had been changed as a result of the ferocious inter-ethnic fighting.

Similarly, the 1999 agreement under which NATO forced President Milosovic to withdraw the Yugoslav army from Kosovo, constitutionally an integral part of the then Yugoslav Republic, was careful to avoid support for the Kosovo Liberation Army's (KLA) secessionist ambitions. Admittedly in both cases provision was made for democratic elections, but since it was unclear how, in countries that remained deeply divided along ethnic lines, democracy would necessarily ensure territorial integrity, it is difficult to avoid the conclusion that in both cases the powers were hoping, Micawber-like, that something would turn up.

Not surprisingly *uti possidetis* proved less problematic in the cases of state recognition that arose in the former colonial world than in Europe, although even here there was not complete consistency. Both Eritrean and East Timorese (Timor Leste) nationalists had always claimed to be supporting the conventional interpretation of self-determination as decolonization, not rejecting it.[23] Eritrea had been colonized by the Italians and then administered by the British during the Second World War, only being attached to Ethiopia by the General Assembly when the Great Powers could not agree among themselves about the fate of the former Italian colonies. Its status had then been changed unilaterally by Ethiopia in defiance of the agreement with the UN, leading to the protracted civil war that was finally brought to an end in the closing stages of the Cold War. East Timor also claimed the right to self-determination as decolonization on the grounds that it was a former Portuguese colony, not a Dutch colony like the rest of Indonesia. On this view the Indonesian annexation of 1974 was illegal.

Two observations should be made about these relatively recent cases of colonial self-determination. The first is that both required a democratic test of opinion prior to international recognition. The majorities in favour of independence were impressive in both cases, but in view of the turmoil that characterized the early years of their independent statehood, whether they should be regarded as a rite of passage or as evidence for a democratic world order is an open question. The second observation is that the decisive issue was not the legal and political arguments about democratic consent but the enabling international environment, which created the opportunities for change: the decision of the two superpowers to cooperate in closing down regional conflicts after the Cold War in the first case; the Asian financial crisis, which precipitated the fall of the Indonesian president, Suharto, in the second.

Had the intellectual debate been decisive, it would presumably have led to the recognition of the Republic of Somaliland, whose leaders can and do make exactly the same case as the Eritreans and East Timor but to no effect. This is not to say that these debates will have no influence on future conflict resolution in disputes over self-determination. Indeed, in two recent cases—the Sudan and Papua New Guinea—where self-determination disputes were the subject of international mediation, there was a deliberate attempt to resolve the conflict by constitutional means. The relative weight of legal theory and international norms as against power-political considerations has recently been tested in South Sudan, which voted in January 2011 by over 98 per cent to secede from the Republic of Sudan in July 2011, although several intractable issues remained unresolved. It is due to be tested again if and when the agreed referendum on the secession of Bourganville from Papua New Guinea is allowed to go ahead.

Democracy and Self-Determination

It was Anthony Lake, President Clinton's first National Security Advisor, who proposed enlargement—by which he meant democracy and open-market economics—as the new grand strategic framework for international society.[24] It was intended to replace George Kennan's idea of containment that had governed Western strategic thought throughout the Cold War. Its implementation faced formidable obstacles from the start, not least in relation to the attempt to reformulate the criteria for exercising self-determination and securing admission to international society.

The problem is one of logic, not of constructive imagination or even political will. Ivor Jennings's observation quoted earlier remains as true in 2016 as when he wrote it in 1956. A democratic test requires a population to be polled within an established and demarcated territory in which they reside. It also raises the question as to which dissatisfied groups should theoretically be entitled to a democratic test on their political affiliations. There was no serious international pressure on Russia to entertain the possibility of secession in Chechnya, or on Indonesia in relation to Aceh, yet in the first instance the substantive case was not obviously different from those Soviet Republics that had been allowed to secede, or in the second from East Timor. Democratization, in other words, cannot reach deep inside an established state whose legal personality is not in doubt. China is unlikely to put its sovereignty over Tibet to the test, and even democratic India is not expected to honour its fifty-year-old pledge to hold a plebiscite in Kashmir in the foreseeable future.

In his polemical essay *The Return of History* Robert Kagan identified the return of Great Power nationalism as one of the defining contours of the new international landscape.[25] He argues persuasively that three of the Great Powers—Russia, China, and India—do not seem at all likely to favour any change in the existing interpretation of self-determination, except where a change in the political map happens to coincide with their national interests. Nor is it clear that either the United States or the European Union will actively seek to reopen so contentious a question, even though it is amongst Western international lawyers and political analysts that there has been the most vigorous debate on the issue.

In support of this conclusion let us briefly review the events of 2008, first in relation to the unilateral declaration of independence by Kosovo in February, and second, Russia's intervention in Georgia in August and subsequent recognition of the break-away provinces of South Ossetia and Abkhazia. The question of whether the 1999 NATO intervention in Kosovo was justified need not detain us here. Suffice it to say that lawyers and political analysts remain divided over whether it was legal, illegal but morally justified, or immoral because illegal. After the United Nations had established its transitional protectorate, it was hoped that by working with moderate Kosovar Albanians and Serbs the territory would settle into a pattern of stable inter-ethnic coexistence, and that the UN would then be able to steer the province into an accommodation with Belgrade, under which the prospect of EU membership would be sufficient to persuade Serbia from any attempt to reassert its hegemony, or alternatively arrange for a peaceful divorce on the Czech/Slovak model.

None of this worked out, so that the UN, which had originally intervened to prevent the Serb army ethically cleansing the majority, found itself effectively presiding over the ethnic cleansing of the Serb minority. By 2007 frustration within the UN was building rapidly and both the United States and the EU were impatient with Russia, which had made it clear that it would veto any attempt by the Security Council to recognize the independence of Kosovo. Kosovo's unilateral declaration of independence was effectively orchestrated by the Western Powers, even though some of them such as Spain, facing potential secessionists of their own, were far from happy.

Kosovo's supporters were able to mobilize over fifty states to support its independence but, in the face of Russian opposition, this was largely academic. Moreover, when the Georgians unwisely attempted to enforce their control of the breakaway province of South Ossetia, the Russians invaded Georgia itself and, following a ceasefire and withdrawal brokered by the then French president, Nicolas Sarkozy, recognized the independence of South Ossetia and Abkhazia, the Black Sea provinces of Georgia, whose inhabitants have been in rebellion against Tiblisi since the disintegration of the Soviet Union. Both the Russians and Kosovo's Western supporters argue that these are all special cases, which do not establish a precedent, but that, of course, remains to be seen.

Some international lawyers have argued that there is no comparison, and that the recognition of Kosovo's declaration of independence is justified on at least three grounds. It is justified, in their view, firstly because it meets the criterion of remedial self-determination, in view of the massive human-rights abuses suffered by the Albanian population in the past; secondly it meets the criterion for constitutional self-determination, namely that the Serbian government (in its previous incarnation as the Federal Republic of Yugoslavia) had forfeited its claim to be the protector of the entire population through its policy of ethnic cleansing; and thirdly it is justified by Kosovo's international administration as an entity separate from Serbia, thus making its situation analogous to a former European colony.[26]

These are all compelling arguments, even if they are also open to the charge of special pleading. The jury is quite literally out on whether they will convince the majority of uncommitted members of the United Nations to recognize Kosovo. In 2009 the Serbs succeeded in obtaining General Assembly approval by a large majority for an Advisory Opinion from the World Court on the legality of Kosovo's unilateral secession. The Court's Advisory Opinion was delivered in July 2010. It did not rule on the substance of the question before it, but by a majority of ten to four found that the text of Kosovo's declaration of independence was not itself illegal because 'international law contains no prohibitions on declarations of independence'. The number of states that have recognized Kosovo rose to 108 by the end of 2015, but two of the five permanent members of the Security Council, China and Russia, still oppose recognition and have argued for continued negotiation between the parties. It is not clear when, or even if, Kosovo will obtain formal admission into international society.

The impasse over the recognition of Kosovo, South Ossetia, and Abkhazia provides a fitting note on which to end this survey of the ways in which the principle of national self-determination has been accommodated within international society. There are strong voices in favour of linking self-determination to democratic choice but the conservatism of both the Great Powers and the small ones on this issue should not be underestimated. It is difficult to say with any certainty, therefore, to what extent the conventional interpretation has been modified since the end of the Cold War.

NOTES

1. H. Bull (1977) *The Anarchical Society: A Study of Order in World Politics*, London, 23–52.
2. T. Hobbes, *Leviathan* (numerous editions), ch. 21.
3. F. Tonnies (2001) *Community and Civil Society*, trans. Jose Harris and Margaret Hollis, and ed. Jose Harris, Cambridge.
4. J. Mayall (2000) *World Politics: Progress and its Limits*, Cambridge, 11–12.
5. A. Cobban (1945) *National Self-Determination*, London, revised as (1969) *The Nation-State and National Self-Determination*, London.
6. The text of this speech is published electronically by Fordham University's Modern History sourcebook, <http://www.fordham.edu/halsall/mod/1918wilson.html>. For its wider appeal, see also, E. Manela (2007) *The Wilsonian Moment and the International Origins of Anti-Colonial Nationalism*, New York.
7. J. Jackson Preece (1998) *National Minorities and the European States System*, Oxford, 1–198.
8. The Bolsheviks were caught in the same dilemma but they postponed the reckoning by adopting a different tactic, reconstituting the Tsarist Empire as a Union of Soviet Soviet Republics all of which in theory were based on acts of self-determination.
9. E. H. Carr (2001) *The Twenty Years' Crisis, 1919–1939*, Basingstoke: an introduction to the study of international relations.
10. J. Mayall (1990) *Nationalism and International Society*, Cambridge, 46.
11. W. I. Jennings (1956) *The Approach to Self-Government*, Cambridge, 56.
12. J. Mayall (2000) 'Nationalism and the International Order: The Asian Experience', in M. Leifer (ed.) *Asian Nationalism*, London, 187–96.
13. The nineteenth-century revival of the concept was intended to prevent European powers from re-entering Latin America after the departure of the Spanish and Portuguese in search of *terra nullius* (a concept that was no longer relevant in the 1960s) and to prevent a rash of irredentist claims leading to conflict. This was the main parallel with Africa, although of course it did not prevent the terrible war (1866–70) between Brazil, Uruguay, and Paraguay that decimated the Paraguyan population in particular.
14. I. M. Lewis (ed.) (1983) *Nationalism and Self-Determination in the Horn of Africa*, London.
15. Mayall, *Nationalism and International Society*, 58–9.
16. 'Tanzania's Memorandum on Biafra's Case'; for text see, A. H. M. Kirk-Greene (ed.) (1971) *Crisis and Conflict in Nigeria: A Documentary Sourcebook, Vol 2, July 1967–January 1970*, Oxford, 429–39.
17. M. Glenny (1992) *The Fall of Yugoslavia*, Harmondsworth.
18. See Chapter 28 by Richard Caplan.
19. B. Boutros-Ghali (1993) *Agenda for Peace*, text in A. Roberts and B. Kinsbury (eds.) *United Nations, Divided World: The UNs Roles in International Relations*, Oxford, appendix A, 468–98.
20. M. Weller (2008) *Escaping the Self-Determination Trap*, Leiden, 46–58.
21. *Agenda for Peace*, paragraph 19.
22. Department of Justice, Canada, Backgrounder, 37 February 1997.
23. Mayall, 'Nationalism and the International Order: The Asian Experience', 71–2 and 139–42.

24. 'From Containment to Enlargement', speech delivered at Johns Hopkins University, 21 September 1993, <www.fas.org/news/1993/usa-930–921.htm>.
25. R. Kagan (2008) *The Return of History and the End of Dreams*, New York, 10–53.
26. B. Stankovski (n.d.) 'Implications of Kosovo Independence on the Doctrine of Constitutional Self-Determination', unpublished MPhil thesis, University of Cambridge.

Suggested Further Reading

Bull, H. (1977) *The Anarchical Society: A Study of Order in World Politics*, London.

Bull, H. and Watson, A. (eds.) (1984) *The Expansion of International Society*, Oxford.

Cobban, A. (1945) *National Self-Determination*, London, issued under the auspices of the Royal Institute of International Affairs; revised (1969) as *The Nation-State and National Self-Determination*, London.

Connor, W. (1984) *The National Question in Marxist-Leninist Theory and Strategy*, Princeton, NJ.

Higgins, R. (1995) *Problems and Process: International Law and How we Use it*, Oxford, ch. 7.

Jackson, R. (ed.) (2000) *Sovereignty at the Millenium*, Oxford.

Jackson Preece, J. (2005) *Minority Rights*, Cambridge.

Mayall, J. (1990) *Nationalism and International Society*, Cambridge.

Mill, J. S. (1910, 1957) *Representative Government*, London, ch. 16. Numerous editions of this text are available.

Weller, M. (2008) *Escaping the Self-Determination Trap*, Leiden.

Weller, M. and Metzger, B. (eds.) (2008) *Settling Self-Determination Disputes: Complex Power-sharing in Theory and Practice*, Leiden, published under the Auspices of the Centre for Constitutional Studies, University of Cambridge.

CHAPTER 28

INTERNATIONAL INTERVENTIONS IN NATIONALIST DISPUTES

RICHARD CAPLAN

Introduction

Nationalist disputes in the twentieth century have been widespread. There is not a region of the world that has not experienced conflict—violent or otherwise—arising from nationalist contestation in this period. Not all of these disputes have attracted significant interest beyond the borders of the states in question. A myriad nationalist insurgencies have beset some states for decades, generating little more than mild concern abroad. Other disputes, however, have not only attracted interest but have also prompted international interventions of various kinds and to varying degrees. These interventions have often been controversial because, unless undertaken at the request of the host government, they have been seen by many states as having violated fundamental principles of international relations, notably the inviolability of national boundaries and non-interference in the domestic affairs of a sovereign state. The controversy is compounded by the fact that while some interventions seem to have contributed to the mitigation of conflict, other interventions have not only failed to alleviate the underlying problems but in some cases may even have aggravated them.

This chapter examines historical developments in relation to international interventions in nationalist disputes. It focuses on developments since the Second World War, with particular emphasis on international interventions in the post-Cold War era. The first section looks at the shifts in international relations in this period that account for the marked increase in third-party interventions in nationalist disputes. The second section looks at the various kinds of interventions that have been undertaken, by whom, and for what purposes, highlighting innovations in practice. The third section examines some of the key issues and debates associated with international interventions in this period. I leave the origins of nationalist disputes unaddressed, instead concentrating on the nature of the international responses.

For the purposes of this chapter, a nationalist dispute is understood to be a conflict arising either between states or within states involving one or more self-identified national communities—which a government or an opposition movement may claim to represent—over matters that are deemed by the communities in question to be fundamental to their existence. This definition is wider than many conventional definitions[1] in so far as it does not limit nationalist disputes to armed conflicts and it does not reduce nationalist disputes to contests for (or against) the establishment of sovereign statehood for a nation. Nationalist disputes may arise, additionally, over the treatment of co-nationals in another state, demands for recognition and the collective rights or privileges of national communities within states, and claims by one nation state to the territory of another (irredentism), among other motivations. Conflicts may also be mixed in character: for instance, they may embody elements of power competition together with nationalism (as with German expansionism under Hitler) or have a basis in ascriptive differences such as religion in addition to national ones (as with the Northern Ireland conflict).

Changing Patterns of Intervention

The twentieth century represents the first time in history that the society of states has been organized on a permanent basis to undertake collective actions of various kinds, including interventions in conflicts between and within states. Prior to the establishment of the League of Nations in 1919, there were no international bodies that could have taken the decision to intervene, the nearest equivalent being coordinated action by the major powers in the form of 'congress' diplomacy, as with the 1815 Congress of Vienna and the 1878 Congress of Berlin. The League and its successor body, the United Nations, created a normative framework and an institutional infrastructure that have facilitated international interventions of many kinds in response to conflicts, nationalist or otherwise, that have threatened or actually disturbed the peace.

For a long time after the Second World War, however, the tendency among states was to refrain from intervention in nationalist disputes. Most of those disputes had been conflicts within states, in which cases other states were constrained generally by the norms of non-interference and territorial integrity.[2] During the Cold War, states were further constrained by the bipolar competition waged in the shadow of nuclear war, whereby an intervention by one superpower (or its allies) risked being seen by the other as a threat to the precarious balance of power. There were exceptions: in 1964, for instance, the United Nations Security Council authorized the deployment of UN peacekeepers—including British forces—to Cyprus, with the consent of the Cypriot government, to prevent a recurrence of fighting between the Greek and Turkish communities on the island state.[3] More exceptional still was the acceptance by the international community of the unilateral secession of East Pakistan from Pakistan in 1971, which achieved its independence (as the People's Republic of Bangladesh) in the wake of a campaign of violence directed against the Bengali-majority province by the Pakistan authorities. States did sometimes support nationalist insurgencies—the Cold War era is rife with covert meddling of this kind—but most nationalist disputes did not attract significant overt intervention.[4]

One broad exception to the Cold War pattern of constraint was the nationalist disputes associated with decolonization which, after the Second World War, enjoyed growing (and eventually universal) support among all states, as reflected in the UN General Assembly's 'Declaration on the Granting of Independence to Colonial Countries and Peoples' adopted on 14 December 1960. The declaration proclaimed the 'necessity of bringing to a speedy and unconditional end colonialism in all its forms and manifestations'.[5] Support for decolonization did not extend to support for independence demands within former colonies, however, which virtually all states opposed, the East Pakistan/Bangladesh case notwithstanding.[6] '[C]rucial to any common international progress', UN Secretary General Boutros Boutros-Ghali would later observe in *An Agenda for Peace*, is respect for 'the fundamental sovereignty and integrity' of the state. '[I]f every ethnic, religious or linguistic group claimed statehood, there would be no limit to fragmentation, and peace, security and economic well-being for all would become ever more difficult to achieve.'[7] Precisely with an eye towards avoiding such fragmentation, it was generally accepted that the national boundaries of the newly independent states would coincide with the boundaries of the former colonial entities—a principle known as *uti possidetis juris*. The principle would also be applied later to the break-up of Yugoslavia and the Soviet Union, in which cases the boundaries of the constituent republics became the boundaries of the newly independent states.[8]

While non-intervention has remained the norm and the practice of international relations, the end of the Cold War has witnessed a steady erosion of both. Already by 1992, when Boutros-Ghali issued his *Agenda for Peace*, the European Community (as it was then known) had elected to intervene in the nationalist disputes in the former Yugoslavia that erupted in 1991—through mediation efforts, sanctions, the deployment of unarmed monitors, and the recognition of the Yugoslav republics as independent states, among other measures. What was to follow, within the space of just a few years, was an unprecedented degree of international interventionism in nationalist disputes—unprecedented, at least, with respect to post-Second World War international relations—that was, moreover, unanticipated by the UN Charter.[9] Azerbaijan, Bosnia-Herzegovina, Burundi, Georgia, Iraq, Macedonia, Rwanda, Serbia, Sri Lanka, Sudan, and Tajikistan, among other states, all suffered ethno-nationalist conflicts in this period that would be the focus of international intervention efforts of various kinds. (The nature of these efforts is discussed in the following section.) Other, non-nationalist disputes—among them Albania, Haiti, Sierra Leone, and Somalia—were also targets of international intervention.

A number of developments account for this significant shift in international relations. The first development is the end of the Cold War. The collapse of communism spurred a wave of nationalist conflicts, particularly in Europe. In some cases (for example, the Baltic states and Armenia and Azerbaijan) the collapse of communism allowed for the re-emergence of nationalist conflicts that communist authoritarianism had managed to suppress but not to resolve.[10] In these and other cases (for example, Croatia and Serbia) the collapse of communism also inaugurated a phase of democratization that fuelled nationalist conflicts as political leaders sought to mobilize public support on the basis of sometimes militant nationalist agendas.[11] The end of the Cold War left its mark on Africa as well, where it attenuated superpower patronage of authoritarian regimes and thus enabled cleavages along tribal, ethnic, and national lines to harden into battle lines.

The end of the Cold War contributed to the rise in interventionism for another reason: it led to the removal of impediments to cooperation among major powers in the United Nations (and elsewhere) and thus facilitated the adoption of new forms of international engagement in conflicts of all kinds. During the Cold War the UN Security Council was often paralyzed because either the United States or the Soviet Union would use its veto to prevent actions favoured by the other party in response to international crises. In the first forty-three years of the Organization—from 1946 to 1989—a total of 228 vetoes were cast, most of them by Washington or Moscow. By contrast, in the first 15 years since the end of the Cold War—from 1990 to 2005—only 18 vetoes were cast.[12] Interventions by major powers that in the past would have been strongly resisted by the other major powers, and might even have triggered a Third World War, were realistic options in the post-Cold War era—at least initially—because the geostrategic stakes were decidedly lower. Thus it would have been inconceivable during the Cold War that the Soviet Union would ever have allowed the deployment of forces from the North Atlantic Treaty Organization (NATO) in response to the outbreak of nationalist conflict in strategically important Yugoslavia. Yet in 1992 NATO—with the tacit support of Russia and China—established a joint naval operation with the Western European Union (WEU) to patrol the Adriatic in an effort to help enforce the UN's regime of economic sanctions against Serbia and Montenegro. This was the first of several UN-mandated roles for the two Western military organizations in the Balkan regional conflicts.[13]

The second development that accounts for greater international intervention in nationalist disputes has been a reconceptualization of sovereignty and a concomitant rise in humanitarian activism. Boutros-Ghali claimed in *An Agenda for Peace* that the 'time of absolute and exclusive sovereignty... has passed'.[14] While that claim may have been overstated, there could be no doubt that the importance attached to respect for human rights and humanitarian law—both often flouted in the context of violent nationalist disputes—was beginning to override traditional conceptions of sovereign authority, as humanitarian crises were seen increasingly to be threats to international peace and security and thus grounds for Chapter VII (enforcement) actions by the Security Council. SC Resolution 688 in April 1991 had already provided the basis for France, Britain, and the United States to intervene forcefully against the government of Saddam Hussein in defence of the embattled Kurdish population of northern Iraq.

Eight years later NATO member states would intervene in Kosovo, on behalf of the Albanian population but without authorization from the Security Council, in a war that many viewed as legitimate for humanitarian reasons, its apparent illegality notwithstanding.[15] Speaking before the UN General Assembly later that year, Secretary General Kofi Annan could claim—this time without exaggeration—that state sovereignty was being 'redefined' such that the state was now widely understood to be 'the servant of its people, and not vice versa'.[16] This thinking would culminate in the adoption by world leaders, meeting at the high-level Plenary Meeting of the General Assembly in September 2005, of a World Summit Outcome Document that affirmed the view that all states have a 'responsibility to protect' their populations from genocide, war crimes, ethnic cleansing, and crimes against humanity, and that the failure to afford such protections could provide grounds for the Security Council to intervene on behalf of beleaguered populations.[17]

While the shifts identified above have been consequential ones, it would be a mistake to suggest that they have resulted in the universal acceptance of new rules of the game. Many states that approved the 2005 World Summit Outcome Document, for instance—including China, India, and Russia—have been extremely wary of efforts to facilitate greater international intervention. These and other states have therefore resisted efforts to operationalize the 'responsibility to protect' principle, as would be achieved, for instance, by restricting the exercise of the veto in cases where there is considerable support on the Security Council for international intervention.[18] Moreover, states continue to exhibit a lack of political will to intervene even where there is manifest evidence of a humanitarian emergency—as international reaction to the ethno-tribal war in Darfur (Sudan) and the civil war in Syria in the twenty-first century would show.

Forms of Intervention

Interventions in nationalist disputes have been undertaken by a variety of international actors, have assumed many different forms, and have had diverse aims as their purpose. In the narrowest use of the term, intervention is understood to mean a military intervention in a state, without the approval of that state's authorities, with the humanitarian aim of preventing or alleviating widespread suffering of the civilian population implicated in a violent conflict and/or with the strategic aim of bringing about an end to the conflict. This definition fails to capture many important non-military forms of intervention, however, and while there is a danger in employing terms too elastically, the analysis below relies on a broader notion of intervention so as to be able to encompass a wide range of relevant instruments. It is also important to bear in mind that the nature of international interventions in nationalist disputes has not been different necessarily from that of interventions in non-nationalist disputes, with the exception of some of the political remedies that have been sought. In the discussion that follows, therefore, a distinction is not always made between nationalist and non-nationalist conflicts.

To generalize, international interventions in nationalist disputes—whether militarily or non-militarily—have been undertaken with three broad aims in mind: to prevent, to mitigate, or to resolve the disputes in question. These are not discrete categories; indeed, they often overlap. Moreover, the aims associated with each category are often pursued in tandem.

Conflict Prevention. Considerable intellectual stock has been invested in conflict prevention in the post-Cold War period—the scholarly literature on the subject is now quite substantial—but significantly new policy initiatives in this area have been relatively few, despite the emphasis that Boutros-Ghali placed on this notion in his tenure as UN Secretary General.[19] One notable exception was the establishment in December 1992 of a UN preventive deployment force in Macedonia (UNPROFOR, later UNPREDEP)—the first and, to date, only such deployment of its kind—for the purpose of monitoring and reporting on developments in the border areas that could undermine confidence and stability in the only former republic of Yugoslavia that had not succumbed to fighting involving Serbian or Serbian-backed forces.[20] UNPREDEP also contributed arguably to the containment of an incipient nationalist conflict between ethnic Albanians and Slav Macedonians within the territory—a conflict that would erupt into violence several years after the UNPREDEP operation was terminated in February 1999.[21] Other, more conventional forms of preventive intervention in nationalist disputes employed in this period have included mediation efforts, confidence- and security-building measures, and fact-finding. The effectiveness of conflict prevention can be difficult to gauge as it often entails proving a counterfactual. Would Macedonia have remained peaceful in the absence (earlier) and presence (later) of UN forces? In addition, preventive diplomacy is frequently conducted outside of the public view so that these efforts, and any successes associated with them, have not always been widely known.

Non-governmental conflict prevention efforts in this period have also been noteworthy, in particular those of the International Crisis Group (ICG). A non-governmental organization (NGO) created in 1995 in the wake of the international community's failure to anticipate and respond effectively to the brutal wars that erupted in Somalia, Bosnia-Herzegovina, and Rwanda in the early 1990s, ICG has sought to function as an early warning system with regard to impending complex emergencies, relying on an influential board of former statesmen and stateswomen to mobilize international action. Calls for the United Nations to expand its own early warning systems, and for greater intelligence sharing by states within the Organization, have been hampered by concern on the part of some member states that such mechanisms could facilitate international interventions to which they would be opposed.

Conflict Mitigation. International efforts to mitigate nationalist conflicts, or at least the effects of such conflicts, have been extensive in this period—a reflection, in part, of the severity of these conflicts in terms of their toll on civilian lives.[22] (The erosion of respect for humanitarian law has also manifested itself in the increasing number of attacks on humanitarian workers, who historically have enjoyed formal legal protection and de facto immunity from attack by belligerent parties.) Intrastate wars have largely been responsible for the steady increase in refugee flows in this period—rising from 2.4 million in 1975 to 18.2 million in 1993[23]—many of whom have been the victims of forced displacements by warring parties in an era that witnessed the introduction of 'ethnic cleansing' to the diplomatic lexicon. The high civilian toll of violent nationalist disputes explains why the principal activities associated with conflict mitigation efforts have been humanitarian in character: aid delivery and the protection of refugees and internally displaced persons (IDPs) in particular. One measure of the dramatic rise in humanitarian assistance—and an indication of the magnitude of the problem that it has sought to address—is the expenditure by the UN High Commissioner for Refugees (UNHCR), which increased more than 150 per cent in the twenty-year period from 1975 to 1995.[24]

One innovation emerging from the challenges associated with these humanitarian emergencies has been the provision of security through the establishment of so-called safety zones. While provisions for such zones have long existed in international conventions, the post-Cold War era saw the application of this idea in novel and ambitious ways, with the establishment of a 'safe haven' in northern Iraq in 1991, six 'safe areas' in Bosnia-Herzegovina in 1993, and 'safe humanitarian zones' in Rwanda in 1994.[25] In a departure from historic norms and practice, which have stressed the importance of securing the consent of the warring parties to the establishment of protected areas, these safety zones were imposed and maintained militarily by outside bodies without the consent of the warring parties—and, in the case of Iraq, without the explicit authorization of the UN Security Council. Adding to the controversy, these zones were not demilitarized (in Iraq and Rwanda especially),[26] thus affording protection to both civilians *and* combatants, although in the case of Bosnia-Herzegovina they failed ultimately to provide very much protection at all.[27]

Another significant development associated with international efforts to mitigate nationalist conflicts in this period has been the dramatic expansion of the number and the nature of UN peacekeeping operations. In the forty years from 1948 until 1988, there were a total of thirteen such operations; in the next fifteen years an additional forty-six operations were launched. UN peacekeeping operations were conceived originally with interstate wars in mind, the idea being that impartial, international forces deployed between two armies could help keep the peace, thus facilitating diplomatic efforts to achieve a negotiated settlement. With the end of the Cold War, however, the vast majority of peacekeeping deployments were to intrastate conflicts—many of them nationalist disputes. At the same time, and again reflecting the peculiar challenges posed by internal conflicts, the nature of peacekeeping has changed. More than just keepers of the peace, peacekeepers were now mandated to carry out such disparate tasks as ensuring the delivery of humanitarian aid, repatriating refugees and internally displaced persons, monitoring compliance with human-rights obligations, organizing and holding elections, overseeing the demobilization and reintegration of armed forces, and reconstituting and training police forces, among other responsibilities.[28] This expansion of tasks would culminate in the United Nations and other international bodies serving as 'surrogate sovereigns' or 'titular trustees' in the administration of some war-torn territories (Bosnia-Herzegovina, Kosovo, and East Timor) not unlike such bygone institutions as the International Control Commission for Albania (1913–14) and the League of Nations administrations of the Saar Basin (1920–35), the Free City of Danzig (1920–39), and the Colombian town and district of Leticia (1933–4).[29]

Conflict Resolution. Some of the more significant innovations in international practice have occurred with respect to efforts at conflict resolution. It is also in this area where the distinctive features of nationalist conflicts, as opposed to other kinds of conflicts, have influenced the choice and character of intervention tools.

Nationalist disputes often revolve around self-determination claims. As noted above, there is an inherent conservatism in international relations with regard to self-determination claims of national communities that entail the right to choose one's own sovereignty (what is known as 'external' self-determination), as these claims threaten a fundamental principle of international order: the inviolability of national boundaries. The two general exceptions have been with respect to the external self-determination claims of colonial peoples and boundary changes achieved consensually, as with the creation of new states emerging from the former Soviet Union, the unification of Germany, and the separation of Eritrea from Ethiopia. By contrast, there has been greater willingness to accommodate 'internal' self-determination claims that entail the right to meaningful participation in the political process, as discussed below.[30]

The post-Cold War era has seen a dramatic challenge to this conservatism. When nationalist fighting erupted in Yugoslavia in 1991, the European Community sought to broker a peace between Serbia and the other republics, but when this proved fruitless the EC member states chose to recognize the republics as independent states.[31] The EC was arguably bowing to the inevitable—only massive violence could have kept Yugoslavia together—but the Community also seized what it saw as an opportunity to mould the strategic environment by requiring the emerging states to accept extensive provisions for safeguarding the rights of vulnerable national minorities within their borders and thus eliminate one of the presumed sources of the conflict: ethno-national insecurity.[32] More than a decade later, in 2008, the European Union (EU) would adopt a similar approach to the nationalist conflict in Kosovo, an autonomous province of Serbia, although this time it would be argued that Serbia had forfeited its sovereign authority over the territory because of its sustained and systematic repression of Kosovar Albanians who, as a consequence, had earned the right to secede.[33] The international community was at pains to emphasize the uniqueness of the Kosovo case and, indeed, comparable cases (e.g., Chechnya in Russia, Tibet in China) have not received comparable treatment. International law and practice continue to proscribe any actions by states aimed at the dismemberment of another state, including support for non-consensual secession. However, Russia, invoking international support for Kosovo statehood, would later recognize the independence claims of the sub-state nationalist entities South Ossetia and Abkhazia in Georgia, while nationalist insurgents elsewhere have been encouraged by the Kosovo 'non-precedent'.

The nationalist conflicts in Yugoslavia spawned another important innovation in international efforts at conflict resolution: the establishment of ad hoc tribunals for the prosecution of genocide, war crimes, and crimes against humanity. The first of these—the International Criminal Tribunal for the former Yugoslavia (ICTY)—was created by the UN Security Council in 1993; the second—the International Criminal Tribunal for Rwanda (ICTR)—was established by the Council in 1994 in reaction to the crimes committed in the context of the ethnic conflict between Hutus and Tutsis. These tribunals represent the first international attempts since the Nuremberg and Tokyo trials, following the Second World War, to hold individuals responsible for grave violations of international humanitarian law, thereby undermining charges of collective responsibility for egregious crimes and thus, it has been hoped, facilitating reconciliation between the affected national and ethnic communities. The two tribunals also represent the first time that the crime of genocide has been tried by an international court and—consistent with the emerging principle of 'responsibility to protect'—the first time that an indictment has been filed against an acting head of state (Yugoslav President Slobodan Milošević) for crimes allegedly committed while he was in office. The two ad hoc tribunals would pave the way for the establishment of the permanent International Criminal Court (ICC) in 1998 and for the establishment of 'hybrid' national-international war-crimes tribunals in Sierra Leone (2002) and Cambodia (2006).[34]

Several other approaches to the resolution of nationalist conflicts have been employed by third parties, among these the promotion of minority rights. In a manner reminiscent of the League of Nations era, the post-Cold War period has seen a significant expansion in the development of collective minority rights and of instruments to protect those rights. This expansion stands in marked contrast to the early post-Second World War era when Western states in particular, mindful of the abuse of minority rights by kin-states (notably Germany) in the interwar period,[35] placed the emphasis instead on the development of protections for *individual* human rights. The expansion of minority rights protections has been most evident in, but not limited to, Europe, where the Organization for Security and Cooperation in Europe (OSCE), the Council of Europe (CoE), the EU, and NATO, among other bodies, have all undertaken major initiatives in this area. These initiatives have either been pan-regional in scope (for example, the CoE's Framework Convention for the Protection of National Minorities) or they have been directed towards the resolution of specific conflicts (for example, the Constitution of Bosnia and Herzegovina). In addition to formal enforcement mechanisms, which also existed (albeit limitedly) in the interwar period, the allure of membership in the European 'club' has also helped considerably to induce compliance with the new minority rights norms.

What explains, in part, this shift in support of national minority rights is the threat and the actual outbreak of ethno-national conflict in Europe with the end of the Cold War and the belief that the promotion of national minority rights could help to prevent, contain, and resolve these conflicts. The expansion of minority rights has also reflected a belief in liberal ideals of multiculturalism—in the prospect of diverse societies achieving or maintaining stability through the inculcation of tolerance and the accommodation of difference—that have gained ground in Western societies especially since the end of the Second World War. These ideals would be called into question, however, with the terrorist attacks originating from within and directed against those societies in the early twenty-first century.[36]

Other international (and domestic) strategies employed to resolve nationalist disputes have been power-sharing arrangements and territorial solutions short of secession.[37] Power sharing—often also referred to as consociationalism—is predicated on the idea that conflicts between national and other groups can be managed when arrangements are in place to ensure that no decision bearing on a vital interest can be taken without the consent of the relevant parties. Power-sharing arrangements have been adopted in response to nationalist conflict or competition in Belgium (Flemish and Walloons), Northern Ireland (Protestants and Catholics), Bosnia and Herzegovina (Serbs, Croats, and Muslims), Kosovo (Serbs and Albanians), Macedonia (Albanians and Macedonians), Iraq (Kurds, Sunnis, and Shiites), Sudan (Muslims and Christians/Animists), and Sri Lanka (Tamils and Hindus), among other nationalist disputes. Various kinds of power-sharing arrangements have been established as a consequence of international interventions, notably power sharing at the executive level, proportional representation in all branches of government, and the introduction of special veto rights. While these arrangements help to ensure that government decisions are taken on a consensual basis, they can be unwieldy and in some instances have led to decision-making paralysis or have been rendered anachronistic, as occurred in Lebanon, because of demographic changes that have left major national communities under-represented.

Territorial solutions for nationalist disputes have largely entailed various forms of autonomy, in which one or more national groups are allowed to exercise a significant degree of self-government. The autonomous province of Alto Adige/South Tyrol in northern Italy has served as a model for international interventions in many nationalist disputes, especially in Europe. South Tyrol had been ceded by Austria to Italy after the First World War, but because of its large German-speaking population it was to be a seat of unrest and a source of tension for the next seven decades.[38] Encouraged by the UN General Assembly, Italy and Austria negotiated autonomy arrangements for the region that, together with further Italian constitutional reforms adopted in 2001, granted the province a large measure of control over its fiscal, economic, social, cultural, and educational affairs, thus diffusing tensions that, in the past, had occasionally erupted in violence.

Certain other strategies, it is interesting to note, that third parties employed in response to nationalist disputes in the early twentieth century were no longer considered acceptable practices in the late twentieth century. One such strategy is 'voluntary' population transfers or exchanges, as occurred, for instance, between Turkey and Greece in 1923 when, with the support of the League of Nations, the 'Muslim inhabitants of Greece' and the 'Greek inhabitants of Turkey', as the League defined the two communities, were forcibly relocated to their respective 'homelands'. The action was seen at the time as making a major contribution to peace—Fridtjof Nansen, the League High Commissioner and architect of the plan, was awarded the Nobel Peace Prize for his efforts—but such actions today would be seen to violate fundamental human rights, notably the right to freedom of movement.[39]

Similarly, partition has been resorted to in the past to resolve communal conflicts—as with the partition of Ireland in 1920, India in 1947, and Palestine (attempted) in 1947. Proponents of this approach maintain that national, ethnic, and other cleavages in a society can be so great as to render peaceful coexistence among different communal groups impossible, in which case partition may offer the best prospect for conflict reduction. While there have been latter-day advocates of partition—with respect to nationalist disputes in South Africa, Bosnia and Herzegovina, Russia, and Kosovo, for instance—this approach has generally fallen out of favour among international policymakers both because of the practical difficulty, if not impossibility, of achieving a just partition but also because partition violates the principle of territorial integrity.[40]

Key Issues and Debates

The various international strategies outlined above have not been without controversy. Of course, international intervention—in the classical sense of a military intervention—is inherently controversial for the simple reason that it constitutes a violation of the principle of non-intervention, and the humanitarian activism of the late twentieth century that has led to increased interventionism has only heightened that controversy. This was nowhere more apparent than with the US-led invasion of Saddam Hussein's Iraq in March 2003, which the Bush administration justified partly, but ultimately unconvincingly, on humanitarian grounds, given that there was no ongoing or imminent genocide or comparable mass slaughter or loss of life—the standard threshold criteria for a humanitarian intervention. The invasion confirmed the fears of many, especially in the Third World, that legitimization of humanitarian intervention in the post-Cold War era risked unleashing a new Frankenstein's monster, notwithstanding the contribution that interventions had arguably made to the enhancement of human security in Kosovo, Liberia, Sierra Leone, Côte d'Ivoire, and elsewhere. As Ken Roth, the director of Human Rights Watch, warned in the wake of the Iraq invasion:

> If its defenders continue to try and justify it [intervention] as humanitarian when it is not, they risk undermining an institution that, despite all odds, has managed to

> maintain its viability in this new century as a tool for rescuing people from slaughter.[41]

In the broader sense of the term 'intervention', international interventions in nationalist disputes in the post-Cold War era have raised a number of other critical issues. The first of these concerns the role and the effect of humanitarian action in the context of violent nationalist wars. Humanitarian action, some critics charged in the 1990s, was being used by states and international organizations to alleviate public pressure on them to take more effective political and military action to stop the fighting. Indeed, the vulnerability of humanitarian assistance to disruption by combatants was often invoked by states and organizations as a reason for their cautious and even-handed treatment of the warring parties, which, it was claimed, was necessary to ensure continued combatant cooperation. The appropriateness of the even-handedness of humanitarian agencies was also called into question. For more than a century humanitarian engagement in violent conflict has been guided by the principles of impartiality and neutrality, and while there are sound reasons for this approach, humanitarian assistance, some now argued, was having the perverse effect of prolonging conflict—and the human suffering caused by it—because it was enabling combatants and civilian populations to continue their resistance whereas without such assistance they might have capitulated earlier. These were not new arguments—similar charges had been levelled against Save the Children during the First World War—but the scale of the humanitarian disasters associated with the wars of the 1990s gave these arguments renewed force. In addition, these same critics argued, humanitarian assistance was making it more likely that the strategic outcome of these conflicts would be a stalemate rather than a decisive victory by one side, thus diminishing the prospects for a viable peace settlement.[42]

Peacekeeping was subject to related criticism in this period. Like humanitarian action, peacekeeping is governed by the view that peacekeepers must implement their mandates without favour or prejudice to any party in order to ensure the consent and cooperation of all parties. In the face of blatant violations of humanitarian law by warring parties, however, peacekeeping impartiality can and did sometimes convey the impression of passivity or moral indifference. As the 2000 Panel on United Nations Peace Operations observed in the wake of genocidal acts of violence in Rwanda and Bosnia and Herzegovina, which UN peacekeepers were criticized for failing to prevent:

> where one party to a peace agreement clearly and incontrovertibly is violating its terms, continued equal treatment of all parties by the United Nations can in the best case result in ineffectiveness and in the worst may amount to complicity with evil. No failure did more to damage the standing and credibility of United Nations peacekeeping in the 1990s than its reluctance to distinguish victim from aggressor.[43]

Such criticisms would lead the United Nations to make significant changes in its peacekeeping doctrine, acknowledging the need not to be neutral in the execution of peacekeeping mandates.[44]

A related issue concerns peacekeeping and the use of force. Traditionally peacekeepers have been lightly armed with a mandate to use force only in self-defence. Self-defence can be variously interpreted—in a limited sense to mean the defence of peacekeepers, in a wider sense to mean the defence of the mandate.[45] The expansion of peacekeeping discussed above has resulted not only in a multiplication of tasks but also, given the nature of some of those tasks, a greater need for UN forces to be equipped with 'robust' mandates to implement them. As a result, the post-Cold War period would see the Security Council authorizing peacekeepers to use 'all necessary means' to conduct their operations. Peacekeeping operations, however, have not always been equipped to use force effectively or at all: troop contributions, for instance, may not have reached required levels, which, anyway, may have been inadequate for a robust mandate, or national governments have been reluctant to put their forces in harm's way. As a result, there have been heightened expectations of what peacekeepers should achieve and repeated failures to meet these expectations, further contributing to the crisis in UN peacekeeping in the 1990s noted above.

Along with an expansion of peacekeeping activities, the post-Cold War period has witnessed a significant expansion in the number of actors—regional organizations in particular—intervening in nationalist and non-nationalist conflicts. This expansion has been welcomed, to the extent that it has alleviated burdens on the United Nations, but it has not been without controversy as these actors have often assumed roles that differed markedly from their original mandates. NATO, for instance, which was conceived with the defence of Western Europe, Turkey, and North America in mind, has seen its scope of active engagement extend to 'out-of-area' conflicts in the Western Balkans (Bosnia and Herzegovina, Kosovo, and Macedonia), the Middle East (Iraq), Asia (Afghanistan), and Africa (Sudan/Darfur). The EU in this same period would also begin to undertake significant out-of-area police and military operations, in the context of its European Security and Defence Policy (ESDP), first in the Western Balkans and then farther afield in the Democratic Republic of Congo, Afghanistan, and the Palestinian Territories. Overcoming historic inhibitions against intervention on the African continent, member states of the African Union (AU)—established in 2002 as the successor to the Organization for African Unity (OAU)—would confer on the Union a right to intervene when 'grave circumstances' warrant such action, namely, in the event of war crimes, genocide, crimes against humanity, and 'a serious threat to legitimate order'.[46] Although Chapter VIII of the UN Charter envisions a role for regional organizations in the maintenance of peace and security, these new undertakings—actual and potential—raise questions about the precise role of the United Nations in non-UN interventions, particularly with respect to the use of force.

A further, but by no means final, issue raised by international interventions in the post-Cold War era concerns the relationship between the pursuit of peace and the prosecution of justice. Efforts to prosecute war criminals, some have argued, can complicate or even undermine efforts to achieve a negotiated settlement, as alleged criminals may be reluctant to accept a settlement fearing that it will render them vulnerable to prosecution, especially if amnesty is ruled out as an option. On the other hand, there is a danger that accommodation of political and military leaders tolerant of, if not actually responsible for, the commission of war crimes may have the effect of encouraging further violence and atrocities. There is no evidence to suggest that states have impeded prosecutions in the interest of securing a negotiated settlement, but they have not always been forthcoming in their support of the judicial processes.[47] The threat of prosecution represented by a permanent International Criminal Court may succeed in deterring future violations of humanitarian law, but its effectiveness in this regard remains to be proved.

Conclusion

The post-Cold War era, in contrast to the period from 1945 to 1989, has been characterized by considerable international intervention in nationalist disputes—whether the aim has been to prevent, to mitigate, or to resolve these disputes. This increased interventionism is not only the result of the changing face of global conflict engendered by the end of the Cold War—notably the prevalence of violent civil wars and failed states—but also a consequence of major normative shifts in international relations that have seen a reconceptualization of state sovereignty and associated state responsibilities. It is difficult to generalize about the effectiveness of interventions as varied and various as those discussed in this chapter: it is fair to say that these interventions have achieved some noteworthy successes with respect to each of the three broad aims but also some notorious failures. While there have been important innovations in practice in this period, by and large the international community does not have significantly more instruments at its disposal now than it has had in the past. The difference is that with the end of the Cold War there has often, but not always, been a greater willingness to deploy these instruments.

Notes

1. See, for instance, E. Gellner (2006) *Nations and Nationalism*, 2nd edn., Oxford; E. J. Hobsbawm (1992) *Nations and Nationalism Since 1790*, 2nd edn., Cambridge; and A. D. Smith (1986) *The Ethnic Origins of Nations*, Oxford.
2. Most violent disputes of any kind since 1946 have been intrastate conflicts. The number of interstate conflicts has been consistently low notwithstanding the threefold increase in the number of states (and thus potential warring parties) in the international system. For a discussion of global war trends since 1946, see Human Security Centre (2005) *Human Security Report 2005*, New York.
3. United Nations Security Council Resolution 186, 4 March 1964.
4. J. Mayall (1990) *Nationalism and International Society*, Cambridge, ch. 4.
5. United Nations General Assembly Resolution 1514 (XV), 14 December 1960.

6. Five states (Ivory Coast, Gabon, Haiti, Tanzania, and Zambia), however, recognized Biafra in 1968 in its bid to achieve independence from Nigeria, although not one of these states established formal diplomatic relations with Biafra. See 'Why We Recognised Biafra', *The Observer*, 26 April 1968.
7. B. Boutros-Ghali (1992) *An Agenda for Peace: Preventive Diplomacy, Peacemaking and Peacekeeping*, UN Doc. A/47/277 (1992), paragraph 17.
8. The exception was Kosovo, which was a province of the Yugoslav republic of Serbia.
9. Article 2(7) of the Charter expressly proscribes intervention by the United Nations in matters 'which are essentially within the domestic jurisdiction of any state'.
10. R. Caplan and J. Feffer (eds.) (1996) *Europe's New Nationalism: States and Minorities in Conflict*, New York.
11. E. D. Mansfield and J. Snyder (1995) 'Democratisation and the Danger of War', *International Security*, 20 (Summer), 5–38.
12. 'Changing Patterns in the Use of the Veto in the Security Council', *Global Policy Forum*, <http://www.globalpolicy.org/security/data/vetotab.htm>.
13. The Security Council repeatedly requested states, nationally or through regional agencies or arrangements, to take measures necessary to ensure compliance with its resolutions on Yugoslavia without, however, mandating any specific bodies to take action.
14. Boutros-Ghali, *An Agenda for Peace*, paragraph 17.
15. See, for instance, International Independent Commission on Kosovo (2000) *The Kosovo Report*, Oxford; House of Commons 'Foreign Affairs Committee, Session 1999–2000 (2000)', *Kosovo*, HC 28–1, London: The Stationery Office.
16. 'Secretary-General Presents his Annual Report to General Assembly', Press Release, UN Doc SG/SM/7136 and GA/9596, 20 September 1999. Little known is Tanzania's use of similar yet even more far-reaching language thirty years earlier to justify its recognition of Biafran statehood, when the Nigerian government was employing large-scale and indiscriminate violence to suppress the Biafran rebellion: 'States are made to serve people.... When the state ceases to stand for the honour, the protection, and the well-being of all of its citizens, then it is no longer the instrument of those it has rejected. In such a case the people have the right to create another instrument for their protection—in other words, to create another state.' Statement by the Government of Tanzania, 13 April 1968, in A. H. M. Kirk-Greene (ed.) (1971) *Crisis and Conflict in Nigeria: A Documentary Sourcebook 1966–1970*, London, vol. 2, 209–10.
17. 2005 World Summit Outcome, UN General Assembly Doc. A/60/L.1, 20 September 2005, paragraphs 138–9.
18. The International Commission on Intervention and State Sovereignty (ICISS), which pioneered efforts for adoption of the 'responsibility to protect' doctrine, argued for such a proposal to ensure that the Council would respond more effectively to humanitarian crises. See *The Responsibility to Protect: Report of the International Commission on Intervention and State Sovereignty* (Ottawa: International Development Research Centre, 2001), paragraph 8.29.
19. Boutros-Ghali, *An Agenda for Peace*, paragraphs 23–33.
20. United Nations Security Council Resolution 795 (1992) of 11 December 1992 authorized the extension of UN peacekeeping operations in the former Yugoslavia to Macedonia; United Nations Security Council Resolution 983 (1995) of 31 March 1995 established UNPREDEP to replace UNPROFOR.

21. China vetoed the Security Council resolution that would have renewed UNPREDEP's mandate after Macedonia established diplomatic relations with Taiwan.
22. S. Chesterman, 'Introduction', in S. Chesterman (ed.) (2001) *Civilians in War*, Boulder, CO, 2.
23. Figures from A. Roberts (1996) *Humanitarian Action in War*, Adelphi Paper no. 305, Oxford, 12. These figures do not include the very large number of internally displaced persons (IDPs), which in some years have been twice the number of refugees.
24. Roberts, *Humanitarian Action in War.*
25. C. McQueen (2006) *Humanitarian Intervention and Safety Zones: Iraq, Bosnia and Rwanda*, London.
26. Claims that the Bosnian 'safe areas' were not demilitarized—which the Bosnian Serbs used as a pretext to attack the areas—were largely overstated. See 'The Fall of Srebrenica', Report of the Secretary General Pursuant to Resolution 53/35, UN Doc. A/54/549, 15 November 1999, paragraphs 475–9.
27. 'The Fall of Srebrenica'.
28. M. Berdal, 'The Security Council and Peacekeeping', in V. Lowe, A. Roberts, J. Welsh, and D. Zaum (eds.) (2008) *The United Nations Security Council and War*, Oxford, ch. 7.
29. R. Caplan (2005) *International Governance of War-torn Territories: Rule and Reconstruction*, Oxford.
30. A. Cassese (1995) *Self-Determination of Peoples: A Legal Reappraisal*, Cambridge, chs. 4 and 5.
31. The EC's apparent transgression was mitigated by the view expressed by the EC Arbitration Commission (Badinter Commission) that the crisis in Yugoslavia was so acute that the state's legal personality was being extinguished and that Yugoslavia was dissolving into its constituent units. EC recognition, therefore, was merely an acknowledgement of this fact.
32. R. Caplan (2005) *Europe and the Recognition of New States in Yugoslavia*, Cambridge.
33. The notion of remedial secession is discussed in L. C. Bucheit (1978) *Secession: The Legitimacy of Self-Determination*, New Haven, CT, 222. For a discussion of this concept as it applies to the Kosovo case, see C. Tomuschat (2006) 'Secession and Self-Determination', in M. G. Kohen (ed.) *Secession: International Law Perspectives*, Cambridge, 23–45.
34. For a discussion of the major war-crimes tribunals, see W. A. Schabas (2006) *The UN International Criminal Tribunals: The Former Yugoslavia, Rwanda and Sierra Leone*, Cambridge.
35. J. Jackson Preece (1998) *National Minorities and the European Nation-States System*, Oxford, ch. 5.
36. W. Kymlicka (2007) *Multicultural Odysseys: Navigating the New International Politics of Diversity*, Oxford, chs. 1 and 2.
37. U. Schneckener (2004) 'Models of Ethnic Conflict Regulation: The Politics of Recognition', in U. Schneckener and S. Wolff (eds.) *Managing and Settling Ethnic Conflicts*, London, ch. 2.
38. M. Toscano (1975) *Alto-Adige—South Tyrol*, Baltimore, MD.
39. Universal Declaration of Human Rights (1948), Article 13.
40. B. O'Leary (2006) 'Debating Partition: Justifications, Critiques & Evaluation', MFPP Working Paper No. 28, Institute for British-Irish Studies, University College Dublin.

41. K. Roth (2004) 'War in Iraq: Not a Humanitarian Intervention', *Human Rights Watch World Report 2004*, New York, 34.
42. R. K. Betts (1994) 'The Delusion of Impartial Intervention', *Foreign Affairs*, 73, no. 6, 20–33.
43. United Nations General Assembly and Security Council (2000) Report of the Panel on United Nations Peace Operations ('Brahimi Report'), UN Doc. A/55-305-S/2000/809, 21 August, ix.
44. United Nations, Department of Peacekeeping Operations (2008) *United Nations Peacekeeping Operations: Principles and Guidelines*, 33–4.
45. T. Findlay (2002) *The Use of Force in Peace Operations*, Oxford.
46. Constitutive Act Establishing the African Union (2000), Article 4(h) and Protocol on Amendments to the Constitutive Act (2003).
47. P. R. Williams and M. P. Scharf (2002) *Peace with Justice? War Crimes and Accountability in the Former Yugoslavia*, Lanham, MD, and Oxford.

Suggested Further Reading

Bellamy, A. J.; Williams, P. D. and Griffin, S. (2004) *Understanding Peacekeeping*, Polity.
Brown, M. E. (ed.) (1996) *The International Dimensions of Internal Conflict*, Cambridge.
Caplan, R. (2005) *International Governance of War-Torn Territories: Rule and Reconstruction*, Oxford.
Hannum, H. (1990) *Autonomy, Sovereignty and Self-Determination: The Accommodation of Conflicting Rights*, Philadelphia, PA.
International Commission on Intervention and State Sovereignty (2001) *The Responsibility to Protect*, Ottawa.
Kaldor, M. (2006) *New and Old Wars: Organised Violence in a Global Era*, 2nd edn., London.
Kymlicka, W. (2007) *Multicultural Odysseys: Navigating the International Politics of Diversity*, Oxford.
Mayall, J. (1990) *Nationalism and International Society*, Cambridge.
McGarry, J. and O'Leary, B. (eds.) (1993) *The Politics of Ethnic Conflict Regulation*, London.
Roberts, A. (1996) *Humanitarian Action in War*, Adelphi Paper 305, London.
Schneckener, U. and Wolff, S. (eds.) (2004) *Managing and Settling Ethnic Conflicts*, London.
Schabas, W. A. (2006) *The UN International Criminal Tribunals: The former Yugoslavia, Rwanda and Sierra Leone*, Cambridge

CHAPTER 29

FASCISM AND RACISM

ROGER EATWELL

Introduction

The first self-styled fascist movement, the *Fasci di combattimento*, was founded in 1919 by Benito Mussolini and an eclectic group of radical nationalists, who sought to defeat the divisive left and liberals at home and win new empire for Italy abroad. The movement took its name from the word *fasci*, meaning 'union', and adopted as its symbol the imperial Roman *fasces*, denoting authority. By the early 1920s the movement had metamorphosed into the National Fascist Party (PNF), which quickly gathered mass support. By the late 1920s this was the only legal party in a self-proclaimed 'totalitarian' state, headed by Mussolini as 'Il Duce'.[1]

Whilst early historiographical debates raged about the relative importance of agency and structure in the origins and development of fascism, few questioned that interwar Europe witnessed the birth of a broad family of such movements, and to a lesser extent regimes. The most important of these was the German National Socialist Workers' Party (NSDAP), which came to power in 1933 with Adolf Hitler as its Führer. This quickly established a more pervasive and ultimately radical dictatorship than Mussolini was ever to lead.[2]

However, following an explosion of research on these and other putative fascisms (relatively few outside Italy termed themselves 'fascist'), many historians came to stress difference rather than genetic similarity. In particular, by the 1970s the Nazi regime came to be widely seen as 'without precedent or parallel' on account of its biological racism, which culminated in barbaric expansionism into Slavic states and the Holocaust.[3]

During the 1990s a 'cultural turn' in historiography portrayed 'generic fascism' as a distinctive form of revolutionary nationalist ideology, a conceptualization that allowed Nazism to be reinterred in the fascist Pantheon. This was commonly linked to the claim that fascism was a political religion, which helps to offer insights into its support and especially its fanaticism.[4] However, this one-sided emphasis glosses over the major economic dimension to the Third Way (between capitalism and socialism) ideology and propaganda of fascism, as well as the role of economic motives in the Holocaust.[5]

Moreover, in the new millennium many historians continue to claim that Nazi racism made it *sui generis*.[6] Whilst it is important not to understate the specificities of fascism, more perceptively the growing transnational school of history has pointed to the genocidal similarities between modern colonialism more generally. Indeed, a much-neglected aspect of fascist thought is the impact of the expansion of other great powers.

In order to probe more deeply into the nature of generic fascism, and especially its relationship with racism, this chapter is divided into three main sections. The first two deal with the paradigmatic cases of Italian Fascism and German National Socialism. The third section more briefly considers two other forms. In France, which had witnessed notable manifestations of political anti-Semitism prior to 1914, fascist groups like the Faisceau and Parti Populaire Français (PPF) tended to focus on socioeconomic radicalism, although they were far from immune to stereotyping Jews and accepted the right to rule over lesser colonial peoples. In Romania, anti-Semitic traditions ran even deeper and Jew-baiting was a central theme in by far the most important fascist group, the Iron Guard, though socioeconomic issues also featured in its campaigns.

Together, these case studies demonstrate that racism was central to all forms of fascism. However, there were different views among fascists about nation and the more elusive concept of race. Moreover, emphasizing their centrality to fascist ideology and practice does not necessarily mean that overt racism was always central to propaganda, let alone to understanding mass support.

Italian Fascism

Mussolini was a prominent socialist and opponent of colonial expansion prior to 1914. But even before his conversion to the cause of Italy's entry into the First World War (May 1915) it is possible to discern crucial developments that led to apostasy. Although different roads led individuals to Fascism, including opportunism after it came to power, Mussolini's journey is especially instructive as he was its leader from its birth to final death throes.

Arguably the main constant in Mussolini's thinking was his conviction that violence was necessary to shape history. However, he was not the mindless activist implied by the stereotypical early Fascist slogan, 'I don't care a damn', which was borrowed from First World War elite shock troops (*arditi*). Although he came from a relatively poor background, Mussolini read widely, and was clearly influenced by both contemporary ideas and political developments.

Another enduring belief concerned the importance of dynamic leadership, organization, and propaganda. Well before 1914 Mussolini was aware of the writings of the

French crowd psychologist Gustave le Bon and the German elite theorist Robert Michels, who was also an early student of the power of charismatic leadership.[7] Mussolini was further greatly influenced by aspects of the growing socialist movement, especially its tendency towards hagiographical worship of leaders, and emotive public ceremonies and marches.

However, the repression of strike waves during 1912–14 led Mussolini to question whether the socialist movement could muster the force to seize power. Whilst similar considerations led some socialists to turn to reformism rather than revolution, they helped push Mussolini towards the belief that nationalism offered a better road to change. By 1919 he was developing a dual strategy to achieve power. This was based upon the formation of a disciplined movement to confront the growing left whilst simultaneously fighting elections, thereby opening up the prospect of an alliance of convenience with the weakly organized liberal Establishment parties and the forces of law and order.

Experience of fighting in the First World War led Mussolini to seek a paramilitary 'trenchocracy', a vanguard of young men who had served courageously in the trenches. This new Blackshirt elite was envisaged not simply as a paramilitary force, but also as the prototype of a 'new man', a priesthood actively committed to collective ideals rather than decadent and self-interested bourgeois ones. However, whilst Mussolini rejected the liberal view of 'economic man', he did not see Fascism as an emotional form of secular religion. Rather, at the heart of Fascism's strategy was a syncretism that sought to combine aspects of religious style with more concrete economic and strategic goals.[8]

Georges Sorel, the French philosopher and theorist, whom Mussolini acknowledged as a major influence, is typically portrayed in terms of his views about mobilizing myths. However, this prophet of the revolutionary general strike was unusual among socialists in his stress on productivism, which became a key element of Mussolini's thought following his conversion to nationalism. Similarly, several leading Fascist theorists, such as the former syndicalist Sergio Panunzio, sought to develop a Third Way between capitalism and socialism that would create prosperity and underpin social unity.

Economic growth was also vital to underpin Fascist aspirations for Italy to become a Great Power. Although Mussolini was a bitter critic of the Italian invasion of Libya in 1911, there was already a national and geopolitical dimension to his thought. While living in the Trentino, northern Italy, he experienced what he saw as Germanic racial arrogance and contempt for Latins. However, Mussolini also came into contact there with Pan-Germanist thought, which reinforced his belief that all Italians should be united within one state. This included not only those in the Alto Adige (South Tyrol) under Austrian rule, but also Italians who were scattered along the eastern Adriatic in what was to become Yugoslavia after 1919.

Mussolini was further influenced by the radical wing of the Italian Nationalist Association (ANI), which held that the Italian nation still needed to be born. In this vein, the writer and later Fascist intellectual Giovanni Papini wrote in 1914: 'Italy of 1860 had been shit dragged kicking and screaming towards unification by a daring minority, and shit it remains.' An important influence on these nationalists was the Japanese victory over Russia in 1905, which led to a quest for the equivalent of the warrior *Bushido* ethic in order to produce a nation capable of fighting modern war by overcoming bourgeois 'decadence'. Just as Japanese nationalists believed they had a right to expansion in Southeast Asia, Italian nationalists looked mainly to North Africa as Italy's rightful 'place in the sun'.[9]

Mussolini wrote in the preamble to the 1921 Fascist programme that 'The nation is . . . the supreme synthesis of all the material and immaterial values of the racial stock'. Although at times there was notable slippage in Mussolini's usage of 'race' (*razza*) and 'nation' (*nazione*), he basically held that Italian stock (*stirpe*) was based on a mixture stemming from historic expansion rather than a single race. Indeed, in 1932 he specifically rejected the existence of 'biologically pure races'. However, Mussolini was also influenced by fashionable early twentieth-century eugenic views, which led to a quest to boost domestic birth rates as part of the preparation for war (though this Battle for Births was also influenced by a desire to keep women within the home).[10] Eugenicism further encouraged fears about miscegenation abroad, which were sharpened after the brutal Italian suppression of opposition in Libya (1931) and the conquest of Abyssinia (1935–6).

In 1912 Italy annexed Tripolitania and Cyrenaica, which was to become Libya, in a renewed effort to join the 'scramble for Africa' that had been started thirty years before by Britain, France, and Germany. Initially Italian forces controlled little more than a few beachheads and townships. After Fascism came to power a ruthless war was waged against those who resisted Italian rule, involving tactics such as poisoning wells and herding civilians into camps. By 1931, opposition had been broken, leaving large numbers dead. However, the governor general, Italo Balbo, subsequently promised equal rights for native peoples. There was new investment and medical facilities that helped the native peoples. Mussolini even adopted the title 'Protector of Islam' and in a typically flamboyant gesture arranged for a jewel-encrusted 'Sword of Islam' to be presented to him in the Libyan capital during 1937.

Nevertheless, what became known as Italy's 'Fourth Shore' was essentially run in the interest of Italians. 'Unproductive' land was seized from the nomadic Bedouin to give to new immigrants, who came largely from Italy's poorer regions, and extensive olive groves were planted for export. The vast majority of investment was spent on infrastructure to help these immigrants. Similarly, after the conquest of Abyssinia in 1935–6, which involved tactics such as the use of poison gas, there was an attempt to promote Islamic institutions. However, these policies were mainly motivated by a desire to court Muslim opinion and destabilize British and French interests in Africa and the Middle East, and were secondary to the attempt to exploit Abyssinia for Italian ends.

Just before achieving victory in Abyssinia there had been tensions between Italy and Germany, including fears about German plans to incorporate Austria into a Greater Reich and wider ambitions in the Balkans that conflicted with Italian aspirations to be the dominant power in this region. However, British and French opposition to the

Abyssinian war had the effect of pushing the two fascist states closer together. So too did joining the German-Japanese anti-Commintern Pact in 1937. Shortly before, Mussolini had made his first state visit to Germany. In 1938 Hitler was feted in Rome, following Italian acceptance of the *Anschluss* with Austria in March.

A new line on race that was adopted during 1938 has often been seen as proof of increasing Nazi influence over Fascism.[11] This included the publication of a *Manifesto of Racial Scientists*, a *Charter of Race*, and the launch of *La difesa della razza*. The first cover of this glossy journal contrasted the faces of a Roman with a Jew and black African (the former set apart by a descending sword blow). New laws banned Jews from many positions; marriages with true Italians were forbidden; Jewish property was liable to confiscation.[12]

The new policy was not the complete break with Mussolini's past that some have claimed. Although he had for many years enjoyed a Jewish mistress, even before 1914 Mussolini had been concerned about Jewish power, a fear heightened by his belief following the imposition of sanctions after the Abyssinian invasion that world Jewry was at the heart of 'anti-fascism' and conspiring against Italy as well as Germany. Nevertheless, whilst a small number of leading Fascists like Roberto Farinacci openly expressed strongly anti-Semitic views from the early days, most did not. Indeed, relatively large numbers of Italy's 40,000–50,000 Jews joined the Fascist Party.[13]

An important aspect of this shift in racial discourse is related to the wider development of the Fascist Party, not least the way in which in spite of the cult of 'Il Duce', Mussolini's role was in many ways more that of a power broker than charismatic visionary. As part of his quest to achieve, and then consolidate, power during the 1920s, he had sought to weaken radical elements in the party. The formal incorporation of the Nationalist Association into the PNF, together with the entry of opportunists, also strengthened conservative forces on the domestic front, especially as social Catholic ideas displaced syndicalist and other more left-wing forms of Third Way thinking.

The decision in 1929 to sign the Concordat and Lateran Pacts with the Vatican, which virtually made the Catholic Church a state religion, marked a further tension with an official discourse that sought to create a 'new man'. Although it is misleading to portray Italy in the 1930s as a traditional authoritarian dictatorship, it was certainly a long way short of the 'ethical' totalitarian state envisaged by the pre-eminent philosopher of Fascism, Giovanni Gentile.[14] Extensive propaganda and new organizations such as the *Dopolavoro* (the National Recreational Club) provided cultural and leisure activities for the masses, but the Fascist message had not penetrated deeply into large sections of Catholic and working-class culture. Whilst victory in Abyssinia appears to have been popular, the regime relied more on conformity and coercion than mass enthusiasm (although the Italian Fascist state killed far fewer domestic opponents during peacetime than the Nazi one, the threat of repression was an omnipresent reality).

Prompted by growing criticisms of both the Fascist Party and regime against a background of economic problems, Mussolini responded to this atrophy by seeking in the late 1930s to relaunch the Fascist revolution through 'three punches to the belly of the bourgeoisie': namely, the anti-*Lei* campaign (*lei* was the formal second-person pronoun), the Nazi-inspired goose-step (disingenuously named the *passo romano*), and the 1938 racial measures. The last were particularly targeted at the Catholic Church. In spite of its important role historically in portraying Jews as Christ-killers (a charge also made by some Protestants), Catholicism was doctrinally opposed to biological racism.

The 1938 racial laws need to be further understood within the context of wider attitudes towards nation and race. There were undoubtedly some who well before 1938 held views similar to Nazism. For example, there were parallels between Fascists who celebrated a mystical relationship between the people and the land on which it lived (*strapaese*) and Nazi views about *Blut und Boden* ('Blood and Soil'). There were even stronger similarities between the geopolitical view that Italy had a right to find living space (*spazio vitale*) and the Nazi quest for *Lebensraum*. Among some scientists there were also clear affinities with Nazi biological racism, especially in eugenics-related fields such as breeding and health (concerns that widely permeated post-nineteenth-century European and American scientific thought).

However, the main school of Italian academic racial thought was influenced by cultural rather than biological thinking. This ridiculed the use of the term 'Aryan' in a racial context, and mocked Nordicists by contrasting the achievements of Ancient Rome with that of 'German' barbarians. In contrast to Nazi biological determinists, these Italianists generally supported a spiritual racism that emphasized the impact of environment or praised the Mediterranean race as the superior product of intermixing. Although Gentile celebrated the power of the 'totalitarian' state to create both a new man and order, he held that nationality was ultimately a moral choice. Gentile specifically rejected the view that biology could shape personal or national destiny as both epistemologically wrong and morally repugnant.[15]

There was also very strong opposition to the racial laws from some leading Fascists such as Balbo. He opposed adopting anti-Semitic laws in Libya partly because of the importance of Jews within the economy, but more generally because this Germanophobe objected on principle. Most Italians too seem to have opposed the 1938 racial measures and closer links with Germany. This helps explain why the vast majority of the Jews living in Italy escaped the fate that befell those who lived in Nazi-occupied Europe during 1939–45.

Nevertheless, it is important to challenge a long-held myth of the good Italian (*italiani brava gente*) who was innately humanitarian and resisted illegitimate laws.[16] Whilst anti-Semitism played no part in the rise of the Fascist movement, many Italians were clearly happy to concur with colonial expansion in Africa. Moreover, extensive anti-Semitic propaganda does seem to have had some effect on attitudes. This was especially the case during the death throes of Mussolini's Salò Republic after 1943, when the Duce tried to relaunch a more radical vision of Fascism amid the chaos of war. Whilst it was usually German troops who rounded up Jews for deportation, Fascists often participated and many Italians appeared indifferent to the fate of their fellow nationals.

NAZISM

Prior to the First World War, Hitler was not politically active, living as a marginal artist in Vienna until moving to Munich in 1913 and joining the Germany army in 1914. However, he read widely, including Arthur Schopenhauer, whose views about the 'will' influenced Friedrich Nietzsche, and the best-selling works of Houston Stewart Chamberlain, a British Germanophile (and son-in-law of Richard Wagner) who argued that 'Aryan' (a term borrowed from linguistics, primarily to refer to modern north European) civilization was threatened by alien influences and inferior races.[17]

It remains unclear whether Hitler's virulent anti-Semitism stemmed mainly from this period, as he claimed in *Mein Kampf* (1925–6), or more from the traumas of defeat in 1918 and its aftermath. Nevertheless, there seems little doubt that whilst living in the Austrian capital he underwent a fertile political apprenticeship. He learned about the use of anti-Semitism by new parties, and more generally became familiar with the populist styles of Karl Lueger and Georg Ritter von Schönerer, who used a 'low' politics language to distance themselves from the established political elite.[18]

After the war, Hitler did not wish to see a return to the old elite-dominated *Kaiserreich* and possibly had sympathies for moderate social democrats who had supported the German cause in 1914. However, his fervent pan-Germanism and hostility to 'Jewish' Marxism induced his military superiors to retain him as an anti-'Bolshevik' propagandist in Munich. During September 1919 this led him to join the new German Workers' Party (DAP), which in 1920 changed its name to the National Socialist German Workers' Party. A year later, Hitler's oratorical talents helped him to become party leader.

Initially, Hitler saw his mission as that of the drummer boy of nationalist revolution, not as a national saviour. The Nazis were a small party that mainly sought to appeal to ex-combattants across the class divide. Symbolic of this strategy was the adoption by the paramilitary brown-shirted *Sturmabteilung* (SA), and later the black-shirted *Schutzstaffel* (SS), of the death-head emblem (*Totenkopf*) that had been used by elite 'Stormtroops' who drew their members from all classes by the end of the First World War. It was, therefore, a symbol both of militarism and a new egalitarian-elitism that 'front experience' writers like Ernst Jünger celebrated as 'blood socialism'.

However, after the failure of the violent 1923 Munich *Putsch*, Hitler's views changed. During his trial and brief imprisonment he increasingly saw himself as the future *Führer*, and a growing Hitler cult developed within the party. Linked to this was a new electoral strategy. An important figure in this change was the First World War fighter ace, Hermann Göring, who after the Munich *Putsch* fled to Italy and came to appreciate the Fascists' dual strategy of violence against the left, accompanied by growing success at the polls, as a way of pressuring the Establishment and Janus-faced state without provoking it into repression.

Following disappointing election results in 1928, more emphasis was placed on broadening the Nazi Party's appeal. A key part of this strategy stressed economic issues that acquired greater importance with the onset of the Depression in 1929. There had always been members of the party who had taken a strong interest in economics. Notable in the party's early days was Gottfried Feder, who had lectured to Hitler while an army propagandist. Feder stressed an old *völkisch* trope that distinguished between 'rapacious' and 'productive' capital, which appealed to Hitler, especially as the former could be associated with Jews in professions such as banking.

The new economic strategy involved targeting specific groups, such as farm workers who made up almost 30 per cent of the German labour force. The approach also focused on the local level, which involved the training of speakers, the dissemination of propaganda, and the infiltration of existing groups as well as the setting up of new Nazi ones. A key figure in planning the rural campaign was Walther Darré, who popularized the phrase *Blut und Boden* ('Blood and Soil') and advocated an almost medieval form of peasant corporatism. However, in the urban areas propaganda focused more on 'Work and Bread', and was targeted at the working class.

This was supported by a major national campaign focusing on Hitler, who travelled by aeroplane to make two or more major speeches in a day at times during 1932. Propaganda portrayed the Führer in almost God-like terms, as a man sent by providence to save Germany. Revealingly, by this time the Nazis were widely referred to as the 'Hitler Party', and there seems little doubt that Hitler appealed to a wide range of voters. This charismatic appeal, together with the local campaigns, was crucial to the Nazis gaining easily the largest vote in the 1932 Reichstag elections, reaching almost 40 per cent in July.

Behind the scenes, more respectable members of the Nazi leadership like Göring courted business and Establishment support for the Nazis' entry into government by stressing their anti-left credentials. Anti-Semitism was also played down in most campaigning, partly because it was not popular in some areas but also because rabble-rousing threatened the strategy of courting Establishment support. Eventually in early 1933 President Hindenburg appointed Hitler as Chancellor in the hope that this would provide stability.

In his first broadcast as Chancellor, Hitler began by hailing fellow Germans with the revealing compound term 'national-comrade' (*Volksgenossen*). The Nazis promised a *Volksgemeinshaft*, a racially pure national community that would transcend divisions. However, it is important to note that there were notable differences within the Nazi Party concerning racism.

Among the rank and file, hostility to Jews does not appear to have been a major factor leading people to join the party, although paranoid anti-Semites were strongly represented among older members who held leading party offices by the 1930s.[19] Among the political leadership, there was a widespread tendency to Manichaeanism, but the key enemy was not always the Jews, as some focused more on the left and even the Establishment. For example, Gregor Strasser, who had played a key role in the party reorganization after 1928, and Joseph Goebbels, who became Propaganda Minister in 1933, saw the idea of National Socialism itself as more important than race. There were also different forms of anti-Semitism within the Nazi leadership, and differences over the relative importance of race.

Hitler held that the Jews were responsible for Germany's defeat; he also believed that Jews were behind communist revolution and rapacious capitalism, both of which threatened the nation. He believed that there was a widespread Jewish conspiracy against the Aryan peoples of the type portrayed by *The Protocols of the Elders of Zion*, a Tsarist forgery that enjoyed widespread sales in Germany after 1918 and reinforced the Manichaean fears. This claim figured prominently in the 1940 Nazi propaganda film *The Eternal Jew*, which held that the Jews believed they were the master race!

Hitler's views about the Jewish nature of Bolshevism were reinforced by Alfred Rosenberg, who saw himself as the NSDAP's main theorist of race. However, whilst Rosenberg's book *The Myth of the Twentieth Century* was the second most distributed Nazi book after *Mein Kampf*, Hitler does not appear to have read *Der Mythos* (nor do many other Germans!). Indeed, he rejected Rosenberg's spiritual rather than biological view of race. Hitler also opposed Rosenberg's quest for a 'new religion' of the blood, partly because he sought to avoid conflict with the Christian churches. During the Nazi rise to power, many in the Protestant churches had helped the cause, and after the Nazis achieved power some Catholic priests aligned traditional Christian anti-Semitism with National Socialism and especially supported the anti-Bolshevik crusade.[20]

Hitler's quest for an accommodation with these churches occasionally led to tensions with Heinrich Himmler, the leader of the elite corps known as the SS (abbreviation of *Schutzstaffel*) who sought to suppress Christian festivals such as Christmas and promote new forms of secular worship. When Himmler joined the Nazi Party in 1925 he was already a member of the Thule Society, which preached that the greatness of Germany reached back to the Teutonic tribes' defeat of the Romans. Himmler's views were further influenced by influential Nordicist academics such as H. F. K. Günther, who sought the preservation of the Aryan race under German leadership against the threat from Jews and inferior Slavs. This led to the development of a SS German-led Europeanism, which can be seen most clearly in the propaganda surrounding the wartime *Waffen* SS divisions recruited in occupied countries both to fight communism and for the preservation of the Aryan race. The idea of a post-war German-led new Aryan Europe can also be found among some economic planners and technocrats, though for most the primary concern was securing German prosperity.

There were differences too among the academics who supported Nazism. The friend-foe dichotomy of the eminent legal-political theorist, Carl Schmitt, led him to see Jews as an alien threat and his concept of *Grossraum* legitimated German expansion to the east. However, he saw the nation as an ethnic-cultural community based on history rather than biology and he was denounced by some Nazis as an opportunist Catholic. Among anthropologists and especially scientists there was a tendency to see race more in terms of biology, although there were differences over issues such as whether cross-breeding could be beneficial.[21] Such eugenicist thinking, which was strong long before the Nazis came to power, influenced the post-1933 sterilization programme of women who were deemed mentally infirm or disabled.[22] Other policies to boost the healthy Aryan population and its martial qualities included improved welfare provision for 'German' mothers of young children (though as in Italy, this was also linked to views about the role of women).

In spite of differences of opinion over race, anti-Semitism was a core driving principle of the Nazi regime. Initially, Jews were forced out of influential fields, such as the media and the universities. The 1935 Nuremberg Laws banned marriages and sexual liaisons between Germans and Jews. Revealing confusions about racial science, Jewishness was judged on religious affiliation going back to the grandparents rather than biology. These Laws also removed German citizenship from those who were not considered of German blood. Whilst specifically aimed at Jews, in practice these laws also encompassed Roma and Sinti who were declared to be of 'alien blood'. By 1939 fewer than 200,000 of the 500,000 Jews who had lived in pre-Hitler Germany remained. The vast majority had emigrated, usually having had their assets largely stolen by Nazi Party members and those who had competed with these Jews.

In *Mein Kampf* Hitler had argued that the state's highest task was 'the preservation and intensification of the race'.[23] This involved not merely making Germany 'Jew free', but territorial expansion to the east. In part this sought to rectify major losses imposed by the Versailles Treaty of 1919. However, expansion was also seen in geopolitical terms—a quest for colonial resources that would underpin Germany's destiny as a Great Power without bringing down the ire of the Western Great Powers, especially the British.

Hitler in many ways admired the British achievement in ruling over nearly a quarter of the world's land mass. Although Hitler's view of the USA was in general more hostile, he was impressed by the way in which the early settlers had tamed new lands by settling them with superior stock. Indeed, he sometimes talked of the Volga as Germany's Mississippi, with clear allusions to ethnic cleansing of Native Americans as well as economic dynamism. This parallel arguably had a far stronger influence on Hitler than that claimed for Soviet mass killings, though Hitler publicly referred in the early 1930s to mass starvations in the Ukraine and was aware of Stalin's later great purges.

In a speech in January 1939 Hitler had prophesied that if international Jewish bankers again plunged the nations into world war, the result would not be the triumph of Bolshevism but the annihilation of the Jewish race in Europe. However, at this time there was no specific policy of extermination. Prior to late 1939, concentration camps were used mainly for political prisoners and other targets such as homosexuals. Some Jews were even allowed to leave for Palestine. Indeed, unlike in the Soviet Union where millions had been directly or indirectly killed by the state, 'only' about 10,000 German Jews had died at the hands of the Nazis before war began against Poland.

The conquest of Poland in 1939, and especially the invasion of Russia in 1941, brought large numbers of Slavs, several million Jews, and a far smaller number of Roma, Sinta, and other inferior peoples under Nazi rule. Initially, there were several plans for the Jewish population, including deportation to Madagascar. However, with no serious hope of major forced emigration, planning quickly came to focus on the ghettoization of Jews and the development of concentration camps within the new borders. This was seen as especially important for limiting Jewish access to scarce food and other supplies and in exploiting the Jews as forced labour, plans that were often initiated at a local level.[24]

The precise steps that led to the general decision to commit genocide remain contested. Some historians point to the way in which the 'euthanasia' programme developed after 1939 provided the core staff and means for mass killing by gassing. Others have stressed the importance of technocratic issues about public health in the ghettoes and camps, which escalated into plans for genocide through a process of 'cumulative radicalization'. However, there seems little doubt that Hitler exerted a charismatic authority over his inner circle who sought to implement his will. Genocide thus stemmed more from the top down, through a process of key figures like Himmler vying for favour by 'working towards the Führer' in a polyocracy where the formal executive structure of government had long since broken down, though the state retained a veneer of legality.[25]

Hitler's racism was further crucial in failing to exploit anti-communist sentiment as the Nazis swept forward in 1941. The Führer thought that only a minority of Slavs who had some link with earlier waves of expansion could be re-Germanized; the rest were to remain at best an underclass to serve their new masters. A few leading Nazis wanted to recruit Slavs to help the German cause, and some were deployed to help massacre Jews and to staff the concentration camps. Such help sometimes emerged spontaneously, given the traditions of anti-Semitism in these areas, though there is little doubt that the prospect of spoils added to the number of volunteers (among collaborationist elites the motivation was more geopolitical support of Germany against the Soviet Union).[26] This meant that genocide was locally aided and abetted in a way lacking in other forms of colonialism.

However, there was no serious attempt to turn this into a wider anti-Bolshevik crusade until it was too late to stem the advancing tide of the Red Army. As well as prejudice against Slavs, such collaboration ran counter to Himmler's policy of settling Germans in parts of conquered Eastern Europe. 'Blood Is Our Frontier', a common slogan among SS intellectuals, reveals that what was sought was not simply geopolitical 'space' in which to exploit inferior peoples and provide buffer zones. It was more an ethnically cleansed *Lebensraum*, requiring the forced removal of the Slavic population, which was often undertaken with great brutality towards these racial inferiors. Indeed, many died, most commonly through starvation. This encouraged the surviving population to support the Resistance, whose activities in turn were met by a spiral of violent reprisals.

These deportations, and the mass killings of Jews by shooting before the gassing programme was fully in operation in 1942, were often carried out by ordinary soldiers rather than special units (*Einsatzgruppen*). Again, this marks a notable difference from most forms of modern colonialism where territorial aggrandizement was achieved by limited armed forces using new technology such as the rifle and machine gun against 'natives' (a major exception was the bloody Japanese geopolitical-racist expansionism after 1930).[27]

The involvement of many 'ordinary Germans' in mass killings raises major questions about the attitudes and motivations of those involved.[28] Were most Germans imbued with a deep racist ideology, dating back to early Christian anti-Semitism, nineteenth-century nationalism, and the rise of racial science?[29] Or did conformity to orders among Germans stem more from what has been termed the 'banality of evil', the ability to engender compliance with 'legitimate' orders, especially among those not directly involved in killing?[30]

Certainly the evidence points to the fact that anti-Semitism was not a significant element contributing to the electoral triumph of the Nazis in 1933, although some Germans later appreciated the economic benefits that ensued thereafter as Jews were increasingly eliminated from economic life. Many Germans also endorsed a war against communism, which Nazi propaganda had closely linked with Jews. However, the main general impact of propaganda appears to have been more to inure Germans to the fate of Jews and racial inferiors, rather than creating a nation of fanatics who saw killing as part of a racial crusade.

French and Romanian Fascism

France's first fascist party was the *Faisceau*, founded in 1925 by Georges Valois. Born into the working class, Valois had been a leading theorist of the pre-war authoritarian-nationalist and overtly Catholic *Action Française* (AF), founded at the time of the Dreyfus Affair (1894–early 1900s), which had bitterly divided France over the false imprisonment of a Jewish army officer.

Immediately prior to the First World War, Valois had come together with Sorel and other syndicalists to form the *Cercle Proudhon*, which has been portrayed as setting out the first fully fledged fascist ideology.[31] However, whilst this was a notable harbinger of attempts to synthesize socialism, nationalism, and religion, it was Valois's experience of fighting in the First World War that provided the final push in his conversion to clearly fascist views. This led him to place great emphasis on the need for new young leadership, which would create a technocratic-modernizing state, and drive forward the economic regeneration needed to divert the working class from communism and finance the armed forces necessary to withstand a future resurgent Germany.

In spite of his earlier anti-Semitic views, Valois declared after 1918 that Jews had an 'incontestable creative fever'. He was also affected by the sacrifices of the many Jews who fought for France during 1914–18. However, the old paranoia and rhetoric about Jewish plots and power never completely disappeared from Faisceau propaganda. Indeed, this slant grew as internally the party became plagued by divisions over policy, not least between its Catholic corporatists and more radical exponents of a Third Way.

Although there were only about 200,000 Jews in France, some leading members of the Faisceau argued for their expulsion claiming that they held excessive influence in the corridors of economic and political power. Nevertheless, for at least a decade after the First World War anti-Semitism proved a less powerful rallying cry among a notable section of the French people than it had been a generation earlier. Lacking the charisma to exert a wider appeal, or to unite the Faisceau's burgeoning factions, Valois wound the movement up in 1928 and began a journey to the left. (He later joined the Resistance and died in a German concentration camp.)

It is commonly argued that neither the economic nor political conditions were present in France to spawn a mass-based fascist movement.[32] The trajectory of the *Parti Populaire Français*, founded in 1936 by the former young communist leader Jacques Doriot, illustrates these problems well. The PPF's programme initially was based on Third Way economics and attacks on the growing Communist Party, but propaganda about 'Judeo-bolshevik' and other Jewish conspiracies quickly became more prominent. Some hoped that this would boost the PPF's fortunes, though other factors behind this development included hostility to the Popular Front's Jewish prime minister, Léon Blum, and financial support from anti-Semitic business interests.

As was the case with the Faisceau, association with 'capitalists' added to the difficulties of appealing to left-wing constituencies, whilst France's *notable*-dominated conservative parties were rooted in strong, locally based patron-client ties. Moreover, unlike in Italy and Germany, there was little sympathy for the radical right within key groups such as the police and judiciary, which helped prevent street confrontations escalating into a spiral of abuse and violence, simultaneously heightening the fear that the mainstream parties and liberal democratic state could not withstand the new challengers.

Whilst the numbers were not large, the PPF attracted some major intellectuals, though they were attracted to fascism via different routes. One was the novelist Pierre Drieu La Rochelle, who saw himself as a member of a race rather than a nation, holding that the French had at least three identities: Nordic, Celtic, and Mediterranean. He thus preached a form of ethno-regionalism within a federal Europe, which he further saw as vital to the defence against both the American and Soviet menaces. Drieu's novels associated Jews with decadence, weak parliamentary government, and crass materialism—though like Doriot, his most extreme statements came after becoming a Nazi collaborator following the fall of France in 1940.

Another writer who, having begun his political life in the anti-German *Action Française*, was to end it as a Nazi collaborator, was Robert Brasillach. Brasillach broke with the small *Action Française*, led by the ageing Charles Maurras, in a quest for more youthful leadership and Third Way socioeconomic polices. He regarded himself as only a 'moderate' anti-Semite, but this 'moderation' encompassed advocating laws to exclude Jews from the national community, including French-born Jews as well as recent arrivals, who were the focus of growing anti-Semitism in the 1930s. Brasillach also blamed the Jews for the onset of war!

The defeat of France was accompanied by the establishment of a regime based in the town of Vichy in unoccupied France and headed by Marshall Pétain, the feted 'saviour of Verdun' in the First World War. Members of this regime came from eclectic political backgrounds, though there were notable links with the *Action Française* and increasingly after 1940 with those who had been active in fascist politics during the 1930s. The policies of the Vichy regime were a mixture of reactionary attempts to roll back liberalization and secularization with more technocratic planning for a 'New Order'. This complex and dynamic mix helps explain why there have been major debates about whether it should be seen as a form of authoritarian rather than fascist regime, with most commentators tending towards the former categorization.[33]

There have also been notable debates about the Vichy regime's racial policy. It quickly introduced laws debarring Jews from many offices and professions, though war veterans were an initial exception. During 1942 French police helped round up foreign Jews for deportation to the concentration camps in eastern Europe, though later attempts to round up French nationals ran into notably more opposition. Some have defended the Vichy regime's policies, arguing that it acted as a shield against more radical German policies and/or was ultimately forced into compliance. However, it is now more correctly held that Vichy was in many ways the culmination of a deep racist strand in French politics that had first become clear during the late nineteenth century (and which was not confined entirely to the right). Certainly in the Italian-occupied part of France, Jews stood a much greater chance of survival, as in general the occupiers refused to hand them over to the Germans.

There has also been notable debate about how to classify the Romanian Iron Guard, which many have argued was populist or clerico-fascist rather than truly fascist.[34] Certainly politics were in many ways different in a country that was largely rural and where levels of illiteracy were higher than in Germany and even Italy. Nevertheless, it is possible to identify forms of fascism in Romania, of which what is commonly termed the Iron Guard movement was by far the most prominent.

It was founded in 1927 by Corneliu Codreanu, a law graduate who heard Hitler speak while a student in Germany, where he also learned of the 'March on Rome' in October 1922 by Mussolini's Fascists. Codreanu claimed his movement was not a copy of either. Certainly a key difference compared to early Italian Fascism was the Iron Guard's strident anti-Semitism. However, Codreanu claimed that Mussolini would have been anti-Semitic if he had lived in a country where Jewish elites exercised immense power, and ordinary Jews separated themselves through dress and language! Moreover, the Guard developed a cult of modern-day Romanians as direct descendants of the Dacians, establishing a link with the glories of Ancient Rome in the same manner as the Italian Fascists.

A major difference compared to both Fascism and Nazism was that the Iron Guard was overtly Orthodox Christian.[35] Initially known as the Legion of the Archangel Michael, the Guard was organized like a religious order, and its style was in many ways irrational and mystical. Its young members, known as Legionnaires, were officially asked 'to embrace death'. Given that Romania had gained significant new territory after the First World War, this was not part of an attempt to create a militaristic culture in order to expand, though force was seen as necessary to keep ethnic minorities in check and especially to defend the expanded frontiers. Rather, this was a mixture of cult and political tactic, in which Legionaries embraced a willingness to assassinate their enemies, risk their own lives, and even the salvation of their own souls.

However, it is important not to see the Guard as simply a millenarian movement led by a charismatic individual, or a movement largely exploiting anti-Semitic traditions that ran deep in Orthodox culture. The Guard attracted several notable intellectuals, including two who later achieved major international reputations, Mircea Eliade and E. M Cioran. The latter was symptomatic of many who turned to fascism, focusing on the alleged degeneracy of contemporary culture, which he saw as requiring a radical new regime to reverse. Another intellectual supporter of the Iron Guard was the corporatist economist Mihail Manoilescu, who sought to develop a 'national-Christian socialism'. This encompassed policies to prevent the workers turning to communism, including the creation of national syndicates and public works.[36]

Corporatism was a notable aspect of the Guard's attempt to appeal to workers at a time of economic instability. There was also an economic dimension in its appeal to the parochial peasantry, who appear to have been less attracted to nationalist arguments than the urban middle class and more concerned with parochial issues. For example, Codreanu promised a cow to some, a patch of land to others, and even told some peasants before the 1937 elections that they would be given free merchandise.

By the time of these elections, the Guard had proportionally more members than the PNF before the March on Rome, or the NSDAP before Hitler became Chancellor. Running under the name 'Totul pentru Ţară' ('Everything for the Country'), it officially won 16 per cent of the vote, though its true support was much higher as the elections were partly rigged.[37]

During 1938, King Carol decided to suspend the democratic Constitution, using rising violence between groups as the pretext (even some liberals saw this as preferable to an Iron Guard-led government). Codreanu and several other fascist leaders were arrested, accused of being in the pay of Germany, and killed 'while trying to escape'. Although authoritarian, Carol had no sympathy for the Guard, which in turn bitterly attacked the monarch on account of his Jewish mistress and clique of friends. Moreover, Carol had learned from the Italian and especially the German experience that seeking to tame fascism for Establishment purposes was playing with fire.

By 1940, the Axis victories made the Romanian political situation more favourable to the remaining Guard leadership and Codreanu's successor, Horia Sima, was invited to become the first Legionary minister. Shortly afterwards the Legion allied with General Ion Antonescu to create a National Legionary State, which forced the abdication of Carol. However, in early 1941 Antonescu suppressed a Legion coup, following growing lawlessness. Although Sima was forced to flee to Germany, the anti-Jewish campaign continued to gather pace under the authoritarian-nationalist Antonescu regime. What had started in the late 1930s with Nuremberg-style laws, followed by persecution and even killings, escalated into mass killings after Romania joined the invasion of the Soviet Union (Operation Barbarossa) in June 1941, often through localized pogroms of Roma as well as Jews.

The vast majority of these killings took place in territories acquired after the break up of the multi-ethnic Austro-Hungarian and Russian empires following the First World War, or within the new multi-ethnic Soviet Empire during Operation Barbarossa. Although Jews in the rump of Romania suffered badly, some appear to have been protected by a sense of residual citizenship, though others effectively purchased their survival.

None of these policies were initiated at the request of the Nazi Germans. And whilst members of the Iron Guard played a prominent part in the murders, unduly focusing on their role glosses over the far wider set of historical and social forces that led to genocide in Romania.

Conclusion

One leading student of nationalism has argued that Nazism cannot be considered a member of part of the nationalist family on account of its pursuit of a racial 'Aryan' order, which far transcended Germany's pre-1914 borders and even the Germanic parts of the Austrian Empire.[38]

However, as the above case studies show, the lines between nationalism and racism are complex and fluid. Hitler was both a nationalist and racist, holding that Germany was in the vanguard of the defence of a wider Aryan people, which meant geopolitical expansion and war with Soviet communism in order to ensure German-led prosperity. Mussolini did not believe that an Italian nation had yet been formed, and later turned on the Jews partly in an attempt to create a Fascist 'new man' who would ensure Italian hegemony over a new empire, which would similarly underpin Great Power status.

Maurice Bardèche, Brasillach's brother-in-law and a rare intellectual who after 1945 accepted the label 'fascist', has written that: 'There is not the slightest logical, necessary, automatic link between fascism and racism.'[39] Bardèche was seeking to rehabilitate a movement based on its early Italian form, rightly pointing to the fact that there was no necessary connection between fascism and hostility to Jews. However, written out of Bardèche's history was the tendency of fascisms to turn to anti-Semitism at critical junctures. Moreover, whilst there were forms of fascism that did not advocate military expansion, all accepted that war between nations and races was a driving force of history—that some peoples were more fit to rule than others.

In this sense fascism and racism are intimately intertwined. Nevertheless, there are dangers in overstressing the link in terms of explaining why fascism arose and gathered support because, in the paradigmatic cases of Italy and Germany, overt racism, especially anti-Semitism, was not crucial to gaining either elite or mass support.[40]

NOTES

1. Following Anglophone common practice, this chapter uses 'F' to refer to the specifically Italian variant and 'f' to refer to 'generic' fascism.
2. For a more general treatment of these nationalist movements, see Chapter 21 by Oliver Zimmer.
3. M. Burleigh and W. Wipperman (1992) *The Racial State: Germany 1933–45*, Cambridge, 306.
4. See especially R. Griffin (ed.) (2005) *Fascism, Totalitarianism and Political Religion*, London.
5. R. Eatwell (2009) 'On Defining Generic Fascism: The "Fascist Minimum" and the "Fascist Matrix"', in C. Iordachi (ed.) *Comparative Fascist Studies: New Approaches*, Abingdon.
6. For example, R. Bessel (2005) *Nazism and War*, London, esp. 3.
7. R. Eatwell (2009) 'Propaganda, Violence and the Rise of Fascism', in A. Costa-Pinto (ed.) *Rethinking the Nature of Fascism*, Basingstoke.
8. B. Mussolini (1935) *Fascism: Doctrine and Institutions*, Rome, 59.
9. On Japanese nationalism, see Chapter 14 by Rana Mitter and on its broader ideological influence, see Chapter 34 by Cemil Aydin.
10. V. de Grazia (1992) *How Fascism Ruled Women: Italy, 1922–45*, Berkeley, CA.
11. M. Michaelis (1978) *Mussolini and the Jews: German-Italian Relations and the Jewish Question in Italy, 1922–1945*, Oxford.
12. J. D. Zimmerman (2005) *Jews in Italy under Fascist and Nazi Rule, 1922–1945*, Cambridge.
13. A. Gillette (2002) *Racial Theories in Fascist Italy*, London, 44.
14. D. Roberts (2006) *The Totalitarian Experiment in Twentieth-Century Europe*, London; cf. R. Bosworth (1998) *The Italian Dictatorship*, London.
15. A. J. Gregor (2005) *Mussolini's Intellectuals*, Princeton, NJ.
16. M. Sarfatti (2006) *The Jews in Mussolini's Italy: From Equality to Persecution*, Madison, WI.
17. For links between Nietzsche and earlier nationalist ideas, see Chapter 3 by Erica Benner.
18. B. Hamann (1999) *Hitler's Vienna: A Dictator's Apprenticeship*, New York.
19. P. H. Merkl (1975) *Political Violence under the Swastika: 581 Early Nazis*, Princeton, NJ.
20. K. P. Spicer (2008) *Hitler's Priests: Catholic Clergy and National Socialism*, DeKalb, IL.
21. C. M. Hutton (2005) *Race and the Third Reich*, Cambridge.
22. P. Weindling (1989) *Health, Race and German Politics between National Unification and Nazism, 1870–1945*, Cambridge.
23. A. Hitler (1925–6, 1969) *Mein Kampf*, London, 355.
24. C. Browning (2004) *The Origins of the Final Solution: The Evolution of Nazi Jewish Policy September 1939–March 1942*, London; and A. Kallis (2008) *Fascism and Genocide in Inter-War Europe*, London.
25. I. Kershaw (1997) *Hitler, 1896–1936: Hubris*, London.
26. D. Stone (2010) *Histories of the Holocaust*, Oxford.
27. Cf. its portrayal in the nationalist Yasukuni Museum in Tokyo, where expansion is portrayed as liberation from racist Europeans.
28. C. Browning (2001) *Ordinary Men: Reserve Police Battalion 101 and the Final Solution in Poland*, London.
29. D. Goldhagen (1996) *Hitler's Willing Executioners*, London.
30. H. Arendt (1994) *Eichmann in Jerusalem: A Report on the Banality of Evil*, London.

31. Z. Sternhell et al. (1992) *The Birth of Fascist Ideology*, Princeton, NJ.
32. B. Jenkins (ed.) (2007) *France in the Era of Fascism*, Oxford.
33. On this simple and at times misleading heuristic distinction, see J. Linz (2000) *Totalitarian and Authoritarian Regimes*, London.
34. For a good survey of different types of fascism, see S. G. Payne (1995) *A History of Fascism, 1914–45*, Madison, WI.
35. C. Iordachi (2004) *Charisma, Politics and Violence: The Legion of the 'Archangel Michael' in Inter-War Romania*, Trondheim.
36. L. Volovici (1991) *Nationalist Ideology and Antisemitism: The Case of Romanian Intellectuals in the 1930s*, Oxford.
37. For more on fascist electoral support in Italy, Germany, and Romania, see M. Mann (2002) *Fascists*, Cambridge.
38. A. D. Smith (1979) *Nationalism in the Twentieth Century*, New York.
39. M. Bardèche (1961) *Qu'est-ce-que le fascisme?*, Paris, 53.
40. I am grateful to John Breuilly, Aristotle Kallis, and James Eatwell for comments on earlier drafts.

Suggested Further Reading

Browning, C. R. (2004) *The Origins of the Final Solution: The Evolution of Nazi Jewish Policy September 1939–March 1942*, Lincoln. A detailed historical account of the origins of the Final Solution, which whilst recognizing the role of lower orders and technocrats, takes on board the recent focus on more ideological and Hitler-centric accounts.

Burleigh, M. and Wippermann, W. (1991) *The Racial State: Germany 1933–45*, Cambridge. A powerful statement of the uniqueness of Nazism, especially on account of its racism and ultimate policy of genocide.

Gillette, A. (2002) *Racial Theories in Fascist Italy*, London. This shows the different strands in Italian racism, including a Mediterranean one that is contrasted to Nazi Nordicism.

Gregor, A. J. (2005) *Mussolini's Intellectuals*, Princeton, NJ. This attempts to show that none of the key intellectuals within Italian Fascism was racist, but glosses over issues such as Italian racial science and imperial practice.

Hutton, C. M. (2005) *Race and the Third Reich: Linguistics, Racial Anthropology and Genetics in the Dialectic of Volk*, Cambridge. This focuses on academic racial anthropology, human biology, and linguistics, showing that many race theorists rejected the idea of an Aryan race.

Kallis, A. (2008) *Genocide and Fascism: The Eliminationist Drive in Fascist Europe*, London. An excellent general survey, though it overstresses the role of Fascism's utopian emphasis on national/racial rebirth in the realm of concrete events.

Kershaw, I. (1997) *Hitler, 1896–1936: Hubris*, London, and (2000) *Hitler, 1936–45: Nemesis*, London. The best biography of Hitler, by a German specialist who accepts that Nazism was fascist (whilst challenging how useful the concept of 'generic fascism' is theoretically).

Sarfatti, M. (2006) *The Jews in Mussolini's Italy: From Equality to Persecution*, Madison, WI. An important general study and corrective to the belief that the vast majority of Italians were repulsed by anti-Semitism and the myth of the good Italian (*brava gente*).

Stone, D. (2010) *Histories of the Holocaust*, Oxford. This highlights the importance of economic gain as well as anti-Semitic ideology for many perpetrators; also stresses the impact of global imperialism on wider racial thought and genocide.
Zimmerman, J. D. (ed.) (2005) *Jews in Italy under Fascist and Nazi Rule 1922–1945*, Cambridge. A good collection of essays covering Mussolini, the impact of the racial laws, the post-1943 German occupation, the Vatican, et cetera.

CHAPTER 30

NATIONALISM WITHOUT STATES

MONTSERRAT GUIBERNAU

INTRODUCTION

Do all nationalisms seek their own state? Are all nationalisms separatist? To date the main Catalan nationalist parties have not been secessionist; nor have the Galician, Welsh, and Corsican ones. Even in Scotland popular support for independence is recent, linked to the Scottish National Party governing Scotland since 2007. Should these non-secessionist 'nationalisms' be redefined as 'regionalisms'? Surely not, since all these parties seek the protection, enhancement, and development of the 'nations' they claim to represent.

Not all nationalisms pursue secessionist aims; not all nations have a state of their own. Some scholars consider that nationalism without states is synonymous with 'regionalism' or 'federalism' and should never be referred to as 'nationalism'. I challenge this approach, which fails to make clear-cut distinctions between the concepts of nation, state, and nationalism.

The state is a political institution. According to Max Weber the state is 'a human community that (successfully) claims the monopoly of the legitimate use of physical force within a given territory.'[1] By 'nation' I refer to a human group conscious of forming a community, sharing a common culture, attached to a clearly demarcated territory, having a common past and a common project for the future, and claiming the right to decide upon its political destiny. This definition attributes five dimensions to the nation: psychological, cultural, territorial, political, and historical.[2] Not all nations have a state of their own and not all states are coextensive with a nation.

Nationalism is both sentiment and political ideology. It refers to the sentiment of belonging to a community—the nation—whose members identify with a culture, history, and territory, and have the will to decide upon their common political destiny.

It also refers to the political ideology whose objective is to secure the nation's 'right to decide' upon its political destiny. While some nations are happy to maintain the status of region, province, member of a federation, or autonomous community, others demand independence. Within a single nation we find different views concerning the nation's future, including its political status.

Nationalism, the State, and the Nation

Most so-called nation states are not constituted by a single nation, which is coextensive with the state;[3] internal diversity is the rule. The nations or parts of nations included within a single state do not share similar levels of national awareness. Nations are not unique and fixed, and history records the disintegration of some nations, which have played a prominent role during a particular period, and the creation of new ones.

The state tends to absorb functions and to resist delegating any it considers integral to its sovereignty. The argument for state centralization is closely connected to the idea of state sovereignty understood as full control over all matters concerning the social, political, and economic life of its citizens. The increasing number of international organizations, multinational companies, supranational social movements, and the technical sophistication of modern warfare currently challenge this classic concept of state sovereignty.

In addition to these external pressures the state is under pressure to modify its centralized form and acknowledge internally the existence of territorially circumscribed cultural communities that show varying degrees of national self-consciousness while advancing different sociopolitical demands. The origins of most of these communities pre-date the formation of the nation state.

The nationalism of nations without states emerges as a sociopolitical movement that defends the right of peoples to decide upon their own political destiny. Some forms of nationalism endorse democratic means in this quest, others employ violence, just as some states are democratic and others violent and authoritarian. However, all these movements share the will to develop their specific culture and language, whenever it exists, and to be represented in the institutions that decide their future. The number of people involved in a movement indicates the strength of such nationalism; a massive following is more difficult to ignore if the state wants to maintain democratic credibility.

Romanticism and the Nation: The Preservation of Language and Culture

The primary conviction of Romantic nationalism is that culture, a particular way of life, and important social institutions are essentially formed and shaped by the nation.[4] They are expressions of a unitary force usually referred to as the soul, mind, or spirit of a people. Alongside an interest in language, there emerges a specific interest in history—the glorious past, myths of origin, customs, ways of life, and ideas of a particular people.

Contemporary forms of nationalism in nations without states also invoke the pre-eminence of the nation and value of its culture and language. However, while Romantic nationalism provided justifications for cultural claims on behalf of small nations, contemporary nationalisms extend beyond the defence of minority languages and cultures to make claims for political autonomy that may or may not involve independence.

According to Thomas Nipperdey, Romantic nationalism was a reaction to intellectual hegemony based on the Enlightenment, as well as to the imperial uniformity threatened by the expansion of Napoleonic France.[5] In an analogous way, the nationalism of nations without states is a response to the perceived threat of cultural homogenization associated with contemporary globalization. Americanization of culture and the rise of English as a dominant language have prompted reactions in various nation states as well as in nations without states. They are all concerned about their cultures being replaced by an increasingly pervasive global culture that permeates public life and even intrudes into the private sphere.

Romantic nationalism contributed to the creation of new nation states, such as Germany and Italy in 1870–1.[6] It also achieved prominence among the peoples of western Europe who lived in national states, as was the case with the French; and had a profound effect in nations without states such as Catalonia, where it favoured the revitalization of their vernacular cultures and languages. The nationalism of nations without states contribute to the generation of new political institutions and structures formed by representatives of smaller nations, which prove to be economically viable and possess a strong sense of national identity. For Catalan, Scottish, Welsh, and Basque people, among many other European national minorities, the prospect of a Europe of the Regions stands as a pioneering political structure within which they could enjoy a substantial degree of autonomy. A Europe of the Regions would encourage regional development and allow for sub-state cultures to be preserved.

Romanticism sought to protect relatively untouched traditions at a time when cultural isolation was still possible. In the global age, interdependence and awareness of difference have resulted in the creation of complex societies engaged in constant dialogue, competition, and confrontation with other cultures. They welcome some new influences, they reject others, they clash and constantly adapt to a changing socio-political environment. Only cultures with sufficient power and resources are equipped to survive in the global age.

The Quest for Political Recognition

In what follows, I focus on democratic nationalism within nations lacking a state of their own that do not make secession their objective but instead advocate alternative forms of national coexistence such as political autonomy and federation. There are many studies of political violence that highlight the pernicious character of nationalism.[7] However, a significant number of democratic nationalisms have emerged in nations lacking a state of their own such as Catalonia, Quebec, and Scotland, and this type of nationalism merits specific and separate analysis.[8]

This democratic nationalism currently employs two major sets of arguments to legitimize its claims. First, there are political arguments stemming from the French and American Revolutions. They concern the endorsement of democracy and popular sovereignty as legitimations of the modern state.[9] Second, there are cultural arguments based on Romanticism.

Recognition by the state in the first instance, and then by the international community, are the foremost goals of nations without states, since most of them are included within the boundaries of states, which are reluctant or bluntly opposed to acknowledge their status as nations. The main objective of nearly all state-elites in the last two hundred years has been to generate a single nation within the state's territory in order to legitimize their power over an originally culturally and linguistically heterogeneous population.

The democratic nationalism of nations without states is often confronted with the ignorance, neglect, or hostility of the state, which tends to resist pressure to grant self-determination to national minorities living within its borders. In most cases, nations without states possess memories of a past in which they enjoyed autonomous institutions. The processes which brought that time to an end are not free from conflict and experiences of oppression. Isaiah Berlin defines nationalism as 'the result of wounds inflicted by someone or something, on the natural feelings of a society, or of artificial barriers to its normal development'.[10] In the nationalist discourses of nations without states that are currently seeking recognition, it is common to find a detailed description of grievances against the state. In Berlin's words: 'Nationalism springs, as often as not, from a wounded or outraged sense of human dignity, the desire for recognition.'[11]

Nationalism without States: Catalonia, Scotland, and Quebec

Introductory Comments

The democratic nationalism of nations without states seeks to halt a relationship with the state that is often marked by:

1. political dependence (sometimes involving also economic dependence)
2. limited or non-existent access to power and resources

3. restricted or even absent financial powers
4. a constant effort aimed at the cultural and linguistic homogenization of the nation
5. in many cases, a restrained capacity to develop and promote one's own culture and language.

Nations without states claim the right to be recognized as political actors and to have a voice in international organizations such as the EU and the UN.

The citizens of nations without states often feel dissatisfied with their present situation. They tend to regard the state within which they are included as 'alien', as an 'obstruction' to the development of their nation, or as a 'burden' that takes many of their resources while providing insufficient benefits. The articulation of such feelings generates the emergence of nationalist movements with differing political aims ranging from devolution and autonomy to secession and independence. Such movements are based upon the denunciation of an unsatisfactory situation related to economic, social, political, or security matters stemming from the relationship between the state and its national minority or minorities. The particular nature of the state, which differs in each case, determines the status of the national minority, while the strength of the minority's nationalist movement heavily influences a possible reshaping of its relationship with the state.

In what follows I offer an outline of the making of the Catalan, Scottish, and Quebec nations, and the subsequent emergence of contemporary forms of nationalism within the three.

The Historical Roots of Contemporary Nationalism

Catalonia

Until the mid-eighteenth century, Catalonia enjoyed a good deal of autonomy. The union with Aragon in 1137 recognized separate political identities including their territorial integrity, laws, institutions, and rulers. This was enshrined in the Catalan *Usatges* of 1150 whose very title (the *uses* and established customs and practices) suggests that the laws the document proclaimed had existed for a long time. During the thirteenth and fourteenth centuries Catalonia built up a powerful Mediterranean empire of a primarily commercial character. When Martin the Humane (*Martí l'Humà*) died without a successor in 1410, Fernando de Antequera (*Fernando I*) from the Castilian family of the Trastámara was elected to the throne (Compromise of Casp, 1412).

The joint rule of Isabel, Queen of Castile, and Fernando, King of the Crown of Aragon (which is referred to as *Reyes Católicos*), over their territories from 1479 placed two very different nations under the same monarchs.[12] As a result, apart from sharing common sovereigns, neither Castile nor the Crown of Aragon underwent any radical institutional alteration. However, Castile soon came to overshadow the other territories. A radical change in the Castilian policy towards Catalonia took place when Philip IV appointed the Count Duke of Olivares as chief minister in March 1621. Their objective was to create a powerful absolutist state. In 1640 the increasing tension between Castile and Catalonia reached its climax in the Revolt of the Reapers, treated by scholars of Catalan history as one of the first nationalist revolutions in Europe.[13]

In the Spanish War of Succession (1701–14), Catalonia supported the Austrians against the Bourbon claimant Philip V. The Treaty of Utrecht (1713) confirmed Philip V as King of Spain. After a massive Franco-Spanish attack that followed a siege of fourteen month, Barcelona surrendered on 11 September 1714. Philip V ordered the dissolution of Catalan political institutions and a regime of occupation. Catalan was forbidden and Castilian (Spanish) proclaimed as the official language, although the majority of the population could not understand it.

The industrialization of Catalonia and the Basque country generated a scenario in which the most economically developed parts of the state were politically subject to underdeveloped Castile.[14] By the end of the nineteenth century and influenced by German Romanticism, the *Renaixença*—a movement for national and cultural renaissance—prompted demands for Catalan autonomy, first in the form of regionalism and later a federal state. Catalan nationalism did not emerge as a unified phenomenon. Rather diverse political ideologies and cultural influences gave rise to different types of nationalism: the conservative nationalism of the Catholic priest Jaime Balmes, the federalism of the liberal politician and writer Pi i Margall, the Catholic nationalism of Bishop Torres i Bages, the Catalan Marxism of the revolutionary Andreu Nin, among many others.[15] Only in the early twentieth century did a pro-independence Catalan Nationalist Party obtain significant electoral support.[16]

Catalonia enjoyed some autonomy under the administrative government of the *Mancomunitat* (1913–23). This was halted in 1923 by the coup d'état of Miguel Primo de Rivera. Autonomy was granted again during the Second Spanish Republic—*Generalitat* (1931–8)—but abolished by General Francisco Franco's decree of 5 April 1938 after the coup d'état of 18 July 1936 that initiated the Spanish Civil War (1936–9). After almost forty years of Franco's dictatorship, Catalonia recovered its autonomous government, *Generalitat*, in 1977 and sanctioned a new Statute of Autonomy in 1979. The president of the Catalan government in exile, Josep Tarradellas, returned from France in 1977. Jordi Pujol, leader of the Convergence and Union coalition (*Convergència i Unió* or CiU) became the first president of the *Generalitat* after the first democratic Catalan election, in 1980.

Scotland

Scotland was independent until the Act of Union of 1707, and preserved many of its institutions—notably in law, religion, and education—from that time forward.

In 1320 the Scots nobles had sent a letter to Pope John XXII trying to persuade him of the legitimacy of King Robert the Bruce. This patriotic address known as the Declaration of Arbroath is invariably quoted as the first nationalist statement in western Europe: 'For as long as one hundred of us shall remain alive we shall never in any wise consent to submit to the rule of the English, for it is not for glory we fight, for riches, or for honours, but for freedom alone, which no good man loses but with his life.'[17] The Declaration referred to Robert the Bruce as 'king of Scots', not King of Scotland, thus portraying him as a limited monarch of the people and not as 'owner' of the land. It was not until 1328 that Robert the Bruce was fully absolved by the Pope who had excommunicated him when he was crowned King of the Scots. By that time Scotland had finally gained independence.

James VI, king of Scotland, also became James I of England in 1603 and adopted by proclamation in October 1604 the title of 'King of Great Britain, France and Ireland'.[18] This was a personal union of the Crowns of England and Scotland, though it was legally recognized that subjects born in Scotland and England shared a common nationality.

Following the execution of Charles I in 1649, England was proclaimed a free Commonwealth. Scotland reacted by immediately proclaiming his son King Charles II. Oliver Cromwell invaded Scotland, which was finally defeated in 1652. A Declaration of the English Parliament stated that Scotland and England were to be made into one Commonwealth. The Scots soon found that they were to be seriously underrepresented in the joint Parliament in London and other Commonwealth institutions.

In 1706 violent protest against the Union's draft Treaty broke out in Edinburgh, Glasgow, and Dumfries. Concern about the future of the Kirk (the Scottish Church) was raised and numerous petitions were presented to the Scottish Parliament. In response to this, the Parliament passed an Act for Securing the Protestant Religion and Presbyterian Church Government, which was to be regarded as part of the Treaty, at the same time as the English Parliament passed an Act for Securing the Church of England. The Scots lost political independence after the Treaty of Union in 1707. The degree to which Scots willingly consented to the Union is a matter of debate.[19]

The Act of Union preserved the Kirk, much of Scotland's educational system, the old land laws and a distinctive judicial organization.[20] According to John Duncan Mackie, 'in theory after 1 May 1707 there was no English Parliament, but a wholly new "British" legislature, in practice, the English Parliament simply absorbed the Scottish one'.[21] In his view, hostility to England among the Scottish governing classes increased after the English showed a patronizing attitude towards Scotland, often misinterpreting and sometimes even ignoring the Treaty of Union. The idea that Scotland was 'sold' spread among opponents of the Union who argued that the sums Scotland had received when signing the Union Treaty constituted an act of bribery of the Scottish Parliament.

The Jacobites—adherents of James II (after his overthrow by William of Orange in 1688) and his heirs—sought unsuccessfully to regain the throne in 1715 and again in 1745. In the eighteenth century, Scottish culture flourished and Scotland stood in the forefront of the European Enlightenment.[22] The economy took off and by the end of the eighteenth century cotton spinning and weaving on the new power machinery of the Industrial Revolution became Scotland's leading industries. Also shipping and shipbuilding and a range of heavy industries developed around Glasgow.

Quebec

Europeans first came to North America in the sixteenth century. At that time Iroquois, Cree, Algonquin, Huron, and Montagnais were the main Indian nations living on the territory of present-day Quebec. Jacques Cartier, sponsored by Francis I, King of France (1515–47), explored the Gulf of St Lawrence and stopped at the Indian settlements of Stadacona (Quebec City) and Hochelaga (Montreal). It was not until 1608 that Samuel Champlain established a permanent French settlement in Quebec City.

In the late eighteenth century, France and England were engaged in a protracted war (in Europe called the Seven Years War, 1756–63, in America known as the French and Indian War, 1754–63). On 13 September 1759 English forces under General James Wolfe defeated French troops commanded by Louis, Marquis de Montcalme, at the Plains of Abraham just outside Quebec City. Montreal was conquered within a year. From then on until 1982 the English monarch was Canada's head of state.

By the Treaty of Paris (1763) Quebec became a British colony and was ruled under the terms of a Royal Proclamation (7 October 1763). Catholics (in other words the French) were barred from public office because of the oath requiring allegiance to the British monarch as Head of the Church.

The 1774 Quebec Act allowed French Canadians to cultivate their language, maintain their old civil law—although English criminal law was imposed—and gave them freedom to practise their religion; it explicitly forbade the creation of an elected assembly. Instead an appointed council to advise the governor was established. The demand for an elected assembly therefore united the English and French Canadians against London and the local administrative elite.

The Constitutional Act of 1791 imperfectly divided the English-speaking and the French-speaking populations into Upper and Lower Canada, respectively. The Act allowed for elected assemblies but appointed governors and councils. It soon became clear that the governor's executive authority extended as far as overriding decisions of the colonial parliaments. In Lower Canada, English speakers constituted a minority, though they had considerable influence on political decisions, while the French-speaking rural majority, the *Canadiens* as they were often referred to, were marginalized.

The Act of Union of 1841 united Upper and Lower Canada into a single colony; Kingston became its capital. French was denied official status as a language either of public record or of debate in the assembly, though this policy was reversed in 1848. A very high property qualification was established for eligibility to run for election, resulting in the exclusion of most French Canadians. Governor and council were appointed. French civil law and the religious rights of the Catholic Church were respected. Education was under local control.

The uprising of the Métis (people of half-French and half-Indian descent) in 1885 was viewed by nationalist French Canadians as an uprising for French Canadian rights beyond Quebec's territory. The rebellion concluded with the hanging of its leader Louis Riel, a Métis. This caused a bitter division between French and English Canadians, which sparked off nationalist feelings strong enough to defeat the Conservative provincial government in Quebec and ruin the federal Conservative Party in Quebec for almost one hundred years.[23]

In the First World War, Canada, which was a Dominion of Britain, automatically entered the war. French Canadians opposed conscription. There were riots in Quebec City (29 March–2 April 1918), martial law was declared, and a battalion of English-Canadian soldiers from Toronto was sent there; five civilians were killed in the confrontations.

In the Second World War, initially there was no conscription in Canada, but pressure increased and the then prime minister, Mackenzie King, held a plesbicite in which English Canada (ROC or the rest of Canada without Quebec) gave a resounding 80 per cent in favour of conscription and Quebec voted 73 per cent against it. Only volunteers were sent overseas until 1944 when King agreed to send conscripts to the front to reinforce the British army's infantry units.

Comparisons

In all three cases there is a significant history of political independence or autonomy and cultural distinctiveness. Catalonia and Scotland were independent kingdoms through much of the medieval period and maintained autonomous institutions and laws until the early eighteenth century (1714 and 1708 respectively). Quebec, though under French colonial control until the late eighteenth century, was distinct from English possessions in North America. Even after the end of independence, Scotland and Catalonia enjoyed periods of political autonomy and managed to preserve a distinct cultural identity, as did Quebec within British Canada. Arguably it was the desire to recover autonomy, together with a strong sense of separate cultural identity, that animated resistance against a centralized state.

The basis for popular nationalism came in the modern period. The socioeconomic basis for this differed in the three cases. Catalonia was one of the more industrialized and modern parts of Spain and resented what it saw as exploitation by a more backward centre. Parts of Scotland shared in a more general British industrialization and imperial expansion that delayed the emergence of a distinct political nationalism. Quebec remained a largely agricultural society until after the 1960s, delaying the onset of a modern, urban-based politics. However, in all three cases a distinct culture—in the cases of Catalonia and Quebec also linked to a distinct language and literature, in the case of Scotland to a distinct set of institutions—connected to an earlier history of separate statehood from that of the modern central state and provided the basis for a widely shared sense of national identity on which a democratic nationalism could build.

The Rise of Modern Nationalism

Catalonia

Franco's coup d'état against the legitimate government of the Second Spanish Republic (18 July 1936) and his subsequent victory after the Civil War led to the suppression of Catalan political institutions, the banning of the Catalan language, and the proscription of expressions of Catalan identity, from the flag (the *senyera*) to the national anthem (*Els Segadors*).[24]

After the Civil War, the most important representatives of the democratic political parties banned by the regime went into exile, were imprisoned, or executed. The authoritarian state designed by Franco did not accept dissent, and used brute power toward the historical nations included within its territory. The regime's aim was to annihilate them as nations.

In February 1939 members of the institutions of the *Generalitat* went into exile.[25] In 1940 the Gestapo arrested the president of the *Generalitat,* Lluís Companys, and handed him over to the Spanish authorities. In Madrid he was interrogated and tortured, and subsequently sent to Barcelona, where he was court martialled and executed in Montjuïc Castle on 15 October 1940.

The Allied countries did not take any action to overthrow the Francoist dictatorship,[26] with the exception of two United Nations resolutions. The first (12 December 1946) recommended withdrawing ambassadors from Spain, and the second (17 November 1947) denounced the Franco regime because it had been created with the collaboration of the Axis powers. The disappointment of the Catalan resistance emphasized the political discrepancies between the firm defenders of the re-establishment of the Republic—ERC (*Esquerra Republicana de Catalunya* or Catalonia's Republican Left) and the PSUC (*Partit Socialista Unificat de Catalunya* or Unified Socialist Party of Catalonia)—and those who proposed beginning a provisional period of reflection to discuss the future organization of the state and the status of Catalonia.[27] The threat of a foreign intervention to restore democracy in Spain evaporated and it was not long before Franco received economic support from the United States (1951) and signed the Concordat with the Vatican (1953).

From 1959, with the awareness that the future of Francoism was guaranteed, a widening gap between most of Catalan society and the regime emerged. Only those members of the bourgeoisie who had renounced their national identity to protect their status and class interests were still satisfied.[28] In this new stage, the homogenizing policies imposed by the dictatorship encountered the opposition of those who wanted to recover democracy and protect Catalan identity. As a threatened national minority, the Catalans devised several kinds of counter-strategies aimed at rejecting the uniformity dictated by the regime.

Armed struggle did not take root among the anti-Franco opposition in Catalonia, which preferred non-violent tactics. The only exception was the *maquis*, approximately 12,000 armed men who operated mainly in the Pyrenees[29] and were active primarily in the 1950s.

Cultural resistance, that is, the use of all kinds of symbols of Catalan identity in both the public and the private sphere, evolved from the performance of isolated risky actions to the achievement of numerous activities enlisting mass support.[30] Acts of resistance culminated in 11 September 1977, when one million demonstrators demanded a Statute of Autonomy for Catalonia. Franco had died in 1975 and the political reform proposed by Adolfo Suárez, then prime minister of Spain, had been ratified by an overwhelming majority. The Catalans, through this display of strength, manifested their outright rejection of mere administrative decentralization and demanded political autonomy.

On 7 November 1971 about three hundred people representing different political, social, and professional sectors of Catalonia founded the Assembly of Catalonia, a clandestine organization that soon became the broadest and most important unitary Catalan movement since the Civil War. No unitary movement of comparable scope and relevance was created elsewhere in Spain. The Assembly, initially founded by the socialists and, in particular, the communists, received the economic support of the group led by Jordi Pujol (president of the Catalan government, 1980–2003), which subsequently joined it.[31] The MSC (Catalonia's Socialist Movement) and the PSUC won over the support of significant sectors of the working class and of a high number of Castilian-speaking immigrants. They all voiced the need to bring together democracy, left-wing policies, and autonomy for Catalonia.

The mobilizing action of the Assembly continued until the first democratic parliamentary election held on 15 June 1977. The unity of the democratic front was now replaced by competing 'images' of Catalonia, including its status within Spain. Jordi Pujol was elected as president of Catalonia in 1980, was re-elected and governed the country until 2003, when he decided not to stand again for office. Pujol led the CiU, a social-democratic nationalist party, and played a key role in building Catalan institutions, language, and culture after forty years of repression. Radical political change was initiated after the 16 November 2003 Catalan election when the new PSC (PSC-PSOE)-ERC-ICV government, under the leadership of Pasqual Maragall, ended twenty-three years of CiU's government at the *Generalitat*.[32] Instability generated by the differences among coalition members forced early elections. Maragall was prevented from standing as leader by the pro-PSOE sector in his own party. José Montilla became president of the *Generalitat* after repeating the coalition with ERC and ICV. In 2010, Artur Mas (CiV) became president.

Scotland

In 1853 the Association for the Vindication of Scottish Rights was created.[33] It was the first concerted 'nationalist' protest whose main aim was to defend the place of Scotland in British politics, thus defending a brand of nationalism without state.

In 1885 a Secretary for Scotland was appointed. However, he did not command a place in the Cabinet until 1892 and the office did not become a full Secretaryship of State until 1926. The so-called Scottish Renaissance in letters developed in the 1920s and reflected a period of notable nationalist re-emergence in politics and literature culminating in the creation of the National Party of Scotland in 1928; a precursor of today's Scottish National Party. However, Scottish politics throughout the nineteenth and the first half of the twentieth century was entirely dominated by parties committed to the Union, first the Liberal Party and later the Labour Party.

The movement for home rule for Scotland received an impetus after the Second World War when the Scottish Liberal Party published a scheme for the establishment of a Parliament for Scotland. In 1954 the Royal Commission on Scottish Affairs recommended increased powers for the Secretary of State for Scotland, but rejected devolution. The nationalist movement gained prominence in 1966 with the discovery of North Sea oil.

In the 1979 Referendum the Scots voted in favour of the Labour government's proposals to establish a Scottish Assembly. This was never implemented because of a requirement that at least 40 per cent of the registered electorate vote in favour. A majority of those voting supported the measure but this was only 32.9 per cent of the electorate.

Since 1988 the Scottish Constitutional Convention comprising Labour, Liberal Democrats, Scottish Nationalists, churches, unions, and other civic groups have campaigned for change. Once in power, the Labour government decided to hold a referendum (11 September 1997); 74 per cent of Scots voted for the re-establishment of a Scottish Parliament and 63 per cent voted to give it tax-varying powers. The First Minister of the newly created Scottish Executive was the Labour leader Donald Dewar. The SNP initially formed in 1928 came to the fore under the leadership of Alex Salmond, who led his party to victory in the 2007 Scottish election while defending a pro-independence manifesto. For the first time ever, Scotland was led by a secessionist political party.

Quebec

Traditional Quebec nationalism was conservative and strongly influenced by Catholic values. It was not separatist, but possessed a strong ethnic orientation and aimed at preserving French-Canadian specificity within the federation. It considered Canada as founded by two equal nations and did not want French Canada to disappear under the political, economic, and social might of English-speaking Canadians all over Canada, including Quebec.

The key components of Quebec identity were the French language, Catholic religion, a common history, and territory.[34] Its main ideologist was the Abbé Groulx and its most clear expression can be found in the Tremblay Report (1954). Traditional Quebec nationalism 'was an ideology opposed both to individualist liberalism and to collectivist socialism, emphasizing instead the Catholic social doctrines of personalism and subsidiarity, anti-materialist and imbued with spiritual values'.[35]

A radical shift in Quebec nationalism took place in the 1960s and gave rise to the so-called *Revolution Tranquille* (Quiet Revolution), which coincided with the election of a Liberal government led by Jean Lesage. Demands for socioeconomic change resulted in a modernization programme that strengthened and redefined nationalism. Language remained a key identity-marker of Quebeckers,[36] but substantial transformations affected civil society. Among those were the secularization of nationalism, the spread of liberal values, the rise of a francophone middle class, the expansion of organized labour, and the wish to take control over their own affairs, encapsulated in Lesage's slogan *maîtres chez nous* (masters in our own house).[37]

The 1960s Quiet Revolution[38] took place in Quebec, thus awakening a nationalist movement that denounced the second-class treatment received by French Canadians within the federation.[39] Education, employment, and language appeared as three major areas in which French Canadians were discriminated against.

In 1971 Pierre E. Trudeau, then prime minister, declared Canada to be a multicultural state, a claim strongly disputed in Quebecois circles who argued that multiculturalism was an instrument to water down their nationalist claims and the primarily bilingual and bicultural nature of the Canadian federation.

A constitutional amendment that affected Quebec, the Canadian Charter of Rights and Freedoms, was enacted in 1982 when Canada patriated its Constitution without the consent of the people of Quebec through their representatives in the provincial assembly. This constituted an injustice from the Quebecois' perspective because it violated one of the fundamental rules of federation: what affects all must be agreed to by all or by their representatives.

In A. Gagnon's words: 'attempts at reducing Quebecois to the status of one minority among others in Canada simply denies the fact that Quebec forms one of the main pillars upon which Canada was established in the Confederation agreement of 1867'.[40] The relationship between Quebec and the Canadian federal state illustrates the dynamic character of federation. Change is intrinsic to federation as a political arrangement that is not only based upon respecting diversity but which also acknowledges its non-permanent nature.[41]

Comparisons

In the modern period these nationalist movements have largely employed democratic political methods to advance their cause and have generally confined their demands to respect for a distinct culture, language, and political autonomy within the larger state.

Certain modern developments conditioned these features. First, it was not possible to maintain a democratic movement under conditions of authoritarian or dictatorial rule as was the case in Francoist Spain. Under those circumstances nationalists had to operate in exile and underground. The strength of the Catalan democratic and pro-European nationalist movement exemplified by the Assembly of Catalonia played a key role in the process that culminated in the democratization of Spain after Franco's death in 1975.

Nationalists did not confront such problems in Britain and Canada. The late emergence of democratic nationalism in these places therefore has to be linked to other conditions. In Scotland the dominant political forces in the nineteenth and first half of the twentieth centuries supported the Union. It was the faltering in economic growth combined with the prospects opened up by North Sea oil that encouraged a strengthening of demands for greater autonomy. Within the SNP there has always been a secessionist current but this was never able to dominate until the early twenty-first century. In the case of Quebec it was the rapid modernization of the region from the 1960s that created the basis for a nationalist movement building on modern, urban social groups and more secular in its character than traditional, social Catholic Quebecois politics. Currently the Party Quebecois (founded in the 1960s) and the Bloc Quebecois (founded in the 1990s) are strong supporters of Quebec's independence while maintaining some kind of partnership with Canada. Finally, this kind of democratic, autonomist nationalism in Catalonia and Scotland has been strengthened by the development of the European Union, which provides a political pole of attraction beyond Madrid and London and which makes claims to autonomy or even a separate state appear more achievable as located within a broader political structure.

Nationalism without States: Different Political Scenarios

Cultural recognition, political autonomy, and federation are three possible political responses to the nationalism of nations without states. All presuppose the acceptance of democracy and the readiness of the state to accept internal differences. I will consider regionalization, devolution, and decentralization as variations either within cultural recognition or political autonomy, depending upon each case.

Cultural Recognition

The acknowledgement of certain cultural traits as specific characteristics of a territorially based national minority that the state may refer to as 'region', 'province', or '*département*' stands as a 'soft' option in the state's process of recognizing its internal diversity. Cultural recognition presupposes the existence of a unitary state that recognizes only one nation and promotes a common language and culture through more or less efficient national education and media systems. Internal differences are not perceived as a threat to the state's integrity; rather, they are incorporated into the state's culture.

Cultural recognition seems to work wherever national minorities have a weak sense of identity, or are unwilling to articulate or prevented from articulating social and political movements in defence of their specificity. There are five main reasons for such a weak sense of identity: 1) a successful assimilation programme implemented by the state resulting in a considerable degree of integration of the national minority (for example, the homogenization of French Catalans, Bretons, and Occitans, and of the Welsh);[42] 2) repression, whether or not using physical force, of a national minority over a substantial period[43]; 3) historical accident, such as the need to find a new monarch outside the nation;[44] 4) a high level either of immigration or emigration (as in South Wales, which received a large contingent of English- speaking immigrants resulting in the weakening of Welsh identity and a much more limited use of the Welsh language than in the North); and 5) upward mobility and assimilation of the kind that arguably made Lowland Scots into political Britons.

Cultural recognition involves little, if any, decentralization. The state may appoint a special representative to distribute state subsidies and administer the region. There are no regional elections, sovereignty is exercised at a single level and is not devolved. The integrity of the state is well preserved since the possibility of internal challenges is ruled out by a firm unitary state structure. Cultural recognition usually involves the protection and promotion of the regional language, if there is one, and culture. For instance, the two major achievements of Welsh nationalism prior to devolution were the 1967 Welsh Language Act promoting the use and teaching of Welsh and the establishment of the Welsh language TV station, S4C—Sianel Pedwar Cymru—or Channel Four Wales, which had to confront, among other things, the opposition of the then prime minister, Margaret Thatcher.[45]

Political Autonomy

Political autonomy refers to a situation in which a unitary state implements some decentralization by devolving certain powers and functions to all or some of its constituent regions, provinces, or nations—the terminology varies but key concepts connected with political autonomy include subsidiarity, decentralization, and devolution. They all refer to the transformation of a unitary state into a political institution able to delegate some functions while retaining key powers and functions.

Political autonomy requires constitutional amendments and clear principles concerning the allocation of resources to the devolved authorities. Sovereignty is not shared, as in a federation. Instead, the state transfers functions to newly created regional institutions with or without an historical past, which remain accountable to the state. Matters relating to culture and welfare are easier to transfer than those concerning taxation, security, and international relations. There is no fixed rule of how much power might be devolved when autonomy is conferred upon regions.

For instance, Catalonia shares Scotland's history of having been independent until the early eighteenth century and subsequently integrated within a larger state. A separate sense of identity based on a particular culture, which in the case of Catalonia includes a distinct language, and the desire for political recognition, have been at the heart of Catalan and Scottish nationalist demands. Both nationalisms experienced significant cultural developments in the eighteenth and the nineteenth centuries. A shift towards claims for greater political recognition became significant during the twentieth century. Currently, the major difference between the two concerns the status of Catalonia as a net contributor to the Spanish coffers, which contrasts with Scotland's economic dependence on the British state.

Federation

Federation is constitutionally established and guaranteed. It offers the greatest degree of autonomy that a nation without a state can enjoy without becoming independent. However, there are major differences between different federal structures. Graham Smith argues that federalism is both a political ideology and an institutional arrangement.[46] Federation exemplifies a particular articulation of political power within a clearly demarcated territory, which is informed by the desire to acknowledge, protect, and encourage diversity within, while at the same time maintaining the territorial integrity of the state. The constituent units of a federation are not mere local authorities subordinate to a dominant central power.[47] As Daniel Elazar puts it, 'the very essence of federation as a particular form of union is self-rule plus shared rule'.[48]

As the case of Quebec shows, there is often a tension between some members of the federation's desire to expand the scope of self-determination and the state's wish to increase central control. The intensity of such tension depends a great deal on the reasons that prompted the creation of the federation. Ideally, federations should be the outcome of an agreement between independent states that freely decide to start a federal project which will allow them to shoulder common interests jointly while dealing separately with their domestic affairs.

In Switzerland, most cantons are linguistically fairly homogeneous. Ethnonationalism within language communities is discouraged by primary powers being vested in the cantons. Political parties do not correspond to language regions and the voting behaviour of cantons on constitutional issues is primarily associated with sociopolitical patterns rather than language. A further cross-cutting cleavage in Switzerland derives from the division between Protestants and Catholics.[49]

Quite often, however, federations arise from the pressure exerted by territorially circumscribed ethnic groups that are dissatisfied with the treatment they receive from the unitary state, and have enough power to force its transformation. This is the case in Belgium where a strong Flemish nationalist movement, which initially displayed a cultural character, progressively developed a political agenda. Pressure for change resulted in the transformation of Belgium—once a unitary state—into a federation to accommodate Flemish nationalist demands. The country evolved into a federal structure through five state reforms (1970–2001). Currently it is not clear whether the Belgian federation will withstand mounting nationalist pressure or finally break up. In other cases, federations are not the result of pressures from below but are created from above, as with the Soviet Union and India.

An exception is the regionalization of the German political system and the role of the *Länder*. Here federalism today does not reflect a society divided by significant ethnic, social, cultural, or religious tension; rather it is designed to reduce the power of the central government and guarantee a stable democracy.[50] This explains the greater emphasis that the German Basic Law places on the sharing of powers, responsibilities, and resources compared to the Constitution of the United States, which stipulates a separation of powers between the federation and the states. In Germany, federal and *Länder* (state) governments are forced to collaborate by a system of joint policy-making or 'interlocking politics'. The cultural or historical basis of the *Länder* is weak due to the vicissitudes of German history throughout which the territorial patchwork was in constant flux. Arthur Benz emphasizes the role of the two World Wars in overturning the territorial boundaries of the state and its parts. 'After the Second World War, the regional structures of the German state were re-established in a territorial setting primarily defined by the artificially created occupation zones. The *Länder* which formed the Federal Republic after 1949, as well as those which existed in the GDR until 1952 and which were re-established in 1990, were for the most part pragmatic creations of the Allies and lacked traditions.'[51] Cultural regions exist but they are more fiction than reality from a political point of view since the *Länder* do not coincide with them, except in a few cases like Bavaria. Thus federation is employed not only to protect and promote a diversity of nations or ethnic groups, but also to promote the interest of territories turned into 'regions' by the state or external powers.

The success of federal systems is not to be measured in terms of the elimination of social conflicts but, instead, in their capacity to regulate and manage such conflicts.[52] Federations seek to resolve conflict through democratic means, by encouraging tolerance and respect for ethnic, national, and cultural diversity. This is why successful federations cannot be the result of force or imposition from above.

To prevent disintegration, federations must combine strong but minimal federal government with a genuine policy of decentralization and respect for its members.

Decisions need to be taken collectively and the relations between the federal state and its constituents clearly established in a Constitution sanctioned by all. A state may adopt some federal elements, but it cannot be referred to as a federation unless the federal principle is stated in its Constitution. Once a federation is established, in principle, all its members hold equal rights and duties.

Does Devolution Foster Separatism?

Most Western nation states have embraced federal political structures or some type of devolution. Nevertheless, both the rationales and the mechanisms vary.[53] Britain, Canada, and Spain have opted for various devolution models encompassing federation, symmetrical and asymmetrical devolution. These have not remained static but, so far, none of them has encountered a separatist movement sufficiently robust to achieve independence for the region it claims to represent. These movements have been somehow accommodated through particular devolution structures. The main nationalist political parties do not seek outright independence; rather they advocate greater devolution or some form of 'qualified independence' such as the 'sovereignty and partnership' model defended by some Quebeckers.

Does devolution act as an antidote to secession and, if so, why? Secession empowers people to decide upon their political destiny by drawing up their own laws and constructing their political institutions and national identity. Nation states are strongly opposed to the possibility of new states emerging within their own territories and are often ready to fight secessionist demands, even if these are democratically based. Nation states fear that one successful secessionist movement could trigger a domino effect. National minorities are aware of this and often demand cultural and political recognition within the boundaries of the nation state, which is altogether a much harder claim to resist if the nation state in question defines itself as democratic.

Does such hostility towards secession prompt nation states to regard devolution as a remedial strategy to placate nationalist demands? A cautious response is needed since each case study is subject to specific nuances. Pro-independence nationalist movements in Catalonia and the Basque country favour maintaining some kind of partnership with Spain and membership of the EU, while Scottish and Welsh nationalist parties demand greater autonomy—independence in the case of Scotland— but contemplate some kind of relationship with Britain and membership of the EU. Similarly, the Quebec pro-independence movement supports 'sovereignty and partnership' with Canada.

The Outcomes of Devolution

The cases considered suggest that devolution does not fully satisfy claims to self-determination but does tend to weaken them. It locks regional movements and political parties into a dynamic, which involves an almost permanent tension with the central state grounded on ongoing demands for greater autonomy and recognition. Yet, devolution also enables national minorities to enjoy substantial powers. I list here some of the outcomes of devolution, which help explain its deterrent power against secession:

1. The creation of devolved institutions contributes to the dynamism of civil society for two main reasons. First, it requires the reallocation of resources to facilitate distinct policies and regional budget planning. These processes, in turn, help revitalize civil society, encouraging local and regional initiatives including cultural, economic, and social projects. Second, among other endeavours, devolved institutions tend to promote regional businesses, restore and preserve the regional heritage, and create regional cultural networks such as universities, museums, and libraries. None of this is necessarily inconsistent with sustaining an overall national identity.
2. The constitution of devolved institutions invariably tends to foster a sense of common regional identity where it did not previously exist, as is the case in the non-historical Spanish autonomous communities. In those cases where a pre-existing sense of identity was already in place, devolved institutions tend to strengthen it by promoting the culture, language, art, and selected meaningful landscapes of the area in question. But while some of these elements originate in the local cultures, others are the products of recent invention. Whether indigenous or invented, old or new, cultural distinctiveness both generates and restores regional collective identities.
3. Devolution generally results in the emergence of dual identities, regional and national. The promotion of regional identity seems to be compatible with holding an overall national identity.
4. Devolution reinforces the sentiment of forming a community at the regional level. Citizens can participate in decisions concerning their common political destiny and usually feel better represented by their own regional leaders. Furthermore, projects to promote the culture, economy, and well-being of the region's citizens tend to increase individual self-esteem This is not to ignore the disappointment that some may sense when faced with insufficiently funded devolution settlements, self-interested politicians, occasional corruption, and a growing bureaucracy.
5. Devolution enables the construction and consolidation of a regional political elite enjoying various degrees of power and prestige.[54] A substantial degree of devolution when accompanied by sufficient—or even moderately generous—resources automatically raises the profile of regional political elites. Members of the regional government, key figures among the indigenous bourgeoisie—if there is one—and some distinguished intellectuals dominate the elite. Moreover, selected political leaders representing various tendencies are almost invariably incorporated within the regional elite. Furthermore, devolution tames secessionist leaders by enticing them with doses of political power and prestige. There is a certain 'comfort'

arising from devolution, which tends to turn secessionist aims into never-ending demands for greater power and recognition.

6. Devolution tends to strengthen democracy as it brings decision-making closer to the people. Problems are identified, analysed, and resolved where they emerge. Regional politicians usually have greater awareness of the needs and aspirations of their electorates.

Conclusion

The objective of democratic nationalism is to foster an integral development of the nation. Not all nations choose the secessionist route. Why is this so? There is not a single answer valid for all cases, however among the reasons to explain this are the following:

- Lack of sufficient resources on behalf of the nation, for instance, Galicia in North West Spain.
- Lack of interest in becoming an independent state; for instance, Frantisek Palacky argued that an independent Czech state would inevitably fall under the domination of Russia or Germany and that therefore federal autonomy within the Habsburg Empire was the best bet.
- In Catalonia, some political elites have accommodated to a limited devolution of powers and financial resources in order to maintain the support of a large section of the Catalan population who would not support a more radical stance against Madrid. In 2012, the 1.5 million strong demonstration in favour of Catalan independence has challenged this idea.
- A nation's determination to defend its own culture, language, and identity while, at the same time, feeling part of a wider political unit. It could be argued that this is the case in contemporary Catalonia.
- Fear of being portrayed as 'radical', 'undemocratic', or even as a 'terrorist' while posing a threat to the state and the status quo; in some instances this generates not only hostility within the state but also in the international arena. Sometimes the Quebec nationalist movement has been portrayed in this light from Ottawa, in particular around the 1995 sovereignty referendum.
- Secessionist movements are more likely to be associated with the use of political violence, something that undermines their cause.
- Claims for some form of devolution are hard to oppose if a state wishes to appear democratic. Pragmatically, devolution can appear as a legitimate right of nations seeking recognition, while secession can be dismissed as violating the state's Constitution and laws.

The key question is whether a nation—including its culture, language, and resources—can be fully developed without having a state of its own or whether, on the contrary, as

Ernest Gellner argued, 'a nation/culture cannot normally survive without its own political shell, the state'.[55]

Notes

1. M. Weber (1946) *From Max Weber: Essays in Sociology*, ed. H. Gerth and C. Wright Mills, New York, 78.
2. M. Guibernau (1999) *Nations without States*, Cambridge, 14.
3. M. Guibernau (1996) *Nationalisms*, Cambridge, 47.
4. See Chapter 3 above by Erica Benner for a detailed consideration of these intellectual sources of nationalism.
5. See T. Nipperdey (1983) 'In Search of Identity', in J. C. Eade (ed.) *Romantic Nationalism in Europe*, Humanities Research Centre, Australian National University. For the political process, see Chapter 7 above by Michael Rowe.
6. See Chapter 8 above by John Breuilly.
7. E. J. Hobsbawm (1990) *Nations and Nationalism since 1780*, Cambridge; E. Kedourie (1960) *Nationalism*, London.
8. Henceforth I will use the term 'democratic nationalism' to refer to these nationalisms of nations without states.
9. See the chapters above by Benner (3), Doyle (6), and Rowe (7) for further details.
10. I. Berlin (1996) *The Sense of Reality: Studies in Ideas and their History*, London, 248.
11. Berlin, *The Sense of Reality*, 252.
12. J. H. Elliott (1963) *The Revolt of the Catalans: A Study in the Decline of Spain (1598–1640)*, Cambridge, 7.
13. Elliott, *The Revolt of the Catalans*, 45. See also P. Vilar (1987) *Història de Catalunya*, vol. III by C. Batlle, Barcelona, 217ff.
14. For an analysis of the process of industrialization of Catalonia, see P. Vilar (1977) *La Catalogne dans l'Espagne moderne*, Paris.
15. A. Balcells (1996) *Catalan Nationalism*, London.
16. This refers to *Esquerra Republicana de Catalunya* (Catalan Republican Left).
17. Quoted in J. K. Mackie (1964, 1991) *A History of Scotland*, London, 77.
18. Mackie, *A History of Scotland*, 188.
19. Mackie, *A History of Scotland*, 261, for the essential points of the Treaty.
20. Mackie, *A History of Scotland*, 333.
21. Mackie, *A History of Scotland*, 264.
22. See M. Lynch (1991, 1997) *Scotland: A New History*, London.
23. J. C. Conway (1992) *Debts to Pay: English Canada and Quebec from Conquest to Referendum*, Toronto, 42.
24. See J. Benet (1973) *Catalunya sota el règim franquista*, Paris, and M. Guibernau (2004) *Catalan Nationalism: Francoism, Transition and Democracy*, London.
25. For a detailed version of the activities of the *Generalitat* in exile illustrated with key documents from that period, see M. Ferré (1977) *La Generalitat de Catalunya a l'exili*, Barcelona.
26. D. Díaz Esculíes *El catalanisme polític a l'exili (1939–59)*, Barcelona, 129–35.

27. B. de Riquer and J. B. Culla (1989) 'El franquisme i la transició democràtica (1939–1988)', in P. Vilar (ed.) *Història de Catalunya*, Barcelona, 8 vols., VII, 153.
28. See I. Riera (1998) *Els catalans de Franco*, Barcelona, 1998; R. Aracil et al. (1999) *Empresarios de la post-guerra. La Comisión de incorporación industrial y mercantil número 2, 1938–1942*, Barcelona, and F. Cabana (2000) *37 anys de franquisme a Catalunya*, Pòrtic, Barcelona.
29. See F. Sánchez Agustí (1999) *Maquis a Catalunya. De la invasió de la Vall d'Aran a la mort de Caracremada*, Lleida.
30. See J. Fabré, J. M. Huertas, and A. Ribas (1978) *Vint anys de resistència catalana (1939–1959)*, Barcelona; J. Colomines (1999) *El compromís de viure*, Barcelona; P. Carbonell (1999) *Tres Nadals empresonats*, Barcelona; and H. Raguer (1999) *Gaudeamus Igitur*, Barcelona.
31. See Balcells, *Catalan Nationalism.*
32. At the election, the PSC (PSC-PSOE)-CpC obtained 42 seats, corresponding to 31.17 per cent of the vote. Against all predictions, the CiU, with its new leader Artur Mas, managed to obtain 30.93 per cent of the vote, which corresponded to 46 seats. As well as the PSC, it had also lost 10 seats when compared to 1999. The key to political change in Catalonia was then in the hands of the ERC, which obtained a record 23 seats corresponding to 16.47 per cent of the vote. In the 1999 election it had obtained 8.7 per cent of the vote corresponding to 12 seats. The ICV achieved a significant recovery, obtaining 9 seats (it had 5 previously), and the PP obtained 15 seats, 3 more than in 1999.
33. See M. Lynch (1991, 1997) *Scotland: A New History*, London, 357.
34. M. Keating (2001) *Nations against the State: The New Politics of Nationalism in Quebec, Catalonia and Scotland*, 2nd edn., London, 78.
35. Keating, *Nations against the State*, 78–9.
36. In Quebec the term 'Quebecois' refers to Quebec nationalists, whereas 'Quebecker' refers to all francophones living within the province of Quebec.
37. Keating, *Nations against the State*, 80.
38. J. Fitzmaurice (1985) *Quebec and Canada: Past, Present and Future*, London, 201–39.
39. See J. L. Brown (1990) 'The Meech Lake Accord in Historical Perspective', in M. Burgess (ed.) *Canadian Federalism: Past, Present and Future*, Leicester, 72–93.
40. A. G. Gagnon (1996) 'From Nation State to Multinational State: Quebec and Canada Facing the Challenge of Modernity', Keynote speech delivered before the British Association of Canadian Studies, 12 April, 16.
41. See A. Gagnon and D. Iacovino (2006) *Federalism, Citizenship and Quebec*, Toronto.
42. See P. Sahlins (1989) *Boundaries: The Making of France and Spain in the Pyrenees*, Berkeley and Los Angeles. See also E. Weber (1979) *Peasants into Frenchmen*, London.
43. For an account of the Kurdish case, see M. Ignatieff (1993) *Blood and Belonging*, London; E. O'Ballance (1996) *The Kurdish Struggle 1920–1994*, London. For an account of the linguistic homogenization of France and the consolidation of the nation state, see S. Citron (1992) *L'Histoire de France. Autrement*, Paris.
44. Martin the Humane, king of Aragon and count of Barcelona, died without a successor in 1410. Fernando de Antequera from the Castilian family of the Trastámara was elected to the throne (1412). This event signalled the end of the Catalan-Aragonese dynasty and resulted in the progressive weakening of the Crown of Aragon traditionally led by the Counts of Barcelona.

45. See J. A. Davies (1995) *A History of Wales*, London; R. Rawlings (2003) *Delineating Wales: Constitutional, Legal and Administrative Aspects of National Devolution*, Cardiff.
46. G. Smith (1995) *Federalism: The Multiethnic Challenge*, London, 4.
47. M. Burgess and A. G. Gagnon (1993) *Comparative Federalism and Federation*, London, 5.
48. D. Elazar (1987) *Exploring Federalism*, Tuscaloosa, AL, 12.
49. See A. Koller (ed.) (2003) *Federalism in a Changing World: Learning from Each Other*, Montreal.
50. A. Gunlicks (1989) 'Introduction', *Publius*, 19, no. 4, special edn., in A. Gunlicks (ed.) *Federalism and Intergovernmental Relations in West Germany*.
51. A. Benz, 'German Regions in the European Union', in P. Le Galès and R. Lesquene (eds.) (1998) *Regions in Europe*, London, 111–29, 113.
52. Burgess and Gagnon, *Comparative Federalism and Federation*, 18.
53. M. Keating (1999) 'Asymmetrical Government: Multinational States in an Integrating Europe', *Publius: The Journal of Federalism*, 29, no. 1 (Winter), 71–86. See also M. Seymour (2004) *The Fate of the Nation State*, Montreal, Kingston, London, and Ithaca, NY.
54. M. Guibernau (2000) 'Nationalism and Intellectuals in Nations without States: The Catalan Case', *Political Studies*, 48, no. 5 (December), 989–1005, see 1003–4.
55. E. Gellner (1983) *Nations and Nationalism*, Oxford, 143.

Suggested Further Reading

Balcells, A. (1995) *Catalan Nationalism: Past and Present*, London.
Bogdanor, V. (2001) *Devolution in the United Kingdom*, Oxford.
Brown, A. (1998) *Politics and Society in Scotland*, London.
Gagnon, A. and Iacovino, D. (2006) *Federalism, Citizenship and Quebec*, Toronto.
Gellner, E. (2008) *Nations and Nationalism*, 2nd edn., Ithaca, NY.
Guibernau, M. (1999) *Nations without States*, Cambridge.
Guibernau, M. (2004) *Catalan Nationalism: Francoism,Transition and Democracy*, London.
Guibernau, M. (2007) *The Identity of Nations*, Cambridge.
Rex, J. (2010) *The Ethnicity Reader*, 2nd edn., Cambridge.
Gunlicks, A. (2003) *The Lander and German Federalism*, Manchester.
Hobsbawm, E. J. (1992) *Nations and Nationalism since 1780*, Cambridge.
Koller, A. (ed.) (2003) *Federalism in a Changing World: Learning from Each Other*, Montreal.
McCrone, D. (2001) *Understanding Scotland: The Sociology of a Nation*, London.
McDowall, D. (2001) *A Modern History of the Kurds*, London.
Rawlings, R. (2003) *Delineating Wales: Constitutional, Legal and Administrative Aspects of National Devolution*, Cardiff.
Smith, A. D. (1998) *Nationalism and Modernism*, London.
Trench, A. (2008) *The State of the Nations 2008: Into the Third Term of Devolution in the UK*, London.

CHAPTER 31

NATIONAL IDENTITY AND EVERYDAY LIFE

YVES DÉLOYE

INTRODUCTION

To consider nationalism from the point of view of everyday life is to recognize that the ability of citizens to identify permanently with a nation does not result solely from the work of political nation-builders—educational, symbolic, military, et cetera—or from the actions of nationalist intellectuals. It also, and perhaps especially, depends on a series of social micro-processes of identification that suffuse social and political life and lead ordinary citizens to see themselves, in a commonplace way, as members of what Benedict Anderson has called an 'imagined community', the nation.[1] This line of research owes a great deal to Michael Billig's important work, *Banal Nationalism*. Billig introduced the term 'banal nationalism' to refer to:

> the ideological habits which enable the established nations of the West to be reproduced. It is argued that these habits are not removed from everyday life, as some observers have supposed. Daily, the nation is indicated, or 'flagged', in the lives of its citizenry. Nationalism, far from being an intermittent mood in established nations, is the endemic condition.[2]

This approach, now widely adopted,[3] is based essentially on a study of the rhetoric of the media (in this case, the British press in the 1990s), and it demonstrates the political importance of the way the media presents information to the public. Through the choice of cognitive categories it makes (national versus international, us versus them), by the framing effects it uses in presenting the current political situation, by internalizing 'a textual structure, which uses the homeland's national boundaries, dividing the world into "homeland" and "foreign", *Heimat* and *Ausland*',[4] information conveyed by the mass media powerfully contributes to the normalization of national identity and to making such identity seem 'natural' to citizens who are induced to reproduce mentally, in an apparently spontaneous way, the territorial and political divisions that reflect the principles on which a world composed of nation states are based. In a way, Michael Billig continues the work of earlier writers like Karl Deutsch or, more recently, Benedict Anderson, both of whom agree that communication plays a central role in the birth and reproduction of the feeling of belonging to a nation. Anderson argues in *Imagined Communities* that the nation has historically succeeded in substituting itself for older forms of community identification because it brings together mentally individuals who do not know each other, and who probably will never know each other, 'yet in the minds of each lives the image of their communion'.[5] The development of the press and of modern techniques of publication made a decisive contribution to the emergence of this 'imaginative faculty'. By eliciting the same thoughts at the same time among members of a national culture, whose language often delimits its borders, the press provokes a troubling but powerful result:

> The significance of this mass ceremony—Hegel observed that newspapers serve modern man as a substitute for morning prayers—is paradoxical. It is performed in silent privacy, in the lair of the skull. Yet each communicant is well aware that the ceremony he performs is being replicated simultaneously by thousands (or millions) of others of whose existence he is confident, yet of whose identity he has not the slightest notion. Furthermore, this ceremony is incessantly repeated at daily or half-daily intervals throughout the calendar.... At the same time, the newspaper reader, observing exact replicas of his own paper being consumed by his subway, barbershop, or residential neighbours, is continually reassured that the imagined word is visibly rooted in everyday life.[6]

In order to demonstrate the heuristic advantage of such a perspective, we will first discuss the theoretical contribution of this routinized approach of the nation, and then introduce the political, but mainly economical and cultural, sources of this national identification that is often compatible with other scales of identity. We will finally present in detail two historical aspects of this banal nationalism: architecture and music.

A Daily Plebiscite

This kind of analysis has the advantage of emphasizing the forms of interactions at the heart of contemporary societies that shape national identifications. As John B. Thompson has shown,[7] the rapid urbanization and substantial geographical mobility that have characterized Western societies since the beginning of the twentieth century have made a major contribution to detaching the individual from certain primary social ties (family, village, religion, et cetera) and exposing him or her to more abstract and changing ways of life. The decline of direct forms of interaction and 'communal patriotism' characteristic of traditional communities is reinforced when they are replaced by indirect or mediated interactions and identification, which promote the emergence of an 'abstract patriotism', to use Benjamin R. Barber's term.[8] Concern for reciprocity, interdependence, loyalty, organic solidarity, empathy, the valorization of individual sacrifice for the benefit of the national collectivity ('*pro patria mori*'): these are the constitutive elements of this 'abstract patriotism' that unites and connects those who see themselves as participating in the 'everyday plebiscite' ('une plébiscite de tous les jours') to which Ernest Renan so judiciously referred in the famous lecture 'Qu'est-ce qu'une nation?' ('What is a nation?') that he delivered at the Sorbonne in March 1882.[9] The approach in terms of 'banal nationalism' is therefore an invitation to see nationalism as more than something imposed from above upon a passive and credulous public for ideological and political reasons. To be sure, national narratives have been represented and disseminated on a large scale by novels, operas, paintings, and engravings, historical works scholarly and popular,[10] and in the form of school textbooks, as well as by street names, statues in public spaces, public commemorations,[11] the construction of historical monuments, new festive calendars,[12] et cetera. What matters in this incomplete list is the constant 'advertising' effort that accompanies the promotion of the 'national habitus',[13] especially in the course of the nineteenth and twentieth centuries. The daily affirmation of national identity, which is revealed in particular by the study of the media of mass communication, becomes *an active social co-production of a commonplace national identity* that combines not only the work of nationalization carried out by nationalist elites but also the everyday activity of identifying, receiving, and reappropriating undertaken by the populations concerned. The concrete, direct, and reciprocal interaction that was characteristic of rural communities in villages and small towns[14] comes to be replaced by mass communications (the press, popular literature, television, et cetera) and the apparatuses of 'exo-education' (public and private schools, military conscription) that today create in individuals the feeling of intimacy, subjectively shared community, and solidarity through the opinions, information, representations, and collective emotions that they disseminate and encourage. It is clear that this process of collective identification does not occur in the same way, at the same speed, with the same intensity, or with the same result in every country; each national group 'imagines itself' differently, notably because of its history, the form and strength of its government,[15] its cultural or religious composition, and the modalities of its involvement on the international scene. Nonetheless, this *bottom-up approach* changes the way we view nationalism and how we study it seriously.

The first decentring of the perspective involves encouraging observers to elaborate a kind of 'micro-physics' of nationalism. Making liberal use of a vocabulary borrowed from Michel Foucault, this chapter will emphasize the multiple *invisible practices* that create the modern national subject. Far from being only the result of the voluntary action of elites, nationalist movements, or the state ideological apparatuses that the latter control, the spread of the feeling of belonging to a nation as the ability to identify with an 'imagined community' proceeds along various, ambiguous lines, based on largely unconscious processes, even often without easily identifiable actors. What is at stake here is the emergence of a national identification that is on the whole an unintended result. Thus it is not the rare direct experiences connected with national civic membership such as occasional participation in the electoral ritual,[16] the often distanced spectacle of a commemoration or national holiday, physical involvement in a military conflict, et cetera, that are privileged here. Rather the focus is upon a vast set of everyday interactions such as reading a national newspaper; collective participation in sporting events that are often coloured by chauvinism and sometimes by xenophobia;[17] living in a neighbourhood with a national architectural style; treating the landscape as a trope for the nation; repeated visits to an exhibition or special place; intimate contact with material objects bearing the national imprint;[18] listening to a song expressing the 'harmony of peoples'; and so on. It is such interactions and experiences that are capable of anchoring this deep feeling of a 'community of destiny'[19] that constitutes membership in a nation. This 'micro-physics' of nationalism operates in a kind of *perpetual motion*, a play of complex and mobile interactions whose terms are never truly acquired or stabilized. As in the case of Foucault's approach to the question of power,[20] here we are concerned to advocate not so much a new 'theory' of nationalism as an 'analytical' approach to nationalism that makes the *functioning* of national identifications central. Attention needs to be given to these identifications, and to their everyday implementation (not to their institutional or ideological foundation). Thus through a set of ordinary practices,[21] usually diffuse and repetitive, nationalism can increase its symbolic and political efficacy.

A second change in perspective involved in this approach is the priority given to routinized situations of national identification. For Michael Billig, understanding everyday nationalism presupposes a distinction between moments of 'hot nationalism', in which the assertion of national identity 'is extraordinary, politically charged and emotionally driven', and 'cool nationalism', in which identification with the national community results from a series of routine, common behaviours and feelings that are distant from moments of nationalist effervescence and conflict. Whereas with hot nationalism, which is often given priority in scholarly literature, nationalism is perceived as something exceptional, even as a social pathology, with cool nationalism it becomes the rule, the banal result of a constant and often unconscious expression of membership in a nation. This approach fills an important gap in the literature on nationalism: 'All over the world, nations display their flags, day after day. Unlike the flags on the great days, these flags are largely unwaved, unsaluted, unnoticed.'[22] This decentring of the perspective encourages us in particular to qualify an interpretation of nationalism as a kind of 'collective effervescence'—an interpretation proposed by the young Émile Durkheim[23] in 1880, on the occasion of the first time 14 July was celebrated in the streets of Paris as the French national holiday. Durkheim drew the perhaps hasty conclusion that popular enthusiasm is capable of producing, in a punctual and exceptional way, a strong feeling of membership in a collectivity that would give rise to a genuine civic religion of the nation whose roots sank deep into modern French history.[24] Rather than adopt this approach, which focuses on the passionate character of nationalism, it seems preferable to adopt that proposed by

Durkheim's nephew, the anthropologist Marcel Mauss, an author who has unfortunately been neglected in much of the literature on nationalism. In his works on the techniques of the body, Mauss offers a point of view very different from that of his uncle. Drawing on his empirical observations, Mauss notes that the body, by means of the incorporated know-how that constitutes it, is able to analyse effectively the largely interiorized influences that govern the diversity of national affiliations. Because socialization, like communication and imitation, plays a central role in the transmission of ways of being and acting—in short, in the existence of 'social habitus' that is often deeply marked by the national context—it is important to pay attention to the way in which people 'know how to make use of their bodies', to the national *forms* taken by these techniques of the body, and to the body language that reproduces *ad infinitum* ways of being that are strongly influenced by their national imprint. It was especially his experience of the First World War that led Mauss, who had enlisted in the French army, to develop this very useful theory for understanding the deep mechanisms of interiorization and inscription in bodies (at least as much as in consciousness) of affiliations with this or that national entity. Taking as his example the 'British infantry, [whose] march step differs from ours', Mauss recounts an anecdote that reveals the latent qualities and inertias that make any switch from one national technology to another improbable:

> The Worcester regiment, having achieving great feats during the battle of the Aisne alongside the French infantry, requested royal authorisation to have a band of French buglers and drummers. The result was not encouraging. For almost six months . . . I often witnessed the following spectacle: The unfortunate regiment of big Englishman could not march. Everything was off. When they tried to keep pace, the music was out of synch with them. So the Worcester regiment was forced to get rid of its French buglers.[25]

This failure shows in reverse the force of 'national habitus' and still more the capacity of such habitus to diffuse itself into the most ordinary behaviours and gestures, in everyday postures and external bodily manifestations.

Mauss's anthropological analysis converges with the results of some contemporary work in political demography. In an innovative study devoted to pregnancies on the Franco-Belgian border, Morgane Labbé has shown that the geographical distribution of fertility is governed chiefly by a national factor: on each side of a border that is nonetheless largely porous from linguistic, cultural, and historical points of view, fertility still is strongly affected by the administrative division of the two populations into nation states.[26] In other words, the reproduction of 'bodies' is governed by an interiorized state-national logic that asserts itself historically as the nationalization of the two societies grows deeper and leads to a persistent difference between the birth rates in the two countries. In this historical case, the 'political border' was coupled with a 'population border' that attests to the influence of the national factor on family and demographic behaviours in border areas. As the process of nationalization of the Belgian and French societies grew deeper (especially after the First World War), the intranational differences in terms of fertility have faded away (in particular affecting the Flemish population, historically more fertile than the Walloons), whereas the gaps between the national fertility rates have increased and led to a contrast that is still present today.

Economy, Culture, Politics: The Sources of the Banalization of Nationalism

These two ways of decentring the perspective lead us to qualify the degree to which the process of national identification is politicized. Max Weber argued that this process is based on the ability of the national identity, which he identified with a form of 'ethnic communitarian relations, "to be" subjectively perceived as a common trait'.[27] For Weber, it was not an objective resemblance that provides the basis for the national bond, but rather the actors' perception of the borderline between the similar and the different. More precisely, it is the *feeling* of sharing certain values and representations that grounds the subjective reality of the nation. That is because the nation is the object of an investment of meaning and, frequently, of an intense psychological valorization (which Anthony Giddens later designated as the essential dimension of nationalism),[28] and because it is taken for granted in everyday life. The shift of view Weber carried out is, as we know, particularly fertile. His perspective makes nationalism a phenomenon of *belief* and makes the *sense* of national affiliation an object of analysis. His approach thus accords a central role to the subjective dimension of 'communalization' (*Vergemeinschaftung*). If the nation has no univocal material reality, and still less an essence, it nonetheless exists in the consciousness of those whom it brings together. This perspective led Weber to grant a crucial role to political activity in promoting and, still more, in maintaining this national consciousness, which is often conceived in terms of family relationships and blood: 'All history shows how easily political action can give rise to the belief in blood relationship . . . '.[29] Borrowing his illustrations from the history of ancient Greece and from the contemporary history of the United States, Weber repeatedly refers to the artificial and politically constructed nature of identity-related national cleavages. Like the 'tribe', the nation is only an artificial product of the political community. The arbitrary aspect of such delimitations does not exclude, nonetheless, the existence 'of a strong sense of identity'. Thus 'it is also not rare that families travel from New York to Richmond to make an expected child a "Virginian"'.[30] Although this theoretical formulation is largely in agreement with that proposed by Michael Billig, the approach in terms of 'banal nationalism' has the advantage of qualifying this political origin of the feeling of belonging to the national community. If for Max Weber, 'time and again we find that the concept of "nation" directs us to political power',[31] we must also emphasize here the significant contribution made by other matrices of national communalization. This common way of acting and thinking must also be related to the mechanisms of economic and monetary communalization that helped 'implicate' citizens when economic modernization was undertaken in European countries from the middle of the nineteenth century. As many works on social history have shown, integration into national networks of monetary and economic exchange strongly promotes the development of a national feeling that is all the stronger for being based on a series of intersecting interests that lead citizens to become economically dependent on each other. This 'implication' (the term is borrowed from the American historian Eugen Weber) leads us to take into consideration the peculiarly material factors that promote national integration and, still more, its banalization: the development of the highway network, starting in the middle of the nineteenth century; the construction of railways; the standardization of time by means of the invention and spread of clockmaking at the end of the eighteenth century; the broad diffusion of material objects bearing the national stamp (furniture, for instance); the rise of sports that encourage the expression and maintenance of the national consensus; the development of means of mass communication (the press, popular literature, radio, et cetera); and integration into a 'market culture'[32] that reinforces the division of labour and financial and economic interdependence. As Eugen Weber has shown in the case of France,[33] the (belated) success of this nationalization of society must be connected with the conjunction of these different innovations that overturned the whole social system, both on the political level and on the cultural and economic levels, although in my view this process is more unpredictable than Weber, who is sometimes imprisoned in a top-down analysis, presents it. When this process of national assimilation was completed, the citizen became aware of belonging to a whole whose borders—although intangible—became just as important as the immediate ones that defined the horizon of his everyday life. It is only at the price of this particular 'implication' that citizens learn to interiorize the abstract borders of national space-time and gradually to project part of their behaviours and opinions into an ideal whole: that of the nation to which they adhere in a way that has become unconscious because it is interiorized.

From this point of view, culture is also an important source of national communalization. Whereas Max Weber's approach attributes to the state a decisive place in the construction of the national community, the approach in terms of 'banal nationalism' also grants an important place to peripheral cultural contributions, to hybrid forms of nationalization, and to makeshift meanings that clearly attest to the *co-produced character* of the feeling of belonging to a nation.[34] Thus Peter Sahlins suggests that the appearance of national identity-related consciousness should be understood not on the basis of the 'political centre', as the main result of the state's public intentions and public actions, but rather in relation to that of the 'periphery', as the effect of local cultural practices of national identity. Taking as his starting point the example of the valley of Cerdanya, which has been shared by France and Spain since the Treaty of the Pyrenees (1659), Sahlins describes a situation in which the interaction between the local and the national gradually inscribes the border on ordinary culture and political necessity. Far from being a product of the state, the border and the identity-related cleavage that accompanies it are constructed, from the end of the eighteenth into the nineteenth century, in the action and dynamism of local communitarian relationships. In the framework of local conflicts, national identity becomes, for example, a resource that can be mobilized by villagers to oppose themselves to neighbouring communities. It is in the everyday borrowings and translations involving national identity on each side of the border that the feeling of belonging to the nation crystallizes: 'It appeared less as a result of state intentions than from a local process of adopting and appropriating the nation without abandoning local interests, a local sense of place, or a local identity. At once opposing and using the state for its own ends, local society brought the nation into the village.'[35] The interest of this kind of microscopic view is to encourage us to take into account the diversity of the historical ways in which the feeling of belonging to a nation can emerge; to examine carefully its diverse temporalities (which are not always identical with those of the state and its elites); and thus to remain attentive to the local conditions of the reception of national identity and to locate the differing itineraries (which are sometimes in conflict) taken by the nationalization of societies.

From One Identity to Another: The Strata of the 'Social Habitus'

The two decentrings proposed above offer another heuristic advantage. They lead us to consider the *cumulative* nature of political identities that classical theories of nationalism too often conceive as being in conflict with each other. From this point of view, the most novel analyses are probably those that bear on the functioning (and development) of national identifications in the European Union. To be sure, as we have already said, historians have proposed the hypothesis of a continuity between local identities (the famous 'little homelands' that were so praised in nineteenth-century Europe) and national identities currently under construction. Communitarian integration nonetheless offers an unprecedented example that we can observe and analyse to understand the logic of the functioning and interlocking of scales of identification. Initially, a conflict between identification with the European Union and identifications with its member nations, which were more deeply anchored in memories and habits, was hypothesized, especially for the countries that were the most jealous of their national particularities (France, the United Kingdom, Denmark, et cetera). The most recent comparative investigations tend to refute this hypothetical conflict and to demonstrate the cumulative (though partial) nature of the relationship between identifying with a nation and with the European Union. Just as in everyday life it is possible to reconcile a subnational identity with a national identity, so it is possible to conceive national and European identities on the model of Russian nested dolls. Far from being reducible to a zero-sum game (in which everyday identification at a territorial level would come at the expense of another level of identification), the two levels of belonging might even reinforce each other. As Sophie Duchesne and André-Paul Frognier have clearly shown, there is no 'inverse relationship between European and national identifications'. Moreover, these authors demonstrate that outside electoral periods, during which Eurosceptics enjoy particular influence, European pride is positively correlated with national pride. That is, for instance, what is indicated by the *Eurobarometer* poll taken in the autumn of 2000 (that is, after the 1999 European elections): of those who are very proud of their nationality, 31.7 per cent are very proud of being European, 36.9 per cent are proud, 15.2 per cent are not very proud, and only 9.6 per cent are not proud at all. Conversely, 2.4 per cent of those who are not proud of their nationality are very proud to be European, 19 per cent are rather proud, 14.8 per cent are not very proud, and 58.7 per cent are not proud of being European.[36] In other words, the prouder people are of their own nation, the more they are proud of being Europeans. Using new questionnaire data on three European Union countries (the United Kingdom, France, and Holland), Michael Bruter has confirmed this hypothesis: there is a positive correlation between the different levels of identification he investigated (local, regional, national, and European). For Bruter, it is clear that these positive correlations are strongest between the closest territorial levels, that is, between European and national identities and especially between regional and local identities.[37] In a complementary way, the broader investigation carried out by Richard Robyn's team (the investigation concerned seven European countries: Germany, Denmark, France, Italy, Holland, the United Kingdom, and Sweden) also demonstrate that national pride is not an obstacle to the emergence of an identification (still relative and fragile) with the European Union—with the notable exception of Germany, where national pride is significantly weaker than in the rest of the European Union. Moreover, this last investigation suggests that Europeans are capable of taking on 'multiple identities'.[38] This cumulative functioning of contemporary identifications attests to the importance of considering 'banal nationalism' as the result of a 'social habitus' composed of several superimposed strata, including one related to the national community. In other words, the ability to identify on a scale of post-national affiliation seems strikingly confirmed by the popularized, naturalized dimension of national identification, which far from being an obstacle to a supranational identification becomes one of its commonplace conditions. Upon reading this research, it seems that people who ordinarily project themselves in a serene, proud way in relation to their national community often find it easier to see themselves as 'European' as well.

Latency and the Social Morphology of Ordinary Nationalism

National and Other Identities

Nonetheless, it remains that identification with Europe still suffers from a certain number of 'drag effects' that have to do in part with the antiquity, diversity, and latency of social micro-processes of national identification that still ensure a real predominance of the 'community of understanding' (to use Max Weber's term) that constitutes the nation. The notion of 'drag effects' is borrowed from Norbert Elias, for whom communitarian construction must be resituated in a long-term historical perspective that sees the sequence of human interdependencies extending as the process of individualization deepens: 'This structure of relationships demands of the individual a greater circumspection, more conscious forms of self-control, reduced spontaneity in action and speech in the forming and management of relationships.' But Elias immediately adds that this advance of the individual 'has not extinguished the basic human need for impulsive warmth and spontaneity in relationships with other people. It has not caused the desire for security and constancy in the emotive affirmation of one's own person by others, and its counterpart, the desire for the company of people one likes, to disappear.'[39] This 'affective' desire explains in part the 'drag effect' that Elias mentions when he tries to understand the everyday development of the 'national habitus' confronted by this process of extending the sequences of interdependency and the increased individualism to which it leads. There probably resides Elias's main lesson: 'Such changes do not take place overnight. They involve processes that often take many generations.'[40] He reminds us that in Europe, the 'national' layer of social habitus occupies a particular place because of its history and the 'emotional tonality' that is attached to it. Because it is 'very deeply and firmly anchored into the personality structure of the individual', because it results from an ancient and intense politics of 'manipulation of feelings in relation to state and nation, government and political system',[41] the 'national tradition' helps delay the arrival, and still more the awareness, of a supranational level of political and civic inclusion. The approach adopted in this chapter allows us to complete this theoretical perspective by discussing the multiple vectors and processes that provide the emotional anchorage of banal nationalism. Without claiming to make an exhaustive inventory here, it is appropriate at this point to define functional modalities by examining some of their symbolic and memorial frameworks and by analysing some of the routine social and cultural practices that make national identity so intimate and banal that it is often permanently 'embodied' by citizens.

Architecture and Landscape

Architectural style is one of the most interesting vectors for understanding the territorial dissemination of a distinctive feeling of commonplace identification with a nation. If studies on this subject are still rare[42] and often monographic, they nonetheless tend to demonstrate the importance of 'national' architectural styles and 'landscape tropes for the nation' (to adopt the title of François Walter's book) in the development of this 'imaginative faculty' that serves as a base for banal nationalism.[43] And this is so less because in the second half of the nineteenth century these national forms of architecture were the object of a series of 'identity-related exhibitions' at the time of the Universal Expositions (or World Fairs) and other international expositions that were open to the general public,[44] or because they were theorized, even codified by a technical literature and professional journals that made it easier to disseminate these forms and to make them permanent, than because they succeeded in occupying citizens' visual fields and becoming genuine identity landmarks, veritable 'social frameworks' of national memory.[45] Reproduced in numerous media of communication and education (school textbooks, postcards, tourist posters and guides, postage stamps, et cetera), these national styles succeeded above all in putting a durable imprint on the space citizens lived in and traversed, both in the city and in the countryside. The study of the 'Romanian national style' recently published by Carmen Popescu allows us to describe more precisely the conditions of the social efficacy of this national construction through architecture. Dealing with the period between the proclamation of the Romanian monarchy in 1881 and the end of the Second World War, this study demonstrates the ability of a certain architectural style, which claimed to be a legitimate continuation of traditional Romanian art, to cover the territory of the new state that had been freed in 1878 from the tutelage of the Ottoman Empire. The essential point is that this national architecture did not concern solely the new state's official, symbolic buildings: schools, city halls (notably the Bucharest city hall erected at the end of the nineteenth century), museums, and the palaces of the state archives; but also a whole series of 'typical' houses in both the urban habitat (low-cost housing, villas) and the rural habitat (farmhouses, country houses). An emblem of Romanian identity, 'architecture discovers that it has a privileged role: it affects both the private level (it is a second nature) and the public level (it lays out cities, erects monuments), while at the same time having the power to manipulate symbolic languages'.[46] Such languages are all the more effective among the people because they are neither doctrinaire nor ideological, but aesthetic, and therefore easy to understand. The invariable characteristics of the architectural style also ensure its efficacy: 'a picturesque composition, with a tendency to asymmetry, often realized by the accent provided by towers, the picturesque use of shadow derived from the use of numerous openings treated in decorative ways . . . the frequent use of rustic elements in wood . . . '.[47] Often based on local historical sources, this national style spread all the more rapidly because it developed at a time when the real-estate sector of private homes was undergoing a remarkable economic boom in Romania. This development concerned not only exterior architecture but also interior decoration (chairs, dining tables, beds, et cetera), which was then the object of an ambitious national reflection. A veritable manner of 'living in the Romanian way' spread and helped set its aesthetic and intimate stamp on the framework of Romanian families' everyday lives. This ability to appeal across class lines resulted from the simplification and plasticity of a national style which produced not only masterpieces (for example, those of the Cotroceni Palace in Bucharest) that are now preserved in museums, but also ordinary furniture that incarnates several architects' desires to construct 'Romanian interiors, furniture, and clothes . . . '.[48]—in short, a whole series of familiar material objects capable of referring to 'a way of being common to many people',[49] and of deeply imbuing the private lives of citizens with banalized references to and markers of national identity. The importance of this spatialization of feeling can be gauged more accurately if we recall the arguments of Maurice Halbwachs about the functioning of the collective memory. The importance he accords to the localization of memories leads him to claim that 'there is no collective memory that does not take place in a spatial framework'. 'A reality that lasts', space anchors images and memories deeply in communal affiliations. In such a perspective, each national group succeeds in persisting because it inscribes its shape on the ground and offers citizens an everyday spatial framework that helps national memory 'immobilize itself'.[50] In a complementary way, we must here mention the 'landscape tropes for the nation', that is, the set of landscape schemes that have historically contributed, and still contribute today, to the creation of a collective sensory experience that, because of the spatial and national stereotypes it deploys, is crucial for the development and maintenance of a routinized feeling of belonging to a nation.[51] It would also be appropriate to mention the important role played by the images on postage stamps—which often reproduce landscapes or architectural figures symbolizing the nation—in the construction of the national narrative, of the collective memory, and of a self-image. Produced on the state's initiative, they are massively distributed in everyday life and reflect historically the transformations of the relationship between the nation and its citizens.[52]

Music

While the visual field is an effective everyday medium for conveying and inscribing on individual memories the distinctive feeling of belonging to a nation, we should also mention the importance of the nationalization of citizens' auditory fields. The development of national schools of music in the nineteenth and twentieth centuries, the regular use of national anthems in schools, in military barracks, and on the occasion of publicly staged sporting or commemorative events, the instrumentalization of national or ethnic musical themes in films—all these are so many social occasions for federating citizens and making the simultaneous communion of minds heard. More than the 'national' literature, which is often reserved for a literate elite, music—whether popular or classical—'helps reveal what is most secret and least translatable in the collective soul of a people'.[53] Of course, the musical investment in the nation is expressed in different ways, depending on whether we are concerned with a more or less homogeneous state or with a country struggling to gain autonomy. But in many cases, as Halbwachs also noted, music is one of the ordinary frameworks of the collective memory of social and national groups. The phonetic habits of a national group, the memory of a musical sound evoking a system of notes or an assemblage of signs issuing from a convention transmitted from one generation to another, the sensory experience elicited by repeatedly listening to an 'original' popular song: there is an abundance of examples showing the identity-related effects of playing and listening to music. Naturally, these kinds of 'national music' composed in accord with international aesthetic genres (think of Grieg in Norway, Granados and de Falla in Spain, Dvorak and Smetana in Czechoslovakia, Bartok and Kodaly in Hungary, and so on) take on a colouration of their own, which often relies on reference to popular melodies that are supposed to express 'the national genius'—the importance of which was so strongly emphasized by Johann Gottfried Herder in the eighteenth century—and its versions in culture, history, and landscape. These are so many 'authentic' components that music seeks to inscribe on citizens' auditory memory and thus to root them in the depths of the awareness of belonging. The most interesting European example of this is probably Germany at the turn of the twentieth century. Celia Applegate has shown, for instance, the 'felicity conditions'—to use Max Weber's term—for this affinity between musical creation and the ordinary affirmation of German nationalism. Applegate persuasively argues for the importance of social mechanisms in disseminating national musical standards that gradually left their privileged site of production and spread throughout the society by establishing a set of auditory landmarks that promoted identification with the German nation. This contributed to creating a sense of self-awareness amongst politically fragmented Germans. Like architecture and literature, music gives rise to a veritable aesthetic revolution that had a nationalist impact: 'if German national identity emerged in the salons and singing societies of musically inclined Germans, then we must reposition nationalism in the intersection of a public and a private realm, a male world and a female world. In the end, we may hear the same music, but perhaps we will hear it with a more finely tuned awareness of what it can mean.'[54]

Concluding Remarks

Thus it is in these interstices of social life that we should finally seek, more than the modalities of the formation of nationalism, the 'felicity conditions' of its power of identification. As Max Weber suggested, 'aesthetically conspicuous differences of the physical appearance' are also the most effective ones, because they are 'perceptible differences in the *conduct of everyday life*'.[55] Perhaps this is part of the ordinary mystery of national identity. Far from being only the reflection of an ideology borne by intellectuals or the mechanical result of an instrumental and manipulative policy from political elites, banal nationalism results from a series of social micro-processes of identification that historically lead individuals to identify themselves with the nation just as they feel they are members of other, often closer, human groups. For such an abstract process of identification to happen, national allegiance has to become banal, made concrete—through architecture, music, sport, media, popular literature—so that the individuals make it their own often unknowingly and sometimes unwillingly. In that perspective, the historical formation of the state, the construction of national unity, and the assertion of national civic identity are the result of a complex to-and-fro movement, which dates back several centuries, between the political and the social, state and society. The purpose of this process remains historically as open today as it ever was.

NOTES

1. B. Anderson (1983, 1991) *Imagined Communities: Reflections on the Origin and Spread of Nationalism*, London.
2. M. Billig (1995) *Banal Nationalism*, London, 6.
3. A lot of literature uses this approach. See for instance A. Law's critical paper (2001) 'Near and Far: Banal Nationalism Identity and the Press in Scotland', *Media, Culture & Society*, 23, no. 3, 299–317. It was also used to describe mechanisms of infranational identification: K. Crameri (2000) 'Banal Catalanism?', *National Identities*, 2, no. 2 (July), 145–57.
4. Billig, *Banal Nationalism*, 119.
5. Anderson, *Imagined Communities*, 6.
6. Anderson, *Imagined Communities*, 35–6.
7. J. B. Thompson (1995) *The Media and Modernity: A Social Theory of the Media*, Cambridge.
8. B. R. Barber (1974) *The Death of Communal Liberty: A History of Freedom in a Swiss Mountain Canton*, Princeton, NJ, ch. IX.
9. E. Renan (1882, 1994) 'What is a Nation?', in J. Hutchinson and A. D. Smith (eds.) *Nationalism*, Oxford, 17–18.
10. There is an abundant literature; see in particular S. Berger, K. Donovan, and K. Passmore (eds.) (1999) *Writing National Histories: Western Europe since 1800*, London.
11. J. R. Gillis (1994) *Commemorations: The Politics of National Identity*, Princeton, NJ.
12. For a general overview, see A.-M. Thiesse (1999) *La création des identités nationales. Europe XVIIIe–XXe siècle*, Paris.
13. This notion of 'national habitus' is taken from N. Elias (1996) *The Germans: Power Struggles and the Development of Habitus in the Nineteenth and Twentieth Centuries*, New York, esp. 2–15 and 157–8.
14. Historical literature has studied this process of political transformation in great depth. On the French case, the main source remains E. Weber's (1975) *Peasants into Frenchmen*, Stanford, CA. Weber argued in favour of a late nationalization of French society and of an approach contrasting the centre and the periphery. However, the American historian J. R. Lehning (1995) improved on this thesis in his book *Peasant and French: Cultural Contact in Rural France During the Nineteenth Century*, Cambridge, where he outlines a process of negotiation on identity between a rural society that remains culturally active and a French national identity open to diversity. O. Zimmer (2003) takes a similar approach in the Swiss case, where he highlights a conflictive process of national affirmation, in *A Contested Nation: History, Memory and Nationalism in Switzerland, 1761–1891*, Cambridge.
15. On the importance of this state-dependent variable, see J. Breuilly (1992) *Nationalism and the State*, Manchester.
16. Like the national flag, universal suffrage brings together—often on an emotional level—people who have little in common, including the political orientation of their vote. The ritualized scenic design of the electoral body as well as its homogenization when the

results are proclaimed pertain to the same necessity: to assert the presence of an electoral and national community of destiny. The aggregation of votes on the evening of the election symbolically reveals the existence of a national space of political representation unified by the act of voting. Insofar as it triggers similar thoughts in citizens who cast their vote at exactly the same time, the act of voting becomes a rite of assertion of identity. On this topic, see Y. Déloye (1998) 'Rituel et symbolisme électoraux. Réflexions sur l'expérience française', in R. Romanelli (ed.) *How Did They Become Voters? The History of Franchise in Modern European Representation*, The Hague, 61–5.

17. They are common expressions of nationalism and have been relatively extensively treated in scholarly literature. See Billig, *Banal Nationalism*, 119–25, and especially M. Cronin's (1999) research, *Sport and Nationalism in Ireland: Gaelic Games, Soccer and Irish Identity since 1884*, Dublin. For a comparative perspective, see M. Cronin and D. Mayall (eds.) (1998) *Sporting Nationalisms*, London. See also H. Dauncy and G. Hare (1999) *France and the 1998 Word Cup: The National Impact of a World Sporting Event*, London.
18. For a good illustration, see K. M. Guy (2003) *When Champagne Became French: Wine and the Making of a National Identity*, Baltimore, MD.
19. The concept of 'community of destiny' is borrowed from O. Bauer ('Le concept de nation', 1907), who contrasts it with the 'community of character', such as social class, and considers that 'it is only destiny lived in deep reciprocal interaction and mutual rapport that creates the nation', quoted by P. Birnbaum (ed.) (1997) *Sociologie du nationalisme*, Paris, 8.
20. M. Foucault (1990) *The History of Sexuality: An Introduction*, New York, Part Four.
21. C. Palmer (2000) 'From Theory to Practice', *Journal of Material Culture*, 3, no. 2, 175–99.
22. Billig, *Banal Nationalism*, 44 and 46.
23. See G. Davy (1919) 'Emile Durkheim', *Revue de métaphysique et de morale*, 26, no. 2, 188.
24. D. A. Bell (2001) *The Cult of the Nation in France: Inventing Nationalism, 1680–1800*, Cambridge.
25. M. Mauss (1950) *Sociologie et anthropologie*, Paris, 367.
26. M. Labbé (2000) *La population à l'échelle des frontières. Une démographie politique de l'Europe contemporaine*, Paris, 150–4.
27. M. Weber (1978) *Economy and Society*, Berkeley, CA, 385.
28. A. Giddens (1985) *The Nation-State and Violence*, Cambridge, 116.
29. Weber, *Economy and Society*, 393.
30. Weber, *Economy and Society*, 393.
31. Weber, *Economy and Society*, 398.
32. T. L. Haskell and R. F. Teichgraeber (eds.) (1993) *The Culture of the Market: Historical Essays*, Cambridge.
33. Weber, *Peasants into Frenchmen.*
34. Apart from J. L. Lehning's work cited above, see C. Ford (1993) *Creating the Nation in Provincial France: Religion and Political Identity in Brittany*, Princeton, NJ; and D. Reed-Danahay (1996) *Education and Identity in Rural France: The Politics of Schooling*, Cambridge.
35. P. Sahlins (1989) *Boundaries: The Making of France and Spain in the Pyrenees*, Berkeley, CA, 9.
36. S. Duchesne and A.-P. Frognier (2002) 'Sur les dynamiques sociologiques et politiques de l'identification à l'Europe', *Revue française de science politique*, 52, no. 4, 363–4. See more recently, S. Duchesne and A.-P. Frognier (2008) 'National and European Identifications: A Dual Relationship', *Comparative European Politics*, no. 6, 143–68.

37. M. Bruter (2005) *Citizens of Europe. The Emergence of a Mass European Identity*, Basingstoke, 114–16.
38. R. Robyn (ed.) (2005) *The Changing Face of European Identity*, London, 229.
39. N. Elias (1991) *The Society of Individuals*, Oxford, 204.
40. Elias, *The Society of Individuals*, 229.
41. Elias, *The Society of Individuals*, 209 and 210.
42. See P. Jones's overview (2003) 'Architecturing Modern Nations: Architecture and the State', in G. Delanty and E. F. Isin (eds.) *Handbook of Historical Sociology*, London, 301–11.
43. F. Walter (2004) *Les figures paysagères de la nation. Territoire et paysage en Europe, 16e–20e siècle*, Paris.
44. Thiesse, *La création des identités nationales*, 197–206.
45. S. Daniels (2001) *Fields of Vision: Landscape Imagery and National Identity in England and the United States*, London; and M. Morgan (2001) *National Identities and Travel in Victorian Britain*, Basingstoke.
46. C. Popescu (2004) *Le style national roumain. Construire une nation à travers l'architecture 1881–1945*, Rennes, 18. For a comparative perspective on this architectural and spatial symbolic frame, see M. Facos and S. L. Hirsh (eds.) (2003) *Art, Culture and National Identity in Fin de Siècle Europe*, Cambridge.
47. Popescu, *Le style national roumain*, 177.
48. Popescu, *Le style national roumain*, 180.
49. Maurice Halbwachs (1950, 1997) *La mémoire collective*, Paris, 195.
50. Halbwachs, *La mémoire collective*, 209, 232.
51. Walter, *Les figures paysagères de la nation*. There is abundant literature on this: see also T. Cusack (2001) 'A "Countryside Bright with Cosy Homesteads": Irish Nationalism and the Cottage Landscape', *National Identities*, 3, no. 3 (November), 221–38; and M. Häyrynen (2000) 'The Kaleidoscopic View: The Finish National Landscape Imagery', *National Identities*, 2, no. 1 (March), 5–19. For a stimulating study on how architecture is able to express post-national European identity, see G. Delanty and P. R. Jones (2002) 'European Identity and Architecture', *European Journal of Social Theory*, 5, no. 4, 453–66.
52. See recently P. Reanto and S. D. Brunn (2008) 'Picturing a Nation: Finland on Postage Stamps, 1917–2000', *National Identities*, 10, no. 1 (March), 49–75.
53. The phrase is borrowed from a French music critic (René Dumesnil) cited in B. Fournier et al. (2006) *L'harmonie des peuples. Les écoles musicales nationales aux XIXe et XXe siècles*, Paris, 31.
54. C. Applegate (1992) 'What Is German Music? Reflections on the Role of Art in the Creation of the Nation', *German Studies Review*, no. 15, 30.
55. Weber, *Economy and Society*, 390, emphasis by Weber.

Suggested Further Reading

Anderson, B. (1983) *Imagined Communities: Reflections on the Origin and Spread of Nationalism*, London.

Berger, S., Donovan K. and Passmore, K. (eds.) (1999) *Writing National Histories: Western Europe since 1800*, London.

Billig, M. (1995) *Banal Nationalism*, London.

Confino, A. (1997) *The Nation as a Local Metaphor: Württemberg, Imperial Germany, and National Memory, 1871–1918*, Chapel Hill, NC.
Cronin, M. (1999) *Sport and Nationalism in Ireland: Gaelic Games, Soccer and Irish Identity since 1884*, Dublin.
Elias, N. (1996) *The Germans: Power Struggles and the Development of Habitus in the Nineteenth and Twentieth Centuries*, New York.
Facos, M. and Hirsh, S. L. (eds.) (2003) *Art, Culture and National Identity in Fin-de-Siècle Europe*, Cambridge.
Gillis, John R. (1994) *Commemorations: The Politics of National Identity*, Princeton, NJ.
Labbé, M. (2000) *La population à l'échelle des frontières. Une démographie politique de l'Europe contemporaine*, Paris.
Linz, J. J. (1993) 'State Building and Nation Building', *European Review*, 1, no. 4, 355–69.
Mauss, M. (2006; 1950) *Techniques, Technology and Civilisation*, New York.
McCrone, D. (1998) *The Sociology of Nationalism*, London.
Popescu, C. (2004) *Le style national roumain. Construire une nation à travers l'architecture 1881–1945*, Rennes.
Thiesse, A.-M. (1999) *La création des identités nationales. Europe XVIIIe–XXe siècle*, Paris.
Throssell, K. (2015) *Child and Nation: A Study of Political Socialisation and Banal Nationalism in France and England*, Bruxelles.
Walter, F. (2004) *Les figures paysagères de la nation. Territoire et paysage en Europe, 16e–20e siècle*, Paris.
Weber, E. (1975) *Peasants into Frenchmen*, Stanford, CA.
Weber, M. (1978) *Economy and Society*, Berkeley, CA.
Zimmer, O. (2003) *A Contested Nation: History, Memory and Nationalism in Switzerland, 1761–1891*, Cambridge.

PART V

CHALLENGES TO THE WORLD OF NATION STATES

CHAPTER 32

NATIONALISM AND SOCIALIST INTERNATIONALISM*

JOHN SCHWARZMANTEL

INTRODUCTION

THE purpose of this chapter is to consider the relationship between nationalism and socialist internationalism in historical perspective, emphasizing the ways in which each of these forces was changed by its interaction with the other. Socialist internationalism can be considered as historically the main challenger to nationalism, being its main rival in the field of political ideologies and in terms of movements inspired by those ideologies. One can thus start from a simplistic antithesis between socialist internationalism and nationalism. The former aspired to be a movement aiming to create and develop solidarity between workers (and others) spanning national boundaries. The latter can be viewed as an ideology and movement emphasizing the community and identity of the nation transcending class divisions. 'Class' on the one hand, 'nation' on the other: this stark antithesis can form the starting point of the analysis, which of course has to be qualified and made more complex as the historical development proceeds.

It is possible to tell the story of the relationship between nationalism and socialist internationalism in terms of the latter's 'rise and fall', with the crucial dates marking the apparent demise of socialist internationalism being those of 1914 and 1991. The first epochal blow to the aspiration to create a supra-national community of workers came with the rallying to the flag of national defence on the part of the majority of socialist

* I am most grateful to the editor of this volume, Professor John Breuilly, and to Professor Ernst Wangermann (Salzburg University) for their extremely helpful comments on an earlier draft of this chapter.

parties and their followers in August 1914. The appeal of 'Union Sacrée' or 'Burgfrieden' generally prevailed over the resolution to make 'war on war' and turn war into a catalyst for revolution. The second, and, in the opinion of some, final crisis of socialist or proletarian internationalism came with the collapse of Communism as represented by the USSR in 1991. Founded in 1919, the Communist International (Comintern or Third International) brought together newly formed Communist parties, which were rigidly organized on the model of the Russian Bolshevik Party. This International proclaimed itself as the agent of international revolution, and the USSR as the base from which, in the first instance, this revolution would proceed. The dissolution of the Comintern in 1943 and its rather short-lived replacement by the Cominform at the early stages of the Cold War (from 1947 to 1956) did not change the formal commitment of the USSR to be a beacon of international revolution, to represent an alternative form of society that was to be an aspiration for exploited classes and colonized peoples everywhere. The dissolution of the Soviet Union can thus be seen as ringing down the curtain on the idea of world revolution with its directing centre in Moscow, even if the last phase of international communism showed a far higher degree of diversity and pluralism following on from the Sino-Soviet split and from the assertion by Western European communist parties of their autonomy in the name of 'polycentrism' and of 'national roads to socialism'.

While there is no doubting the significance of those two dates of 1914 and 1991 in the history of the relationship between socialist internationalism and nationalism, that relationship is more complex than the one of simple antithesis presented above ('class' versus 'nation'). Furthermore, a narrative of socialist internationalism couched in terms of 'rise and fall' is both too simplistic and possibly premature in its obituary of the ideals and aspirations of socialist internationalism, since those ideals are still relevant to contemporary politics. Any study of this subject has to examine the changing ways in which socialist internationalism and nationalism have modified and affected each other, as well as the diverse understandings of what was meant by 'socialist internationalism' in theory and practice. Accordingly, this chapter starts with some general considerations on the meaning of socialist internationalism and its relationship to nationalism, before dealing with the period of the Second International from 1889 to 1914 and then, after the watershed of 1914, considering the changed nature of socialist internationalism in the period of the Comintern and after. A final concluding section discusses whether socialist internationalism really is 'dead and buried', or whether it has survived as an ideal transformed by the experience of its chequered history.

What is Socialist Internationalism?

Socialist internationalism needs to be seen in various ways, in the first instance as an ideal related to yet also distinct from the concept of cosmopolitanism stemming from

Enlightenment heritage. This heritage found expression in Utopian socialism, for example Henri de Saint-Simon's scheme for the 'reorganization of European Society'. He called for members of a European Parliament to be people whose activities 'extend beyond their own country, make them better able to achieve the universal outlook, which should make up the European *esprit de corps*...'.[1] Yet the distinctiveness of *socialist* internationalism in contrast to other forms of internationalism rests on the idea of a particular agency or vehicle for realizing the goal of an international community. That agency was seen as the working-class or labour movement, whose internationalism was in some sense intrinsic to its very nature. At least in the classical Marxist perspective, the working class was viewed as a new formation, being at once the product of capitalist society and the agent of its transcendence. Since capitalism was bound through its inherent dynamism to extend its area across national boundaries and realize itself as a world system, so too the working class as the rebellious child of that system was by its nature international. In the dramatic words of Karl Marx, 'The nationality of the worker is neither French, nor English, nor German, it is *labour, free slavery, self-huckstering.* His government is neither French, nor English, nor German, it is capital. His native air is neither French, nor German, nor English, it is *factory air.*'[2] This socialist internationalism thus was not a mere idealistic aspiration. It could be demonstrated by a sociological analysis to be part of contemporary reality. Capitalism was conceived as an economic and social system that would spread throughout the world, creating a working class whose conditions would be primarily defined by their need to sell their labour power to the capitalist class, irrespective of particular local conditions or cultures. The expectation of classical Marxism was that the awareness of such similarity of conditions would increase over time, and hence link workers of one nation with those of another in mutual recognition of their shared condition. Hence derives the statement of *The Communist Manifesto* that 'the working men have no country. We cannot take from them what they have not got.'[3] This oft-quoted sentence was not meant to deny that workers lived in a particular nation, but that their awareness of their common conditions would come to outweigh any distinct national identity and local culture. The analysis provided by classical Marxism was therefore that class struggle would necessarily develop on an international level, since the interests of the workers of one country were the same as those of workers from other countries. Improvement and ultimately transformation of their condition required joint action with workers everywhere. This in turn required international organizations and institutions to coordinate and foster such joint action in their common interest.

In a recent essay entitled 'Internationalism: A critique' the Scottish writer Tom Nairn presents internationalism as a ghost or 'noble spectre which has haunted the whole development of socialism'. He argues that 'It has been clear since 1871 that he (i.e. internationalism) is not the body of socialism.'[4] In Nairn's words, 'Internationalism poses a moral alternative to the way the world has actually gone, since the Franco-Prussian War, the end of the First International[5] and (more emphatically) since 1914. Because this option has been so rarely and partially translatable into practice, one must ask whether the apparent aspiration was always the real one.'[6] Nairn's line of argument suggests that it is nationalism that is in reality 'the way the world has actually gone', and that internationalism was a form of false consciousness developed primarily by intellectuals as a way of averting their gaze from this reality that belied their aspirations. However, a more fruitful approach seems to be to probe the dilemma faced by the socialist movement as it developed, which was that the aspiration to develop a consciousness of international solidarity coexisted with the reality of the nation state. The nation state and the undoubted existence of different national identities and cultures constituted the framework within which socialist parties and movements had to act. Whatever might be the shape of the future society brought into being first by the capitalist world-market and then by joint socialist action, in the here and now (speaking of the formative period of mass socialist parties before 1914) it was within real existing nation states that socialist movements had to establish their base and achieve their immediate objectives. The problem which Nairn raises, that of the difficulty of realizing internationalism in practice, can be further explored by discussing how socialism reacted, in theory and practice, to the reality of the nation state and the appeal of nationalism. In turn, the history of nationalism and the politics of nationalists have been shaped by the challenge of socialist internationalism, so that the fate of socialist internationalism and the changing nature of nationalism have been intertwined. Neither can be understood without the other. This is all the more true since the democratization of the modern nation state in such countries as France took place in the same historical period as the development of mass working-class organizations and the growth of socialist parties. In the pithy formulation of the historian E. H. Carr, coined in 1945, 'the socialisation of the nation has as its natural corollary the nationalisation of socialism',[7] and it is this reciprocal interaction of socialist internationalism and nationalism that needs further investigation.

Socialism as a body of thought and as a movement sought to make a reality of the common interests that linked workers of different nations, and to embody this in institutions that expressed such international solidarity. Internationalism in socialist thought and practice has been the aspiration to heighten awareness of the common interest between workers of different nations, and to deploy this practically against the dangers of heightened nationalism, most notably in the struggle against war. This suggests then that internationalism was to be seen as the realization of common interests, and ultimately as the aspiration to a supranational community, expressing a form of solidarity that transcended the borders of the nation state. The hope was that this supranational community would be a powerful vehicle opposing the elevation of the nation as the supreme focus of loyalty. In practical terms this meant the attempt to deploy the international union of the workers as a force against war between nations. However, in line with the sociological realism mentioned above, socialist movements existed in a world of nation states. This meant not only that they had to take the reality of national cultures and histories into account, but that in very practical terms labour movements operated politically in a national context. Socialist parties sought to mobilize workers for political action within the framework of the nation, using the opportunities, the language, and the political institutions of their particular nation state. The *Communist Manifesto*, despite the dramatic statement quoted above that 'The working men have no country', emphasized the national context of socialist action in another passage: 'Since the proletariat must first of all acquire political supremacy, must rise to be the leading class of the nation, must constitute *the* nation, it is, so far, itself national, though not in the bourgeois sense of the word.'[8] This argument was also developed, as will be shown below, by theorists like Otto Bauer and Karl Renner writing in the context of a multinational state, the Austro-Hungarian Empire. Their perspective was that by sharing in the culture of the nation, hitherto the property of the ruling classes, the working class would in this cultural sense 'constitute the nation' and no longer be excluded from it.

Historically, the relationship between nationalism and socialist internationalism was therefore a reciprocal one, in that each affected the other. Socialists had to accept that they worked, though not exclusively, in a national context. Their problem was how to accept this, and seek to gain and extend national citizenship for the working class, while at the same time developing and heightening an awareness of the need for political action transcending national boundaries. It was the 'revisionist' Eduard Bernstein who wrote that the task of social democracy was 'to raise the worker from the social position of a proletarian to that of a citizen (*Bürger*) and thus to make citizenship universal'.[9] This citizenship was, however, a national citizenship, in which workers would gain full admission to the rights and privileges of a member of the national community. At the same time the task of socialist parties was to heighten a sense of belonging to an international community of workers whose sense of solidarity had to be mobilized when nationalists, among others, tried to make the nation the sole or overriding source of identity, for example when war threatened. Thus socialists were concerned to recognize the national framework of action while at the same time transcending it. As will be shown in more detail below, different socialists grappled in contrasting ways with this dilemma, ranging from an acceptance and indeed welcoming of the diversity of national cultures (the Austro-Marxists) to those like Rosa Luxemburg who sought to warn of the dangers of giving too much significance to national culture and distinctiveness at the expense of the joint action of a working-class movement seen as international by its very nature. The topic thus has to be treated historically, with the two dates of 1914 and 1991 seen as closing two distinct periods, that of the Second International and that dominated by international communism.

The Period of the Second International

While it is true that the beginnings of socialist internationalism can be traced to the relatively short-lived existence of the First International, the IWMA, or International Workingmen's Association (1864–76), it was the period of the Second International (1889–1914) that saw the development of distinctively socialist perspectives on problems of nationalism and the nation state, and witnessed a sustained effort to create practical means to give effect to international labour solidarity and the prevention of war. The reciprocal interaction of socialist internationalism and nationalism in this period can best be understood within two different contexts, both of which found representation in the organization of the Second International. The first was that of 'established' nation states, whether such unification had long since been accomplished in a nation such as France, or whether it was of very recent date, such as Germany. The second problem area was that of multinational empires, those of Austro-Hungary, Russia, and the Ottoman Empire, which saw the development of nationalist movements of what Ernest Gellner calls 'the classical Habsburg (and points south and east) form of nationalism'.[10] These movements sought to make explicit a distinct national culture and were in search of that desideratum of modernity, a political roof (state) for the cultural unit of the nation.[11] The problem of socialist internationalism and its relationship to nationalism presented itself differently in each of these two types of situation.

The Second International, formed in 1889, proclaimed its aspiration to develop an international community of workers, whose practical achievement would be to combat the most devastating result of nationalism, war between nations. This was made most explicit at its Stuttgart congress of 1907, which committed socialist parties to develop their joint action against the threat of war. If war nevertheless broke out, the famous amendment of Lenin, Luxemburg, and Martov instructed the socialist parties of the International to use the weapon of the general strike and to oppose war through revolution.[12] In congresses of the International, as one recent analysis makes clear in an illuminating way, the attempt was made to symbolize and enact through performance and representation an international culture of proletarian solidarity, which was, however, based on an acceptance of national traditions and cultures: 'the reality of the structure of the Second International', Kevin Callahan argues, was one of 'socialist identities rooted in national traditions underpinning an international identification, or simply an international identity'.[13] The aim of the parties of the Second International, of which the German party, the *Sozialdemokratische Partei Deutschlands* (SPD), was the leading light, could thus be summarized as a twofold one: of seeking on the one hand to integrate the workers into the citizenship and more broadly into cultural membership of the nation (the 'socialisation of the nation' spoken of by E. H. Carr), while aiming on the other hand to broaden this national identity or complement it by an international identity. The latter was not purely symbolic, but the aspiration was to realize it in practical terms through international congresses and by a political commitment to oppose the threat of war and, if war broke out, by the refusal to fight for the nation. It is obvious that there was a tension between these two aims. The first (integrating the workers into the nation and in general socializing the nation) represented not so much a concession to nationalism as an attempt to turn the reality of the nation state and the national context of socialist action into a positive asset for socialist parties and movements. Yet it does show the impact of nationalism on socialist internationalism. Indeed, one theme of socialist ideology, well illustrated in the French case, was the claim that socialists were genuine patriots in ways which the self-proclaimed nationalist parties of the Right or 'revolutionary Right'[14] could never be. Socialist leaders and ideologues, such as Paul Lafargue, son-in-law of Marx, denounced the 'patriotism of the bourgeoisie' as a hypocritical pretence, since the bourgeoisie and property-owning classes in general were happy to invest their money and capital wherever they could make most profit, irrespective of the interests of their own nation, and were perfectly happy with employing foreign workers if they could pay them lower wages.[15] The argument deployed by socialists was therefore that bourgeois patriotism was a sham, a mask for encouraging workers to manifest solidarity with their employers and exploiters in the name of national solidarity, while the capitalists themselves followed their interests wherever there was profit to be made.[16] In opposition to such false patriotism and the exaggerated aggressive and anti-republican nationalism of the patriotic leagues baying for 'revenge' against Germany, French socialists proclaimed that they were the true patriots who had the interests of the working masses of the nation at heart, and who were continuing the revolutionary traditions of the French nation that the right-wing nationalists were betraying.

There was of course a danger here that such an attempt at 'socialist nationalism' could turn out to be nationalism *tout court*, privileging French (in this example) workers against workers of other countries, and thus potentially undermining the internationalism that the ideology of socialist internationalism was meant to be inculcating. Socialist parties moved within a national context. The statement of the *Communist Manifesto* that 'the working man has no country' was bound to seem increasingly irrelevant when it was precisely within the national context that citizenship rights were demanded and to some extent acquired. Workers' parties could fight for social reforms through the national ballot: there was universal male suffrage in France and also in Germany, despite the severe limitations on the power of the national Parliament, while in England most male workers had gained the right to vote following the second and third Reform Acts of 1867 and 1884. In Austria universal male suffrage had been gained in 1907 after hard-fought struggles. Furthermore, the extension of national education and conscription into the army provided powerful agencies of political and national socialization to which workers were no more immune than any other class of society. One of the leaders of French socialism, Jules Guesde, asserted at a congress (Limoges, 1906) of the recently (in 1905) unified Socialist Party, whose full title of *Section française de l'Internationale Ouvrière* (SFIO) announced its internationalist vocation, that it was erroneous to proclaim to peasants and workers that they had no country. However true that might have been in 1848, he argued, 'Since 1848, since universal suffrage has been put into his hands as a weapon, the proletarian has a country, and if he does not profit from it that is his fault.'[17] Through universal suffrage exercised on the national terrain of the republic the workers could conquer power, according to the analysis of Guesde. This clearly led to a form of 'socialist nationalism' in which the international vocation of Second International socialism became slanted to give more emphasis to the working-class movement making the nation *their* nation, with clear implications for loyalty to the nation in the case of war.

While the examples given so far are taken from the French case, which may be particularly exemplary because of the influence that France's revolutionary history and memories of 1789 exercised on the French Left, such a socialist nationalism was not peculiar or specific to France. French socialists could pride themselves on their citizenship of a republic and the historical legacy of 1789, both of which they opposed to German socialists who had neither. German socialists, who were subject to an imperfectly constitutional empire, could for their part lay emphasis on the unique strength and organizational cohesion of German social democracy, and (after 1894 and the Franco-Russian alliance) maintained that the French republic was allied with Tsarism, that bastion of reaction throughout Europe. In his lifetime Engels[18] linked the success of socialist revolution in general to the fate of the German party (SPD), and warned that if war broke out it would be 'above all a war against the strongest party, best prepared for action, in all Europe'.[19] He drew the conclusion that German socialists would have no other option but to oppose any aggressor nation, even republican France, especially if allied with Russia. In the same vein, the eminent leader of the SPD, August Bebel, acknowledged in 1891 that the SPD might in the event of war collaborate with the class enemy ('with those who today are our opponents'), however this would not be in order to help them or their social and political order but to defend the nation, 'to save ourselves and to liberate from a barbarian a territory on which we aim one day to realize our own ideal society'.[20] The 'barbarian' in this case was clearly Russia. Hence if French socialists saw themselves as, in the event of war, defending the terrain of the democratic republic, German socialists could and did invoke their advanced organization and its national terrain as essential to the international socialist revolution, and therefore as requiring defence if the need arose. Similarly in Britain, as a recent analysis makes clear, 'While shocked by the irrationality of jingoism, the left refused to give up patriotism and the opposition' (the author is speaking here of opposition to the Boer War) 'in most cases was based on a radical version of patriotism, and again and again they stressed their loyalty to "their" country, opposing a radical version of its interests to the official version of the "national interest".'[21]

The implication of this analysis is that in the period of its most rapid growth, in terms of mass-organized parties seemingly marching to electoral victory, socialist internationalism was affected, or infected, by nationalism, in the following sense. The national context of socialist action and the achievement, in however stunted and inadequate a form, of political rights (suffrage) and social rights (welfare and social citizenship rights), meant that workers and their socialist leaders were not and could not be indifferent to the nation within which their activities took place. Indeed, they claimed in certain respects to be better patriots and more concerned with the welfare of the nation than the self-proclaimed patriots and nationalists of the Right, who used nationalism as a device to contain class conflict but who were always prone to neglect the nation and national interest when it was a question of pursuing their class economic interests in the search for profit. By the same token, nationalism became, if not socialist in any genuine sense, then at least populist, since nationalist parties and movements sought to integrate the workers into the national community, often by channelling their discontent against a scapegoat of the foreign worker and the immigrant. The French nationalist Maurice Barrès and the evolution of '*le parti national*' in France provide good examples of this process. In the context of fin-de-siècle France, as one historian notes, '. . . socialists and national socialists vied for the same constituency, the "popular masses". Ultra-nationalists entered this contest determined to tear the working class from socialism's embrace.' The 'champions' of French national socialism 'fought to "nationalize" the proletariat'.[22] With respect then to the nations of western Europe in the period of the Second International, socialist parties attempted to develop a sense of international solidarity but this was more abstract and weaker than their necessary involvement in a national context that often led them to stress their loyalty to 'their' nation, albeit a loyalty couched in different terms from that of their bourgeois or nationalist rivals. In turn, those nationalist rivals attempted to develop a populist or would-be socialist form of nationalism, claiming to address the problems of the workers and cement their loyalty to the nation by opposing national solidarity to an 'Other' consisting of foreign workers stealing the jobs of the workers of the nation in question. The whole debate and struggle thus was moved on to the terrain of the nation, and the idea of the nation became a contested concept of which Left and Right, socialists and nationalists respectively, sought to impose their version as hegemonic or dominant. Right-wing defenders of the nation sought also to attract a working-class constituency by suggesting that imperial expansion and the conquest of colonies would pay for projects of social reform and improve the conditions of the metropolitan working class.

With regard to eastern and central Europe, where socialist parties operated in the context of multinational empires in which the 'national question' presented itself in a more acute form, the debate developed in a different way. Yet here too socialism with its international vocation was sharply affected by its necessary recognition of the force of nationalism. The most extensive theoretical interrogation of nationalism from within the Marxist and socialist tradition in general remains Otto Bauer's great study, *The Question of Nationalities and Social Democracy*, for many years after its initial publication in 1907 unavailable in English translation, a situation happily remedied by its appearance in 2000 in an English version.[23] One of the distinctive features of Bauer's treatment of the issue of nationalism was that he rejected the argument that there was no such thing as national character, thus implicitly challenging such statements as that of Marx quoted above to the effect that the worker's 'native air' was 'factory air', irrespective of the nation to which that worker belonged: 'For although there may be relationships based on interaction between German and English workers,' Bauer wrote, 'these are much more tenuous than the relationships that link the English worker with the English bourgeoisie.'[24] In Bauer's view (and that of the Austro-Marxists more generally), national character was a significant reality in its own right, not however functioning as a causal explanatory factor, but as something that had itself to be explained: 'the national character itself is not an explanation of the behaviour of any given individual, but merely the recognition of the relative similarity of the behaviour of the members of a nation in a particular era. It does not constitute an explanation—it requires explanation.'[25] Such an explanation, in Bauer's view, could be provided through the tools of Marxist theory, seeing the nation as the product of a series of historical developments, as a 'community of fate' (*Schicksalsgemeinschaft*) from which, so far, the working class had been excluded by the power of the ruling class. Through a shared language and the common culture it expressed, there existed a cross-class national community that would become more rather than less significant as socialism grew in strength and the workers could share in the cultural goods of their nation.

The nation was thus envisaged as a cultural community, and it was this distinctive cultural perspective on the nation that marks out the Austro-Marxist approach. Socialists in eastern and central Europe had both to accept the power of nationalism, and at the same time seek to transcend this in the name of an international solidarity that socialist parties sought to articulate. Nowhere was this 'double game' more problematic than in those multinational empires where members (including working-class members) of different ethnic or national groups lived together on the same territory, and where therefore any neat linking of 'one nation, one state' was impossible. The solution proposed by Austro-Marxism attempted to achieve such a double act of recognition of the nation combined with a practical attempt to unite workers and socialists of different nations in international solidarity. The sphere of the nation was, for these theorists, the sphere of national culture, which would be secured in practical terms through non-territorial national cultural autonomy. Individuals could inscribe themselves as members of a particular nation, and these nations would be cultural associations recognized by law, with rights of local self-government and rights to express the culture of the nation through schooling and through the different cultural practices that manifested the life of the nation. Yet this was different from the life of the state, which, at least as the Austro-Marxists understood it, was to be a multinational state, within which the socialist party was to bring together workers of different nations in a '*Gesamtpartei*', or a unified party that would transcend national allegiance in a supranational movement fighting for economic and social rights common to workers of all nations. Part of the reason for the Austro-Marxists' desire to maintain the multinational framework of the Austro-Hungarian monarchy was also their belief, in line with Marxist orthodoxy, that such a larger state would favour economic development. In that way it would hasten the coming of that stage of capitalist maturity which would lay down the preconditions for socialism. The aim was thus to separate 'state' from 'nation' through the policy of national cultural autonomy.[26]

This can be seen as another strategy or theoretical perspective developed by socialists to unify the movement along the lines of international solidarity while at the same time recognizing the significance of demands for the recognition of national culture and identity. It is well-known how this Austro-Marxist strategy was attacked by Lenin and the Bolsheviks for giving too much importance to distinct national cultures, to which Lenin denied any lasting validity. He claimed that there was no such thing as 'national culture', since, as he maintained, 'our slogan is: the international culture of democracy and of the world working-class movement'.[27] The Austro-Marxist theorists, of whom the most prominent were Otto Bauer and Karl Renner, were in a very different situation from that of Lenin. As leaders of a mass working-class party, they had to deal with nationalist conflicts within the ranks of that party, above all the tensions between German-speaking and Czech workers. The Austro-Marxists attempted to defuse nationalist squabbles that were often of a very trivial sort over such issues as the naming of roads and other symbolic offences to national pride. Such issues undermined the unity of the working-class movement and blocked social legislation in Parliament. The Austro-Marxists attempted to calm such nationalist passions by conceding autonomy at the cultural level to nationalist associations, and through giving nations a degree of power at the local level. In this respect their policies can bear comparison with more contemporary models of multiculturalism and also with proposals by contemporary social scientists for 'containing nationalism' by conceding a limited degree of power at sub-central level.[28] The problem with their analysis, however attractive in theoretical terms, was that it proved more difficult than they envisaged to separate 'nation' from 'state', to confine the national question to questions of culture that were distinct from political, economic, and social questions on which workers of different nationalities were supposed to come together in pursuit of their common interests. Once recognition of cultural autonomy was conceded, the dynamic of nationalism could and did break the bounds confining it to that sphere, since it is precisely the force of nationalism to link politics and culture and to connect questions of state membership with cultural identity, for as one modern analyst of nationalism observes, 'all nationalism is cultural'.[29] With no less truth could it be said that 'all nationalism is political', concerned with securing a share of political state power to protect a particular national culture. The Austro-Marxist attempt to separate out the political unit of the multinational state from the cultural (as they saw it) unit of the nation was thus highly problematic.

The conclusion therefore is that socialist internationalism was changed through its unavoidable engagement with nationalism. It was transformed by the fact that the parties and movements that tried to articulate such internationalism moved within the ambit of a 'world of nation states', or, in the context of eastern and central Europe (though not, at this stage, in Russia), nations aspiring to be states and achieve nation statehood. It would indeed be simplistic to conclude that in August 1914 'nation' won out over 'class' in a straightforward way. It is hard, however, to avoid the conclusion that attempts to make a reality of the international solidarity of the working class had to yield to the appeal of national identity, the more the socialist parties succeeded in achieving some of their immediate objectives. This appeal was of course reinforced by the ideas inculcated through the school, the army, and through historical narratives steeped in nationalist ideology that overshadowed alternative narratives. The temporary eclipse of socialist internationalism in August 1914 thus leads on to the next chapter in the history of this ideal, that represented by its successor in the shape of the Communist International, formed in 1919 in the aftermath of the collapse of the (Second) Socialist International in August 1914 and the coming to power of the Bolsheviks in the Russian Revolution of October 1917.

The Period of the Third International

The period that runs from the formation of the Third (Communist) International in 1919 to the collapse of the Soviet Union in 1991 can be considered, with all its variations, as marking the 'second coming' of socialist internationalism after the blow it received in August 1914. The questions that need investigation are, first, whether and in what ways socialist internationalism in this period differed from that of the earlier phase, and second, how it reacted to the changing face of nationalism in this period. With regard to the first question, some differences are immediately obvious. What emerges from one thorough study of the formation of the Communist International is that 'the policy of 4 August made it necessary to confront the question of whether the visionary internationalism based upon proletarian class consciousness to which Marxism laid claim could ever be more than a chimera'.[30] However drastic the defeat of socialist internationalism, the same author, R. Craig Nation, also observes justly of the events following on from August 1914 that 'What was remarkable, under the circumstances, was the pace at which a socialist left committed to an internationalist alternative reappeared.'[31] This internationalist socialist Left was indeed a small minority. The accounts by Craig Nation (and others) make it clear that Lenin's 'Zimmerwald Left' grouping was a minority of a minority, and that those socialists who met at the Zimmerwald conference in Switzerland in September 1915 had plenty of divergences among themselves. They were divided between those who wanted to revive the Second International and unite socialists of combatant nations in that way, those like the Russian socialist Julius Martov who saw peace as the immediate objective, and the intransigent minority represented by Lenin and a few others who insisted not only that the Second International was a 'stinking corpse' but that 'the conversion of the present imperialist war into a civil war is the only correct proletarian slogan', as was stated in Lenin's article 'The War and Russian Social-Democracy' written as early as the end of September 1914.[32] In letters to his fellow Bolshevik Inessa Armand, Lenin explained that the message of *The Communist Manifesto* that 'the working man has no fatherland' was 'a basic truth of socialism', and that the conclusion had to be 'that international unity of the proletariat is *more important than* national unity'.[33] For one French socialist, the Zimmerwald conference was 'the flame of hope in which we have once more placed our faith'.[34]

In what ways then did Third International internationalism differ from that of its predecessor, which Lenin so contemptuously dismissed in the light of its failure when it came to the real test of August 1914? In a broad sense the ideals of each form of internationalism were of course the same, to bring about an international community based on the working class and radically different from the capitalist society out of which that working-class movement had developed: 'Communist internationalism was conceived as a radical alternative to a capitalist world system presumed to be responsible for an unprecedented paroxysm of violence and destruction.'[35] Yet such an ideal of a radical alternative was also held by socialists of the pre-1914 era. What differentiated communist internationalism from its pre-1914 predecessor were two factors, one of agency, the second of the base, homeland, or model of the 'radical alternative' to nationalism and capitalism. Each of these factors was problematic, and exhibited the same reciprocal influence between internationalism and nationalism that characterized the Second International. The first factor was that the agent to whom the task of realizing this radical alternative was entrusted was the Bolshevik Party and the other parties of the Communist International organized on the model of that party. This was the rationale behind the 'Bolshevization' of parties of the Comintern. The Communist International, or Comintern, was to be itself tightly centralized, in contrast to its predecessor that had essentially been a loose federation of independent parties in no way dependent, ideologically or financially, on a directing centre. But beyond that, the individual parties that constituted the Comintern were themselves to be organized on the Bolshevik model of 'democratic centralism', so that organizational uniformity was to be achieved, both of the Communist International overall and of its constituent parties. In this way one 'national' model of party organization was seen as of universal or international validity. Lenin himself made this explicit in his pamphlet *Left-Wing Communism—An Infantile Disorder*, when he stated that 'We now possess quite considerable international experience, which shows very definitely that certain fundamental features of our revolution have a significance that is not local, or peculiarly national, or Russian alone, but international.'[36]

Thus from the beginning the Communist International was given a 'national' inflection, in so far as one national party, which had been successful in the context of Russia, was imposed as a model, acceptance of which became the 'entrance condition' to the Communist International. However, this was not a 'nationalist' phenomenon, since it was believed to be a necessary precondition for an international objective, namely the extension on a world scale of what had taken place in Russia in and after October 1917, in other words a project of world revolution. Yet it meant that the aspiration to world revolution was envisaged as the repetition of a scenario which had evolved in a particular national context (that of Russia), whose specific characteristics were seen as the 'recipe' for victory. It thus came up against particular national traditions of socialist organization that were, at least in the heyday of the 'Bolshevization' of Communist parties, ruthlessly suppressed, only to return at a later stage with the demands for the recognition of 'national roads to socialism' and 'polycentrism'. Such recognition was implicit in the (now) famous analysis of Antonio Gramsci in his *Prison Notebooks*, written in 1930–2. Gramsci noted that 'In Russia the State was everything, civil society was primordial and gelatinous.'[37] Such an analysis suggested that international revolution could not be promoted by the application of the Russian model to societies of very different political traditions and structures. Yet Gramsci's thought only became widely known after the Second World War, and found some degree of practical realization in the late 1960s and 1970s with the phenomenon (short-lived though it was) of 'Eurocommunism'. Communist parties such as the Italian and French parties then insisted that they had to develop a path to socialism that took account of the specificities of their nation and, more generally, of Western liberal-democratic societies and the opportunities their institutions offered for socialist advance. In the period of the Third International, however, one model (the Bolshevik one) was imposed as the only realistic one. The internationalism of the Comintern entailed the conviction that a repetition of what had occurred in Russia could be brought about, an extension to Europe of the Bolshevik Revolution, with the same agency of a party based on democratic centralism as the crucial factor.

If internationalism came in orthodox communism to denote a specific model of the party as the tool or agent of revolution, the second factor that distinguished communist internationalism was evidently the insistence that international revolution had a base, a homeland, indeed a model in the Soviet Union. As the expectation of imminent revolution throughout Europe receded, the interpretation of 'proletarian internationalism' came to mean increasingly the defence of the Soviet Union as the homeland of Communism and the ideal to which communist parties worldwide had to subscribe. While the Second International had had a 'leading party', namely the German SPD, whose influence as a model was extended particularly in eastern and central Europe,[38] there was no question of socialist internationalism in the pre-1914 era meaning the attachment to one nation as the model to be followed internationally. Yet by the time of the final years of the Comintern, as E. H. Carr writes, 'the promotion of revolution no longer occupied a central place in its (Comintern's) agenda. World revolution continued to figure in the perorations of Comintern pronouncements on every solemn occasion; it was no longer thought of as the primary condition of the survival of the Soviet regime. "Socialism in one country" had taken its place.'[39] This is certainly true, yet internationalism in the period of the Comintern did not mean the total abandonment of any aspiration to world revolution. If Carr is right to say that promoting revolution was not 'central' to the agenda of the Comintern, the defence of the Soviet Union still went hand in hand with a perspective of aiding and assisting communist parties elsewhere and fostering revolution—as long as this was on lines approved by the USSR and compatible with its defence and with its image as the homeland, the hallowed terrain, of socialist revolution. Hence the record of the USSR in the Spanish Civil War (1936–9) was one of assistance to the International Brigades but opposition to those anarchist, syndicalist, and Trotskyite movements like the POUM, which rejected the Soviet model of the party and its strict subordination to Moscow.[40]

It is thus possible to expound the history of internationalism in the period of the Communist International as one of the defeat or rather distortion of the ideal of internationalism, as is done by most orthodox accounts. Such a version of the story suggests that after the vehement resurrection of an ideal of international solidarity in the years after the debacle of 1914, the idea of proletarian internationalism became degraded to an ideological weapon in the armoury of the Soviet state. The Stalinist mantra of 'socialism in one country' took precedence over any genuine form of international solidarity. However, in line with the general analysis given in this chapter, it is more convincing to present a more nuanced account in which the reciprocal reaction of nationalism and internationalism is given greater explanatory power, so that it is not just a one-sided picture of the fall or degeneration of socialist or communist internationalism.

In the first place, and remaining still for the moment within the European context, even in the period of the Stalinized Comintern, national parties were able to assert some autonomy, especially in the period of the 'turn' to the Popular Front strategy after 1935. This can be viewed, especially in the French case, as showing the way in which internationalism and nationalism blended in a movement of mutual influence, with the French Communist Party laying claim to be the defender of specifically French traditions and expressing itself in a particular patriotic discourse, even a nationalist one. The rhetoric of the Popular Front was one that asserted an earlier tradition of socialist nationalism, suggesting that the bourgeoisie were those ready to betray the true interests of the nation for the sake of their selfish class interests ('rather Hitler than Blum'), while it was communists and socialists who truly spoke for the nation. This suggests not so much that nationalism distracted the Left from the path of socialist internationalism, but rather that even in its most Bolshevized time the parties of the Third International were not totally immune or insensitive to the fact that they existed in a particular national context which could be mobilized or exploited for internationalist ends. One can interpret this as showing the irreducible power of nationalism, but it would be better to suggest that socialist internationalism and some form of nationalism of the Left are not incompatible and that the idea of the nation is so malleable that it can under certain circumstances be harnessed to socialist and internationalist ends.[41] In a strange sense, it could be said, the Comintern policy of the Popular Front rejoined Otto Bauer, since his idea that the progress of socialism consisted of integrating the workers into the national culture from which the structure of class society excluded them was not so different from the Popular Front ideology that played up the theme of a socialist concept of the nation as part of an international movement against fascism. This idea of a 'left nationalism' in which the Left proclaimed itself as the true inheritor of national revolutionary traditions was given all the more impetus in the era of fascism, since fascism showed the dangerous power of a 'radical right' form of extreme nationalism to rally workers to a movement totally opposed to socialist ideals and working-class interests.

Secondly, the perspective of the Communist International recognized the significance of nationalism in its policy towards movements of national liberation and anti-colonial nationalism, seen as playing a crucial role in the process of world revolution. Lenin maintained that international socialist revolution could be initiated not in the most developed centres of the capitalist world system, but on the periphery, in 'the weakest link of the imperialist chain'. This opened the way for a concept of internationalism that included movements of national liberation as an integral part of this process. In colonial and semi-colonial countries it was the task of communist revolutionaries to assist nationalist movements struggling for independence, since this was a stage on the way to world revolution. It is true that the Second International had not entirely neglected the colonial question, with a spectrum of positions ranging from the French socialist Jean Jaurès' criticism of French colonial policy in Morocco to those socialists who defended colonialism and even imperialism in a paternalist way by seeing it as bringing civilization to developing countries. Yet socialist internationalism before 1914 never integrated movements of national liberation into a perspective of world revolution in the way in which this was done, at least in theoretical terms, by theorists of the Third International. In the period after the Second World War, and indeed after the dissolution in 1956 of the Cominform, the successor institution to the Comintern, Soviet aid to countries of the Third World continued this policy. It is true that in the Cold War period this was part of a struggle with the USA and its allies for 'spheres of influence', and could again be seen as part of the process by which genuine internationalism was subordinated to the dictates of Great Power politics. Some authors[42] see the type of internationalism represented by the Third International and its successors as a form of 'nation-building', where the sponsorship of anti-colonial nationalism was viewed as contributing to world revolution. The implication is that instead of a genuine internationalism it was nationalism (albeit of an anti-colonial kind) that occupied the centre stage. This yet again illustrates the complex reciprocal relationship between nationalism and socialist internationalism. The latter, in its communist form, sought to incorporate nationalism as a subordinate partner in an alliance with the aspiration to world revolution. Yet the danger of this accommodation with movements of national liberation could be that of 'riding the tiger', in other words that an instrumental attitude could end up with the 'instrument' leading the 'user', the tail wagging the dog. Fred Halliday notes that the whole of the internationalist tradition 'had an uneasy relation to nationalism . . . ', and that while 'later thinkers, beginning with Lenin, sought to recruit nationalism to their cause', 'revolutionary nationalism proved to be the source of much more international conflict and competitive focus on national interest, than an assumption of any revolutionary harmony of interests would have suggested'.[43] Speaking of communist revolutions of the twentieth century in China, Vietnam, and Yugoslavia, Perry Anderson observes rightly that 'all triumphed under the banner of the nation, whereas the Russian Revolution in the hour of its victory had been exempt from any nationalist connotation'.[44]

Socialist Internationalism—Alive or Dead?

The collapse of the Soviet Union can be seen as justifying an obituary of the aspiration to revolutionary internationalism, however distorted that aim became because of the contortions imposed on it by Stalinism and the idea of the Soviet Union as the model socialist society. Perry Anderson notes some of the paradoxes of the present situation, in which, as he argues, internationalism now means 'an affirmative ideal—the reconstruction of the globe in the American image, *sans phrases*', whereas he sees 'the most salient form of nationalism' as 'the type of conflict whose pattern has been set by the post-Communist secessions, but which extend far into the post-colonial world itself'.[45] This would seem in an ironic way to deepen the message of the victory of nationalism over internationalism: internationalism has been separated from any socialist or revolutionary concerns and has been transmuted into globalization or US hegemony, a world modelled on the American image. Nationalism on the other hand has shown its continued vitality, but chiefly in an envenomed and ethnic form, finding expression in secessionist movements that in turn create new problems as minorities victimized by ethnic nationalism in turn wish to secede or seek the protection of some external homeland. The recent independence of Kosovo could be viewed as the latest exemplification of such a process. Socialist internationalism started its career as the main challenger to nationalism and to the 'pulling power' of the nation state, yet it seems to have tried (in its communist form) to co-opt nationalism as part of the process of international revolution. The present conjuncture seems to witness the demise of internationalism in any recognizable socialist form, and the survival of nationalism in an ethnic and fissiparous form far removed from ideas of national liberation or popular sovereignty in an inclusive and civic sense. This in turn stimulates attempts to 'steer' nationalism back onto a more democratic path, in recognition of the fact that, in the words of one social scientist, the nation state is 'the framework in which the modern era produced history's most enduring and successful experiments in large-scale democracy'.[46]

Yet such a focus on nationalism may lead one to write the obituary of internationalism prematurely, if by internationalism is meant a critical concept associated with a movement aiming, in the phrase used by Marx and Engels to describe their concept of Communism, to be 'the real movement which abolishes the present state of things'. Such a movement still exists. Some authors speak of a 'cosmopolitanism from below', represented by the alternative globalization movement, which would assert internationalist ideals in an oppositional way.[47] While this alternative globalization movement is very different in its social basis from that of socialist and communist movements of the nineteenth and twentieth centuries, it breathes new life into the ideal of internationalism for which socialism was so long the standard bearer. In this case a new challenger to the excesses of an ethnic nationalism would take over and rejuvenate (in a literal generational as well as metaphorical sense) the banner of socialist internationalism, including a reconstituted labour movement as one component in its very diverse ranks. The story of the reciprocal relationship between nationalism and socialist internationalism is still an unfinished one: it may well have started a new chapter, with the protagonists of each side appearing in a new form.

NOTES

1. H. de Saint-Simon (1976) 'On the Reorganisation of European Society', in G. Ionescu (ed.) *The Political Thought of Saint-Simon*, Oxford, 89.
2. K. Marx (1975) 'Draft of an Article on Friedrich List's book *Das Nationale System der Politischen Oekonomie*', in K. Marx and F. Engels (eds.) *Collected Works*, vol. 4, London, 280.
3. K. Marx (2002) *Selected Writings*, ed. David McLellan, Oxford, 260.
4. T. Nairn (1997) *Faces of Nationalism: Janus Revisited*, London and New York, 25.
5. The First International, or International Working Men's Association, was formed in September 1864, on an initiative of English and French workers. It was severely affected by the repression following the defeat of the Paris Commune in May 1871, and divided by disputes between Marxists and Anarchists over questions of political action and autonomy of individual sections of the International. After bitter disputes at the Hague Congress of 1872, its seat was transferred to New York, and it was formally dissolved in 1876.
6. Nairn, *Faces of Nationalism*, 30.
7. E. Carr (1968) *Nationalism and After*, London, 19. The first edition of this book, including the words quoted here, appeared in 1945.
8. Marx, *Selected Writings*, 260.
9. E. Bernstein (1993) *The Preconditions of Socialism*, ed. and trans. Henry Tudor, Cambridge, 146.
10. E. Gellner (2006) *Nations and Nationalism*, 2nd edn., intro. J. Breuilly, Oxford, 94.
11. Gellner, *Nations and Nationalism*, 96.
12. J. Braunthal (1966) *History of the International 1864–1914*, London, 337.
13. K. Callahan (2000) '"Performing Inter-Nationalism" in Stuttgart in 1907: French and German Socialist Nationalism and the Political Culture of an International Socialist Congress', *International Review of Social History*, 45, 71.
14. Z. Sternhell (2000) *La Droite Révolutionnaire, 1885–1914. Les origines françaises du fascisme*, Paris.
15. P. Lafargue, 'Le patriotisme de la bourgeoisie', *Le socialiste*, 16 December 1905.
16. R. Stuart (2006) *Marxism and National Identity: Socialism, Nationalism, and National Socialism during the French Fin de Siècle*, Albany, NY, 81–92.
17. J. Guesde (1906) *Parti Socialiste (SFIO), 3ème Congrès National tenu à Limoges*, November, 243.
18. Friedrich Engels (1820–95) outlived Karl Marx by twelve years, and in the final years of his life became a central point of reference and adviser to the socialist movement throughout Europe, especially through his contacts with the leaders and theoreticians of the SPD.
19. H.-J. Steinberg (1971) 'Friedrich Engels' revolutionäre Strategie nach dem Fall des Sozialistengesetzes', in Hans Pelger (ed.) *Friedrich Engels 1820–1970. Referate, Diskussionen, Dokumente*, Hanover, 118.
20. Steinberg, 'Friedrich Engels', 120.
21. P. Ward (1998) *Red Flag and Union Jack: Englishness, Patriotism and the British Left, 1881–1924*, Woodbridge, 75.
22. Stuart, *Marxism and National Identity*, 145.
23. O. Bauer (2000) *The Question of Nationalities and Social Democracy*, ed. E. Nimni, trans. J. O'Donnell, London and Minneapolis, MN.
24. Bauer, *The Question of Nationalities and Social Democracy*, 101.

25. Bauer *The Question of Nationalities*, 24.
26. K. Renner (2005) 'State and Nation', in E. Nimni (ed.) *National Cultural Autonomy and its Contemporary Critics*, London, 15–48.
27. V. I. Lenin (1964) 'Critical Remarks on the National Question', *Collected Works*, vol. 20, Moscow, 23.
28. M. Hechter (2000) *Containing Nationalism*, Oxford.
29. J. Leerssen (2006) 'Nationalism and the Cultivation of Culture', *Nations and Nationalism*, 12, Part 4 (October), 559–78.
30. R. C. Nation (1989) *War on War: Lenin, the Zimmerwald Left, and the Origins of Communist Internationalism*, Durham and London, 25.
31. Nation, *War on War*, 30.
32. V. I. Lenin (1964) 'The War and Russian Social-Democracy', *Collected Works*, vol. 21, Moscow, 34.
33. Nation, *War on War*, 37.
34. A. Kriegel (1964) *Aux origines du communisme français 1914–1920. Contribution à l'histoire du mouvement ouvrier français*, Paris and The Hague, 120.
35. Nation, *War on War*, 235.
36. V. I. Lenin (1969) *Selected Works*, London, 516.
37. A. Gramsci (1971) *Selections from the Prison Notebooks*, ed. and trans. Q. Hoare and G. Nowell-Smith, London, 238.
38. G. Haupt (1986) *Aspects of International Socialism 1871–1914*, Cambridge, 48–80.
39. E. H. Carr (1982) *The Twilight of Comintern 1930–1935*, London, 4.
40. K. McDermott and J. Agnew (1996) *The Comintern: A History of International Communism from Lenin to Stalin*, Basingstoke, 139–42.
41. J. Schwarzmantel (1991) *Socialism and the Idea of the Nation*, Hemel Hempstead.
42. M. Forman (1998) *Nationalism and the International Labour Movement: The Idea of the Nation in Socialist and Anarchist Theory*, University Park, PA.
43. F. Halliday (1999) *Revolution and World Politics: The Rise and Fall of the Sixth Great Power*, Basingstoke, 92.
44. P. Anderson (2002) 'Internationalism: A Breviary', *New Left Review, Second Series*, 14 (March–April), 17.
45. Anderson, 'Internationalism', 24.
46. C. Calhoun (2007) *Nations Matter: Culture, History, and the Cosmopolitan Dream*, London and New York, 4.
47. F. Kurasawa (2004) 'A Cosmopolitanism from Below: Alternative Globalisation and the Creation of a Solidarity without Bounds', *European Journal of Sociology*, XLV, no. 2, 233–55.

Suggested Further Reading

Bauer, O. (2000) *The Question of Nationalities and Social Democracy*, ed. E. Nimni, trans. J. O'Donnell, London and Minneapolis, MN.

Berger, S. and Smith, A. (eds.) (1999) *Nationalism, Labour and Ethnicity 1870–1939*, Manchester.

Haupt, G. (1986) *Aspects of International Socialism 1871–1914*, Cambridge.

Holthoon, F. van and Linden, M. van der (eds.) (1988) *Internationalism in the Labour Movement 1830–1940*, 2 vols., Leiden.
Löwy, M. (1998) *Fatherland or Mother Earth? Essays on the National Question*, London.
McDermott, K. and Agnew, J. (1996) *The Comintern: A History of International Communism from Lenin to Stalin*, Basingstoke.
Nation, R. Craig (1989) *War on War: Lenin, the Zimmerwald Left, and the Origins of Communist Internationalism*, Durham and London.
Nimni, E. (1991), *Marxism and Nationalism: theoretical origins of a political crisis*, London.
Pasture, P. and Verberckmoes, J. (eds.) (1998) *Working-Class Internationalism and the Appeal of National Identity: Historical Debates and Current Perspectives*, Oxford.
Schwarzmantel, J. (1991) *Socialism and the Idea of the Nation*, Hemel Hempstead.
Stuart, R. (2006) *Marxism and National Identity: Socialism, Nationalism, and National Socialism during the French Fin de Siècle*, Albany, NY.
Szporluk, R. (1988) *Communism and Nationalism: Karl Marx versus Friedrich List*, New York and Oxford.
Ward, P. (1998) *Red Flag and Union Jack: Englishness, Patriotism and the British Left, 1881–1924*, Woodbridge.

CHAPTER 33

NATIONALISM AND RELIGION

PETER VAN DER VEER

Modernity and Nationalism

Nationalism is generally interpreted as a quintessentially modern phenomenon. According to that interpretation, it consists of a transformation of culture that is directly connected to the formation of modern states in Europe. The modern concept of 'culture' itself can be seen as the very product of the transformation of traditions into a national culture. The emergence of the European nation state is commonly seen to depend on three connected processes of centralization: the emergence of supralocal identities and cultures (the 'nation'); the rise of powerful and authoritative institutions within the public domain (the 'state'); and the development of particular ways of organizing production and consumption (the 'economy').[1] However, this direct connection between modernity as a particular European phenomenon and nationalism is difficult to maintain if one argues, as Benedict Anderson has done, that the settlers in the Americas had pioneered nationalism.[2] From that perspective it is not state formation in Europe that produces the nation but it is rather the moving away from the traditional social restrictions of Europe that creates the possibility of imagining oneself as a national community. Regardless of whether Anderson is right or wrong in his argument about pioneer nationalism, the important point is that nationalism can emerge in societies that are far from developing a nation state.

Another problem with the idea of Europe as the cradle of nationalism is that it leaves countries from the rest of the world outside the West in the role of mere recipients of a model from elsewhere and thus having derivative nationalisms. While it seems undeniable that European colonialism has brought modern European ideas and institutions to the rest of the world, it is often not taken into account that European modernity itself is very much a product of the European encounters with other civilizations and traditions. Therefore a number of crucial European nationalisms, such as those of Britain, France, and Holland, have been imagined in relation to imperialism. At the same time anti-colonial nationalisms are hardly derivative in their creative transformation of traditions of community and heritage. Just as one has begun to think in historical sociology in terms of multiple modernities, one needs to consider a variety of nationalist imaginings that go beyond European models or blueprints.[3]

When one abandons the necessity of direct connection between a particular modern state formation and nationalism, this opens up a realm of possible forms of nationalism, one of which not only delinks nationalism from state formation but also from modernity itself. Obviously, there has always been great difficulty in demarcating modernity in history, since modernity is not a clear-cut historical period with a beginning and an end, but an ideological notion that values the new and devalues the old by making a sharp opposition between modern and traditional. Confronted with notions of modernity historians are therefore always at pains to show continuities that lie under the surface of ideologically assumed rupture. The study of nationalism shows the inverse problematic. One of the ideological tasks of nationalism is to show continuities over the long history of a particular people, while professional historians are often able to point out that nationalism invents and constructs that continuous past in modern history. Ironically, therefore, historians are often both bridging the great divide between the pre-modern and the modern, while at the same time debunking nationalist myths of the continuity of the modern nation.

In this chapter I will examine the relation between nationalism and religion. After a discussion of secularization and nationalization, I will focus on the colonial phase of globalization and its effects on religious and secular nationalisms specifically in South Asia and China. In this phase imperial interactions are crucial to the formation of religion and nationalism both in Europe and in Asia.

Nationalism, Religion, and Secularization

While nationalism is seen as modern, religion is commonly seen as either ancient or transcending history. According to some philosophers and historians of ideas, modernity clashes with religion. In their view the harbinger of modernity is the European Enlightenment and its critique of religion.[4] This view has been accepted by leading students of nationalism who have argued that modern, national society is by definition secular and depends therefore on the disappearance or marginalization of religious world views and communities.[5] Similarly, an important distinction is made between civic identity, based on citizenship in a territorially defined nation state, and primordial identity, based on kinship, language, or religion, or a combination of these elements. According to this view civic identity should replace primordial identity in modern nation-building.[6] The historical process producing modernity by replacing religious identity with civic identity is called secularization.

Much sociological attention and imagination has gone, first, into the development of the secularization thesis, and more recently its dismantling. The secularization thesis has three propositions, namely the decline of religious beliefs, the privatization of religion, and the differentiation of secular spheres and their emancipation from religion. The causality of these connected processes is to be found in modernization.[7] In Europe one can certainly find ample evidence for one or the other of these propositions, but it is hardly possible to combine them in one convincing narrative of secularization, let alone connect them to stages of political or economic modernization.[8] While generally there is an *unchurching* in Europe, that process is highly uneven, both geographically and historically. At the same time, Christian Democratic parties are still important in the politics of a number of European nation states and, especially, the highly advanced political economies of Western Europe, as in Germany, the Netherlands, and Belgium. The process of unchurching that can be found in Europe in various stages, however, cannot be found in the USA, another highly advanced modern society. While the USA has had secular arrangements of the relations between Church and State from the late eighteenth century, it does not show evidence of unchurching. Interestingly enough, it seems that the uncoupling of Church and State in the USA has had a positive effect on the growth of different Churches. The narrative of decline of religion in the face of modernization does not fit the American case, while in Europe it is a much more diverse narrative that cannot be connected to modernization per se. In the rest of the world the secularization thesis makes even less sense.

Nationalizing Religion

While one cannot anymore accept many of the assumptions implicit in modernization theory, one can still argue that both nationalism and religion are modern transformations of pre-modern traditions and identities. Indeed, there are continuities and sometimes really deep histories. First of all, proto-nationalist formations in ethnicity, language, or religion provide the material for nationalism. National traditions can be 'invented' and nations are 'imagined', but this is not done from scratch. Moreover, they do not form a seamless whole, a monolithic culture, but rather a discourse in which different versions compete with each other in social debate and conflict. But, deeper than proto-nationalism that precedes nationalism, there are ancient understandings of linguistic, religious, and ethnic unity, coupled with notions of territorial sovereignty, that can be found among the ancient Hebrews, Greeks, Indians, and Chinese, for instance.[9] These ancient understandings of sacred geographies together with sacred histories of particular peoples provide much of the material used in nationalist imaginings. All of this material has to be transformed to serve the nationalist cause. Religion thus has to be nationalized in the modern period.

In societies where religions were pitted against each other they had to be cleansed of their divisive potential by being encapsulated in nationalism. They have to be made part and parcel of national identity, and histories of religious conflict have to be tailored to fit a tale of national unity. Religious worship comes to be connected to moments of national glory and national remembrance. This process of homogenization is never entirely successful, because nationalism not only unifies but also diversifies by sprouting alternative nationalisms or regional identities. Since in modern nation states a politics of numbers, producing majorities and minorities, is important, religion can be used as the foundation of majority nationalism as well as the foundation of minority identities. For example, Hindu nationalists in India had constantly to attempt to transcend caste boundaries as well as linguistic differences. Their efforts, however, also created deeper divisions between Hindus and Muslims. In Britain and the Netherlands, which since the Reformation had legally discriminated against Catholics, it was only during the nineteenth century that such laws were removed. At the same time the British and the Dutch acquired a sense of religious and racial superiority towards the colonized peoples in their empires.[10] These struggles are never completed and by their very instability are important in the production of nationalism.

Secular Nationalism and Religion

Besides nationalized religion we find secular nationalism in the modern period. At a theoretical level secular nationalism has sometimes been seen as a replacement for religion and as the religion of the nation state, while modern statecraft can be seen as a secularized, political theology.[11] Even according to this view, however, religious communities are never entirely absorbed by nationalism and continue to be the object of secular regulation, such as in the separation of Church and State. Secular nationalism as an ideology is important in creating and defining the spheres in which religions are allowed to operate. Forms of separation of Church and State are defined in ways that are different in France, Britain, and the USA, and Turkey and India, to mention just a few cases. The extent to which science is separated from religion differs greatly, although the power of science is such that it defines the spaces in which religious arguments can be allowed. In the political sphere it is often argued that democracy is secular or that it ought to be secular, but it is not. There are several possible connections between democracy and secularity, but there is no necessary one. Secularity can be promoted in a society by democratic means, but also, as in communist regimes, by dictatorial means.

Democracy, however, by no means depends on secularization. In fact, there are hardly any secular democracies in the world, because there are hardly any secular societies. As a form of political participation and representation, democracy is characteristic of the modern nation state. Liberal secularists may demand that the state be secular and that it treat religions equally and neutrally, but they will have to acknowledge that, if one allows freedom of religious expression, religion more often than not will play an important role in the democratic process. One therefore needs to distinguish between the relative secularity of the state and the relative secularity of society, and make clear how one defines that secularity. Modern states like England, Holland, and the USA all have had their own specific arrangements for guaranteeing a certain secularity of the state, but these states have found their legitimation in societies in which religion plays an important public role. To give one clear example: It can be safely said that the wall of separation in the USA is a demand that has emerged not from secularists, but from religious minorities that were persecuted in England, and therefore that, at least in this case, the secularity of the state is in fact a religious demand. Such a religious demand for the separation of Church and State can also be found in the Netherlands among Protestant dissenters in the second half of the nineteenth century who wanted to have an education system that was not controlled by the established state Church.

The role of the secular in relation to the religious is not only limiting, since religious traditions that are interpreted in a nationalist way are crucial in the formation of relations between state and society, and society and individual, in the modern nation. These traditions become fields of disciplinary practice in which the modern civil subject is formed. They are also important in creating the modern public. In Britain Evangelicals were instrumental in the eighteenth and early nineteenth centuries in mobilizing a large public into joining anti-slavery societies as well as global mission societies. An entire spectrum of societies of 'moral uplift' targeted the working class during the Industrial Revolution.[12] On the one hand religious institutions enable notions of individual conscience and civilized conduct; on the other hand notions of public awareness, the public, and public opinion are produced by religious movements.

Religious Themes in Nationalism

Nationalism does not have to be secular. It can also be explicitly religious in nature. Religious nationalism may amount to no more than a civil religion in the sense that national leaders, for instance in the USA, express their belief that the nation is 'a nation under God'. Themes of death, sacrifice, and rebirth as well as that of a mission in the world are celebrated in a religious fashion in national holidays and with national monuments. This is especially the case when war and death are involved, in relation to which the nation has to acquire a metaphysical existence beyond individual life. Important theological notions like that of being the 'Chosen' of God can be used to fuel nationalist projects abroad and at home. As important is the notion of rebirth or revival of the nation, which is connected to the Protestant metaphor of Awakening. Finally, there is the notion of the coming of a messiah, a leader who is leading his people to the

Promised Land. This important notion is shared by Judaism, Christianity, and Islam, but variations of it are also found in Hinduism, Buddhism, and forms of Chinese religion. A religious symbolic repertoire of divine election, of ordeals to test one's convictions, conversion to higher truth, and martyrdom is routinely applied to the biographies of great, nationalist leaders.

Globalization, Nationalism, and Religion

Nationalism and the nation state are not singular phenomena, but emerged during a process of European expansion and the creation of a world-system of economies and states. Although sovereignty and self-determination are important elements of nationalism, they are conceptualized in a larger framework of international relations on a global scale. Similarly, so-called 'world religions' like Christianity can never be entirely captured by individual nationalisms, since they have a global mission. Europe has been globalizing and has been globalized over many centuries, depending on which starting point one wants to take for which kind of globalization. In a recent exhibition about Venice and the Islamic World at the Metropolitan Museum of Art in New York, one is shown a Koran that was printed in sixteenth-century Venice as well as portraits of the Ottoman sultan Mehmud by Gentile Bellini that closely resemble the painter's portraits of Venetian doges.[13] This reflects the globalization of technology and art and trade, closely connected to the globalization of religions such as Christianity and Islam. These religions have spread through expansion and conversion along trading routes and military campaigns within Europe and outside of Europe. This larger history of both competition and contact between Muslim and Christian expansionists is certainly important and can be told in many ways that would confound recent depictions of Christian Europe as a bulwark against Islam.

From the nineteenth century the global Christian mission was transformed by the emergence of a world-system of nation states in which a Christian is at the same time a member of a worldwide community and a citizen of a nation state. Members of Christian minorities all over the world have been constantly questioned about their national loyalties. This is clearest in the case of nineteenth-century ultramontanism, the Catholic doctrine of the supremacy of the pope, a doctrine seen both, positively, as an allegiance to the pope and, negatively, as an accusation of national disloyalty. The nationalist question of loyalty concerned Catholics in nineteenth-century Britain as much as it concerns Coptic Christians in Egypt today. Particularly, conversion to Christianity in nations that consider themselves to be non-Christian, like India and China, is often considered to be anti-national. One strategy to cope with that is to show the deep, historical roots of Christianity in periods of national history that are important to the nationalist imagination.

The global character of Christianity allows it to transcend nationalism while being aligned to it. Although Protestant state Churches are directly connected to nation states, the religious cause is always seen as expanding beyond the boundaries of the nation state, especially in missionary activities and theologies of dialogue. The Christian mission may be as old as Christianity itself, yet missionary activities received new salience and new challenges due to the emergence of nationalism. In the contemporary phase of globalization transnational Christian movements, such as Evangelicalism and Charismatic Catholicism, align themselves with nationalism in different parts of the world, while simultaneously remaining outside of the control of national states.[14]

The Concept of Religion

Undoubtedly the crucial fact about the globalization of religion in the age of nationalism is that the entire category of 'religion' acquires a different meaning. The question raised in relation to religion is the same as with nationalism: is religion manufactured, invented, or constructed? And if it is, is it any different from other categories in social thought, such as society or economy?[15] Important in these reflections is Michel Foucault's genealogical method.[16] First of all, it shows that a concept like religion does not have a transhistorical essence, but that the term is configured and transformed throughout history in relation to a conceptual field. Does one have to assume a transhistorical, transcultural essence of the concept of 'religion' in order to be able to compare religions over time and across cultures? This is what many historians and anthropologists who work on religion seem to think, but others have rightly pointed out that it might be more useful to analyse historically the shifts in discursive grammar that make certain world views and actions possible.[17] Secondly, the genealogical method does not need to come up with a historical narration that shows perfect closure, but instead can focus on struggles, on the emergence of dominant meanings, on the marginalization of other meanings. By its very nature it is a fragmentary narration and the focus on struggle implies immediately an understanding that the definition of religion is related to a history of power.

More than usual in the study of society this perspective, when developed in the case of religion, has to be informed by a critical understanding of one's own historical position. Christianity can be studied by Buddhist scholars and Islam by Christian scholars, but the adherence to a particular religious point of view may obscure a clear view of the object of study. This is a difficulty that always occurs in the study of human practices, but it is very obvious and tenacious in religious studies, partly because of its institutional location in Departments of Theology. The answer to this is not to find a purely secular point of view, as some want to argue forcefully, since the secular alone should not be taken for granted as presenting a neutral view. More than anything else, the secular frames our understanding of religion and needs to be analysed itself.

Religion and Nationalism in the Colonized World

The effects of religion on nationalism can be shown best by examining their relationship in the colonized world. The encounter of Western power with Asian religions in the modern period is one that has been preceded by pre-colonial missionary and political encounters, but also by a long history of the expansion and spread of religious denominations within Asia. The presence of Christianity, Islam, and Judaism in Asia long precedes European expansion. Moreover, there is a long history of the development and spread of Asian religions, like Buddhism and Hinduism. One could, of course, mention that Judaism, Christianity, and Islam all originate in West Asia and that they are also Asian religions, but then we would also have to ask from which period the notion of 'Asia' becomes a meaningful category. Obviously, the encounter of Christianity with Islam is of very long standing, as Pope Benedict XVI has recently reminded us when he referred to hostile comments made by a fourteenth-century Byzantine emperor about Islam, but the encounter of Hinduism and Buddhism with Islam is just as old.[18] There is no objective reason why Islam and Christianity should not be considered indigenous to Asian societies in much the same way as Buddhism and Hinduism, although there exists a strong Hindu nationalist urge in India and Buddhist nationalist urge in Thailand and Sri Lanka, for example, to argue for such a fundamental difference. These ideological claims are far from harmless, as we know from the history of communalism in India as well as from the history of anti-Semitism in Europe.

However long and important the history of religious encounters in Asia may have been, the modern period of imperialism and nationalism provides a specific rupture with the past, because of the pervasive influence of imperial power and the ideological emphasis on the difference of modern society from both its own past and from other, so-called backward, societies. Certainly earlier empires like those of Rome and China made a distinction between civilized and barbarian, but in modern empires these cultural distinctions have been presented as universally valid and scientific ones. Comparison and an evolutionary perspective on difference became crucial in the high days of empire. One form this took was in the construction of the 'science' of Orientalism. As Edward Said rightly argued, the assumptions and findings of Orientalism also provided the colonized with a new understanding of their traditions.[19] Hinduism, Buddhism, Confucianism, Daoism were discovered and evaluated by philologists, archeologists, and other historians while traders, missionaries, and colonial officers tried to deal with the contemporary forms of these traditions. It is this apparatus of imperial knowledge that has created an archive which is still crucial for any understanding of Asian traditions and the modern transformation of religion, both in Asia and in the West.

One element of the modern transformation of religion is 'the invention of world religions'. The term 'world religions' came into real fashion only in the 1920s together with world religion courses in North America, but it was developed in late nineteenth-century discussions in the context of the new discipline of 'science of religion'.[20] Buddhism came to be recognized in the nineteenth century as existing in various parts of Asia and thus as a 'world religion' like Christianity. In contrast to the old enemy, Islam, Buddhism was also regarded as an ethically upstanding religion with universal pretensions like Christianity. Some would even argue that Buddhism was a philosophy or system of morality, but not a religion. This is certainly an important issue that has been debated over and over again even up to the present day, but besides such important discussions as to what constituted a true religion, there were also crucial developments in Asia. Above all, there were attempts by nineteenth-century archeologists in India to excavate for evidence of ancient Buddhist sites and artefacts under layers of Hindu ones. Major General Alexander Cunningham (1814–93), the founder of the Indian Archeological Survey, indeed found Buddhist sites in India, such as the famous Sarnath. These findings were an important element in establishing a version of ancient Indian history in which Buddhism was portrayed as the enemy of Brahmanism, came to be destroyed by Islam, and was ultimately supplanted by Hinduism. This was essential to the grand narrative of Indian history in which Buddhism was also seen as an alternative to caste-ridden Hinduism and taken up as such by egalitarian reformers like Ambedkar. It is this simultaneous reinvention of Buddhism, as both a religion native to India and a world religion that should be universally respected for its modern, egalitarian message, that has endowed India with such an important legacy.

In Sri Lanka something quite different happened. Here Buddhism was reconfigured first by the Pali Text Society of Rhys Davids, then by Theosophists like Colonel Olcott who designed the Sri Lankan flag and created a Buddhist catechism, and most importantly by the reformist monk Anagarika Dhammapala. It is precisely the reconfiguration in Western scholarship of Buddhism as a world religion within the imperial framework that has enabled it to become such an important element of religious nationalism among the Sinhalese in Sri Lanka. The dialectics of Orientalism and nationalism are of great importance on both sides of the imperial imagination. In big cities especially, the development of a universal spirituality, of which Buddhism is seen as a prime example, fits the marginalization of institutionalized religion in a secularizing society.[21]

An interesting case in this regard is Dutch scholarship on religion. Besides Friedrich Max Muller (1823–1900), Cornelis Petrus Tiele (1830–1902) is often mentioned as a founder of *Religionswissenschaft* (the 'science of religion'). Again the national context is interesting, just as much as in the case of India, Sri Lanka, or Britain, since the Dutch separated theological subjects that were to be taught by Church-appointed professors from the scientific history of religion, to be taught by State-appointed professors. This development was directly related to a process of religious mobilization that led to a nation state characterized by pillarization (denominational segregation) and to the formation of special universities for a certain kind of Calvinist (Free University of Amsterdam) and for Catholics (first Nijmegen and later also Tilburg).

At the same time that Buddhism was accepted as a world religion in the discipline of science of religion, Islam was rejected as a particularistic creed rather than a universalistic one. In the Netherlands this was not merely an academic discussion. The Dutch Ministry of Colonies supported scholarship on Islam in Arabia with a clear view to gathering information on Muslims from Aceh who were living in Mecca. The colonial theory of Pan-Islamism was operative then, as it is today, whether scientists of religion thought Islam to be universalistic or not. Christiaan Snouck Hurgronje (1857–1936) began as a student of Theology at Leiden University in 1874 and went on to become one of the most prominent scholars of Islam. He stayed in Mecca in 1884–5 and came into close touch with pilgrims from the Netherlands Indies. In 1891–2 Snouck stayed in Aceh as an advisor to the colonial government. His analysis of local forms of insurgency led in 1898 to the bloodiest military expedition of the Dutch in the Indies, the war in Aceh that left 60,000 to 70,000 dead out of a population of about 500,000. While Snouck's work is a good illustration of Said's account of Orientalism, it is also fundamental for imperial understandings of Islam as a rather recent layer of religion that has grown on top of earlier, more harmless layers of Hindu-Buddhism. Islam was seen as an aggressive, dangerous religion while Javanese and Balinese cultures were seen as suffused by a more quietist and mystical Hindu-Buddhism. There is an uncanny relation between the Dutch colonial need for depoliticized law and order and Suharto's need for a similar New Order, and the interpretation of Hindu-Buddhist culture as a deep structure of quietist civilization in the Netherlands Indies.[22] The archeological recovery of the Burubudur as a world monument of Indonesian Buddhism from under the veil of a superficial Islam signifies this colonial theory. It is within the imperial context of Dutch control of the Dutch Indies and British control of British India that knowledge—whether archeological, philological, orethnographic—was acquired about religions that became the subject of the science of religion.

Like the category 'nation', the category 'religion' is universalized in the modern era. Where the Christian Churches had always been involved in distinguishing superstition and false belief from true religion, in the seventeenth century attempts were made to define *natural religion*, that is, beliefs, practices, and ethics said to exist in all societies, in all religions. As Talal Asad argues, 'the emphasis on belief meant that henceforth religion could be conceived as a set of propositions to which believers gave assent, and which therefore could be judged and compared between different religions and as against natural science'.[23] This makes the theoretical exercises of anthropology and comparative religion possible in the nineteenth century, but also a modern Christianity (or a Christian modernity) that is located firmly in activities in the secular world and affirms the laws of nature that can be 'read' as God's Creation. Central in the nineteenth century is the inclusion of non-Christian traditions in the category of religion in order to make them both understandable and amenable to modernity.

For Christian missionaries the recognition of these traditions as forms of religion made it possible to recognize elements in them that could lead to Christian conversion. Attempts to convert Christians to other forms of Christianity, say Catholics to Protestantism, became marginal, because they were all seen as forms of Christianity within the emerging nation states. Conversion became more and more a conversion to modernity, that is, a transformation of the lives and practices of both the lower classes in the metropolitan societies and the entire populations of the non-Christian colonies. The effect of missionary projects in India and China as well as in the Islamic world was much less conversion to Christianity than the modern transformation of other religious traditions.

The conceptual difficulties in translating non-Christian traditions into religions are huge. In India the dominant tradition was called 'Hinduism' by colonial intellectuals in the eighteenth century. The term *Hindu* is derived from Sanskrit *Sindhu* and refers to the people who live near the great river Indus. *Al-Hind* is an early Arabic term used by Muslims who settled in this area. Hindu was thus a term used by outsiders to refer to this area and its inhabitants. It was European Orientalism of the eighteenth century that gradually systematized knowledge about the people of India and their various beliefs and practices into an integrated, coherent religion called Hinduism. It is often argued that Hinduism as such does not exist, since one finds in India a great variety of heterogeneous devotions and rituals as well as metaphysical schools that are merely lumped together by the foreign term Hinduism in the nineteenth century. This is true not only for Hinduism but also for Buddhism and, as we will see later, for Chinese religions such as Confucianism.

Hinduism, thus constructed, has become the national religion of India. Attempts continue to this day to streamline Hindu traditions (in the plural) into what is called *Hindutva* (Hindu-ness) so that they come to resemble Semitic religions like Christianity and Islam (one book, one God, one nation). Such attempts emphasize the opposition between indigenous Hinduism and 'foreign' religions in India, such as Islam and Christianity, although they create all kinds of contradictions. To see Hinduism as indigenous one needs to abolish the idea that it has been a creation of Aryan invaders, members of the Indo-European family; and to see Islam and Christianity as alien one has to ignore their millennial or even longer presence on Indian soil.

Since the late nineteenth century there has been a struggle in India between those who want to nationalize Hinduism as the tolerant civilization that is the basis of a secular state and those who want to nationalize Hinduism as the national religion that makes non-Hindus in India second-class citizens. This struggle is, to an extent, symbolized by the differences between Mahatma Gandhi, the leader of the Independence struggle, and his assassin Nathuram Godse, a religious nationalist of an extremist persuasion who killed Gandhi in 1948 for betraying Hindus.

The Case of China

Chinese traditions have been as difficult as Hinduism to translate into the category of 'religion', but it has been even harder to make one, homogenized set of traditions into the national religion. The best candidate to become the national religion of China was

Confucianism. In the World Parliament of Religions in Chicago in 1893 Peng Guanyu, the First Secretary of the Chinese Legation in Washington, DC, was invited as a representative of Confucianism. He gave the orthodox view of scholar-officials in the Qing dynasty that Confucianism is not a religion (*zongjiao*, a modern term that was adopted from Japan at the end of the nineteenth century) but the law and the teaching (*jiao*) of proper human relations by the ruler and his officials. The notion that also existed for centuries in China that there were three teachings (*sanjiao*)—namely Buddhism, Daoism, and Confucianism—assumed a certain equality between these teachings that in orthodox circles of scholar-officials was not accepted. Peng Guangyu argued that the term 'religion' could be best translated in Chinese not as 'teaching' (*jiao*) but as Shamanism (*wu*). Christianity could thus be seen as a form of Shamanism. Shamanism had to be controlled by the state, because it was a superstition, created by a clergy, that could lead to millenarian rebellions.

Peng's arguments reveal an uncanny connection between modern secularism as an ideological project and Confucian thought. In his view religion was something dangerous and primitive that should be, if not overcome, at least controlled by proper government. It is imperial rule, based on Confucian principles in the Qing dynasty, that sets the norms according to which religious believers in Buddhism, Daoism, or Christianity have to conform.[24] All those religious teachings have fundamental flaws, but as long as they did not violate the political order they could be tolerated. An interesting element of this transformation was a movement to promote Confucianism (*kongjiao*) as part of a Qing-led official nationalism. The important Qing reformer Kang Youwei (1858–1927) initiated this project. Confucius was taken out of the context of imperial ritual into the realm of nationalism. In the schools Confucius should be worshipped as a fount of wisdom, learning, and moral rectitude. These were the beginnings of turning Confucianism into a form of moral nationalism, or national moralism, that became the ideology of the Nationalist Party, the Kuomintang. As in all state-led attempts to create a civil religion, demonstrated by attempts in the French Revolution to replace the Christian calendar with a secular calendar, the real problem was to infuse it with ritual and cosmological significance. This significance could not be adopted from the collapsing world of imperial ritual but had to be reconfigured.[25] One may argue that this reconfiguration of religious elements in a form of secular nationalism also implied a competition with other forms of ritual and signification for the hearts of the people. To put it bluntly, this battle was lost by the Kuomintang in Mainland China and increasingly too after 1960 in Taiwan, whereas the communists succeeded with a combination of Maoist millenarianism and radical destruction of local religion until the 1970s, but they too are now in retreat. It turned out to be extremely difficult to turn Confucianism into a civil religion that could perform the affective and instrumental functions that a variety of religious forms had performed in China over centuries. Much of this history resembles France's failed experiments with invented traditions after the Revolution.

Peng Guangyu's presentation at the World Parliament of Religions in 1893 cannot be separated from the intellectual ferment in which Confucianism became on the one hand a world religion through its incorporation in the Oxford project of *Sacred Books of the East*, initiated by Friedrich Max Muller, and on the other hand a civil religion, unmoored from imperial ritual but attached to a moral nationalism. The transnational context in which Peng had to present his case was predetermined by the translation of the term 'religion' into *zongjiao* and by the standards of morality to which comparative religion subjected 'religion'. Transnational audiences, as in the World Parliament of Religions, were very important for the establishment of the status of a society and its religion in the eyes of the world. Also important as a transnational audience were Chinese overseas communities who were particularly interested in a respectable religion that could unify and symbolize their communities in multicultural dialogues. Confucianism became ultimately more important among them than in Mainland China. This explains the emphasis on Confucian values in a place like Singapore.[26]

China is not only a perfect example of both the difficulties and the keen need to define religion, but also of secularist nationalism as a project to destroy popular forms of worship that are felt to be obstacles to progress. Secularism as an ideology and as a practice in China is in the first place a form of anti-clericalism.[27] Anti-clericalism has deep roots in Chinese history, but at the end of the nineteenth century it gained both the attention of the popular media and of intellectuals who grappled with modern, Western ideas. Intellectuals separated Buddhism and Taoism from their clerical roots and made them into national moralities that could serve the modernization of China. Buddhist leaders and Taoist modernists went to great efforts to bring their religions under the rubric of secular nationalism. The popular press was also not opposed to religion as such but instead to Buddhist and Taoist clerics who were described not only as ignorant buffoons, but also as criminals, drunkards, gluttons, and, foremost, as sexually debauched. Temples and monasteries were described in the emergent press in the Late Qing period as dungeons for sexual debauchery, places of great pornographic potentiality. Clerics are portrayed in stories as visiting houses of pleasure. The main theme here is in fact that monastic celibacy and techniques of self-improvement are a disguise for a lawless, unbridled sexuality. This theme of sexual scandal is certainly crucial in the emergence of the popular press in the nineteenth century everywhere, but the Chinese focus on clerics recalls especially the pornography that was printed in the Netherlands but distributed in revolutionary circles in France in the decades before the Revolution. Here we see a genealogy of *laicité* (secularity) in the underbelly of the Enlightenment that connects religion with sexuality in ways that are never made explicit, but which are, in my view, also behind the social energy in anti-Islamic gestures today in France.

Clerics in China were also seen as dangerously violent, since their ascetic disciplines and martial arts capable of inflicting violence on their own bodies can be turned against others for criminal or rebellious purposes. This theme, obviously, gained prominence in the late nineteenth century during the failed Boxer rebellion (1899–1901). Clerics were able to organize secret societies that threatened the state monopoly of violence, but could also be used by factions of the declining Qing Empire against the Western powers. They combined fighting techniques with magic that made the believers think they were invincible and thus extremely dangerous. Despite the widespread killing of missionaries and the popular xenophobia, the Boxer rebellion failed. This failure showed Chinese intellectuals that there was no future in using magical means to defeat the imperial powers. Again, the themes of delusion and disguise emerge here with the notion that the illiterate masses are led into meaningless and ultimately fruitless violence by cunning clerics.

Besides being a form of anticlericalism Chinese secularism is a form of scientism and rationalism. From a nineteenth-century enlightened and evolutionary perspective it pitches scientific rationality against magical superstition. Secularism is thus a battle against the misconceptions of natural processes that keep the illiterate masses in the dark and in the clutches of feudal rulers and clerics. The Chinese term for superstition (*mixin*) comes from Japanese, as do many other terms that are employed in the discourse of modernity, including indeed the term 'religion' (*zongjiao*) itself. Such neologisms make a distinction between religion that contributes to the morality of the state and superstition that is detrimental to modern progress. These views are shared by intellectuals of all persuasions, including the nationalists and the communists, but also by many reformist religious thinkers. This is both a discursive and an institutional shift as an aspect of the transition from the *ancien régime* of the Qing Empire to the modern Republic. The traditional system of three teachings (*sanjiao*), Confucian, Buddhist, and Daoist, in which Confucian state ritual defined the framework for the other two, was transformed in the Republic by the notion that there were now five acceptable world religions: Buddhism, Taoism, Catholicism, Protestantism, and Islam. Confucianism was kept outside of this arrangement, because it was considered to be both national instead of global and in essence secular rather than religious. Confucian intellectuals did try to turn it into a secular civil religion, but this met with little success outside of the nationalist elite. The five religions that are officially recognized today in China are being organized along the model of Christianity in nationwide associations that are ultimately controlled by the state. What remains outside of this is what is often called popular religion (*minjian xinyang*), namely all those cults that are in fact closely connected to Confucianist, Buddhist, and Taoist ideas and practices but are not part of these associations. Moreover, many of the Buddhist and Taoist local cults are hard to transform into nationwide associations. The opposition between officially approved religion and local forms of superstition gives authorities great latitude for controlling and repressing all kinds of religious expression.

Anticlericalism and scientism together in China were deeply connected to Western, enlightened ideas about progress, in which magic had to be replaced by scientific rationality and by moral religion as the basis of national identity. Major currents of Western thought, like social Darwinism, neo-Kantianism, and Marxism, were absorbed in China. Not only prescriptive thought about society came to stand in the light of rationality, but also descriptive social science, such as sociology and anthropology, which lost their ability to describe the effects of these ideologies on society since they could not distance themselves from them. Chinese intellectuals played an important role in the secularist projects of nationalizing and rationalizing religion and, crucially, they were part and parcel of large-scale state interventions to produce a modern, national identity. While Buddhism and Taoism were to some extent sources for the creation of a national religion, Confucianism was itself being considered as already both a national and rational secular religion. The attempts to transform Confucian traditions into a civil, national religion were extremely interesting as a form of social engineering, but ultimately they failed, largely because Confucian teachings could encompass Daoist and Buddhist teachings but not the social energy that local Daoist and Buddhist cults could mobilize.

I do not want to detail the sordid history of state persecution of clerics and the destruction of temples both before and during communist rule in China. I only want to draw attention to the fact that under communism the campaigns against superstition and clericalism were combined with those against feudalism. The 1950s not only saw the brutal elimination of millenarian movements like Yiguandao, but also the destruction of feudalism and thus the redistribution of temple land and temple property; secularization in its original sense. Mao Tse-tung, as a good Marxist, predicted the decline of religion as part of the creation of a socialist China in the following words: 'The gods were erected by peasants. When the right time comes, the peasants themselves will throw away these gods with their own hands.' But, as a matter of fact, Mao and the Communist Party did everything to destroy what the peasants tried to protect.

Concluding Remarks

Nationalism and religion are products of a multiplicity of modernities in different parts of the world. This multiplicity cannot be any longer easily understood in terms of modernization and secularization. The many different historical trajectories are, however, connected to each other through imperialism and the universalization of conceptual categories, such as 'nation' and 'religion'. In that sense Europe cannot be seen as a model of future developments in the world, but rather as a historical instance of global processes that affect the entire world. The post-colonial world, with its global traffic of trade and information that incorporates but transcends the earlier imperial itineraries, has inherited many of its problems from the imperial encounters that were engendered in the nineteenth century. While commonly an opposition between the secular and the religious is assumed, the argument of this essay has been that these categories are simultaneously produced and complement each other. Nationalism is, historically, a force that produces a nation by subsuming previous cleavages. It does not necessarily incorporate religious identities within a secular frame, although secular ideas, such as the separation of Church and State, do transform the status of religion in society. It is perhaps better to see nationalism as a modern force that shapes and is shaped by important available symbolic traditions, be they religious, ethnic, or regional. In the contemporary world we can observe an increasing global interaction between forms of nationalism and religion that cannot be understood within the confines of the nation state. Neither nationalism nor religion are disappearing, but their globalization is transforming them drastically.

Notes

1. R. Grillo (ed.) (1966) *'Nation' and 'State' in Europe: Anthropological Perspectives*, London.
2. B. Anderson (1991) *Imagined Communities: Reflections on the Origin and Spread of Nationalism*, London. See Chapter 6 in this volume by Don Doyle and Eric van Young on the origins of nationalism in the Americas.
3. S. N. Eisenstadt (2000) 'Multiple Modernities', *Daedalus*, 129, 1–27.
4. P. Gay (1966, 1969), *The Enlightenment: An Interpretation*, 2 vols., New York; J. Israel (2001) *Radical Enlightenment: Philosophy and the Making of Modernity 1650–1750*, Oxford.
5. E. Gellner (1983) *Nations and Nationalism*, Oxford; Anderson, *Imagined Communities.*
6. C. Geertz (1973) 'The Integrative Revolution: Primordial Sentiments and Civil Politics in the New States', in *The Interpretation of Cultures*, New York, 255–311.
7. S. Bruce (2002) *God is Dead: Secularization in the West*, Oxford.
8. J. Casanova (1994) *Public Religions in the Modern World*, Chicago, IL.
9. A. Roshwald (2006) *The Endurance of Nationalism*, Cambridge.
10. P. van der Veer (2001) *Imperial Encounters: Religion and Modernity in India and Britain*, Princeton, NJ.
11. H. de Vries and L. Sullivan (eds.) (2006) *Political Theologies: Public Religions in a Post-Secular World*, New York.
12. Van der Veer, *Imperial Encounters.*
13. For a reproduction of this portrait, see the exhibition catalogue, *Turks: A Journey of 1000 years, 600–1600*, ed. D. Roxburgh Royal Academy of Arts, London, 2005, 273.
14. P. van der Veer (ed.) (1996) *Conversion to Modernities: The Globalization of Christianity*, New York; J. Scott and G. Griffith (eds.) (2005) *Mixed Messages: Materiality Textuality, Missions*, New York.
15. D. Peterson and D. Walhof (eds.) (2002) *The Invention of Religion*, New Brunswick.
16. M. Foucault (1986) 'Nietzsche, Genealogy, History', in P. Rabinow (ed.) *The Foucault Reader*, Harmondsworth.
17. Central in this debate is the path-breaking work of T. Asad (2003) *Genealogies of Religion*, Baltimore, MD, as well as (2003) *Formations of the Secular: Christianity, Islam, Modernity*, Stanford, CA.
18. Lecture given by Pope Benedict XVI at the University of Regensburg on 12 September 2006: <www.vatican.va>, accessed 24 November 2008.
19. E. Said (1978) *Orientalism*, New York. See Chapter 34 on pan-nationalism in this volume by Cemil Aydin where non-European responses to the orientalism of Ernest Renan are considered.
20. T. Masuzawa (2005) *The Invention of World Religions*, Chicago, IL.
21. R. Gombrich and G. Obeyesekere (1990) *Buddhism Transformed: Religious Change in Sri Lanka*, Princeton, NJ.
22. J. Pemberton (1994) *On the Subject of 'Java'*, Ithaca, NY.
23. T. Asad (1993) *Genealogies of Religion*, Baltimore, MD.
24. Hsi-yuan Chen (2005) 'At the Threshold of the Pantheon of Religions: Confucianism and the Emerging Religious Discourse at the Turn of the Twentieth Century', Paper given at the Conference on Chinese Religiosities, Santa Barbara, CA.

25. See Ya-Pei Kuo (2008) 'Redeploying Confucius: Imperial State and Nation Imaging in Modern China, 1901–1911', in M. Mei-hui Yang (ed.) *Chinese Religiosities: Afflictions of Modernity and State Formation*, Berkeley, CA.
26. Tu Wei-Ming (2005) 'Cultural China: The Periphery as Center', *Daedalus* (Fall), 145–67.
27. V. Goossaert (2002) 'Anatomie d'un discours anticléricale. Le Shenbao, 1872–1878', *Extreme-Orient-Extreme-Occident*. 24, 113–31.

Suggested Further Reading

Appadurai, A. (1995) *Modernity at Large*, Minneapolis, MN.
Asad, T. (1993) *Genealogies of Religion*, Baltimore, MD.
Asad, T. *Formations of the Secular: Christianity, Islam, Modernity*, Stanford, CA.
Casanova, J. (1994) *Public Religions in the Modern World*, Chicago, IL.
Duara, P. (1995) *Rescuing History from the Nation: Questioning Narratives of Modern China*, Chicago, IL.
Gladney, D. (1996) *Muslim Chinese: Ethnic Nationalism in the People's Republic*, Cambridge.
Hervieu-Leger, D. (2000) *Religion as a Chain of Memory*, New Brunswick.
Roshwald, A. (2006) *The Endurance of Nationalism*, Cambridge.
Taylor, C. (2007) *A Secular Age*, Cambridge.
Veer, P. van der (1994) *Religious Nationalism: Hindus and Muslims in India*, Berkeley, CA.
Veer, P. van der (2001) *Imperial Encounters: Religion and Modernity in India and Britain*, Princeton, NJ.
Veer, P. van der and Lehmann, H. (eds.) (1999) *Nation and Religion*, Princeton, NJ.
Wolffe, J. (1994) *Godand Greater Britain: Religion and National Life in Britain and Ireland 1843–1945*, London.
Yang, M. Mei-hui (ed.) (2008) *Chinese Religiosities: Afflictions of Modernity and State Formation*, Berkeley, CA.

CHAPTER 34

PAN-NATIONALISM OF PAN-ISLAMIC, PAN-ASIAN, AND PAN-AFRICAN THOUGHT

CEMIL AYDIN

Introduction

Any history of modern nationalism(s) has to face a major puzzle about nationalism's involvement with pan-nationalist projects. The history of almost all nationalist movements, especially in the colonized world, was intertwined with a pan-nationalist discourse, vision, or project. We cannot understand the histories of Egyptian, Indonesian, and Turkish nationalisms independent of pan-Islamism, nor the histories of Indian, Japanese, and Chinese nationalisms without the influence of pan-Asianist visions. Similarly, many of the nationalist movements in Africa were linked to pan-African nationalism. Moreover, various forms of pan-nationalism (from pan-Slavism, pan-Islamism, pan-Asianism, and pan-Africanism, to pan-Arabism and pan-Americanism) were highly attractive to both anti-colonial nationalist movements and various empires and great powers (Russian, Ottoman, Japanese, American) that were not necessarily in agreement with anti-colonial assumptions. In fact, pan-nationalism could be utilized as an instrument, justification and propaganda for hegemonic imperial projects. How should we see the world-historical significance and legacy of pan-nationalism for the formation of the modern world order, as well as for the history of nationalism and decolonization? How can we understand the contradictory reflections of the political projects of pan-nationalism in modern history?

We do know that the story of nationalism is partly related to contradictory forces of globalization. Yet, in the literature about the interactions between globalization and nationalism, we often overlook the fact that, for a significant period of time, pan-national identities and ideals were as important as other kinds of national ones in moulding the political imagination, which in turn shaped the nature of globalization in the twentieth century. The origins of pan-nationalisms have to be understood in terms of the diverse ways political communities have been imagined in a rapidly globalizing imperial world order since the middle of the nineteenth century.

To illustrate the world-historical significance of pan-nationalisms, this chapter will focus on the case studies of pan-Islamism, pan-Asianism, and pan-Africanism, three major pan-nationalist movements that interacted with nationalist thought and projects in Asia and Africa from the 1880s to the 1960s. While outlining the origins of the three pan-nationalisms taken as case studies, the chapter will discuss how they produced important critiques of globalization, empires, international law, and struggles for justice. Then, the chapter will assess how the political trajectories and intellectual content of these three pan-nationalist visions became transformed during the interwar period, accommodating the challenges by Wilsonian and socialist internationalism. Although pan-nationalism adjusted its vision to the idea of national self-determination and a world order beyond the community of empires, it could still be utilized by various imperial projects, as can be seen in the case of pan-Asianism sponsored by the Japanese Empire. In the final section, the chapter will examine the role played by these three pan-nationalist movements in the process of decolonization, with close attention to their post-Second World War reconfigurations. Paying close attention to the intellectual content and impact of pan-nationalist ideas might also help us understand the seeming revival of pan-nationalism in the aftermath of the Cold War and its new institutional versions in the age of nation states.

By examining the appeal and persistence of pan-nationalist ideas, this chapter suggests that we evaluate the historical formation of the modern international order, with the legitimacy of the sovereign nation states loosely cooperating under the umbrella of the United Nations, in the light of its alternative historical possibilities. Nationalism and nation states are constructs of global modernity in its world-order dimension. Yet, there were other constructs, such as civilizations, races, continents, and cultures, which also have had significant influence on contemporary international formations. Pan-nationalism should be understood as one of these modern constructs of imaginations, and the resultant political projects, that preceded, accompanied, aided, resisted, and perpetuated the ideal of nationalism and the formation of sovereign nation states.

The Genesis of Pan-Nationalisms during the Age of High Imperialism, 1882–1919

Pan-nationalisms are generally defined as 'politico-cultural movements seeking to enhance and promote the solidarity of peoples bound together by common or kindred language, cultural similarities, the same historical traditions, and/or geographical proximity. They postulate the nation writ large in the world's community of nations.'[1] Yet, this definition of pan-nationalism based on the shared assumptions of a supra-national community has to account for when and how a globally constructed notion of continental, racial, and cultural community emerged.

There were regional, religious, and cultural identities connecting different communities in Asia and Africa before the experiences of Eurocentric globalization in the nineteenth century. However, these transregional links in the Asian and African continents, and Muslim societies, never produced any pan-nationalist vision. For example, during the medieval and early modern periods, the predominantly Muslim parts of West and Central Asia, together with the Muslim populations of South Asia and China, shared various levels of Muslim networks of trade, education, literature, and pilgrimage, which also extended to Africa. Similar to the networks fostered by the Islamic faith and the Arabic language, Buddhism and more importantly China-centered Confucianism and Chinese literary culture created powerful networks in East Asia, facilitating the exchange of ideas, goods, and human travel in a large region extending from Korea and Japan to India and Southeast Asia. Yet, until the late nineteenth century, there was no shared consciousness of being Asian or African in the sense of a pan-nationalist feeling of belonging to a specific continent or race, nor were there any signs of pan-Islamism. Rather than pan-national identities, imperial identities were very important. In fact, we must see empires, not religion, civilization, race, ethnicity, as the main actors of world history.[2] Even in the first half of the nineteenth century, imperial units were taken as the basic actors of the rapidly globalizing world order, in a diplomatic arrangement symbolized by the Congress of Vienna of 1815. According to the logical outcomes of this system, as embodied in the alliances of the Crimean War (1853–6), the Ottoman Empire, for example, would not be associated with either Turkish nationality or pan-Islamic solidarity.[3]

During the second half of the nineteenth century, when the Eurocentric notions of continents, races, and civilizations became globalized and spread to different societies in Asia and Africa, various geopolitical and continental identities began to be shared and embraced by individuals and social groups from Morocco and Egypt to China, Japan, and Mongolia. Some of these pan-national identities could be overlapping, as Indian Muslims or Muslims under the Dutch Rule in East Indies could share both a pan-Asian and a pan-Islamic identification, while Egyptian nationalists could be proud of being Muslim and African (and still sympathize with Japan and China). Moreover, the racial nature of some of the geopolitical identities of Asia and Africa (which were loosely tied to yellow and black race constructions) made members of the African diaspora in America strong advocates of pan-Africanism, while the Chinese diaspora was linked to a pan-Asian identity. By the turn of the twentieth century, the geopolitical identities of race, civilization, and continent were so entrenched in the global public sphere that nationalist and reformist intellectuals all over the world had to envision their future and destiny in terms of this dominant narrative about pan-national identities.

Thus, it was the spread of Eurocentric categories of knowledge about human geography, coupled with the intense process of globalization in the second half of the nineteenth century, that led to the emergence of Asian, Islamic, and African identities, a precondition for the rise of pan-nationalist thought. For example, a global Asian-Buddhist identity was created not only by travels within the Buddhist world but also through familiarity with the emerging European literature of the history of Buddhism. Thanks to these intra-Asian Buddhist travels and dialogues, Buddhists from Japan to Sri Lanka contributed to the formation of a modern Buddhist canon and facilitated a new pan-Asian Buddhist identity that was best reflected in the 1893 Chicago World Parliament of Religions.[4] Similarly, although pre-modern Muslim networks already existed, it was only during the mid-nineteenth century that the Muslims of West Asia began to visit, write, and read about Muslims in China or Southeast Asia, leading to the formation of a new consciousness about a global Muslim World.[5] African identity also reflected this dimension of movement of peoples coupled with intellectual history, and it was individuals from the African diasporas in America and Europe who became the most vocal advocates of early pan-Africanism.[6]

Due to its crucial global nature and intellectual component, pan-nationalism was never just a natural response to European expansion in Asia and Africa, which had already been taking place since the late eighteenth century. In fact, at the time of the French invasion of Algeria in 1830, the Opium Wars in China (1839–60), or Indian Mutiny in 1857, there was no developed notion of Asian, African, or Islamic solidarity as a response. Instead, many intellectuals from the existing non-Western empires (Ottoman, Chinese, Japanese, and Persian) accepted the idea of a universal European civilization and even the benevolence of European imperialism in offering to uplift the level of civilization in the rest of the world.[7] Formulated in the paradigm of liberal civilizationism, this ideology allowed the non-Western imperial elites to challenge the new European international society to be more inclusive, by asking European powers to accept the multi-religious Ottoman State and Iran ruled by a Muslim dynasty, or the non-Christian Chinese and Japanese empires ruled by non-Christian emperors as equal members of the new system, upon the fulfillment of the required reforms. Appropriation of the notion of a Eurocentric but universal civilization by the Ottoman, Chinese, Egyptian, Persian, and Japanese elites also empowered these same elites in domestic politics, as they could justify centralizing radical reforms over their own populations as a civilizing mission.[8] Self-civilizing projects in Cairo, Istanbul, or Tokyo meant that peasants had to pay more taxes and families had to send their male children to the army, while diverse sub-national lifestyles had to be sorted out for the homogenizing projects of the central government.

While the globalizing world order of the nineteeth century was shaped by cooperation among various European empires, and non-Western empires trying to join this club of civilized empires, a gradual yet radical change began to occur from the 1850s to the 1880s in terms of the rise of racial, cultural, and continental identities demarcating humanity. The Ottoman Empire initially hoped to become a civilized empire composed of Muslim, Christian, and Jewish subjects, but it increasingly became identified with Islam and the Muslim world. The Russian Empire began to champion the cause of Slavic races and Orthodox Christianity, although it had a substantial Muslim population, many of whom were loyal to the czar. Both the Japanese and Chinese empires began to be associated with yellow race. More importantly, European empires were embracing the ethos of the superiority of the white race over coloured races, or the superiority of Christianity over Islam in its legitimacy claims during a more intense and competitive imperial expansion symbolized by the post-1882 division of Africa by various European empires.

It is in the period from the 1880s to the First World War that world public opinion witnessed the popularization of geopolitics as the predominant paradigm for interpreting international politics. The full colonization of Africa and more aggressive imperialism by European powers were sustained by more systematic theories of Orientalism and race ideology, establishing permanent identity-walls between Christian white Europeans on the one hand and the Muslim world or the coloured races on the other. In that sense, Muslim responses to the invasion of Tunisia and Egypt in the early 1880s were different from their response to the invasion of Algeria some fifty years earlier. In the early 1880s European expansion and hegemony were seen as part of a global pattern of uneven and unjust relationships. Similarly, when European empires were dividing Africa between themselves, the emphasis on the mission of the white race to civilize the 'dark continent' became stronger over the years, prompting African-American intellectuals to reflect on the global politics of their race. By the turn of the twentieth century, the global consciousness of supranational identities was already well established in various educated reformist communities all over the world, whether in the form of the strong white Western pride of American Ivy League elites and globalized black consciousness of African Americans, or Chinese, Ottoman, and Japanese intellectuals' perceptions of themselves as Asians and Orientals. Non-Western reformists who were enthusiastic about executing Westernizing reforms began to perceive a non-transcendable racial and cultural barrier between their own societies and Europe, and expressed a strong sense of being pushed away by the European centre to which they were looking for inspiration. During the high age of imperialism, the anti-Muslim racist statements of British Prime Minister William Gladstone or the anti-yellow race remarks of German Emperor Kaiser Wilhelm were not scandals of rarity, but mainstream European discourses supported by a multitude of racial and cultural theories in European social sciences and humanities.

It is in this context that pan-Islamic, pan-African, and pan-Asian ideas were produced as a rethinking of the relationship between civilizing processes, the international order, and predominant forms of racial and religious identities. The first pan-Islamic magazine, *al-'Urwat al-Wuthqa*, was published in Paris by Jamal ad-Din Afghani (1838–97) and Muhammad 'Abduh (1849–1905) in the early 1880s.[9] Similarly, the first pan-Asian organization, Kôakai, was established in 1880.[10] Pan-Islamic and pan-Asian ideas gradually entered into the vocabulary of writings about international affairs, often paralleling the ideas of pan-Slavism, pan-Germanism, and later pan-Europeanism. Similarly, around the same period, pan-Africanism started as a political project calling for the solidarity and potential union of all Africans into a single African federation to which those in the African diaspora could return. The earliest notions of a pan-African vision of unity were developed by a wide range of African-American intellectuals, such as Martin R. Delany (1812–85), Alexander Crummell (1822–98), and Edward Blyden (1832–1912), who all influenced the more systematic ideas of African identity and unity in the writings of W. E. B. Du Bois (1868–1963). Their 'negro race'-based pan-Africanism rested in large part on a critique of Western civilization and white supremacism.[11] Initially, well-educated non-Western or non-white intellectuals had to think of themselves as members of a single 'Negro' race, yellow race, Oriental or Muslim world, before they could envision a program of pan-nationalism. These global level supranational identity markers could overlap and sometimes contradict each other. For example, by picking race as the primary key to identity, early pan-Africanists excluded the lighter-skinned, Arabic-speaking North African populations, who were mostly Muslim, from their vision of unity. Similarly, some early pan-Asianists would see Muslim empires in India as an outside force.[12] Yet, gradually, pan-nationalists would become more inclusive and internationalist.

All the pan-nationalist visions of Asian, African, or Muslim solidarity had to rely on a set of assumptions about the seemingly natural division of humanity into various supranational groups. For example, pan-Asianists of different shades and colours were of one mind on the question of why they were pan-Asianists, which was that 'Asia is one' but 'Asia was weak', and Asians have to cooperate to get Asia out of its state of weakness and subjugation.[13] Similarly, Muslims all over the world began to perceive the Islamic world as a geopolitical and cultural unit, unjustly oppressed by the Christian West and in need of revival. These assumptions of the unity of black race, yellow race, Asia, Africa, Muslim world, America, was always accompanied by a geopolitical vision and a comparison to the assumed unity and superiority of the white race, Christian West, or Europe. Based on this comparison to the unity of the West, there was a desire to assert the moral, historical, and racial equality of Asians, Muslims, Africans, or coloured races, with the additional implication of a need for solidarity to overcome the existing weakness of the transnational group of identification.

Political projects of union, federation, or solidarity advocated by different pan-nationalist ideals were not very realistic, because there was no imperial or international power that could implement these projects, even though advocates of pan-nationalist ideals were looking for a power centre to support their projects. The political and intellectual elites of the Ottoman, Chinese, Japanese, or Persian empires would agree with the basic assumptions of their Muslim, yellow race, or Asian identities, and like their counterparts in Europe and America, they shared the Eurocentric notions of world geography and geopolitics. However, these imperial elites could not officially endorse nor were they interested in any notion of pan-national and anti-Western solidarity. Elites of these non-Western polities were very careful in fostering friendly cooperation with Western powers while attempting to prevent Western suspicions that they could be behind a 'reactionary' alliance against the West. At certain times and in certain locations pan-nationalist projects could have a pro-Western modernist imperial twist and could actually be supported by a European empire. For example, the advocates of the Ottoman support for the Aceh Sultanate (against the Dutch attacks) during the 1870s made the argument that it should be the duty of the Ottoman Empire to civilize the backward Muslim peripheries. Similarly, there were pan-Africanists in the US who could consider getting Western support to 'civilize' the African continent by bringing Western technology there.[14] As pan-ideologies were linked to geopolitical thinking, during the First World War the German Empire could contemplate using pan-Islamism against the British and Russian empires.

More important than its political projects, pan-nationalism produced important cultural achievements and was instrumental in the formation of anti-colonial counter-public opinion. Muslim intellectuals attended Orientalist congresses in Europe to counter the discourses of their inferiority by European scholars.[15] Pan-Asian intellectuals produced important critiques of Euro-American discourses on yellow race, Confucianism, Buddhism, and Asia.[16] Pan-Africanism encouraged and inspired a body of shared literature, artistic projects, and historical writings about black Africans in a truly transnational intellectual sphere.[17] It was already a great achievement to argue for and insist on the equality of black and white races, and to demonstrate their rights for political independence via new narratives of African and other forms of black cultural achievements. Pan-Asianism and pan-Islamism were similarly instrumental in the formation of counter-narratives against the Eurocentric view of human history and the global future, with strong arguments against racism.

From the 1880s to the 1910s, pan-nationalist non-Western intellectuals offered internal critiques and revisions of Eurocentric race and cultural theories and world-history narratives, if possible in dialogue with European intellectuals. It is in this context that the very flexibility of the concepts of Asian, African, Eastern, Islamic civilizations, and their achievements as compared to an idealized European civilization, allowed pan-nationalist intellectuals to inject their own visions and subjectivity into these European-originated notions. The response of Muslim modernist intellectuals to the views of the French philosopher and religious scholar Ernest Renan on Islam and progress showed how a pan-nationalist view of Islamic history and civilization could emerge in the truly global public sphere of the 1880s. Renan championed the intellectual trend to 'Hellenize Christianity and Semitize/Arabize Islam'.[18] Before the 1870s, Muslim reformists thought that the Muslim world shared the same cultural legacy with modern Europe (Hellenism and monotheism), and thus believed that they had stronger innate capacities for progress and civilization along European lines than black Africans. If the Arab-Muslim civilization had preserved the Hellenistic legacy of science and philosophy and passed it on to modern Europe, there could not be anything contradictory in being a Muslim and being civilized and progressive.[19] Being aware of these optimistic Muslim modernist ideas, Renan argued that science in the medieval Muslim world had developed despite Islam and the Arabs, not because of them. For Renan, as Islam was the religion of Semitic Arabs, it could never be compatible with modernity and progress, and Muslims would have to shed their religion in order to adapt to modern life.[20] As a scholar of Islam, Renan noted that if there were great scientific and cultural achievements in medieval Islam, this was either due to Christian Arabs, whose Hellenistic Christian faith controlled their Semitic Arab side, or due to Iranian Muslims whose Aryan race overshadowed the negativities of their Semitic faith.

Muslim intellectuals perceived Renan's ideas as the most eloquent formulation of the prevalent European image of the Islamic world as an inferior race, justifying European colonialism in the Muslim world just a few years after the invasions of Tunisia and Egypt in 1881 and 1882. Many Muslim intellectuals published refutations of Renan's ideas; they also searched for venues and means to engage in a dialogue with European intellectuals, especially through attendance at Orientalist congresses. In fact, the Ottoman government sponsored trips of prominent intellectuals or sent bureaucrats to read semi-official papers.[21] These efforts to support their intellectual heritage were creating a new pan-Islamic narrative of the golden age of Islamic history, the compatibility of Islam with modernity, the humiliation of the Muslim world by unjust colonial subjugation, and the necessity of reviving Islamic pride, which would all support demands by Muslims for political equality.

Non-Muslim Asians also struggled with similar discourses of Christianity's superiority over Buddhism and Hinduism, or the white race's superiority over the coloured races. The Chicago World Parliament of Religions in 1893 as well as the 1911 London Universal Races Congress became forums where Asians and Africans intellectually and eloquently refuted Western racial superiority with their own narratives about Islamic, Asian, and African civilization.[22] Pan-African intellectuals were especially successful in formulating their critique of racism, as most of its leading advocates in the diaspora could write in the English language. In addition to influential figures in the United States such as W. E. B. Dubois, before the First World War, most of the pan-African intellectual and political activism was organized by African students in Britain. They used the name 'Ethiopianism', a pre-First World War movement best depicted in J. E. Casely Hayford's (1866–1930) autobiographical novel *Ethiopia Unbound* (published in London in 1911). All of these activities aimed at 'race emancipation' while proudly claiming Africa as the 'cradle of civilization'.[23] Various pan-African, pan-Islamic, and pan-Asian engagements with Orientalism and race ideologies demonstrate that Orientalist and racist notions at that time were omnipresent but not omnipotent. They could be redefined and re-employed for diverse purposes very different from the intentions of the original European formulators of the dichotomy between Eastern and Western civilizations, or white-coloured race divisions.

Pan-nationalist ideas were most visible in the perception of international affairs and world history by non-Western intellectuals and reformists. Around the turn of the twentieth century, Muslim intellectuals began to perceive international relations as a global encirclement of the Muslim world by the Christian West in an illegitimate manner.[24] Similarly, East Asian intellectuals were emphasizing the conflict between the white and yellow races, while African and African-American intellectuals were emphasizing the unjust oppression of the black race internationally and domestically by the white race.[25] The Japanese politician and journalist Konoe Atsumaro, in an article written in 1898 upon his return from Germany, predicted an inevitable racial struggle in East Asia between the white and yellow races, with the Chinese and the Japanese siding with each other as sworn enemies of the white race. It is important to emphasize that all these theories about the clash of civilizations relied on the literature of international affairs produced and read in European and American universities, and reproduced in the Western media. Thus, it is not surprising that the major pan-nationalist texts on Islam versus the West or the white-yellow race conflict were produced by Muslim or Asian thinkers who had received academic training in Europe or America. Halil Halid's book *The Crescent versus the Cross* is based on a master's thesis at Cambridge University, and Kodera Kenichi's 1,000-page-long *Treatise on Pan-Asianism* is based on his PhD at George Washington University (then Columbian University).[26] Similarly, a white supremacist with a PhD from Harvard, Lothrop Stoddard, was closely read and followed by pan-Islamic and pan-Asian thinkers precisely because of Stoddard's use of categories of cultural and racial conflict in his realist writings on international affairs.[27] The Arabic translation of Stoddard's book *The World of Islam* contains long dissenting commentaries by the leading pan-Islamist Shakib Arslan on issues of detail, but agrees on the basic framework of interpreting world affairs as a conflict between the Muslim world and the West.[28] Sun Yat-sen's famous 1924 speech in Kobe on Great Asianism also starts with a reference to the title of Stoddard's book, by evoking a 'rising tide of color against the worldwide white supremacy'.[29]

We should not assume that pan-nationalists during the age of high imperialism, namely from the 1880s to the 1920s, were against Westernization. On the contrary, they formulated some of the most advanced theoretical reflections on why non-Westerners had to embrace European conceptions of modernity while deploying their cultural distinctiveness in an insecure world defined by imperial competition and geopolitical visions. Writings by intellectuals like Ziya Gokalp, Tokutomi Soho, Muhammad Iqbal, W. E. Dubois, or Rabindranath Tagore reflect their ambivalence as well as sophistication in rethinking the basic parameters of Eurocentric modernity in relation to nationalism, imperialism, and pan-national identities.[30]

Their shared experience of European imperialism while engaging European ideas of Orient-Occident or race hierarchies brought the advocates of different pan-nationalist identities together around the notion of a shared Asian-Eastern identity or global non-Western identity, and prompted their alternative form of internationalism. Pan-Asianism began to include the Islamic world via the concept of the shared destiny of non-Western Asians.[31] The sympathy of pan-Asianists for pan-African thinkers prepared the ground for broader Japanese public sympathy for Ethiopians during the Italian invasion of that country in 1935, even though Italy and Japan had good diplomatic relations at that time. Similarly, W. E. B. Dubois visited Japan in 1936 partly as a product of this mutual sympathy. Meanwhile, pan-Islamists developed great interest in the fate of non-Muslim Asia and the coloured races. Initially, Japan and even China were outside the scope of the Muslim transnational imagination, as Ottoman, Iranian, and Egyptian elites saw monotheistic Christian Europeans, with whom they shared the

Hellenistic legacy, as being closer to them than East Asians. The Asianization or Easternization of Muslim identities toward the 1890s allowed them to link the destinies of China and Japan with their own.

Anti-colonial pan-nationalists were not immune to contradictions and internalized racism: in fact, pan-Islamists like Halil Halid noted that if European racism and the civilizing mission ideology had been limited to the natives of Australia, the Caribbean, and Africa, he would not have had any objections to it.[32] He was, however, noting the unacceptability of the civilizing mission ideology for Muslim, Indian, and Chinese societies, whose greatness lay in bygone civilizations and who maintained a continuing legacy of higher moral values. Many pan-nationalist intellectuals took very seriously racial thinking in the European social sciences, especially the issue of race classification in the writings of Charles Darwin, Herbert Spencer, and Gustave Le Bon. Non-Western pan-nationalists generally preferred the theories of Spencer, in particular his notion of racial self-responsibility, because they could accept that in reality the coloured races were underdeveloped, but denied that this was a permanent inferiority.[33] It is against the backdrop of this engagement with the European discourses about the Orient and race that the Russo-Japanese War of 1905 became a turning point in the history of pan-nationalist thought around pan-Africanism, pan-Asianism, and pan-Islamism, because it disproved all previous European discourses on the inferiority of the Asian and yellow races. In fact, the reconsideration of the scientific literature on race characteristics, to which the Japanese victory contributed immensely, would lead to the 1911 Universal Races Congress, an event that testified to the global impact of the ideas and critiques of non-Western intellectuals.[34] The slogans of the 'Awakening of the East' or 'awakening of the coloured races' associated with the Russo-Japanese War are indicative of the achievements of pan-nationalist thought. Western civilization or the 'white race' did not have to 'decline' for Asia and Africa to gain liberation from Western hegemony.

Political Projects and Influences

The most significant political influence of pan-nationalist ideas was in the way they shaped the perception of international affairs by political actors. For example, the pan-Islamic perception of a modern Western imperial encirclement of the Muslim world did play a role in garnering Ottoman public support for entering the First World War on the side of Germany.[35] In the aftermath of the Italian invasion of Libya, and the Balkan Wars from 1911 to 1913, many leaders of Ottoman public opinion reasoned that the diplomacy of cooperation with Western powers was not working and there was indeed a clash of civilizations. Beyond this diplomatic calculation, through which the Ottoman government secured a formal alliance with the German Empire, popular notions of pan-Islamic solidarity provided Ottoman policymakers with the vision that, upon entering the war, they could utilize the contradictions and weak points in the legitimacy of the imperial world order by encouraging Muslim disobedience, and if possible open revolt, against the British, French, and Russian empires. All of the European empires took this threat, epitomized by the Ottoman caliph's declaration of *jihad* against them, very seriously.

Despite the Ottoman Empire's defeat, and the emergence of Wilsonian and socialist internationalism as important alternatives during the interwar period, the pan-Islamic movement continued to play an important role in the aftermath of the First World War. In fact, as a reaction to the perceived harsh treatment of the Ottoman Empire at the Paris Peace Conference in 1919, a new transnational pan-Islamic movement emerged in the form of the Khilafat Movement. Established by Indian Muslims, and supported by leading Hindu nationalists such as Mahatma Gandhi, the Khilafat Movement symbolized a paradoxical merger between the ideals of Islamic solidarity, anti-colonial nationalism, and Wilsonian notions of legitimacy. While collecting enormous sums of material donations for the Turkish War of Independence, the Khilafat Movement leaders asked the British government, the colonial rulers of India, to recognize the right to self-determination of the Muslim majority in Turkey. Ultimately, the Turkish national movement achieved its goals, partly due to moral and material support from the pan-Islamic movement. Nevertheless, the elite of the new Turkish Republic decided to abolish the caliphate and disavow its pan-Islamic claims to leadership in the Muslim world, thus indicating their own self-conscious preference for a Wilsonian and nationalist direction in the interwar international order. Turkey's decision to abolish the caliphate ended the high moment of post-1918 pan-Islamic *Realpolitik*.[36] The Muslim identity of the Turkish leaders and population did not change, yet the new Turkish Republic focused its energies on modernizing and Westernizing a predominantly Muslim population, which also inspired non-Turkish Muslim nationalists to take a similar path.

The Japanese Empire, as an ally of the British Empire, had no reason to flirt with pan-Asian ideas. Yet, pan-Asianist intellectuals were very active in Japan and elsewhere in Asia during the First World War, emphasizing the primacy of Western subjugation of the coloured Asian races as the main conflict in international affairs, and urging the Japanese Empire to break its alliance with Britain in order to become the natural leader of rising Asian nationalism. Although Japan's pan-Asianists were in opposition during the war, they did conduct a successful public opinion campaign in cooperation with Asianists in China and India, underlining the continuing racial discrimination by whites even against their Japanese allies, and emphasizing that it was better for Japanese national interests to be the leader of a free Asia than to be a discriminated member of the all-white superpowers club.[37] This perception of a racial war and race discrimination was partly a reason behind the Japanese government's proposal for the abolishment of race discrimination in international affairs during the Paris Peace Conference. By securing an international legal document against race discrimination, Japanese leaders hoped to enlist more domestic support for their alliances with the Western powers and for Japan's leadership in the establishment of a League of Nations. Pan-Asianists were not only supportive of this Japanese proposal for race equality; they also mobilized strong protests against the 'hypocrisy' of the League of Nations toward the coloured races when the Japanese proposal was rejected.

Pan-African intellectuals were also very active during the Paris Peace Conference: They not only supported the Japanese proposal, but also showed their global vision by convening their first international pan-African Congress. During the first pan-African Congress, convened by Du Bois in Paris in February 1919, fifty delegates from Africa, the Caribbean, and the United States managed to put forward a proposal for the creation of a new state in Africa based on Germany's former colonies, and asked the League of Nations to protect the rights of Africans and those of African descent in the colonies.[38]

During the interwar period, pan-nationalist movements had to face the challenge of a revived socialist internationalism, inspired by the Bolshevik Revolution of 1917 and later on backed by a powerful state in the form of the Soviet Union, as their new rival, offering a different path to overcome imperial subjugation. Initially, the Bolsheviks tried to benefit from the accumulated anti-Western sentiments of earlier pan-nationalist trends of pan-Islamism and pan-Asianism by organizing the 1920 Eastern People's Congresses in Baku on the Caspian Sea, where leading pan-Islamic personalities such as Enver Paşa appeared.[39] Yet, the Bolsheviks could not accept the idea of an alternative Eastern civilization entrenched with pan-Islamic and pan-Asian discourses, and gradually, they distanced themselves from pan-Islamic and pan-Asian movements, due to their fear that instead of using these two rival internationalisms, the Bolsheviks could become their instruments.[40] With regard to pan-Africanism, however, the Comintern did have a more positive relationship of support.[41]

During the interwar period, the pan-African movement was represented by the growth of the Universal Negro Improvement Association (UNIA) led by Marcus Garvey, a Jamaican immigrant to the United States. At its height in the early 1920s, the UNIA had an estimated two million members and sympathizers, and approximately one thousand chapters in forty-three countries and territories, becoming the largest black movement in the African diaspora and the most widespread black-led movement in world history. The movement proclaimed 'the inherent right of the Negro to possess himself of Africa', with the goal of establishing a 'Negro independent nation on the continent of Africa' to which all diaspora Africans could return. Even though the UNIA goals exhibited a surprising unawareness of the diversity and multiplicity of African cultures or peoples, it did have some following in Africa, especially in South Africa.[42] In addition to UNIA's activism, cultural ideas emanating from the Caribbean and francophone West Africa in the 1920s and the 1930s, known as *Negritude*, became influential in creating a transnational African-black consciousness. Although it never turned into a formal organization, the Negritude cultural project emerged out of transnational African student groups with a shared colonial background, and was best represented by the achievements of Léopold Sédar Senghor (later first president of Senegal), Aimé Cesairé (author and politician from Martinique), and Léon-Gontran Damas (author and politician from French Guiana).[43] Moreover, pan-Africanism was strongly influenced by the international Communist movement and Soviet-supported anti-imperialist work. Led by the Trinidadian author and journalist George Padmore, this Comintern-connected pan-African movement contributed to the international mobility of African nationalists and provided moral and intellectual support for the cause of decolonization. Whether exemplified by Garvey, Sengor, or Padmore, these politically active and well-connected diaspora communities contributed immensely to the formation of a new generation of nationalist leaders who challenged Western hegemony with counterclaims about Africa's racial equality, cultural legacy, and the potential for modernization.

Pan-Asianist nationalism received great political support from the Japanese Empire during the 1930s. Japan began to demonstrate a vision of pan-Asian solidarity at this time, but only in the context of a crisis of legitimacy in the aftermath of its invasion of Manchuria in September 1931.[44] Pan-Asianism was used to justify Japanese imperial rule in East Asia as a project of liberating Asia from Western rule. Japan's call for Asian solidarity under its leadership during the late 1930s showed both the limitations and partial effectiveness of Asian identity in creating political cooperation. While some nationalists in India, Indonesia, China, and other areas cooperated with the Japanese efforts, the majority of Asian nationalists underlined the hypocrisy of Japan's declaration of Asian solidarity when the Japanese Empire was simultaneously colonizing large territories in China and Korea. Japanese imperial propaganda about an Asian pan-nationalism did recognize the reality of self-determination of different national units and in fact, gradually, a realistic vision of a League of Asian Nations was imagined as Japan's alternative to the Atlantic Charter and the United Nations. The Japanese Empire sponsored several instances of a Greater East Asia Conference as a coordinating intergovernmental body for Asian solidarity, while Japanese intellectual propaganda entrenched among the Japanese population a strong identity of being Asian and having a mission and responsibility within Asia.[45] Indian nationalist leaders like Subhas Chandra Bose and Indonesian nationalist leaders like Sukarno cooperated with the Japanese Empire's pan-Asian projects during the Second World War partly out of their conviction that pan-Asian solidarity represented the only viable alternative to the perpetuation of European colonial rule in Asia.

Pan-Nationalism in the Age of the United Nations

After the end of the Second World War, the Allied Powers established the United Nations, partly as their response to the challenge of anti-colonial pan-nationalist critiques. American leaders were especially cognizant of the lack of legitimacy of Western empires in Asia, and the appeal of anti-Western pan-Asianism propagated by the Japanese Empire, an assessment confirmed through reports collected by the US government's Office of Strategic Studies during the war.[46] In the new post-war context of decolonization and the emergence of new African and Asian nations, all three anti-colonial pan-nationalisms left their mark on post-colonial historical memory and nationalist identities during the Cold War.

The memory of imperial-era injustice of the white race against the coloured races or of Christian injustice against Muslims, emphasized by pan-Asian and pan-Islamic discourses, became part of the narratives of state-building and nationalist reconstructions in Asia. As these nationalist narratives about the imperial domination of the West over the East have been taught to new generations in post-colonial Asia, from Turkey, Egypt, and Iran to India, China, and even Japan, the memory of Western outsiders' humiliation of the yellow race or Muslims was kept alive throughout the post-colonial period. For example, when the leaders of the newly decolonized African and Asian nations met at the Afro-Asian Conference at Bandung in 1955, their speeches and statements reflected the continuing relevance of historical memories of colonial-era cultural identities. Many delegates at the Bandung Conference advocated the solidarity of non-Western peoples against the political collectivity called the West in a new pan-Arabic and pan-Asian rhetoric. Richard Wright, who attended the conference as the only African-American journalist, expressed his astonishment at the speeches, characterizing the ideology of the conference in terms of a 'Color Curtain', which, in his observation, had taken precedence in Asian politics even over the 'Iron Curtain' of the Cold War.[47] In the post-colonial period, the image of an untrustworthy and sinister West continued to exist as a trope in the intellectual histories of Asian societies, despite the fact that the international context that created this image had been radically transformed with the end of the Western empires. New post-1945 visions of Asian solidarity, associated with the names of Mao Zedung and Jawaharlal Nehru, were generally part of a broader concept of Third World solidarity and included cooperation with the newly independent African countries as well.

During the Cold War, Asian countries became politically divided into different blocs. But, especially after the Cold War, many Asian intellectuals have continued to debate new forms of potential Asian cooperation in a multipolar world where Asia could emerge as a regional power counterbalancing Europe and the United States. There are currently several international organizations, activities, and NGOs based on this Asian concept, such as the Asian Development Bank, Asian Games, the Asian News Network, the Network of Asian Think Tanks, the Asian Football Federation, et cetera. For example, international sports associations still use the continent of Asia as a single unit for tournaments and qualifications, and thus countries in two distant parts of Asia, such as Japan and Bahrain, play games with each other regularly despite the geographical distance between their countries. More importantly, the imagined connectivity and unity of a shared Asian culture or the remnant exoticism associated with it are still used by the tourism industry to promote travel to different parts of Asia. For example, the Japanese tourist industry revived a certain level of nostalgic Asian identity in special Silk Road tours from the 1970s onwards, while trips to Turkey are being presented as seeing the other end of Asia. Finally, the concept of Asia appeared in the Asian-American identity of various diaspora communities living the United States. While Asian-American identity was used and recognized, facilitating communication and interactions among various communities originating from different parts of Asia, in reality the stark diversity of Asian-American communities created sharply different diaspora cultures, experiences, and organizations in the United States, ranging from Chinese Americans to Americans of Indian, Vietnamese, or Korean descents.

The Second World War had a more profound impact on the decolonization of Africa. When the fifth pan-African Congress gathered in Manchester in 1945, the leadership was handed from the diaspora community to the actual leaders of new nationalism on the African continent such as Kwame Nkrumah. After Nkrumah became the first prime minister of independent Ghana, he declared that 'the independence of Ghana is meaningless unless it is linked up with the total liberation of the African continent'.[48] It was on this mid-twentieth-century stage, when intellectuals born in Africa took more leading roles in pan-African thought, that a race-based African identity was challenged in favour of a more geographical, continental idea of African identity and solidarity that included North African Arabs. When post-colonial African leaders such as Nkrumah and Gamal Abdel Nasser of Egypt established the Organization of African Unity (OAU) in 1963, they defined the scope of the organization according to the continental boundaries, though the idea of African unity continued to include those 'blacks' whose ancestors had left the continent as traded slaves. African diaspora continued to be engaged in pan-African ideals, best evidenced by the fact that W. E. B. Dubois himself lived and died in independent Ghana. Moreover, in the process of the decolonization of Africa, especially during the Algerian Revolution (1954–62), the idea of free Africa turned into a powerful transnational concept, and pan-Africanist diaspora intellectuals such as Frantz Fanon helped shape the content of global post-colonial thought. The Asian-African Conference in Bandung in 1955 became a symbol of this post-colonial moment, which was then followed by the prominent role of African countries in the Non-Aligned Movement.

The OAU did encourage further decolonization of the continent and played a significant role in mediating border disputes. But, in the various Cold War conflicts in Africa, it became highly divided. During the 1970s the OAU did not play any important role or function in African affairs, when decolonized Africa plunged into problems of nation-building and competing ideologies in highly diverse experiences of reform. While pan-Africanism today may have lost much of its political influence, it could be said that, for much of the twentieth century, the very complex and diverse pan-Africanist networks played a crucial role in the decolonization of the African continent and in the transnational imagination of both the African diaspora's civil-rights movements and national movements on the African continent.

In the post-1945 period, pan-Islamism seemed very weak and irrelevant, while pan-Arabism emerged as a subset of earlier pan-Islamic identity around a more secular language and culture-based pan-nationalism, which could incorporate both the reality of sovereign nation states and the nationalist feelings of Christian Arab populations.[49] Although the roots of the idea of Arab unity can be traced back to the British-backed Arab revolt against the Ottoman Empire during the First World War, and interwar secular Arab nationalism, the first significant pan-Arab organization was the League of

Arab States established in 1945 in Cairo with the participation of six Arab states (Egypt, Iraq, Jordan, Saudi Arabia, Syria, and Lebanon). With the process of decolonization, the number of members in the Arab League reached twenty by the 1980s. Beyond the intragovernmental activities of the Arab League, the idea of pan-Arabism gained great popularity with the presidency of Nasser in Egypt. Especially during the decade from the time of the Suez Crisis in 1956 to the Arab-Israeli War in 1967, Nasser became identified with the hopes of pan-Arab solidarity, as someone who could lead the Arab world to end the long period of colonial humiliation, and as a leader who could bring about both modernization and political dignity. Pan-Arabism was incorporated as a principle of foreign policy in almost all the Arab nationalist ideologies in the 1950s and the 1960s, expressing hope that with efficient coordination, Arab populations could use their own resources to reach higher levels of economic development while achieving full political independence from Western domination and Israeli threats. In 1958, at the request of the Syrian leaders to Nasser, Egypt and Syria formed a pan-Arab union, called the United Arab Republic. Although there were hopes of adding more countries to this unity, the United Arab Republic did not survive beyond 1961, when Syria left the Union after complaints about Egyptian policies towards Syria. The Algerian War of Liberation and the Palestinian struggle kept the desires and activism around pan-Arab solidarity very much alive. After Nasser's defeat in 1967 against Israel, however, early high hopes for pan-Arab solidarity gradually faded away and pan-Arabism lost its momentum, especially when President Anwar El Sadat of Egypt signed a separate peace treaty with Prime Minister Menachem Begin of Israel in 1979.

While the Arab League continued its activities in encouraging cooperation among Arab countries, a broader notion of Islamic solidarity was revived both in its ideological versions in various Islamist ideologies and in general public opinion during the 1970s. When the Organization of the Islamic Conference (OIC) was established in 1971 as an international organization of Muslim solidarity, all Arab countries became members of this new organization as well. Iran's Islamic Revolution in 1979, and the Afghan resistance to Soviet Invasion during the 1980s, strengthened the transnational ideal of Muslim solidarity including but also extending beyond the Arab world. Currently, the OIC has fifty-seven members and in some vague manner represents a form of inter-governmental pan-Islamic cooperation. However, both the Arab League and the OIC are rather weak international organizations, falling far behind the ideological expect-ations of pan-Arabism and pan-Islamism. For all practical purposes, the post-1945 settlement in a world order aimed at sovereign nation states, with easy membership access to the UN and a set of international norms, prevented any feasible notion of pan-nationalist mergers. In terms of alternative ideologies, however, pan-Islamism is espoused by a strand of new Islamist ideologies all over the Muslim world, although they have yet to create any visible result beyond condemnations of Muslim humiliation by the West and discrimination against Muslims in international affairs. Organizations like al-Qaida appeal to this historical memory of humiliation and pan-Islamic identity, yet they are devoid of any truly significant social support and a firm base in Muslim societies.

Conclusion

A brief overview of the three pan-nationalist trends of thought around African, Islamic, and Asian identities shows that pan-nationalism became possible as part of globalizing discourses during the high age of imperialism from the 1880s to the 1920s. This was a period of imperialism-driven globalization that facilitated a truly worldwide debate on the division of humanity into developed and underdeveloped, whites and coloured, or belonging to different cultural legacies. It is in this context that a set of racial, transnational, and cultural categories of knowledge, mostly Eurocentric in their basic outline, became globally diffused, gradually inspiring pan-nationalist identities, intellectual visions, and political projects. During the high age of globalization and colonial expansion, when nationalism itself was merely in a formative period compared with strong imperial visions, there did emerge a set of shared themes and ideas characterizing transnational Asian, Muslim, and African thinking about the conditions of the societies and peoples concerned, especially in their relationship to the imperialism of the imagined unit identified as the West. The fact that a transnational identity of 'Muslim', 'Asian', or 'African' emerged by the turn of the twentieth century indicates a process of 'geopolitization of globalization', as a result of which mainstream thinking about world politics involved pan-nationalist categories of knowledge. The appeal of pan-Islamic, pan-Asian, and pan-African ideas for both nationalist movements and various empires of that time demonstrate the power of transnational identities associated with this new geopolitical thinking.

By examining their genesis, content, and legacies, this chapter has emphasized that we should see the three forms of pan-nationalism discussed primarily as a narrative about the moral foundations of the globalized imperial world order from the 1870s to the late 1940s. As the Eurocentric imperial order relied on a meta-narrative of the superiority of Christian and white Europeans over the rest of humanity, the challenge to its legitimacy has to offer its own alternative narratives, which often were and had to be pan-nationalist. The long-lasting legacy and impact of the intellectual content of such pan-nationalist projects are often overlooked as scholarly and non-scholarly literature tends to focus on the non-viability and failure of the various political projects of Asian, Islamic, or African solidarity. Even though what came after the imperial world order was something unexpected for the anti-colonial nationalists who espoused a pan-nationalist vision of solidarity, their counter-narratives of Islamic, Asian, and African civilization contributed to the erosion of imperial legitimacy and speeded the decolonization process. Any history of pan-nationalism has to consider its achievements as a challenge to the imperial-racial world order even if the system of nation-state sovereignty that emerged in the post-1945 period rendered projects of pan-nationalist polity impractical.

Pan-Asian, pan-Islamic, and pan-African ideas evolved in relation to the structural transformation in the international order through the two World Wars, a transformation to which they contributed greatly. While pan-Asianism, pan-Islamism, and pan-Africanism developed as strong intellectual currents dealing with issues of history, racism, and cultural identity, they also contributed to the decolonization of Asia and Africa by challenging the moral foundations of the imperial world order. The practical political projects of Asian, Islamic, and African solidarity did not reach a level that advocates of these pan-nationalisms hoped for. Yet, in terms of eroding the legitimacy of an uneven and imperial international order based on colonial hegemony and race discrimination, these three pan-nationalisms left their mark on the modern global history of decolonization. Moreover, they encouraged and strengthened broader intra-Asian, intra-African, and intra-Islamic sympathies, a kind of Third World consciousness throughout Asia and Africa, for example, that allowed Chinese intellectuals to feel closer to Turks in their War of Independence, and Turkish and Iranian nationalists to exhibit sympathies for Chinese and Indian nationalists. The narratives of history and culture produced by pan-nationalists such as W. E. B. Dubois, Jamaladdin Al-Afghani, Okakura Tenshin, and many others also inspired and solidified the universalist aspirations of nationalism, exemplifying the close ties between anti-colonial nationalist thought and various pan-nationalist ideals. On an intellectual and emotional level, there is still a strong belief in the shared narratives of Islamic, African, and Asian history, as well as in the identities sustained by the notion of particular Islamic, African, and Asian values. Thus, it should not be surprising to witness the legacies and persistence of pan-nationalist ideas through the period of decolonization and the Cold War up to the present day.

NOTES

1. L. Snyder (1984) *Macro-Nationalisms: A History of the Pan-Movements*, Westport, CT, 5
2. For an example of intellectual, cultural, and economic networks among Muslim societies of the fourteenth century, without any Pan-Islamic identity, see R. E. Dunn (2008) *The Adventures of Ibn Battuta: A Muslim Traveler of the Fourteenth Century*, Berkeley, CA; For the importance of empires in world history, see T. Hopkins (1999) 'Back to the Future: From National History to Imperial History,' *Past & Present*, 164, no. 1, 198–243.
3. For the importance of imperial cooperation in the first half of the nineteenth-century international order, see E. Weitz (2008) 'From the Vienna to the Paris System: International Politics and the Entangled Histories of Human Rights, Forced Deportations, and Civilizing Missions', *American Historical Review*, 113, no. 5, 1313–43; see also S. Deringil (2003) '"They Live in a State of Nomadism and Savagery": The Late Ottoman Empire and the Post-Colonial Debate', *Comparative Studies in Society and History*, 45, no. 2, 311–42.
4. R. Jaffe (2004) 'Seeking Sakyamuni: Travel and the Reconstruction of Japanese Buddhism', *Journal of Japanese Studies*, 30, no. 1 (Winter), 65–96.
5. C. Aydin (2007) *The Politics of Anti-Westernism in Asia: Visions of World Order in Pan-Islamic and Pan-Asian Thought*, New York, ch. 2.
6. A. Eckert (2007) 'Bringing the "Black Atlantic" into Global History: The Project of Pan-Africanism', in *Competing Visions of World Order: Global Moments and Movements, 1880s–1930*, eds. S. Conrad and D. Sachsenmaier, New York, 237–57.

7. For a formulation of a universal theory of civilization by the most prominent early Meiji-era intellectual, see F. Yukichi (1973) *An Outline of a Theory of Civilization*, Bunmeiron no Gairyaku, trans. D. A. Dilworth and G. C. Hurst, Tokyo. For the broader Ottoman context of Westernization during the nineteenth century, see S. Hanioglu (2008) *A Brief History of the Late Ottoman Empire*, Princeton, NJ.
8. For aspects of the Ottoman civilizing mission to its own populations, in the form of reapplying European Orientalism for domestic political purposes, see U. Makdisi (2002) 'Ottoman Orientalism,' *American Historical Review*, 107, no. 3, 768–96. For the Japanese version of the same process, see S. Tanaka (1993) *Japan's Orient: Rendering Past into History*, Berkeley, CA.
9. N. Keddie (1968) *An Islamic Response to Imperialism*, Berkeley, CA.
10. V. Tikhonov (2002) 'Korea's First Encounters with Pan-Asianism Ideology in the Early 1880s', *The Review of Korean Studies*, 5, no. 2 (December), 195–232.
11. K. A. Appiah (1999) 'Pan-Africanism', in K. A. Appiah and H. L. Gates Jr. (eds.) *Africana: The Encyclopedia of the African and African American Experience*, New York, 1485.
12. For a profile of a early twentieth-century Pan-Asianist organization, composed of Japanese, Chinese, and Indian members, that saw the Muslims as alien invaders of Asia, see R. Karl (1998) 'Creating Asia: China in the World at the Beginning of the Twentieth Century', *American Historical Review*, 103, no. 4 (October), 1096–118.
13. See E. Hotta (2007) *Pan-Asianism and Japan's War, 1931–1945*, New York, 49.
14. A. Zimmerman (2005) 'A German Alabama in Africa: The Tuskegee Expedition to German Togo and the Transnational Origins of West African Cotton Growers', *American Historical Review*, 110, 1362–98.
15. C. V. Findley (1998) 'An Ottoman Occidentalist in Europe: Ahmed Midhat Meets Madame Gulnar, 1889', *American Historical Review*, 103, no. 1, 15–49.
16. J. Snodgrass (2003) *Presenting Japanese Buddhism to the West: Orientalism, Occidentalism, and the Columbian Exposition*, Chapel Hill, NC.
17. P. O. Esedebe (1994) *Pan-Africanism: The Idea and Movement, 1776–1991*, Washington, DC.
18. For a broader world-historical assessment of E. Renan's ideas on Aryan race, see V. Kaiwar (2003) 'The Aryan Model of History and the Oriental Renaissance: The Politics of Identity in an Age of Revolutions, Colonialism and Nationalism', in S. Mazumdar and V. Kaiwar (eds.) *The Antinomies of Modernity*, Durham, NC, 13–61.
19. M. Adas (1989) *Machines as the Measure of Man: Science, Technology and Ideologies of Western Dominance*, Ithaca, NY, 11–12.
20. Renan gave his speech on 'Islam and Science' in 29 March 1883 at the Sorbonne, and published it in the 30 March 1883 issue of *Journal des Debates*. Later that same year, the speech was published as a 24-page-long separate booklet. For its English-language translation, see E. Renan, 'Islamism and Science', in B. S. Turner (ed.) (2000) *Orientalism: Early Sources, Volume I: Readings in Orientalism*, London and New York, 199–217.
21. N. K. Bey (2002) 'Islamiyet ve Devlet-i Aliyye-i Osmaniye Hakkinda Doğru bir Söz: Cenevre'de Müsteşrikin Kongresi'nde İrad Olunmuş bir Nutkun Tercümesidir', in Ismail Kara (ed.) *Hifet Risaleleri 1*, Istanbul, 353–71. For the French version of the paper presented at the Congress, see N. K. Bey (1894) 'Vérité sur l'Islamisme et l'Empire Ottoman', *Présentée au X. Congrés International des Orientalistes a Genève*, Paris.
22. J. E. Ketelaar (1990) *Of Heretics and Martyrs in Meiji Japan*, Princeton, NJ, 136–220.
23. J. E. Casely Hayford (1911; 1969) *Ethiopia Unbound: Studies in Race Relations*, London.

24. H. Halid (1907) *The Crescent versus the Cross*, London.
25. Tokutomi Sohô (1863–1957) advocated the term 'Yellow Man's Burden', giving voice to an alternative to the idea of 'The White Man's Burden' (based on Rudyard Kipling's famous poem of 1899). See H. Sukehiro (1987) 'Modernizing Japan in Comparative Perspective', *Comparative Studies of Culture*, no. 26, 29.
26. A Pan-Islamist Ottoman who published extensively in England about issues of the Muslim World, H. Halid studied and taught at Cambridge University. See S. T. Wasti (1993) 'Halil Halid: Anti-Imperialist Muslim Intellectual', *Middle Eastern Studies*, 29, no. 3 (July), 559–79. For Halil Halid's own autobiography, see H. Halid (1903) *The Diary of a Turk*, London. Similarly, the first comprehensive book on Pan-Asianism was written by a Japanese graduate of Columbian College of Law in Washington, DC, around the turn of the century: K. Kenkichi (1916) *Dai Ajiashugi Ron*, Tokyo.
27. L. Stoddard (1921) *The New World of Islam*, New York.
28. For its Arabic translation, see L. Stûdard (1924) *Hadir al-Alam al-Islami*, trans. 'Ajjâj Nuwayhid, ed. al-Amîr Shakîb Arslân, Cairo. For the Ottoman translation of the same work (1922), *Yeni Alem-i Islam*, trans. A. R. Seyfi, Istanbul.
29. For a good sourcebook and evaluation of Sun Yat-sen's speech in Kobe on Pan-Asianism in 1924, see C. Tokujin and Y. Sankichi (eds.) (1989) *Sonbun Kôen Dai Ajia Shugi Shiryôshû: 1924 nen, 11 Gatsu Nihon to Chûgoku no Kiro*, Kyoto. In this talk, Sun Yat-sen refers to L. Stoddard's (1920) *The Rising Tide of Color Against the White World Supremacy*, New York.
30. See A. Davison (2006) 'Ziya Gokalp and Provincializing Europe', *Comparative Studies of South Asia, Africa and the Middle East*, 26, no. 3, 377–90.
31. For the development of a shared Eastern identity in different parts of Asia around the turn of the century, see R. Karl (2002) *Staging the World: Chinese Nationalism at the Turn of the Twentieth Century*, Durham, NC. For the development of cooperation between Japanese Asianists and Muslim activists around the notion of shared Eastern identity, see S. Esenbel (2004) 'Japan's Global Claim to Asia and the World of Islam: Transnational Nationalism and World Power, 1900–1945', *The American Historical Review*, 109, no. 4 (October), 1140–70.
32. H. Halid (1907) *Hilal ve Salib Münazaasi*, Cairo, 185–8.
33. See Chapter 14 by Rana Mitter in this volume.
34. R. J. Holton (2002) 'Cosmopolitanism or Cosmopolitanisms? The Universal Races Congress of 1911', *Global Network*, 2 (April), 153–70. For a recent reassessment of the London Universal Races Congress of 1911, see the special Forum section in *Radical History Review*, 92 (Spring 2005), 92–132.
35. M. Aksakal (2008) *The Ottoman Road to WWI: The Ottoman Empire and the First World War*, Cambridge.
36. For examples of the post-WWI Pan-Islamic movement and its ideas, see S. M. H. Kidwai (1919) *The Future of the Muslim Empire: Turkey*, London; and (1919) *The Sword against Islam or a Defence of Islam's Standard-Bearers*, London, 1919. G. Minault (1982) *The Khilafat Movement: Religious Symbolism and Political Mobilization in India*, New York.
37. T. Das (1917) *Is Japan a Menace to Asia?*, Shanghai; and (1918) *An Asian Statesman: The Isolation of Japan in World Politics*, Tokyo.
38. S. A. Adejumobi (2001) 'The Pan-African Congress', in Nina Mjagkij (ed.) *Organizing Black America: An Encyclopedia of African American Associations*, New York.

39. J. Riddell (ed.) (1993) *To See the Dawn: Baku, 1920: First Congress of the Peoples of the East*, New York.
40. For the separation between communism and Pan-Islamism, see T. Malaka (2001) 'Communism and Pan-Islamism', in *What Next: Marxist Discussion Journal*, no. 21, which can be found at the following web link: <http://www.whatnextjournal.co.uk/Pages/Back/Wnext21/Panislam.html>.
41. G. Padmore (1956) *Pan-Africanism or Communism: The Coming Struggle for Africa*, London. Ho Chi Minh's biography illustrates the appeal of both Woodrow Wilson's principle of self-determination and socialist internationalism. See M. Bradley (2000) *Imagining Vietnam and America: The Making of Postcolonial Vietnam, 1919–1950*, Chapel Hill, NC. See also Chapter 32 by John Schwartzmantel in this volume.
42. R. Lewis (1988) *Marcus Garvey: Anti-Colonial Champion*, Tenton.
43. G. Wilder (2005) *The French Imperial Nation-State: Negritude and Colonial Humanism between the Two World Wars*, Chicago, IL, and London.
44. See Chapter 14 by Rana Mitter in this volume.
45. For a recent assessment of Pan-Asianism during the 1930s, see Hotta, *Pan-Asianism and Japan's War*, and also Sven Saaler and Victor Koschmann (eds.) (2007) *Pan-Asianism in Modern Japanese History: Colonialism, Regionalism and Borders*, London. It is important to note that Nazi Germany did not appeal to Pan-Islamic notions of solidarity during WWII—a big contrast to Imperial Germany's Pan-Islamic propaganda during WWI.
46. C. Thorne (1978) *Allies of a Kind: The United States, Britain and the War Against Japan, 1941–1945*, New York, 157–9.
47. R. Wright (1995) *The Color Curtain: A Report on the Bandung Conference*, Jackson, MI.
48. D. Birmingham (1998) *Kwame Nkrumah: Father of African Nationalism*, Athens, OH.
49. See in this volume Chapter 11 by Aviel Roshwald on nationalism in the Middle East up to 1945 and Chapter 22 by Fred Halliday on Arab nationalism after 1945.

Suggestions for Further Reading

Aydin, C. (2007) *The Politics of Anti-Westernism in Asia: Visions of World Order in Pan-Islamic and Pan-Asian Thought*, New York.

Duara, P. (2001) 'The Discourse of Civilization and Pan-Asianism', *Journal of World History*, 12, no. 1 (Spring), 99–130.

Eckert, A. (2007) 'Bringing the "Black Atlantic" into Global History: The Project of Pan-Africanism', in S. Conrad and D. Sachsenmaier (eds.) *Competing Visions of World Order: Global Moments and Movements, 1880s–1930*, ed. S. Conrad and D. Sachsenmaier, New York, 237–57.

Esedebe, P. O. (1994) *Pan-Africanism: The Idea and Movement, 1776–1991*, Washington, DC.

Geiss, I. (1974) *The Pan-African Movement*, London.

Griffith, C. E. (1975) *The African Dream: Martin Delany and the Emergence of Pan-African Thought*, University Park, PA.

Halid, H. (1907) *The Crescent versus the Cross*, London.

Hotta, E. (2007) *Pan-Asianism and Japan's War, 1931–1945*, New York.

Karl, R. (2002) *Staging the World: Chinese Nationalism at the Turn of the Twentieth Century*, Durham, NC.

Landau, J. M. (1990) *The Politics of Pan-Islam: Ideology and Organization*, Oxford.
Özcan, A. (1997) *Pan-Islamism: Indian Muslims, the Ottomans and Britain (1877–1924)*, Leiden.
Reid, A. (1967) 'Nineteenth-Century Pan-Islam in Indonesia and Malaysia', *Journal of Asian Studies*, 26, no. 2 (February), 275–6.
Saaler, S. and Koschmann, V. (eds.) (2007) *Pan-Asianism in Modern Japanese History: Colonialism, Regionalism and Borders*, London.
Wilder, G. (2005) *The French Imperial Nation-State: Negritude and Colonial Humanism between the Two World Wars*, Chicago and London.
Wright, R. (1995) *The Color Curtain: A Report on the Bandung Conference*, Jackson, MI.

CHAPTER 35

NATIONALISM AND GLOBALIZATION

JÜRGEN OSTERHAMMEL

Theories and Histories of Nationalism and Globalization

The theories and histories of nationalism on the one hand and globalization on the other hand are difficult to reconcile. Although 'nationalism' remains a contested topic, there is broad agreement about the basic issues facing any theory of nationalism, about a canon of classical authors, texts, and references, and about the possible uses of theory in historical analysis and of history in theoretical arguments. This kind of consensus is lacking for 'globalization'. The term itself continues to be an instrument of polemics. It is closely bound up with political and cultural diagnoses of the present state of the world. To speak about globalization is likely to evoke the vast problem of modernity. 'Anti-globalizers' still deny the usefulness and legitimacy of the word as an analytical concept or warn against its indiscriminate application.[1] Since the nature of globalization is still a matter of fundamental dispute, the tasks of theorizing about the subject are difficult to define. No single body of outstanding theoretical statements has attained the authoritative status enjoyed by the major writers on nationalism from Ernest Renan to Anthony D. Smith.[2] The discourse on globalization is fissiparous, polycentric, and highly susceptible to any new turn in world affairs and any new fashion in the social and cultural sciences. It tends to be descriptive and to avoid explanations about origins.

As far as globalization theory has dealt with theories of nationalism at all, it has limited itself to the question of the expected demise or survival of the nation state. Implicit in this concern is the idea that nationalism and nation state came first and then globalization came second. The first-generation literature on globalization, mainly in the 1990s, tended to emphasize the imminent death of the nation state. At a second stage, more sceptical and nuanced assessments prevailed, distinguishing between various types and levels—the global, the regional, the national, and the local—and stressing the connections and the interpenetration between these levels.[3] Most observations of this kind care little for the historical evidence and do not assume the form of fully articulated theory. There is thus an obvious asymmetry between the theories of nationalism and of globalization. The two of them are in no position to engage in an even-handed dialogue.

Something similar is true for the respective histories. While debates about the history of nationalism focus on individual cases and particular topics and rarely see a need to doubt the established parameters of time and space, it has never been settled what a history of globalization should be about. Debates are raging, for example, about the temporal shape of globalization: When is it supposed to begin? What should a sensible periodization look like? One group of authors, close to the social sciences, fail to discover any evidence for globalization before the 1950s or even the 1970s. At the other extreme, advocates of 'big history' detect traces of globalization as far back as the Iron Age. In between these polar opposites, three schools of thought have attracted a roughly equal share of support. The first school is impressed by the unification of much of Eurasia through the Mongol world empire in the thirteenth century.[4] A second school prefers the maritime unification of the globe in the decades after Christopher Columbus as the threshold to emerging globality.[5] A third school insists on the causative importance of industrialized traffic and electric telecommunication (and sometimes also of the doctrine of free trade), and therefore places the cut-off point between archaic and modern globalization in the 1860s or 1870s, with a transitory phase beginning around 1820.[6] Narratives of globalization and of 'nationalization', in other words, the rise of nationalism, are difficult to synchronize. An overarching history of 'modernity' might smooth the differences, but it remains to be elaborated.[7] The development of 'national' solidarities and the intensification of worldwide connections are certainly elementary processes that characterize the past two centuries. But they do not touch, interact, intermingle, or coincide in an orderly and patterned way. Nor are they logically coterminous. Sometimes 'nationalism' is the wider concept: In certain cases, nationalism has historically arisen under circumstances only slightly and indirectly connected to globalization, economic or otherwise. In other respects, 'globalization' is more encompassing: The worldwide diffusion of nationalism from its European places of origin can be seen as but one instance and facet of globalization. Nationalism was globalized, whereas only in exceptional cases does it make sense to speak of globalization being 'nationalized'.

Levels of Integration and Fragmentation

Nationalism as a set of beliefs, attitudes, and rhetorical strategies corresponds to 'globalism', a somewhat artificial term, rather than to globalization. The proper counterpart to globalization as a particular type of macro-societal change is the formation and transformation of nation states. Both processes can be conceived of as different kinds of integration, operating at varying spatial scales.[8] They assemble larger entities from a multitude of smaller elements and imbue them with the spirit and practices of homogenization. There is, however, at least one important difference. The nation state, as Saskia Sassen has put it, is 'the most complex institutional architecture' ever invented by mankind.[9] Historical globalization, by contrast, has produced a broad range of markets, networks (of migration or cultural exchange), and international organizations rather than a world state, a world society, or a cultural ecumene of planetary extent. Globalization is a process, or a bundle of processes, of integration; yet, the integrative density of its outcome has so far been lower than that of the quintessential nation state. Globalization and the formation of nation states are not necessarily discrete and independent processes. As Sassen points out, globalization works through the nation state and often manifests itself in macro-processes within an individual national state and society.[10] Conversely, elites engaged in building nation states have often attempted to appropriate and employ resources from outside the boundaries of their emerging state: economic resources through trade, imperialist exploitation, or, in the post-colonial era, developmental aid, and also the symbolic resources of an international idiom of sovereignty and recognition. 'World languages', to give another example, can be seen as colonial impositions. At the same time they open up spaces of communication that increase the capacities of nationalist movements and of emerging nation states. From its very beginning, Indian nationalism relied on English to overcome parochialism and to counter the communicative advantages of the British Raj.

Other levels of integration intervene between the world and the nation: empires, large regions of multicultural interaction such as Eurasia or the Atlantic, or the international system. The modern ('Westphalian', to use a convenient cliché) international system contains in itself contradictory tendencies of stabilization and destabilization, of integration and fragmentation. Nationalism, as Ian Clark observes, has in the past worked both ways, integrative and disintegrative.[11] It has helped to bring about 'great powers' with a stake in the proper functioning of international mechanisms, such as alliances and balance-of-power constellations, while at the same time sharpening rivalries and aggressiveness.

Not infrequently, transformations leading to modernity occurred in the core areas of empires. Several of the oldest nationalisms and nation states in Europe developed within contexts of a pre-industrial or 'archaic' globalization that was mediated through empire.[12] Earlier ideas about English distinctiveness and superiority were strengthened around 1800 during the simultaneous conflict with France *and* with Indian princes, a conflict that involved coalitions across continental Europe and into the Americas. Confronting France or India, the English (and also the Scottish and Irish) upper classes persuaded themselves that they belonged to a 'higher civilization'.[13] The relationship between national and imperial integration does not follow a straightforward tendency or rule. The inaugural phase of revolutionary nation-building in France coincided with the construction of (a very brief) hegemony over vast parts of Europe and a dramatic contraction of overseas empire: Saint-Domingue (Haiti) was lost, 'Louisiana' sold to the United States, and a brief French foothold in Egypt failed to perpetuate itself. In the Spanish case, by contrast, an even more cataclysmic collapse of imperial dominion in the western hemisphere, ultimately triggered by the French invasion of Spain, did not accompany a comparable upsurge of nationalist sentiments and nation-building policies in the metropole.

The period from the 1860s to, at least, the First World War is unique in modern history for the equidirectional advance of integration at various levels. The paths to nation-building were diverse, but the results were similar. The number of independent or semi-independent political entities in the world sank to an all-time low. Germany, Italy, Japan, and the United States were transformed into consolidated nation states. By the turn of the century, each of these countries had forcibly acquired its own overseas possessions. Mosaics of colonies in Canada and Australia amalgamated into vast federations. In Africa, thousands of more or less autonomous units were absorbed into fewer than forty European colonies, many of whom had, by 1914, acquired some kind of recognizable statehood. All this happened at a time when markets across the world were becoming interconnected to a degree unprecedented in history. A spectacular increase in 'factor mobility', especially of labour and capital, accompanied by diminishing price differentials on markets all over the globe, has prompted economic historians to speak of the first great wave of economic globalization and the rise of global capitalism.[14] The same period was characterized by the absence of full-scale war between major powers in Europe—in marked contrast to the military turmoil of 1792 to 1815 and 1914 to 1918.

Fragmentation and de-globalization of the world economy during the First World War and after, ending an age of free trade and investment that had easily survived tariff protection since the late 1870s, went hand in hand with the persistence of the West European colonial empires and even with attempts to raise their degree of integration with the metropolitan economies. In spite of the new geopolitical mapping of Eastern and Southeastern Europe and of the post-Ottoman Middle East, achieved at the Paris Peace Conference in 1919, empire rather than the nation state seemed to be the appropriate political form to ensure success under conditions of intensified international rivalry, a belief shared by political elites of widely differing ideological persuasions. International anarchy was not effectively restrained by the flimsy agreements and institutions created in the aftermath of the Great War—the Versailles and Washington systems, the League of Nations, or, later, the Briand Kellogg Pact. No comprehensive international order offered solutions to the perceived security problems of nation states and empires, not even the strongest among them. The unspoken moral and ideological assumptions that had underwritten the actions of European political elites from 1815 to 1913 were replaced by conflicts between sharply divergent world views and by a lack of trust in any rules of the game. In the mid-1930s, the growing vacuum in international governance began to be filled by the competitive dynamics of national rearmament. The enlightened motto of 'national self-determination', originally intended to help former imperial peripheries on the road to autonomy or even independence, proved its worth as an instrument of revisionist nationalism. Step by step, Adolf Hitler expanded the German Reich to incorporate adjacent areas with German-speaking majorities who expressed a will to join the mother country. In conditions of weak political globalization, a universalist principle was applied to ultranationalist purposes.

The new imperialisms of Japan, Italy, and Germany abandoned the programme of the civilizing mission that had served as the main justification for European imperialism throughout the long nineteenth century.[15] The fascist imperialist ideologies of the 1930s and early 1940s were built around the three elements of suprematist nationalism, economic autarky, and racial hierarchy. While they were intended to resist and challenge the alleged global hegemony of the liberal-capitalist West, they transcended the limits of pre-1914 nationalism even in its integral forms. The insulated imperial *Grossraum* or, in Japan's case, 'Co-prosperity Sphere' rather than the classical nation state seemed to offer the best guarantee for the security and prosperity of nations that redefined themselves as master races with a self-appointed historical mission to build 'new orders'. Less aggressively and without overt racism, the Soviet Union, having resuscitated the Tsarist empire in (almost) its pre-1914 borders, followed a similar model of macro-integration at a level between the nation and the world. The Second World War, more than any other conflict in the past, was a clash of empires. At the same time, it led to a military re-globalization of the international system, generating genuinely global strategies, forms of cooperation, and, on the Allied side, blueprints for the post-war order.

After 1945, empires lost their integrative capacities, being overlaid by the new lines of political solidarity and military allegiance characteristic of a global Cold War. Shorn of their multi-ethnic overseas empires, the countries of Western Europe, for the first time ever, approached the nineteenth-century ideal of the homogeneous nation state free from imperial distractions—only to surrender, voluntarily, part of their national sovereignty to new and historically unprecedented supra-national institutions. The new Europe, founded in the late 1950s and growing ever since, was neither a neo-imperial realm under the control of any one preponderant state nor a mere mediator of globalization or instrument of Pax Americana. The pre-1945 language of strident nationalism and chauvinism disappeared from West European politics and gave way to moderate and peaceful bargaining about national interests. Consensual integration on the basis of continuing though less than absolute national sovereignties took the place of coercive integration as attempted by Napoleon, Hitler, and, more cautiously, Stalin.[16]

It is open to debate whether supra-national integration or global integration, constricted as it mainly is to the economy and communications, has been the more potent force in shaping the development of Europe from the 1950s onwards. In other parts of the world, the nation state became the general norm and was not downsized in importance by overarching integrative structures. An organization like the Association of South East Asian Nations (ASEAN) is not even remotely comparable to the European Union in its ability to transcend the nation state. Forces of transnational coordination, let alone integration, are even weaker in Africa, the Middle East, and Latin America. The disintegration of empires, beginning in 1947 in South Asia and coming to a close with the dissolution both of the Soviet-controlled satellite sphere between Berlin and Ulan Bator and finally of the Soviet Union itself, led to an enormous pluralization of the political map of the world. Since this process unfolded at a time of accelerated economic globalization, Benedict Anderson justly speaks of a 'paradoxical double movement of integration and disintegration' in Asia and Africa since the Second World War.[17] An interesting point about this unsurprising paradox is the relative strength of the countervailing tendencies. The shift from imperial to national integration during the process of decolonization created new opportunities for nationalist foreign policies within unstable regional systems of power, for example, in South Asia or Africa. The nineteenth-century European model of the nation state and nationalism advancing hand in hand was, however, seldom repeated. Many of the new states owed their continued existence less to successful 'national' integration in terms of institutions and ideologies than to the capacity of the international system to prevent boundary changes being made.

The self-pacification of Europe under the steadying influence of the United States, which ended an epoch of militant nationalism, has as yet found no parallel elsewhere. The lack of intermediate layers of integration between nation and world in much of the globe outside Europe may also render it more difficult to cushion national states and economies from some of the negative effects of economic globalization. Through a common currency, through shared policies on tariffs and trade, and through the redistribution of resources between wealthier and poorer members of the Union, Europe is in a comparatively strong position to influence the terms of globalization without resorting to nationalist defensiveness. The partial surrender of national sovereignty in favour of an augmented supra-national capacity to shape an emerging world society seems to be a good deal for nation states, especially if they are economically well structured and politically stable.

Nineteenth-Century Nation States and the Terms of Globalization

The constant tension between the national and the global should not be misconstrued as a basic antagonism. Early modern dynastic states possessed only blunt instruments for influencing long-distance flows of trade and for profiting from them. They could tax trade (either directly or, more characteristically, through revenue farming), grant monopolies to particular groups of private merchants, or provide legal frameworks for the coercion of subordinate people like slaves, indentured servants, and convicts. Some types of economic activity such as the movement of bullion almost entirely eluded their grasp. Port cities on the coasts of the Mediterranean, the Atlantic, the Indian Ocean, and the China Seas were often insulated and only loosely enmeshed in their hinterlands. Even after the rise of nation states, these nodal points of vast commercial networks were difficult to include in national economic systems. It took some time after the founding of the German Reich in 1871 to integrate Hanseatic cities like Hamburg and Bremen fully into German economic circuits.[18] During the early modern period, certain organized private interests, certain regions, and certain enclaves specializing in the export of commodities and people were active in weaving together the delicate networks of 'archaic' globalization. Governments were not systematically involved, and larger territorial systems seldom benefited from interactions that were mostly seaborne and had little impact on the rural societies which almost everywhere predominated over the maritime fringes.

This relationship between globalization and the state underwent a profound transformation in nineteenth-century Europe. The nation state, as Siegfried Weichlein has pointed out, was among the great profiteers from globalization.[19] It created legal frameworks, technological infrastructures, and extended spaces of communication that matched the functional needs of an intensified circulation of migrants, commodities, capital, and information. Older political forms like city states or multi-ethnic continental empires found it increasingly hard to keep up with the demands of regular and frequent mobility. Where nation states did not already exist, far-sighted intellectuals sometimes envisaged a national economy as the best way to adapt to a new age of growing international trade and mounting industrial competition. Friedrich List (1789–1846), a German economist and politician with some first-hand experience of the United States, advocated economic integration among the German states through modern means of communication; he became famous on every continent for his championing of moderate protective tariffs as a precondition of industrialization under the shadow of British economic supremacy. List's aim was not autarchy, but market-building on spatial levels below the British-dominated world economy as it had been taking shape since the 1820s.[20] Similarly, in colonial India half a century later, as Manu Goswami has suggested, 'the first sustained articulations of nationalism crystallized around the notion of a territorially delimited economic collective, a national economy'.[21] In India, such visions had to wait for their fulfilment until the end of colonial rule. By contrast, national economies became the norm in Europe during the second half of the nineteenth century. They were congruent with nation states and ultimately provided a basis for national systems of welfare. When towards the end of the century the social consequences of industrialization in conjunction with economic globalization prodded governments to offer basic social security to their most vulnerable citizens, the nation state proved to be the format best suited to organizing and financing such novel tasks of public authority. In immigration and frontier societies like the United States, Australia, and (somewhat less successfully) Argentina, but also in France and Germany, the nation state created concepts of nationhood and citizenship that turned immigrants and refugees into accepted members of the vast and somewhat abstract community of the nation. New arrivals from abroad were no longer, as in early modern times, treated as alien minorities living permanently under special laws. They were now selected and administered according to new criteria for inclusion and exclusion. Subjects or inhabitants previously otherwise defined (e.g. by estate or locality) were transformed into national citizens.

Governments of nation states that had successfully removed *internal* tariffs increasingly felt the pressure to shield their national economies from uncontrollable influences originating outside their own borders. Especially in continental Europe after 1879 and in the United States, tariffs were no longer used mainly for revenue purposes but as tools regulating access to markets. When Western imperial power imposed free-trade regimes, as it did in China or the Ottoman Empire, this was a factor inhibiting the development of national political institutions in those countries. European governments were caught between the conflicting expectations of industrialists, agrarian producers, and the labouring masses for whom the cheapness of daily consumption continued to matter.[22] Tariff protection can be, but is not necessarily, an expression of economic nationalism. One does not have to be a 'nationalist' when one cares for the viability of a country's productive basis. Seen in a different light, agricultural protection not only serves the interests of landlords and agrobusiness, but follows logically from advancing democratization: Rural voters enter the political arena.[23] In no major case before 1914 were anti-globalist policies pushed to extremes. Tariffs before 1914 remained moderate when compared to what happened after the First World War, and large-scale expropriation of foreign business in the name of revolutionary nationalism was first practised by the victorious Bolsheviks from November 1917, becoming a feature not of the nineteenth but of the twentieth century.

Globalization in the nineteenth century was not an inexorable juggernaut leaving no choice beyond adaptation or doom. National policies and legislation were in principle able to influence the terms of globalization. To what extent they succeeded depended above all on the position of a particular nation state in the international hierarchy. Thus, for example, any measure by the Westminster Parliament lowering British tariffs reverberated around the world, while a similar decision taken by the government of Greece, Persia, or Uruguay was unlikely to cause a stir outside those countries. However, this was even as the world's most powerful country, Britain, was not strong enough to prevent the major powers on the European continent from abandoning the doctrine and practice of radical free trade from the late 1870s onwards. British hegemony was of the 'weak' variety operating less through overt coercion than through compliance brought about by obeying general rules (of free trade) and submitting to threats (of naval intervention). It provided an international framework by which other states could orient themselves, while it was vulnerable to challenges by rising powers with a more self-centred agenda. The leading nation states of the *fin de siècle* did not yet possess a post-Keynesian repertoire of tools for managing domestic and international economies. Still, they did not allow global connections to develop untamed. They concluded agreements on common standards from money to railway gauges and world time, collaborated on the unification of international and civil law, and upheld, through the tacit conformity with unwritten rules, such a fragile though effective construction as the gold standard.[24] Nevertheless, far from being under firm political control and guidance, economic globalization during the six or seven decades before 1914 did not subvert the principal European nation states and the newly arrived USA and Japan. They were, by and large, able to use globalization to their own advantage. The challenge from transnational corporations, those powerful globalizers of the twentieth century, was not yet as threatening as it would become later. Weak countries reacted defensively to globalizing tendencies rather than putting their stamp on them. If their governments were lucky and wise enough, such countries might survive or even prosper on the margins of the international system. Countries like Switzerland and Belgium, minor players in a constellation of Great Power 'anarchy', carved niches for themselves where they sponsored world organizations (such as the Red Cross) and offered the services of internationalism.[25]

As a general rule, only well-organized nation states were able to capitalize on economic globalization. By the 1900s, many political entities had lost their independence and were subject to the political decisions of colonial masters. For the remaining countries outside Europe, it was an important variable whether their incorporation into the world economy occurred simultaneously with the construction of state structures or at some other time. Japan was an exception in that the economic 'opening' of the country was, even during the final years of the Tokugawa Shogunate, closely monitored by a political elite with a strong sense of national interest, determined to defend and assert the economic sovereignty of the archipelago. After the onset of the Meiji Restoration in 1868, state-building and the insertion of the country into global structures were two sides of a comprehensive national policy. The situation was different in Latin America, a continent of autonomous post-colonial countries. There the entanglement with global capitalism typically preceded the emergence of coherent and effective political institutions. When nation states consolidated from about the 1880s onwards, they often had little scope to modify the structures that already tied their economies to global networks of trade. They saw their task as deepening and strengthening the existing arrangements for export production.[26]

Global Mobility and Defensive Nationalism

No other aspect of the ubiquitous mobility that globalization is all about is more closely related to nationalism than migration. In the long nineteenth century, more than ever before, new nations owed their existence to large-scale migration: the United States, Australia, New Zealand, Argentina, and several others. These societies were 'global' before they came 'national', and when they began to develop visions of a national bond transcending ethnic and religious differences, this was still a long way from a purposeful nationalism. The most extreme case is Australia: a 'new' nation without a defining national moment, apart from the less than heroic arrival of the First Fleet in January 1788, without external enemies and even without evil colonial oppressors.[27] Australians never turned violently against the British the way the Irish did. Until the Pacific War,

Australia would not confront a single external foe. In the course of the nineteenth century, Australians slowly developed a kind of patriotic pride, but neither the explicit political programme nor the feeling of superiority then characteristic of European nationalism. Australia never stood at the centre of economic and migratory globalization. Nevertheless, it was a product of long-distance mobility, a 'global' nation without a clear demarcation between what was indigenous and what was alien. The discrimination and persecution of the aboriginal population was a weak equivalent to the energetic attempts of the European nations to underline their differences and distances.

Australians lived in colonies, but under a comparatively mild colonial regime. They harboured no expansionist aims of their own. Australia was the terminal point of expansion, not its origin. This was different with the United States, the largest and greatest of all the immigrant nations of modern times. Here, the dynamics of immigration and frontier settlement translated into the hemispheric hegemonism of 'manifest destiny', a doctrine directed against weaker neighbours on the American continent, be they Native American tribes or post-colonial Mexicans. Migratory dynamics shaded into military conquest to an extent unknown elsewhere in the areas of 'white settlement'. Until late in the nineteenth century, the nationalism of 'manifest destiny' carried no overt universalist overtones in spite of lingering residues of Jeffersonian rhetoric. A global nation denied itself the task of spreading a global mission. The United States formulated a national vision almost at the same time as this happened in several European countries. The cleavage between the slave-holding South, aspiring to its own brand of national self-definition, and the 'free labour' North postponed the implementation of this kind of nationalism until the aftermath of the Civil War.[28] It finally turned global in the late 1890s when the white elites of the United States began to see themselves as unrivalled custodians of liberty, enterprise, and civilization with a duty to spread these virtues abroad.

Whereas the United States nationalized global flows of people by devising institutions and symbols that made it possible for immigrants from many different backgrounds to live together peacefully, the same processes, from a different point of view, could be interpreted as a globalization of the national. For those parts of the world that became major sources of emigration, the national experience had to accommodate the new realities of diaspora. Irish nationalism in an age of the massive transatlantic exodus had a strong anti-colonialist streak and step by step developed a secessionist orientation aiming at an independent nation state. But it was clear from the very beginning that a considerable part of the nation would be living permanently in America and other far-away places and would never belong to the future Irish nation state. Moreover, such states would never be strong enough to protect their overseas expatriates.

Diasporic nationalism assumed many different forms. In the case of Greece, for example, a nation state, however fragile, already existed at the time when the great transatlantic migrations began. Greeks had long been used to living scattered around the Mediterranean. In contrast to Ireland, which formed part of the United Kingdom, the Ottoman province of Lebanon had no militant national movement. Even so, the departure of a great proportion of its population gave rise to the idea of a Lebanese nation spread over three continents. When the so-called 'coolie trade' from China increased after the middle of the nineteenth century, the Qing government assumed the role of protector of the overseas Chinese, especially in Southeast Asia. Continuing the traditional concept that the Chinese emperor was father to all his subjects, this could just as well be read as the first instance of China making nationality an issue in its foreign relations. The Qing dynasty itself later became a target of anti-Manchu nationalism. It is worth remembering that, a few decades earlier, it had pioneered Chinese nationalism by giving it an ethnic meaning. In all these cases, nationalism assumed the form it did in direct response to processes of globalization. Ideas of citizenship were sometimes difficult to reconcile. Did expatriates or emigrants retain their original status of citizens of their mother country, or was the host country strong enough to demand and enforce unqualified allegiance?

Immigrants are strangers, and therefore they always pose a challenge to nations that invariably, and also in immigrant societies, have a low tolerance for difference and strive to attain homogeneity. Societies and states have developed innumerable ways of insulating or integrating newcomers. The options range from uninhibited assimilation to strict exclusion. Access is typically controlled through law. Since the late nineteenth century, the regulation of immigration has been one of the most important domains for the exercise of sovereignty in 'new' nations. A turning point of worldwide consequences occurred in the 1880s, when the neo-European countries of 'white settlement', especially the United States, Canada, and Australia, took steps to exclude and deter Asian immigrants. At a time of mounting racism, 'whites-only' policies were not just adopted on pragmatic grounds, but called forth all sorts of claims about the inferiority of Asians and their will and capacity to undermine 'civilized' and well-ordered 'white' societies. Such an exclusionist vision of white purity and yellow peril became the hallmark of North American and antipodean nationalisms during the decades around 1900.[29]

Whenever the state arrogates to itself decisions about racial and cultural hierarchies, the question of who represents 'the nation' moves to the centre of political contestation. A racialization of nationalism has not remained restricted to areas of 'white' dominance. Racialized versions of citizenship sometimes developed a long time after the end of political decolonization as a result of complex social processes. Thus, 'blackness' can replace, as it did in Jamaica, the idea of victimization by colonialism as a dominant source of national identity.[30]

The exclusion of Chinese, Japanese, and to some extent, Indians from areas under white hegemony triggered violent reactions on the Asian side. The restriction of immigration was a major issue of diplomatic conflict between the US and Japanese governments in the late nineteenth century. In China the first nationwide popular protests against a foreign country were sparked by the maltreatment of Chinese labourers in the United States.[31] Chinese nationalism has a number of roots. One of them was a reaction against discrimination of Chinese abroad during the years after 1900. This was a stronger impulse than a pure anti-colonialist resentment against the West. It was intimately bound up with the question of 'national honour' that has been a driving force of Chinese attitudes toward the international community ever since. The principal weapon of the early Chinese protests was the boycott, an instrument still used today, mainly against individual firms, by anti-globalization activists.

Nationalism contains elements of an ideology of resistance: resistance against imperial rulers and over-mighty neighbours, against economic exploitation or cultural hegemony. Even in a position of objective strength, nationalism is fuelled by anxieties of subversion or, as in the case of Germany after 1904, of military 'encirclement'.[32] Many or perhaps most of the threats to the national community are seen as approaching from the outside, sometimes from a vast and mysterious outer world that harbours dark forces of destruction. In extreme cases, this can lead to mass hysteria and a paranoid style of politics. Minorities are then treated as 'fifth columns' and instruments of hostile powers. Huge numbers of Jews, Armenians, and Chinese (in Southeast Asia) have fallen victim to this kind of purifying obsession.

Under conditions of globalization, nationalist politicians and voices of public opinion face a dilemma. While it is imperative for the well-being of a nation or the stability of a regime to engage in economic relations with the outside world, that external sphere is perceived as a source of destabilization. Globalized China trying to control the Internet is a current manifestation of this contradiction inherent in modern nationalism. Nationalist resistance against what is seen as global capitalism menacing local ways of life covers a broad spectrum from conspiracy theories and firm rejection of anything 'alien' or 'strange' to a well-considered defence of national and local preferences. The banning of Coca Cola from India by the Hindu-nationalist Janata Party in 1977 tended to the first extreme;[33] the safeguarding of traditional quality standards in food production against neo-liberal legislation in the European Union exemplifies a position of a more moderate anti-globalism. Today, globalization is often equated with cheap and uniform mass production, with aggressive tourism and ruthless exploitation of the environment. This was not entirely different during the first great wave of globalization before 1914. In both periods, the process can be understood as having stimulated a new attachment to local practices and problems.[34] The result has rarely been a fully developed nationalist programme. At the same time, a mild assertion of cultural difference and specificity has opposed the homogenizing tendencies of globalization, insisting on the need for and the right to identity. One's own nation, or 'Europe', 'Africa', and so forth, carries with it particular values and forms of life, different from those of other imagined or socially integrated communities. Globalization does not encourage identification. It offers little in the way of emotional attachment. 'Cosmopolitanism', based on a general and abstract idea of freedom and unlimited choice, has historically been a poor substitute for the attractions of community life.[35]

Nationalism and Normative Universalism

Nationalism has been played out in an ever-expanding arena. During much of the nineteenth century, nationalisms interacted merely within Europe. Apart from embryonic ideas like the 'nativism' of a few thinkers in late Tokugawa Japan, Asian nationalisms emerged slowly from the 1880s onwards. In the early twentieth century, they challenged European colonial rule. In at least one instance, the epochal conflict between Japan and China in the 1930s and early 1940s, they clashed with one another. As late as 1945, the various nationalisms had not met on a world stage, although some of them had formed the non-territorial solidarities of Asian, African, Turkic, and other 'pan' movements.[36] From then onward, the United Nations would offer such a stage, especially after decolonization and the ensuing proliferation of the model of the nation state. A 'global nationalism' has already been identified for Germany around 1900.[37] German nationalism at that time imagined Germany's improving (and threatened) position in the world economy and the global political order. It envisaged Germany as a colonial power and as a *Kulturnation* of worldwide attractiveness.

A century later, nationalism has become global in a more profound sense. The United Nations and numerous other international organizations and conferences assemble representatives of many nations, each of them operating within a tension between national objectives and the need for international compromise. The rise of international television has turned gigantic sports events like the Olympic Games or the football World Cups into symbolic spaces where national identities come together in peaceful competition. At the same time, nations are reviving their 'national' sports, whether genuine or invented. Audiences in the same countries identify just as much with 'global' sports as with national peculiarities like Irish 'hurling'.[38] Even the smallest nation state nowadays struggles for diplomatic and media attention in a way inconceivable a hundred years ago.

One last manifestation of globalism to be considered in a discussion of globalization and nationalism is the universalism of generally accepted international norms. Before the First World War, such norms existed only in a most rudimentary form, be it as a limited body of international law or as a hazy 'standard of civilization' to which non-European states were expected to conform regardless of their own traditions. Normative universalism then grew in the course of the twentieth century. By the final quarter of that century nationalist policies, rhetoric, and attitudes were facing the new and immensely powerful force of 'world opinion'. Earlier nationalisms, especially if they had a strong political foundation, sometimes attempted to universalize their own principles by casting them in the language of a civilizing mission or, as in the German case after Hitler's rise to power in 1933, of the natural superiority of a particular race.

Such strategies became difficult to pursue after 1945. The norm of national self-determination, first publicized during the 'Wilsonian moment' of 1919, enjoys an unprecedented degree of acceptance.[39] Small states are easily admitted as viable newcomers to the community of nations if they can claim territorial jurisdiction and show some degree of cultural coherence. With self-determination comes the accompanying principle of non-intervention by foreign powers into the domestic affairs of a recognized nation state.[40] This principle, however, stands in stark contrast to a new thinking in terms of human rights. The behaviour of governments towards their own citizens and subjects, in particular as regards minorities, comes under close scrutiny by international and non-governmental institutions. Around 1900 or 1930, nationalist politicians could do within their own borders whatever they pleased. Towards the end of the twentieth century, the normative power of global standards of political behaviour increased tremendously, more so in the case of smaller states than with large and powerful ones. Sovereignty is no longer as absolute as it used to be, at least in theory.[41] Serious violations of human rights have caused 'humanitarian' interventions, although in many other cases regimes were left undisturbed to commit crimes against their own population. Nationalism has not been cancelled or rendered obsolete by this kind of normative universalization. But it has lost its prestige as a form of politics that was 'natural' and unaccountable to any higher authority.

NOTES

1. For a survey of the debate, see D. Held and A. McGrew (2007) *Globalization/Anti-Globalization: Beyond the Great Divide*, 2nd edn., Cambridge.
2. For the full range of theories of globalization, see R. Robertson and K. E. White (eds.) (2003) *Globalization: Critical Concepts in Sociology*, 6 vols., London and New York.
3. R. J. Holton (2005) *Making Globalization*, Basingstoke, 105–6.
4. J. L. Abu-Lughod (1989) *Before European Hegemony: The World System A.D. 1250–1350*, New York and Oxford.
5. J. Osterhammel and N. P. Petersson (2005) *Globalization: A Short History*, trans. D. Geyer, Princeton, NJ.
6. M. D. Bordo, A. M. Taylor, and J. G. Williamson (eds.) (2003) *Globalization in Historical Perspective*, Chicago and London.
7. Elements of such a (historical) theory are assembled in C. A. Bayly (2004) *The Birth of the Modern World 1780–1914: Global Connections and Comparisons*, Oxford.
8. A seminal theoretical statement is offered by J. P. Arnason, 'Nationalism, Globalization and Modernity', in M. Featherstone (ed.) (1990) *Global Culture: Nationalism, Globalization and Modernity*, London and New Delhi, 207–36.
9. S. Sassen (2006) *Territory, Authority, Rights: From Medieval to Global Assemblages*, Princeton, NJ, 1.
10. Sassen, *Territory*, 23.
11. I. Clark (1997) *Globalization and Fragmentation: International Relations in the Twentieth Century*, Oxford, 27. Another important theorist is James N. Rosenau, who has coined the term 'fragmegration'. See James N. Rosenau (2003) *Distant Proximities: Dynamics beyond Globalization*, Princeton, NJ, 11.
12. See C. A. Bayly, '"Archaic" and "Modern" Globalization in the Eurasian and African Arena, *c.*1750–1850', in A. G. Hopkins (ed.) (2002) *Globalization in World History*, London, 47–73.
13. L. Colley (1992) *Britons: Forging the Nation 1707–1837*, New Haven, CT. For a differently nuanced view, see P. Mandler (2006) *The English National Character: The History of an Idea from Edmund Burke to Tony Blair*, New Haven, CT.
14. J. A. Frieden (2006) *Global Capitalism: Its Fall and Rise in the Twentieth Century*, New York.

15. See J. Osterhammel (2006) *Europe, the 'West' and the Civilizing Mission: The 2005 Annual Lecture at the German Historical Institute London*, London.
16. J. J. Sheehan (2008) *Where Have All the Soldiers Gone? The Transformation of Modern Europe*, New York.
17. B. R. O'G. Anderson (1998) *The Spectre of Comparisons: Nationalism, Southeast Asia, and the World*, New York, 59.
18. D. K. Buse (1993) 'Urban and National Identity: Bremen, 1860–1920', *Journal of Social History*, 26, no. 4 (summer), 521–37, esp. 527–30.
19. S. Weichlein (2006) 'Nationalismus und Nationalstaat in Deutschland und Europa. Ein Forschungsüberblick', *Neue Politische Literatur*, 51, no. 2 (summer), 265–352, at 267.
20. M. Metzler (2006) 'The Cosmopolitanism of National Economics: Friedrich List in a Japanese Mirror', in A. G. Hopkins (ed.) *Global History: Interactions Between the Universal and the Local*, Basingstoke, 98–130, esp. 119.
21. M. Goswami (2004) *Producing India: From Colonial Economy to National Space*, Chicago and London, 209.
22. C. Torp (2005) *Die Herausforderung der Globalisierung. Wirtschaft und Politik in Deutschland 1860–1914*, Göttingen.
23. S. Yoichiro (2001) 'Agricultural Nationalism in the Age of Globalization: The Opening of Japan's Rice Market in the 1990s', in R. Starrs (ed.) *Asian Nationalism in an Age of Globalization*, London, 34–64, esp. 35, 40.
24. M. H. Geyer and J. Paulmann (eds.) (2001) *The Mechanics of Internationalism: Culture, Society, and Politics from the 1840s to the First World War*, Oxford.
25. C. N. Murphy (1994) *International Organization and Industrial Change: Global Governance since 1850*, Cambridge, 76–81; Madeleine Herren (2000) *Hintertüren zur Macht. Internationalismus und modernisierungsorientierte Aussenpolitik in Belgien, der Schweiz und den USA, 1865–1914*, Munich.
26. R. G. Williams (1994) *States and Social Evolution: Coffee and the Rise of National Governments in Central America*, Chapel Hill, NC, 236, 247. See also Chapter 19 by Nicola Miller on Latin America and Chapter 14 by Rana Mitter on East Asia, including Japan.
27. M. Wesley (2000) 'Nationalism and Globalization in Australia', in L. Suryadinata (ed.) *Nationalism and Globalization: East and West*, Singapore, 175–99, at 175–6.
28. See Chapter 20 by Susan-Mary Grant.
29. A comprehensive survey is M. Lake and H. Reynolds (2008) *Drawing the Global Colour Line: White Men's Countries and the International Challenge of Racial Equality*, Cambridge; see also C. Geulen (2007) 'The Common Grounds of Conflict: Racial Visions of World Order 1880–1940', in S. Conrad and D. Sachsenmaier (eds.) *Competing Visions of World Order: Global Moments and Movements, 1880s–1930s*, New York and Basingstoke, 69–96.
30. D. A. Thomas (2004) *Modern Blackness: Nationalism, Globalization and the Politics of Culture in Jamaica*, Durham, NC, 11.
31. See Chapter 14 by Rana Mitter.
32. U. Daniel (2005) 'Einkreisung und Kaiserdämmerung. Ein Versuch, der Kulturgeschichte der Politik vor dem Ersten Weltkrieg auf die Spur zu kommen', in B. Stollberg-Rilinger (ed.) *Was heisst Kulturgeschichte des Politischen?*, Berlin, 279–328.
33. C. Six (2001) *Hindu-Nationalismus und Globalisierung. Die zwei Gesichter Indiens. Symbole der Identität und des Anderen*, Frankfurt am Main, 36.

34. A. D. Smith (2001) *Nationalism: Theory, Ideology, History*, Cambridge, 137.
35. N. P. Petersson (2007) 'Globalisierung und Globalisierungsdiskurse: Netzwerke, Räume, Identitäten', in R. Marcowitz (ed.) *Nationale Identität und transnationale Einflüsse. Amerikanisierung, Europäisierung, Globalisierung in Frankreich nach dem Zweiten Weltkrieg*, Munich, 87–103.
36. See Chapter 34 by Cemil Aydin.
37. S. Conrad (2006) *Globalisierung und Nation im Deutschen Kaiserreich*, Munich, 319.
38. A. Bairner (2001) *Sport, Nationalism, and Globalization: European and North American Perspectives*, Albany, NY, 167.
39. See E. Manela (2007) *The Wilsonian Moment: Self-Determination and the International Origins of Anticolonial Nationalism*, Oxford.
40. See Chapter 28 by Richard Caplan and Chapter 27 by James Mayall.
41. On the weakness of criteria for sovereign statehood, see S. D. Krasner (1999) *Sovereignty: Organized Hypocrisy*, Princeton, NJ, 220.

Suggested Further Reading

Arnason, J. P. (1990) 'Nationalism, Globalization and Modernity', in M. Featherstone (ed.) (1990) *Global Culture: Nationalism, Globalization and Modernity*, London and New Delhi, 207–36.

Bayly, C. A. (2004) *The Birth of the Modern World 1780–1914*, Oxford.

Clark, I. (1997) *Globalization and Fragmentation: International Relations in the Twentieth Century*, Oxford.

Frieden, J. A. (2006) *Global Capitalism: Its Fall and Rise in the Twentieth Century*, New York.

Held, D., McGrew, A., Goldblatt, D., and Perraton, J. (1999) *Global Transformations: Politics, Economics and Culture*, Cambridge.

Hopkins, A. G. (ed.) (2002) *Globalization in World History*, London.

Osterhammel, J., and Petersson, N. P. (2005) *Globalization: A Short History*, trans. D. Geyer, Princeton, NJ.

Ritzer, G. (ed.) (2007) *The Blackwell Companion to Globalizatio*, Malden, MA, and Oxford.

Rossi, I. (ed.) (2008) *Frontiers of Globalization Research: Theoretical and Methodological Approaches*, New York.

Sassen, S. (2006) *Territory, Authority, Rights: From Medieval to Global Assemblages*, Princeton, NJ.

Smith, A. D. (1995) *Nations and Nationalism in a Global Era*, Cambridge.

Suryadinata, L. (ed.) (2000) *Nationalism and Globalization: East and West*, Singapore.

PART VI

NATIONALIST HISTORIOGRAPHY

CHAPTER 36

NATIONALISM AND HISTORICAL WRITING

PAUL LAWRENCE

INTRODUCTION

NATIONALISM has always been intimately connected to a sense of the past. Whether defined generally as identification with a putative cultural collectivity known as a nation, or more specifically as the notion that a given 'nation' deserves and can rightly seek self-government, nationalism is invariably bound up with perceptions of the past, and with claims for the present and future made on the basis of those perceptions. As Ronald Suny notes, 'there can be no nation without a sense of its own history'.[1]

Certainly, a sense of a shared past is a feature of many contemporary definitions of both nations and nationalism. Anthony Smith, for example, argues that nations always share 'common myths and memories', while Steven Grosby describes a nation as an extensive, bounded territory which, among other attributes, possesses 'a history that both asserts and is expressive of temporal continuity'.[2] Even among theorists who believe nationalism to be a rather more modern phenomenon, a shared sense of the past remains significant. While perhaps stressing more overtly the way in which history can be distorted or selectively remembered, modernists concerned with the 'invention of tradition', or the way in which the political doctrine of nationalism produces nations (rather than the other way around), still concede the power of historical memory in shaping national sentiment.[3]

However, while there is general agreement that the remembrance of things past has had a great deal of influence on the nature and development of national sentiment, it is only comparatively recently that specific research has been conducted into the mechanics of how the 'sense of a shared past' of a given community relates to nationalism.[4] In this chapter, the nature of the links between historians, the development of the historical profession, history writing and nationalism will be explored. This focus should not be taken as a claim that it is only professional historians who have been concerned with depicting the past in national terms. Philosophers, artists, playwrights, composers, and literary figures have all often incorporated historical themes into their work. In early nineteenth-century France, for example, even wallpaper manufacturers sought to present the past to the public, producing designs depicting historical events such as the Battle of Austerlitz in 1805 and the July Revolution of 1830.[5] Many cultural products other than the written word can and do provide populations with a sense of a shared past. However, written history produced by acknowledged specialists has often been privileged in nationalist discourses, partly due to the success of the historical profession's own claims to scientific objectivity and partly due to the close links between historians and emergent states forged during the nineteenth century.

This chapter first outlines and analyses the links between the development of history writing and the evolution of nationalism (as both cultural sentiment and political doctrine). It then seeks to consider why there have always been such close links between history writing and the nation, to analyse what it is that makes history so indispensable to nationalists, and to ask overall whether nationalism *requires* certain types of history.

Historical Writing and Nationalism before *c.*1750

For much of the latter half of the twentieth century, there was a tendency in the field of nationalism studies to discount the idea that nations and nationalism were socially significant in the pre-modern period. More recently, however, there has been renewed interest in the possibility of locating recognizable nations and national sentiment much earlier. Steven Grosby, for example, has claimed that 'throughout history man has considered . . . environments which are considerably more extensive than those of the family and the home to be his "own", hence, integral to his life', while Anthony Smith argues that, even in antiquity, 'ethnic communities expressing a clear cultural unity persisted for long periods in several parts of the world'.[6] In these debates, early modern and medieval historians have often been prominent. They have frequently regarded England as the archetypal 'first nation', with Adrian Hastings asserting that, from the early fourteenth century, 'Englishmen felt themselves to be a nation', and Liah Greenfeld arguing that England became 'the first nation in the world' in the late sixteenth century.[7]

Very often, part of the evidence used to assert these claims of pre-modern nations and nationalism have been works of history. Hastings, for example, argues that Bede's *Ecclesiastical History of the English People* (*c.*730) takes for granted a 'single nation'. Stefan Berger notes that the Duke of Malmesbury's *Deeds of the Kings of the English*, written during the twelfth century, 'conveys a clear idea of the political and cultural unity of a nation called England'.[8] On mainland Europe, Regino of Prüm (writing around 900) felt able to differentiate between 'different peoples' on the basis of 'descent, manners, language and laws'.[9] Later European humanists also adopted the topic of the nation, creating values and symbols oriented towards a spatial entity known as the nation, even where this did not yet exist, with the Bavarian historian and philosopher Johannes Aventinus asserting a recognizable sixteenth-century German nationalism.[10] A similar situation can be discerned outside of Europe in parts of the world with settled, literate populations. As Q. Edward Wang notes, 'in China... we encounter ideas of nation and national enemies as early as the Han period and again in the Song period' (960–1279).[11]

However, while it is possible to locate instances of historians writing forms of national history in the medieval and early modern periods, there are limits to the significance of this. In the first place, it is extremely difficult to assess with any certainty the reception and impact of these early histories. Most would have had a very small circulation. Although this is not necessarily indicative of minimal impact if the readership was influential and the histories served as 'the texts in which an elite defines itself', their significance in relation to what the majority thought and felt was likely to have been minor.[12]

Secondly, those writing these 'national' histories may have been working with a rather different notion of 'the nation' to those writing history in the modern period. While Susan Reynolds has claimed that early writers conceptualized nations as 'communities with collective political rights as well as shared histories and cultures', John Breuilly has highlighted differences in usage such that, in his view, 'there is no significant continuity between pre-modern and modern national identity'.[13]

Finally, the nature and intent of these histories were very different from those of the more recent past. Early historians were often working with the concept of *historia magistra*. Inherited from antiquity, this was the notion that history should serve an exemplary purpose, guiding men as to how they should act in the present. Thus, history writing essentially attempted to highlight universal, unchanging truths about mankind, rather than trace developments unique to particular times and places.[14]

From about 1750 onwards, however, as the national principle gained decisively over its rivals—religion, dynastic principle, and feudalism—important changes occurred in both the practice of writing history and in its social and political significance. If before about 1750 history writing was primarily intended to draw examples from the past as a guide to behaviour in the present, during the apogee of the nationalist period (*c*.1750–1945) the exemplary gave way to the unique. Rather than cyclical or constant, the human condition came to be seen as amenable to progress, a trope that was to become particularly significant to the narrative national histories of the post-1750 period.[15]

Writing National Histories, *c*.1750–1945

While it is arguably possible to locate evidence of national sentiment before 1750, there is general agreement that the period 1750–1945 was particularly significant for the development of both nations and nationalism. There have been protracted debates about the origins, nature, and precise extent of the rapid spread of national sentiment that took place during this period.[16] However, a number of points are relatively, although not entirely, uncontentious. In the period from around 1750 onwards, 'the nation' became the focus of increasing intellectual debate in Europe. During the nineteenth century, national sentiment moved from being primarily of cultural significance to one of increasing political import, evidenced by the general shift from multi-ethnic empires to nation states as the 'normal' form of governance, at least in Europe. While the rise of the nation-state principle was relatively unproblematic in some cases (such as England), in other instances it generated violent conflict. The ideal that culturally defined 'nations' should rule themselves was gradually exported, via European colonialism, to other parts of the world. By the early twentieth century, national identity (which had been weak, or confined largely to elite groups) had become a primary identity for large swathes of the world's population.

This period also witnessed the development of the academic historical profession as we know it today. The first university chairs in history were created in Berlin (1810) and Paris (1812), and within a decade historical societies had been created to collect and publish historical documents, and historians had founded their own professional journals. The new professionals of history sought, via an innovative focus on the objective use of archival material, to portray the past, in Leopold von Ranke's famous phrase, *wie es eigentlich gewesen* ('as it actually was'). However, it is readily apparent that many of these new professionals became closely connected to the states in which they lived and worked, and that 'material dependence on the state corresponded with strong intellectual ties to the nation state'.[17]

Nineteenth-century historians were often highly partisan advocates of the interests of their own particular nation states, who 'went into the archives to find evidence that would support their nationalistic and class preconceptions and thus give them the aura of scientific authority'.[18] This point can readily be illustrated with reference to Germany, where historians quickly became, in Thomas Nipperdey's words, the 'main speakers of the nation (*Festredner der Nation*)'.[19] Heinrich von Treitschke, for example, one of the foremost historians of nineteenth-century Germany, had enormous contemporary influence. Following German unification in 1871, he held a seat in the Reichstag and observed with growing apprehension the decline of the patriotic movement. It was in this context that he began work on his *Deutsche Geschichte im Neunzehnten Jahrhundert* (*German History in the Nineteenth Century*), published between 1879 and 1894. This work was never finished but its relevance here lies in the fact that, as well as describing 'the context of the events', Treitschke's expressed aim in the work was to arouse in the hearts of his readers 'the pleasure of living in the Fatherland'.[20]

Such an aim was by no means unusual, and the subjective idealization by historians of their own particular nations was not confined to Germany. In France, too, widely published historians customarily wrote in lyrical, emotive terms. Jules Michelet, for example, initially an archivist at the *Archives Nationales* before being appointed to a chair at the *Collège de France* in 1838, believed that the French Revolution had demonstrated that his 'glorious motherland' was destined to become 'the pilot vessel of humanity'.[21] Ernest Lavisse, editor of a huge twenty-seven-volume *Histoire de France* (published between 1900 and 1911), claimed that 'the long memory of ancestors, the joy of finding my soul in their thoughts and their actions, in their history and in their legends' provided him with his 'main reason for living'.[22]

Nor were such sentiments confined to historians of nations that already possessed a state structure. Historians also often sought to provide a historical basis for the *claims* to nationhood and political independence of states that did not yet exist. As Berger notes, 'creating national historical consciousness was widely seen as the most important precondition for engendering true national feeling in the wider population'.[23] Historians were even, on occasion, involved politically in nationalist struggles. František Palacký, for example, was passionately committed to the idea of a Czech nation, an aim that he pursued equally vigorously via his historical writing and his political career.[24] Many other examples of European historians actively constructing national histories, often from the flimsiest of evidence, can be unearthed.[25]

Different traditions of national history writing began to emerge during the nineteenth century. In France, the significance of the Revolution and the role of 'the people' in disseminating universal notions of liberty were often stressed. In Germany, the importance of the state was a prominent trope, while England was often viewed by its historians as the natural home of democracy and liberty. Within these broad trends there were often competing versions of national history. In Germany, for example, Treitschke's work represented a distinctively 'Prussian' version of German history, which minimized the contribution of Austria and the smaller German states. In England, the imperial themes addressed by historians such as John Seeley offered a focus other than liberty and democracy for the 'story' of England's development.[26] However, aside from a narrative approach based heavily on political and military archival sources, what most nineteenth-century histories had in common was that they sought to highlight the specificity and significance of the historian's own nation state. As the historical profession developed during the nineteenth century, it did so in tandem with new conceptions of the national in the cultural and political life of Europe. The two processes were intimately intertwined, with nineteenth-century historians providing the justification for the founding of new nation states, and for the expansion and consolidation of existing states, while often relying on these very states for their livelihoods and prestige.

This process was not confined to Europe. During the latter part of the nineteenth century it is possible to trace the transmission of the new European ideal of history writing (and the concomitant evolution of national histories) further afield. This transmission is closely related to European imperialism. In Brazil, for example, Francisco Adolfo de Varnhagen's multivolume *História Geral do Brasil* sought to portray Brazilian independence as a continuation of monarchic rule rather than a break with Portugal, thus justifying the colonial elite's right to supremacy.[27]

Countries whose histories came to be written by non-original, predominantly white-settler inhabitants, such as the USA and Australia, had different problems with historical time. Unable to locate the origins of their nation in a dim and distant past but keen to efface the significance of original, non-European inhabitants, early 'Romantic' visions of American history (such as George Bancroft's *History of the United States of America*) portrayed the gradual 'ripening' of a wholly new nation, while later historians chose to focus on the uniqueness of a nation based on progress and growth.[28] History writing became an important part of the process of consolidating national identity and asserting nationalist claims, both in Europe and further afield, during the latter half of the nineteenth century.

Of course, not all historians were writing teleological national histories. Henry Buckle's *History of Civilization in England*, published in two volumes in 1857 and 1861, sought to consider the history of medieval civilization via a comparison between England, France, Spain, and Scotland. Equally, Thomas Maitland's *Constitutional History of England* shows a clear awareness of the 'constructed' nature of historical knowledge, noting that the term 'feudal system' was coined long after the institutions which comprised it had ceased to be.[29] In addition, throughout the nineteenth century, certain key thinkers were critical of nationalist interpretations of history. The assertion by Lord Acton (Regius Professor of Modern History at Cambridge University) that nationalism was both a modern development and 'a retrograde step in history', the spread of which would be marked with 'material as well as moral ruin', is well known.[30] Equally, as the social sciences developed in the early decades of the twentieth century, they also often attacked the historical profession on the basis of its preoccupation with narrative national histories.[31]

It is tempting to assume therefore that, whereas nineteenth-century historians contributed to the development of the nation-state principle via the eulogistic national histories they wrote, the turn of the twentieth century saw increasing criticism of this approach to the subject and the gradual development of higher standards of 'objectivity'. Certainly, during the early part of the twentieth century the discipline of history as it developed in Europe did indeed see initiatives that turned away from the prior focus on the nation state. The French historians Lucien Febvre and Marc Bloch, for example, founders of the *Annales* school, aimed to set aside the concept of linear time and the grand narratives of national development in favour of a focus on mentalities and regional and/or supranational history.

In fact, however, national history remained the norm during the first half of the twentieth century. This was particularly apparent during periods of conflict. On the outbreak of the First World War, historians mobilized alongside other intellectuals to promote their own nation's cause and denigrate the enemy's national past. In September 1914, for example, a group of Oxford historians published the justificatory tract *Why we are at War*, a move countered by the publication in Germany of *Aufruf an die Kulturwelt* (*Appeal to the Cultured World*), signed by ninety-three academics, including historians.[32]

Many historians agreed with Friedrich Thimme's assertion that 'if one can't serve the Fatherland with the sword, then at least it should be done with the pen'.[33]

Traditions of national history writing were further mobilized during the interwar period to justify the outcome in all combatant nations and, certainly up until the Second World War, history writing remained largely focused on 'the nation', which was treated as an unproblematic given, and served to bolster national sentiment and pride among readers by interpreting the past of their nation state as unique and special.

The Persistence of National Histories after the Second World War

A glance at an historical atlas shows that, while the number and distribution of nation states in Europe remained *relatively* stable after the Second World War (at least compared to the previous century), there was significant change in most other parts of the world, as the process of decolonization unleashed new waves of nationalism and created wholly new state formations. The differing political fortunes of nation states in Europe and elsewhere were both reflected in and, in some ways, shaped by, historiographical developments.

Within Europe, the relative stability of borders, the long consolidation of the nation-state principle since 1750, and the role of the Second World War in highlighting (for many historians, at least) the dangers inherent in nationalism, meant that 1945 arguably marked the 'beginning of the end' for the type of unreflective national history writing described in the preceding section. Historiography in Europe gradually began to move away from seeing the nation as a given, with history's purpose to trace its development and illuminate its future trajectory. However, this process has been protracted and is by no means complete.

In the immediate post-war period attempts were made to restabilize and reconnect to traditional national narratives, particularly in West Germany and Italy, but the late 1950s onwards saw a genuine pluralization of historical discourse in Europe and the Americas. In many countries, the 1960s saw a turning away from the prior, almost exclusive, focus on political history and the state, towards social and cultural history. It became common to seek the authentic experience of the ordinary man, and for historians such as those of the *Annales* school in France, or the members of the Communist Party Historians' Group in the United Kingdom, the development of everyday life and thought became more significant to the history they wrote than the actions of politicians and key decision makers.[34]

Equally, from the 1970s onwards it is possible to trace the increasing influence of the social sciences in the historical field. Typified by initiatives such as the Bielefeld school in Germany, engagement with another discipline helped engender a shift from narrative, event-oriented history to social science-influenced historiographical approaches, which both emphasized and problematized social structures and processes of change. Also from the 1970s onwards, the growth of postmodernism or what is often known as the 'linguistic turn', with its emphasis on the constructed nature of historical knowledge, led historians increasingly to question the very category of the nation, and the viability of writing any kind of coherent national history. More recently, the growing popularity of transnational history, defined as 'the study of movements and forces that cut across national boundaries', has also served to make purely national histories seem parochial and naive.[35]

However, some qualification is needed. In the first place, of course, even in Western countries with stable states, historians did not entirely eschew national history. For example, whilst there was a vast expansion in the numbers of university-based historians (tripling in France and West Germany between the 1960s and the end of the century), most of these historians were still appointed to posts associated with the study of one particular country. Thus the national paradigm remained dominant in institutional terms, even while it was being eroded within the historiography.

Moreover, there are some notable exceptions to the general trends outlined above. The Cold War was a particular complicating factor. As Karl Erdmann notes, 'in the 1980s, the East-West conflict was the most important single factor in structuring international relations, and it had a deep impact on the study and writing of history, too.'[36] In East Germany, for example, history writing retained a strong national tendency during the Cold War. Special 'Institutes for the History of the German People' were founded at key universities, and a new multivolume German history was published with the intention of narrating the story of the German people from a Marxist-Leninist perspective.[37] A variety of communist regimes preserved a national frame in writing about the struggles of peasants and workers. Equally, following the disintegration of the USSR in the early 1990s, historians either busied themselves actively constructing national identities (in regions such as Kazakhstan where an imposed identity had been in place), or in reinforcing notions of nationalism as a primordial given (in regions with relatively ethnic homogenous populations, such as Armenia).[38]

Overall, therefore, while the 'nation' was perhaps no longer assumed by many European and American historians to be a given, primordial entity, while nationalism as a political doctrine had become intellectually tainted after the Second World War, and while the pluralization of the discipline meant that no single approach to interpreting the past dominated the field, it is still fair to state that the national paradigm remained significant both in practical terms, in that most historians still studied a particular country (usually their own), and in historiographical terms, in that most histories were still very much reflective of the national frameworks in which they were written.

Moreover, outside of Europe and America, these links remained even clearer. The process of decolonization resulted in many former colonies gaining independence, via a range of violent and negotiated transfers of power. In the forty years following the end of the Second World War, former colonies gained independence across Africa, the Middle East, and Asia. While by no means all of these new states could map themselves directly onto a European nation-state model, many at least claimed to do so. History writing was often crucial in delineating new, 'national' identities, on the basis of which claims to independence were often made.

For example, in India, history writing was an integral part of the process of moving towards independence. James Mill's *History of British India* (1817) had made a strong case justifying British rule in India due to the stagnation and inability of Indians to change. Hence, indigenous history writing as it developed in the early part of the twentieth century set out both to 'restore to Indians their lost past, and instil in them a sense of pride in their own ancient heritage', and also, explicitly, to prove 'that India had traditions, especially of government, no less than those of Britain, and therefore was capable of governing itself'.[39] In Africa, too, the writing of history was often undertaken with explicitly political aims in mind, as historians 'aligned their research with anti-colonial struggles from the very outset'.[40] Settler nations also often felt the need retrospectively to construct a national history in order to consolidate a fledgling national identity. In Australia, for example, 'notions of a separate Australianness only began to enter academic discussions about national history in the inter-war period'.[41]

Overall, therefore, for much of the period since 1945, national history writing has remained significant. It is possible to argue for the evolution of an inquisitive, self-aware form of national history in certain parts of the world, with a more strident, declamatory, justificatory historiography in some other regions. Such is the varied nature of historical writing, however, that it is problematic to make any such sweeping claims. In particular, as was the case during the nineteenth century, national histories were certainly not always consensual. For example, the academic debate that developed during the latter half of the twentieth century over the existence of a German *Sonderweg* (special path), while still very much contained within the paradigm of national history, proposed radically new versions of German national history.[42] Equally, minority nationalisms in Europe, such as those of Scotland and Catalonia, sought during the same period to construct their own national pasts as part of a political challenge to the dominant national narratives of Britain and Spain.

Historiography certainly diversified over the course of the twentieth century and 'faith in the grand narratives focused on the modernization of the Western world as the culmination of a coherent historical process' has arguably been 'irredeemably lost'.[43] Yet history writing, albeit often typified by competing national narratives, still served to reinforce nationalism in many parts of the globe during the twentieth century, even if the link was not as significant at the end of the century as at the start. Given this continued association between nationalism and history writing, the final section of this chapter will inquire more closely into the specific nature of the link between the two.

The Link between Historiography and Nationalism

It would appear that there are clear links between nationalism, in both its cultural and political forms, and the writing of history. While different traditions of national history writing emerged, particularly during the nineteenth and early twentieth centuries, national histories shared many common tropes. As Suny summarizes, a national history was normally 'one of continuity, antiquity of origins, heroism and past greatness, martyrdom and sacrifice, victimization and overcoming of trauma . . . a story of the empowerment of the people, the realization of the ideals of popular sovereignty'.[44] These similarities point to a common function—national histories served to enhance and sustain nationalism in both its political and cultural forms. However, to recognize this link between history writing and nationalism is one thing, to explain it is quite another. Why should a sense of a 'national' past be particularly relevant to an individual's sense of identity or political affiliations in the present? In one sense, the answer to this question very much depends on which interpretation of nationalism is adopted. Different groups of theorists have proposed very different explanations for the genesis and functioning of nationalism, and hence they have all tended to find history writing significant in different ways.

During the first half of the twentieth century, when nationalism first came under sustained intellectual scrutiny, historians such as Carlton Hayes and Hans Kohn were very much concerned with the 'idea' of nationalism. Their analyses were based on the assertion that, while nations might be old, nationalism was a relatively new intellectual concept. Hence, what philosophers, playwrights, politicians, and others wrote in the period from 1750 was accorded key significance. Hayes, for example, posited a three-stage process via which the new doctrine of nationalism was disseminated, the first stage of which was its elaboration 'by an eminent company of "intellectuals"—philologists, historians, anthropologists, economists, philosophers, and litterateurs'.[45] This doctrine was subsequently adopted by political elites and then spread downward to the mass of the population. The significance of history writing in such analyses is apparent, but such idealist interpretations of nationalism later came under criticism because (in addition to being Eurocentric) they did not provide a convincing explanation as to why this particular doctrine rose to prominence or found such popular resonance.

From the 1960s onwards, partly due to the influence of the social sciences on the field, some writers came to see nationalism primarily as a functional component or product of 'modernity', rather than as an abstract idea or doctrine. Theorists such as Karl Deutsch and Ernest Gellner viewed the rise of both nations and nationalism as intimately bound up with industrialization. Gellner, for example, argued that a new type of education ('exo-socialization') was required to cope with the task of providing the transferable skills required for modern, industrial societies. This education could no longer be supplied at the village level (as it had been during feudal, agrarian periods) because only states had the necessary resources. Hence, in the industrial age, it became important that cultural and political boundaries were congruous and this, for Gellner, was the key to understanding the birth of both nations and nationalism. In the work of 'classical modernists', therefore, history writing holds little explicatory significance. Gellner's focus on the evolution of state-based education systems in engendering national consciousness does perhaps leave a role to play for historians, as the suppliers of the raw materials for school history textbooks, but Gellner himself never mentioned history writing and modernists in general saw cultural factors as subordinate to underlying economic and industrial shifts.[46]

However, this modernist position came under attack from the 1980s onwards by writers who, while still asserting the modernity of both nations and nationalism, stressed rather the diverse mechanisms of their construction, invention, or imagination. Scholars such as Eric Hobsbawm and Benedict Anderson, rather than seeing nationalism as a predestined product of industrialization, sought to highlight the ways in which nationalism was (both consciously and unconsciously) manufactured. Hobsbawm, for example, initially investigated the way in which 'traditions which appear or claim to be old are often quite recent in origin, and sometimes invented'.[47] The role of historians in constructing nationalism 'from above' was here readily apparent. Although nationalism emerged as a more multifaceted construction in Hobsbawm's later work, a coalescence of the needs of elites and desires and practices of their newly enfranchized populations, the role of history writing in actively constructing a sense of continuity during periods of rapid social change remained significant.

Clearly, though, nationalism is never entirely 'invented', or constructed out of thin air. Even those seeking consciously to manufacture national sentiment can only succeed by working with pre-existing customs and ideas that have a public resonance. Hence, while initially striking, the wave of research on the theme of invention and imagination came to be seen as insufficiently nuanced and unable to explain why nationalism has such emotive power. A consideration of the deep roots and antecedents of modern nationalism was the primary focus of 'ethno-symbolists' such as John Armstrong and Anthony Smith during the 1980s and early 1990s. They argued that, contrary to the modernist position, the precursors to modern nations (often termed *ethnies*, or ethnic groups) had a strong sense of group identity and past continuity. While not supplied by written history, *ethnies* were bound together by what Armstrong referred to as 'myth-symbol' complexes, which featured many of the themes (the election of a people, the notion of a homeland, and the remembrance of a past golden age) of later national histories.[48] Yet, while successful in challenging the dominance of modernist conceptions of nationalism, ethno-symbolism was never able adequately to answer the 'how' and 'why' questions attached to the shift from loose ethnic groups to much more coherent nations and nationalism.

Thus the main approaches to date, while often conceding some significance to history writing in their interpretations of nationalism, do not give more than fragmentary accounts of the nature of the link between history writing and nationalism.

A satisfactory answer to the question—how does history writing inform nationalism?—is yet to be supplied. However, one fruitful way of thinking about this topic might be to focus on 'identity', and the role that a sense of the past plays in providing individuals and groups with both a potent and satisfying sense of community in the present, and a feeling of continuity with both past and future.

The idea that nationalism—cultural and/or political attachment to the nation—provides a deep sense of purpose and stability that is otherwise denied by the flux of modern life is not new. Early sociologists such as Émile Durkheim, while writing little explicitly about nationalism, wrote extensively about the sense of social dislocation (*anomie*) produced by the abrupt transition to modernity. Durkheim was also interested in the similarities between religious and national rituals, claiming that 'it is by uttering the same cry, pronouncing the same word, or performing the same gesture in regard to some object that they [the people] become and feel themselves to be in unison'.[49] Thus it might be argued that, in the transition to industrial society which occurred during the period 1750–1900, traditional allegiances and identities broke down and the nation arose as a way for increasingly secular societies to 'worship themselves brazenly and openly'.[50] Certainly, the prose of many of the national histories produced during the nineteenth century supports the idea that they serviced a quasi-religious need for purpose and order in a turbulent era of declining faith. Michelet, for example, noted explicitly that he turned to writing about his 'noble country' to 'fill the incommensurable void which Christianity left when it died'.[51]

This line of argument gives the start of a general answer to our question. Written history became important to cultural nationalism because it supplied an authoritative sense of continuity with an (often imaginary) past, and hence a sense of group identity in the present, during a period of rapid social change—often precipitated by conflict between and within states, as well as by socioeconomic developments. The projection of the nation forward into a glorious, united future, which was a theme of many national histories, also helps to explain the emotive power generated by nationalist ideology. The usefulness of this emotive power to politicians and other elites in turn helps to account for the connection that developed between nationalism as cultural sentiment and nationalism as political doctrine. Thus, as Peter Mandler notes, it was the very 'narrativity' of the nation, the sense of a story unfolding over time, of individuals united by a common fate, that gave national identity a 'special salience' over and above other types of identity, which are usually rooted much more strongly in the present.[52] This same narrativity, however, also gave nationalism a degree of abstraction that enabled its flexible deployment by cultural and political elites.

Although some recent work on identity (often postmodernist in approach) has stressed the multiplicity of identities in the modern world, and the fragmentary nature of national identity in particular, it does seem likely that national histories (particularly as developed during the nineteenth century) were uniquely placed to provide individuals with a sense of identity, group solidarity, and location in time. This common function may account for some of the similarities in structure and approach between different national histories. As Berger notes, national histories 'operated routinely with models of rise and decline, golden ages, lost homelands and national revivals'.[53] Debate over foundational moments, the roles of national heroes, and the unique properties of individual nations were also common to many texts. National histories were often very similar at a structural level, and their popular resonance was at least partly due to the identity-reinforcing function of their underlying narratives.

In addition, however, it is also likely that national histories were peculiarly successful because they drew on popular imagery surviving from pre-national eras, and perhaps even the 'myth-symbol complexes' identified by Armstrong and Smith. As Berger notes, 'many of the tropes of national belonging and identity, which were prominent ingredients of national histories, went back to medieval and early modern times'.[54] In this way, national histories functioned as 'master narratives', that is to say, 'attempts to answer important questions about cultural identity'.[55] Berger sees master narratives as ways of thinking about and conceptualizing the world that are vital for the successful functioning of societies. Arguably, the national master narrative came to be the most powerful of all, reaching back to the distant past and allowing individuals to find a place 'not only in the world in which he or she live[d], but also in an uninterrupted chain of being . . . thus carrying a promise of immortality'.[56]

Thus, while this topic is the subject of ongoing, much more detailed research (see note 4), it appears that the particular salience of national histories to nationalism, especially in the period from 1750, is twofold. In the first place (drawing on well-established cultural motifs) they helped to provide individuals with a powerful sense of identity in the present, supporting the development of 'cultural nationalism' during a period of very rapid social change. This statement holds true whether nationalism is viewed primarily as an intellectual doctrine or as a by-product of industrialization. Then, this sense of cultural identity came to be very useful politically in binding populations to their states. Hence national histories were very often sponsored and encouraged by political and power elites, often to the extent of invention or construction. National history arose in response to the need for new forms of identity in a changing world but then became politically useful, thus both reflecting and helping to augment nationalism.

Conclusion

The writing of history has always been intertwined with the development of nationalism in both its cultural and political forms. However, the nature and strength of the links between the two have varied across time and place. Before about 1750, while some 'national' histories were written, these remained largely the preserve of a limited, elite readership, and were often of more cultural than political significance. In the period since 1750, and particularly in nineteenth-century Europe, new forms of academic history writing became closely associated with the spread of nationalism as both a significant, mass form of cultural identification and a pervasive ideology of power politics. While the prevalence of teleological national histories gradually declined in areas such as Europe and America during the twentieth century, national histories remained very important in other parts of the world throughout the period of decolonization.

While by no means defunct, national histories have now become sufficiently unfashionable within the historical profession for some to raise the possibility of their eventual decline. Stuart Woolf, for example, has considered the possibility of a supranational 'history of Europe', the continuation of a tradition of history writing that was in many ways interrupted by the era of the nation state.[57] Charles Maier has argued that, with hindsight, the period *c.*1860–*c.*1980 can be viewed as one in which 'territoriality'—the attribution of significance to the control of bordered political space'—was a novel and defining characteristic. For Maier, territoriality has begun to lose its significance during the past several decades, with the result that 'the once-reassuring congruence between identity space and decision space has weakened'.[58] If this is true, it is at least plausible that national histories will further lose their purchase on group identities. Certainly, among historians at least, there has been a rise in interest in the possibility of writing genuinely transnational history.[59]

However, to paraphrase Mark Twain, it may be that the reports of the death of national history have been exaggerated. While it is certainly true that this is the general picture to be gleaned from the perusal of historical journals, it is also important to consider the function that national narratives (broadly defined) have in supplying both group and individual identity in the present. If, as Berger has claimed, national histories are cultural 'master narratives', strongly woven into the fabric of everyday life and drawing on metaphors and imagery that have strong public purchase, they are unlikely to be successfully dismantled just because historians point out their inherent flaws. After all, nineteenth-century national histories were powerful not because they were true but because of popular belief in their truth.

While academic historians have increasingly moved away from interpreting the past for mass public consumption into an arena of specialized and rarefied professional debate, this does not mean that the popular appetite for national narratives has waned. Indeed, Jay Winter has argued for what he calls a 'memory boom'—increased consumption of cultural products that confer/confirm identity—at the end of the twentieth century.[60] Rather, it is simply the case that national stories are no longer being provided primarily by professional historians. Other cultural products such as television narratives of national pasts, filmic representations of key national events, and novels set in specific historical contexts have flowed into the vacuum created by the withdrawal of professional historians. The challenge for professional historians today is to represent the new post-national versions of history they are developing in ways that will engage with the wider public.

NOTES

1. R. G. Suny (2002) 'Constructing Primordialism: Old Histories for New Nations', *The Journal of Modern History*, 73, no. 4 (December), 862–96, 869.
2. A. D. Smith (2000) *The Nation in History*, Oxford, 3; S. Grosby (2005) *Nationalism: A Very Short Introduction*, Oxford, 20.
3. E. Hobsbawm and T. Ranger (eds.) (1983) *The Invention of Tradition*, Cambridge; J. Breuilly (1993) *Nationalism and the State*, Manchester.
4. An early work on this topic was Anthony Smith's (1992) 'Nationalism and the Historians', *International Journal of Comparative Sociology*, 33, nos. 1–2, 58–80. A new wave of scholarship began with the publication of S. Berger, M. Donovan, and K. Passmore (1999) *Writing National Histories: Western Europe since 1800*, London. Berger is a key figure in the field, coordinating a large European Science Foundation research project—'Representations of the Past: The Writing of National Histories in Europe'—and editing an accompanying series of books with Palgrave Macmillan.
5. M. Samuels (2004) *The Spectacular Past: Popular History and the Novel in Nineteenth-Century France*, Ithaca, NY, and London, 4–5.
6. S. Grosby (1995) 'Territoriality: The Transcendental, Primordial Feature of Modern Societies', *Nations and Nationalism*, 1, no. 2, 143–62, 144; A. D. Smith (1986) *The Ethnic Origins of Nations*, London, 69.
7. A. Hastings (1997) *The Construction of Nationhood: Ethnicity, Religion and Nationalism*, Cambridge, 15; L. Greenfeld (1992) *Nationalism: Five Roads to Modernity*, Cambridge, MA, 6.
8. S. Berger (2007) 'The Power of National Pasts: Writing National History in Nineteenth- and Twentieth-Century Europe', in Berger (ed.) *Writing the Nation: A Global Perspective*, London, 30.
9. S. Reynolds (1997) *Kingdoms and Communities in Western Europe, 900–1300*, Oxford, 38.
10. C. Hirschi (2005) *Wettkampf der Nationen: Konstruktionen einer deutschen Ehrgemeinschaft an der Wende vom Mittelalter zur Neuzeit*, Göttingen.
11. Q. E. Wang (2007) 'Between Myth and History: The Construction of a National Past in Modern East Asia', in Berger (ed.) *Writing the Nation*, 3.
12. R. McKitterick (2004) *History and Memory in the Carolingian World*, Cambridge, 7.
13. See the essays by S. Reynolds and J. Breuilly in L. Scales and O. Zimmer (eds.) (2005) *Power and the Nation in European History*, Cambridge, quotes from 54 and 68.
14. R. Torstendahl and I. Veit-Brause (eds.) (1996) 'History-Making: The Intellectual and Social Formation of a Discipline', *Konferenser* 37, Stockholm, 95–113, 98ff.
15. R. Koselleck (2004) *Futures Past: On the Semantics of Historical Time*, New York.
16. For a concise summary, see U. Özkirimli (2000) *Theories of Nationalism*, London.
17. L. Raphael (2000) 'Flexible Response? Strategies of Academic Historians Towards Larger Markets for National Historiographies and Increasing Scientific Standards', in R. Torstendahl (ed.) *An Assessment of Twentieth-Century Historiography—Konferenser 49*, Stockholm, 127–47, 127–8. On the development of the historical profession, see G. Iggers (1997) *Historiography in the Twentieth Century*, London; and B. Stuchtey and P. Wende (eds.) (2000) *British and German Historiography, 1751–1950*, Oxford.
18. Iggers, *Historiography*, 28.
19. S. Berger (1997) *The Search for Normality: National Identity and Historical Consciousness in Germany since 1800*, Oxford, 4.

20. P. Winzen (1981) 'Treitschke's Influence on the Rise of Imperialist and anti-British Nationalism in Germany', in P. Kennedy and A. Nicholls (eds.) *Nationalist and Racialist Movements in Britain and Germany before 1914*, London, 155.
21. J. Michelet (1967) *The History of the French Revolution*, ed. G. Wright, Chicago, IL.
22. Cited in P. Nora (ed.) (1997) 'L'histoire de France de Lavisse', in *Les lieux de mémoire, II. La nation*, Paris, 322.
23. Berger, *Writing the Nation*, 1.
24. R. Plaschka (1974) 'The Political Significance of Frantisek Palacky', in W. Laqueur and G. L. Mosse (eds.) *Historians in Politics*, London, 91–111.
25. For example, on the retrospective construction of 'Finnishness', see D. Fewster (2006) *Visions of Past Glory: Nationalism and the Construction of Early Finnish History*, Helsinki. On the importance of historians in relation to Central European nationalism, see M. Baar (2009) *Historians and the Nation in the Nineteenth Century: The Case of East Central Europe*, Oxford.
26. G. Iggers (1968) *The German Conception of History*, Middletown, CT; J. Seeley (1883) *The Expansion of England*, London.
27. E, de Freitas Dutra (2007) 'The Mirror of History and Images of the Nation: The Inventions of a National Identity in Brazil and its Contrasts with Similar Enterprises in Mexico and Argentina', in Berger (ed.) *Writing the Nation*, 84–102.
28. A. Smith (2007) 'Seven Narratives in North American History', in Berger (ed.) *Writing the Nation*, 63–83.
29. On this, see P. Burke, ed. (2002) *History and Historians in the Twentieth Century*, Oxford, 3.
30. Lord Acton (1956) 'Nationality', in *Essays on Power and Freedom*, London, 169.
31. See, for example, I. McLaughlin (1926) 'History and Sociology: A Comparison of their Methods', *The American Journal of Sociology*, 32, no. 3, 379–95.
32. K. D. Erdmann (2005) *Towards a Global Community of Historians: The International Historical Congresses and the International Committee of Historical Sciences, 1898–2000*, Oxford, 68–9.
33. Cited in P. Lambert (1998) 'Paving the "peculiar path": German Nationalism and Historiography since Ranke', in G. Cubitt (ed.) *Imagining Nations*, Manchester, 99.
34. For an overview, see J. Burrow (2007) *A History of Histories*, London, 478–94.
35. A. Iriya (2004) 'Transnational History', *Contemporary European History*, 13, no. 2, 211–22, 213. On the influence of the social sciences and the challenge of postmodernism, see Iggers, *Historiography*.
36. Erdmann, *Towards a Global Community*, x.
37. S. Berger (2005) 'A Return to the National Paradigm? National History Writing in Germany, Italy, France, and Britain from 1945 to the Present', *The Journal of Modern History*, 77 (September), 629–78, 644.
38. Suny, 'Constructing Primordialism'. See also S. Antohi, B. Trencsényi, and P. Apor (eds.) (2007) *Narratives Unbound: Historical Studies in Post-Communist Eastern Europe*, Budapest.
39. R. Seshan (2007) 'Writing the Nation in India: Communalism and Historiography', in Berger (ed.) *Writing the Nation*, 155–78.
40. I. Thioub (2007) 'Writing National and Transnational History in Africa: The Example of the Dakar School', in Berger (ed.) *Writing the Nation*, 197.
41. Thioub, 'Writing National and Transnational History in Africa', 12.
42. D. Blackbourn and G. Eley (1984) *The Peculiarities of German History*, Oxford.
43. Iggers, *Historiography*, 139.

44. Suny, 'Constructing Primordialism', 870.
45. C. Hayes (1926) *Essays on Nationalism*, New York, 62. For a more recent, and more sophisticated, cultural history of the idea of nationalism, see J. Leerssen (2008) *National Thought in Europe: A Cultural History*, Amsterdam.
46. K. Deutsch (1956) *Nationalism and Social Communication*, Cambridge, MA; E. Gellner (2006) *Nations and Nationalism*, Oxford.
47. Hobsbawm and Ranger, *Invention of Tradition*, 1.
48. J. Armstrong (1982) *Nations before Nationalism*, Chapel Hill, NC; A. D. Smith (1986) *The Ethnic Origins of Nations*, London.
49. Cited in M. Guibernau (1996) *Nationalisms: The Nation-State and Nationalism in the Twentieth Century*, Cambridge, 84.
50. E. Gellner (1984) *Nations and Nationalism*, New York, 56.
51. Cited in C. Crossley (1993) *French Historians and Romanticism: Thierry, Guizot, the Saint-Simonians, Quinet, and Michelet*, London and New York, 198.
52. P. Mandler (2006) 'What is "National Identity"? Definitions and Applications in Modern British Historiography?', *Modern Intellectual History*, 3, no. 2, 271–97, 280.
53. Berger (ed.) *Writing the Nation*, 9.
54. Berger (ed.) *Writing the Nation*, 31.
55. S. Berger and A. Mycock (eds.) (2006) 'Europe and its National Histories', *Storia della storiografia*, 50, 9.
56. Y. Tamir (1995) 'The Enigma of Nationalism', *World Politics*, 47 (April), 418–40, 437.
57. S. Woolf (2003) 'Europe and its Historians', *Contemporary European History*, 12, no. 3, 323–37.
58. C. S. Maier (2000) 'Consigning the Twentieth Century to History: Alternative Narratives for the Modern Era', *American Historical Review* (June), 807–31, 823.
59. C. Bayly et al. (2006) '*AHR* Conversation: On Transnational History', *American Historical Review*, 111, no. 5 (December), 1440–64.
60. J. Winter (2000) 'The Generation of Memory: Reflections on the "Memory Boom" in Contemporary Historical Studies', *Bulletin of the GHI*, 27 (fall), 69–92.

Suggested Further Reading

Berger, S. (2005) 'A Return to the National Paradigm? National History Writing in Germany, Italy, France, and Britain from 1945 to the Present', *The Journal of Modern History*, 77 (September), 629–78.

Berger, S. and Mycock, A. (eds.) (2006) 'Europe and its National Histories', *storia della storiografia*, vol. 50, 629–78.

Berger, S., Donovan, M., and Passmore, K. (eds.) (1999) *Writing National Histories: Western Europe Since 1800*, London.

Berger, S. (ed.) (2007) *Writing the Nation: A Global Perspective*, Basingstoke.

Breuilly, J. (2002) 'Historians and the Nation', in Burke, P. (ed.) *History and Historians in the Twentieth Century*, Oxford, 55–87.

Iggers, G. (1997) *Historiography in the Twentieth Century: From Scientific Objectivity to the Postmodern Challenge*, London.

Lawrence, P. (2005) *Nationalism: History and Theory*, Harlow.

Smith, A. D. (1992) 'Nationalism and the Historians', *International Journal of Comparative Sociology*, XXXIII, nos. 1–2, 58–80.
Torstendahl, R. and Veit-Brause, I. (eds.) (1996) *History-Making: The Intellectual and Social Formation of a Discipline—Konferenser 37*, Stockholm.
Woolf, S. (2003) 'Europe and its Historians', *Contemporary European History*, 12, no. 3, 323–37.

Index

Lightning Source UK Ltd.
Milton Keynes UK
UKHW031009150619
344490UK00001B/1/P